STREET ATLAS
South Hampshire

First published in 1991 by

Philip's, a division of
Octopus Publishing Group Ltd
2–4 Heron Quays, London E14 4JP

Second colour edition 2002
Third impression 2004

ISBN 0-540-08105-1 (hardback)
ISBN 0-540-08106-X (spiral)

© Philip's 2003

This product includes mapping data licensed
from Ordnance Survey® with the permission of
the Controller of Her Majesty's Stationery Office.
© Crown copyright 2003. All rights reserved.
Licence number 100011710.

Printed and bound in Spain
by Cayfosa-Quebecor

Contents

III   **Key to map symbols**

IV   **Key to map pages**

VI   **Route planning**

VIII   **Administrative and Postcode boundaries**

1   **Street maps** at 3½ inches to 1 mile

215   **Street map of Portsmouth city centre** at 7 inches to 1 mile

216   **Town maps** of Winchester, Andover, Basingstoke, Farnborough and Newbury

219   **Index** of towns and villages

220   **Index** of streets, hospitals, industrial estates, railway stations, schools, shopping centres, universities and places of interest

Digital Data

The exceptionally high-quality mapping found in this atlas is available as digital data in TIFF format, which is easily convertible to other bitmapped (raster) image formats.

The index is also available in digital form as a standard database table. It contains all the details found in the printed index together with the National Grid reference for the map square in which each entry is named.

For further information and to discuss your requirements, please contact Philip's on 020 7644 6932 or james.mann@philips-maps.co.uk

Motorway with junction number	**Railway station**
Primary route – dual/single carriageway	**Private railway station**
A road – dual/single carriageway	**Bus, coach station**
B road – dual/single carriageway	**Ambulance station**
Minor road – dual/single carriageway	**Coastguard station**
Other minor road – dual/single carriageway	**Fire station**
Road under construction	**Police station**
Pedestrianised area	**Accident and Emergency entrance to hospital**
Postcode boundaries	**Hospital**
County and unitary authority boundaries	**Place of worship**
Railway	**Information Centre** (open all year)
Railway under construction	**Parking**
Tramway, miniature railway	**Park and Ride**
Rural track, private road or narrow road in urban area	**Post Office**
Gate or obstruction to traffic (restrictions may not apply at all times or to all vehicles)	**Camping site**
Path, bridleway, byway open to all traffic, road used as a public path	**Caravan site**
The representation in this atlas of a road, track or path is no evidence of the existence of a right of way	**Golf course**
	Picnic site
Adjoining page indicators	**Important buildings, schools, colleges, universities and hospitals**
The map area within the pink band is shown at a larger scale on the page indicated by the red block and arrow	**Water name**
	River, stream
	Lock, weir
	Water
	Tidal water
	Woods
	Houses
	Non-Roman antiquity
	Roman antiquity

Walsall · Prim Sch · River Medway · Church · ROMAN FORT

Acad	**Academy**	Mkt	**Market**
Allot Gdns	**Allotments**	Meml	**Memorial**
Cemy	**Cemetery**	Mon	**Monument**
C Ctr	**Civic Centre**	Mus	**Museum**
CH	**Club House**	Obsy	**Observatory**
Coll	**College**	Pal	**Royal Palace**
Crem	**Crematorium**	PH	**Public House**
Ent	**Enterprise**	Recn Gd	**Recreation Ground**
Ex H	**Exhibition Hall**	Resr	**Reservoir**
Ind Est	**Industrial Estate**	Ret Pk	**Retail Park**
IRB Sta	**Inshore Rescue Boat Station**	Sch	**School**
		Sh Ctr	**Shopping Centre**
Inst	**Institute**	TH	**Town Hall/House**
Ct	**Law Court**	Trad Est	**Trading Estate**
L Ctr	**Leisure Centre**	Univ	**University**
LC	**Level Crossing**	Wks	**Works**
Liby	**Library**	YH	**Youth Hostel**

■ The small numbers around the edges of the maps identify the 1 kilometre National Grid lines ■ The dark grey border on the inside edge of some pages indicates that the mapping does not continue onto the adjacent page

The scale of the maps on the pages numbered in blue is 5.52 cm to 1 km • 3½ inches to 1 mile • 1: 18103

0 ¼ ½ ¾ 1 mile
0 250 m 500 m 750 m 1 kilometre

The scale of the maps on pages numbered in red is 11.04 cm to 1 km • 7 inches to 1 mile • 1: 9051.4

0 220 yards 440 yards 660 yards ½ mile
0 125 m 250 m 375 m ½ kilometre

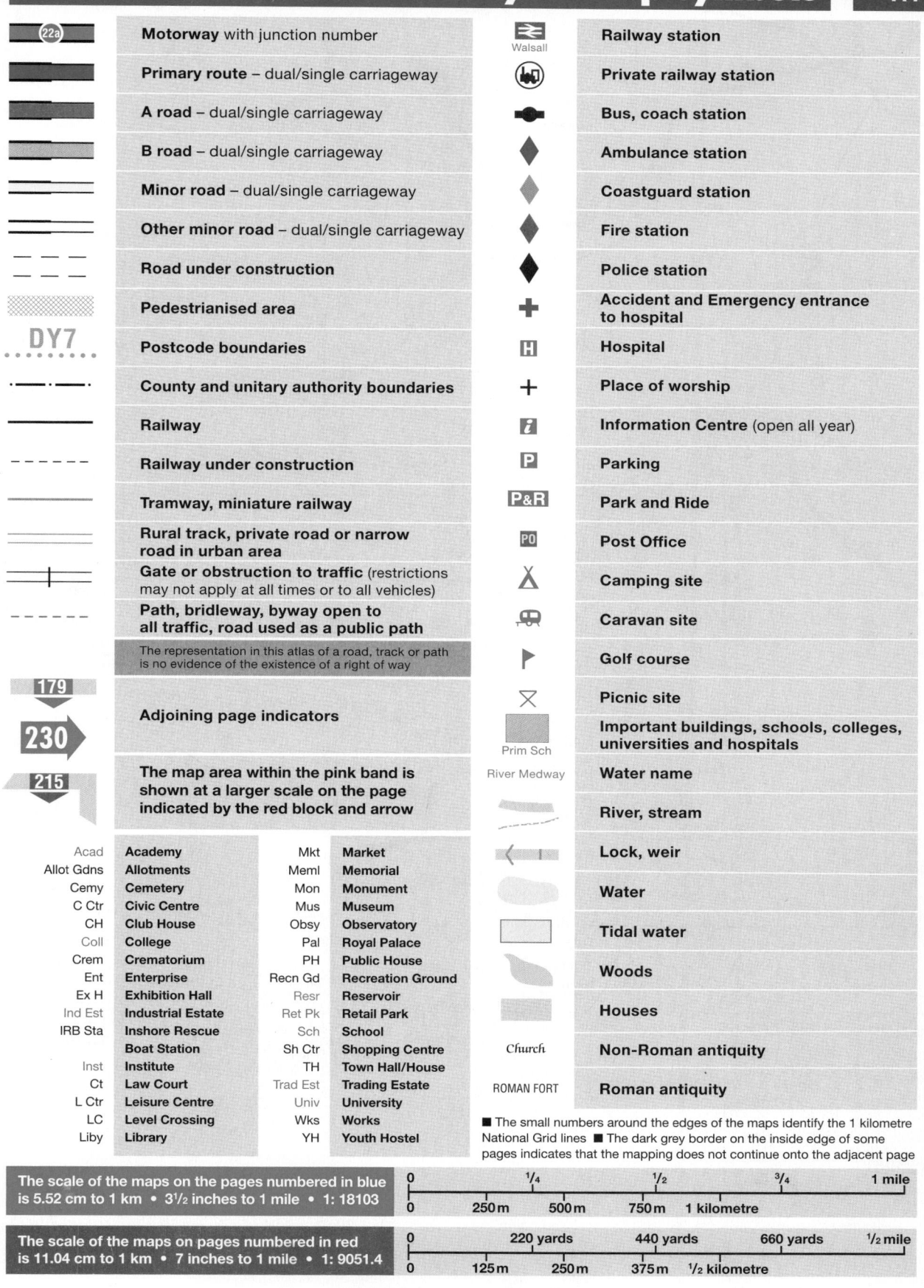

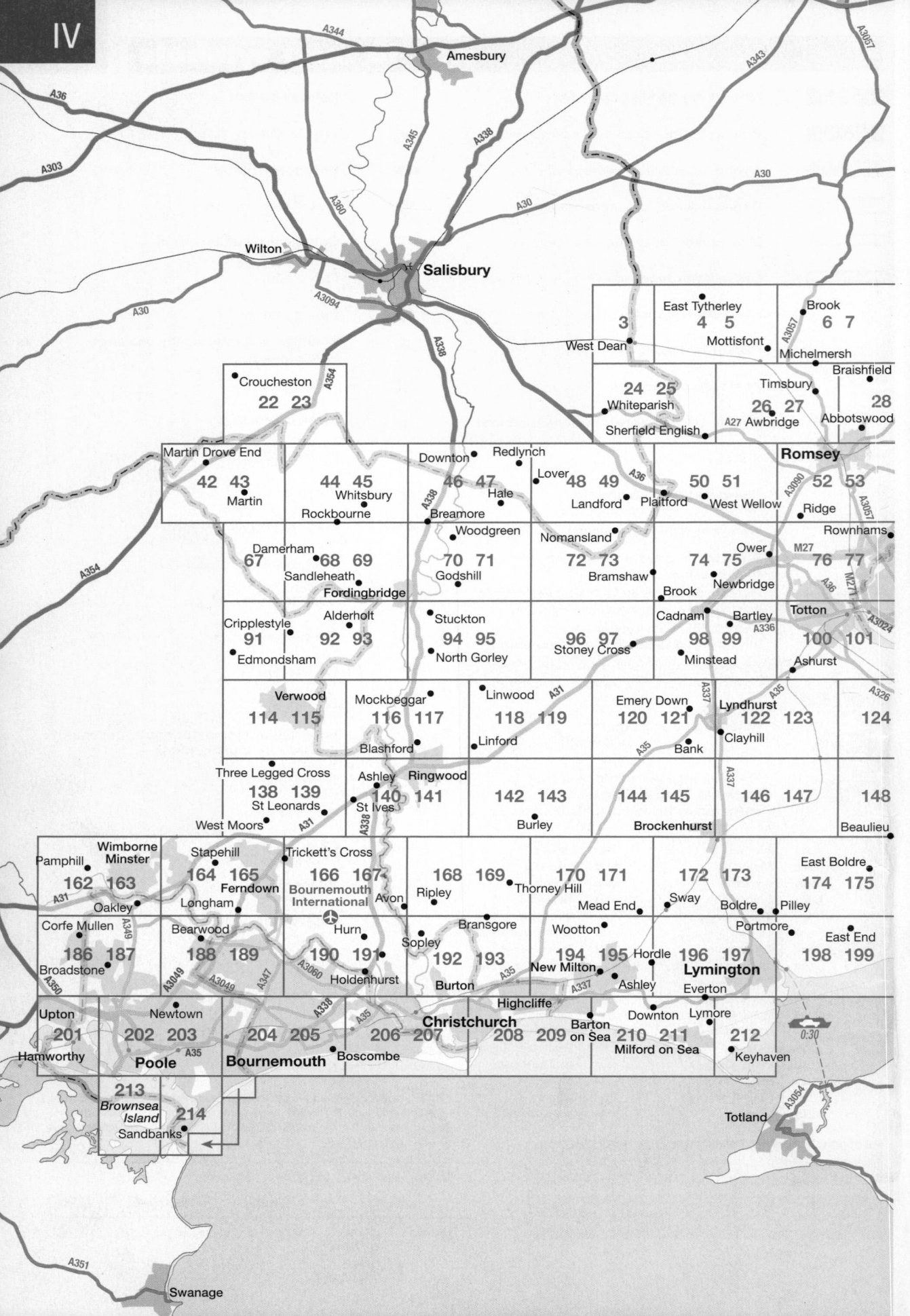

A344
Amesbury
A345
A338
A343
A3057
A36
A303
A30
A30
A360
A30
Wilton
Salisbury
A3094
A345
A338
A30

Croucheston
22 23
A354

3 East Tytherley **4 5** Brook **6 7**
West Dean Mottisfont Michelmersh
A3057
Braishfield
24 25 Timsbury **26 27 28**
Whiteparish A27 Awbridge Abbotswood
Sherfield English **Romsey**

Martin Drove End
42 43 Downton Redlynch Lover **48 49** **50 51** **52 53**
Martin Whitsbury **44 45** **46 47** Hale Landford Plaitford West Wellow Ridge
Rockbourne Breamore A36 A3090 A3057
Woodgreen Nomansland Rownhams
Damerham Ower M27
67 68 69 **70 71** **72 73** **74 75** **76 77**
Sandleheath Godshill Bramshaw Newbridge A5
Fordingbridge Brook M271
Cripplestyle Alderholt Stuckton Cadnam Bartley Totton A3024
91 92 93 **94 95** **96 97** **98 99** A336 **100 101**
Edmondsham North Gorley Stoney Cross Minstead Ashurst
Verwood Mockbeggar Linwood A31 Emery Down Lyndhurst A326
114 115 **116 117** **118 119** **120 121** A337 **122 123** **124**
Blashford Linford A35 Bank Clayhill
Three Legged Cross Ashley Ringwood A337
138 139 **140 141** **142 143** **144 145** **146 147** **148**
St Leonards St Ives Brockenhurst Beaulieu
West Moors A31 A338 Burley

Wimborne Stapehill Trickett's Cross East Boldre
Pamphill Minster **164 165** **166 167** **168 169** **170 171** **172 173** **174 175**
162 163 Ferndown Bournemouth Ripley Thorney Hill Sway Boldre Pilley
A31 Longham International Avon Mead End Portmore
Oakley Hurn Bransgore Wootton East End
Corfe Mullen Bearwood Sopley **192 193** **194 195** Hordle **196 197** **198 199**
186 187 **188 189** **190 191** Burton New Milton Ashley **Lymington**
Broadstone A3049 A3049 A347 A3060 Holdenhurst A35 Everton
A350 Highcliffe A337 Downton Lymore
Upton Newtown Christchurch Barton **210 211** **212**
201 **202 203** **204 205** **206 207** **208 209** on Sea Milford on Sea 0:30
Hamworthy **Poole** A35 **Bournemouth** Boscombe Keyhaven
Totland
213 Brownsea A3054
Island **214**
Sandbanks
Swanage A351

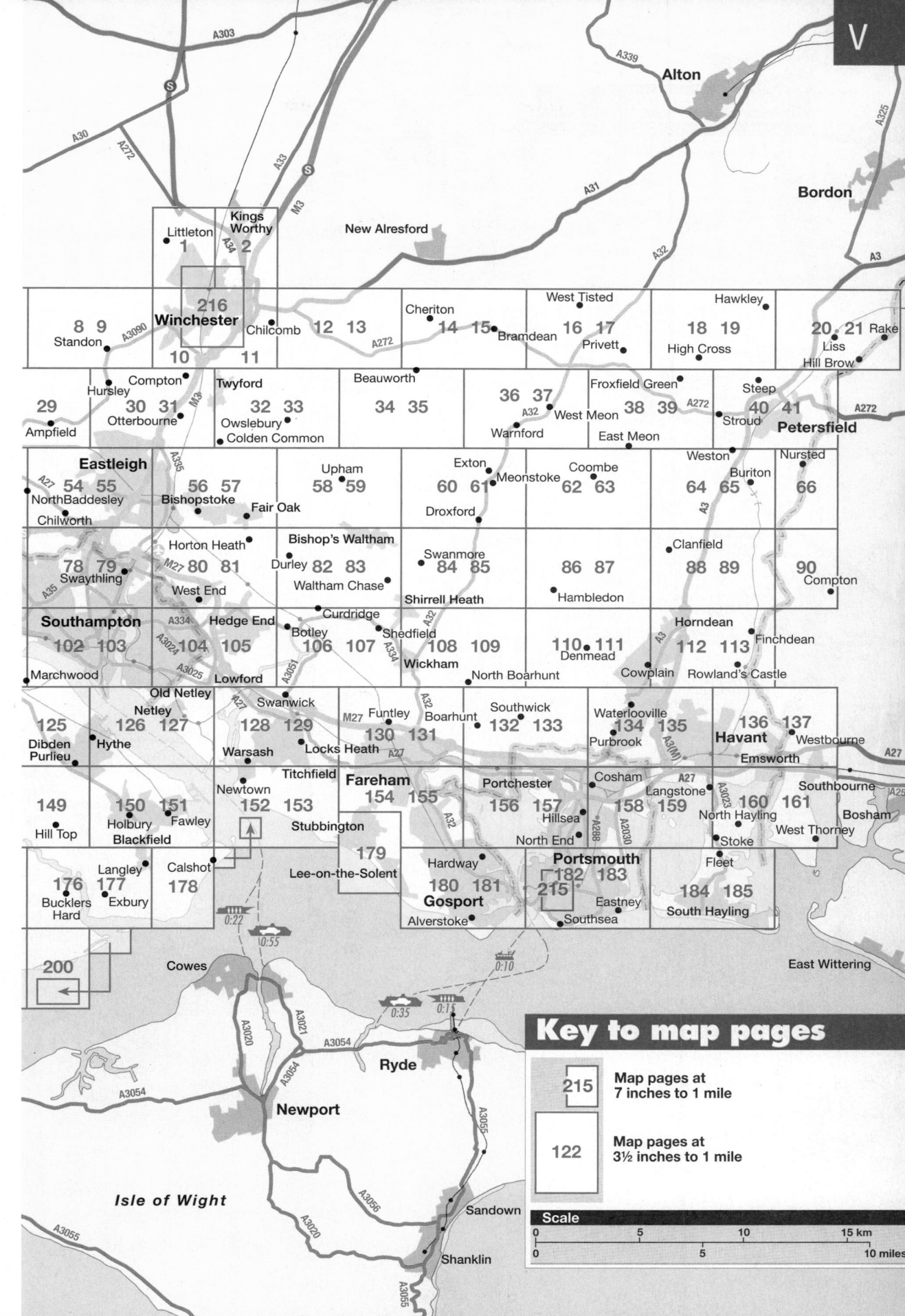

V

Alton

Bordon

A303

A339

A325

A30

A272

A31

A3

A33

M3

Littleton
1

Kings
Worthy
2

New Alresford

West Tisted

Hawkley

216
Winchester

Chilcomb

12 13

Cheriton

14 15
Bramdean

16 17
Privett

18 19
High Cross

20 21 Rake
Liss
Hill Brow

8 9
Standon

10

11

A272

West Meon

A272

Stroud

Steep

40 41
Petersfield

29
Ampfield

Compton
Hursley

30 31
Otterbourne

M3

Twyford

32 33
Owslebury
Colden Common

Beauworth

34 35

36 37
A32
Warnford

Froxfield Green

38 39
East Meon

54 55
North Baddesley
Chilworth

Eastleigh

A335

56 57
Bishopstoke
Fair Oak

Upham

58 59

Exton

60 61
Droxford

Meonstoke

Coombe

62 63

Weston

64 65
Buriton

A3

Nursted

66

78 79
Swaythling

M27

80 81
West End

Horton Heath

Bishop's Waltham

82 83
Durley
Waltham Chase

Swanmore

84 85
Shirrell Heath

86 87
Hambledon

Clanfield

88 89

90
Compton

Southampton

A334

102 103
Marchwood

A3024

A3025

104 105
Lowford

Hedge End
Botley

A3051

Curdridge

106 107
Wickham

Shedfield

A334

108 109
North Boarhunt

110 111
Denmead

A3

Cowplain

112 113
Rowland's Castle

Horndean

Finchdean

125
Dibden
Purlieu

Old Netley
Netley

126 127
Hythe

A27

128 129
Warsash

Swanwick

M27

Funtley

130 131
Locks Heath

A27

Boarhunt

132 133

Southwick

Waterlooville

134 135
Purbrook

136 137
Havant
Westbourne
Emsworth

A27

149
Hill Top

150 151
Holbury
Blackfield

Fawley

Titchfield

Newtown

152 153
Stubbington

Fareham

154 155

A32

Portchester

156
Hillsea
North End

Cosham

157

A288

Langstone

A2030

158 159

A27

A3023

North Hayling

160 161
Stoke

West Thorney

Southbourne

Bosham

A27

176 177
Bucklers
Hard
Exbury

Langley

Calshot

178

179
Lee-on-the-Solent

Hardway

180 181
Gosport
Alverstoke

Portsmouth

182 183
215
Eastney
Southsea

Fleet

184 185
South Hayling

200

Cowes

0:22

0:55

0:35

0:15

0:10

East Wittering

A3020

A3021

A3054

Ryde

A3054

A3055

A3054

Newport

A3055

A3020

A3056

A3055

Sandown

Shanklin

Isle of Wight

Key to map pages

| **215** | Map pages at 7 inches to 1 mile |
| **122** | Map pages at 3½ inches to 1 mile |

Scale

| 0 | | 5 | | 10 | | 15 km |

| 0 | | 5 | | 10 miles |

Major administrative and Postcode boundaries

County and unitary authority boundaries
District boundaries
Postcode boundaries
Area covered by this atlas

Scale

0   5   10   15 km

0   5   10 miles

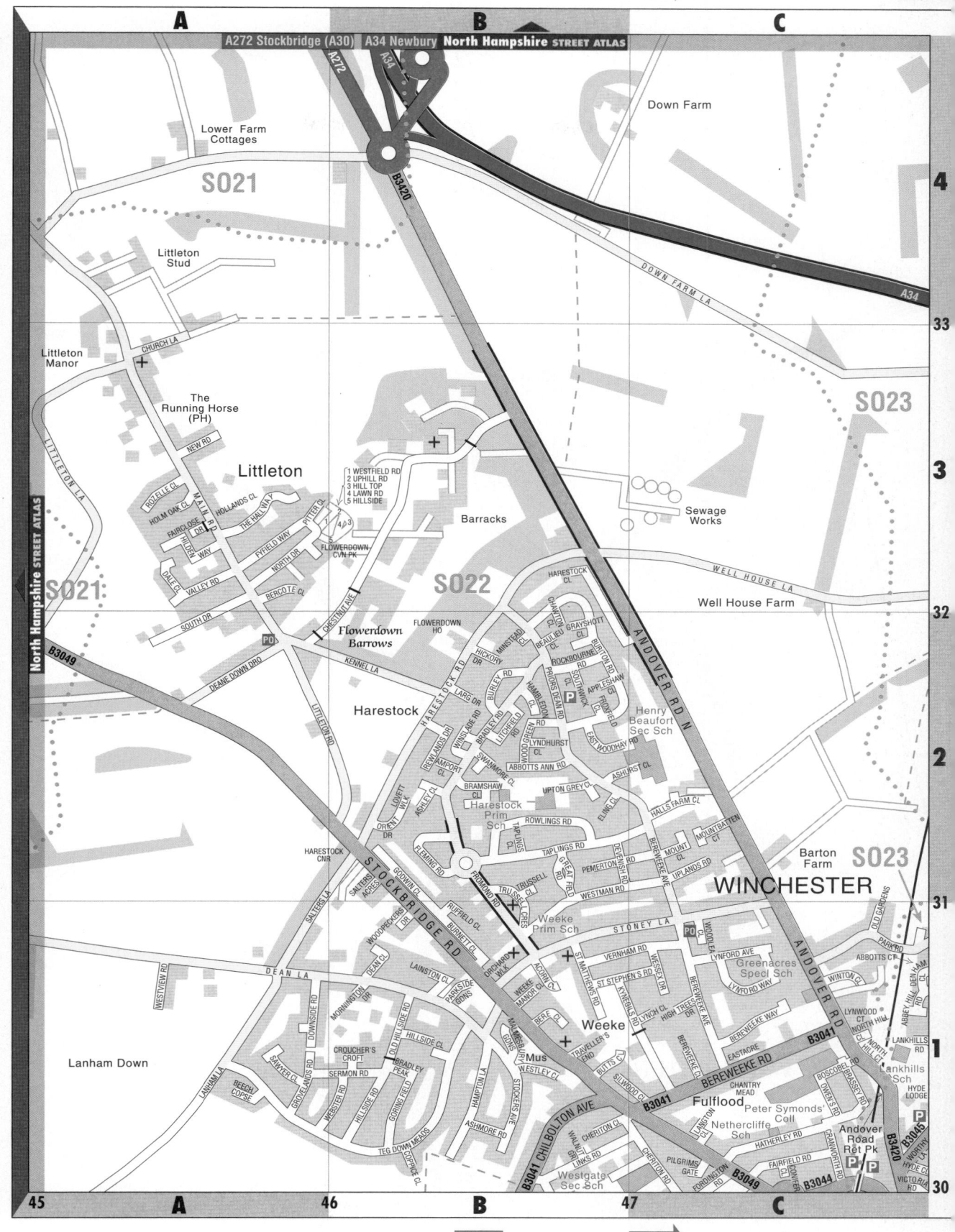

1

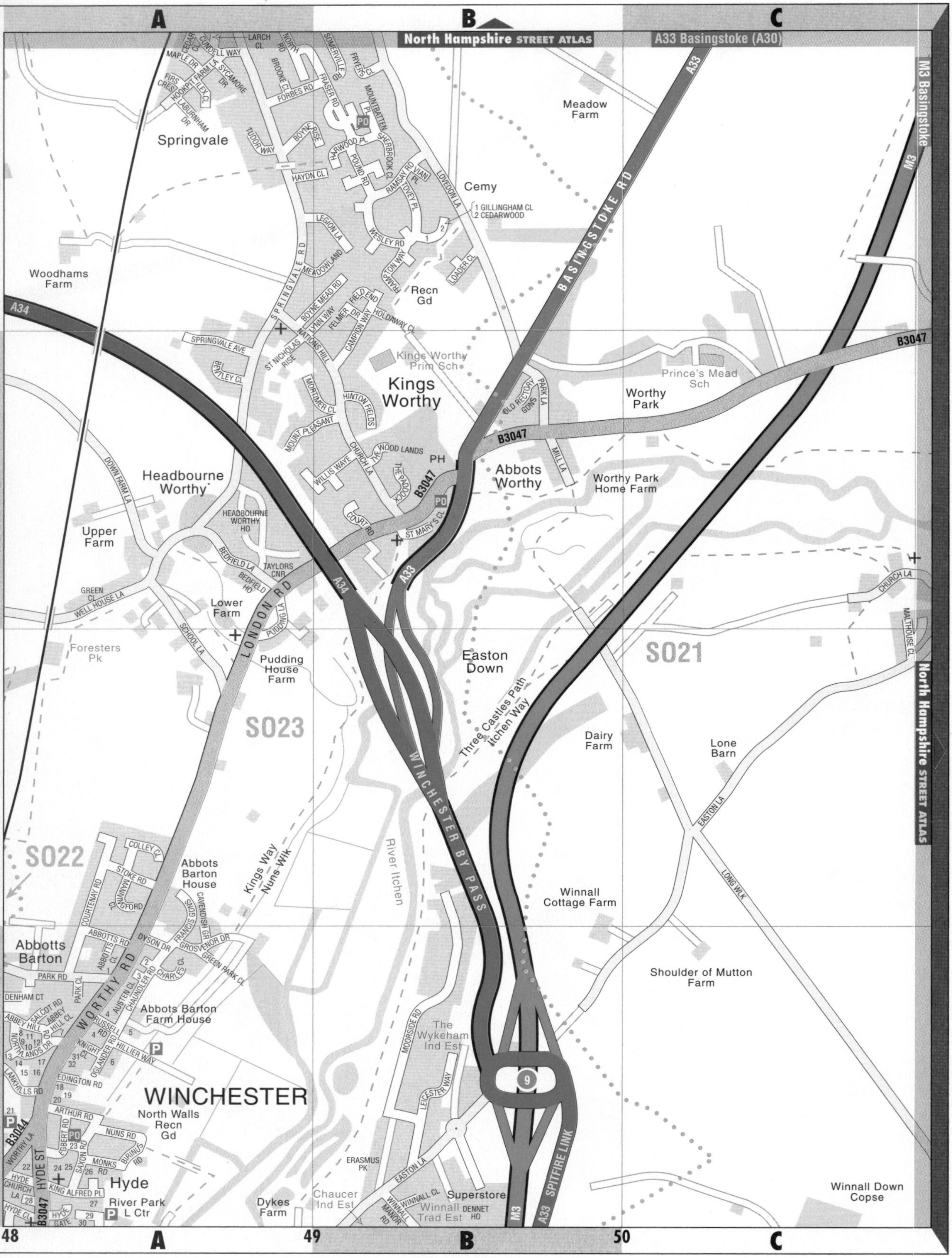
A
B
C
North Hampshire STREET ATLAS
A33 Basingstoke (A30)
M3 Basingstoke
Springvale
Meadow Farm
Cemy
1 GILLINGHAM CL
2 CEDARWOOD
Woodhams Farm
Recn Gd
Kings Worthy Prim Sch
Kings Worthy
Prince's Mead Sch
Worthy Park
Headbourne Worthy
Abbots Worthy
Worthy Park Home Farm
Upper Farm
Lower Farm
Foresters Pk
Pudding House Farm
Easton Down
SO21
SO23
SO22
Three Castles Path
Itchen Way
Dairy Farm
Lone Barn
Abbots Barton House
Kings Way
Nuns Wlk
River Itchen
WINCHESTER BY PASS
Winnall Cottage Farm
Abbotts Barton
Shoulder of Mutton Farm
Abbots Barton Farm House
The Wykeham Ind Est
WINCHESTER
North Walls Recn Gd
Hyde
River Park L Ctr
Dykes Farm
Chaucer Ind Est
ERASMUS PK
Superstore
Winnall Trad Est
Winnall Down Copse
BASINGSTOKE RD
LONDON RD
WORTHY RD
HYDE ST
SPITFIRE LINK
A34
A33
M3
B3047
B3044
EASTON LA
LONG WLK
CHURCH LA
MALTHOUSE CL
48
49
50
4
33
3
32
2
31
1
30

A1
1 PARK CT
2 HUSSEY CL
3 CORAM CL
4 CONEY GN
5 SIMONDS CT
6 COLBOURNE CT
7 COVENTRY CT
8 KENILWORTH CT
9 STRATFORD CT
10 MERIDEN CT
11 WARNER CT
12 ALTON CT
13 WARWICK CL
14 WARWICK CT
15 TWYFORD CT
16 FARINGDON CT
17 REGENT CT
18 WOODLANDS CT
19 DONNINGTON CT
20 THE TOLLGATE
21 HYDE LODGE
22 HYDE HOUSE GDNS
23 DANES RD
24 HYDE CHURCH PATH
25 BARTHOLOMEW CL
26 ST BEDE'S CT
27 ALSWITHA TERR
28 ROSEWARNE CT
29 KING ALFRED TERR

1

A1
30 ARLINGTON PL
31 DALZELL
32 YORK HO

11

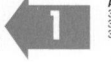

North Hampshire STREET ATLAS

A   B   C

Coalpits Copse

Park Lane

Park Copse

Redridge Copse

Bentley Wood

Beechwood
Copse

Barnridge
Copse

Duck
Ponds

Home
Farm

STANDING HILL

Elm's
Copse

Cole's Pond
Farm

RED LA

4

Howe Copse East

Howe
Cottage

Hatchers
Farm

South
Lodge

Tytherley
Common

29

Howe
Farm

Heath Copse

Drove
Farm

DEAN RD

3

Howe Copse
West

Dean Copse

Frenchmoor
Farm

SP5

Rosewood
Farm

28

Hawks
Grove

FRENCHMOOR LA

Fine
Wood

Glebe Farm

2

ROOKERY
COTTS

Church
Farm

PO

Park Farm

+ West Dean

Dean

RECTORY HILL

LC

27

DEAN RD

Green Acre

Windrush

MOODY'S HILL

MOODY'S HILL

The Red Lion
(PH)
Sawmills

HILLSIDE CL

FRENCHMOOR LA

Old
Brewers
(PH)

1

ASHMORE LA

26

Wiltshire STREET ATLAS

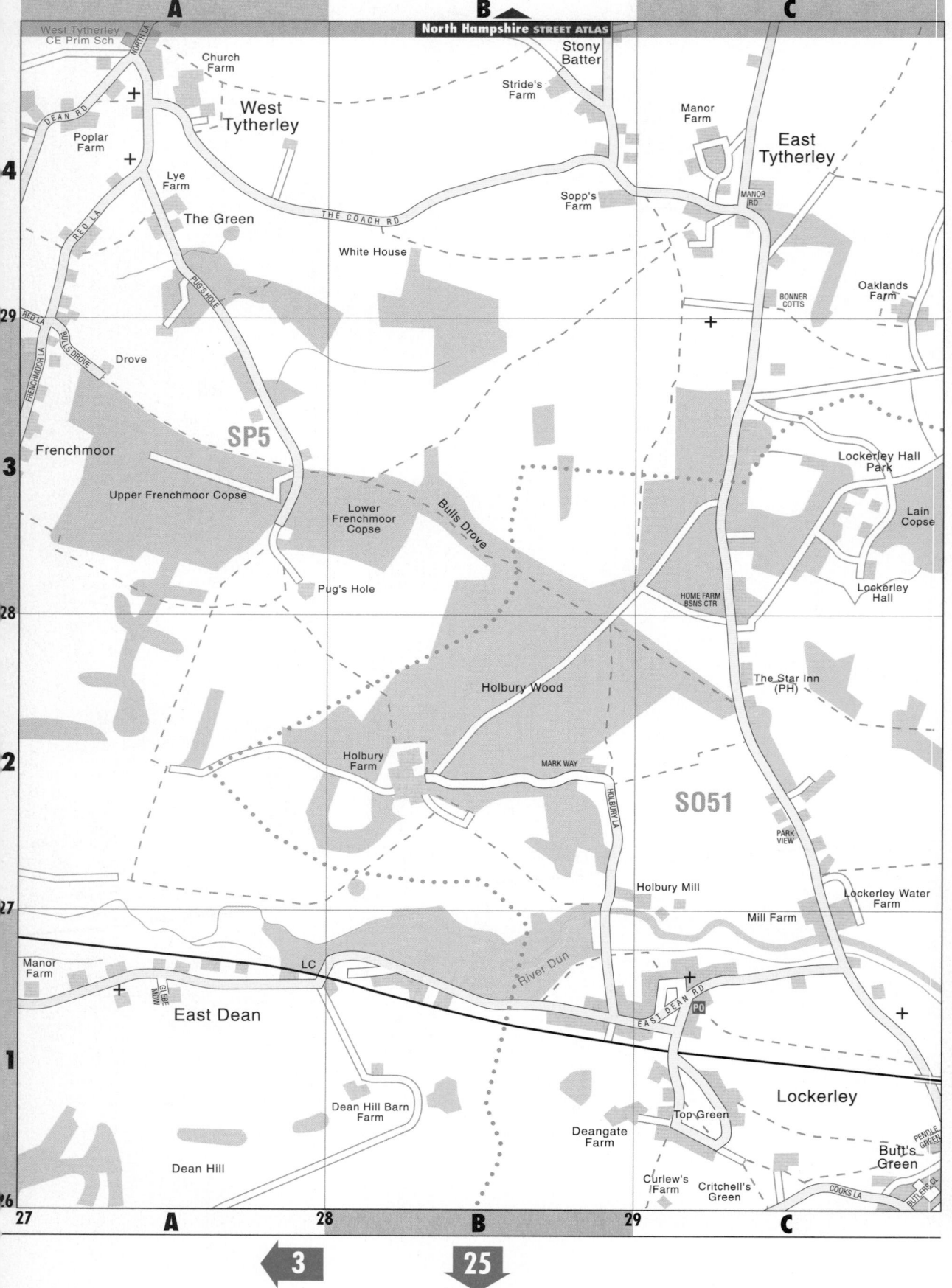

West Tytherley CE Prim Sch

Church Farm

West Tytherley

Stony Batter

Stride's Farm

Manor Farm

East Tytherley

DEAN RD

Poplar Farm

NORTH LA

Lye Farm

The Green

THE COACH RD

Sopp's Farm

MANOR RD

RED LA

White House

BULL'S DROVE

PUG'S HOLE

BONNER COTTS

Oaklands Farm

29

RED LA

FRENCHMOOR LA

Drove

SP5

Frenchmoor

Upper Frenchmoor Copse

Lower Frenchmoor Copse

Bulls Drove

Lockerley Hall Park

Lain Copse

3

Pug's Hole

HOME FARM BSNS CTR

Lockerley Hall

28

Holbury Wood

The Star Inn (PH)

2

Holbury Farm

MARK WAY

HOLBURY LA

SO51

PARK VIEW

27

Holbury Mill

Mill Farm

Lockerley Water Farm

Manor Farm

GLEBE MDW

LC

River Dun

EAST DEAN RD

PO

East Dean

1

Dean Hill Barn Farm

Deangate Farm

Top Green

Lockerley

Dean Hill

Curlew's Farm

Critchell's Green

Butt's Green

PENDLE GREEN

COOKS LA

BUTLERS CL

26

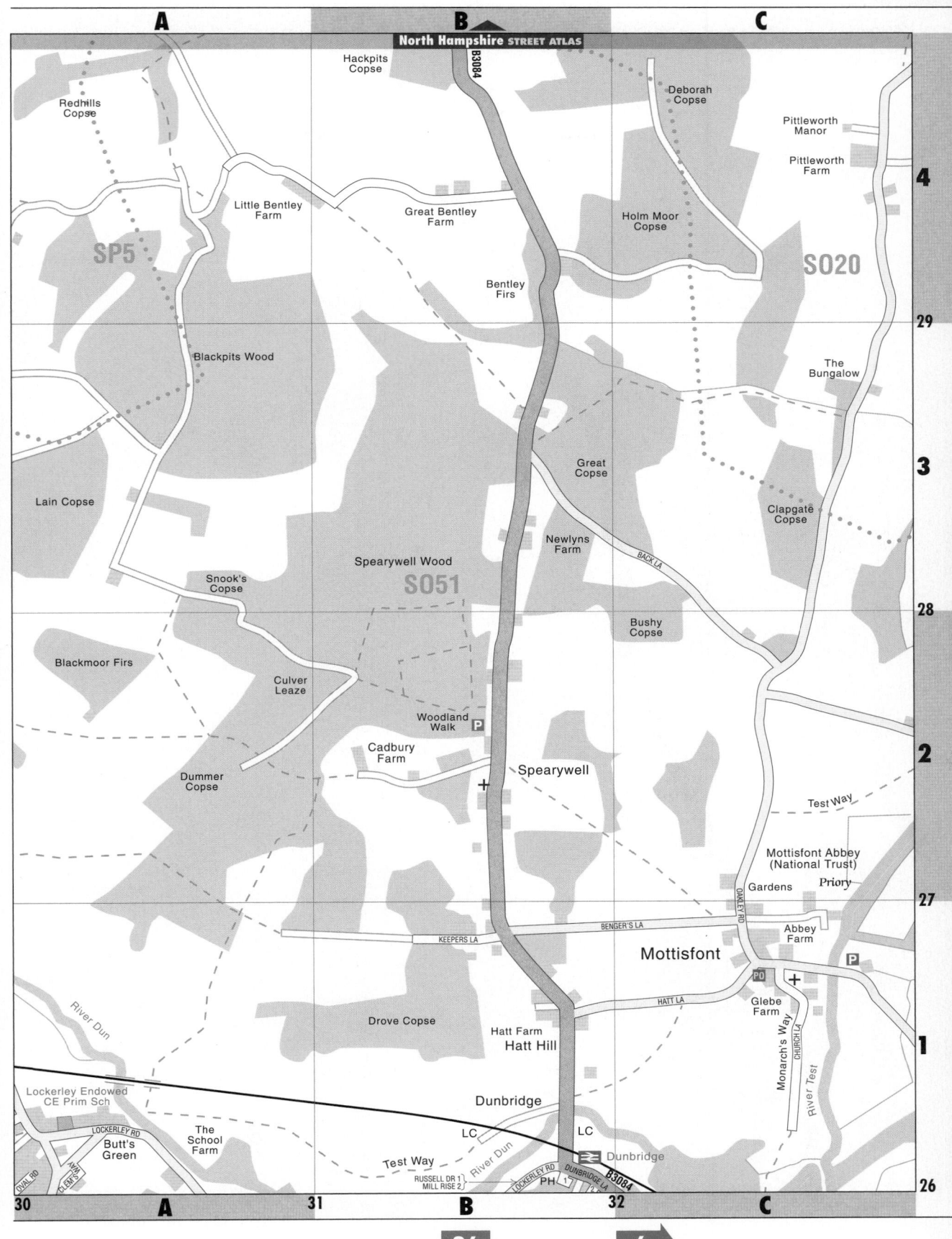

North Hampshire STREET ATLAS

Redhills Copse

Hackpits Copse

Deborah Copse

Pittleworth Manor

Pittleworth Farm

Little Bentley Farm

Great Bentley Farm

Holm Moor Copse

4

SP5

SO20

Bentley Firs

29

Blackpits Wood

The Bungalow

3

Lain Copse

Great Copse

Clapgate Copse

Snook's Copse

Spearywell Wood

SO51

Newlyns Farm

BACK LA

28

Blackmoor Firs

Bushy Copse

Culver Leaze

Woodland Walk P

Dummer Copse

Cadbury Farm

Spearywell

Test Way

2

Mottisfont Abbey (National Trust)

Gardens

Priory

OAKLEY RD

27

BENGER'S LA

Abbey Farm

KEEPERS LA

Mottisfont

P

River Dun

Drove Copse

HATT LA

PO

Glebe Farm

Monarch's Way

CHURCH LA

River Test

Hatt Farm

Hatt Hill

1

Lockerley Endowed CE Prim Sch

Dunbridge

LOCKERLEY RD

Butt's Green

The School Farm

LC

LC

Dunbridge

26

OVAL RD

Test Way

River Dun

LOCKERLEY RD

DUNBRIDGE LA

PH

B3084

RUSSELL DR 1
MILL RISE 2

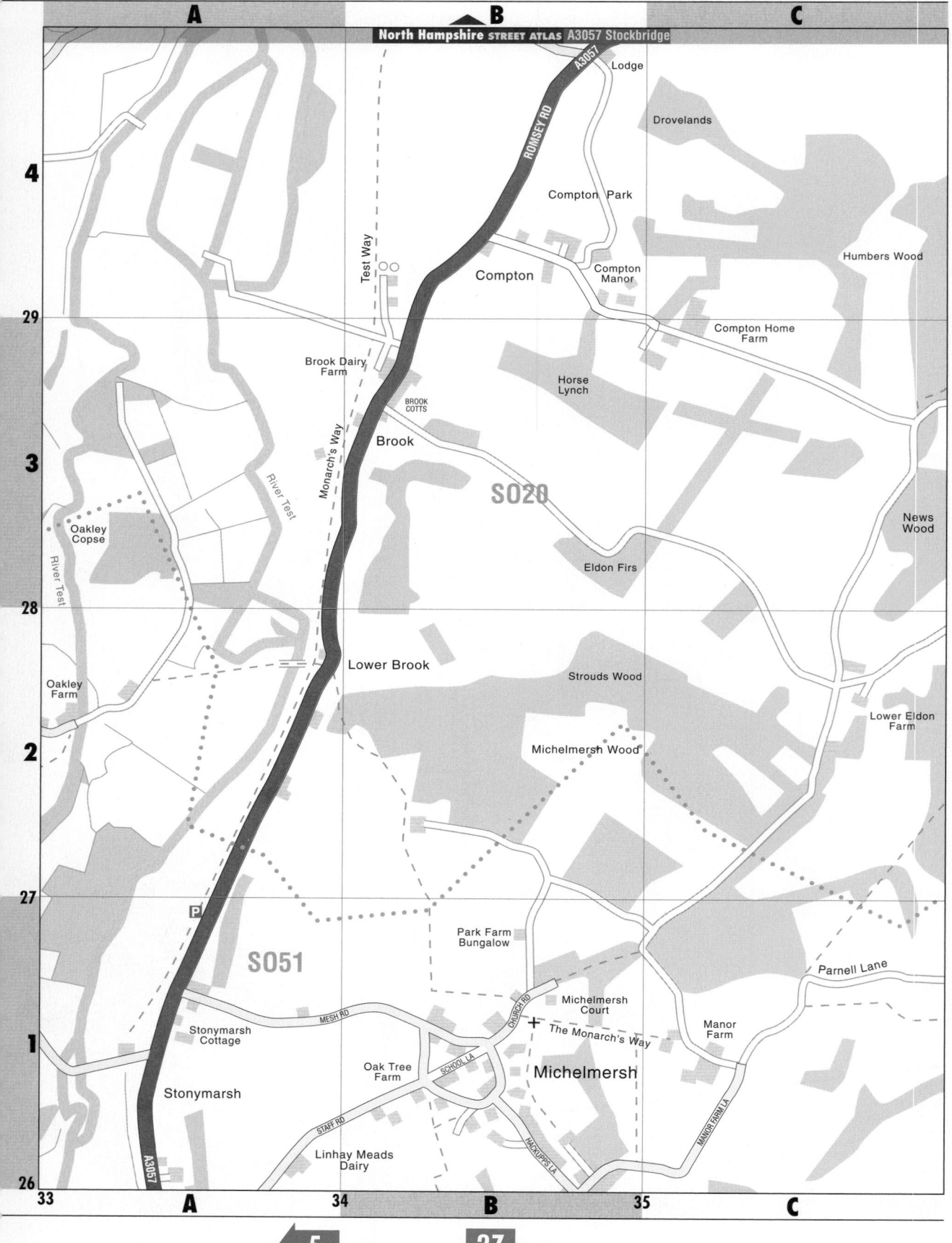

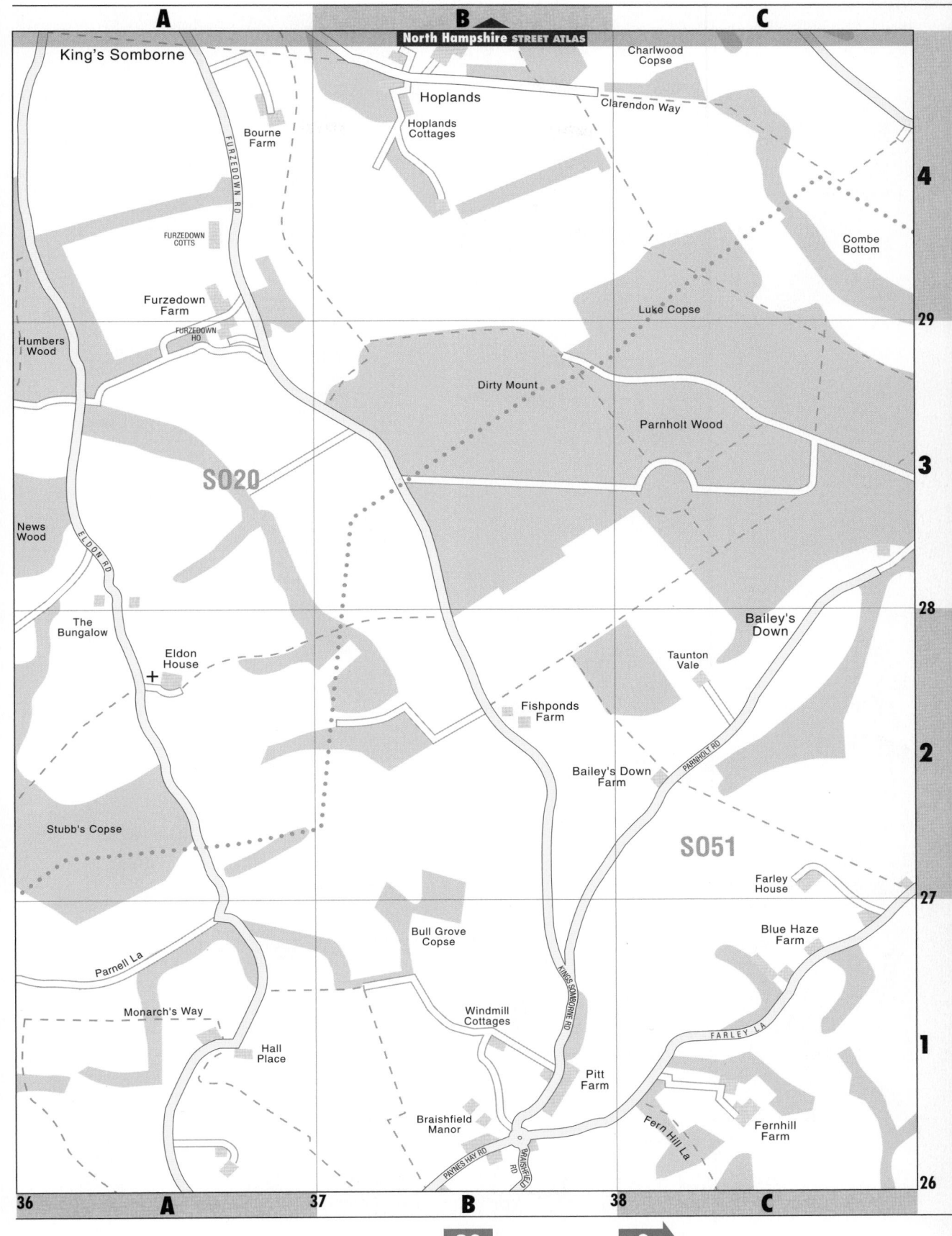

North Hampshire STREET ATLAS

King's Somborne

Hoplands

Charlwood
Copse

Clarendon Way

Bourne
Farm

Hoplands
Cottages

FURZEDOWN
COTTS

Combe
Bottom

Furzedown
Farm

Luke Copse

Humbers
Wood

FURZEDOWN
HO

Dirty Mount

Parnholt Wood

SO20

News
Wood

ELDON RD

FURZEDOWN RD

The
Bungalow

Bailey's
Down

Eldon
House

Taunton
Vale

Fishponds
Farm

Bailey's Down
Farm

PARNHOLT RD

Stubb's Copse

SO51

Farley
House

Parnell La

Bull Grove
Copse

Blue Haze
Farm

Monarch's Way

Windmill
Cottages

KINGS SOMBORNE RD

FARLEY LA

Hall
Place

Pitt
Farm

Braishfield
Manor

Fern Hill La

Fernhill
Farm

PAYNES HAY RD

BRAISHFIELD RD

North Hampshire STREET ATLAS

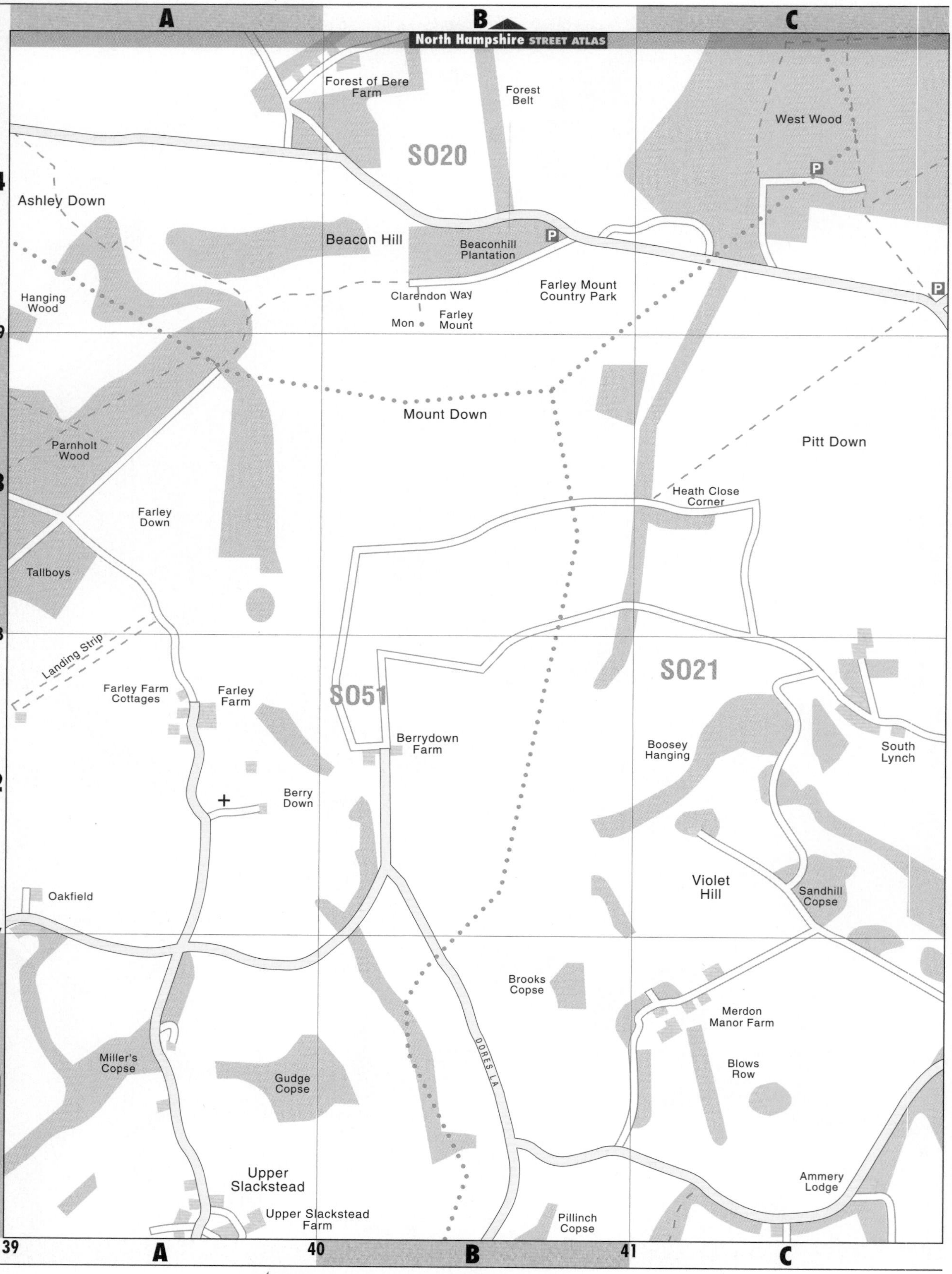

A **B** **C**

Forest of Bere
Farm

Forest
Belt

West Wood

SO20

P

4

Ashley Down

Beacon Hill

Beaconhill
Plantation

P

Farley Mount
Country Park

Hanging
Wood

Clarendon Way

P

Mon

Farley
Mount

29

Mount Down

Pitt Down

Parnholt
Wood

3

Heath Close
Corner

Farley
Down

Tallboys

28

Landing Strip

SO51

SO021

Farley Farm
Cottages

Farley
Farm

Berrydown
Farm

Boosey
Hanging

South
Lynch

2

+

Berry
Down

Oakfield

Violet
Hill

Sandhill
Copse

27

Brooks
Copse

Merdon
Manor Farm

Miller's
Copse

Gudge
Copse

DORES LA

Blows
Row

1

Ammery
Lodge

Upper
Slackstead

Upper Slackstead
Farm

Pillinch
Copse

26

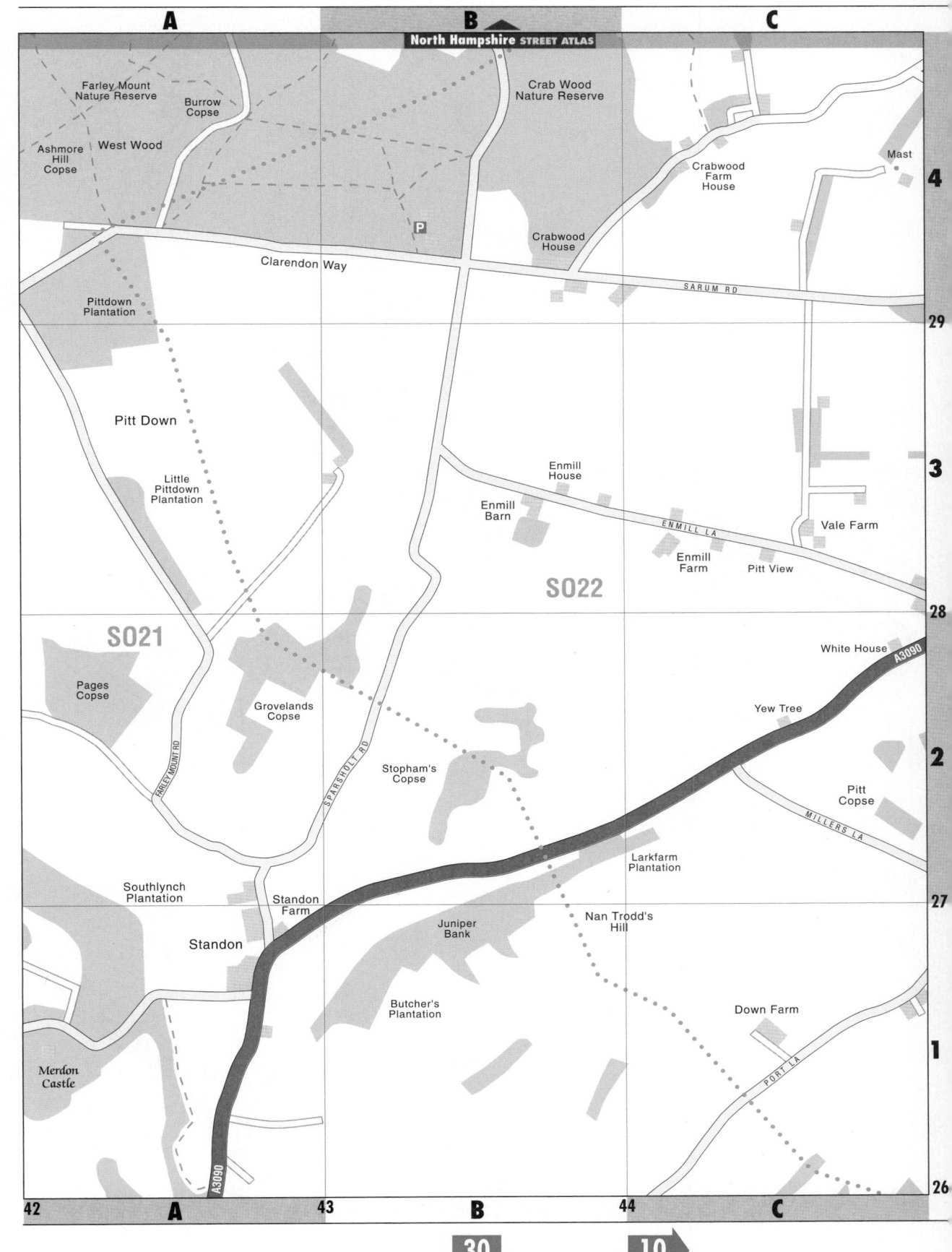

North Hampshire STREET ATLAS

A

B

C

Farley Mount
Nature Reserve

Burrow
Copse

Crab Wood
Nature Reserve

Ashmore
Hill
Copse

West Wood

Crabwood
Farm
House

Mast

4

P

Crabwood
House

Clarendon Way

SARUM RD

29

Pittdown
Plantation

Pitt Down

Enmill
House

3

Little
Pittdown
Plantation

Enmill
Barn

ENMILL LA

Vale Farm

Enmill
Farm

Pitt View

SO22

SO21

28

White House

A3090

Pages
Copse

Grovelands
Copse

Yew Tree

2

FARLEY MOUNT RD

SPARSHOLT RD

Stopham's
Copse

Pitt
Copse

MILLERS LA

Larkfarm
Plantation

Southlynch
Plantation

Standon
Farm

27

Standon

Juniper
Bank

Nan Trodd's
Hill

Down Farm

Butcher's
Plantation

PORT LA

1

Merdon
Castle

A3090

26

42

A

43

B

44

C

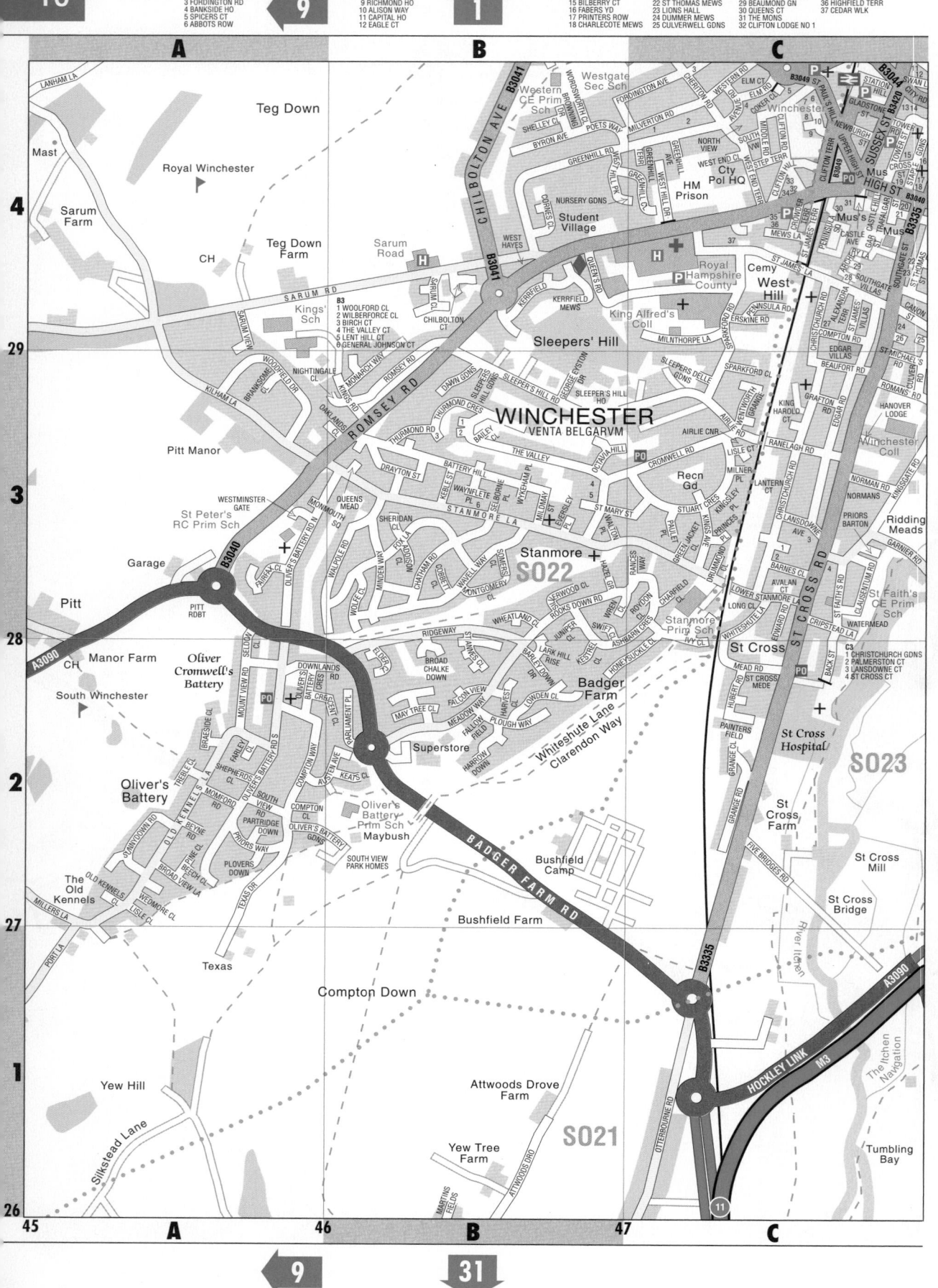

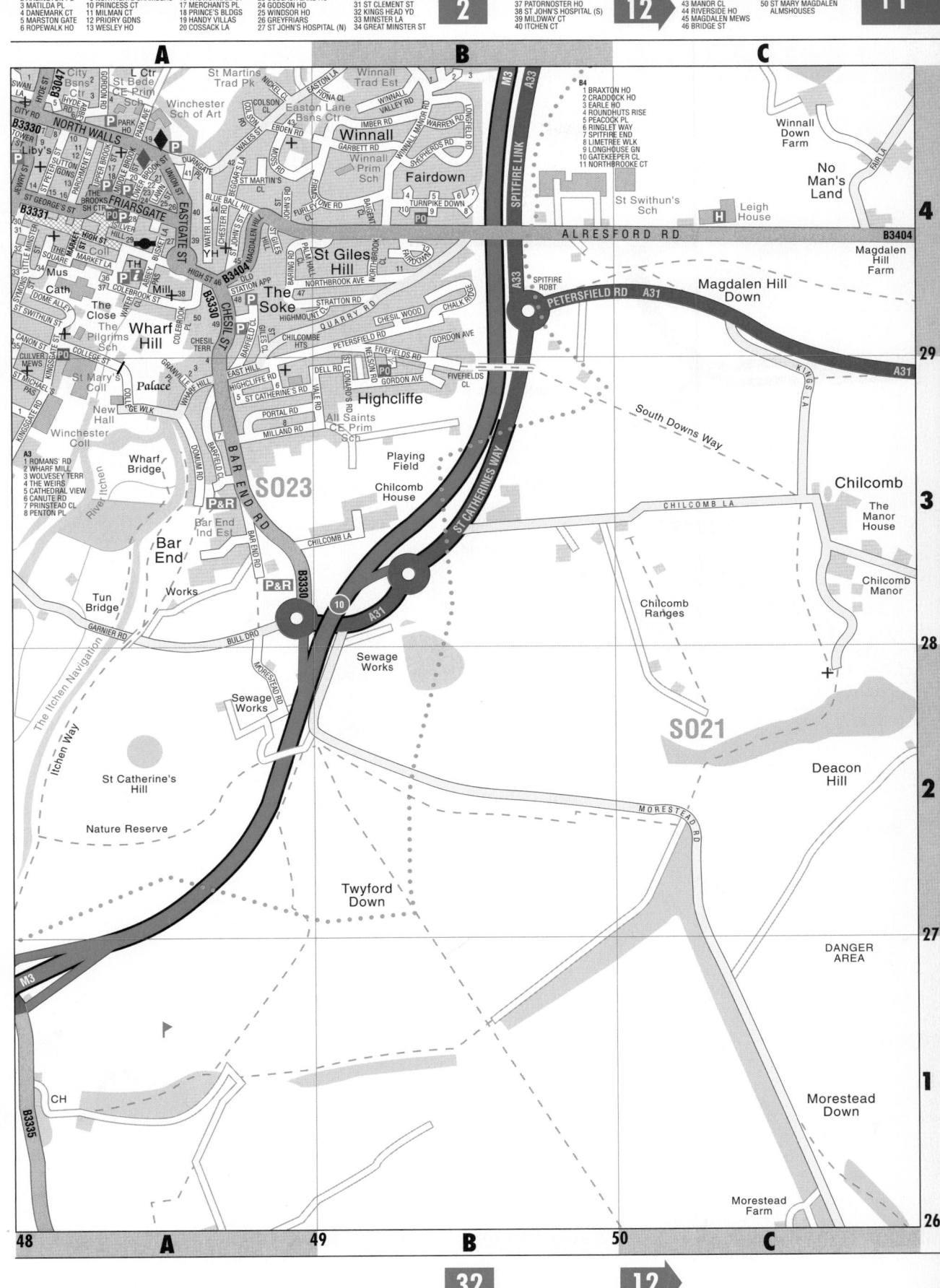

2
12
32
12

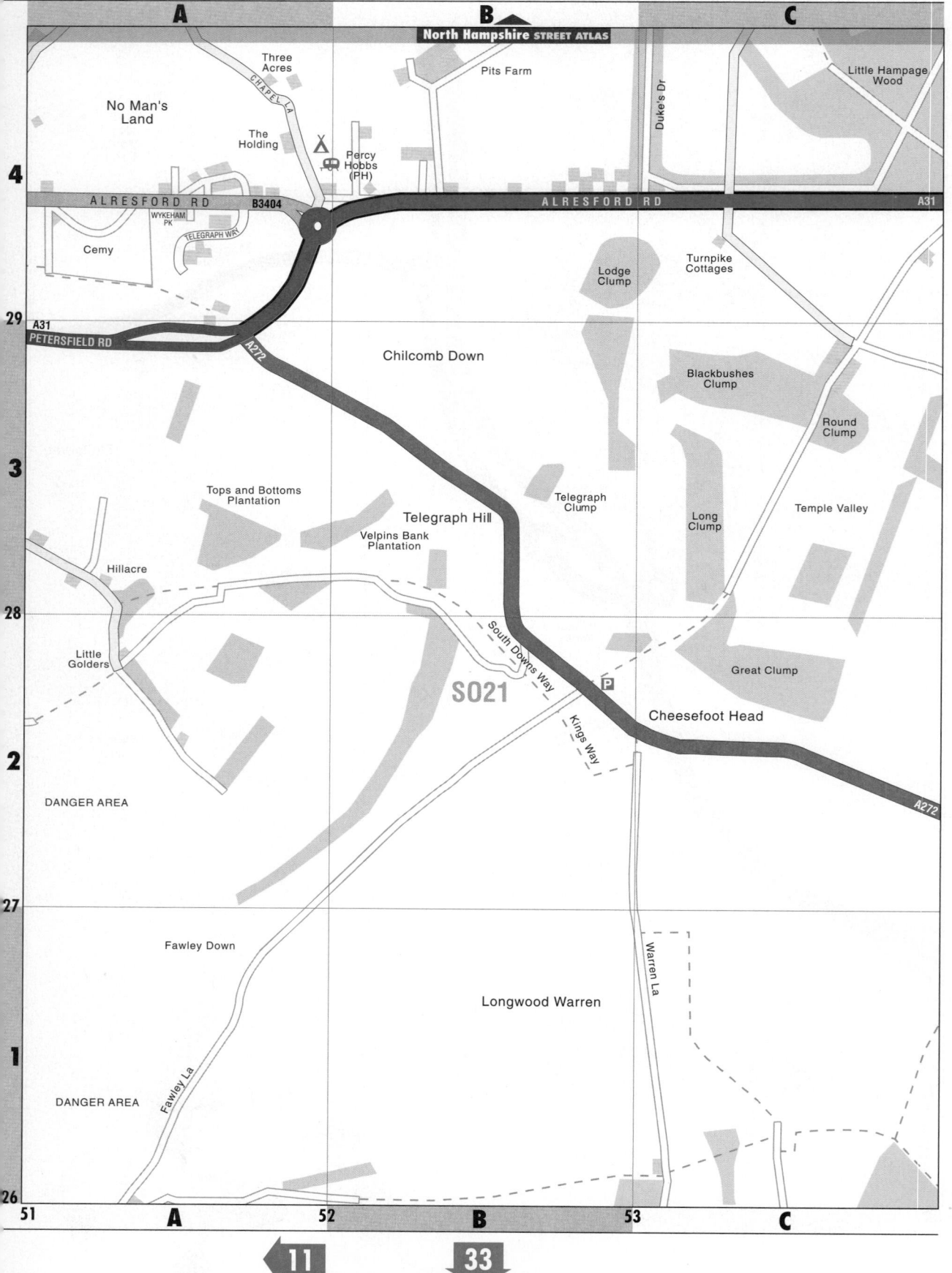

North Hampshire STREET ATLAS

A   B   C

Three Acres
Pits Farm
Little Hampage Wood

No Man's Land
CHAPEL LA
The Holding
Duke's Dr

Percy Hobbs (PH)

4

ALRESFORD RD   B3404   ALRESFORD RD   A31

WYKEHAM PK
Cemy
TELEGRAPH WAY
Lodge Clump
Turnpike Cottages

29
A31
PETERSFIELD RD
A272
Chilcomb Down
Blackbushes Clump
Round Clump

3
Tops and Bottoms Plantation
Telegraph Clump
Temple Valley
Telegraph Hill
Velpins Bank Plantation
Long Clump

Hillacre

28
Little Golders
South Downs Way
Great Clump
SO21
P
Cheesefoot Head
Kings Way

2
DANGER AREA
A272

27
Fawley Down
Warren La

Longwood Warren

1
Fawley La
DANGER AREA

26
51   A   52   B   53   C

14

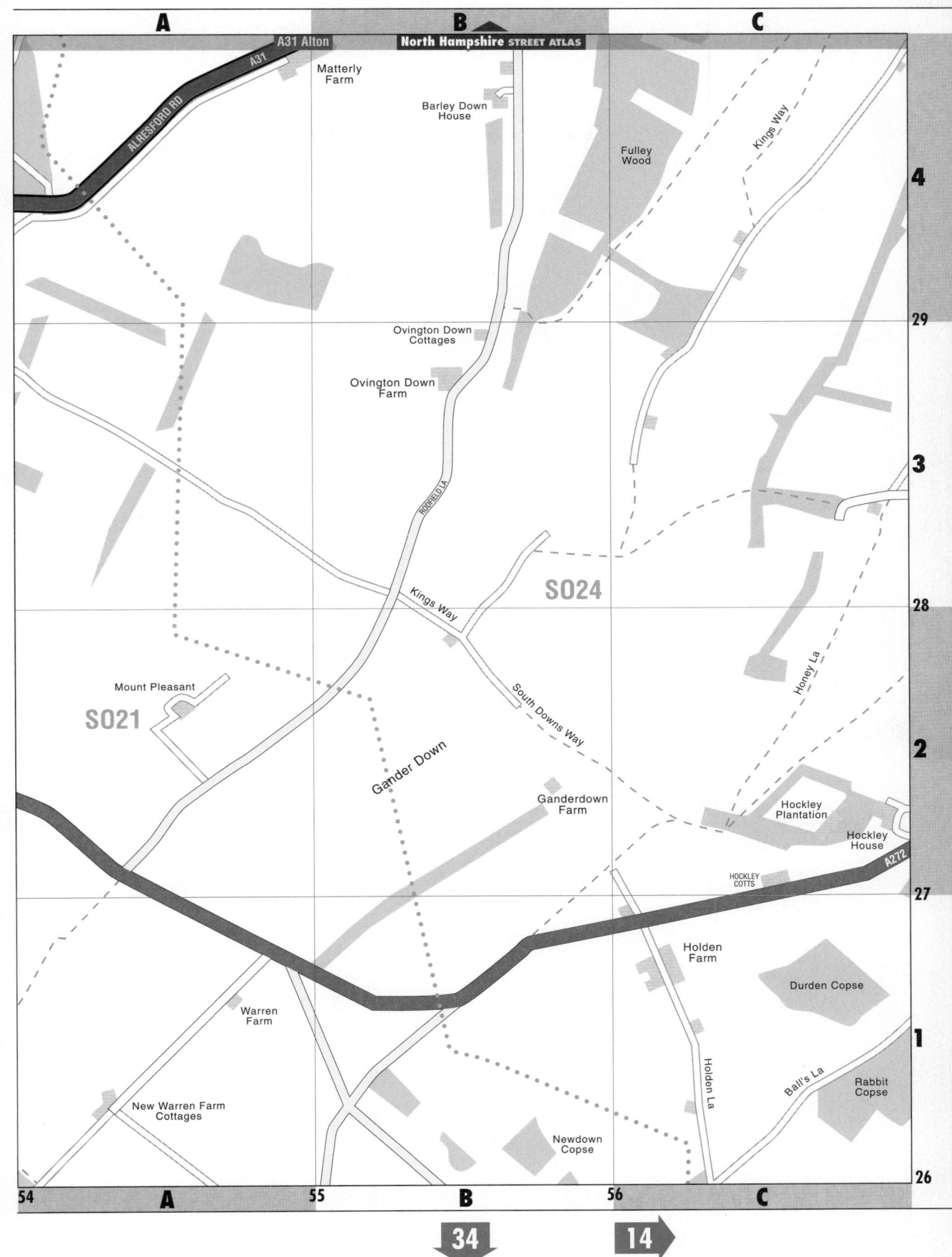

A31 Alton

A31

ALRESFORD RD

Matterly Farm

Barley Down House

Fulley Wood

Kings Way

4

Ovington Down Cottages

29

Ovington Down Farm

ROPFIELD LA

3

SO24

Kings Way

28

Mount Pleasant

South Downs Way

SO21

Gander Down

Honey La

2

Ganderdown Farm

Hockley Plantation

Hockley House

A272

HOCKLEY COTTS

27

Holden Farm

Durden Copse

Warren Farm

1

New Warren Farm Cottages

Holden La

Ball's La

Rabbit Copse

Newdown Copse

26

54   A   55   B   56   C

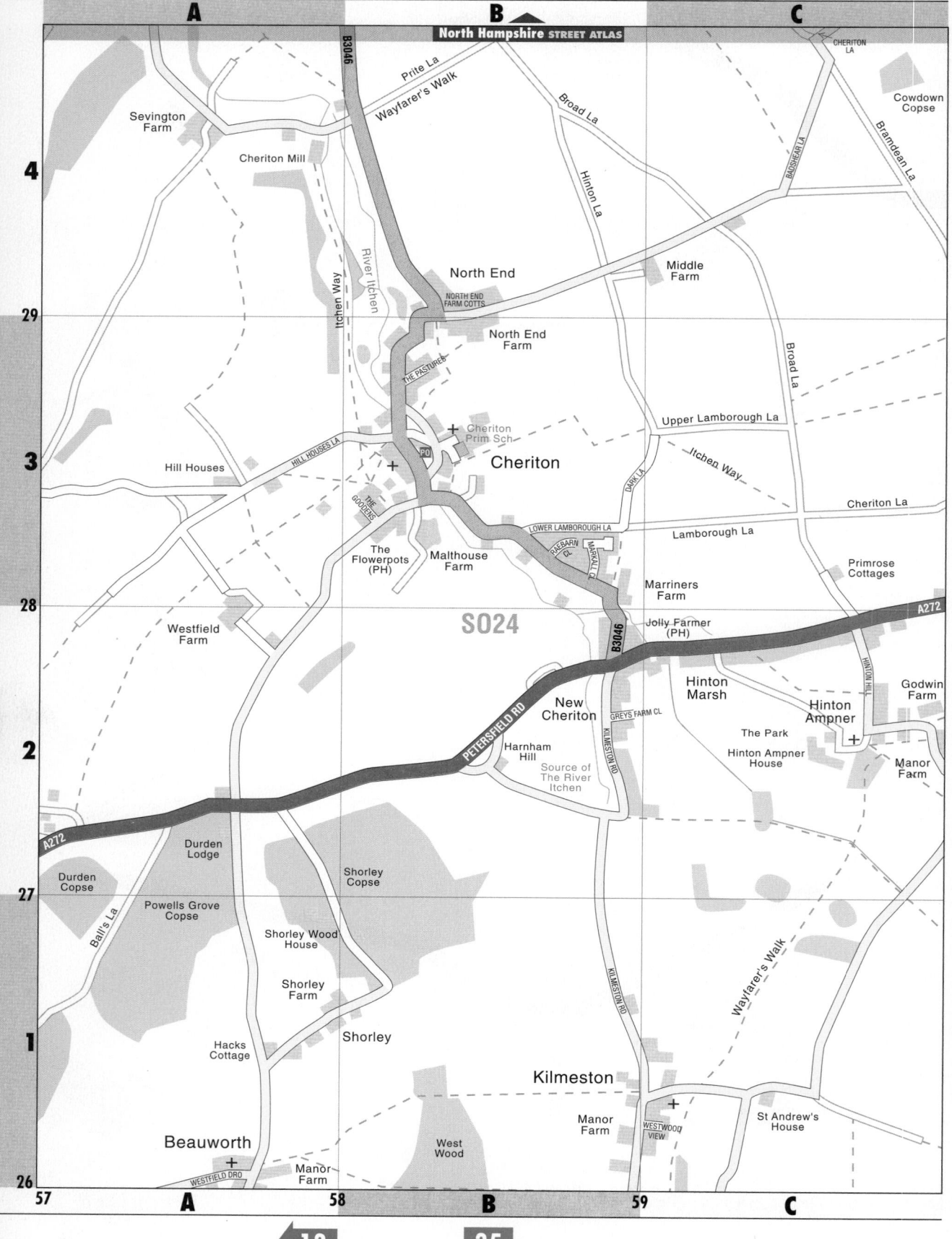

B3046

Prite La
Wayfarer's Walk

Broad La

Hinton La

Sevington
Farm

Cheriton Mill

4

River Itchen

Itchen Way

North End

NORTH END
FARM COTTS

29

North End
Farm

THE PASTURES

Cheriton
Prim Sch

PO

Hill Houses La

3

Hill Houses

THE GOODENS

Cheriton

Cheriton La

Middle
Farm

Bagshear La

Cowdown
Copse

Bramdean La

Cheriton La

Upper Lamborough La

Itchen Way

Dark La

Broad La

The Flowerpots
(PH)

Malthouse
Farm

Lower Lamborough La

Raeborn Cl

Markall Cl

Lamborough La

Marriners
Farm

Primrose
Cottages

28

Westfield
Farm

SO24

B3046

Jolly Farmer
(PH)

A272

Hinton Hill

Hinton
Marsh

Godwin
Farm

Petersfield Rd

New
Cheriton

Greys Farm Cl

Kilmeston Rd

Hinton
Ampner

The Park

Hinton Ampner
House

Manor
Farm

2

Harnham
Hill

Source of
The River
Itchen

A272

Durden
Lodge

Durden
Copse

Ball's La

Shorley
Copse

27

Powells Grove
Copse

Shorley Wood
House

Wayfarer's Walk

Shorley
Farm

1

Shorley

Hacks
Cottage

Kilmeston

Manor
Farm

Westwood
View

St Andrew's
House

Beauworth

Westfield Dro

Manor
Farm

West
Wood

26

57 A 58 B 59 C

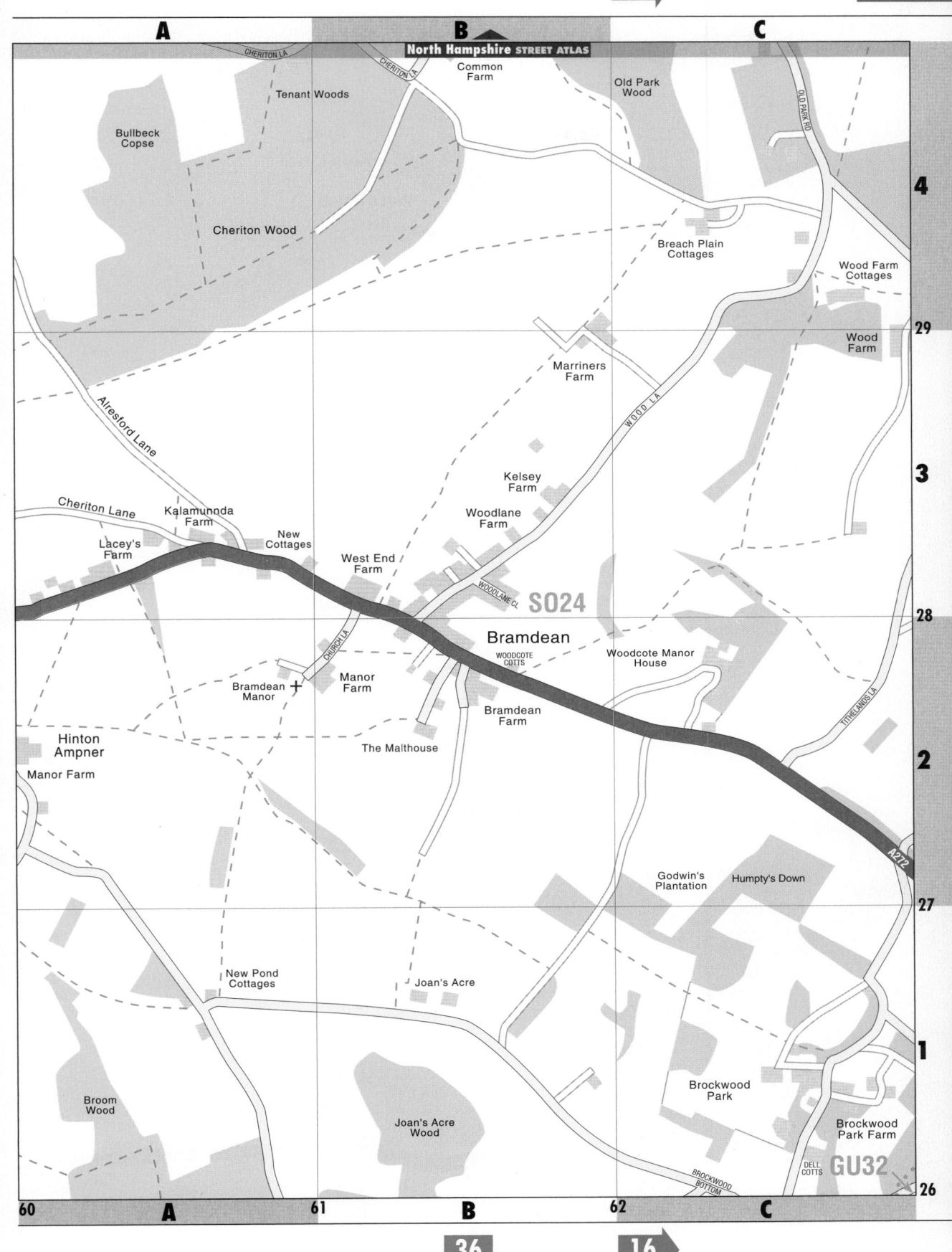

North Hampshire STREET ATLAS

A B C

4

CHERITON LA

Common Farm

Tenant Woods

Old Park Wood

OLD PARK RD

Bullbeck Copse

Cheriton Wood

Breach Plain Cottages

Wood Farm Cottages

29

Marriners Farm

Wood Farm

WOOD LA

Alresford Lane

3

Cheriton Lane

Kalamunnda Farm

Kelsey Farm

Woodlane Farm

Lacey's Farm

New Cottages

West End Farm

WOODLANE CL

SO24

28

Bramdean

Manor Farm

WOODCOTE COTTS

Woodcote Manor House

CHURCH LA

Bramdean Manor

Bramdean Farm

TITHELANDS LA

Hinton Ampner

The Malthouse

2

Manor Farm

Godwin's Plantation

Humpty's Down

27

A272

New Pond Cottages

Joan's Acre

1

Broom Wood

Brockwood Park

Joan's Acre Wood

Brockwood Park Farm

BROCKWOOD BOTTOM

DELL COTTS

GU32

26

60 A 61 B 62 C

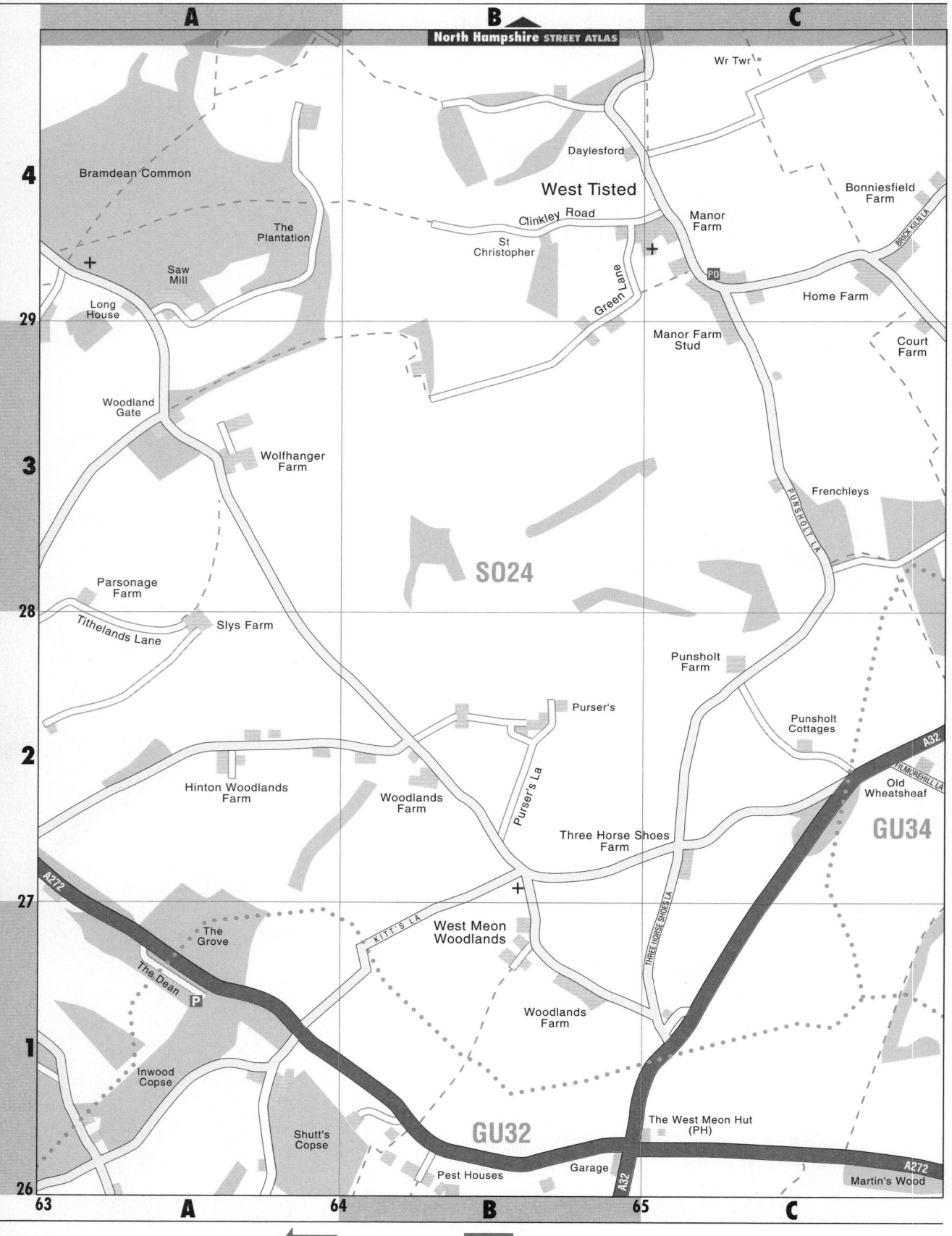

North Hampshire STREET ATLAS

A

B

C

Wr Twr

Daylesford

Bonniesfield
Farm

West Tisted

4

Bramdean Common

The
Plantation

Clinkley Road

Manor
Farm

St
Christopher

Home Farm

Saw
Mill

PO

Long
House

Manor Farm
Stud

Court
Farm

29

Woodland
Gate

BRICK KILN LA

GREEN LANE

Wolfhanger
Farm

Frenchleys

3

PUNSHOLT LA

SO24

Parsonage
Farm

28

Tithelands Lane

Slys Farm

Punsholt
Farm

Purser's

Punsholt
Cottages

Hinton Woodlands
Farm

Woodlands
Farm

Purser's La

Three Horse Shoes
Farm

A32

Old
Wheatsheaf

FILMOREHILL LA

2

GU34

A272

27

The Grove

KITT'S LA

West Meon
Woodlands

THREE HORSE SHOES LA

The Dean

P

1

Woodlands
Farm

Inwood
Copse

Shutt's
Copse

GU32

The West Meon Hut
(PH)

Garage

A32

A272

Pest Houses

Martin's Wood

26

63

A

64

B

65

C

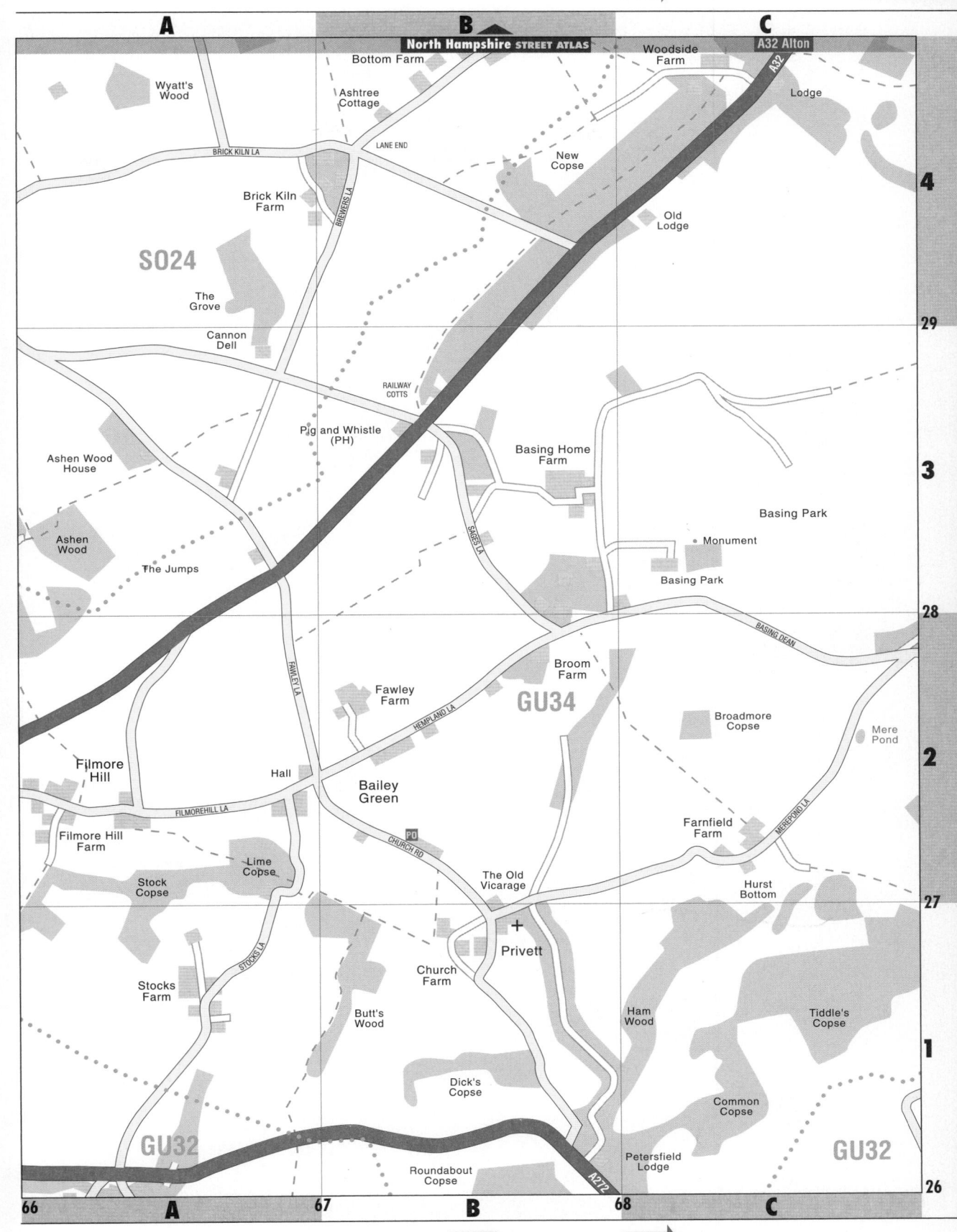

Woodside Farm

A32 Alton

Bottom Farm

Ashtree Cottage

Lodge

LANE END

New Copse

BRICK KILN LA

4

Brick Kiln Farm

BREWERS LA

Old Lodge

SO24

The Grove

29

Cannon Dell

RAILWAY COTTS

Pig and Whistle (PH)

Basing Home Farm

3

Ashen Wood House

SAGES LA

Basing Park

Monument

Ashen Wood

Basing Park

The Jumps

28

BASING DEAN

FAWLEY LA

Broom Farm

Fawley Farm

GU34

Broadmore Copse

HEMPLAND LA

Mere Pond

2

Filmore Hill

Hall

Bailey Green

Farnfield Farm

MEREPOND LA

Filmore Hill Farm

FILMOREHILL LA

PO

CHURCH RD

Hurst Bottom

Lime Copse

The Old Vicarage

27

Stock Copse

STOCKS LA

✝
Privett

Stocks Farm

Church Farm

Ham Wood

Tiddle's Copse

Butt's Wood

1

Dick's Copse

Common Copse

GU32

A272

Petersfield Lodge

GU32

Roundabout Copse

26

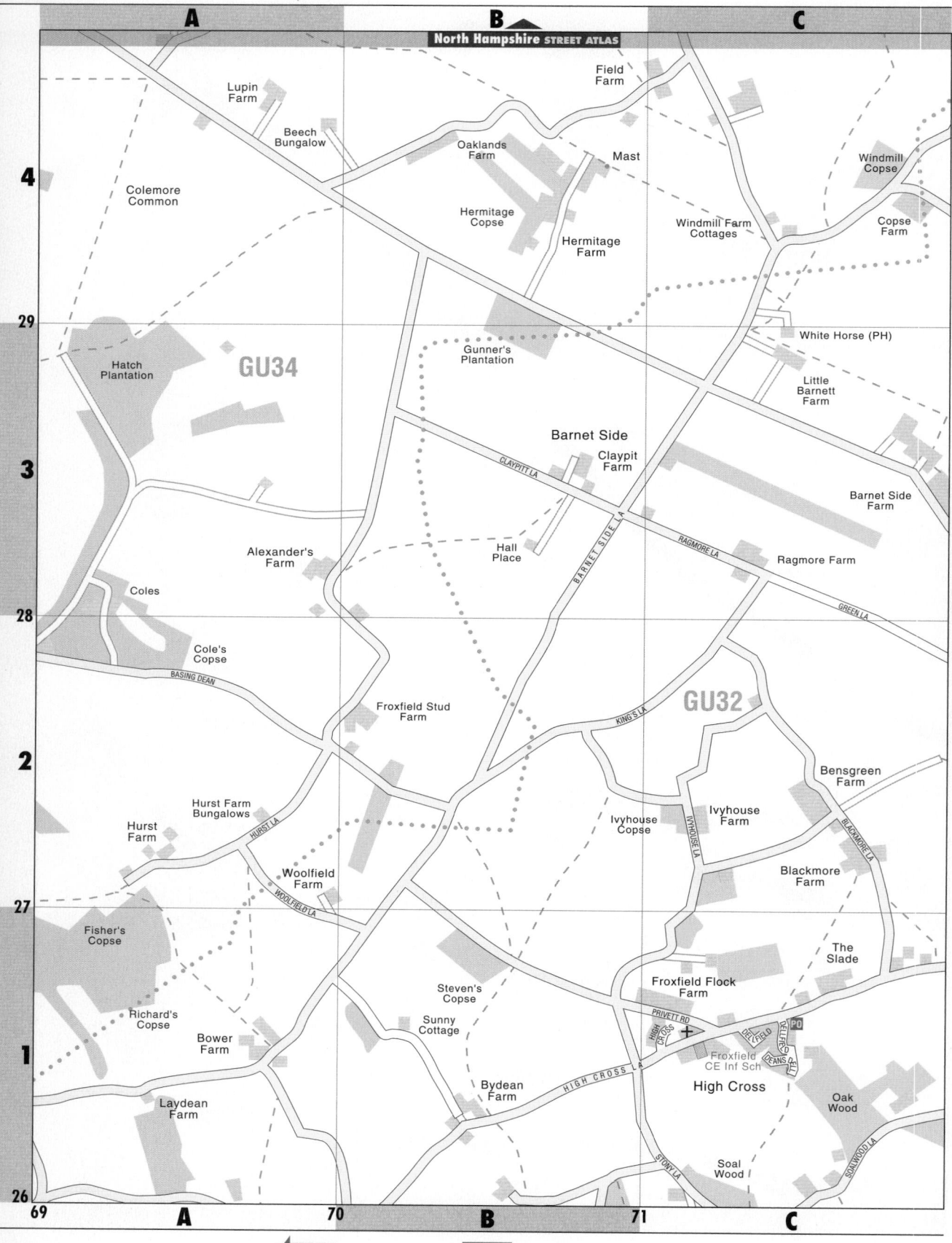

North Hampshire STREET ATLAS

A   **B**   **C**

Field Farm

Lupin Farm

Beech Bungalow

Oaklands Farm

Mast

Windmill Copse

4

Colemore Common

Hermitage Copse

Windmill Farm Cottages

Copse Farm

Hermitage Farm

29

White Horse (PH)

Hatch Plantation

GU34

Gunner's Plantation

Little Barnett Farm

Barnet Side

Claypit Farm

3

CLAYPITT LA

Barnet Side Farm

RAGMORE LA

Alexander's Farm

Hall Place

BARNET SIDE LA

Ragmore Farm

Coles

GREEN LA

28

Cole's Copse

BASING DEAN

KING'S LA

GU32

Froxfield Stud Farm

2

Bensgreen Farm

Hurst Farm Bungalows

Ivyhouse Farm

Hurst Farm

HURST LA

Ivyhouse Copse

IVYHOUSE LA

BLACKMORE LA

Blackmore Farm

Woolfield Farm

WOOLFIELD LA

27

The Slade

Fisher's Copse

Froxfield Flock Farm

Steven's Copse

PRIVETT RD

PO

Richard's Copse

Sunny Cottage

HIGH CROSS

DELFIELD

DELFIELD

ILEANS

Bower Farm

Froxfield CE Inf Sch

Oak Wood

1

Bydean Farm

HIGH CROSS LA

High Cross

Laydean Farm

STONY LA

Soal Wood

SOALWOOD LA

26

69   **A**   70   **B**   71   **C**

17   39

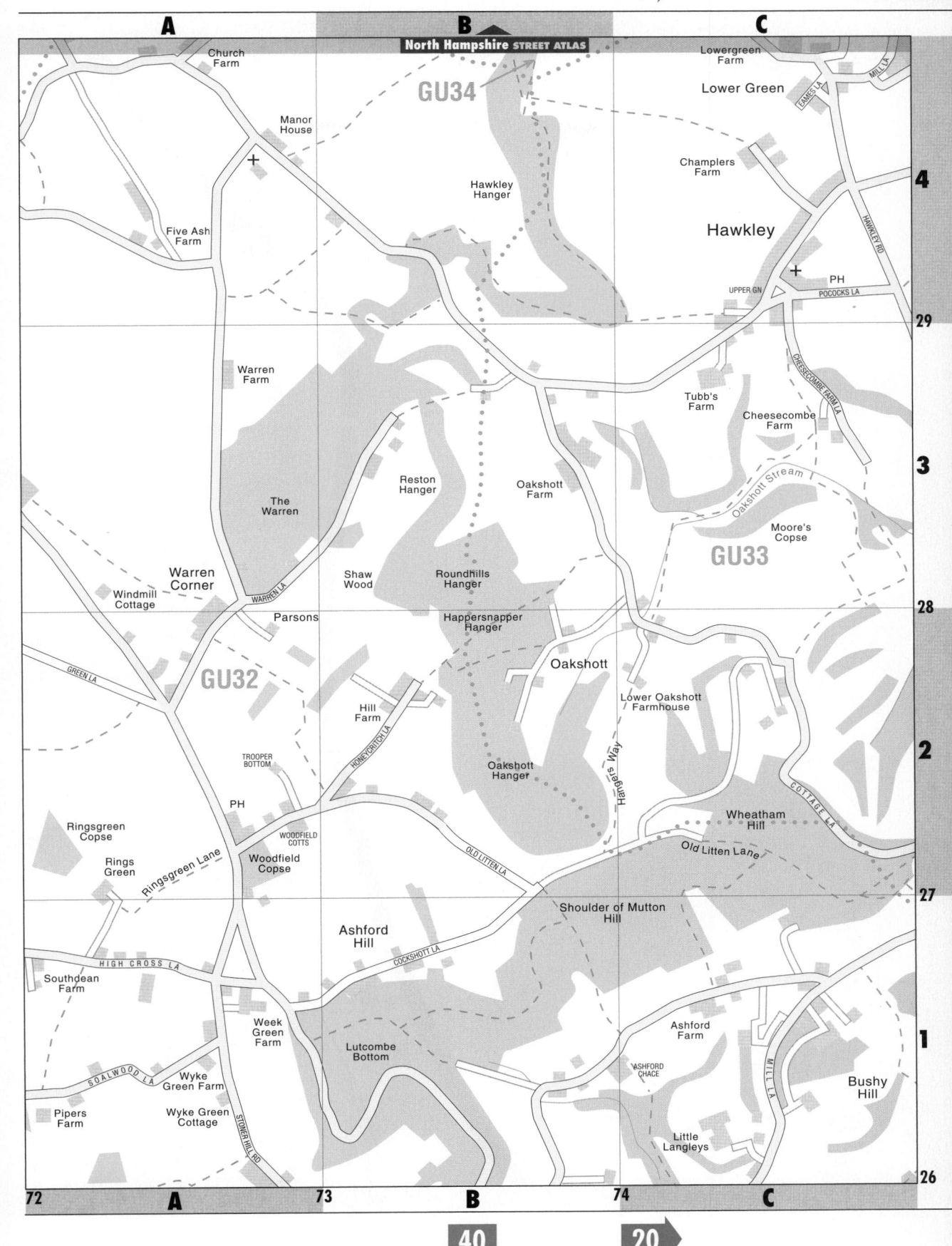

North Hampshire STREET ATLAS

A

Church Farm
Manor House
Five Ash Farm

GU34

Hawkley Hanger

Lowergreen Farm
Lower Green

Champlers Farm

Hawkley

UPPER GN
PH
POCOCKS LA

Warren Farm

Tubb's Farm
Cheesecombe Farm

The Warren

Reston Hanger
Oakshott Farm

Oakshott Stream

Moore's Copse

GU33

Warren Corner
Windmill Cottage

Shaw Wood
Roundhills Hanger

WARREN LA

Parsons

Happersnapper Hanger

Oakshott

GREEN LA

GU32

Hill Farm

Lower Oakshott Farmhouse

HONEYCRITCH LA

TROOPER BOTTOM

PH

Oakshott Hanger

Hangers Way

Wheatham Hill

COTTAGE LA

Ringsgreen Copse

WOODFIELD COTTS

OLD LITTEN LA

Old Litten Lane

Rings Green

Ringsgreen Lane

Woodfield Copse

Shoulder of Mutton Hill

HIGH CROSS LA

Southdean Farm

Ashford Hill

COCKSHOTT LA

Week Green Farm

Ashford Farm

Lutcombe Bottom

ASHFORD CHACE

MILL LA

SOALWOOD LA

Wyke Green Farm

Pipers Farm

Wyke Green Cottage

STONER HILL RD

Little Langleys

Bushy Hill

A   **B**   **C**

4
29
3
28
2
27
1
26

19

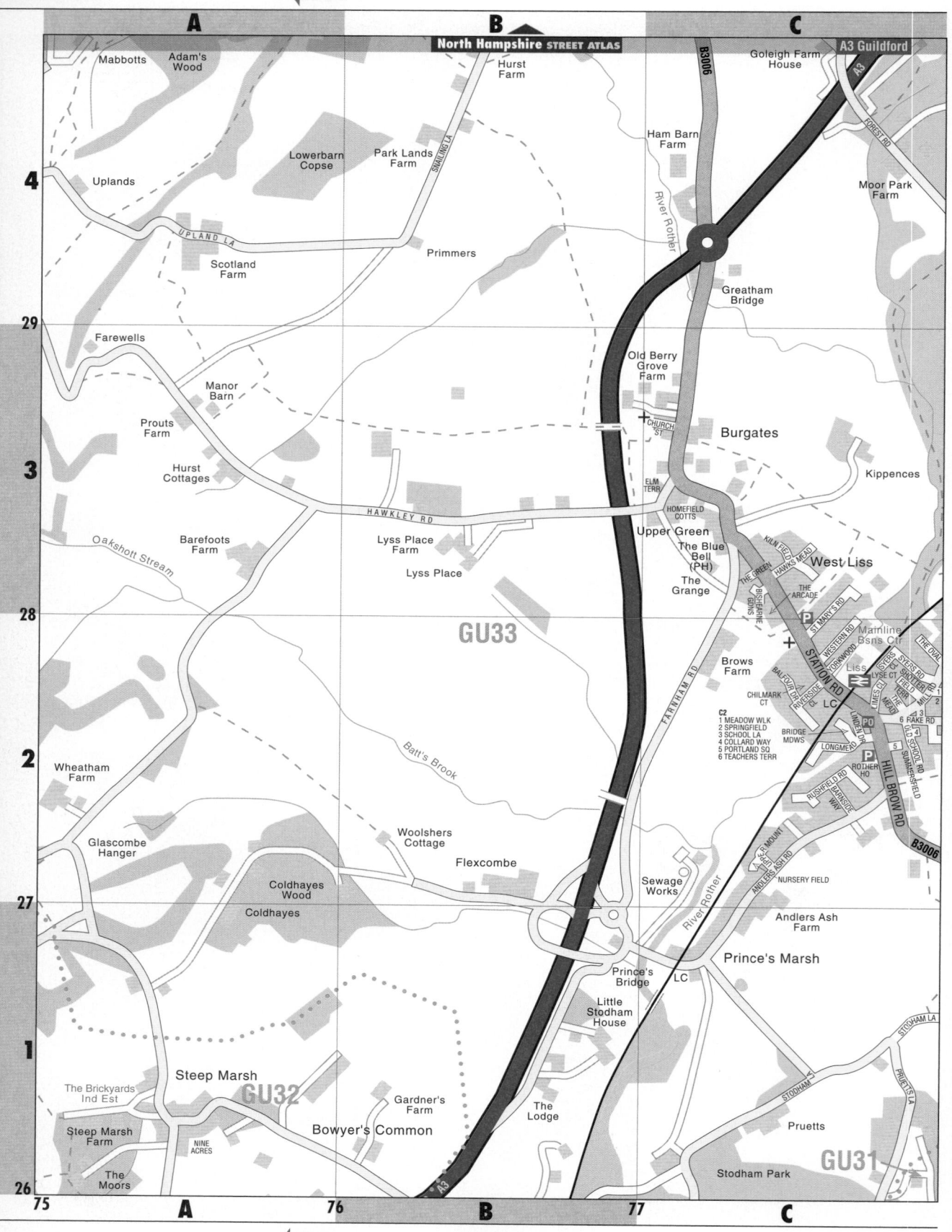

North Hampshire STREET ATLAS

A

Mabbotts
Adam's Wood
Uplands
UPLAND LA
Scotland Farm
Farewells
Manor Barn
Prouts Farm
Hurst Cottages
Barefoots Farm
Oakshott Stream
Wheatham Farm
Glascombe Hanger
Coldhayes Wood
Coldhayes

The Brickyards Ind Est
GU32
Steep Marsh
Steep Marsh Farm
NINE ACRES
The Moors

B

Hurst Farm
Lowerbarn Copse
Park Lands Farm
SHALLING LA
Primmers
HAWKLEY RD
Lyss Place Farm
Lyss Place
GU33
Batt's Brook
Woolshers Cottage
Flexcombe
Gardner's Farm
Bowyer's Common
The Lodge

River Rother
B3006
Ham Barn Farm
Greatham Bridge
Old Berry Grove Farm
CHURCH ST
ELM TERR
HOMEFIELD COTTS
Upper Green
The Blue Bell (PH)
The Grange
Brows Farm
CHILMARK CT
FARNHAM RD
BRIDGE MDWS
Sewage Works
River Rother
Prince's Bridge
Little Stodham House

C

A3 Guildford
Goleigh Farm House
A3
FOREST RD
Moor Park Farm
Burgates
Kippences
THE GREEN
BISCHARNE GDNS
KILN FIELD
HAWKS MEAD
West Liss
THE ARCADE
ST MARY'S RD
WESTERN RD
CORNWOOD
RIVERSIDE
BALFOUR DR
STATION RD
Mainline Bsns Ctr
THE OVAL
SISTERS RD
STROTTER RD
LYSE CT
RAKE RD
MILL LA
Liss
LC
C2
1 MEADOW WLK
2 SPRINGFIELD
3 SCHOOL LA
4 COLLARD WAY
5 PORTLAND SQ
6 TEACHERS TERR
LONGMEAD
RUSHFIELD RD
ROTHER HO
LINDEN RD
PO
PARKSIDE WAY
F MOUNT
ANDLERS ASH RD
NURSERY FIELD
HILL BROW RD
SUMMERSFIELD
B3006
Andlers Ash Farm
Prince's Marsh
LC
Stodham Park
Pruetts
STODHAM LA
PRUETTS LA
GU31

Wheatham Farm

4
29
3
28
2
27
1
26

75
76
77

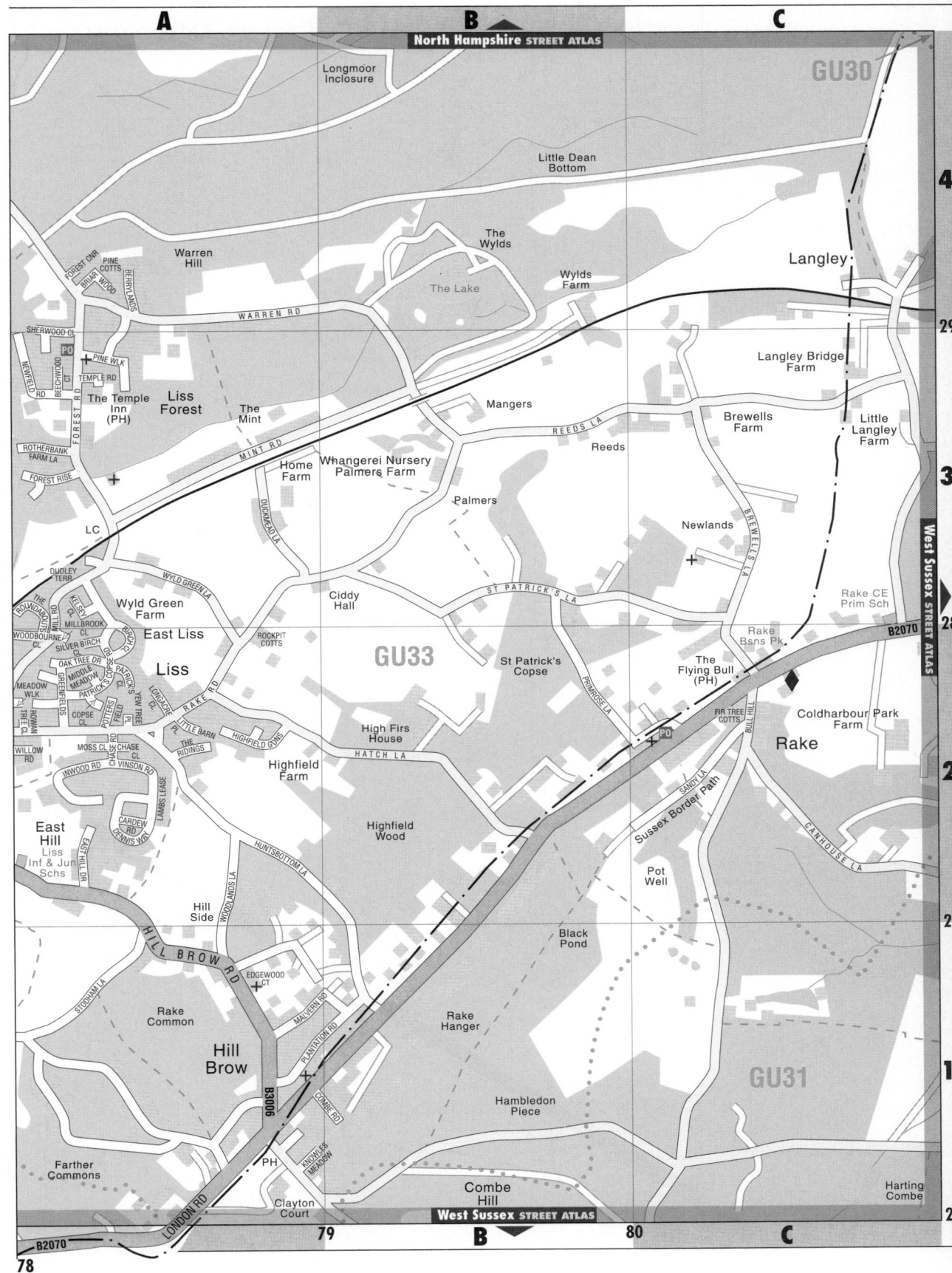

GU30

A   B   C

4

Longmoor
Inclosure

Little Dean
Bottom

The Wylds

Langley

29

Warren
Hill

The Lake

Wylds
Farm

Langley Bridge
Farm

FOREST CNR
PINE COTTS
BRIAR
WOOD
BERRYLANDS

WARREN RD

SHERWOOD CL
PO
NEWFIELD RD
BEECHWOOD CT
PINE WLK
TEMPLE RD

The Temple
Inn
(PH)

Liss
Forest

The Mint

Mangers

REEDS LA

Reeds

Brewells
Farm

Little
Langley
Farm

ROTHERBANK
FARM LA

FOREST RISE

MINT RD

Home
Farm

Whangerei Nursery
Palmers Farm

Palmers

Newlands

BREWELLS LA

3

LC

DUCKMEAD LA

West Sussex STREET ATLAS

DUDLEY
TERR

ROUNDABOUTS
THE OLD THE
KELSEY
MILLBROOK
SILVER BIRCH CL
WOODBOURNE CL

WYLD GREEN LA

Wyld Green
Farm

East Liss

Liss

ROCKPIT
COTTS

Ciddy
Hall

ST PATRICK'S LA

St Patrick's
Copse

Rake CE
Prim Sch

Rake
Bsns Pk.

B2070

28

OAK TREE DR
GREENFIELDS
MEADOW
WLK
ROWAN
MEADOW
TREE CL
PATRICK'S
YEW TREE CL
COPSE CL
POTTERS
PL
LONGACRE
RAKE RD
LITTLE BARN

GU33

The
Flying Bull
(PH)

Rake

WILLOW
RD
MOSS CL
CHASE CL
VINSON RD
INWOOD RD
CHASE RD
THE
RIDINGS
HIGHFIELD GDNS

High Firs
House

PRIMROSE LA

PO

Coldharbour Park
Farm

2

CARDEW
RD
DENNIS WAY
LAMBS LEASE

Highfield
Farm

HATCH LA

FIR TREE
COTTS

BULL HILL

SANDY LA

East
Hill
Liss
Inf & Jun
Schs

EAST HILDR
EAST HILL DR

Highfield
Wood

Sussex Border Path

Pot
Well

2?

Hill
Side

HILL BROW RD

STODHAM LA

EDGEWOOD
CT

WOODLANDS LA

HUNTSBOTTOM LA

Black
Pond

CANHOUSE LA

GU31

Rake
Common

MALVERN RD

Rake
Hanger

1

Hill
Brow

B3006

PLANTATION RD

COMBE RD

Hambledon
Piece

Farther
Commons

PH

KNOWLES
MEADOW

Clayton
Court

LONDON RD

Combe
Hill

Harting
Combe

2?

B2070

78   79   B   80   C

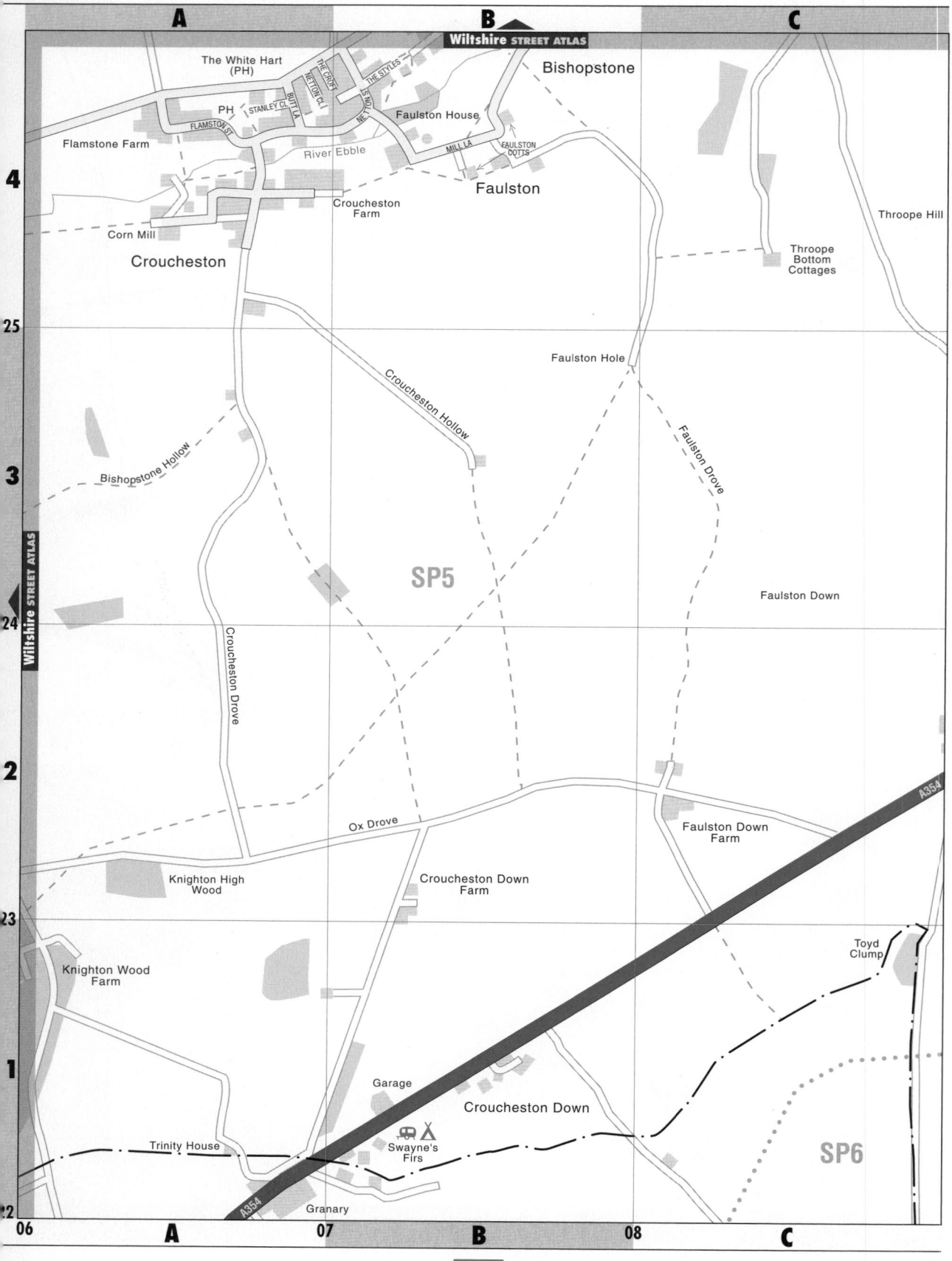

Bishopstone

The White Hart (PH)

THE CROFT

NETTON CL

THE STYLES

Faulston House

PH

STANLEY CL

BUTT LA

NETTON CL

Flamstone Farm

FLAMSTONE ST

River Ebble

MILL LA

FAULSTON COTTS

Faulston

Corn Mill

Croucheston Farm

Throope Hill

Croucheston

4

Throope Bottom Cottages

25

Faulston Hole

Croucheston Hollow

Faulston Drove

Bishopstone Hollow

3

SP5

Faulston Down

Croucheston Drove

24

2

A354

Ox Drove

Faulston Down Farm

Knighton High Wood

Croucheston Down Farm

23

Toyd Clump

Knighton Wood Farm

1

Garage

Croucheston Down

SP6

Trinity House

Swayne's Firs

A354

Granary

Wiltshire STREET ATLAS

06   A   07   B   08   C

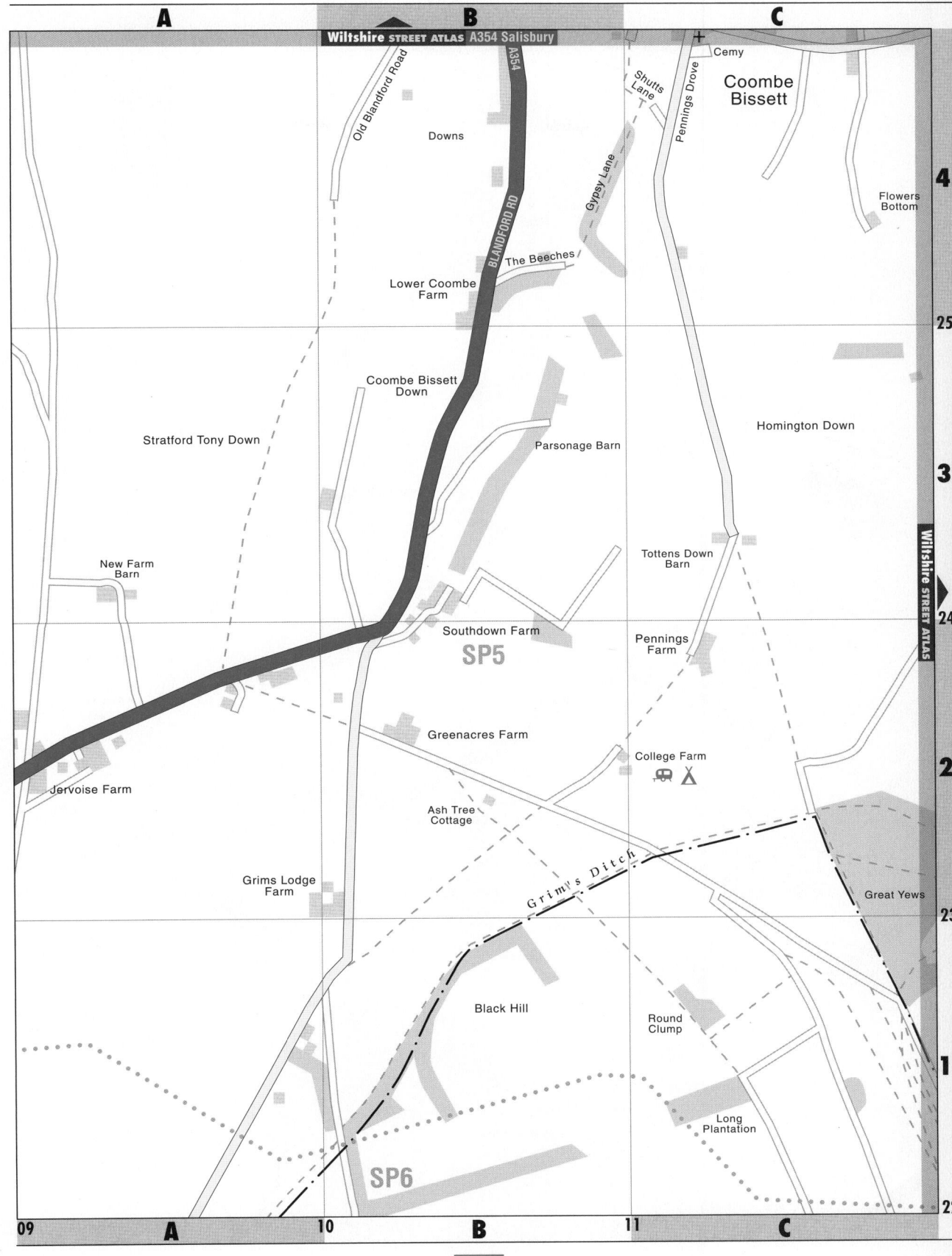

Coombe Bissett

Old Blandford Road

Downs

Shutts Lane

Pennings Drove

Cemy

Gypsy Lane

BLANDFORD RD

A354

The Beeches

Lower Coombe Farm

Flowers Bottom

Coombe Bissett Down

Stratford Tony Down

Parsonage Barn

Homington Down

New Farm Barn

Tottens Down Barn

Southdown Farm

SP5

Pennings Farm

Greenacres Farm

College Farm

Jervoise Farm

Ash Tree Cottage

Grims Lodge Farm

Grim's Ditch

Great Yews

Black Hill

Round Clump

Long Plantation

SP6

4

25

3

24

2

23

1

09 · A · 10 · B · 11 · C ·

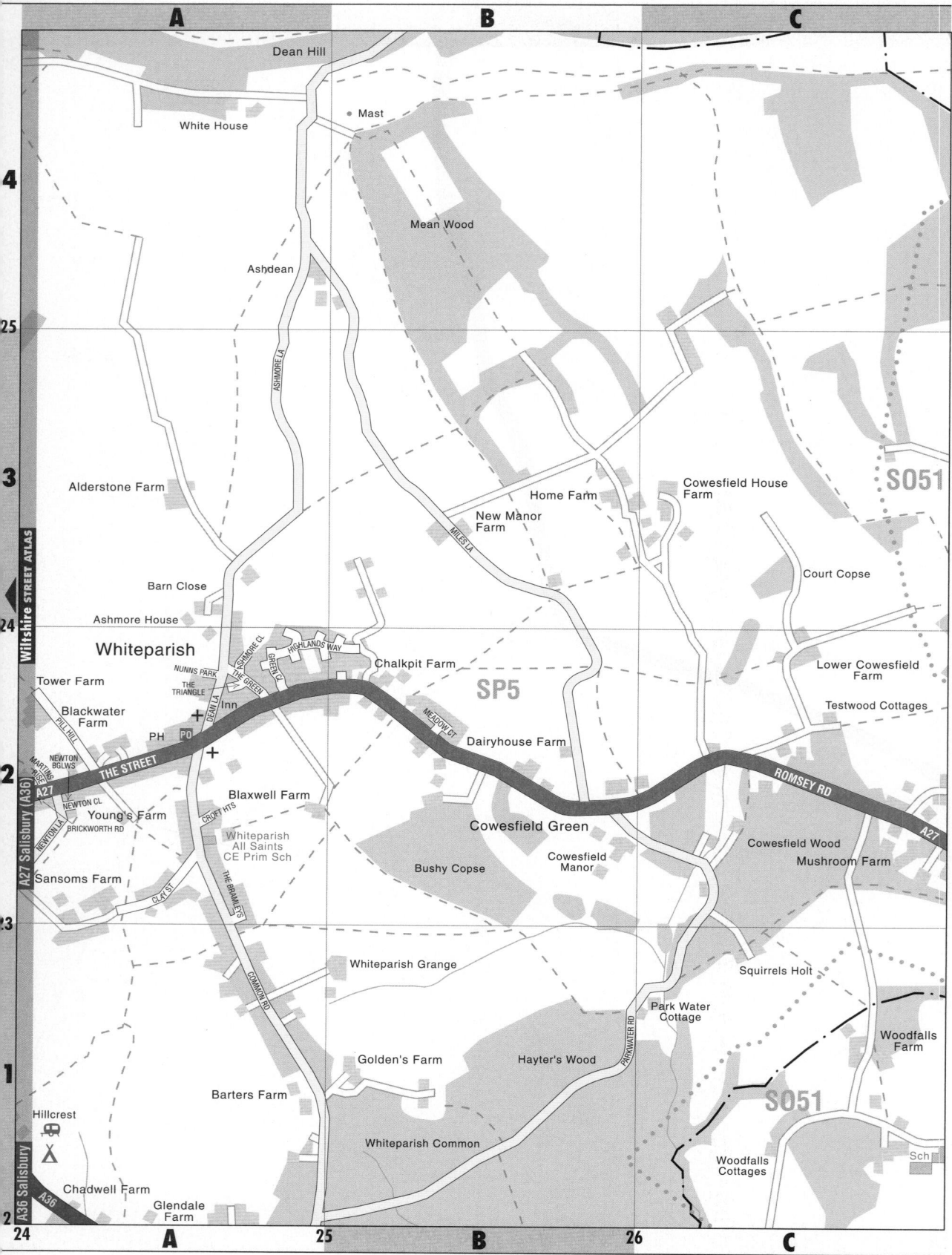

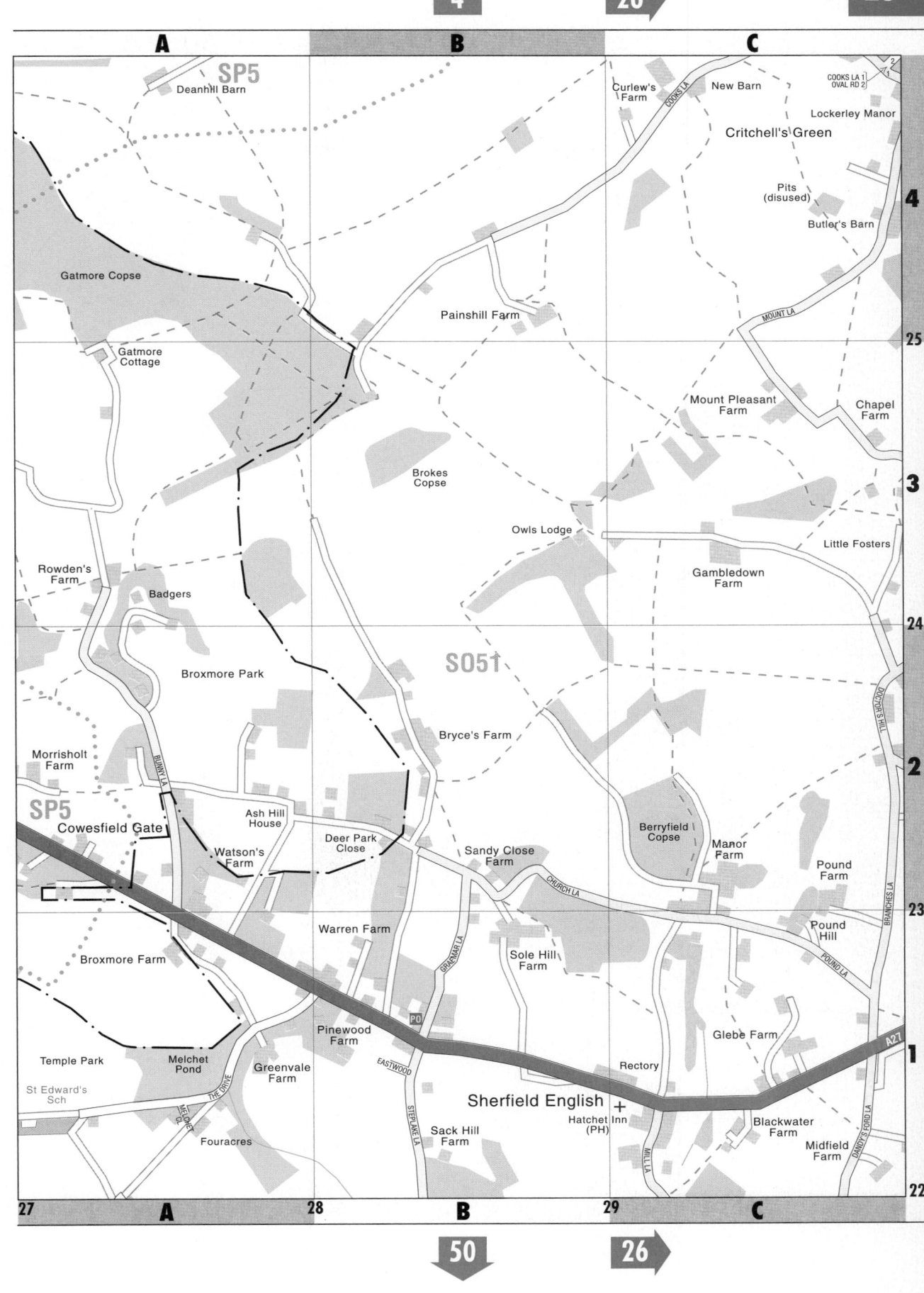

SP5
Deanhill Barn

Gatmore Copse

Gatmore Cottage

Curlew's Farm
COOKS LA
New Barn
COOKS LA 1
OVAL RD 2
Lockerley Manor
Critchell's Green

Pits (disused)
Butler's Barn

Painshill Farm
MOUNT LA

Mount Pleasant Farm
Chapel Farm

Brokes Copse

Owls Lodge

Gambledown Farm
Little Fosters

Rowden's Farm
Badgers

Broxmore Park

SO51

Bryce's Farm

Morrisholt Farm
BUNNY LA

Ash Hill House
Deer Park Close
Sandy Close Farm
Berryfield Copse
Manor Farm
Pound Farm

DUCK'S... HILL

SP5
Cowesfield Gate
Watson's Farm
Warren Farm
GRAMMAR LA
Sole Hill Farm
CHURCH LA
Pound Hill
POUND LA
BRANCHES LA

Broxmore Farm
PO
Glebe Farm
A27

Temple Park
Melchet Pond
THE DRIVE
MELCHET CL
Greenvale Farm
EASTWOOD
Pinewood Farm
Rectory
Sherfield English
Hatchet Inn (PH)
MILL LA
Blackwater Farm
DANDY'S FORD LA

St Edward's Sch
Fouracres
STEPLAKE LA
Sack Hill Farm
Midfield Farm

4
25
3
24
2
23
1

A   B   C

PH
COOKS LA
MOUNT LA

River Dun

LOCKERLEY RD

Canefield

Dunbridge Hill

B3084

Dunbridge Copse

River Dun

School Farm

Barley Hill Wood

Kimbridge Farm

4

Canefield Copse

Mount Copse

Monarch's Way

LC

KIMBRIDGE LA

Mount Farm

DUNBRIDGE LA

Kimbridge

25

Mount Farm

Hatchers Farm

Carter's Clay

John's Hill Copse

Kents Oak Farm

SAUNDERS LA

3

CHAPEL LA

THE BANKS

New Farm

Hyde Farm

Awbridge Farm

Tote Hill

CARTER'S CLAY RD

COUNCIL HOS

Butler's Wood Farm

THE BEECHES

COWLEAS CL

COWLEAS DOTTS

Yew Tree Farm

SO51

Kent's Oak

Awbridge Prim Sch

24

DOCTOR'S HILL

Hazelwood Farm

Wood Farm

Hansard Poultry Farm

B3084

THE SQUARE

PH

Awbridge

Horseshoe Farm

Doctor's Hill

Newtown

Upper Ratley

2

NEWTOWN RD

CHURCH LA

🚐 🏕

Doctor's Hill Farm

DOCTOR'S HILL

Lower Ratley

COOMBE LA

Danes Farm

Awbridge Danes

Awbridge Danes Lake

Test Way

23

CH

Dunwood Manor

Dunwood Fruit Farm

Baldwin's Copse

Croylands

A27

Birchwood House Farm

The Frenches

OLD SALISBURY LA

Dellens Farm

1

FRENCHES LA

Frenchwood Farm

Dunwood Hill

The Frenches Farm

Stanbridge-Ranvilles Farm

Lower Frenchwood Farm

Lower Shootash Farm

Shootash

Winacres Farm

TANNERS LA

A27

22

30   A   31   B   32   C

A   B   C

Meadow Farm

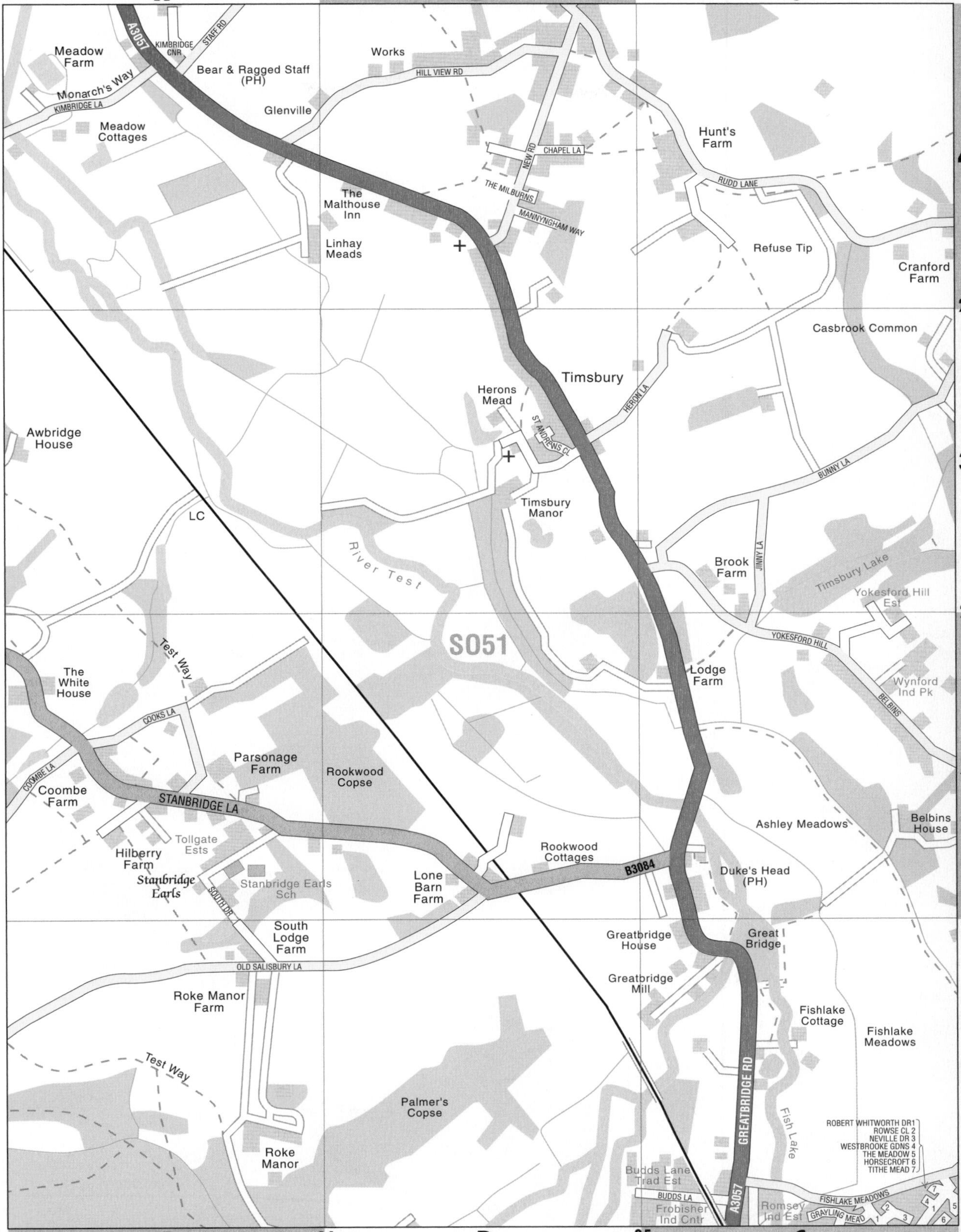

A3057

KIMBRIDGE CNR

STAFF RD

Monarch's Way

KIMBRIDGE LA

Bear & Ragged Staff (PH)

Glenville

Meadow Cottages

The Malthouse Inn

Linhay Meads

Works

HILL VIEW RD

NEW RD

CHAPEL LA

THE MILBURNS

MANNYNGHAM WAY

Hunt's Farm

RUDD LANE

Refuse Tip

Cranford Farm

4

25

Awbridge House

LC

River Test

Herons Mead

ST ANDREWS CL

Timsbury

Timsbury Manor

HERON LA

Casbrook Common

BUNNY LA

JIMMY LA

Brook Farm

3

Timsbury Lake

Yokesford Hill Est

24

SO51

YOKESFORD HILL

Lodge Farm

BELBINS

Wynford Ind Pk

Test Way

COOKS LA

The White House

COOMBE LA

Coombe Farm

Parsonage Farm

STANBRIDGE LA

Rookwood Copse

Hilberry Farm

Tollgate Ests

Stanbridge Earls

SOUTH DR

Stanbridge Earls Sch

South Lodge Farm

OLD SALISBURY LA

Roke Manor Farm

Test Way

Roke Manor

Palmer's Copse

Lone Barn Farm

Rookwood Cottages

B3084

Greatbridge House

Greatbridge Mill

GREATBRIDGE RD

Ashley Meadows

Belbins House

Duke's Head (PH)

Great Bridge

Fishlake Cottage

Fishlake Meadows

Fish Lake

Budds Lane Trad Est

BUDDS LA

Frobisher Ind Cntr

A3057

Romsey Ind Est

FISHLAKE MEADOWS

GRAYLING MEAD

ROBERT WHITWORTH DR 1
ROWSE CL 2
NEVILLE DR 3
WESTBROOKE GDNS 4
THE MEADOW 5
HORSECROFT 6
TITHE MEAD 7

2

23

1

22

A   **B**   **C**

Malthouse Farm

Paynes Hay Farm

Merrie Meade Farm

Fern Hill Lane

ELDON RD

PAYNES HAY RD

Monarch's Way

WHITE LADIES

4

Sharpes Farm

Braishfield

CHURCH LA

Hawkes Farm

Churchers Barn

LOWER ST

DUMMER RD

Monarch's Way

DORES LA

Pucknall

BUNNY LA

25

NEWPORT LA

The Newport Inn (PH)

CHAPEL CL

HILL VIEW RD

P

PO

COMMON HILL RD

Braishfield Prim Sch

Pucknall Farm

Fairbourne Lake

KILN LA

The Wheatsheaf Inn (PH)

3

Round Copse

Fairbournes Farm

The Homestead

S051

Dog & Crook (PH)

MEGANA WAY

24

Abbotswood Farm

BRAISHFIELD RD

Crookhill Farm

Sir Harold Hillier Gardens & Arboretum

The Bog

Jermyns House

Outwood Lodge

BELBINS

2

SANDY LA

Belbins Bsns Pk

P

Cemy

JERMYNS LA

Bracken Wood

A3090

Nursery

23

Abbotswood

Abbotswood House

WOODLEY CLOSE FLATS

WOODLEY CL

Ganger Farm

South Holmes Copse

CUPERNHAM LA

Oxlease

Cupernham

ROMSEY

GANGER FARM WAY

GANGER RD

FOOTNER CL

ANDERSON CL

NORRIS CL

Woodley

Woodlands

THE STRAIGHT MILE

1

THE MEADOW

BROOK WAY

WOODLEY LA

CAVENDISH CL

STAPLEFORD CL

WARREN GDNS

ANSTEY RD

HORSESHOE DR

OAKWOOD CL

ABBOTS WOOD CL

SHORT HILL

NORTH RD

SOUTH RD

HUNTERS CRES

THE GREEN

DIBBEN WLK

PEEL CL

Ganger Wood

Crampmoor Farm

GRIDLEY WAY

KINVER CL

RICHMOND CL

BRANSLEY CL

PINEWOOD CL

BEVERLEY GDNS

CEDAR LAWN

THE COPSE

1 GRANGE MEWS
2 COWSLIP WAY
3 HALTERWORTH LA
4 ST SWITHUN'S CL

CRAMPMOOR LA

Crampmoor

FISHLAKE MDWS

OXLEASE

FIELD

CANAL RD

SMITH'S FIELD

DURBAN CL

CUPERNHAM CL

Cupernham Schs

P

ADDISON CL

WAVERLEY RD

LINCOLN CL

WINTERBOURNE RD

WESTERING

WINCHESTER HILL

A3090 WINCHESTER RD

COLTSFOOT WLK

BRAISHFIELD

CONFREY CL

CAMPION DR

BRAMBLE

GREEN LA

FAIRVIEW DR

FAIRVIEW CL

BRIAR WAY

PRIMROSE WAY

SORREL CL

CLOVER WAY

CARISBROOKE

RALPH LA

22

36   **A**   **37**   **B**   **38**   **C**

A1
1 RIMINGTON GDNS
2 HALDEN CL
3 SELBORNE CT
4 TAVISTOCK CL
5 WINCHESTER CT
6 SUTHERLAND CL
7 HOGARTH CL
8 WOODLANDS GDNS
9 SAVERNAKE CL

10 CLARENDON CL

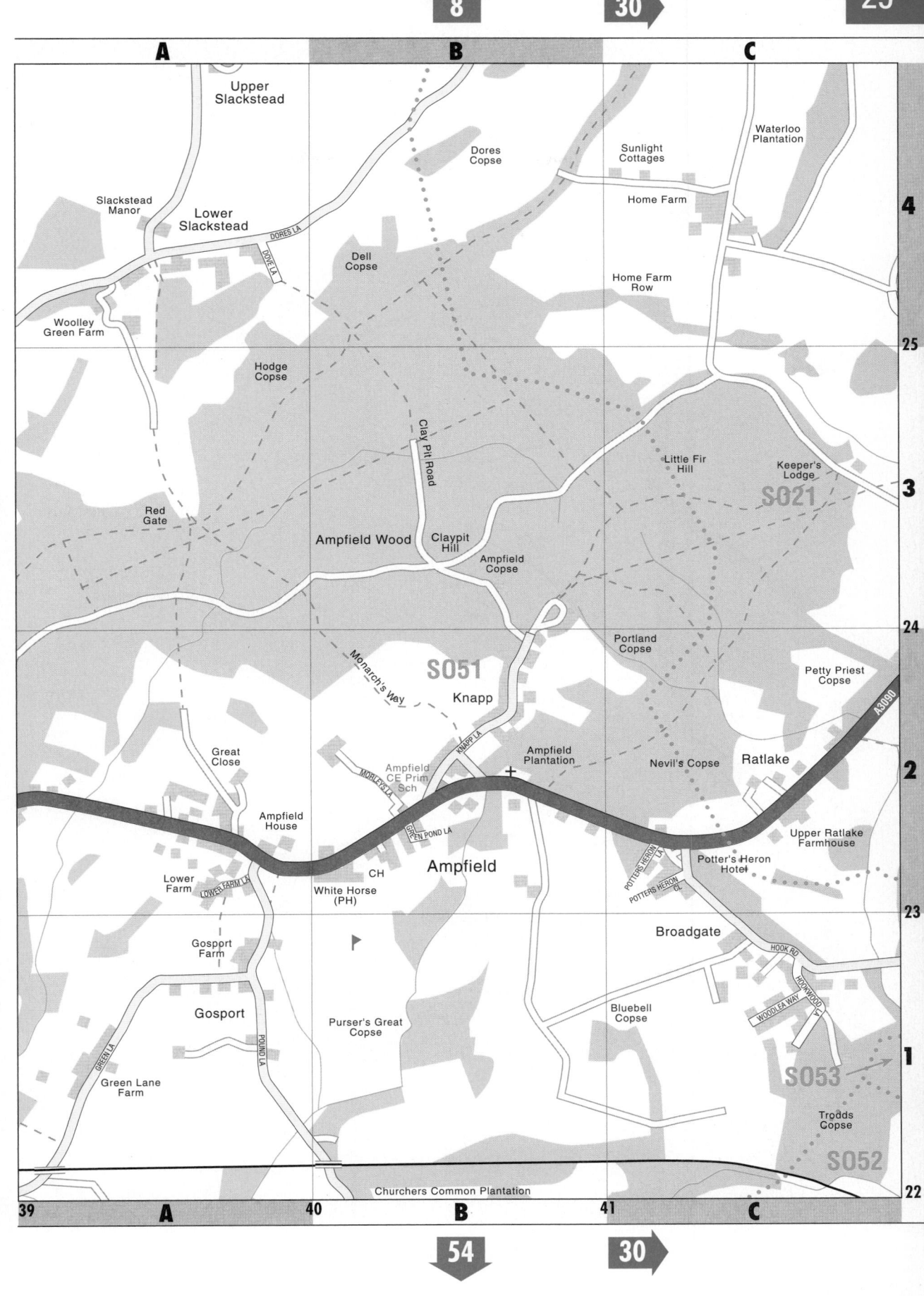

SO22

A3090

PORT LA

KEBLE CL

King's Head Inn

CATWAYS

HEATHCOTE PL

Hursley Park Rd

COLLINS LA

Shawlands Farm

SILKSTEAD LA

4

Hursley Park

PELICAN CT

PO

Cemy

Parsonage Farm

BUNSTEAD LA

Monarch's Way

Shepherds Lane

Hursley

MEREDOW CL

SOUTH END CL

25

Hursley Park Rd

Keble Meml CE Prim Sch

Bunstead

Upper Silkstead Farm

POLES LA

Silkstead

3

B3043

Brooks Copse

SO21

Weedacre Copse

Lower Silkstead Farmhouse

A3090

Hursley Forest

Windmill Copse

24

Red House

Ladwell

Strowdens Copse

Freemantles Copse

Kent's Copse

Wells Row

2

Field House

Cranbury Park

Hawstead Farm

Home Farm

Cranbury House

Great Pond

Hocombe Plantation

SO53

Castle Copse

Upper Pond

23

Hocombe Upper Plantation

Hocombe

ROTHVILLE PL

Hocombe Bridge

Lower Pond

The Castle

HOOK RD

HOOK WATER CL

HOOK WATER RD

HURSLEY RD

Hocombe Park Cl

HOCOMBE RD

SO51

HOOK CL

HOOK CRES

HOCOMBE WOOD RD

ASHDOWN DR

CHARNWOOD GDNS

ASHDOWN CL

HEATHFIELD CL

MAYTREE RD

RANDALL RD

Castle Copse

BEECHWOOD CRES

TITHEWOOD CL

CHARNWOOD CRES

ASHDOWN RD

HEATHFIELD RD

NICHOL RD

WOODLANDS CL

COULTAS RD

1

CHARNWOOD CL

CLEVELAND CT

RICHMOND CL

WALNUT

ELM CT

HAZEL CL

LAKEWOOD RD

MALCOLM RD

SHERWOOD RD

MARLBOROUGH RD

THORNBURY WOOD

THE GLADE

BEECH CL

BEECHWOOD CL

Hursley Ct 1
Ashton Pl 2
Hiltingbury Ct 3
Vanburgh Way 4

PO

Stewart Ho

SYCAMORE AVE

Queen's Rd

GORDON RD

WESTERN RD

KINGSWAY

ST MARK'S HTS

FLEXFORD CL

BADDESLEY RD

AVEBURY GDNS

RAMSDOWN GDNS

BRIDGE RISE

ROSEMOOR GR

1 2 3
4 5 Chillington Gdns
6 Cranborne Gdns
7 Lauriston Dr
8 Ormesby Dr
9 Stratfield Dr
10 Albury Rd
11 Apsley Pl
12 Oaklands

Hiltingbury

HILTINGBURY RD

HILTINGBURY CL

HEATHERDENE RD

THOROLD RD

GROSVENOR RD

FRESHWATER CT

THORNBURY HTS

SO52

THE WOODLANDS

N. MILLERS DALE

KINGS TANYARDS

MILLERS DALE

Recn Gd

PINE RD

B3043

Cemy

Cuckoo Bushes

Hiltingbury Inf Sch

Hiltingbury Jun Sch

OAKWOOD

OAKWOOD CL

OAKWOOD RD

PINE CRES

PINE RD

BROXBURN CL

MALBRES RD

WINCHESTER RD

22

42 43 44

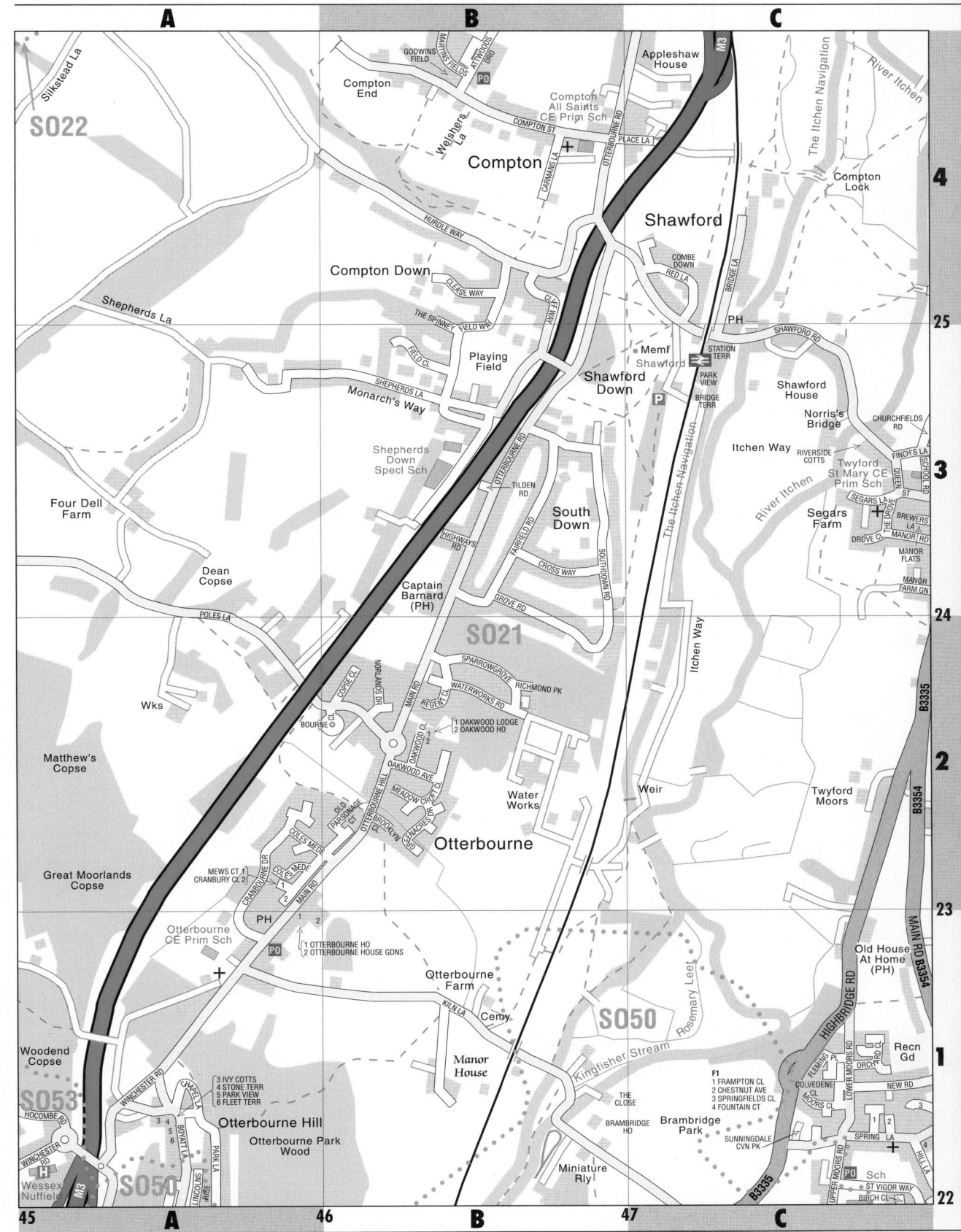

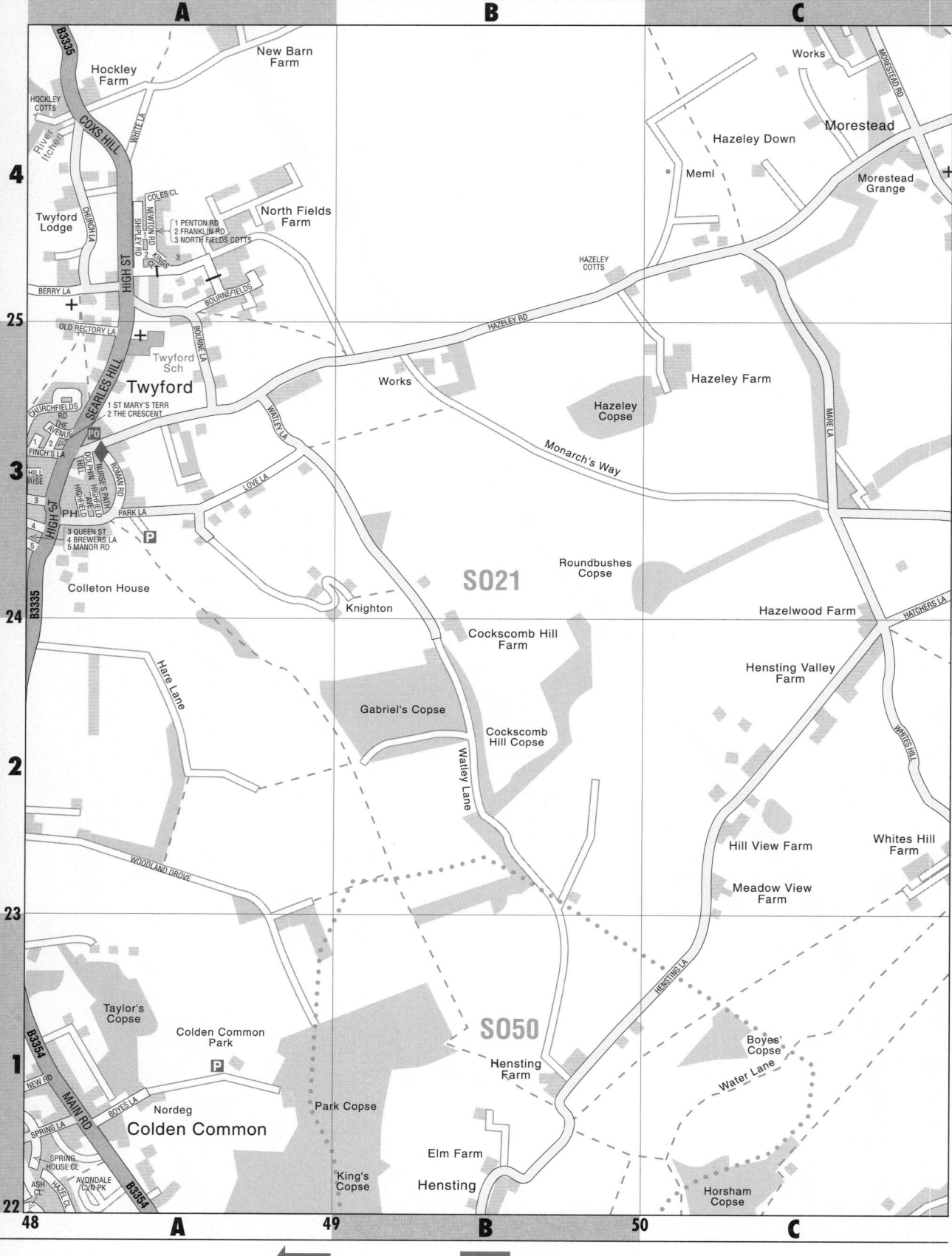

A   B   C

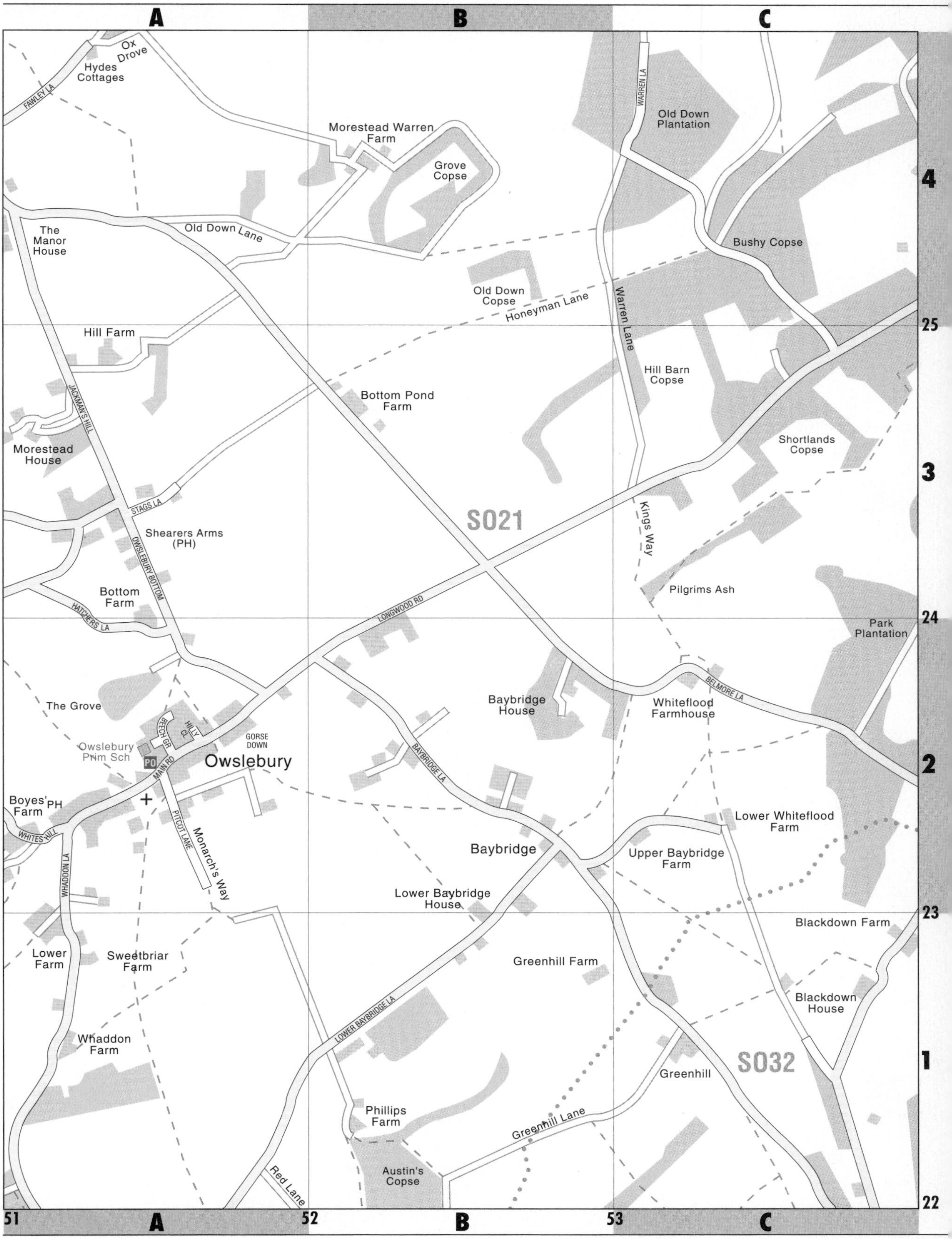

4

Ox Drove
Hydes Cottages
FARLEY LA

Morestead Warren Farm

Grove Copse

Old Down Plantation

WARREN LA

Bushy Copse

The Manor House

Old Down Lane

Old Down Copse

Honeyman Lane

WARREN LANE

25

Hill Farm

Hill Barn Copse

JACKMAN'S HILL

Bottom Pond Farm

Shortlands Copse

3

Morestead House

STAGS LA

OWSLEBURY BOTTOM

Shearers Arms (PH)

SO21

Kings Way

HATCHERS LA

Bottom Farm

LONGWOOD RD

Pilgrims Ash

24

Park Plantation

The Grove

BEECH GR

HILLY CL

Owslebury Prim Sch

PO

GORSE DOWN

MAIN RD

Owslebury

Baybridge House

BAYBRIDGE LA

Whiteflood Farmhouse

BELMORE LA

2

Boyes' Farm

PH

WHITES HILL

WHADDON LA

PITCOT LANE

Monarch's Way

Baybridge

Upper Baybridge Farm

Lower Whiteflood Farm

23

Lower Baybridge House

Blackdown Farm

Lower Farm

Sweetbriar Farm

Greenhill Farm

Blackdown House

Whaddon Farm

LOWER BAYBRIDGE LA

1

SO32

Greenhill

Phillips Farm

Greenhill Lane

Red Lane

Austin's Copse

22

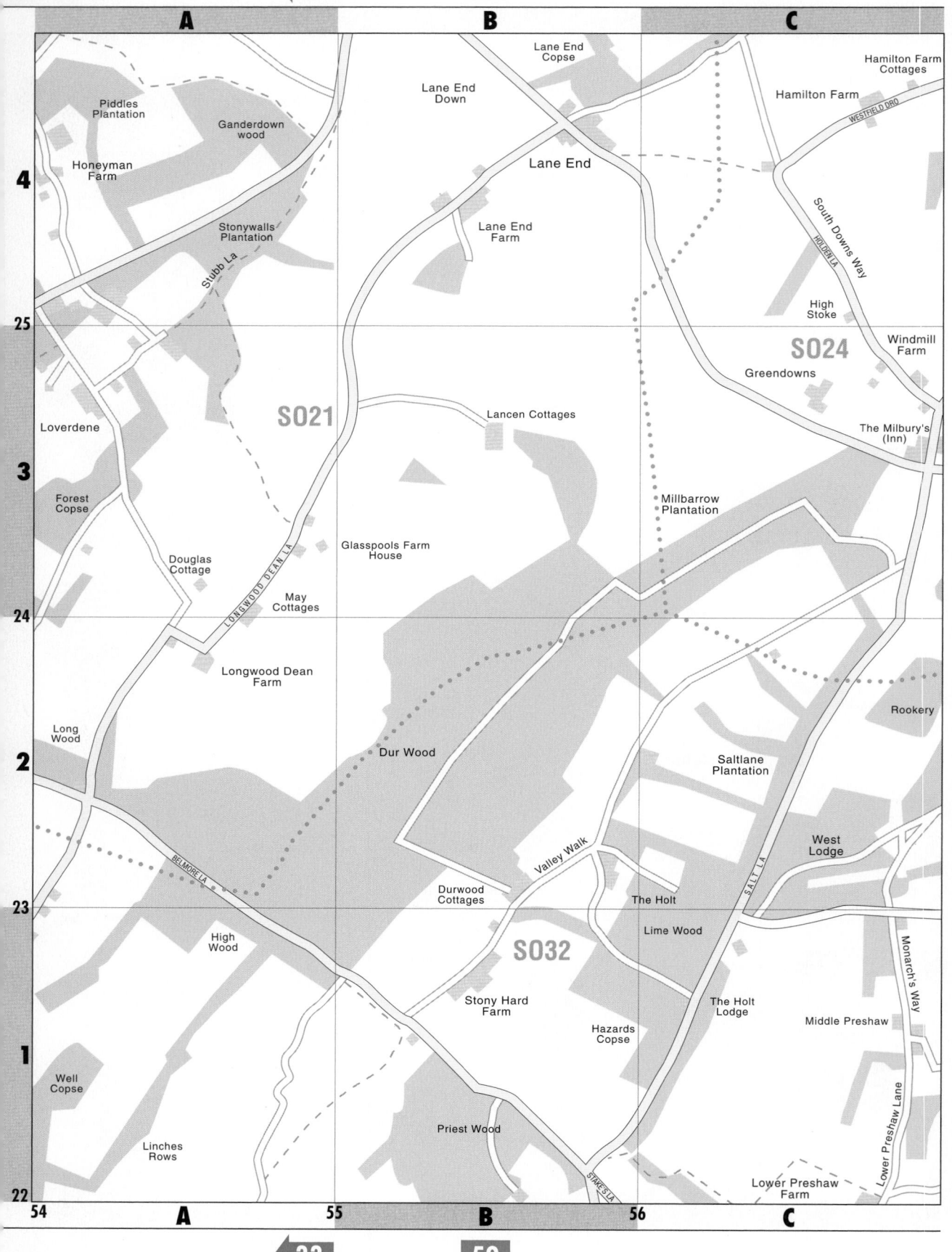

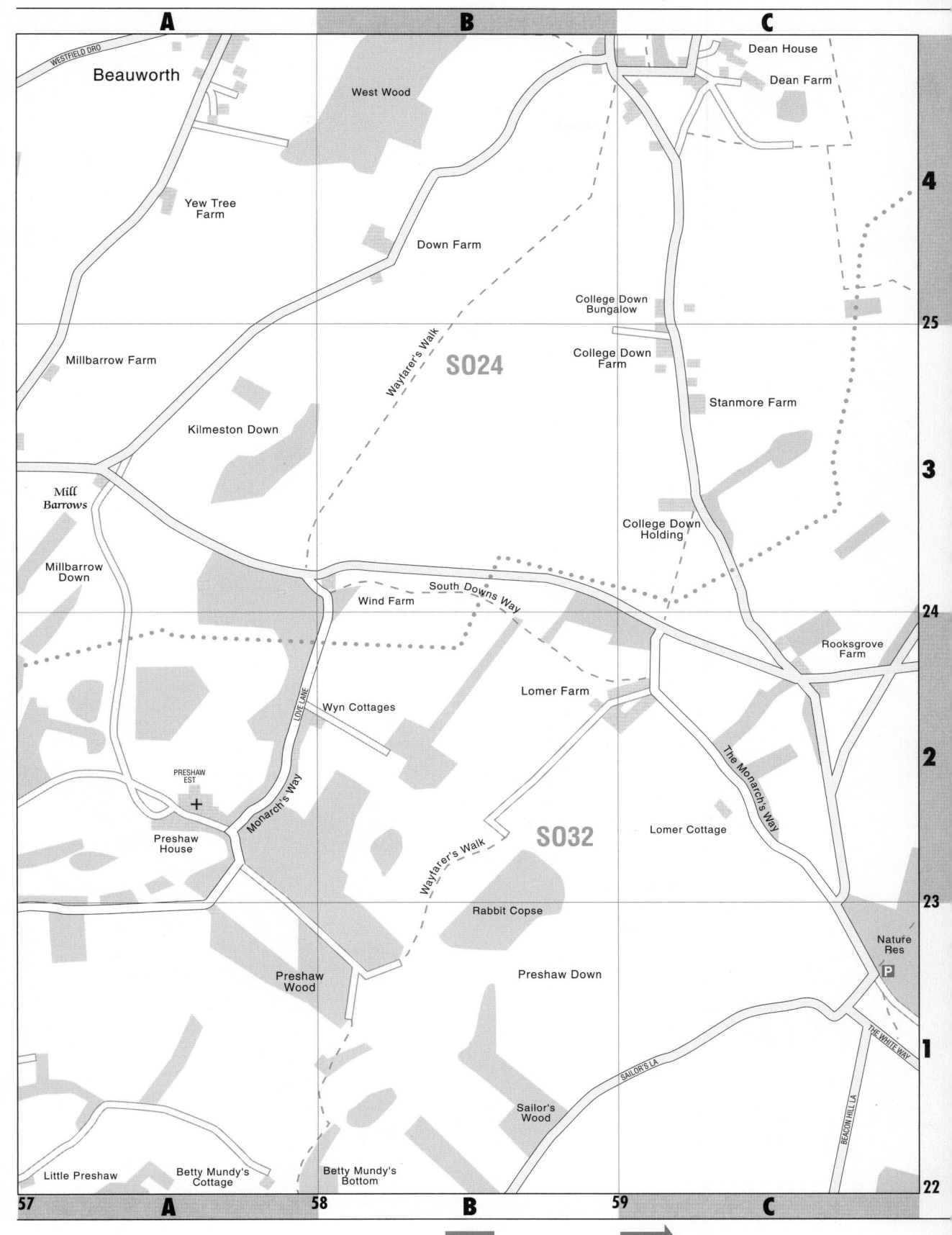

A   **B**   **C**

WESTFIELD DRO

Beauworth

West Wood

Dean House

Dean Farm

Yew Tree Farm

Down Farm

College Down Bungalow

4

Wayfarer's Walk

SO24

College Down Farm

25

Millbarrow Farm

Stanmore Farm

Kilmeston Down

Mill Barrows

College Down Holding

3

Millbarrow Down

Wind Farm

South Downs Way

24

Rooksgrove Farm

LOVE LANE

Wyn Cottages

Lomer Farm

The Monarch's Way

2

PRESHAW EST

Monarch's Way

Preshaw House

Wayfarer's Walk

SO32

Lomer Cottage

23

Rabbit Copse

Nature Res

P

Preshaw Wood

Preshaw Down

THE WHITE WAY

SAILOR'S LA

1

BEACON HILL LA

Little Preshaw

Betty Mundy's Cottage

Betty Mundy's Bottom

Sailor's Wood

22

57   **A**   58   **B**   59   **C**

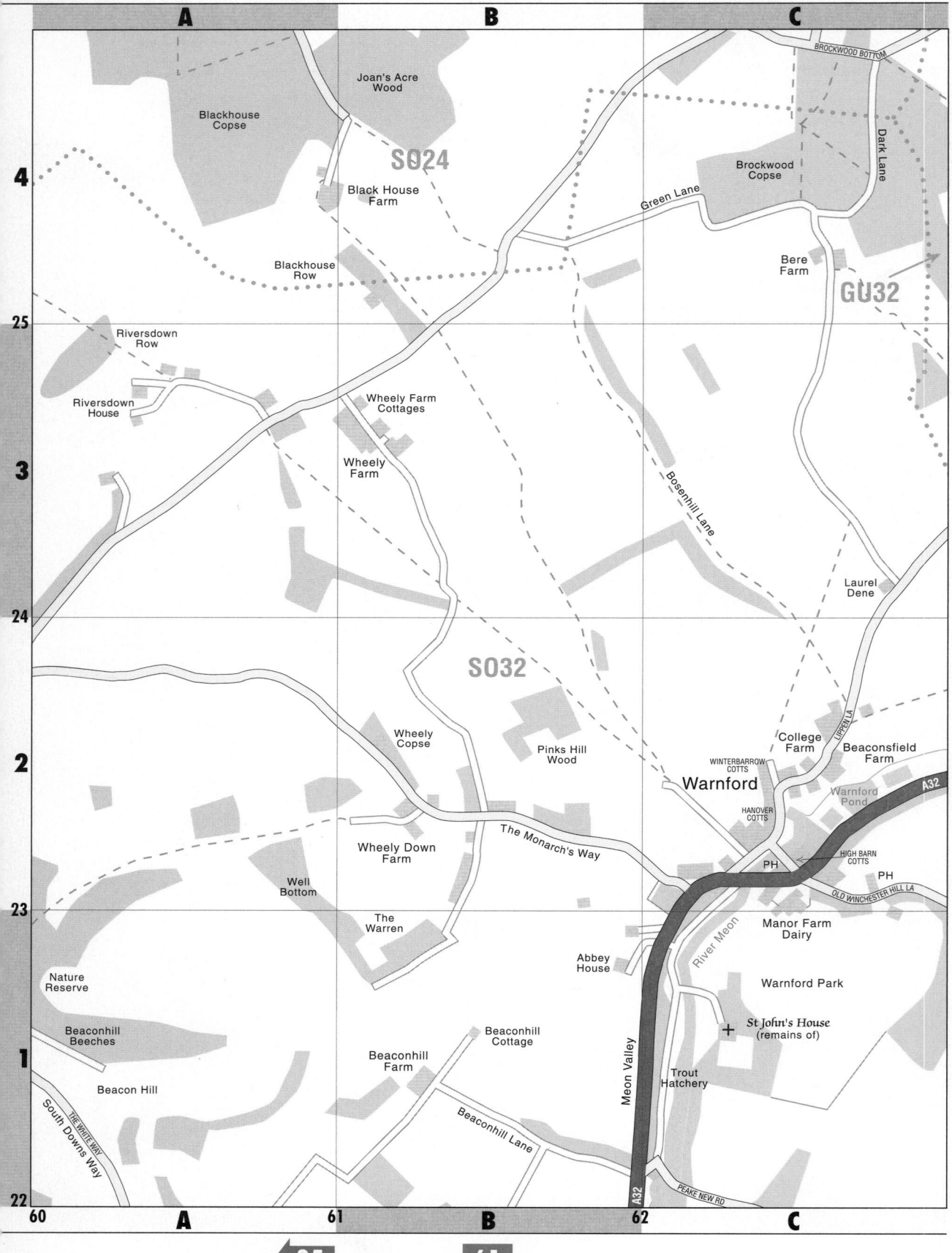

A   B   C

BROCKWOOD BOTTOM

Joan's Acre
Wood

Blackhouse
Copse

SO24

Dark Lane

Brockwood
Copse

Black House
Farm

Green Lane

Bere
Farm

4

Blackhouse
Row

GU32

25

Riversdown
Row

Riversdown
House

Wheely Farm
Cottages

Bosenhill Lane

Wheely
Farm

3

Laurel
Dene

24

SO32

Wheely
Copse

Pinks Hill
Wood

College
Farm

LIPPEN LA

Beaconsfield
Farm

2

WINTERBARROW
COTTS

Warnford

Warnford
Pond

A32

HANOVER
COTTS

The Monarch's Way

Wheely Down
Farm

HIGH BARN
COTTS

PH

PH

Well
Bottom

OLD WINCHESTER HILL LA

23

The
Warren

Manor Farm
Dairy

Abbey
House

River Meon

Warnford Park

Nature
Reserve

Beaconhill
Beeches

Beaconhill
Cottage

St John's House
(remains of)

1

Beaconhill
Farm

Beacon Hill

Meon Valley

Trout
Hatchery

THE WHITE WAY

South Downs Way

Beaconhill Lane

A32

PEAKE NEW RD

22

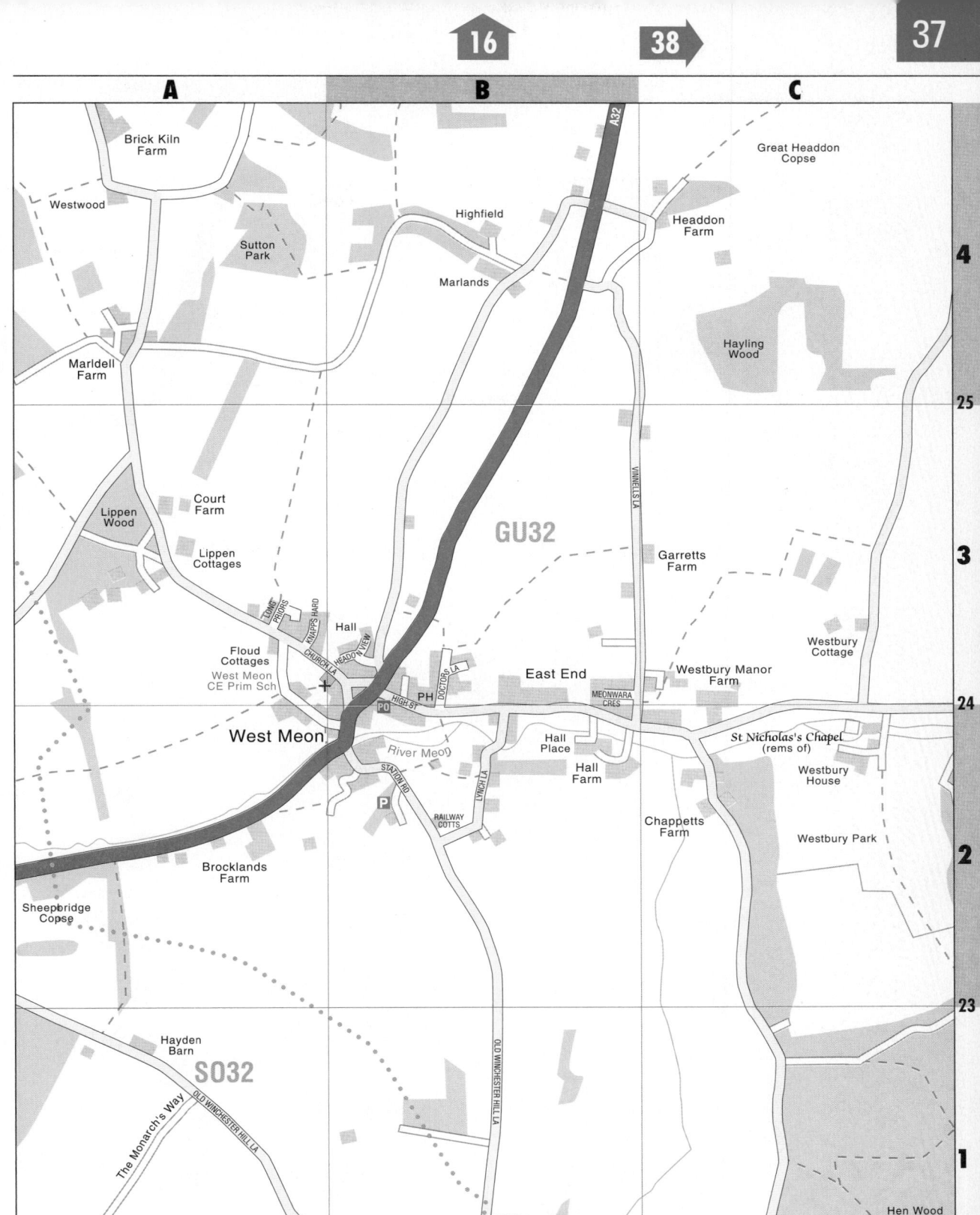

A   B   C

Brick Kiln
Farm

Westwood

Sutton
Park

Highfield

Great Headdon
Copse

Headdon
Farm

4

Marlands

Hayling
Wood

Marldell
Farm

25

Court
Farm

Lippen
Wood

GU32

Garretts
Farm

3

Lippen
Cottages

LONG PRIORS
KNAPPS HARD
HEADON VIEW
CHURCH LA

Hall

Westbury
Cottage

Floud
Cottages

East End

Westbury Manor
Farm

West Meon
CE Prim Sch

DOCTORS LA

HIGH ST

PH

MEONWARA
CRES

St Nicholas's Chapel
(rems of)

24

PO

West Meon

River Meon

Hall
Place

Westbury
House

STATION RD

Hall
Farm

Westbury Park

Chappetts
Farm

2

Brocklands
Farm

LYNCH LA

RAILWAY
COTTS

Sheepbridge
Copse

23

Hayden
Barn

SO32

OLD WINCHESTER HILL LA

The Monarch's Way

OLD WINCHESTER HILL LA

1

Hen Wood

Whitewool
Hanger

Peake Farm

22

63   A   64   B   65   C

A   B   C

Arbor Trees Farm

Redwood Cottage

Red Wood

Peak Farm

Kingsland Copse

Great Copyhold Copse

GU34

Old Down

War Hill

Park House

Upper Bordean House

Upper Bordean Farm

Bordean Barn

Warhill Cottage

Old Down Farm

Tigwell Copse

Mare Pond

Trenleygrove Plantation

Trenley Grove

Tigwell Cottages

Tigwell Farm

East Lodge

Burrow Plantation

GU32

Bereleigh Cottage

Orchard Plantation

Riplington

Park Cottages

River Meon

Drayton House

Bereleigh House

Park Farm

Riplington Hanger

Drayton Farm

Park Cottages

Drayton Cottages

Drayton

Horsedown Farm

Drayton Mill

Mascoombe Bottom

Park Hill

Emmet's Down

Drayton Down

Chalk Dell Cottages

Hen Wood

Halnaker Lane

Middle Down

Sewage Works

Vineyard Hole

Gravel Lane

Frogmore

Yew Down

EAME'S COTTS

Court House PH

PO

GREENWAY

East Meon

PARK VISTA

WORKHOUSE LA

THE CROSS

CHIDDEN

CHAPEL ST

HILL VIEW

CHURCH ST

GLENTHORNE MEADOW

HIGH ST

TEMPLE LA

East Meon CE Prim Sch

66   A   67   B   68   C

4

25

3

24

2

23

1

22

A

B

C

High Cross La

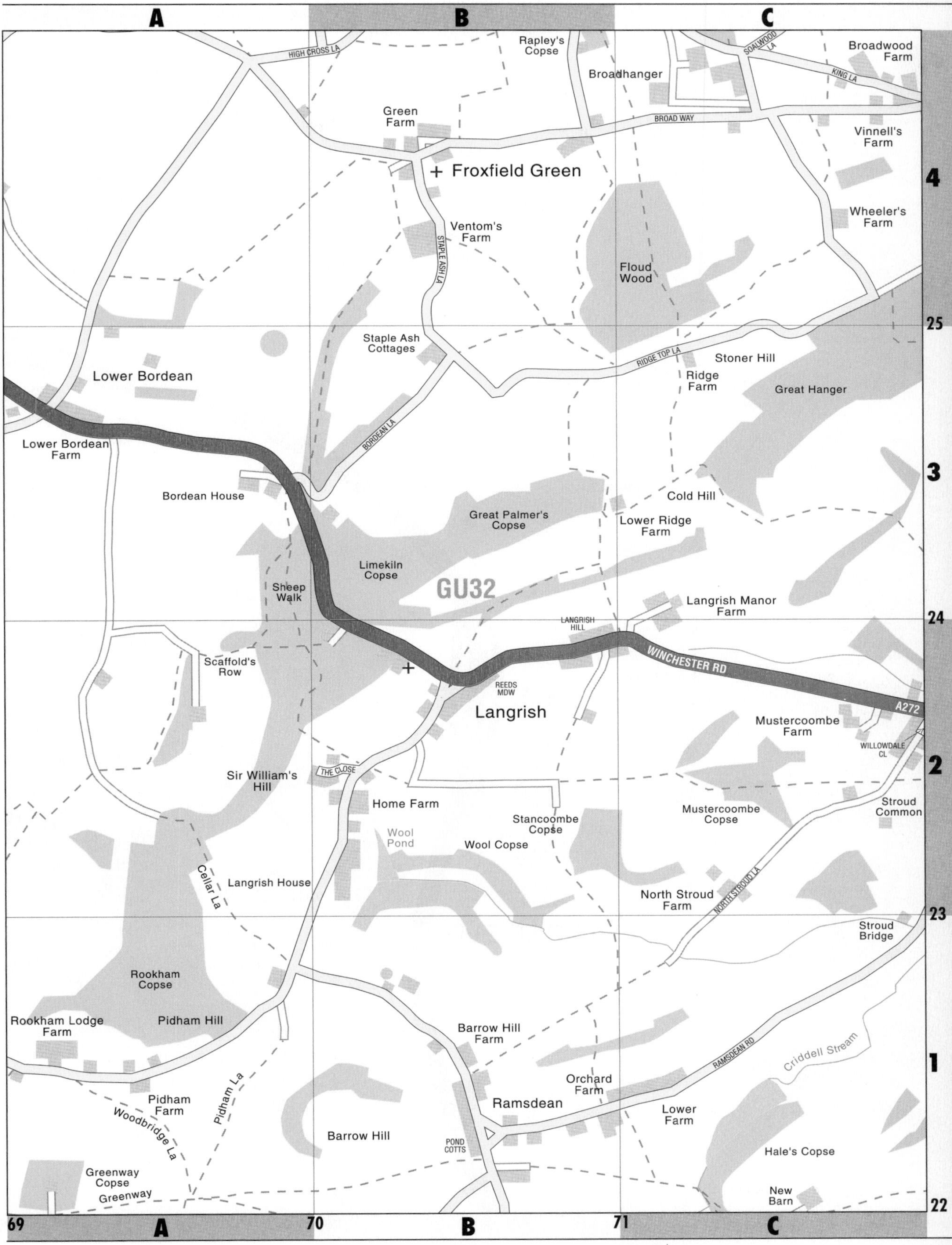

Rapley's Copse

Broadhanger

Broadwood Farm

SOALWOOD LA

KING LA

Green Farm

Broad Way

Vinnell's Farm

+ Froxfield Green

4

Ventom's Farm

Floud Wood

Wheeler's Farm

STAPLE ASH LA

Staple Ash Cottages

RIDGE TOP LA

25

Stoner Hill

Lower Bordean

Ridge Farm

Great Hanger

BORDEAN LA

Lower Bordean Farm

Bordean House

Great Palmer's Copse

Cold Hill

3

Lower Ridge Farm

Limekiln Copse

Sheep Walk

GU32

Langrish Manor Farm

Scaffold's Row

LANGRISH HILL

Langrish Manor Farm

24

WINCHESTER RD

Langrish

+

REEDS MDW

Langrish

A272

Mustercoombe Farm

WILLOWDALE CL

Sir William's Hill

THE CLOSE

Home Farm

Mustercoombe Copse

2

Stroud Common

Wool Pond

Stancoombe Copse

CELLAR LA

Wool Copse

NORTH STROUD LA

Langrish House

North Stroud Farm

23

Stroud Bridge

Rookham Copse

Pidham Hill

Barrow Hill Farm

RAMSDEAN RD

Criddell Stream

Rookham Lodge Farm

PIDHAM LA

1

WOODBRIDGE LA

Pidham Farm

Orchard Farm

Ramsdean

Lower Farm

Barrow Hill

POND COTTS

Hale's Copse

Greenway Copse Greenway

New Barn

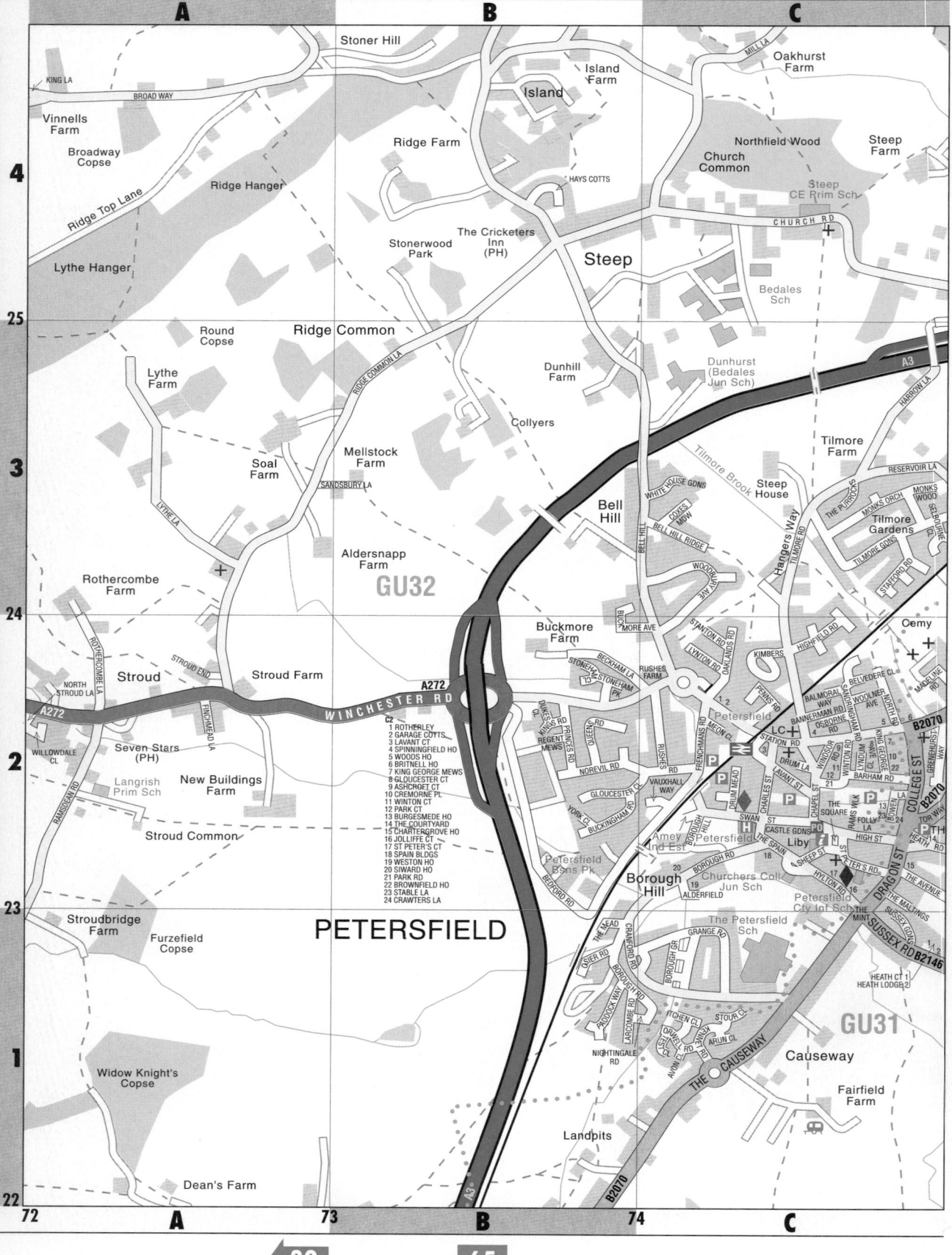

A   B   C

Stoner Hill

King La

BROAD WAY

Vinnells Farm

Broadway Copse

Ridge Top Lane

Ridge Hanger

Lythe Hanger

4

Island Farm

Island

Ridge Farm

HAYS COTTS

Stonerwood Park

The Cricketers Inn (PH)

Steep

Oakhurst Farm

Northfield Wood

Church Common

Steep Farm

Steep CE Prim Sch

CHURCH RD

Bedales Sch

MILL LA

25

Round Copse

Ridge Common

Lythe Farm

RIDGE COMMON LA

Ridge Common La

Soal Farm

Mellstock Farm

SANDSBURY LA

LYTHE LA

Dunhill Farm

Collyers

Dunhurst (Bedales Jun Sch)

A3

HARROW LA

Tilmore Farm

RESERVOIR LA

3

Rothercombe Farm

Aldersnapp Farm

GU32

Bell Hill

WHITE HOUSE GDNS

COXES MDW

BELL HILL RIDGE

Tilmore Brook

Steep House

Hangers Way

TILMORE RD

The Purrocks

MONKS ORCH

MONKS WOOD

SELBOURNE CL

Tilmore Gardens

TILMORE GDNS

STATEFORD RD

ROTHERCOMBE LA

Stroud

NORTH STROUD LA

STROUD END

Stroud Farm

Buckmore Farm

BUCKM

MORE AVE

WOODRAIL

STANTON RD

OAKLANDS RD

HIGHFIELD RD

Cemy

BELVEDERE CL

MADELINE R

24

A272

A272

FINCHMEAD LA

WINCHESTER RD

Petersfield Bsns Pk

BEDFORD RD

PETERSFIELD

23

Stroudbridge Farm

Furzefield Copse

PETERSFIELD

Borough Hill

ALDERFIELD

The Petersfield Sch

Grange Rd

GU31

1

Widow Knight's Copse

Causeway

Fairfield Farm

22

Dean's Farm

Landpits

THE CAUSEWAY

B2070

72   A   73   B   74   C

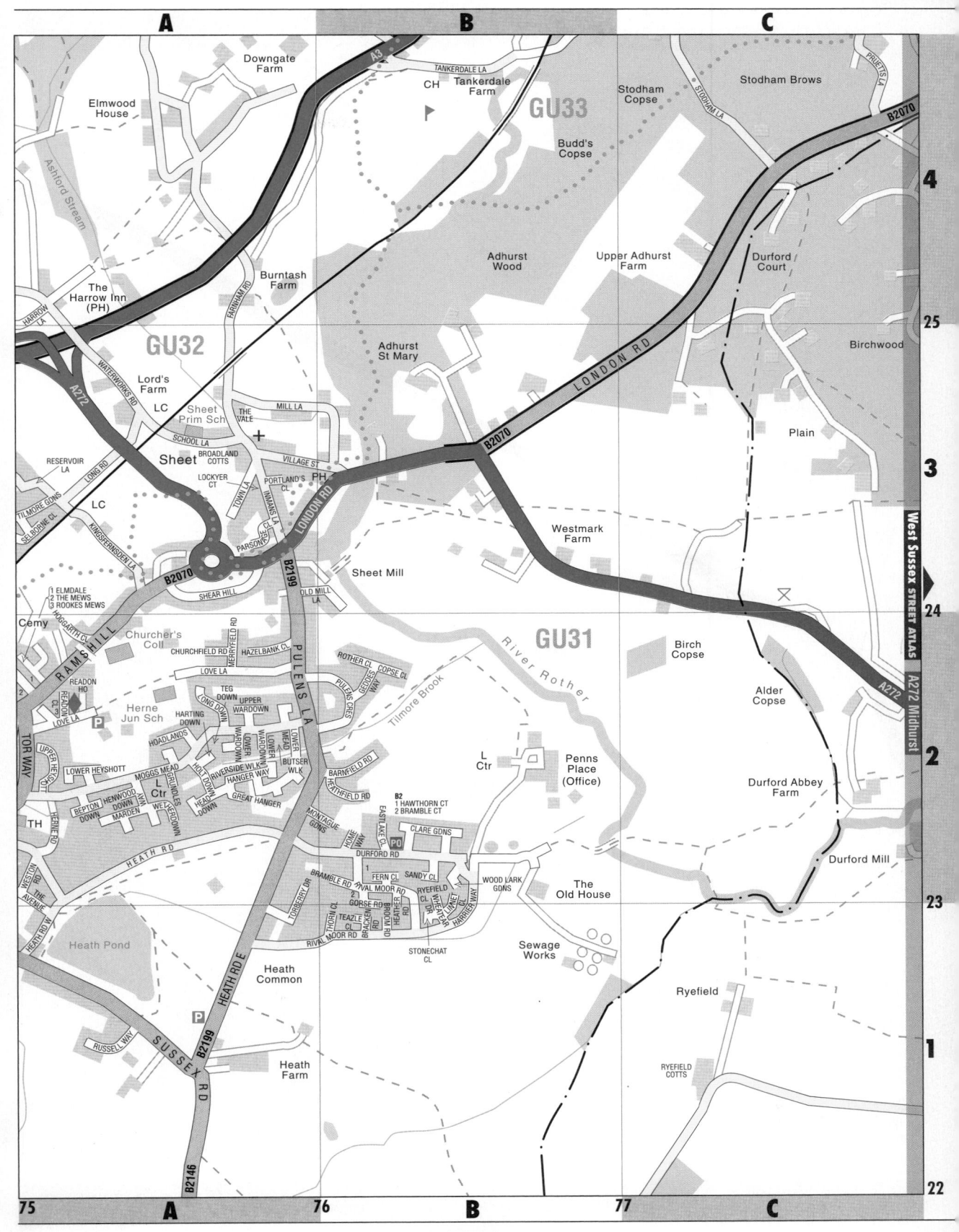

A 75 76 **B** 77 **C**

- A Downgate Farm
- Elmwood House
- Tankerdale Farm
- TANKERDALE LA
- CH
- GU33
- Stodham Copse
- Stodham Brows
- STODHAM LA
- PRIETTS LA
- B2070
- Budd's Copse
- 4
- Adhurst Wood
- Upper Adhurst Farm
- Durford Court
- Burntash Farm
- FARNHAM RD
- The Harrow Inn (PH)
- HARROW LA
- 25
- Birchwood
- GU32
- LONDON RD
- Lord's Farm
- WATERWORKS RD
- A272
- LC
- Adhurst St Mary
- Sheet Prim Sch
- MILL LA
- THE VALE
- Plain
- SCHOOL LA
- RESERVOIR LA
- LONG RD
- Sheet
- BROADLAND COTTS
- VILLAGE ST
- PH
- 3
- TILMORE GDNS
- SELBORNE CL
- LC
- LOCKYER CT
- PORTLAND'S CL
- TOWN LA
- INMANS CL
- LONDON RD
- B2070
- Westmark Farm
- KINGSFERNSDEN LA
- PARSONS CL
- B2199
- OLD MILL LA
- Sheet Mill
- GU31
- 24
- Cemy
- 1 ELMDALE
- 2 THE MEWS
- 3 ROOKES MEWS
- SHEAR HILL
- River Rother
- A272 Midhurst
- A272
- West Sussex STREET ATLAS
- RAMSHILL
- Churcher's Coll
- READON HO
- CHURCHFIELD RD
- MERRYFIELD RD
- HAZELBANK RD
- ROTHER CL
- COPSE CL
- GEDDES WAY
- Tilmore Brook
- Birch Copse
- Alder Copse
- Durford Abbey Farm
- 2
- READON CL
- Love LA
- LOVE LA
- TEG DOWN
- LONG DOWN
- UPPER WARDOWN
- PULENS CRES
- PULENS LA
- L Ctr
- Penns Place (Office)
- Herne Jun Sch
- HARTING DOWN
- LOWER WARDOWN
- LOWER MEAD
- LOWER BUTSER WLK
- RIVERSIDE WLK
- HANGER WAY
- Durford Mill
- TOR WAY
- UPPER HEYSHOTT
- HOADLANDS
- HOLT DOWN
- GREAT HANGER
- BARNFIELD RD
- HEATHFIELD RD
- B2 1 HAWTHORN CT 2 BRAMBLE CT
- EASTLAKE CL
- L Ctr
- LOWER HEYSHOTT
- MOGGS MEAD
- GRUNDLES GROWN
- HEATH DOWN
- MONTAGUE GDNS
- CLARE GDNS
- The Old House
- 23
- BEPTON DOWN
- HENWOOD DOWN
- MARDEN
- WELLS GROWN
- DURFORD RD
- PO
- FERN CL
- SANDY CL
- Wood Lark Gdns
- TH
- HERNE RD
- THE AVENUE
- HEATH RD
- BRAMBLE RD
- RIVAL MOOR RD
- GORSE CL
- THORN CL
- TEAZLE CL
- HEATHER RD
- BROOM RD
- Ryefield
- WHEATER'S LA
- HARRIER WAY
- Sewage Works
- HEATH RD W
- Heath Pond
- TORBERRY DR
- RIVAL MOOR RD
- STONECHAT CL
- Ryefield
- Heath Common
- Ryefield Cotts
- RUSSELL WAY
- P
- SUSSEX RD
- B2199
- HEATH RD E
- Heath Farm
- 1
- B2146
- 22

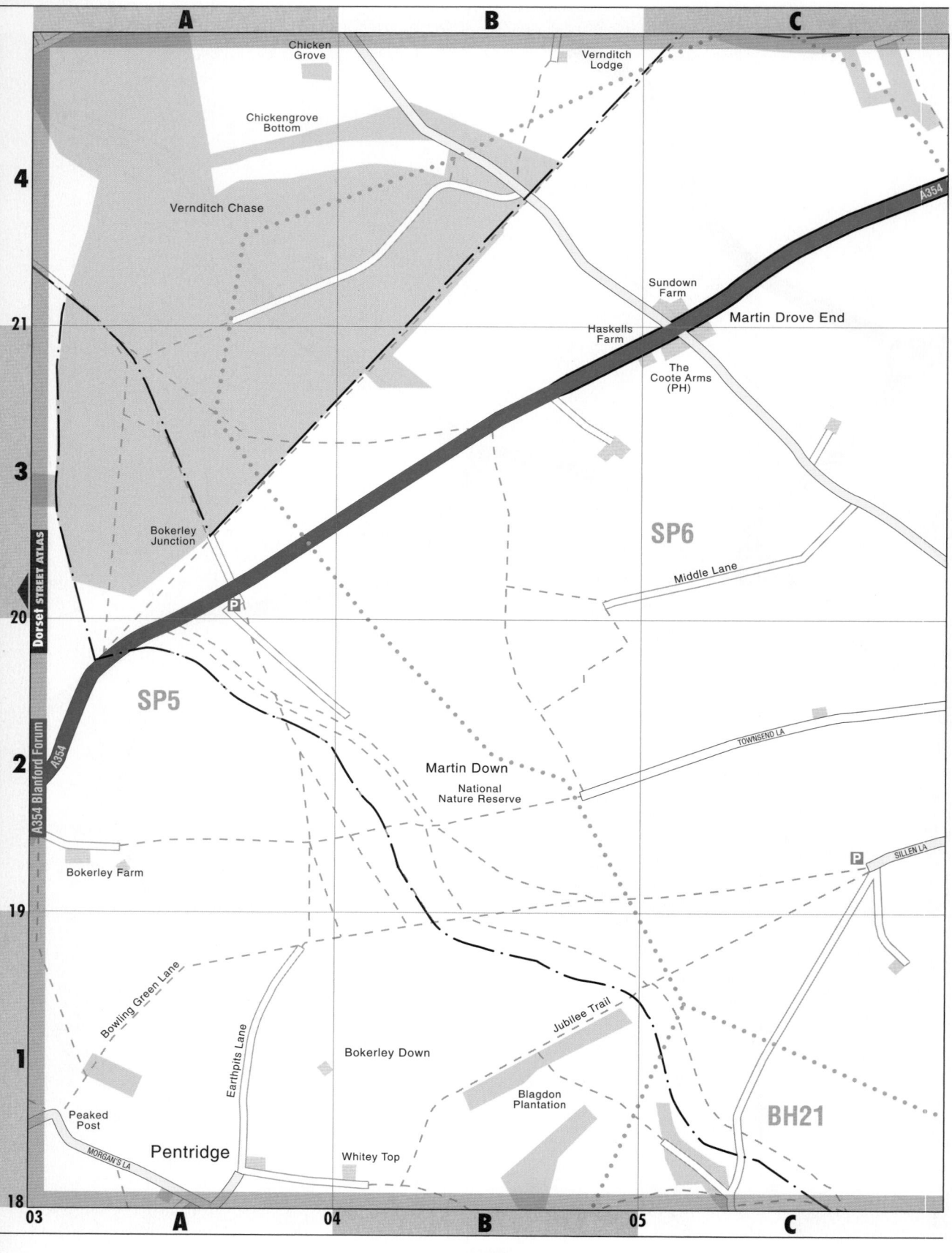

Dorset STREET ATLAS

A354 Blanford Forum

Chicken Grove

Verndity Lodge

Chickengrove Bottom

Verndity Chase

Sundown Farm

Martin Drove End

Haskells Farm

The Coote Arms (PH)

SP6

Middle Lane

Bokerley Junction

SP5

TOWNSEND LA

Martin Down

National Nature Reserve

Bokerley Farm

SILLEN LA

Bowling Green Lane

Earthpits Lane

Jubilee Trail

Bokerley Down

BH21

Blagdon Plantation

Peaked Post

Pentridge

MORGAN'S LA

Whitey Top

A354

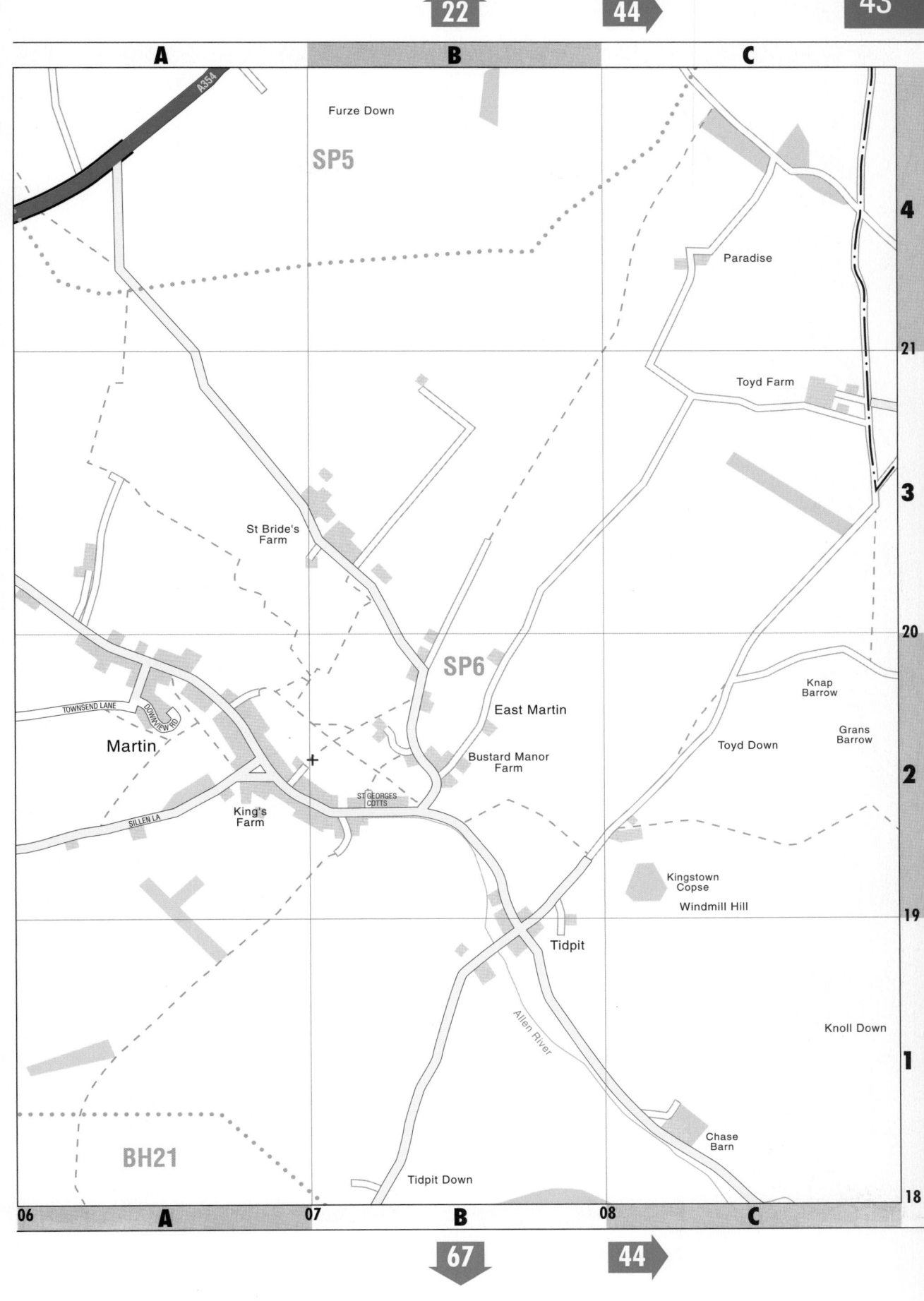

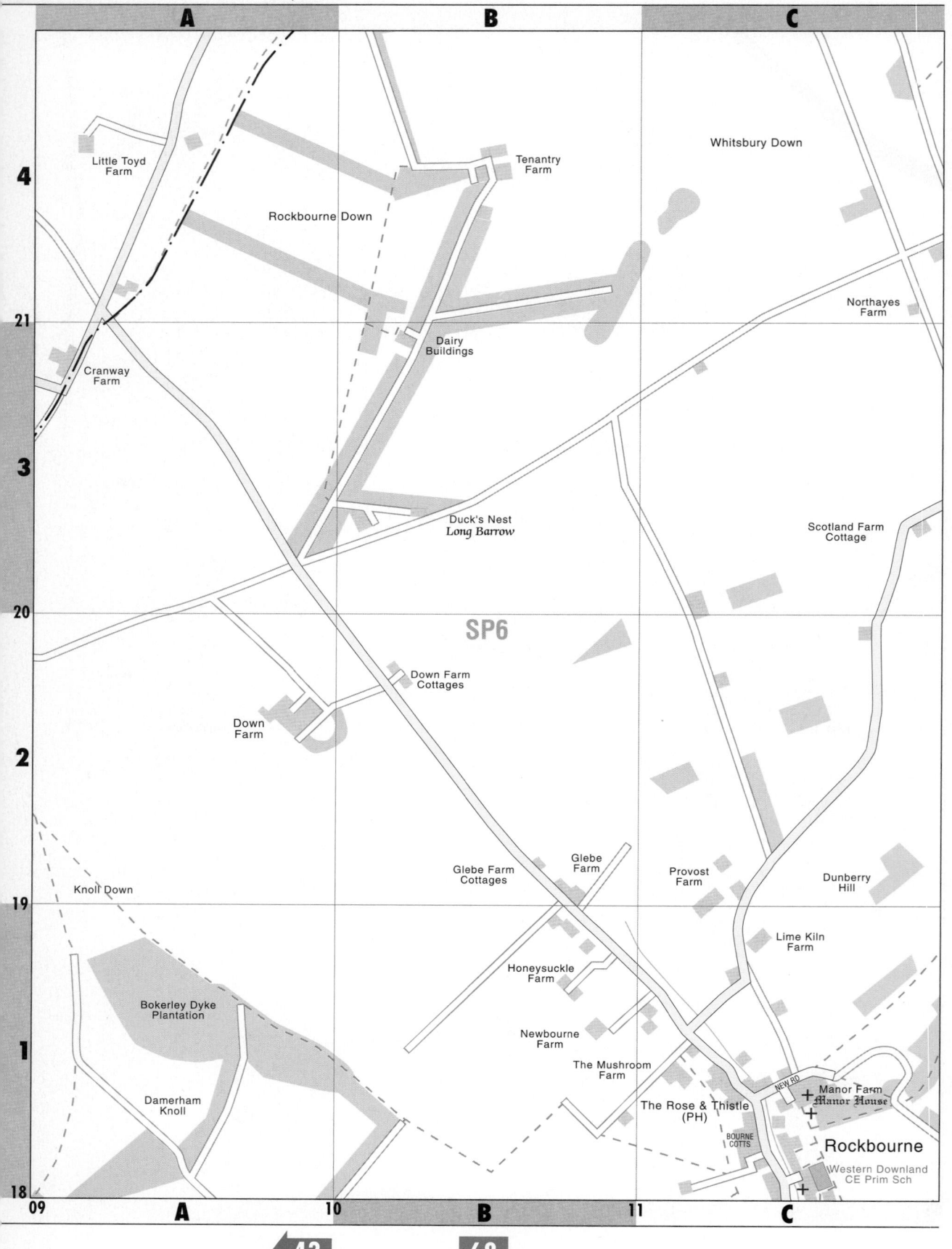

A   B   C

Little Toyd
Farm

4

Rockbourne Down

Whitsbury Down

Northayes
Farm

21

Dairy
Buildings

Cranway
Farm

3

Duck's Nest
Long Barrow

Scotland Farm
Cottage

20

SP6

Down Farm
Cottages

Down
Farm

2

Glebe
Farm

Glebe Farm
Cottages

Provost
Farm

Dunberry
Hill

Knoll Down

19

Lime Kiln
Farm

Honeysuckle
Farm

Bokerley Dyke
Plantation

Newbourne
Farm

1

The Mushroom
Farm

NEW RD
Manor Farm
Manor House

Damerham
Knoll

The Rose & Thistle
(PH)

BOURNE
COTTS

Rockbourne

Western Downland
CE Prim Sch

18

09   A   10   B   11   C

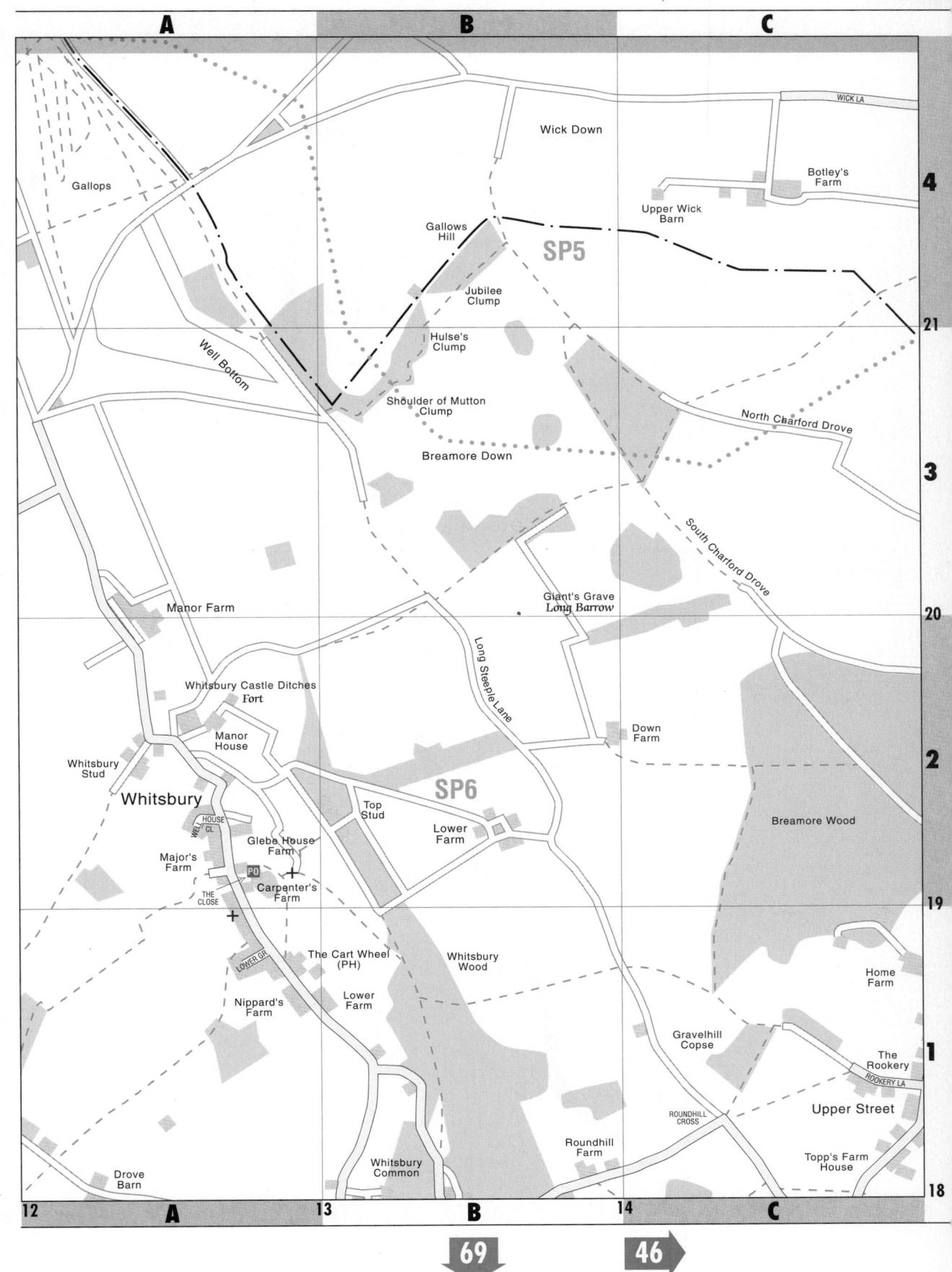

WICK LA

Wick Down

Botley's
Farm

Gallops

Upper Wick
Barn

4

Gallows
Hill

SP5

Jubilee
Clump

21

Hulse's
Clump

Well Bottom

Shoulder of Mutton
Clump

North Charford Drove

Breamore Down

3

South Charford Drove

Manor Farm

Giant's Grave
Long Barrow

20

Whitsbury Castle Ditches
Fort

Long Steeple Lane

Down
Farm

Whitsbury
Stud

Manor
House

2

SP6

Breamore Wood

Whitsbury

Top
Stud

HOUSE
CL

WELL

Glebe House
Farm

Lower
Farm

Major's
Farm

PO

THE
CLOSE

Carpenter's
Farm

19

LOWER GR

The Cart Wheel
(PH)

Whitsbury
Wood

Home
Farm

Nippard's
Farm

Lower
Farm

Gravelhill
Copse

The
Rookery

ROOKERY LA

1

ROUNDHILL
CROSS

Upper Street

Roundhill
Farm

Topp's Farm
House

Drove
Barn

Whitsbury
Common

18

12   **A**   13   **B**   14   **C**

45

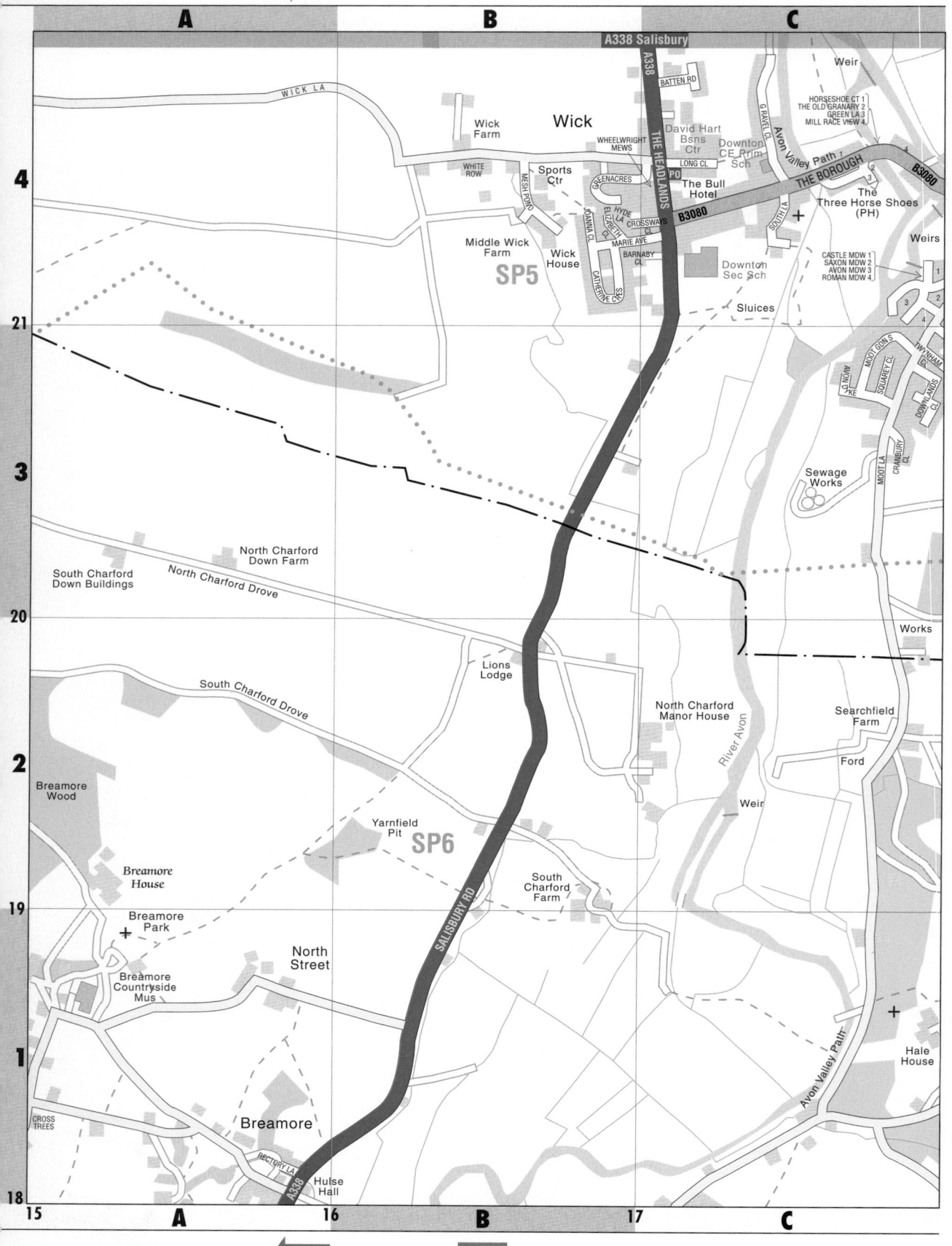

45

70

A   B   C

4

Cemy
BARFORD LA
Parsonage
Farm
HAMILTON PK
THE SLOMES
Liby
CHURCH HATCH
HIGH ST
B3080
PO
Downton
LODE HILL

Templeman's
Old Farmhouse
LANG FORD LA
Templeman
Farm
THE ROW
PH
Grove Copse
SANDY LA
PETTICOAT LA
GROVE LA
Cemy

Down
House
MUDDYFORD RD

Gdn
CASTLE MDW
Moot
Farm
MOOT LA
SAXONHURST
SAXON MDW
EASTMAN CL
TWYNHAM CL

Paccombe
Farm

CHALK CL
APPLETREE RD
RISE RD
MORGANS
THE CLOSE
BOUNDARY RD
DOWNTON HILL
CRAB TREE CL
ORCHARD RD
MORGANS VALE RD
VICARAGE PK
Morgan's Vale
& Woodfall's
Prim Sch
Morgan's
Vale

BOWERS HILL
NUN LA
PRINCES HILL
PRINCES CL
Redlynch
QUAVEY RD
CHAPEL LA
GOGGS LA
Pensworth
Farm

21

SLAB LA
PRIMROSE LA
HILBERT RD
BIRDNG IS
MITCHELLS CL
GREEDS MEADE
CASTLE WOODS
HILLCROFT
VALE RD
VALLEY CL
ELMFIELD CL
SP5

THE RIDGE
HARTHILL DRO
CHURCH HILL

3

Church Close
Copse
Lodge Farm
House

Woodfalls
Farm

KINGSFORD CL
Woodfalls
HIGHFIELD LA
Inn
The
Drove
PO

Lock's
Farm
Lover

Lodge
Copse
Rye Hill
Copse

Ridge
Farm
SPRINGFIELD CRES
Little Woodfalls
Farmhouse
LITTLE WOODFALLS DR
PINE VIEW
TINNEY'S
Tinney's Firs

BESSMER DRO
ST MARY'S CL
SCHOOL RD

20

Avon Valley Path
LODGE DRO

WHITESHOOT
WHITESHOOT HILL
Whiteshoot
Farm
Bohemia

2

Hookers Copse

North
Charford

Hatchet
Green
HATCHET CL
CARTER'S CL
TETHERING DRO

LOOSEHANGER
BOHEMIA LA

HALE LA
Cemy
Hale
Prim Sch
ST GEORGE'S
COTTS

FOREST RD

19

Home
Farm

Hale
SP6

Hale
Farm
QUEEN ST
Hale

MAYS FIRS
B3080
Maydene

1

Hale
Park

Folly Drove

Hale Purlieu

18

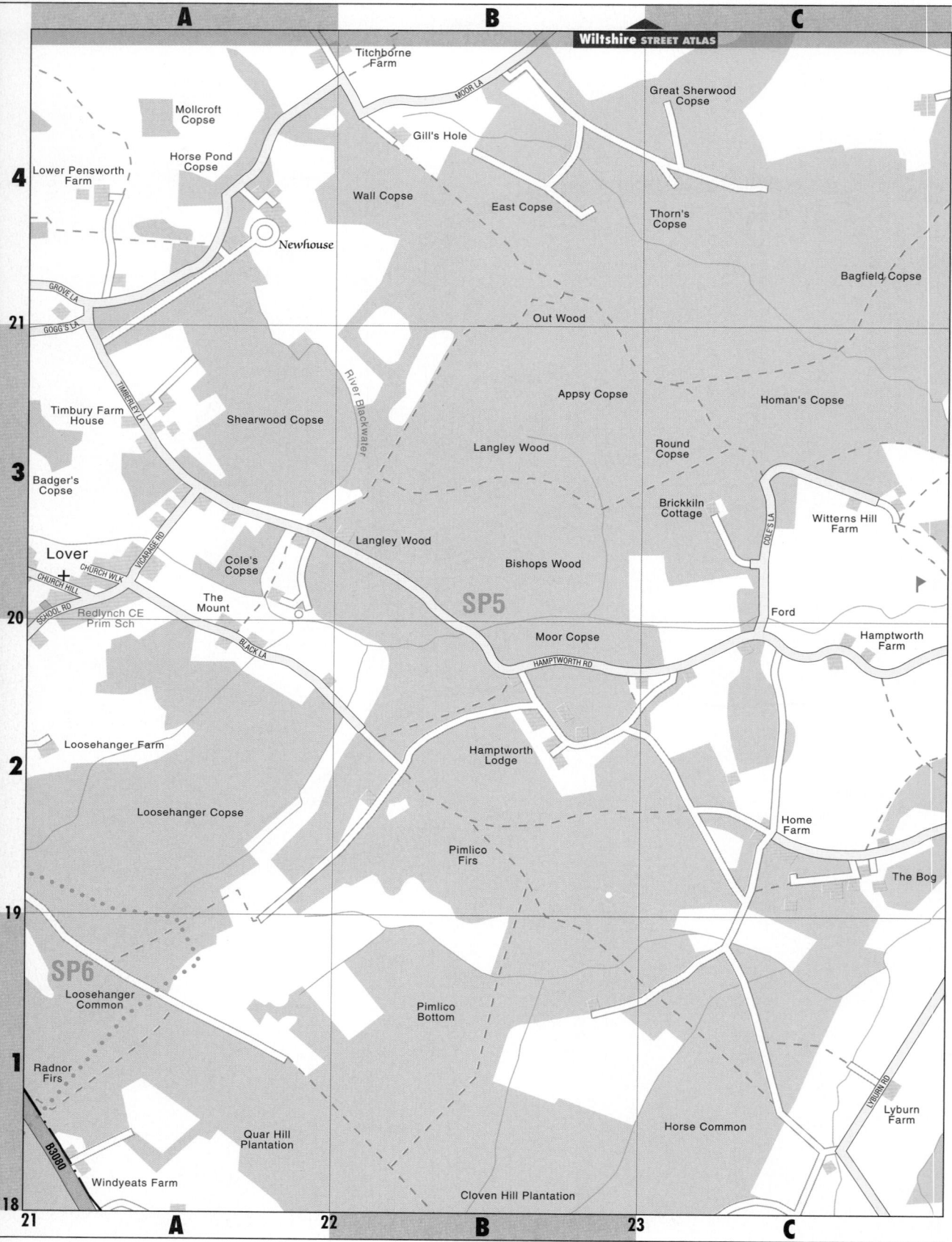

A   B   C

Titchborne Farm

MOOR LA

Great Sherwood Copse

Mollcroft Copse

Gill's Hole

Horse Pond Copse

4

Lower Pensworth Farm

Wall Copse

East Copse

Thorn's Copse

Bagfield Copse

Newhouse

GROVE LA

Out Wood

21

GOGG'S LA

River Blackwater

Appsy Copse

Homan's Copse

Timbury Farm House

TIMBERLEY LA

Shearwood Copse

Langley Wood

Round Copse

3

Badger's Copse

Brickkiln Cottage

Witterns Hill Farm

COLE'S LA

VICARAGE RD

Lover

CHURCH WLK

Cole's Copse

Langley Wood

Bishops Wood

CHURCH HILL

20

SCHOOL RD

Redlynch CE Prim Sch

The Mount

SP5

Ford

Hamptworth Farm

Moor Copse

BLACK LA

HAMPTWORTH RD

Loosehanger Farm

Hamptworth Lodge

2

Loosehanger Copse

Home Farm

Pimlico Firs

The Bog

19

SP6

Loosehanger Common

Pimlico Bottom

1

Radnor Firs

LYBURN RD

Lyburn Farm

B3080

Quar Hill Plantation

Horse Common

Windyeats Farm

18

Cloven Hill Plantation

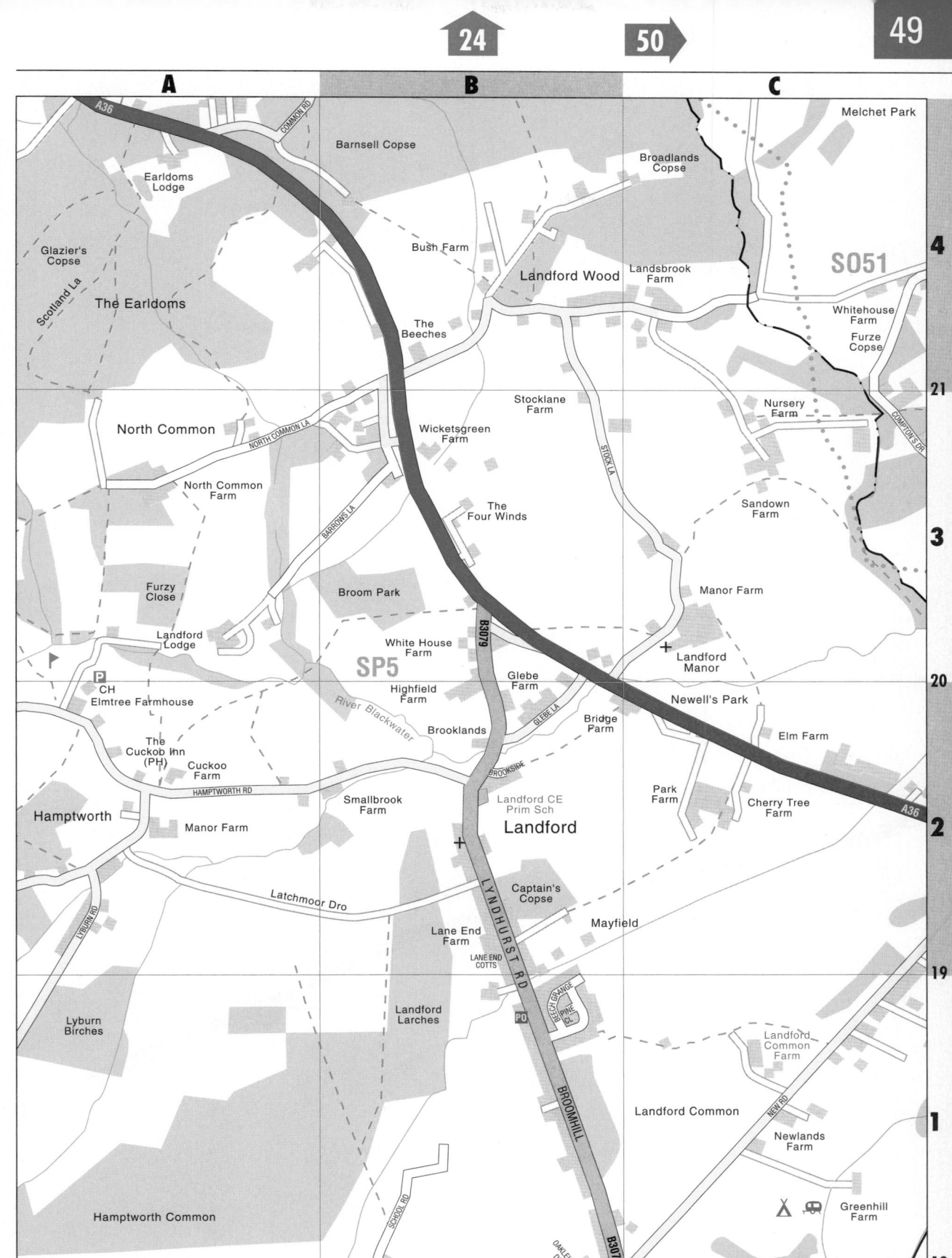

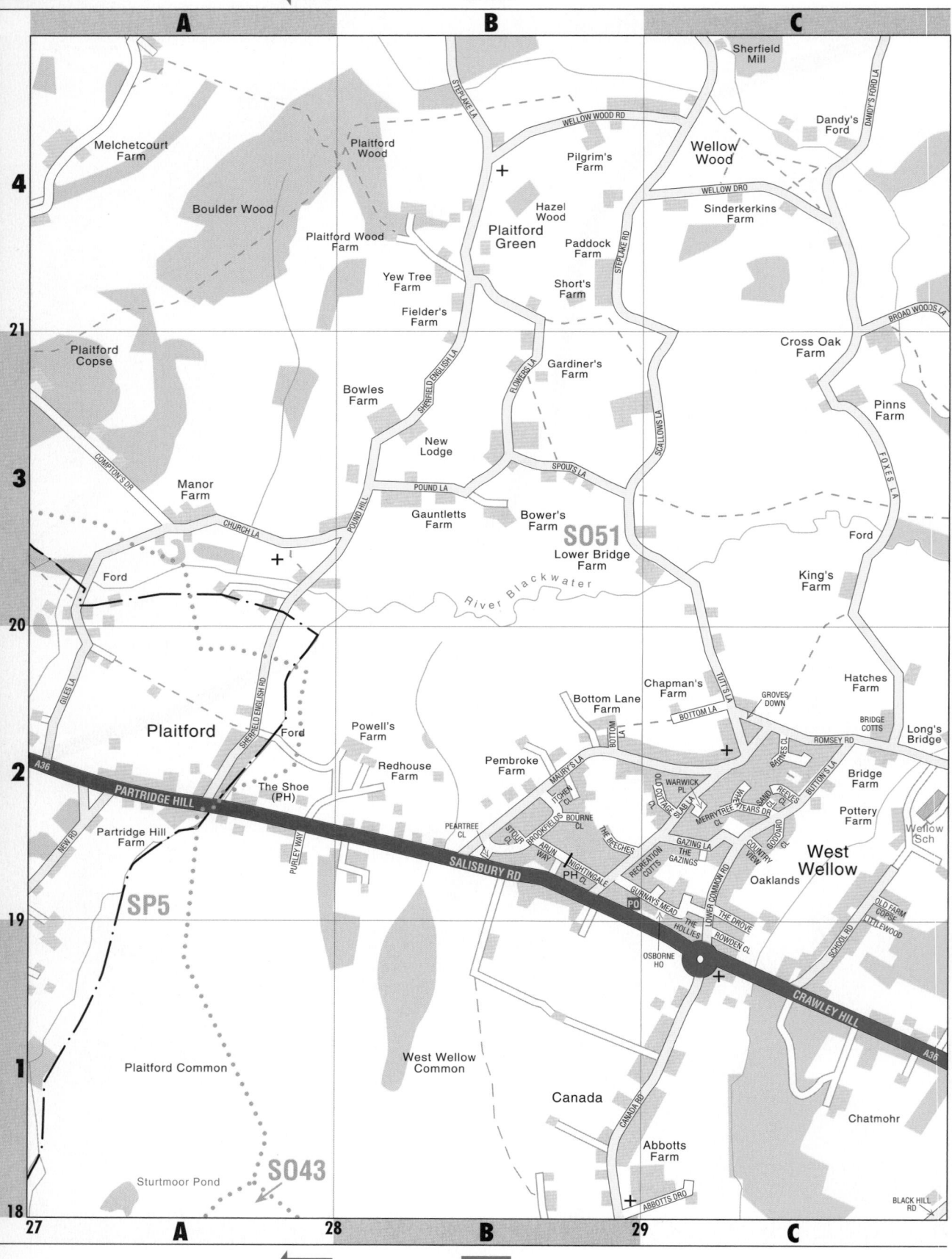

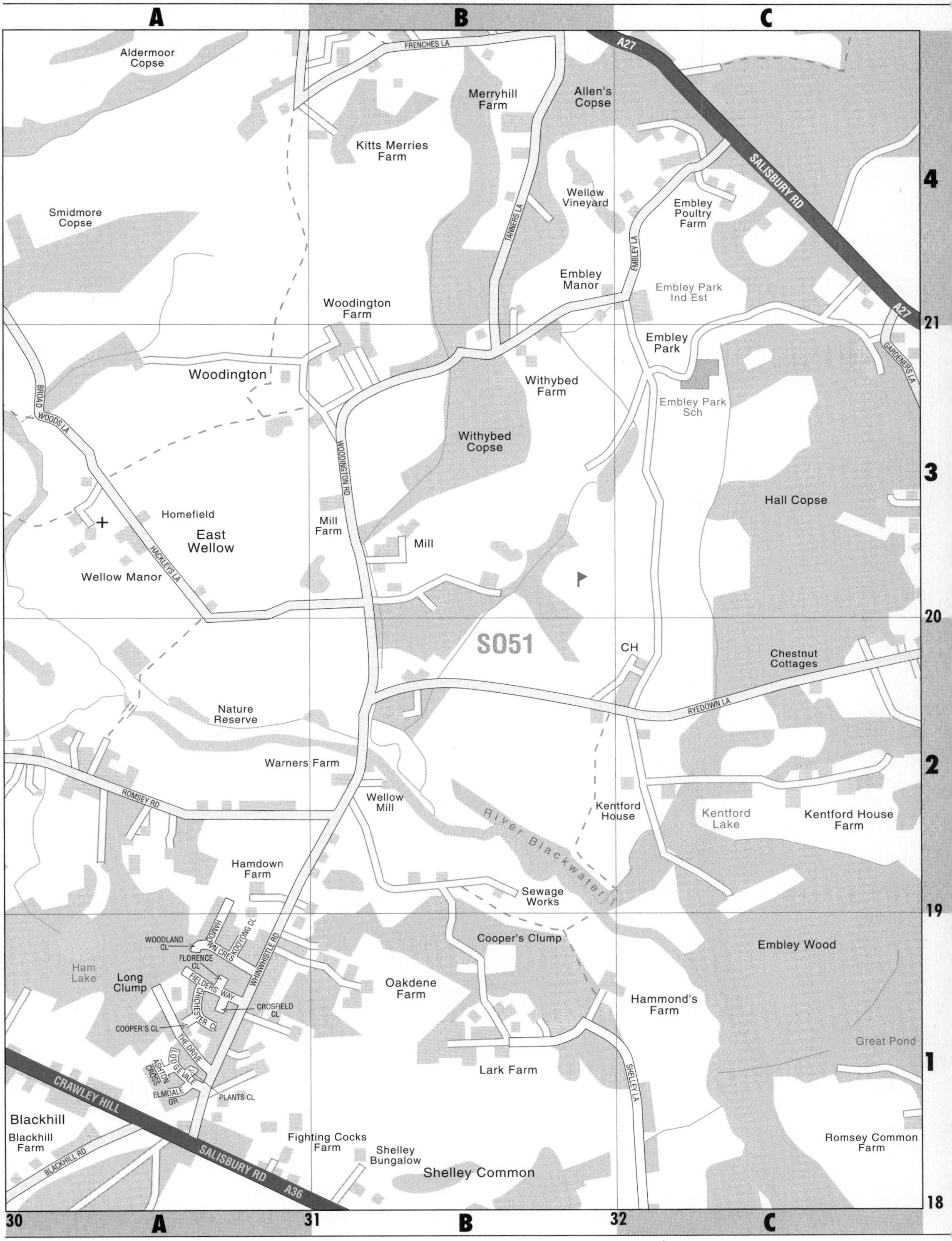

A B C

Aldermoor
Copse

FRENCHES LA

Merryhill
Farm

Allen's
Copse

A27

Kitts Merries
Farm

SALISBURY RD

Smidmore
Copse

Wellow
Vineyard

Embley Poultry
Farm

4

TANNERS LA

Woodington
Farm

Embley
Manor

EMBLEY LA

Embley Park
Ind Est

A27

Embley
Park

GARDENERS LA

21

Woodington

Withybed
Farm

Embley Park
Sch

BROAD WOODS LA

WOODINGTON RD

Withybed
Copse

Hall Copse

3

Homefield

Mill
Farm

Mill

East
Wellow

+

HACKLEYS LA

Mill

Wellow Manor

20

Nature
Reserve

SO51

CH

Chestnut
Cottages

RYEDOWN LA

Warners Farm

2

ROMSEY RD

Wellow
Mill

River Blackwater

Kentford
House

Kentford
Lake

Kentford House
Farm

Hamdown
Farm

Sewage
Works

19

WINWHISTLE RD

WOODLAND CL

OWN CRES

CROYDONS CL

Cooper's Clump

Embley Wood

Ham
Lake

Long
Clump

FLORENCE CL

FIELDERS WAY

CHICHESTER CL

CROSFIELD CL

Oakdene
Farm

Hammond's
Farm

Great Pond

COOPER'S CL

THE DRIVE

ASHTON CROSS

COPSE VALE

ELMDALE GR

PLANTS CL

Lark Farm

SHELLEY LA

1

Blackhill

CRAWLEY HILL

Blackhill
Farm

BLACKHILL RD

SALISBURY RD

A36

Fighting Cocks
Farm

Shelley
Bungalow

Shelley Common

Romsey Common
Farm

18

30 A 31 B 32 C

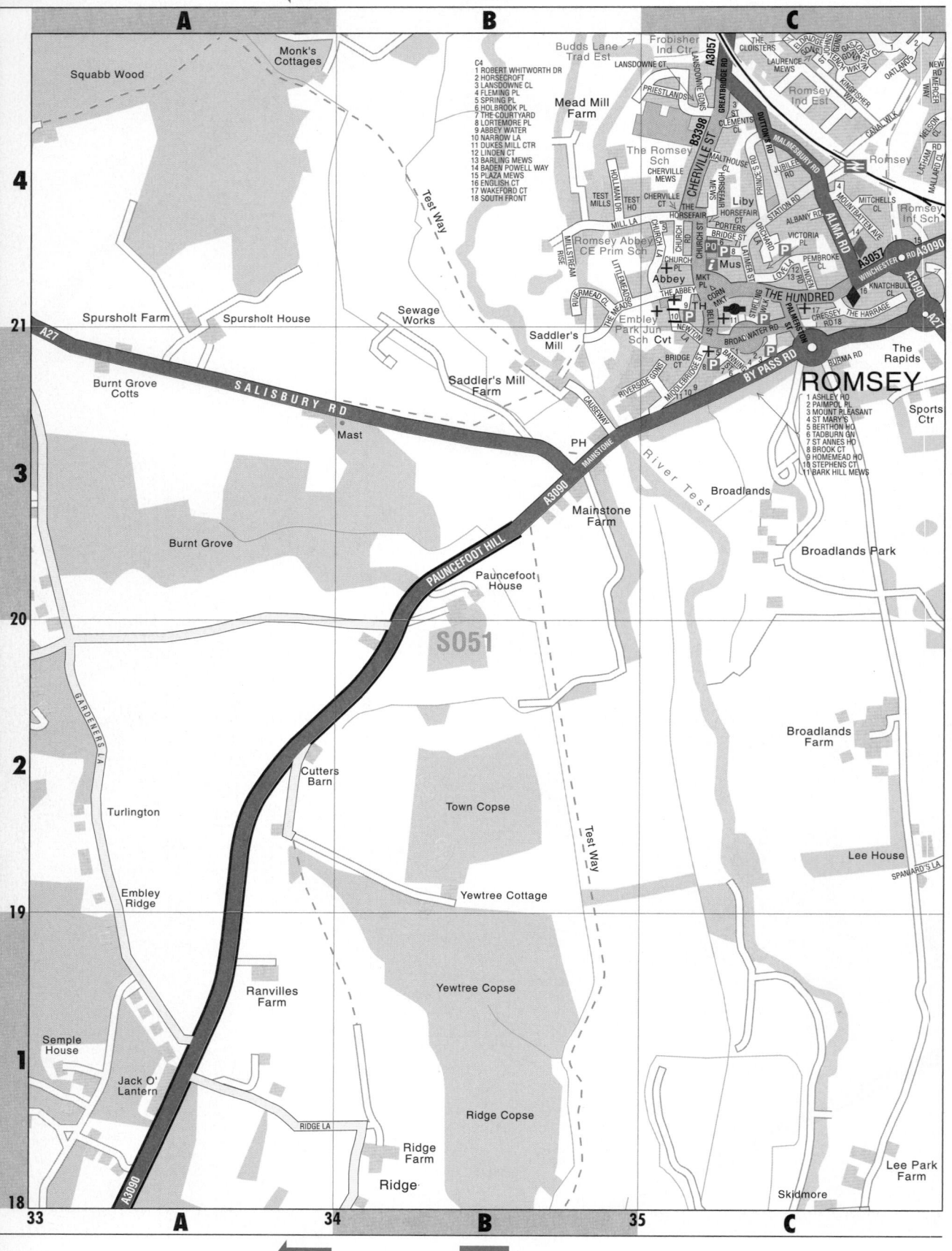

C4
1 ROBERT WHITWORTH DR
2 HORSECROFT
3 LANSDOWNE CL
4 FLEMING PL
5 SPRING PL
6 HOLBROOK PL
7 THE COURTYARD
8 LORTEMORE PL
9 ABBEY WATER
10 NARROW LA
11 DUKES MILL CTR
12 LINDEN CT
13 BARLING MEWS
14 BADEN POWELL WAY
15 PLAZA MEWS
16 ENGLISH CT
17 WAKEFORD CT
18 SOUTH FRONT

Squabb Wood
Monk's Cottages
Frobisher Ind Ctr
THE CLOISTERS
Budds Lane Trad Est
LANSDOWNE CT
Romsey Ind Est
Romsey
Mead Mill Farm
PRIESTLANDS
The Romsey Sch
CHERVILLE MEWS
Romsey Int Sch
Test Way
MILLSTREAM RISE
RIVERMEAD CL
Sewage Works
Saddler's Mill
Liby
Romsey Abbey CE Prim Sch
Mus
Abbey
THE ABBEY
Spursholt Farm
Spursholt House
SALISBURY RD
A27
Saddler's Mill Farm
CAUSEWAY
Embley Park Jun Sch
Cvt
ROMSEY
Burnt Grove Cotts
PH
MAINSTONE
A3090
River Test
Broadwater RD
BY PASS RD
BURMA RD
The Rapids
Sports Ctr
1 ASHLEY HO
2 PAIMPOL PL
3 MOUNT PLEASANT
4 ST MARY'S
5 BERTHON HO
6 TADBURN GN
7 ST ANNES HO
8 BROOK CT
9 HOMEMEAD HO
10 STEPHENS CT
11 BARK HILL MEWS
Mast
Mainstone Farm
Broadlands
Burnt Grove
PAUNCEFOOT HILL
Pauncefoot House
Broadlands Park
GARDENERS LA
S051
Broadlands Farm
Cutters Barn
Turlington
Town Copse
Lee House
SPANWARD'S LA
Embley Ridge
Yewtree Cottage
Test Way
Ranvilles Farm
Yewtree Copse
Semple House
Jack O' Lantern
RIDGE LA
Ridge Copse
Lee Park Farm
Ridge Farm
Ridge
Skidmore
A3090

28
54

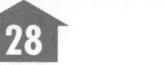

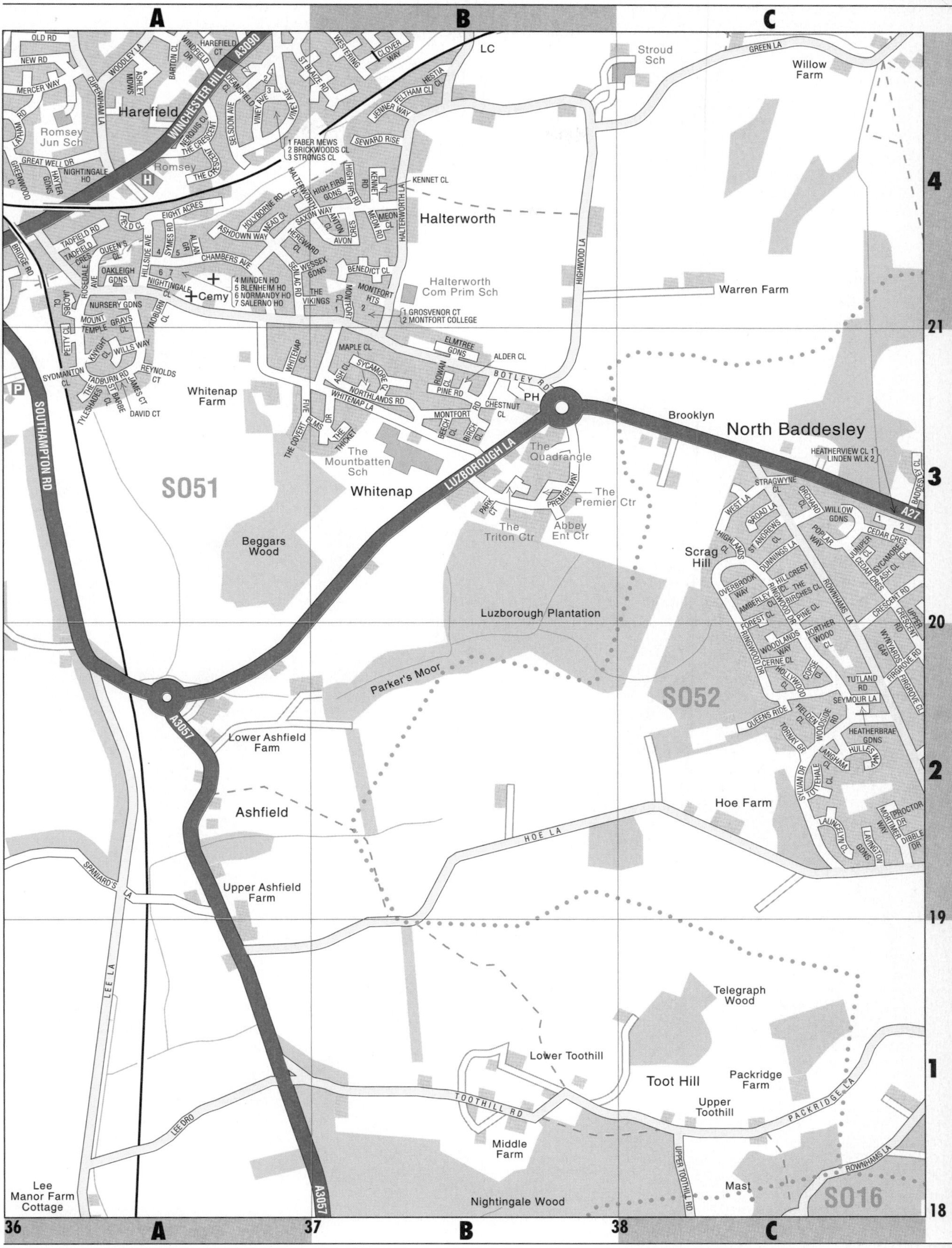
A
B
C
OLD RD
NEW RD
MERCER WAY
CUPERNHAM LA
WOODLEY LA
ASHLEY MDWS
BARTON CL
WINDFIELD DR
HAREFIELD CT
A3090
WINCHESTER HILL
Harefield
Romsey Jun Sch
LATHAM RD
GREAT WELL DR
NIGHTINGALE HO
HAYTER GDNS
GREENWOOD CL
Romsey
THE CRESCENT
NERQUIS CL
SELSDON AVE
DEANSFIELD CL
VINEY AVE
ST BLAIZE RD
WESTERING
CLOVER WAY
HESTIA
FELTHAM CL
JENNER WAY
1 FABER MEWS
2 BRICKWOODS CL
3 STRONGS CL
SEWARD RISE
HALTERWORTH CL
HIGH FIRS GDNS
HIGH FIRS RD
KENNET RD
KENNET CL
LC
Stroud Sch
GREEN LA
Willow Farm
4
EIGHT ACRES
HOLYBORNE RD
SAXON WAY
ANTON CL
AVON
AVON CRES
MEON RD
MEON CL
HALTERWORTH LA
Halterworth
TADFIELD RD
TADFIELD CRES
QUEEN'S CL
BRIDGE RD
HILLSIDE AVE
SYMES RD
ALLAN GR
CHAMBERS AVE
ASHDOWN WAY
MEAD CL
HEREWARD CL
WESSEX GDNS
SENLAC RD
BENEDICT CL
HIGHWOOD LA
ROSEDALE AVE
OAKLEIGH GDNS
NIGHTINGALE CL
4 MINDEN HO
5 BLENHEIM HO
6 NORMANDY HO
7 SALERNO HO
Cemy
THE VIKINGS
MONTFORT CL
MONTFORT HTS
Halterworth Com Prim Sch
Warren Farm
JACOBS CL
NURSERY GDNS
MOUNT TEMPLE
GRAYS CL
TADBURN CL
1 GROSVENOR CT
2 MONTFORT COLLEGE
21
PETTY CL
KNYGHT CL
WILLS WAY
ELMTREE GDNS
ALDER CL
MAPLE CL
SYDMANTON CL
REYNOLDS CT
TADBURN RD
ST BARBE CL
JAMES CT
TYLESHADES
DAVID CT
Whitenap Farm
WHITENAP CL
SYCAMORE CL
ASH CL
NORTHLANDS RD
WHITENAP LA
ROWAN CL
PINE RD
BOTLEY RD
PH
CHESTNUT CL
MONTFORT CL
BEECH CL
BIRCH CL
FIVE ELMS DR
THE COVERT
THE THICKET
SOUTHAMPTON RD
The Mountbatten Sch
LUZBOROUGH LA
The Quadrangle
Brooklyn
North Baddesley
HEATHERVIEW CL 1
LINDEN WLK 2
BADDESLEY CL
3
S051
Whitenap
PARK CT
The Triton Ctr
PREMIER WAY
The Premier Ctr
Abbey Ent Ctr
STRAGWYNE CL
ORCHARD CL
WEST LA
BROAD LA
WILLOW GDNS
A27
CEDAR CRES
Beggars Wood
Scrag Hill
HIGHLANDS CL
ST ANDREWS CL
DUNNINGS LA
POPLAR WAY
JUNIPER CL
CEDAR CRES
SYCAMORE CL
ASH CL
OVERBROOK WAY
HILLCREST
AMBERLEY CL
THE BIRCHES CL
RINGWOOD DR
PINE CL
ROWNHAMS LA
CRESCENT RD
UPPER CRESCENT RD
Luzborough Plantation
FOREST CL
NORTHER WOOD CL
WYNYARDS GAP
FIRGROVE RD
20
Parker's Moor
WOODLANDS WAY
CERNE CL
HOLLYWOOD CL
CORSE CL
TUTLAND RD
FIRGROVE CL
S052
SEYMOUR LA
QUEENS RIDE
FIELDEN CL
WOODSIDE RD
A3057
Lower Ashfield Farm
TORNAY GR
HEATHERBRAE GDNS
LANGHAM CL
HULLES WAY
2
SYLVAN DR
TOTTEHALE CL
Ashfield
Hoe Farm
HOE LA
LAUNCELYN CL
LAVINGTON GDNS
MORTIMER WAY
PROCTOR DR
DIBBLE DR
SPANIARD'S LA
Upper Ashfield Farm
19
LEE LA
Telegraph Wood
Lower Toothill
1
Toot Hill
Packridge Farm
Upper Toothill
TOOTHILL RD
PACKRIDGE LA
LEE DRO
Middle Farm
UPPER TOOTHILL RD
ROWNHAMS LA
Mast
S016
Lee Manor Farm Cottage
Nightingale Wood
A3057
18
36
37
38

77
54

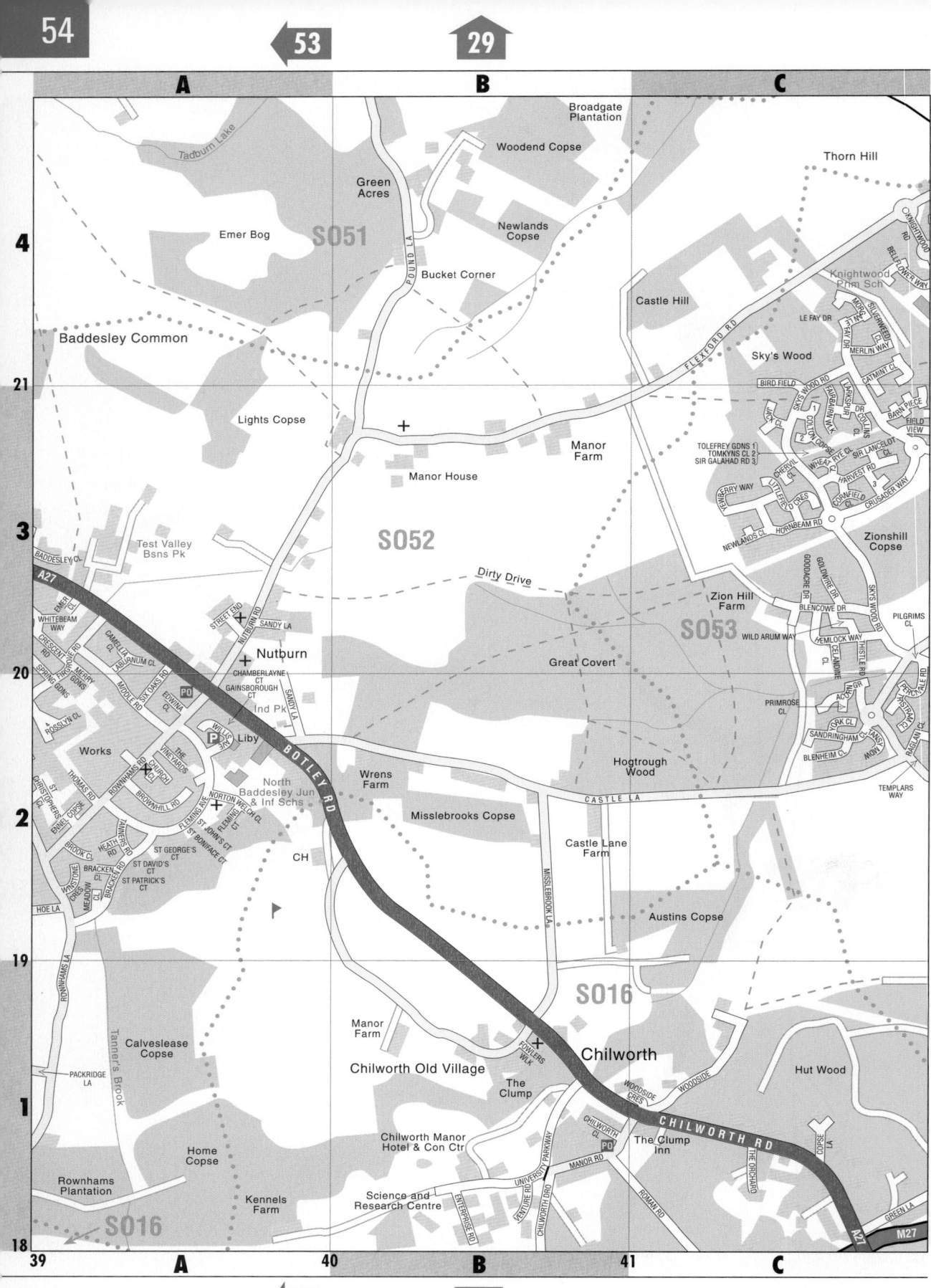

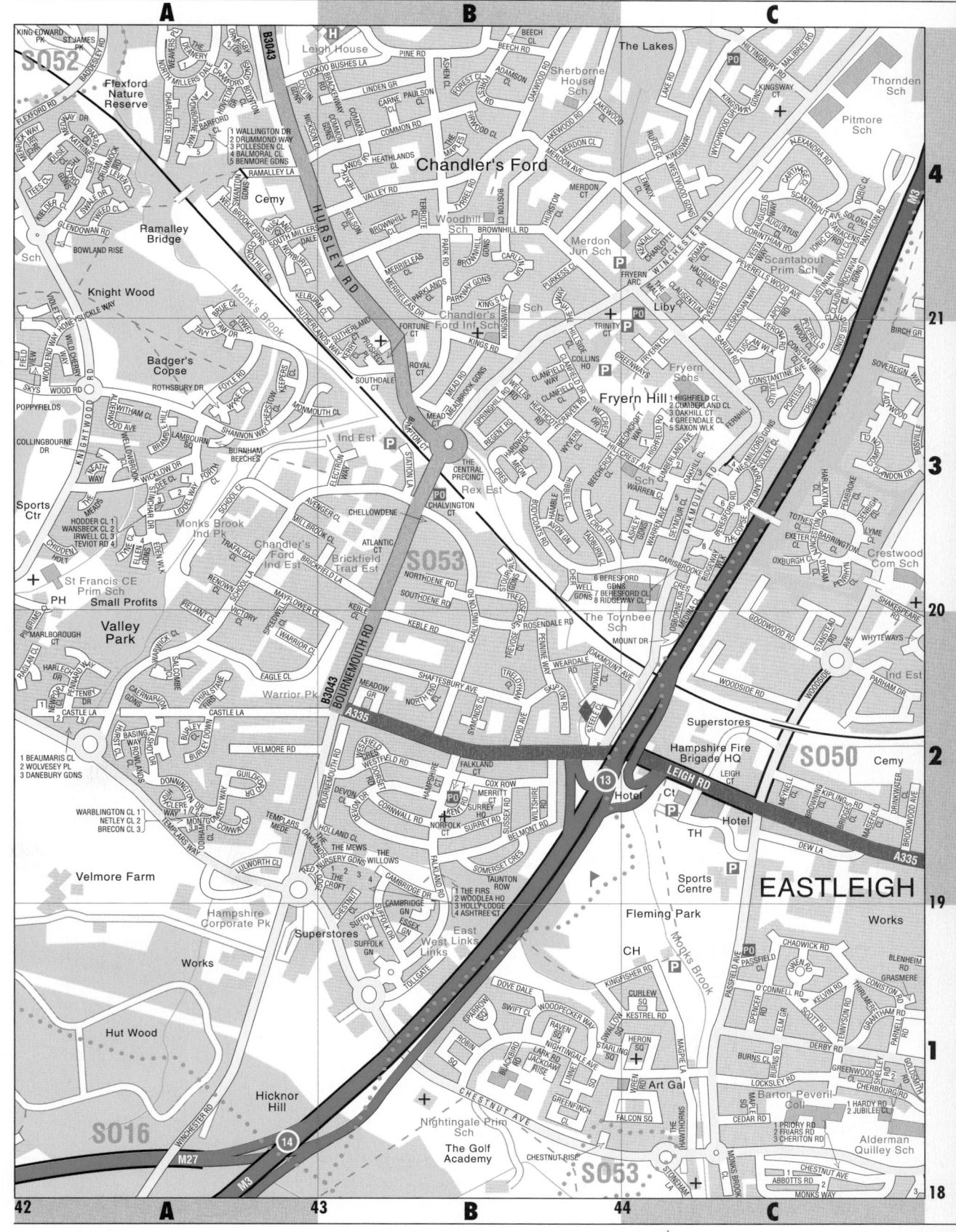

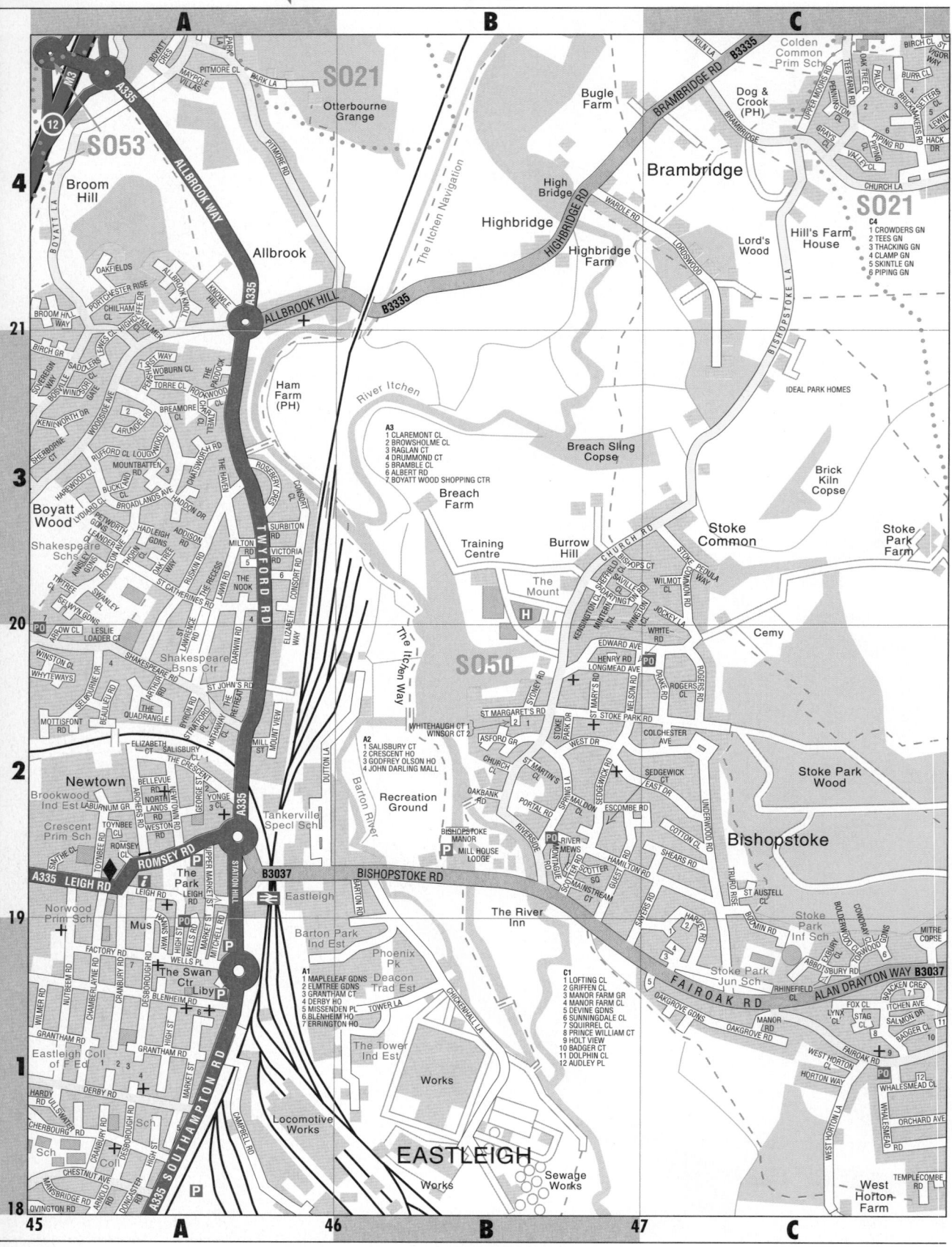

A **B** **C**

B3354
Cvn Pk

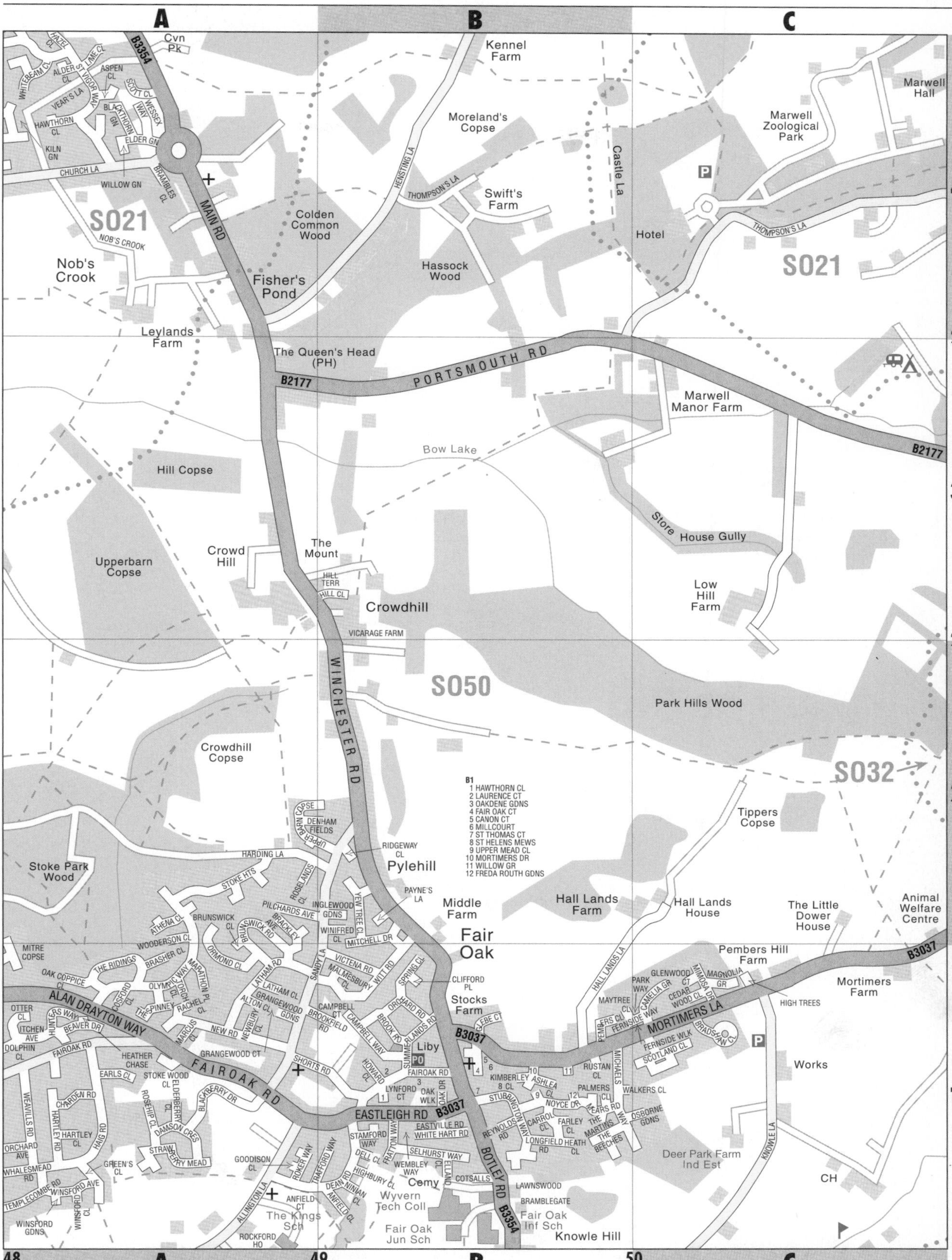

WHITEBEAM CL · HAZEL CL · ALDER CL · VIGOR WAY · SCOTT CL · VESSEX CL · ASPEN CL
YEAR'S LA · HAWTHORN CL · BLACKTHORN GN · ELDER GN
KILN GN · BRAISHES CL · CHURCH LA · WILLOW GN

Kennel Farm

Moreland's Copse

SO21

NOB'S CROOK

Nob's Crook

Colden Common Wood

HENSTING LA · THOMPSON'S LA
Swift's Farm

Hassock Wood

Castle La

Marwell Hall

Marwell Zoological Park

Hotel

P

SO21

Fisher's Pond

Leylands Farm

The Queen's Head (PH)

B2177

PORTSMOUTH RD

THOMPSON'S LA

B2177

Marwell Manor Farm

Hill Copse

Bow Lake

Store House Gully

Low Hill Farm

Upperbarn Copse

Crowd Hill

The Mount

HILL TERR · HILL CL

Crowdhill

VICARAGE FARM

SO50

Park Hills Wood

SO32

Crowdhill Copse

WINCHESTER RD

COPSE · DENHAM FIELDS

Tippers Copse

B1
1 HAWTHORN CL
2 LAURENCE CT
3 OAKDENE GDNS
4 FAIR OAK CT
5 CANON CT
6 MILLCOURT
7 ST THOMAS CT
8 ST HELENS MEWS
9 UPPER MEAD CL
10 MORTIMERS DR
11 WILLOW GR
12 FREDA ROUTH GDNS

Hall Lands Farm

Hall Lands House

The Little Dower House

Animal Welfare Centre

Stoke Park Wood

HARDING LA · STOKE HTS · ROSKLANDS · YEW TREE LA · RIDGEWAY CL

Pylehill

PAYNE'S LA

Middle Farm

Fair Oak

Pembers Hill Farm

B3037

Mortimers Farm

MITRE COPSE · THE RIDINGS · OAK COPPICE CL · BRUNSWICK · WOODERSON CL · BRASHER CL · ORMOND CL · WHARTON RD · SWICK RD · PILCHARDS AVE · CRACKLE · INGLEWOOD GDNS · WINIFRED CT · MITCHELL DR

ATHENA CL · MARATHON WAY · OLYMPIA WAY · RACHEL CL · LATHAM CL · VICTENA RD · WITT RD · SPRING CL

ALAN DRAYTON WAY
OAK CL · OXFORD · THE SPINNEY · ALTON CL · GRANGEWOOD GDNS · BROOKFIELD · CAMPBELL WAY · CAMPBELL RD · ORCHARD RD · CLIFFORD PL

Stocks Farm

GLENWOOD CT · PARK WAY · MAYTREE · MINNS RD · CAMELIA GR · MAGNOLIA GR · CEDAR WOOD CL · HIGH TREES

HINES WAY · BEAVER DR · OLYMPIA WAY · MAUD CL · NEW RD · GRANGEWOOD CT · HOWARD CL · LYNFORD CT · OAK WLK · FAIROAK RD

FAIROAK RD
Liby PO

B3037

GLEBE CT · FERNSIDE WAY · SCOTLAND CL · BRADSHAW CL · RUSTAN CL · MICHAELS · WALKERS CL

MORTIMERS LA

P

Works

OTTER CL · ITCHEN AVE · DOLPHIN CL · WEAVILLS RD · EARLS CL · CHARDEN RD · HEATHER CHASE · STOKE WOOD CL · ELDERBERRY CL · DAMSON CRES · BLACKBERRY DR · SHORTS RD

HARTLEY CL · HAIG RD · GOODISON CL · ROWER WAY · DELL CL · HIGHBURY CL

ORCHARD AVE · WHALESMEAD RD · TEMPLECOMBE RD · WINSFORD AVE · WINSFORD GDNS · GREEN'S CL · STRAWBERRY MEAD · DEAN NINIAN CL · ANFIELD CT · ANFIELD CL · ALLINGTON LA · ROCKFORD HO

FAIROAK RD

EASTLEIGH RD

B3037

STAMFORD WAY · FRATTON WAY · WHITE HART RD · SELHURST WAY · WEMBLEY WAY · COTSALLS CL · LAWNSWOOD · BRAMBLEGATE

Cemy

KIMBERLEY RD · ASHLEA CL · REYNOLDS WAY · CARROL CL · NOYCE DR · STUBBINGTON WAY · FARLEY CL · LONGFIELD HEATH RD · THE MARTINS · THE BEECHES · OSBORNE GDNS · PALMERS · THE PEARS RD · MARTIN WAY

BOTLEY RD

B3354

Wyvern Tech Coll

The Kings Sch

Fair Oak Jun Sch

Fair Oak Inf Sch

Deer Park Farm Ind Est

CH

Knowle Hill

A 48 49 **B** 50 **C**

4
21
3
20
2
19
1
18

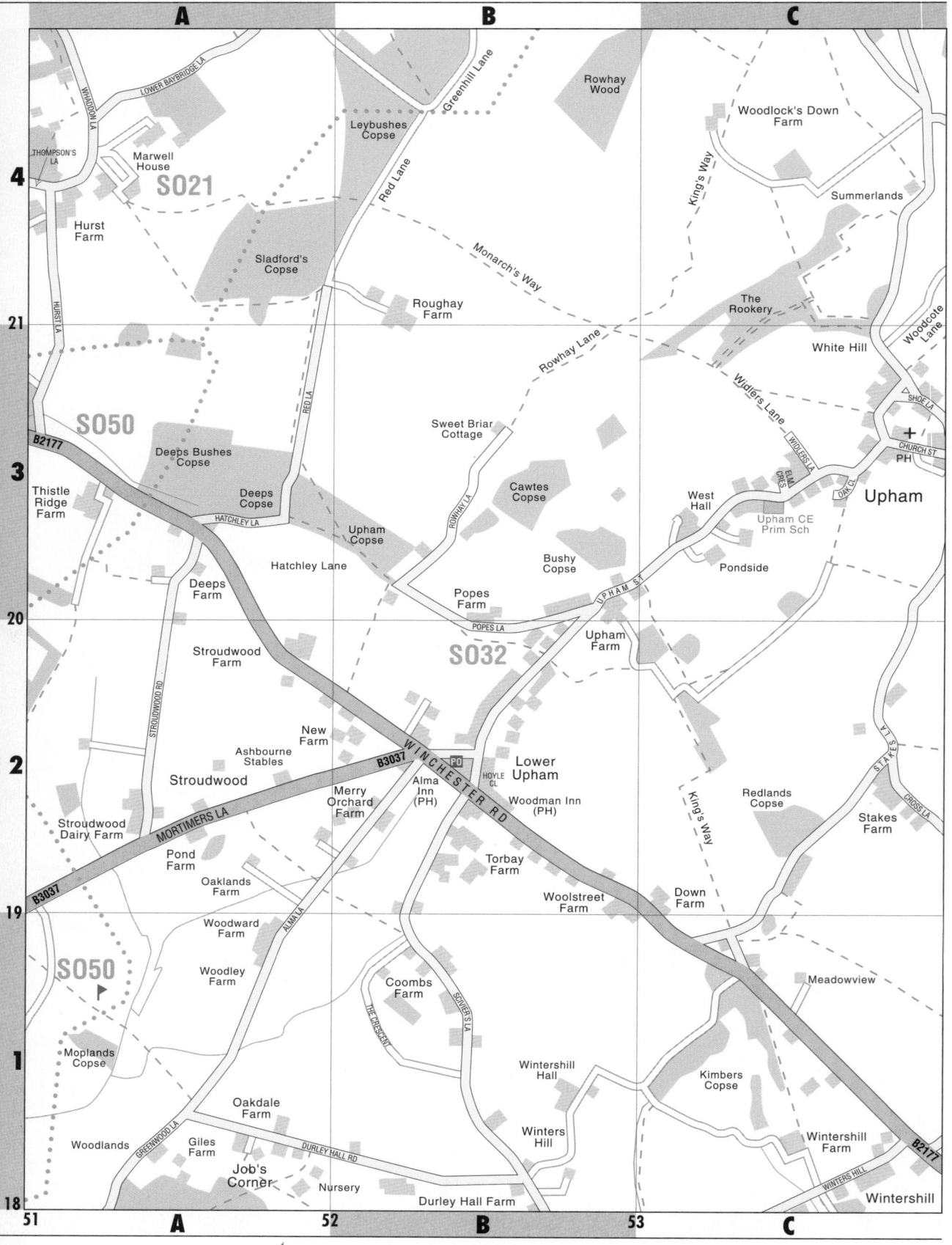

4

THOMPSON'S LA

WHADDON LA

LOWER BAYBRIDGE LA

Marwell House

SO21

Greenhill Lane

Leybushes Copse

Red Lane

Rowhay Wood

Woodlock's Down Farm

King's Way

Summerlands

Hurst Farm

Sladford's Copse

Roughay Farm

Monarch's Way

The Rookery

Woodcote Lane

HURST LA

21

Rowhay Lane

White Hill

Widlers Lane

SO050

B2177

RED LA

Deeps Bushes Copse

Sweet Briar Cottage

Cawtes Copse

SHOE LA

WIDLERS LA

CHURCH ST

PH

3

Thistle Ridge Farm

Deeps Copse

HATCHLEY LA

Upham Copse

ROWHAY LA

Bushy Copse

West Hall

Upham CE Prim Sch

ELMA CRES

OAK CL

Upham

Hatchley Lane

Popes Farm

UPHAM ST

Pondside

Deeps Farm

POPES LA

20

Stroudwood Farm

SO032

Upham Farm

STROUDWOOD RD

New Farm

King's Way

Redlands Copse

STAKES LA

CROSS LA

2

Ashbourne Stables

Stroudwood

MORTIMERS LA

Merry Orchard Farm

B3037

WINCHESTER RD

PO

Alma Inn (PH)

HOYLE CL

Lower Upham

Woodman Inn (PH)

Stakes Farm

Stroudwood Dairy Farm

B3037

Pond Farm

Oaklands Farm

Torbay Farm

Woolstreet Farm

King's Way

Down Farm

19

Woodward Farm

ALMA LA

Meadowview

SO050

Woodley Farm

Coombs Farm

THE CRESCENT

SERVIERS LA

Wintershill Hall

Kimbers Copse

1

Moplands Copse

Winters Hill

Wintershill Farm

B2177

Woodlands

GREENWOOD LA

Giles Farm

Oakdale Farm

DURLEY HALL RD

Job's Corner

Nursery

Durley Hall Farm

WINTERS HILL LA

Wintershill

18

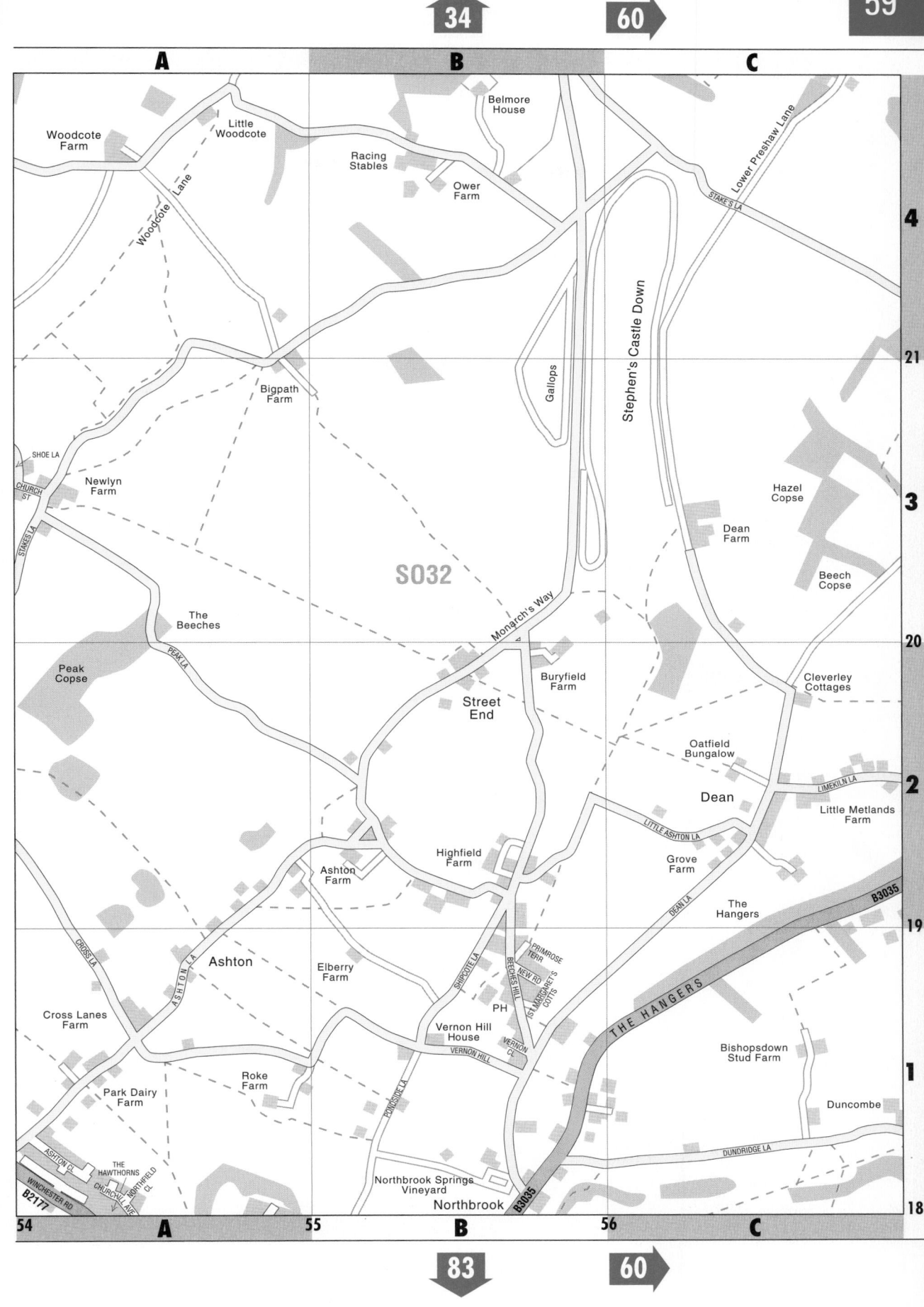

A B C

Woodcote Farm
Little Woodcote
Woodcote Lane
Belmore House
Racing Stables
Ower Farm

4

Bigpath Farm

21

Galops

Stephen's Castle Down

Lower Preshaw Lane

STAKE'S LA

SHOE LA
CHURCH ST
Newlyn Farm
STAKES LA

Hazel Copse

Dean Farm

3

Beech Copse

SO32

Monarch's Way

The Beeches

PEAK LA

Peak Copse

20

Buryfield Farm

Street End

Cleverley Cottages

Oatfield Bungalow

LIMEKILN LA

Dean

2

Little Metlands Farm

Ashton Farm

Highfield Farm

LITTLE ASHTON LA

Grove Farm

The Hangers

Ashton
CROSS LA
ASHTON LA

Elberry Farm

SHIPCOTE LA
NEW RD
BEECHES HILL
PRIMROSE TERR
ST MARGARET'S
COUTTS

PH

Vernon Hill House
VERNON CL
VERNON HILL

DEAN LA

THE HANGERS

B3035

19

Bishopsdown Stud Farm

1

Cross Lanes Farm

Park Dairy Farm

Roke Farm

PONDSIDE LA

Duncombe

DUNDRIDGE LA

ASHTON CL
THE HAWTHORNS
CHURCHILL
WINCHESTER RD
NORTHFIELD CL
B2177

Northbrook Springs Vineyard

Northbrook

B3035

18

54 A 55 B 56 C

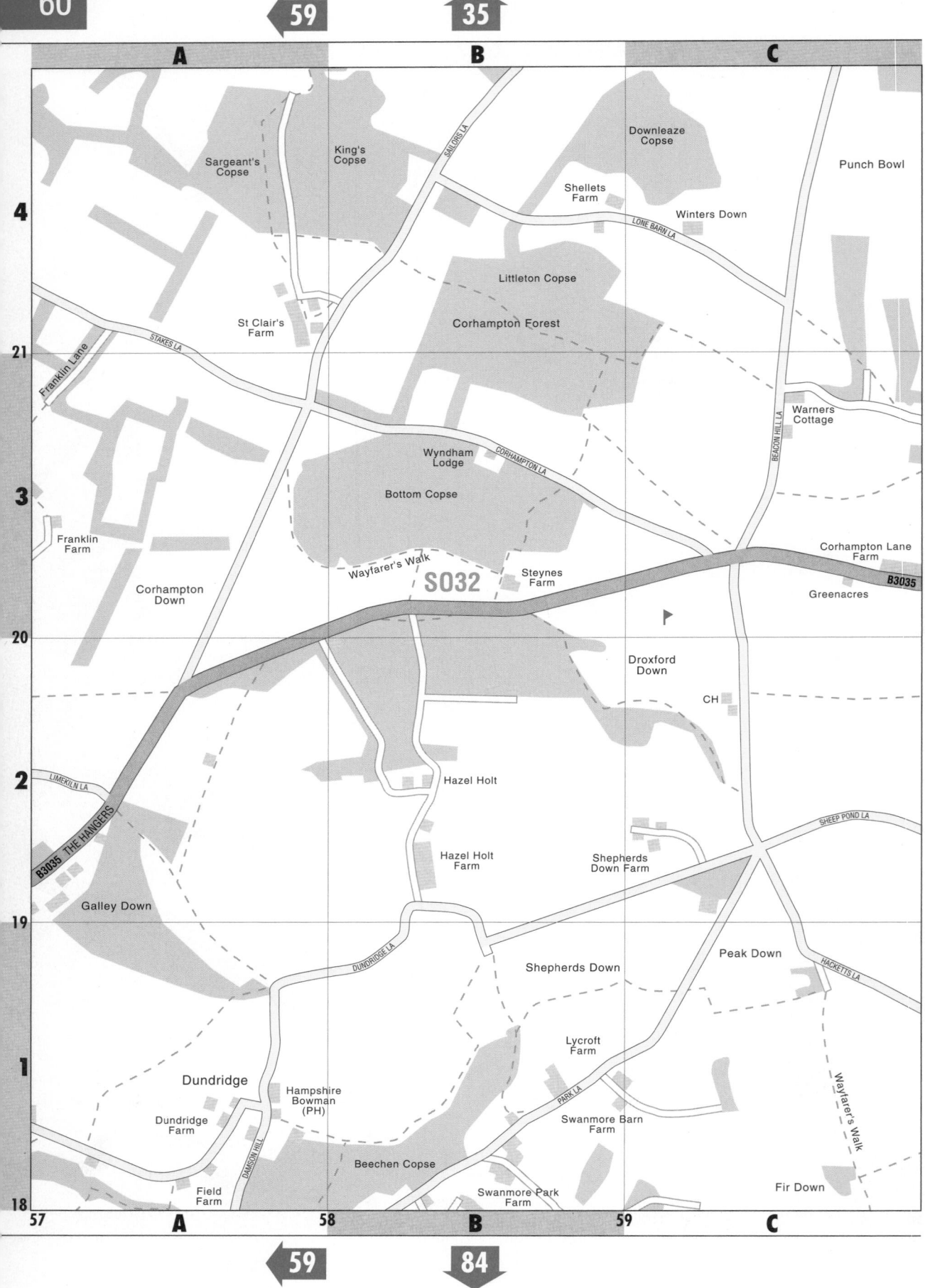

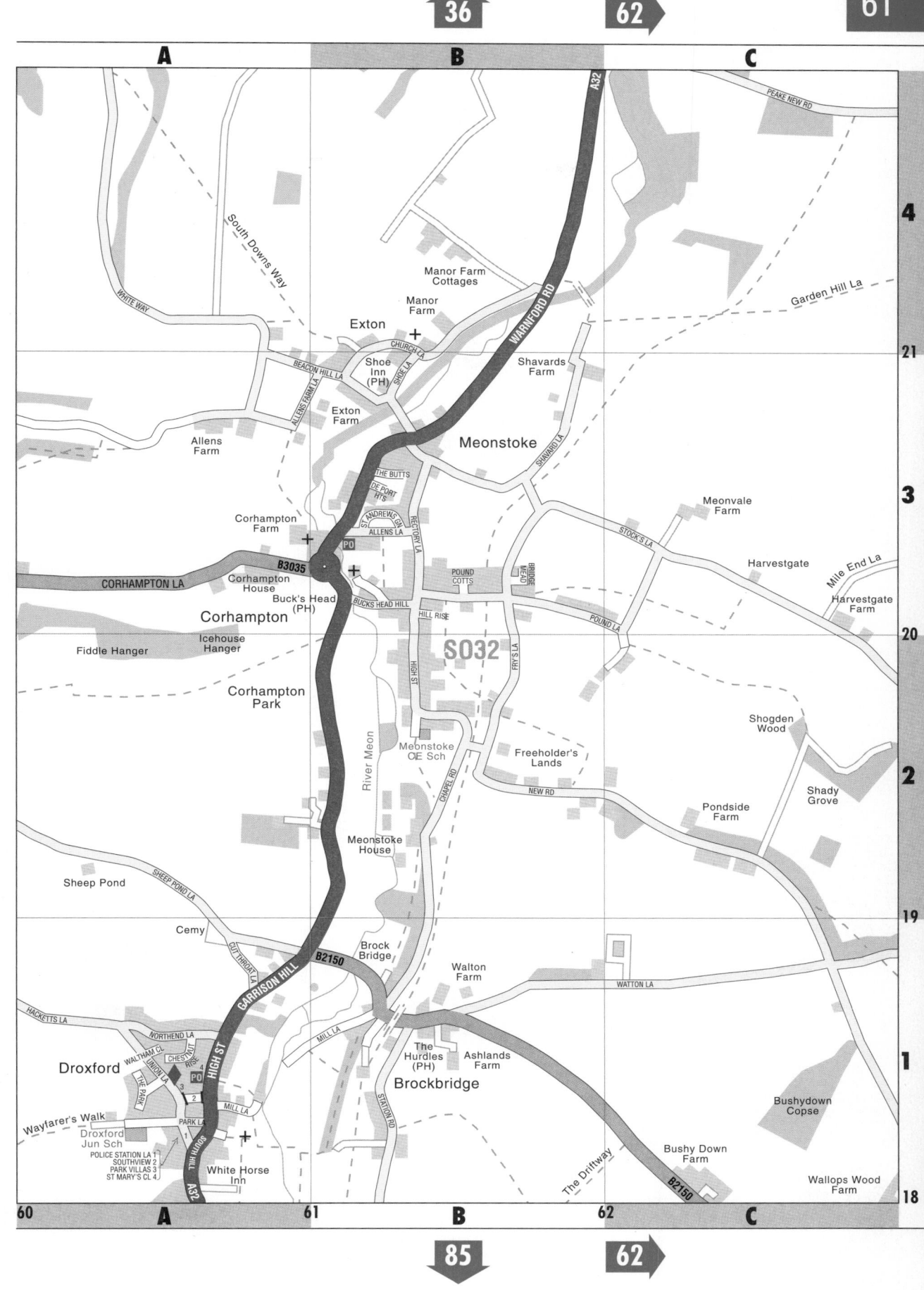

61
37

A
B
C
4
21
3
20
2
19
1
18
63
64
65
Peake Farm
PEAKE NEW RD
Bullshead Copse
OLD WINCHESTER HILL LA
OLD WINCHESTER HILL LA
Hen Wood
Peake Wood
Whitewool Hanger
Whitewool Farm
P
Roll's Copse
South Downs Way
Nature Trail
GU32
Old Winchester Hill
Nature Reserve
Monarch's Way
Castle Cottages
Mile End La
SO32
Stocks Farm
STOCK'S LA
Teglease Down
Little West End Farm
Teglease Copse
PO7
Westend Down
Teglease Farm
Sheepbarn Copse
SHEARDLEY LA
Little Sheardley Wood
WHITELEAF LA
Stoke Wood
Wallops Wood Farm

61
86

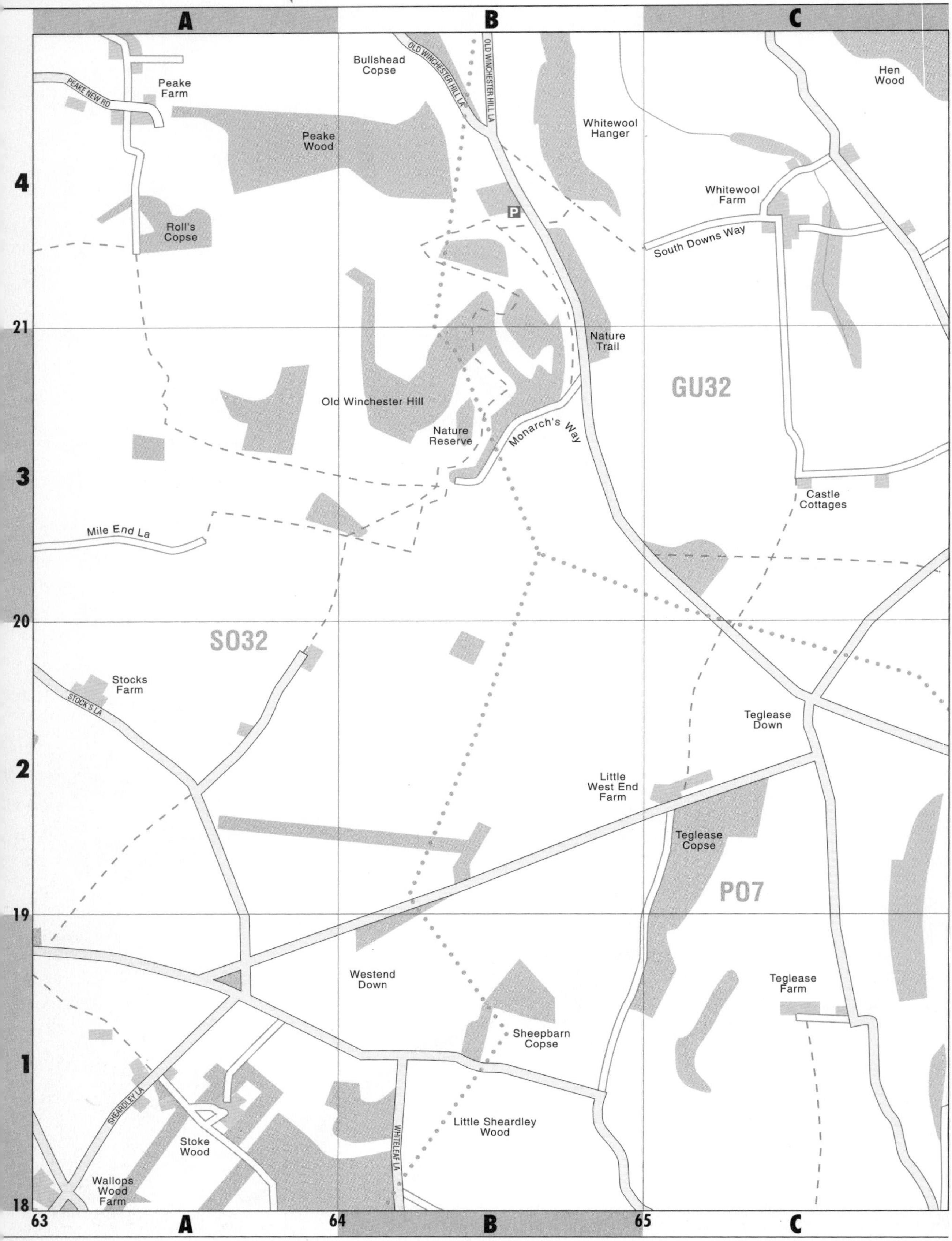

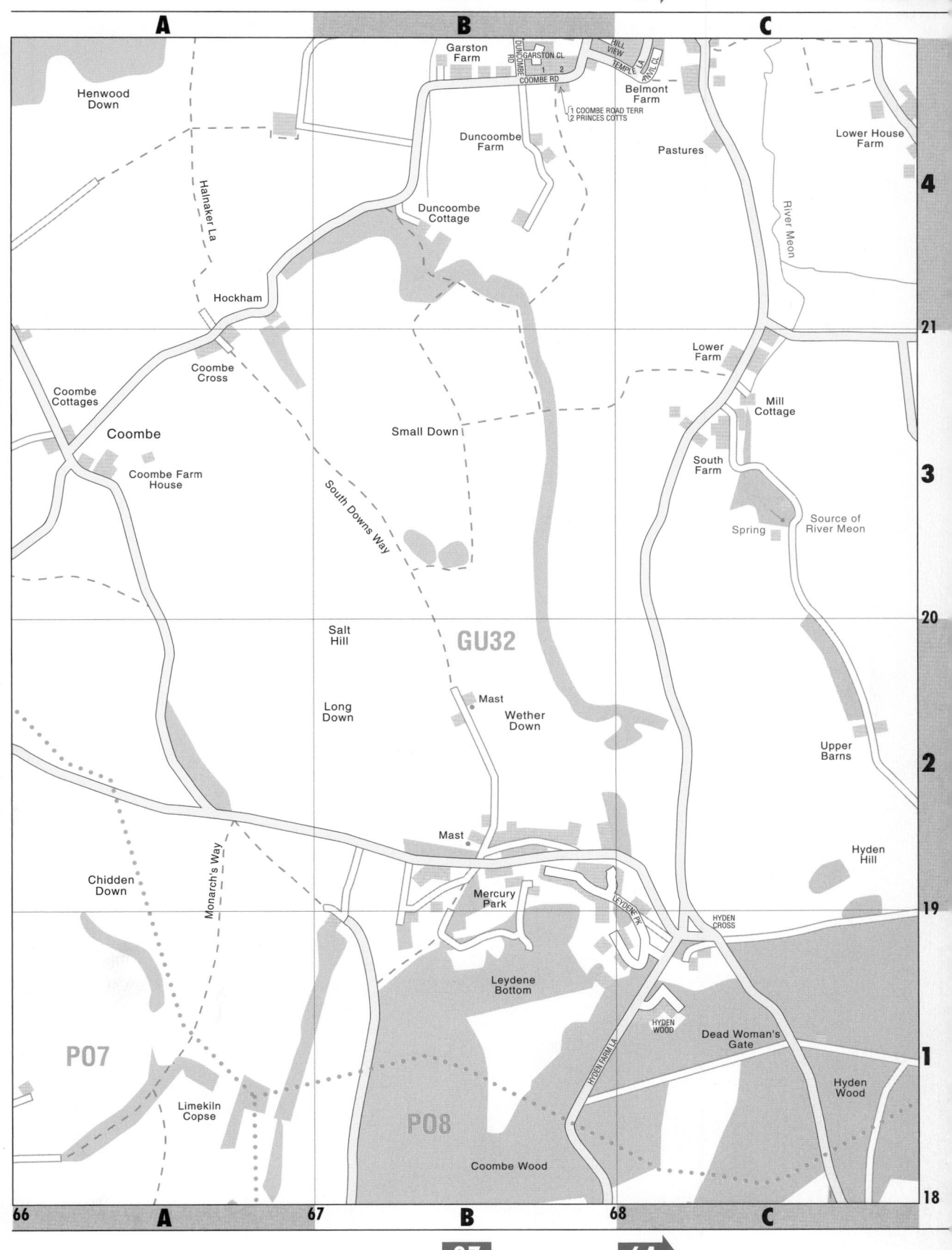

Henwood
Down

Garston
Farm

GARSTON CL

DUNCOMBE RD

COOMBE RD

HILL
VIEW

TEMPLE LA

RVIL CL

Belmont
Farm

Lower House
Farm

Duncoombe
Farm

1 COOMBE ROAD TERR
2 PRINCES COTTS

Pastures

Halnaker La

Duncoombe
Cottage

River Meon

4

Hockham

21

Lower
Farm

Coombe
Cottages

Coombe Cross

Mill
Cottage

Coombe

South
Farm

3

Coombe Farm
House

South Downs Way

Small Down

Spring

Source of
River Meon

20

Salt
Hill

GU32

Long
Down

Mast

Wether
Down

Upper
Barns

2

Mast

Chidden
Down

Monarch's Way

Mercury
Park

LEYDENE PK

HYDEN
CROSS

Hyden
Hill

19

P07

Leydene
Bottom

HYDEN FARM LA

HYDEN
WOOD

Dead Woman's
Gate

1

Limekiln
Copse

Hyden
Wood

P08

Coombe Wood

18

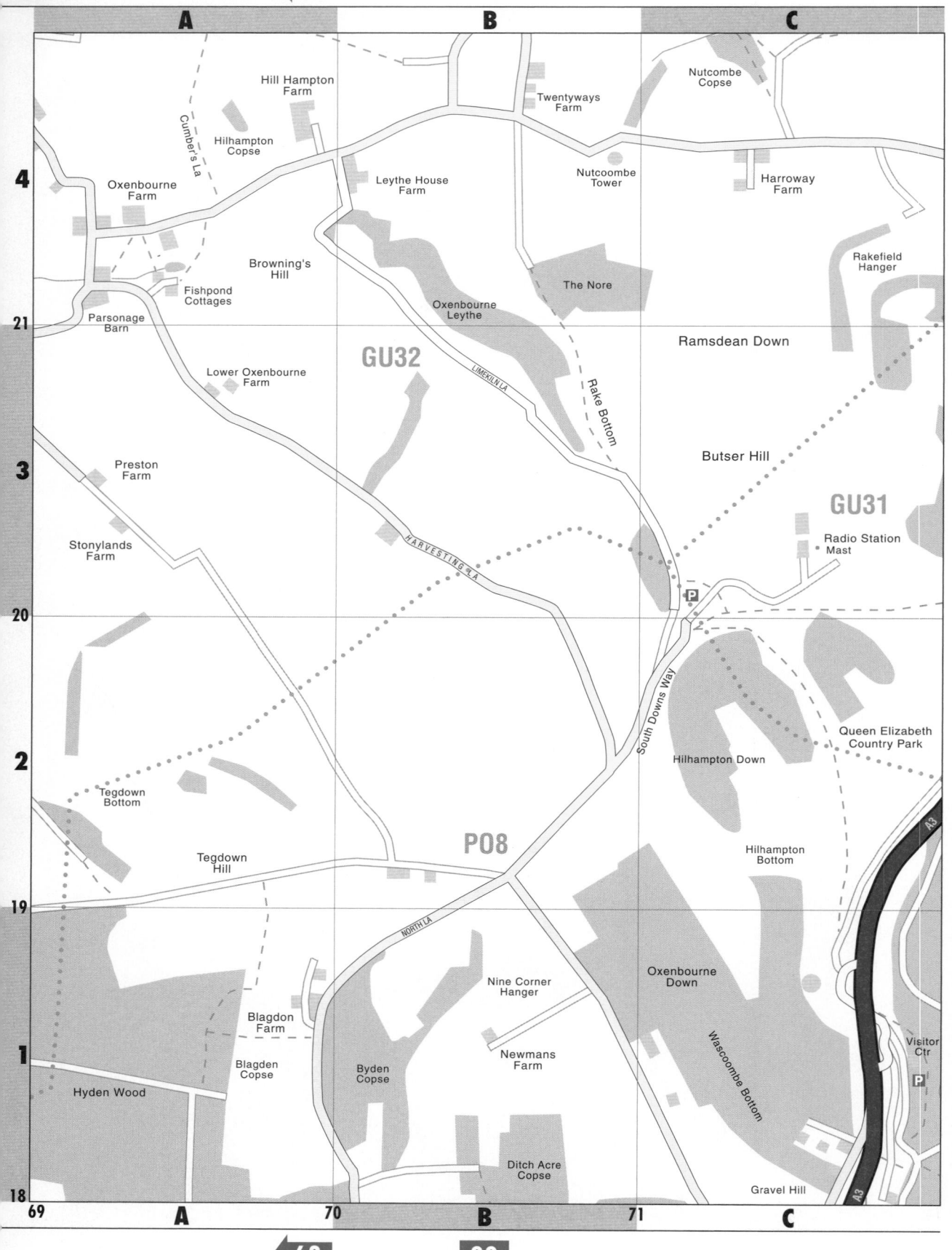

A B C

4

Cumber's La

Hill Hampton Farm

Hilhampton Copse

Oxenbourne Farm

Browning's Hill

Fishpond Cottages

Leythe House Farm

Twentyways Farm

Nutcoombe Tower

Oxenbourne Leythe

The Nore

Nutcombe Copse

Harroway Farm

Rakefield Hanger

21

Parsonage Barn

GU32

LIMEKILN LA

Rake Bottom

Ramsdean Down

Lower Oxenbourne Farm

Butser Hill

GU31

3

Preston Farm

HARVESTING 4 A

Radio Station Mast

Stonylands Farm

20

P

South Downs Way

Tegdown Bottom

2

Hilhampton Down

Queen Elizabeth Country Park

PO8

Hilhampton Bottom

A3

Tegdown Hill

19

NORTH LA

Oxenbourne Down

Nine Corner Hanger

Blagdon Farm

Wascoombe Bottom

Visitor Ctr

1

Blagden Copse

Byden Copse

Newmans Farm

P

Hyden Wood

Ditch Acre Copse

Gravel Hill

A3

18

69 A 70 B 71 C

A **B** **C**

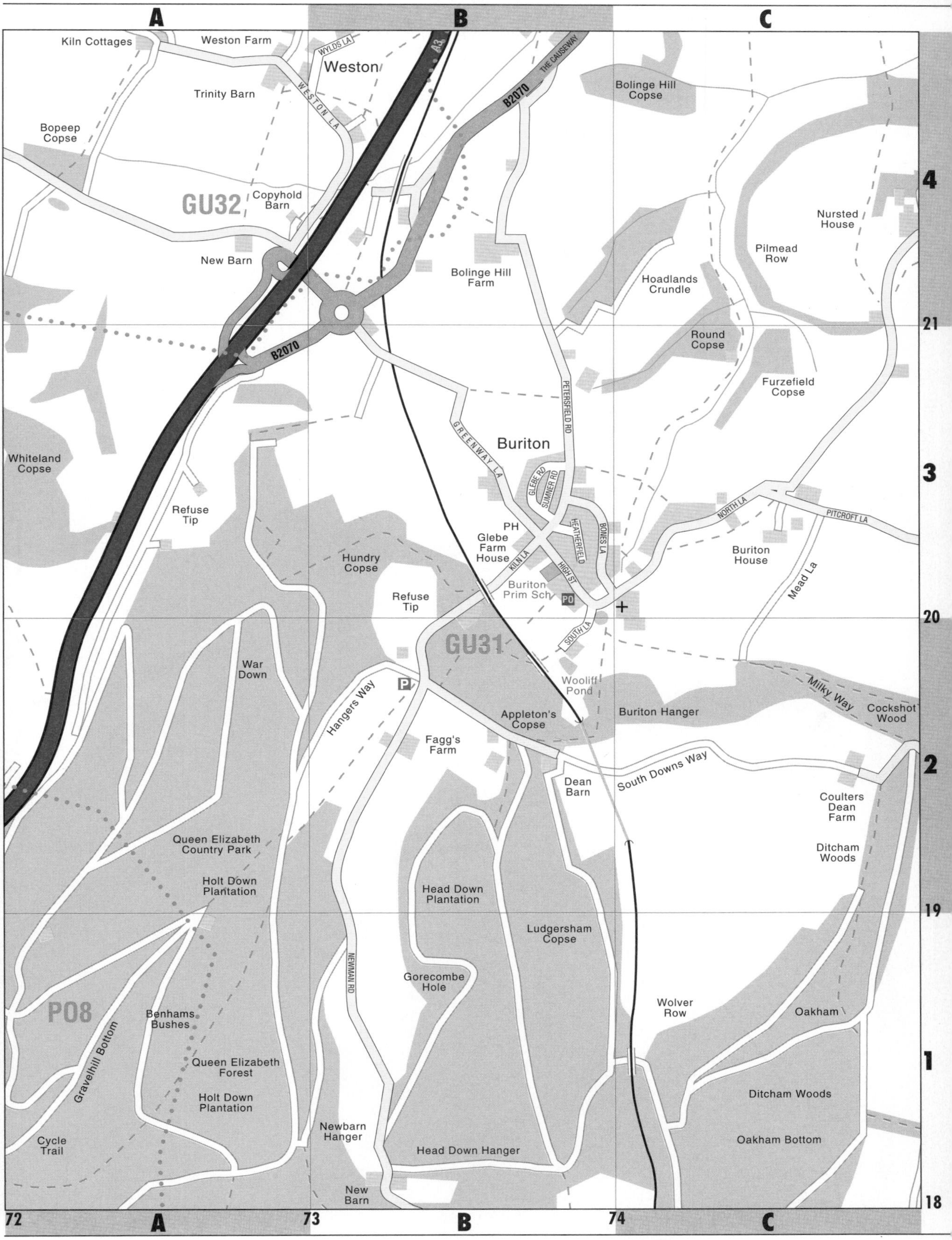

Kiln Cottages
Weston Farm
WYLDS LA
Weston
Trinity Barn
WESTON LA
B2070
THE CAUSEWAY
Bolinge Hill
Copse

Bopeep
Copse

GU32
Copyhold
Barn

New Barn

Bolinge Hill
Farm

Hoadlands
Crundle

Nursted
House

Pilmead
Row

4

A3

B2070

21

Round
Copse

Furzefield
Copse

Whiteland
Copse

Buriton

PETERSFIELD RD

GREENWAY LA

Refuse
Tip

Hundry
Copse

Refuse
Tip

GLEBE RD
SUMNER RD

PH
Glebe
Farm
House

KILN LA

HEATHERFIELD

BONES LA

NORTH LA
PITCROFT LA

Buriton
House

3

Buriton
Prim Sch

HIGH ST

PO

+

Mead La

GU31

SOUTH LA

Woolitt
Pond

20

War
Down

Hangers Way

P

Fagg's
Farm

Appleton's
Copse

Buriton Hanger

Milky Way

Cockshot
Wood

Dean
Barn

South Downs Way

Coulters
Dean
Farm

2

Queen Elizabeth
Country Park

Holt Down
Plantation

NEWMAN RD

Head Down
Plantation

Ludgersham
Copse

Ditcham
Woods

19

PO8

Gravelhill Bottom

Benhams
Bushes

Queen Elizabeth
Forest

Gorecombe
Hole

Wolver
Row

Oakham

Holt Down
Plantation

1

Ditcham Woods

Cycle
Trail

Newbarn
Hanger

Head Down Hanger

Oakham Bottom

New
Barn

18

72 **A** 73 **B** 74 **C**

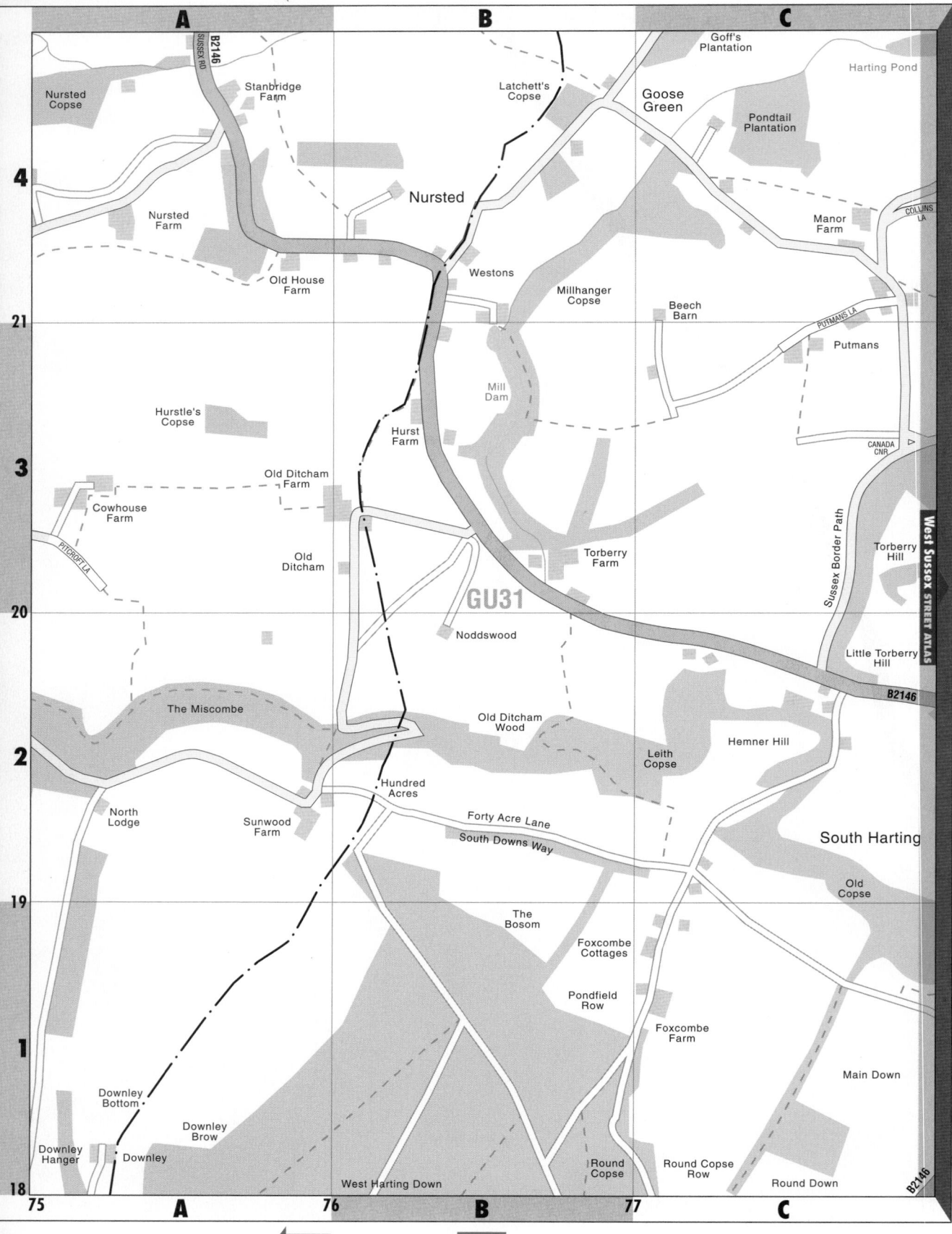

A **B** **C**

Nursted Copse

Stanbridge Farm

Latchett's Copse

Goff's Plantation

Harting Pond

Goose Green

Pondtail Plantation

B2146

SUSSEX RD

4

Nursted

Nursted Farm

Old House Farm

Westons

Millhanger Copse

Beech Barn

Manor Farm

COLLINS LA

21

Mill Dam

PUTMANS LA

Putmans

Hurstle's Copse

Hurst Farm

CANADA CNR

3

Cowhouse Farm

Old Ditcham Farm

Old Ditcham

Torberry Farm

Sussex Border Path

Torberry Hill

PITCROFT LA

GU31

20

Noddswood

Little Torberry Hill

B2146

The Miscombe

Old Ditcham Wood

Leith Copse

Hemner Hill

2

North Lodge

Sunwood Farm

Hundred Acres

Forty Acre Lane

South Downs Way

South Harting

Old Copse

19

The Bosom

Foxcombe Cottages

Pondfield Row

Foxcombe Farm

1

Main Down

Downley Bottom

Downley Brow

Round Copse

Round Copse Row

Round Down

B2146

Downley Hanger

Downley

18

West Harting Down

75 **A** 76 **B** 77 **C**

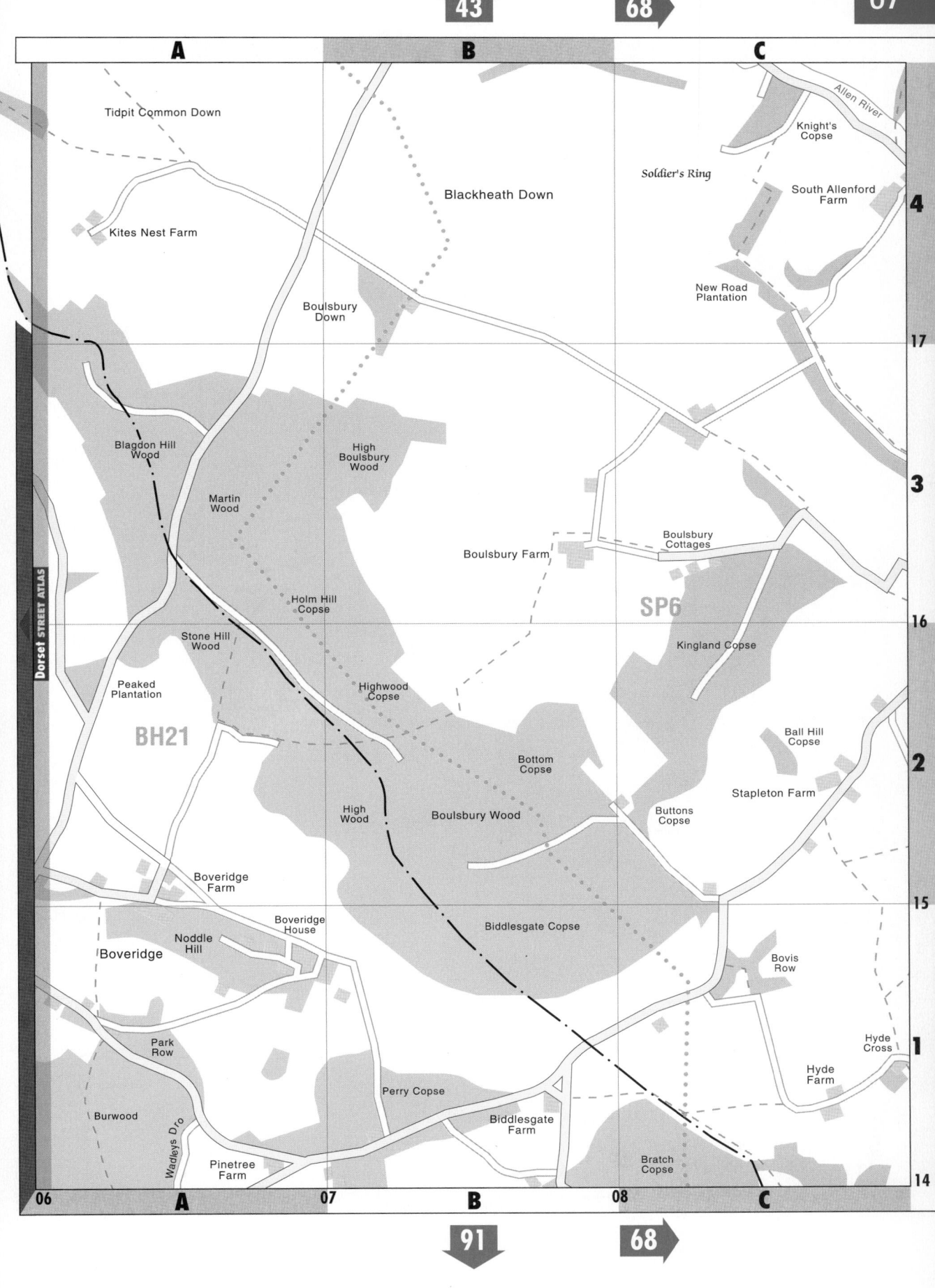

A   **B**   **C**

Tidpit Common Down

Blackheath Down

Allen River

Knight's Copse

Soldier's Ring

South Allenford Farm

4

Kites Nest Farm

Boulsbury Down

New Road Plantation

17

Blagdon Hill Wood

High Boulsbury Wood

Martin Wood

3

Boulsbury Cottages

Boulsbury Farm

SP6

Holm Hill Copse

Stone Hill Wood

16

Kingland Copse

Peaked Plantation

Highwood Copse

BH21

Ball Hill Copse

Bottom Copse

2

Stapleton Farm

High Wood

Boulsbury Wood

Buttons Copse

Boveridge Farm

15

Boveridge House

Biddlesgate Copse

Noddle Hill

Bovis Row

Boveridge

Park Row

Hyde Cross

1

Hyde Farm

Burwood

Perry Copse

Wadleys Dro

Biddlesgate Farm

Pinetree Farm

Bratch Copse

14

Dorset STREET ATLAS

06   **A**   07   **B**   08   **C**

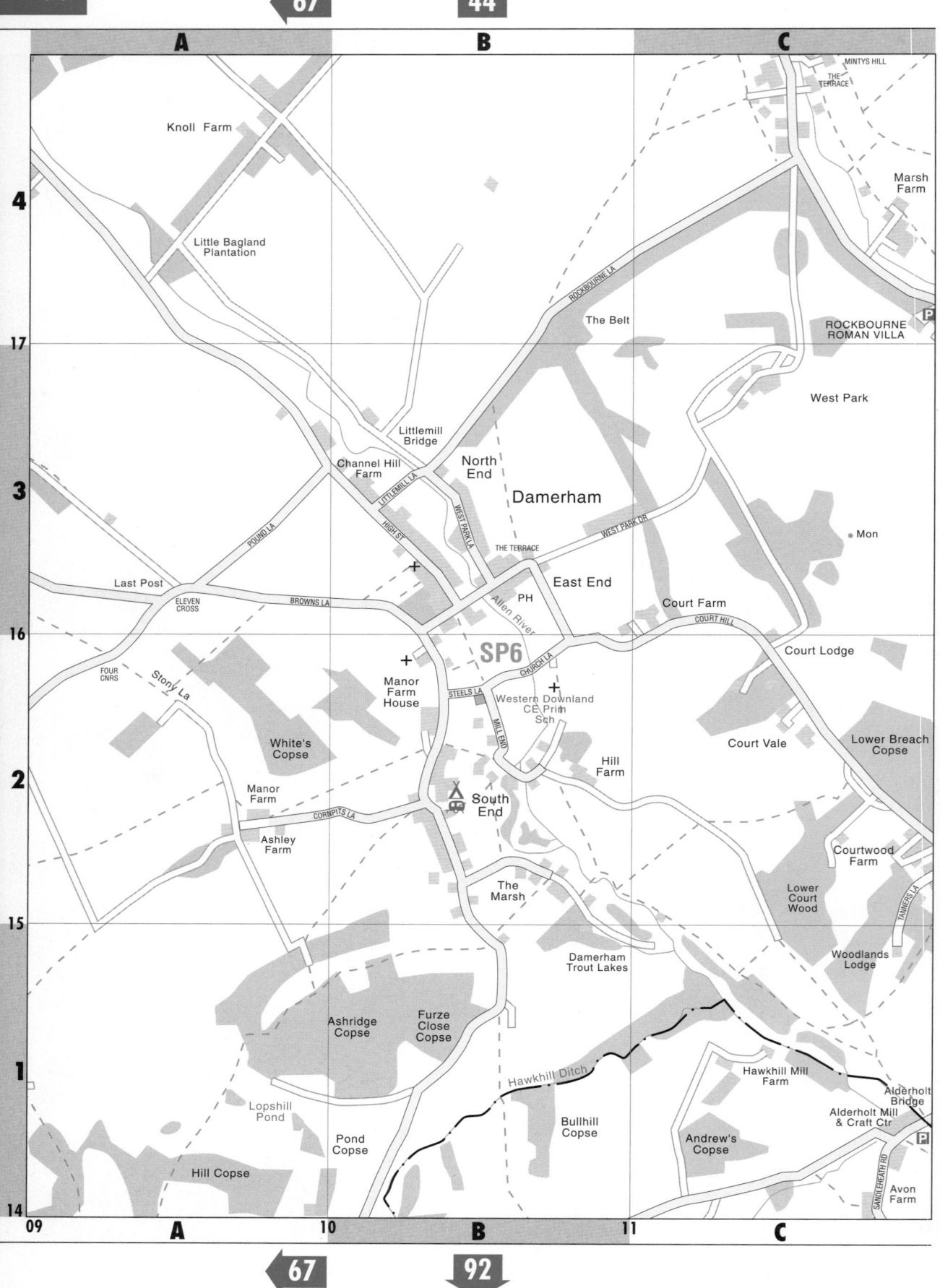

A B C

4

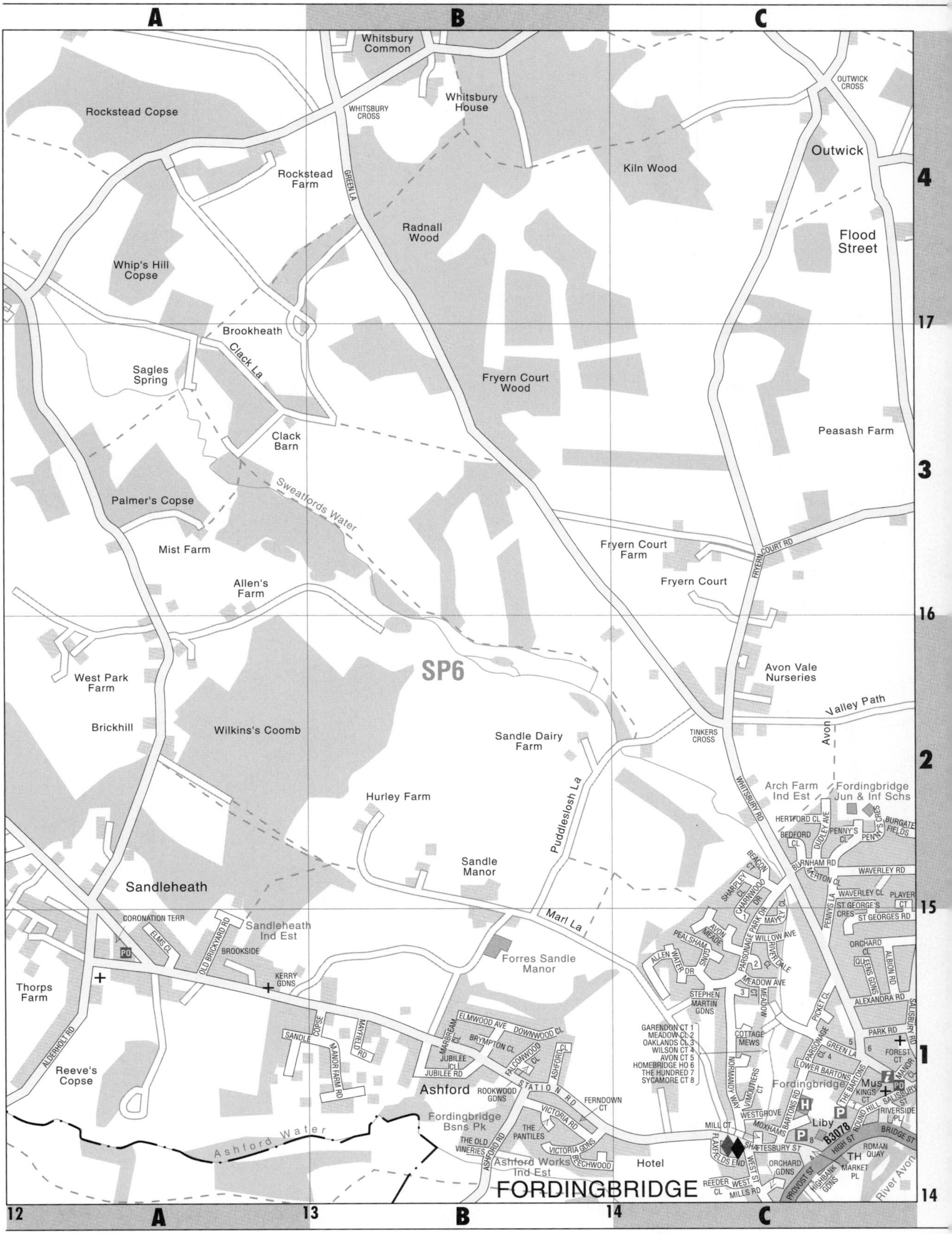

Rockstead Copse

Whitsbury Common

Whitsbury House

WHITSBURY CROSS

Kiln Wood

OUTWICK CROSS

Outwick

Flood Street

Rockstead Farm

GREEN LA

Radnall Wood

17

Brookheath

Clack La

Sagles Spring

Fryern Court Wood

Peasash Farm

3

Clack Barn

Sweatfords Water

Palmer's Copse

Fryern Court Farm

FRYERN COURT RD

Mist Farm

Allen's Farm

Fryern Court

16

West Park Farm

SP6

Avon Vale Nurseries

Brickhill

Wilkins's Coomb

Sandle Dairy Farm

Avon Valley Path

TINKERS CROSS

2

Hurley Farm

PUDDLESLOSH LA

WHITSBURY RD

Arch Farm Ind Est

Fordingbridge Jun & Inf Schs

HERTFORD CL
BEDFORD CL
DUDLEY AVE
PENNY'S CL
BURGATE FIELDS

BURNHAM RD
WAVERLEY RD

Sandleheath

Sandle Manor

Marl La

BEACON
SHARPLEY CL
CARPINWOOD
MAYE'S
PENNYS LA
WAVERLEY CL
ST GEORGE'S CRES
PLAYER CT
ST GEORGES RD

15

CORONATION TERR
ELMS CL
OLD BRICKYARD RD
BROOKSIDE

Sandleheath Ind Est

KERRY GDNS

Forres Sandle Manor

AVON MEAD
WILLOW AVE
RIVERDALE
ORCHARD CL
QUEENS GDNS
ALBION RD
ALEXANDRA RD

Thorps Farm

ALDERHOLT RD

PEALSHAM GDNS
ALLEN WATER DR
PARSONAGE PARK DR
MEADOW AVE
STEPHEN MARTIN GDNS

PO

MANOR FARM RD
SANDLE
MAYFIELD RD

ELMWOOD AVE
DOWNWOOD CL
BRYMPTON CL
FIR
TREE

COTTAGE MEWS

GARENDON CT 1
MEADOW CL 2
OAKLANDS CL 3
WILSON CT 4
AVON CT 5
HOMEBRIDGE HO 6
THE HUNDRED 7
SYCAMORE CT 8

PICKET CL
PARSONAGE GREEN LA
NORMANDY WAY
VINJUITERS
WESTGROVE
MOXHAMS

FOREST CT
PARK RD

Reeve's Copse

JUBILEE CL
JUBILEE RD
MARBREAM

CORNWOOD
ASHFORD
CL
FERNDOWN CT

Fordingbridge

LOWER BARTONS
THE BARTONS
KINGS
Mus
PO

1

STATION RD
Ashford

ROOKWOOD GDNS
VICTORIA RD

RIVERSIDE PL
Liby

H
P
B3078
HIGH ST

Ashford Water

Fordingbridge Bsns Pk

THE OLD VINERIES

THE PANTILES
VICTORIA GDNS
BEECHWOOD

Hotel

MILL CT
FLAXFIELDS END
SHAFTESBURY ST

MOXHAMS
SALISBURY ST
MILL ST

ORCHARD GDNS
HIGHBANK GDNS
MARKET PL
TH
ROMAN QUAY

Ashford Works Ind Est

FORDINGBRIDGE

REEDER CL
PROVOST ST
WEST ST

River Avon

14

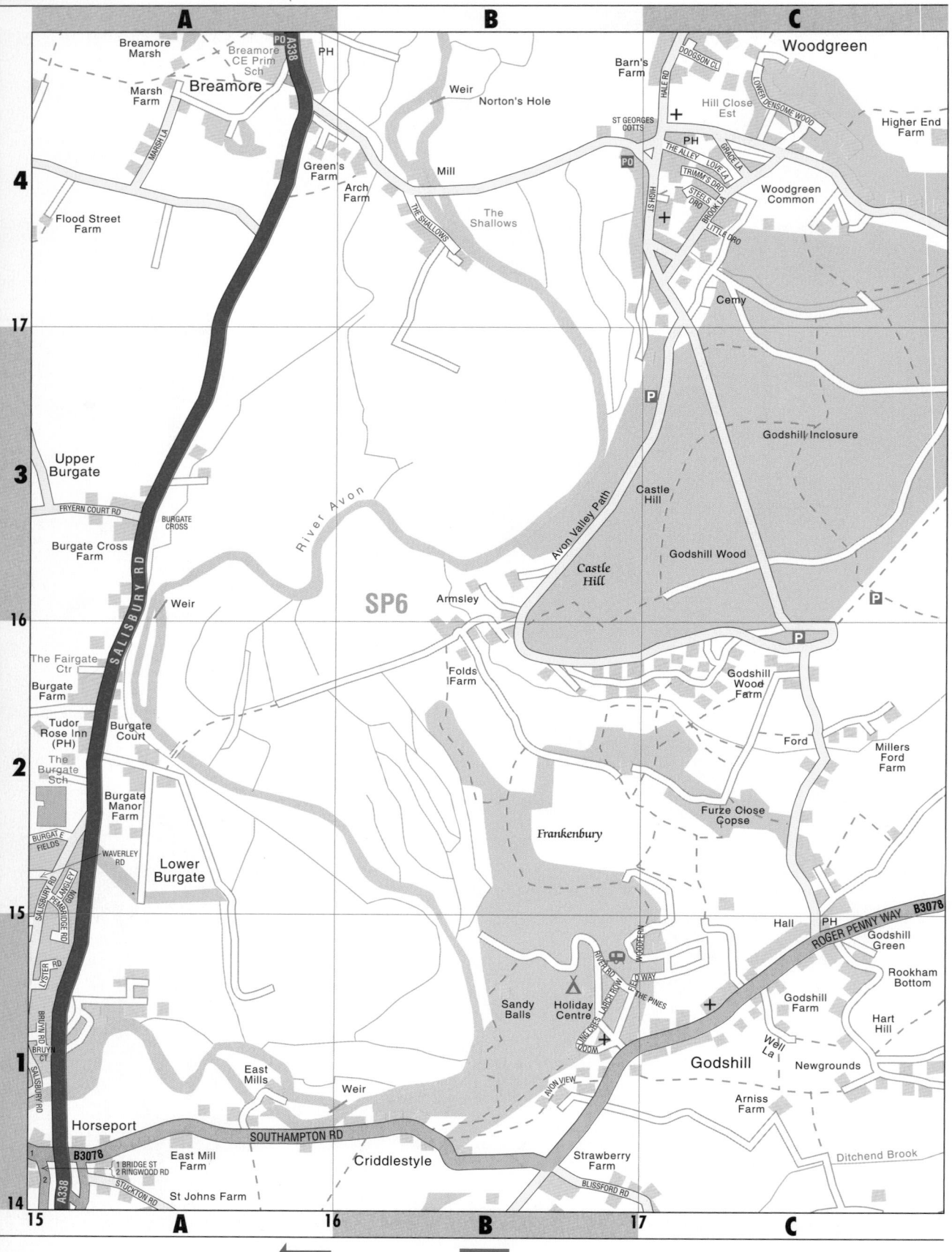

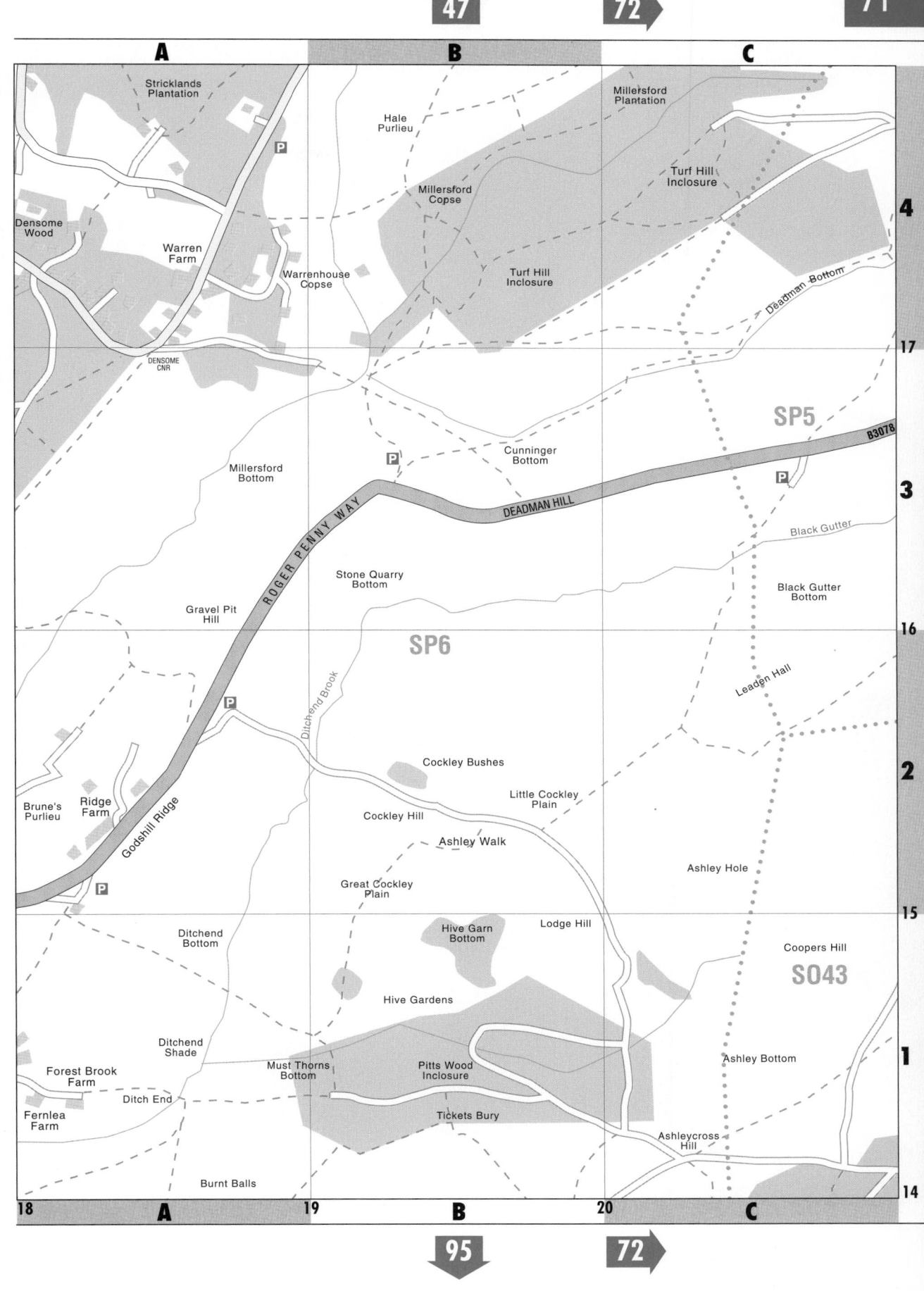

A   **B**   **C**

B3080

Golden Cross
Jacob's Barrow

LYBURN RD

Pound
Bottom

Cloven Hill Plantation

Franchises
Common

Tinney's
Plantation

P

4

Rushy
Flat

P

FOREST RD

Burnt Ground Wood

Franchises
Lodge

Franchises
Wood

17

B3080

ROGER PENNY WAY

Hope
Cottage

Firs Hill
Copse

B3078

SP5

Bramshaw
Telegraph

Tucker's
Hat

Picket
Corner

Studley
Head

P

3

Black Gutter

Bur
Bushes

Studley
Wood

Claypits Bottom

Homy Ridge

16

Studley
Castle

The Butts

2

Howen Bottom

Eyeworth Wood

Islands Thorns Inclosure

15

SO43

Crock Hill

Latchmore Brook

Eyeworth
Pond

1

Eyeworth
Lodge

P

Howen
Bushes

Fritham
Farm

Fritham
Bridge

The Royal Oak
(PH)

Fritham

14

Gorley Bushes

P

21   **A**   **22**   **B**   **23**   **C**

B3078

A **B** **C**

LYBURN RD

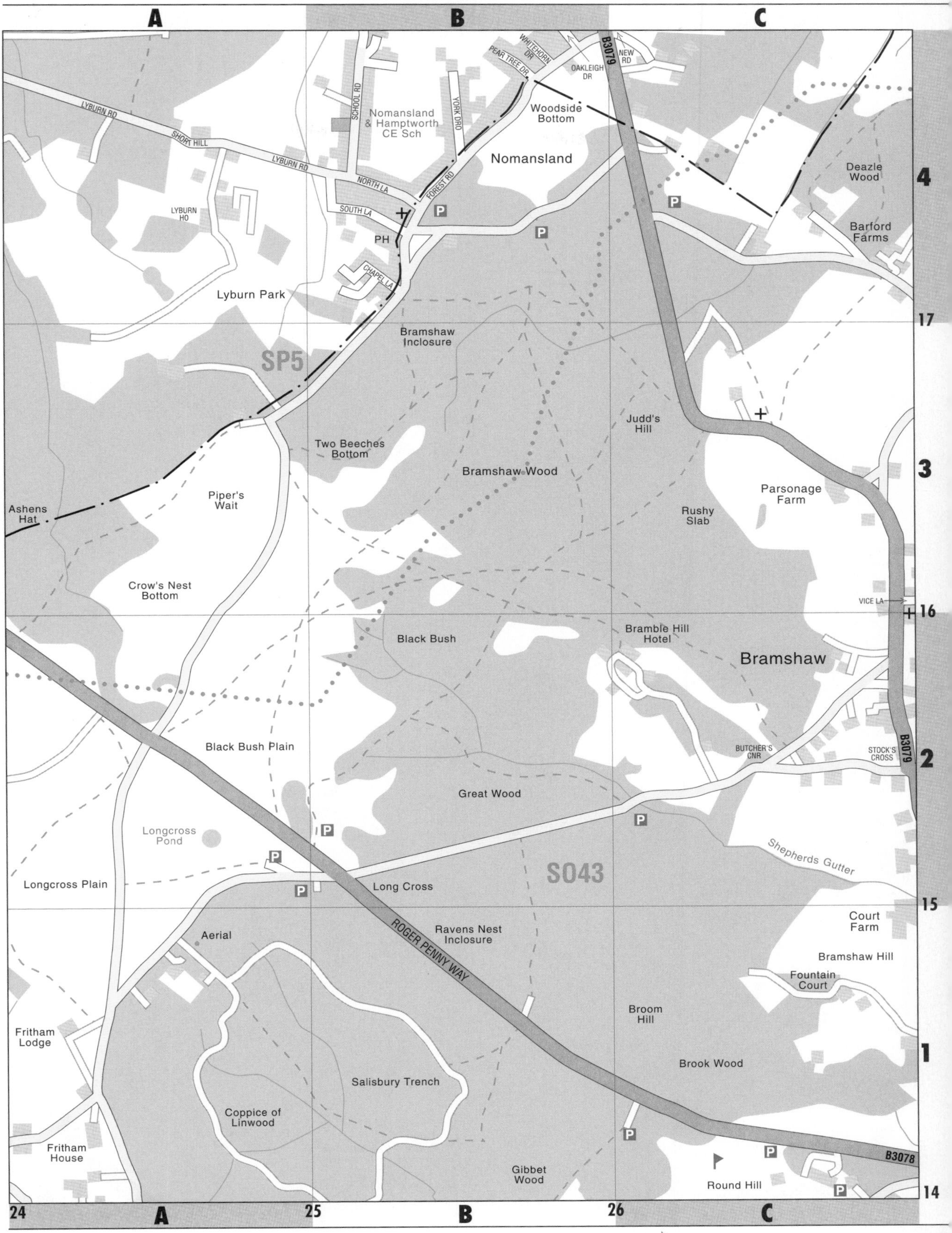

SHORT HILL

LYBURN RD

SCHOOL RD

Nomansland & Hamptworth CE Sch

YORK DRO

PEAR TREE DR

WHITEHORN DR

OAKLEIGH DR

NEW RD

B3079

Woodside Bottom

Nomansland

NORTH LA

SOUTH LA

FOREST RD

LYBURN HO

PH

CHAPEL LA

P

P

P

Deazle Wood

Barford Farms

4

Lyburn Park

Bramshaw Inclosure

SP5

17

Two Beeches Bottom

Bramshaw Wood

Judd's Hill

Parsonage Farm

Piper's Wait

Rushy Slab

3

Ashens Hat

Crow's Nest Bottom

VICE LA

16

Black Bush

Bramble Hill Hotel

Bramshaw

Black Bush Plain

BUTCHER'S CNR

STOCK'S CROSS

B3079

2

Great Wood

P

Shepherds Gutter

S043

Longcross Pond

Longcross Plain

P

P

P

Long Cross

15

Court Farm

Aerial

Ravens Nest Inclosure

ROGER PENNY WAY

Bramshaw Hill

Fountain Court

Broom Hill

1

Fritham Lodge

Salisbury Trench

Brook Wood

Coppice of Linwood

P

Fritham House

Gibbet Wood

Round Hill

P

P

B3078

14

SP5

Rockingham Arms (PH)

Black Hill

CANADA RD

P

PLANTATION RD

Canada Common

SO51

Pitts Farm

Swallow Fields

BLACKHILL RD

4

Wicksmoor Farmhouse

Penn Common

17

Hungerford Farm

Cooper's Lane

Furzley

FURZLEY LA

Furzley Farm

Half Moon Common

Penn Farm

3

SO43

Furzley Common

Mark's Farm

Penn Copse

Duck Hill

16

Stagbury Hill

VICE LA

Porters Farm

Crock Hill

Furzley Rd

Newbridge

2

Blenmans Farm

Cadnam Common

NEWBRIDGE RD

B3079

Warren's House

15

Warren's Park

Storm's Farm

Cadnam River

PO

SO40

Brook Hill

Warren's Farm

Cadnam Green

CADNAM LA

Withers Farm

1

BROOK CRE

KENLANE LA

Manor Farm

Dairyhouse Farm

B3079

CH

The Bell Inn Hotel

Brook

Springer's Farm

Manor Farm

M27

OLD LYNDHURST RD

A31

B3078

B3079

Ford

WITTENSFORD LA

14

27   A   28   B   29   C

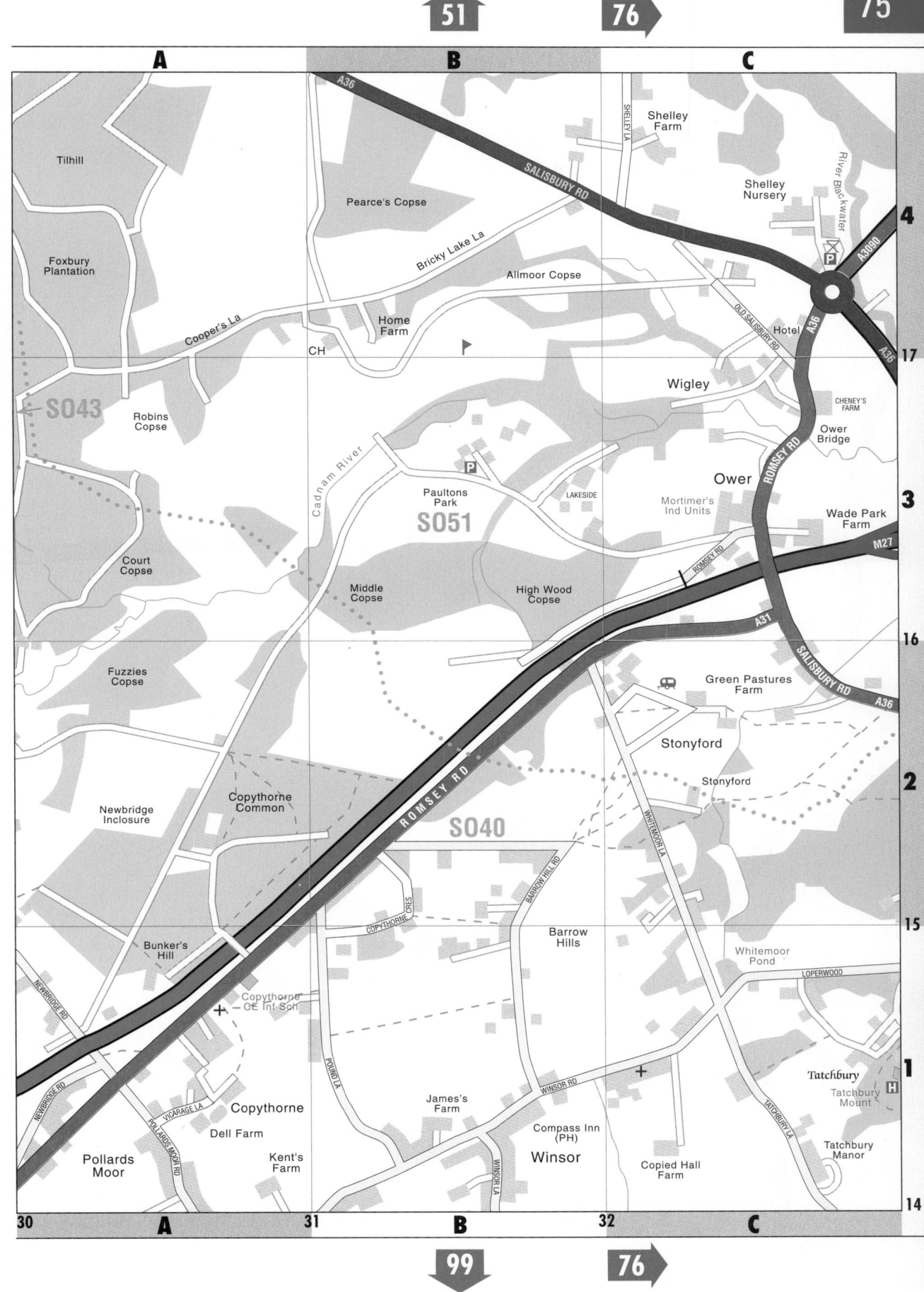

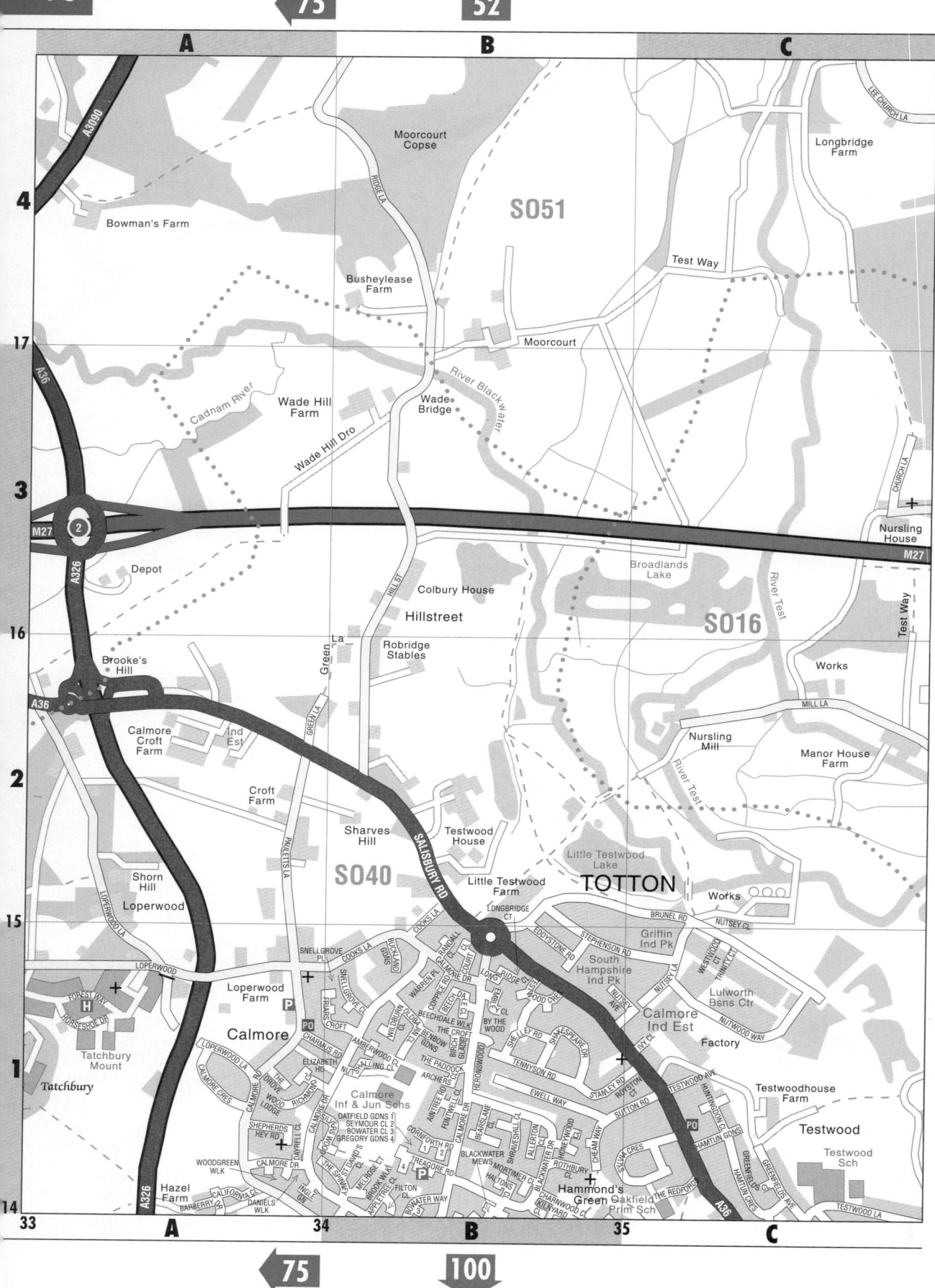

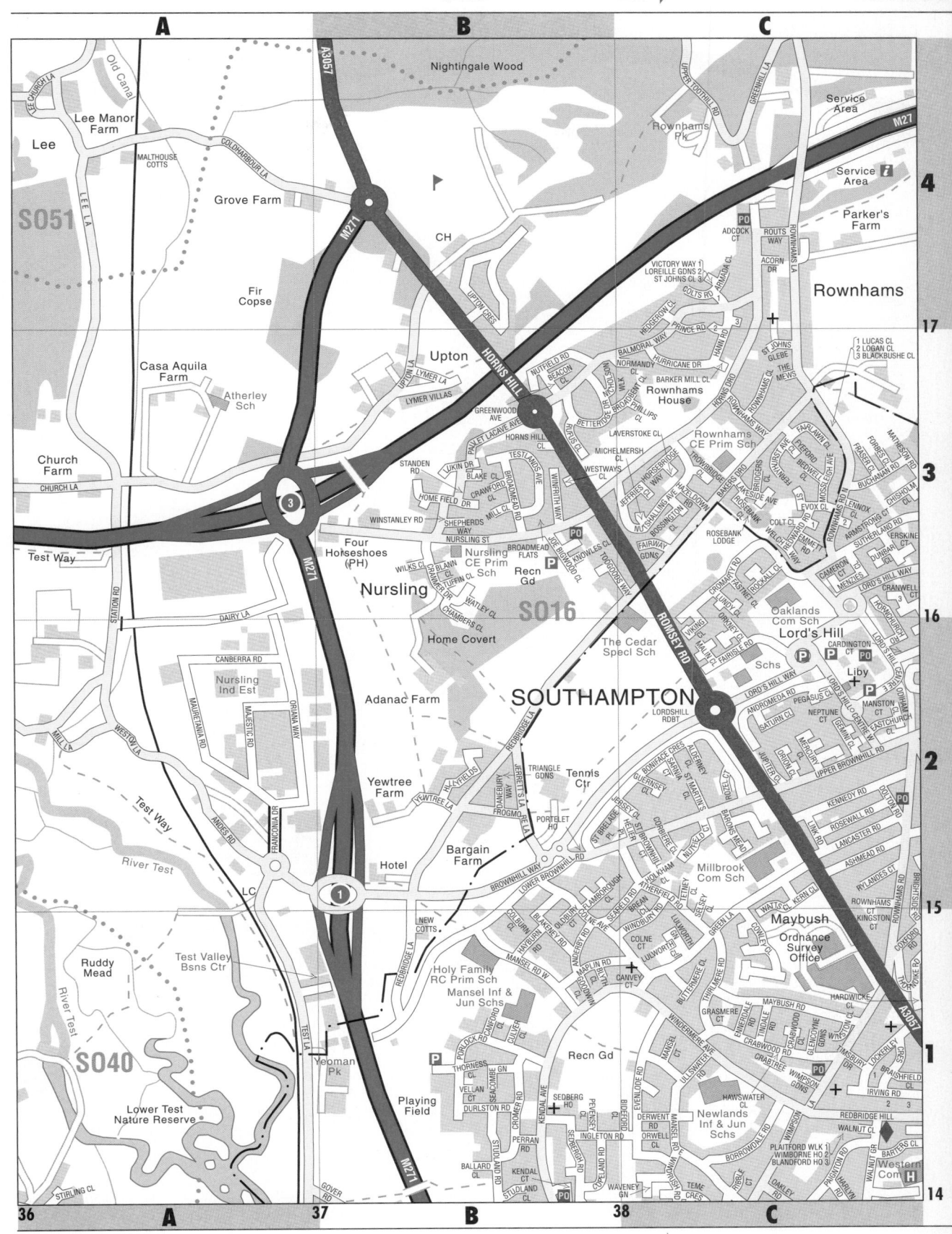

A B C

SO52

M27

Chilworth Common

Chilworth Tower

Dymer's Wood

4

Chilworth Common

HEATHERLANDS RD
PINELANDS RD
ROMAN RD
GREENBANK RD

CHILWORTH RD A27

PINE WAY
LITTLE TOLLER
FITZROY
A33

17

Lord's Wood

Tanner's Brook

Castle Hill

Chilworth Ring

HADRIAN WAY
PINE WLK
DENE CL
PINE WLK
THE RING
PINE HO
WILLIAM CL
ROMAN DR

BASSETT HEATH AVE
BIRCH HO
LINKS VIEW WAY
SAXHOLM WAY
SAXHOLM DALE
SAXHOLM
BASSETT ROW
BASSETT DALE

3

MATHESON RD
SUTHERLAND RD
SINCLAIR RD
Sinclair Jun Sch
Sinclair Inf Sch

WHINCHAT
SANDPIPER RD
WARWICK
LAWRENCE
FIRECREST
HARRIER
WIDGEON CL
BRAMBLING CL

SHELDRAKE
WARBLER CL
TINTAGEL DR
Oakwood Schs
WOBURN RD
DUNVEGAN DR
DUNSTER DR
MELVILLE CL
BALMORAL CL

GOLF COURSE RD
CH
GREENBANK CRES
RIDGEMOUNT LA 1
CHELWOOD GATE 2
BRAMPTON TWR 3
BRAMPTON MANOR 4
RIDGEMOUNT GDNS
ARDNAVE CRES
GABLES CT
HOLLY HILL
HOLLY HILL CL
BELL CL

SO16

Lordswood

BASSETT AVE
GLEN EYRE RD
BEECHMOUNT
BEECHMOUNT
CHETWYND RD

16

PEMBREY CL
KINLOSS
NORTHOLT GDNS
TANGMERE DR
CATWICK GDNS
CROYDON CL
GATWICK GDNS
LEWIS SILKIN WAY
COLERAISTOR
ALDERMOOR RD
NIGHTINGALE CT

BEAULIEU CL
PETWORTH GDNS
BRAMSBURY CL
WALTHAM CRES
SALERWO RD
KELLY CT
TARANTO RD
CURZON CT
LORDSWOOD
LORDSWOOD GDNS
DUNKIRK CT

Vermont Gdn
Red Lodge Sch
LITTLE OAK RD
THE FIRS
VERMONT CL
OVERCLIFF GDNS
A35
A33

Univ
A35

2

CONIFER RD
LINDEN RD
OUTER CIRC
HOLLY OAK RD
BEECH RD
PALM RD
WILLOW RD
LARCH RD
ROWAN RD

SPRINGFORD CL
LANGRISH RD
SHALDEN RD
LYBURN CL
GREYWELL AVE
PRESTW
STELLA CT
JEX BLAKE CL
SPRINGFORD RD
WINSTON RD
BRADLEY
1 GREYWELL CT
2 PINELANDS CT
3 LYBURN CT

ARNHEIM CL
DUNKIRK RD
LORDSWOOD RD
HIGHCLERE RD
THORNHILL
ROCKLEIGH RD

REDHILL CL
RED HILL CRES
RED HILL WAY
ABINGDON GDNS
WYKEHAM RD
OAKTREE RD
POINTOUT CL
POINTOU
BEAUMONT CL
FERNLEA
BUTTERFIELD RD
MEADOWHEAD RD
HORDER CL
OAKLANDS WAY
BASSETT CRES E
TUDOR WOOD
BASSETT MDW
TALBOT CT

Cutthorn

15

Tanner's Brook
Princess Anne
Aldermoor
VINE RD
SPRINGFORD GDNS
COXFORD RD
Northbrook Ind Est
Southampton Gen
Shirley Warren

Cemy
Holly Brook
DALE VALLEY RD
SEYMOUR
HOLLYBROOK AVE
MALVERN CRES
NORMAN AVE
VINCENT
Malvern Bsns Ctr
BURGESS RD

SOUTHAMPTON

Coronation Ave
Southampton Common
The Lake

HIGHFIELD RD
OAKMOUNT AVE
OAKMOUNT MANS
SO17

BURGESS RD
A3035 HIGHFIELD AVE
THE AVENUE

1

Coxford
Old Shirley

WARREN AVE
CHESTNUT RD
SYCAMORE RD
BINDON
BURNS
ROSS GDNS
THORNDIKE
BIRCH RD
ELMWOOD CT
TREMONA RD
Chalybeate
CHALYBEATE
Super store
WINCHESTER RD
ST JAMES PARK RD
BLAGON CT
Bellemoor Sec Sch (Boys)
Malvern Terr
WARWICK RD
MELROSE RD
LUCCOMBE RD
SHANKLIN RD
LEICESTER RD
LINCOLN CT
SHANKLIN CRES

Upper Shirley
Taunton Coll

SO15

The Cowards (PH)

14

WILLIAM MACLEOD WAY
ROMSEY RD
A35 TEBOURBA WAY
A3057
REDBRIDGE HILL
BEULAH RD
KINGS EDWARD AVE
PERTH RD
CECIL AVE
VICTOR ST
Wordsworth Inf Sch
VAUDREY
UPPER SHIRLEY AVE
DARLINGTON GDNS
CRANBOURNE
KINETON RD
RADWAY RD
Cemetery Lake

BLENHEIM GDNS
GALLIA RD
A33

39 A 40 B 41 C

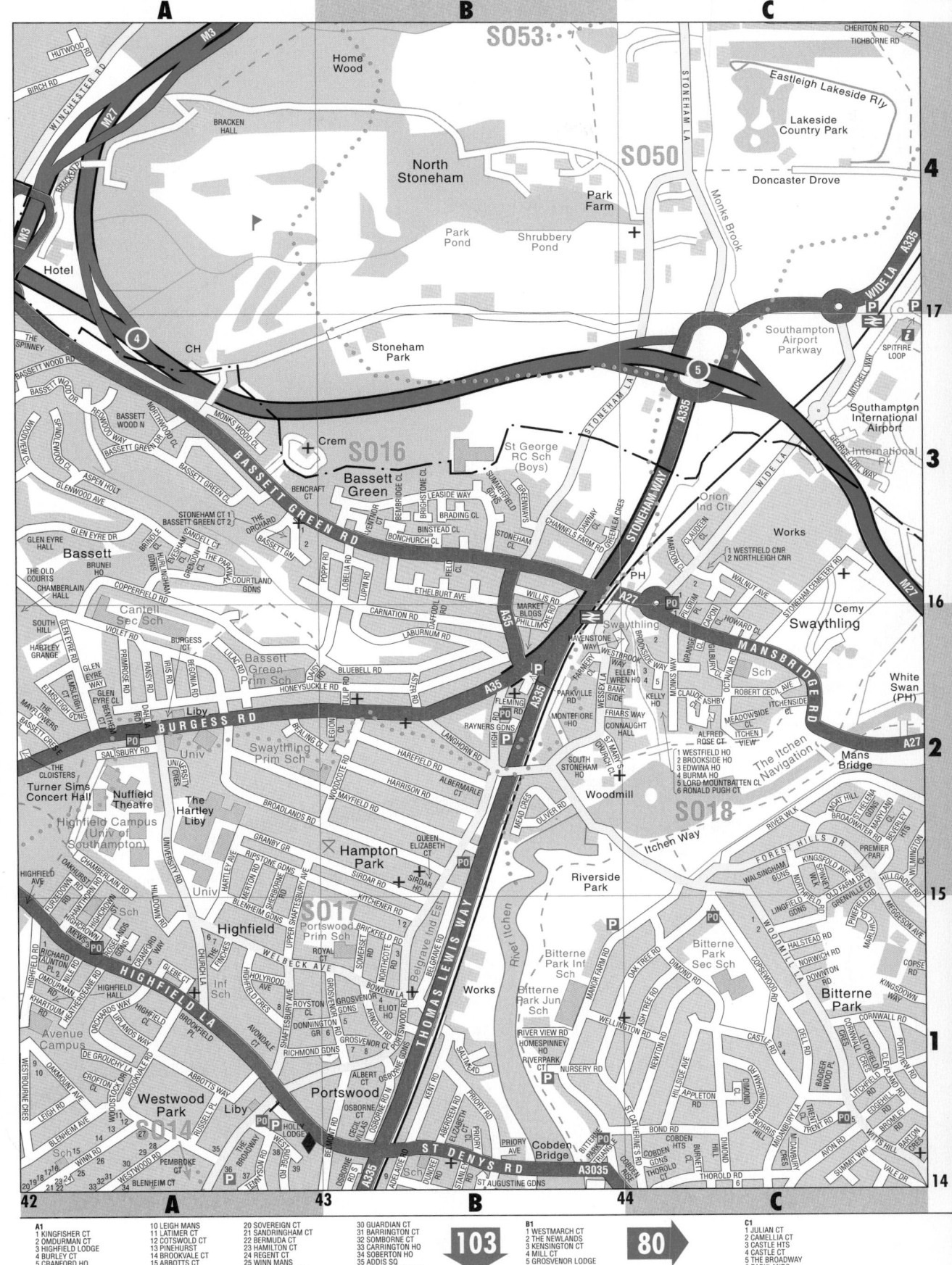

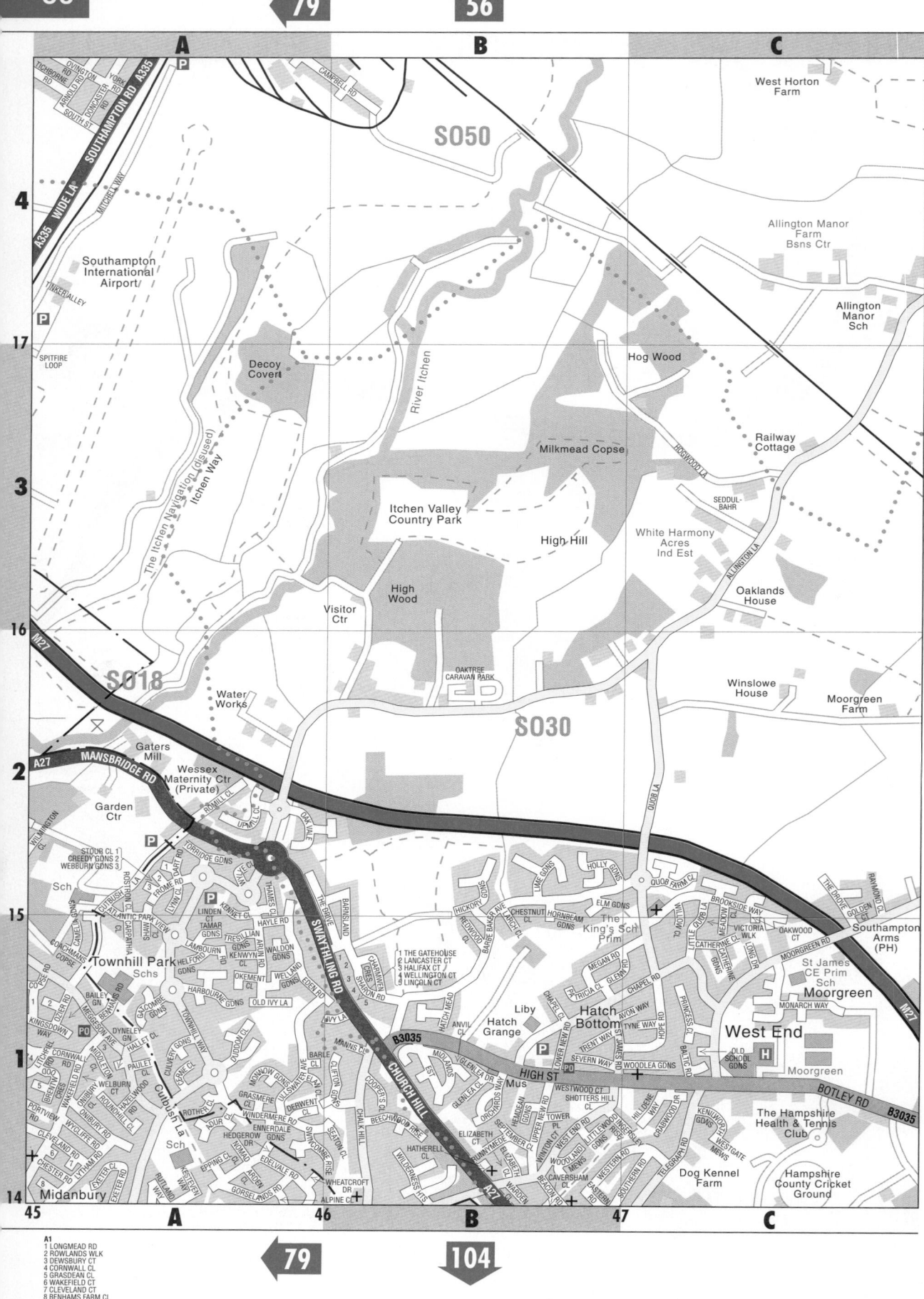

A1
1 LONGMEAD RD
2 ROWLANDS WLK
3 DEWSBURY CT
4 CORNWALL CL
5 GRASDEAN CL
6 WAKEFIELD CT
7 CLEVELAND CT
8 BENHAMS FARM CL

57
82

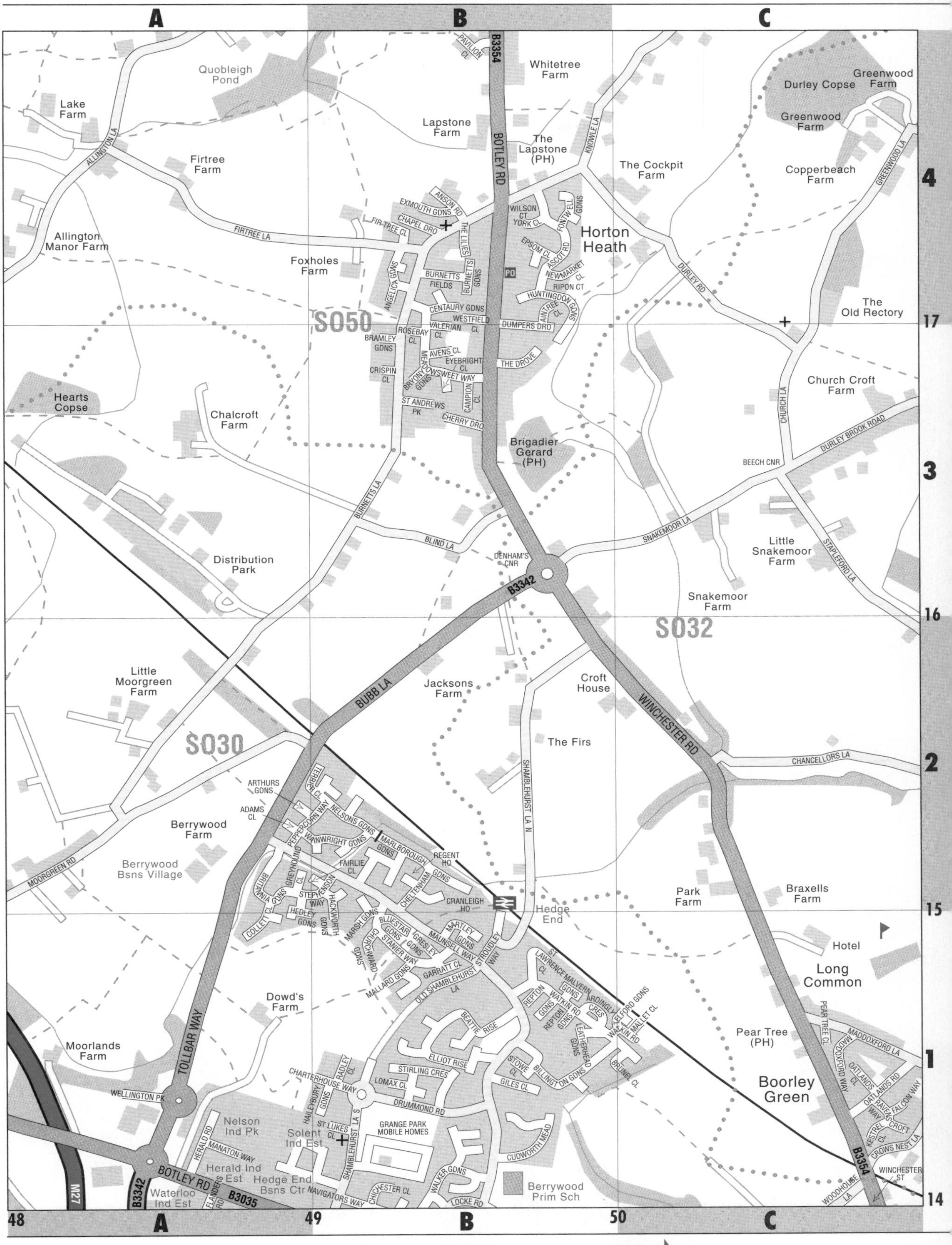
A
B
C
4
17
3
16
2
15
1
14
48
49
50
Quobleigh Pond
Lake Farm
Whitetree Farm
Lapstone Farm
The Lapstone (PH)
Greenwood Farm
Durley Copse
Greenwood Farm
Copperbeach Farm
The Cockpit Farm
Firtree Farm
Allington Manor Farm
Foxholes Farm
Horton Heath
The Old Rectory
SO50
Hearts Copse
Chalcroft Farm
Church Croft Farm
Brigadier Gerard (PH)
BEECH CNR
Little Snakemoor Farm
Distribution Park
DENHAM'S CNR
Snakemoor Farm
SO32
Little Moorgreen Farm
Jacksons Farm
Croft House
The Firs
SO30
Berrywood Farm
Berrywood Bsns Village
Park Farm
Braxells Farm
Hedge End
Hotel
Long Common
Dowd's Farm
Moorlands Farm
Pear Tree (PH)
Boorley Green
Nelson Ind Pk
Solent Ind Est
GRANGE PARK MOBILE HOMES
Herald Ind Est
Hedge End Bsns Ctr
Waterloo Ind Est
Berrywood Prim Sch
B3354
BOTLEY RD
ALLINGTON LA
FIRTREE LA
KNOWLE LA
DURLEY RD
GREENWOOD LA
CHURCH LA
DURLEY BROOK ROAD
SNAKEMOOR LA
STAPLEFORD LA
BURNETTS LA
BLIND LA
B3342
BUBB LA
WINCHESTER RD
CHANCELLORS LA
SHAMBLEHURST LA N
MOORGREEN RD
TOLLBAR WAY
WELLINGTON PK
BOTLEY RD
B3035
M27
PAVILION CL
EXMOUTH GDNS
ANSON RD
CHAPEL DRO
FIR TREE CL
THE LILIES
WILSON CT
YORK CL
FONTWELL GDNS
EPSOM CL
ASCOT RD
NEWMARKET CL
RIPON CT
HUNTINGDON GDNS
AINTREE CL
DUMPERS DRO
THE DROVE
ANGELICA GDNS
BURNETTS FIELDS
BURNETTS GDNS
CENTAURY GDNS
WESTFIELD
VALERIAN CL
ROSEBAY CL
BRAMLEY GDNS
AVENS CL
EYEBRIGHT CL
MEADOWSWEET WAY
BRYONY GDNS
CRISPIN CL
ST ANDREWS PK
CAMPION CL
CHERRY DRO
ARTHURS GDNS
ADAMS CL
TERRIER CL
PEPPERCORN WAY
NELSONS GDNS
WAINWRIGHT GDNS
MARLBOROUGH GDNS
REGENT HO
FAIRLIE CL
CHELTENHAM GDNS
CRANLEIGH HO
BRITANNIA GDNS
GREYHOUND CL
STEPHENSON WAY
HACKWORTH GDNS
COLLETT CL
HEDLEY GDNS
MARSH GDNS
BLUESTAR GDNS
GRESLEY GDNS
CHURCHWARD GDNS
STANIER WAY
MARTLEY GDNS
MAUNSELL WAY
STROUDLEY WAY
GARRATT CL
MALLARD GDNS
OLD SHAMBLEHURST LA
ST LAWRENCE CL
MALVERN GDNS
REPTON GDNS
WATKIN RD
ARDINGLY CRES
TELFORD GDNS
MALLET CL
BEATTIE RISE
ELLIOT RISE
LEATHERHEAD GDNS
STOWE CL
BILLINGTON GDNS
BRUNEL CL
GILES CL
STIRLING CRES
LOMAX CL
CHARTERHOUSE WAY
RADLEY CL
HAILEYBURY GDNS
DRUMMOND RD
ST LUKES CL
SHAMBLEHURST LA S
CUDWORTH MEAD
WALKER GDNS
HERALD RD
MANATON WAY
FLANDERS RD
NAVIGATORS WAY
CHICHESTER CL
LOCKE RD
PEAR TREE CL
MADDOXFORD LA
MADDOXFORD WAY
OATLANDS CL
OATLANDS RD
FALCON WAY
RAVEN WAY
CROFT
KESTREL CL
CROWS NEST LA
WINCHESTER ST
WOODHOUSE LA
PO

105
82

81
58

A **B** **C**

Greenwood

GREENWOOD LA

4

SOMERS LA

WINTERS HILL

Laurel
Farm

Kings Way

Woodlea
Nursery

Trullingham
Farm

Wintershill

THE DROVE

Robin Hood
(PH)

Durley
Street

MANOR
TERR

TANGIER LA

MANOR RD

Durley Manor
Farm

Tangier
Farm

DURLEY ST

17

VICTORIA
CT

DURLEY BROOK RD

Perlins
Farm

Durley
Lodge

Durley CE
Prim Sch

KYTES LA

Broom
Farm

3

Lower
Farm

Durley

Millstone
Farm

MINCINGFIELD LA

Mincingfield
Farm

PARSONAGE LA

MILLWAY

Brownheath
Park

WHITE GATES

THE SAWMILL

Brown Heath

Farmer's Home
(PH)

MINCINGFIELD
TERR

Brokes Copse

16

STAPLEFORD LA

Stapleford
Farmhouse

HEATHEN ST

Gregory
Farm

GREGORY LA

SO32

CHANCELLORS LA

Blundell's
Copse

Brokes
Farm

River Hamble

Harfields
Bungalow

B3035

2

Hill
Farm

Netherhill
Farm

MILL LA

Calcot
House

Calcot
Farm

CALCOT LA

Harfields
Farm

15

Ford Lake

NETHERHILL LA

Durley
Mill

BLIND LA

Frogmill
Farm

Maddoxford
Farm

Breach Hill

Cricketer's Inn
(PH)

CURDRIDGE LA

1

CROWS NEST LA

MADDOXFORD LA

Long Acres
Farm

Boorley
Green

Holly Tree
Farm

WANGFIELD LA

The
Paddocks

Lower
Wangfield
Farm

Parklands

THE PLANTATION

Hill
Farm

CAPERS END LA

BOTLEY RD

Curdridge
Firs

Firs
Farm

LOCKHAMS RD

GORDON RD

FIR LA

Boorley Green
Farm

SO30

14

B3035

CHAPEL LA

51 **A** **52** **B** **53** **C**

A B C

B2177
Claylands Road Ind Est
Hermitage
Albany CL
MARLOW RD
CLAYLAND CL
Works
FOUNDSCLA
BEAUFORT DR
ANDREWES
GARFIELD CL
B3035
LOWER LA
Albany DR
Albany RD
CUNNINGHAM
Battery Hill
MARKS TERR
Langton RD
Brooklands RD
FREE ST
PARK LA
BUTTS
EDMOND CL
MERLIN CL
Kestrel CL
Siskin CL
WINCHESTER RD
BLANCHARD RD
MORLEY RD
St Bonnet DR
LOWER RD
St Peter's LA
Roman Row
COLVILLE DR
CEDAR CT
ELMDEN RD
LAWSON
WORDSWORTH
BROOM CL
Highfield CT
Greens CL
PO
POUNDSIDE LA
Southfields CT
Brook St
Bank St
Malvern
HELICONIA RD
Sch
PINE RD
ELM RD
RARERIDGE LA
Cemy
Hoe
Ambleside
Park RD
The Avenue
Princes RD
Victoria RD
Priory CT
PO
P
Bastings LA
Little Shore LA
Cres
Shore LA
Willow CL
OAK RD
Sycamore RD
GUNNERS RD
Hoe RD
WEST HOE LA
JERVIS COURT LA
Newtown
Tangier LA
Mallard
Leopold DR
Elizabeth WAY
Albert RD
Martin ST
STATION RD
PALACE MEWS
Eastways
Malt LA
Green LA
Cherry GDNS
Cricklemede
Hamble Springs
Godfrey PINK
Swanmore RD
Little Hoe Farm
17

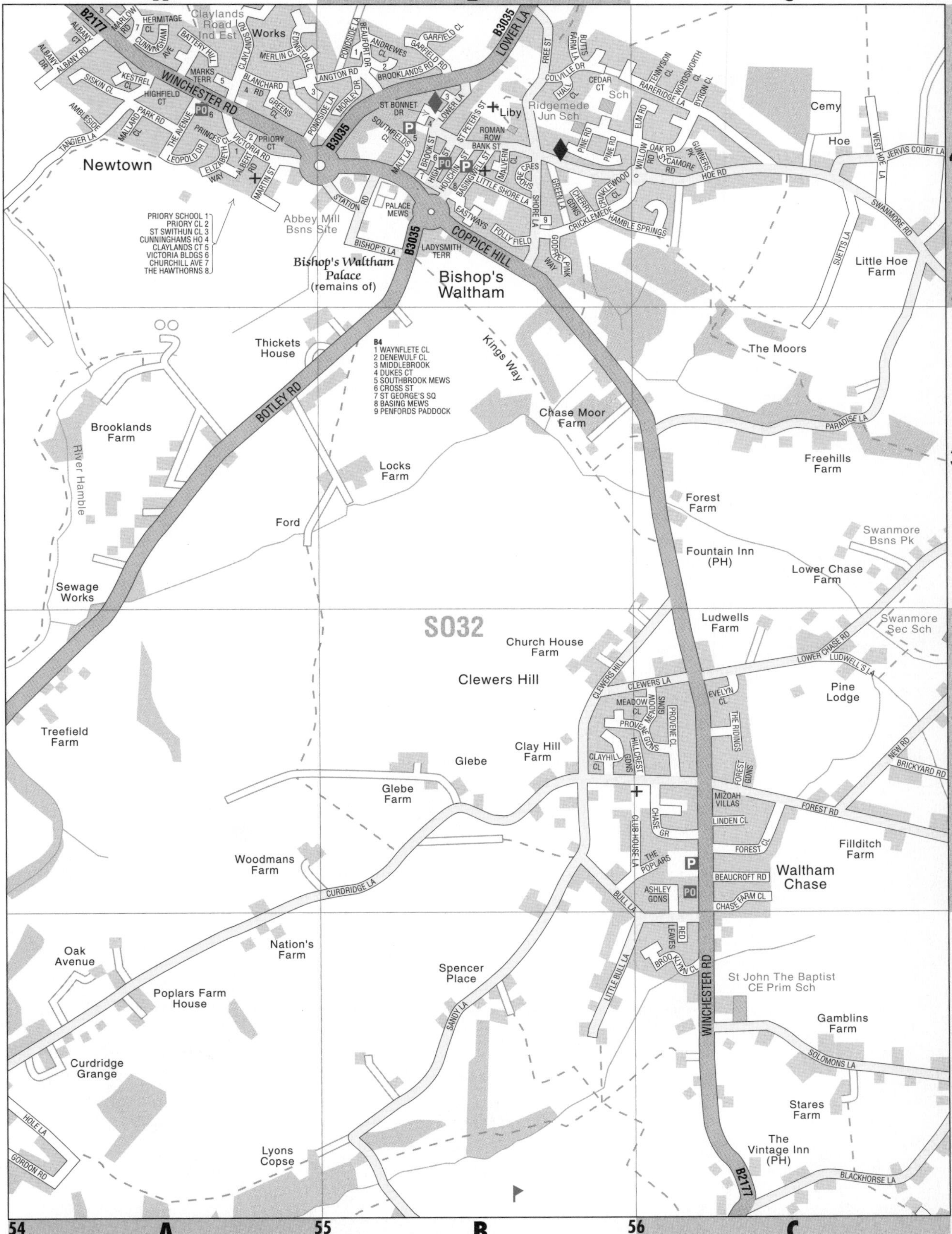

PRIORY SCHOOL 1
PRIORY CL 2
ST SWITHUN CL 3
CUNNINGHAMS HO 4
CLAYLANDS CT 5
VICTORIA BLDGS 6
CHURCHILL AVE 7
THE HAWTHORNS 8

Abbey Mill Bsns Site
Bishop's Waltham Palace (remains of)
BISHOP'S LA
B3035
LADYSMITH TERR
COPPICE HILL
Bishop's Waltham
Folly Field
WAY

Thickets House
BOTLEY RD
B4
1 WAYNFLETE CL
2 DENEWULF CL
3 MIDDLEBROOK
4 DUKES CT
5 SOUTHBROOK MEWS
6 CROSS ST
7 ST GEORGE'S SQ
8 BASING MEWS
9 PENFORDS PADDOCK
Kings Way
Chase Moor Farm
The Moors
PARADISE LA
Freehills Farm
3

Brooklands Farm
River Hamble
Locks Farm
Ford
Forest Farm
Fountain Inn (PH)
Lower Chase Farm
Swanmore Bsns Pk
16

Sewage Works
SO32
Church House Farm
Clewers Hill
Ludwells Farm
LOWER CHASE RD
Swanmore Sec Sch
LUDWELL'S LA

Treefield Farm
Glebe
CLEWERS HILL
CLEWERS LA
MEADOW CL
SNUG
PROVENE GDNS
EVELYN CL
THE RIDINGS
FOREST
SNUG
Pine Lodge
NEW RD
BRICKYARD RD
2

Glebe Farm
Clay Hill Farm
CLAYHILL CL
HILLCREST
HILL GDNS
MIZOAH VILLAS
LINDEN CL
FOREST RD
Fillditch Farm

Woodmans Farm
CURDRIDGE LA
CHASE GR
CLUB HOUSE LA
THE POPLARS
BULL LA
P
ASHLEY GDNS
PO
FOREST CL
BEAUCROFT RD
CHASE FARM CL
Waltham Chase
15

Oak Avenue
Nation's Farm
Poplars Farm House
Spencer Place
SANDY LA
RED LEAVES
LITTLE BULL LA
BROOK LYNDEN CL
WINCHESTER RD
St John The Baptist CE Prim Sch
Gamblins Farm
SOLOMONS LA
1

Curdridge Grange
HOLE LA
GORDON RD
Lyons Copse
Stares Farm
The Vintage Inn (PH)
B2177
BLACKHORSE LA
14

54 A 55 B 56 C

A B C

4

DAMSON HILL
PARK LA
Hill Top
SWANMORE PARK HO
Mayhill Copse
Swanmore Park
Upper Swanmore
Wyches Farm
GREEN LA
MAYHILL LA
OXFORD LA
MIDLINGTON HILL
JERVIS COURT LA
Jervis Court Farm
VICARAGE LA
Laurel Cottage
Mayhill Farm
Mayhill Stud Farm
WELL LA
SWANMORE RD

17

Hampton Farm
MOORLANDS RD
SWANMORE RD
DONIGERS CL
BELL
DONIGERS CL
HAMPTON HILL
CHURCH RD
VICARAGE LA
CUT THROAT LA
Upper Hill Farm

3

LOWER CHASE RD
FOXCOMBE CL
Swanmore CE Prim Sch
FULLEGAR COTTS
BUCKETTS FARM CL
CHURCH LA
DROXFORD RD
Hill Place
Bottom Copse
BROAD LA
PO
MEON GDNS
Swanmore
Hill Farm Orchards
S032

Swanmore Sec Sch
LARKSPUR CL
CROFTON WAY
NEW RD
MYERS CL
LEACOCK CL
CHAPEL RD
SPRING VALE
SPRING LA
DODDS LA
Hill Grove
HILL GROVE LA
1 BEVERLEY GDNS
2 CORONATION RD
3 GREENWAYS
4 THE DROVE

16

P
SPRING VALE
RUSSET CL
ROWAN CL
SPRING LA
Hunters Inn (PH)
Kings Way
MARTIN CL
COTT WAY
GLENVALE
The Bungalow
COTT ST
Tudor Cottage
Oxford Cottages
COTT STREET LA
Cott Street Farm
PH
Hillpound Farm

THE LAKES
Hillpound
Waltham Bsns Pk

2

BRICKYARD RD
ORCHARDLEA
HUNTERS CHASE
Dirty Copse
Ragnals Copse
Forest Farm
GRAVEL HILL
Holywell House
FOREST RD
Longridge Farm
MISLINGFORD RD

15

Bishopsmore
WESTFIELD DR
A32
Gravel Hill
Bishop's Inclosure
Bishopswood Farm
BISHOP'S WOOD RD

1

BLACKHORSE LA
SOLOMONS LA
HEARNE GDNS
Hawksnest Farm
P017
Soberton Mill
HIGH ST
WINTERS RD
HOSPITAL RD
BISHOPS LA
Shirrell Heath
NEWMANS HILL
River Meon
Timber Yard
A32
BUDDEN'S LA
P017

14
Mislingford

57 A **58** B **59** C

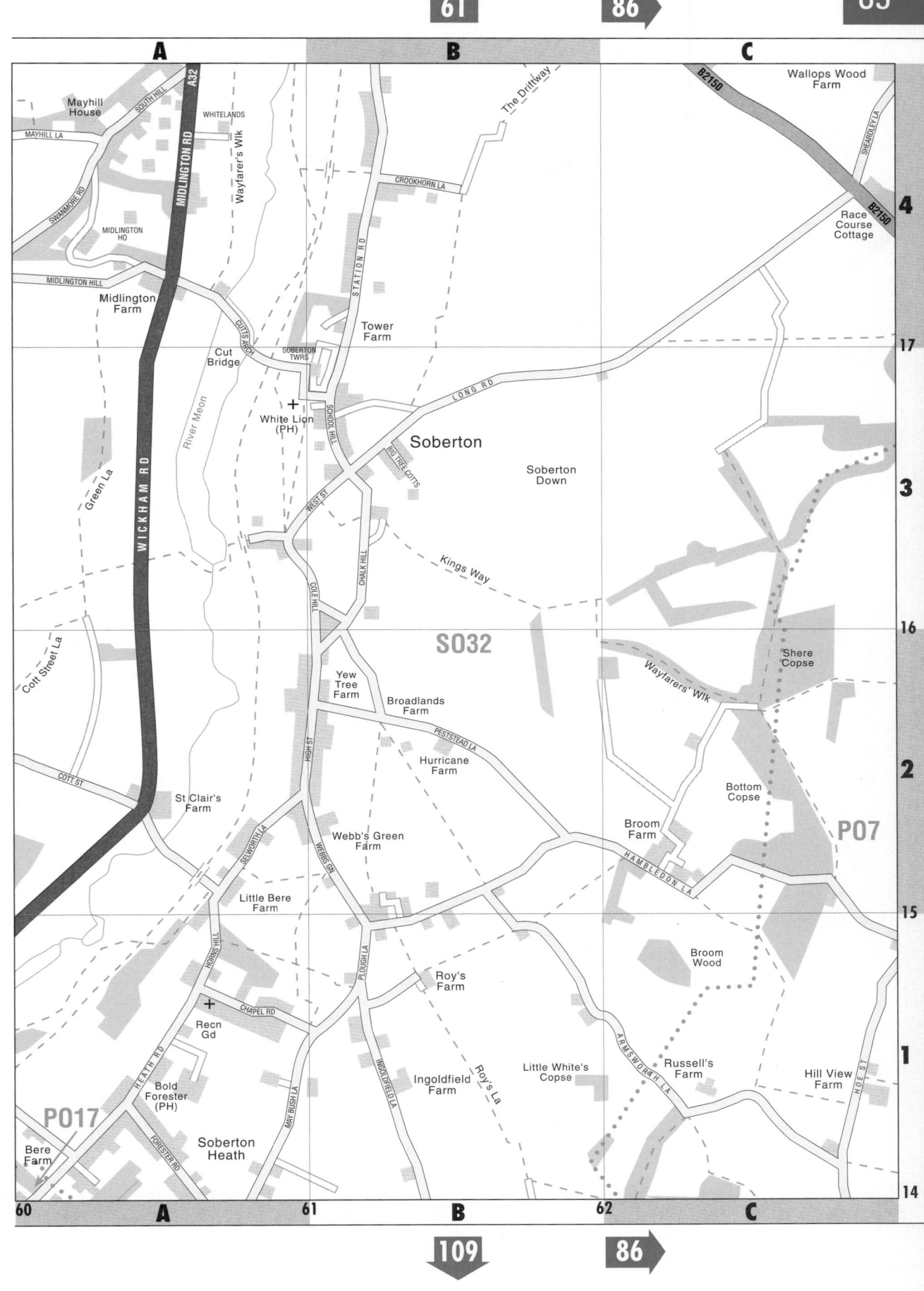

A   B   C

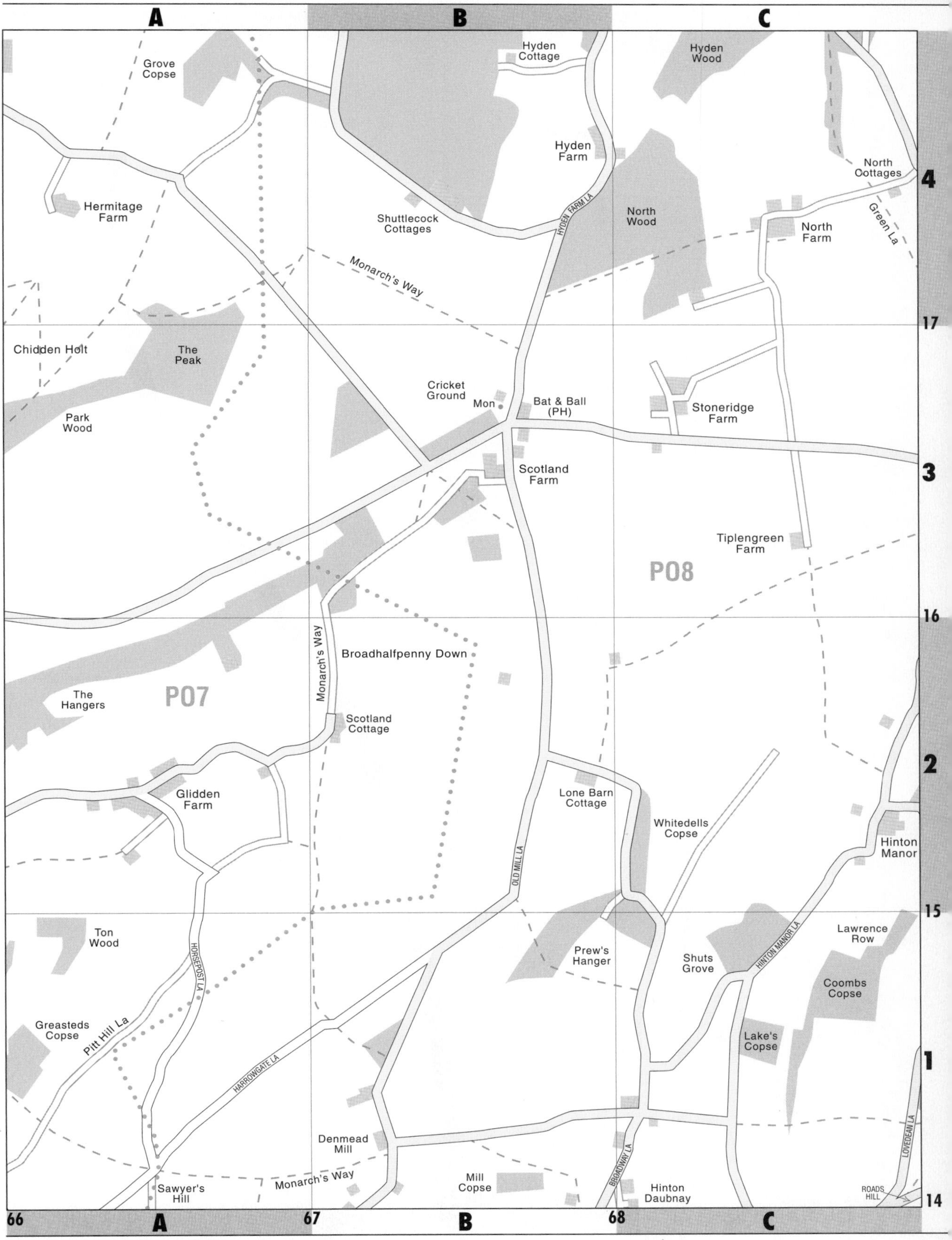

Grove
Copse

Hyden
Cottage

Hyden
Wood

Hermitage
Farm

Hyden
Farm

North
Cottages   4

Shuttlecock
Cottages

North
Wood

North
Farm

Green La

Monarch's Way

HYDEN FARM LA

17

Chidden Holt

The
Peak

Cricket
Ground

Bat & Ball
(PH)

Stoneridge
Farm

Mon

Park
Wood

Scotland
Farm

3

PO8

Tiplengreen
Farm

Monarch's Way

16

The
Hangers

PO7

Broadhalfpenny Down

Scotland
Cottage

Glidden
Farm

Lone Barn
Cottage

2

Whitedells
Copse

Hinton
Manor

OLD MILL LA

15

Ton
Wood

HORSEPOST LA

Lawrence
Row

HINTON MANOR LA

Prew's
Hanger

Shuts
Grove

Coombs
Copse

Greasteds
Copse

Pitt Hill La

HARROWGATE LA

Lake's
Copse

1

Denmead
Mill

BROADWAY LA

Sawyer's
Hill

Monarch's Way

Mill
Copse

Hinton
Daubnay

LOVEDEAN LA

ROADS
HILL

14

66   67   68

A   B   C

A   B   C

Smith's Copse

Lowton's Copse

Ditch Acre Copse

Chapel Farm

Thieves' Lane

Hog's Lodge La

New Buildings

Hog's Lodge Inn (PH)

Petersfield Rd

Green La

Green Lane

4

BRAMBLE LA
Clanfield Jun Sch
SWALLOW CT
EAST MEON RD
IVY ORCH
PH
CHURCH CL
KINGSBURY CT
WILKINS
MOREFIELD WAY
POND LA
NICKLEY RD

Manor Farm

PO8

CHALTON LA

CHALTON LA

17

HAMBLEDON RD
SWORD CL
SOUTH LA
DRY PEAK

Clanfield

MAPLE CRES
BEECH RD
SYCAMORE CL
OAK RD
HAZEL RD
WHIT BEAM RISE
WINDMILL CL
SUNDERTON LA
ROSEWOOD GDNS
SANDLEWOOD CL
ALDRIDGE CL
NEW RD
HAZEL GR
JOHNSONS WAY

Down Farm

Clanfield Down

Butser Ancient Farm

3

PIPERS MEAD

HINTON MANOR LA

FARM VIEW AVE
JACOBS CL
ST DAVID'S RD
RIDGE CL
REDWING RD
FIELDFARE CL
KESTREL CL
PINE DR
GREEN LA

STORRINGTON RD
GORING AVE
WARBURTON WAY
SINGLETON GDNS
GORING AVE
BLACKBERRY
LININGTON RD

Meadow Croft Farm

1 SLINDON CL
2 AMBERLEY RD
3 MIDDLETON RISE
4 HEYSHOTT GDNS

Chalton Windmill

Windmill Hill

16

CHILWORTH GDNS
ST JAMES CL
HARTING CL
LONSWORTH CL
VALLEY PARK DR
ELDERBERRY CL

Petersgate Inf Sch

Windmill Hill Farm

Windmill Down

2

DOWNHOUSE RD

Charity Farm

Kennels

WHITE DIRT LA
WATKIN CRES
NIXON CL
DRIFT RD
MEON RD
ARLE CL
FIRST AVE
CHALK RIDGE
BUTSER CT

PO

Snell's Corner

Horndean Down

Blendworth Down

HILLSIDE CL
DRAYCOTE CL
VIKING WAY
WESSEX RD
HILL TOP GDNS

LONDON RD

A3

15

GLAMORGAN RD
WREXHAM GR
CATHERINGTON HILL

WHITE DIRT LA
SOUTHDOWN RD
WODE CL
FRANCIS RD
BELMONT CL
ROMSEY RD

White Dirt Farm

Munday's Row

LOVEDEAN LA

Old Lane

DERWENT CL
THORPFIELD CL
NORTHFIELD CL
TRAIN RISE
ESCOMBE CL
HAWTHORN RD
ST GILES WAY
ST MICHAELS WAY
ST ANDREW CL
ENNERDALE CL
NORTH RD
ST HUBERT RD
CLAIRE GDNS
LONDON RD
ST HILDA AVE

New Barn Farm

1

Catherington Down

Nature Reserve

CATHERINGTON LA

P

Catherington CE Inf Sch

PH

Kings Court Sch

St Catherines

Catherington

Stubbins Down

SOUTHDOWN RD
THE VALE
DOWN RD
COPSE CL
WELL
SOUTH RD
CHERVIL CL
JUNIPER CL
DOOMS
MUNDAYS
COTTAGE WAY
DOWNWOOD WAY
LOVAGE WAY
COMFREY CL
DOWN FARM PL

A3
A3(M)
A3

Blendworth Lith

Crabden Row

CRABDEN LA

14

69   A   70   B   71   C

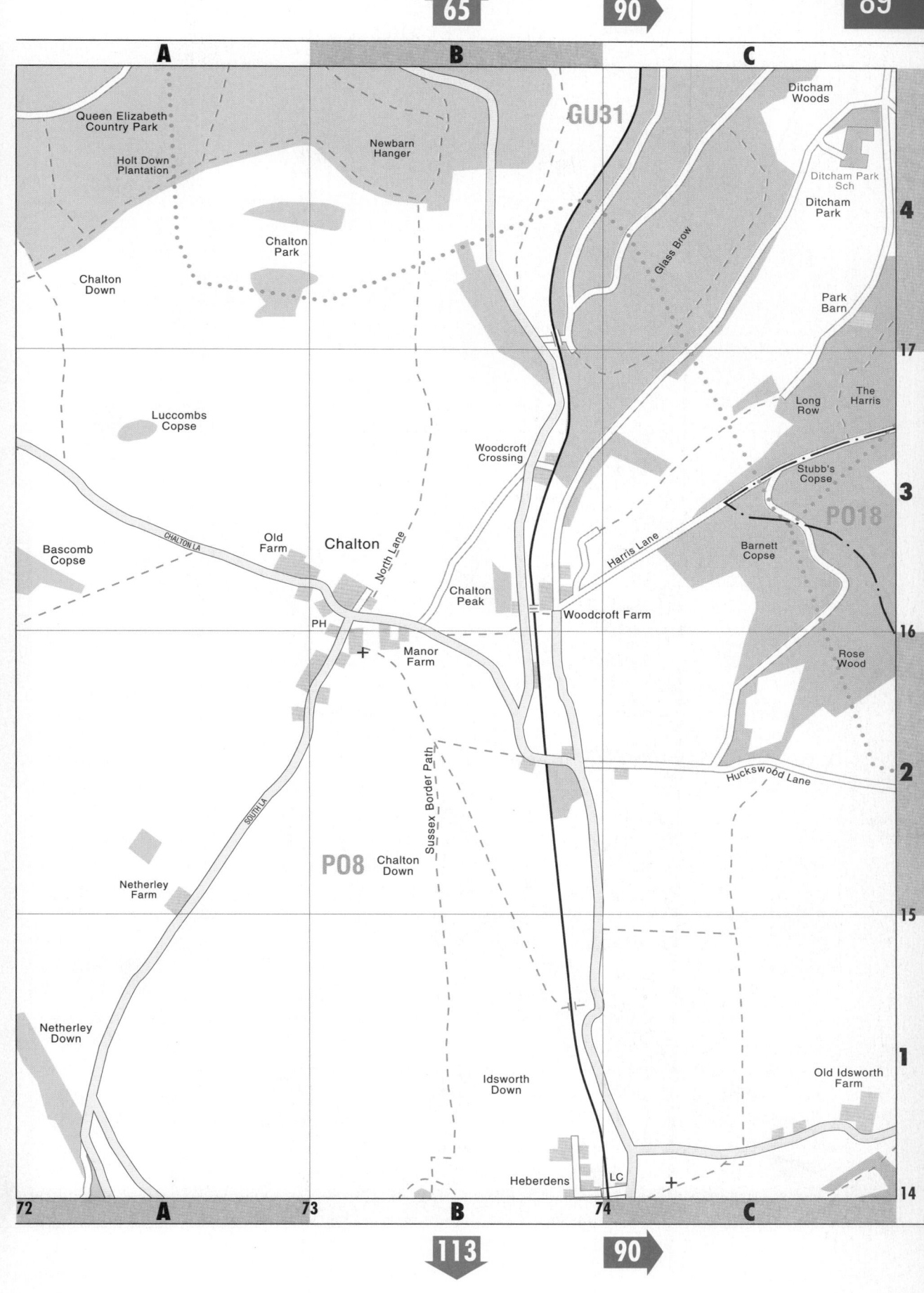

A **B** **C**

GU31

Ditcham
Woods

Queen Elizabeth
Country Park

Holt Down
Plantation

Newbarn
Hanger

Ditcham Park
Sch

Chalton
Park

Ditcham
Park

4

Chalton
Down

Glass Brow

Park
Barn

17

Luccombs
Copse

Woodcroft
Crossing

Long
Row

The
Harris

Stubb's
Copse

3

Bascomb
Copse

CHALTON LA

Old
Farm

Chalton

North Lane

Harris Lane

Barnett
Copse

PO18

Chalton
Peak

Woodcroft Farm

PH

Manor
Farm

16

Rose
Wood

SOUTH LA

Sussex Border Path

Huckswood Lane

2

PO8

Chalton
Down

Netherley
Farm

15

Netherley
Down

1

Old Idsworth
Farm

Idsworth
Down

Heberdens

LC

14

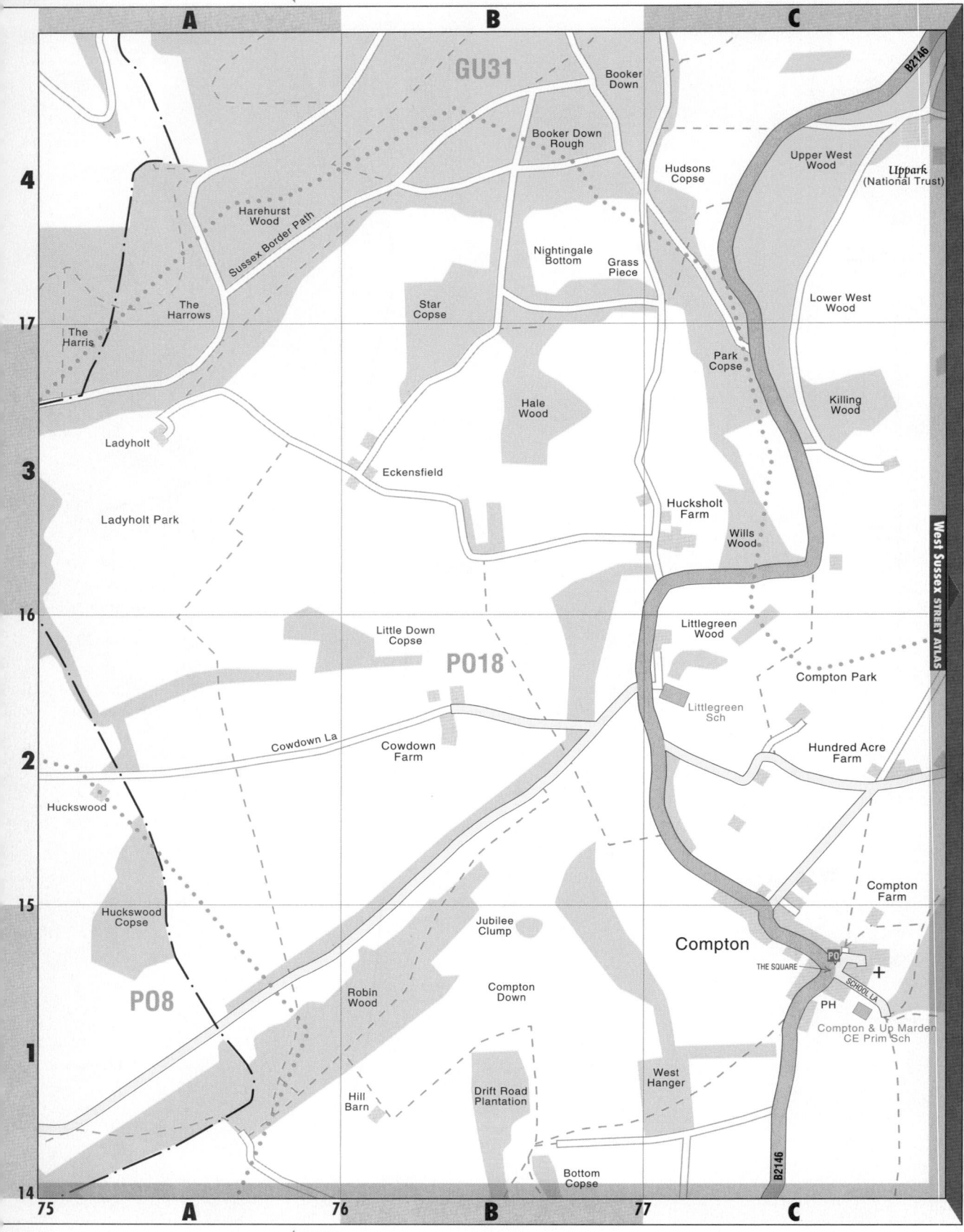

GU31

Booker
Down

Booker Down
Rough

Hudsons
Copse

Upper West
Wood

Uppark
(National Trust)

Harehurst
Wood

Sussex Border Path

Nightingale
Bottom

Grass
Piece

Lower West
Wood

The Harrows

Star
Copse

The
Harris

Park
Copse

Killing
Wood

Hale
Wood

Ladyholt

Eckensfield

Hucksholt
Farm

Ladyholt Park

Wills
Wood

Littlegreen
Wood

Little Down
Copse

Compton Park

PO18

Littlegreen
Sch

Cowdown La

Cowdown
Farm

Hundred Acre
Farm

Huckswood

Huckswood
Copse

Compton
Farm

Jubilee
Clump

Compton

PO8

THE SQUARE

Robin
Wood

Compton
Down

PH

Compton & Up Marden
CE Prim Sch

West
Hanger

Hill
Barn

Drift Road
Plantation

Bottom
Copse

B2146

West Sussex STREET ATLAS

75
76
77

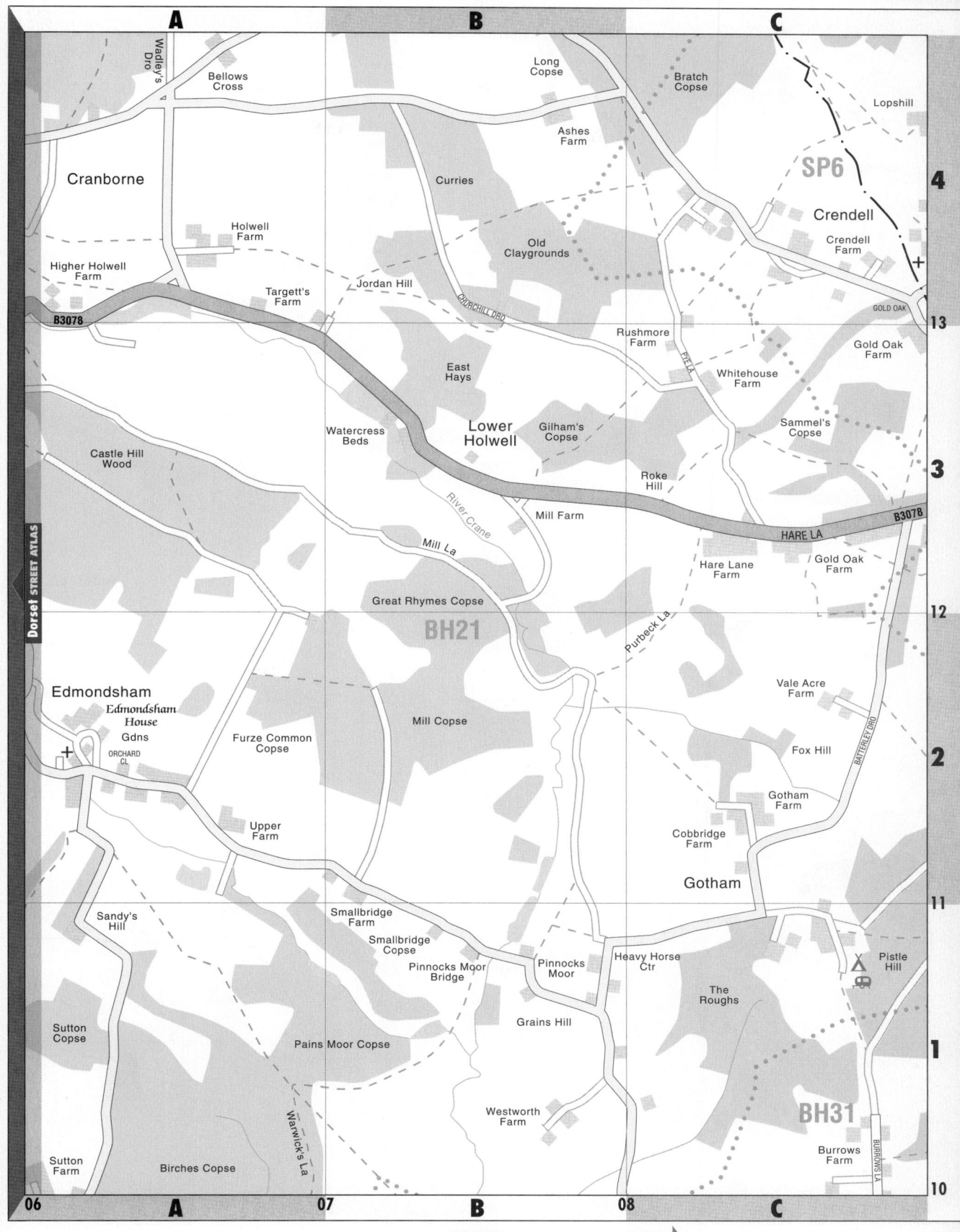

A   B   C

Cutts Copse

Higher Bullhill
Farm

Pond Close

Lopshill
Farm

Cheater's Gate

CHEATER'S LA

Alderholt
Park

4

Lopshill Common

Lower Daggons

High
Wood

Park Farm

Hill Cottage
Farm

Hart's
Farm

13

Hither Daggons
Wood

Further Daggons
Wood

Vicarage
Farm

Churchill Arms
(PH)

APPLE TREE
RD

B3078

STATION RD

PARK LA

STATION CL

OLD FORGE
CL

STATION RD

LIME TREE CL

PEAR TREE
CL

3

Bittersweet
Farm

Daggons

DAGGONS RD

HIGHWOOD CL

PO

ALDER DR

EARLSWOOD DR

B3078

CRANBORNE RD

SP6

CHURCHILL CL

BLACKWATER GR

ATTWOOD CL

STATION RD

PINE RD

OAK RD

Cripplestyle

King
Barrow

Charing Cross

RINGWOOD RD

Alderholt

12

Cross Roads
Plantation

Sleepbrook
Farm

2

Ringwood Forest

Stanford
Point

Alderholt Common

BH21

Telegraph
Plantation

Cranborne
Common

11

Sleep Brook

Decoy
Pond

Sleep Bottom

Mast

BH31

Plumley Wood

1

BH24

Mount
Ararat

10

09   A   10   B   11   C

A   **B**   **C**

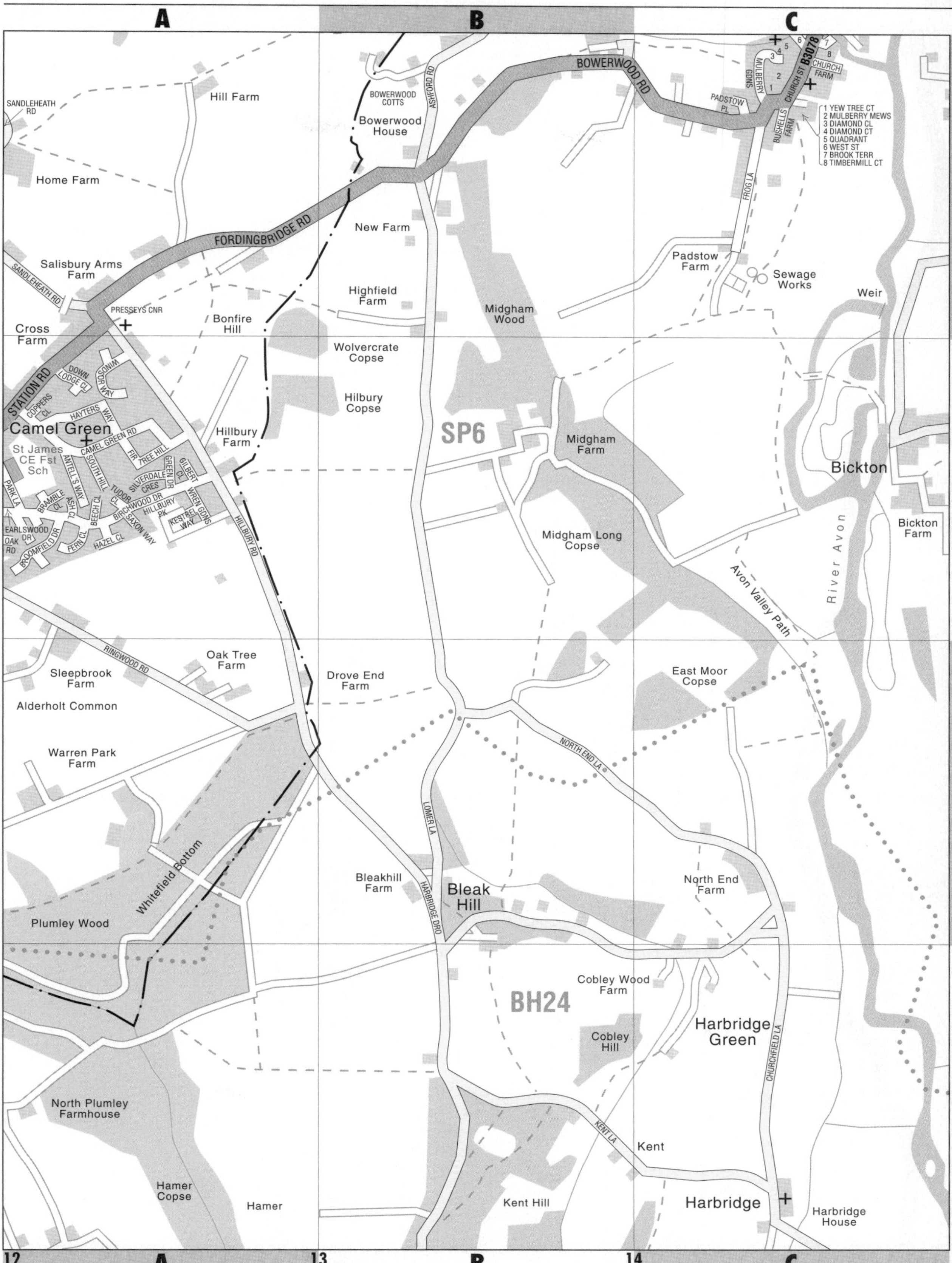

SANDLEHEATH RD

Hill Farm

Bowerwood COTTS

Bowerwood House

BOWERWOOD RD

Home Farm

PADSTOW PL

1 YEW TREE CT
2 MULBERRY MEWS
3 DIAMOND CL
4 DIAMOND CT
5 QUADRANT
6 WEST ST
7 BROOK TERR
8 TIMBERMILL CT

CHURCH ST B3078

BUSHELLS FARM

MULBERRY GDNS

CHURCH FARM

4

FORDINGBRIDGE RD

Salisbury Arms Farm

New Farm

Padstow Farm

Sewage Works

Weir

SANDLEHEATH RD

PRESSEYS CNR

Highfield Farm

Midgham Wood

FROG LA

13

Cross Farm

Bonfire Hill

Wolvercrate Copse

STATION RD

DOWN LODGE CL

SOPER WAY

COPPERS CL

HAYTERS WAY

CAMEL GREEN RD

FIR TREE HILL

Hilbury Copse

Midgham Farm

SP6

Bickton

3

Camel Green

St James CE Fst Sch

PARK LA

ANTELLS WAY

BRAMBLE CL

BEECH CL

ASH CL

SOUTH HILL

TUDOR RD

GILBERT GDNS

GREEN DR

SILVERDALE CRES

BIRCHWOOD DR

Hillbury Farm

Midgham Long Copse

River Avon

Bickton Farm

EARLSWOOD DR

OAK RD

BROOMFIELD DR

FERN CL

HAZEL CL

Hillbury Pk

WREN CL

KESTREL WAY

SAXON WAY

HILLBURY RD

Avon Valley Path

Oak Tree Farm

Drove End Farm

East Moor Copse

12

Sleepbrook Farm

RINGWOOD RD

Alderholt Common

NORTH END LA

2

Warren Park Farm

LOMER LA

North End Farm

Whitefield Bottom

HARBRIDGE DRO

Bleakhill Farm

Bleak Hill

11

Plumley Wood

Cobley Wood Farm

Harbridge Green

CHURCHFIELD LA

BH24

Cobley Hill

North Plumley Farmhouse

1

KENT LA

Kent

Hamer Copse

Hamer

Kent Hill

Harbridge

Harbridge House

10

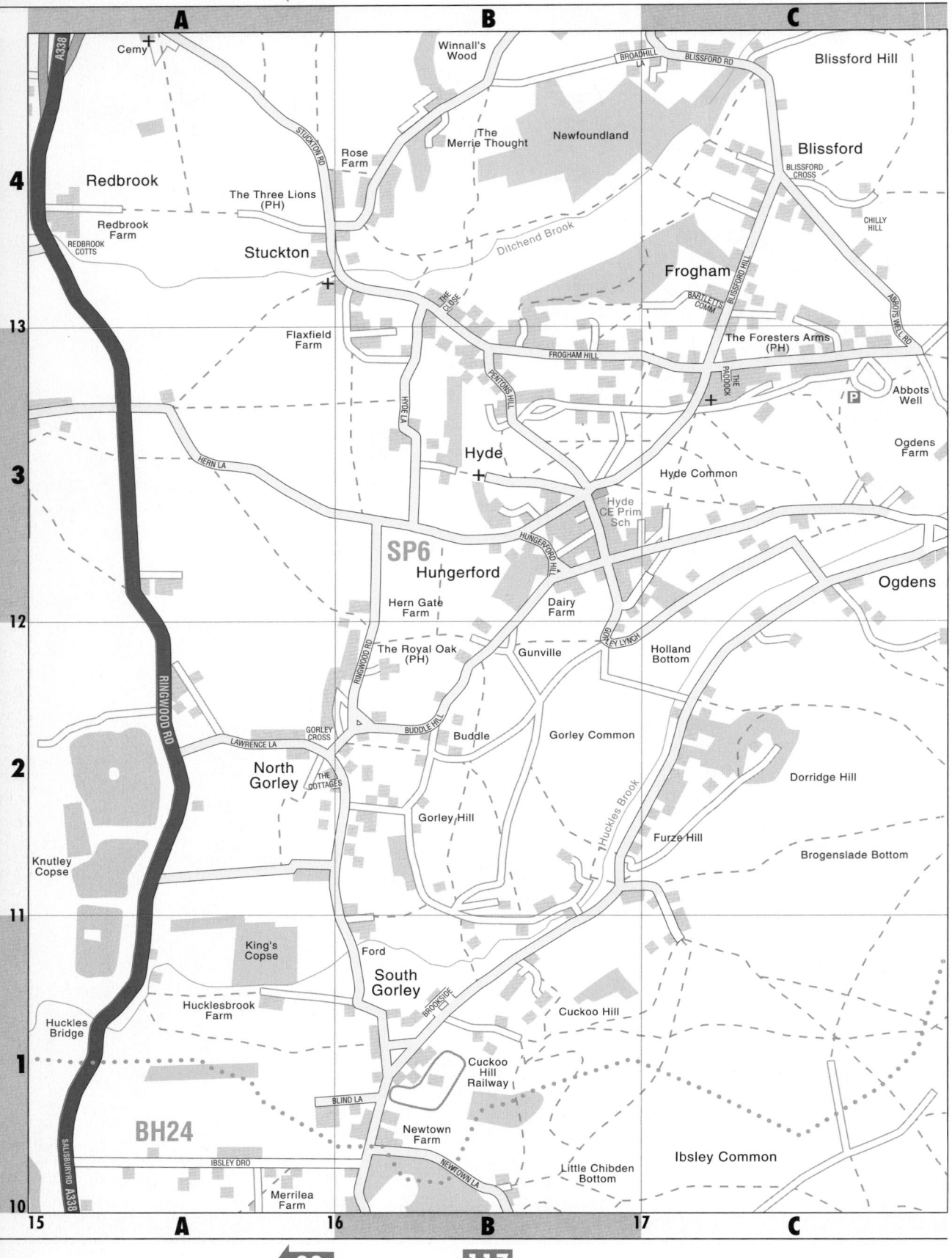

A338

Cemy

A
B
C

Winnall's Wood

Redbrook

Rose Farm

The Merrie Thought

Newfoundland

BROADHILL LA

BLISSFORD RD

Blissford Hill

4

The Three Lions (PH)

Redbrook Farm

STUCKTON RD

Blissford

BLISSFORD CROSS

REDBROOK COTTS

Stuckton

Ditchend Brook

CHILLY HILL

Flaxfield Farm

Frogham

BARTLETTS COMM

13

HYDE LA

FROGHAM HILL

The Foresters Arms (PH)

THE PADDOCK

Abbots Well

P

Hern La

HERN LA

FENTONS HILL

Hyde

Ogdens Farm

3

Hyde Common

HUNGERFORD HILL

Hyde CE Prim Sch

SP6

Ogdens

Hungerford

Hern Gate Farm

Dairy Farm

RINGWOOD RD

12

The Royal Oak (PH)

Gunville

GORLEY LYNCH

Holland Bottom

BUDDLE HILL

Buddle

Gorley Common

GORLEY CROSS

Dorridge Hill

2

LAWRENCE LA

North Gorley

THE COTTAGES

Huckles Brook

RINGWOOD RD

Gorley Hill

Furze Hill

Brogenslade Bottom

Knutley Copse

11

King's Copse

Ford

South Gorley

BROOKSIDE

Cuckoo Hill

Hucklesbrook Farm

Huckles Bridge

Cuckoo Hill Railway

1

BH24

BLIND LA

Newtown Farm

Ibsley Common

SALISBURY RD A338

IBSLEY DRO

NEWTOWN LA

Little Chibden Bottom

Merrilea Farm

10

15
A
16
B
17
C

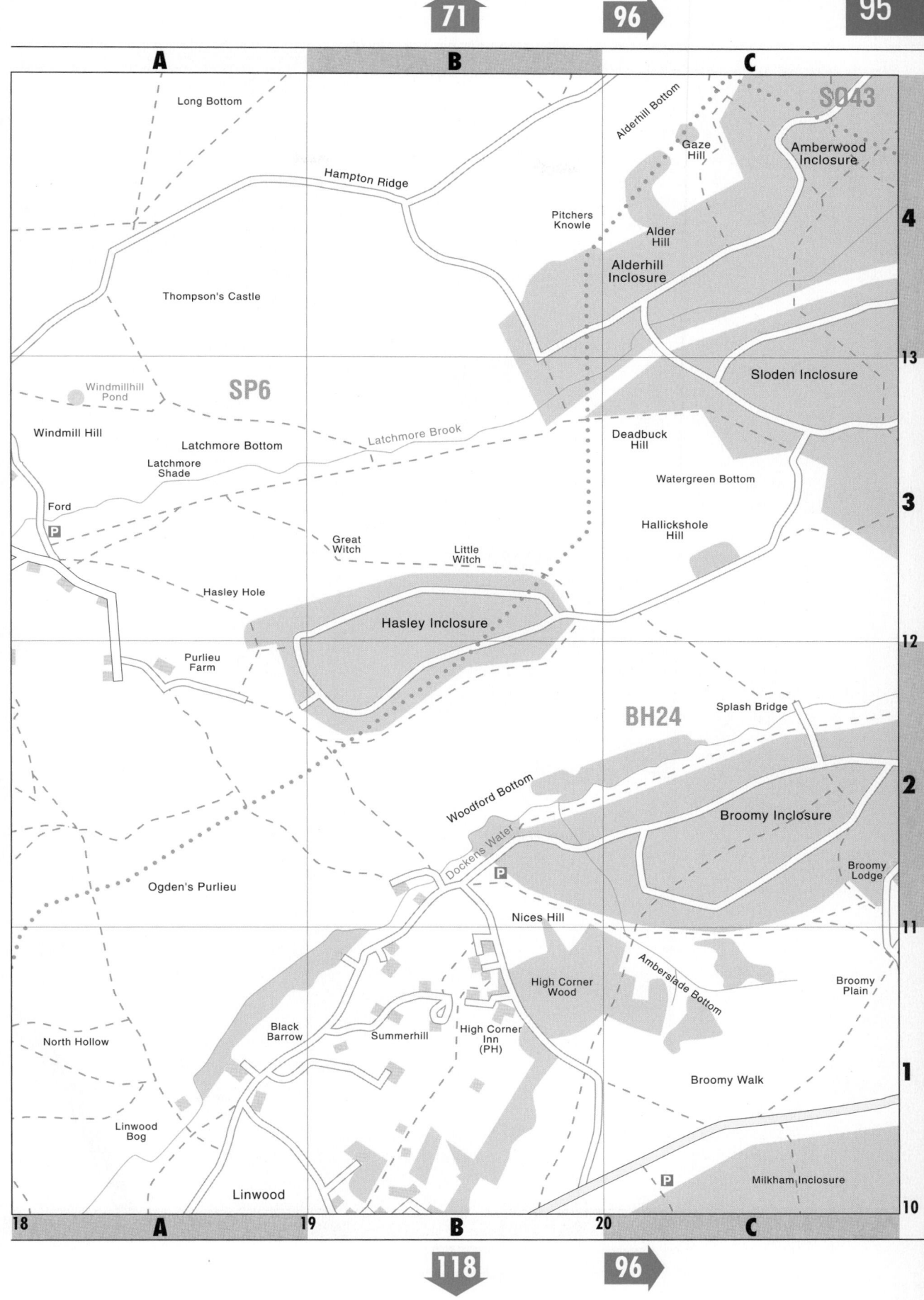

A
Long Bottom

Hampton Ridge

Thompson's Castle

Windmillhill Pond

SP6

Windmill Hill

Latchmore Bottom
Latchmore Shade

Ford
P

Hasley Hole

Great Witch

Purlieu Farm

Ogden's Purlieu

North Hollow

Black Barrow

Summerhill

Linwood Bog

Linwood

B
Alderhill Bottom

Gaze Hill

Pitchers Knowle

Alderhill Inclosure

Latchmore Brook

Little Witch

Hasley Inclosure

Woodford Bottom

Dockens Water
P

Nices Hill

High Corner Wood

High Corner Inn (PH)

C
SO43

Amberwood Inclosure

Alder Hill

Sloden Inclosure

Deadbuck Hill

Watergreen Bottom

Hallickshole Hill

BH24

Splash Bridge

Broomy Inclosure

Broomy Lodge

Amberslade Bottom

Broomy Plain

Broomy Walk

Milkham Inclosure

P

4

13

3

12

2

11

1

10

A

B

C

Latchmore Brook

Whiteshoot
Bottom

Hiscocks
Hill

P

Fritham
Grange

Amberwood
Inclosure

Green
Pond

North Bentley
Inclosure

4

Queen North
Wood

Fritham Plain

Sloden
Inclosure

13

Freeworms
Hill

South Bentley
Inclosure

Rakes Brakes
Bottom

SO43

Dockens Water

3

Anses
Wood

Ragged Boys
Hill

Cadmans
Pool

P

P

Ocknell
Pond

12

Holly Hatch
Inclosure

Holly Hatch
Cottage

P

BH24

2

P

Ocknell Plain

Broomy
Lodge

11

Broomy
Bottom

Winding
Stonard

Bratley Water

Spreading
Oak

Broomy Plain

1

Slufters
Inclosure

Slufters
Bottom

A31

P

Fritham
Cross

10

21		22		23	
	A		B		C

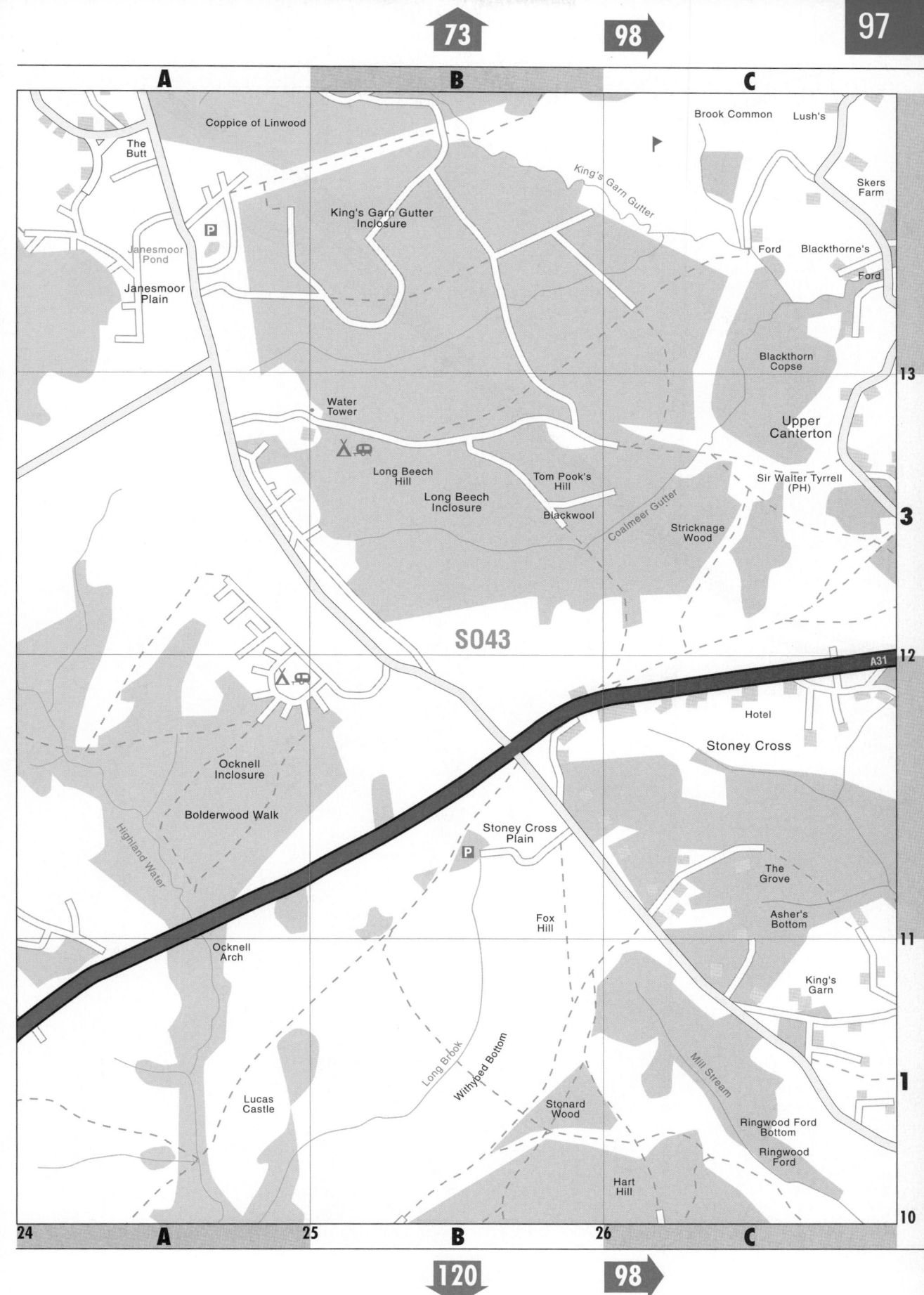

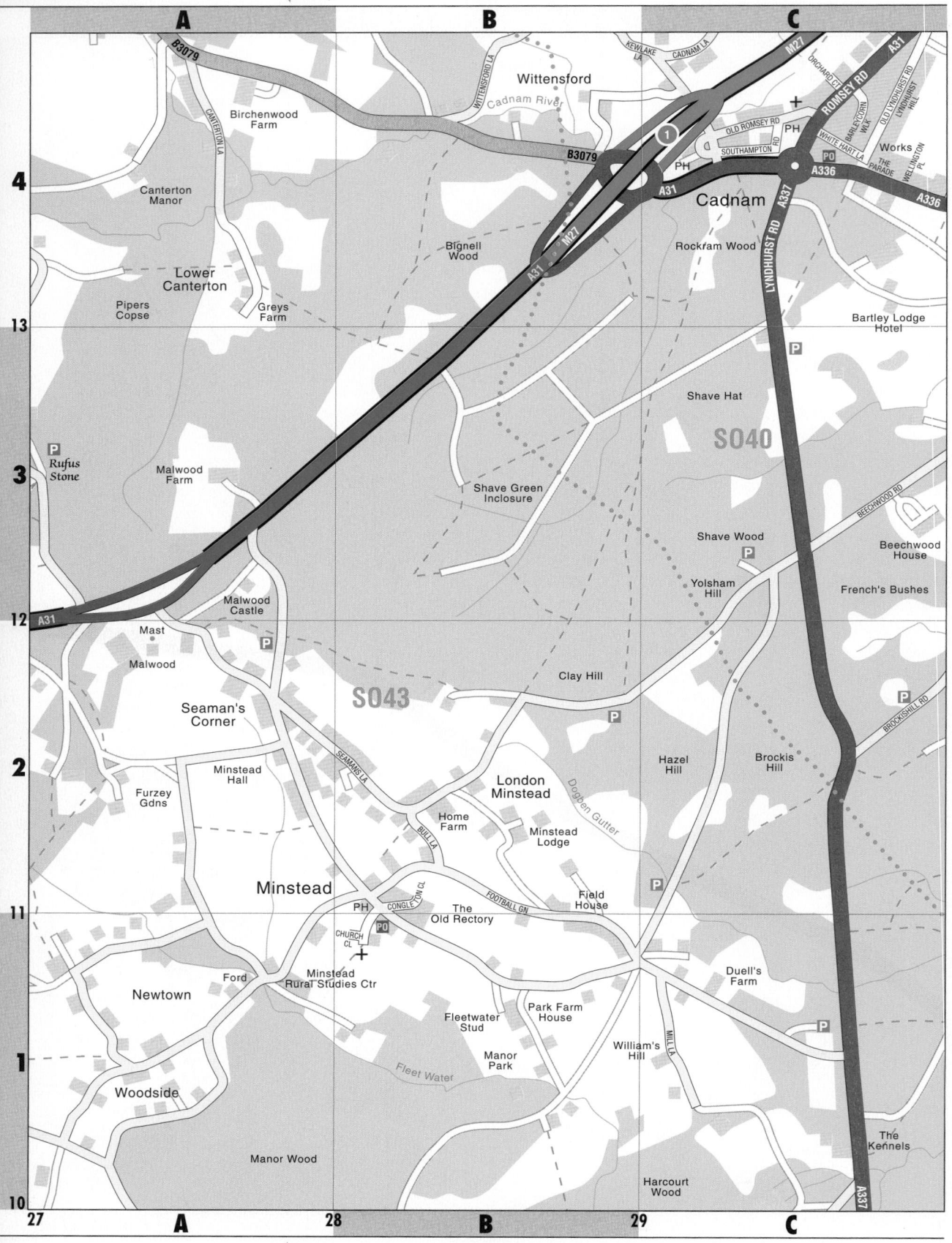

B3079

Wittensford

KEWLAKE LA   CADNAM LA

WITTENSFORD LA

M27   A31

ROMSEY RD   A31

Cadnam River

Birchenwood
Farm

B3079

ORCHARD CT

Old Romsey Rd

WHITE HART LA   SOUTHAMPTON RD   PH

HARETHORN WLK

OLD LYNDHURST RD

LYNDHURST HILL

CANTERTON LA

4

Canterton
Manor

Bignell
Wood

A31

PH

A31   Cadnam

Works

THE PARADE

PO

WELLINGTON PL

A336

A336

Rockram Wood

Lower
Canterton

Greys
Farm

LYNDHURST RD

A337

Bartley Lodge
Hotel

13

Pipers
Copse

M27

Shave Hat

SO40

P

BEECHWOOD RD

P   Rufus
Stone

3

Malwood
Farm

Shave Green
Inclosure

Shave Wood

P

Beechwood
House

French's Bushes

Yolsham
Hill

12

A31   Malwood
Castle

Clay Hill

SO43

BROCKISHILL RD

P

Mast

P

Malwood

Hazel
Hill

Brockis
Hill

P

2

Seaman's
Corner

SEAMANS LA

London
Minstead

Dogben Gutter

Furzey
Gdns

Minstead
Hall

Home
Farm

BULL LA

Minstead
Lodge

Field
House

P

FOOTBALL GN

Minstead

PH

CONGLETON CL

PO

The
Old Rectory

11

CHURCH CL

Duell's
Farm

Newtown

Ford

Minstead
Rural Studies Ctr

Fleetwater
Stud

Park Farm
House

William's
Hill

MILL LA

P

1

Woodside

Fleet Water

Manor
Park

A337

The
Kennels

Manor Wood

Harcourt
Wood

10

A · B · C

Homestead
Oakhill
POLLARDS MOOR RD
THE BRICKYARD
WINSOR RD
Budds Farm
St Helen's Farm
Manor Farm
Judds Farm
Stamford Hill Farm
TATCHBURY LA
Burnards Copse
WINSOR LA

FIR TREE RD
PH
BARNEY HAYES LA
KENSINGTON LA
Bartley CE Jun Sch
4
Garden Centre
ROCKRAM CL
SOUTHAMPTON RD
NEW INN RD
PH
OAKFIELD RD
NEW INN LA
ABBOTSFORD
PO
Bartley Grange
EADENS LA
Saw Mill
Carlton House
RINGWOOD RD
A336
13

Forest House
Bartley
CHINHAM RD
PUNDLE GREEN EST
RIVERSIDE CL
SHEPHERDS CL
SHEPHERDS CL
SHEPHERDS RD
Bourne Farm
BOURNE RD
PARADISE LA
BOURNE LA
Ford
Ridge Farm
WOODLANDS RD
3

Beechwood Park
BROCKISHILL RD
Bartley Manor
+
The Copse Caravan Park
The Orchard Caravan Park
ROSSITERS LA
Rossiters La
Rossiters Copse
LANESBRIDGE CL
GREEN CL
12

Nicholas Corner
PURKISS CL
BARTLEY RD
Moorlands Farm
PH
MILLVINA CL

Goldenhayes
SO40
Woodlands

Eaves Hill
Goldenhayes Park
Foyers
Hotel
2

Brockishill Inclosure
P
The Woodlands Lodge Hotel
WOODLANDS RD
THE CRESCENT
ALPINE RD
HAZEL GR
WOODLANDS DRO
FLETCHWOOD LA
11

Busketts Wood

Busketts Lawn Inclosure
Ford
Ford
Costicles Inclosure
1

SO43
Bartley Water

Furzy Lawn Inclosure
Gutter Heath
Ironshill Lodge
A35
10

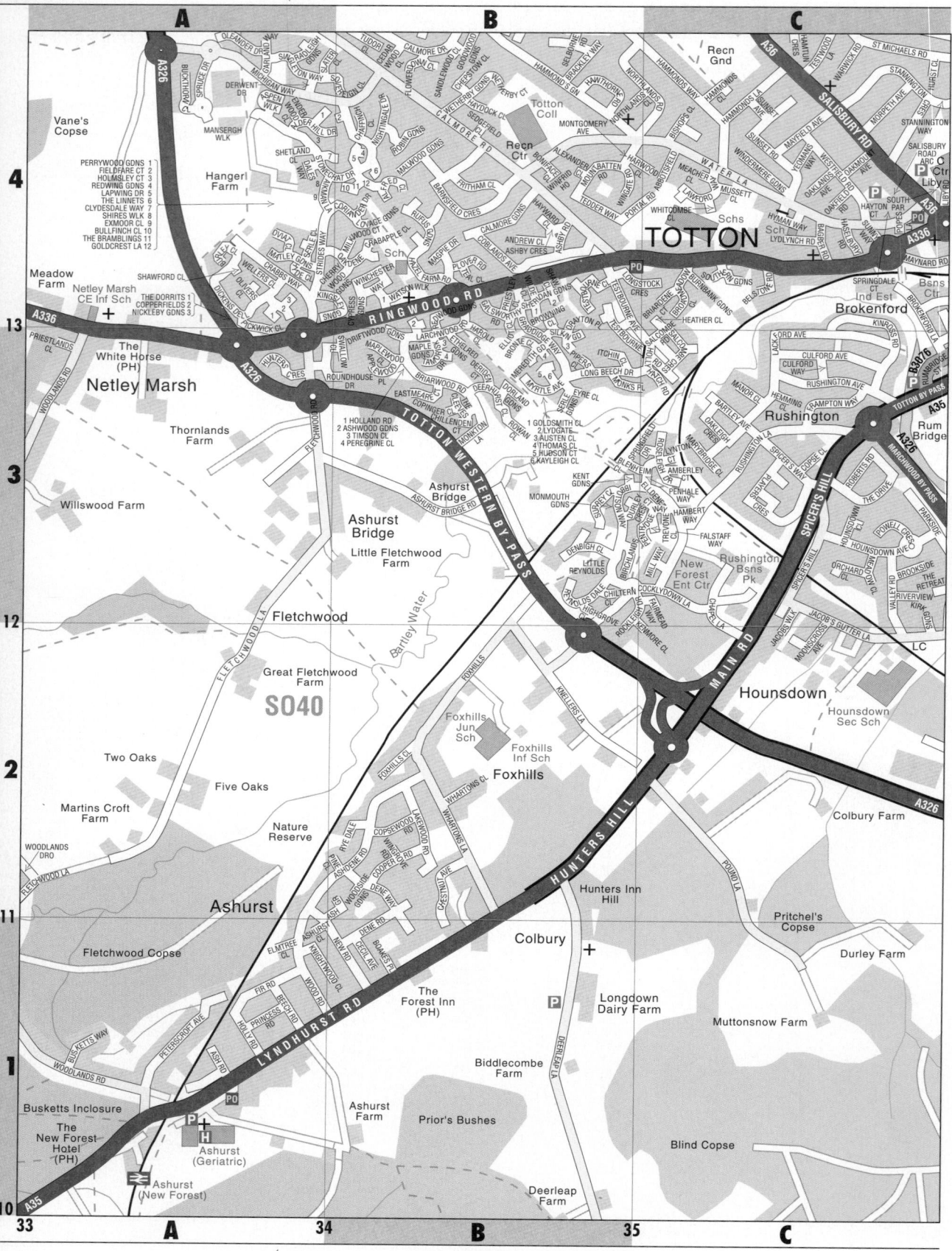

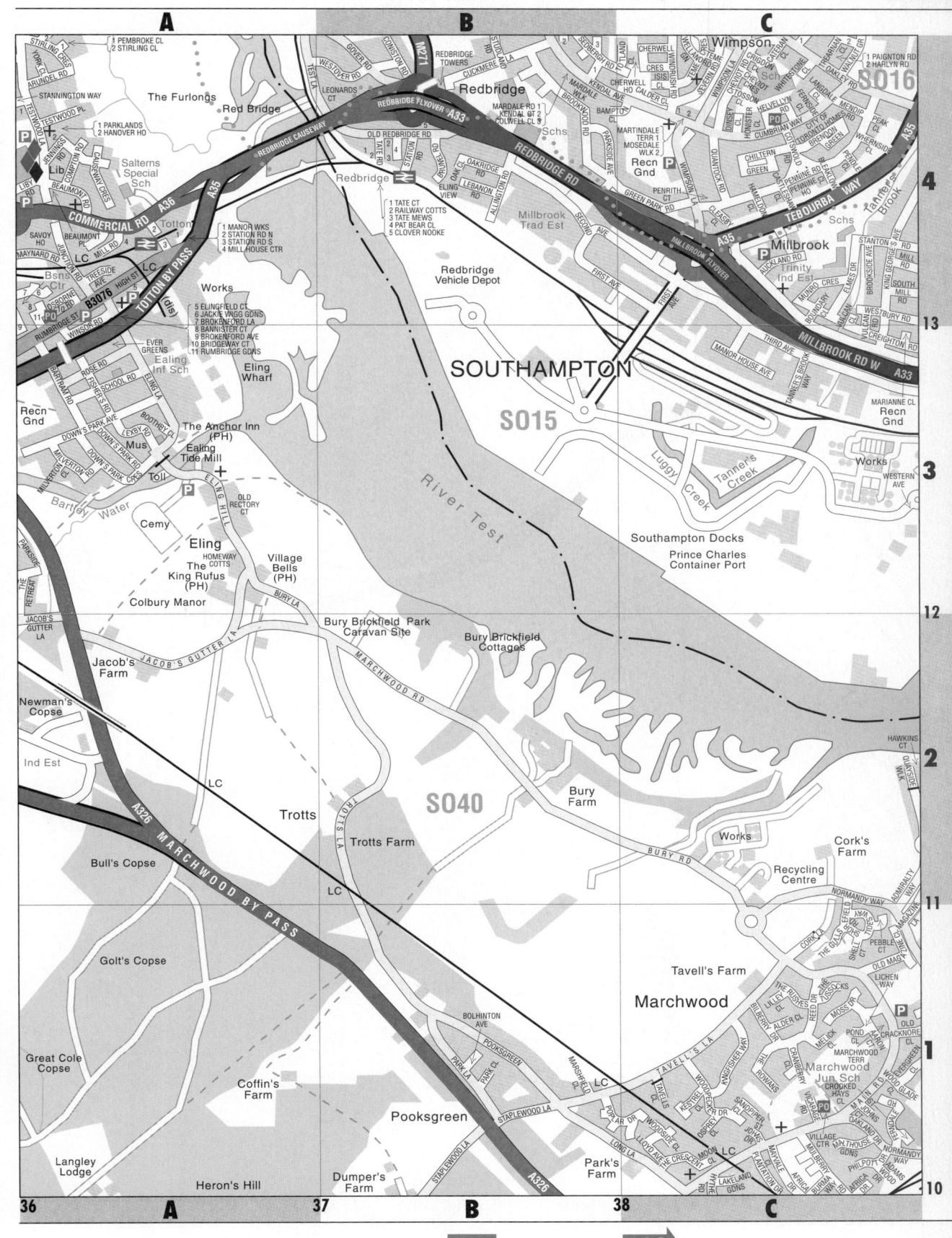

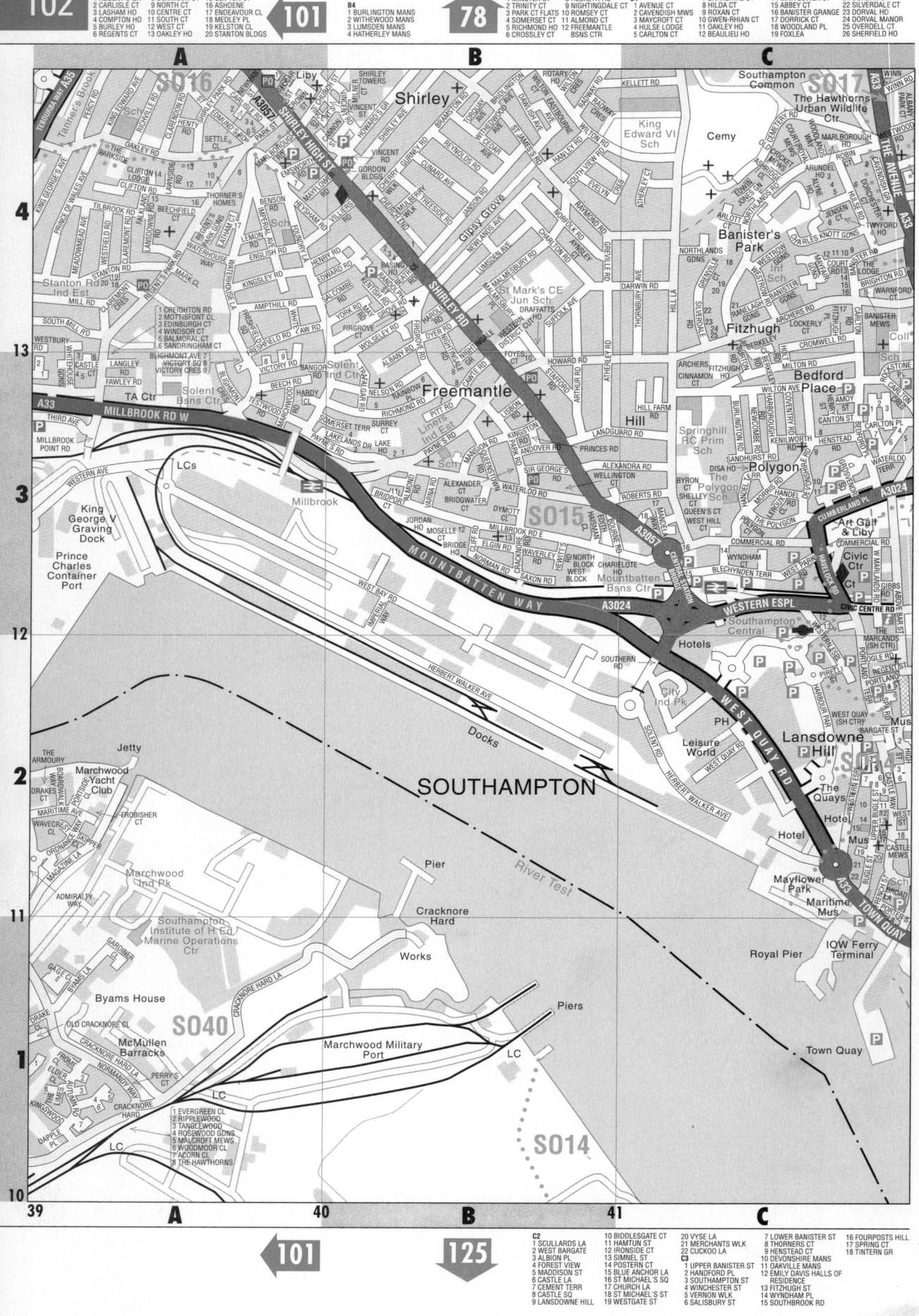

A4
1 REGENT'S GR
2 CARLISLE CT
3 LASHAM HO
4 COMPTON HO
5 BURLEY HO
6 REGENTS CT
7 LEIGHTON AVE
8 DENNISON CT
9 NORTH CT
10 CENTRE CT
11 SOUTH CT
12 WEST CT
13 OAKLEY HO
14 CLIFTON GDNS
15 CLIFTON CT
16 ASHDENE
17 ENDEAVOUR CL
18 MEDLEY PL
19 KELSTON CL
20 STANTON BLDGS

101

B4
1 BURLINGTON MANS
2 WITHEWOOD MANS
3 LUMSDEN MANS
4 HATHERLEY MANS

78

B3
1 MINSTER CT
2 TRINITY CT
3 PARK CT FLATS
4 SOMERSET CT
5 RICHMOND HO
6 CROSSLEY CT
7 CHERITON CT
8 HESKETH HO
9 NIGHTINGDALE CT
10 ROMSEY CT
11 ALMOND CT
12 FREEMANTLE BSNS CTR
13 BROOK CT

C4
1 AVENUE CT
2 CAVENDISH MWS
3 MAYCROFT CT
4 HULSE LODGE
5 CARLTON CT

C
6 ST MARGARETS HO
7 BARKSHIRE CT
8 HILDA CT
9 ROXAN CT
10 GWEN-RHIAN CT
11 OAKLEY HO
12 BEAULIEU HO
13 BANISTER CT
14 MAYFLOWER CT
15 ABBEY CT
16 BANISTER GRANGE
17 DORRICK CT
18 WOODLAND PL
19 FOXLEA
20 PAVILION CT
21 DURBAN CT
22 SILVERDALE CT
23 DORVAL HO
24 DORVAL MANOR
25 OVERDELL CT
26 SHERFIELD HO

101
125

C2
1 SCULLARDS LA
2 WEST BARGATE
3 ALBION PL
4 FOREST VIEW
5 MADDISON ST
6 CASTLE LA
7 CEMENT TERR
8 CASTLE SQ
9 LANSDOWNE HILL
10 BIDDLESGATE CT
11 HAMTUN ST
12 IRONSIDE CT
13 SIMNEL ST
14 POSTERN CT
15 BLUE ANCHOR LA
16 ST MICHAEL'S SQ
17 CHURCH LA
18 ST MICHAEL'S ST
19 WESTGATE ST
20 VYSE LA
21 MERCHANTS WLK
22 CUCKOO LA

C3
1 UPPER BANISTER ST
2 HANDFORD PL
3 SOUTHAMPTON ST
4 WINCHESTER ST
5 VERNON WLK
6 SALISBURY ST
7 LOWER BANISTER ST
8 THORNERS CT
9 HENSTEAD CT
10 DEVONSHIRE MANS
11 OAKVILLE MANS
12 EMILY DAVIS HALLS OF RESIDENCE
13 FITZHUGH ST
14 WYNDHAM ST
15 SOUTHBROOK RD
16 FOURPOSTS HILL
17 SPRING CT
18 TINTERN GR

A4				
1 CLIFFORD DIBBEN MEWS	7 BALMORAL CT	14 WINDSOR CT	21 ST ANDREWS HO	28 CHARLES WYATT HO
2 BUCKINGHAM CT	8 WESSEX CT	15 PARKLAND PL	22 ST GEORGES HO	29 TEMPLAR CT
3 LINGDALE PL	9 RANELAGH CT	16 CHERRY CT	23 WOODSIDE CT	30 LAMWARD MANS
4 MINSTEAD CT	10 KINTERBURY CT	17 CAMBRIDGE CT	24 ASCUPART HO	C4
5 HARTLEY CT	11 ELFIN CT	18 ST ANNES MEWS	25 BEVOIS MANS	1 MIDANBURY WLK
6 WINDSOR CT	12 WESTWOOD CT	19 HYNES CT	26 BEVOIS MEWS	2 KELLY CT
	13 CANDLEMAS PL	20 BARTLETT HO	27 DARNAN HO	3 FLORENCE CT

C4		C4		C2
4 DEAN CT		10 MIDANBURY CT	16 ROSEBROOK CT	
5 BINDON CT		11 WELLOW CT	17 JUNIPER CT	
6 CAUSEWAY CT		12 THE GATEHOUSE	A2	
7 ABBEYFIELD HO		13 WINDSOR CT	1 ALBION TWRS	
8 BIRCHWOOD CT		14 MANOR PARK HO	2 JOHNSON ST	
9 CHRISTINE CT		15 COBBETT CT	3 KINGSLAND SQ	
			4 KINGSLAND CT	

79 ↑   **104** ↑   **103**

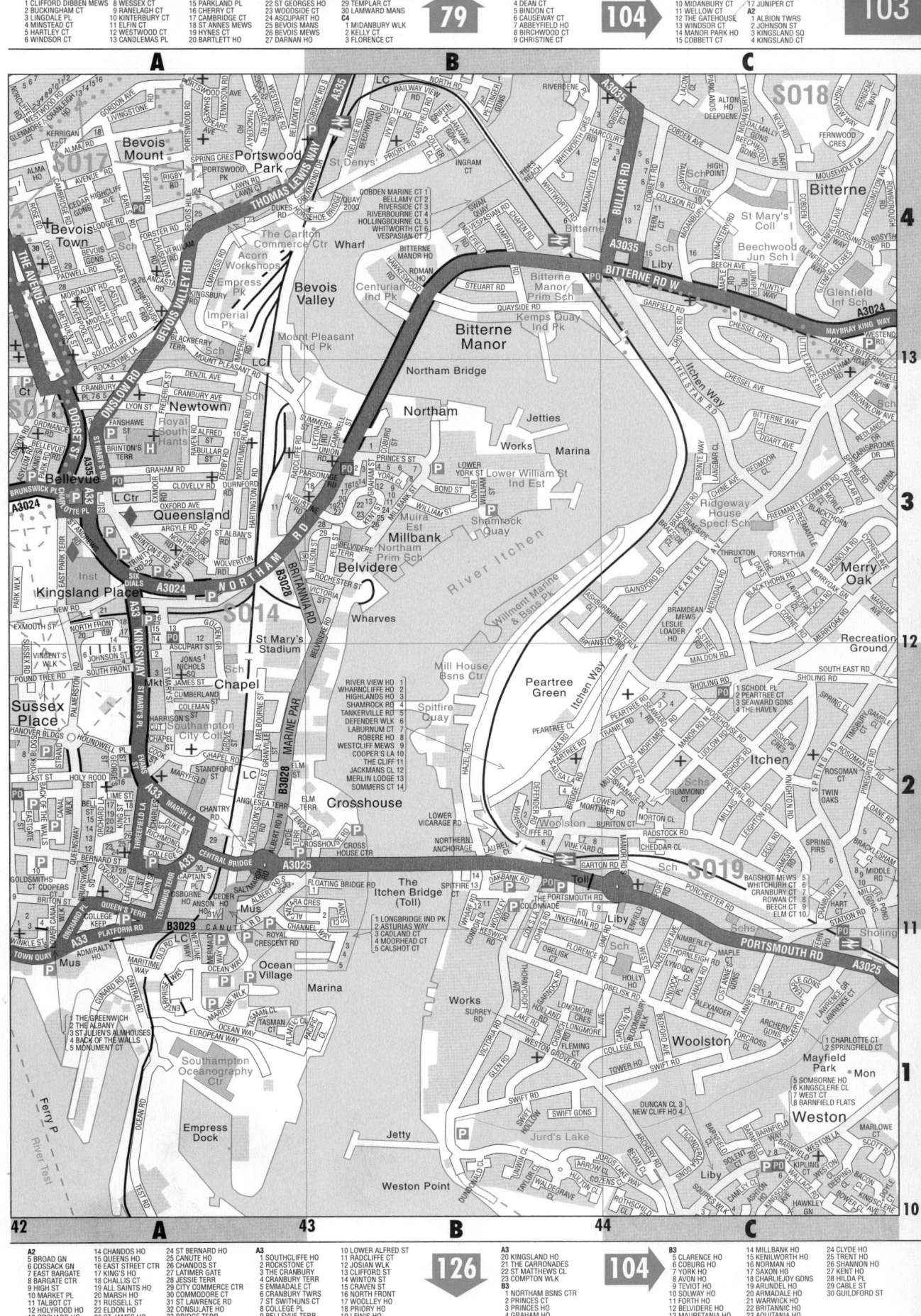

42   A   **43**   B   **44**   C

A2				B3	
4 BROAD GN	14 CHANDOS HO	24 ST BERNARD HO	A3	5 CLARENCE HO	14 MILLBANK HO	24 CLYDE HO
5 COSSACK GN	15 QUEENS HO	25 CANUTE HO	20 KINGSLAND HO	6 COBURG HO	15 KENILWORTH HO	25 TRENT HO
6 EAST BARGATE	16 EAST STREET CTR	26 CHANDOS ST	21 THE CARRONADES	7 YORK HO	16 NORMAN HO	26 SHANNON HO
7 EAST BARGATE	17 KING'S HO	27 LATIMER GATE	22 ST MATTHEWS CL	8 AVON HO	17 SAXON HO	27 KENT HO
8 BARGATE CTR	18 CHALLIS CT	28 CRANBURY TERR	23 COMPTON WLK	9 TEVIOT HO	18 CHARLIEJOY GDNS	28 HILDA PL
9 HIGH ST	19 ALL SAINTS HO	29 CITY COMMERCE CTR	C4	10 SOLWAY HO	19 ARUNDEL HO	29 CABLE ST
10 MARKET PL	20 MARSH HO	30 COMMODORE CT	1 SOUTHCLIFFE HO	11 FORTH HO	20 ARMADALE HO	30 GUILDFORD ST
11 TALBOT CT	21 RUSSELL ST	31 ST LAWRENCE RD	2 ROCKSTONE CT	12 BELVIDERE HO	21 WARWICK HO	
12 HOLYROOD HO	22 ELDON ST	32 CONSULATE ST	3 THE CRANBURY	13 MAURETANIA HO	22 BRITANNIC HO	
13 ORCHARD HO	23 ST JAMES RD	33 BRIDGE TERR	4 CRANBURY TERR		23 AQUITANIA HO	
			5 EMMADALE CT			
A3		10 LOWER ALFRED ST	6 CRANBURY TWRS			
1 SOUTHCLIFFE HO		11 RADCLIFFE CT	7 ST SWITHUNS CT			
2 ROCKSTONE CT		12 JOSIAH WLK	8 COLLEGE PL			
3 THE CRANBURY		13 CLIFFORD ST	9 BELLEVUE TERR			
4 CRANBURY TERR		14 WINTON ST				
5 EMMADALE CT		15 CRAVEN ST	B3			
6 CRANBURY TWRS		16 NORTH FRONT	1 NORTHAM BSNS CTR			
7 ST SWITHUNS CT		17 WOOLLEY HO	2 PRINCES CT			
8 COLLEGE PL		18 PRIORY HO	3 PRINCES HO			
9 BELLEVUE TERR		19 LEWIS HO	4 GRAHAM HO			

126 ↓   **104** ↓

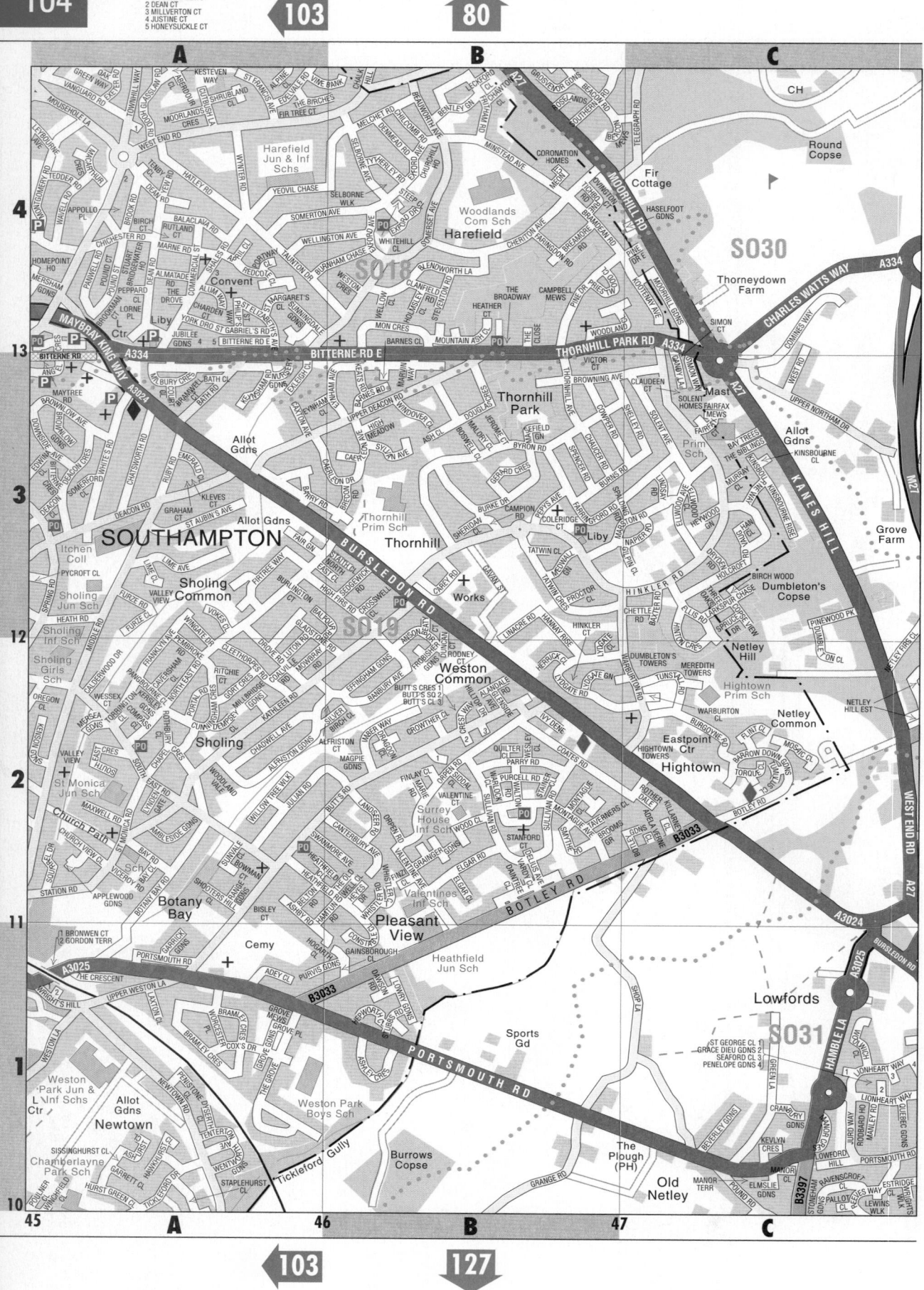

A B C

Place names and labels

Waterloo Ind Est Flander Ind Pk
ROYAL LONDON PK
Shopping Centre
Superstore
CHARLES WATTS WAY
Shamblehurst Prim Sch
Wildern
Wildern Sec Sch
Sports Ctr
Botleigh Grange Hotel
GRANGE RD
Broadway Farm
Holmesland
Broadoak
BROAD OAK A334 HIGH ST
Woodhill Sch
Recn Gd
Southbrook
Liby
UPPER NORTHAM RD
LOWER NORTHAM RD
St John's
SO30
Fir Tree Farm
Hatts Copse Farm
Gould Copse
Manor Lodge
Hedge End
Kings Copse Prim Sch
Manor Farm Mus
Paling Bsns Pk
Sports Ground
Piland's Copse
Netley Hill
Sunday's Hill
Bursledon Common SO19
Kings Copse Farm
Dock Copse
Hunters Ct
Dodwell Farm
Manor Farm Country Park
River Hamble
Bursledon Windmill
Hoe Moor House SO31
Catland Copse
Lowford
Bursledon Hall
Swanwick Wood SO31
Brixedone Farm
Works
Lynwood
PROVIDENCE HILL
OAKHILL BRIDGE RD A27
Claypits
M27

Street index insets

1 BIRCHWOOD GDNS
2 NAVIGATOR'S WAY
3 HARRIS AVE
4 LAKE FARM CL

ROWLEY CT 1
ROWLEY CL 2
CHESTNUT WLK 3
HOLMESLAND WLK 4
LIME WLK 5
RECTORY CT 6
SYCAMORE WLK 7

1 FOWLERS RD
2 DOWDS CL
3 FORSYTHIA CL

1 BUTTERCUP CL
2 LAMBOURNE HO
3 RUSSET HO
4 BRAMLEY HO

5 FOUNTAIN CT
6 LITTLE PARK CL
7 CHAPEL DRO

THE SHIRES 8
THE BARTONS 9

1 TAMELLA RD
2 MONTROSE CL

B3
1 FREEGROUNDS CL
2 SPEGGS WLK
3 LITTLE KIMBLE WLK
4 FERRYBRIDGE GN
5 MELBOURNE RD
6 MELBOURNE GDNS
7 LARKSPUR GDNS
8 MEDLAR CL
9 HORNBEAM CL
10 BARWELL TERR

1 CAMBRIAN CL
2 PHOENIX CL
3 DILIGENCE CL
4 QUEBEC GDNS
5 SUNNYFIELD RISE
6 SHERLEY GN
7 CUMMINS GN

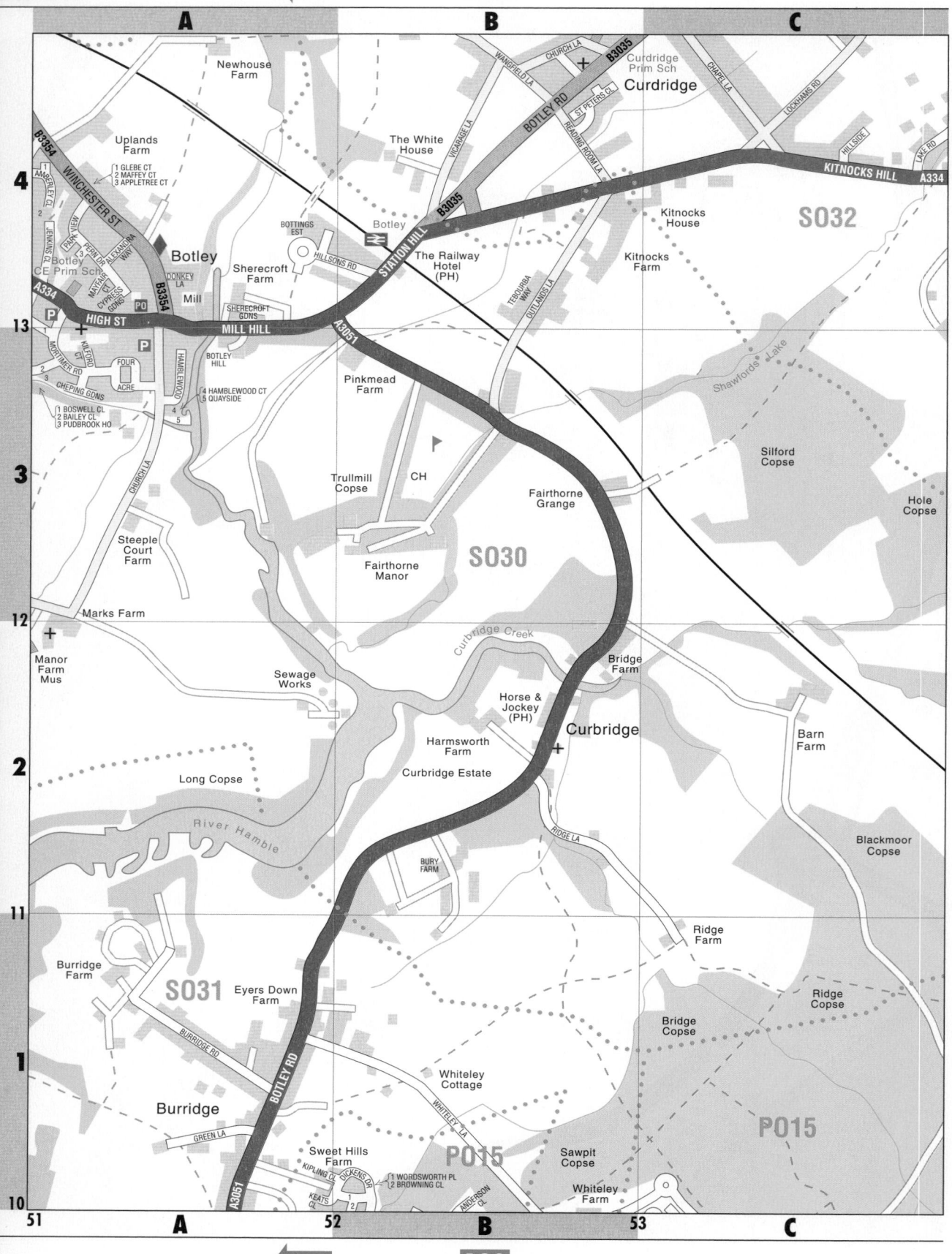

A   B   C

Newhouse Farm

B3354

Uplands Farm

1 GLEBE CT
2 MAFFEY CT
3 APPLETREE CT

WINCHESTER ST

4

The White House

CHURCH LA

B3035
BOTLEY RD

Curdridge Prim Sch

Curdridge

ST PETERS CL

VICARAGE LA

WANGFIELD LA

READING ROOM LA

KITNOCKS HILL

A334

Kitnocks House

SO32

1 AMBERLEY CL

Botley

BOTTINGS EST

HILLSONS RD

STATION HILL

B3035

Botley

Railway Station

The Railway Hotel (PH)

Kitnocks Farm

Botley CE Prim Sch

Sherecroft Farm

PARK VIEW DR
PENN DR
ALEXANDRA WAY

Donkey LA

DONKEY LA

JENKINS CL
MAYFLY CL
CYPRESS GDNS

Mill

SHERECROFT GDNS

TEBOURBA WAY

OUTLANDS LA

13

A334

P

HIGH ST

MILL HILL

A3051

MILL HILL

MORTIMER RD
KILFORD CT

P

Botley Hill

Pinkmead Farm

Shawfords Lake

FOUR ACRE

HAMBLEWOOD

4 HAMBLEWOOD CT
5 QUAYSIDE

CHEPING GDNS

CH

Silford Copse

1 BOSWELL CL
2 BAILEY CL
3 PUDBROOK HO

4
5

Trullmill Copse

Fairthorne Grange

Hole Copse

3

CHURCH LA

Steeple Court Farm

Fairthorne Manor

SO30

12

Marks Farm

Curbridge Creek

Manor Farm Mus

Sewage Works

Bridge Farm

Barn Farm

2

Long Copse

Horse & Jockey (PH)

Harmsworth Farm

Curbridge Estate

Curbridge

RIDGE LA

River Hamble

BURY FARM

Blackmoor Copse

11

Ridge Farm

Burridge Farm

SO031

Eyers Down Farm

BURRIDGE RD

Bridge Copse

Ridge Copse

1

BOTLEY RD

Whiteley Cottage

WHITELEY LA

PO15

Burridge

GREEN LA

Sweet Hills Farm

KIPLING CL
DICKENS DR

KEATS CL

PO15

1 WORDSWORTH PL
2 BROWNING CL

ANDERSON CL

Sawpit Copse

Whiteley Farm

PO15

10

A3051

51   A   52   B   53   C

A   **B**   **C**

LAKE RD

Row Ash

Rowash
Farm House

Wickham
Vineyard

Raglington
Farm

Ferny
Copse

HALL CT

SO32

Shedfield Grange

Country Club

Shedfield
House

Shedfield
Lodge

SANDY LA

B2177

Sandy Hills
House

SMITHS LA

HIGH ST

GAMBLINS LA

NIGHTINGALE
CRES

ST ANNES LA

ST JOHNS LA

UPPER CHURCH RD

4

Turkey
Island

THE OLD
FORGE

MURRAY
COTTS

CHURCH RD

CANCESO CL

SLOANE
PARK

PO

Shedfield

Fairlands
Montessori Sch

Shedfield
Common

CHURCH
VIEW

PRICKETT HILL

13

CULVERLANDS
CL

WINCHESTER RD

Hallcourt
Wood

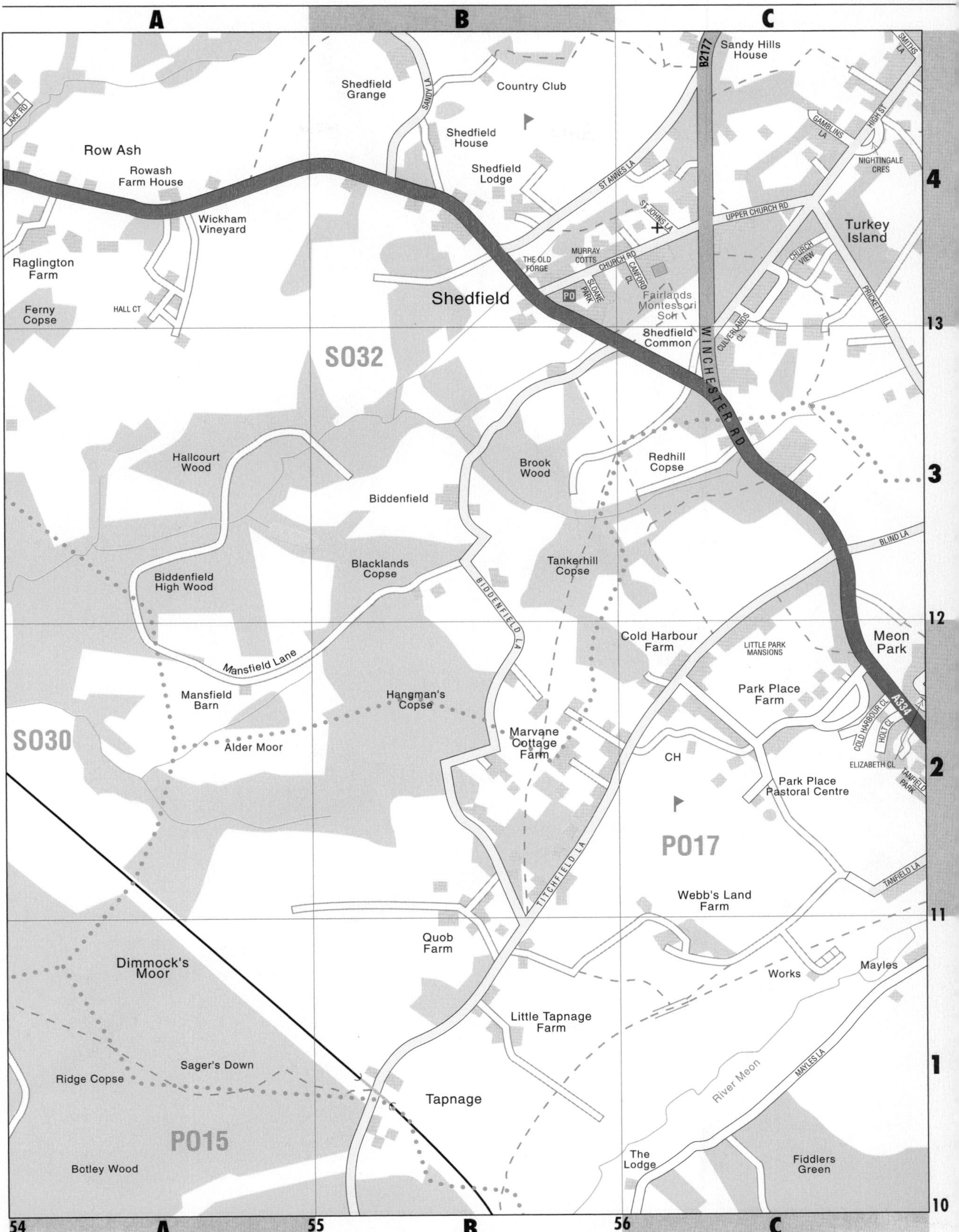

Biddenfield

Brook
Wood

Redhill
Copse

3

BLIND LA

Biddenfield
High Wood

Blacklands
Copse

Tankerhill
Copse

Cold Harbour
Farm

LITTLE PARK
MANSIONS

Meon
Park

12

Mansfield Lane

BIDDENFIELD LA

Park Place
Farm

A334

Mansfield
Barn

Hangman's
Copse

Marvane
Cottage
Farm

CH

COLD HARBOUR CT

HOLT CL

ELIZABETH CL

TANFIELD
PARK

2

SO30

Alder Moor

Park Place
Pastoral Centre

PO17

TITCHFIELD LA

Webb's Land
Farm

TANFIELD LA

11

Dimmock's
Moor

Quob
Farm

Works

Mayles

Little Tapnage
Farm

Sager's Down

Ridge Copse

River Meon

MAYLES LA

1

PO15

Tapnage

The
Lodge

Fiddlers
Green

Botley Wood

10

107
84

A B C

HIGH ST
WINTERS RD
Ollys Farm
Highridge Farm
HOSPITAL RD
TWYNHAMS HILL

Shirrell Heath
SO32

FRITH LANE END
FRITH LA

NEWMANS HILL
Bishop's Wood
Kingsmead Farm
KINGSMEAD

A32
Upperford Copse
BUDDEN'S LA
HEATH RD

Woodend

4

Kingsmead

P

West Walk (North) Forest Walk
P

The Roebuck Inn (PH)

Close Wood

13

West Walk

Frith Farm

PRICKETTS HILL
BLIND LA

West Lodge

3

Northfields Farm House
NORTHFIELDS FARM LA

Cutlers
Cycle Route

River Meon

West Walk (South) Forest Walk
P

12

Meon Park
THE SPUR
THE CIRCLE
Wickham CE Prim Sch
GARNIER PK
DICKSON PK
STATION RD
NORMANDY CT
MILL LA

Rookesbury Park Farm

HUNDRED ACRES RD
HUNDRED ACRES

ELIZABETH CT
BUDDENS RD
TANNERS RD
ROBERTS CL
PO
P
WARWICK WAY
Mill
Rookesbury Park
Rookesbury Park Sch

1 SPRINGFIELD CL
2 CASES BAKERY CL
3 LION HO
4 WATERSEDGE

PO17

2

A334 WINCHESTER RD
UPPER HOUSE CT
TANFIELD CT
TANFIELD LA
WICKHAM CROFT
STAR COTTS
BRIDGE ST
ST NICHOLAS ROW
RIVERSIDE MEWS
GLEBE CT
B2177

SOUTHWICK RD

Wickham
SCHOOL RD
A334
WYKEHAM FIELD
FAREHAM RD
PARK COTTS 1
MANOR VILLAS 2
MAYLES CL
MANOR CL

11

Winscombe

B2177

Mayles Farm
MAYLES LA

Wickham Common
Mellishes Bottom

FIRSGROVE LA
Mount Folly Farm

Castle Farm
CASTLE FARM LA

HOAD'S HILL

1

Birchfrith Copse

Water Tower

A32

FOREST LA
Bonhams
Crockerhill Farm

Birching Copse

Orchard Copse

BERE FARM LA

10

57 A 58 B 59 C

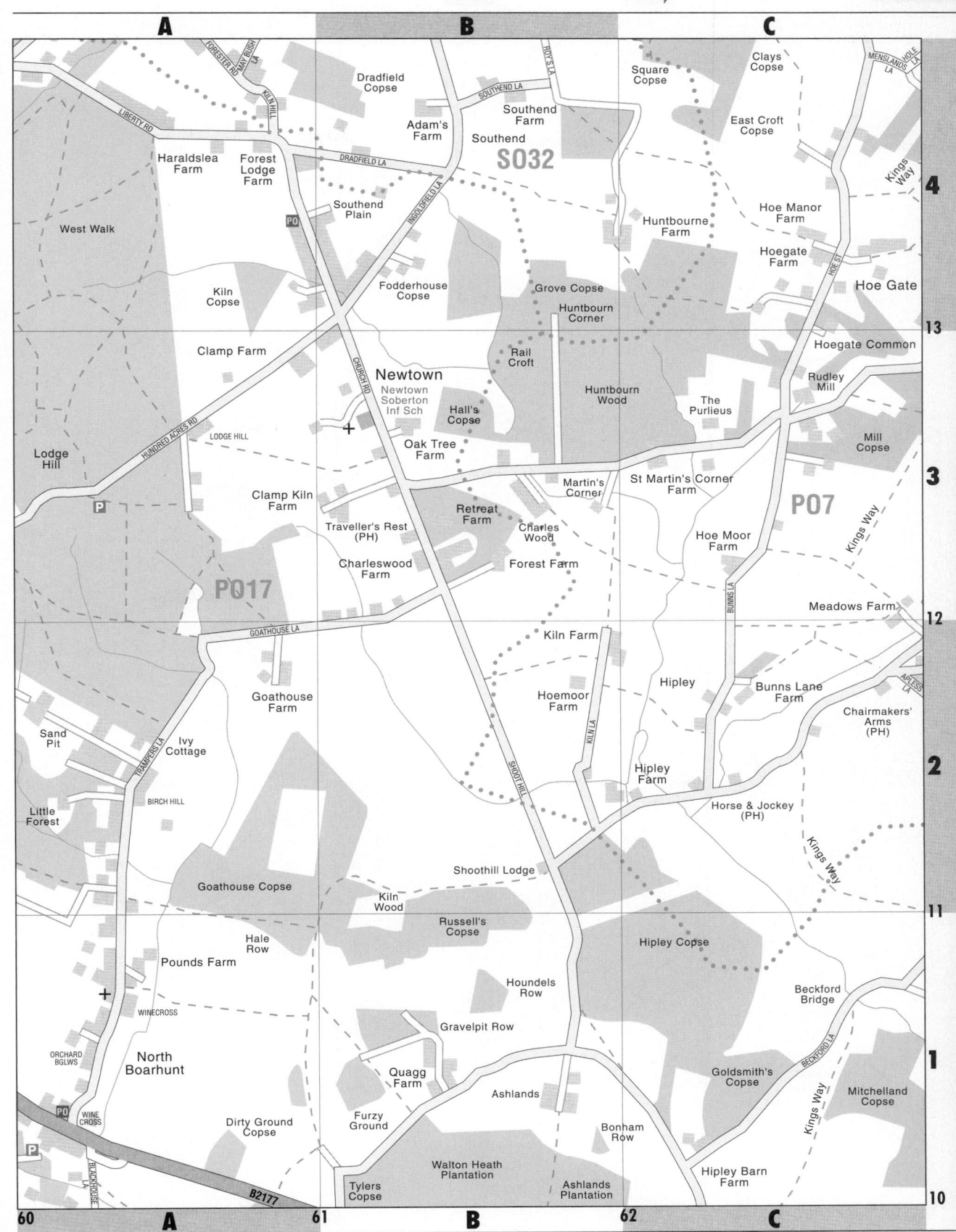

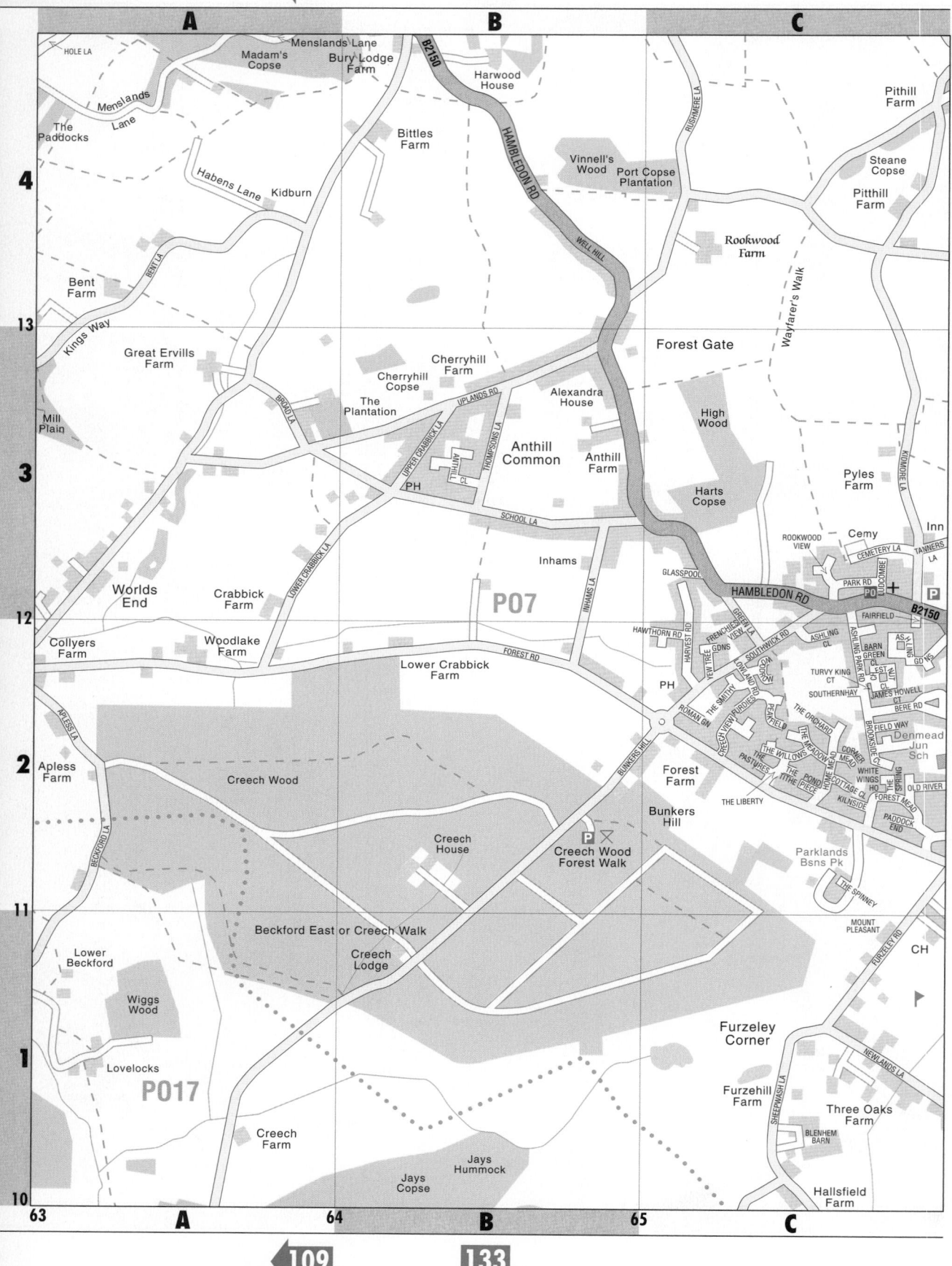

A B C

HOLE LA
Menslands Lane
Madam's Copse
Bury Lodge Farm
Harwood House
B2150
HAMBLEDON RD
Menslands Lane
The Paddocks
Bittles Farm
Vinnell's Wood
Port Copse Plantation
Pithill Farm
4
Habens Lane
Kidburn
Steane Copse
Pitthill Farm
WELL HILL
RUSHMERE LA
Rookwood Farm
Bent Farm
BENT LA
Wayfarer's Walk
13
Kings Way
Great Ervills Farm
Cherryhill Farm
Forest Gate
Cherryhill Copse
UPLANDS RD
Alexandra House
KIDMORE LA
Mill Plain
BRAD LA
The Plantation
Anthill Common
High Wood
Pyles Farm
Inn
3
UPPER CRABBICK LA
ANTHILL CL
THOMPSONS LA
Anthill Farm
Harts Copse
TANNERS LA
Cemy
PH
SCHOOL LA
ROOKWOOD VIEW
CEMETERY LA
LUDCOMBE
PARK RD
PO
Worlds End
Crabbick Farm
LOWER CRABBICK LA
Inhams
INHAMS LA
GLASSPOOL
HAMBLEDON RD
PO
B2150
FAIRFIELD
12
Collyers Farm
Woodlake Farm
Lower Crabbick Farm
FOREST RD
PO7
HAWTHORN RD
HARVEST RD
PH
Apless Farm
APLESS LA
Creech Wood
ROMAN GN
BUNKERS HILL
Forest Farm
Denmead Jun Sch
2
BECKFORD LA
Creech House
Bunkers Hill
THE LIBERTY
Parklands Bsns Pk
THE SPINNEY
11
Beckford East or Creech Walk
MOUNT PLEASANT
Lower Beckford
Creech Lodge
FURZELEY RD
CH
Wiggs Wood
Furzeley Corner
1
Lovelocks
PO17
Furzehill Farm
SHEEPWASH LA
NEWLANDS LA
Three Oaks Farm
Creech Farm
BLENHEM BARN
Jays Copse
Jays Hummock
Hallsfield Farm
10

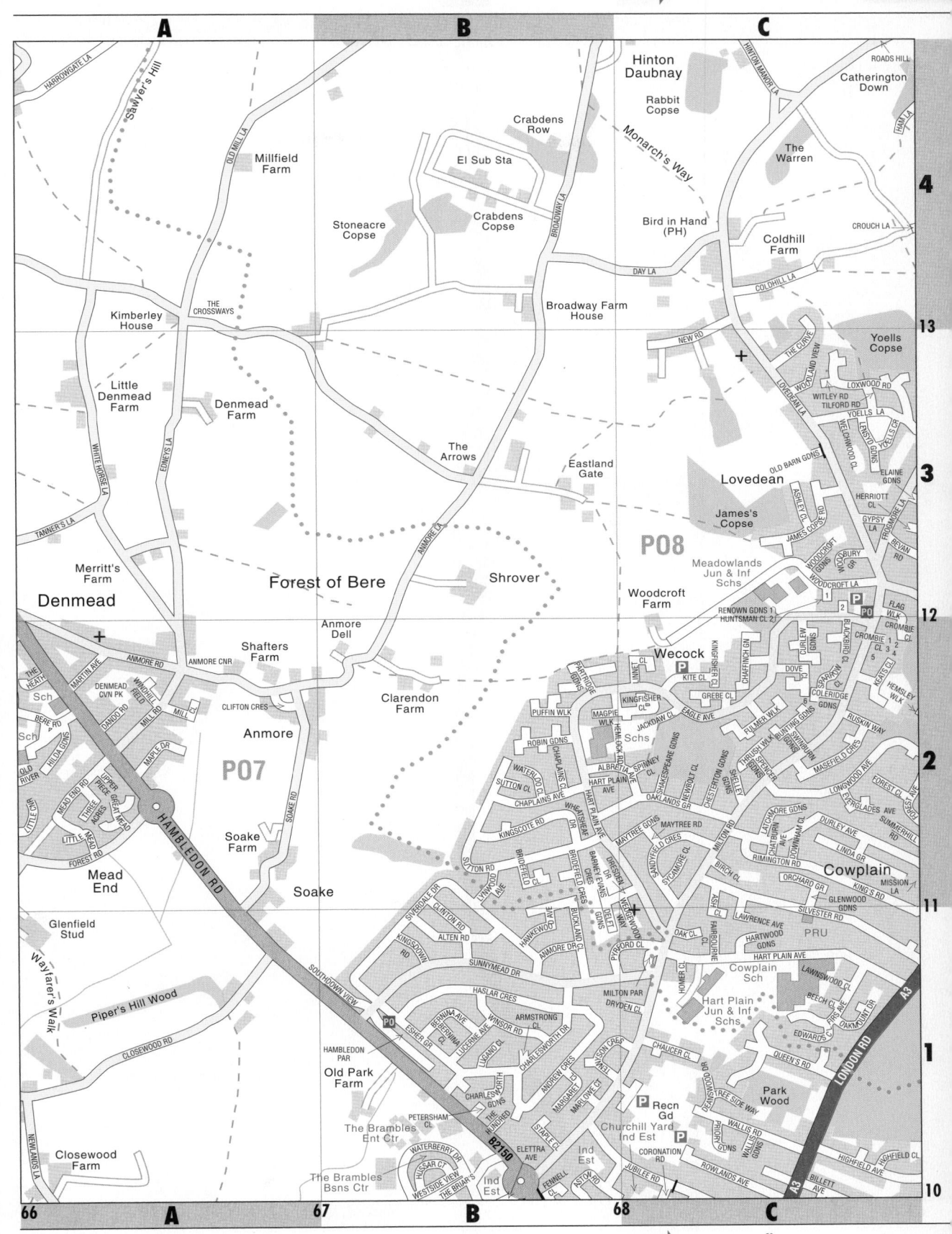

C2
1 THAMES CT
2 AVON CT
3 HAMBLE CT
4 ITCHEN CT
5 BEAULIEU CT
6 PATRICK HOWARD -DOBSON CT

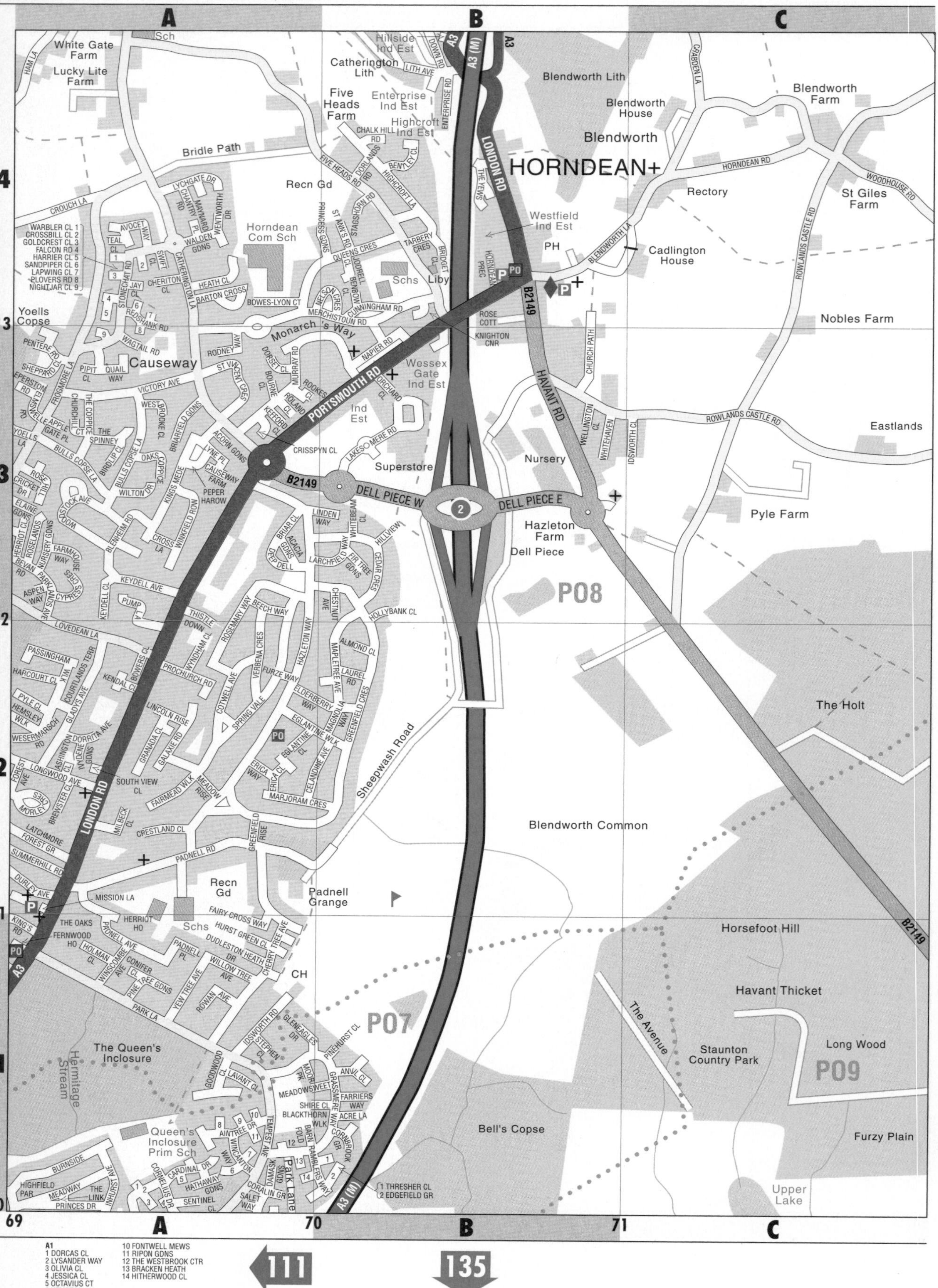

A1
1 DORCAS CL
2 LYSANDER WAY
3 OLIVIA CL
4 JESSICA CL
5 OCTAVIUS CT
6 KEMPTON PK
7 PLUMPTON GR
8 HAYDOCK MEWS
9 CHEPSTOW CT
10 FONTWELL MEWS
11 RIPON GDNS
12 THE WESTBROOK CTR
13 BRACKEN HEATH
14 HITHERWOOD CL

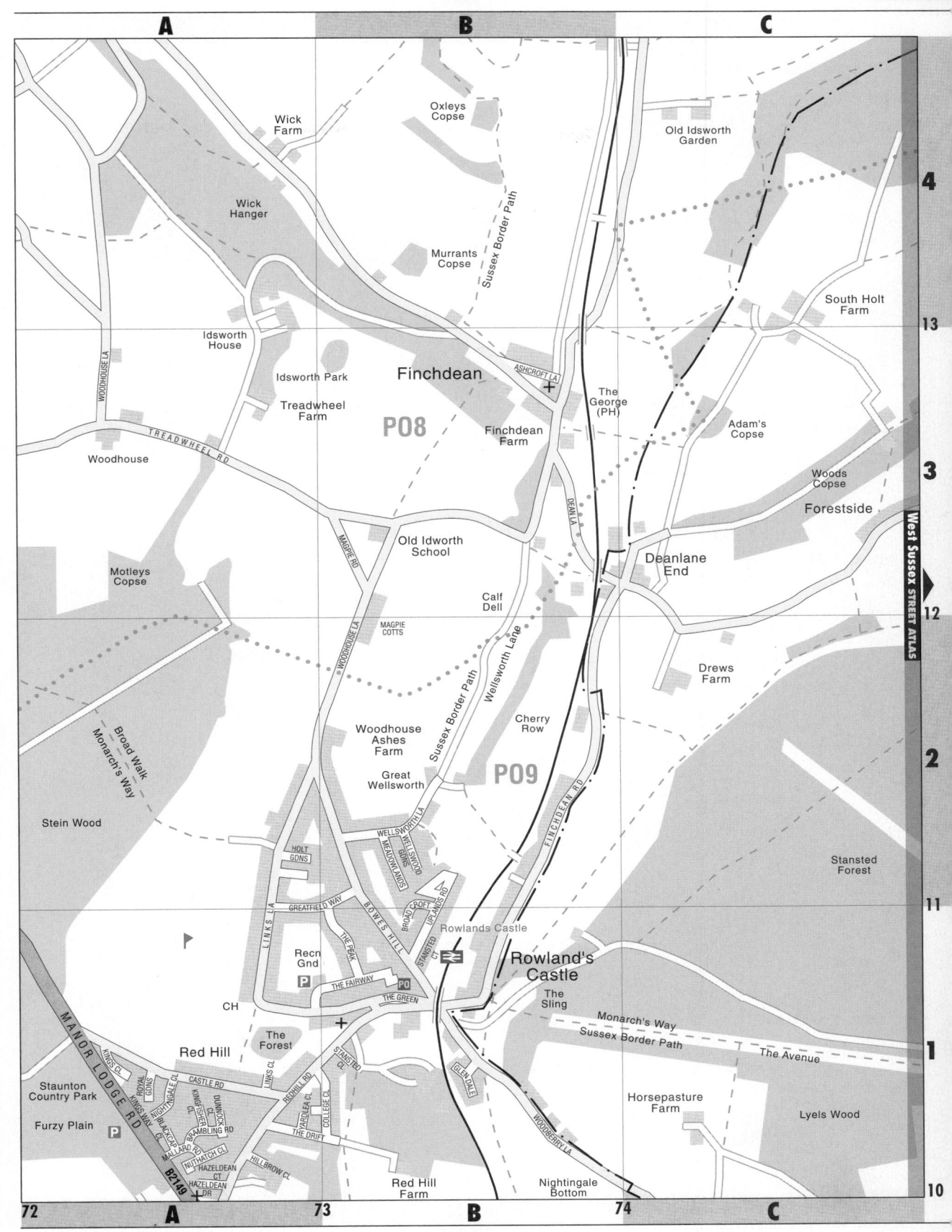

A B C

Wick
Farm

Oxleys
Copse

Old Idsworth
Garden

Wick
Hanger

4

Murrants
Copse

Sussex Border Path

South Holt
Farm

13

Idsworth
House

Finchdean

ASHCROFT LA

The George
(PH)

Adam's
Copse

Idsworth Park

Treadwheel
Farm

PO8

Finchdean
Farm

DEAN LA

Woods
Copse

3

TREADWHEEL RD

Woodhouse

Forestside

Deanlane
End

Old Idworth
School

Calf
Dell

MAGPIE RD

Motleys
Copse

12

Drews
Farm

MAGPIE
COTTS

WOODHOUSE LA

Wellsworth Lane

Sussex Border Path

Broad Walk
Monarch's Way

Stein Wood

Woodhouse
Ashes
Farm

PO9

Cherry
Row

2

Great
Wellsworth

FINCHDEAN RD

Stansted
Forest

WELLSWORTH LA
WELLSWOOD GDNS
MEADOWLANDS

HOLT
GDNS

GREATFIELD WAY

BROADCROFT
UPLANDS RD

LINKS LA

BOWES HILL

Rowlands Castle

11

STANSTED CT

THE PEAK

Recn
Gnd

P

Rowland's
Castle

The
Sling

Monarch's Way

Sussex Border Path

THE FAIRWAY

PO

THE GREEN

CH

The
Forest

The Avenue

1

MANOR LODGE RD

Red Hill

LINKS CL

STANSTED CL

Horsepasture
Farm

Lyels Wood

Staunton
Country Park

KINGS CL
ROYAL GDNS
KINGS WAY
NIGHTGALE CL
DUNNOCK CL
KINGFISHER
BLACKCAP
CASTLE RD
REDHILL RD

YARDLEA CL
COLLEGE CL

REDHILL RD

GLEN DALE

Furzy Plain

P

MALLARD
NUTHATCH CL
HAZELDEAN
CT
HAZELDEAN DR

THE DRIFT

HILLBROW CL

WOODBERRY LA

B2149

Red Hill
Farm

Nightingale
Bottom

10

72 A 73 B 74 C

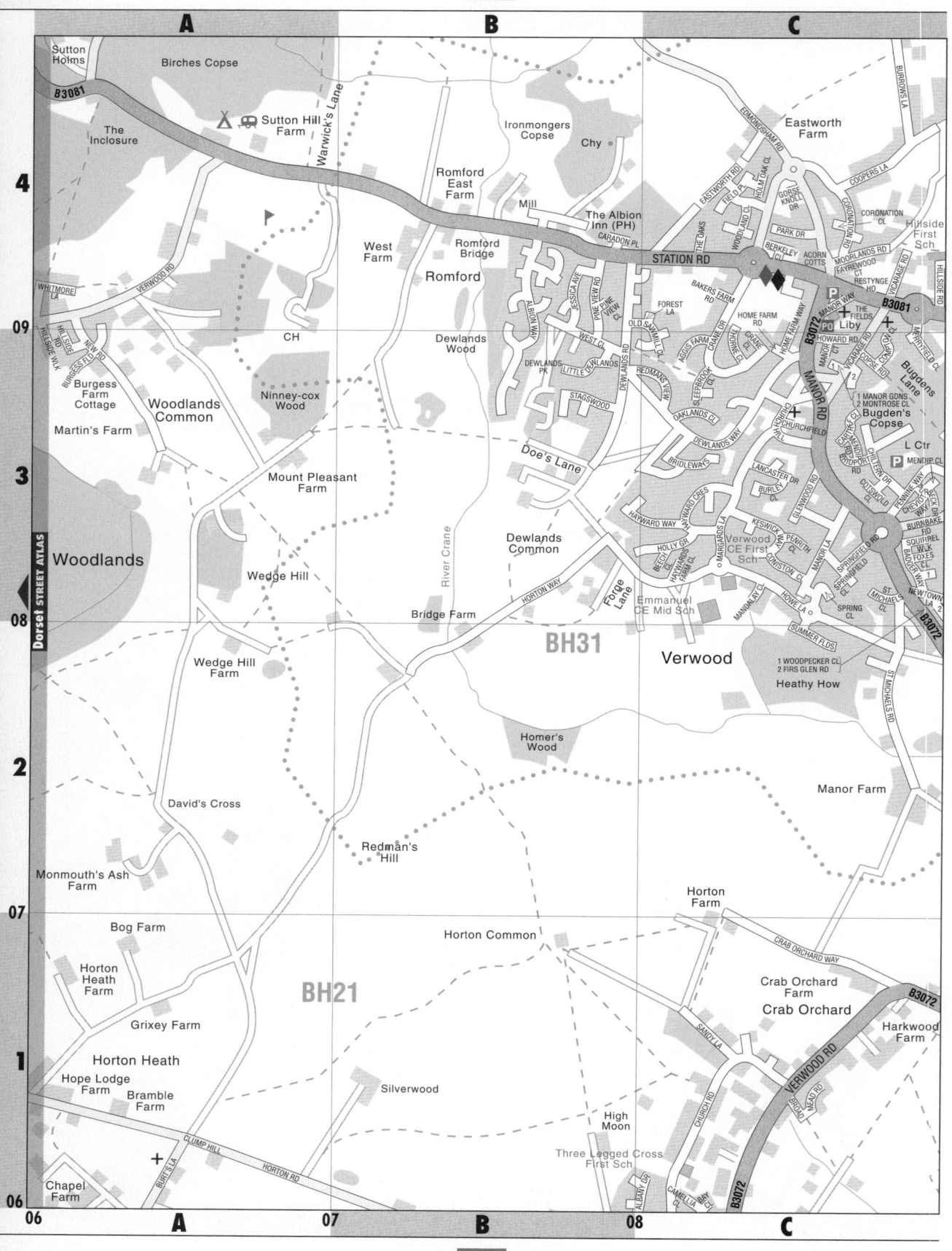

Boveridge Heath

Wiggs Copse

Plumley Wood

Stephen's Castle

Bailey's Plantation

Harefield Plantation

Stephen's Castle Nature Reserve

Wild Church Bottom

4

Noon Hill House

Noon Hill

Numbers

SCHOOL CL
STARLIGHT FARM CL
ST STEPHENS LA
SILVERWOOD DR
STRATHMORE DR
NOON HILL DR
NOON GORSE CL
FOXHILLS RD
NOON HILL RD
HEATHLANDS CL
SHARD CL
BLACK HILL
CRESCENT RD
SOUTHERNHAY RD

Reservoir Cottage

09

HILLSIDE RD
ACORN WAY
NEWTOWN RD
TAYLOR WAY
SHETLAND VIEW
SHIRES MEAD
OAKS MEAD
PAULT DR
BUGDENS LA
RAYMOND CL
SANDY LA

Verwood Ind Est

RINGWOOD RD

THE CHASE

BH31

Ringwood Forest

3

BELMONT CL
THE GROVE
BITTERNE WAY
BURNBAKE RD
STANLEY CL
VERNE RD
PADDOCK GR
OWLS RD
ORCHARD CT
THE LEN
MEADOW WAY
LAKE RD
THE KINGCUPS
THE CURLEWS
NIGHTINGALE CL
CLAYLAKE DR
NEWTOWN LA
FIRST GLEN RD
HILL MEADOW
LAKE RD
BINGHAM RD
BINGHAM DR
MONMOUTH DR
ASPEN DR
LOMBARDY CL
PINE VIEW
BLACKTHORN WAY
WHITEBEAM WAY
WOOD LINDEN DR
FAIRWOOD RD
PRIMROSE WAY
LAVENDER CL
BARBERRY WAY
HUNTERS CL
THE FORESTSIDE
ROSEBERY CL

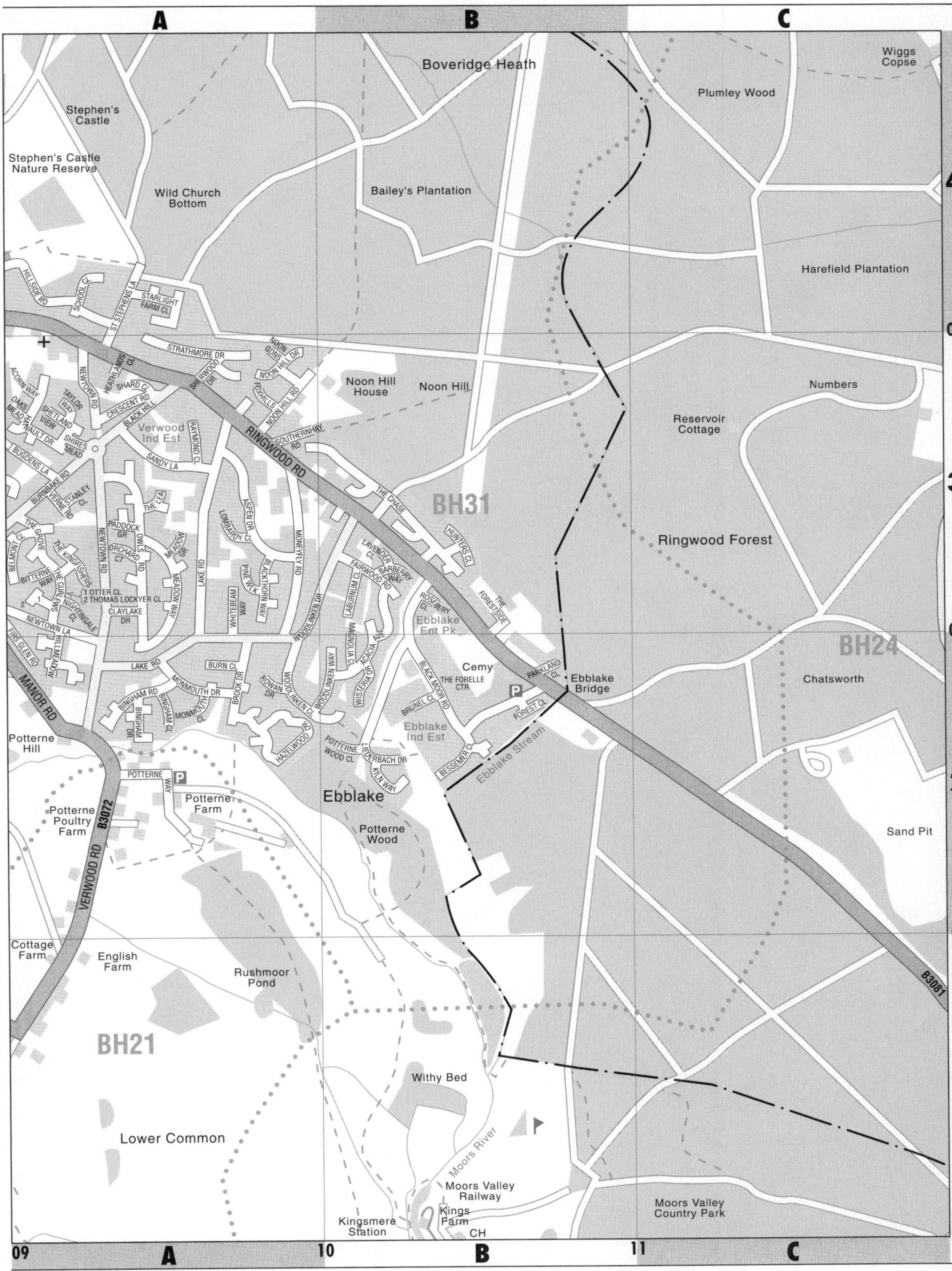

1 OTTER CL
2 THOMAS LOCKYER CL

MANOR RD

BURN CL
ROWAN DR
WOOD LINKEN DR
WISTERIA CL
MAGNOLIA CL
ROMOA AVE
BLACK MOOR RD
BRUNEL CL
BESSEMER CL

Ebblake Ent Pk

Cemy
THE FORELLE CTR

PARKLAND CL

Ebblake Bridge

BH24

Chatsworth

08

Ebblake Ind Est

FOREST CL

Ebblake Stream

Potterne Hill

B3072

HAZELWOOD

POTTERNE WAY

Potterne Farm

KILN WAY
LEVERBACH DR
POTTERNE WOOD CL

Ebblake

2

Potterne Poultry Farm

VERWOOD RD

Potterne Wood

Sand Pit

07

Cottage Farm

English Farm

Rushmoor Pond

B3081

BH21

Withy Bed

1

Lower Common

Moors River

Moors Valley Railway

Moors Valley Country Park

Kingsmere Station

Kings Farm

CH

06

A | B | C

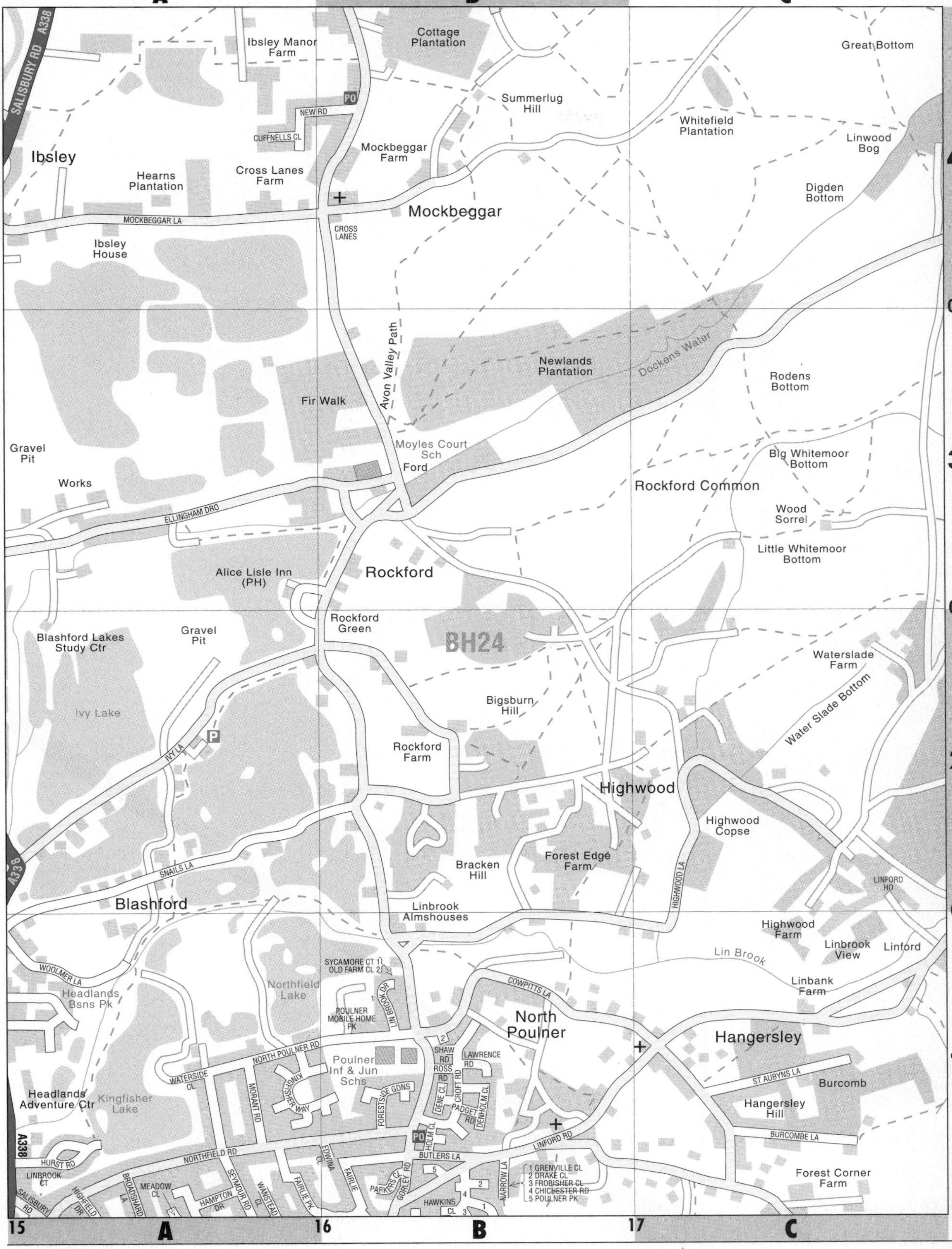

SALISBURY RD A338

Ibsley Manor Farm

Cottage Plantation

Great Bottom

4

Summerlug Hill

Whitefield Plantation

Linwood Bog

NEW RD

PO

Mockbeggar Farm

CUFFNELLS CL

Ibsley

Hearns Plantation

Cross Lanes Farm

Digden Bottom

✛

CROSS LANES

Mockbeggar

MOCKBEGGAR LA

Ibsley House

09

Avon Valley Path

Newlands Plantation

Dockens Water

Rodens Bottom

3

Fir Walk

Big Whitemoor Bottom

Gravel Pit

Moyles Court Sch

Ford

Rockford Common

Works

ELLINGHAM DRO

Wood Sorrel

Little Whitemoor Bottom

Alice Lisle Inn (PH)

Rockford

08

Rockford Green

BH24

Waterslade Farm

Blashford Lakes Study Ctr

Gravel Pit

Ivy Lake

P

IVY LA

Bigsburn Hill

Water Slade Bottom

2

Rockford Farm

Highwood

Highwood Copse

SNAILS LA

A338

Blashford

Bracken Hill

Forest Edge Farm

HIGHWOOD LA

LINFORD HO

Linbrook Almshouses

07

WOOLMER LA

Lin Brook

Highwood Farm

Linbrook View

Linford

SYCAMORE CT 1
OLD FARM CL 2

Northfield Lake

COWPITTS LA

Linbank Farm

Headlands Bsns Pk

LIN BROOK DR

POULNER MOBILE HOME PK

North Poulner

Hangersley

1

NORTH POULNER RD

WATERSIDE CL

Poulner Inf & Jun Schs

SHAW RD

LAWRENCE RD

ROSS RD

✛

ST AUBYNS LA

Burcomb

Headlands Adventure Ctr

Kingfisher Lake

KINGFISHER WAY

FORESTSIDE GDNS

DENE CL

CROFT CL

PADGET RD

DENHOLM CL

LINFORD RD

Hangersley Hill

BURCOMBE LA

HURST RD

MOZART RD

NORTHFIELD RD

EDWINA CL

FAIRLIE PK

PO

HOLT CL

✛

A338

LINBROOK CT

HIGHFIELD DR

BROADSWARD

MEADOW CL

HAMPTON DR

SEYMOUR RD

WINSTEAD

PARKSIDE

ORLEY RD

BUTLERS LA

HAWKINS CL

1 GRENVILLE CL
2 DRAKE CL
3 FROBISHER CL
4 CHICHESTER RD
5 POULNER PK

Forest Corner Farm

06

SALISBURY RD

15 | A | 16 | B | 17 | C

117
95

A **B** **C**

Milkham
Inclosure

Amie's
Wood

Linwood

Webb's
Copse

Toms
Farm

TOMS LA

King's
Garden

Appleslade
Farm

The
Red Shoot Inn
(PH)

Linwood
Farm

Amie's
Corner

4

Appleslade
Bottom

Lin Wood

Mount
Hill

Castle
Piece

Roe
Inclosure

09

Appleslade
Inclosure

Linford Brook

3

Red Shoot
Plain

Red Shoot
Wood

Green
Ford

Buckherd
Bottom

Greenford
Bottom

08

Great Linford
Inclosure

White
Hill

BH24

Pinnick
Wood

Collier's
Thorns

Handy
Cross

A31

2

Linford Bottom

Akercombe
Bottom

Little Linford
Inclosure

Marrowbones
Hill

Handy Cross Plain

07

Linford

Picket
Bottom

Ridley Plain

1

Brook
Farm

Picket
Hill

Old
Gate

Little
Wood

Harvest
Slade

Shobley

Ridley
Bottom

Shobley
Bottom

Picket
Post

Ridley
Wood

06

18 **A** **19** **B** **20** **C**

A31

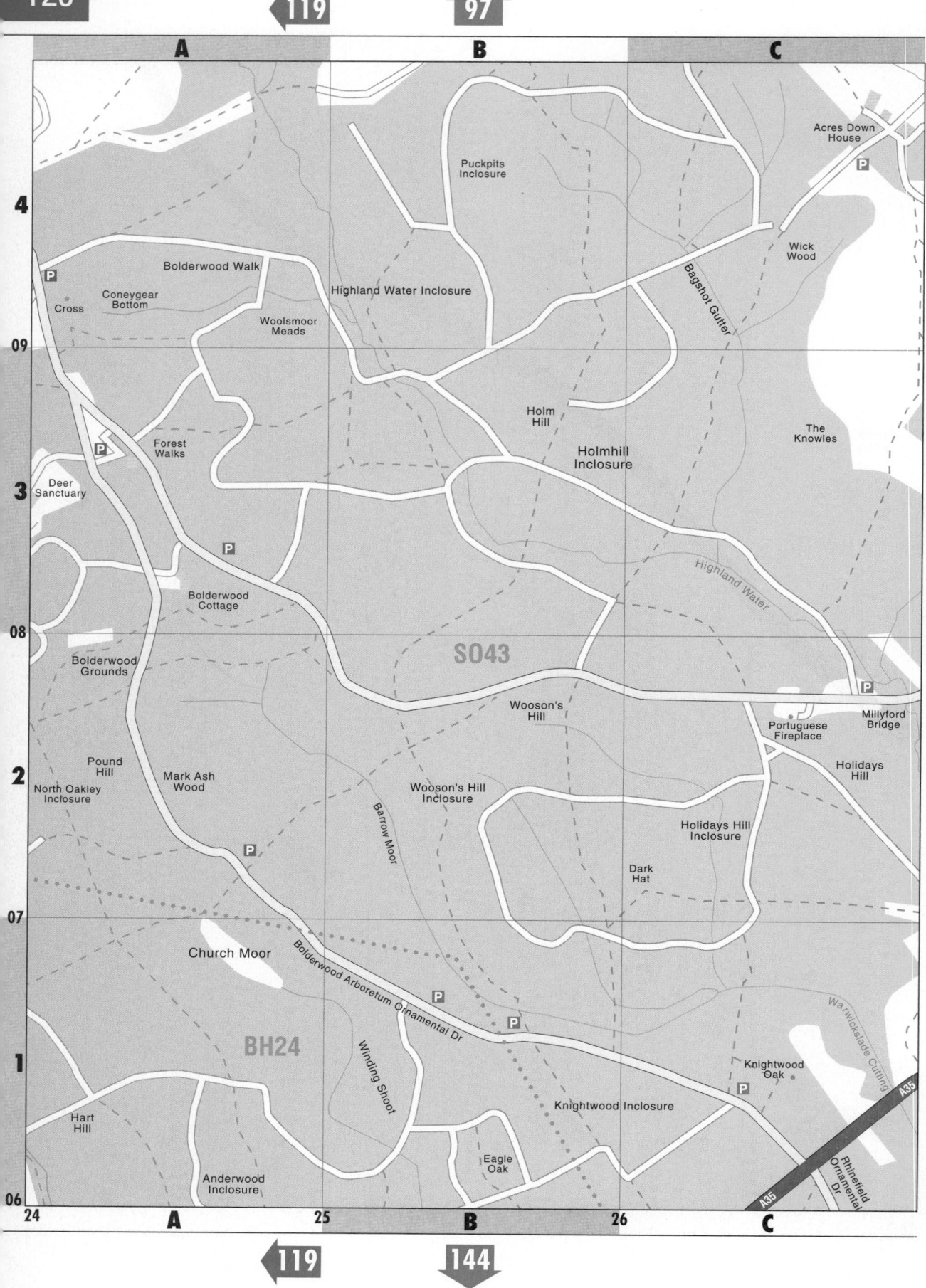

A B C

4

Acres Down House

P

Puckpits Inclosure

Wick Wood

Bagshot Gutter

Bolderwood Walk

Highland Water Inclosure

P
Cross

Coneygear Bottom

Woolsmoor Meads

09

Holm Hill

Holmhill Inclosure

The Knowles

P
Forest Walks

3

Deer Sanctuary

P

Highland Water

Bolderwood Cottage

08

Bolderwood Grounds

SO43

Wooson's Hill

Portuguese Fireplace

Millyford Bridge

P

2

Pound Hill

Mark Ash Wood

Wooson's Hill Inclosure

Holidays Hill

North Oakley Inclosure

Barrow Moor

Holidays Hill Inclosure

P

Dark Hat

07

Church Moor

Bolderwood Arboretum Ornamental Dr

Warwickslade Cutting

BH24

Winding Shoot

P

P

1

Knightwood Oak

P

Hart Hill

Knightwood Inclosure

A35

Rhinefield Ornamental Dr

Anderwood Inclosure

Eagle Oak

06

24 A 25 B 26 C

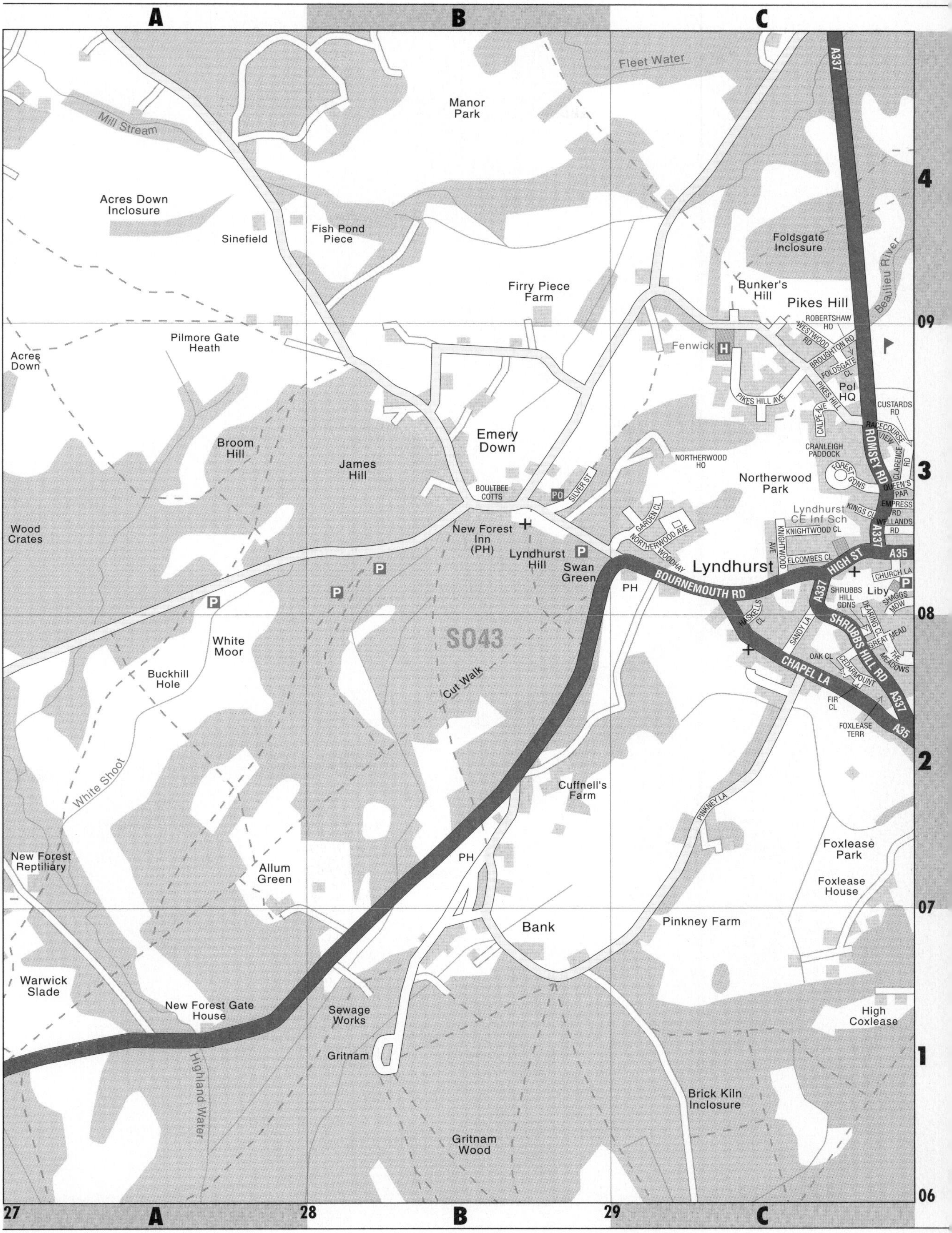

121
99
121
146

Fox Hill

Redbridge Hill

Ironshill Inclosure

Lodgehill Inclosure

A35

Rushpole Wood

Whitebridge Hill

Lodgehill Cottage

Mallard Wood

SO40

Fair Cross

Beaulieu River

Dunces Arch Inclosure

Beaulieu River

CH

Dunces Arch

Fox Hill

Row Hill

Longwater Lawn

THE CUSTARDS

Custards

SOUTHAMPTON RD

1 QUEEN'S PAR
2 EMPRESS RD

PEMBERTON RD

QUEENS RD

PRINCES CT

PRINCES CT

WELLANDS RD

HOLMFIELD

PO

HIGH ST

A35

B3056

Meml

Cemy

White Moor

SO43

RUFUS CT

Hotel

Mus

Bolton's Bench

SHAGES MDW

Goose Green

The Bench

The Ridge

GOSPORT LA

A35

BEAULIEU RD

Brooklands

Irons Hill Walk

A337

Matley Ridge

Clayhill

BEECHEN LA

HILARY CL

PARK CL

Pondhead Inclosure

Parkhill (Hotel)

Pondhead

The Crown & Stirrup (PH)

Holmhill Passage

CLAY HILL

Beechen La

Parkhill Lawn

Little Holmhill Inclosure

Park Ground Inclosure

Denny Inclosure

Little Holmhill

A337

Park Hill

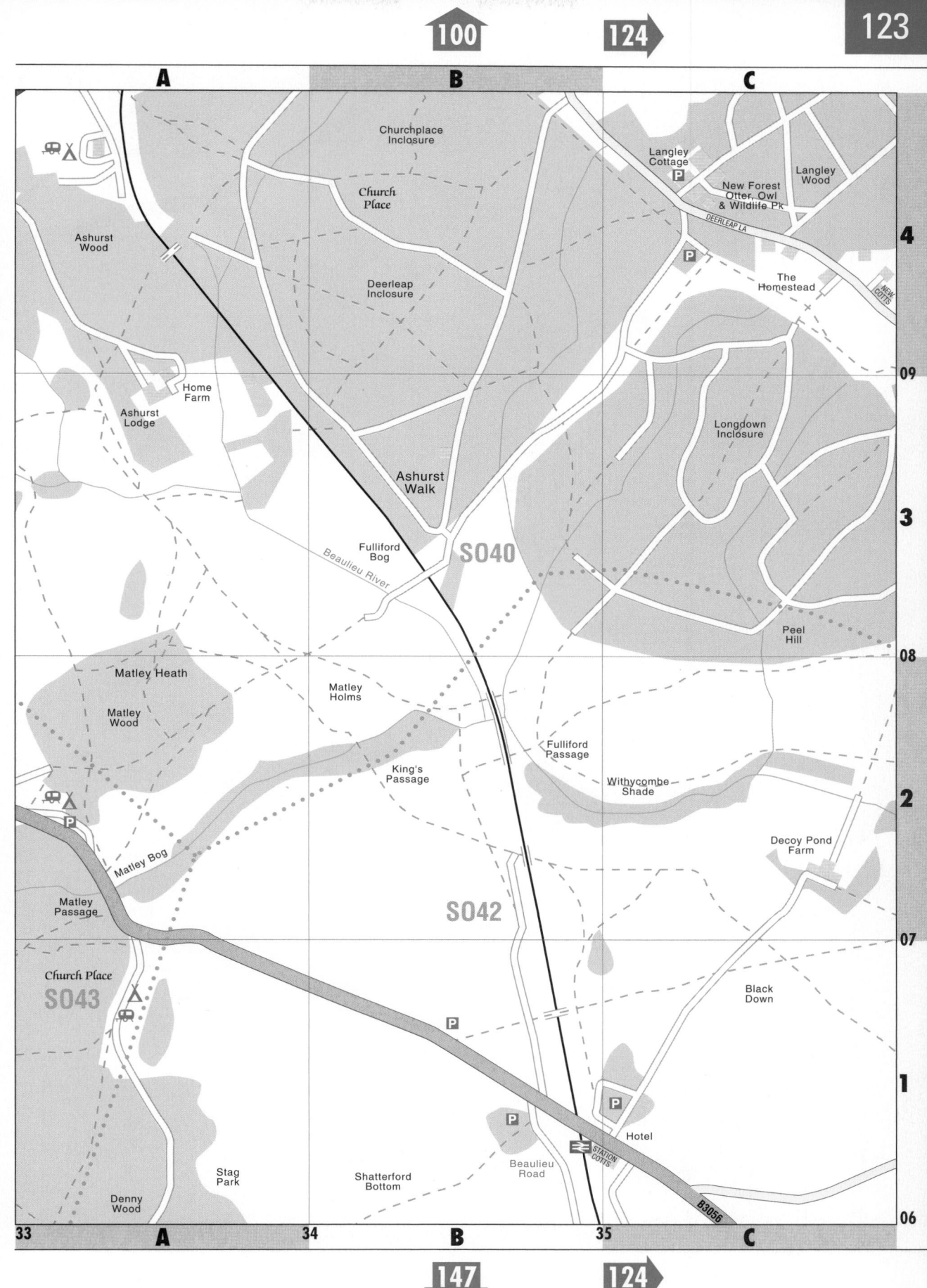

Churchplace Inclosure

Church Place

Ashurst Wood

Deerleap Inclosure

Langley Cottage

New Forest Otter, Owl & Wildlife Pk

Langley Wood

DEERLEAP LA

The Homestead

NEW COTTS

4

Home Farm

Ashurst Lodge

Longdown Inclosure

09

Ashurst Walk

Fulliford Bog

SO40

Beaulieu River

Peel Hill

3

08

Matley Heath

Matley Holms

Matley Wood

Fulliford Passage

King's Passage

Withycombe Shade

2

Decoy Pond Farm

Matley Bog

Matley Passage

SO42

07

Church Place

SO43

Black Down

P

P

Hotel

P

STATION COTTS

1

Stag Park

Shatterford Bottom

Beaulieu Road

Denny Wood

B3056

06

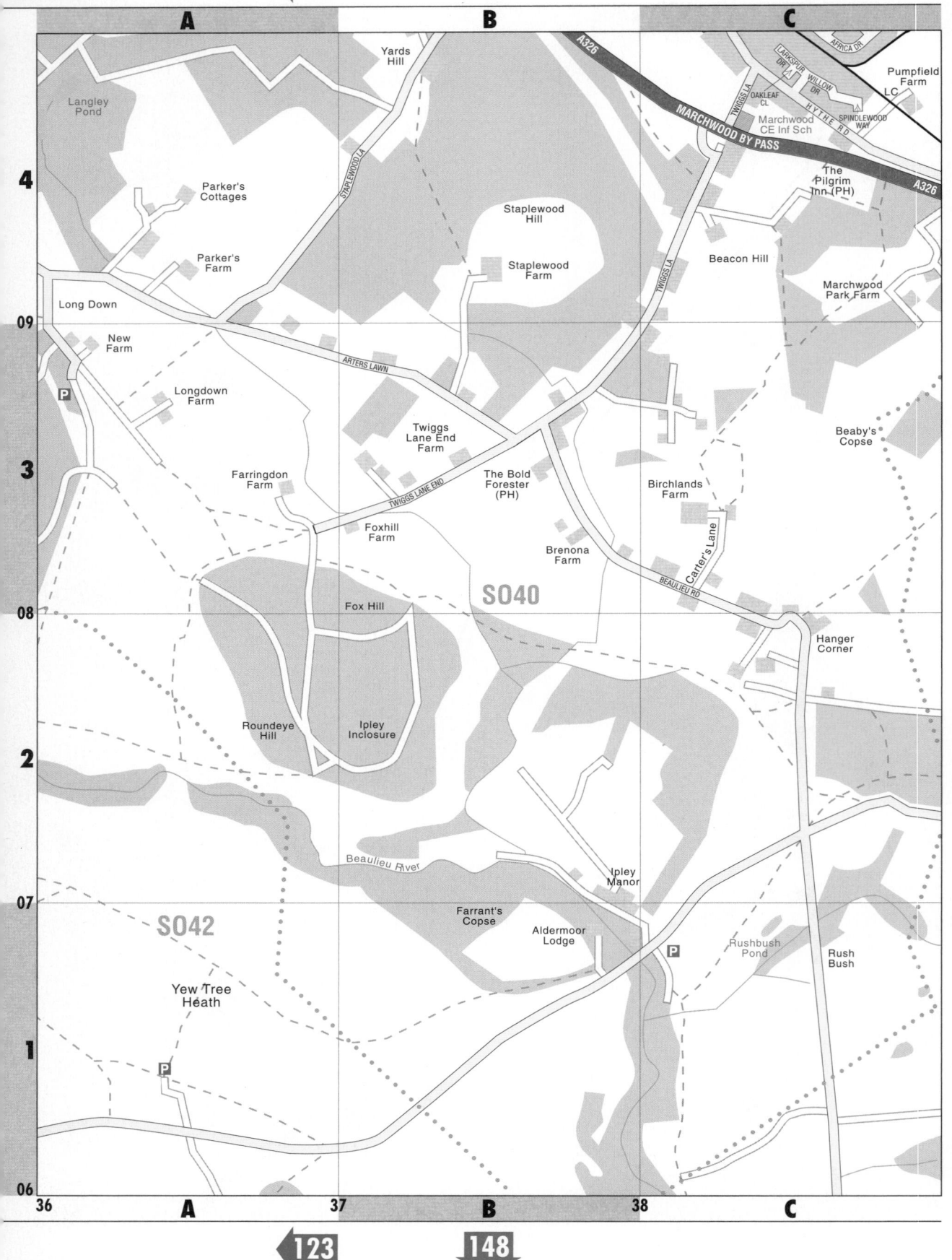

A B C

4

09

3

08

SO40

2

07

SO42

1

06

36 A 37 B 38 C

Langley Pond

Yards Hill

A326

MARCHWOOD BY PASS

AFRICA DR

LARKSPUR DR

WILLOW DR

Pumpfield Farm

OAKLEAF CL

TWIGGS LA

HYTHE RD

Marchwood CE Inf Sch

SPINDLEWOOD WAY

LC

The Pilgrim Inn (PH)

A326

Parker's Cottages

Staplewood Hill

Beacon Hill

Marchwood Park Farm

Parker's Farm

STAPLEWOOD LA

Staplewood Farm

TWIGGS LA

Long Down

New Farm

ARTERS LAWN

Longdown Farm

Twiggs Lane End Farm

The Bold Forester (PH)

Birchlands Farm

Beaby's Copse

Farringdon Farm

TWIGGS LANE END

Foxhill Farm

Carter's Lane

Brenona Farm

BEAULIEU RD

Fox Hill

Hanger Corner

Roundeye Hill

Ipley Inclosure

Beaulieu River

Ipley Manor

Farrant's Copse

Aldermoor Lodge

Rushbush Pond

Rush Bush

Yew Tree Heath

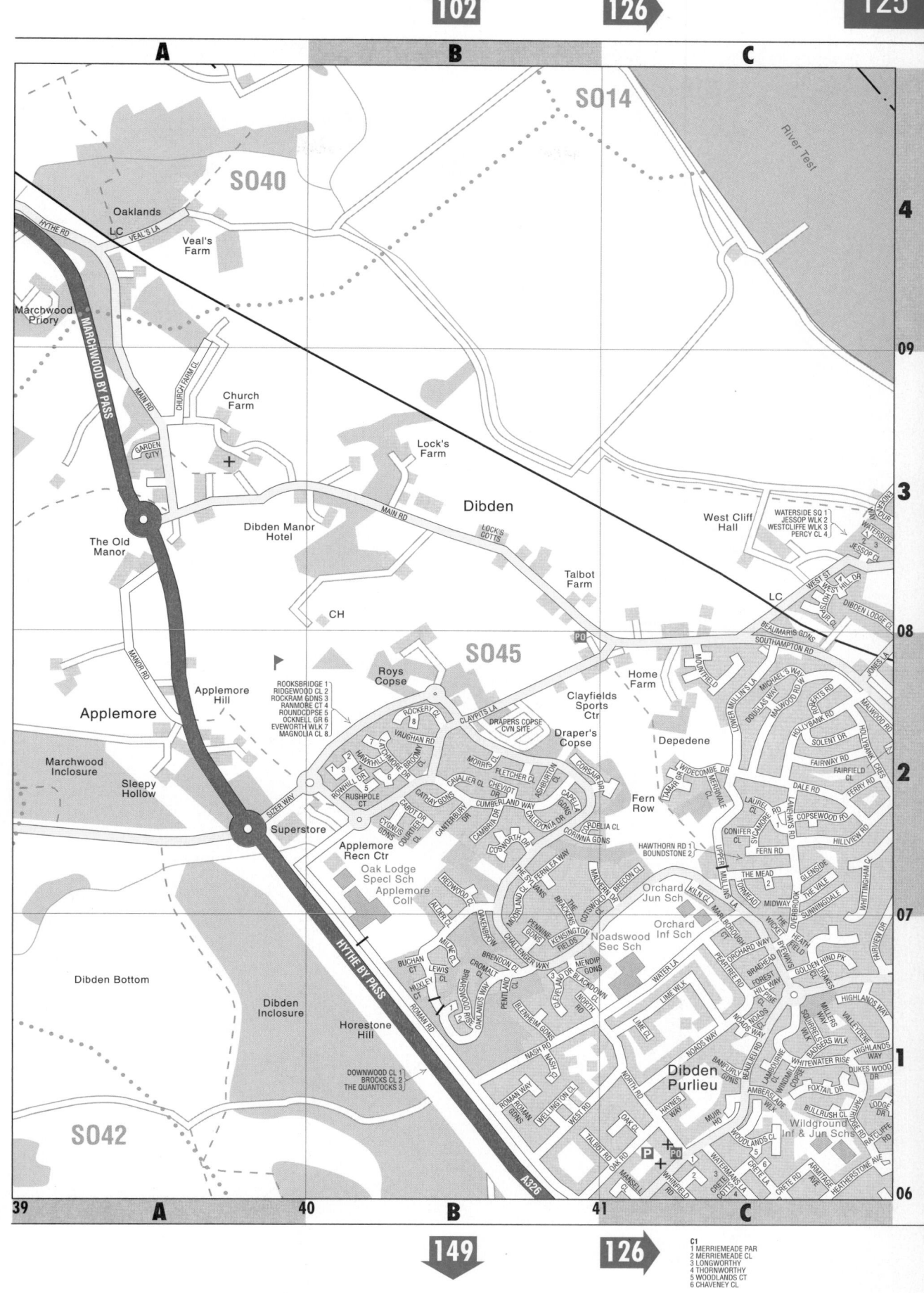

A   B   C

S014

Docks

Mast

Weston Shelf

Weston Hard

ROTHSCHILD CL

S019

Weston Par

Solent Way

HURSTBOURNE PL

CANBERRA TWRS

Weston Shore Inf Sch

Weston Park

S031

MARINA VIEW

ABBEY HILL

C4
1 SQUIRES WLK
2 HAMPTON TWRS
3 HAVRE TWRS
4 OSLO TWRS
5 COPENHAGEN TWRS
6 ROTTERDAM TWRS
7 WESTON HOMES
8 GRATELEY CL
9 DRAYTON CL

Ferry

09

Hythe Marina

Southampton Water

3

Hythe Pier Rly   Hythe Pier

Hythe Hard

Hythe

A3
1 WHITE HEATHER CT
2 VELSHEDA CT
3 ASTRA CT
4 WATERSIDE
5 MOUNT HOUSE CL
6 HAZELDALE VILLAS
7 HOMEBOROUGH HO
8 DRUMMOND CT
9 ADMIRALS WAY

08

Hythe Prim Sch

Liby

Pier

A2
1 MARSH PAR
2 NEW MARSH HO
3 DRUMMOND RD
4 COURT HOUSE CL
5 SIR CHRISTOPHER CT
6 LAWRENCE HO
7 MARINERS MEWS
8 HANOVER CT
9 THE SYCAMORES
10 FAIRFIELD CL
11 GREEN CL
12 HOLLYBANK CL

2

S045

Langdown Jun Sch

Howard Oliver Ho

Solent Way

07

Langdown

Furzey Piece

Langdown Inf Sch

Hythe

1

Furzedown Farm

Frostlane

Kitcher's Copse

Forest Lodge

Crampool Copse

Works

06

42   A   43   B   44   C

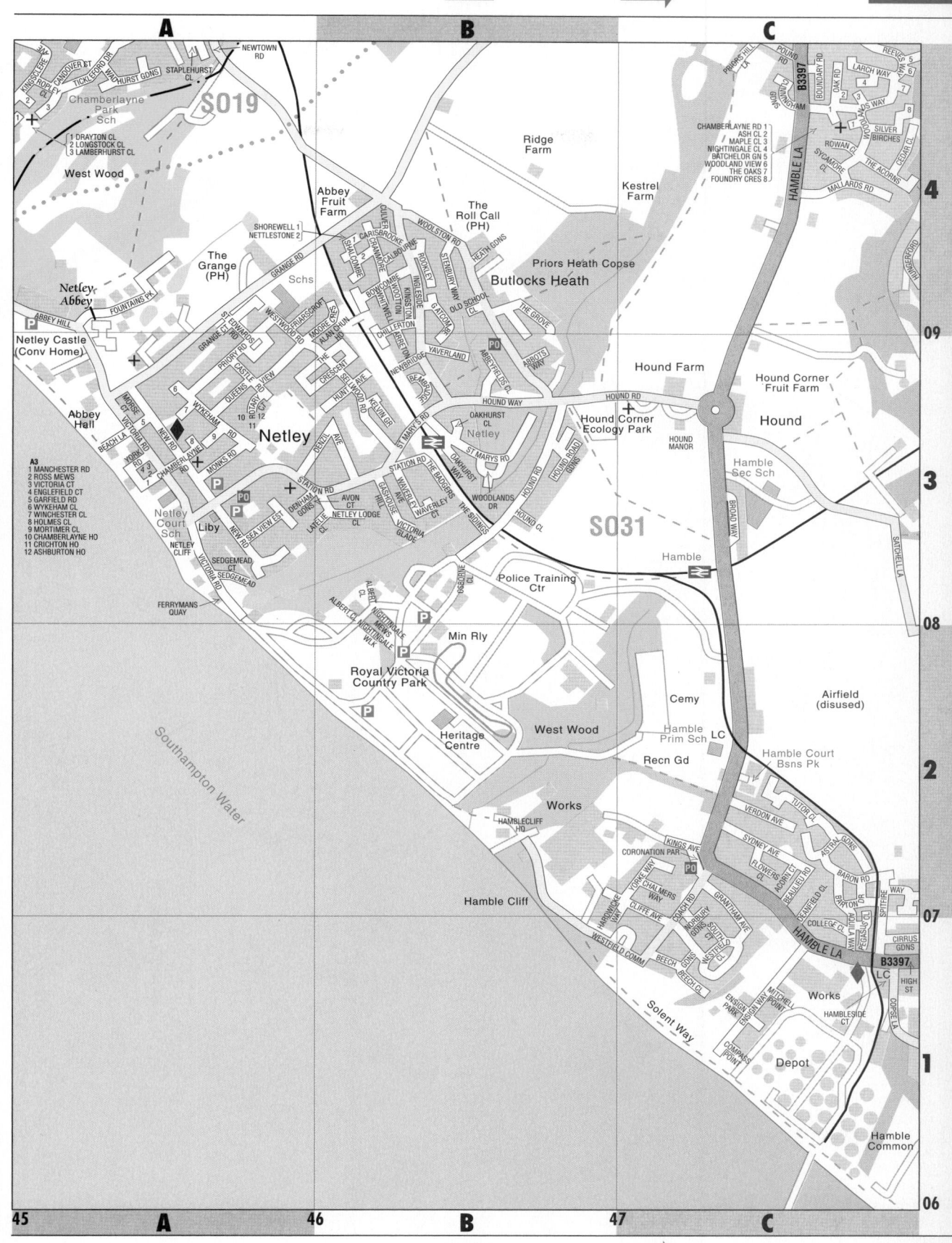

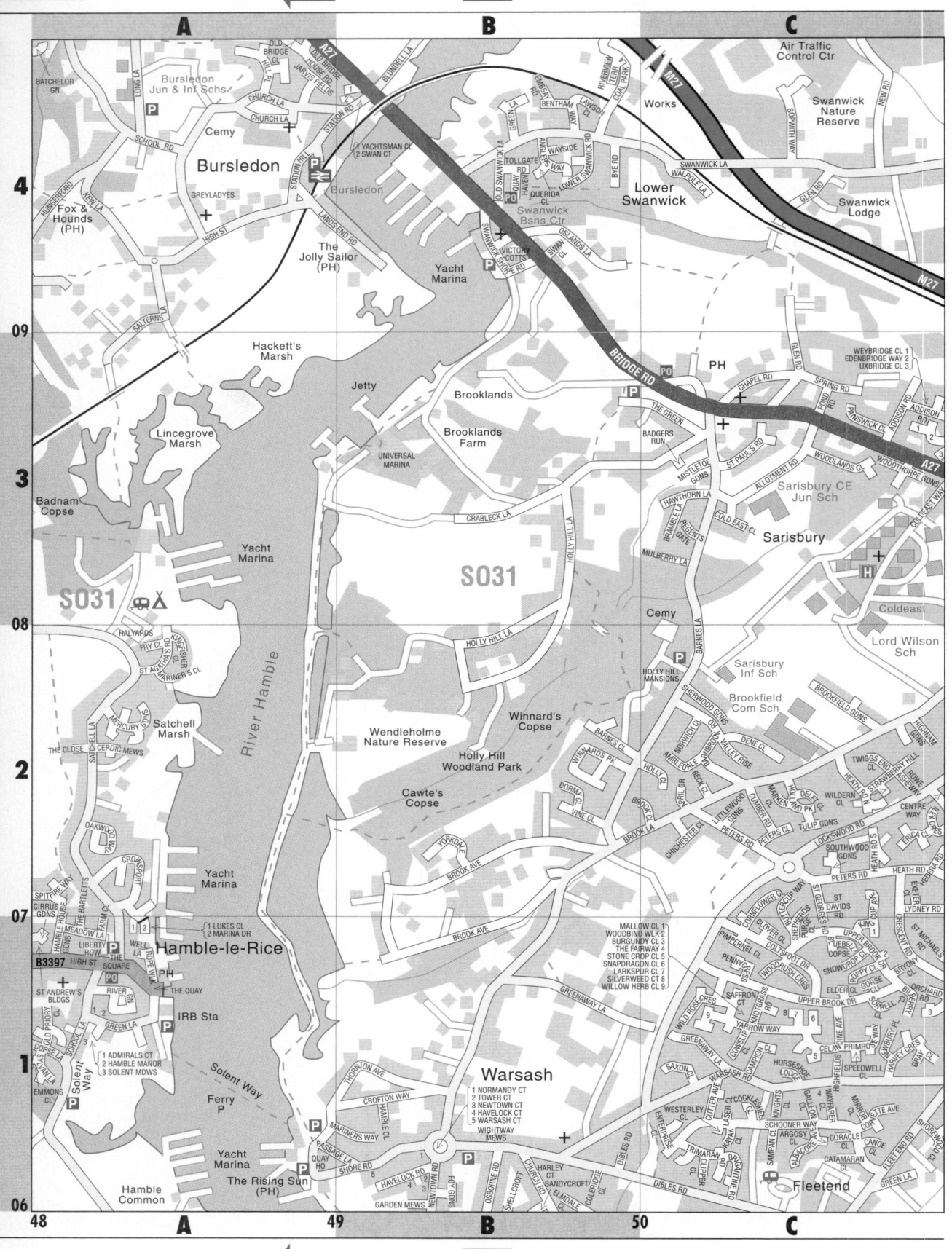

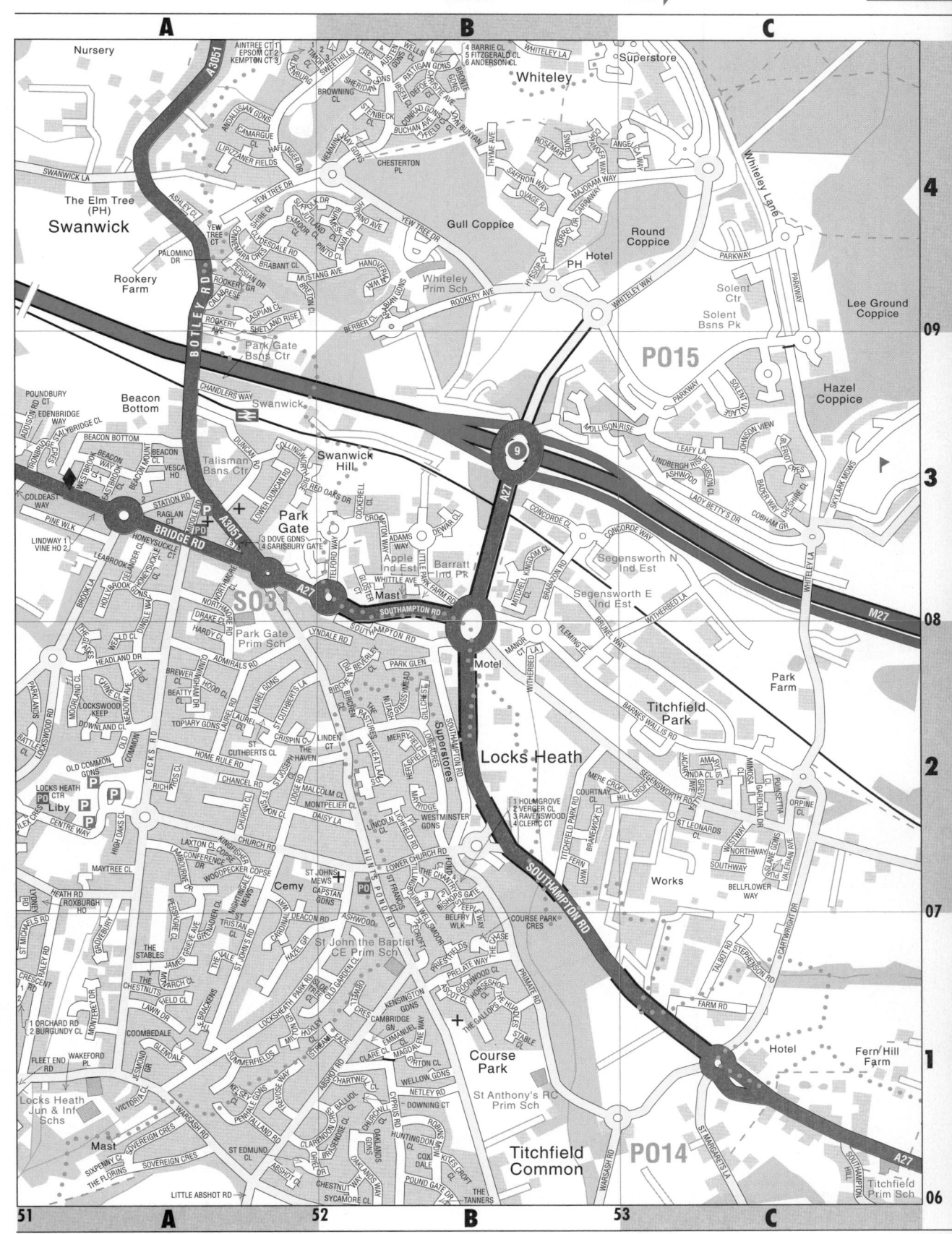

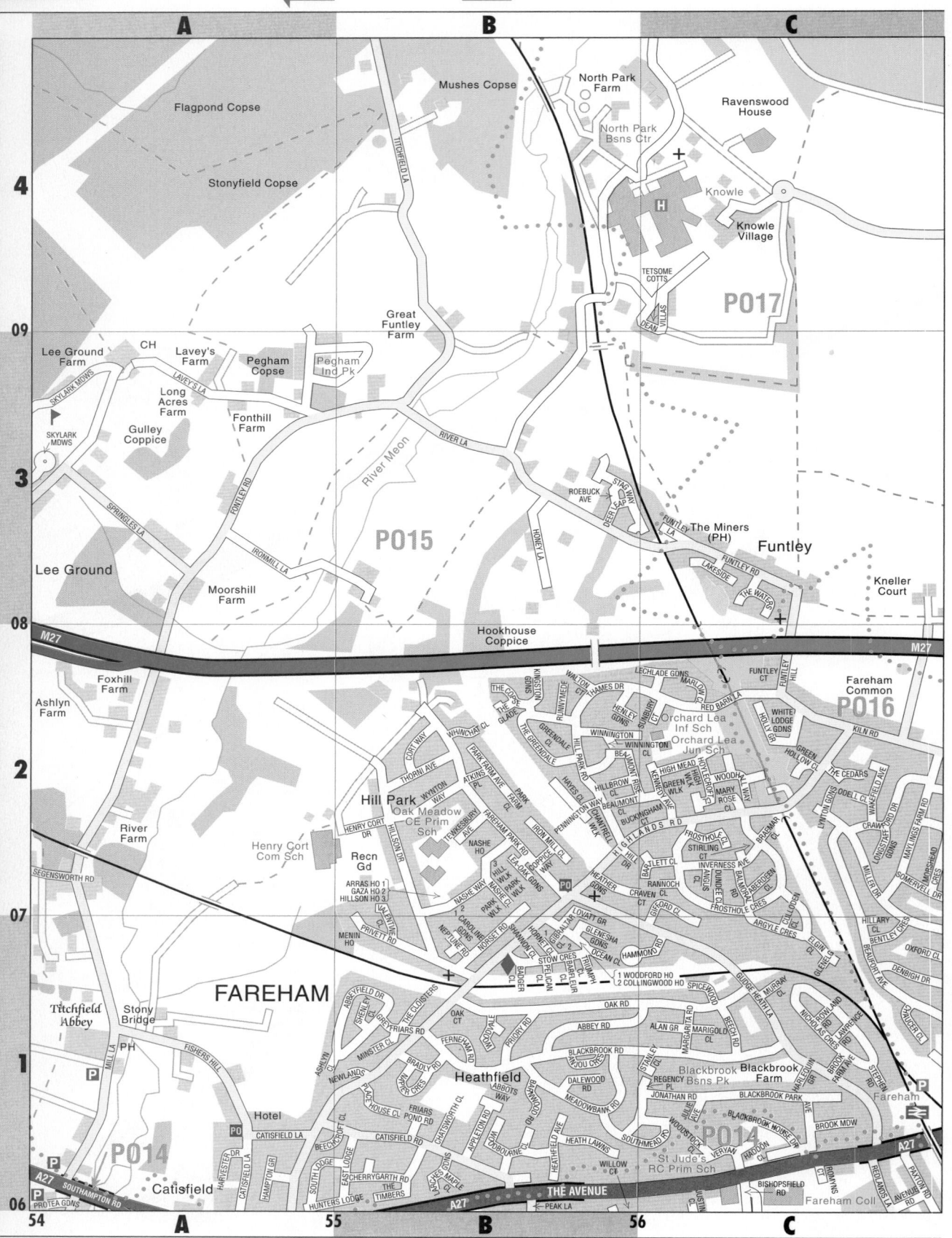

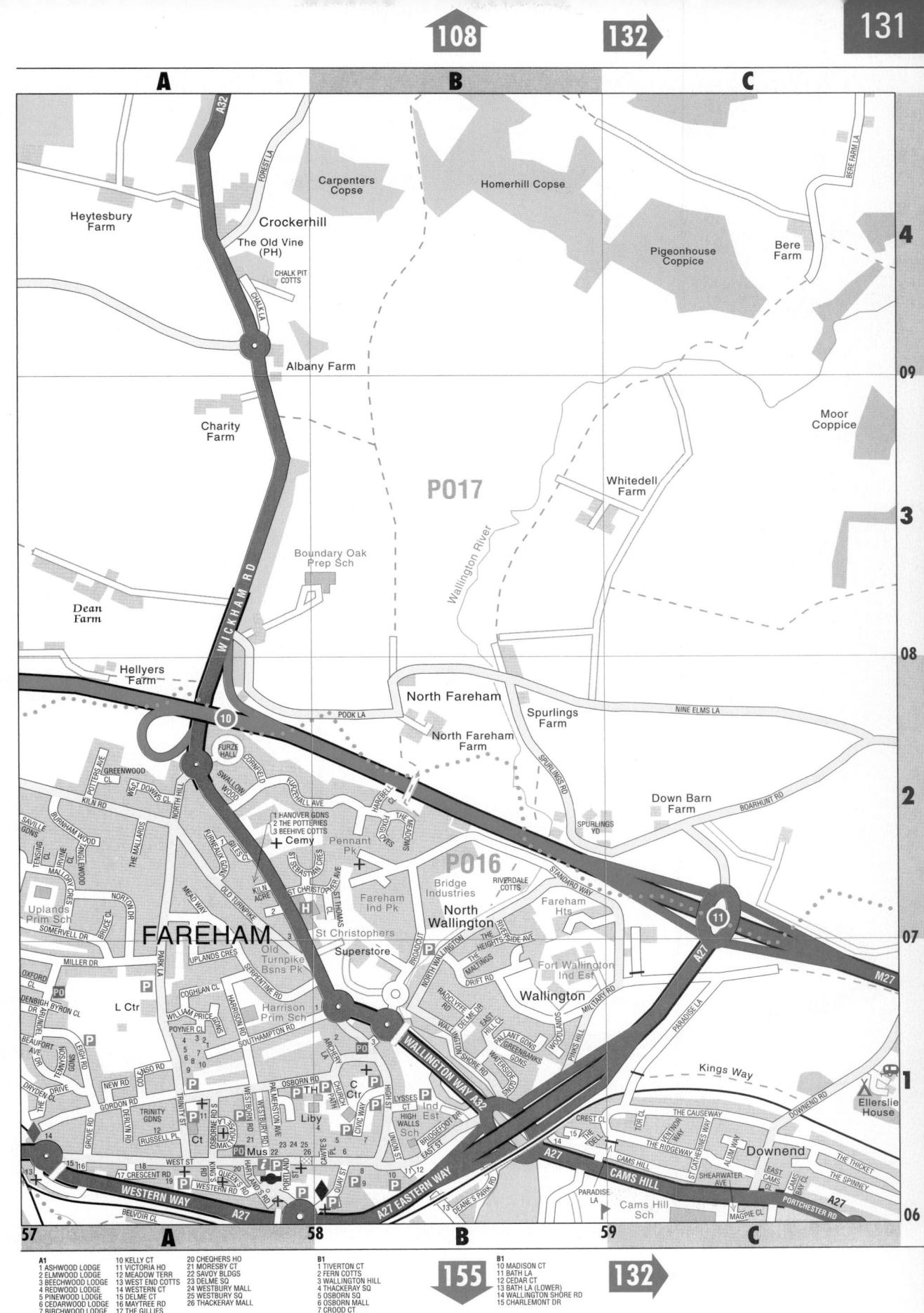

A1
1 ASHWOOD LODGE
2 ELMWOOD LODGE
3 BEECHWOOD LODGE
4 REDWOOD LODGE
5 PINEWOOD LODGE
6 CEDARWOOD LODGE
7 BIRCHWOOD LODGE
8 NORTHWOOD SQ
9 DARREN CT

10 KELLY CT
11 VICTORIA HO
12 MEADOW TERR
13 WEST END COTTS
14 WESTERN CT
15 DELME CT
16 MAYTREE RD
17 THE GILLIES
18 BURY HO
19 HOMEFAYRE HO

20 CHEQHERS HO
21 MORESBY CT
22 SAVOY BLDGS
23 DELME SQ
24 WESTBURY MALL
25 WESTBURY SQ
26 THACKERAY MALL

B1
1 TIVERTON CT
2 FERN COTTS
3 WALLINGTON HILL
4 THACKERAY SQ
5 OSBORN SQ
6 OSBORN MALL
7 CROOD CT
8 WESTQUAY HO
9 ADELAIDE PL

B1
10 MADISON CT
11 BATH LA
12 CEDAR CT
13 BATH LA (LOWER)
14 WALLINGTON SHORE RD
15 CHARLEMONT DR

A B C

4

Carmans Copse
STAPLE CROSS
B2177
Staplecross Copse
Walton Heath
Mitchelland
BLACKHOUSE LA
Carmans Farm
Lodge Farm
Vernons Farm
Prior's Hold Farm
Lodge Coppice
Friar's Coppice
COMMON LA

Wallington River
Boarhunt Mill
09
Grub Coppice
Mill Coppice
Ham Coppice
Newman's Bridge
Castle Farm
BRIDGE ST
NORTON RD
Kings Way
Dirtystile Copse
Ham Farm
BACK LA
CASTLE LA
NORTON CL
Royal Naval Cotts
WEST ST
HIGH ST
PO

3
Ashleydown Coppice
Southwick
The Wilderness
Manor Farm
Boarhunt
Ashley Down Farm
Stroud Coppice
Southwick Park Lake
FAREHAM RD
Perrige's Coppice
B2177
P

PO17
Marls Rows
BOARHUNT RD
MONUMENT LA

08
Offwell Farm

2
Damson Row
PORTCHESTER LA
CROOKED WALK LA
Monument Farm
SWIVELTON LA
Mountemoor's Coppice
Fort Southwick

Mus
Fort Nelson
P
Nelson's Monument
JAMES CALLAGHAN DR
Mast
07
DOWNEND RD
Mast
PORTSDOWN HILL RD
M27
P
Ports Down
SKEW RD
High Tor
PO6
The Mount
NELSON LA
WINTERBOURNE RD
KINGSCOTE RD
ALMONDSBURY RD
HILLSLEY RD
RIDGEWAY CL
Upper Cornaway La
LECKFORD CL
CAER PERIS VIEW
NYEWOOD AVE
ANSON GR
BENEDICT WAY
BROWNING AVE

1
PO16
TUDOR CL
KILMISTON DR
WALTHAM CL
WEYHILL
ROGATE GDNS
CARLTON RD
KEATS AVE
CHAUCER AVE
WORDSWORTH AVE
COLERIDGE RD
MACAULAY AVE
Winnham Farm
LANCASTER CL
DANES RD
SAXON CL
MERLIN GDNS
DORE AVE
HIGH
HARTING GDNS
FROXFIELD CL
BURITON CL
SHELLEY AVE
MASEFIELD AVE
BRIDGES AVE
FALMOUTH RD
Porchester
NORTHFIELD PK
CAMS LOT
JUTE CL
ISLAND VIEW WLK
SOLENT VIEW
GRINDLE
RICHMOND RISE
LAVEROCK LEA
MORNINGSIDE AVE
SEAVIEW AVE
DRYDEN AVE
NEWBOLT RD
BUDE CL
HELSTON RD
Cams Bridge
THE PINES
THE THICK
TAMAR
WINNALL
Crem
BOXWOOD CL
HAWTHORN CL
RED BARN LA
Northern Schs
ROBINSON CT
CANNON'S BARN CL
LINDEN LEA
HILL VIEW RD
CONIFER MEWS
PORT SVIEW GDNS
LEITH AVE
SAUNDERS HO
PO
RAYMOND RD
ROWLAND
CONNAUGHT RD
PAMELA AVE
HILLSIDE CRES
THIRD RD
MOUSEHOLE RD
PENDERS
M27

60 A 61 B 62 C

131 156

C1
1 TRINIDAD HO
2 ST LUCIA HO
3 BERMUDA HO
4 ST KITTS HO
5 ANTIGUA HO
6 FOXCOTE HO
7 KINGSCOTE HO
8 ALMONDSBURY HO
9 OAKLANDS HO
10 THORNBURY HO
11 PARKFIELD HO

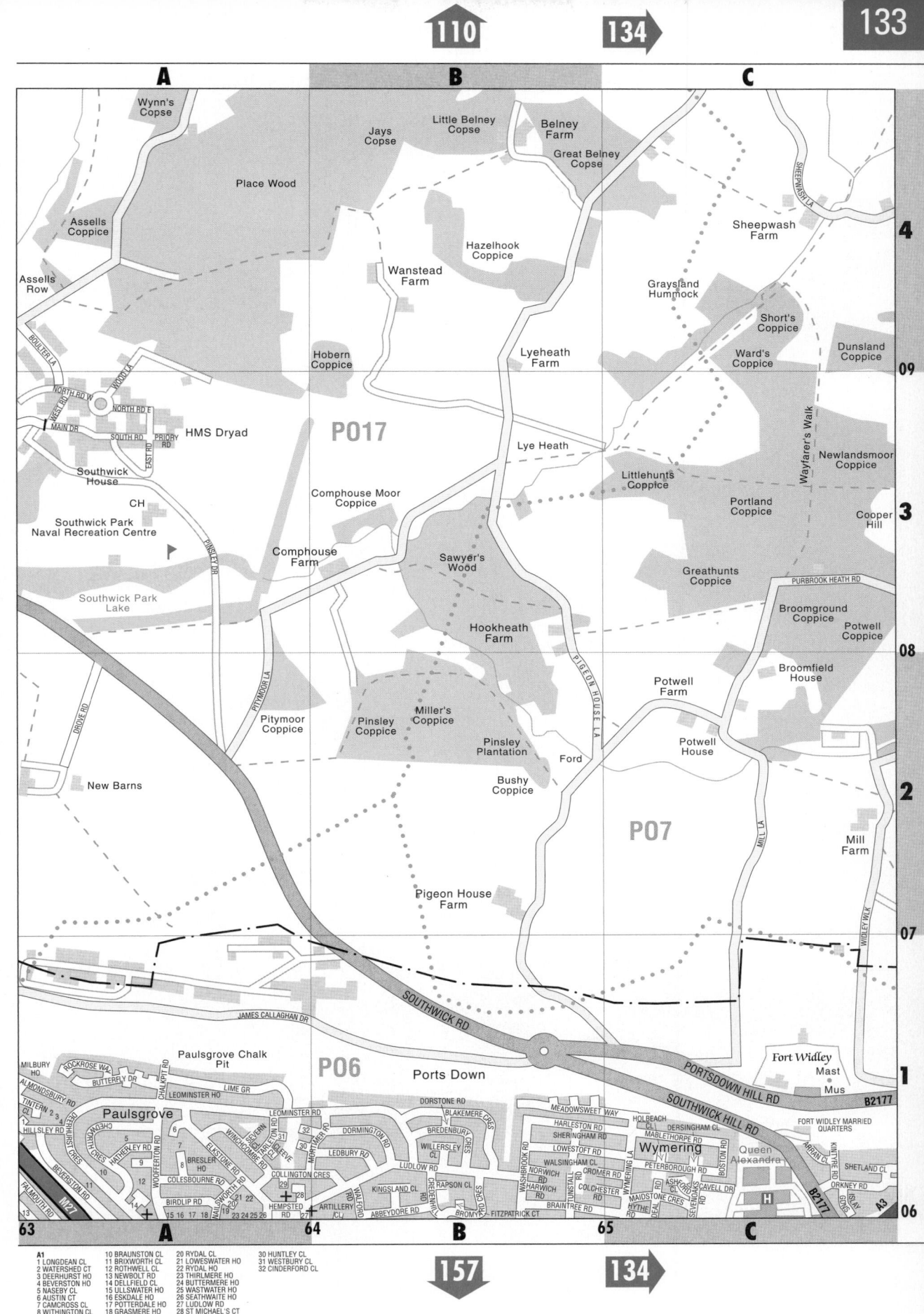

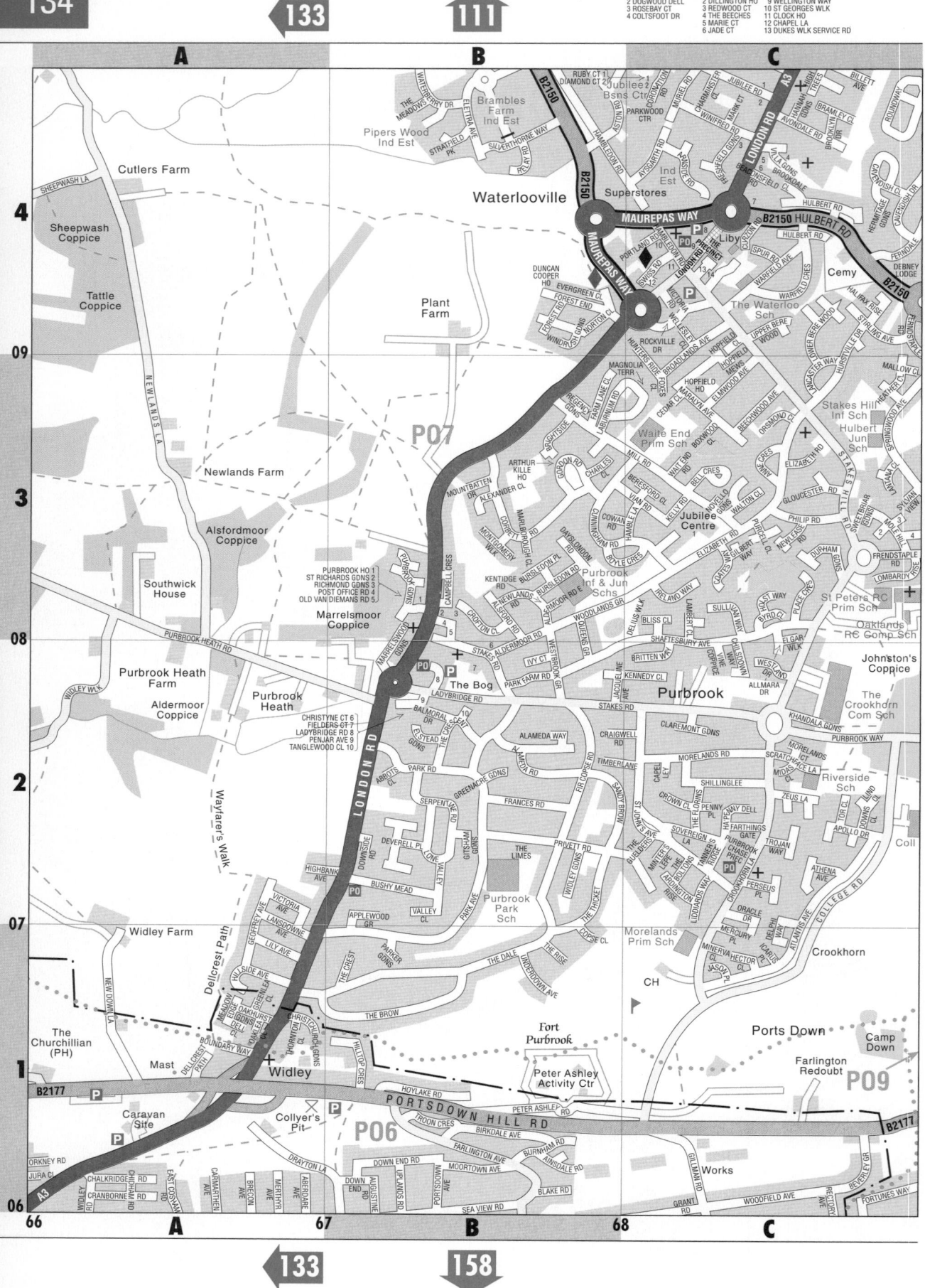

14 DUKES WLK

C3
1 MILLENNIUM CT
2 DOGWOOD DELL
3 ROSEBAY CT
4 COLTSFOOT DR

C4
1 HINTON HO
2 DILLINGTON HO
3 REDWOOD CT
4 THE BEECHES
5 MARIE CT
6 JADE CT

7 HOMEWATER HO
8 QUEEN'S PAR
9 WELLINGTON WAY
10 ST GEORGES WLK
11 CLOCK HO
12 CHAPEL LA
13 DUKES WLK SERVICE RD

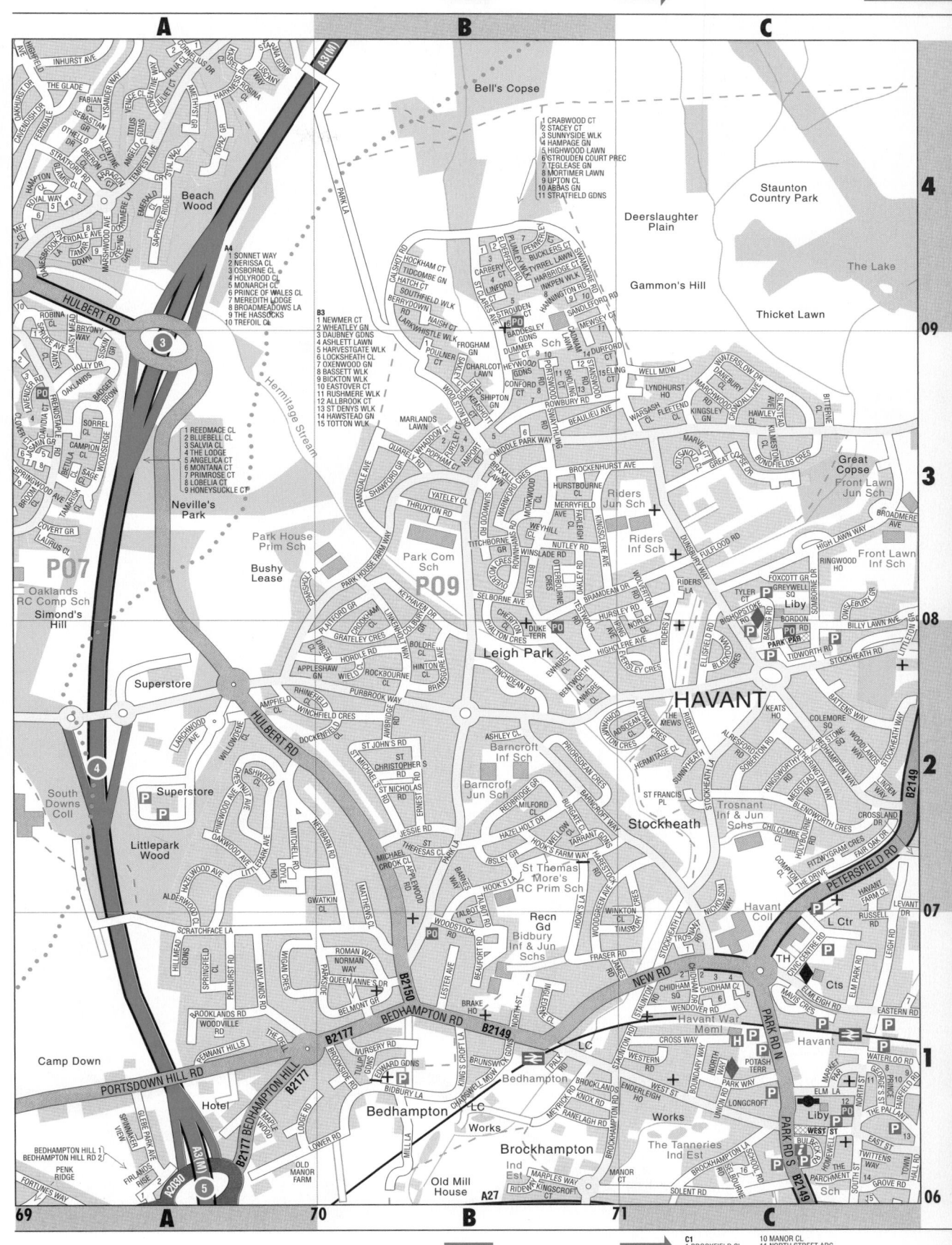

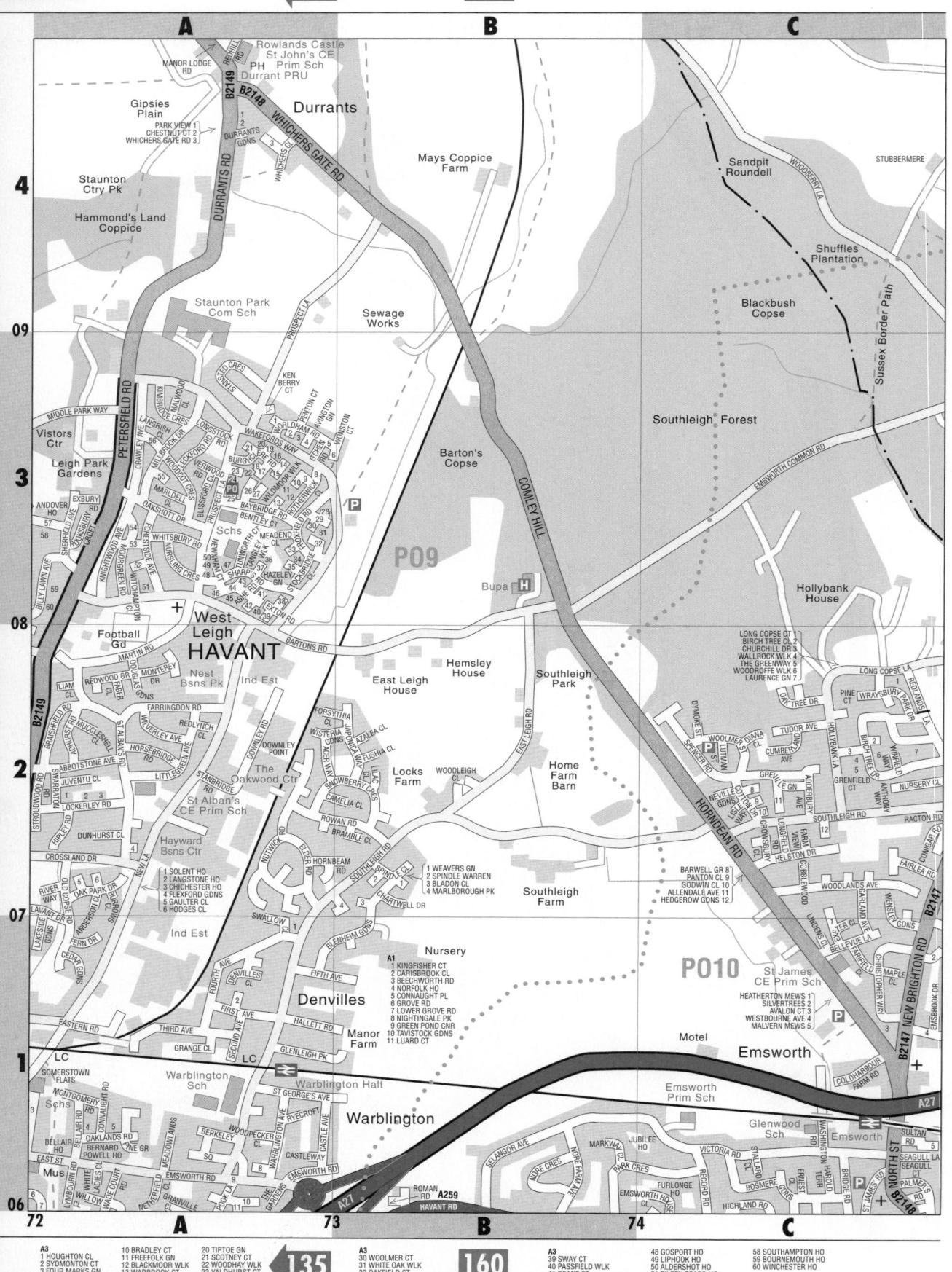

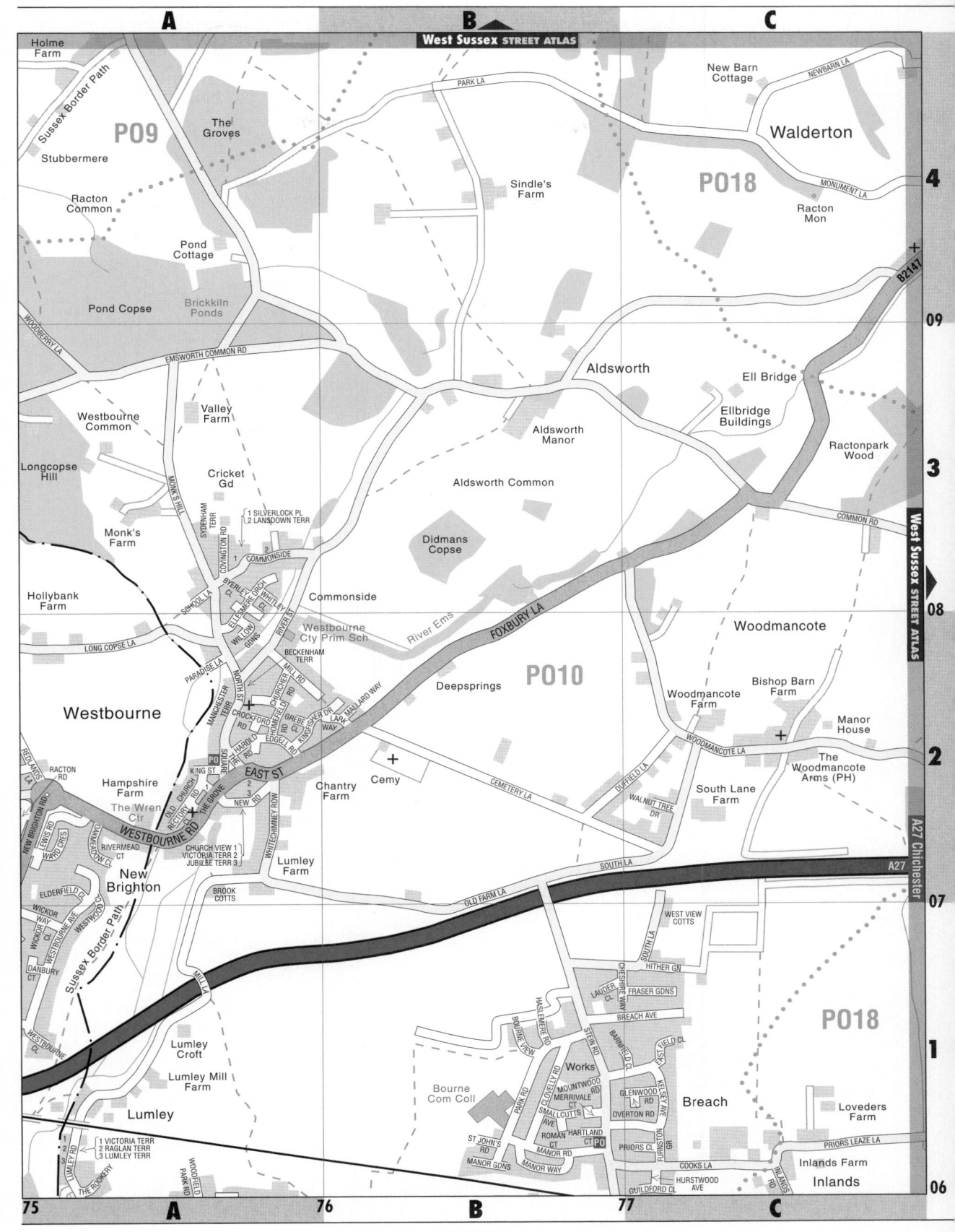

West Sussex STREET ATLAS

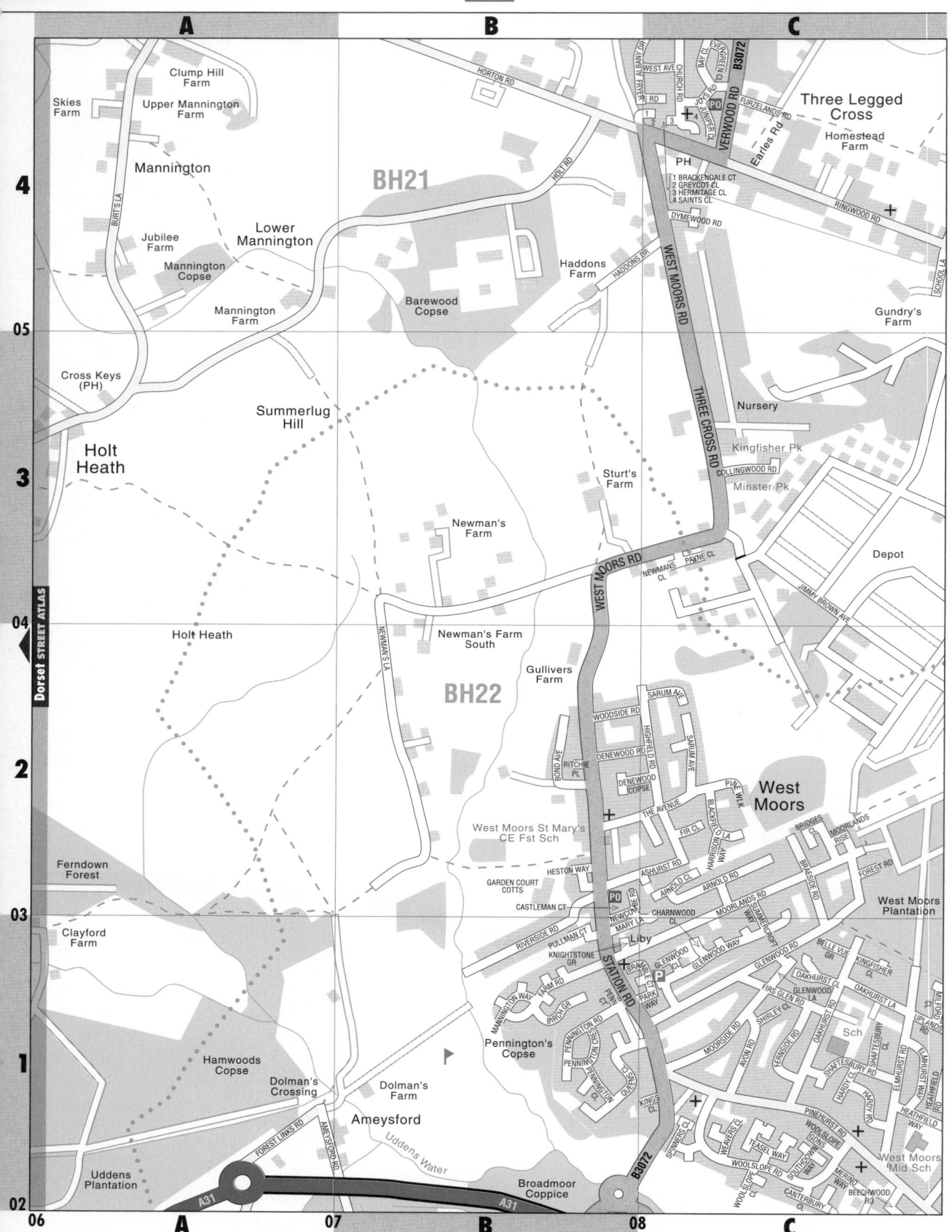

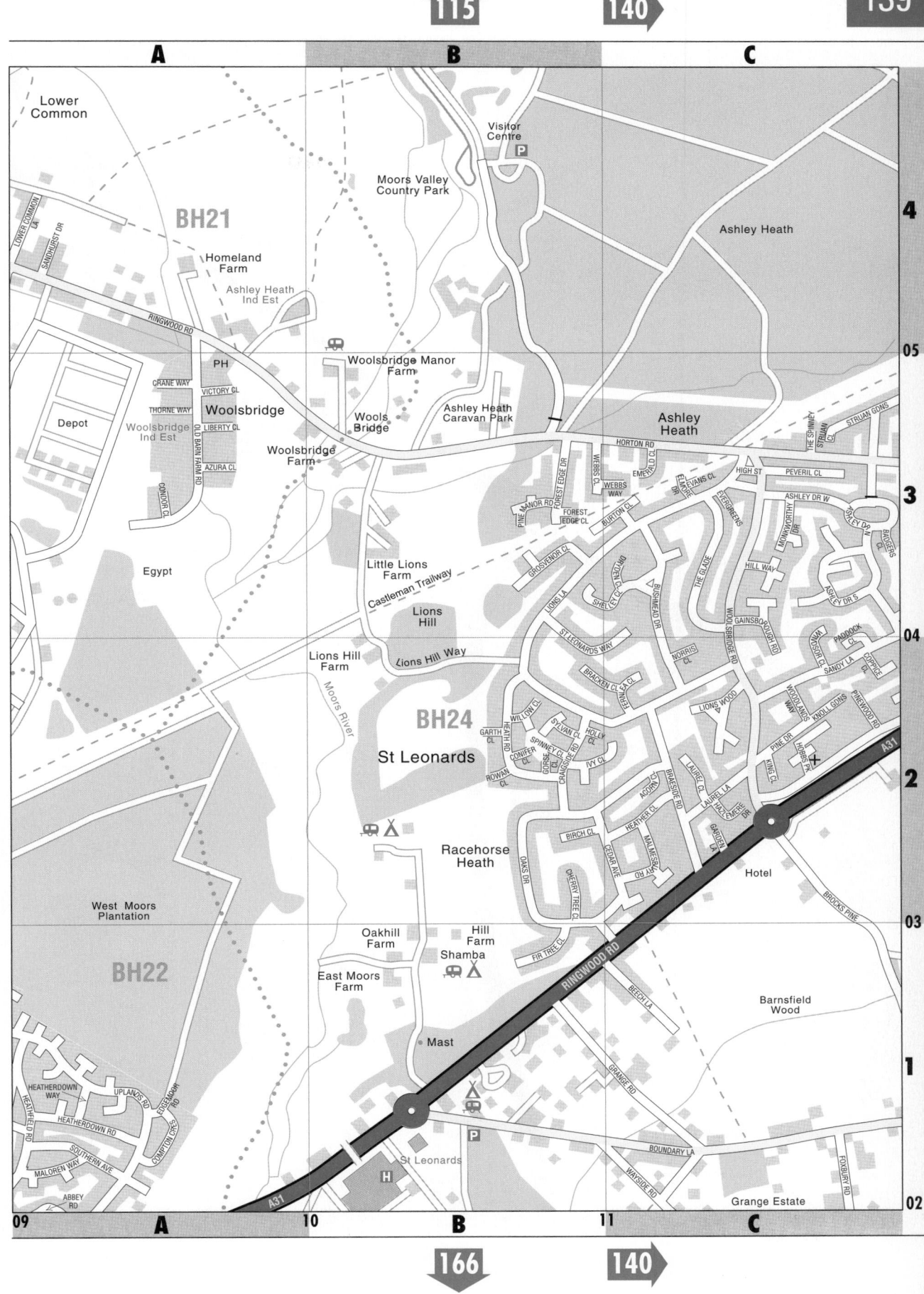

A B C

Lower
Common

BH21

Homeland
Farm

Ashley Heath
Ind Est

Ashley Heath

SANDHURST DR
LOWER COMMON LA

RINGWOOD RD

PH

CRANE WAY

THORNE WAY

VICTORY CL

LIBERTY CL

Woolsbridge

Depot

Woolsbridge
Ind Est

CONIFER CL

OLD BARN FARM RD

AZURA CL

Woolsbridge
Farm

Egypt

Woolsbridge Manor
Farm

Wools
Bridge

Ashley Heath
Caravan Park

Ashley Heath
Caravan Park

Visitor
Centre
P

Moors Valley
Country Park

Ashley
Heath

HORTON RD

WEBBS CL

WEBBS WAY

EMERY CL
EVANS CL

HIGH ST

PEVERIL CL

The SPINNEY
STRUAN CL
STRUAN GDNS

ASHLEY DR W

ASHLEY DR N

BADGERS CL

PINE MANOR RD
FOREST EDGE DR

FOREST
EDGE CL

BURTON CL

ELMERS DR

EVERGREENS

MINKWORTHY DR

HILL WAY

The GLADE

ASHLEY DR S

Little Lions
Farm

GROSVENOR CL

Castleman Trailway

SHELLEY CL
LIONS LA

BUSHMEAD DR

WOOLSBRIDGE RD

GAINSBOROUGH RD

PADDOCK CL

SANDY LA

COPPICE

Lions
Hill

ST LEONARDS WAY

NORRIS CL

GARSTON
LA

WOODLANDS

KNOLL GDNS

PINEWOOD RD

Lions Hill
Farm

Lions Hill Way

BRACKEN CL

FRANCIS CL

Lions Wood

PINE DR

HOBBS PK

KING CL

A31

Moors River

BH24

St Leonards

WILLOW CL

HEATH RD

GARTH
CL

SYLVAN CL

SPINNET CL

GORSE
CL

CRANSIDE RD

HOLLY
CL

IVY CL

ACORN
WAY

BRACSIDE RD

HALL
RD

LAUREL CL

GARDEN
RD

KING CL

Hotel

ROWAN
CL

OAKS DR

Racehorse
Heath

CHERRY TREE CL

HEATHER CL

CEDAR AVE

MALMESBURY RD

BIRCH CL

West Moors
Plantation

BH22

Oakhill
Farm

East Moors
Farm

Hill
Farm

Shamba

FIR TREE CL

RINGWOOD RD

BEECH LA

Barnsfield
Wood

BROCKS PINE

Mast

A31

P

St Leonards

H

GRANGE RD

BOUNDARY LA

WAYSIDE RD

Grange Estate

FOXBURY RD

HEATHERDOWN
WAY

UPLANDS RD

EDGEMOOR RD

HEATHERDOWN RD

COMPTON CRES

SOUTHERN AVE

HEATHFIELD RD

MALOREN WAY

ABBEY
RD

4
05
3
04
2
03
1
02

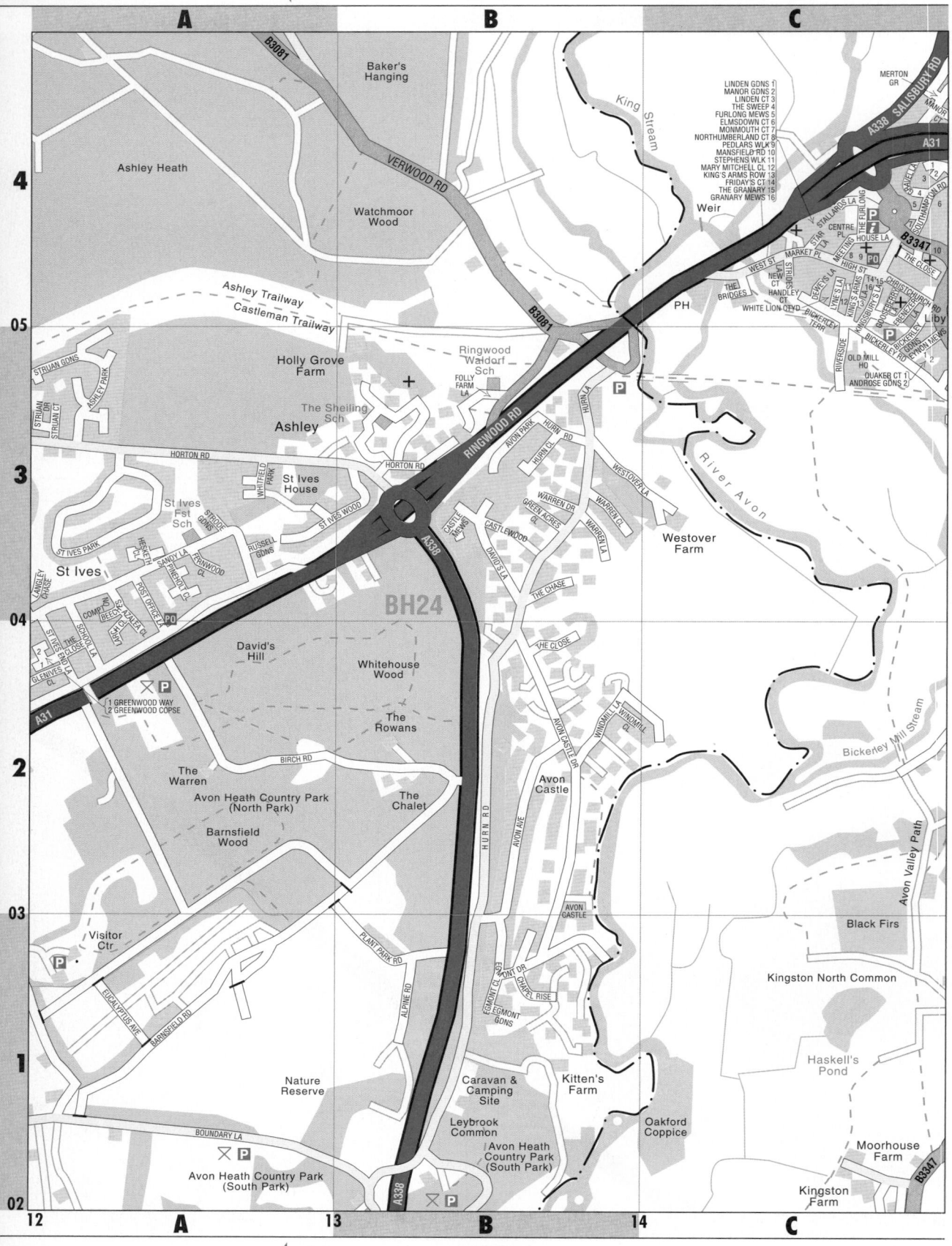

A3
1 HARRY BARROW CL
2 COXSTONE LA
3 YEW TREE GDNS
4 MINTYS YD
5 DUCK ISLAND LA
6 SOUTHFIELD MEWS

A4
1 SOMERLEY VIEW
2 BEECHCROFT MEWS
3 LUMBY DRIVE CARAVAN PARK
4 CAVENDISH CORNER CARAVAN PARK
5 ORCHARD MEAD
6 ORCHARD MOUNT

7 MOUNT PLEASANT
8 ELM COTTS

B4
1 PILGRIM PARK HOMES
2 WHITEHART FIELDS
3 MERRYWEATHER EST
4 PIPERS ASH

RINGWOOD

Poulner

Forest Corner

Dunain Farm

POULNER HILL A31

Poulner Hill Farm

Long Barn

Hazy Down Farm

Old Forest Farm

Lynes Farm

Hightown Lower Copse

Hightown

Elm Tree (PH)

Lane End Farm

Forest Hills

Hightown Copse

Ringwood Sch

Recn Ctr

Cemy

Ringwood Jun Sch

Hightown Ind Est

Hightown Lake

The Holdings

Moortown

Sabines Farm

Owl Sanctuary

Crow

BH24

Crow Hill

Crow Hill Farm

Charles Copse

Gaddens Close Farm

Millstream Trad Est

Stag Bsns Pk

Crow Arch Lane Ind Est

Moortown LA

STREETS LA

Upper Kingston

Upper Kingston Farm

Barrack La

Crow Cotts

Charles Farm

Gaddens

Moortown Farm

Sewage Works

Lakes Farm

North Kingston

Bagnum

Little Bagnum Farm

Kingston

Castleman's Farm

Brixey's Farm

Bagnum Farm

Park Hill

Sandford Copse

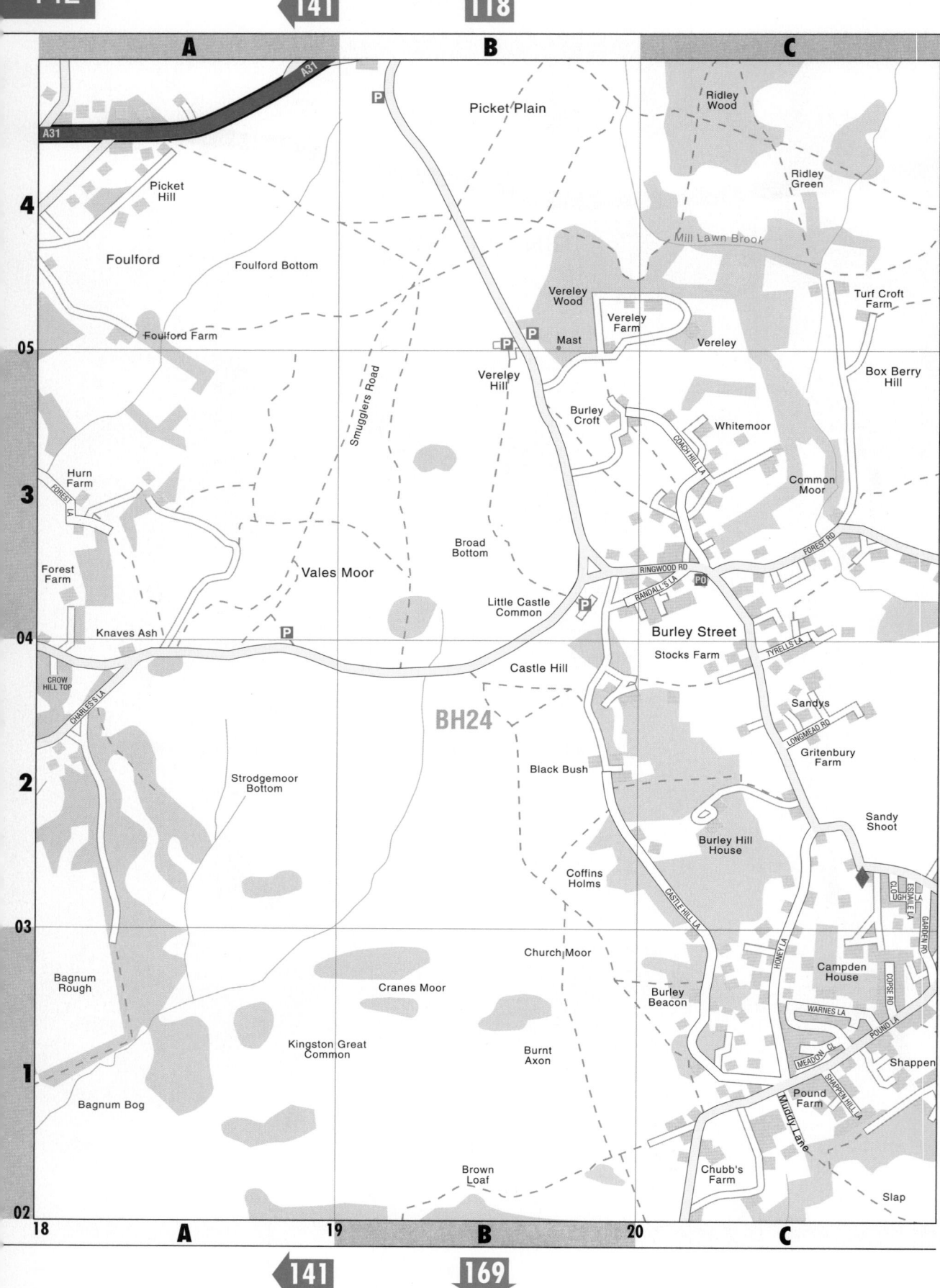

A31

A
B
C

Picket Plain

Ridley Wood

4

Picket Hill

Ridley Green

Foulford

Foulford Bottom

Mill Lawn Brook

Vereley Wood

Turf Croft Farm

05

Foulford Farm

Vereley Farm

Mast

Vereley

Box Berry Hill

Vereley Hill

Smugglers Road

Burley Croft

Whitemoor

3

Hurn Farm

Common Moor

FOREST LA

Forest Farm

Vales Moor

Broad Bottom

Little Castle Common

RINGWOOD RD

FOREST RD

04

Knaves Ash

CHARLES'S LA

P

RANDALL'S LA

PO

Burley Street

TYRELL'S LA

CROW HILL TOP

Castle Hill

Stocks Farm

BH24

Sandys

LONGMEAD RD

Gritenbury Farm

2

Strodgemoor Bottom

Black Bush

Sandy Shoot

Burley Hill House

CLOUGH LA
ESDAILE LA
GARDEN RD

03

Coffins Holms

CASTLE HILL LA

HONEY LA

Campden House

COPSE RD

Bagnum Rough

Church Moor

Burley Beacon

WARNES LA

POUND LA

Cranes Moor

MEADOW CL
SHAPPEN HILL LA

Shappen

1

Kingston Great Common

Burnt Axon

Pound Farm

MUDDY LANE

Bagnum Bog

Brown Loaf

Chubb's Farm

Slap

02

18
A
19
B
20
C

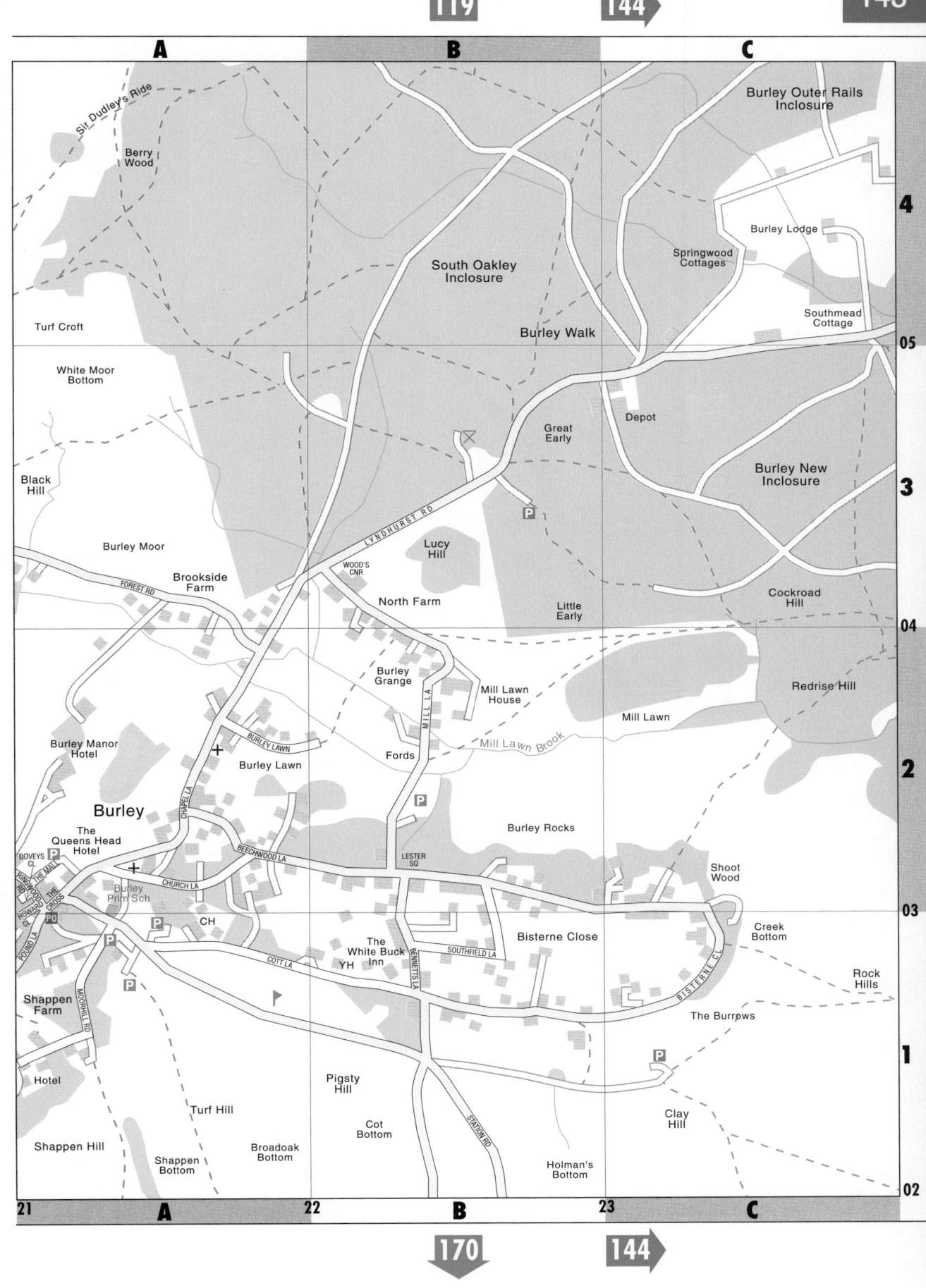

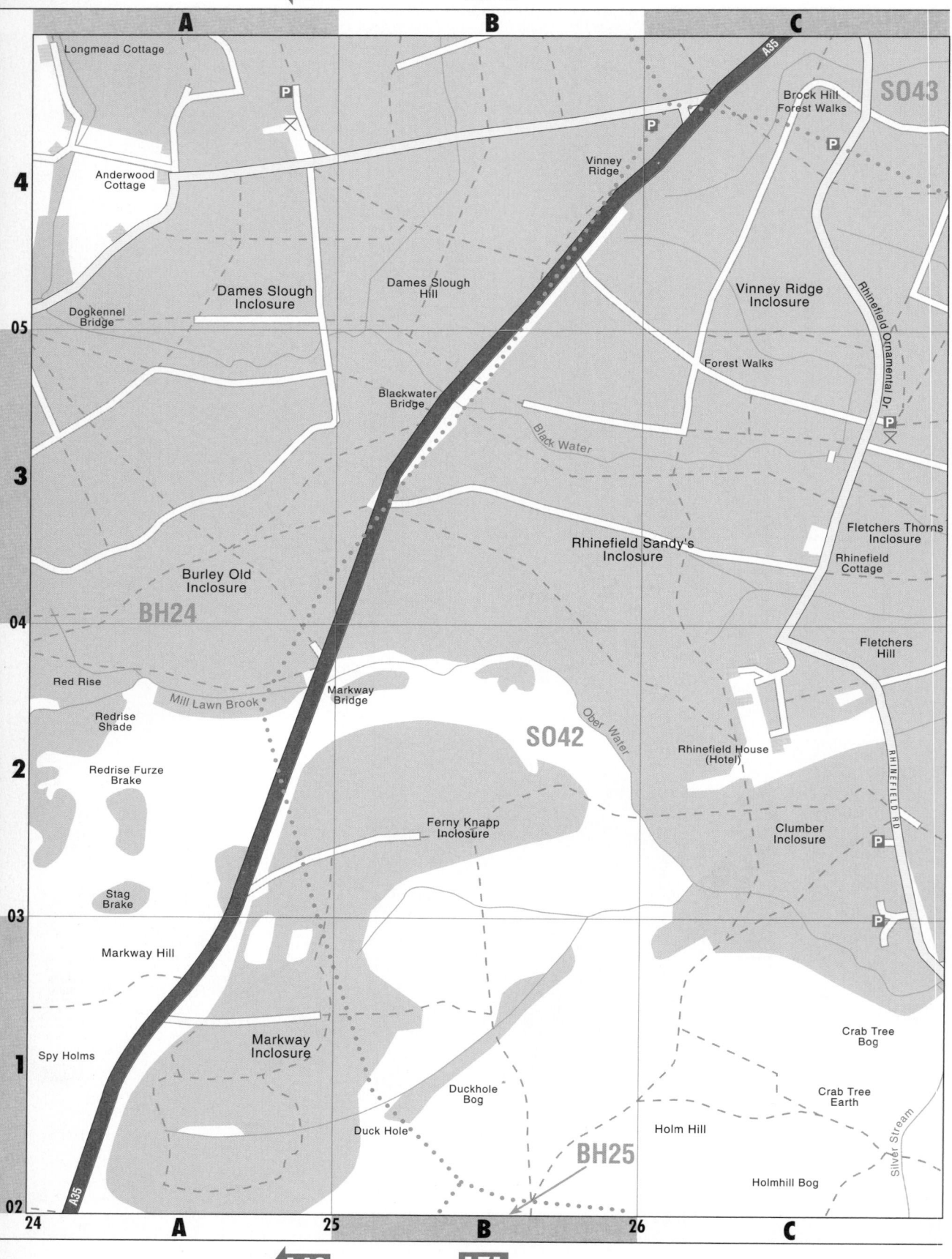

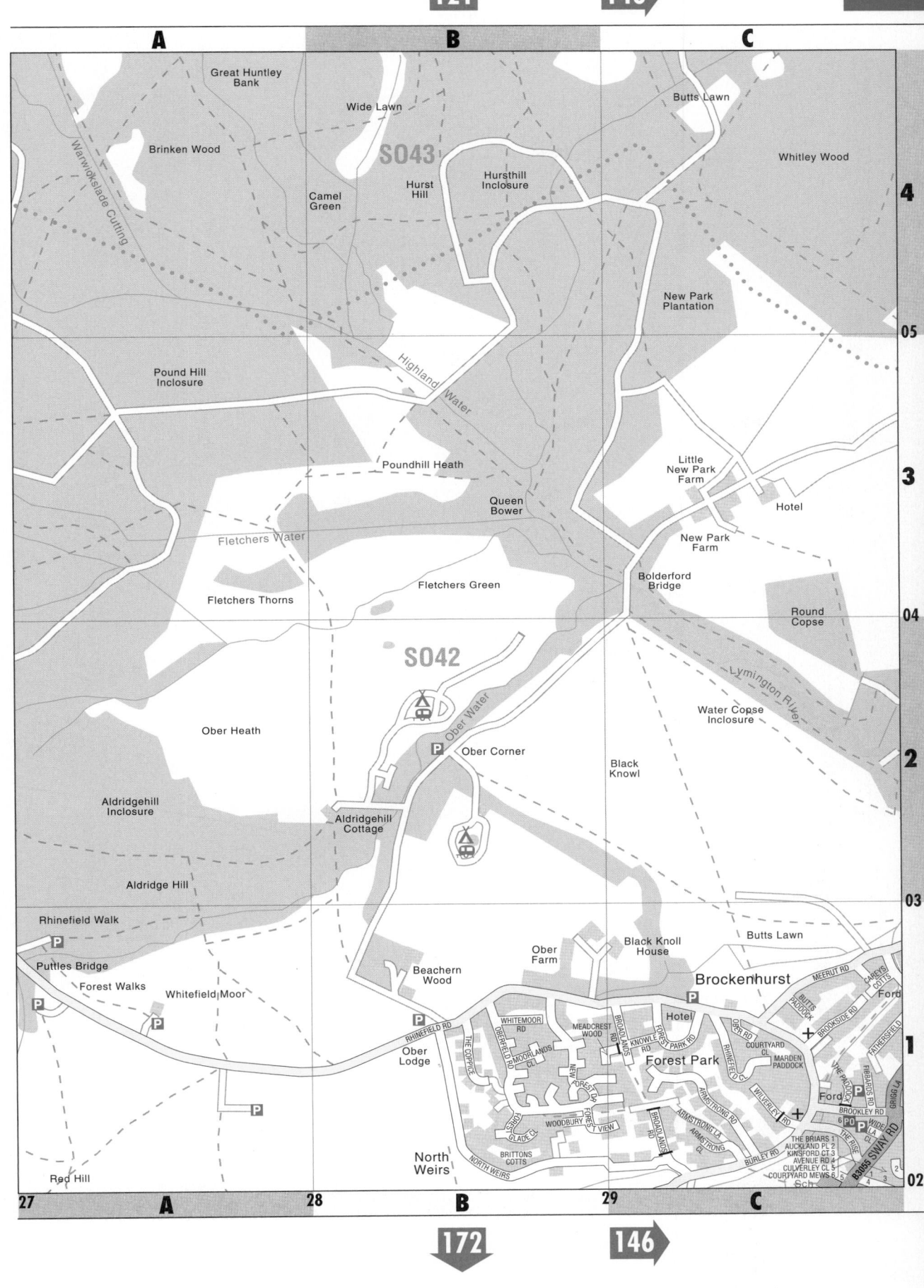

Great Huntley Bank

Wide Lawn

Butts Lawn

SO43

Brinken Wood

Whitley Wood

Warwickslade Cutting

Hurst Hill

Hursthill Inclosure

Camel Green

4

New Park Plantation

05

Pound Hill Inclosure

Highland Water

Poundhill Heath

Little New Park Farm

3

Queen Bower

Hotel

Fletchers Water

New Park Farm

Fletchers Green

Bolderford Bridge

Fletchers Thorns

Round Copse

04

SO42

Lymington River

Ober Water

Water Copse Inclosure

2

Ober Heath

Ober Corner

Black Knowl

Aldridgehill Inclosure

Aldridgehill Cottage

03

Aldridge Hill

Rhinefield Walk

Butts Lawn

Puttles Bridge

Ober Farm

Black Knoll House

Forest Walks

Beachern Wood

Brockenhurst

MEERUT RD

Whitefield Moor

Hotel

Forest Park

Rhinefield Rd

Ober Lodge

North Weirs

Red Hill

THE BRIARS 1
AUCKLAND PL 2
KINSFORD CT 3
AVENUE RD 4
CULVERLEY CL 5
COURTYARD MEWS 6

A B C

4

05

3

04

2

03

1

02

30 31 32

A B C

S043

Spaniards
Hole

King's
Hat

Parkhill
Inclosure

Hollands
Wood

Ramnor
Inclosure

Stubby Copse
Inclosure

Pignal
Inclosure

S042

Balmer
Lawn

Standing
Hat

Pound

Perrywood
Haseley
Inclosure

Victoria
Tilery
Cottage

Pignalhill
Inclosure

Ford

Hotel

B3055

BALMER LAWN RD

Jacks
Wood

New Copse
Inclosure

Balmerlawn

Bridge
Farm

Warren
Farm

Whitley Ridge

Hotel

MEERUT RD

RINGWOOD
TERR

Hotel

Brockenhurst

1 FATHERSFIELD
2 WATERS GN
3 WATERS GREEN CT

Old Mill
House

Perrywood
Ivy
Inclosure

B3055

Brockenhurst
Coll

Lymington River

Longbow

HOMEFORDE
HO

GREEN
WAYS RD

Irons
Hill

MILL LA

Ivy
Wood

A337

B3055

1 STATION APP
2 LYMINGTON RD

Perrywood
Ironshill
Inclosure

LYNDHURST RD

B3055

A337

A **B** **C**

Denny Wood

Denny Lodge

B3056

B3056

Stephill Bottom

4

Woodfidley Passage

Furzy Brow

05

Bishop of Winchester's Purlieu

Denny Lodge Inclosure

Penny Moor

3

Woodfidley

SO42

Rowbarrow

04

LC

Frame Heath Inclosure

2

Frame Wood

03

Ladycross Inclosure

Moon Hill

Ladycross Lodge

1

Worts Gutter

Hawkhill Inclosure

Lodge Heath

B3055

Stockley Inclosure

Little Wood

02

33 **A** 34 **B** 35 **C**

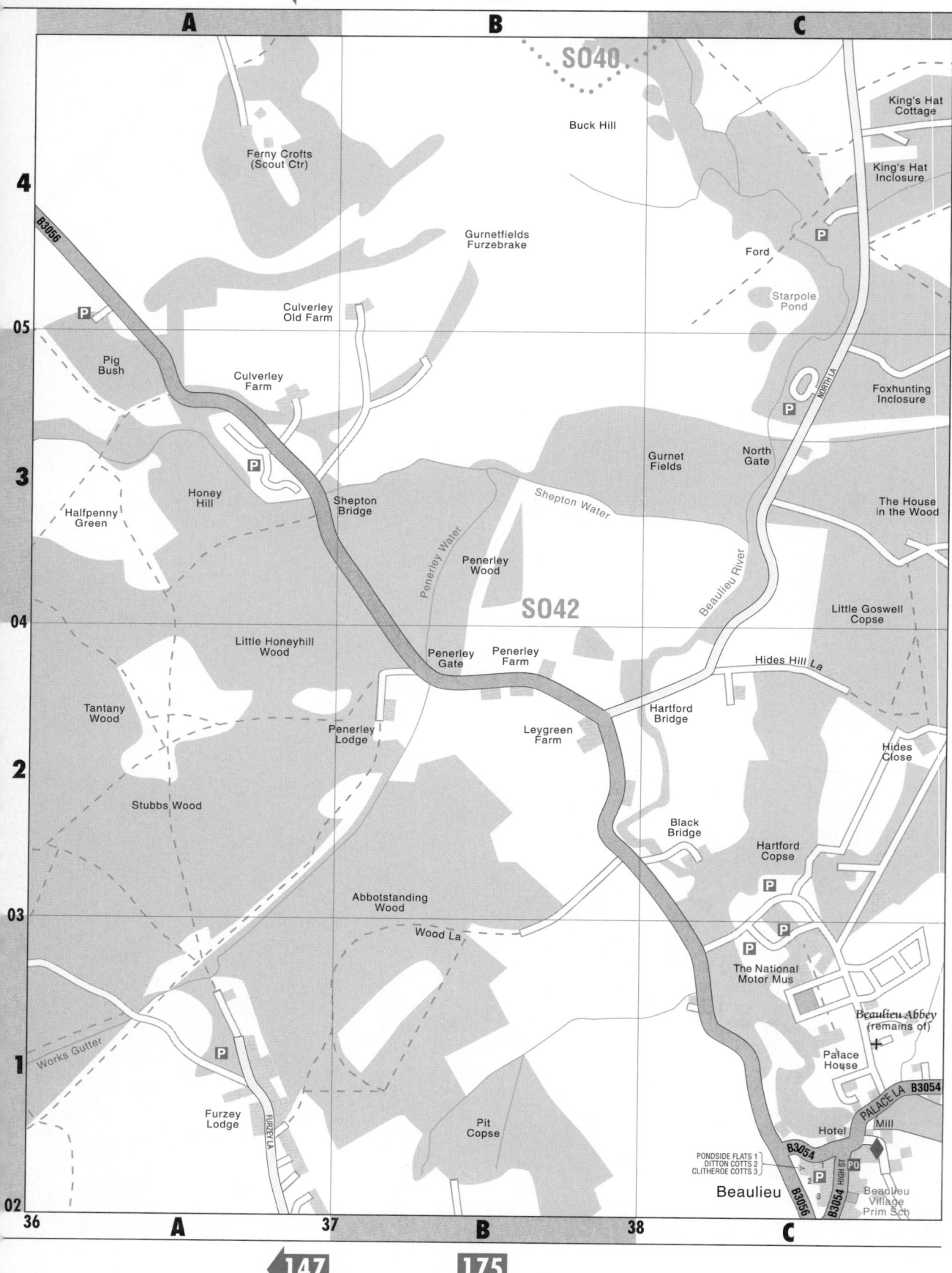

SO40

A   B   C

Buck Hill

King's Hat
Cottage

Ferny Crofts
(Scout Ctr)

King's Hat
Inclosure

4

Gurnetfields
Furzebrake

Ford

P

Starpole
Pond

B3056

05

P

Culverley
Old Farm

P

Foxhunting
Inclosure

Pig
Bush

Culverley
Farm

Gurnet
Fields

North
Gate

3

Honey
Hill

Shepton
Bridge

Shepton Water

The House
in the Wood

Halfpenny
Green

Penerley Water

Penerley
Wood

Beaulieu River

Little Goswell
Copse

04

SO42

Little Honeyhill
Wood

Penerley
Gate

Penerley
Farm

Hides Hill La

Tantany
Wood

Penerley
Lodge

Leygreen
Farm

Hartford
Bridge

Hides
Close

2

Stubbs Wood

Black
Bridge

Hartford
Copse

P

Abbotstanding
Wood

P

P

03

Wood La

The National
Motor Mus

Beaulieu Abbey
(remains of)

Works Gutter

Palace
House

1

P

PALACE LA   B3054

FURZEY LA

Furzey
Lodge

Pit
Copse

Hotel

Mill

B3054

PONDSIDE FLATS 1
DITTON COTTS 2
CLITHEROE COTTS 3

P

HIGH ST

PO

B3054

Beaulieu
Village
Prim Sch

02

Beaulieu

B3056

36   A   **37**   B   **38**   C

A   B   C

Dibden
Inclosure

P

A326

BEAULIEU RD

B3054

BEAULIEU RD
WHINFIELD RD
CRETE COTTS
CRETE RD
DEVILLIERS AVE
ASHWOOD
HAYLEY RD

PRU

LUNDALE RD
MONTAGUE CT
SOLENT RD
HEATHERSTONE RD
CORBOULD RD
BEVERLEY RD
BARCLAY MEWS
BUTTS ASH LA
FOREST FRONT

ROMAN RD

MONKS WLK

HYTHE BY PASS

Solent Way

A326

Nature
Reserve

The
Noads

4

Fawley
Inclosure

Crabhat
Inclosure

Flash Pond

05

Harford
House

Solent Way

Beaulieu Heath

SO45

3

Holbury
Purlieu

Hartford Heath

Stonyford
Pond

SO42

04

Great Goswell
Copse

Hilltop
Farm

2

Hill Top

Hilltop
Wood

Hilltop
House

03

Boarman
Pond

Royal Oak
(PH)

MOONHILLS LA

Moonhills
Gate

P

PALACE LA

Home
Farm

Moonhills
Copse

1

Otterwood
Gate

Stock Water

Carpenters
Cottage

DOCK LA

SUMMER LA

Otterwood
Farm House

Cowleys La

Cowleys
Copse

Otterwood

02

39
A
40
B
41
C

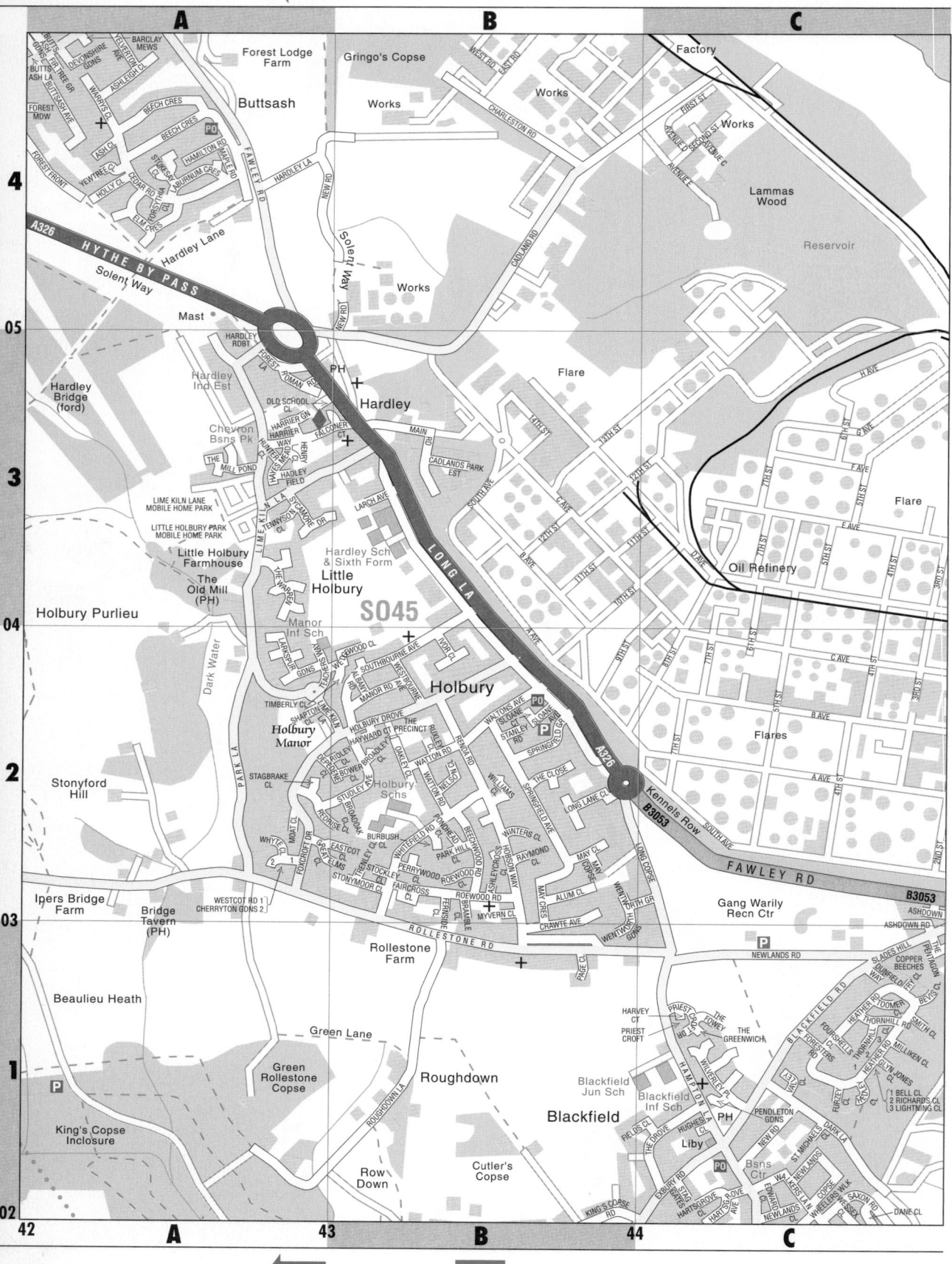

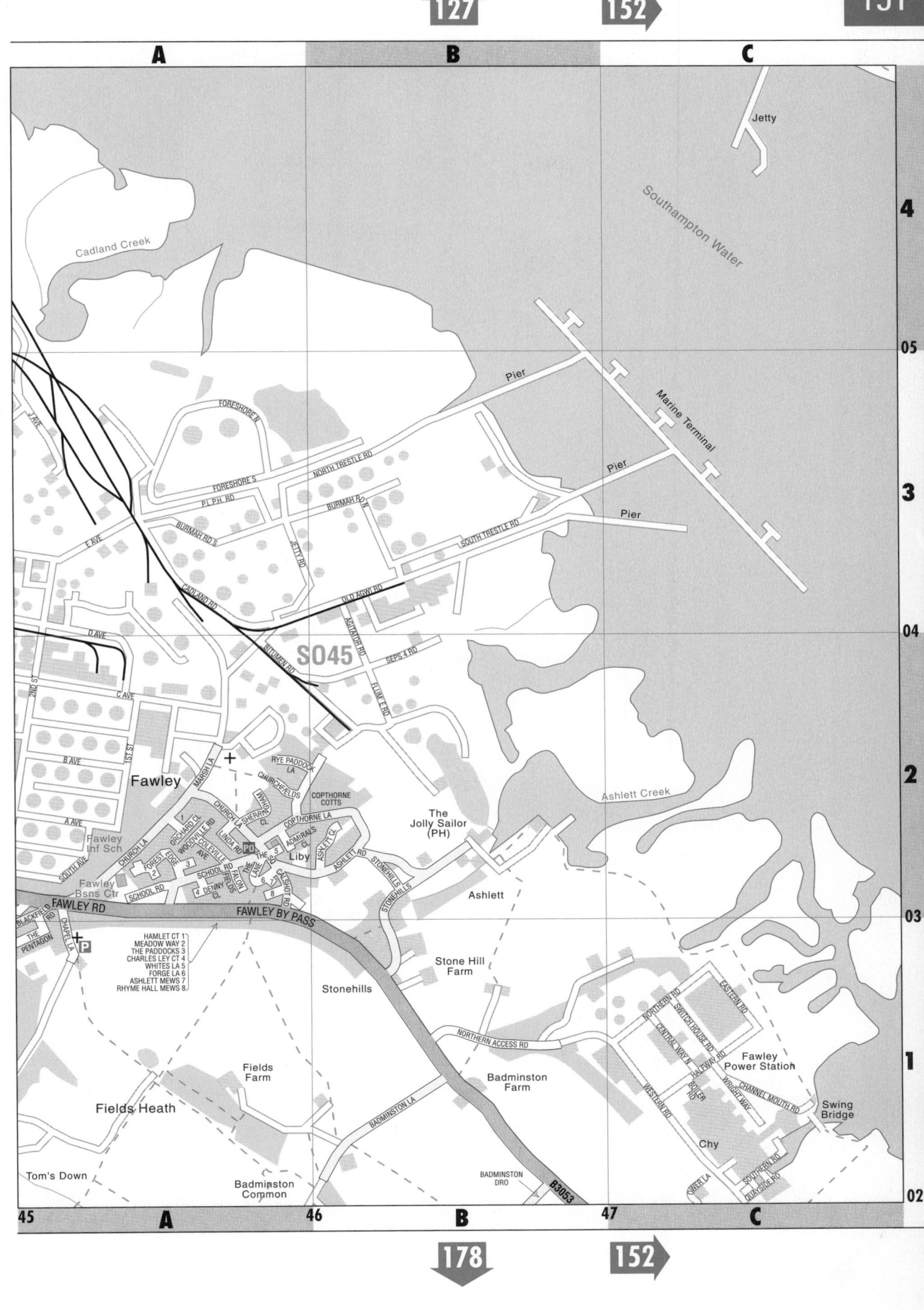

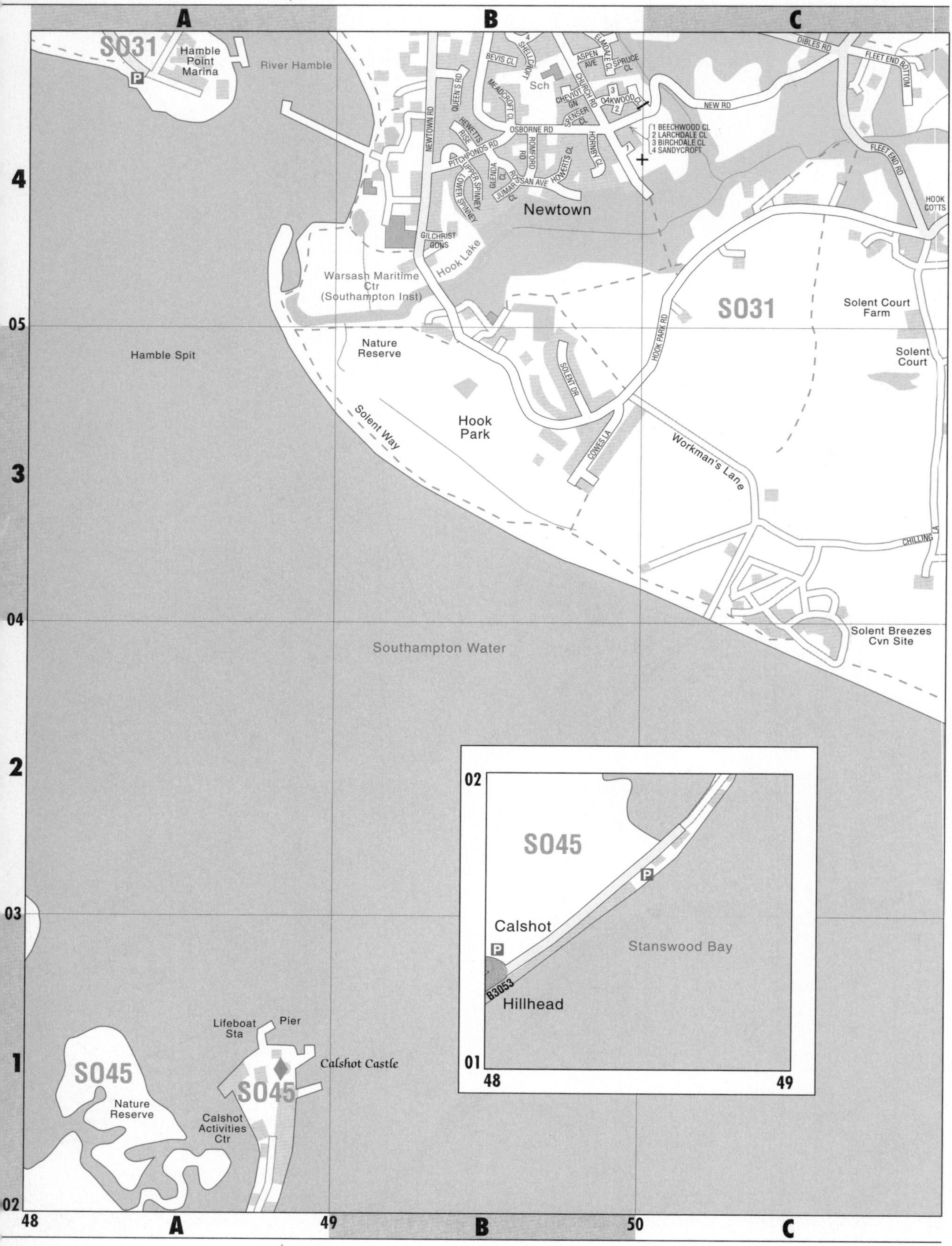

A   **B**   **C**

SO31

Hamble Point Marina

P

River Hamble

DIBLES RD

FLEET END BOTTOM

4

Newtown

NEW RD

Sch

BEVIS CL

SHELLCROFT

ASPEN CL

ELMDALE CL

SPRUCE CL

QUEEN'S RD

NEWTOWN RD

MEADCROFT CL

CHURCH RD

CHEVIOT GN

OAKWOOD CL

HEWETTS RISE

OSBORNE RD

SPENSER CL

1 BEECHWOOD CL
2 LARCHDALE CL
3 BIRCHDALE CL
4 SANDYCROFT

PITCHPONDS RD

ROMFORD RD

HORNBY CL

FLEET END

Hook Cotts

LOWER SPINNEY

GLENDALE

JUMAR SUSAN AVE

HOWLETTS CL

GILCHRIST GDNS

Warsash Maritime Ctr (Southampton Inst)

Hook Lake

SO31

Solent Court Farm

Hook Park Rd

05

Hamble Spit

Nature Reserve

SOLENT DR

Solent Court

Solent Way

Hook Park

COWES LA

Workman's Lane

3

CHILLING

04

Southampton Water

Solent Breezes Cvn Site

02

SO045

P

2

Calshot

P

Stanswood Bay

03

B3053

Hillhead

Lifeboat Sta

Pier

Calshot Castle

01

48   **49**

1

SO045

Nature Reserve

SO045

Calshot Activities Ctr

02

A   49   **B**   50   **C**

48

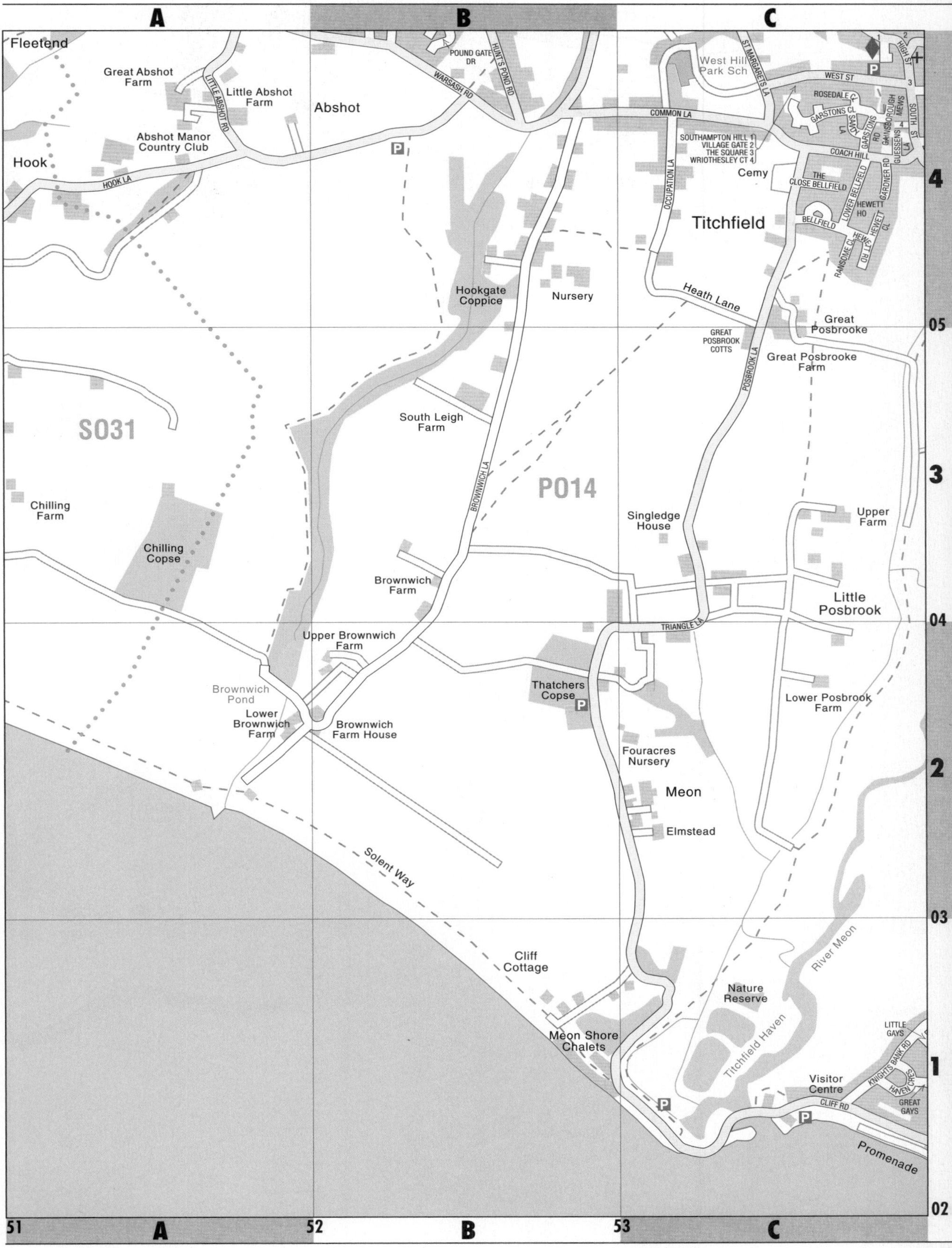

A B C

Fleetend

Great Abshot Farm

Little Abshot Farm

Abshot

Hook

Abshot Manor Country Club

HOOK LA

LITTLE ABSHOT RD

POUND GATE DR

HUNT'S POND RD

WARSASH RD

P

COMMON LA

West Hill Park Sch

P

WEST ST

ST MARGRETS LA

HIGH ST

SOUTH ST

ROSEDALE C

GARSTONS CL

GARSTONS RD

GAINSBOROUGH MEWS

GLESSENS LA

COACH HILL

SOUTHAMPTON HILL 1
VILLAGE GATE 2
THE SQUARE 3
WRIOTHESLEY CT 4

Cemy

THE CLOSE BELLFIELD

BELLFIELD

HEWETT HO

RANSOME CL

LOWER BELLFIELD

HEWS LA

HEWETT CL

GARDNER RD

Titchfield

Hookgate Coppice

Nursery

OCCUPATION LA

Heath Lane

GREAT POSBROOK COTTS

POSBROOK LA

Great Posbrooke

Great Posbrooke Farm

05

SO31

South Leigh Farm

PO14

Singledge House

Upper Farm

Little Posbrook

BROWNWICH LA

Chilling Farm

Chilling Copse

Brownwich Farm

Upper Brownwich Farm

TRIANGLE LA

3

04

Brownwich Pond

Lower Brownwich Farm

Brownwich Farm House

Thatchers Copse

P

Lower Posbrook Farm

Fouracres Nursery

Meon

Elmstead

2

Solent Way

03

Cliff Cottage

Nature Reserve

River Meon

Meon Shore Chalets

Titchfield Haven

LITTLE GAYS

KNIGHTS BANK RD

HAVEN CRES

Visitor Centre

GREAT GAYS

CLIFF RD

P

P

Promenade

1

02

51 A 52 B 53 C

A4
1 QUAYSIDE COMMERCE CTR
2 MILLERS QUAY HO
3 THE ROPE WLK
4 ST GEORGES CT
5 SOLENT HO
6 HAMBLE HO
7 NEEDLES HO
8 MEON HO
9 SPITHEAD HO
10 MEDINA HO
11 LANGSTONE HO
12 YOUNGBRIDGE CT
13 TRAFALGAR WAY

131
156
180
156

The Gillies · The Boatyard Ind Est · Town Quay · Upper Quay · Upper Wharf · Lower Quay · Salterns Quay · Works · The Moorings · Delta Bsns Pk · Newgate Lane Ind Est

Home Farm Office Village · North Park · Cams Hall · Carnac House · Cams Hill Sch · South Park · Cunigre Pond

PO16 · Portsmouth Harbour · Wicor Hard · Pier · Foxbury Point · Kings Way · Sports Gd

Sports Ctr · Fort Fareham · Palmerston Bsns Pk · Fort Fareham Ind Est · Superstore · Collingwood Ret Pk · Speedfields Pk · Superstore · Apex Ctr · Superstores · Solent Gate

PO14 · Fleetlands · PO16 · RNAD Gosport · The Leisure

Woodcot · Woodcot Prim Sch · Peel Farm · Peel Common · Peel Common Jun & Inf Schs · Bridgemary · Holbrook Prim Sch · Bridgemary Com Sch · Liby · Bedenham Prim Sch · Frater Lake · Fort Elson

GOSPORT · PO13 · PO12 · Rowner Jun & Inf Schs · Chark Common · River Alver · Recn Ctr · Holbrook · Fort Brockhurst · Mus · Brockhurst Ind Est

B1
1 LYDDEN CT
2 KIEDER GR
3 BIRCHMORE CL
4 ST CHRISTOPHERS GDNS
5 PEMBROKE CT
6 ALLIANCE CL
7 LANDON RD
8 LAWN CL

Rooksway Gr 1 · Goldcrest Cl 2 · Hawkwell 3 · Cygnet Ct 4 · Cormorant Cl 5 · Wrenway 6 · Teal Ct 7 · Kingfishers 8 · Romsey Ave 9

1 Lombardy Cl
2 Sycamore Cl
3 The Hoe
4 The Thicket
5 The Chine
6 The Mount
7 Aspengrove
8 The Glen
9 Vineside

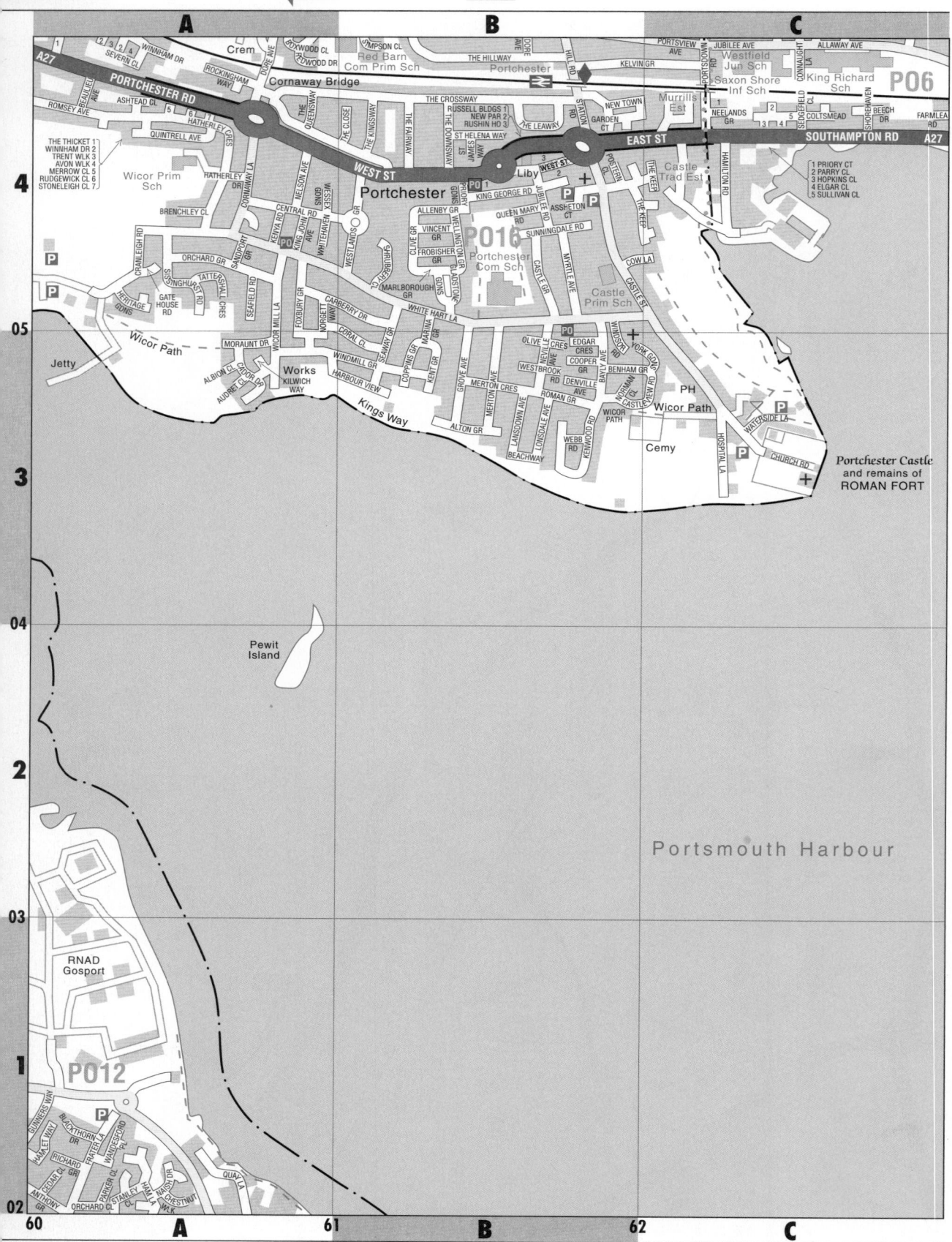

A   B   C

P06

A27

PORTCHESTER RD

Crem

Cornaway Bridge

Red Barn Com Prim Sch

Portchester

THE HILLWAY

PORTSVIEW AVE

Westfield Jun Sch

King Richard Sch

JUBILEE AVE

ALLAWAY AVE

CONNAUGHT LA

Saxon Shore Inf Sch

NEW TOWN

Murrills Est

NEELANDS GR

COLTSMEAD

SEDGEFIELD CL

SHOREHAVEN

BEECH DR

FARMLEA RD

SOUTHAMPTON RD   A27

THE THICKET 1
WINNHAM DR 2
TRENT WLK 3
AVON WLK 4
MERROW CL 5
RUDGEWICK CL 6
STONELEIGH CL 7

WEST ST

Portchester

Liby

WEST ST

EAST ST

Castle Trad Est

THE KEEP

HAMILTON RD

1 PRIORY CT
2 PARRY CL
3 HOPKINS CL
4 ELGAR CL
5 SULLIVAN CL

4

Wicor Prim Sch

PO16

Portchester Com Sch

Castle Prim Sch

P016

KING GEORGE RD

QUEEN MARY RD

SUNNINGDALE RD

ASSHETON CT

CASTLE GR

MYRTLE AVE

COW LA

CASTLE ST

05

Wicor Path

Jetty

Works
KILWICH WAY

Windmill Rd

Harbour View

WHITE HART LA

OLIVE CRES

EDGAR CRES

COOPER GR

WINDSOR RD

YORK CRES

BAVY CL

BENHAM GR

PH

Wicor Path

WATERSIDE LA

3

Kings Way

BEACHWAY

WEBB RD

KENWOOD RD

Cemy

HOSPITAL LA

CHURCH RD

Portchester Castle
and remains of
ROMAN FORT

04

Pewit Island

2

Portsmouth Harbour

03

RNAD Gosport

1

PO12

GUNNERS WAY

BLACKTHORN DR

FRATER LA

WANDESFORD PL

RICHARD GR

PARKER CL

STANLEY RD

CHESTNUT

QUAY LA

ANTHONY GR

ORCHARD CL

NAISH

HAM LA

02

60   A   61   B   62   C

B4
1 ARTILLERY CL
2 DOWNTON HO
3 COTSWOLD HO
4 MELLOR CL
5 MALDON RD
6 HADLEIGH RD

7 HOCKLEY CL
8 PEBMARSH RD
9 WYMERING MANOR CL
10 BLACKWATER CL
C1
1 GLEBEFIELD GDNS
2 TANKERTON CL

133

C4
3 DYMCHURCH HO
4 NEPTUNE HO
5 MALLOW CT
6 ELIZABETH CT
7 STUART CT
8 TUDOR CT

158

C4
9 WINDSOR CT
10 ODEON BLDGS
11 CHIPSTEAD RD
12 CHIPSTEAD RD
13 NORTHERN BLDGS
14 ALDROKE ST

15 BEATRICE MEWS
16 VICTORIA TERR
17 ORFORD CT
18 GLENLEIGH CT
19 GLENLEIGH AVE
20 MEGAN CT
21 SELWYN CT
22 VINE CT

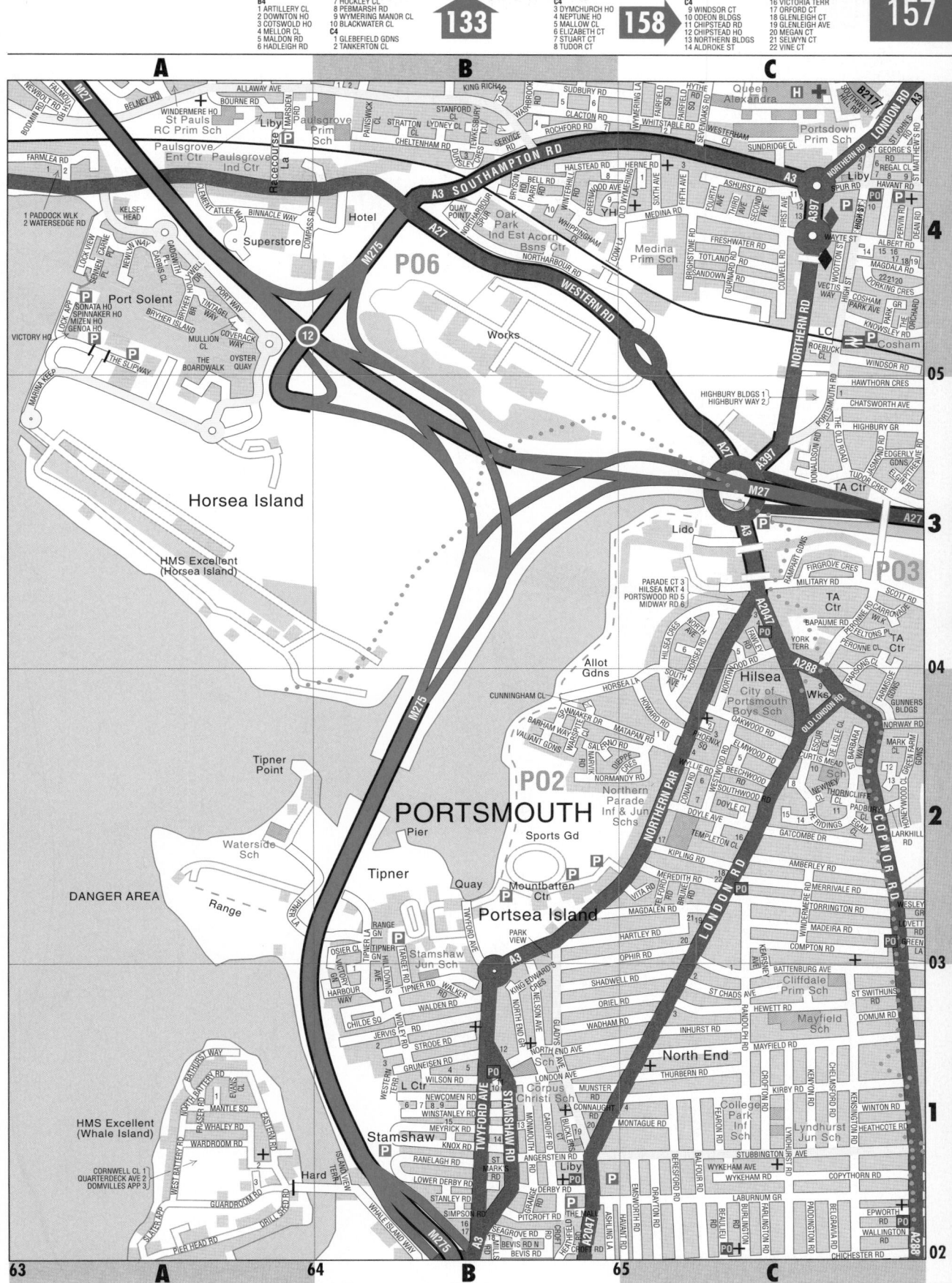

B1
1 SOMERVILLE PL
2 SCOTT HO
3 HASTINGS HO
4 OAK LODGE
5 STAMPSEY CT
6 BILL STILLWELL CT
7 SMEATON ST
8 NEWCOMEN CT
9 SHADWELL CT

10 EDEN TERR
11 PENROSE CL
12 HARRISON HO
13 WEYMOUTH RD
14 STAMSHAW CT
15 MEYRICK HO
16 ST JOHN'S CT
17 RUDMORE CT
18 ST NICHOLAS FLATS
19 WHITES CT

20 THE PROMENADE

182

158

C1
1 BURGUNDY TERR
2 SHACKLETON CT
3 VERNON CT
4 KIRBY CT
C2
1 FALKLANDS RD
2 ST FRANCIS CT
3 DAME ELIZABETH KELLY CT
4 CORONATION EVENTIDE HOMES

5 EASTWOOD RD
6 GERARD HO
7 LORING HO
8 OLDGATE GDNS
9 WALBERANT BLDGS
10 KNIGHTSTONE CT
11 GARRICK HO
12 BREECH CL
13 BENHAM DR
14 WHITECROSS GDNS

15 BALDERTON CL
16 DOYLE CT
17 PARK ROYAL
18 KIPLING BLDGS
19 MAGDALEN CT
20 BRIGHAM CL
21 HAIG CT
22 WOODFIELD HO

158

A4
1 WALBERTON CT
2 DORNEY CT
3 PARK MANS
4 WIDLEY CT

◀ **157** ▲ **134**

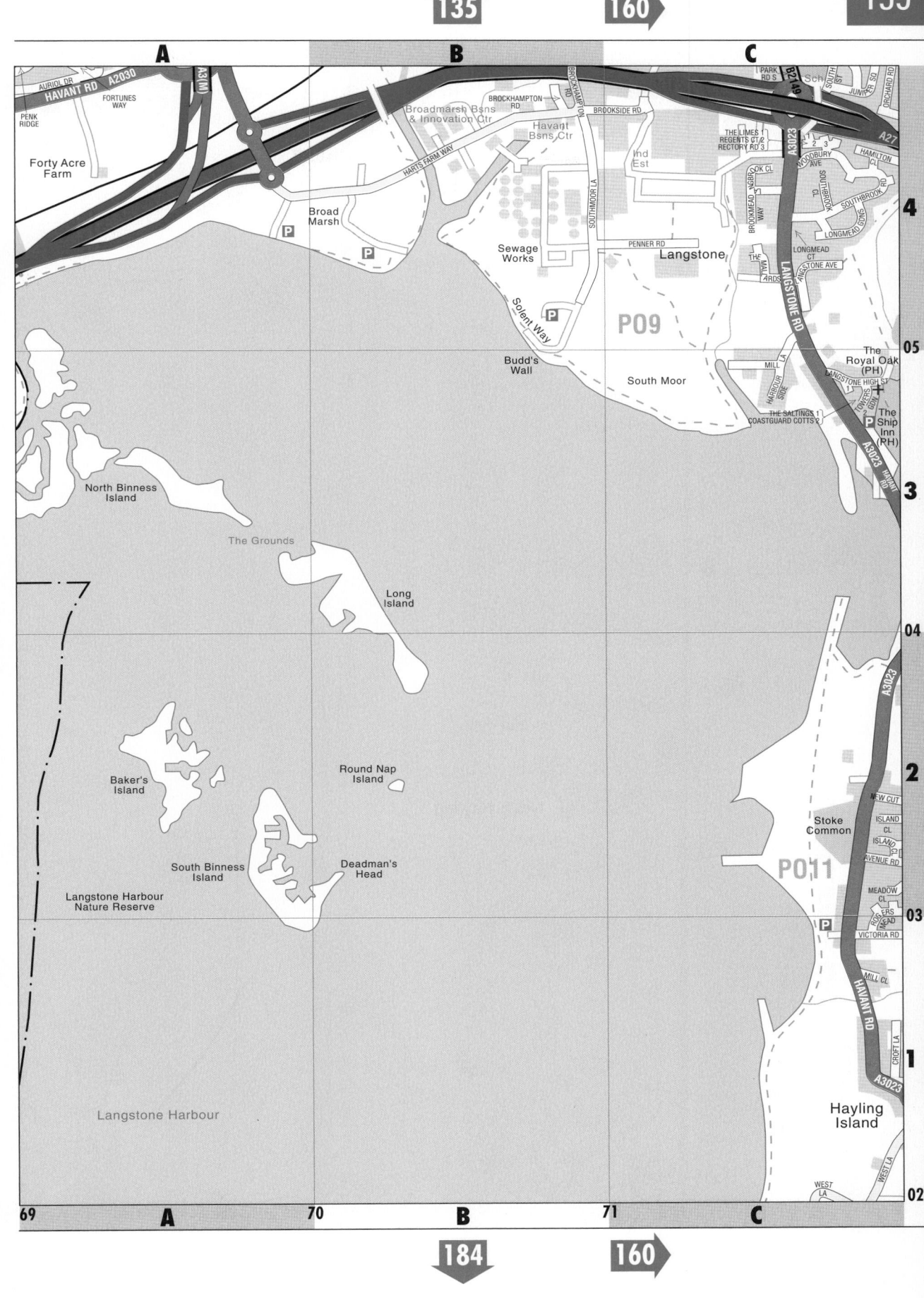

A · B · C

AURIOL DR · HAVANT RD · A2030 · A3 (M)
PENK RIDGE
FORTUNES WAY

Forty Acre Farm

Broadmarsh Bsns & Innovation Ctr
BROCKHAMPTON RD
BROCKHAMPTON
BROOKSIDE RD
Havant Bsns Ctr
PARK RD S
B2149
South
JUNIOR SQ
ORCHARD RD
The Limes
REGENTS CT
RECTORY RD
A27
HAMILTON CL
WOODBURY AVE
A3023
1 2 3
HARTS FARM WAY
SOUTHMOOR LA
Ind Est
BROOKMEAD
CL
SOUTHBROOK
LONGMEAD GDNS
SOUTHBROOK
LONGMEAD AVE

Broad Marsh
P
P

Sewage Works
PENNER RD
Langstone
THE MALLARDS
LONGMEAD CT
LANGSTONE RD
LANGSTONE AVE

4

Solent Way
P
PO9

Budd's Wall
South Moor
MILL
LANGSTONE RD
HARBOUR SIDE
The Royal Oak (PH)
LANGSTONE HIGH ST
05

The Saltings
Coastguard Cotts
TOWERS GDNS
A3023
HAVANT RD
P
The Ship Inn (RH)

North Binness Island

3

The Grounds

Long Island

04

Baker's Island

Round Nap Island

Stoke Common
A3023
NEW CUT
ISLAND CL
ISLAND
AVENUE RD
MEADOW CL
ROGERS MEAD
PO11

2

South Binness Island
Deadman's Head

Langstone Harbour Nature Reserve
VICTORIA RD
P

03

MILL CL
HAVANT RD

Langstone Harbour

CROFT LA
A3023

Hayling Island

1

WEST LA
WEST LA
02

69 · A · 70 · B · 71 · C

A B C

Warblington

PO10

PO9

Wade
Court

ORCHARD
RD

Cemy

Solent Way

Church Path

Wayfarer's Walk

WESTERN
PAR

C4
1 KING'S TERR
2 MEADOW CT
3 CHURCH PATH
4 WARWICK CT
5 OYSTER MEWS
6 ST PETER S SQ
7 FROBISHER GDNS

Swimming
Pool

Conigar Point

Nore Rithe

Fowley Rithe

Fowley
Island

New Cut

Duckard Point

Marina

Langstone
Bridge

Hotel

North
Common

Boating
Lake

Sweare Deep

Wickor
Point

Northney

Spinnaker Grange

NORTHNEY RD

NORTHNEY LA

CLOVELLY RD

North Hayling

PYCROFT CL

PO11

CHURCH LA

Church
Farm

ST PETER'S AVE

Thorney
Island

Emsworth Channel

Victoria Rd

THORNEY
VIEW

Northwood
Farm

Upper Tye
Farm

CHICHESTER RD

Tye

GUTNER LA

Marker Point

Northwood
Farm

NORTHWOOD LA

WEST LA

Stoke

Finchwood Farm
Ind Units

CORSE LA

WOODGASTON LA

Gutner
Farm

HAVANT RD

A3023

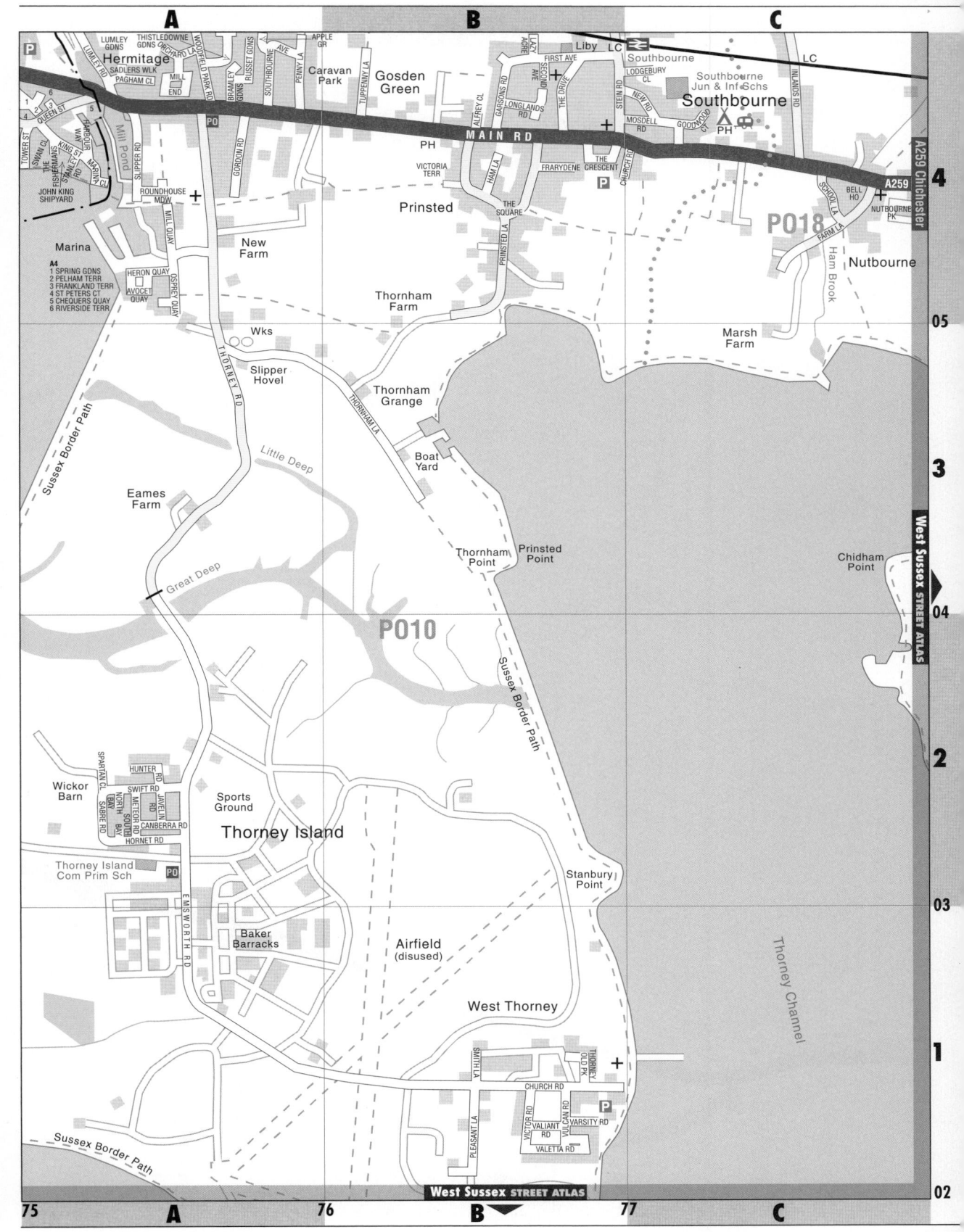

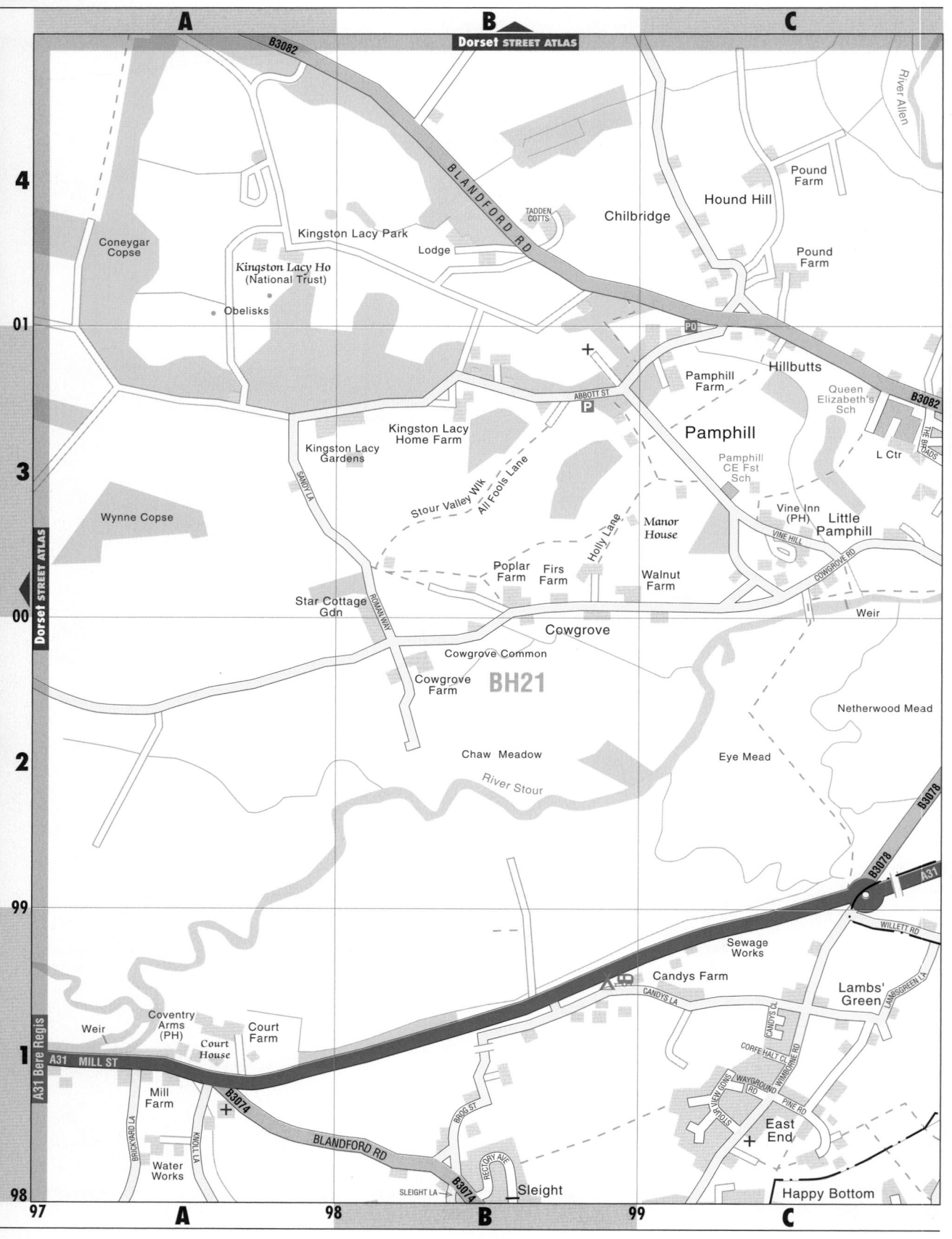

B3082

4

Coneygar
Copse

Kingston Lacy Park

Lodge

Kingston Lacy Ho
(National Trust)

Obelisks

01

Kingston Lacy Home Farm

Kingston Lacy
Gardens

3

Wynne Copse

SANDY LA

Stour Valley Wlk

All Fools Lane

BLANDFORD RD

TADDEN
COTTS

Chilbridge

ABBOTT ST

P

Pamphill
Farm

Pamphill

Pamphill
CE Fst
Sch

Hound Hill

Pound
Farm

Pound
Farm

PO

Hillbutts

Queen
Elizabeth's
Sch

B3082

L Ctr

THE BROADS

Vine Inn
(PH)

Little
Pamphill

VINE HILL

COWGROVE RD

Holly Lane

Manor
House

Walnut
Farm

Weir

00

Star Cottage
Gdn

ROMAN WAY

Poplar
Farm

Firs
Farm

Cowgrove

Cowgrove Common

Cowgrove
Farm

BH21

Netherwood Mead

Eye Mead

2

Chaw Meadow

River Stour

B3078

99

Sewage
Works

B3078

A31

WILLETT RD

Candys Farm

CANDYS LA

Lambs'
Green

LAMBSGREEN LA

A31 Bere Regis

Weir

Coventry
Arms
(PH)

Court
House

Court
Farm

CANDYS CL

CORFE HALT CL

WIMBORNE RD

1

MILL ST

A31

B3074

BROG ST

Mill
Farm

STOUR VIEW GDNS

WAYGROUND RD

PINE RD

East
End

BRICKYARD LA

KNOLL LA

Water
Works

BLANDFORD RD

B3074

RECTORY AVE

SLEIGHT LA

Sleight

Happy Bottom

98

97   A   98   B   99   C

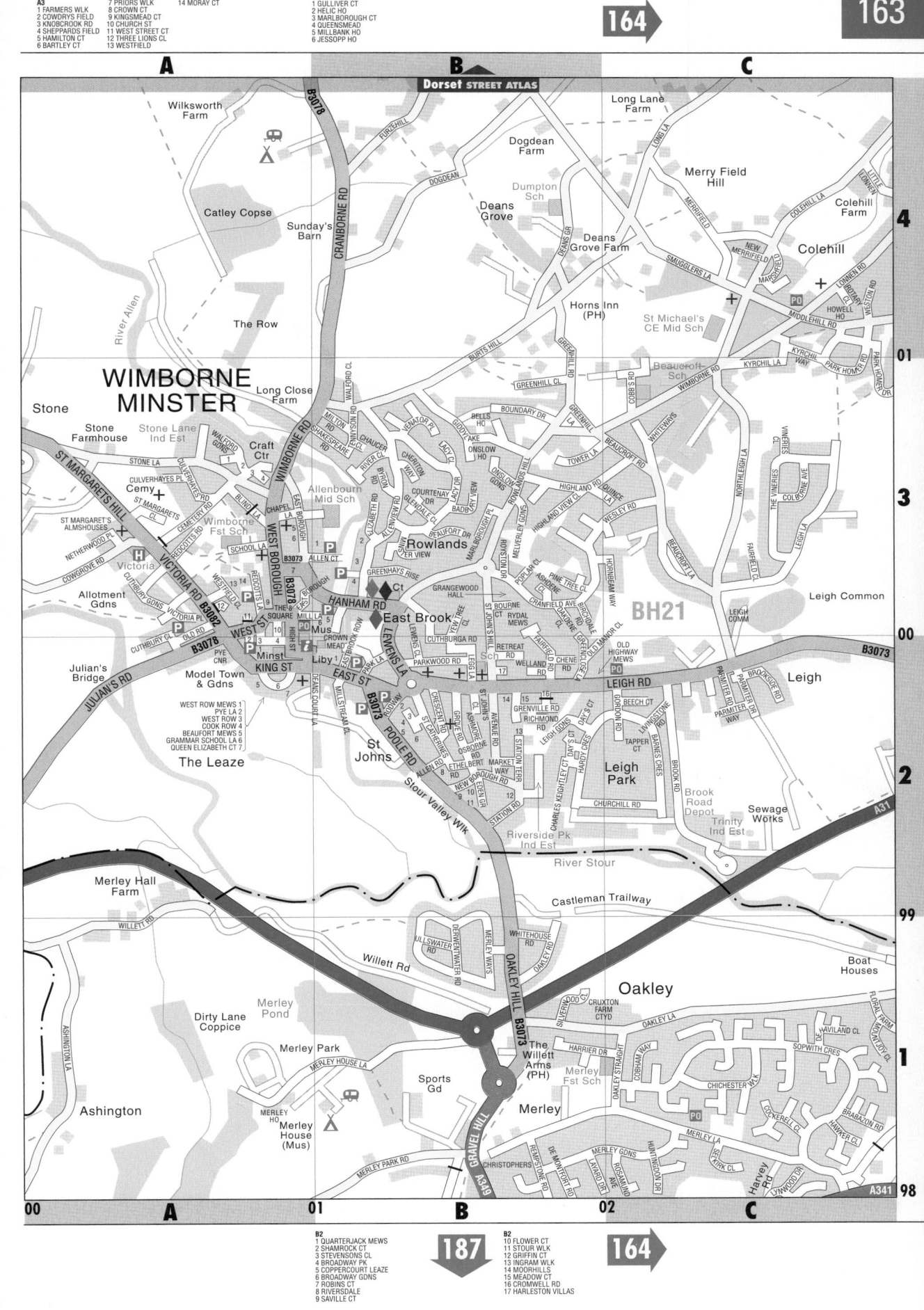

Dorset STREET ATLAS

WIMBORNE MINSTER

Wilksworth Farm

Catley Copse

Sunday's Barn

The Row

Stone

Stone Farmhouse

Stone Lane Ind Est

Craft Ctr

Long Close Farm

River Allen

St Margaret's Almshouses

Allotment Gdns

Victoria

Julian's Bridge

Julian's Rd

Model Town & Gdns

The Leaze

St Johns

Merley Hall Farm

Willett Rd

Ashington

Dirty Lane Coppice

Merley Pond

Merley Park

Merley House (Mus)

Sports Gd

Merley

Wilksworth Farm

Dogdean Farm

Dumpton Sch

Deans Grove

Deans Grove Farm

Horns Inn (PH)

St Michael's CE Mid Sch

Long Lane Farm

Merry Field Hill

Colehill

Colehill Farm

New Merrifield

Beaucroft Sch

Rowlands

East Brook

Grangewood Hall

BH21

Leigh Common

Leigh

Leigh Park

Brook Road Depot

Trinity Ind Est

Sewage Works

Riverside Pk Ind Est

River Stour

Castleman Trailway

Oakley

Boat Houses

The Willett Arms (PH)

Merley Fst Sch

A31

A341

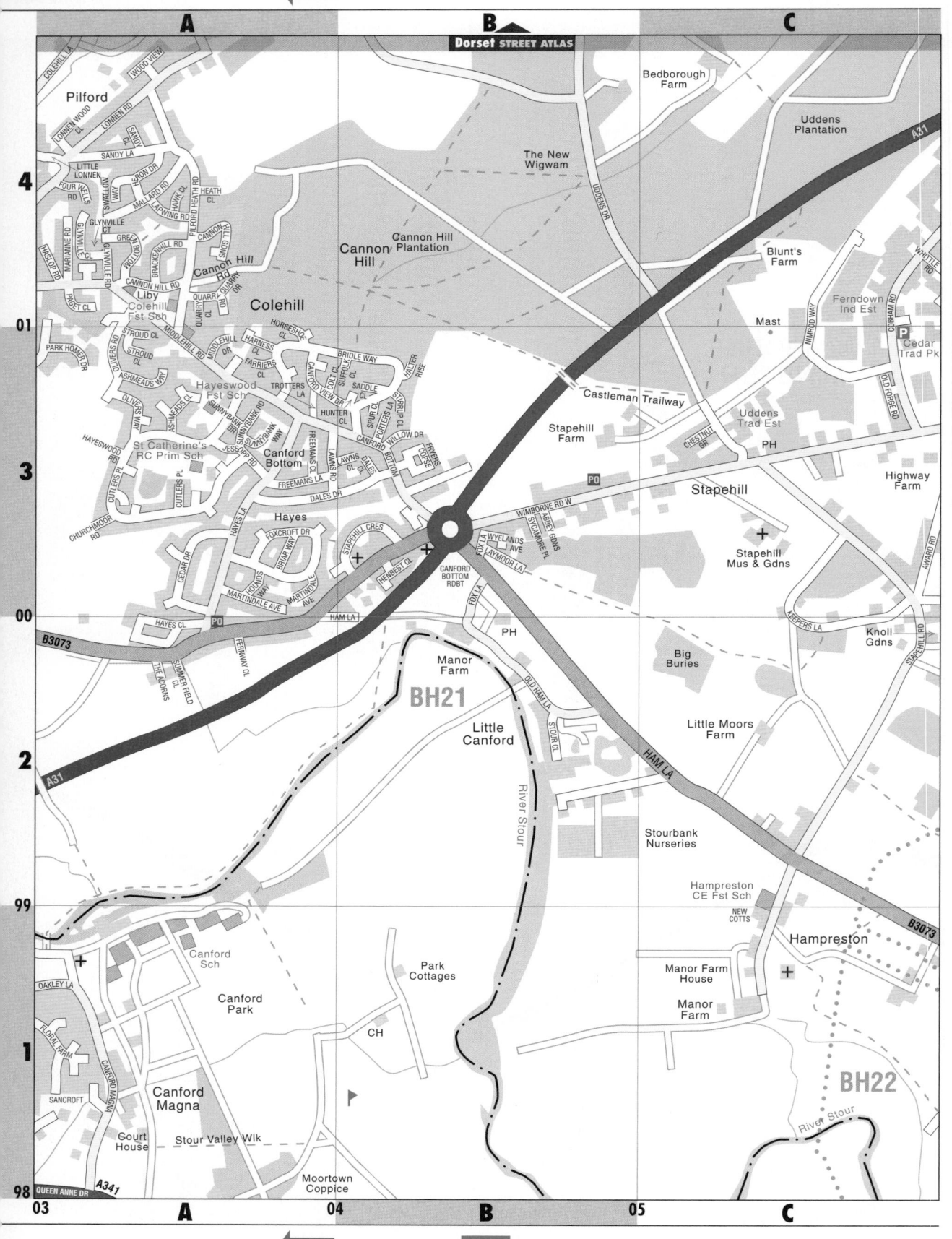

A   **B**   **C**

A31

Uddens Plantation

B3072

Uddens Water   Cemy

4

COBHAM RD   JOHNSON RD   LANCASTER RD   LINDBERGH RD   MITCHELL RD   TELFORD RD   HAVILAND RD   WHITTLE RD

Ferndown Ind Est

LEESON DR   KINGSWAY   STONECHAT CL   BUNTING CL   SISKIN CL   KESTREL   CURLEW CL   BRACKEN RD   CLAYFORD AVE   COPPICE AVE   WARREN WLK   RED OAKS CL   HILLTOP CL   HILLTOP RD

PINE GLEN AVE   PRUNUS CL   PRUNUS DR   LARKS RISE   LARKS CL   HILLVEN   THE LAURELS   ELFIN DR

JUNIPER   REDWOOD DR   SCAR WAY   KINGSWAY   HILLCREST AVE   LARCH WAY   WILLOW WAY   PINE CL   RYAN CL   RYAN GDNS   CLIVEDEN AVE   BEAUFOYS AVE   BEAUFOYS CT   WIMBORNE RD E

HAZEL DR   ROBINSWOOD DR   QUEENS RD   QUEENSDOWN DR   FEATHER DR   HIGH TREES WLK   LYNWOOD   PINEWOOD GDNS

EVERGLADES   WEST MOORS RD   MARTINS DR   MARTINS CL   MARTINS WAY   STEWARTS WAY   GARDEN WLK   WOODLAND WLK   BADGERS WLK   WHINCROFT CL   WHINCROFT DR

GLADELANDS MOBILE HOME PK   Superstore   Motel   Trickett's Cross   A347

B3072   A31

WOODLAND   LYNX   FORD CL   TURBARY RD   TURBARY CT   PICKARD   AMEYS LA   TRICKETTS LA   LOOKERS RD   DUDDELL CL   GLENEAGLES CL   GREENSOME DR   FAIRWAYS

01

PH   Ferndown Upper Sch   Sports Ctr   Playing Field   **Ferndown**

STANFIELD RD   CASTER CL   CHERRY GR   MAYFIELD CL   MAYFIELD DR   WESTWOOD AVE   SOUTHWK   PENROSE RD

BRAMLEY CT   BRAMLEY RD   MAFIELD CT   RUSSEL CT   VICTORIA RD   VICTORIA GDNS   PRINCES   GLENDALE AVE   EASTWOOD AVE   WICKHAM RD   WOODSIDE RD   GREENWOOD AVE

SUMMERLANDS 1   MOORHAVEN 2   SUNRISE CT 3   SHELLEY CT 4   BYRON CT 5   SPINNEY'S LA 6

PETER GRANT WAY   OLD SCHOOL   ALBERT RD   MILTON CT   LIBRARY RD   MANOR CT   HOMELANDS HO   BROOMHILL   APPLE TREE GR   PRINGLES DR

Ferndown Mid Sch   Ferndown Fst Sch   **BH22**   MOUNTBATTEN DR   ST MARY'S RD   HIGH BROW   Liby   PO   B3072   A347   ORCHARD CL   CARROLL AVE   PENNY'S CT

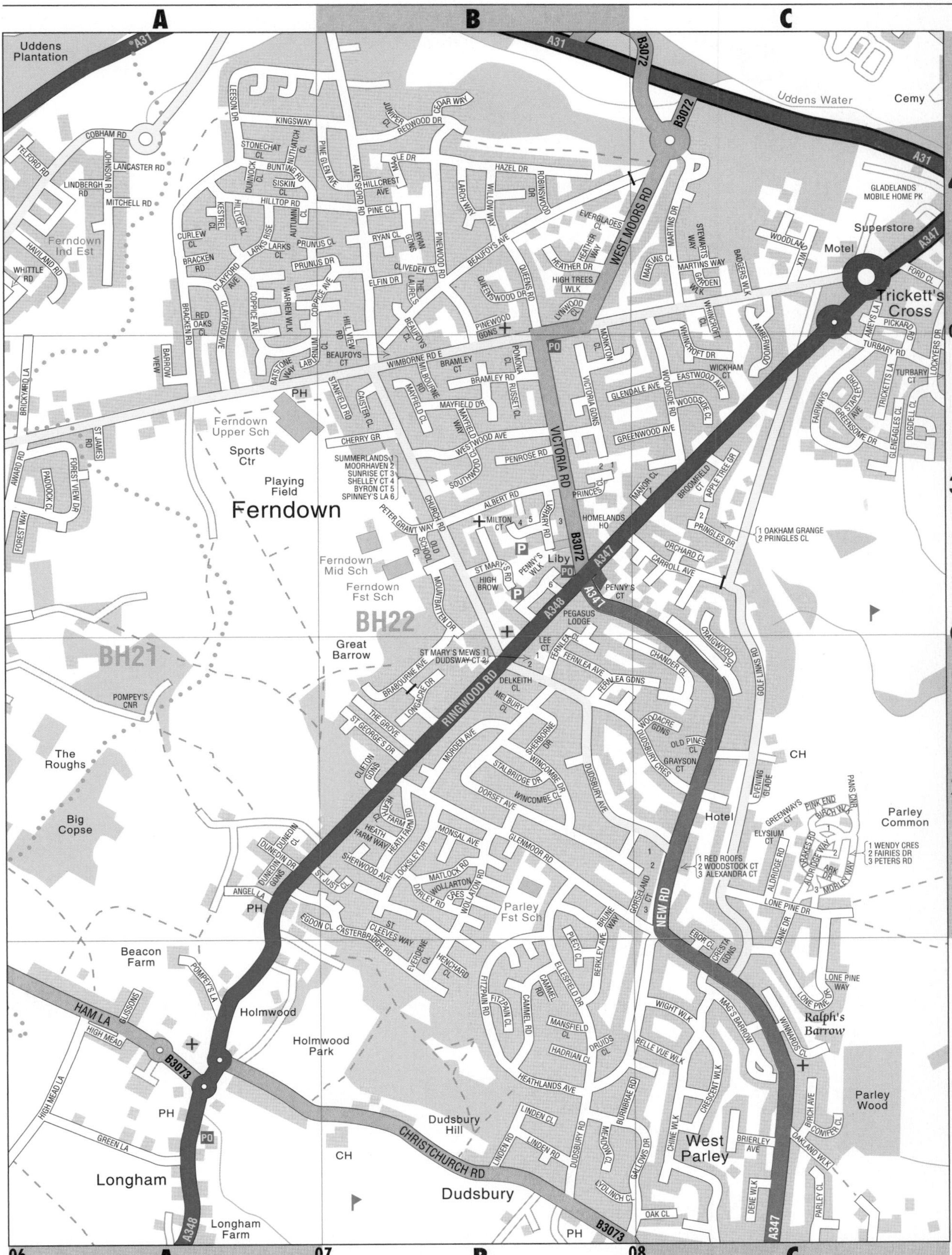

1 OAKHAM GRANGE   2 PRINGLES CL

3

Great Barrow   **BH21**   POMPEY'S CNR

The Roughs   Big Copse

ST MARY'S MEWS 1   DUDSWAY CT 2   BRABOURNE CL   LONGACRE DR   THE GROVE   ST GEORGE'S DR   CLIFTON GDNS   MORDEN AVE   WINCOMBE DR   SHERBORNE DR   STALBRIDGE DR   DORSET AVE   WINCOMBE CL

RINGWOOD RD   A348   PEGASUS LODGE   LEE CT   FERNLEA CT   FERNLEA AVE   FERNLEA GDNS   CHANDLER CL   DELKEITH CL   MELBURY CL   WOODACRE GDNS   DUDSBURY CRES   OLD PINES CL   GRAYSON CT   GOLF LINKS RD

CH   Hotel   Parley Common   PANS DNR   BIRCH WAY   PINK END   GREENWAYS CT   STAKES RD   ELYSIUM CT   EVENING GLADE   MORLEY WAY

1 WENDY CRES   2 FAIRIES DR   3 PETERS RD

2

HEATH FARM WAY   NEW FARM RD   OLD FARM RD   HEATHLAND   DUNEDIN DR   DUNEDIN CL   DUNEDIN GDNS   ANGEL LA   PH   ST JUST CL

SHERWOOD AVE   LOCKSLEY DR   MONSAL AVE   MATLOCK RD   GLENMOOR RD   WOLLARTON RD   DARLEY RD   CPES   Parley Fst Sch

WOODSTOCK   1 RED ROOFS   2 WOODSTOCK CT   3 ALEXANDRA CT

NEW RD   A347   GORSELAND   ALDRIDGE RD   LONE PINE DR   Hotel

Beacon Farm   HAM LA   GLISSONS   HIGH MEAD   POMPEY'S LA   B3073   Holmwood   Holmwood Park

ST CLEEVES WAY   CASTERBRIDGE RD   EGDON CL   EVERHENE   HENCHARD CL   FITZMAN RD   FITZPAIN CL   BELLE VUE WLK   BERKLEY AVE   PELCY CL   CAMMEL RD   ELLESFIELD DR   DRUIDS CL   HADRIAN CL   MANSFIELD RD

BRUNE DR   MAG'S BARROW   WIGHT WLK   WINWARDS CL   LONE PINE WAY   DANE DR   EBOR RD   CRESTA GDNS   Ralph's Barrow   LONE PINE

99

HIGH MEAD LA   GREEN LA   PH   PO   **Longham**   Longham Farm   A348

Dudsbury Hill   CH   CHRISTCHURCH RD   **Dudsbury**   B3073   PH

LINDEN CL   LINDEN RD   MEADOW CL   DUDSBURY RD   BUTTERNE RD   CHINE WLK   CRESCENT WLK   LYDLINCH CL   GALTONS CL   OAK CL   DENE WLK

West Parley   Parley Wood   BIRCH AVE   BRIERLEY AVE   PARLEY CL   OAKLAND WLK   COMPER CL   A347

1

98

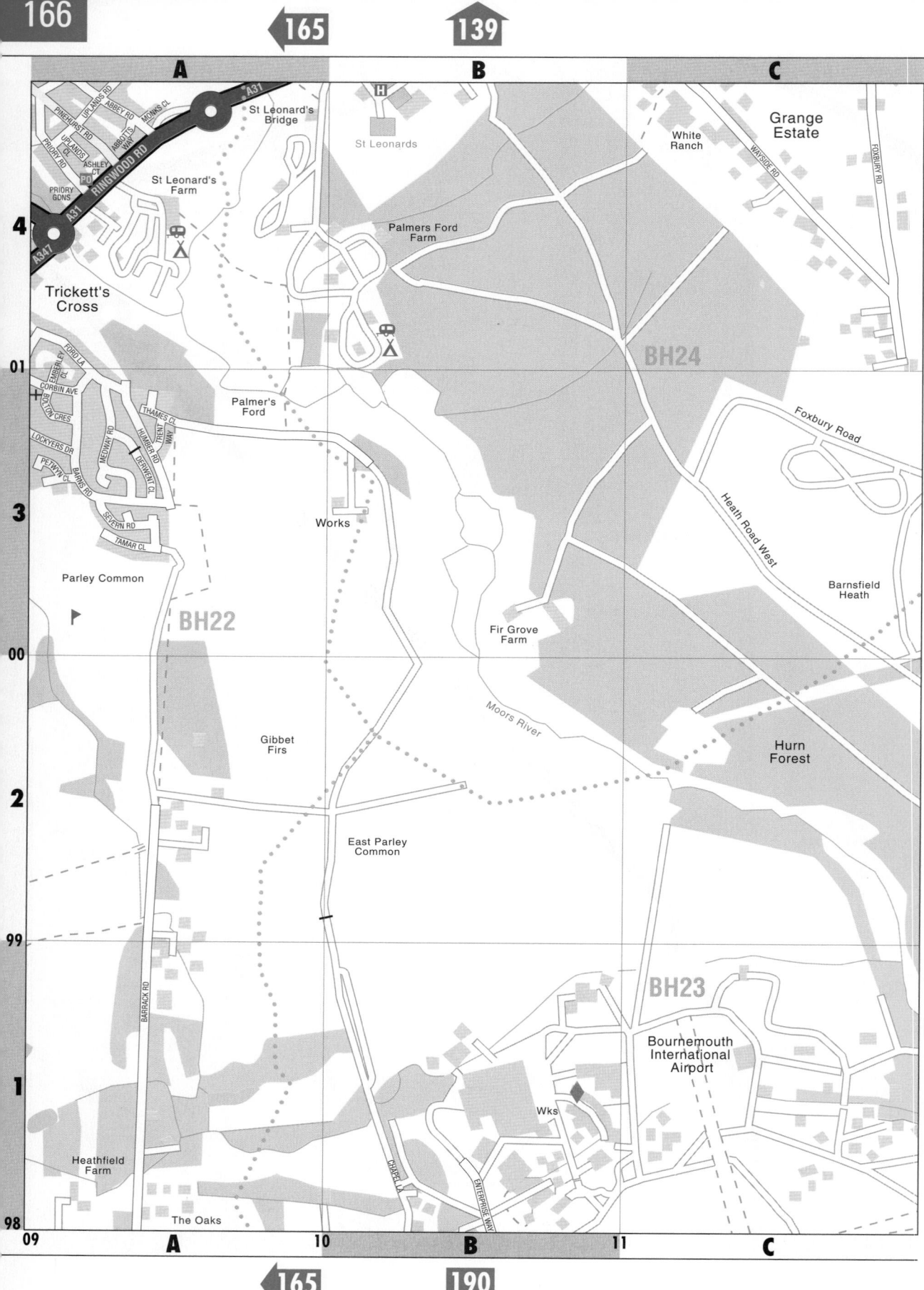

165
139
165
190

A31
St Leonard's Bridge
H
St Leonards
White Ranch
Grange Estate
WAYSIDE RD
FOXBURY RD
PINEHURST RD
UPLANDS RD
ABBEY RD
MEONS CL
ABBOTS WAY
UPLANDS CL
ASHLEY CT
PRIORY RD
PO
RINGWOOD RD
St Leonard's Farm
Palmers Ford Farm
PRIORY GDNS
A31
A347
4
Trickett's Cross
BH24
01
EMBERLEY CL
CORBIN AVE
BOLTON CRES
FORD LA
THAMES CL
MEDWAY RD
HUMBER RD
TRENT RD
TRENT WAY
DERWENT CL
Palmer's Ford
Foxbury Road
LOCKYERS DR
BAINS RD
PETWYN CL
SEVERN RD
TAMAR CL
Works
Heath Road West
3
Barnsfield Heath
Parley Common
BH22
Fir Grove Farm
00
Moors River
Gibbet Firs
Hurn Forest
2
East Parley Common
99
BH23
BARRACK RD
Bournemouth International Airport
1
Wks
Heathfield Farm
CHAPEL LA
ENTERPRISE WAY
98
The Oaks

09
A
10
B
11
C

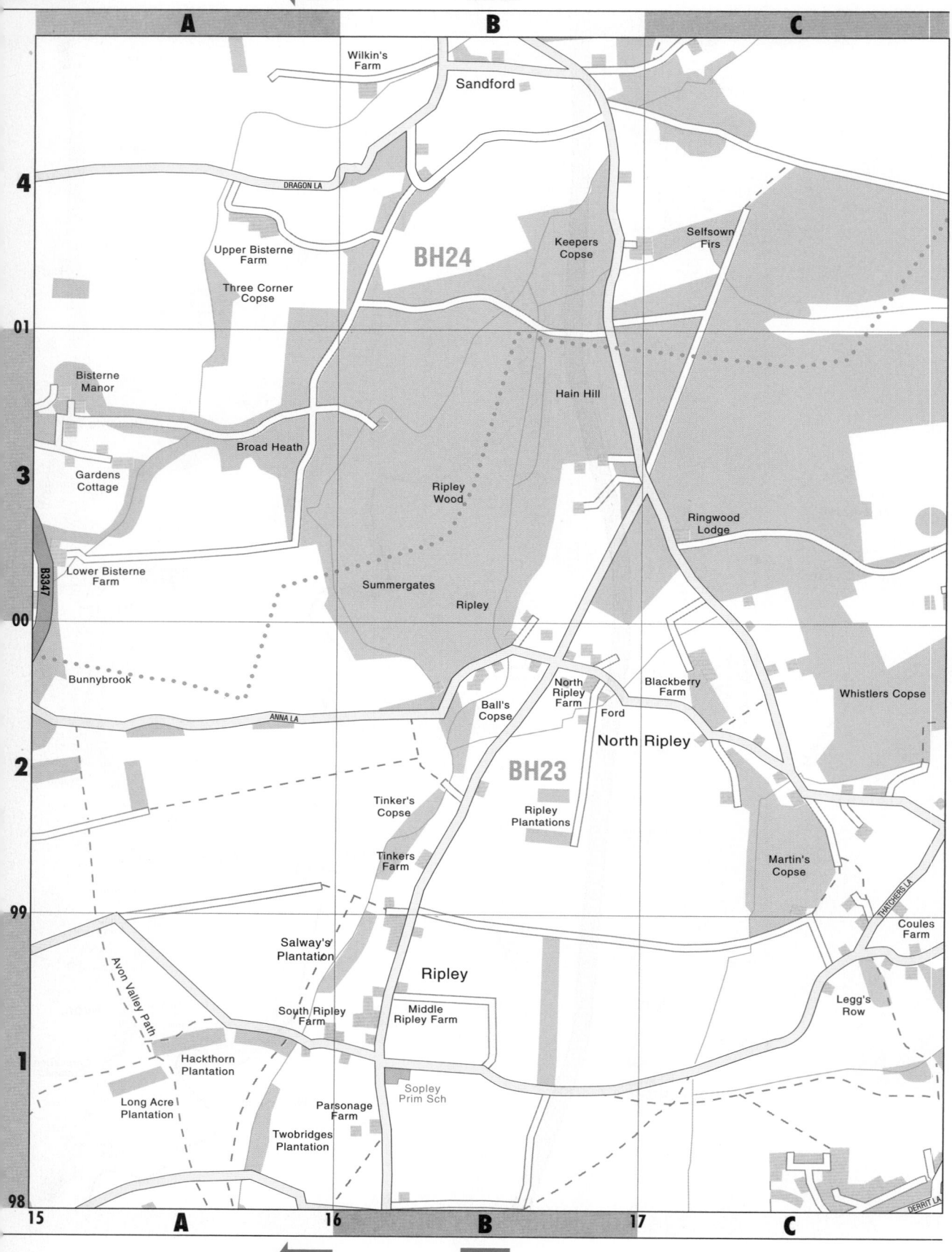

A   B   C

Wilkin's
Farm

Sandford

DRAGON LA

4

BH24

Keepers
Copse

Selfsown
Firs

Upper Bisterne
Farm

Three Corner
Copse

01

Bisterne
Manor

Hain Hill

Broad Heath

3

Gardens
Cottage

Ripley
Wood

Ringwood
Lodge

B3347

Lower Bisterne
Farm

Summergates

Ripley

00

Bunnybrook

ANNA LA

North
Ripley
Farm

Blackberry
Farm

Whistlers Copse

Ball's
Copse

Ford

North Ripley

2

BH23

Tinker's
Copse

Ripley
Plantations

Martin's
Copse

THATCHERS LA

Tinkers
Farm

99

Coules
Farm

Avon Valley Path

Salway's
Plantation

Ripley

Legg's
Row

South Ripley
Farm

Middle
Ripley Farm

1

Hackthorn
Plantation

Sopley
Prim Sch

Long Acre
Plantation

Parsonage
Farm

Twobridges
Plantation

DERRIT LA

98

15   A   16   B   17   C

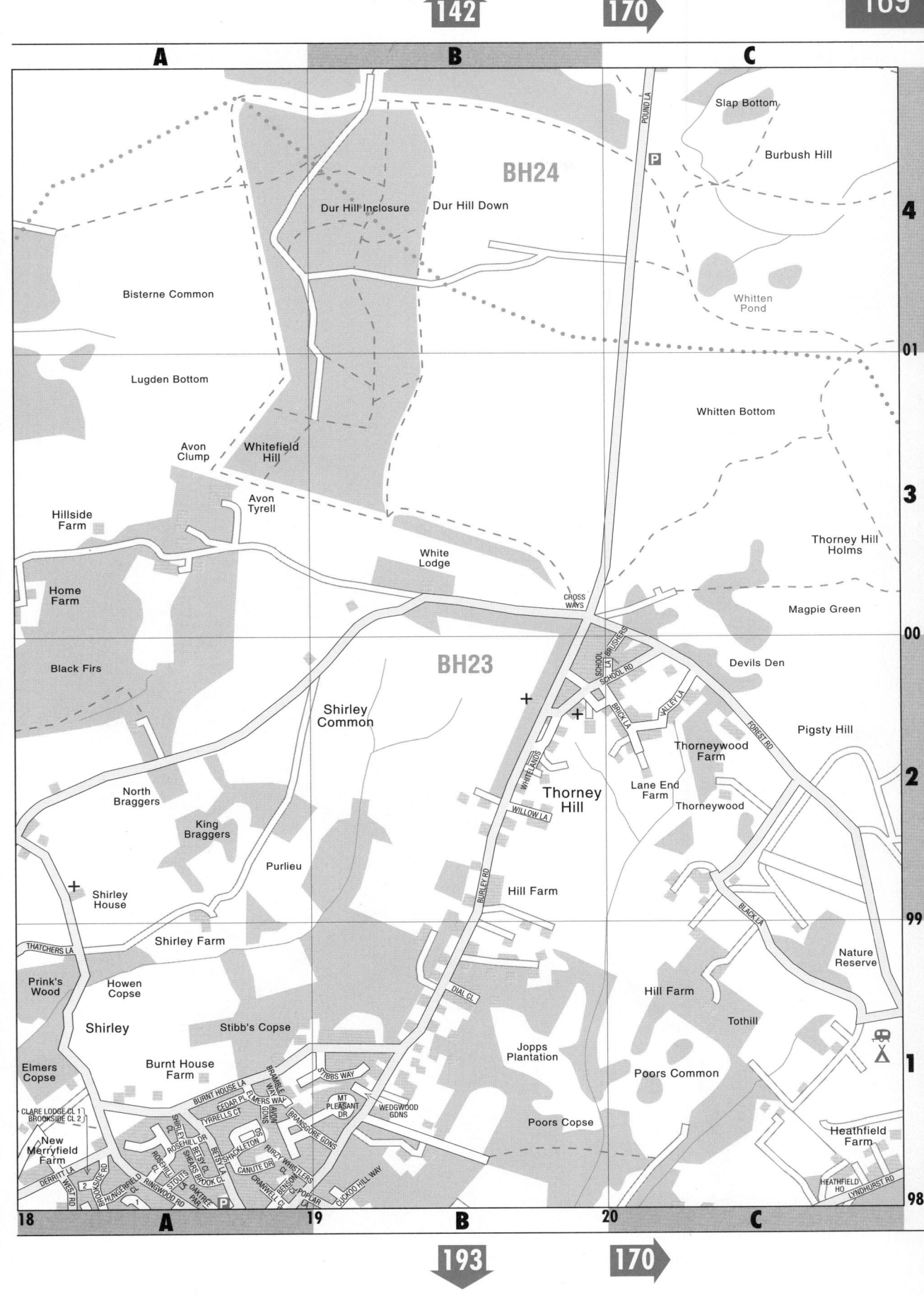

169
143

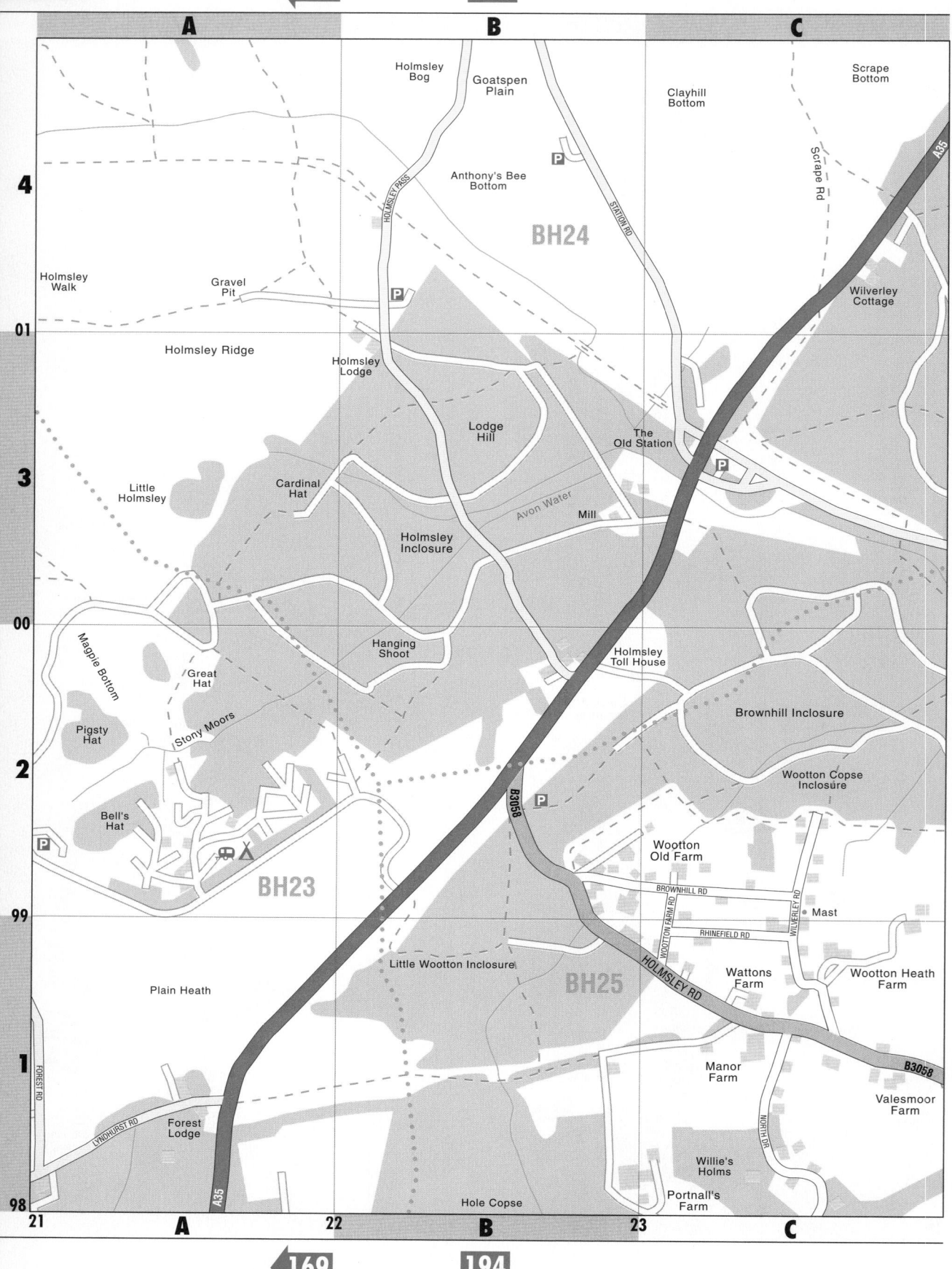

A B C

169
194

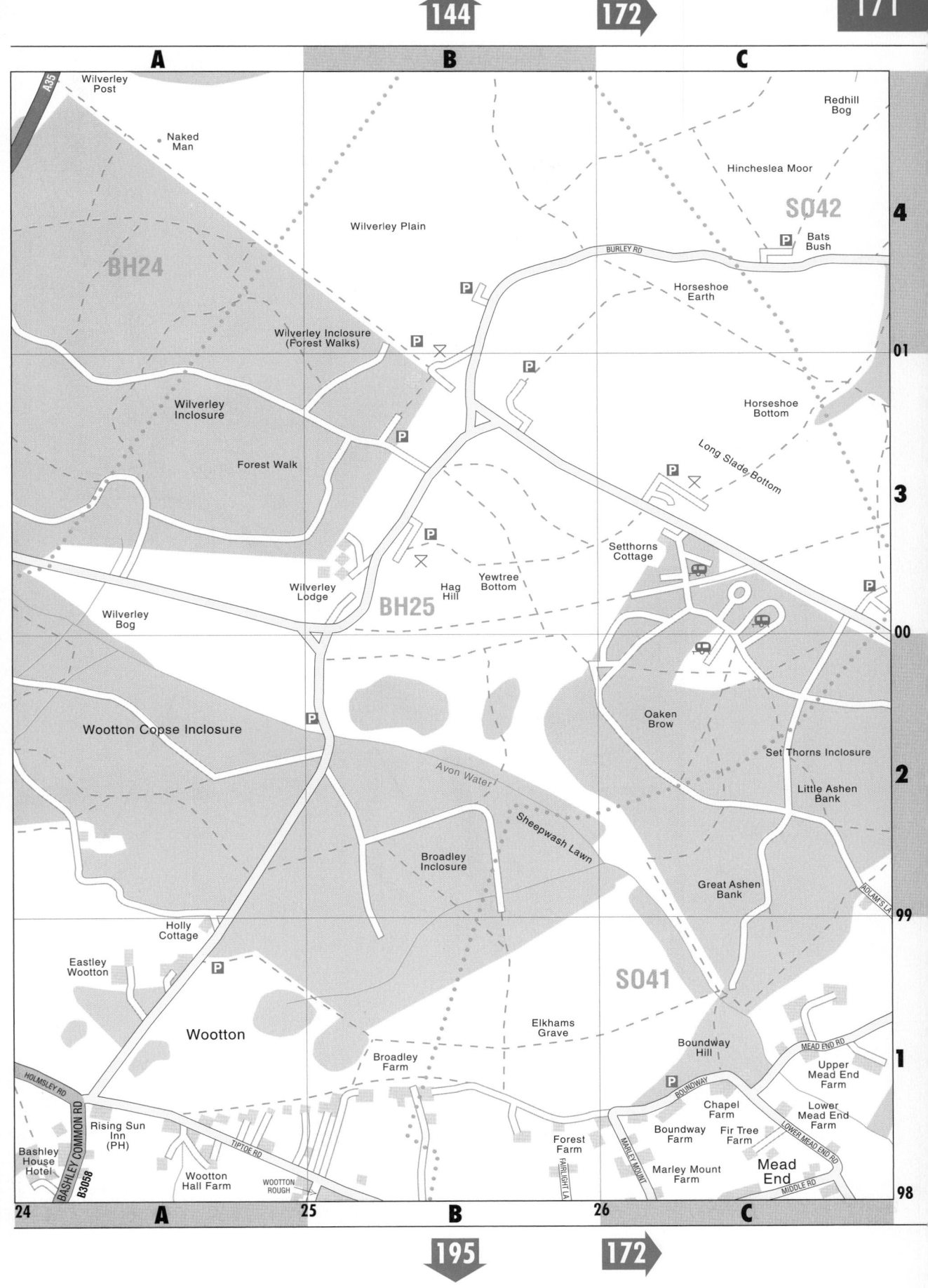

Wilverley Post

Naked Man

Wilverley Plain

BH24

Wilverley Inclosure
(Forest Walks)

Wilverley Inclosure

Forest Walk

Wilverley Lodge

Wilverley Bog

BH25

Hag Hill

Yewtree Bottom

Wootton Copse Inclosure

Avon Water

Broadley Inclosure

Sheepwash Lawn

Holly Cottage

Eastley Wootton

Wootton

Bashley House Hotel

Rising Sun Inn (PH)

B3058

HOLMSLEY RD

BASHLEY COMMON RD

TIPTOE RD

Wootton Hall Farm

WOOTTON ROUGH

Broadley Farm

Elkhams Grave

Forest Farm

FAIRLIGHT LA

SO41

Marley Mount Farm

MARLEY MOUNT

Boundway Farm

Chapel Farm

Fir Tree Farm

Boundway Hill

Boundway

MEAD END RD

Upper Mead End Farm

Lower Mead End Farm

Mead End

MIDDLE RD

LOWER MEAD END RD

Redhill Bog

Hincheslea Moor

SO42

Bats Bush

BURLEY RD

Horseshoe Earth

Horseshoe Bottom

Long Slade Bottom

Setthorns Cottage

Oaken Brow

Set Thorns Inclosure

Little Ashen Bank

Great Ashen Bank

ADLAM'S LA

171
145

A   B   C

White Moor

Furzey Cottage

Pound Farm

Brockenhurst CE Prim Sch

Brookley Farm

RAILWAY TERR 1
AVENUE RD 2

PARTRIDGE RD

HIGHWOOD RD

Highwood PRU

TATTENHAM RD

THE LAURELS

Five Thorns Hill

Furzy Hill

South Weirs

ADDISON RD

BURLEY RD

SOUTH WEIRS

COLLYERS RD

WOODLANDS RD

SWAY RD

B3055

4

Worthys Farmhouse

Westbeams Stables

Brokenhurst Copse

01

Trenley Lawn

Farm Cottage

SO42

Blackhamsley House

CH

Brokenhurst Manor Golf Club

Hincheslea Wood

Lymington Junction

TILEBARN LA

3

Hincheslea Bog

BH25

Cater's Cottage

Latchmoor House

Blackhamsley Hill

B3055

Setley Plain

00

Three Beech Bottom

Milking Pound Bottom

2

Cemy

QUARR HO

Widden Bottom

SO41

BUILDOWNE WLK

MANCHESTER RD

FOREST EDGE CL

BRIGHTON RD

ISLAND VIEW

BOND CL

JORDANS LA

99

OAKENBROW

GILPIN HILL

RUNNERS CL

LITTLE BURN

HIGH CL

DURRANT WAY

OXFORD TERR

HIGHFIELD GDNS

THE CLOSE

HAWTHORN CL

ASHFORD RISE

MIDDLE RD

WIDDEN CL

NORMANDY CL

STANLEY RD

ANDERWOOD DR

DURNSTOWN

ST JAMES CL

Durns Town

ADAM'S LA

CRUSE CL

HYDE CL

BADGERS CL

CENTENARY CL

SET THORNS RD

PH

BACK LA

SHIRLEY HOLMS

MEAD END RD

HERON CL

St Luke's CE Prim Sch

WESTBEAMS RD

CAPTAL CL

PITMORE LA

1

Rushcroft Farm

Hotel

STATION RD

ROWAN CL

CHURCH LA

BIRCHY HILL

COOMBE LA

CHAPEL LA

Little Purley Farm

Hilltop

Sway

P.O.

Sway Park Ind Est

HOLLIES CL

JUBILEE CL

TEBOURBA COTTS

B3055

OLD VICARAGE LA

Manor Farm

Eastwoods

98

27   A   28   B   29   C

171
196

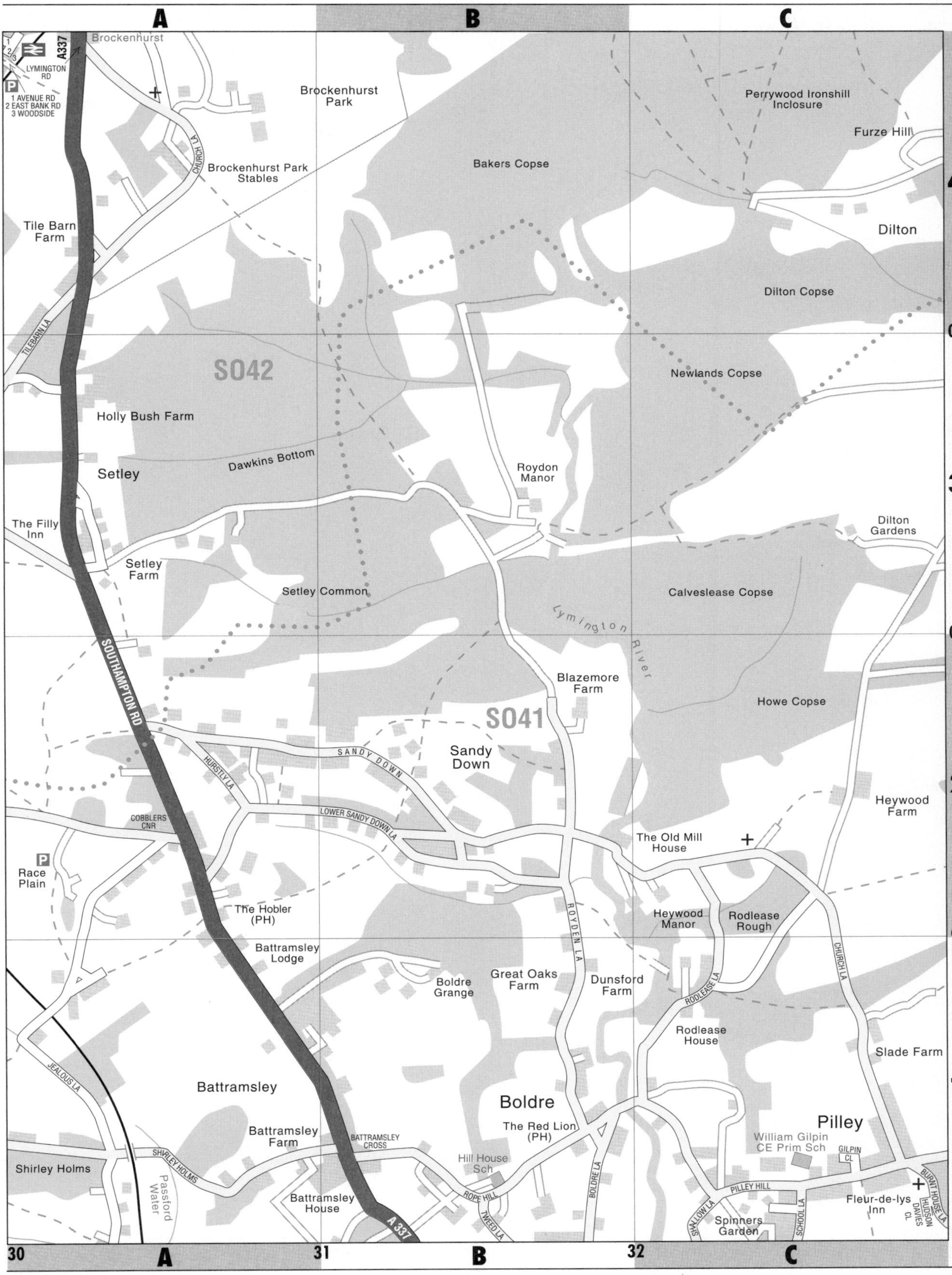

A   B   C

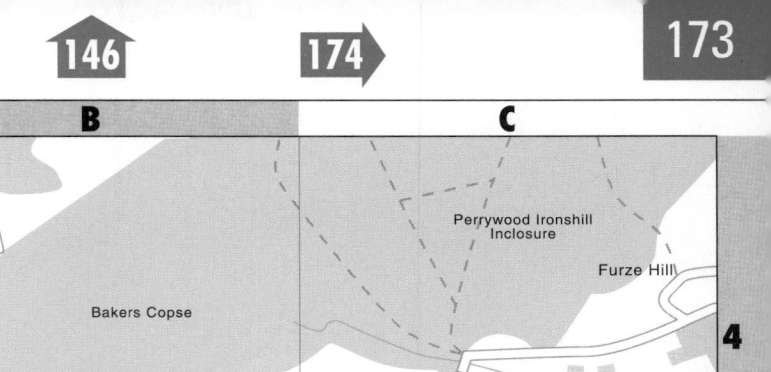

Brockenhurst

A337

LYMINGTON RD

P
1 AVENUE RD
2 EAST BANK RD
3 WOODSIDE

Brockenhurst
Park

Brockenhurst Park
Stables

CHURCH LA

Tile Barn
Farm

Perrywood Ironshill
Inclosure

Bakers Copse

Furze Hill

4

Dilton

TILEBARN LA

Dilton Copse

01

SO42

Newlands Copse

Holly Bush Farm

Dawkins Bottom

Roydon
Manor

3

Setley

Dilton
Gardens

The Filly
Inn

SOUTHAMPTON RD

Setley
Farm

Setley Common

Calveslease Copse

Lymington River

00

Blazemore
Farm

Howe Copse

SO41

HURSTLY LA

SANDY DOWN

Sandy
Down

COBBLERS
CNR

LOWER SANDY DOWN LA

Heywood
Farm

2

P
Race
Plain

The Old Mill
House

ROYDEN LA

The Hobler
(PH)

Heywood
Manor

Rodlease
Rough

RODLEASE LA

CHURCH LA

99

Battramsley
Lodge

Boldre
Grange

Great Oaks
Farm

Dunsford
Farm

Rodlease
House

Slade Farm

JEALOUS LA

Battramsley

Boldre

Pilley

1

SHIRLEY HOLMS

Battramsley
Farm

The Red Lion
(PH)

William Gilpin
CE Prim Sch

GILPIN
CL

BURNT HOUSE LA

HUDSON DAVIES CL

Shirley Holms

Passford
Water

Battramsley
House

BATTRAMSLEY
CROSS

A337

Hill House
Sch

ROPE HILL

TWEED LA

BOLDRE LA

PILLEY HILL

SHALLOW LA

SCHOOL LA

Spinners
Garden

Fleur-de-lys
Inn

98

30   A   31   B   32   C

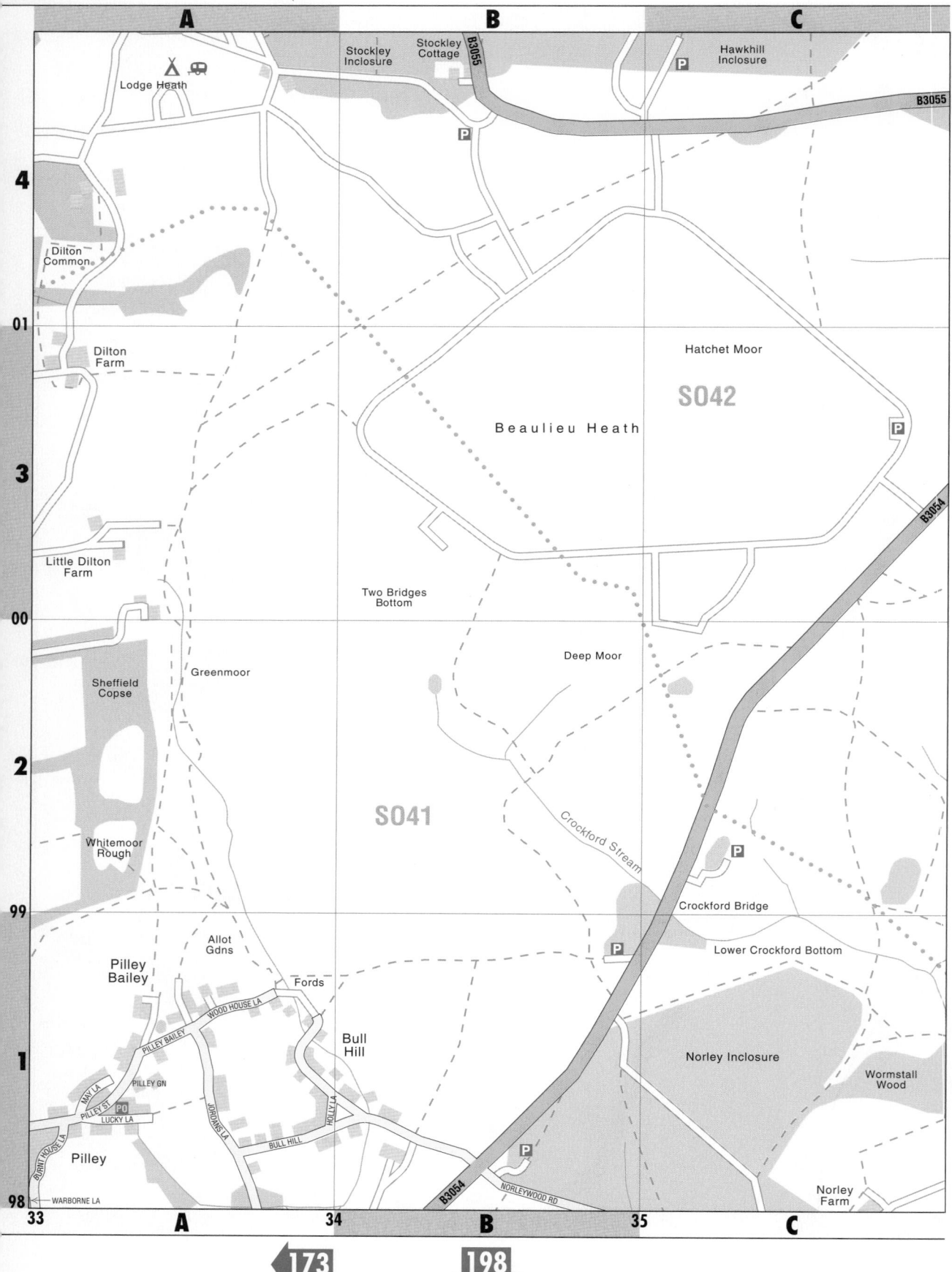

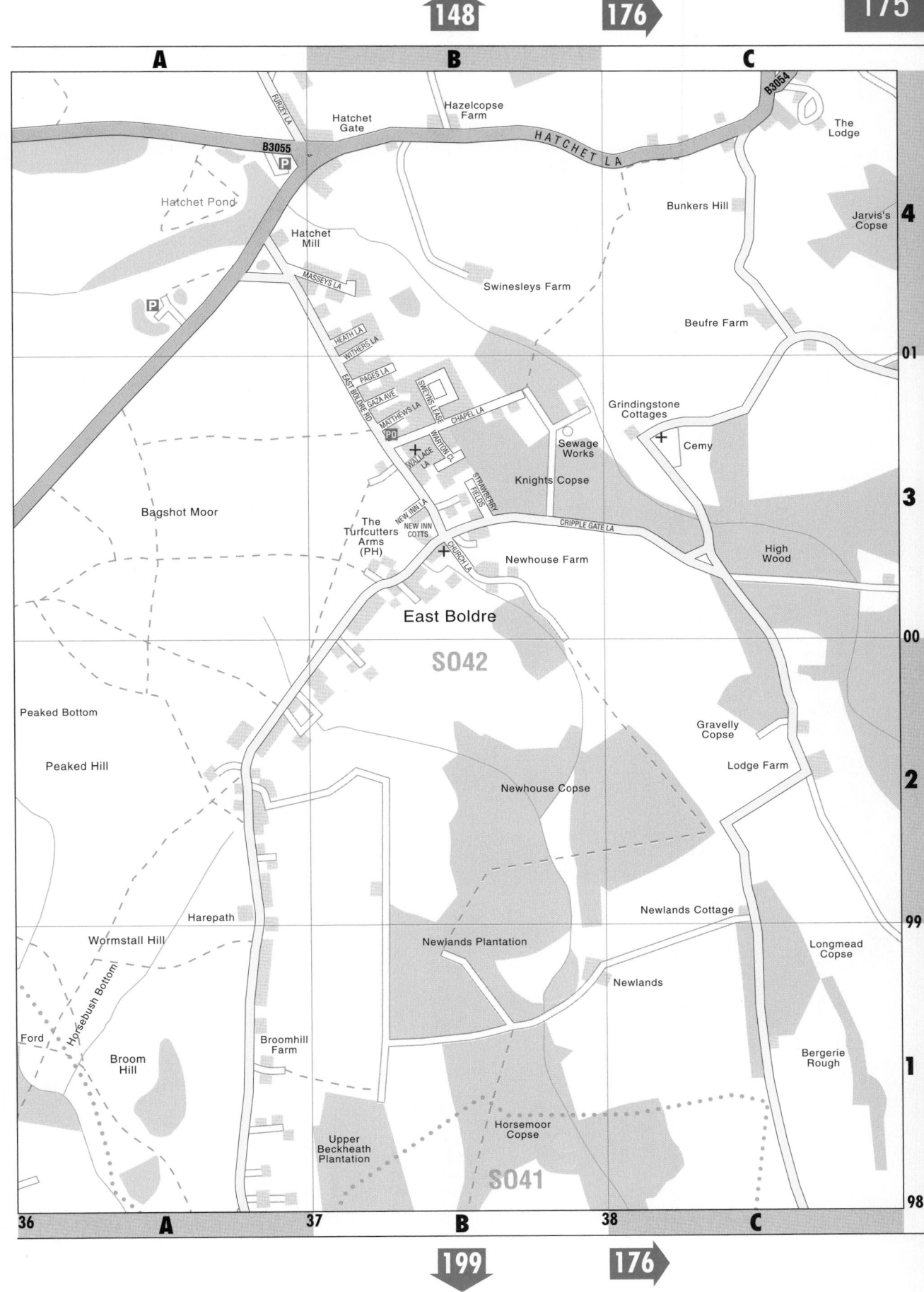

A B C

FIRZEY LA
Hatchet Gate
Hazelcopse Farm
HATCHET LA
B3055
P
B3054
The Lodge
Hatchet Pond
Bunkers Hill
Jarvis's Copse
4
Hatchet Mill
MASSEYS LA
Swinesleys Farm
Beufre Farm
P
HEATH LA
WITHERS LA
PAGES LA
GAZA AVE
EAST BOLDRE RD
MATTHEWS LA
SWEINS EASE
CHAPEL LA
Grindingstone Cottages
01
Cemy
Sewage Works
Bagshot Moor
PO
WALLACE LA
WHARTON CL
Knights Copse
3
NEW INN LA
STRAWBERRY FIELDS
CRIPPLE GATE LA
High Wood
The Turfcutters Arms (PH)
NEW INN COTTS
CHURCH LA
Newhouse Farm
East Boldre
SO42
00
Peaked Bottom
Gravelly Copse
Peaked Hill
Lodge Farm
2
Newhouse Copse
Harepath
Newlands Cottage
99
Wormstall Hill
Newlands Plantation
Longmead Copse
Horsebush Bottom
Newlands
Ford
Broom Hill
Broomhill Farm
Bergerie Rough
1
Upper Beckheath Plantation
Horsemoor Copse
SO41
98

36 A 37 B 38 C

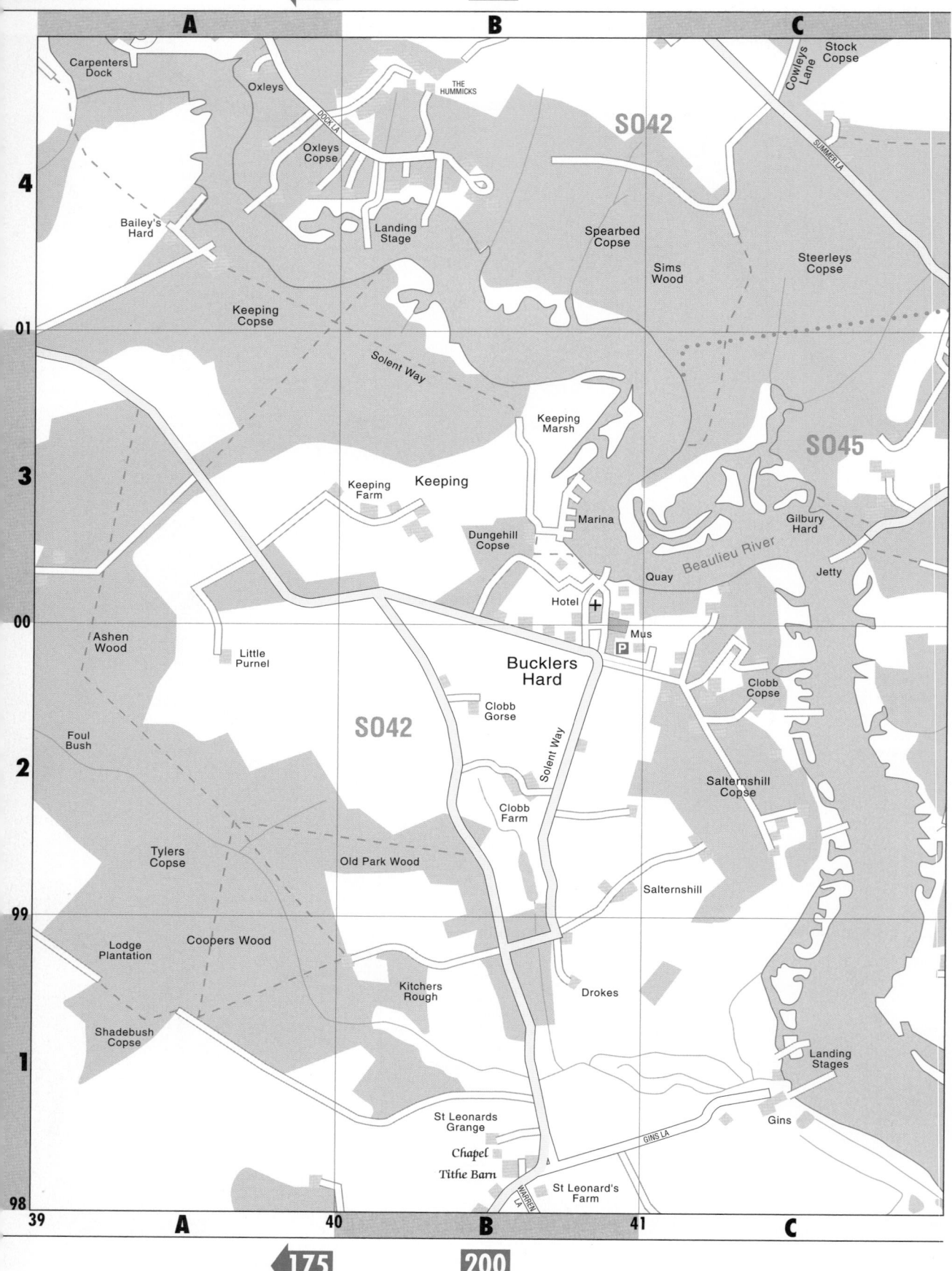

150
178

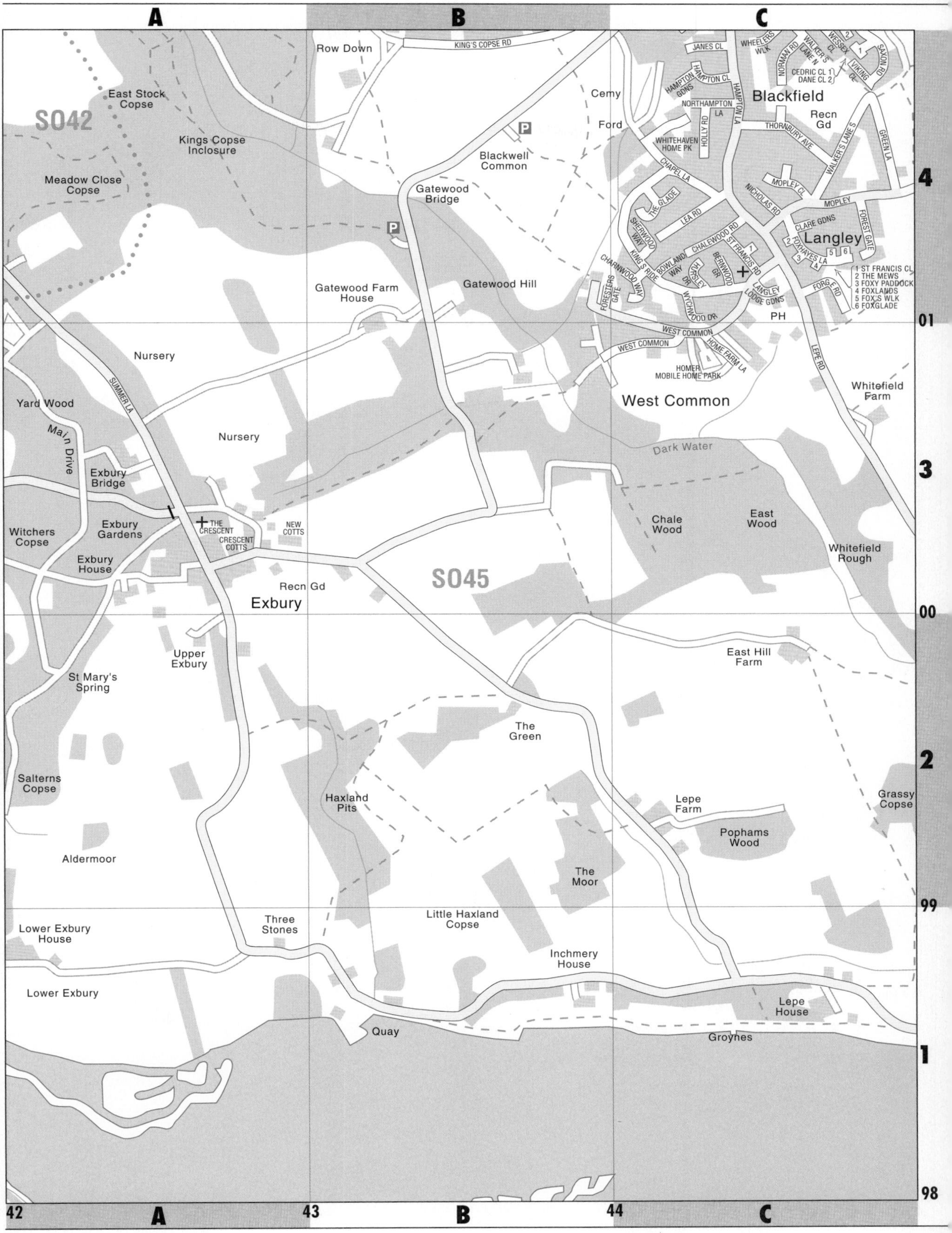
A
B
C
Row Down
KING'S COPSE RD
East Stock Copse
SO42
Kings Copse Inclosure
Meadow Close Copse
Cemy
Ford
Blackwell Common
Gatewood Bridge
Gatewood Farm House
Gatewood Hill
JANES CL
WHEELERS WLK
NORMAN RD
WALKER'S LANE N
WESSEX CL
SAXON RD
VIKING CL
CEDRIC CL 1
DANE CL 2
HAMPTON GDNS
HAMPTON CL
HAMPTON LA
NORTHAMPTON LA
HOLLY RD
Blackfield
Recn Gd
THORNBURY AVE
WHITEHAVEN HOME PK
GREEN LA
WALKER'S LANE S
CHAPEL LA
MOPLEY CL
MOPLEY
NICHOLAS RD
THE GLADE
LEA RD
SHERWOOD WAY
CLARE GDNS
FOREST GATE
Langley
FOXHAYES LA
CHALEWOOD RD
ST FRANCIS RD
BOWLAND WAY
KING'S RIDE
CHARNWOOD WAY
HURSLEY DR
BERNWOOD GR
WYCHWOOD DR
LANGLEY LODGE GDNS
FORGE RD
FORESTERS GATE
1 ST FRANCIS CL
2 THE MEWS
3 FOXY PADDOCK
4 FOXLANDS
5 FOX'S WLK
6 FOXGLADE
PH
WEST COMMON
HOME FARM LA
HOMER MOBILE HOME PARK
LEPE RD
Whitefield Farm
West Common
Nursery
SUMMER LA
Yard Wood
Main Drive
Nursery
Dark Water
Exbury Bridge
Witchers Copse
Exbury Gardens
THE CRESCENT
CRESCENT COTTS
NEW COTTS
Chale Wood
East Wood
Whitefield Rough
Exbury House
Recn Gd
SO45
Exbury
Upper Exbury
St Mary's Spring
East Hill Farm
The Green
Salterns Copse
Haxland Pits
Lepe Farm
Pophams Wood
Grassy Copse
Aldermoor
The Moor
Lower Exbury House
Three Stones
Little Haxland Copse
Inchmery House
Lower Exbury
Quay
Lepe House
Groynes
4
01
3
00
2
99
1
98
42
43
44

178

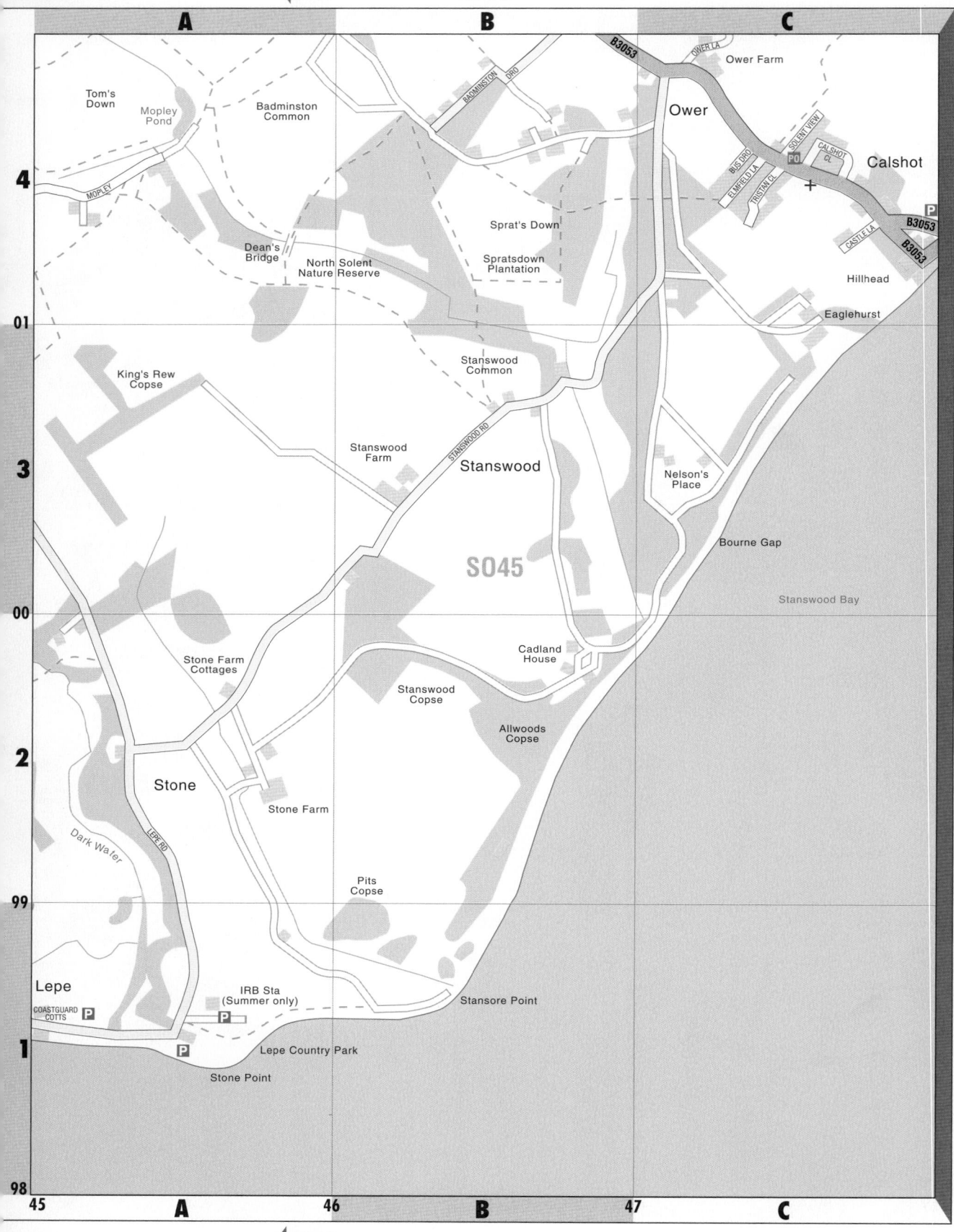

A B C

Tom's Down

Mopley Pond

Badminston Common

B3053

OWER LA

Ower Farm

Ower

SOLENT VIEW

CALSHOT CL

Calshot

4

MOPLEY

BUS DRO

ELMFIELD LA

TRISTAN CL

PO

+

P

B3053

Dean's Bridge

North Solent Nature Reserve

Sprat's Down

Spratsdown Plantation

CASTLE LA

B3053

Hillhead

01

Eaglehurst

King's Rew Copse

Stanswood Common

3

Stanswood Farm

STANSWOOD RD

Stanswood

Nelson's Place

Bourne Gap

SO45

Stanswood Bay

00

Stone Farm Cottages

Cadland House

2

Stanswood Copse

Stone

Stone Farm

Allwoods Copse

Dark Water

LEPE RD

Pits Copse

99

Lepe

IRB Sta (Summer only)

Stansore Point

COASTGUARD COTTS

P

P

1

P

Lepe Country Park

Stone Point

98

45 A 46 B 47 C

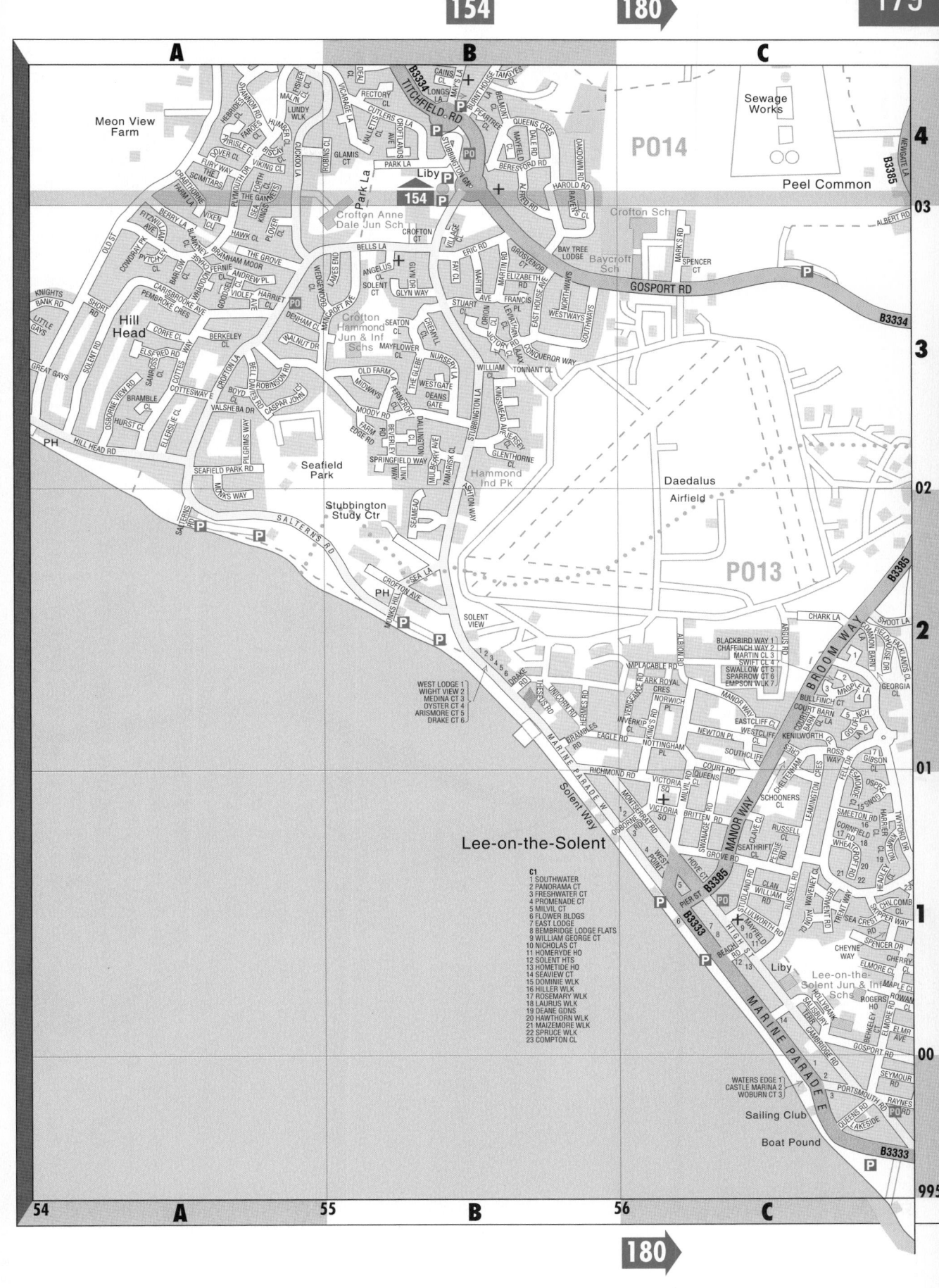

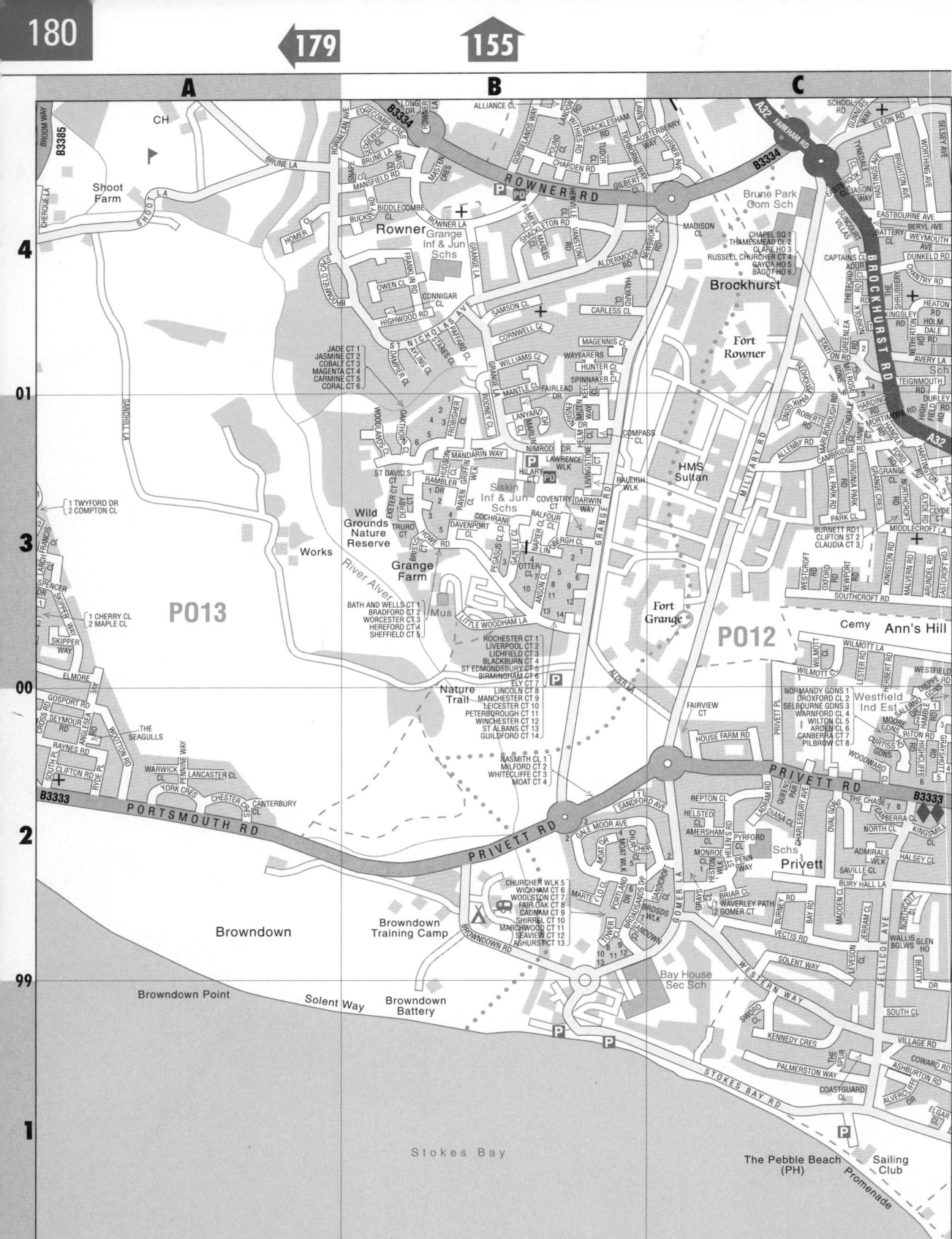

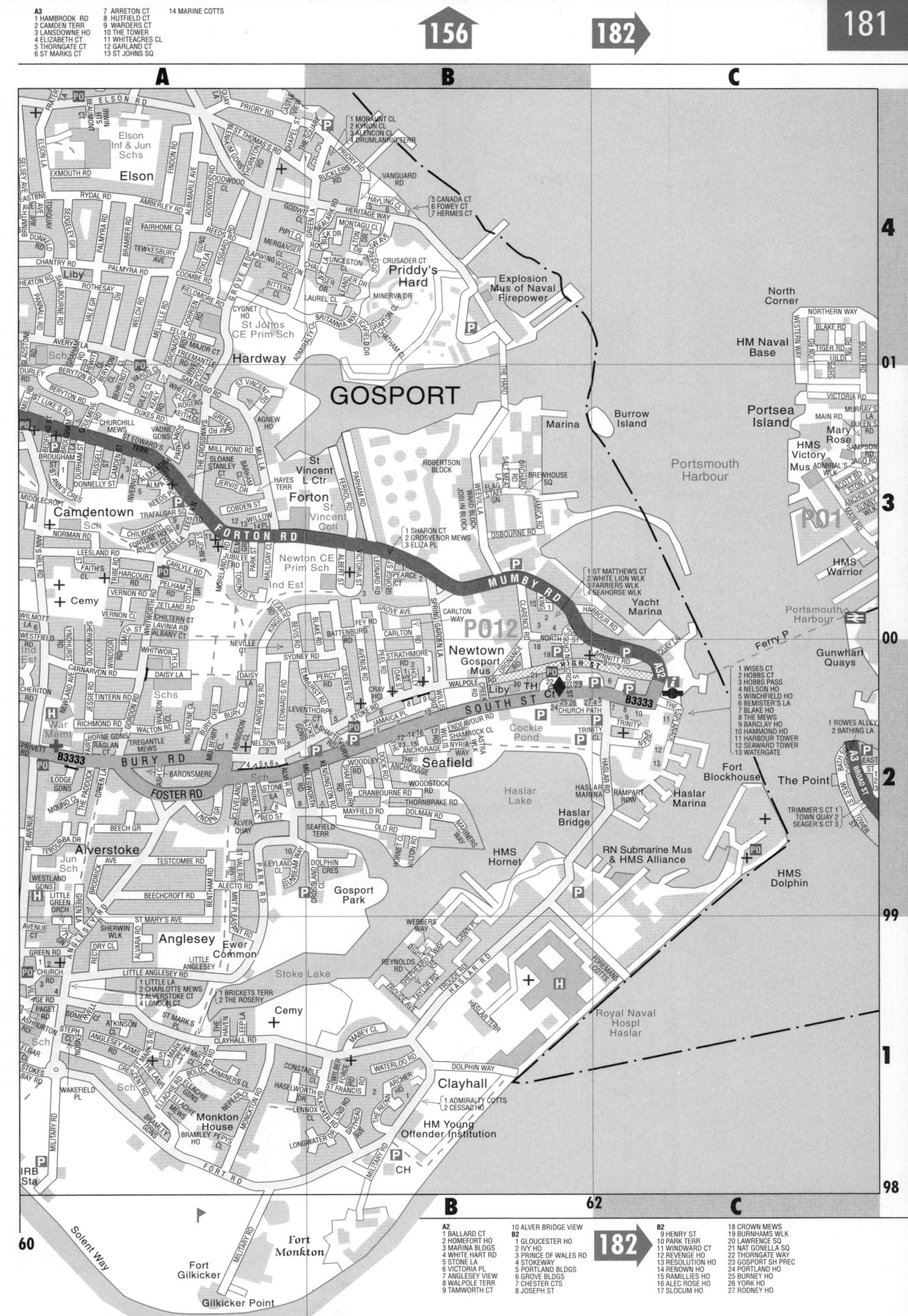

A3
1 STATION APP
2 HALF MOON ST
3 OLD STAR HO
4 DRAKE HO
5 BENBOW PL
6 BENBOW HO
7 CARTER HO
8 UNION ST
9 FROBISHER HO
10 CLOCK ST
11 POWELL SQ
12 SHIP LEOPARD HO
13 CRADDOCK HO
14 BENEFICIAL ST
15 COCHRANE HO
16 COLLEGE LA
17 VICTORY RD
18 ROSEMARY LA
19 MILL GATE HO
20 MARGERY'S CT
21 THREE TUN CL
22 GRENVILLE HO
23 DUCKWORTH HO
24 SEA MILL GDNS
25 RALEIGH HO
26 EVA ALLAWAY CT
27 DAVIDSON CT
28 ST GEO BSNS CTR
29 TED KELLY CT
30 JOSEPH NYE CT
31 ROBERT MACK CT
32 MONTAGUE WALLIS CT
33 FRANK JUDD CT
34 RICHMOND HO
35 DELAVAL HO
36 FOUNDRY CT
37 WILLIAM BOOTH HO
38 MAUD HO
39 SARAH ROBINSON HO

B4
1 SILVERLOCK CL
2 HASLEGRAVE HO
3 FLYING BULL CL
4 GLADSTONE PL
5 KILBRIDE PATH
6 KILPATRICK CL
7 CHAPEL CT
8 CONSORT HO
9 NORRISH HO
10 NICKLEBY HO
11 BARKIS HO
12 MICAWBER HO
13 PICKWICK HO
14 MAITLAND ST
15 BLACKWOOD HO
16 WELLER HO
17 PEGGOTTY HO
18 TUPMAN HO
19 CHEERYBLE HO
20 BRISBANE HO
21 COPPERFIELD HO
22 PROVIDENCE CT
23 BARRINGTON CT
24 THE LION BREWERY

157

A2
1 MARTELLS CT
2 WARBLINGTON CT
3 A'BECKETT CT
4 SOUTH NORMANDY
5 ST THOMAS'S CT
6 HIGHBURY ST
7 HANOVER CT
8 LOMBARD ST
9 KING CHARLES ST
10 WALTON CT
11 HAYWARDS CT
12 REGENCY CT
13 OYSTER MEWS
14 FRENCH ST
15 CAPTAINS ROW
16 SPICE QUAY
17 LAMBER PL
18 THE RELDAS
19 THE GEORGE CT
20 LINGFIELD CT

B1
1 CUNNINGHAM CT
2 THEATRE MEWS
3 DOCK MILL COTTS
4 ADMIRAL'S CNR
5 GARDEN TERR
6 RAVENSWOOD GDNS
7 CHILTERN CT
8 PALM CT
9 TUDOR CT
10 CLARENDON CT
11 BEAUFORT RD
12 FURNESS RD
13 FASTNET HO
14 JACK COCKERILL WAY
15 ST MARTIN'S HO
16 PALM CT
17 QUEENS KEEP
18 HAMILTON CT
19 ADMIRALS CT
20 NETLEY TERR
21 NETLEY RD
22 PARK HO
23 HOMEHEIGHTS
24 CLIFTON TERR
25 CLIFTON RD
26 CLIFTON PL
27 PORTLAND TERR
28 PALMERSTON MANS
29 PALMERSTON RD PREC
30 THE FRIARY
31 FRIARY CL
32 FONTWELL RD
33 TRAFALGAR CT
34 CHESTER PL
35 LINDSAY HO
36 FREESTONE RD

C1
1 KING COTE VILLAS
2 MANSION CT
3 ROSTREVOR LA
4 CRANESWATER GATE
5 CRANESWATER MEWS
6 NORMAN CT
7 DOLPHIN CT
8 CHARMINSTER
9 SOLENT GATE
10 CRESTA CT

181

For full street detail of the highlighted area see page 215.

158
184

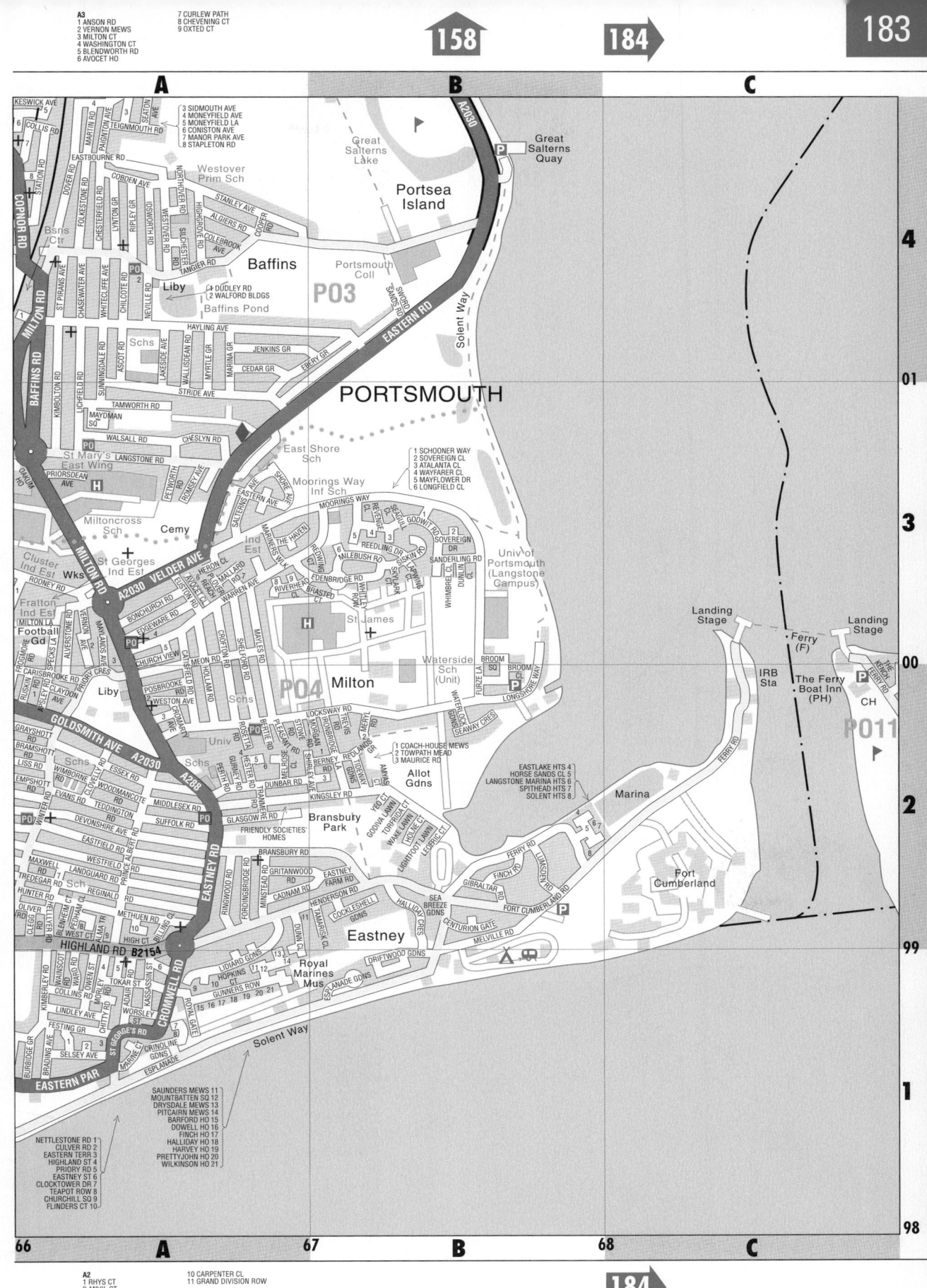

184

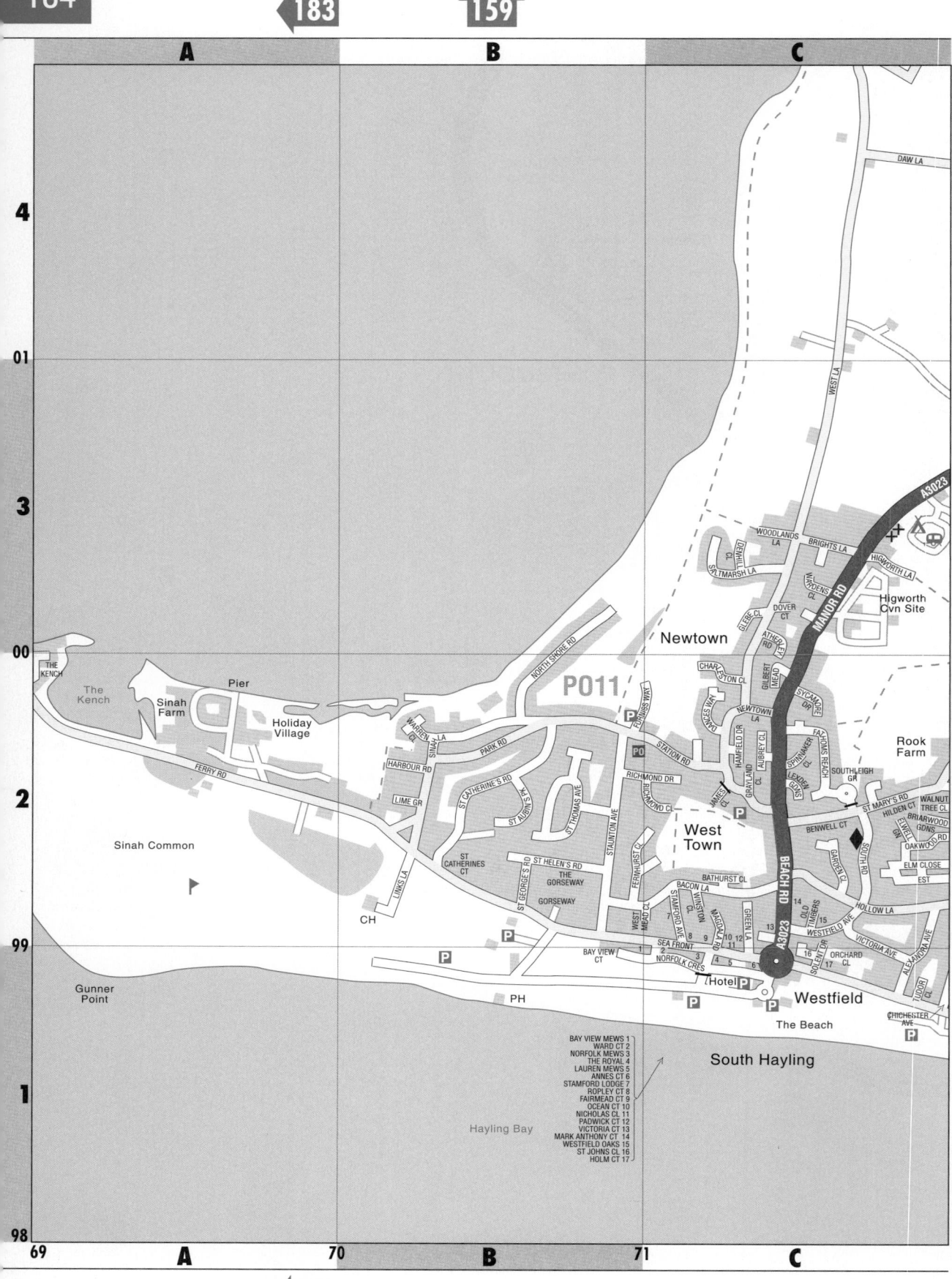

BAY VIEW MEWS 1
WARD CT 2
NORFOLK MEWS 3
THE ROYAL 4
LAUREN MEWS 5
ANNES CT 6
STAMFORD LODGE 7
ROPLEY CT 8
FAIRMEAD CT 9
OCEAN CT 10
NICHOLAS CL 11
PADWICK CT 12
VICTORIA CT 13
MARK ANTHONY CT 14
WESTFIELD OAKS 15
ST JOHNS CL 16
HOLM CT 17

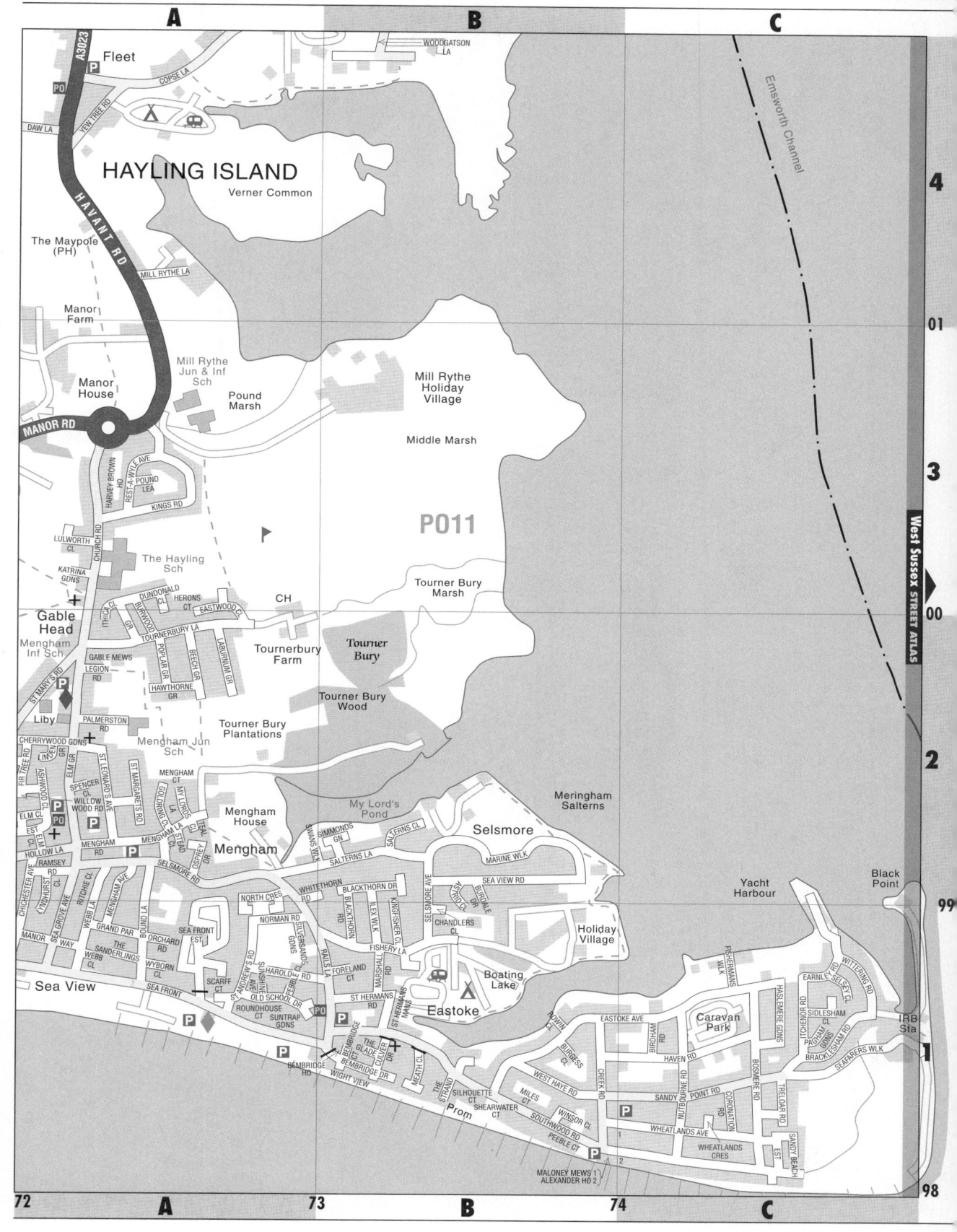

HAYLING ISLAND

Verner Common

Fleet

The Maypole (PH)

Manor Farm

Manor House

Gable Head

Mengham Inf Sch

Liby

Mengham Jun Sch

Mengham House

Mengham

Tournerbury Farm

Tourner Bury

Tourner Bury Wood

Tourner Bury Plantations

Pound Marsh

Mill Rythe Jun & Inf Sch

The Hayling Sch

Mill Rythe Holiday Village

Middle Marsh

Tourner Bury Marsh

PO11

My Lord's Pond

Meringham Salterns

Selsmore

Holiday Village

Yacht Harbour

Black Point

Sea View

Eastoke

Boating Lake

Caravan Park

IRB Sta

Sea View

Prom

Emsworth Channel

West Sussex STREET ATLAS

4

01

3

00

2

99

1

98

72   73   74

A   B   C

162

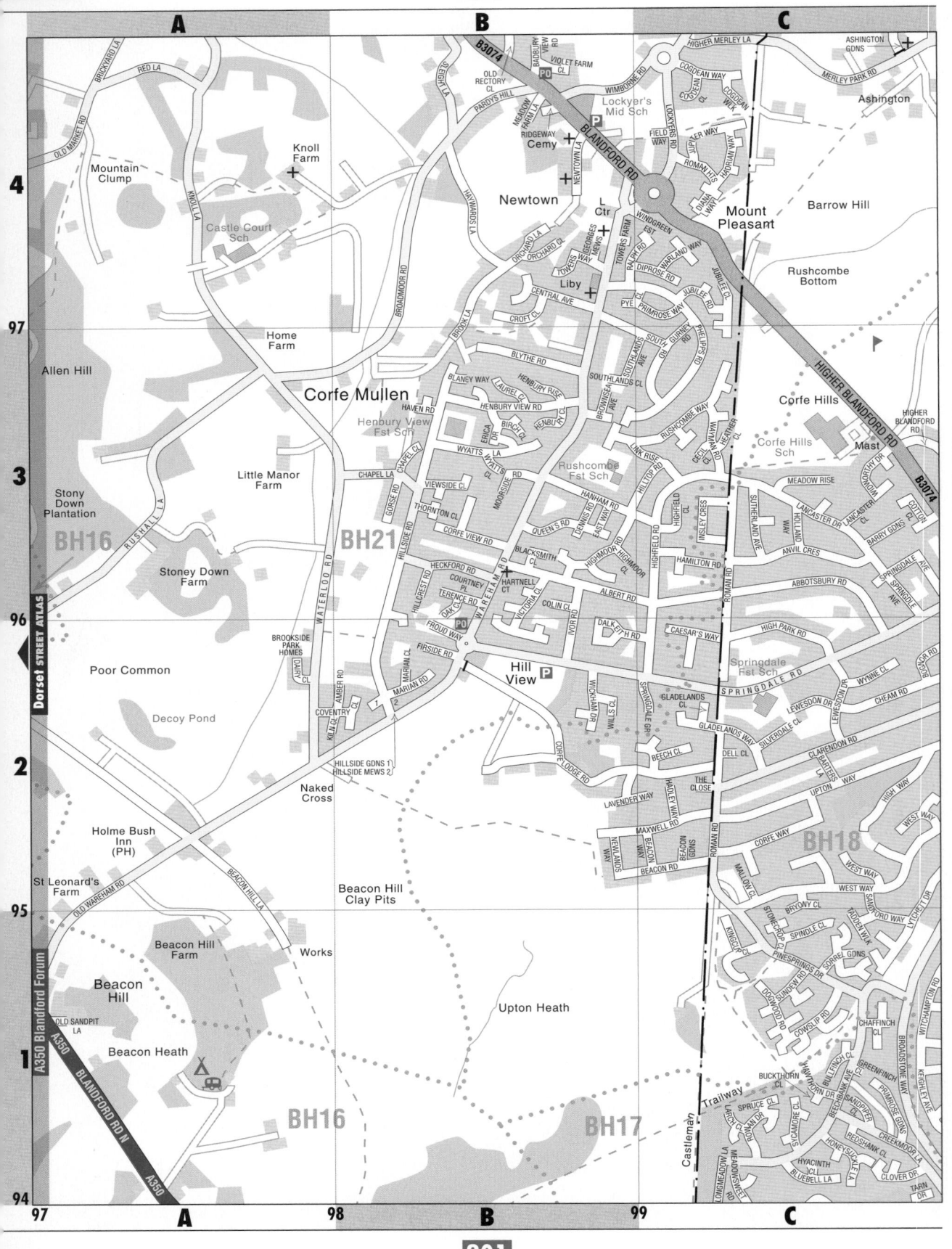

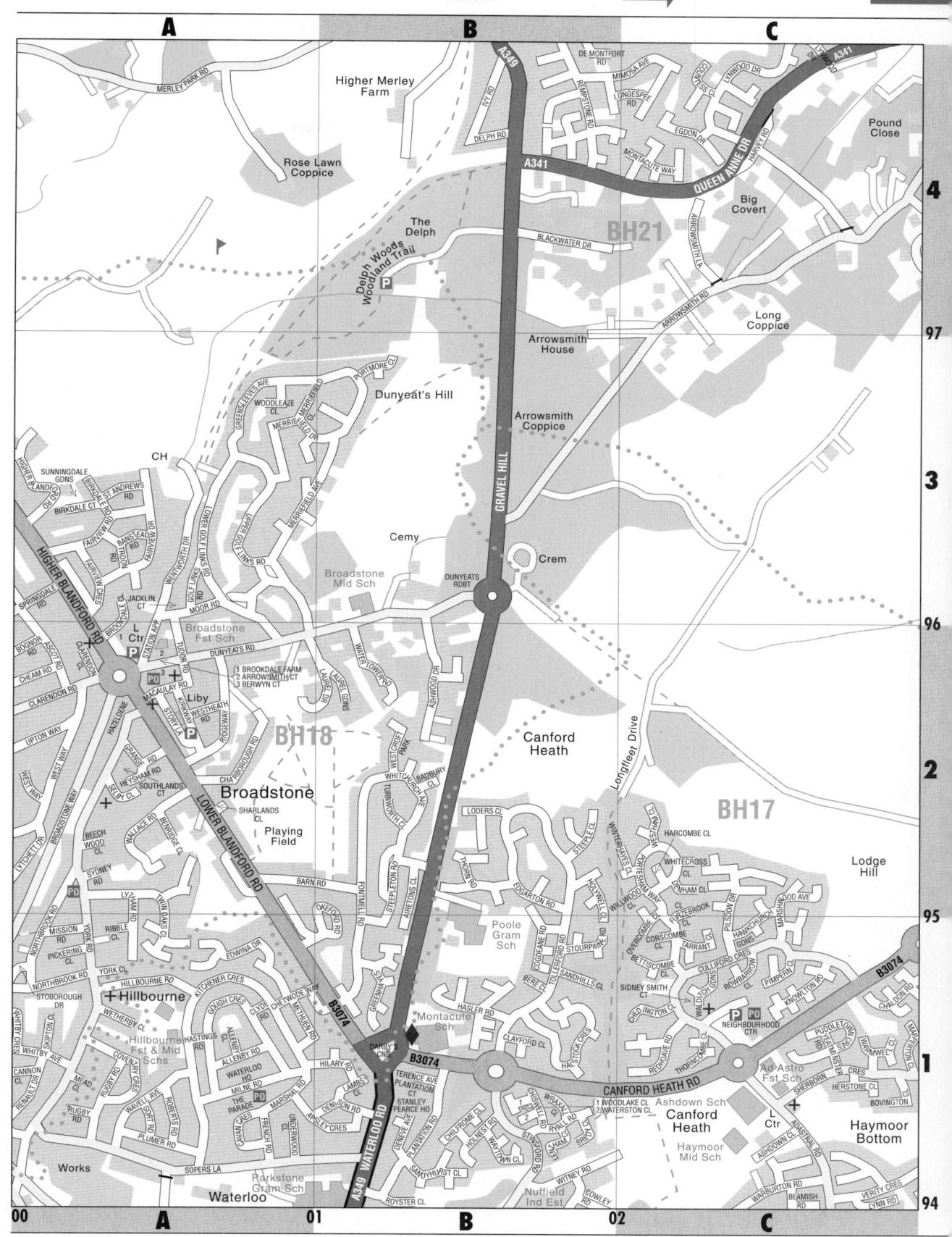

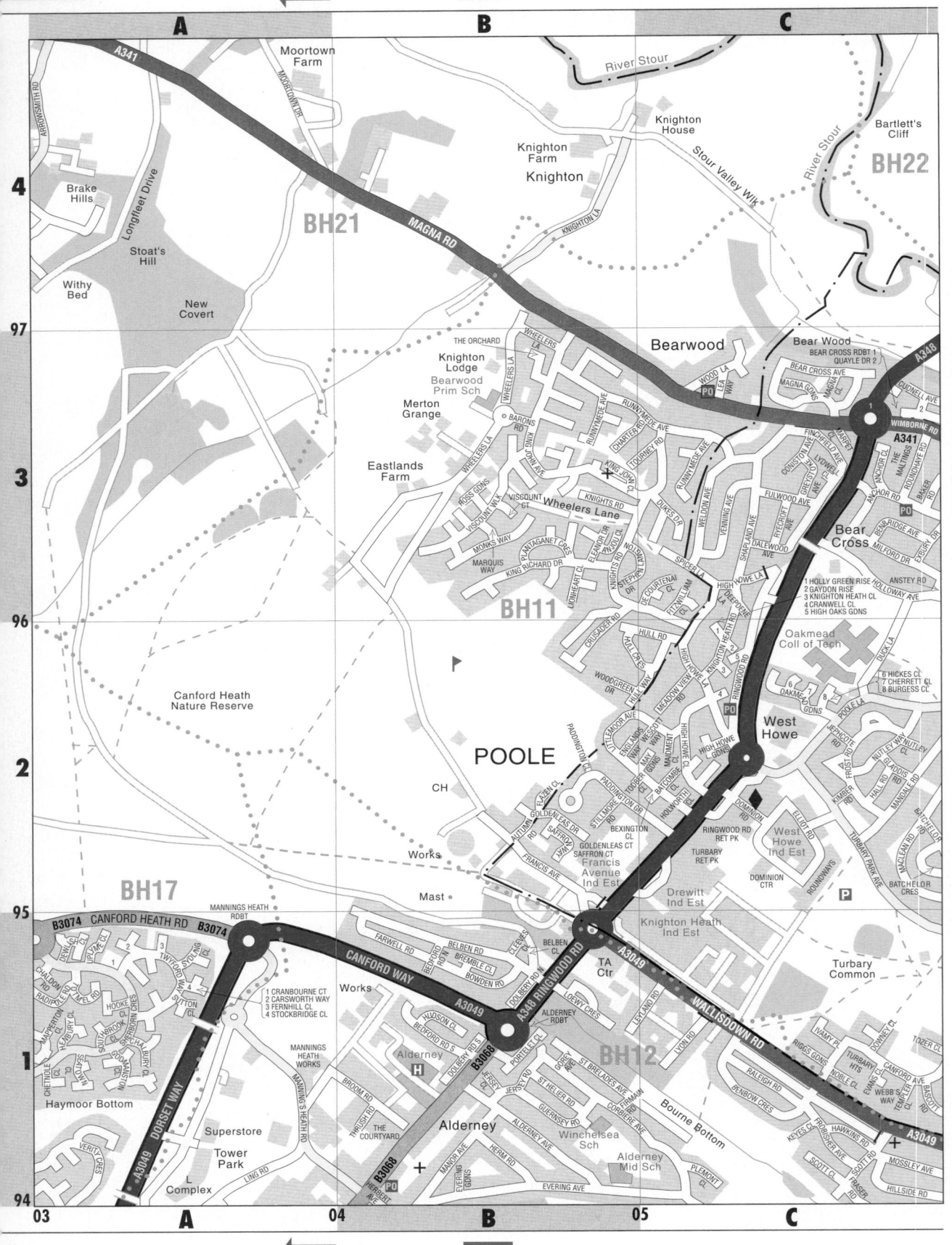

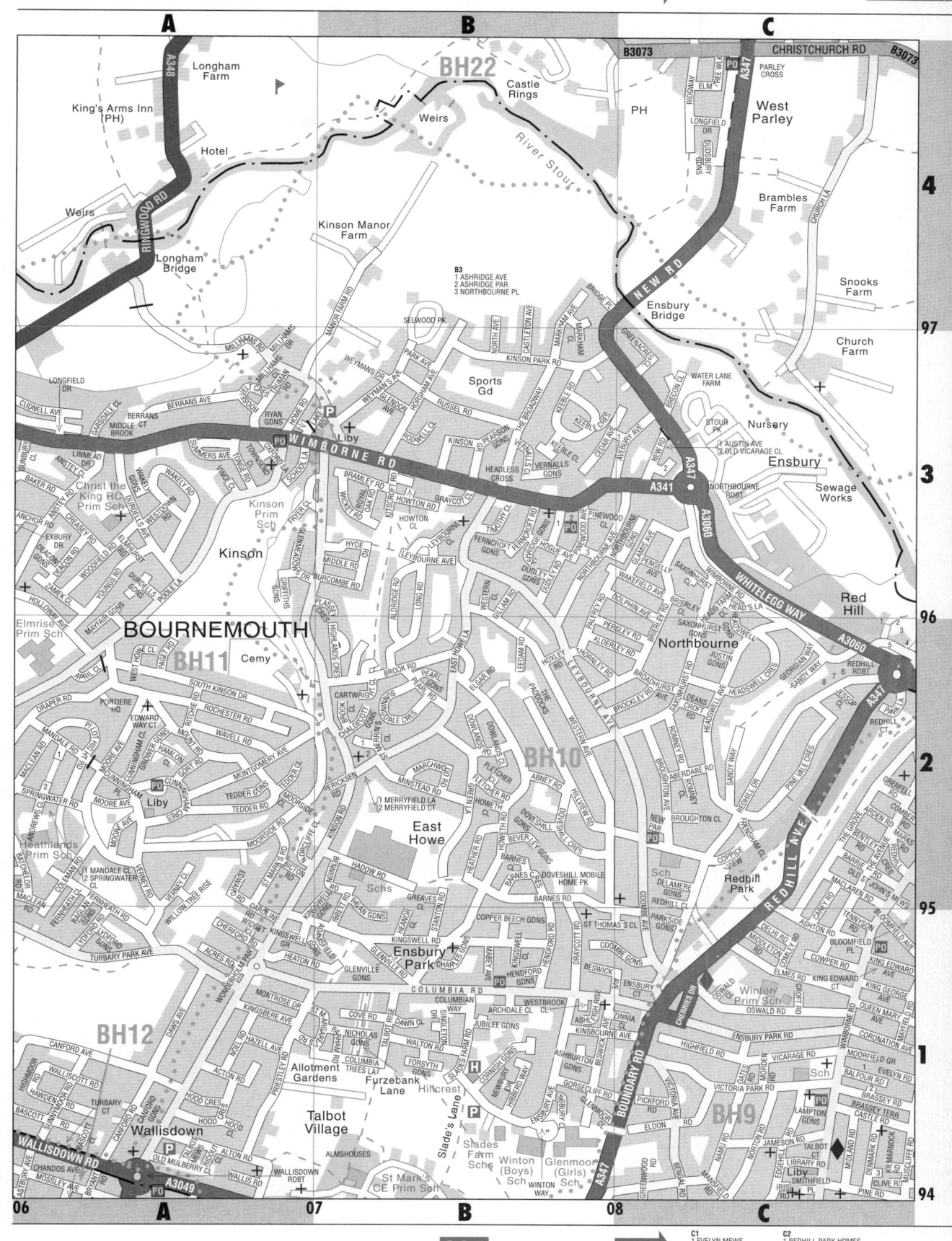

C1
1 EVELYN MEWS
2 ST JOHN'S GDNS
3 NORWAY CL

C2
1 REDHILL PARK HOMES
2 WHEATPLOT PARK HOMES
3 KINGFISHER PARK HOMES
4 RIVERSIDE
5 WIMBORNE RD
6 MAGNOLIA HO
7 WISTERIA HO
8 LABURNUM HO

189 166

A B C

B3073 CHRISTCHURCH RD
BARRACK RD

East Parley

Bournemouth Sports Club

CHAPEL LA
ENTERPRISE WAY
CHAPEL GATE

Bournemouth International Airport

4

PARLEY LA

BH22

New Cottages

BH23

College of Air Traffic Control

MERRITOWN LA

Alice in Wonderland Family Park

Merritown

B3073

Parley Court

Parley Green

DALES LA

West Hurn

River Stour

97

HURN COURT LA

Hurn Court Farm

PIG SHOOT LA

3

A2
1 REDHILL CT
2 PORTSWOOD DR
3 THE CIRCLE
4 THE AVENUE
5 COMBER RD
6 MEADOW CT
7 PRIORY VIEW PL
8 CHARNWOOD AVE
9 WARMWELL CL
10 STURMINSTER RD
11 SIDNEY GDNS

BH10

Works

Muccleshell Farm

West Lodge

Berry Hill

Leaden Stour

BH9

THE FRANK WAREHAM COTTAGE HOMES

MUSCLIFFE LA

Hicks Farm

WOOD ROW

Weir

96

Throop Mill

Nursery

NEWMORTON RD
STRATHMORE RD
GRANBY RD
EDIFRED RD

SANDRINGHAM GDNS
SANDRINGHAM RD

Sch

SUSSEX CL

THROOPSIDE AVE

LAVENDER LA

STOUR WLK

River Farm

Throop

BH8

BOURNEMOUTH

Muscliffe Prim Sch

Muscliffe

TAYLOR DR

1 DOWNTON CL
2 CALMORE CL
3 FRITHAM GDNS
4 BRAMSHAW GDNS

Cemy

VICARAGE COTTS

HOLDEAHURST RD

2

A3060

THE GROVE
MOORDOWN
LAWFORD RD
WIMBORNE RD

Blue Roof Farm

Nurseries

THROOP RD

MOUNTBATTEN GDNS 1
IBBERTSON CL 2
BOURNEMOUTH MEMORIAL HOMES 3

YEOMANS WAY

PETIT RD
PRIORY VIEW
COBHAM RD
FRANKLIN RD

MALVERN RD
WEST WAY

LUCKHAM GDNS

MILL RD W

YEOMANS RD

STACEY GDNS

The Hampshire Ctr

Yeomans Ind Pk

95

B3063

CASTLE LA W

BELMONT RD

SHAWFORD GDNS 1
MICHELMARSH GN 2
SHERFIELD CL 3
WHITSBURY CL 4

Bournemouth Gram Sch (Girls)

CASTLE GATE

BRENDON CL

Eventide Homes

Moordown

CHARMINSTER RD

Charminster

Bournemouth Gram Sch (Boys)

Sports Ctr

EAST WAY

MALLARD RD

CURLEW RD

Strouden

Liby

INGLEWOOD

A3060

1

Summerbee First & Jun Schs

Summerbee Comp Sch

Haddon Hill

WORDSWORTH AVE

NORMANHURST AVE

FEVERSHAM AVE

PARKWAY DR

COPSEWOOD AVE

COOPER DEAN DR

WESSEX WAY

PORTLAND RD
STROUDEN RD
MURLEY RD

B3063

MORTIMER RD
STROUDEN AVE

Cemy

94

09 A 10 B 11 C

A1
1 ROSEBUD AVE
2 MC WILLIAM RD
3 MINTERNE RD
4 MALVERN CT
5 CHARMINSTER CL

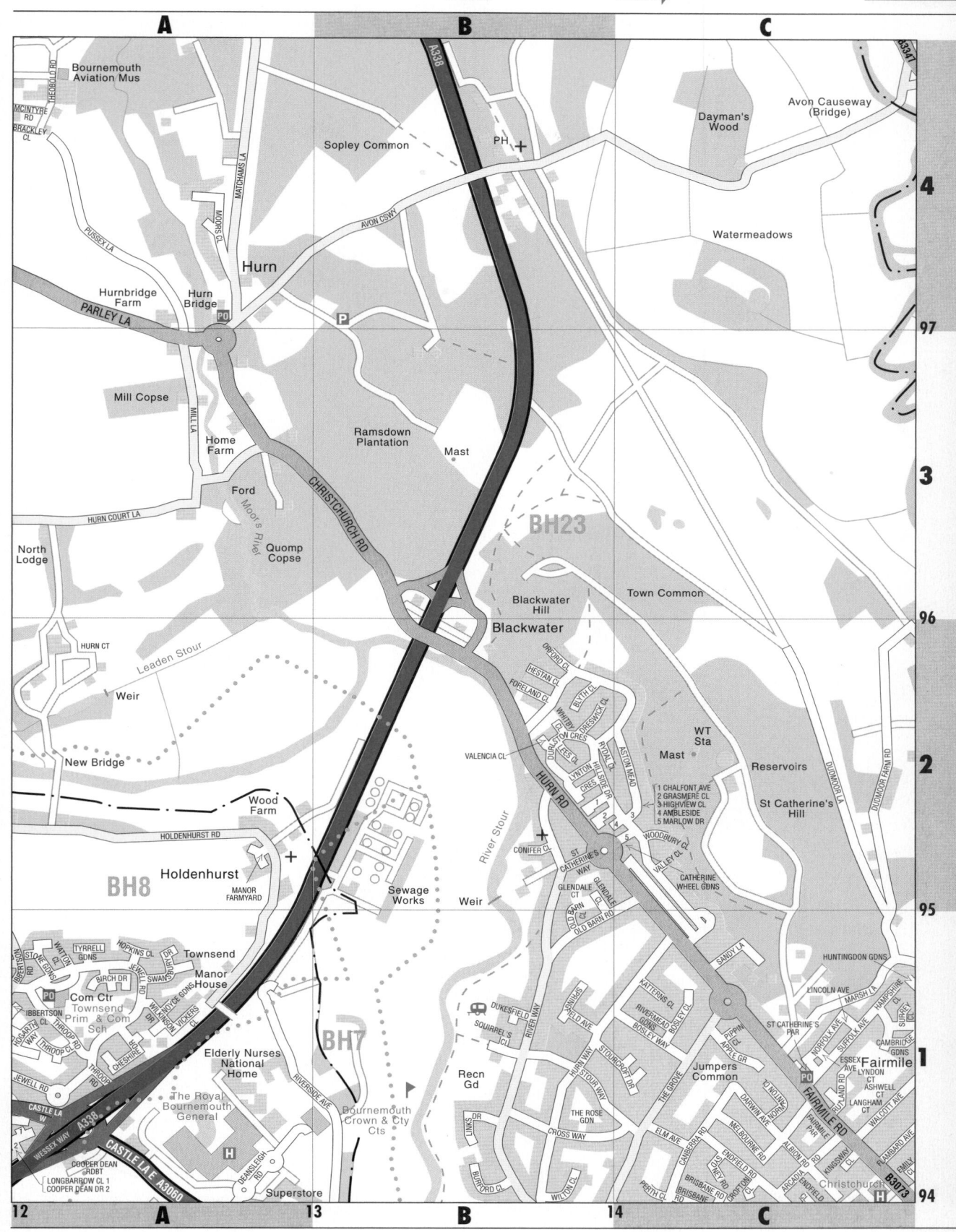

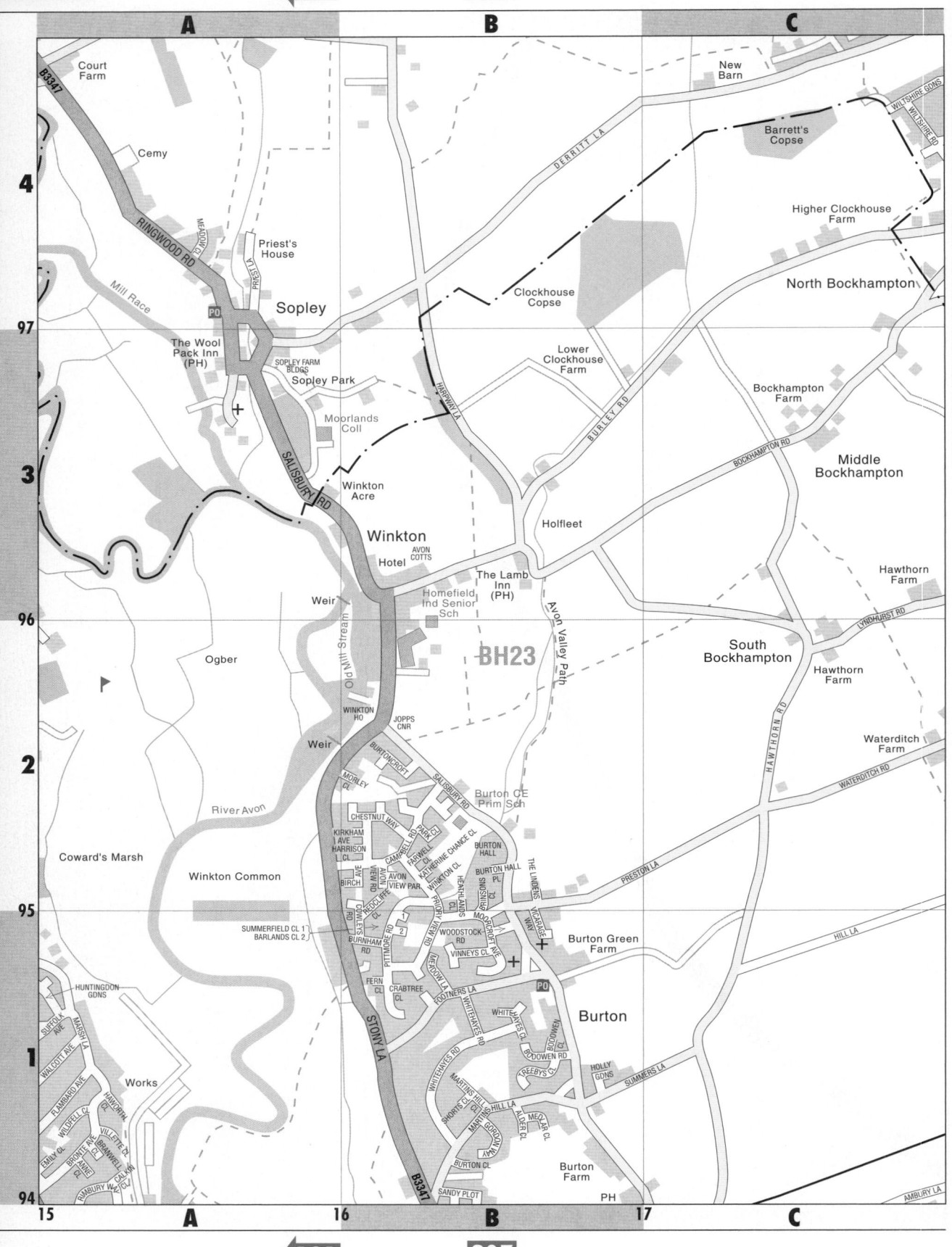

A   B   C

4

97

3

96

BH23

2

95

1

94

15   A   16   B   17   C

Court Farm
B3347
Cemy
RINGWOOD RD
Mill Race
MEADOW CL
PO
The Wool Pack Inn (PH)
Priest's House
PRIEST LA
Sopley
SOPLEY FARM BLDGS
Sopley Park
Moorlands Coll
SALISBURY RD
Winkton Acre
Winkton
Hotel
AVON COTTS
Weir
Homefield Ind Senior Sch
The Lamb Inn (PH)
Holfleet
Ogber
Old Mill Stream
WINKTON HO
JOPPS CNR
Weir
River Avon
Coward's Marsh
Winkton Common
BURTONCROFT
MORLEY CL
SALISBURY RD
Burton CE Prim Sch
CHESTNUT WAY
KIRKHAM AVE
HARRISON CL
CAMPBELL RD
FAGWELL CL
PARK CL
KATHERINE CHANCE CL
WILMTON CL
Burton Hall
BIRCH AVE
AVON VIEW PAR.
PRIORY VIEW RD
HEATHLANDS CL
MOORCROFT AVE
Burton Hall PL
SINSINGTON RD
THE LINDERS
VICARAGE WAY
SUMMERFIELD CL 1
BARLANDS CL 2
BURNHAM RD
PITTMORE RD
WOODSTOCK RD
VINNEYS CL
Burton Green Farm
Burton
HILL LA
HUNTINGDON GDNS
FERN CL
CRABTREE CL
FOOTNERS LA
MEADOW WAY
PO
SUFFOLK AVE
MARSH LA
WALCOTT AVE
Works
WHITEHAYES RD
WHITEHAYES RD
WHITEHAYES CL
BODOWEN CL
BODOWEN RD
HOLLY GDNS
SUMMERS LA
FLAMBARD AVE
HAWORTH CL
WILDFELL CL
VILLETTE CL
FAMILY CL
BRONTE AVE
ANNE CL
BRANWELL CL
CALVIN
RUMBURY W.
MARTINS HILL CL
SHORTS CL
MARTINS HILL LA
GORDON AVE
ALDER CL
MEDOR CL
BURTON CL
SANDY PLOT
PH
Burton Farm
B3347
AMBURY LA

New Barn
WILTSHIRE GDNS
WILTSHIRE RD
DERRITT LA
Barrett's Copse
Higher Clockhouse Farm
North Bockhampton
Clockhouse Copse
Lower Clockhouse Farm
HARPWAY LA
BURLEY RD
Bockhampton Farm
BOCKHAMPTON RD
Middle Bockhampton
Hawthorn Farm
Avon Valley Path
South Bockhampton
LYNDHURST RD
Hawthorn Farm
HAWTHORN RD
Waterditch Farm
WATERDITCH RD
PRESTON LA

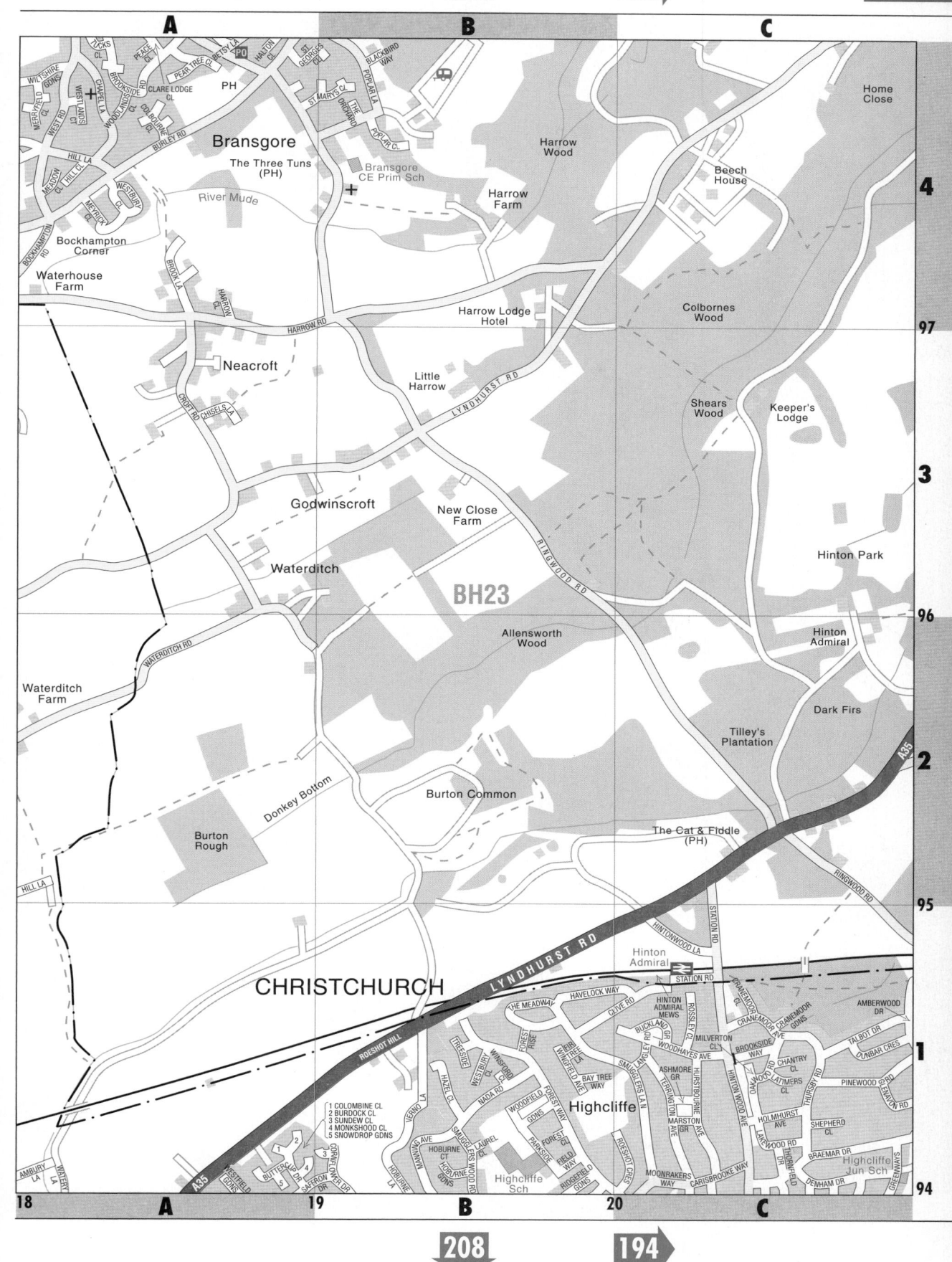

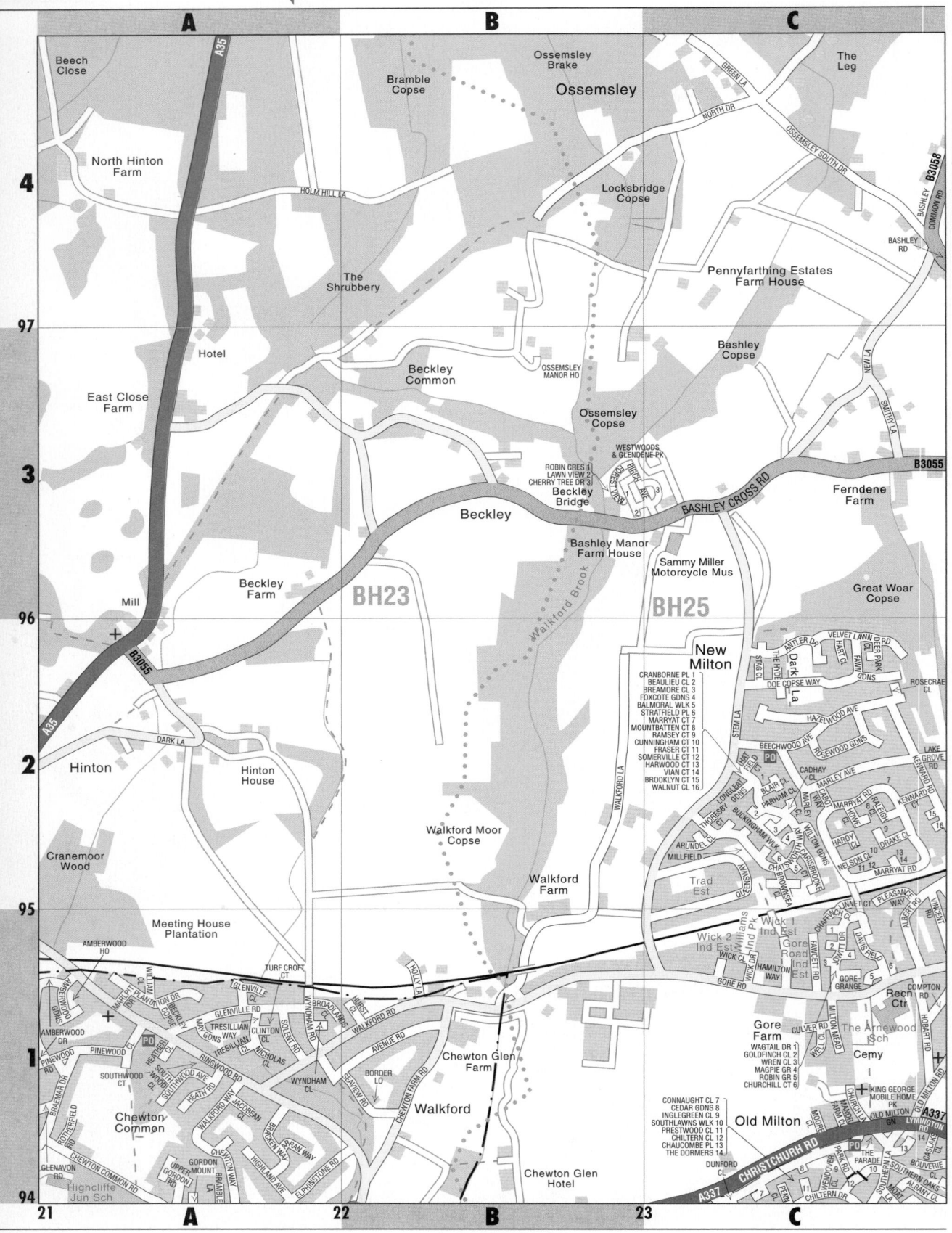

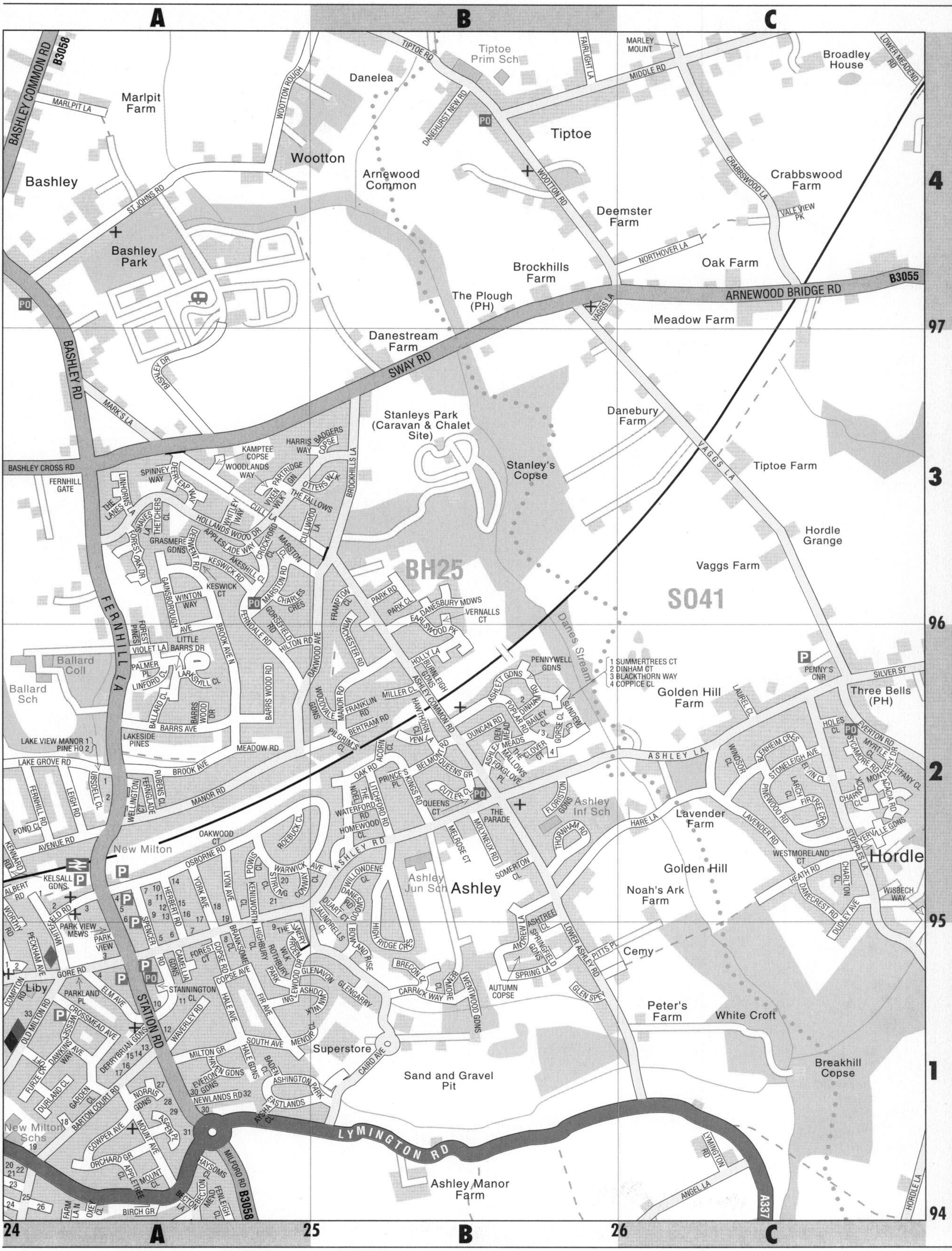

A1
1 VINCENT RD
2 VINCENT CL
3 CHARLOTTE CL
4 ELM CT
5 SPENCER CT
6 ORCHARD LEIGH
7 CORNERWAYS CT
8 JACMAR CT
9 ASHLEY ARNEWOOD CT
10 WESTCROFT PAR
11 ELIZABETH CT
12 WAVERLEY HO
13 HOMEFIELD HO
14 ELIOT HO
15 SHELLEY HO
16 BYRON HO
17 KEATS HO
18 SHENSTONE CT
19 CLIFTON CT
20 WINSTON CT
21 SOLENT LO
22 WINSTON PAR
23 BOUVERIE CL
24 EDMUNDS CL
25 BARTON COURT AVE
26 SPINDLEWOOD CL
27 HAZEL CT
28 ST DENYS
29 DUDLEY PL
30 YEW TREE CT
31 CHERRY TREE CT
32 GREENWOODS
33 CASSELLES CT

A2
1 WHITEFIELD LO
2 HEATHER LO
3 RUSSELL CT
4 OSBOURNE HO
5 HOMEMILL HO
6 MALLARD BLDGS
7 RICHMOND CT
8 PEGASUS CT
9 BEAU CT
10 ORCHARD CT
11 TANGLEWOOD CT
12 ALVANDI GDNS
13 ASHTON CT
14 MORANT CT
15 TREVONE
16 FREMINGTON CT
17 YORK PL
18 FAIRCOURT
19 MERLEWOOD CT
20 CONWAY CT
21 STIRLING CT

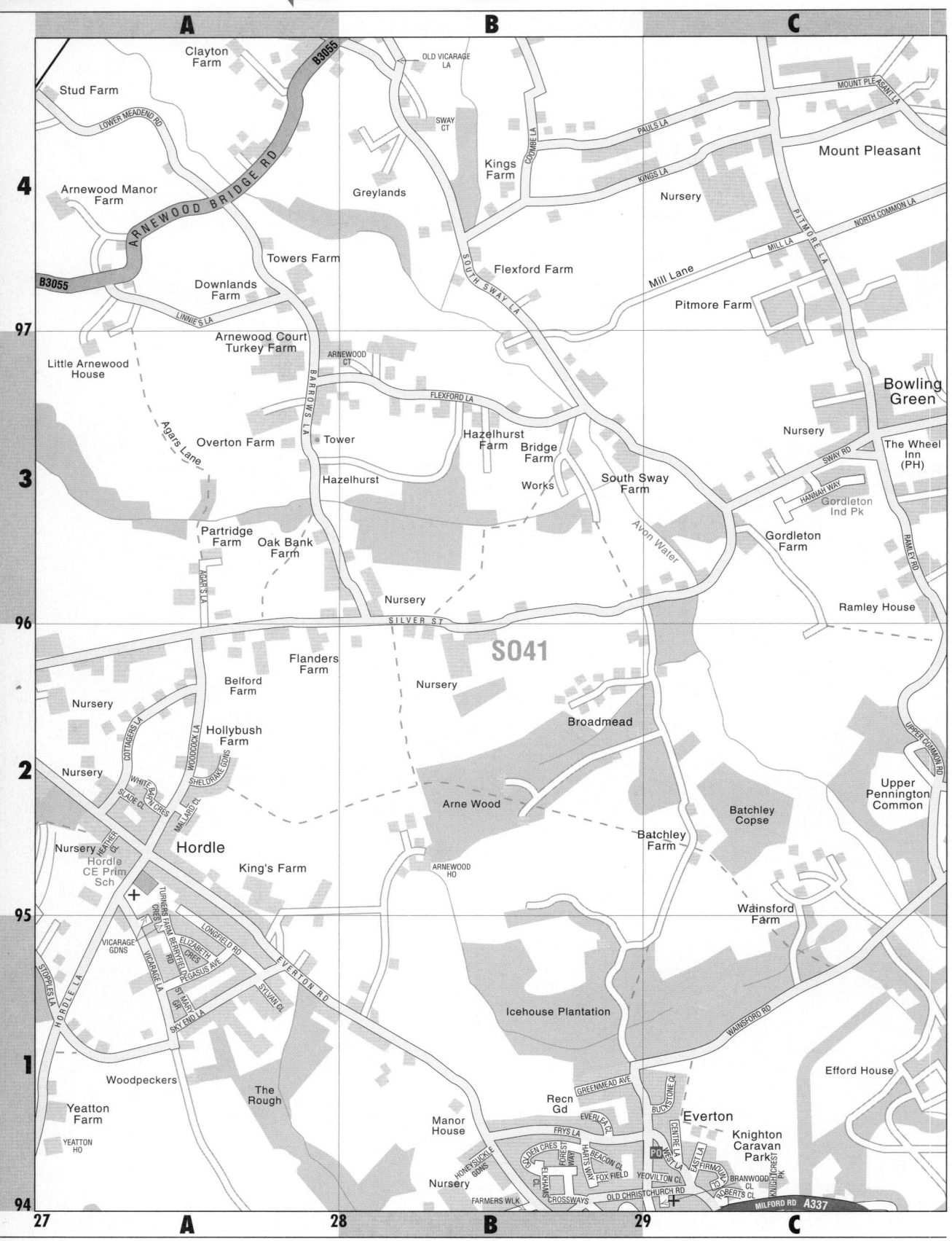

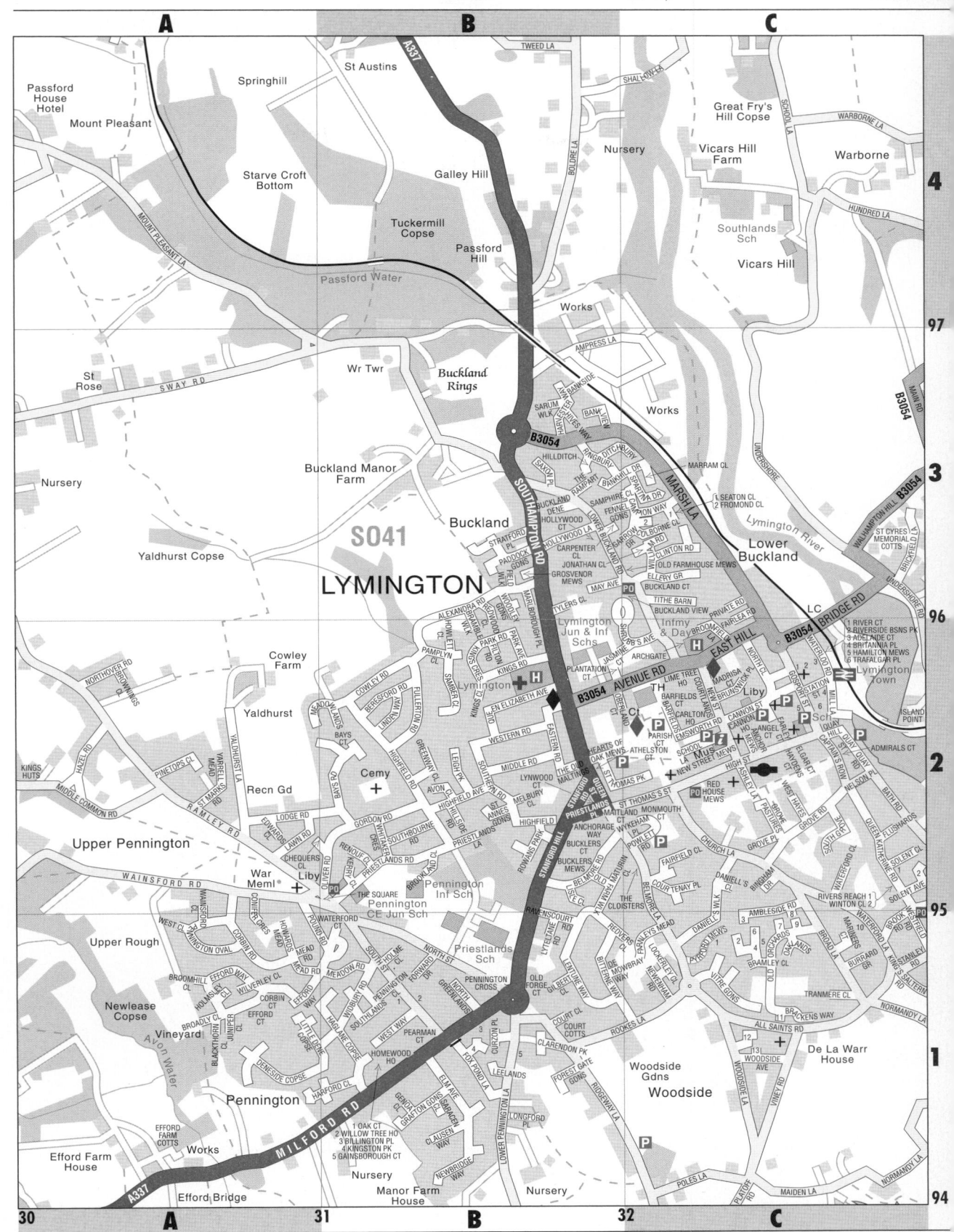

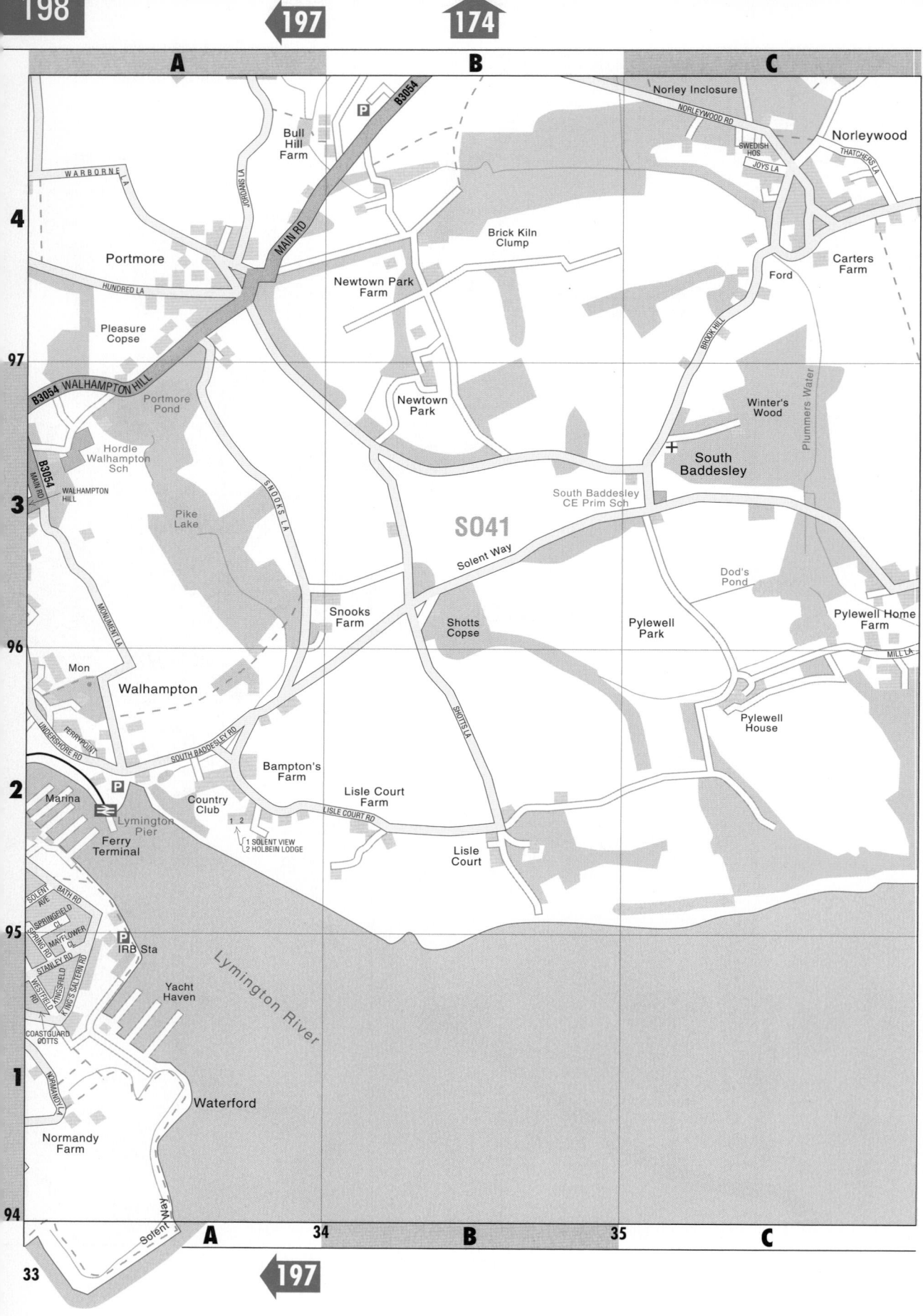

A   B   C

Norley Inclosure

NORLEYWOOD RD

Norleywood

SWEDISH HOS

THATCHERS LA

JOYS LA

WARBORNE LA

Bull Hill Farm

P

B3054

Portmore

4

Brick Kiln Clump

Carters Farm

Ford

HUNDRED LA

MAIN RD

JORDANS LA

Newtown Park Farm

Pleasure Copse

BROCK HILL

97

B3054 WALHAMPTON HILL

Portmore Pond

Newtown Park

Winter's Wood

Plummers Water

South Baddesley

Hordle Walhampton Sch

B3054 MAIN RD

WALHAMPTON HILL

SNOOKS LA

South Baddesley CE Prim Sch

3

Pike Lake

SO41

Dod's Pond

Solent Way

Pylewell Home Farm

MONUMENT LA

Snooks Farm

Shotts Copse

Pylewell Park

MILL LA

96

Mon

Walhampton

Pylewell House

SHOTTS LA

FERRY POINT

UNDERSHORE RD

SOUTH BADDESLEY RD

Bampton's Farm

2

Marina

P

Lymington Pier

Country Club

1 2

Lisle Court Farm

LISLE COURT RD

Ferry Terminal

1 SOLENT VIEW
2 HOLBEIN LODGE

Lisle Court

SOLENT AVE

BATH RD

SPRINGFIELD CL

SPRING RD

MAYFLOWER CL

95

P

STANLEY RD

IRB Sta

KINGSFIELD

Yacht Haven

Lymington River

WESTFIELD RD

KING'S SALTERN RD

COASTGUARD COTTS

1

NORMANDY LA

Waterford

Normandy Farm

94

A   34   B   35   C

SOLENT WAY

SO42
Upper Beckheath Plantation
Beck Farm House
Thorns Corner Cottages
Norley Copse
Beck Farm
SO42
4
NORLEYWOOD RD
MAIN RD
ST LEONARDS RD
Hardings Wood
Thorns Cottages
Forestside Farm
LYMINGTON RD
Coombes Gate Farm Kennels
BROOM HILL
ROWES LA
East End
Solent Way
Thorns Farm
East End Bridge
Ravensbeck Farm
97
Bridge Farm
THORNS LA
East End Arms (PH)
3
Sowley Pond
Whitehouse Copse
SO42
Sowley Brooms
SO41
SOWLEY LA
New Cotts
Solent Way
Sowley House
MILL LA
Sowley Farm
SANDPIT LA
96
Colgrims
PITTS DEEP LA
BROWNS LA
Otters Hill Copse
Boscoppa
TANNERS LA
Pitts Deep
2
Quay
95
1
94

SO41

SO42

A B C

4

97

3

2

1

96

95

94

Bergerie Farm

Solent Way

The Log House

Gins House

Black Water

Park

Rye Errish

Black Water House

WARREN LA

Thorns Copse

Rye Errish Copse

Warren Farm

Park Farm

Gravelly Marsh

Great Marsh

Thorns Marsh

Warren House

Thorns Beach

Park Shore

THORNS LA

Little Marsh

Beaulieu River

Gull Island

Bird Sanctuary

Needs Ore Cottages

Needs Ore Point

WARREN LA

Bird Sanctuary

97 42 43

39 A 40 B 41 C

PARK LA

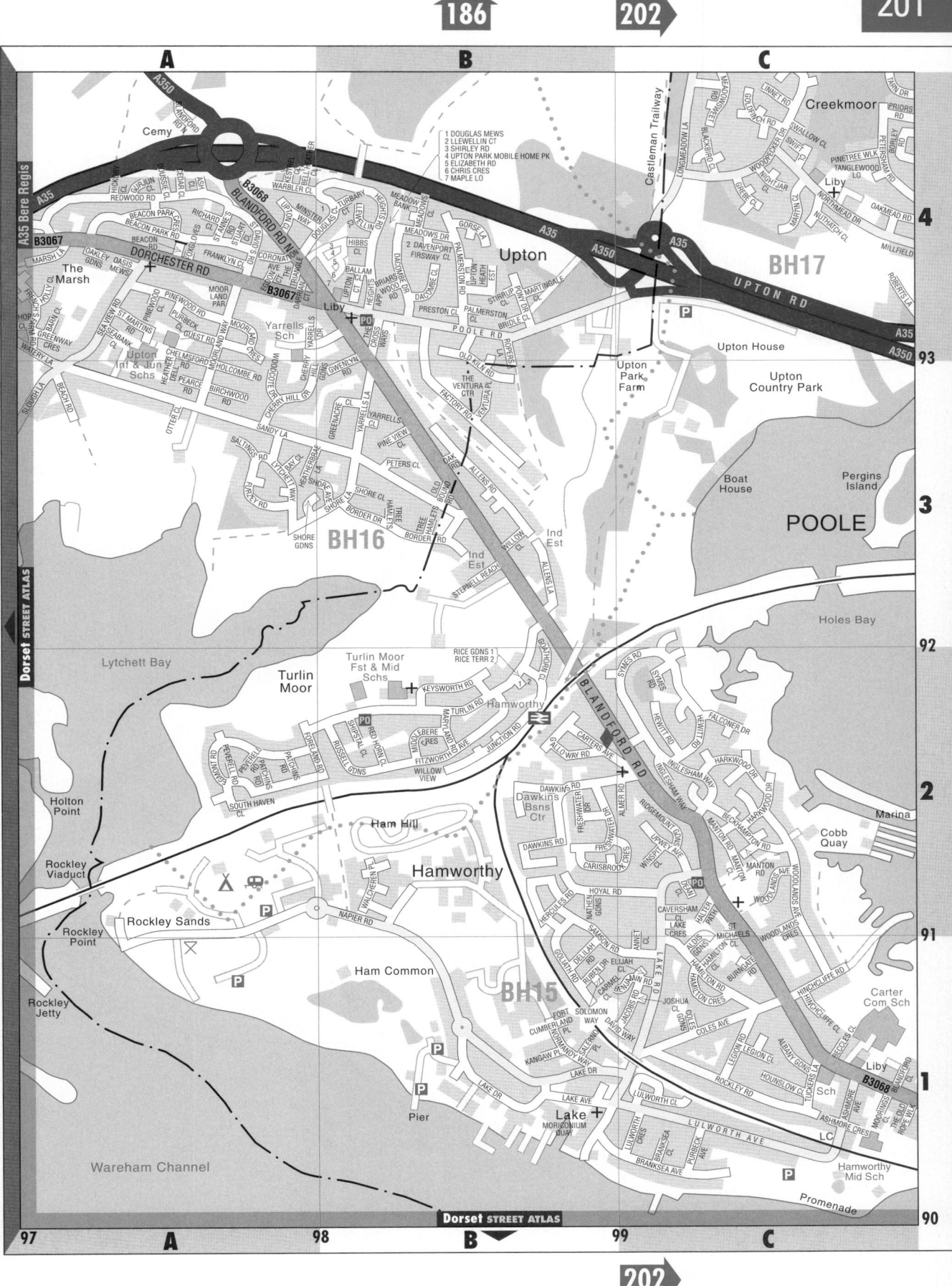

1 DOUGLAS MEWS
2 LLEWELLIN CT
3 SHIRLEY RD
4 UPTON PARK MOBILE HOME PK
5 ELIZABETH RD
6 CHRIS CRES
7 MAPLE LO

Creekmoor

Upton

BH17

UPTON RD

Upton House

Upton Park Farm

Upton Country Park

Boat House

Pergins Island

POOLE

Holes Bay

The Marsh

DORCHESTER RD

Yarrells Sch

Upton Inf & Jun Schs

BH16

Lytchett Bay

Turlin Moor

Turlin Moor Fst & Mid Schs

Hamworthy

Holton Point

Rockley Viaduct

Rockley Sands

Rockley Point

Rockley Jetty

Ham Hill

Ham Common

Hamworthy

BH15

Dawkins Bsns Ctr

Cobb Quay

Marina

Carter Com Sch

Wareham Channel

Pier

Lake

Morconium Quay

Hamworthy Mid Sch

Promenade

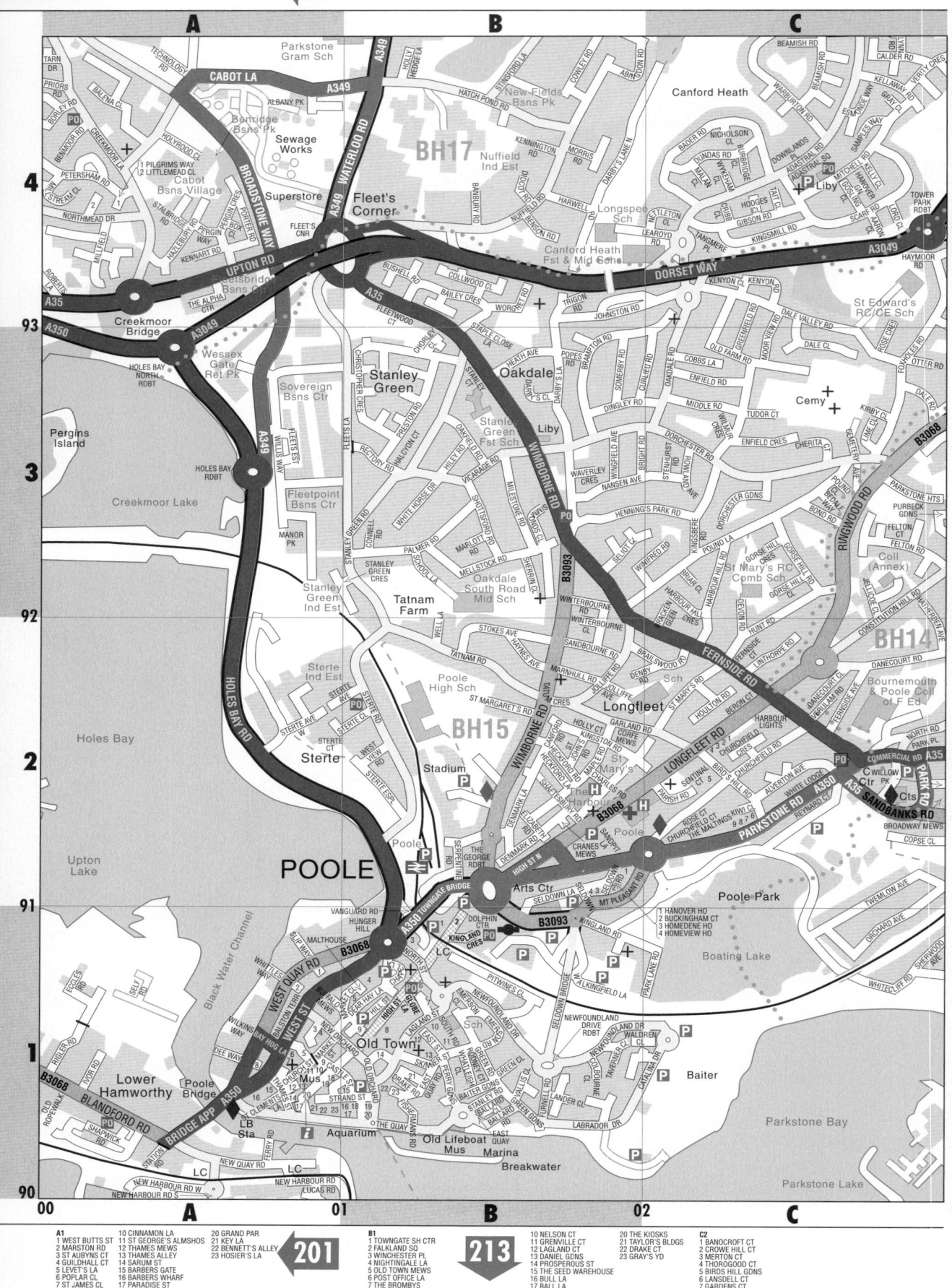

A1
1 WEST BUTTS ST
2 MARSTON RD
3 ST AUBYNS CT
4 GUILDHALL CT
5 LEVET'S LA
6 POPLAR CL
7 ST JAMES CL
8 BARBERS PILES
9 NEW ST
10 CINNAMON LA
11 ST GEORGE'S ALMSHOS
12 THAMES MEWS
13 THAMES ALLEY
14 SARUM ST
15 BARBERS GATE
16 BARBERS WHARF
17 PARADISE ST
18 BELL LA
19 DENNETTS LA
20 GRAND PAR
21 KEY LA
22 BENNETT'S ALLEY
23 HOSIER'S LA

B1
1 TOWNGATE SH CTR
2 FALKLAND SQ
3 WINCHESTER PL
4 NIGHTINGALE LA
5 OLD TOWN MEWS
6 POST OFFICE LA
7 THE BROMBYS
8 WESTONS LA
9 CARTER'S LA
10 NELSON CT
11 GRENVILLE CT
12 LAGLAND CT
13 DANIEL GDNS
14 PROSPEROUS ST
15 THE SEED WAREHOUSE
16 BULL LA
17 BALL LA
18 BUTTON'S LA
19 QUAY POINT
20 THE KIOSKS
21 TAYLOR'S BLDGS
22 DRAKE CT
23 GRAY'S YD

C2
1 BANOCROFT CT
2 CROWE HILL CT
3 MERTON CT
4 THOROGOOD CT
5 BIRDS HILL GDNS
6 LANSDELL CT
7 GARDENS CT
8 SUNNINGDALE
9 PARK VIEW

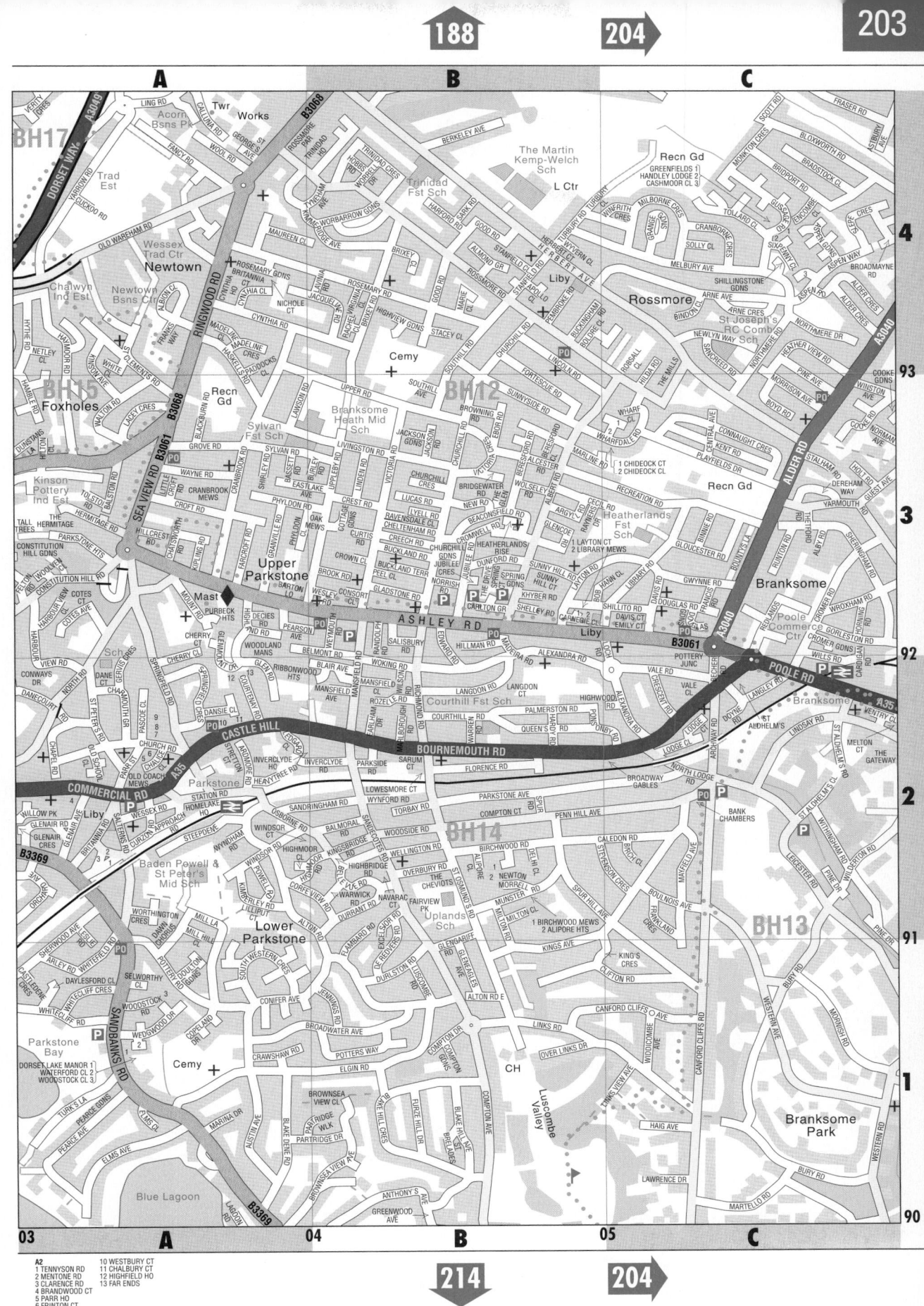

A2
1 TENNYSON RD
2 MENTONE RD
3 CLARENCE RD
4 BRANDWOOD CT
5 PARR HO
6 FRINTON CT
7 ST PETER'S CT
8 SINCLAIR CT
9 ELDON CT
10 WESTBURY CT
11 CHALBURY CT
12 HIGHFIELD HO
13 FAR ENDS

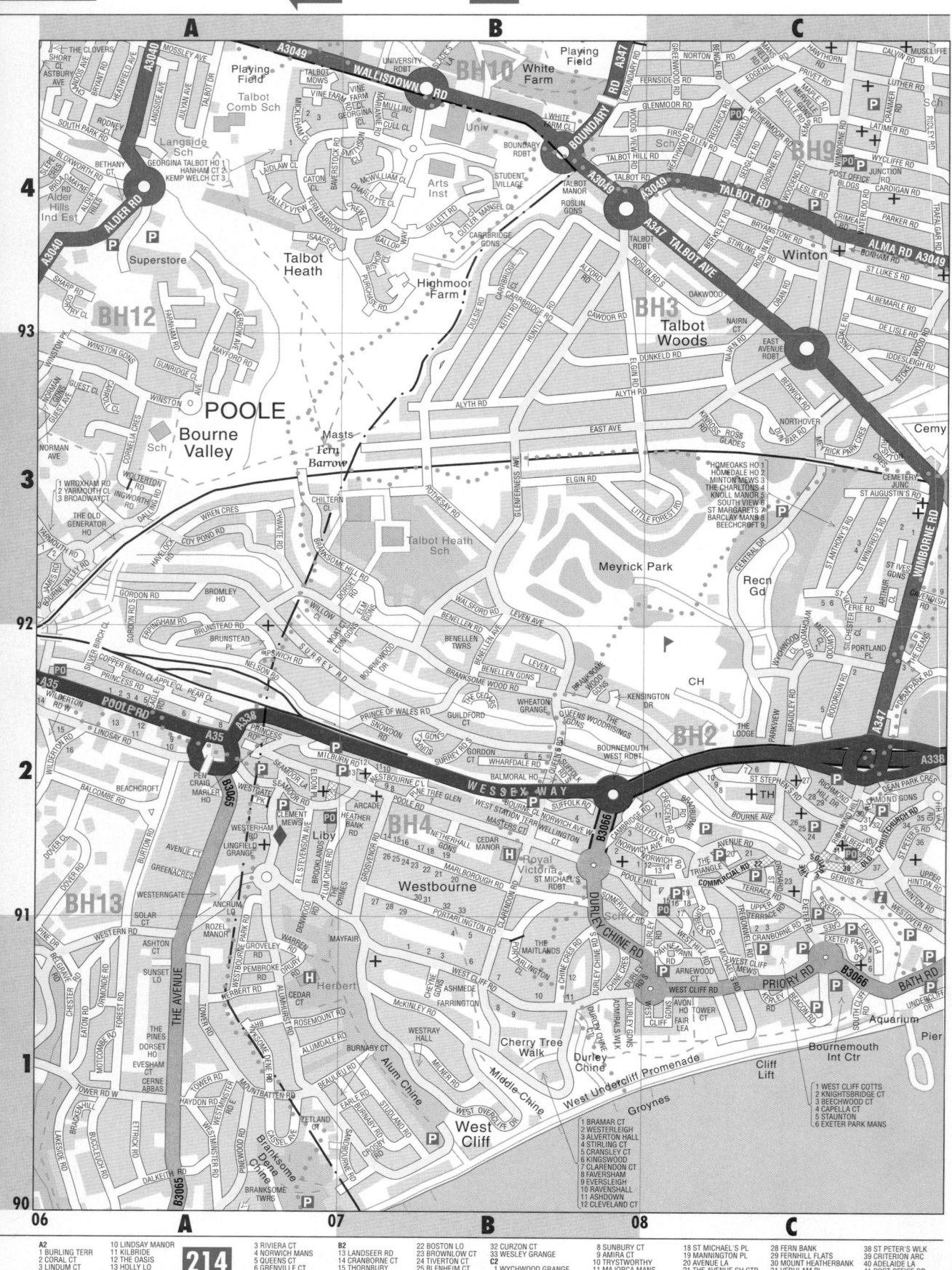

A3
1 CULFORD CT
2 APSLEY CT
3 TRELOEN CT
4 RAVANA CT
5 HOMELEIGH HO
6 BEECHY CT

7 WELLINGTON CT
8 MORINGTON CT
9 PARSONAGE CT
10 HAMILTON CT
11 MOORLEA
12 PORCHESTER CT

B3
1 OPHIR GDNS
2 METHUEN CT
3 LOWTHER GDNS
4 THE LANE
5 STEWART CL
6 HENVILLE RD

7 MALMESBURY PARK PL
8 WESLEY CL

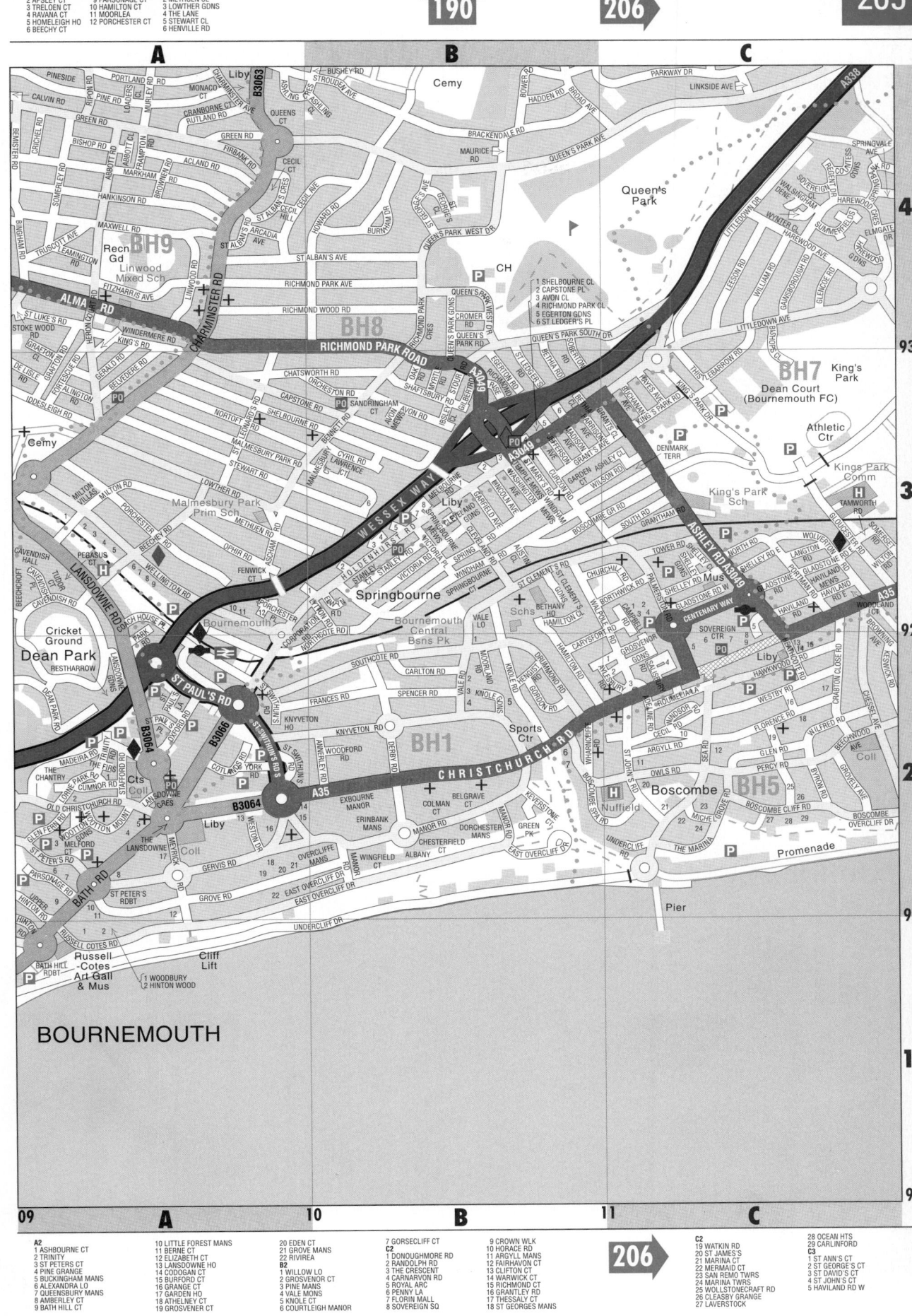

A2
1 ASHBOURNE CT
2 TRINITY
3 ST PETERS CT
4 PINE GRANGE
5 BUCKINGHAM MANS
6 ALEXANDRA LO
7 QUEENSBURY MANS
8 AMBERLEY CT
9 BATH HILL CT

10 LITTLE FOREST MANS
11 BERNE CT
12 ELIZABETH CT
13 LANSDOWNE HO
14 CODOGAN CT
15 BURFORD CT
16 GRANGE CT
17 GARDEN HO
18 ATHELNEY CT
19 GROSVENER CT

20 EDEN CT
21 GROVE MANS
22 RIVIERA

B2
1 WILLOW LO
2 GROSVENOR CT
3 PINE MANS
4 VALE MONS
5 KNOLE CT
6 COURTLEIGH MANOR

7 GORSECLIFF CT
C2
1 DONOUGHMORE RD
2 RANDOLPH RD
3 THE CRESCENT
4 CARNARVON RD
5 ROYAL ARC
6 PENNY LA
7 FLORIN MALL
8 SOVEREIGN SQ

9 CROWN WLK
10 HORACE RD
11 ARGYLL MANS
12 FAIRHAVON CT
13 CLIFTON CT
14 WARWICK CT
15 RICHMOND CT
16 GRANTLEY RD
17 THESSALY CT
18 ST GEORGES MANS

C2
19 WATKIN RD
20 ST JAMES'S
21 MARINA CT
22 MERMAID CT
23 SAN REMO TWRS
24 MARINA TWRS
25 WOLLSTONECRAFT RD
26 CLEASBY GRANGE
27 LAVERSTOCK

28 OCEAN HTS
29 CARLINFORD
C3
1 ST ANN'S CT
2 ST GEORGE'S CT
3 ST DAVID'S CT
4 ST JOHN'S CT
5 HAVILAND RD W

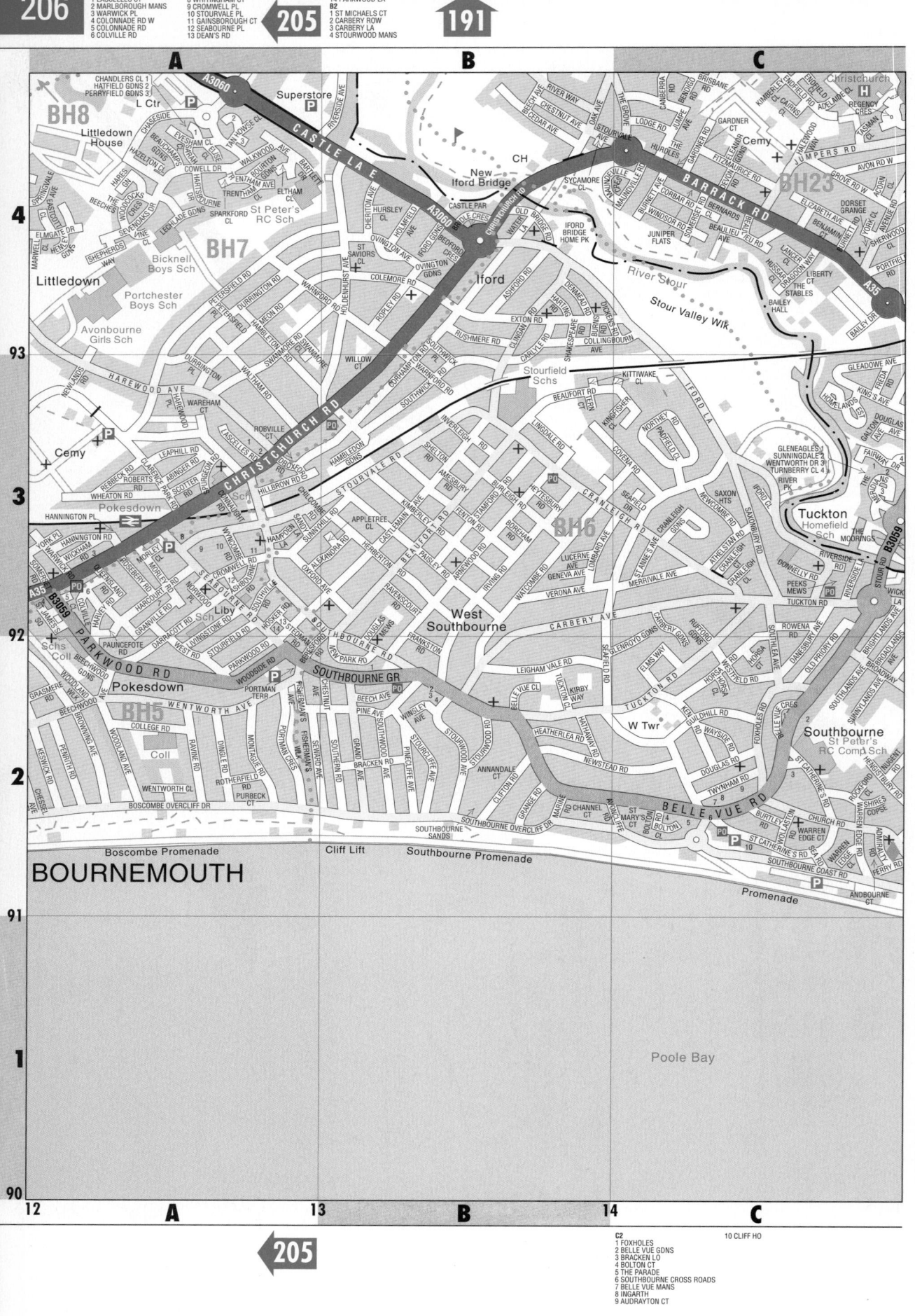

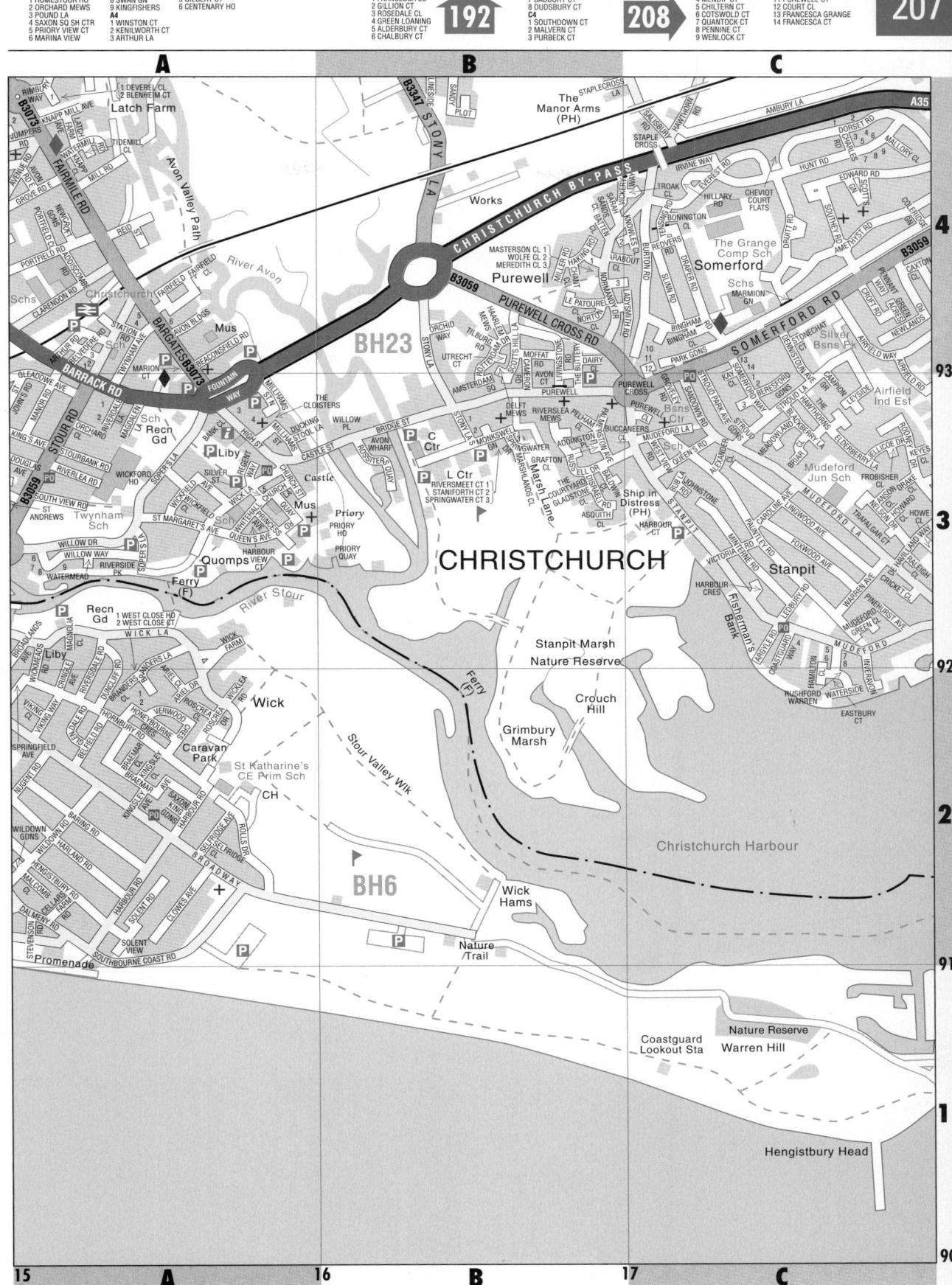

A4
1 LAVENDER VILLAS
2 BUCKINGHAM CT
3 CASTLE CT
4 CARISBROOKE CT
5 WINDSOR CT
6 HURST CT
7 BALMORAL CT
8 MERTON CT
9 BERMUDA CT
10 EXETER CT
11 PEMBROKE CT
12 HERTFORD CT
13 FRANCES CT
14 ROSEMARY CT
15 KENNETH CT
16 ALAN CT
17 WILLIAM CT
18 PENELOPE CT
19 STELLA CT

209
195

209

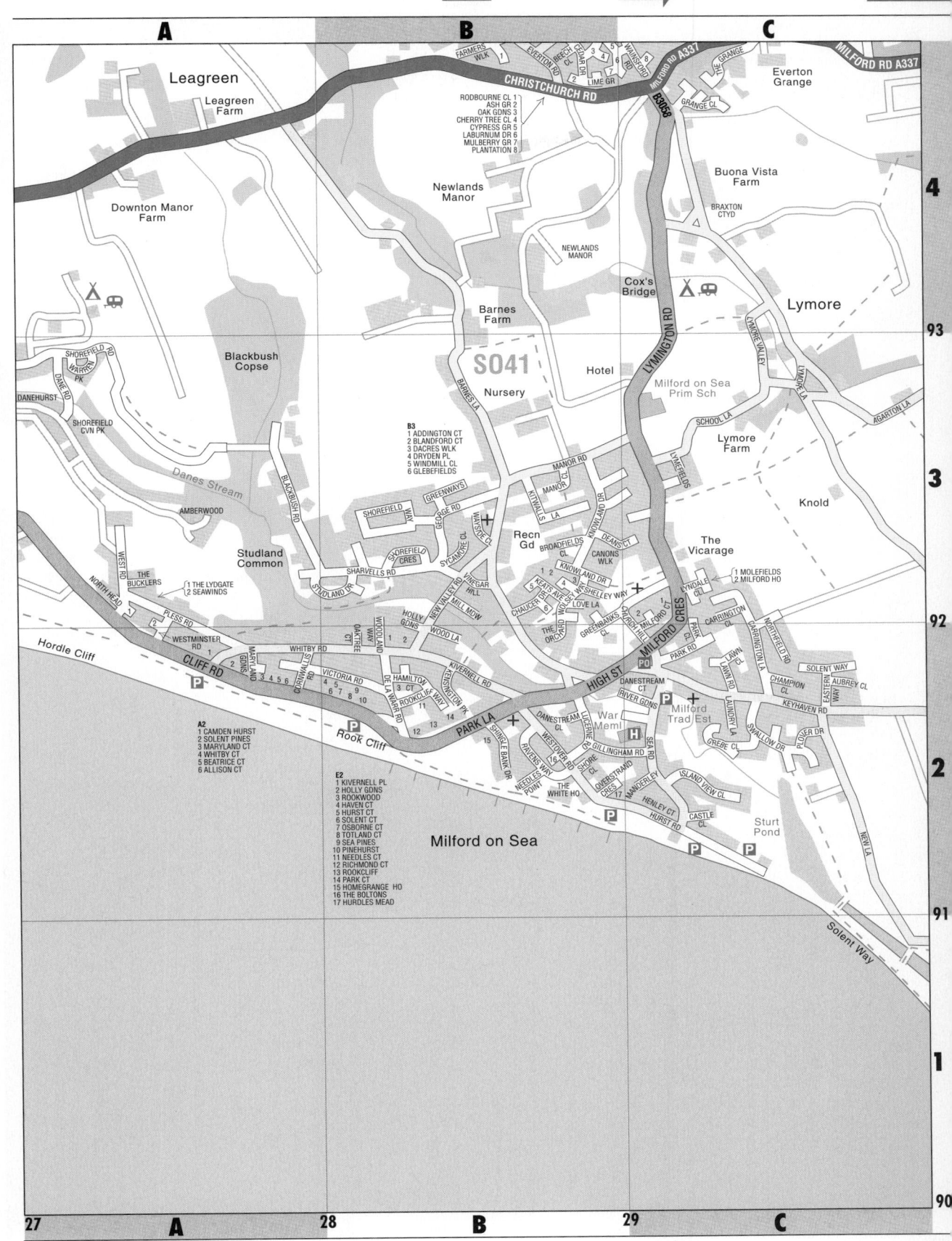

Leagreen

Leagreen
Farm

FARMERS WLK
EVERTON RD
BEECH
CEDAR DR
WAINSFORD RD
MILFORD RD A337
GRANGE

EVERTON RD
LIME GR

CHRISTCHURCH RD

RODBOURNE CL 1
ASH GR 2
OAK GDNS 3
CHERRY TREE CL 4
CYPRESS GR 5
LABURNUM DR 6
MULBERRY GR 7
PLANTATION 8

MILFORD RD A337

B3058

GRANGE CL

Everton
Grange

Downton Manor
Farm

Newlands
Manor

Buona Vista
Farm

BRAXTON
CTYD

SHOREFIELD
WARREN PK

SHOREFIELD RD
DANE RD

DANEHURST

SHOREFIELD
CVN PK

Blackbush
Copse

Newlands
Manor

Barnes Farm

Cox's
Bridge

Lymore

SO41

Nursery

Hotel

Milford on Sea
Prim Sch

LYMORE VALLEY

LYMORE LA

AGARTON LA

LYMINGTON RD

LYMEFIELDS

SCHOOL LA

Lymore
Farm

Danes Stream

AMBERWOOD

BLACKBUSH RD

B3
1 ADDINGTON CT
2 BLANDFORD CT
3 DACRES WLK
4 DRYDEN PL
5 WINDMILL CL
6 GLEBEFIELDS

BARNES LA

MANOR RD

MANOR LA

KINWALLS LA

KNOWLAND DR

DEANS CT

Knold

The
Vicarage

1 MOLEFIELDS
2 MILFORD HO

WEST RD

THE
BUCKLERS

Studland
Common

1 THE LYDGATE
2 SEAWINDS

SHOREFIELD
WAY

GEORGE RD

GREENWAYS

SHOREFIELD
CRES

SYCAMORE CL

WAYSIDE RD

Recn
Gd

BROADFIELDS
CL

CANONS
WLK

LYNDALE

MILFORD CRES

CARRINGTON LA

NORTH HEAD

PLESS RD

STUDLAND RD

SHARVELLS RD

VINEGAR CL

NEW VALLEY RD

MILL MDW

KNOWLAND
CL

KEATS AVE

SHELLEY WAY

CHAUCER DR

WILLIS LA

LOVE LA

GREENBANKS
CL

CHURCH LA

MILFORD
CL

PARK RD

PO

LAWN RD

SOLENT WAY

NORTHFIELD RD

EASTERN
WAY

AUBREY CL

WESTMINSTER
RD

MARYLAND
GDNS

GUNNVILLS RD

OAKTREE
CT

WOODLAND
WAY

HOLLY
GDNS

WOOD LA

THE
ORCHARD

CHAMPION

LAUNDRY LA

CARRINGTON LA

KEYHAVEN RD

Hordle Cliff

CLIFF RD

WHITBY RD

VICTORIA RD

DE LA WARR RD

KENSINGTON PK

HAMILTON
CT

KIVERNELL RD

ROOKCLIFF
WAY

HIGH ST

DANESTREAM
CT

RIVER GDNS

P

Milford
Trad Est

SWALLOW DR

PLOVER DR

A2
1 CAMDEN HURST
2 SOLENT PINES
3 MARYLAND CT
4 WHITBY CT
5 BEATRICE CT
6 ALLISON CT

P

Rook Cliff

PARK LA

SHINGLE BANK DR

NEEDLES
POINT

DANESTREAM
CL

LUCERNE RD

WESTOVER RD

SHORE
RD

GILLINGHAM RD

SEA RD

War
Meml

H

GREBE CL

CASTLE
CL

Sturt
Pond

NEVIL LA

E2
1 KIVERNELL PL
2 HOLLY GDNS
3 ROOKWOOD
4 HAVEN CT
5 HURST CT
6 SOLENT CT
7 OSBORNE CT
8 TOTLAND CT
9 SEA PINES
10 PINEHURST
11 NEEDLES CT
12 RICHMOND CT
13 ROOKCLIFF
14 PARK CT
15 HOMEGRANGE HO
16 THE BOLTONS
17 HURDLES MEAD

THE
WHITE HO

RAVENS WAY

OVERSTRAND
CRES

HENLEY CT

HURST RD

MANDERLEY

ISLAND VIEW CL

Milford on Sea

P

P

P

Solent Way

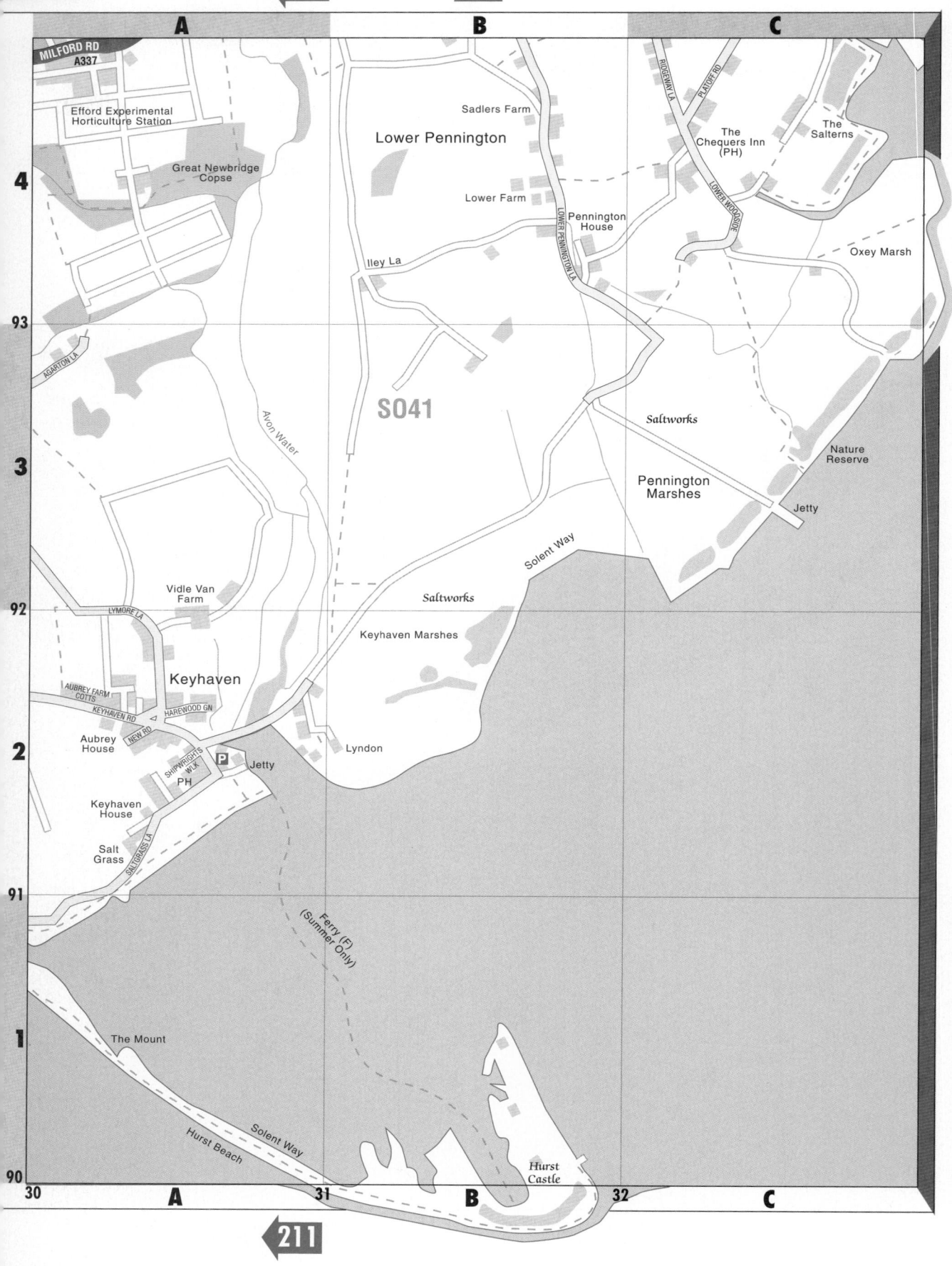

MILFORD RD
A337

Efford Experimental
Horticulture Station

Great Newbridge
Copse

Sadlers Farm

Lower Pennington

Lower Farm

The Chequers Inn
(PH)

The Salterns

Pennington
House

RIDGEWAY LA

PLATOFF RD

LOWER MOORSIDE

Iley La

Oxey Marsh

4

93

AGARTON LA

Avon Water

SO41

Saltworks

LOWER PENNINGTON LA

Nature
Reserve

3

Pennington
Marshes

Jetty

Solent Way

Saltworks

92

LYMORE LA

Vidle Van
Farm

Keyhaven Marshes

Keyhaven

AUBREY FARM
COTTS

KEYHAVEN RD

HAREWOOD GN

NEW RD

Aubrey
House

Lyndon

2

SHIPWRIGHTS
WLK

P

Jetty

PH

Keyhaven
House

SALTGRASS LA

Salt
Grass

91

Ferry (F)
(Summer Only)

1

The Mount

Solent Way

Hurst Beach

Hurst
Castle

90

30   A   31   B   32   C

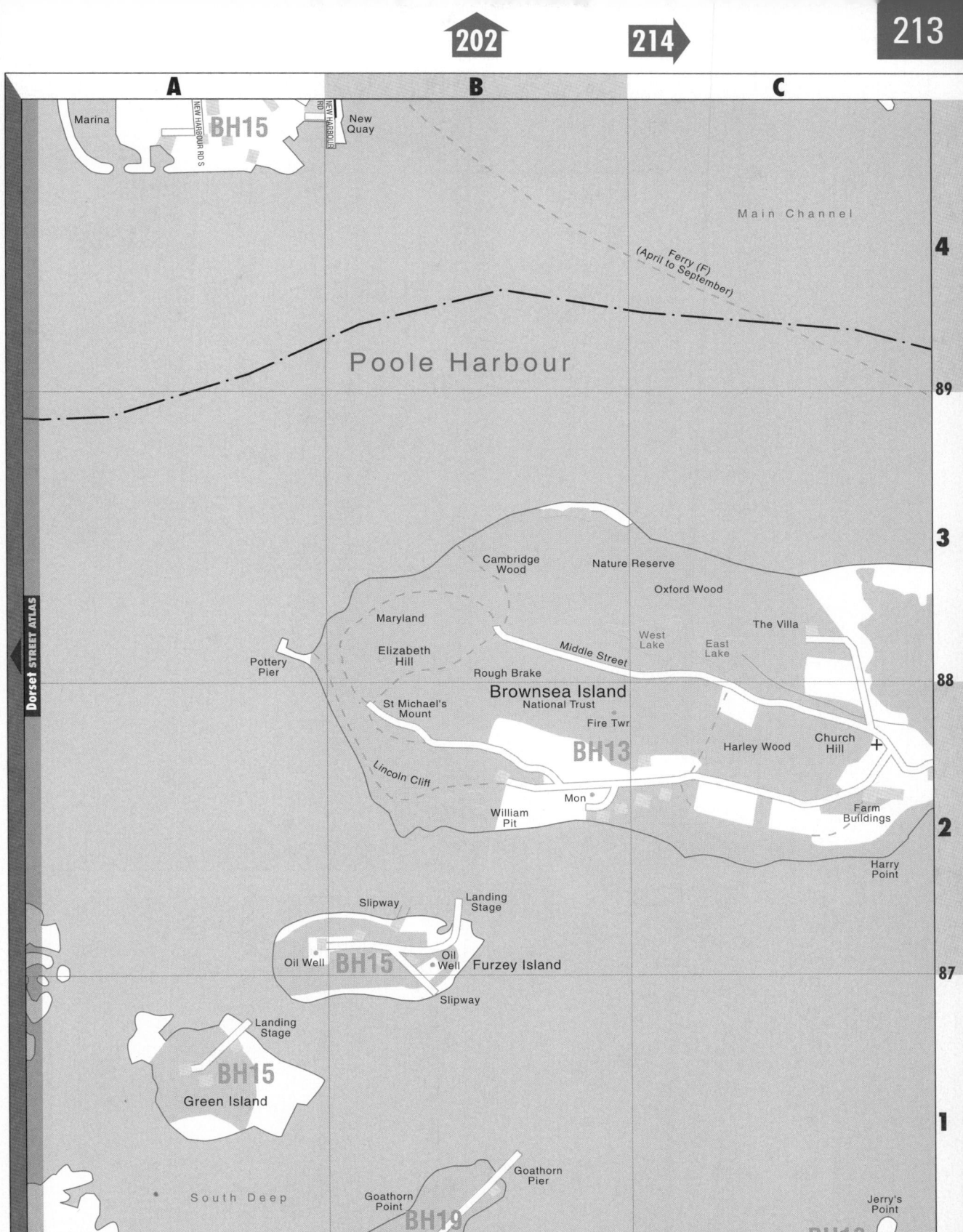

A | B | C

Marina

BH15

NEW HARBOUR RD S

NEW HARBOUR RD

New Quay

Main Channel

4

Ferry (F)
(April to September)

Poole Harbour

89

Dorset STREET ATLAS

3

Cambridge Wood

Nature Reserve

Oxford Wood

Maryland

West Lake

The Villa

East Lake

Elizabeth Hill

Middle Street

Pottery Pier

Rough Brake

Brownsea Island

88

St Michael's Mount

National Trust

Fire Twr

BH13

Harley Wood

Church Hill

Lincoln Cliff

Mon

William Pit

Harry Point

Farm Buildings

2

Slipway

Landing Stage

Oil Well

BH15

Oil Well

Furzey Island

87

Slipway

Landing Stage

BH15

Green Island

1

South Deep

Goathorn Pier

Jerry's Point

BH20

Goathorn Point

Goathorn Plantation

BH19

Brand's Bay

BH19

86

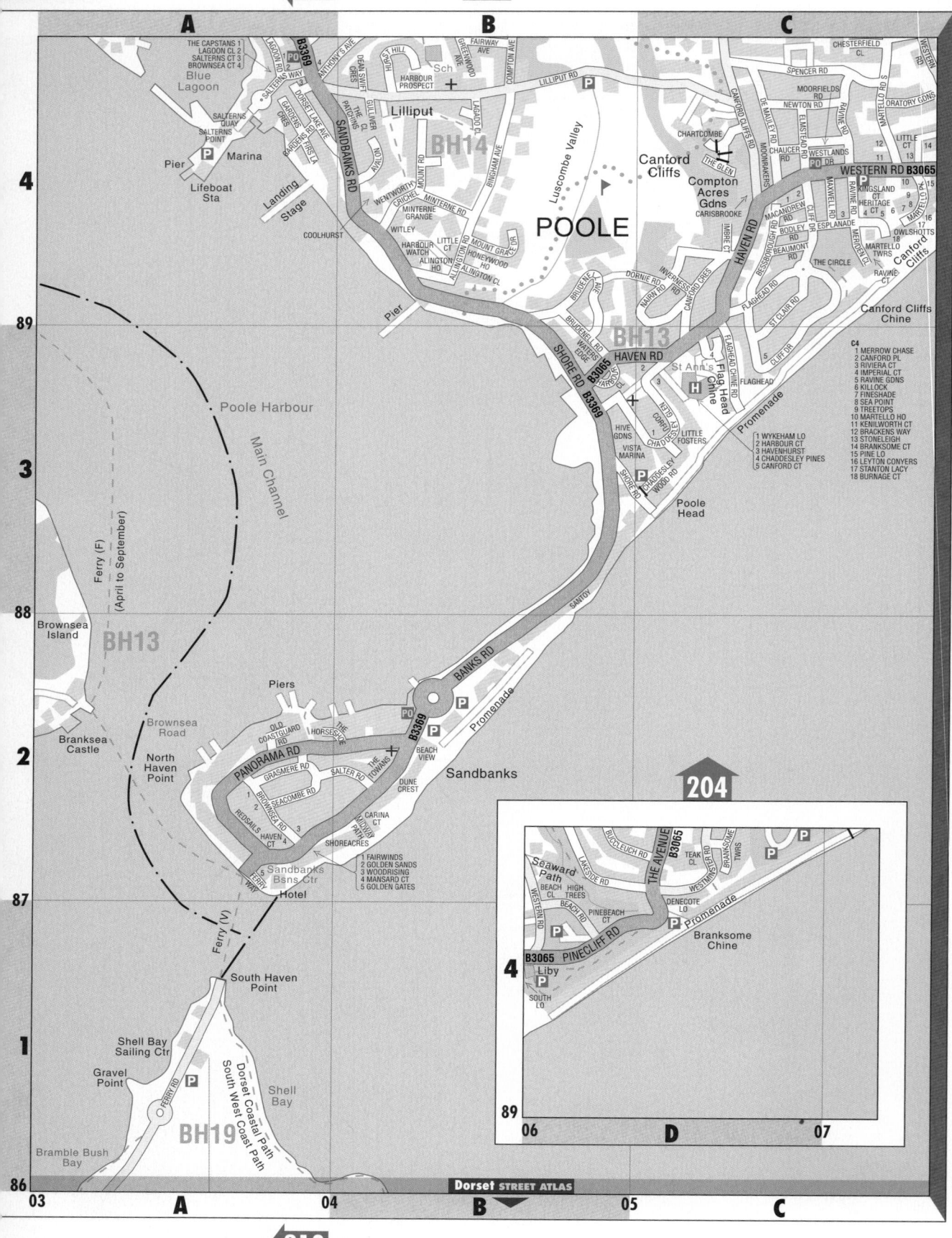

A B C

4

Blue
Lagoon

THE CAPSTANS 1
LAGOON CL 2
SALTERNS CT 3
BROWNSEA CT 4

Marina

Pier

Lifeboat
Sta

Landing
Stage

SALTERNS
QUAY
SALTERNS
POINT

COOLHURST

SANDBANKS RD

B3369

ANTHONY'S AVE

FAIRWAY
AVE

GREENWOOD
AVE

COMPTON AVE

Lilliput

LILLIPUT RD

BH14

Sch

Harbour
PROSPECT

Luscombe Valley

Canford
Cliffs

Compton
Acres
Gdns

CARISBROOKE

POOLE

CHARTCOMBE

THE GLEN

CHESTERFIELD
CL

SPENCER RD

MOORFIELDS
RD

NEWTON RD

WESTLANDS

WESTERN RD B3065

KINGSLAND

HERITAGE

OWLSHOTTS

MARTELLO
TWRS

CANFORD CLIFFS RD

RAVINE RD

Canford
Cliffs

THE CIRCLE

89

Poole Harbour

Main Channel

Pier

SHORE RD

B3065

B3369

HAVEN RD

BH13

HAVEN RD

St Ann's

H

Flag
Head
Chine

Promenade

Canford Cliffs
Chine

C4
1 MERROW CHASE
2 CANFORD PL
3 RIVIERA CT
4 IMPERIAL CT
5 RAVINE GDNS
6 KILLOCK
7 FINESHADE
8 SEA POINT
9 TREETOPS
10 MARTELLO HO
11 KENILWORTH CT
12 BRACKENS WAY
13 STONELEIGH
14 BRANKSOME CT
15 PINE LO
16 LEYTON CONVERS
17 STANTON LACY
18 BURNAGE CT

1 WYKEHAM LO
2 HARBOUR CT
3 HAVENHURST
4 CHADDESLEY PINES
5 CANFORD CT

HIVE
GDNS

VISTA
MARINA

Little
FOSTERS

Poole
Head

3

Ferry (F)
(April to September)

Brownsea
Island

BH13

SANTOY

88

Branksea
Castle

Brownsea
Road

North
Haven
Point

Piers

OLD
COASTGUARD
RD

PANORAMA RD

GRASMERE RD

SEACOMBE RD

REDSAILS

HAVEN
CT

SHOREACRES

THE
HORSESHOE

SALTER RD

THE
TOWANS

BEACH
VIEW

DUNE
CREST

CARINA
CT

B3369

PO

P

P

Promenade

Sandbanks

1 FAIRWINDS
2 GOLDEN SANDS
3 WOODRISING
4 MANSARD CT
5 GOLDEN GATES

BANKS RD

204

2

Sandbanks
Bsns Ctr

Hotel

FERRY
WAY

Seaward
Path

BEACH
CL

HIGH
TREES

BEACH
RD

PINEBEACH

DENECOTE
LO

Promenade

Branksome
Chine

THE AVENUE

B3065

BUCCLEUCH
CL

LAKESIDE RD

WESTMINSTER RD

TEAK
CL

BRANKSOME
TWRS

P

P

87

Ferry (V)

South Haven
Point

B3065 PINECLIFF RD

Liby

SOUTH
LO

4

89

06 D 07

1

Shell Bay
Sailing Ctr

Gravel
Point

FERRY RD

P

BH19

Bramble Bush
Bay

Shell Bay

Dorset Coastal Path
South West Coast Path

86

03 A 04 B 05 C

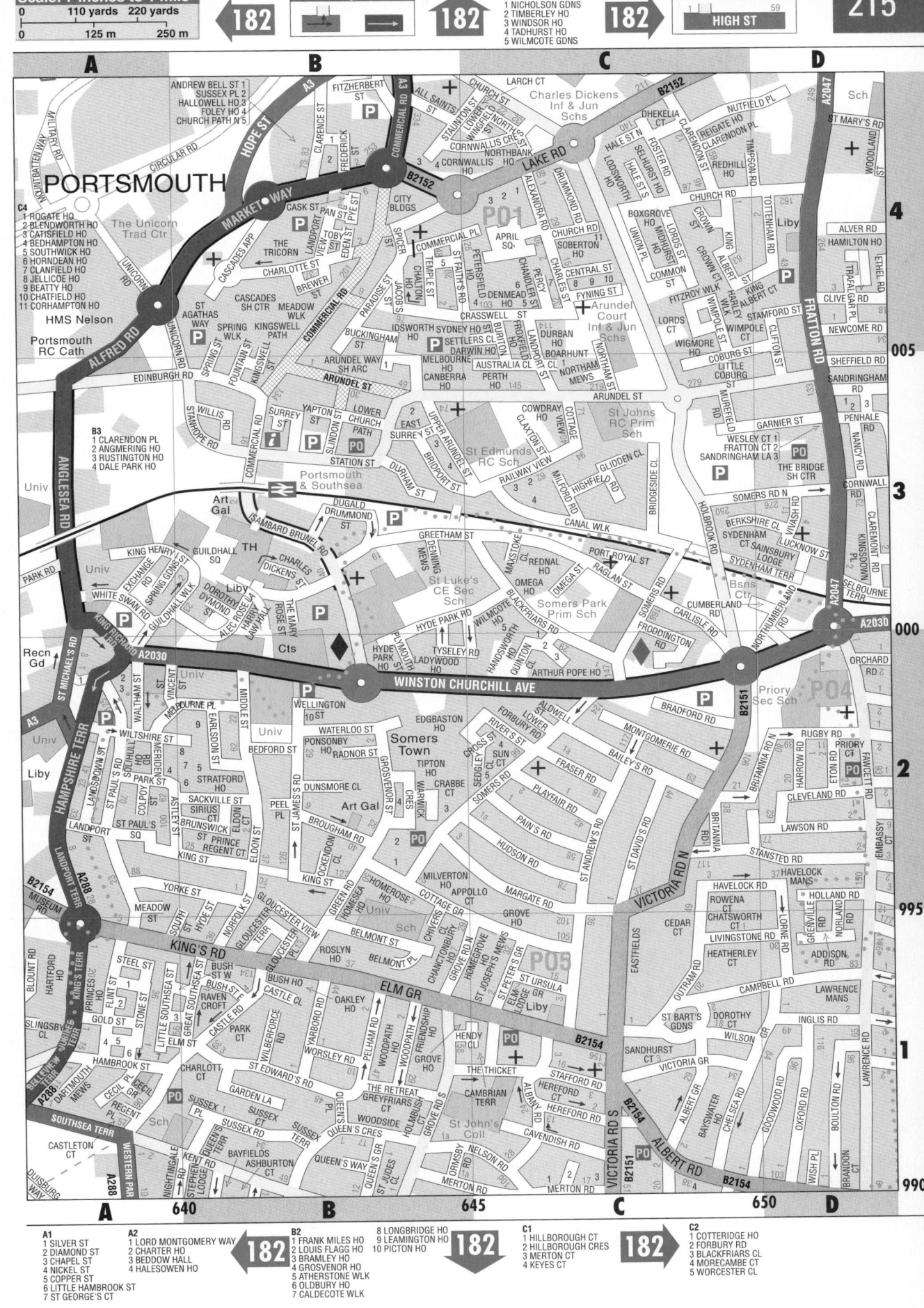

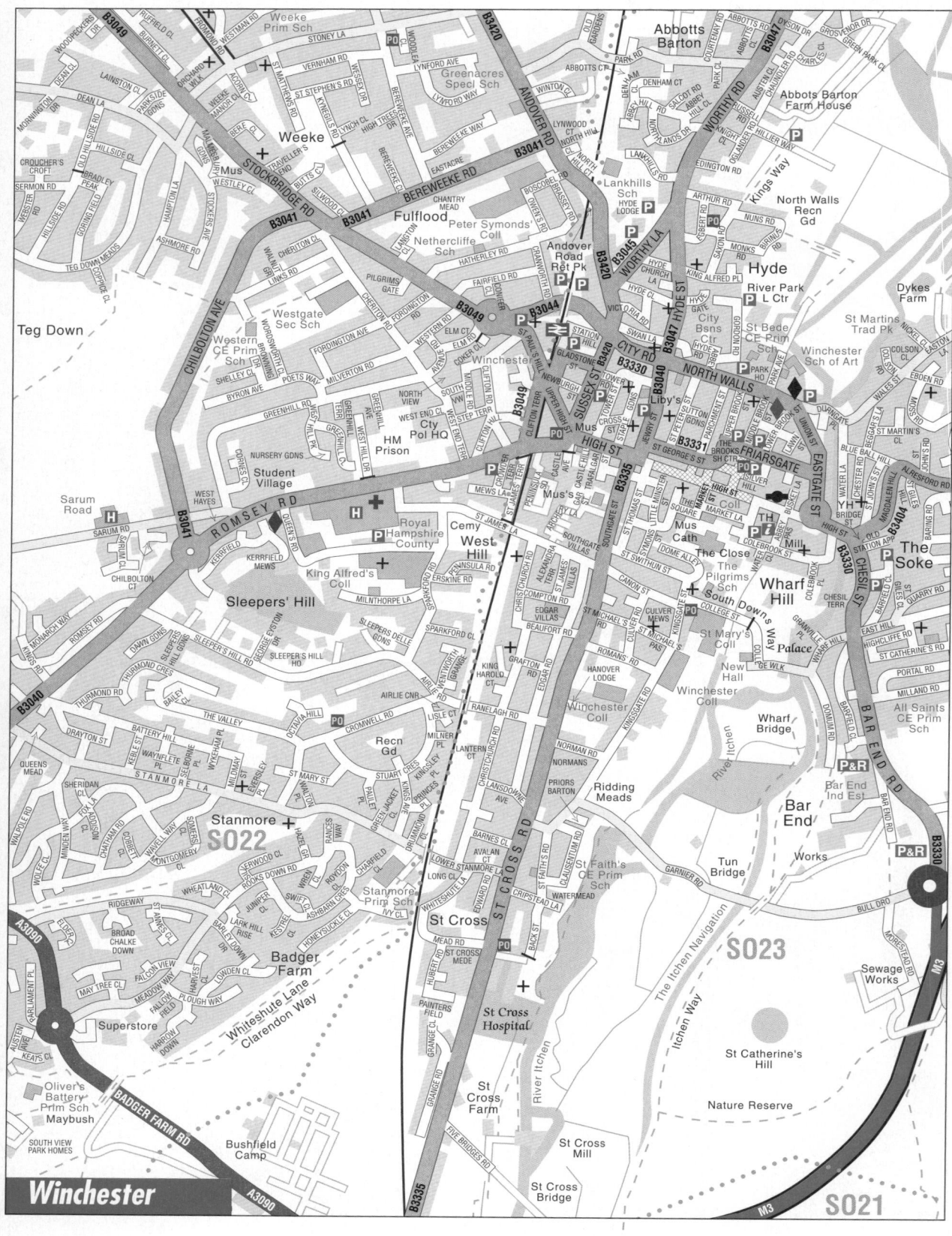

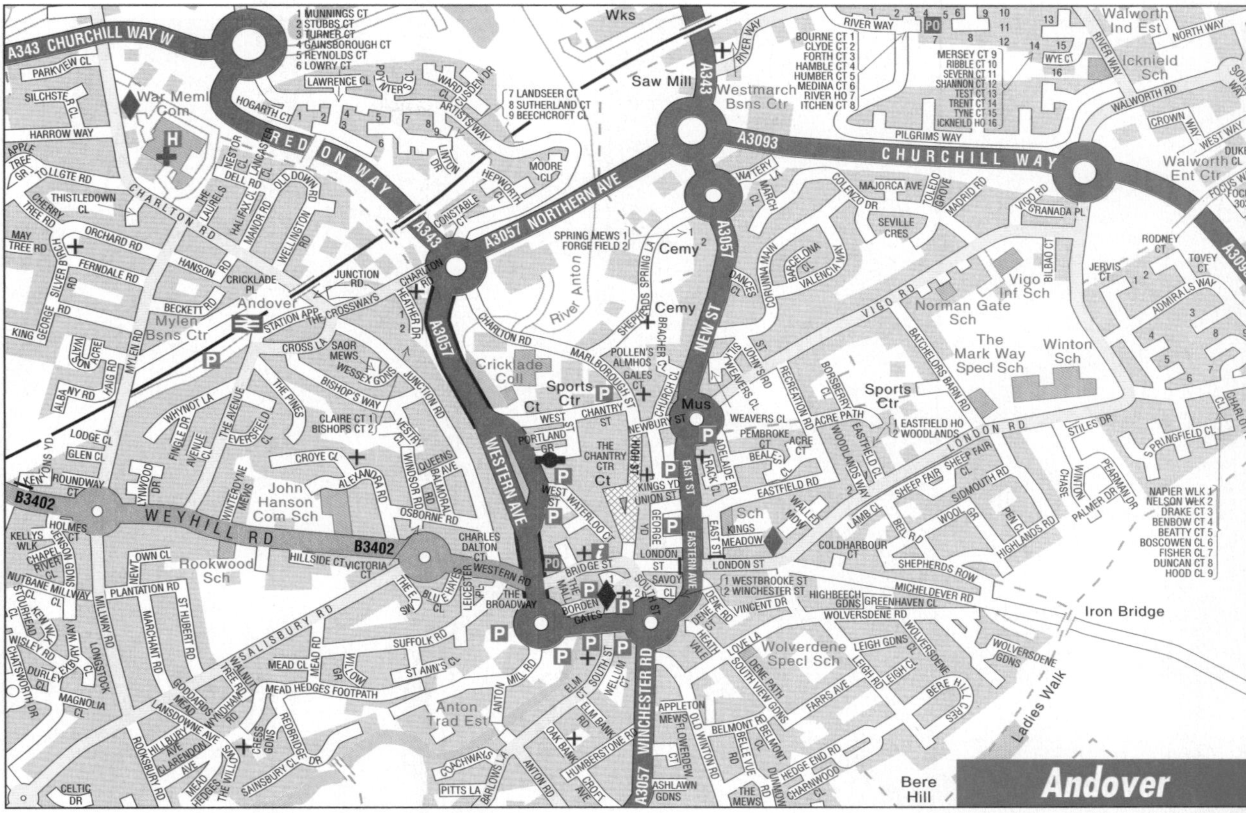

Andover

A343 CHURCHILL WAY W · PARKVIEW CL · SILCHSTE · HARROW WAY · War Meml Com · War Meml Com · APPLE · CHERRY · MAY TREE RD · ORCHARD RD · THISTLEDOWN CL · TOLLGTE RD · CHARLTON RD · HOGARTH CT · LAWRENCE CL · ARTIST WAY · REDON WAY · A343 · A3057 NORTHERN AVE · A3093 · CHURCHILL WAY · Wks · Saw Mill · Westmarch Bsns Ctr · RIVER WAY · BOURNE CT 1 · CLYDE CT 2 · FORTH CT 3 · HAMBLE CT 4 · HUMBER CT 5 · MEDINA CT 6 · RIVER HO 7 · ITCHEN CT 8 · PILGRIMS WAY · MERSEY CT 9 · RIBBLE CT 10 · SEVERN CT 11 · SHANNON CT 12 · TRENT CT 13 · TYNE CT 14 · ICKNIELD HO 15 · WYE CT 16 · Icknield Sch · Walworth Ind Est · NORTH WAY · SOUTH WAY · WEST WAY · CROWN WAY · DUKE · Walworth Ent Ctr · FOCUS 003

1 MUNNINGS CT · 2 STUBBS CT · 3 TURNER CT · 4 GAINSBOROUGH CT · 5 REYNOLDS CT · 6 LOWRY CT · 7 LANDSEER CT · 8 SUTHERLAND CT · 9 BEECHCROFT CT

Andover Mylen Bsns Ctr · CROSS LN · WESSEX CT · BISHOP'S WAY · CLAIRE CT 1 · BISHOPS CT 2 · CROYE CL · John Hanson Com Sch · Rookwood Sch · Hillside Victoria · The Broadway · Cricklade Coll · Sports Ctr · Mus · WEAVERS CL · Sports Ctr · The Mark Way Specl Sch · Winton Sch · Norman Gate Sch · MAJORCA AVE · GRANADA PL · SEVILLE CRES · BILBAO CT · VALENCIA · CELOMA · Vigo Inf Sch · RODNEY CT · TOVEY CT · JERVIS CT · ADMIRALS WAY · NAPIER WLK 1 · NELSON WLK 2 · DRAKE CT 3 · BENBOW CT 4 · BEATTY CT 5 · BOSCOWEN CL 6 · FISHER CL 7 · DUNCAN CT 8 · HOOD CL 9

WEYHILL RD · B3402 · B3402 · SALISBURY RD · Anton Trad Est · WINCHESTER RD · Kings Meadow · Iron Bridge · Wolverdene Specl Sch · Ladies Walk · Bere Hill · Ashlawn Gdns

River Anton · Cemy · Cemy · SPRING MEWS · FORGE FIELD · DANES · NEW ST · A3057 · HOOK · A3057 WINCHESTER RD

Basingstoke

KNIGHTS PARK · Depot · COLLEGE RD 1 · MAY ST 2 · CROMWELL RD · KINGSCLERE RD · SHERBORNE RD · WEALE RD · BURGESS RD · LYFORD RD · DOSWELL WAY · GRESLEY RD · A339 · RINGWAY · BASING RD · LANCASTER RD 1 · KINGFISHER CT 2 · Cemy · Basingstoke · PHOENIX PARK · BUNNIAN PL · BASING VIEW · THE PARADE · BASING VIEW

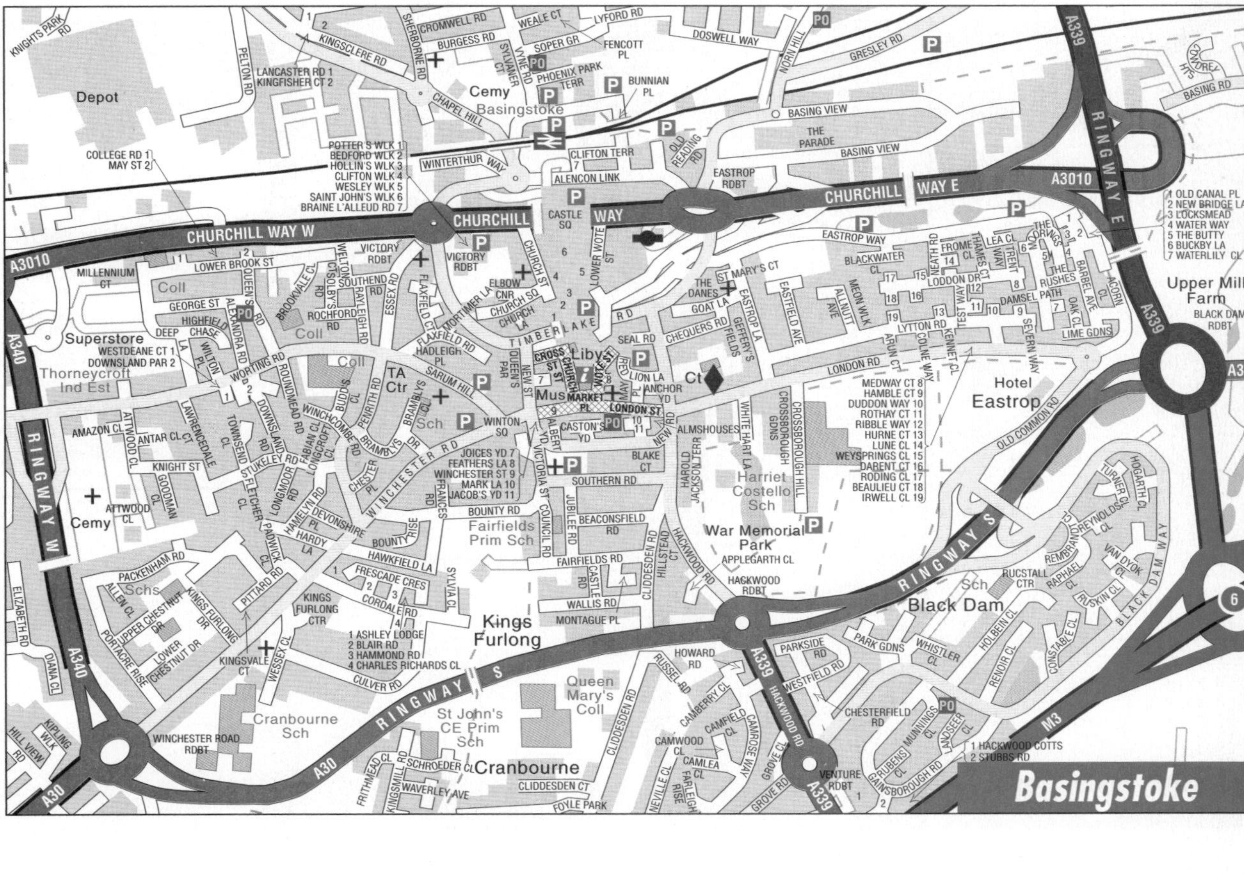

CHURCHILL WAY E · A3010 · RINGWAY E · POTTER'S WLK 1 · BEDFORD WLK 2 · HOLLIN'S WLK 3 · CLIFTON WLK 4 · WESLEY WLK 5 · SAINT JOHN'S WLK 6 · BRAINE L'ALLEUD WLK 7 · WINTERTHUR WAY · CLIFTON TERR · ALENCON LINK · EASTROP RDBT · Upper Mill Farm · BLACK DAM RDBT

1 OLD CANAL PL · 2 NEW BRIDGE LA · 3 LOCKSMEAD · 4 WATER WAY · 5 THE BUTTY · 6 BUCKBY LA · 7 WATERLILY CL

CHURCHILL WAY W · A3010 · VICTORY RDBT · CASTLE SQ · CASTLE SQ · MILLENNIUM CT · Superstore · Thorneycroft Ind Est · A340 · RINGWAY W · LOWER BROOK ST · GEORGE ST · Coll · Coll · Coll · TA Ctr · Lib · Mus · MARKET · LONDON ST · Hotel Eastrop · Harriet Costello Sch · Black Dam · A339 · A30 · M3 · 6

WESTDEANE CT 1 · DOWNSLAND PAR 2 · AMAZON CL · ANTAR CL · KNIGHT ST · ATTWOOD CL · Cemy · PACKENHAM RD · Schs · KINGS FURLONG CTR · KINGSVALE CT · Cranbourne Sch · WINCHESTER ROAD RDBT · St John's CE Prim Sch · Cranbourne · Queen Mary's Coll · Kings Furlong

1 ASHLEY LODGE · 2 BLAIR RD · 3 HAMMOND RD · 4 CHARLES RICHARDS CL

MEDWAY CT 8 · HAMBLE CT 9 · DUDDON WAY 10 · ROTHAY CT 11 · RIBBLE WAY 12 · HURNE CT 13 · LUNE CL 14 · WEYSPRINGS CL 15 · DABENT CT 16 · RODING CL 17 · BEAULIEU CT 18 · IRWELL CL 19

War Memorial Park · Fairfields Prim Sch · HACKWOOD RDBT · PARKSIDE RD · VENTURE RDBT · A339 · 1 HACKWOOD COTTS · 2 STUBBS RD

1 EASTFIELD HO · 2 WOODLANDS · 1 WESTBROOKE ST · 2 VINCENT ST

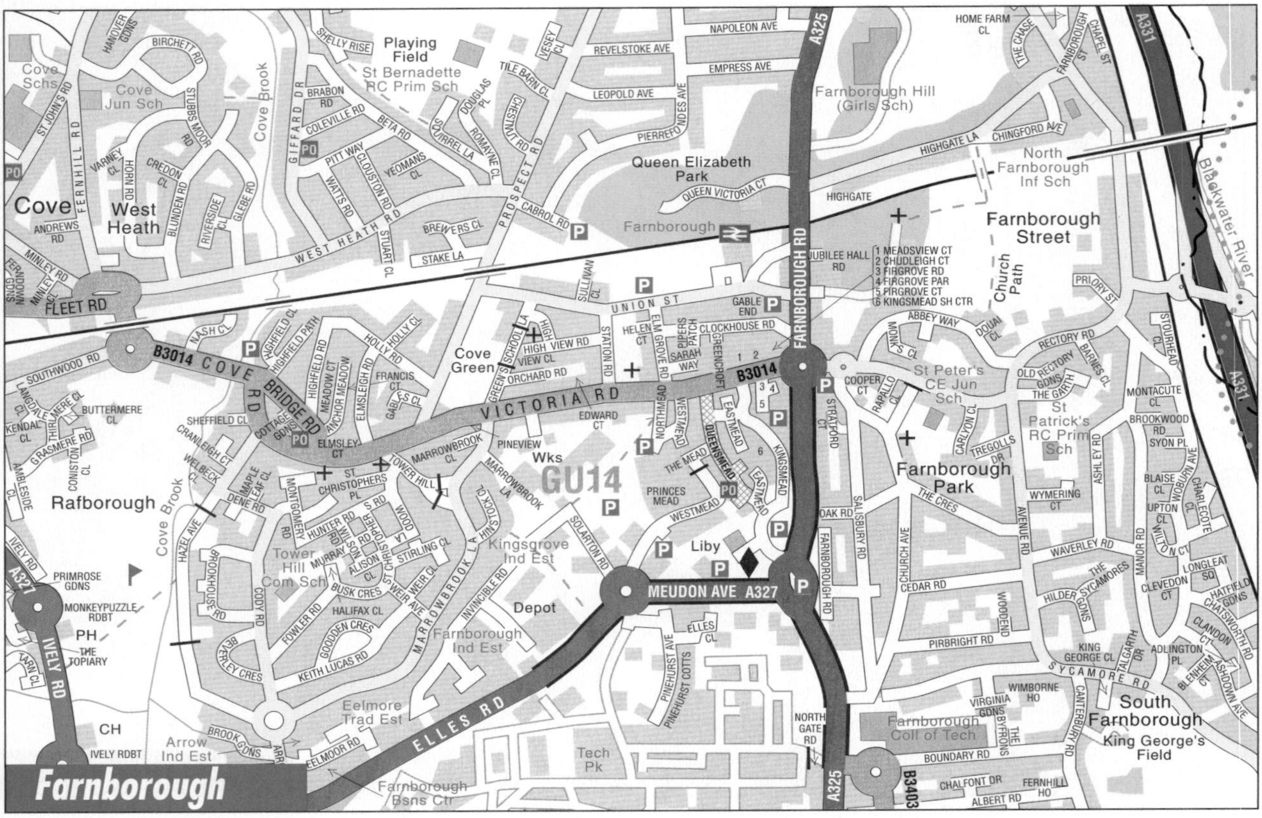

Farnborough

Cove Schs • Cove Jun Sch • Cove • West Heath • Rafborough • Fleet Rd • B3014 Cove Bridge Rd • Cove Green • Victoria Rd • GU14 • Tower Hill Com Sch • Kingsgrove Ind Est • Depot • Farnborough Ind Est • Meudon Ave A327 • Liby • Elles Rd • Eelmore Trad Est • Arrow Ind Est • Farnborough Bsns Ctr • Ively Rd A327 • Ively Rdbt • Monkeypuzzle Rdbt • Primrose Gdns • The Topiary • Playing Field • St Bernadette RC Prim Sch • Queen Elizabeth Park • Farnborough • Napoleon Ave • Empress Ave • Farnborough Hill (Girls Sch) • North Farnborough Inf Sch • Farnborough Street • Church Path • St Peter's CE Jun Sch • St Patrick's RC Prim Sch • Farnborough Park • South Farnborough • King George's Field • Farnborough Coll of Tech • Farnborough Rd A325 • Blackwater River • A331 • B3403

1 Meadsview Ct
2 Chudleigh Ct
3 Firgrove Rd
4 Firgrove Par
5 Firgrove Ct
6 Kingsmead Sh Ctr

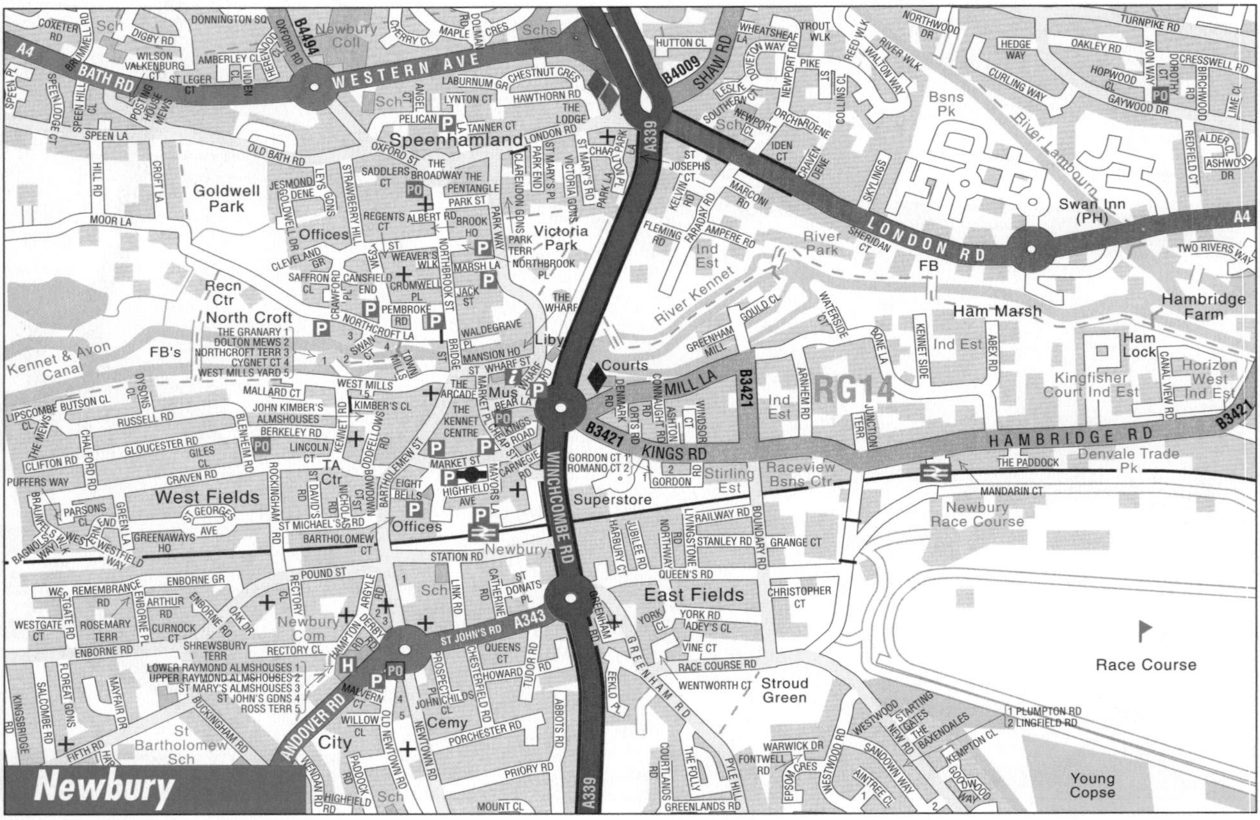

Newbury

A4 Bath Rd • B4494 • Western Ave • Newbury Coll • Speenhamland • Goldwell Park • North Croft • Kennet & Avon Canal • West Fields • The Granary • Dolton Mews • Northcroft Terr • Cygnet Ct • West Mills Yard • Recn Ctr • Victoria Park • The Wharf • River Kennet • River Park • Liby • Courts • Mus • Winchcombe • B3421 Kings Rd • Mill La • RG14 • Superstore • Newbury • Offices • East Fields • Andover Rd A343 • City • Cemy • St Bartholomew Sch • Newbury Com Sch • Stroud Green • B4009 Shaw Rd • Bsns Pk • River Lambourn • Swan Inn (PH) • London Rd A4 • Ham Marsh • Hambridge Farm • Ham Lock • Kingfisher Court Ind Est • Horizon West Ind Est • Hambridge Rd B3421 • Denvale Trade Pk • Newbury Race Course • Raceview Bsns Ctr • Race Course • Young Copse • A339

Church Rd **6** Beckenham BR2..........**53** C6

Place name	**Location number**	**Locality, town or village**	**Postcode district**	**Page and grid square**
May be abbreviated on the map	Present when a number indicates the place's position in a crowded area of mapping	Shown when more than one place has the same name	District for the indexed place	Page number and grid reference for the standard mapping

Public and commercial buildings are highlighted in magenta   **Places of interest** are highlighted in blue with a star★

Abbreviations used in the index

Acad	**Academy**	Comm	**Common**	Gd	**Ground**	L	**Leisure**	Prom	**Prom**
App	**Approach**	Cott	**Cottage**	Gdn	**Garden**	La	**Lane**	Rd	**Road**
Arc	**Arcade**	Cres	**Crescent**	Gn	**Green**	Liby	**Library**	Recn	**Recreation**
Ave	**Avenue**	Cswy	**Causeway**	Gr	**Grove**	Mdw	**Meadow**	Ret	**Retail**
Bglw	**Bungalow**	Ct	**Court**	H	**Hall**	Meml	**Memorial**	Sh	**Shopping**
Bldg	**Building**	Ctr	**Centre**	Ho	**House**	Mkt	**Market**	Sq	**Square**
Bsns, Bus	**Business**	Ctry	**Country**	Hospl	**Hospital**	Mus	**Museum**	St	**Street**
Bvd	**Boulevard**	Cty	**County**	HQ	**Headquarters**	Orch	**Orchard**	Sta	**Station**
Cath	**Cathedral**	Dr	**Drive**	Hts	**Heights**	Pal	**Palace**	Terr	**Terrace**
Cir	**Circus**	Dro	**Drove**	Ind	**Industrial**	Par	**Parade**	TH	**Town Hall**
Cl	**Close**	Ed	**Education**	Inst	**Institute**	Pas	**Passage**	Univ	**University**
Cnr	**Corner**	Emb	**Embankment**	Int	**International**	Pk	**Park**	Wk, Wlk	**Walk**
Coll	**College**	Est	**Estate**	Intc	**Interchange**	Pl	**Place**	Wr	**Water**
Com	**Community**	Ex	**Exhibition**	Junc	**Junction**	Prec	**Precinct**	Yd	**Yard**

Index of localities, towns and villages

Abbotswood 28 A2	Compton (Sussex) 90 C1	Hayling Island 185 A4	New Milton 194 C2	Standon 9 A1
Alderholt 92 C3	Coombe Bissett 23 C4	Hedge End 105 B3	Nomansland 73 B4	Steep 40 B4
Ampfield 29 B2	Corfe Mullen 186 B3	Hermitage 161 A4	North Baddesley ...53 C3	Steep Marsh 20 A1
Ashington 163 A1	Cosham 158 A3	Highcliffe 208 C4	North Boarhunt ...109 A1	Stubbington 154 B2
Ashurst 100 A2	Cowplain 111 C2	High Cross 18 C1	North Hayling 160 B2	Swanmore 84 B3
Awbridge 26 C2	Cranborne 91 A4	Hill Brow 21 A1	Nursling 77 B3	Swanwick 129 A4
Barton on Sea 209 C3	Croucheston 22 A4	Holbury 150 B2	Oakley 163 C1	Sway 172 A1
Beaulieu 148 C1	Curdridge 106 B4	Holt Heath 138 A3	Otterbourne 31 B2	Thorney Island 161 A2
Beauworth 35 A4	Damerham 68 B3	Hordle 195 C2	Ower 75 C3	Three Legged Cross .138 C4
Bishopstoke 56 C2	Dean 59 C2	Horndean 112 B4	Owslebury 33 A2	Timsbury 27 B3
Bishop's Waltham ...83 B4	Denmead 111 A3	Horton Heath 81 B4	Pamphill 162 C3	Titchfield 153 C4
Blackfield 177 C4	Dibden Purlieu ...125 C1	Hurn 191 A4	Pentridge 42 A1	Totton 100 C4
Blashford 117 A2	Downton 47 A4	Hursley 30 A4	Petersfield 40 B2	Twyford 32 A3
Boldre 173 B1	Droxford 61 A1	Hythe 126 A3	Plaitford 50 A2	Upham 58 C3
Botley 106 A4	Durley 82 A3	Ibsley 117 A4	Poole 202 A2	Upton 201 B4
Bournemouth 206 A2	East Boldre 175 B3	Keyhaven 212 A2	Portchester 156 B4	Verwood 114 C2
Braishfield 28 B4	East Dean 4 A1	Kilmeston 14 B1	Portmore 198 A4	Walderton 137 C4
Bramdean 15 B2	East End 199 A4	Kingston 167 C4	Portsea Island 182 C3	Waltham Chase 83 C2
Bramshaw 73 C2	Eastleigh 55 C2	Kings Worthy 2 B3	Portsmouth 157 B2	Warnford 36 C2
Bransgore 193 A4	East Meon 38 B1	Landford 49 B2	Privet 17 B1	Warsash 128 B1
Breamore 70 A4	East Tytherley 4 C4	Langrish 39 B2	Purbrook 134 C2	Waterlooville 134 B4
Broadstone 187 A2	East Wellow 51 A3	Langstone 159 C4	Rake 21 C2	Westbourne 137 A2
Brockbridge 61 B1	Edmondsham 91 A2	Lee-on-the-Solent ..179 B1	Ramsdean 39 B1	West Dean 3 B3
Brockenhurst 145 C1	Emery Down 121 B3	Lepe 178 A1	Redlynch 47 C3	West End 80 C1
Brook 74 A1	Emsworth 136 C1	Linwood 118 A4	Ringwood 141 B4	West Meon 37 A2
Bucklers Hard 176 B2	Exbury 177 A3	Liss 21 A2	Ripley 168 B1	West Moors 138 C2
Buriton 65 B3	Fair Oak 57 B1	Littleton 1 A3	Rockbourne 44 C1	West Parley 189 C4
Burley 143 A2	Fareham 131 A2	Lockerley 4 C1	Romsey 52 C3	West Tisted 16 B4
Bursledon 128 A4	Fawley 151 A2	Locks Heath 129 B2	Rowland's Castle ..113 B1	West Tytherley 4 A4
Burton 192 B1	Ferndown 165 A3	Lover 48 A3	Rownhams 77 C4	West Wellow 50 C2
Cadnam 98 C4	Finchdean 113 B3	Lymington 197 B3	St Leonards 139 B2	Whiteparish 24 A2
Calshot 178 C4	Fordingbridge 69 C1	Lyndhurst 121 C3	Sandleheath 69 A2	Whitsbury 45 A2
Chalton 89 B3	Fratton 182 C2	Marchwood 101 C1	Shedfield 107 B4	Wick 46 B4
Chandler's Ford ...55 B4	Fritham 72 C1	Martin 43 A2	Sherfield English ...25 B1	Wickham 108 A2
Cheriton 14 B3	Froxfield Green 39 B4	Meonstoke 61 B3	Soberton 85 B3	Wimborne Minster ..163 A3
Chilcomb 11 C3	Godshill 70 C1	Michelmersh 6 B1	Sopley 192 A4	Winchester 10 B3
Chilworth 54 B1	Gosport 181 B3	Milford on Sea 211 B2	Southampton 102 B2	Woodgreen 70 C4
Christchurch 207 B3	Hambledon 86 B1	Minstead 98 A2	Southbourne 161 C4	Woodlands 114 A3
Clanfield 88 B3	Hamble-le-Rice ...128 A1	Mottisfont 5 C1	South Harting 66 C2	Wootton 171 A1
Colden Common 32 A1	Hamworthy 201 B2	Netley 127 A3	South Hayling 184 C1	
Colehill 164 A4	Havant 135 C2	Netley Marsh 100 A3	Southsea 182 B1	
Compton (Hants) ...31 B4	Hawkley 19 C4	Newbridge 74 C2	Southwick 132 C3	

1

1st St SO45 .....151 A2

2

2nd St SO45 .....151 A2

3

3rd St SO45 .....150 C2

4

4th St SO45 .....150 C2

5

5th St SO45 .....150 C2

6

6th St Fawley SO45 .....150 C2
Fawley SO45 .....150 C3

7

7th St SO45 .....150 C2

8

8th St SO45 .....150 C2

9

9th St SO45 .....150 B2

1

10th St SO45 .....150 B3
11th St SO45 .....150 B3
12th St SO45 .....150 B3
13th St SO45 .....150 B3
14th St SO45 .....150 B3
17th Century Experience Mus★ PO13 .....180 B3

A

A Ave SO45 .....150 B2
A'beckett Ct 3 PO1 .....182 A2
Aaron Cl BH17 .....202 C4
Aaron Ct SO40 .....101 C1
Abbas Gr PO9 .....135 B4
Abbey Cl SO45 .....126 A2
Abbey Ct 15 SO15 .....102 C4
Abbey Ent Ctr SO51 .....53 B3
Abbey Gdns BH21 .....164 B3
Abbey Hill SO31 .....127 A4
Abbey Hill Cl SO23 .....2 A1
Abbey Hill Rd SO23 .....1 C1
Abbey Mill Bsns Site SO32 .....83 A4
Abbey Pas SO23 .....11 A4
Abbey Rd Fareham PO15 .....130 B1
West Moors BH22 .....166 A4
Abbey The SO51 .....52 C4
Abbey Water 9 SO51 .....52 C4
Abbeyfield Dr PO15 .....130 B1
Abbeyfield Ho 7 SO18 .....103 C4
Abbeyfields Cl SO31 .....127 B3
Abbots Cl
Christchurch BH23 .....208 C4
Waterlooville PO7 .....134 B2
Abbots Row 6 SO22 .....10 C4
Abbots Way
Fareham PO15 .....130 B1
Netley SO31 .....127 B3
Abbots Well Rd SP6 .....94 C4
Abbotsbury Rd
Bishopstoke SO50 .....56 C1
Broadstone BH18 .....186 C3
Abbotsfield SO40 .....100 C4
Abbotsfield Cl SO16 .....78 B3
Abbotsford SO40 .....99 A3
Abbotstone Ave PO9 .....136 A2
Abbotswood Cl SO51 .....28 B1
Abbotswood Jun Sch SO40 .....100 C4
Abbott Cl BH9 .....205 A4
Abbott Rd BH9 .....205 A4
Abbott St BH21 .....162 B3
Abbotts Ann Rd SO22 .....1 B2
Abbotts Cl SO23 .....2 A1
Abbotts Ct
15 Southampton SO17 .....79 A1
Winchester SO22 .....1 C1
Abbotts Dro SO51 .....50 C1
Abbotts Rd Eastleigh SO50 55 C1
Winchester SO23 .....2 A1
Abbotts Way
Southampton SO17 .....79 A1
West Moors BH22 .....166 A4
Abercrombie Gdns SO16 .78 A2
Aberdare Ave PO6 .....158 A4
Aberdare Rd BH10 .....189 C2
Aberdeen Cl PO15 .....130 C2
Aberdeen Rd SO17 .....79 B1
Aberdour Cl SO18 .....104 A4
Abingdon Cl PO12 .....181 A2
Abingdon Dr BH23 .....209 B4
Abingdon Gdns SO16 .....78 C2
Abingdon Rd BH17 .....202 B4
Abinger Rd BH7 .....206 A3
Abney Rd BH10 .....189 B2
Above Bar St SO14 .....102 C3
Abraham Cl SO30 .....105 B3
Abshot Cl PO14 .....129 A1
Abshot Rd PO14 .....129 B1
Acacia Ave BH31 .....115 B2
Acacia Gdns PO8 .....112 A3
Acacia Rd Hordle SO41 .....195 C2
Southampton SO19 .....103 C3
Acer Way PO9 .....136 A2
Ackworth Rd PO3 .....158 A3
Acland Rd BH9 .....205 A4
Acorn Bsns Ctr PO6 .....157 B4
Acorn Bsns Pk BH12 .....203 A4
Acorn Cl
Christchurch BH23 .....206 C4
Cosham PO6 .....158 C4
Gosport PO13 .....155 B1
Marchwood SO40 .....102 A1
New Milton BH25 .....195 B2
St Leonards BH24 .....139 C2
Acorn Cotts BH31 .....114 C4
Acorn Ct SO31 .....127 C2
Acorn Dr SO16 .....77 C4
Acorn Gdns PO8 .....112 A3
Acorn Gr SO53 .....54 C2
Acorn Way BH31 .....115 A3
Acorn Workshops SO14 103 A4
Acorns The
Bursledon SO31 .....127 C4
Wimborne Minst BH21 .....164 A2
Acre La PO7 .....112 B1
Acres Rd BH11 .....189 A1
Acton Rd BH10 .....189 A1
Ad Astro Fst Sch BH17 .....187 C1
Adair Rd PO4 .....183 A1
Adames Rd PO1 .....182 C3
Adams Cl SO30 .....81 A2
Adams Rd SO45 .....126 A1
Adams Terr PO6 .....158 B3
Adams Way PO15 .....129 B3
Adams Wood Dr SO40 .....101 C1
Adamsfield Gdns BH10 .189 B1
Adamson Cl SO53 .....55 B4
Adastral Rd BH17 .....202 C4
Adastral Sq BH17 .....202 C4
Adcock Ct SO16 .....77 C4
Adderbury Ave PO10 .....136 C2
Addington Ct 1 SO41 .....211 B3
Addington Pl BH23 .....207 B3
Addis Sq 35 SO17 .....79 A1
Addiscombe Rd BH23 .....207 A4
Addison Cl Romsey SO51 .....28 A1
Winchester SO22 .....10 B3
Addison Rd
Brockenhurst SO42 .....172 C4
Eastleigh SO50 .....56 A3
Locks Heath SO31 .....128 C3
Portsmouth PO5 .....215 D1
Addison Sq BH24 .....141 A4
Adelaide Cl BH23 .....206 C4
Adelaide Ct SO41 .....197 C2
Adelaide La 40 BH1 .....204 C2
Adelaide Pl 9 PO16 .....131 B1
Adelaide Rd SO17 .....103 B4
Adeline Rd BH5 .....205 C2
Adey Cl SO19 .....104 A1
Adhurst Rd PO9 .....136 A2
Adlam's La SO41 .....172 A1
Admiral Lord Nelson Sch PO3 .....158 A1
Admiral Park The PO3 .....158 A2
Admiral's Cnr 4 PO5 .....182 B1
Admiral's Wlk PO1 .....181 C3
Admirals Cl SO45 .....151 A2
Admirals Ct
Hamble-le-Rice SO31 .....128 A1
Lymington SO41 .....197 C2
19 Portsmouth PO5 .....182 B1
Admirals Rd SO31 .....129 A2
Admirals Way 9 SO45 .....126 A3
Admirals Wlk
Bournemouth BH2 .....204 B1
Gosport PO12 .....180 C2
Admiralty Cl PO12 .....181 B4
Admiralty Cotts PO12 .....181 B3
Admiralty Ho SO14 .....103 A1
Admiralty Rd
Bournemouth BH6 .....206 C2
Portsmouth PO1 .....182 A3
Admiralty Way SO40 .....101 C2
Adsdean Cl PO9 .....135 C2
Adstone La PO3 .....158 B2
Adur Cl Gosport PO12 .....180 C4
West End SO18 .....80 A1
Aerodrome Rd PO13 .....155 C2
Africa Dr SO40 .....124 C4
Agar's La SO41 .....196 A3
Agarton La SO41 .....211 C3
Aggis Farm BH31 .....114 C3
Agincourt Rd PO2 .....182 B4
Agitator Rd SO45 .....151 B2
Agnew Ho PO12 .....181 A3
Agnew Rd PO13 .....155 B2
Aikman La SO40 .....100 A4
Ailsa La SO19 .....103 B2
Ainsdale Rd PO6 .....134 B1
Ainsley Gdns SO50 .....56 A3
Aintree Cl SO50 .....81 B4
Aintree Ct SO31 .....129 A4
Aintree Dr PO7 .....112 A1
Aintree Rd SO40 .....76 B1
Airetons Cl BH18 .....187 B2
Airfield Ind Est BH23 .....207 C3
Airfield Rd BH23 .....207 C3
Airfield Way BH23 .....207 C4
Airlie Cnr SO22 .....10 C3
Airlie Rd SO22 .....10 C3
Airport Service Rd PO3 158 A2
Airspeed Rd
Christchurch BH23 .....208 A4
Portsmouth PO3 .....158 B1
Ajax Cl PO14 .....179 B3
Akeshill Cl BH25 .....195 A3
Alameda Rd PO7 .....134 B2
Alameda Way PO7 .....134 B2
Alan Chun Ho SO31 .....127 B4
Alan Ct 16 BH23 .....209 A4
Alan Drayton Way SO50 .56 C1
Alan Gr PO15 .....130 C1
Alandale Rd SO19 .....104 B2
Albacore Ave SO31 .....128 C1
Albany BH1 .....205 B2
Albany Cl BH25 .....194 C1
Albany Ct
Bishop's Waltham SO32 .....83 A4
Gosport PO12 .....181 A3
Albany Dr
Bishop's Waltham SO32 .....83 A4
Three Legged Cross BH21 114 C1
Albany Gdns BH15 .....201 C1
Albany Park Ct SO17 .....102 C4
Albany Pk BH17 .....202 A4
Albany Rd
Bishop's Waltham SO32 .....83 A4
Holbury SO45 .....150 B2
Portsmouth PO5 .....215 C1
Romsey SO51 .....52 C4
Southampton SO15 .....102 B3
Albany The SO14 .....103 A2
Albatross Wlk PO13 .....155 A1
Albemarle Ave PO12 .....181 A4
Albemarle Rd BH3 .....204 C4
Albermarle Ct SO17 .....79 B2
Albert Cl SO31 .....127 B3
Albert Ct SO17 .....79 B1
Albert Gr PO5 .....215 C1
Albert Rd
Bishop's Waltham SO32 .....83 A4
Bournemouth BH1 .....204 C2
Corfe Mullen BH21 .....186 B3
Cosham PO6 .....157 C4
6 Eastleigh SO50 .....56 A3
Ferndown BH22 .....165 B3
Hedge End SO30 .....105 A3
New Milton BH25 .....194 C1
Poole BH12 .....203 B3
Portsmouth PO4, PO5 .....182 C1
Stubbington PO14 .....179 C3
Albert Rd N SO14 .....103 A2
Albert Rd S SO14 .....103 A2
Albert St PO12 .....181 B3
Albion Cl Poole BH12 .....203 A4
Portchester PO16 .....156 A3
Albion Pl 3 SO14 .....102 C2
Albion Rd
Christchurch BH23 .....191 C1
Fordingbridge SP6 .....69 C1
Lee-on-the-Solent PO13 .....179 C2
Albion Twrs 1 SO14 .....103 A2
Albion Way BH31 .....114 B4
Albretia Ave PO8 .....111 C2
Albury Pl SO53 .....30 A1
Alby Rd BH12 .....203 C3
Alcantara Cres SO14 .....103 A2
Alcester Rd BH12 .....203 B3
Alchorne Pl PO3 .....158 A2
Aldbury Ct BH25 .....210 A4
Alder Cl Burton BH23 .....192 B1
Colden Common SO21 .....57 A4
Hythe SO45 .....125 B2
Marchwood SO40 .....101 C1
Romsey SO51 .....53 B3
Alder Cres BH12 .....203 C4
Alder Dr SP6 .....92 C3
Alder Hill Dr SO40 .....100 A4
Alder Hills BH12 .....204 A4
Alder Hills Ind Est BH12 204 A4
Alder La PO12,PO13 .....180 B3
Alder Rd Poole BH12 .....203 C3
Southampton SO16 .....78 A2
Alderbury Ct 5 BH23 .....207 C3
Alderfield GU32 .....40 C2
Alderholt Mill & Craft Ctr★ SP6 .....68 C1
Alderholt Rd SP6 .....69 A1
Alderley Rd BH10 .....189 C2
Alderman Quilley Sch SO50 .....55 C1
Alderman Quilley Sch The SO50 .....56 A1
Aldermoor Ave SO16 .....78 A2
Aldermoor Cl SO16 .....78 B2
Aldermoor Rd
Gosport PO13 .....180 B4
Southampton SO16 .....78 A2
Waterlooville PO7 .....134 B2
Aldermoor Rd E PO7 .....134 B3
Alderney Ave BH12 .....188 B1
Alderney Cl SO16 .....77 C2
Alderney Hospl BH12 .....188 B1
Alderney Mid Sch BH12 188 B1
Alderney Rdbt BH12 .....188 B1
Alders Rd PO16 .....155 A4
Aldershot Ho 50 PO9 .....136 A3
Alderwood Ave SO53 .....55 A3
Alderwood Cl PO9 .....135 A2
Aldis Gdns BH15 .....201 C1
Aldrich Rd PO1 .....182 A3
Aldridge Cl PO8 .....88 B3
Aldridge Rd
Bournemouth BH10 .....189 B3
Ferndown BH22 .....165 C2
Aldridge Way BH22 .....165 C2
Aldroke St 14 PO6 .....157 C4
Aldsworth Cl PO6 .....158 B4
Aldsworth Gdns PO6 .....158 B4
Aldwell St PO5 .....215 C2
Alec Rose Ho 16 PO12 .....181 B2
Alec Rose La PO1 .....215 B3
Alec Wintle Ho PO2 .....182 B4
Alecto Rd PO12 .....181 A2
Alencon Cl PO12 .....181 B4
Alexander Cl
Christchurch BH23 .....207 C3
Totton SO40 .....100 B4
Waterlooville PO7 .....134 B3
Alexander Ct
Southampton SO15 .....102 B3
Southampton, Woolston SO19 .....103 C1
Alexander Gr PO16 .....155 A4
Alexander Ho PO11 .....185 C1
Alexandra Ave PO11 .....184 C1
Alexandra Cl SO45 .....126 A2
Alexandra Lo 6 BH1 .....205 A2
Alexandra Rd
Bournemouth BH6 .....206 B3
Chandler's Ford SO53 .....55 C4
Fordingbridge SP6 .....69 C1
Hedge End SO30 .....105 A3
Hythe SO45 .....126 A2
Lymington SO41 .....197 B3
Poole BH14 .....203 C2
Portsmouth PO1 .....215 C4
Southampton SO15 .....102 C3
Alexandra St PO12 .....181 A3
Alexandra Terr SO23 .....10 C4
Alexandra Way SO30 .....106 A4
Alexandria Ct BH22 .....165 C2
Alford Rd BH3 .....204 B4
Alfred Cl SO40 .....100 B4
Alfred Rd
Portsmouth PO1 .....215 A4
Stubbington PO14 .....154 B2
Alfred Rose Ct SO18 .....79 C2
Alfred St SO14 .....103 A3
Alfrey Cl PO10 .....161 B4
Alfriston Ct SO19 .....104 B2
Alfriston Gdns SO19 .....104 A2
Algiers Rd PO3 .....183 A4
Alhambra Rd PO4 .....182 C1
Alice in Wonderland Family Pk★ BH23 .....190 C4
Alington 18 BH4 .....204 B2
Alington Cl BH14 .....214 B4
Alington Ho BH14 .....214 B4
Alington Rd BH3 .....205 A3
Alipore Cl BH14 .....203 B2
Alipore Hts BH14 .....203 B2
Alison Way 10 SO22 .....10 C4
All Saints CE Prim Sch SO23 .....11 A3
All Saints Ho 19 SO14 .....103 A2
All Saints Rd SO41 .....197 C1
All Saints' Rd PO1 .....182 B4
All Saints' St PO1 .....215 B4
Allan Gr SO51 .....53 A4
Allaway Ave PO6 .....157 A4
Allbrook Ct 12 PO9 .....135 B3
Allbrook Hill SO50 .....56 A4
Allbrook Knoll SO50 .....56 A4
Allbrook Way SO50 .....56 A4
Allcot Rd PO3 .....158 A1
Allen Ct BH21 .....163 B3
Allen Rd Hedge End SO30 105 B4
Wimborne Minst BH21 .....163 B2
Allen Water Dr SP6 .....69 C1
Allen's Rd PO4 .....182 C1
Allenbourn Mid Sch BH21 .....163 B3
Allenby Cl BH17 .....187 A1
Allenby Gr PO16 .....156 B4
Allenby Rd Gosport PO12 180 C3
Poole BH17 .....187 A1
Allendale Ave PO10 .....136 C2
Allens Farm La SO32 .....61 A3
Allens La Meonstoke SO32 .61 B3
Upton BH16 .....201 B3
Allens Rd BH16 .....201 B3
Allenview Rd BH21 .....163 B3
Allerton Cl SO40 .....76 B1
Alley The SP6 .....70 C4
Alliance Cl PO13 .....180 B4
Allington La SO30 .....80 C3
Allington Manor Farm Bsns Ctr SO50 .....80 C4
Allington Rd Poole BH14 214 B4
Southampton SO15 .....101 B4
Allison Ct 6 SO41 .....211 A2
Allison Ho SO30 .....105 B4
Allmara Dr PO7 .....134 C2
Allotment Rd
Hedge End SO30 .....105 A3
Locks Heath SO31 .....128 C3
Alma Ho SO14 .....103 A4
Alma La SO32 .....58 A1
Alma Rd
Bournemouth BH9 .....205 A4
Romsey SO51 .....52 C4
Southampton SO14 .....103 A4
Alma St PO12 .....181 A3
Alma Terr PO4 .....183 A2
Almatade Rd SO18 .....104 A4
Almer Rd BH15 .....201 C2
Almond Cl Cosham PO9 .....158 C4
Waterlooville PO8 .....112 B2
Almond Ct 11 SO15 .....102 B3
Almond Gr BH12 .....203 B4
Almond Rd SO15 .....102 B3
Almondsbury Ho 8 PO6 .....132 C1
Almondsbury Rd PO6 .....132 C1
Almondside PO13 .....155 C1
Almshouses BH10 .....189 B1
Alpha Ctr The BH17 .....202 A4
Alphage Rd PO12 .....155 C1
Alpine Cl SO18 .....104 A4
Alpine Rd Ashurst SO40 .....99 C2
St Leonards BH24 .....140 B1
Alresford Rd
Chilcomb SO21, SO23 .....12 B4
Havant PO9 .....135 C2
Winchester SO21, SO23 .....11 B4
Alsford Rd PO7 .....134 B3
Alswitha Terr 27 SO23 .....2 A1
Alten Rd PO7 .....111 B1
Althorpe Dr PO3 .....158 B2
Alton Cl SO50 .....57 A1
Alton Ct 12 SO23 .....2 A1
Alton Gr PO16 .....156 B3
Alton Ho SO18 .....103 C4
Alton Rd
Bournemouth BH10 .....189 A1
Poole BH14 .....203 B2
Alton Rd E BH14 .....203 B1
Alum Chine Rd BH4 .....204 A2
Alum Cl SO45 .....150 B2
Alum Way
Portchester PO16 .....131 C1
Southampton SO18 .....104 A4
Alumdale Rd BH4 .....204 A1
Alumhurst Rd BH4 .....204 A1
Alvandi Gdns 12 BH25 .....195 A2
Alvara Rd PO12 .....181 A1
Alver Bridge View 10 PO12 .....181 A2
Alver Quay PO12 .....181 A2
Alver Rd Gosport PO12 .....181 A2
Portsmouth PO1 .....182 C3
Alvercliffe Dr PO12 .....180 C1
Alverstoke CE Jun Sch PO12 .....181 A2
Alverstoke Ct PO12 .....181 A1
Alverstoke Inf Sch PO12 .....181 A1
Alverstone Rd PO4 .....183 A3
Alverton Ave BH15 .....202 C2
Alverton Hall BH4 .....204 B1
Alveston Ave PO14 .....154 B4
Alyne Ho SO15 .....102 C4
Alyth Rd BH3 .....204 B3
Amarylis Cl PO15 .....129 C2
Ambassador Cl BH23 .....208 A3
Ambassador Ind Est BH23 .....208 A3
Amber Rd BH21 .....186 B2
Amberley Cl Botley SO30 106 A4
Christchurch BH23 .....208 C4
North Baddesley SO52 .....53 C3
Amberley Ct
8 Bournemouth BH1 .....205 A2
Totton SO40 .....100 C3
Amberley Rd Clanfield PO8 88 B3
Gosport PO12 .....181 A4
Portsmouth PO2 .....157 C2
Amberslade Wlk SO45 .....125 C1
Amberwood
Ferndown BH22 .....165 C3
Milford on Sea SO41 .....211 A3
Amberwood Cl SO40 .....76 B1
Amberwood Dr BH23 .....193 C1
Amberwood Gdns BH23 194 A1
Amberwood Ho BH23 .....194 A1
Ambledale SO31 .....128 C2
Ambleside
Bishop's Waltham SO32 .....83 A4
Christchurch BH23 .....191 C2
Hedge End SO30 .....105 B3
Ambleside Gdns SO19 .....104 A2
Ambleside Rd SO41 .....197 C2
Ambury La BH23 .....207 C4
Amersham Cl PO12 .....180 C2
Amesbury Rd BH6 .....206 B3
Amethyst Gr PO7 .....135 A4
Amethyst Rd BH23 .....207 C4
Amey Ind Est GU32 .....40 C2
Ameys La BH22 .....165 C4
Ameysford Rd BH22 .....165 B4
Amira Ct 9 BH2 .....204 C2
Amoy St SO15 .....102 C3
Ampfield CE Prim Sch SO51 .....29 B2
Ampfield Cl PO9 .....135 A2
Ampfield Rd BH8 .....190 B2
Amport Cl SO22 .....1 B2
Amport Ct PO9 .....135 B3
Ampress La SO41 .....197 B3
Ampthill Rd SO15 .....102 A4
Amsterdam Sq BH23 .....207 B3
Amyas Ct PO4 .....183 B2
Ancasta Rd SO14 .....103 A4
Anchor Cl
Bournemouth BH11 .....188 C3
Christchurch BH23 .....208 A3
Anchor La PO1 .....182 A3
Anchor Mews SO41 .....197 C2
Anchor Rd BH11 .....188 C3
Anchorage Rd PO3 .....158 A2
Anchorage The PO12 .....181 B2
Anchorage Way SO41 .....197 B2

Ancrum Lo BH4 ......204 A2
Andalusian Gdns SO31 .129 A4
Andbourne Ct BH6 ....206 C2
Anderby Rd SO16 ......77 B1
Anderson Cl Havant PO9 136 A2
 Romsey SO51 ....28 B1
 Swanwick PO15 ....129 B4
Anderson's Rd SO14 ..103 A2
Anderwood Dr SO41 ...172 A1
Andes Cl SO14 ....103 B2
Andes Rd SO16 ....77 A2
Andlers Ash Rd GU33 ..20 C2
Andover Ct BH23 ......208 A4
Andover Ho PO9 ....136 A3
Andover Rd
 Portsmouth PO4 ......182 C1
 Southampton SO15 ...102 B3
 Winchester SO21, SO22,
 SO23 ....1 A1
Andover Rd N SO22 .....1 C2
Andover Road Ret Pk
 SO23 ....1 C1
Andree Ct BH23 ....209 A4
Andrew Bell St PO1 ...215 B4
Andrew Cl
 7 Hythe SO45 ....126 A1
 Portsmouth PO1 ......182 C3
 Totton SO40 ....100 B4
Andrew Cres PO7 ......111 B1
Andrew La BH25 ....195 B1
Andrew Pl PO14 ....179 A3
Andrewes Cl SO32 .....83 B4
Andrews Cl BH11 ......189 A2
Andromeda Rd SO16 ...77 C2
Androse Gdns BH24 ...140 C3
Anfield Cl SO50 ....57 B1
Anfield Ct SO50 ....57 A1
Angel Cres SO18,SO19 .104 A3
Angel Ct SO41 ....197 C2
Angel La
 Barton on Sea BH25 ..210 B4
 Ferndown BH22 ....165 A2
Angelica Ct PO7 ......135 A3
Angelica Gdns SO30 ...81 B4
Angelica Way PO15 ...129 C4
Angeline Cl BH23 .....208 C4
Angelo Cl PO7 ....135 A4
Angelus Ct PO14 ......179 B3
Angerstein Rd PO2 ...157 B1
Anglers Way SO31 ....128 B4
Anglesea Ct SO15 .....78 A1
Anglesea Rd
 Lee-on-the-Solent PO13 .180 A2
 Portsmouth PO1 ......215 A3
 Southampton SO15 ...78 A1
Anglesea Terr SO14 ..103 A2
Anglesey Arms Rd
 PO12 ....181 A1
Anglesey Rd PO12 ....181 A1
Anglesey View 7 PO12 .181 A2
Anglewood Mans 9
 BH4 ....204 B2
Anglo-European Coll of
 Chiropractic BH5 ....206 A2
Angmering Ho 2 PO1 .215 B3
Angus Cl PO15 ....130 C2
Anjou Cl BH11 ....188 B2
Anjou Cres PO15 .....130 B1
Anker La PO14 ....154 C1
Ankerwyke PO13 ......155 A1
Anmore Cl PO9 ....135 B2
Anmore Cnr PO7 ......111 A2
Anmore Dr PO7 ....111 B2
Anmore La PO7,PO8 ..111 B3
Anmore Rd PO7 ......111 A2
Ann's Hill Rd PO12 ..181 A3
Anna La BH23 ....168 A2
Annandale Ct BH6 ...206 B2
Anne Cl BH23 ....192 A1
Anne Cres PO7 ....134 C3
Annerley Rd BH1 .....205 B2
Annes Ct PO11 ....184 C1
Annet Rd BH15 ....201 C1
Anson Cl
 Christchurch BH23 ...207 C3
 Gosport PO13 ....180 B3
 Ringwood BH24 ....141 B4
Anson Dr SO19 ....104 B3
Anson Gr PO16 ....132 C2
Anson Ho SO14 ....103 A2
Anson Rd
 Horton Heath SO50 ...81 B4
 1 Portsmouth PO4 ...183 A4
Anstey Cl BH11 ......189 A3
Anstey Rd
 Bournemouth BH11 ...189 A3
 Romsey SO51 ....28 A1
Antell's Way SP6 .....93 A3
Anthem Cl PO7 ....110 B3
Anthony Gr PO12 .....156 A1
Anthony Way PO10 ...136 C2
Anthony's Ave BH14 .203 B1
Antigua Ho 5 PO6 ...132 C1
Antler Dr BH25 ....194 C2
Anton Cl SO51 ....53 B4
Anvil Cl East Meon GU32 .63 C4
 Waterlooville PO7 ....112 C1
 West End SO30 ....80 B1
Anvil Cres BH18 .....186 C3
Anvil Ct 2 PO4 ......183 A2
Anzac Cl PO14 ....154 B2
Apex Ctr PO14 ....155 A4
Apless La PO7 ....110 A2
Apollo Cl BH12 ......203 B4
Apollo Dr PO7 ....134 C2
Apollo Rd SO53 ......55 C4
Apple Cl BH12 ....204 A2

Apple Gr
 Christchurch BH23 ...191 C1
 Emsworth PO10 ......161 A4
Apple Ind Est PO15 ..129 B3
Apple Tree Cl SP5 ....47 B4
Apple Tree Gr BH22 .165 C3
Apple Tree Rd SP6 ...92 C3
Applegate Pl PO8 ....112 A3
Applemore Coll SO45 .125 B2
Applemore Recn Ctr
 SO45 ....125 B2
Appleshaw Cl SO22 ....1 B2
Appleshaw Gn PO9 ...135 B2
Appleslade Way BH25 .195 A3
Appleton Rd
 Fareham PO15 ....130 B1
 Southampton SO18 ..79 C1
Appletree Cl
 Bournemouth BH6 ...206 B3
 New Milton BH25 .....195 A1
 Totton SO40 ....76 B1
Appletree Ct SO30 ...106 A4
Appletree Rd SP5 ....47 B4
Applewood Gdns SO19 .104 A2
Applewood Gr PO7 ..134 B2
Applewood Pl SO40 ..100 B3
Applewood Rd PO9 ..135 B2
Appollo Ct PO5 ......215 B2
Appollo Pl SO18 .....104 A4
Approach Rd BH14 ..203 A2
Approach The PO3 ...158 A1
April Cl
 Bournemouth BH11 ..189 A2
 Southampton SO18 ..104 A4
April Gr SO31 ....128 C2
April Sq PO1 ....215 C4
Apsley Cres BH17 ....187 B1
Apsley Ct 2 BH8 .....205 A3
Apsley Pl SO53 ......30 A1
Apsley Rd PO4 ....183 A1
Aquila Way SO31 ....127 C1
Aquitania 23 SO14 ..103 B3
Arabian Gdns PO15 ..129 B4
Aragon Way BH9 ....190 A2
Arbour Ct BH4 ....204 A2
Arcade BH4 ....204 A2
Arcade The
 37 Bournemouth BH1 .204 C2
 Liss GU33 ....20 C3
Arcadia Ave BH8 ....205 A4
Arcadia Cl SO16 .....78 B2
Arcadia Rd BH23 ....191 C1
Arch Farm Ind Est SP6 .69 C2
Archdale Cl BH10 ...189 B1
Archer Ho PO12 .....181 B1
Archers SO15 ....102 C3
Archers Cl SO40 .....76 B1
Archers Rd Eastleigh SO50 56 A3
 Southampton SO15 ..102 C4
Archery Gdns SO19 ..103 C1
Archery Gr SO19 ....103 C1
Archery La
 Fareham PO16 ....131 B1
 Winchester SO22 ....10 C4
Archery Rd SO19 ....103 C1
Archgate SO41 ......197 C2
Archway Rd BH14 ...203 C2
Arden Cl Gosport PO12 .180 C2
 Southampton SO18 ..80 A1
Arden Rd BH9 ....189 C2
Arden Wlk BH25 ....195 A1
Ardingly Cres SO30 .81 B1
Ardington Rise PO7 .134 C2
Ardmore Rd BH14 ...203 A2
Ardnave Cres SO16 ..78 C3
Argosy Cl SO31 .....128 C3
Argus Rd PO13 .....179 C2
Argyle Cres PO15 ...130 C1
Argyle Rd
 Christchurch BH23 ..207 C3
 Southampton SO14 .103 A3
Argyll Mans 11 BH5 .205 C2
Argyll Rd
 Bournemouth BH5 ...205 C2
 Poole BH12 ....203 B3
Ariel Cl BH6 ....207 A2
Ariel Dr BH6 ....207 A2
Ariel Rd PO1 ....182 C3
Arismore Ct PO13 ..179 B2
Ark Dr BH22 ....165 C2
Ark Royal Cres PO13 .179 C2
Arle Cl PO8 ....88 B2
Arley Rd BH14 ......203 A1
Arlington Ct BH25 ..210 A4
Arlington Pl 2 SO23 ..11 A4
Arliss Rd SO16 .....78 A1
Arlott Ct SO15 ......102 C4
Armada Cl SO16 ....77 C4
Armada Dr SO45 ....125 C1
Armadale Ho 20 SO14 .103 B3
Arminers Cl PO12 ...181 A1
Armitage Ave SO45 .125 C1
Armory La PO1 .....182 A2
Armoury The SO40 .102 A2
Armstrong Cl
 Brockenhurst SO42 .145 C1
 Waterlooville PO7 ...111 B1
Armstrong Ct SO16 .77 C3
Armstrong La SO42 .145 C1
Armstrong Rd SO42 .145 C1
Armsworth La PO7,SO32 .85 C1
Arnaud Cl PO2 ......182 B4
Arne Ave BH12 .....203 C4
Arne Cres BH12 ....203 C4
Arnewood Bridge Rd
 SO41 ....196 A4
Arnewood Ct
 Bournemouth BH2 ...204 C1

Arnewood Ct continued
 Sway SO41 ....196 B3
Arnewood Ho SO41 .196 B2
Arnewood Rd BH6 ..206 B2
Arnewood Sch The
 BH25 ....194 C1
Arnheim Cl SO16 ....78 B2
Arnheim Rd SO16 ...78 B2
Arnold Cl BH22 .....138 C2
Arnold Rd Eastleigh SO50 80 A4
 Southampton SO17 ..79 B1
 West Moors BH22 ...138 C2
Arnolds Cl BH25 ....209 C4
Arnside Rd PO7 ....134 C4
Arnwood Ave SO45 .149 C4
Arragon Ct PO7 ....135 A4
Arran Cl PO6 ....133 C1
Arran Way BH23 ....194 A1
Arras Ho PO15 .....130 B2
Arreton SO31 ....127 B3
Arreton Ct 7 PO12 .181 A3
Arrow Cl Eastleigh SO50 .56 A2
 Southampton SO19 ..103 B1
Arrowsmith Ct BH18 .187 A2
Arrowsmith La BH21 .187 C4
Arrowsmith Rd BH21 .187 C4
Arters Lawn SO40 ..124 B3
Arthur Cl BH2 ......204 C3
Arthur Kille Ho PO7 .134 C4
Arthur La 3 BH23 ..207 A4
Arthur Pope Ho PO5 .215 C2
Arthur Rd
 Christchurch BH23 ..207 A4
 Eastleigh SO50 .....56 A2
 Southampton SO15 .102 B3
 Winchester SO23 ...2 A1
 Swanwick SO31 ....129 A4
 Winchester SO22 ...1 B2
Arthur St PO1 ......182 C4
Arthurs Gdns SO30 .81 A2
Artillery Cl 11 PO7 .157 B4
Artillery Terr 4 PO4 .183 A2
Arts Inst of Bournemouth The
 BH12 ....204 B4
Arun Cl GU31 ......40 C1
Arun Rd SO18 ......80 A1
Arun Way SO51 .....50 B2
Arundel Cl BH25 ....195 B2
Arundel Ct Inf Sch PO1 215 C4
Arundel Ct Jun Sch
 PO1 ....215 C4
Arundel Dr PO16 ...131 A1
Arundel Ho
 Southampton, Banister's Pk
 SO15 ....102 C4
 19 Southampton, Northam
 SO14 ....103 B3
Arundel Rd Eastleigh SO50 56 A3
 Gosport PO13 ......180 C3
 Totton SO40 ....101 A3
Arundel St PO1 .....215 C3
Arundel Way BH23 .208 C4
Arundel Way Sh Arc
 PO1 ....215 B3
Ascham Rd BH8 ....205 A3
Ascot Cl PO14 .....129 B1
Ascot Rd
 Broadstone BH18 ..187 A2
 Fair Oak SO50 ....81 B4
 Portsmouth PO3 ...183 A4
Ascupart Ho 24 SO17 .103 A4
Ascupart St SO14 ..103 A2
Asford Gr SO50 ....56 B2
Ash Cl Alderholt SP6 .93 A3
 Bursledon SO31 ...127 C4
 Colden Common SO21 .32 A1
 Fareham PO14 .....154 C4
 Gosport PO12 .....181 A2
 Hythe SO45 ....150 A4
 North Baddesley SO52 .53 B3
 Romsey SO51 .....53 B3
 Southampton SO19 .104 B3
 Upton BH16 ......201 A4
 Waterlooville PO8 .111 C1
Ash Gr Ashurst SO40 .100 B2
 Hordle SO41 ......211 B4
 Ringwood BH24 ...141 B4
Ash Rd SO40 ......100 A1
Ash Tree Rd SO18 ..79 C1
Ashbarn Cres SO22 .10 C3
Ashbourne Ct 1 BH1 .205 A4
Ashbourne Rd BH5 .206 A4
Ashbridge Rise SO53 .30 A1
Ashburn Garth BH24 .141 B3
Ashburnham Cl SO19 .103 B3
Ashburton Cl SO45 ..125 B2
Ashburton Ct PO5 ..215 B1
Ashburton Gdns BH10 .189 B1
Ashburton Ho 12 SO31 .127 A3
Ashburton Rd
 Gosport PO12 .....180 C1
 Portsmouth PO5 ...182 B1
Ashby Cres SO40 ..100 B4
Ashby Pl PO5 ......182 B1
Ashby Rd
 Southampton SO19 .104 A2
 Totton SO40 ......100 B4
Ashcroft 9 GU32 ..40 C2
Ashcroft La PO8 ..113 B2
Ashdene 16 SO15 ..102 A4
Ashdene BH21 ....163 B1
Ashdene Rd SO40 ..100 B2
Ashdown
 Bournemouth BH2 ...204 B1
 Fawley SO45 ......150 C2
 Gosport PO13 .....155 C2
Ashdown Cl
 Chandler's Ford SO53 .30 B1
 Poole BH17 ....187 C1
Ashdown Dr SO53 ..30 B1

Ashdown Rd
 Blackfield SO45 ....150 C1
 Chandler's Ford SO53 .30 B1
Ashdown Sch BH17 .187 C1
Ashdown Way SO51 .53 A4
Ashdown Wlk BH25 .195 B1
Ashe Rd PO9 ......136 A3
Ashen Cl SO53 ....55 B4
Ashford Chace GU32 .19 C1
Ashford Cl Cosham PO6 .133 C1
 Fordingbridge SP6 ..69 B1
Ashford Cres SO45 ..126 A2
Ashford Rd
 Bournemouth BH6 ...206 B4
 Fordingbridge SP6 ..93 B4
Ashington Cl PO8 ...112 A2
Ashington Gdns BH21 .186 C4
Ashington La BH21 ..163 A1
Ashington Pk BH25 .195 A1
Ashlea Cl SO50 .....57 B1
Ashleigh Cl SO45 ..150 A4
Ashleigh Rise BH10 .189 B1
Ashlett Cl SO45 ....151 B2
Ashlett Gdns BH25 ..195 B2
Ashlett Lawn 4 PO9 .135 B2
Ashlett Mews SO45 .151 A2
Ashlett Rd SO45 ...151 B2
Ashley Arnewood Ct 9
 BH25 ....195 A1
Ashley Cl
 Bournemouth BH1 ...205 B2
 Havant PO9 ....135 B2
 Horndean PO8 .....111 C3
 Ringwood BH24 ...141 B3
 Swanwick SO31 ...129 A4
 Winchester SO22 ...1 B2
Ashley Common Rd
 BH25 ....195 B2
Ashley Cres SO19 ..104 B1
Ashley Ct
 Bursledon SO31 ...105 C3
 Gosport PO12 .....181 A3
 West Moors BH22 .166 A4
Ashley Dr BH24 ....116 B2
Ashley Drive N BH24 .139 C3
Ashley Drive S BH24 .139 C3
Ashley Drive W BH24 .139 C3
Ashley Gdns
 Chandler's Ford SO53 .55 C3
 Waltham Chase SO32 .83 C2
Ashley Heath Ind Est
 BH21 ....139 A4
Ashley Ho SO51 ...52 C3
Ashley Inf Sch BH25 .195 B2
Ashley Jun Sch BH25 .195 B2
Ashley La Hordle SO41 .195 C2
 Lymington SO41 ...197 C2
 New Milton BH25 ..195 C2
Ashley Mdws SO51 .53 A4
Ashley Meads BH25 .195 B2
Ashley Park BH24 ..140 A3
Ashley Rd
 Bournemouth BH1, BH7 .205 C2
 New Milton BH25 ..195 B2
 Poole BH14 ....203 B3
Ashleycross Cl SO45 .150 B2
Ashling Cl
 Bournemouth BH8 ...205 A4
 Denmead PO7 ....110 C2
Ashling Cres BH8 ..205 A4
Ashling Gdns PO7 ..110 C2
Ashling La PO2 ....157 B1
Ashling Pk Rd PO7 ..110 C2
Ashlyn Cl PO15 ....130 B1
Ashmead Rd SO16 ..77 C2
Ashmeads Cl BH21 ..164 B1
Ashmeads Way BH21 .164 B1
Ashmede BH4 .....204 B1
Ashmore BH21 ....163 B1
Ashmore Ave
 Barton on Sea BH25 .210 A4
 Hamworthy BH15 ..201 C1
Ashmore Cl SP5 ...24 C2
Ashmore Cres BH15 .201 C1
Ashmore Gr BH23 .193 C1
Ashmore La
 West Dean SP5 ...24 A3
 Whiteparish SP5 ..24 A3
Ashmore Rd BH12 .203 C4
Ashridge Ave 1 BH10 .189 B1
Ashridge Cl SO15 ..102 C4
Ashridge Gdns BH10 .189 B1
Ashridge Par 2 BH10 .189 B3
Ashtead Cl PO16 ..156 A4
Ashton Cl SO32 ...59 A1
Ashton Cross SO51 .51 A1
Ashton Ct
 13 New Milton BH25 .195 A2
 Poole BH13 ....204 A1
Ashton Ho SO19 ..103 C1
Ashton La SO32 ...59 A1
Ashton Pl SO53 ...30 A1
Ashton Rd BH9 ...189 C1
Ashton Way PO14 ..179 B2
Ashtree Cl BH25 ..195 B1
Ashtree Ct SO53 ..55 B4
Ashurst (New Forest) Sta
 SO40 ....100 A1
Ashurst Bridge Rd SO40 100 B3
Ashurst Cl Ashurst SO40 .100 A1
 Southampton SO19 .104 A1
 Winchester SO22 ...1 A1
Ashurst Ct PO12 ..180 B2
Ashurst Hospl (Geriatric)
 SO40 ....100 A1

Ashurst Rd
 Bournemouth BH8 ...190 B2
 Cosham PO6 ....157 C4
 West Moors BH22 ..138 C2
Ashwell Ct BH23 ..191 C1
Ashwood
 Swanwick, Whiteley PO15 .129 C3
 Titchfield SO31 ...129 C3
Ashwood Cl Havant PO9 .135 A2
 South Hayling PO11 .185 A2
Ashwood Dr BH18 ..187 B2
Ashwood Gdns
 15 Southampton SO16 ..78 C2
 Totton SO40 ......100 A3
Ashwood Lodge 1
 PO16 ....131 A1
Aspen Ave SO31 ..152 B4
Aspen Cl
 Colden Common SO21 .57 A4
 Hedge End SO30 ..105 B4
Aspen Dr BH31 ...115 A3
Aspen Gdns BH12 ..203 C4
Aspen Holt SO16 ..79 A3
Aspen Pl BH25 ...195 A1
Aspen Rd BH12 ...203 C4
Aspen Way Poole BH12 .203 C4
 Waterlooville PO8 .112 A3
Aspen Wlk SO40 ..100 A4
Aspengrove PO13 ..155 C1
Asquith Cl BH23 ..207 B3
Assheton Ct PO16 .156 B4
Astbury Ave BH12 .189 A1
Aster Rd SO16 ....79 B2
Astley St PO5 .....215 A2
Aston Mead BH23 .191 C2
Aston Rd
 Portsmouth PO4 ..182 C2
 Waterlooville PO7 .134 B4
Astra Ct 3 SO45 ..126 A3
Astra Wlk PO12 ..181 B2
Astral Gdns SO31 ..127 C2
Astrid Cl PO11 ....185 B2
Asturias Way SO14 .103 B2
Asylum Rd SO15 ..103 A3
Atalanta Cl PO4 ..183 B3
Atheling Rd SO45 ..126 A3
Athelney Ct 18 BH1 .205 B2
Athelstan Rd
 Bournemouth BH6 ..206 C3
 Southampton SO19 .103 C3
Athelston Ct SO41 .197 B2
Athena Ave PO7 ..134 C2
Athena Cl SO50 ..57 A2
Atherfield Rd SO16 .77 C2
Atherley Ct SO15 ..102 C4
Atherley Rd
 South Hayling PO11 .184 C3
 Southampton SO15 .102 C4
Atherley St SO15 ..77 A3
Atherstone Wlk 5 PO5 .215 B2
Atkins Pl PO15 ...130 B2
Atkinson Cl PO12 ..181 A1
Atlantic Cl SO14 ..103 A1
Atlantic Ct SO53 ..55 B3
Atlantic Park View SO18 .80 A1
Atlantis Ave PO7 ..134 C1
Attwood Cl SP6 ...92 C3
Attwoods Dro SO21 .10 B1
Aubrey Cl
 Milford on Sea SO41 .211 C2
 South Hayling PO11 .184 C2
Aubrey Farm Cotts
 SO41 ....212 A2
Auckland Ave SO42 .146 A1
Auckland Pl SO42 .146 A1
Auckland Rd
 Christchurch BH23 .208 B4
 Southampton SO15 .101 C4
Auckland Rd E PO5 .182 B1
Auckland Rd W PO5 .182 B1
Audemer Ct BH24 ..141 B4
Audley Pl 12 SO50 .56 C1
Audrayton Ct 9 BH6 .206 C2
Audret Ct PO16 ...156 A3
Augustine Rd
 Cosham PO6 ....158 B4
 Southampton SO14 .103 A3
Augustus Cl SO53 ..55 C4
Augustus Way SO53 .55 C4
Auriol Dr PO9 .....159 A4
Aust Rd PO14 .....154 B4
Austen Ave
 Bournemouth BH10 .189 C3
 Winchester SO22 ..10 B2
Austen Cl Totton SO40 .100 B3
 Winchester SO23 ..2 A1
Austen Gdns PO15 .129 B4
Auster Cl BH23 ...208 A4
Austerberry Way PO13 .180 C4
Austin Ave BH14 ..203 A1
Austin Cl BH1 ....205 B3
Austin Ct 6 PO6 ..133 A1
Australia Cl PO1 ..215 C3
Autumn Cl BH22 ..165 A4
Autumn Copse BH25 .195 B1
Autumn Pl 18 SO17 .79 A1
Autumn Rd
 Bournemouth BH11 .188 B2
 Marchwood SO40 ..102 A1
Avalan Cl SO23 ...10 C2
Avalon BH14 ......214 B4
Avalon Ct PO10 ..136 C1
Avebury Ave BH10 .189 C3
Avebury Gdns SO53 .30 A1
Avenger Cl SO53 ..55 A3

Avens Cl SO50 ....81 B3
Avenue C SO45 ......150 C4
Avenue Campus (Univ of
Southampton) SO17 ...79 A1
Avenue Ct Gosport PO12 .181 A1
Poole BH13 ....204 A2
1 Southampton SO17 ..102 C4
Avenue D SO45 ......150 C4
Avenue De Caen PO5 ..182 B1
Avenue E SO45 ......150 C4
Avenue La 20 BH2 ...204 C2
Avenue Rd
Bournemouth BH2 ....204 C2
Brockenhurst SO42 ...172 C4
Christchurch BH23 ...206 C4
Christchurch, Walkford
BH23 ....194 B1
Fareham PO14 ....130 C1
Gosport PO12 ....181 B2
Lymington SO41 .....197 C2
New Milton BH25 ....195 A2
North Hayling PO11 ...160 A2
Southampton SO14 ...103 A4
Wimborne Minst BH21 .163 B2
Winchester SO22 ......10 C1
Avenue Sh Ctr The 21
BH2 ....204 C2
Avenue The
Bishop's Waltham SO32 ..83 A4
Bournemouth BH9 ....189 C2
Fareham PO14 ....130 B1
Gosport PO12 ....181 A2
Petersfield GU31 ......40 C2
Poole BH13 ....204 A1
Southampton SO17 ...102 C4
Twyford SO21 ....32 A3
West Moors BH22 ....138 C2
Avery La PO12 ......181 A4
Avington Cl SO50 .....56 B3
Avington Ct SO16 .....78 C2
Avington Gn PO9 ....136 A3
Avocet Cl PO4 ......183 A3
Avocet Ho 6 PO4 ....183 A3
Avocet Quay PO10 ...161 A4
Avocet Way PO8 .....112 A4
Avocet Wlk PO13 ....155 A1
Avon Ave BH24 ......140 B2
Avon Bldgs BH23 ....207 A4
Avon Castle BH24 ....140 B2
Avon Castle Dr BH24 .140 B2
Avon Cl
Bournemouth BH8 ....205 B3
Lee-on-the-Solent PO13 .179 C1
Lymington SO41 .....197 B2
Petersfield GU31 ......40 C1
Avon Cotts BH23 ....192 B3
Avon Cres SO51 ......53 B4
Avon Cswy BH23 ....191 A4
Avon Ct
Christchurch BH23 ...207 B3
Fordingbridge SP6 ....69 C1
Netley SO31 ....127 B3
2 Waterlooville PO8 ..111 C2
Avon Dyke SP5 ....46 C3
Avon Farm Cotts BH23 .167 C2
Avon Gdns BH23 ....169 A1
Avon Gn SO53 ....55 B3
Avon Heath Ctry Park Visitor
Ctr ★ BH24 ....140 A1
Avon Heath Ctry Pk (North
Pk) BH24 ....140 A2
Avon Heath Ctry Pk (South
Pk) BH24 ....167 A4
Avon Ho
Bournemouth BH2 ...204 C2
8 Southampton SO14 .103 B3
Avon Mdw SP5 ....46 C4
Avon Meade SP6 .....69 C1
Avon Mews BH8 .....205 B3
Avon Park BH24 .....140 B2
Avon Rd
Bournemouth BH8 ....205 B3
Southampton SO18 ...79 C1
West Moors BH22 ....138 C1
Avon Rd E BH23 .....207 A4
Avon Rd W BH23 ....206 C4
Avon Run Cl BH23 ...208 A3
Avon Run Rd BH23 ..208 A3
Avon View SP6 ....70 B1
Avon View Par BH23 .192 B2
Avon View Rd BH23 .192 B2
Avon Way SO30 ......80 C1
Avon Wharf BH23 ....207 B3
Avon Wlk PO16 ......156 A4
Avonborne Way SO53 ..55 A4
Avonbourne Girls Sch
BH7 ....206 A4
Avoncliffe Rd BH6 ...206 C2
Avondale Cl SO17 .....79 A1
Avondale Cvn Pk SO21 ..32 A1
Avondale Rd
Portsmouth PO1 .....182 C4
Waterlooville PO7 ....134 C4
Avonlea Sch BH24 ...141 A4
Award Rd BH21 .....164 C3
Awbridge Prim Sch SO51 26 B3
Awbridge Rd PO9 ...135 B2
Axford Cl BH8 ....190 B2
Aylen Rd PO3 ....158 A1
Aylesbury Rd
Bournemouth BH1 ...205 C2
Portsmouth PO2 .....182 C4
Ayling Cl PO13 ......180 B4
Aylward St PO1 .....182 A3
Aynsley Ct SO15 .....102 B4

Aysgarth Rd PO7 ....134 C4
Aysha Cl BH25 ......195 A1
Azalea Cl Havant PO9 .136 B2
Azalea Cl BH24 .....140 A3
Azura Cl BH21 ......139 A3

B

B Ave Fawley SO45 ...150 B3
Fawley SO45 ....150 C2
Back La Mottisfont SO51 ..5 C3
Southwick PO17 .....132 C3
Sway SO41 ....172 B1
Back of the Walls
Southampton SO14 ...103 A3
Southampton SO14 ...103 A3
Back St SO23 ....10 C2
Bacon Cl SO19 ......103 C1
Bacon La PO11 ......184 C2
Badbury Cl BH18 ....187 B2
Badbury Ct 7 BH21 ..207 C3
Badbury View BH21 ..163 B3
Badbury View Rd BH21 .186 B4
Baddesley Cl SO52 ...53 C3
Baddesley Gdns PO9 .135 B3
Baddesley Rd SO53 ...30 A1
Baden Powell & St Peter's
Mid Sch BH14 ......203 A2
Baden Powell Way 14
SO51 ....52 C4
Bader Cl SO30 ......105 B4
Bader Rd PO14 ......202 C4
Bader Way PO15 ....129 C3
Badger Brow PO7 ...135 A3
Badger Cl
Bishopstoke SO50 ....56 C1
Fareham PO15 ......130 B1
Badger Ct 10 SO50 ...56 C1
Badger Farm Rd SO22,
SO23 ....10 B2
Badger Rd PO14 ....154 C2
Badger Way BH31 ...114 C3
Badger Wood Pl SO18 ..79 C1
Badgers Cl
St Leonards BH24 ...139 C4
Sway SO41 ....172 B1
Badgers Copse BH25 .195 A3
Badgers Run SO31 ..128 C3
Badgers The SO31 ...127 B3
Badgers Wlk
Ferndown BH22 .....165 C4
Hythe SO45 ....125 C1
Badminston Dro SO45 .178 B4
Badminston La SO45 .151 B1
Badshear La SO24 ...14 C4
Baffins Rd PO3 ......183 A4
Bagber Rd SO40 ....100 C4
Bagot Ho PO12 .....180 C3
Bagshot Mews SO19 .103 C2
Baigent Cl SO23 ......11 B4
Bailey Cl Botley SO30 .106 A3
New Milton BH25 ....195 B2
Winchester SO22 .....10 B3
Bailey Cres BH15 ....202 B4
Bailey Dr SO31 ......206 C4
Bailey Gn SO18 ......80 A1
Bailey Hall BH23 ....206 C4
Bailey's Rd PO5 .....215 C2
Baiter Gdns BH15 ...202 B1
Baker Rd BH11 ......189 A3
Baker St PO1 ....182 B4
Bakers Dro SO16 .....77 C3
Bakers Farm Rd BH31 .114 C4
Balcombe Rd BH13 ..204 A2
Balderton Cl 15 PO2 .157 C2
Baldwin Cl BH23 ....207 B3
Balena Cl BH17 .....202 A4
Balfour Cl
Christchurch BH23 ...208 B4
Gosport PO13 ......180 B3
Balfour Dr GU33 .....20 C2
Balfour Rd
Bournemouth BH9 ...189 C1
Portsmouth PO2 .....157 C1
Southampton SO19 ..104 B2
Balfour Red Cross Mus ★
SO22 ....1 B1
Ball La 17 BH15 .....202 B1
Ballam Cl BH16 .....201 B4
Ballard Cl
New Milton BH25 ....195 A2
Poole BH15 ....202 B1
Southampton SO16 ..77 B1
Ballard Coll BH25 ...195 A2
Ballard Cl 1 PO12 ..181 B2
Ballard Rd BH15 ....202 B1
Ballard Sch BH25 ...195 A2
Balliol Cl PO14 .....129 B1
Balliol Rd PO2 ......182 C4
Balmer Lawn Rd SO42 .146 A2
Balmoral Ave BH8 ..190 C1
Balmoral Cl
Chandler's Ford SO53 ..55 A4
Gosport PO13 ......155 B1
Southampton SO16 ..78 B3
Balmoral Ct
7 Christchurch BH23 .209 A4
7 Southampton SO17 .103 A4
Southampton, Millbrook
SO15 ....102 A3
Balmoral Dr PO7 ....134 B2
Balmoral Ho BH2 ...204 B2
Balmoral Rd
Fareham PO15 ......130 C2
Poole BH14 ....203 B2

Balmoral Way
Petersfield GU32 .....40 C2
Rownhams SO16 ....77 C3
Balmoral Wlk BH25 ..194 C2
Balston Rd BH14 ....203 A3
Balston Terr BH15 ...202 A1
Baltic Rd SO30 ......80 C1
Bambridge Pk Gdn Ctr
Miniature Rly ★ SO50 .31 C1
Bamford Ho PO4 ....183 A1
Bampton Cl SO16 ...101 C4
Bampton Ct SO53 ....55 B3
Banbury Ave SO19 ..104 B2
Banbury Rd BH17 ...202 B4
Banfurly Gdns SO45 .125 C1
Bangor Rd SO15 ....102 A3
Banister Ct 13 SO15 .102 C4
Banister Mews SO15 .102 C4
Banister Grange 16
SO15 ....102 C4
Banister Inf Sch SO15 .102 C4
Banister Mews SO15 .102 C4
Banister Rd SO15 ...102 C4
Bank Chambers BH14 .203 C2
Bank Cl BH23 ....207 A3
Bank Side SO18 ......79 B2
Bank St SO32 ....83 B4
Bankhill Dr SO41 ...197 B3
Banks Rd BH13 .....214 B2
Banks The SO51 .....26 A3
Bankside SO41 ......197 B3
Bankside Ho 4 SO22 ..10 C4
Bankside BH9 ....190 A2
Bankview SO41 .....197 B3
Bannerman Rd GU32 ..40 C2
Banning St SO51 .....52 C3
Bannister Ct SO40 ..101 A4
Banocroft Ct 1 BH15 .202 C2
Banstead Rd BH18 ..187 A3
Bapaume Rd PO3 ...157 C3
Bar End Ind Est SO23 ..11 A3
Bar End Rd SO23 ....11 A3
Bar Gate & Guildhall (Mus) ★
SO14 ....102 C2
Barbe Baker Ave SO30 ..80 B1
Barberry Dr SO40 ....76 A1
Barberry Way BH31 .115 B3
Barbers Gate 15 BH15 .202 A1
Barbers Piles 8 BH15 .202 A1
Barbers Wharf 16 BH15 .202 A1
Barclay Ho PO12 ...181 C2
Barclay Mans BH2 ..204 C3
Barclay Mews
Hythe SO45 ....149 C4
Hythe SO45 ....150 A4
Bardon Way PO14 ..154 B4
Barfield Cl SO23 .....11 A3
Barfields SO41 ......197 C2
Barfields Ct SO41 ..197 C2
Barfleur Cl PO15 ...130 B1
Barfleur Rd SO41 ...155 A3
Barford Cl SO53 .....55 A4
Barford La SP5 ......47 A4
Bargate Ctr 8 SO14 .103 A2
Bargate St SO14 ....102 C2
Bargates BH23 ......207 A4
Barham Cl PO12 ....181 A3
Barham Rd GU32 ....40 C2
Barham Way PO2 ...157 B2
Baring Rd
Bournemouth BH6 ..207 A2
Winchester SO23 .....11 A4
Bark Hill Mews SO51 .52 C3
Barker Mill Cl SO16 ..77 C3
Barkis Ho SO19 .....104 B2
Barkshire Ct 7 SO15 .102 C4
Barlands Cl BH23 ...192 B1
Barle Cl SO18 ....80 A1
Barley Down Dr SO22 ..10 B2
Barleycorn Wlk SO40 ..98 C4
Barling Mews 13 SO51 .52 C4
Barlow Cl PO14 .....179 A3
Barn Cl Emsworth PO10 .160 B4
Upton BH16 ....201 A4
Barn Fold PO7 ......112 B1
Barn Piece SO53 .....54 C3
Barn Rd BH18 ......187 A2
Barnaby Cl SP5 ......46 B4
Barnbrook Rd SO31 .128 C2
Barncroft Inf Sch PO9 .135 B2
Barncroft Jun Sch PO9 .135 B2
Barncroft Way PO9 ..135 B2
Barnes Cl
Bournemouth BH10 .189 A3
Locks Heath SO31 ..128 B2
Southampton SO18 ..104 B3
West Wellow SO51 ...50 C2
Winchester SO23 .....10 C3
Barnes Cres
Bournemouth BH10 .189 A3
Wimborne Minst BH21 .163 C2
Barnes La
Locks Heath SO31 ..128 C2
Milford on Sea SO41 .211 B3
Barnes Rd
Bournemouth BH10 .189 B2
Portsmouth PO1 .....182 C4
Southampton SO19 ..104 B3
Barnes Wallis Rd PO15 .129 C2
Barnes Way PO9 ....135 B2
Barnet Side La GU32 ..18 B3
Barney Evans Cres PO8 .111 B2
Barney Hayes La SO40 ..99 A4
Barnfield BH23 .....208 B4
Barnfield Cl
Southampton SO19 ..103 C1
Southbourne PO10 ..137 B2

Barnfield Ct
Fareham PO16 ......154 C4
Southampton SO19 ..103 C1
Barnfield Flats SO19 .103 C1
Barnfield Rd
Petersfield GU31 .....41 B2
Southampton SO19 ..103 C1
Barnfield Way SO19 .103 C1
Barnfields Flats SO19 .103 C1
Barns Rd BH22 .....166 A3
Barnsfield Cres SO40 .100 B4
Barnside Rd BH24 ..140 A2
Barnside Way GU33 ..20 C2
Barnsland SO30 ......80 B2
Barnwood Rd PO15 .130 B1
Baron Rd SO31 .....127 C2
Barons Ct 8 BH12 ..204 A2
Barons Mead SO16 ..77 C2
Barons Rd BH11 ....188 B3
Baronsmere PO12 ..181 A4
Barrack La BH24 ...141 B2
Barrack Rd
Christchurch BH23 ..206 C4
Ferndown BH22 ....166 A1
Barratt Ind Pk PO15 .129 B3
Barrie Cl PO15 .....129 B4
Barrie Rd BH9 ......189 C2
Barrington Cl 31 SO17 ..79 A1
Barrington Ho PO1 .182 B4
Barrow Down Gdns
SO19 ....104 C2
Barrow Dr BH8 .....190 C1
Barrow Hill Rd SO40 ..75 B2
Barrow Rd BH8 .....190 C1
Barrow View BH22 ..165 A3
Barrow Way BH8 ...190 C1
Barrowgate Rd BH8 .190 B2
Barrowgate Way BH8 .190 B2
Barrows La Landford SP5 .49 B3
Sway SO41 ....196 A3
Barrs Ave BH25 .....195 A2
Barrs Wood Dr BH25 .195 A2
Barrs Wood Rd BH25 .195 A2
Barry Gdns BH18 ...186 C2
Barry Rd SO19 .....104 A3
Barters Cl SO16 ......77 C1
Barters La BH15 ....186 C2
Bartholomew Cl 28 SO23 ..2 C1
Bartlett Cl PO15 ....130 C2
Bartlett Dr BH7 .....206 A4
Bartlett Ho 20 SO17 .103 A4
Bartletts Comm SP6 ..94 C4
Bartletts The SO31 ..128 A1
Bartley Ave SO40 ...100 B4
Bartley CE Jun Sch SO40 99 A4
Bartley Ct 6 BH21 ..163 A3
Bartley Rd SO40 .....99 B2
Barton Cl SO51 ......53 A4
Barton Common La
BH25 ....210 A4
Barton Common Rd
BH25 ....210 A4
Barton Court Ave BH25 .210 A4
Barton Court Rd BH25 .195 A1
Barton Cres SO18 ...79 C1
Barton Croft BH25 ..210 A4
Barton Cross PO8 ..112 A4
Barton Ct BH25 ....210 A4
Barton Dr
Barton on Sea BH25 .209 A4
Hamble-le-Rice SO31 .127 C2
Hedge End SO30 ...105 B4
Barton Gn BH25 ....210 A3
Barton Gn PO3 .....158 A2
Barton Ho PO3 .....158 A2
Barton Ho BH25 ....209 A4
Barton La BH25 ....209 C4
Barton Lo BH12 ....203 A4
Barton Rd SO50 .....56 B2
Barton Way BH25 ..209 C4
Barton Wood Rd BH25 .209 C4
Bartons Rd
Fordingbridge SP6 ...69 C1
Havant PO9 ....136 A2
Bartons The
Fordingbridge SP6 ...69 C1
Hedge End SO30 ...105 A4
Bartonside Rd BH25 .209 B4
Bartram Rd SO40 ..101 A4
Barwell Gr PO10 ...136 C2
Barwell Terr 10 SO30 .105 B3
Bascott Cl BH11 ....189 A1
Bascott Rd BH11 ...189 A1
Bashley Common Rd
BH25 ....195 A4
Bashley Cross Rd BH25 .194 C3
Bashley Dr BH25 ...195 A3
Bashley Rd BH25 ...195 A3
Basin St PO2 ....182 B4
Basing Dean GU34 ...17 C2
Basing Ho SO15 ....102 B4
Basing Mews 8 SO32 ..83 B4
Basing Rd PO9 .....135 C2
Basing Way SO53 ...55 A2
Basingstoke Rd SO23 ..2 C1
Basingwell St SO32 ..83 B4
Bassett Ave SO16 ...78 C2
Bassett Cl SO16 .....78 C2
Bassett Cres E SO16 .78 C2
Bassett Cres W SO16 .78 C2
Bassett Ct SO16 .....78 C2
Bassett Dale SO16 ..78 C2
Bassett Gdns SO16 ..78 C2
Bassett Gn SO16 ....79 A2
Bassett Green Cl SO16 .79 A2
Bassett Green Rd SO16 .79 A3

Bassett Green Dr SO16 ..79 A3
Bassett Green Prim Sch
SO16 ....79 A2
Bassett Green Rd SO16 .79 A3
Bassett Heath Ave SO16 .78 C3
Bassett Mdw SO16 ..78 C2
Bassett Mews SO16 ..78 C2
Bassett Rd BH12 ...203 A3
Bassett Row SO16 ..78 C2
Bassett Wlk 8 PO9 .135 B3
Bassett Wood Dr SO16 .79 A3
Bassett Wood Mews 7
SO16 ....78 C2
Bassett Wood N SO16 ..79 A3
Bassett Wood Rd SO16 .79 A3
Bastone Way BH22 .165 A3
Batchelor Cres BH11 .188 C2
Batchelor Gn SO31 .127 C4
Batchelor Rd BH11 .188 C2
Batcombe Cl BH11 ..188 C2
Bath & Wells Ct PO13 .180 B3
Bath Cl SO19 ....104 A3
Bath Hill Ct 9 BH1 .205 A2
Bath Hill Rdbt BH1 .205 A1
Bath La 11 PO16 ...131 B1
Bath La (lower) 13
PO16 ....131 B1
Bath Lane Cotts PO16 .155 B4
Bath Rd
Bournemouth BH1 ..205 A2
Emsworth PO10 ....160 C4
Lymington SO41 ...197 C2
Portsmouth PO4 ...182 C2
Southampton SO19 ..104 A3
Bath Sq PO1 ....181 C2
Bath St SO14 ......103 A4
Bathing La PO1 ....181 C2
Bathurst Cl PO11 ..184 C2
Bathurst Way PO2 .157 A1
Batten Cl BH23 ....207 B4
Batten Rd SP5 ......46 C4
Battenburg Ave PO2 .157 C1
Battenburg Rd PO12 .181 B2
Battens Way PO9 ..135 C2
Batterley Dro BH21 ..91 C2
Battery Cl PO12 ...180 C4
Battery Hill
Bishop's Waltham SO32 .83 A4
Winchester SO22 ...10 B3
Battery Row PO1 ..182 A2
Battle Cl SO31 .....129 A2
Battramsley Cross SO41 173 B1
Baverstock Rd BH12 .204 A4
Baxter Rd SO19 ....104 C3
Bay Cl Southampton SO19 104 A2
Three Legged Cross BH21 138 C4
Upton BH16 ....201 A3
Bay Hog La BH15 ..202 A1
Bay House Sec Sch
PO12 ....180 C2
Bay Rd Gosport PO12 .180 C2
Southampton SO19 ..104 A2
Bay Tree Lodge PO14 .179 B3
Bay Tree Way BH23 .193 B1
Bay Trees SO19 ....104 C3
Bay View Ct PO11 ..184 B1
Bay View Mews PO11 .184 B1
Baybridge La SO21 ...33 B2
Baybridge Rd PO9 ..136 A3
Baycroft Sch PO14 .179 C3
Bayfields PO5 ......215 B3
Bayly Ave PO16 ....156 B3
Bays Cl SO41 ......197 B2
Bays Rd SO41 .....197 B2
Bayswater Ho PO5 .215 C1
Baythorn Cl PO2 ...182 B4
Beach Ave SO41 ...209 C4
Beach Cl BH13 .....214 B4
Beach La SO31 ....127 A3
Beach Rd
Emsworth PO10 ....160 C4
Lee-on-the-Solent PO13 .179 C1
Poole BH13 ....214 D4
Portsmouth PO5 ...182 B1
South Hayling PO11 .184 C2
Upton BH16 ....201 A3
Beach View BH13 ..214 B2
Beachcroft BH13 ...204 A2
Beachway PO16 ....156 B3
Beacon Bottom SO31 .129 A3
Beacon Cl Hordle SO41 .196 B3
Locks Heath SO31 ..129 A3
Beacon Ct
Christchurch BH23 ..208 C4
Fordingbridge SP6 ...69 C2
Beacon Dr BH23 ...208 C4
Beacon Gdns BH18 .186 C2
Beacon Hill La
Corfe Mullen BH21 .186 A2
Droxford SO32 ......60 C3
Meonstoke SO32 ....61 B3
Beacon Mews SO30 .104 B4
Beacon Mount SO31 .129 A3
Beacon Park Cres BH16 201 A4
Beacon Park Rd BH16 .201 A4
Beacon Rd
Bournemouth BH2 ..204 C1
Broadstone BH18 ...186 C2
Upton BH16 ....201 A4
West End SO30 .....104 B4
Beacon Sq PO10 ...160 C4
Beacon Way
Broadstone BH18 ...186 C2
Locks Heath SO31 ..129 A3
Beaconsfield Ave PO6 .158 A4
Beaconsfield Rd
Christchurch BH23 ..207 A4

Beaconsfield Rd continued
Fareham PO16 ....155 A4
Poole BH12 ....203 B3
Waterlooville PO7 ......134 C4
Bealing Cl SO16 ....79 A2
Beamish Rd BH17 ....202 C4
Bear Cross Ave BH11 ...188 C3
Bear Cross Rdbt BH11 ..188 C3
Bearslane Cl SO40 ....76 B1
Bearwood Prim Sch
BH11 ....188 B3
Beatrice Ct 5 SO41 ....211 A2
Beatrice Mews 15 PO6 ..157 C4
Beatrice Rd
Portsmouth PO4 ....182 C1
Southampton SO15 ......102 B4
Beatrice Royal Art Gal★
SO50 ....55 C1
Beattie Rise SO30 ....81 B1
Beatty Cl
Locks Heath SO31 ......129 A2
Ringwood BH24 ....141 B4
Beatty Dr PO12 ....180 C2
Beatty Ho 9 PO1 ....215 C4
Beatty Rd BH9 ....190 A1
Beaty Ct SO19 ....104 C3
Beau Ct
31 Bournemouth BH4 ....204 B2
9 New Milton BH25 .....195 A2
Beauchamp Ave PO13 ...155 B1
Beauchamps Gdns BH7 ..206 A4
Beaucroft La BH21 .....163 C3
Beaucroft Rd
Waltham Chase SO32 ....83 C2
Wimborne Minst BH21 ...163 C3
Beaucroft Sch BH21 ....163 C3
Beaufort Ave PO16 .....130 C1
Beaufort Cl BH23 ....208 A4
Beaufort Dr
Bishop's Waltham SO32 ..83 B4
Wimborne Minst BH21 ...163 B3
Beaufort Mews BH21 ...163 A2
Beaufort Rd
Bournemouth BH6 ....206 B3
Havant PO9 ....135 B1
10 Portsmouth PO5 .....182 B1
Winchester SO23 ....10 C3
Beaufoys Ave BH22 .....165 B4
Beaufoys Cl BH22 ......165 B4
Beaufoys Ct BH22 ......165 B4
Beaulieu Abbey★ SO42 .148 C1
Beaulieu Ave
Christchurch BH23 ......206 C4
Havant PO9 ....135 B3
Portchester PO16 ....156 A4
Beaulieu Cl
New Milton BH25 ....194 C2
Southampton SO16 ......78 A3
Winchester SO22 ....1 B2
Beaulieu Ct 5 PO8 .....111 C2
Beaulieu Ho 12 SO15 ...102 C4
Beaulieu Pl PO13 ......155 A1
Beaulieu Rd
Beaulieu SO42,SO45 ....149 B3
Bournemouth BH4 ......204 A1
Christchurch BH23 ......206 C4
Eastleigh SO50 ....56 A2
Hamble-le-Rice SO31 ...127 C2
Hythe SO45 ....125 C1
Lyndhurst SO42 ....122 B2
Marchwood SO40 ....124 C3
Portsmouth PO2 ....157 C1
Beaulieu Road Sta
SO42 ....123 B1
Beaulieu Village Prim Sch
SO42 ....148 C1
Beaumaris Cl SO53 .....55 A2
Beaumaris Gdns SO40 ..125 C3
Beaumond Gn 29 SO22 .10 C4
Beaumont Cl
Fareham PO15 ....130 B2
Southampton SO16 .....78 C2
Beaumont Ct PO12 .....181 A4
Beaumont Pl SO40 .....101 C4
Beaumont Rd
Poole BH13 ....214 C4
Totton SO40 ....101 A4
Beaumont Rise PO15 ...130 B2
Beauworth Ave SO18 ...104 B4
Beaver Dr SO50 ....57 A1
Beaver Ind Est BH23 ...208 A3
Beccles Cl BH15 ....201 C1
Becher Rd BH14 ....203 C2
Beck Cl SO31 ....128 C2
Beck St PO1 ....182 A3
Beckenham Terr PO10 ..137 C2
Beckford La GU32 ......40 B2
Beckham Ct SO16 ......79 A2
Beckhampton Rd BH15 ..201 C2
Beckley Copse BH23 ....194 A1
Becton La BH25 ....210 A4
Becton Mead BH25 .....195 A1
Bedale Way BH15 ......202 C3
Bedales Sch GU32 ......40 C4
Beddow Hall 3 PO5 ....215 C4
Bedenham La PO13 .....155 C2
Bedenham Prim Sch
PO13 ....155 B2
Bedfield Ho SO23 ......2 A3
Bedfield La SO23 ......2 A3
Bedford Ave SO19 ......103 C1
Bedford Cl
Fordingbridge SP6 ......69 C2
Havant PO9 ....160 A4
Hedge End SO30 ....105 B3
Bedford Cres BH7 ......206 B4
Bedford Pl SO15 ....102 C3
Bedford Rd GU32 ......40 B2

Bedford Rd N BH12 .....188 B1
Bedford Rd S BH12 .....188 B1
Bedford St Gosport PO12 181 A3
Portsmouth PO5 ....215 B2
Bedhampton Hill PO9 ...135 A1
Bedhampton Hill Rd
PO9 ....135 A1
Bedhampton Ho 4 PO1 215 C4
Bedhampton Rd
Havant PO9 ....135 B1
Portsmouth PO2 ....182 C4
Bedhampton Sta PO9 ...135 B1
Bedhampton Way PO9 ..135 C2
Bedwell Cl SO16 ....77 C3
Beech Ave
Bournemouth BH6 ......206 B2
Christchurch BH23 .....206 B4
Southampton SO18 .....103 C4
Beech Cl Alderholt SP6 ..93 A3
Broadstone BH18 ......186 C2
Chandler's Ford SO53 ..30 B1
Hamble-le-Rice SO31 ...127 C1
Hordle SO41 ....211 B4
Romsey SO51 ....53 B3
Verwood BH31 ....114 C3
Waterlooville PO8 ......111 C1
Winchester SO22 ......10 A1
Beech Cnr SO32 ....81 C3
Beech Copse SO22 .....1 A1
Beech Cres SO45 ......150 A4
Beech Ct
Southampton SO19 .....103 C2
Wimborne Minst BH21 ..163 C2
Beech Dr PO6 ....156 C4
Beech Gdns SO31 ......127 C1
Beech Gr Gosport PO12 .181 C1
Owslebury SO21 ......33 A2
South Hayling PO11 ....185 A2
Beech Grange SP5 .....49 B1
Beech Ho SO16 ....78 C4
Beech La BH24 ....139 C1
Beech Rd Ashurst SO40 ..100 A1
Chandler's Ford SO53 ..55 B4
Clanfield PO8 ....88 B3
Fareham PO15 ....130 C1
Hedge End SO30 ......105 B4
Southampton SO15 ....102 A4
Beech Way PO8 ....112 A3
Beech Wood BH18 ....187 A2
Beecham Rd PO1 .....182 C4
Beechbank Ave BH17 ..186 C1
Beechcroft BH1 ......205 A3
Beechcroft Cl
Chandler's Ford SO53 ..55 B3
Fareham PO15 ....130 B1
Beechcroft La BH24 ...141 A4
Beechcroft Mews 2
BH24 ....141 A4
Beechcroft Rd PO12 ...181 A2
Beechcroft Way SO53 ..55 B4
Beechdale Cl SO40 ....76 B1
Beechdale Wlk SO40 ...76 B1
Beechen La SO43 .....122 A4
Beeches Hill SO32 .....59 B1
Beeches The
Awbridge SO51 ......26 C3
Bournemouth BH7 ....206 A4
Fair Oak SO50 ....57 B1
4 Waterlooville PO7 ...134 C4
West Wellow SO51 ...50 B2
Beechey Ct 6 PO8 ....205 A4
Beechey Rd BH8 ......205 A3
Beechfield 30 BH4 ....204 B2
Beechfield Ct SO15 ....102 A4
Beechmount SO16 .....78 C3
Beechmount Rd SO16 ..78 C3
Beechwood SP6 ....69 B1
Beechwood Ave
Bournemouth BH5 .....205 C2
New Milton BH25 ......194 C2
Waterlooville PO7 .....134 C3
Beechwood Cl
Chandler's Ford SO53 ..30 A1
Locks Heath SO31 ....152 B4
Beechwood Cres SO53 ..30 A1
Beechwood Ct
Bournemouth BH2 ....204 C1
Liss GU33 ....21 A3
Beechwood Gdns
Bournemouth BH5 ....206 A2
Southampton SO16 ...103 C4
Beechwood Ho SO17 ..103 B4
Beechwood Jun Sch
SO18 ....103 C4
Beechwood La BH24 ...143 A4
Beechwood Lodge 3
PO16 ....131 B2
Beechwood Rd
Cadnam SO40 ....99 A3
Holbury SO45 ....150 B2
Portsmouth PO2 ......157 C2
West Moors BH22 .....138 C1
Beechwood Rise SO18 ..80 B1
Beechwood Way SO45 ..125 B1
Beechworth Rd 3 PO9 ..136 C1
Beehive Cotts PO16 ....131 A2
Beehive Wlk PO1 ......182 A2
Beeston Ct PO1 ....182 C4
Beggar's La SO23 .....11 A4
Begonia Gdns SO16 ....79 A2
Behrendt Cl PO12 .....181 A3
Belben Cl BH12 ....188 B1
Belben Rd BH12 ....188 B1
Belbins SO51 ....27 C2
Belbins Bsns Pk SO51 ..28 A2
Belfield Rd BH6 ......207 A2
Belfry Wlk PO14 ......129 B1
Belgrave Ct BH1 ......205 B2

Belgrave Ind Est SO17 ..79 B1
Belgrave Rd Poole BH13 .204 A1
Southampton SO17 .....79 B1
Belgravia Rd PO2 ......157 C1
Bell Cl SO45 ....150 C1
Bell Cres PO7 ....134 C3
Bell Davies Rd PO14 ...179 A3
Bell Heather Cl BH16 ..201 A4
Bell Hill GU32 ....40 C3
Bell Hill Ridge GU32 ...40 C3
Bell Ho PO18 ....161 C4
Bell La 18 BH15 ......202 A1
Bell Rd PO6 ....157 B4
Bell St Romsey SO51 ...52 C4
Southampton SO14 ....103 A2
Bellair Ho PO9 ....136 A1
Bellair Rd PO9 ....136 A1
Bellamy Ct SO17 .....103 B4
Belle Vue Cl BH6 .....206 B2
Belle Vue Cres BH6 ...206 C2
Belle Vue Gdns 2 BH6 .206 C2
Belle Vue Gr BH22 ....138 C1
Belle Vue Mans 7 BH6 .206 C2
Belle Vue Rd
Bournemouth BH6 .....206 C2
Poole BH14 ....203 B2
Belle Vue Wlk BH22 ...165 C1
Bellemoor Rd SO15 ...78 B1
Bellemoor Sec Sch (Boys)
SO15 ....78 B1
Belleview Terr PO5 ....215 A1
Bellevue La PO10 .....136 C1
Bellevue Terr 9 SO14 ..103 A4
Bellfield PO14 ....153 C4
Bellflower Cl BH23 ....208 A4
Bellflower Way SO53 ...54 C1
Bells Ho BH21 ....163 B3
Bells La PO14 ....179 B3
Belmont Ave BH8 .....190 B1
Belmont Cl Horndean PO8 88 B2
Hythe SO45 ....126 A1
Stubbington PO14 .....154 B2
Verwood BH31 ....115 A3
Belmont Gr PO9 ......135 B1
Belmont Pl PO5 ......215 B1
Belmont Rd
Chandler's Ford SO53 ..55 B2
New Milton BH25 .....195 B2
Poole BH14 ....203 B3
Southampton SO17 ....103 A4
Belmont St PO5 ......215 B1
Belmore Cl PO1 ......182 C4
Belmore La
Lymington SO41 ......197 C2
Owslebury SO21 .....33 C2
Uppham SO32 ....34 A2
Belmore Rd SO41 .....197 B2
Belmour Lo 26 BH4 ...204 B2
Belney Ho PO6 ....157 A4
Belstone Rd SO40 ....100 C4
Belton Rd SO19 ......104 A2
Belvedere Cl GU32 ....40 C2
Belvedere Rd
Bournemouth BH3 ....205 A3
Christchurch BH23 ....207 A4
Hythe SO45 ....126 A1
Belvedere Ho 12 SO14 .103 B3
Belvedere Rd SO14 ....103 B3
Belvedere Terr SO14 ...103 B3
Belvoir Cl PO16 ......155 A4
Bembridge SO31 .....127 B3
Bembridge Cl SO16 ...79 B3
Bembridge Cres PO4 ..182 C1
Bembridge Ct PO11 ...185 B1
Bembridge Dr PO11 ...185 B1
Bembridge Ho PO11 ..185 B1
Bembridge Lodge Flats 8
PO13 ....179 C1
Bemister Ho BH9 .....205 A4
Bemister's La PO12 ...181 C2
Benbow Cl PO8 ......112 B4
Benbow Cres BH12 ...188 C1
Benbow Gdns SO40 ...76 B1
Benbow Ho 6 PO1 ...182 B4
Benbow Pl 5 PO1 ....182 A3
Benbridge Ave BH11 ..188 C3
Bencraft Ct SO16 .....79 B4
Bendigo Rd BH23 .....206 C4
Benedict Cl SO51 ....53 B4
Benedict Way PO16 ...132 C1
Beneficial St 14 PO1 ..182 A3
Benellen Ave BH4 ....204 B2
Benellen Gdns BH4 ...204 B3
Benellen Rd BH4 .....204 B2
Benellen Twrs BH4 ...204 B2
Bengal Rd BH9 ......204 C4
Benger's La SO51 ....5 B1
Benham Dr 18 PO3 ...157 C2
Benham Gr PO6 ......156 B3
Benhams Farm Cl 8
SO18 ....80 A1
Benhams Rd SO18 ....80 A1
Benjamin Ct BH23 ....206 C4
Benjamin Rd BH15 ...201 C1
Benmoor Rd BH17 ....202 A4
Benmore Cl BH25 ....195 B1
Benmore Gdns SO53 ..55 C4
Benmore Rd BH9 .....190 A1
Bennett Ho 11 BH4 ...204 B2
Bennett Rd BH8 ......205 B3
Bennett's Alley 22 BH15 202 A1
Bennetts La BH24 ....143 B1
Bennion Rd BH10 ....189 B1
Benridge Cl BH18 ....187 A2
Benson Cl BH23 ......169 A1

Benson Rd Poole BH17 .202 B4
Southampton SO15 ....102 A4
Bent La PO7 ....110 A4
Bentham Rd PO12 ....181 A2
Bentham Way SO31 ..128 B3
Benthem Ct SO16 ....79 C2
Bentley Cl Horndean PO8 112 B4
Kings Worthy SO23 ...2 A3
Bentley Cres PO16 ...130 C1
Bentley Ct 16 Havant PO9 136 A3
Bentley Gr SO18 .....104 B4
Bentley Rd BH9 .....189 C2
Bentworth Cl PO9 ...135 B2
Benwell Ct PO11 ....184 C2
Bepton Down GU31 ...41 C4
Berber Cl PO15 ......129 B4
Bercote Cl SO22 .....1 A3
Bere Cl
North Baddesley SO52 ..55 A4
Poole BH17 ....187 B1
Winchester SO22 .....1 B1
Bere Farm La PO17 ..131 C4
Bere Rd PO7 ....110 C2
Beresford Cl
Chandler's Ford SO53 ..55 C3
Poole BH12 ....203 B3
Waterlooville PO7 ....134 C3
Beresford Gdns
Chandler's Ford SO53 ..55 C3
Christchurch BH23 ....207 C3
Beresford Rd
Bournemouth BH6 ....206 A2
Chandler's Ford SO53 ..55 C3
Lymington SO41 .....197 B2
Poole BH12 ....203 B3
Portsmouth PO2 .....157 C1
Stubbington PO14 ....154 B2
Bereweeke Ave SO22 ..1 C1
Bereweeke Cl SO22 ...1 C1
Bereweeke Rd SO22 ...1 C1
Bereweeke Way SO22 .1 C1
Bergen Cres SO30 ...105 B3
Berkeley Ave BH12 ...203 B4
Berkeley Cl
Southampton SO14 ....102 C4
Stubbington PO14 ....179 A3
Verwood BH31 ....114 C4
Berkeley Ct PO13 ....179 C1
Berkeley Gdns SO30 ..105 B3
Berkeley Rd
Bournemouth BH3 ....204 C4
Southampton SO15 ...102 C3
Berkeley Sq PO9 .....136 A1
Berkeley The PO5 ....182 C1
Berkley Ave BH22 ....165 B1
Berkshire Cl PO1 .....215 D3
Bermuda Ct
9 Christchurch BH23 ..209 A4
22 Southampton SO17 .79 A1
Bermuda Ho 3 PO6 ..132 C1
Bernard Ave PO6 .....156 A4
Bernard Powell Ho PO9 136 A1
Bernard St SO14 .....103 A2
Bernards Cl BH23 ....206 C4
Berne Ct 11 BH1 .....205 A2
Berney Rd PO4 ......183 B2
Bernina Ave PO7 ....111 B1
Bernina Cl PO7 ......111 B1
Bernwood Gr SO45 ..177 C4
Beron Ct BH15 ......202 C2
Berrans Ave BH11 ...189 A3
Berrans Ct BH11 ....189 A3
Berry Cl SO30 ....105 B3
Berry La
Stubbington PO14 ....179 A3
Twyford SO21 ....32 A4
Berrydown Rd PO9 ..135 B4
Berryfield Rd SO41 ..196 A3
Berrylands SO31 .....21 A4
Berrywood Bsns Village
SO30 ....81 A2
Berrywood Gdns SO30 105 A4
Berrywood Prim Sch
SO30 ....81 B1
Berthon Ho SO51 ....52 C3
Bertie Rd PO4 ....183 A2
Bertram Rd BH25 ....195 B2
Berwick Rd BH3 .....204 C3
Berwyn Cl BH18 .....187 A2
Berwyn Wlk PO14 ...154 C4
Beryl Ave PO14 .....180 C4
Beryton Cl PO12 ....181 A3
Beryton Rd PO12 ....181 A3
Besomer Dro SP5 ....47 C3
Bessborough Rd BH13 .214 C4
Bessemer Cl BH31 ...115 B2
Beswick Ave BH10 ..189 B1
Bethany Ct BH12 ....204 A4
Bethany Ho BH1 .....205 B3
Bethany Jun CE Sch
BH1 ....205 B3
Bethia Cl BH8 ....205 B3
Bethia Rd BH8 ......205 B3
Betsy Cl BH23 ......169 A1
Betsy La BH23 ......169 A1
Betteridge Dr SO16 ..77 B3
Bettesworth Rd PO1 ..182 C4
Bettiscombe Cl BH17 .187 C1
Betula Cl PO7 ......135 A3
Beulah Rd SO16 ....78 A1
Bevan Cl SO19 .....103 C1
Bevan Rd PO8 .....112 A3
Beverley Gdns
Bournemouth BH10 ...189 B2
Bursledon SO31 .....104 C1
Romsey SO51 ....28 A1

Beverley Gdns continued
Swanmore SO32 ....84 A3
Beverley Gr PO6 ......134 C1
Beverley Grange 29
BH4 ....204 B2
Beverley Hts SO18 ...79 C2
Beverley Rd Hythe SO45 .149 C4
Stubbington PO14 .....179 B3
Beverly Cl PO13 ......155 B1
Beverston Ho 4 PO6 ..133 A1
Beverston Rd PO6 ....133 A1
Bevis Cl Blackfield SO45 .150 C1
Locks Heath SO31 ....152 B4
Bevis Rd Gosport PO12 .181 A3
Portsmouth PO2 ......157 B1
Bevis Rd N PO2 .....157 A1
Bevois Gdns SO14 ...103 A4
Bevois Hill SO14 ....103 A4
Bevois Mans 25 SO14 .103 A4
Bevois Mews 26 SO14 .103 A4
Bevois Town Prim Sch
SO14 ....103 A4
Bevois Valley Rd SO14 .103 A4
Bexington Cl BH11 ...188 C2
Beyne Rd SO22 .....10 A2
Bickerley Gdns BH24 ..140 C3
Bickerley Rd BH24 ...140 C3
Bickerley Terr BH24 ..140 C4
Bicknell Boys Sch BH7 .206 A4
Bicknell Ct 10 BH4 ...204 B2
Bickton Wlk 9 PO9 ...135 B3
Bicton Rd BH10 .....189 A2
Bidbury Inf Sch PO9 ..135 B1
Bidbury Jun Sch PO9 ..135 B1
Bidbury La PO9 ......135 B1
Biddenfield La SO32,
PO17 ....107 B3
Biddlecombe Cl PO13 ..180 B4
Biddlesgate Ct 10 SO14 102 C2
Bideford Cl SO16 .....77 C1
Big Tree Cotts SO32 ...85 B3
Biggin Wlk PO14 .....154 C4
Bilberry Cl SO31 .....128 C1
Bilberry Ct 15 SO22 ..10 C4
Bilberry Dr SO40 .....101 C1
Bill Stillwell Ct 6 PO2 .157 B1
Billett Ave PO7 ......134 C4
Billing Cl PO4 ....183 A2
Billington Gdns SO30 ..81 B3
Billington Pl SO41 ....197 B1
Billy Lawn Ave PO9 ...135 C3
Bilton Bsns Pk PO3 ...158 B1
Bilton Way PO3 ......158 B1
Bindon Cl Poole BH12 .203 C4
Southampton SO16 ...78 A1
Bindon Ct 5 SO18 ...103 C4
Bindon Rd SO16 .....78 A1
Bingham Ave BH14 ..214 B4
Bingham Cl
Christchurch BH23 ...207 C4
Verwood BH31 ....115 A2
Bingham Dr
Lymington SO41 .....197 C2
Verwood BH31 ....115 A2
Bingham Rd
Bournemouth BH9 ...205 A4
Christchurch BH23 ...207 C4
Verwood BH31 ....115 A2
Binnacle Way PO6 ...157 A4
Binness Way PO6 ....158 C4
Binnie Rd BH12 .....203 C3
Binstead Ct SO16 ...79 B3
Binsteed Rd PO2 ....182 C4
Birch Ave Burton BH23 .192 B2
Ferndown BH22 .....165 C1
New Milton BH25 .....194 B3
Birch Cl
Colden Common SO21 .56 C4
Corfe Mullen BH21 ...186 B3
Liss GU33 ....21 A2
Poole BH14 ....203 C2
Romsey SO51 ....53 B3
Southampton SO16 ...78 A1
St Leonards BH24 ...139 B2
Waterlooville PO8 ....111 C2
Birch Ct
Southampton SO18 ...104 A4
3 Winchester SO22 ..10 B3
Birch Dale SO45 .....126 A1
Birch Dr
Bournemouth BH8 ...191 A1
Gosport PO13 ....155 B2
Birch Gr Eastleigh SO50 .56 A3
New Milton BH25 .....195 A1
West Moors BH22 ....138 B1
Birch Hill PO17 ......109 A2
Birch Ho SO16 ......78 C4
Birch Rd Chilworth SO16 79 A3
Hedge End SO30 ....105 B4
Southampton SO16 ...78 A2
St Leonards BH24 ...140 A2
Birch Tree Cl PO10 ...136 C2
Birch Tree Dr PO10 ...136 C2
Birch Wlk BH22 .....165 C2
Birch Wood SO19 ...104 A4
Birchdale Cl SO31 ...152 B4
Birchdale Rd BH21 ..163 B3
Birchen Cl SO31 ....129 B2
Birchen Rd SO31 ....129 B2
Birches Cl The SO52 ..53 C3
Birches The SO18 ...104 A4
Birchglade SO40 ....76 B1
Birchlands SO40 ....100 B3
Birchmore Cl 3 PO13 .155 B1
Birchwood Cl BH23 ..208 C4

Birchwood Ct **8** SO18 . . . . .103 C4
Birchwood Dr SP6 . . . . .93 A3
Birchwood Gdns SO30 . . .105 B4
Birchwood Lodge **7**
PO16 . . . . .131 A1
Birchwood Mews BH14 .203 B2
Birchwood Rd
  Poole BH14 . . . . .203 B2
  Upton BH16 . . . . .201 A3
Birchy Hill SO41 . . . . . . .172 B1
Bird Field SO53 . . . . .54 C4
Bird's Hill Rd BH15 . . .202 C2
Birdham Rd PO11 . . . . . .185 C1
Birdlip Cl PO8 . . . . .112 A3
Birdlip Rd PO6 . . . . .133 A1
Birds Hill Gdns **5** BH15 202 C2
Birdwood Gr PO16 . . . . .155 C4
Birinus Rd SO23 . . . . .2 A1
Birkdale Ave PO6 . . . . . .134 B1
Birkdale Ct BH18 . . . . . .187 A3
Birkdale Rd BH18 . . . . . .187 A3
Birmingham Ct PO13 . . .180 B3
Biscay Cl PO14 . . . . .154 A2
Bishearne Gdns GU33 . . . .20 C3
Bishop Cl BH12 . . . . .204 B4
Bishop Ct BH24 . . . . .141 C4
Bishop Rd BH9 . . . . .205 A4
Bishop St PO1 . . . . .182 A3
Bishop's La SO32 . . . . . . .83 B4
Bishop's Waltham Inf Sch
  SO32 . . . . .83 B4
Bishop's Waltham Pal★
  SO32 . . . . .83 B4
Bishop's Wood Rd PO17 .84 B1
Bishops Cl
  Bournemouth BH7 . . . . .205 C4
  Totton SO40 . . . . .100 C4
Bishops Cres SO19 . . . . .103 C2
Bishops Ct SO50 . . . . .56 B3
Bishops Gate PO14 . . . . .129 B2
Bishops La SO32 . . . . .84 A1
Bishops Rd SO19 . . . . . . .103 C2
Bishopsfield Rd PO14 . . .154 C4
Bishopstoke La SO50 . . . .56 C4
Bishopstoke Manor SO50 56 B2
Bishopstoke Rd
  Eastleigh SO50 . . . . .56 B2
  Havant PO9 . . . . .135 C3
Bisley Ct SO19 . . . . .104 A2
Bisterne Cl BH24 . . . . . . .143 C1
Bittern Cl PO12 . . . . .181 A4
Bitterne CE Inf & Jun Sch
  SO19 . . . . .103 C3
Bitterne Cl PO9 . . . . .135 C3
Bitterne Cres SO19 . . . . .104 A3
Bitterne Manor Ho
  SO18 . . . . .103 B4
Bitterne Manor Prim Sch
  SO18 . . . . .103 B4
Bitterne Park Inf Sch
  SO17 . . . . .79 B1
Bitterne Park Jun Sch
  SO17 . . . . .79 B1
Bitterne Park Sec Sch
  SO18 . . . . .79 C1
Bitterne Park Triangle
  SO18 . . . . .79 B1
Bitterne Rd SO18 . . . . . .104 A3
Bitterne Rd E SO18 . . . . .104 B4
Bitterne Rd W SO18 . . . .103 C4
Bitterne Sta SO18 . . . . . .103 B4
Bitterne Way
  Lymington SO41 . . . . . . .197 B3
  Southampton SO19 . . . . .103 C3
  Verwood BH31 . . . . .115 A3
Bitumen Rd SO45 . . . . . .151 A2
Black Hill BH31 . . . . .115 A3
Black La Bransgore BH23 169 C2
  Redlynch SP5 . . . . .48 A1
Black Moor Rd BH31 . . . .115 B2
Black Swan Bldgs **20**
  SO22 . . . . .10 C4
Blackberry Cl PO8 . . . . . . .88 B2
Blackberry Dr SO50 . . . . . .57 A1
Blackberry La BH23 . . . . .207 C3
Blackberry Terr SO14 . . .103 A4
Blackbird Cl
  Broadstone BH17 . . . . . . .201 C4
  Waterlooville PO8 . . . . . .111 C2
Blackbird Rd SO50 . . . . . .55 B1
Blackbird Way
  Bransgore BH23 . . . . . . .193 B4
  Lee-on-the-Solent PO13 . .179 C1
Blackbrook Bsns Pk
  PO15 . . . . .130 C1
Blackbrook House Dr
  PO14,PO15 . . . . .130 C1
Blackbrook Park Ave
  PO15 . . . . .130 C1
Blackbrook Rd PO15 . . . .130 B1
Blackburn Ct SO13 . . . . . .180 B3
Blackburn Rd BH12 . . . . .203 A3
Blackbush Rd SO41 . . . . .211 A3
Blackbushe Cl SO16 . . . . . .77 C3
Blackcap Cl PO9 . . . . . . .113 A1
Blackdown Cl SO45 . . . . .125 B1
Blackdown Cres PO9 . . . .135 C2
Blackfield Inf Sch SO45 150 C1
Blackfield Jun Sch
  SO45 . . . . .150 B1
Blackfield La BH22 . . . . . .138 C2
Blackfield Rd
  Blackfield SO45 . . . . .150 A1
  Bournemouth BH8 . . . . . .190 B2
Blackfriars Cl **3** PO1 . .215 C2

Blackfriars Rd PO1 . . . . .215 C3
Blackhill Rd SO51 . . . . .74 C4
Blackhorse La SO32 . . . . . .83 C1
Blackhouse La PO17 . . . . .109 A1
Blackmoor Wlk **12** PO9 .136 A3
Blackmore La GU32 . . . . . .18 C2
Blacksmith Cl BH21 . . . . .186 B3
Blackthorn Cl
  Lymington SO41 . . . . . . .197 A1
  Southampton SO19 . . . . .103 C3
Blackthorn Dr
  Gosport PO12 . . . . .156 A1
  South Hayling PO11 . . . . .185 B2
Blackthorn Gn SO21 . . . . .57 A4
Blackthorn Rd
  South Hayling PO11 . . . . .185 B1
  Southampton SO19 . . . . .103 C3
Blackthorn Terr PO1 . . . .182 A3
Blackthorn Way
  New Milton BH25 . . . . . .195 B4
  Verwood BH31 . . . . .115 A3
Blackwater Cl **10** PO6 .157 B4
Blackwater Dr
  Oakley BH21 . . . . .187 B3
  Totton SO40 . . . . .76 B1
Blackwater Gr SP6 . . . . . . .92 C3
Blackwater Mews SO40 . .76 B1
Blackwood Ho **15** PO1 .182 B4
Bladon Cl BH23 . . . . .136 B2
Bladon Rd SO16 . . . . .78 B1
Blair Ave BH14 . . . . .203 B2
Blair Cl BH25 . . . . .194 C2
Blake Cl SO16 . . . . .77 B3
Blake Dene Rd BH14 . . . .203 A1
Blake Hill Ave BH14 . . . . .203 B1
Blake Hill Cres BH14 . . . .203 B1
Blake Ho PO12 . . . . .181 C2
Blake Rd Cosham PO6 . . .134 B1
  Gosport PO12 . . . . .181 B3
  Portsmouth PO1 . . . . . . .181 C4
Blakemere Cres PO6 . . . .133 B1
Blakeney Rd SO16 . . . . . . .77 B1
Blakesley La PO3 . . . . . . .158 B2
Blanchard Rd SO32 . . . . . .83 A4
Blandford Cl BH15 . . . . . .201 C1
Blandford Ct **2** SO41 . .211 B3
Blandford Ho SO16 . . . . . .77 C1
Blandford Rd
  Coombe Bissett SP5 . . . . . .23 B4
  Corfe Mullen BH21 . . . . .186 B4
  Hamworthy BH15,BH16 . .201 B2
  Pamphill BH21 . . . . .162 B4
Blandford Rd N BH16 . . .201 A4
Blaney Way BH21 . . . . . . .186 B3
Blankney Cl PO14 . . . . . .179 A3
Blann Cl SO16 . . . . .77 B3
Blashford Lakes Study Ctr
  BH24 . . . . .117 A2
Blaven Wlk **4** PO14 . . .154 C4
Bleaklow Cl SO16 . . . . . .101 C4
Blechynden Terr SO15 . . .102 C3
Blencowe Dr SO53 . . . . . .54 C3
Blendworth Cres PO9 . . .135 C2
Blendworth Ho **2** PO1 .215 C4
Blendworth La
  Horndean PO8 . . . . .112 A4
  Southampton SO18 . . . . .104 B4
Blendworth Rd **5** PO4 .183 A3
Blenheim Ave SO17 . . . . .79 A1
Blenheim Cl
  Chandler's Ford SO53 . . . .54 C2
  Totton SO40 . . . . .100 C3
Blenheim Cres SO41 . . . .195 C2
Blenheim Ct
  25 Bournemouth BH4 .204 B2
  Christchurch BH23 . . . . . .207 A4
  Portsmouth PO4 . . . . . . .183 A2
  Southampton SO17 . . . . . .79 A1
Blenheim Dr BH23 . . . . . .208 A3
Blenheim Gdns
  Gosport PO12 . . . . .181 A4
  Havant PO9 . . . . .136 B1
  Hythe SO45 . . . . .125 B1
  Southampton SO17 . . . . . .79 A1
Blenheim Ho
  6 Eastleigh SO50 . . . . . .56 A1
  Romsey SO51 . . . . .53 A4
Blenheim Rd
  Eastleigh SO50 . . . . .56 A1
  Waterlooville PO8 . . . . . .112 A3
Blenhem Barn PO7 . . . . .110 C1
Bleriot Cres PO15 . . . . . .129 C3
Blighmont Ave SO15 . . . .102 A3
Blighmont Cres SO15 . . .102 A3
Blind La Curdridge SO32 . .82 C1
  Fair Oak SO30 . . . . .81 B3
  Ibsley SP6 . . . . .94 B1
  Wickham PO17 . . . . .107 C3
  Wimborne Minst BH21 . . .163 A3
Bliss Cl PO7 . . . . .134 C3
Blissford Cl PO9 . . . . . . .136 A3
Blissford Cross SP6 . . . . . .94 C4
Blissford Hill SP6 . . . . .94 C4
Blissford Rd SP6 . . . . .94 C3
Bloomfield Ave SO15 . . . .189 C1
Bloomfield Pl BH9 . . . . . .189 C1
Bloomsbury Wlk SO19 . . .103 C1
Blossom Cl SO30 . . . . . . .105 A3
Blount Rd PO1 . . . . .182 A2
Bloxworth Rd BH12 . . . . .203 C4
Blue Anchor La **15**
  SO14 . . . . .102 C2
Blue Ball Hill SO23 . . . . . .11 A4
Bluebell Cl
  Christchurch BH23 . . . . . .208 A4
  Waterlooville PO7 . . . . . .135 A3
Bluebell Copse SO31 . . . .128 C1

Bluebell La BH17 . . . . . . .186 C1
Bluebell Rd SO16 . . . . .79 B2
Blueprint Portfield Rd
  PO3 . . . . .158 A1
Bluestar Gdns SO30 . . . . . .81 B3
Blundell La SO31 . . . . . . .105 B1
Blyth Cl
  Christchurch BH23 . . . . . .191 B2
  Southampton SO16 . . . . . .77 B1
Blythe Rd BH21 . . . . .186 B3
Blythewood Ct BH25 . . . .209 C4
Boakes Pl SO40 . . . . .100 B1
Boardwalk The PO6 . . . . .157 A4
Boardwalk Way SO40 . . . .102 A2
Boarhunt Cl PO1 . . . . .215 C3
Boarhunt Rd PO17 . . . . . .131 C2
Boatyard Ind Est The
  PO16 . . . . .155 A4
Bob Hann Cl BH14 . . . . . .203 B3
Bockhampton Rd BH23 . .192 C3
Bodley Rd BH13 . . . . .214 C4
Bodmin Rd
  Bishopstoke SO50 . . . . . . .56 C1
  Portchester PO6 . . . . . . .157 A4
Bodorgan Rd BH2 . . . . . .204 C2
Bodowen Cl BH23 . . . . . .192 B1
Bodowen Rd BH23 . . . . . .192 B1
Bodycoats Rd SO53 . . . . . .55 B3
Bognor Rd BH18 . . . . . . .186 C2
Bohemia La SP5 . . . . .47 C2
Boiler Rd Fawley SO45 . . .151 C1
  Portsmouth PO1 . . . . . . .181 C4
Bolde Ct PO3 . . . . .158 A2
Boldens Rd PO12 . . . . . . .181 A1
Bolderwood Arboretum
  Ornamental Dr★ SO43 120 B1
Bolderwood Cl SO50 . . . . .56 C1
Boldre Cl
  Barton on Sea BH25 . . . . .209 B4
  Havant PO9 . . . . .135 C2
  Poole BH12 . . . . .203 B4
Boldre La SO41 . . . . .197 B4
Boldrewood Rd SO16 . . . . .78 C4
Boleyn Cl BH9 . . . . .190 A2
Bolhinton Ave SO40 . . . .101 B1
Bolton Cl BH6 . . . . .206 C2
Bolton Cres BH22 . . . . . . .166 A3
Bolton Ct **4** BH6 . . . . . .206 C2
Bolton Dr PO12 . . . . .181 B2
Bolton Rd BH6 . . . . .206 C2
Boltons The
  16 Milford on Sea SO41 .211 B2
  Waterlooville PO7 . . . . . .134 C2
Bonchurch Cl SO16 . . . . . .79 B3
Bonchurch Rd PO4 . . . . . .183 A3
Bond Ave BH22 . . . . .138 B2
Bond Cl SO40 . . . . .172 A2
Bond Rd Poole BH15 . . . . .202 C3
  Southampton SO18 . . . . . .79 C1
Bond St SO14 . . . . .103 B3
Bondfields Cres PO9 . . . .135 C3
Bones La GU31 . . . . .65 B3
Bonfire Cnr PO1 . . . . . . .182 A3
Bonham Rd BH3 . . . . .204 C4
Boniface Cl SO40 . . . . . . .100 B4
Boniface Cres SO16 . . . . . .77 C2
Bonington Cl BH23 . . . . . .207 C4
Bonner Cotts SP5 . . . . .4 C4
Boothby Cl SO40 . . . . . . .101 A4
Border Dr BH16 . . . . .201 B3
Border Lo BH23 . . . . .194 B1
Border Rd BH16 . . . . .201 B3
Bordon Rd PO9 . . . . .135 C3
Boredean La
  Froxfield Green GU32 . . . .39 B3
  Langrish GU32 . . . . .39 B3
Boreham Rd BH6 . . . . . . .206 B3
Borley Rd BH17 . . . . .202 A4
Borough Gr GU32 . . . . . . .40 C1
Borough Hill GU32 . . . . . .40 C2
Borough Rd
  Petersfield GU32 . . . . .40 B1
  Petersfield GU32 . . . . .40 C2
Borough The SP5 . . . . .46 C4
Borrowdale Rd SO16 . . . . .77 C1
Borthwick Rd BH1 . . . . . .205 C3
Boscobel Rd SO22 . . . . .1 C1
Boscombe Cliff Rd BH5 205 C2
Boscombe Gr Rd BH1 . . .205 B3
Boscombe Overcliff Dr
  BH5 . . . . .206 A2
Boscombe Spa Rd BH5 . .205 B2
Bosham Rd PO6 . . . . .182 C4
Bosham Wlk PO13 . . . . . .155 A1
Bosley Cl BH23 . . . . .191 C1
Bosley Way BH23 . . . . . . .191 C1
Bosmere Gdns PO10 . . . .136 C1
Bosmere Jun Sch PO9 . . .159 C4
Bosmere Rd PO11 . . . . . . .185 C1
Bossington Cl SO16 . . . . . .77 C3
Boston Ct SO53 . . . . .55 B4
Boston Lo **22** BH4 . . . . .204 B2
Boston Rd PO6 . . . . .133 C1
Bosuns Cl PO16 . . . . .155 A3
Bosville SO50 . . . . .56 A3
Boswell Cl Botley SO30 . .106 A3
  Southampton SO19 . . . . .104 B3
Bosworth Mews BH9 . . . .190 A2
Botany Bay Rd SO19 . . . .104 A3
Botley CE Prim Sch
  SO30 . . . . .106 A4
Botley Dr PO9 . . . . .135 B3
Botley Gdns SO19 . . . . . .104 C2
Botley Hill SO30 . . . . .106 A3
Botley Rd Curdridge SO32 .82 C1
  Fair Oak SO50 . . . . .57 C1
  Fair Oak, Wildern SO50 . .81 B4
  North Baddesley SO52 . . .53 B3

Botley Rd continued
  Romsey SO51 . . . . .53 B3
  Southampton SO19 . . . . .104 B2
  Swanwick SO31 . . . . .129 A4
  West End SO30 . . . . .81 A1
Botley Sta SO30 . . . . .106 B4
Bottings Est SO30 . . . . . .106 A4
Bottom La SO51 . . . . .50 C2
Boulnois Ave BH14 . . . . . .203 C2
Boultbee Cotts SO43 . . . .121 B3
Boulter La PO17 . . . . .133 A4
Boulton Rd PO5 . . . . .215 D1
Bound La PO11 . . . . .185 A1
Boundary Acre SO31 . . . .105 A2
Boundary Cl SO15 . . . . . .101 C4
Boundary Dr BH21 . . . . . .163 B3
Boundary La PO17 . . . . . .139 C1
Boundary Oak Prep Sch
  PO17 . . . . .131 B3
Boundary Rd
  Bournemouth BH10,BH9 . .189 C1
  Bursledon SO31 . . . . . . .127 C4
Boundary Rdbt BH3,
  BH10 . . . . .204 B4
Boundary Way
  Havant PO9 . . . . .135 C1
  Waterlooville PO6 . . . . . .134 A1
Boundstone SO45 . . . . . . .125 C2
Boundway SO41 . . . . .171 C1
Bountys La BH12 . . . . . . .203 C3
Bourne Ave
  Bournemouth BH2 . . . . . .204 C2
  Southampton SO15 . . . . . .78 B1
Bourne Cl
  Bournemouth BH4 . . . . . .204 B2
  Otterbourne SO21 . . . . . . .31 A2
  Waterlooville PO8 . . . . . .112 A3
  West Wellow SO51 . . . . . .50 A2
Bourne Com Coll PO10 . .137 B3
Bourne Cotts SP6 . . . . .44 C1
Bourne Ct
  24 Bournemouth BH2 .204 C2
  Wimborne Minst BH21 . . .163 B3
Bourne La
  Netley Marsh SO40 . . . . . .99 B3
  Twyford SO21 . . . . .32 A3
Bourne Pines **3** BH1 . .204 C2
Bourne Rd Cosham PO6 . .157 A4
  Netley Marsh SO40 . . . . . .99 B3
  Southampton SO15 . . . . .102 B3
Bourne Valley Rd BH12 . .204 A3
Bourne View PO10 . . . . . .137 B1
Bournefields SO21 . . . . . . .32 A4
Bournemouth & Poole Coll
  Annexe The BH1 . . . . . . .205 B3
Bournemouth & Poole Coll of
  F Ed BH14 . . . . .202 C2
Bournemouth & Poole Coll of
  F Ed (Annex) BH14 . . . . .202 C2
Bournemouth & Poole Coll
  The BH1 . . . . .205 A3
Bournemouth Aquarium★
  BH2 . . . . .204 C1
Bournemouth Ave PO12 181 A4
Bournemouth Aviation Mus★
  BH23 . . . . .191 A4
Bournemouth Central Bsns
  Pk BH1 . . . . .205 B3
Bournemouth Crown & Cty
  Cts BH7 . . . . .191 B1
Bournemouth Gram Sch
  (Boys) BH8 . . . . .190 B1
Bournemouth Gram Sch
  (Girls) BH8 . . . . .190 B1
Bournemouth Ho **59**
  PO9 . . . . .136 A3
Bournemouth Int Airport
  BH23 . . . . .190 C4
Bournemouth Int Ctr★
  BH2 . . . . .204 C1
Bournemouth Meml Homes
  BH8 . . . . .190 C1
Bournemouth Nuffield Hospl
  BH8 . . . . .205 A3
Bournemouth Rd
  Chandler's Ford SO53 . . . .55 B2
  Lyndhurst SO43 . . . . . . .121 C3
  Poole BH14 . . . . .203 B2
Bournemouth Sta BH1 . . .205 B4
Bournemouth Univ
  BH12 . . . . .204 B4
Bournemouth West Rdbt
  BH2 . . . . .204 B2
Bournewood Dr BH4 . . . .204 B4
Bourton Gdns BH7 . . . . . .206 A4
Bouverie Cl **28** BH25 . .195 A1
Boveridge Gdns BH9 . . . .190 A2
Bovington Cl BH17 . . . . . .187 C1
Bowater Cl SO40 . . . . .76 B1
Bowater Way SO40 . . . . . .76 B1
Bowcombe SO31 . . . . .127 B4
Bowden La SO17 . . . . .79 B1
Bowden Rd BH12 . . . . . . .188 B2
Bower Cl Holbury SO45 . .150 B2
  Southampton SO19 . . . . .103 C1
Bower Rd BH8 . . . . .205 B4
Bowers Cl PO8 . . . . .112 A2
Bowers Hill SP5 . . . . .47 C4
Bowerwood Cotts SP6 . . . .93 B4
Bowerwood Rd SP6 . . . . . .93 B4
Bowes Hill PO9 . . . . .113 B2
Bowes-Lyon Ct PO8 . . . . .112 A4
Bowland Rise
  New Milton BH25 . . . . . .195 B1
  North Baddesley SO53 . . . .55 A4
Bowland Way SO45 . . . . . .177 C4
Bowler Ave PO1 . . . . .182 C3
Bowler Ct PO1 . . . . .182 C3

Bowman Ct SO19 . . . . . .104 C2
Box Cl BH17 . . . . .202 A4
Boxgrove Ho PO1 . . . . . .215 C4
Boxwood Cl
  Portchester PO16 . . . . . .132 A1
  Waterlooville PO7 . . . . . .134 C3
Boyatt Cres SO50 . . . . .56 A4
Boyatt La Eastleigh SO50 . .56 A4
  Otterbourne SO21,SO50 . . .31 A1
Boyatt Wood Sh Ctr **7**
  SO50 . . . . .56 A3
Boyd Cl PO14 . . . . .179 A3
Boyd Rd Gosport PO13 . . .155 C2
  Poole BH12 . . . . .203 C3
Boyes La SO21 . . . . .32 A1
Boyle Cres PO7 . . . . .134 B3
Boyne Mead Rd SO23 . . . . .2 B4
Boyne Rise SO23 . . . . .2 A1
Boynton Cl SO53 . . . . .55 A4
Brabant Cl PO15 . . . . . . .129 A4
Brabazon Dr BH23 . . . . . .208 A4
Brabazon Rd
  Locks Heath PO15 . . . . . .129 B3
  Oakley BH21 . . . . .163 C1
Brabourne Ave BH22 . . . .165 B2
Bracken Cl
  North Baddesley SO52 . . . .54 A2
  St Leonards BH24 . . . . . .139 B2
Bracken Cres SO50 . . . . . .56 C1
Bracken Glen BH15 . . . . .202 C3
Bracken Hall SO16 . . . . . . .79 B4
Bracken Heath **13** PO7 .112 A1
Bracken La SO16 . . . . .78 A1
Bracken Lodge **3** BH6 .206 C2
Bracken Pl SO16 . . . . .79 A4
Bracken Rd
  Bournemouth BH6 . . . . . .206 C2
  Ferndown BH22 . . . . .165 A4
  North Baddesley SO52 . . . .54 A2
  Petersfield GU31 . . . . . . .41 B1
Bracken Way BH23 . . . . . .194 A1
Brackendale Ct BH21 . . . .138 C4
Brackendale Rd BH8 . . . . .205 B4
Brackenhill BH13 . . . . . . .204 A1
Brackenhill Rd BH21 . . . .164 A4
Brackens The
  Hythe SO45 . . . . .125 B2
  Locks Heath SO31 . . . . . .129 A1
Brackens Way
  Lymington SO41 . . . . . . .197 C1
  12 Poole BH13 . . . . . .214 C4
Brackenway Rd SO53 . . . . .55 B4
Bracklesham Cl SO19 . . . .103 C2
Bracklesham Rd
  Gosport PO13 . . . . .180 B4
  South Hayling PO11 . . . . .185 C1
Brackley Ave SO50 . . . . . .57 A2
Brackley Cl BH23 . . . . . . .191 A4
Brackley Way SO40 . . . . .100 B4
Bradbourne Rd BH2 . . . . .204 C2
Bradford Ct PO13 . . . . . . .180 B3
Bradford Rd
  Bournemouth BH9 . . . . . .190 B2
  Portsmouth PO5 . . . . . . .215 C2
Brading Ave
  Gosport PO13 . . . . .155 B1
  Portsmouth PO4 . . . . . . .183 A1
Brading Cl SO16 . . . . .79 B3
Bradley Ct **10** PO9 . . . . .136 A3
Bradley Gn SO16 . . . . .78 A2
Bradley Peak SO22 . . . . . . .1 B1
Bradley Rd SO22 . . . . .1 B2
Bradly Rd PO15 . . . . .130 B1
Bradpole Rd BH8 . . . . . . .190 C1
Bradshaw Cl SO50 . . . . . . .57 C3
Bradstock Cl BH12 . . . . . .203 C4
Braehead SO45 . . . . .125 C1
Braemar Ave
  Bournemouth BH6 . . . . . .207 A2
  Cosham PO6 . . . . .158 A4
Braemar Cl
  Bournemouth BH6 . . . . . .207 A2
  Fareham PO15 . . . . .130 C2
  Gosport PO13 . . . . .155 B1
Braemar Dr BH23 . . . . . . .193 C1
Braemar Rd PO13 . . . . . . .155 B1
Braeside Cl
  Southampton SO19 . . . . .103 C3
  Winchester SO22 . . . . . . .10 A2
Braeside Cres SO19 . . . . .103 C3
Braeside Rd
  Southampton SO19 . . . . .103 C3
  St Leonards BH24 . . . . . .139 C2
  West Moors BH22 . . . . . .138 C2
Braidley Rd BH2 . . . . .204 C2
Braintree Rd PO6 . . . . . . .133 B1
Braishfield Cl SO16 . . . . . .77 C1
Braishfield Gdns BH9 . . . .190 B1
Braishfield Prim Sch
  SO51 . . . . .28 B3
Braishfield Rd
  Havant PO9 . . . . .136 A2
  Romsey SO51 . . . . .28 B2
Brake Ho PO9 . . . . .135 C2
Bramar Cl BH4 . . . . .204 B1
Bramber Rd PO12 . . . . . . .181 C2
Bramble Cl Alderholt SP6 . .93 A3
  5 Eastleigh SO50 . . . . . .56 A1
  Havant PO9 . . . . .136 B2
  Holbury SO45 . . . . .150 B2
  Stubbington PO14 . . . . . .179 A3
Bramble Ct
  2 Petersfield GU31 . . . .41 B1
  West Moors BH22 . . . . . .138 C1
Bramble Dr SO51 . . . . .28 C2
Bramble Hill SO53 . . . . . . .55 A3

Bramble La
Christchurch BH23 ......194 A1
Clanfield P08 ......88 A4
Locks Heath SO31 ......128 C3
Bramble Mews 1 SO18 104 A4
Bramble Rd
Petersfield GU31 ......41 B2
Portsmouth PO4 ......182 C2
Bramble Way
Bransgore BH23 ......169 A1
Gosport PO13 ......155 A1
Bramble Wlk SO41 ......197 B3
Bramblegate SO50 ......57 B1
Brambles Bsns Ctr The
PO7 ......111 B1
Brambles Cl SO21 ......57 A4
Brambles Ent Ctr The
PO7 ......111 B1
Brambles Farm Ind Est
PO7 ......134 B4
Brambles Rd PO13 ......179 B2
Brambling Cl SO16 ......78 A3
Brambling Rd PO9 ......113 A1
Bramblings The SO40 ......100 B4
Brambridge SO50 ......56 C4
Brambridge Ho SO21 ......31 B1
Brambridge Rd SO21,
SO50 ......56 C4
Bramdean Dr PO9 ......135 B3
Bramdean Mews SO19 ......103 C3
Bramdean Rd SO18 ......104 B4
Bramham Moor PO14 ......179 A3
Bramley Cl
Lymington SO41 ......197 C1
Waterlooville PO7 ......134 C4
Bramley Cres SO19 ......104 A1
Bramley Ct BH22 ......165 B3
Bramley Gdns
Fair Oak SO50 ......81 B3
Gosport PO12 ......181 A1
Hermitage PO10 ......161 A4
Bramley Ho
Gosport PO12 ......181 A1
Hedge End SO30 ......105 A3
3 Portsmouth PO5 ......215 B2
Bramley Rd
Bournemouth BH10 ......189 B3
Ferndown BH22 ......165 B3
Bramleys The SP5 ......24 A2
Brampton La PO3 ......158 B2
Brampton Manor SO16 ......78 C3
Brampton Rd BH15 ......202 B3
Brampton Twr SO16 ......78 C3
Bramshaw Cl SO22 ......1 B2
Bramshaw Ct 37 PO9 ......136 A3
Bramshaw Gdns BH8 ......190 B2
Bramshaw Way BH25 ......209 B4
Bramshott Rd
Portsmouth PO4 ......182 C2
Southampton SO19 ......126 C4
Bramston Rd SO15 ......102 B4
Bramwell Ct SO18 ......104 A3
Branches La SO51 ......25 C2
Branders Cl BH6 ......207 A2
Branders La BH6 ......207 A3
Brandon Ct PO5 ......215 D1
Brandon Rd PO5 ......182 B1
Brandwood Ct 4 BH14 ......203 A2
Branewick Cl PO15 ......129 B2
Branksea Ave BH15 ......201 C1
Branksea Cl BH15 ......201 C1
Branksome Ave SO15 ......78 B1
Branksome Cl
New Milton BH25 ......195 A1
Winchester SO22 ......10 A3
Branksome Ct 14 BH13 ......214 C4
Branksome Dene Rd
BH4 ......204 A1
Branksome Heath Mid Sch
BH12 ......203 B3
Branksome Hill Rd
Bournemouth BH4 ......204 A3
Poole BH12 ......204 A3
Branksome Sta BH12 ......203 C2
Branksome Twrs BH13 ......214 D4
Branksome Wood Gdns
BH2 ......204 B2
Branksome Wood Rd
Bournemouth BH2,BH4 ......204 B2
Poole BH12 ......204 B2
Bransbury Cl SO16 ......78 B2
Bransbury Rd PO4 ......183 A2
Bransgore Ave PO9 ......135 B2
Bransgore CE Prim Sch
BH23 ......193 B4
Bransgore Gdns BH23 ......169 B1
Bransley Cl SO51 ......28 A1
Branwell Cl BH23 ......192 A1
Branwood Cl SO41 ......196 C1
Brasenose Cl PO14 ......129 B1
Brasher Cl SO50 ......57 A1
Brassey Cl BH9 ......190 A1
Brassey Rd
Bournemouth BH9 ......190 A1
Winchester SO22 ......1 C1
Brassey Terr BH9 ......189 C1
Brasted Ct PO4 ......183 B3
Braunston Cl 10 PO6 ......133 A1
Braxall Lawn PO9 ......135 B3
Braxton Ctyd SO41 ......211 C4
Braxton Ho 1 SO23 ......11 B4
Breach Ave PO10 ......137 C1
Breach La BH24 ......141 C4
Breamore CE Prim Sch
SP6 ......70 A4
Breamore Cl
Eastleigh SO50 ......56 A3
New Milton BH25 ......194 C2
Breamore Countryside Mus*
SP6 ......46 A1
Breamore Ho* SP6 ......46 A2
Breamore Rd SO18 ......104 B4
Brean Cl SO16 ......77 C1
Brearley Ct BH23 ......209 A4
Brecon Ave PO6 ......158 A4
Brecon Cl
Bournemouth BH10 ......189 C3
Chandler's Ford SO53 ......55 A2
Fareham PO14 ......154 C4
Hythe SO45 ......125 C2
New Milton BH25 ......195 B1
Brecon Rd SO19 ......104 B3
Bredenbury Cres PO6 ......133 B1
Bredon Wlk PO14 ......154 C4
Bredy Cl BH17 ......187 B1
Breech Cl 12 PO3 ......157 C2
Bremble Cl BH12 ......188 B1
Brenchley Cl PO16 ......156 A4
Brendon Cl
Bournemouth BH8 ......190 C1
Hythe SO45 ......125 B1
Brendon Gr SO16 ......101 C4
Brendon Rd PO14 ......154 B4
Brent Ct PO10 ......160 C4
Brentwood Cres SO18 ......80 A1
Breton Cl PO15 ......129 A4
Brewells La GU33 ......21 C2
Brewer Cl SO31 ......129 A2
Brewer St PO1 ......215 B4
Brewers La
Gosport PO13 ......155 B1
Twyford SO21 ......31 C3
West Tisted SO24 ......17 B4
Brewhouse Sq PO12 ......181 B3
Brewster Cl PO8 ......112 A2
Briar Cl
Christchurch BH23 ......207 C3
Gosport PO12 ......180 C2
Poole BH15 ......202 C3
Waterlooville PO8 ......112 A3
Briar Way Romsey SO51 ......28 B1
Wimborne Minst BH21 ......164 A3
Briar Wood GU33 ......21 A4
Briar's The PO7 ......111 B1
Briardene Ct SO40 ......100 C4
Briarfield 28 BH4 ......204 B2
Briarfield Gdns PO8 ......112 A3
Briars The SO42 ......145 C1
Briarswood SO16 ......78 A1
Briarswood Rd BH16 ......201 B4
Briarswood Rise SO45 ......125 B1
Briarwood Cl PO16 ......155 A4
Briarwood Gdns PO11 ......184 C2
Briarwood Rd SO40 ......100 B3
Brick Kiln La SO24 ......17 A4
Brick La BH23 ......169 C2
Brickets Terr PO12 ......181 A1
Brickfield La
Chandler's Ford SO53 ......55 B3
Lymington SO41 ......197 C3
Brickfield Rd SO17 ......79 B1
Brickfield Trad Est SO53 ......55 B3
Brickmakers Rd SO21 ......56 C4
Brickwoods Cl SO51 ......53 A4
Brickworth Rd SP5 ......24 A2
Brickyard La
Broadstone BH21 ......162 A1
Ferndown BH21 ......165 A3
Brickyard Rd SO32 ......84 A2
Brickyard The SO40 ......99 A4
Brickyards Ind Est The
GU32 ......20 A1
Bridefield Cl PO8 ......111 B2
Bridefield Cres PO8 ......111 B2
Bridge App BH15 ......202 A1
Bridge Cl SO31 ......105 A1
Bridge Cotts SO51 ......50 C2
Bridge Ct SO51 ......52 C3
Bridge Ho Gosport PO13 ......155 B2
Southampton SO15 ......102 B3
Bridge Industries PO16 ......131 B2
Bridge La SO21 ......31 C4
Bridge Mdws GU33 ......20 C2
Bridge Mead SO32 ......61 B3
Bridge Pl BH10 ......189 B4
Bridge Rd
Emsworth PO10 ......136 C1
Locks Heath SO31 ......128 B3
Lymington SO41 ......197 C3
Romsey SO51 ......53 A4
Southampton SO19 ......103 B2
Bridge Sh Ctr The PO1 ......215 D3
Bridge St
Christchurch BH23 ......207 B3
Fordingbridge SP6 ......69 C1
Southwick PO17 ......132 C3
Titchfield PO14 ......154 A4
Wickham PO17 ......108 A2
46 Winchester SO23 ......11 A4
Bridge Terr
Compton (Hants) SO21 ......31 C3
33 Southampton SO14 ......103 A2
Bridgefoot Dr PO16 ......131 B1
Bridgefoot Path PO10 ......160 C4
Bridgemary Ave PO13 ......155 B2
Bridgemary Com Sch
PO13 ......155 B1
Bridgemary Gr PO13 ......155 B3
Bridgemary Rd PO13 ......155 B2
Bridgemary Way PO13 ......155 B3
Bridgers Cl SO16 ......77 C3
Bridges Ave PO6 ......132 C1
Bridges Cl Eastleigh SO50 ......55 C2
West Moors BH22 ......138 C2
Bridges The BH24 ......140 C4
Bridgeside Cl PO1 ......215 C3
Bridget Cl PO8 ......112 B4
Bridgewater Rd BH12 ......203 B3
Bridgeway Ct SO40 ......101 A4
Bridgwater Ct SO15 ......102 B3
Bridle Cl BH16 ......201 B4
Bridle Cres BH7 ......206 B4
Bridle Way BH21 ......164 B3
Bridleways BH31 ......114 C3
Bridlington Ave SO15 ......102 B4
Bridport Ct SO15 ......102 B3
Bridport Rd Poole BH12 ......203 C4
Verwood BH31 ......114 C3
Bridport St PO1 ......215 B3
Brierley Ave BH22 ......165 C1
Brierley Cl BH10 ......189 C3
Brierley Rd BH10 ......189 C2
Brigantine Rd SO31 ......128 C1
Brigham Cl 20 PO2 ......157 C2
Brighstone Cl SO16 ......79 B3
Bright Rd BH15 ......202 B3
Brightlands Ave BH6 ......206 C3
Brighton Ave PO12 ......180 C4
Brighton Rd
Southampton SO15 ......102 C4
Sway SO41 ......172 A2
Brights La PO11 ......184 C3
Brightside PO7 ......134 B3
Brightside Rd SO16 ......77 C1
Brightstone Rd PO6 ......157 C4
Brindle Cl SO16 ......79 A3
Brinsons Cl BH23 ......192 B2
Brinton La SO45 ......126 A3
Brinton's Rd SO14 ......103 A3
Brinton's Terr SO14 ......103 A3
Brisbane Ho 20 PO1 ......182 B4
Brisbane Rd BH23 ......191 C1
Bristol Ct PO13 ......180 B3
Bristol Rd PO4 ......182 C1
Britain St PO1 ......182 A3
Britannia Ct BH12 ......203 A4
Britannia Gdns SO30 ......81 A2
Britannia Pl SO41 ......197 C2
Britannia Rd Poole BH14 203 A2
Portsmouth PO5 ......215 C2
Southampton SO14 ......103 A3
Britannia Rd N PO5 ......215 C2
Britannia Way
Christchurch BH23 ......208 A4
Gosport PO12 ......181 B4
Britannic Ho 22 SO14 ......103 B3
Britnell Ho 6 GU31 ......40 C2
Briton St SO14 ......103 A2
Britten Rd PO13 ......179 C1
Britten Way PO7 ......134 C2
Brittons Cotts SO42 ......145 B1
Brixey Cl BH12 ......203 B4
Brixey Rd BH12 ......203 B4
Brixworth Cl 11 PO6 ......133 A1
Broad Ave BH8 ......205 B4
Broad Chalke Down
SO22 ......10 B2
Broad Croft PO9 ......113 B2
Broad Gdns PO6 ......158 C4
Broad Gn 5 SO14 ......103 A2
Broad La Denmead PO7 ......110 A3
Lymington SO41 ......197 C1
North Baddesley SO52 ......53 C3
Southampton SO14 ......102 C2
Swanmore SO32 ......84 A3
Broad Mead Rd GU23 ......114 C1
Broad Oak SO30 ......105 C4
Broad St PO1 ......181 C2
Broad View La SO22 ......10 A2
Broad Way
Froxfield Green GU32 ......39 C4
Hamble-le-Rice SO31 ......127 C3
Broad Woods La SO51 ......51 A3
Broadbent Cl SO16 ......77 C3
Broadcut PO16 ......131 B1
Broadfields Cl SO41 ......211 B3
Broadhill La SP6 ......94 B4
Broadhurst Ave BH10 ......189 C2
Broadland Cotts GU32 ......41 A3
Broadlands* SO51 ......52 C3
Broadlands Ave
Bournemouth BH6 ......206 C2
Eastleigh SO50 ......56 A3
Waterlooville PO7 ......134 C4
Broadlands Cl
Bournemouth BH8 ......190 B2
Christchurch BH23 ......194 A1
Broadlands Rd
Brockenhurst SO42 ......145 C1
Southampton SO17 ......79 A2
Broadlaw Walk Prec 14
PO14 ......154 C4
Broadley Cl SO45 ......150 B2
Broadly Cl SO41 ......197 A1
Broadmarsh Bsns &
Innovation Ctr PO9 ......159 B4
Broadmayne Rd BH12 ......204 A4
Broadmead Cl 8 SO41 ......197 C1
Broadmead Flats SO16 ......77 B3
Broadmead Rd SO16 ......77 B3
Broadmeadow Cl SO40 ......100 C4
Broadmeadows La 8
PO7 ......135 A4
Broadmere Ave PO9 ......135 C3
Broadmoor Rd BH21 ......186 B4
Broadoak Cl SO45 ......150 B2
Broads The BH21 ......162 C3
Broadsands Dr PO12 ......180 B2
Broadsands Wlk PO12 ......180 C2
Broadshard La BH24 ......141 A4
Broadstone Fst Sch
BH18 ......187 A2
Broadstone Mid Sch
BH18 ......187 B3
Broadstone Way
Broadstone BH18,NH17 ......186 C1
Broadstone, Fleet's Cnr
BH15,BH17 ......202 A4
Broadwater Ave BH14 ......203 B1
Broadwater Rd
Romsey SO51 ......52 C3
Southampton SO18 ......79 C2
Broadway BH6 ......207 A2
Broadway Ct BH12 ......204 A3
Broadway Gables BH14 ......203 C2
Broadway Gdns 6
BH21 ......163 B2
Broadway La
Bournemouth BH8 ......190 B2
Horndean PO8 ......111 B4
Broadway Mews BH14 ......202 C2
Broadway Pk 4 BH21 ......163 B2
Broadway The
Bournemouth BH10 ......189 B3
5 Southampton, Bitterne Pk
SO18 ......79 C1
Southampton, Portswood
SO17 ......79 A1
Southampton, Thornhill Pk
SO18 ......104 B4
Winchester SO23 ......11 A4
Brock Hill Forest Wlks*
SO43 ......144 C4
Brockenhurst Ave PO9 ......135 B3
Brockenhurst CE Prim Sch
SO42 ......172 C4
Brockenhurst Coll SO42 146 A1
Brockenhurst Rd BH9 ......190 A1
Brockenhurst Sta SO42 ......173 A4
Brockhampton La PO9 ......135 C1
Brockhampton Rd PO9 ......135 B1
Brockhills La BH25 ......195 B3
Brockhurst Ind Est
PO12 ......155 C1
Brockhurst Inf Sch
PO12 ......180 C4
Brockhurst Jun Sch
PO12 ......181 A4
Brockhurst Rd PO12 ......180 C4
Brockishill Rd SO40 ......99 A3
Brocklands PO9 ......135 B1
Brockley Rd BH10 ......189 C2
Brocks Cl SO45 ......125 B1
Brocks Pine BH24 ......139 C2
Brockwood Bottom SO32 36 C4
Brodrick Ave PO12 ......181 A2
Brog St BH21 ......162 B1
Brokenford Ave SO40 ......101 A4
Brokenford Bsns Ctr
SO40 ......100 C4
Brokenford La SO40 ......100 C4
Brombys The 7 BH15 ......202 B1
Bromley Ho BH12 ......204 A3
Bromley Rd SO18 ......79 C1
Brompton Rd PO4 ......182 C2
Bromyard Cres PO6 ......133 B1
Bronte Ave BH23 ......192 A1
Bronte Cl SO40 ......100 B3
Bronte Gdns PO15 ......129 B4
Bronte Way SO19 ......103 C3
Bronwen Ct SO19 ......104 A1
Brook Ave
Locks Heath SO31 ......128 B2
New Milton BH25 ......195 A2
Brook Ave N BH25 ......195 A2
Brook Cl
Bournemouth BH10 ......189 B2
Locks Heath SO31 ......128 C2
North Baddesley SO52 ......54 A2
Brook Cnr SO43 ......74 A1
Brook Cotts
King's Somborne SO51 ......6 B3
Westbourne PO10 ......137 A2
Brook Ct Romsey SO51 ......52 C3
13 Southampton SO15 ......102 B3
Brook Dr BH31 ......115 A2
Brook Farm Ave PO15 ......130 C1
Brook Gdns PO10 ......160 B4
Brook Hill SO41 ......198 C4
Brook La Botley SO30 ......105 C3
Bransgore BH23 ......193 A4
Corfe Mullen BH21 ......186 B3
Hambledon PO7 ......86 B3
Locks Heath SO31 ......128 C2
Woodgreen SP6 ......70 C4
Brook Mdw PO15 ......130 C1
Brook Rd
Bournemouth BH10 ......189 B2
Fair Oak SO50 ......57 B1
Lymington SO41 ......197 C1
Poole BH12 ......203 B3
Southampton SO18 ......104 A4
Wimborne Minst BH21 ......163 C2
Brook Road Depot
BH21 ......163 C2
Brook St SO32 ......83 B4
Brook Terr SP6 ......93 C4
Brook Valley SO16 ......78 A1
Brook Way
Christchurch BH23 ......208 B4
Romsey SO51 ......28 A1
Brook Wlk SO40 ......76 B1
Brookdale Cl
Broadstone BH18 ......187 A2
Waterlooville PO7 ......134 C4
Brookdale Farm BH18 ......187 A2
Brooke Cl SO23 ......2 A4
Brookers La PO13 ......155 A2
Brookfield Cl 1 PO9 ......135 C1
Brookfield Com Sch
SO31 ......128 C2
Brookfield Gdns SO31 ......128 C2
Brookfield Pl SO17 ......79 A1
Brookfield Rd
Fair Oak SO50 ......57 B1
Portsmouth PO1 ......182 C3
Brookfields SO51 ......50 B2
Brookland Cl SO41 ......197 B2
Brooklands
Bournemouth BH4 ......204 A2
Lyndhurst SO43 ......122 A2
Brooklands Rd
Bishop's Waltham SO32 ......83 B4
Havant PO9 ......135 A1
Brookley Rd SO42 ......146 A1
Brooklyn Cl SO21 ......31 B2
Brooklyn Ct BH25 ......194 C2
Brooklyn Dr PO7 ......134 C4
Brooklynn Cl SO32 ......83 C1
Brookman Ct SO18 ......104 A4
Brookmead Way PO9 ......159 C4
Brooks Cl BH24 ......141 A3
Brooks Sh Ctr The SO23 ......11 A4
Brookside
Fordingbridge SP6 ......69 A1
Gosport PO13 ......155 A3
Ibsley SP6 ......94 B1
Landford SP5 ......49 B2
Totton SO40 ......100 C3
Brookside Ave SO15 ......101 C4
Brookside Cl
Bransgore BH23 ......169 A1
Denmead PO7 ......110 C2
Brookside Ho SO18 ......79 C2
Brookside Park Homes
BH21 ......186 A2
Brookside Rd
Bransgore BH23 ......193 A4
Brockenhurst SO42 ......145 C1
Havant, Bedhampton PO9 ......135 B1
Havant, Langstone PO9 ......159 C4
Wimborne Minst BH21 ......163 C2
Brookside Way
Christchurch BH23 ......193 C1
Southampton SO18 ......79 C2
West End SO30 ......80 C2
Brookvale Ct 14 SO17 ......79 A1
Brookvale Rd SO17 ......79 A1
Brookwood Ave SO50 ......55 C2
Brookwood Ind Est SO50 56 A2
Brookwood Rd SO16 ......101 B4
Broom Cl
Portsmouth PO4 ......183 B2
Waterlooville PO7 ......135 A3
Broom Hill SO41 ......199 A4
Broom Hill Way SO50 ......56 A4
Broom Rd
Petersfield GU31 ......41 B1
Poole BH12 ......188 B1
Broom Sq PO4 ......183 B3
Broom Way PO13 ......179 C2
Broomfield Cres PO13 ......180 A4
Broomfield Ct BH22 ......165 C3
Broomfield Dr SP6 ......93 A3
Broomfield La SO41 ......197 C2
Broomhill SP5 ......49 B1
Broomhill Cl SO41 ......197 A1
Brooms Gr SO19 ......104 B2
Broomy Cl SO45 ......125 B2
Brougham La PO12 ......181 A3
Brougham Rd PO5 ......215 B2
Brougham St PO12 ......181 A3
Broughton Ave BH10 ......189 C2
Broughton Cl
Bournemouth BH10 ......189 C2
5 Southampton SO16 ......78 A1
Broughton Ct PO3 ......158 B2
Broughton Rd SO43 ......121 C3
Brow The PO7 ......134 B1
Browndown Rd PO13 ......180 B2
Brownen Rd BH9 ......205 A4
Brownfield Ho 22 GU31 ......40 C2
Brownhill Cl SO53 ......55 B4
Brownhill Ct SO16 ......77 C2
Brownhill Gdns SO53 ......55 B4
Brownhill Rd
Brockenhurst BH25 ......170 C2
Chandler's Ford SO53 ......55 B4
North Baddesley SO52 ......54 A2
Brownhill Way SO16 ......77 B2
Browning Ave
Bournemouth BH5 ......206 A2
Portchester PO6 ......132 C1
Southampton SO19 ......104 B3
Browning Cl
Eastleigh SO50 ......55 C2
Swanwick PO15 ......129 B4
Totton SO40 ......100 B4
Browning Dr SO22 ......10 B4
Browning Rd BH12 ......203 B3
Brownings Cl SO41 ......197 A2
Brownlow Ave SO19 ......104 A3
Brownlow Cl PO1 ......182 B4
Brownlow Ct 23 BH4 ......204 B2
Brownlow Gdns SO19 ......104 A3
Browns La Beaulieu SO41 199 B3
Damerham SP6 ......68 A3
Brownsea Ave BH21 ......186 B3
Brownsea Cl BH25 ......194 C2
Brownsea Ct BH14 ......214 A4
Brownsea Island (NT)*
BH15 ......213 B2
Brownsea Rd BH13 ......214 A2
Brownsea View Ave
BH14 ......203 B1
Brownsea View Cl BH14 203 B1
Brownwich La PO14 ......153 B3

Browsholme Cl **2** SO50 ....56 A3
Broxburn Cl SO53 ......30 C1
Broxhead Rd **56** PO9 ...136 A3
Bruce Cl PO16 ....131 A2
Bruce Rd PO4 ....182 C1
Brudenell Ave BH13 ...214 B4
Brudenell Rd BH13 ....214 B3
Brue Cl SO53 ....55 A4
Brune La Gosport PO13 ..180 A4
Stubbington PO13 ......155 A1
Brune Park Com Sch
PO12 ....180 C4
Brune Way BH22 ......165 B2
Brunei Ho SO16 ....79 A3
Brunel Cl Hedge End SO30 .81 C1
Verwood BH31 ....115 B2
Brunel Rd
Portsmouth PO2 ....157 C2
Southampton SO15 .....101 B4
Totton SO40 ....76 C1
Brunel Way PO15 .....129 B2
Brunstead Pl BH12 ....204 A2
Brunstead Rd BH12 ....204 A2
Brunswick Cl SO50 ....57 A2
Brunswick Gdns PO9 ..135 B1
Brunswick Pl
Lymington SO41 ....197 C2
Southampton SO15 .....103 A3
Brunswick Rd SO50 ....57 A2
Brunswick Sq SO14 ....103 A2
Brunswick St PO5 .....215 B2
Brushers BH23 ....169 C2
Bruyn Ct SP6 ....70 A1
Bruyn Rd SP6 ....70 A1
Bryanston Rd SO19 ....103 C3
Bryanstone Rd BH3 ....204 C4
Bryant Rd BH12 ....204 A4
Bryher Br PO6 ....157 A4
Bryher Island PO6 .....157 A4
Brympton Cl SP6 ......69 B1
Bryony Cl
Broadstone BH18 ......186 C2
Locks Heath SO31 .....128 C1
Bryony Gdns SO50 .....81 B3
Bryony Way PO7 ......135 A4
Bryson Rd PO6 ....157 B4
Bub La BH23 ....207 C3
Bubb La SO32 ....81 B2
Buccaneers Cl BH23 ..207 C3
Buccleuch Rd BH23 ...204 A1
Bucehayes Cl BH23 ...209 A4
Buchan Ave PO15 .....129 B4
Buchan Ct SO45 ......125 B1
Buchanan Ave BH7 ...205 C3
Buckby La PO3 ....158 B2
Bucketts Farm Cl SO43 ..84 A3
Buckingham Ct
2 Christchurch BH23 ..209 A4
Fareham PO15 ....130 C2
Poole BH15 ....202 B2
2 Southampton SO17 ..103 A3
Buckingham Gr PO1 ...182 B4
Buckingham Mans **5**
BH1 ....205 A2
Buckingham Rd
Petersfield GU32 ......40 B2
Poole BH12 ....203 B4
Buckingham St PO1 ...215 B4
Buckingham Wlk BH25 .194 C2
Buckland Cl
Eastleigh SO50 ....56 A3
Waterlooville PO7 .....111 B1
Buckland Ct SO41 ....197 C3
Buckland Dene SO41 ..197 B3
Buckland Gdns SO40 ..76 B1
Buckland Gr BH23 ....193 C1
Buckland Path PO2 ...182 B4
Buckland Rd BH12 ....203 B3
Buckland St PO2 .....182 C4
Buckland Terr BH12 ...203 B3
Buckland View SO41 ..197 C3
Bucklers Ct Havant PO9 .135 B4
Lymington SO41 ......197 B2
Portsmouth PO2 ......157 B1
Bucklers Hard Maritime
Mus ★ SO42 ....176 B3
Bucklers Mews SO41 ..197 B3
Bucklers Rd PO12 ....181 B2
Bucklers The SO41 ....211 A3
Bucklers Way BH8 ....190 B2
Buckley Ct SO16 .....78 A1
Buckmore Ave GU32 ..40 B2
Bucks Head Hill SO32 ..61 B3
Bucksey Rd PO13 ....180 B4
Buckstone Ct SO41 ...196 C1
Buckthorn Cl
Broadstone BH17 .....186 C1
Totton SO40 ....100 A4
Budden's La PO17 ....108 C4
Buddens Rd PO17 ....108 A2
Buddle Hill SP6 ......94 B2
Budds La SO51 ....27 C1
Budds Lane Trad Est
SO51 ....27 C1
Bude Cl PO6 ....132 C4
Buffalo Mews BH15 ...202 A1
Bugdens La BH31 .....115 A3
Bugle St SO14 ....102 C2
Bulbarrow Wlk PO14 ..154 C4
Buldowne Wlk SO41 ..172 A2
Bull Dro SO23 ....11 A3
Bull Hill Boldre SO41 ...174 A4
Rake GU33 ....21 C1

Bull La Minstead SO43 ...98 B2
16 Poole BH15 ....202 B1
Waltham Chase SO32 ...83 B2
Bullar Rd SO18 ......103 C4
Bullar St SO14 ......103 A3
Bullfinch Cl
Broadstone BH17 .....186 C1
Totton SO40 ....100 B4
Bullfinch Ct PO13 ....179 C2
Bullrush Cl SO45 ....125 C1
Bulls Copse La PO8 ..112 A3
Bulls Dro SP5 ....4 A3
Bunkers Hill PO7 ....110 B2
Bunns La PO7 ....109 C3
Bunny La
Michelmersh SO51 ....27 C3
Sherfield English SO51 ..25 A2
Bunstead La SO21 ...30 B4
Bunting Gdns PO8 ...111 C2
Bunting Rd BH22 ....165 A4
Bupa Hospl PO9 .....136 B3
Burbidge Gr PO4 ....183 A1
Burbush Cl SO45 ....150 B2
Burcombe La BH24 ...117 C1
Burcombe Rd BH10 ..189 B3
Burcote Dr PO3 .....158 A2
Burdale Dr PO11 ....185 B2
Burdock Cl BH23 ....193 A1
Bure Cl BH23 ....208 A3
Bure Haven Dr BH23 ..208 A3
Bure Homage Gdns
BH23 ....208 A3
Bure Homage La BH23 .208 A3
Bure La BH23 ....208 A3
Bure Pk BH23 ....208 A3
Bure Rd BH23 ....208 A3
Burford Cl PO9 ......135 B2
Burford Ct **15** BH1 ...205 A2
Burford La SO42 ....146 A1
Burgate Cl PO9 .....135 B2
Burgate Cross SP6 ...70 A3
Burgate Fields SP6 ..70 A2
Burgate Sch The SP6 ..70 A2
Burgesmede Ho **13** GU32 40 C2
Burgess Cl
Bournemouth BH11 ...188 C2
South Hayling PO11 ..185 B1
Burgess Ct SO16 ....79 A4
Burgess Fld BH21 ...114 A3
Burgess Gdns **14** SO16 ..78 C2
Burgess Rd SO16,SO17 .79 A2
Burghclere Rd
Havant PO9 ....136 A3
Southampton SO19 ...126 C4
Burgoyne Rd
Portsmouth PO5 .....182 B1
Southampton SO19 ...104 C2
Burgundy Cl SO31 ...128 C1
Burgundy Terr **1** PO2 .157 C1
Buriton Cl PO16 .....132 B1
Buriton Ct SO19 ....103 C2
Buriton Prim Sch GU31 .65 B3
Buriton Rd SO22 ....1 B2
Buriton St PO1 ......215 C4
Burke Dr SO19 .....104 B3
Burleigh Rd
Bournemouth BH6 ...206 B3
Portsmouth PO1 .....182 C4
Burley Cl Ashurst SO40 .100 A4
Barton on Sea BH25 ..209 B4
Chandler's Ford SO53 ..55 A2
17 Havant PO9 ....136 A3
Verwood BH31 ......114 C3
Burley Ct **4** SO17 ...79 A1
Burley Down SO53 ..55 A2
Burley Ho **5** SO16 ..102 A4
Burley Lawn BH24 ...143 A2
Burley Prim Sch BH24 .143 A2
Burley Rd
Bransgore BH23 ....193 A4
Brockenhurst SO42 ..172 B4
Burton BH23 ....192 B3
Poole BH12 ....203 B3
Winchester SO22 ....1 B1
Burley YH★ BH24 ...143 B1
Burling Terr **1** BH12 .204 A4
Burlington Arc **34** BH1 .204 C2
Burlington Ct SO19 ..104 A3
Burlington Mans **1**
SO15 ....102 B4
Burlington Rd
Portsmouth PO2 .....157 C1
Southampton SO15 ..102 C4
Burma Ho SO18 .....79 C2
Burma Rd SO51 ....52 C3
Burmah Rd N SO45 ..151 B3
Burmah Rd S SO45 ..151 A3
Burmese Ct PO15 ...129 B4
Burn Cl BH31 ......115 A2
Burnaby Ct BH4 ....204 B1
Burnaby Rd
Bournemouth BH4 ...204 B1
Portsmouth PO1 ....182 A2
Burnage Ct **18** BH13 ..214 C4
Burnbake Rd BH31 ..115 A3
Burnbank Gdns SO40 .100 C4
Burnbrae Rd BH22 ..165 B1
Burnett Ave BH23 ...206 C4
Burnett Cl Hythe SO45 .126 A1
Southampton SO18 ..79 C1
Winchester SO22 ....1 B1
Burnett Rd
Christchurch BH23 ..206 C4
Gosport PO12 ......180 C3
Burnetts Fields SO50 ..81 B4
Burnetts Gdns SO50 ..81 B4
Burnetts La SO50,SO30 ..81 B3

Burney Ho **25** PO12 ...181 B2
Burney Rd PO12 ....180 C2
Burngate Rd BH15 ...201 C1
Burnham Beeches SO53 .55 A3
Burnham Chase SO18 .104 B3
Burnham Dr BH8 ....205 B4
Burnham Rd
Burton BH23 ....192 B1
Cosham PO6 ....134 B1
Fordingbridge SP6 ...69 C2
Burnham Wood PO16 .131 A2
Burnhams Wlk **19** PO12 .181 B2
Burnleigh Gdns BH25 .195 B2
Burns Cl SO50 ......55 C1
Burns Pl SO16 ......78 A1
Burns Rd
Bournemouth BH6 ...206 B4
Eastleigh SO50 ......55 C1
Southampton SO19 ..104 B3
Burnside
Christchurch BH23 ..208 B4
Gosport PO13 ......155 A3
Waterlooville PO7 ...112 A1
Burnt House La
Boldre SO41 ....174 A1
Bransgore BH23 ....169 A1
Stubbington PO14 ..154 A3
Burr Cl SO21 ......56 C4
Burrard Gr SO41 ...197 C3
Burrfields Rd PO3 ...158 A1
Burridge Rd SO31 ..106 A1
Burrill Ave PO6 ....158 A4
Burrows Cl PO9 ....136 A2
Burrows La BH31 ...114 C4
Bursledon Hts SO31 .105 A1
Bursledon Jun & Inf Sch
SO31 ....128 A4
Bursledon Pl PO7 ...134 C3
Bursledon Rd
Hedge End SO30 ...105 A3
Southampton SO19,SO31 .104 B3
Waterlooville PO7 ..134 B3
Bursledon Sta SO31 .128 A4
Bursledon Windmill★
SO31 ....105 A1
Burt's La North Heath BH21 138 A4
Verwood BH21 .....138 A4
Burtley Rd BH6 .....206 C2
Burton CE Prim Sch
BH23 ....192 B2
Burton Cl Burton BH23 .192 B1
St Leonards BH24 ...139 C3
Burton Hall BH23 ...192 B2
Burton Hall Pl BH23 .192 B2
Burton Rd
Christchurch BH23 ..207 A4
Poole BH13 ....204 A2
Southampton SO15 ..102 C3
Burtoncroft BH23 ...192 B2
Burts Hill BH21 .....163 B3
Burwood Gr PO11 ..185 A2
Bury Cl PO12 ......181 A2
Bury Cres PO12 ....181 A2
Bury Farm SO30 ...106 B2
Bury Hall La PO12 .180 C2
Bury Ho **16** PO16 ..131 A1
Bury La SO40 ......101 A3
Bury Rd Gosport PO12 .181 A2
Marchwood SO40 ..101 A3
Poole BH13 ....203 C1
Bus Dro SO45 .....178 C4
Bush Ho PO5 ......215 B1
Bush St E PO5 .....215 B1
Bush St W PO5 ....215 B1
Bushell Rd BH15 ..202 B4
Bushey Rd BH9 ...190 B1
Bushmead Dr BH24 .139 C3
Bushy Mead PO7 ..134 B2
Busket La SO23 ...11 A4
Busketts Way SO40 .100 A1
Butcher St PO1 ...182 A3
Butcher's Cnr SO43 ..73 C2
Bute Dr BH23 .....209 A4
Butlers Cl SO51 ...4 C1
Butlers La BH24 ...117 B1
Butser Ancient Farm★
PO8 ....88 C3
Butser Ct PO8 .....88 B2
Butser Wlk
Fareham PO14 .....154 C4
Petersfield GU31 ..41 A2
Butt La SO19 .....22 A4
Butt's Cl SO19 ....104 B2
Butt's Cres SO19 ..104 B2
Butt's Rd SO19 ...104 B2
Butt's Sq SO19 ...104 B2
Buttercup Cl
Hedge End SO30 ..105 A3
Hythe SO45 ......126 A1
Buttercup Dr BH23 .193 A1
Buttercup Way SO31 .128 C2
Butterfield Rd SO16 ..78 C4
Butterfly Dr PO6 ...133 A1
Buttermere Cl SO16 ..77 C1
Buttermere Ho **24** PO6 .133 A1
Buttery The BH23 ..207 B4
Button's La
18 Poole BH15 .....202 B1
West Wellow SO51 ...50 C1
Butts Ash Gdns SO45 .126 A1
Butts Ash La SO45 ..149 C4
Butts Bridge Hill SO45 .126 A1
Butts Farm La SO32 ..83 B4
Butts Paddock SO42 .145 C1
Butts Rd SO22 ....1 B1
Butts The SO32 ...61 B2
Buttsash Ave SO45 ..150 A4
Camelia Cl Havant PO9 .136 A2

Buttsbridge Rd SO45 ..126 A1
By Pass Rd SO51 ...52 C3
By The Wood SO40 ..76 B1
Byams La SO40 ....102 A1
Bye Rd SO31 ......128 B4
Byerley Cl PO10 ...137 A3
Byerley Rd PO1 ...182 C3
Byeways SO45 ....125 C1
Byrd Cl PO7 ......134 C3
Byres The PO14 ...154 B2
Byron Ave SO22 ..10 B4
Byron Cl
Bishop's Waltham SO32 ..83 C4
Fareham PO16 .....131 A1
Byron Ct Ferndown BH22 .165 B3
Southampton SO15 ..102 C3
Byron Ho **16** BH25 ..195 A1
Byron Rd
Barton on Sea BH25 .209 C4
Bournemouth BH5 ...205 C2
Eastleigh SO50 .....56 A2
Portsmouth PO2 ...182 C4
Southampton SO19 ..104 B3
Wimborne Minst BH21 .163 B3

C

C Ave SO45 ....150 C2
Cable St **23** SO14 ..103 B3
Cabot Bsns Village
BH17 ....202 A4
Cabot Cl SO45 ....125 B2
Cabot La BH17 ...202 A4
Cabot Way **15** SO16 ..78 C2
Cadhay Cl BH23 ...194 C2
Cadland Ct SO14 ..103 B3
Cadland Rd Fawley SO45 151 A3
Holbury SO45 .....150 A4
Cadlands Park Est SO45 150 B3
Cadnam Ct PO12 ..180 B2
Cadnam La SO40 ..74 C1
Cadnam Lawn PO9 .135 B3
Cadnam Rd PO4 ..183 A2
Cadnam Way BH8 ..190 B2
Cadogan Rd BH24 ..141 A4
Cador Dr PO16 ....156 A3
Caen Ho **7** PO14 ..154 C4
Caer Peris View PO16 .132 B1
Caerleon Ave SO19 .104 B3
Caerleon Dr SO19 ..104 B3
Caernarvon Gdns SO53 .55 A2
Caesar's Way BH18 ..186 C2
Cains Cl PO14 ....154 B2
Caird Ave BH25 ...195 B4
Cairns Cl BH23 ...206 C4
Cairo Terr PO2 ....182 B4
Caister Cl BH22 ...165 B3
Caistor Cl SO16 ...78 A3
Calabrese SO31 ..129 A4
Calbourne SO31 ..127 B4
Calcot La SO32 ...82 C2
Caldecote Wlk **7** PO5 .215 B2
Calder Cl SO16 ...101 C4
Calder Rd BH17 ..202 C4
Caledon Rd BH14 .203 C2
Calderwood Dr SO19 .104 B3
Caledonia Dr SO45 ..125 B2
Caledonian Cl BH23 .208 A4
California Cl SO40 ..76 A1
Calkin Cl BH23 ...192 A1
Calluna Rd BH12 ..203 A4
Calmore Cl BH8 ...190 B2
Calmore Cres SO40 ..76 A1
Calmore Dr SO40 ..76 A1
Calmore Gdns SO40 .100 A4
Calmore Ind Est SO40 .76 C1
Calmore Inf Sch SO40 .76 B1
Calmore Jun Sch SO40 .76 B1
Calmore Rd SO40 ..100 B4
Calpe Ave SO43 ...121 C3
Calshot Activities Ctr
SO45 ....152 A1
Calshot Castle★ SO45 .152 A1
Calshot Cl SO45 ..178 C4
Calshot Ct SO14 ..103 B3
Calshot Rd Fawley SO45 .151 A2
Havant PO9 ....135 B4
Calshot Way PO13 ..155 A1
Calvin Rd BH9 ....204 C4
Camargue Cl SO31 .129 A4
Camber Pl **17** PO1 ..182 A2
Cambria Dr SO45 ..125 B2
Cambrian Cl SO31 .105 A1
Cambrian Terr PO5 .215 C1
Cambrian Wlk PO14 .154 C4
Cambridge **17** SO14 .103 A4
Cambridge Dr SO53 ..55 B2
Cambridge Gdns BH23 .191 C1
Cambridge Gn
Chandler's Ford SO53 ..55 B1
Titchfield PO14 .....129 B1
Cambridge Junc PO1 .182 A2
Cambridge Rd
Bournemouth BH2 ...204 B2
Gosport PO12 ......180 C3
Lee-on-the-Solent PO13 .179 C1
Portsmouth PO1 ....182 A2
Southampton SO14 ..103 A4

Camelia Cl continued
North Baddesley SO52 ..54 A3
Camelia Gdns SO18 ..80 A1
Camelia Gr SO50 ...57 C1
Camellia Cl BH21 ..114 C1
Camellia Ct **2** SO18 ..79 C1
Camellia Gdns BH25 .195 A1
Camelot Cres PO16 ..132 A1
Cameron Cl PO13 ...155 B2
Cameron Ct SO16 ...77 C3
Cameron Rd BH23 ..207 B4
Camley Cl SO19 ....103 C1
Cammel Rd BH22 ..165 B1
Camp Rd PO13 ....155 B2
Campbell Cres PO7 .134 B3
Campbell Ct SO50 ..57 B1
Campbell Mews SO18 .104 B4
Campbell Rd
Bournemouth BH1 ...205 C3
Burton BH23 ......192 B1
Eastleigh SO50 ....56 A1
Portsmouth PO5 ...215 D1
Campbell St SO14 ..103 B4
Campbell Way SO50 .57 B1
Campion Cl Fair Oak SO50 81 B3
Locks Heath SO31 ..128 C1
Waterlooville PO7 ..135 A3
Campion Dr SO51 ..28 B1
Campion Gr BH23 ..207 C3
Campion Rd SO19 ..104 C3
Campion Way
Kings Worthy SO23 ..2 B4
Lymington SO41 ...197 C3
Cams Bay Cl PO16 ..131 C3
Cams Hill Hambledon PO7 .86 A1
Portchester PO16 ...131 C1
Cams Hill Sch PO16 .155 C4
Canada Cnr GU31 ...66 C3
Canada Ct PO12 ...181 B4
Canada Pl **6** SO16 ..78 C2
Canada Rd
Southampton SO19 ..103 C3
West Wellow SO51 ..50 B1
Canal Cl SO51 ....28 A1
Canal Wlk
Portsmouth PO1 ...215 C3
Romsey SO51 .....52 C4
Southampton SO14 .103 A2
Canberra Cl PO12 ..180 C2
Canberra Ct SO16 ..180 C2
Canberra Ho PO1 ..215 B3
Canberra Rd
Christchurch BH23 ..191 C1
Nursling SO16 ....77 A2
Thorney Island PO10 .161 A2
Canberra Twrs SO19 .126 C3
Candlemas Pl **13** SO17 .103 A4
Candover Ct SO19 ..127 A4
Candy La SO19 ...104 C3
Candys La BH21 ..162 C1
Candys La BH21 ..162 C1
Canford Ave BH11 ..189 A1
Canford Bottom BH21 .164 B3
Canford Bottom Rdbt
BH21 ....164 B3
Canford Cl
Shedfield SO32 ...107 C4
Southampton SO16 .77 C1
Canford Cliffs Ave
BH14 ....203 C1
Canford Cliffs Rd BH13 .203 C1
Canford Cres BH13 .214 C4
Canford Ct BH13 ...214 C4
Canford Gdns BH11 .189 A1
Canford Heath Fst & Mid
Schs BH17 ....202 B4
Canford Heath Nature
Reserve★ BH11 ...188 A2
Canford Heath Rd BH17 187 C1
Canford Magna BH21 .164 A1
Canford Pl **2** BH13 ..214 C4
Canford Rd
Bournemouth BH11 .189 A1
Poole BH15 ......202 B2
Canford Sch BH21 .164 A2
Canford View Dr BH21 .164 A3
Canford Way BH12 ..188 B3
Canhouse La GU33 ..21 C2
Cann Cl BH18 ....187 A1
Cannock Wlk **16** PO14 .154 C4
Cannon Cl BH18 ...187 A1
Cannon Hill Gdns BH21 .164 A4
Cannon Hill Rd BH21 .164 A4
Cannon Ho SO41 ..197 C2
Cannon St
Lymington SO41 ...197 C2
Southampton SO15 .102 B4
Cannon's Barn Cl PO16 .132 B1
Canoe Cl SO31 ...128 C1
Canon Ct **5** SO50 ..57 B1
Canon St SO23 ...10 C4
Canons Wlk SO41 ..211 A3
Cantell Sec Sch SO19 .79 A2
Canterbury Ave SO19 .104 C3
Canterbury Cl
Lee-on-the-Solent PO13 .180 A2
West Moors BH22 ...138 C1
Canterbury Dr SO45 .125 B2
Canterbury Rd
Portsmouth PO4 ...182 C2
Stubbington PO14 ..154 A4
Canterton La SO43 ..98 A4
Canton St SO15 ...102 C3
Canute Dr BH23 ...169 A1
Canute Ho **25** SO14 .103 A2
Canute Rd
Southampton SO14 .103 A2
6 Winchester SO23 ..11 A3
Canvey Ct SO16 ...77 C1

Capel Ley PO7 .....134 C2
Capella Ct BH2 .....204 C1
Capella Gdns SO45 .....125 B2
Capers End La SO32 .....82 C1
Capesthorne BH23 .....208 A3
Capital Ho 11 SO22 .....10 C4
Capon Cl SO18 .....79 C2
Capstan Gdns SO31 .....129 B2
Capstans The BH14 .....214 A4
Capstone Pl BH8 .....205 B3
Capstone Rd BH8 .....205 A3
Captain's Pl SO14 .....103 A2
Captain's Row SO41 .....197 C2
Captains Cl PO12 .....180 C4
Captains Row 15 PO1 .....182 A2
Caradon Pl BH31 .....114 B4
Carberry Dr PO16 .....156 B4
Carbery Ave BH6 .....206 B3
Carbery Ct PO9 .....135 B4
Carbery Gdns BH6 .....206 C3
Carbery La 3 BH6 .....206 B2
Carbery Row 2 BH6 .....206 B2
Carbis Cl PO6 .....157 A4
Cardew Rd GU33 .....21 A2
Cardiff Rd PO2 .....157 B1
Cardigan Rd
Bournemouth BH9 .....204 C4
Poole BH12 .....203 C2
Cardinal Dr PO7 .....112 A1
Cardinal Way SO31 .....129 A1
Cardington Ct SO16 .....77 C2
Carey Rd
Bournemouth BH9 .....189 C2
Southampton SO19 .....104 B3
Careys Cotts SO42 .....145 C1
Careys Rd BH8 .....190 B2
Carina Ct BH13 .....214 B2
Carisbrook Cres BH15 .....201 B2
Carisbrooke Netley SO31 127 B4
Poole BH13 .....214 C4
Carisbrooke Ave PO14 .....179 A3
Carisbrooke Cl 2 PO9 .....136 A1
Carisbrooke Cres SO53 .....55 C3
Carisbrooke Ct
4 Christchurch BH23 .....209 A4
New Milton BH25 .....194 C2
Romsey SO51 .....28 A1
Carisbrooke Dr SO19 .....103 C3
Carisbrooke Rd
Gosport PO13 .....155 B1
Portsmouth PO4 .....183 A2
Carisbrooke Way BH23 .....193 C1
Carless Cl PO13 .....180 B4
Carlinford 29 BH5 .....205 C2
Carlisle Ct 2 SO16 .....102 A4
Carlisle Rd
Portsmouth PO1 .....215 C3
Southampton SO16 .....102 A4
Carlton Ave BH25 .....209 C4
Carlton Commerce Ctr The
SO14 .....103 A4
Carlton Cres SO15 .....102 C3
Carlton Ct 5 SO15 .....102 C4
Carlton Gr BH12 .....203 B3
Carlton Ho SO41 .....197 C2
Carlton Pl SO15 .....102 C3
Carlton Rd
Bournemouth BH1 .....205 B2
Gosport PO12 .....181 B3
Portchester PO16 .....132 C1
Southampton SO15 .....102 C4
Carlton Way PO12 .....181 B3
Carlyle Rd
Bournemouth BH6 .....206 B3
Gosport PO12 .....181 A3
Carlyn Dr SO53 .....55 B4
Carmans La SO21 .....31 B4
Carmarthen Ave PO6 .....158 A4
Carmel Cl BH15 .....201 B1
Carmine Ct PO13 .....180 B3
Carnarvon Rd
4 Bournemouth BH1 .....205 C2
Gosport PO12 .....181 A2
Portsmouth PO2 .....182 C4
Carnation Rd SO16 .....79 B2
Carne Cl SO53 .....55 B4
Carne Pl PO6 .....157 A4
Carnegie Cl BH14 .....203 B3
Caroline Ave BH23 .....207 C3
Caroline Gdns PO15 .....130 B1
Caroline Rd BH11 .....189 A2
Carolyn Cl SO19 .....103 C1
Carpathia Cl SO18 .....80 A1
Carpenter Cl Hythe SO45 126 A2
Lymington SO41 .....197 B3
10 Portsmouth PO4 .....183 A2
Carradale BH23 .....208 A4
Carran Wlk PO14 .....154 C4
Carraway PO15 .....129 B4
Carrbridge Cl BH3 .....204 B4
Carrbridge Gdns BH3 .....204 B4
Carrbridge Rd BH3 .....204 B4
Carrick Way BH25 .....195 B1
Carrington Cl SO41 .....211 C3
Carrington Ho 33 SO17 .....79 A1
Carrington La SO41 .....211 C2
Carrol Cl SO50 .....57 B1
Carroll Ave BH22 .....165 C3
Carroll Cl BH12 .....204 A3
Carronade Wlk PO3 .....157 C3
Carronades The 21
SO14 .....103 A3
Carshalton Ave PO6 .....158 A4
Carsworth Way BH17 .....188 A1
Carter Com Sch BH15 .....201 C1
Carter Ho Gosport PO13 .....155 A3
7 Portsmouth PO1 .....182 A3
Carter's Cl SP6 .....47 B2
Carter's Clay Rd SO51 .....26 A3
Carter's Copse Nature Trail*
PO13 .....180 B3
Carter's La 9 BH15 .....202 B1
Carters Ave BH15 .....201 B2
Carthage Cl SO53 .....55 C4
Cartref Cl BH31 .....114 C3
Cartwright Cl BH10 .....189 B2
Cartwright Dr PO14,
PO15 .....129 C1
Carvers Ind Est BH24 .....141 A4
Carvers La BH24 .....141 A4
Carysfort Rd BH1 .....205 B2
Cascades App PO1 .....215 B4
Cascades Sh Ctr PO1 .....215 B4
Cases Bakery Cl PO17 .....108 A2
Cashmoor Cl BH12 .....203 C4
Cask St PO1 .....215 B4
Caslake Cl BH25 .....194 C1
Caspar John Cl PO14 .....179 A3
Caspian Cl SO31 .....129 A4
Cassel Ave BH13 .....204 A1
Casselles Ct 33 BH25 .....195 A1
Casterbridge Rd BH22 .....165 B2
Castle Ave
Christchurch BH23 .....208 C4
Havant PO9 .....136 A1
Winchester SO23 .....10 C4
Castle Cl
Milford on Sea SO41 .....211 C2
Portsmouth PO5 .....215 B1
Castle Court Sch BH21 .....186 A4
Castle Ct
3 Christchurch BH23 .....209 A4
4 Southampton, Bitterne Pk
SO18 .....79 C1
Southampton, Millbrook
SO15 .....102 A3
Castle Farm La PO17 .....108 A1
Castle Gate Cl BH8 .....190 B1
Castle Gdns GU32 .....40 C2
Castle Gr PO16 .....156 B4
Castle Hill Poole BH14 .....203 A2
Winchester SO22 .....10 C4
Castle Hill La BH24 .....142 C2
Castle Hts 3 SO18 .....79 C1
Castle La
Chandler's Ford SO53 .....55 A2
Fawley SO45 .....178 C4
North Baddesley SO53,SO52 54 B2
6 Southampton SO14 .....102 C2
Castle La E BH7 .....206 B4
Castle La W BH8, BH9 .....190 B1
Castle Marina PO13 .....179 C1
Castle Mdw SP5 .....46 C4
Castle Mews
Southampton SO14 .....102 C2
St Leonards BH24 .....140 B3
Castle Par BH7 .....206 B4
Castle Prim Sch PO16 .....156 B4
Castle Rd
Bournemouth BH9 .....190 A1
Netley SO31 .....127 A3
Portsmouth PO5 .....215 B1
Rowland's Castle PO9 .....113 A1
Southampton SO18 .....79 C1
Southwick PO17 .....132 C3
Castle Sq 8 SO14 .....102 C2
Castle St
Christchurch BH23 .....207 B3
Poole BH15 .....202 B1
Portchester PO16 .....156 B4
Southampton SO14 .....103 A4
Titchfield PO14 .....154 A4
Castle Trad Est PO16 .....156 C4
Castle View PO12 .....181 A4
Castle View Rd PO16 .....156 C3
Castle Way SO14 .....102 C2
Castle Woods SP5 .....47 B3
Castledene Cres BH14 .....203 A1
Castlemain Ave BH6 .....206 B3
Castleman Ct BH22 .....138 B2
Castleman Way BH24 .....141 A3
Castlemans La PO11 .....160 A1
Castleshaw Cl SO16 .....101 C4
Castleton Ave BH10 .....189 B3
Castleton Ct PO5 .....215 A1
Castleway PO9 .....136 A1
Castlewood BH24 .....140 B3
Catalina Cl BH23 .....208 A3
Catalina Dr BH15 .....202 C1
Catamaran Cl SO31 .....128 C1
Cateran Cl SO16 .....101 C4
Cathay Gdns SO45 .....125 B2
Cathedral View 5 SO23 .....11 A3
Catherine Cl SO30 .....80 C1
Catherine Cres SP5 .....46 B4
Catherine Gdns SO30 .....80 C1
Catherine Wheel Gdns
BH23 .....191 C2
Catherington CE Inf Sch
PO8 .....88 A1
Catherington Hill PO8 .....88 A2
Catherington La
Horndean PO8 .....112 A4
Waterlooville PO8 .....112 A4
Catherington Way PO9 .....135 C2
Catisfield Ho 3 PO1 .....215 C4
Catisfield La PO15 .....130 A1
Catisfield Rd
Fareham PO15 .....130 B1
Portsmouth PO4 .....183 A2
Catmint Cl SO53 .....54 C4
Caton Cl BH12 .....204 A4
Cattistock Rd BH8 .....190 C1
Catways SO21 .....30 A4
Causeway SO51 .....52 B3
Causeway Cres SO40 .....101 A4
Causeway Ct 6 SO18 .....103 C4
Causeway Farm PO8 .....112 A3
Causeway The
Petersfield GU31 .....40 C1
Portchester PO16 .....131 C1
Cavalier Cl SO45 .....125 B2
Cavalier Ct PO6 .....158 B4
Cavan Cres BH17 .....187 A1
Cavanna Cl PO13 .....155 A2
Cavell Dr PO6 .....133 C1
Cavendish Cl
Romsey SO51 .....28 A1
Waterlooville PO7 .....134 C4
Cavendish Corner Cvn Pk 4
BH24 .....141 A4
Cavendish Dr PO7 .....134 C4
Cavendish Gr
Southampton SO17 .....102 C4
Winchester SO23 .....2 A2
Cavendish Hall BH1 .....205 A3
Cavendish Mews 2
SO15 .....102 C4
Cavendish Pl BH1 .....205 A3
Cavendish Rd
Bournemouth BH1 .....205 A3
Portsmouth PO5 .....215 C1
Caversham Cl
Hamworthy BH15 .....201 C2
Southampton SO19 .....104 A2
West End SO30 .....80 B1
Cawdor Rd BH3 .....204 B4
Cawte Rd SO15 .....102 B3
Cawte's Pl PO16 .....131 B1
Caxton Ave SO19 .....104 A3
Caxton Cl BH23 .....208 A4
Cecil Ave Ashurst SO40 .....100 B1
Bournemouth BH8 .....205 B4
Southampton SO16 .....78 A1
Cecil Cl BH21 .....186 C3
Cecil Ct BH8 .....205 A4
Cecil Gr PO5 .....215 A1
Cecil Hill BH8 .....205 A4
Cecil Pl PO5 .....215 A1
Cecil Rd
Bournemouth BH5 .....205 C2
Poole BH12 .....203 B3
Southampton SO19 .....103 C2
Cecil Villas SO17 .....79 B1
Cedar Ave
Bournemouth BH10 .....189 B3
Christchurch BH23 .....206 B4
Southampton SO15 .....102 B4
St Leonards BH24 .....139 C2
Cedar Cl Bursledon SO31 127 C4
Gosport PO12 .....156 A1
Hedge End SO30 .....105 B4
Kings Worthy SO23 .....2 A4
Upton BH16 .....201 A4
Waterlooville PO7 .....134 C3
Cedar Cres
North Baddesley SO52 .....53 C3
Waterlooville PO8 .....112 B3
Cedar Ct
Bournemouth BH4 .....204 A1
12 Fareham PO16 .....131 B1
Portsmouth PO5 .....215 C1
Cedar Dr Hordle SO41 .....211 B4
Wimborne Minst BH21 .....164 A3
Cedar Gdns
Barton on Sea BH25 .....194 C1
Havant PO9 .....136 A1
Southampton SO14 .....103 A4
Cedar Gr PO3 .....183 A4
Cedar Lawn SO51 .....28 B1
Cedar Manor BH4 .....204 B2
Cedar Pl BH23 .....169 A1
Cedar Rd Eastleigh SO50 .....55 C1
Hythe SO45 .....150 A4
Southampton SO14 .....103 A4
Cedar Specl Sch The
SO16 .....77 C2
Cedar St SO32 .....83 B4
Cedar Trad Pk BH21 .....164 C3
Cedar Way
Fareham PO14 .....154 C4
Ferndown BH22 .....165 B4
Cedar Wlk 37 SO22 .....10 C4
Cedar Wood Cl
Fair Oak SO50 .....57 C1
Totton SO40 .....100 B4
Cedarmount SO43 .....121 C2
Cedars The
Bournemouth BH4 .....204 B2
Fareham PO16 .....130 C2
Cedarwood SO23 .....2 B4
Cedarwood Lodge 6
PO16 .....131 A1
Ceder Ho SO14 .....103 A2
Cedric Cl SO45 .....177 C4
Celandine Ave
Locks Heath SO31 .....128 C1
Waterlooville PO8 .....112 A2
Celandine Cl
Chandler's Ford SO53 .....54 C3
Christchurch BH23 .....208 A4
Celia Cl PO7 .....135 A4
Cellars Farm Rd BH6 .....207 A2
Cement Terr 7 SO14 .....102 C2
Cemetery Ave BH15 .....202 C3
Cemetery Junc BH2 .....204 C3
Cemetery La
Denmead PO7 .....110 C3
Westbourne PO10 .....137 B2
Cemetery Rd
Southampton SO15 .....102 C4
Wimborne Minst BH21 .....163 A3
Centaur St PO2 .....182 B4
Centaury Gdns SO50 .....81 B4
Centenary Cl SO41 .....172 B1
Centenary Ho 6 BH23 .....207 A4
Centenary Way BH1, ...205 C3
Central Ave
Corfe Mullen BH21 .....186 B4
Poole BH12 .....203 C3
Central Bridge SO14 .....103 A2
Central Dr BH2 .....204 C3
Central Prec The SO53 .....55 B3
Central Rd Cosham PO6 .....158 B4
Portchester PO16 .....156 A4
Southampton SO14 .....103 A1
Central St PO1 .....215 C4
Central Station Bridge
SO15 .....102 C3
Central Way N SO45 .....151 C1
Centre La SO41 .....196 C1
Centre Pl BH24 .....140 C4
Centre Way SO31 .....129 A2
Centurian Ind Pk SO18 .....103 B4
Centurion Gate PO4 .....183 B2
Cerdic Mews SO31 .....128 A2
Cerne Abbas BH13 .....204 A1
Cerne Cl
Bournemouth BH9 .....190 A2
North Baddesley SO52 .....53 C2
West End SO18 .....80 A1
Cessac Ho PO12 .....181 B1
CH La SO32 .....83 C2
Chadderton Gdns PO1 .....182 A2
Chaddesley Glen BH13 .....214 C3
Chaddesley Pines BH13 214 C3
Chaddesley Wood Rd
BH13 .....214 C3
Chadswell Mdw PO9 .....135 B1
Chadwell Ave SO19 .....104 A2
Chadwick Rd SO50 .....55 C1
Chafen Rd SO18 .....103 B4
Chaffey Cl BH24 .....141 B4
Chaffinch Cl
Broadstone BH17 .....186 C1
New Milton BH25 .....194 C1
Totton SO40 .....100 B4
Chaffinch Gn PO8 .....111 C2
Chaffinch Way
Lee-on-the-Solent PO13 .....179 C2
Portchester PO16 .....155 C4
Chalbury Cl BH17 .....188 A1
Chalbury Ct
6 Christchurch BH23 .....207 C3
11 Poole BH14 .....203 A2
Chaldecott Gdns BH10 .....189 B2
Chaldon Rd BH17 .....187 C1
Chale Cl PO13 .....155 B1
Chalewood Rd SO45 .....177 C4
Chalfont Ave BH23 .....191 B2
Chalfont Ct 7 SO16 .....78 A1
Chalice Cl BH14 .....203 A2
Chalice Ct SO30 .....105 A3
Chalk Cl SP5 .....47 B4
Chalk Hill Soberton SO32 .....85 B3
West End SO18 .....80 B1
Chalk Hill Rd PO8 .....112 B4
Chalk La PO17 .....131 A4
Chalk Pit Cotts PO17 .....131 A4
Chalk Ridge Horndean PO8 88 B2
Winchester SO23 .....11 B4
Chalkpit Rd PO6 .....133 A1
Chalkridge Rd PO6 .....134 A1
Challenge Ent Ctr The
PO3 .....158 A2
Challenger Dr PO12 .....181 B4
Challenger Way SO45 .....125 B1
Challis Ct 18 SO14 .....103 A2
Chalmers Way SO31 .....127 C2
Chaloner Cres SO45 .....126 A1
Chalton Cres PO9 .....135 B2
Chalton Ho PO1 .....215 B4
Chalton La PO8 .....88 B3
Chalvington Ct SO53 .....55 B3
Chalvington Rd SO53 .....55 B2
Chalwyn Ind Est BH12 .....203 A4
Chalybeate Cl SO16 .....78 A1
Chalybeate Hospl SO16 .....78 A1
Chamberlain Gr PO14 .....155 A4
Chamberlain Hall SO16 .....79 A2
Chamberlain Rd SO17 .....79 A2
Chamberlayne Ct SO52 .....54 A2
Chamberlayne Ho 10
SO31 .....127 A3
Chamberlayne Park Sch
Southampton SO19 .....104 A1
Southampton SO19 .....127 A4
Chamberlayne Rd
Bursledon SO31 .....127 C4
Eastleigh SO50 .....56 A1
Netley SO31 .....127 A3
Chambers Ave SO51 .....53 A4
Chambers Cl SO16 .....77 B3
Champion Cl SO41 .....211 C2
Chancel Rd SO31 .....129 A2
Chancellors La SO32 .....81 C2
Chanctonbury Ho PO5 .....215 B1
Chander Cl BH22 .....165 C2
Chandler's Ford Ind Est
SO53 .....55 A3
Chandler's Ford Inf Sch
SO53 .....55 B3
Chandler's Ford Inf Sch
(Annexe) SO53 .....55 B4
Chandlers Cl
Bournemouth BH7 .....206 A4
South Hayling PO11 .....185 B1
Chandlers Way SO31 .....129 A3
Chandos Ave BH12 .....204 A4
Chandos Ho 14 SO14 .....103 A2
Chandos St 26 SO14 .....103 A2
Channel Ct
Barton on Sea BH25 .....209 C4
Bournemouth BH6 .....206 B2
Channel Mouth Rd
SO45 .....151 C1
Channel Way SO14 .....103 B2
Channels Farm Rd SO16 .....79 B3
Chant Cl BH23 .....207 B4
Chantrell Wlk PO15 .....130 B2
Chantry Cl BH23 .....193 C1
Chantry Mead SO22 .....1 C1
Chantry Rd
Gosport PO12 .....181 A4
Horndean PO8 .....112 A4
Southampton SO14 .....103 A2
Chantry The
Bournemouth BH1 .....205 A2
Locks Heath PO14 .....129 B2
Chapel Cl Braishfield SO51 28 B3
Corfe Mullen BH21 .....186 B3
West End SO30 .....80 B1
Chapel Cres SO19 .....104 A2
Chapel Ct 7 PO1 .....182 B4
Chapel Dro Fair Oak SO50 .81 B4
Hedge End SO30 .....105 A3
Chapel Gate BH23 .....190 B4
Chapel La
Blackfield SO45 .....177 C4
Bransgore BH23 .....193 A4
Burley BH24 .....143 A2
Chilcomb SO21, SO23 .....12 A4
Corfe Mullen BH21 .....186 B3
Curdridge SO32 .....106 C4
East Boldre SO42 .....175 B3
Fawley SO45 .....151 A1
Hurn BH23 .....190 B4
Lockerley SO51 .....26 A3
Lyndhurst SO43 .....121 C2
Michelmersh SO51 .....27 B4
Nomansland SP5 .....73 B4
Otterbourne SO21 .....31 A1
Poole BH15 .....202 B1
Redlynch SP5 .....47 C3
Sway SO41 .....172 B1
Totton SO40 .....100 C3
13 Waterlooville PO7 .....134 C4
Wimborne Minst BH21 .....163 A3
Chapel Rd Droxford SO32 .....61 B2
Locks Heath SO31 .....128 C3
Poole BH14 .....203 A2
Soberton SO32 .....85 A1
Southampton SO14 .....103 A2
Swanmore SO32 .....84 A3
West End SO30 .....80 C1
Chapel Rise BH24 .....140 B1
Chapel Sq PO12 .....180 C4
Chapel St East Meon GU32 38 B1
Gosport PO12 .....181 A4
Petersfield GU32 .....40 C2
3 Portsmouth PO2 .....215 A1
Southampton SO14 .....103 A2
Chapelside PO14 .....154 A4
Chaplains Ave PO8 .....111 B2
Chaplains Cl PO8 .....111 B2
Charborough Rd BH18 .....187 A2
Charden Ct SO18 .....104 A4
Charden Rd
Bishopstoke SO50 .....57 A1
Gosport PO13 .....180 B4
Charfield Cl
Fareham PO14 .....154 B4
Winchester SO22 .....10 C3
Charielote Ho SO15 .....102 B3
Charing Cl BH24 .....141 A3
Chark La PO13 .....179 C2
Charlcot Lawn PO9 .....135 B3
Charlecote Dr SO53 .....55 A4
Charlecote Mews 18
SO22 .....10 C4
Charlemont Dr 15 PO16 .....131 B1
Charles Cl
Waterlooville PO7 .....134 B3
Winchester SO23 .....2 A1
Charles Cres BH25 .....195 A3
Charles Dickens Birthplace
Mus* PO1 .....182 B4
Charles Dickens Inf Sch
PO1 .....182 B4
Charles Dickens Jun Sch
PO1 .....182 B4
Charles Dickens St PO1 215 B3
Charles Gdns BH10 .....189 B1
Charles Keightley Ct
BH21 .....163 B2
Charles Knott Gdns
SO15 .....102 C4
Charles Ley Ct SO45 .....151 A2
Charles Rd
Christchurch BH23 .....207 C4
Poole BH15 .....202 B2
Charles St
Petersfield GU32 .....40 C2
Portsmouth PO1 .....215 C4
Southampton SO14 .....103 A2
Charles Watts Way
SO30 .....105 A4
Charles Wyatt Ho 28
SO14 .....103 A4
Charles's La BH24 .....141 C2
Charlesbury Ave PO12 .....180 C2
Charleston Cl PO11 .....184 C2
Charleston Rd SO45 .....150 B4
Charlesworth Dr PO7 .....111 B1
Charlesworth Gdns PO7 111 B1

Charliejoy Gdns 18 SO14 103 B3
Charlott Ct PO5 215 B1
Charlotte Cl
 Christchurch BH23 208 A3
 3 New Milton BH25 195 A1
 Poole BH12 204 B4
Charlotte Ct
 Chandler's Ford SO53 55 C4
 Southampton SO19 103 C1
Charlotte Mews PO12 181 A1
Charlotte Pl SO14 103 A3
Charlotte St PO1 215 B4
Charlton Cl
 Bournemouth BH9 190 B2
 Hordle SO41 195 C2
Charlton Rd SO15 102 B4
Charltons The BH2 204 C3
Charminster 8 PO5 182 B1
Charminster Ave BH9 190 A1
Charminster Cl
 5 Bournemouth BH8 190 A1
 Waterlooville PO7 134 C4
Charminster Pl BH8 190 B1
Charminster Rd BH8 205 A4
Charmouth Gr BH14 203 A2
Charmouth Terr 6 SO16 78 A1
Charmus Rd SO40 76 A1
Charmwen Cres SO30 80 B1
Charnock Cl SO41 195 C2
Charnwood PO13 155 B1
Charnwood Ave 8 BH9 190 A2
Charnwood Cl
 Chandler's Ford SO53 30 B1
 Totton SO40 76 B1
 West Moors BH22 138 C1
Charnwood Cres SO53 30 B1
Charnwood Dr SP6 69 C2
Charnwood Gdns SO53 30 B1
Charnwood Way SO45 177 C4
Chartcombe BH13 214 C4
Charter Ho 2 PO5 215 A2
Charter Rd BH11 188 B3
Chartergrove Ho 15 GU31 40 C2
Charterhouse Way SO30 81 B1
Chartwell Cl
 Eastleigh SO50 56 A3
 Titchfield PO14 129 B1
Chartwell Dr PO9 136 B2
Chase Cl GU33 21 A2
Chase Farm Cl SO32 83 C2
Chase Gr SO32 83 C2
Chase Rd GU33 21 A2
Chase The Gosport PO12 180 C2
 Locks Heath PO14 129 B1
 St Leonards BH24 140 B3
 Verwood BH31 115 B3
Chaseside BH7 206 A4
Chasewater Ave PO3 183 A4
Chatburn Ave PO8 111 C2
Chatfield Ho 10 PO1 215 C4
Chatfield Rd PO13 155 B2
Chatham Cl PO12 181 B4
Chatham Dr PO1 182 A2
Chatham Rd SO22 10 B3
Chatsworth Ave PO6 158 A3
Chatsworth Cl PO15 130 B1
Chatsworth Ct PO5 215 C1
Chatsworth Rd
 Bournemouth BH8 205 B3
 Eastleigh SO50 56 A3
 Poole BH14 203 A3
 Southampton SO19 104 A3
Chatsworth Way BH25 194 C2
Chaucer Ave PO6 132 C1
Chaucer Cl
 Fareham PO16 130 C1
 Waterlooville PO7 111 C1
 Wimborne Minst BH21 163 B3
Chaucer Dr SO41 211 B3
Chaucer Ind Est SO23 2 B1
Chaucer Rd Poole BH13 214 C4
 Southampton SO19 104 B3
Chaucombe Pl BH25 194 C1
Chaundler Rd SO23 2 A1
Chaveney Cl 6 SO45 125 C1
Chawton Cl
 Southampton SO18 104 B4
 Winchester SO22 1 B2
Cheam Rd BH18 186 C2
Cheam Way SO40 76 B1
Cheater's La SP6 92 B4
Cheddar Cl SO19 103 C2
Cheddington Rd BH9 190 A2
Chedington Cl BH17 187 C1
Chedworth Cres PO6 133 A1
Cheeryble Ho 19 PO1 182 B4
Cheesecombe Farm La GU33 19 C3
Chellowdene SO53 55 B3
Chelmsford Rd
 Portsmouth PO2 157 C1
 Upton BH16 201 A4
Chelsea Rd PO5 215 C1
Cheltenham Cres PO13 179 C2
Cheltenham Ct 26 SO17 79 A1
Cheltenham Gdns SO30 81 B2
Cheltenham Rd
 Cosham PO6 157 B4
 Poole BH12 203 B3
Chelveston Cres SO16 78 A2
Chelwood Gate SO16 78 C3
Chene Rd BH21 163 B2
Cheney's Farm SO51 75 C3
Cheping Gdns SO30 106 A3
Chepstow Cl
 North Baddesley SO53 55 A3
 Totton SO40 100 B4
Chepstow Ct 9 PO7 112 A1
Chequers Cl SO41 197 B2
Chequers Ho 20 PO16 131 A1
Chequers Quay 5 PO10 161 A4
Cherbourg Prim Sch SO50 56 A1
Cherbourg Rd SO50 56 A1
Cherford Rd BH11 189 A1
Cherita Ct BH15 202 C3
Cheriton Ave
 Bournemouth BH7 206 B4
 Southampton SO18 104 B4
Cheriton Cl Havant PO9 135 B2
 Horndean PO8 112 A4
 Winchester SO22 1 B1
Cheriton Ct 7 SO15 102 B3
Cheriton La SO24 15 A4
Cheriton Prim Sch SO24 14 B3
Cheriton Rd
 Eastleigh SO50 55 C1
 Gosport PO12 180 C2
 Winchester SO22 10 C4
Cheriton Way BH21 163 B3
Cherque La PO13 180 A4
Cherrett Cl BH11 188 C2
Cherries Dr BH9 189 C1
Cherry Blossom Ct 22 PO1 182 B4
Cherry Cl
 Lee-on-the-Solent PO13 180 A3
 Poole BH14 203 A2
Cherry Ct Poole BH14 203 A3
 16 Southampton SO17 103 A4
Cherry Dro SO50 81 B3
Cherry Gdns SO32 83 B4
Cherry Gr BH22 165 B3
Cherry Hill Gdns BH16 201 A3
Cherry Hill Gr BH16 201 A3
Cherry Tree Ave
 Fareham PO14 154 B4
 Waterlooville PO8 112 A1
Cherry Tree Cl
 Hordle SO41 211 B4
 St Leonards BH24 139 B2
Cherry Tree Ct 31 BH25 195 A1
Cherry Tree Dr BH25 194 C3
Cherry Wlk SO15 102 B4
Cherrygarth Rd PO15 130 B1
Cherryton Gdns SO45 150 A2
Cherrywood SO30 105 A3
Cherrywood Gdns
 South Hayling PO11 185 A2
 Totton SO40 100 B4
Chervil Cl
 Chandler's Ford SO53 54 C3
 Horndean PO8 88 B1
Cherville Ct SO51 52 C4
Cherville Mews SO51 52 C4
Cherville St SO51 52 C4
Cherwell Cres SO16 101 C4
Cherwell Gdns SO53 55 B3
Cherwell Ho SO16 101 C4
Cheshire Cl PO15 129 C3
Cheshire Dr BH8 191 A1
Cheshire Way PO10 137 B1
Chesil St SO23 11 A4
Chesil Terr SO23 11 A4
Chesil Wood SO23 11 B4
Chesildene Ave BH8 190 B2
Chesildene Dr BH8 190 B2
Cheslyn Rd PO3 183 A3
Chessel Ave
 Bournemouth BH5 205 C2
 Southampton SO19 103 C3
Chessel Cres SO19 103 C4
Chester Cres PO13 180 A2
Chester Ct SO16 78 B1
Chester Cts 7 PO12 181 B2
Chester Pl 34 PO5 182 B1
Chester Rd Poole BH13 204 A1
 Southampton SO18 80 A1
 Winchester SO23 11 A4
Chesterfield Cl BH13 214 C4
Chesterfield Ct BH1 205 B2
Chesterfield Rd PO3 183 A4
Chesterton Gdns PO8 111 C2
Chesterton Pl SO31 129 B4
Chestnut Ave
 Ashurst SO40 100 B2
 Barton on Sea BH25 210 A4
 Bournemouth BH6 206 B2
 Christchurch BH23 206 B4
 2 Colden Common SO21 31 C1
 Eastleigh SO50,SO53 55 B1
 Havant PO9 135 A2
 Ibsley BH24 116 A3
 Littleton SO22 1 A2
 Portsmouth PO4 182 C2
 Waterlooville PO8 112 B3
Chestnut Cl
 Chandler's Ford SO53 55 B2
 Denmead PO7 110 C2
 Romsey SO51 53 B3
 West End SO30 80 B2
Chestnut Ct
 Rowland's Castle PO9 136 A4
 8 Southampton SO17 79 A1
Chestnut Gr BH21 164 C3
Chestnut Lodge 12 SO16 78 C2
Chestnut Rd
 Brockenhurst SO42 146 A1
 Southampton SO16 78 A1
Chestnut Rise
 Droxford SO32 61 A1
Chestnut Rise *continued*
 Eastleigh SO53 55 B1
Chestnut Way
 Burton BH23 192 B2
 Titchfield PO14 129 B1
Chestnut Wlk
 Botley SO30 105 C4
 Gosport PO12 156 A1
Chestnuts The SO31 129 A1
Chetnole Cl BH17 188 A1
Chettle Rd SO19 104 C3
Chetwode Way BH17 187 A1
Chetwynd Dr SO16 78 C2
Chetwynd Rd
 Portsmouth PO4 182 C2
 Southampton SO16 78 C3
Chevening Ct 8 PO4 183 A3
Cheviot Court Flats BH23 207 C4
Cheviot Cres SO16 101 C4
Cheviot Dr SO45 125 B2
Cheviot Gn SO31 152 B4
Cheviot Rd SO16 101 C4
Cheviot Way BH31 114 C3
Cheviot Wlk PO14 154 C4
Cheviots The BH14 203 B2
Chevron Bsns Pk SO45 150 A3
Chewter Cl PO4 182 C1
Chewton Common Rd BH23 209 A4
Chewton Farm Rd BH23 194 B1
Chewton Lodge BH23 209 A4
Chewton Way BH23 194 A1
Cheyne Gdns BH4 204 B1
Cheyne Way PO13 179 C1
Chichester Ave PO11 185 A2
Chichester Cl
 Gosport PO13 155 A1
 Hedge End SO30 81 B1
 Locks Heath SO31 128 C2
 West Wellow SO51 51 A1
Chichester Ho PO9 136 A2
Chichester Rd
 North Hayling PO11 160 B1
 Portsmouth PO2 182 C4
 Ringwood BH24 117 B1
 Southampton SO18 104 A4
Chichester Way BH23 208 A3
Chichester Wlk BH21 163 C1
Chickenhall La SO50 56 B1
Chickerell Cl BH9 190 A2
Chidden Cl GU32 38 B1
Chidden Holt SO53 55 A3
Chideock Cl BH12 203 C3
Chideock Ct BH12 203 C3
Chidham Cl PO9 135 C1
Chidham Dr PO9 135 C1
Chidham Rd PO6 134 A1
Chidham Sq PO9 135 C1
Chidham Wlk 2 PO9 135 C1
Chigwell Rd BH8 190 A1
Chilbolton Ave SO22 10 B4
Chilbolton Ct
 14 Havant PO9 136 A3
 Winchester SO22 10 B4
Chilcomb Cl PO13 179 C1
Chilcomb La
 Chilcomb SO21 11 C3
 Winchester SO23 11 B3
Chilcomb Rd SO18 104 B4
Chilcombe Cl PO9 135 C2
Chilcombe Hts SO23 11 A4
Chilcombe Rd BH6 206 A3
Chilcote Rd PO3 183 A4
Childe Sq PO2 157 B1
Chilfrome Cl BH17 187 B1
Chilgrove Rd PO6 158 B4
Chilham Cl SO50 56 A4
Chillenden Ct SO40 100 B3
Chillerton SO31 127 B4
Chilling La SO31 152 C3
Chillington Gdns SO53 30 A1
Chilly Hill SP6 94 C4
Chilmark Ct GU33 20 C2
Chilsdown Way PO7 134 C2
Chiltern Cl
 Barton on Sea BH25 194 C1
 Poole BH12 204 A3
 Totton SO40 100 B3
Chiltern Ct
 5 Christchurch BH23 207 C4
 Gosport PO12 181 A3
 7 Portsmouth PO5 182 B1
Chiltern Dr
 Barton on Sea BH25 209 C4
 Verwood BH31 114 C3
Chiltern Gr SO16 101 C4
Chiltern Wlk PO14 154 C4
Chilworth Cl SO16 54 B1
Chilworth Gdns PO8 88 B2
Chilworth Gr PO12 181 A3
Chilworth Rd SO16 54 C1
Chimes The BH4 204 A2
Chine Ave SO19 103 C3
Chine Cl SO31 129 A2
Chine Cres BH2 204 B1
Chine Cres Rd BH2 204 B1
Chine The PO13 155 C1
Chine Wlk BH22 165 C1
Chinham Rd SO40 99 B3
Chipstead Ho 12 PO6 157 C4
Chipstead Rd 11 PO6 157 C4
Chisels La BH23 193 A3
Chisholm Cl SO16 77 C3
Chiswell Rd BH17 187 B1
Chitty Rd PO4 183 A1
Chivers Cl PO5 215 B1
Chorley Cl BH15 202 B3
Chris Cres BH16 201 B4
Christ the King RC Prim Sch BH11 189 A3
Christchurch Bay Rd BH25 209 C4
Christchurch By-Pass BH23 207 B4
Christchurch Castle* BH23 207 B3
Christchurch Cty Jun Sch BH23 207 A4
Christchurch Cty Prim Sch BH23 207 A4
Christchurch Gdns
 Waterlooville PO7 134 A1
 1 Winchester SO23 10 C3
Christchurch Hospl BH23 206 C4
Christchurch Priory* BH23 207 B3
Christchurch Rd
 Barton on Sea BH25 209 B4
 Bournemouth BH1, BH7 205 B2
 Ferndown BH22 165 B1
 Hordle SO41 211 B4
 Hurn BH23 191 B3
 Ringwood BH24 141 A2
 Winchester SO23 10 C3
Christchurch Ski Ctr BH23 167 A2
Christchurch Sta BH23 207 A4
Christie Ave PO15 129 B4
Christine Ct 9 SO18 103 C4
Christopher Cres BH15 202 B3
Christopher Way PO10 136 C1
Christophers BH21 163 B1
Christyne Ct PO7 134 B2
Church Cl
 Bishopstoke SO50 56 B2
 Clanfield PO8 88 A3
 Locks Heath SO31 129 A2
 Minstead SO43 98 B4
 North Baddesley SO52 54 A2
Church End SO15 102 B4
Church Farm SP6 93 C4
Church Farm Cl SO45 125 A3
Church Hatch SP5 47 A4
Church Hill
 Milford on Sea SO41 211 C2
 Redlynch SP5 47 C3
 Verwood BH31 114 C3
 West End SO18,SO30 80 B1
Church La Awbridge SO51 26 C2
 Boldre SO41 173 C1
 Botley SO30 106 A3
 Braishfield SO51 28 B4
 Bramdean SO24 15 B2
 Brockenhurst SO42 173 A4
 Burley BH24 143 A2
 Bursledon SO31 128 A4
 Christchurch BH23 207 A3
 Colden Common SO21 56 C4
 Curdridge SO32 106 B4
 Damerham SP6 68 B2
 Durley SO32 81 C3
 East Boldre SO42 175 B3
 Fawley SO45 151 A2
 Ferndown BH22 189 C4
 Hambledon PO7 86 B2
 Havant PO9 160 A4
 Hedge End SO30 105 A3
 Kings Worthy SO23 2 B3
 Littleton SO22 1 A3
 Lymington SO41 197 C2
 Lyndhurst SO43 121 C3
 Meonstoke SO32 61 B4
 Mottisfont SO51 5 C1
 New Milton BH25 194 C1
 North Hayling PO11 160 B2
 Nursling SO16 76 C3
 Plaitford SO51 50 A3
 Romsey SO51 52 C4
 Sherfield English SO51 25 B2
 17 Southampton SO14 102 C2
 Southampton, Highfield SO17 79 A1
 Swanmore SO32 84 B3
 Sway SO41 172 A1
 Twyford SO21 32 A4
 West Meon GU32 37 B3
 Winchester SO21 2 C3
Church Mead 12 SO41 197 C1
Church Path
 3 Emsworth PO10 160 C4
 Fareham PO16 131 B1
 Gosport PO12 181 B2
 Horndean PO8 112 B3
 Titchfield PO14 154 A4
Church Path N PO1 215 C4
Church Pl SO51 52 C4
Church Rd
 Bishopstoke SO50 56 B3
 Bournemouth BH6 206 C2
 Ferndown BH22 165 B3
 Froxfield GU34 17 B2
 Gosport PO12 181 A1
 Locks Heath SO31 129 A2
 Locks Heath, Newtown SO31 152 B4
 Michelmersh SO51 6 B1
 Poole BH14 203 A2
 Portchester PO16 156 C3
 Portsmouth PO1 215 C4
 Romsey SO51 52 C4
 Shedfield SO32 107 C4
 Soberton PO17 109 B3
 South Hayling PO11 185 A3
 Southampton SO19 103 B1
Church Rd *continued*
 Southbourne PO10 161 C4
 Steep GU32 40 C4
 Swanmore SO32 84 A3
 Thorney Island PO10 161 B1
 Three Legged Cross BH21 114 C1
 Westbourne PO10 137 A2
Church St
 Christchurch BH23 207 A3
 East Meon GU32 38 C1
 Fordingbridge SP6 93 C4
 Liss GU33 20 C3
 Poole BH15 202 A1
 Portsmouth PO1 215 C4
 Romsey SO51 52 C4
 Southampton SO15 78 B1
 Titchfield PO14 154 A4
 Upham SO32 58 C3
 10 Wimborne Minst BH21 163 A3
Church View
 Portsmouth PO4 183 A3
 Shedfield SO32 107 C4
 Westbourne PO10 137 A2
Church View Cl SO19 104 A2
Church Wlk SP5 48 A3
Churcher Cl PO12 180 B2
Churcher Rd PO10 137 A2
Churcher Wlk PO12 180 B2
Churcher's Coll GU31 41 A2
Churchers Coll Jun Sch GU32 40 C2
Churchfield BH31 114 C3
Churchfield Cres BH15 202 C2
Churchfield Ct BH15 202 C2
Churchfield La BH24 93 C1
Churchfield Rd
 Petersfield GU31 41 A2
 Poole BH15 202 C2
Churchfields SO45 151 A2
Churchfields Rd SO21 32 A3
Churchill Ave SO32 59 A1
Churchill Cl Alderholt SP6 92 C3
 Titchfield PO14 129 B1
Churchill Cres BH12 203 B3
Churchill Ct Cosham PO6 158 C4
 New Milton BH25 194 C1
 Waterlooville PO8 112 A3
Churchill Dr PO10 136 C2
Churchill Dro BH21 91 B4
Churchill Gdns BH12 203 B3
Churchill Ho SO18 104 B4
Churchill Mews PO12 181 A3
Churchill Rd
 Bournemouth BH1 205 B3
 Poole BH12 203 B3
 Wimborne Minst BH21 163 C2
Churchill Sq PO4 183 A1
Churchill Yard Ind Est PO7 111 C1
Churchmoor Rd BH21 164 A3
Churchward Gdns SO30 81 B1
Cinderford Cl 32 PO6 133 A1
Cinnamon Ct SO15 102 C3
Cinnamon La 10 BH15 202 A1
Circle The
 3 Bournemouth BH9 190 A2
 Poole BH13 214 C4
 Portsmouth PO5 182 B1
 Wickham PO17 108 A2
Circular Rd PO1 182 B4
Cirrus Gdns SO31 127 C1
City Bldgs PO1 215 B4
City Bsns Ctr SO23 11 A4
City Commerce Ctr 29 SO14 103 A2
City Ind Pk SO15 102 C2
City of Portsmouth Boys Sch PO2 157 C2
City of Portsmouth Girls' Sch PO1 182 C3
City of Toronto Homes SO16 101 C4
City Rd SO23 10 C4
Civic Centre Rd
 Havant PO9 135 C1
 Southampton SO14 102 C3
Civic Way PO16 131 B1
Clacton Rd PO6 157 B4
Claire Ct BH23 209 A4
Claire Gdns PO8 88 B1
Clamp Gn 4 SO21 56 C4
Clandon Dr SO50 55 C3
Clanfield Cl SO53 55 B3
Clanfield Dr SO53 55 B3
Clanfield Ho 7 PO1 215 C4
Clanfield Jun Sch PO8 88 A4
Clanfield Rd SO18 104 B4
Clanfield Way SO53 55 B3
Clanwilliam Rd PO13 179 C1
Clare Cl PO14 129 B1
Clare Gdns
 Blackfield SO45 177 C4
 Petersfield GU31 41 B2
Clare Ho PO12 180 C4
Clare Lodge Cl BH23 169 A1
Claremont Ave BH9 190 A1
Claremont Cl 1 SO50 56 A3
Claremont Cres SO15 102 A4
Claremont Gdns PO7 134 C2
Claremont Rd
 Bournemouth BH9 190 A1
 Portsmouth PO1 215 D3
 Southampton SO15 102 A4
Clarence Espl PO5 182 B1
Clarence Ho 5 SO14 103 B3
Clarence Par PO5 182 B1
Clarence Park Rd BH7 206 A3

Clarence Rd
Gosport PO12 . . . .**181** B3
Lyndhurst SO43 . . . .**121** C3
3 Poole BH14 . . . .**203** A2
Portsmouth PO5 . . . .**182** B1
Clarence St PO1 . . . .**215** B4
Clarendon Cl
Broadstone BH18 . . . . . .**187** A2
10 Romsey SO51 . . . .**28** A1
Clarendon Cres PO14 . .**129** B1
Clarendon Ct
Bournemouth BH2 . . . . . .**204** B1
9 Portsmouth PO5 . . . . .**182** B1
Clarendon Pk SO41 . . . .**197** B1
Clarendon Pl PO1 . . . . .**215** C4
Clarendon Rd
Bournemouth BH4 . . . . . .**204** B2
Broadstone BH18 . . . . . .**186** C2
Christchurch BH23 . . . . . .**207** A4
16 Havant PO9 . . . .**135** C1
Portsmouth PO5 . . . .**182** B1
Southampton SO16 . . . . .**102** A4
Clarendon St PO1 . . . . .**215** C4
Clark's Rd BH24 . . . .**141** A4
Clarke's Rd PO1 . . . .**182** C3
Claude Ashby Cl SO18 . .**79** C2
Claudeen Cl SO18 . . . . . .**79** C3
Claudeen Ct SO19 . . . . . .**104** C3
Claudia Ct PO12 . . . .**180** C3
Claudius Cl SO53 . . . .**55** C4
Claudius Gdns SO53 . . . . .**55** C4
Clausen Way SO41 . . . . .**197** B1
Clausentum Cl SO53 . . . . .**55** C4
Clausentum Rd
Southampton SO14 . . . . .**103** A4
Winchester SO23 . . . .**10** C3
Clave Cl PO13 . . . .**179** C1
Claxton St PO1 . . . .**215** C4
Clay Hill SO43 . . . .**122** A2
Clay St SP5 . . . .**24** A2
Claybank Rd PO3 . . . . . .**158** A1
Claybank Spur PO3 . . . . .**158** A1
Claydon Ave PO4 . . . . . .**183** C2
Clayfields Sports Ctr
SO45 . . . .**125** B2
Clayford Ave BH22 . . . . .**165** A4
Clayford Cl BH17 . . . .**187** B1
Clayhall Rd PO12 . . . . . .**181** A1
Clayhill Cl SO32 . . . .**83** B2
Claylake Dr BH31 . . . . . .**115** A3
Claylands Ct SO32 . . . . . .**83** A4
Claylands Rd SO32 . . . . . .**83** A4
Claylands Road Ind Est
SO32 . . . .**83** A4
Claypit La GU32 . . . .**18** B3
Claypits La SO45 . . . . . .**125** B2
Cleasby Cl SO16 . . . .**101** C4
Cleasby Grange 28 BH5 .**205** C2
Clease Way SO21 . . . .**31** B4
Clee Ave PO14 . . . .**154** B4
Cleethorpes Rd SO19 . . .**104** A2
Cleeve Ct PO6 . . . .**133** A4
Cleeves Cl BH12 . . . .**188** B1
Cleeves The SO40 . . . . . .**100** B3
Clegg Rd PO4 . . . .**183** A2
Clem's Way SO51 . . . .**5** A1
Clematis Cl BH23 . . . . . .**208** B4
Clement Atlee Way PO6 **157** A4
Clement Mews BH4 . . . . .**204** B4
Cleric Ct PO14 . . . .**129** B2
Cleveland Cl BH25 . . . . . .**209** B4
Cleveland Ct
Bournemouth BH2 . . . . . .**204** B1
7 Southampton SO18 . . .**80** A1
Cleveland Dr
Fareham PO14 . . . .**154** B4
Hythe SO45 . . . .**125** B1
Cleveland Gdns BH1 . . . .**205** B3
Cleveland Rd
Bournemouth BH1 . . . . . .**205** B3
Gosport PO12 . . . .**181** A2
Portsmouth PO5 . . . .**215** D2
Southampton SO18 . . . . . .**79** C1
Clevelands Cl SO53 . . . . . .**30** A1
Clewers Hill SO32 . . . .**83** B2
Clewers La SO32 . . . .**83** C2
Cliff Cres BH25 . . . .**209** C4
Cliff Dr
Christchurch BH23 . . . . . .**208** A4
Poole BH13 . . . .**214** C4
Cliff Ho 10 BH6 . . . .**206** C2
Cliff Rd
Milford on Sea SO41 . . . .**211** A2
Southampton SO15 . . . . .**102** B3
Stubbington PO14 . . . . . .**153** C1
Cliff Terr BH25 . . . .**209** C3
Cliff The SO19 . . . .**103** B2
Cliff Way SO21 . . . .**31** B4
Cliffdale Prim Sch PO2 . .**157** C1
Cliffe Ave SO31 . . . .**127** C1
Cliffe Rd BH25 . . . .**209** C4
Clifford Dibben Mews 1
SO14 . . . .**103** A4
Clifford Pl SO50 . . . .**57** B1
Clifford Rd BH9 . . . .**190** A1
Clifford St 13 SO14 . . . . .**103** A3
Clifton Cres PO7 . . . .**111** C3
Clifton Ct
13 Bournemouth BH5 . . .**205** C2
19 New Milton BH25 . . . .**195** A4
15 Southampton SO15 . . .**102** A4
Clifton Gdns
Ferndown BH22 . . . .**165** B2
14 Southampton SO15 . . .**102** A4
West End SO18 . . . .**80** B1
Clifton Hill SO22 . . . .**10** C4
Clifton Lodge SO15 . . . . .**102** A4

Clifton Lodge No 1 32
SO22 . . . .**10** C4
Clifton Lodge No 2 33
SO22 . . . .**10** C4
Clifton Rd
Bournemouth BH6 . . . . . .**206** B2
Lee-on-the-Solent PO13 . .**180** A2
Poole BH14 . . . .**203** C1
25 Portsmouth PO5 . . . . .**182** B1
Winchester SO22 . . . .**10** C4
Clifton St Gosport PO12 . .**180** C3
Portsmouth PO1 . . . .**215** D4
Clifton Terr
24 Portsmouth PO5 . . . . .**182** B1
Winchester SO23 . . . .**10** C4
Clingan Rd BH6 . . . .**206** B4
Clinton Cl BH23 . . . .**194** A1
Clinton Rd
Lymington SO41 . . . .**197** C3
Waterlooville PO7 . . . . . .**111** B1
Clipper Cl SO31 . . . .**128** C1
Clitheroe Cotts SO42 . . . .**148** C1
Clive Ct 19 BH4 . . . .**204** B2
Clive Gr PO16 . . . .**156** B4
Clive Rd
Bournemouth BH9 . . . . . .**189** C4
Christchurch BH23 . . . . . .**193** C1
Portsmouth PO1 . . . .**182** C3
Cliveden Cl BH22 . . . .**165** B4
Clock Ho 12 PO7 . . . .**134** C4
Clock St 10 PO1 . . . .**182** A3
Clocktower Dr PO4 . . . . .**183** A1
Cloisters The
Christchurch BH23 . . . . . .**207** A3
Fareham PO15 . . . .**130** B1
Lymington SO41 . . . .**197** C2
Ringwood BH24 . . . .**141** B3
Romsey SO51 . . . .**52** C4
Southampton SO16 . . . . . .**79** A2
Close Bellfield The
PO14 . . . .**153** C4
Close The
Barton on Sea BH25 . . . .**210** A4
Broadstone BH18 . . . . . .**186** C2
Colden Common SO21 . . . .**31** B1
Cosham PO6 . . . .**158** A4
Fordingbridge SP6 . . . . . .**94** B4
Hamble-le-Rice SO31 . . . .**128** A2
Hedge End SO30 . . . .**105** A3
Holbury SO45 . . . .**150** B4
Langrish GU32 . . . .**39** B2
Portchester PO16 . . . . . .**156** B4
Redlynch SP5 . . . .**47** B4
Ringwood BH24 . . . .**140** C4
Southampton SO18 . . . . .**104** B4
St Leonards, Avon Castle
BH24 . . . .**140** B2
St Leonards, St Ives BH24 **140** A2
Sway SO41 . . . .**172** A1
Whitsbury SP6 . . . .**45** A2
Closewood Rd PO7 . . . . .**111** A1
Clough La BH24 . . . .**142** C2
Clough's Rd BH24 . . . . . .**141** A4
Clovelly Rd
Emsworth PO10 . . . .**160** C4
North Hayling PO11 . . . . .**160** B2
Portsmouth PO4 . . . .**183** A2
Southampton SO14 . . . . .**103** A3
Southbourne PO10 . . . . .**137** B1
Clover Cl
Christchurch BH23 . . . . . .**208** A4
Gosport PO13 . . . .**155** A2
Locks Heath SO31 . . . . . .**128** C1
Clover Ct
New Milton BH25 . . . . . .**195** B2
Waterlooville PO7 . . . . . .**135** A3
Clover Dr BH17 . . . .**186** C1
Clover Nooke SO15 . . . .**101** B4
Clover Way
Hedge End SO30 . . . .**105** A3
Romsey SO51 . . . .**53** B4
Clovers The BH12 . . . . . .**204** A4
Clowes Ave BH6 . . . .**207** A2
Clump Hill BH21 . . . .**114** A1
Cluster Ind Est PO4 . . . .**183** A3
Clyde Ct SO14 . . . .**103** A3
Clyde Ho 24 SO14 . . . . . .**103** A3
Clyde Rd Gosport PO12 . .**180** C3
Poole BH17 . . . .**187** A1
Clydebank Rd PO2 . . . . . .**182** B4
Clydesdale Rd PO15 . . . .**129** A4
Clydesdale Way SO40 . . .**100** A4
Coach Hill PO14 . . . .**153** C4
Coach Hill Cl SO53 . . . . . .**55** A4
Coach Hill La BH24 . . . . .**142** C3
Coach House Pl BH1 . . . .**205** A3
Coach Rd SO31 . . . .**127** C2
Coach Rd The
East Tytherley SP5 . . . .**4** B4
West Tytherley SP5 . . . .**4** B4
Coach-House Mews
PO4 . . . .**183** B2
Coachmans Copse SO18 . .**80** A1
Coachmans Halt PO7 . . . .**86** B1
Coal Park La SO31 . . . . . .**128** B4
Coalville Rd SO19 . . . . . .**104** A2
Coastguard Cl PO12 . . . .**180** C1
Coastguard Cotts
Exbury SO45 . . . .**178** A1
Havant PO9 . . . .**159** C3
Lymington SO41 . . . .**198** A1
Coastguard Way BH23 . . .**207** C3
Coat Gdns SO45 . . . .**126** A2
Coates Rd SO19 . . . .**104** B2
Coates Way PO7 . . . .**134** C4
Cobalt Ct PO13 . . . .**180** B3
Cobb's Rd BH21 . . . .**163** C3

Cobbett Cl SO22 . . . .**10** B3
Cobbett Ct 15 SO18 . . . .**103** C4
Cobbett Rd SO18 . . . . . .**103** C4
Cobbett Way SO30 . . . . .**105** C4
Cobblers Cnr SO41 . . . . .**173** A2
Cobblewood PO10 . . . . . .**136** C2
Cobbs La BH15 . . . .**202** C3
Cobden Ave
Portsmouth PO3 . . . .**183** A4
Southampton SO18 . . . . .**103** C4
Cobden Cres SO18 . . . . .**103** C4
Cobden Ct SO18 . . . .**103** C4
Cobden Gdns SO18 . . . . . .**79** C1
Cobden Hts SO18 . . . .**79** C1
Cobden Marine Ct SO17 **103** B4
Cobden Rise SO18 . . . . . .**79** C1
Cobden St PO12 . . . .**181** A3
Cobham Gr PO15 . . . . . .**129** C3
Cobham Rd
Bournemouth BH9 . . . . . .**190** A2
Ferndown BH21 . . . .**165** A4
Cobham Way BH21 . . . . .**163** C1
Coblands Ave SO30 . . . . .**100** B4
Coburg Ho 6 SO14 . . . . .**103** B3
Coburg St
Portsmouth PO1 . . . .**215** C4
Southampton SO14 . . . . .**103** B3
Cochrane Cl PO13 . . . . . .**180** B3
Cochrane Ho 15 PO1 . . . .**182** A3
Cockerell Cl
Locks Heath PO15 . . . . . .**129** B3
Oakley BH21 . . . .**163** C1
Cockleshell Cl SO31 . . . .**128** C1
Cockleshell Gdns PO4 . . .**183** B2
Cocklydown La SO40 . . . .**100** B3
Cockshott La GU32 . . . . . .**19** B1
Codogan Ct 14 BH1 . . . . .**205** A2
Cogdean Cl BH21 . . . . . .**186** A4
Cogdean Way BH21 . . . . .**186** A4
Cogdean Wlk BH21 . . . . .**186** A4
Cogdeane Rd BH17 . . . . .**187** B1
Coghlan Cl PO16 . . . .**131** A1
Coker Cl SO22 . . . .**10** C4
Colborne Ave BH21 . . . . .**163** C3
Colborne Cl SO41 . . . . . .**197** C3
Colbourne Cl
Bransgore BH23 . . . .**193** A4
Poole BH15 . . . .**202** B1
Colbourne Ct 6 SO23 . . . . .**2** A1
Colburn Cl SO16 . . . .**77** B1
Colbury Gr PO9 . . . .**135** B2
Colchester Ave SO50 . . . . .**56** C2
Colchester Rd PO6 . . . . .**133** C1
Cold East Cl SO31 . . . . . .**128** C1
Cold Harbour 7 PO17 . . .**107** C2
Coldeast Cl SO31 . . . . . .**128** C1
Coldeast Hospl SO31 . . . .**128** C1
Coldeast Way SO31 . . . . .**128** C1
Colden Common Prim Sch
SO21 . . . .**56** C4
Coldharbour Farm Rd
PO10 . . . .**136** C1
Coldharbour La SO16,
SO51 . . . .**77** A4
Coldhill La PO8 . . . .**111** C4
Cole Hill SO32 . . . .**85** B3
Cole's La SP5 . . . .**48** C3
Colebrook Ave
Portsmouth PO3 . . . .**183** A4
Southampton SO15 . . . . . .**78** B1
Colebrook Rd SO23 . . . . . .**11** A4
Colebrook St SO23 . . . . . .**11** A4
Colehill Cres BH9 . . . . . .**190** A2
Colehill Fst Sch BH21 . . .**164** A4
Colehill La BH21 . . . .**163** C4
Coleman Rd BH11 . . . . . .**189** A4
Coleman St SO14 . . . . . .**103** A4
Colemore Rd BH7 . . . . . .**206** B4
Colemore Sq PO9 . . . . . .**135** C2
Colenso Rd PO16 . . . . . .**131** A1
Coleridge Cl SO31 . . . . . .**128** B1
Coleridge Ct SO19 . . . . . .**104** B3
Coleridge Gdns PO8 . . . .**111** C4
Coleridge Gn BH23 . . . . .**207** C4
Coleridge Rd PO6 . . . . . .**132** C1
Coles Ave BH15 . . . .**201** C4
Coles Cl SO21 . . . .**32** A4
Coles Gdns BH15 . . . . . .**201** C4
Coles Mede SO21 . . . .**31** A2
Colesbourne Rd PO6 . . . .**133** A4
Coleson Rd SO18 . . . . . .**103** C4
Coleville Ave SO45 . . . . .**151** A4
Colin Cl BH21 . . . .**186** B3
Colinton Ave PO16 . . . . .**132** B1
Coll of Air Traffic Control
BH23 . . . .**190** C4
Collard Way 4 GU33 . . . .**20** C1
College Cl
Hamble-le-Rice SO31 . . . .**127** C1
Rowland's Castle PO9 . . .**113** B1
College Keep SO14 . . . . .**103** A4
College La 16 PO1 . . . . .**182** A3
College Park Inf Sch
PO2 . . . .**157** C1
College Pl 8 SO15 . . . . .**103** A4
College Rd
Bournemouth BH5 . . . . . .**206** A2
Portsmouth PO1 . . . .**182** A3
Ringwood BH24 . . . .**141** A4
Southampton SO19 . . . . .**103** C1
Waterlooville PO7 . . . . . .**134** C2
College St
Petersfield GU31, GU32 . .**40** C2
Portsmouth PO1 . . . .**182** A3
Southampton SO14 . . . . .**103** A4
Winchester SO23 . . . .**11** A4
College Wlk SO23 . . . .**11** A3
Collett Cl SO30 . . . .**81** C1
Colley Cl SO23 . . . .**2** A2

Collier Cl SO17 . . . .**103** B4
Collingbourne Ave BH6 .**206** B4
Collingbourne Dr SO53 . .**55** A3
Collington Cres PO6 . . . .**133** A1
Collingwood Ho PO15 . . .**130** B1
Collingwood Rd
Portsmouth PO5 . . . .**182** B1
West Moors BH31 . . . . . .**138** C3
Collingwood Ret Pk
PO14 . . . .**155** A3
Collingworth Rise SO31 **129** A3
Collins Cl SO53 . . . .**54** C3
Collins Ho SO53 . . . .**55** B3
Collins La
Ringwood BH24 . . . .**141** A4
South Harting GU31 . . . . .**66** C4
Collins Rd PO4 . . . .**183** A1
Collins' La SO21 . . . .**30** A4
Collis Rd PO3 . . . .**183** A4
Collwood Cl BH15 . . . . . .**202** B4
Collyers Rd SO42 . . . . . .**172** C4
Colman Cl BH1 . . . .**205** B2
Colne Ave SO16 . . . .**77** B3
Colne Ct SO16 . . . .**77** C1
Colombine Cl BH23 . . . . .**193** B1
Colonnade Rd 5 BH5 . . . .**206** A3
Colonnade Rd W 4
BH5 . . . .**206** A3
Colonnade The SO19 . . .**103** B2
Colpoy St PO5 . . . .**215** A2
Colson Cl SO23 . . . .**11** A4
Colson Rd SO23 . . . .**11** A4
Colt Cl Rownhams SO16 . . .**77** C3
Wimborne Minst BH21 . . .**164** C1
Colton Copse SO53 . . . . . .**54** C3
Colts Rd SO16 . . . .**77** C4
Coltsfoot Cl SO30 . . . . . .**105** A4
Coltsfoot Dr
Locks Heath SO31 . . . . . .**128** C1
4 Waterlooville PO7 . . . .**134** C4
Coltsfoot Wlk SO51 . . . . .**28** B1
Coltsmead PO6 . . . .**156** C4
Columbia Rd BH10 . . . . .**189** B1
Columbia Trees La
BH10 . . . .**189** B1
Columbian Way BH10 . . .**189** B1
Colvedene Cl SO21 . . . . . .**31** C1
Colville Cl BH5 . . . .**206** A3
Colville Dr SO32 . . . .**83** B4
Colville Rd
6 Bournemouth BH5 . . .**206** A3
Cosham PO6 . . . .**158** A4
Colvin Gdns SO53 . . . .**55** A4
Colwell Cl SO16 . . . .**101** A4
Colwell Rd PO6 . . . .**157** C4
Combe Down SO21 . . . . . .**31** C4
Combe Rd SO31 . . . .**21** A1
Comber Rd 5 BH9 . . . . . .**190** A2
Comet Way BH21 . . . . . .**208** A3
Comfrey Cl Horndean PO8 .**88** B2
Romsey SO51 . . . .**28** B1
Comines Way SO30 . . . . .**104** C4
Comley Hill PO9 . . . .**136** B3
Comley Rd BH9 . . . .**189** C1
Commercial Pl PO1 . . . . .**215** B4
Commercial Rd
Bournemouth BH2 . . . . . .**204** C2
Poole BH14 . . . .**203** A2
Portsmouth PO1 . . . .**215** A2
Southampton SO15 . . . . .**102** C3
Totton SO40 . . . .**101** C4
Commercial St SO18 . . . .**104** A4
Commodore Ct 30 SO14 **103** A4
Common Barn La PO13 . .**179** C2
Common Cl SO53 . . . .**55** B4
Common Gdns SO53 . . . . .**55** B4
Common Hill Rd SO51 . . . .**28** B3
Common La
Southwick PO17 . . . .**132** C4
Titchfield PO14 . . . .**153** C4
Common Rd
Chandler's Ford SO53 . . . .**55** B4
Westbourne PO10 . . . . . .**137** C3
Whiteparish SP5 . . . .**24** A1
Common St PO1 . . . .**215** C4
Commonside PO10 . . . . . .**137** A3
Compass Cl
Gosport PO13 . . . .**180** B3
Southampton SO19 . . . . .**104** C4
Compass Point
Fareham PO16 . . . .**155** C2
Hamble-le-Rice SO31 . . . .**127** C1
Compass Pk PO6 . . . .**157** A4
Compton & Up Marden CE
Prim Sch PO18 . . . .**90** C1
Compton Acres Gdns★
BH13 . . . .**214** C4
Compton All Saints CE Prim
Sch SO21 . . . .**31** B4
Compton Ave BH14 . . . . .**203** B1
Compton Beeches
BH24 . . . .**140** A3
Compton Cl
Eastleigh SO50 . . . .**55** C3
Havant PO9 . . . .**135** C2
25 Lee-on-the-Solent
PO13 . . . .**179** C1
Verwood BH31 . . . .**114** C3
Winchester SO22 . . . .**10** A2
Compton Cres BH22 . . . .**139** A1
Compton Ct
4 Havant PO9 . . . .**135** C1
Poole BH14 . . . .**203** B2
Compton Dr BH14 . . . . . .**203** B1
Compton Gdns BH14 . . . .**203** B1
Compton Ho 4 SO16 . . . .**102** A4
Compton Rd
New Milton BH25 . . . . . .**195** A1

Compton Rd continued
Portsmouth PO2 . . . .**157** C2
Totton SO40 . . . .**101** A4
Winchester SO23 . . . .**10** C4
Compton St SO21 . . . .**31** B4
Compton Way SO22 . . . . .**10** A2
Compton Wlk 23 SO14 . .**103** A3
Compton's Dr SO51 . . . . .**50** A3
Conan Rd PO2 . . . .**157** C2
Concorde Cl PO15 . . . . . .**129** B3
Concorde Way PO15 . . . .**129** B3
Condor Ave PO16 . . . . . .**155** C4
Condor Cl
Southampton SO19 . . . . .**103** B2
Three Legged Cross BH21 **139** A3
Coney Gn 4 SO23 . . . .**2** A1
Conference Dr SO31 . . . .**129** A2
Conference Pl 11 SO41 . .**197** C1
Conford Ct PO9 . . . .**135** B3
Congleton Cl SO43 . . . . . .**98** B2
Conifer Ave BH14 . . . . . .**203** A1
Conifer Cl
Christchurch BH23 . . . . . .**191** B2
Ferndown BH22 . . . .**165** C1
Hythe SO45 . . . .**125** C2
St Leonards BH24 . . . . . .**139** B2
Waterlooville PO8 . . . . . .**112** A1
Winchester SO22 . . . .**1** C1
Conifer Cres SO41 . . . . . .**197** A3
Conifer Gr PO13 . . . .**155** B2
Conifer Mews PO16 . . . . .**132** B1
Conifer Rd SO16 . . . .**78** A2
Conigar Rd PO10 . . . .**136** C2
Coniston Ave
Bournemouth BH11 . . . . .**188** C3
Portsmouth PO3 . . . .**183** A4
Coniston Cl BH31 . . . . . .**114** C4
Coniston Gdns SO30 . . . .**105** A3
Coniston Ho 19 PO6 . . . .**133** A1
Coniston Rd
Eastleigh SO50 . . . .**55** C1
Ringwood BH24 . . . .**141** A3
Southampton SO16 . . . . .**101** B4
Coniston Wlk PO14 . . . . .**154** C4
Connaught Cl BH25 . . . . .**194** C1
Connaught Cres BH12 . . .**203** C3
Connaught Hall SO18 . . . .**79** B2
Connaught La PO6 . . . . . .**156** C4
Connaught Pl 5 PO9 . . . .**136** A1
Connaught Rd
Bournemouth BH5 . . . . . .**206** A3
Havant PO9 . . . .**136** A1
Portsmouth PO2 . . . .**157** A2
Connell Rd BH15 . . . .**202** B3
Connemara Cres PO15 . . .**129** A4
Connigar Cl PO13 . . . . . .**180** B2
Conqueror Way PO14 . . .**179** B3
Conrad Gdns PO15 . . . . .**129** B4
Conservatory The 48
SO23 . . . .**11** A4
Consort Cl Eastleigh SO50 .**56** A3
Poole BH12 . . . .**203** B3
Consort Ho 9 PO1 . . . . . .**182** B4
Consort Rd SO50 . . . .**56** C2
Constable Cl
Gosport PO12 . . . .**181** B1
Southampton SO19 . . . . .**104** B1
Constables Gate 28 SO22 **10** C4
Constantine Ave SO53 . . .**55** C4
Constantine Cl SO53 . . . . .**55** C4
Constitution Hill Gdns
BH14 . . . .**203** A3
Constitution Hill Rd
BH14 . . . .**203** A3
Consulate Ho 32 SO14 . .**103** A4
Convent Ct PO10 . . . .**160** C4
Convent La PO10 . . . .**160** C4
Conway Cl
Chandler's Ford SO53 . . . .**55** C3
New Milton BH25 . . . . . .**195** A2
Conway Ct 20 BH25 . . . . .**195** A2
Conways Dr BH14 . . . . . .**203** A2
Cook Cl BH24 . . . .**141** B4
Cook Row BH21 . . . .**163** A2
Cook St SO14 . . . .**103** A2
Cooke Gdns BH12 . . . . . .**203** C3
Cooke Rd BH12 . . . .**203** C3
Cooks La Awbridge SO51 . .**27** A2
Lockerley SO51 . . . .**25** C4
Southbourne SO20 . . . . .**137** C1
Totton SO40 . . . .**76** B2
Cooley Ho PO13 . . . .**155** A3
Coolhurst BH14 . . . .**214** B4
Coombe Ave BH10 . . . . .**189** C2
Coombe Farm Ave
PO16 . . . .**155** A4
Coombe Gdns BH10 . . . .**189** C2
Coombe La SO41 . . . .**196** B4
Coombe Rd
East Meon GU32 . . . .**63** B4
Gosport PO12 . . . .**181** A4
Coombe Road Terr GU32 **63** B4
Coombedale SO31 . . . . . .**129** A1
Coombs Cl PO8 . . . .**88** B2
Cooper Dean Dr BH8 . . . .**190** C1
Cooper Dean Rdbt BH7,
BH8 . . . .**191** A1
Cooper Gr PO16 . . . .**156** B3
Cooper Rd Ashurst SO40 .**100** B4
Portsmouth PO3 . . . .**183** A4
Cooper's Cl
West End SO18 . . . .**80** B1
West Wellow SO51 . . . . . .**51** A1
Cooper's La SO19 . . . . . .**103** B2
Coopers Ct SO14 . . . .**103** A2

Coopers La BH31 ......114 C4
Copeland Dr BH14 .....203 A4
Copeland Rd SO16 ......77 B1
Copenhagen Twrs �
SO19 ....126 C4
Copinger Cl SO40 ......100 B3
Copnor Bridge Bsns Ctr
PO3 ....183 A4
Copnor Inf & Jun Sch
PO3 ....158 A1
Copnor Rd PO3 ....157 C2
Copper Beech Cl BH12 .204 A2
Copper Beech Dr PO6 ..158 C4
Copper Beech Gdns
BH10 ....189 B1
Copper Beeches SO45 .150 C1
Copper St 🟢 PO5 .....215 A1
Coppercourt Leaze 🟢
BH21 ....163 B2
Copperfield Ho 🟤 PO1 .182 B4
Copperfield Rd SO16 ....79 A3
Copperfields SO40 .....100 A3
Coppers Cl SP6 ....93 A3
Coppice Ave BH22 .....165 A4
Coppice Cl
New Milton BH25 ......195 B2
St Leonards BH24 .....139 C2
Winchester SO22 ....1 B1
Coppice Hill SO32 ......83 B4
Coppice Rd SO40 ......76 B1
Coppice The
Brockenhurst SO42 ....145 B1
Christchurch BH23 ....208 A3
Gosport PO13 ....155 B1
Waterlooville PO8 ....112 A3
Coppice View BH10 ...189 C2
Coppice Way PO15 ....130 B2
Coppins Gr PO16 ......156 B3
Copse Ave BH25 ......195 A1
Copse Cl Liss GU33 .....21 A1
North Baddesley SO52 ..53 C2
Otterbourne SO21 ......31 B2
Petersfield GU31 ....41 B2
Poole BH14 ....202 C2
Totton SO40 ....100 C3
Waterlooville PO7 ....134 B1
Copse Cvn Pk The SO40 .99 B3
Copse La Chilworth SO16 .54 C1
Gosport PO13 ....155 B1
Hamble-le-Rice SO31 ..127 C1
North Hayling PO11 ...160 A1
Copse Rd Burley BH24 .142 C1
New Milton BH25 ......195 A1
Southampton SO18 .....80 A1
Verwood BH31 ....114 C3
Copse The
Chandler's Ford SO53 ..55 C3
Fareham PO15 ....130 B2
Romsey SO51 ....28 B1
Copse View SO19 .....104 C3
Copse Way BH23 ......208 C4
Copsewood Ave BH8 ..190 C1
Copsewood Rd
Ashurst SO40 ....100 A4
Hythe SO45 ....125 C2
Southampton SO18 .....79 C1
Copsey Cl PO6 ....158 B4
Copsey Gr PO6 ....158 B4
Copthorne Cotts SO45 .151 B2
Copthorne La SO45 ....151 A2
Copythorn Rd PO2 ....157 C1
Copythorne CE Inf Sch
SO40 ....75 A1
Copythorne Cl BH8 ....190 B1
Copythorne Cres SO40 ..75 B1
Coracle Cl SO31 ......128 C1
Coral Cl PO16 ....156 B3
Coral Ct Gosport PO13 .180 B3
🟢 Poole BH12 ....204 A2
Coralin Gr PO7 ....112 A1
Coram Cl 🟥 SO23 ......2 A1
Corbar Rd BH23 ......206 C4
Corbett Rd PO7 ....134 B3
Corbiere Ave BH12 ...188 B1
Corbiere Cl SO16 ......77 C2
Corbin Ave BH22 .....166 A3
Corbin Ct SO41 ......197 A1
Corbin Rd SO41 ......197 A1
Corbould Rd SO45 ....149 C4
Corby Cres PO3 ....158 A2
Cordelia Cl SO45 .....125 B2
Corfe Cl PO14 ....179 A3
Corfe Halt Cl BH21 ...162 C1
Corfe Hills Sch BH18 .186 C1
Corfe Lodge Rd BH18,
BH21 ....186 B2
Corfe Mews BH15 ....202 B2
Corfe View Rd
Corfe Mullen BH21 ...186 B3
Poole BH14 ....203 B2
Corfe Way BH18 ......186 C2
Corfu BH13 ....214 C3
Corhampton Cres PO9 .135 B2
Corhampton Ho 🟤 PO1 215 C4
Corhampton La
Droxford SO32 ....60 B3
Meonstoke SO32 ....61 A3
Corhampton Rd BH6 ..206 B3
Coriander Dr SO40 ...100 B4
Coriander Way PO15 ..129 B4
Corinna Gdns SO45 ...125 B2
Corinthian Rd SO53 ....55 C4
Cork La SO40 ....101 C1
Cormorant Cl PO16 ...155 C4
Cormorant Dr SO45 ...126 B1

Cormorant Wlk PO13 ..155 A1
Corn Mkt SO51 ....52 C4
Cornaway La PO16 ....156 A4
Cornbrook Gr PO7 ....112 B1
Cornel Rd SO19 ......103 C3
Cornelia Cres PO1 ....204 A3
Cornelius Dr PO7 .....112 A1
Corner Mead PO7 .....112 A1
Cornerways Rd 🟤 BH25 195 A1
Cornes Cl SO22 ....10 B4
Cornfield PO16 ....131 A2
Cornfield Cl SO53 ......54 C3
Cornfield Rd PO13 ....179 C1
Cornflower Cl SO31 ...128 C2
Cornflower Dr BH23 ..208 B4
Cornford Way BH23 ..208 B4
Cornforth Rd SO40 ....76 B1
Cornish Gdns BH10 ...189 B1
Cornpits La SP6 ....68 B2
Cornwall Cl 🟤 SO18 ..80 A1
Cornwall Cres SO18 ...79 C1
Cornwall Rd
Chandler's Ford SO53 ..55 B3
Portsmouth PO1 ......182 C3
Southampton SO18 .....79 C1
Cornwallis Cres PO1 ..215 C4
Cornwallis Ho PO1 ...215 B4
Cornwallis Rd SO41 ..211 A2
Cornwell Cl
Gosport PO13 ....180 B4
Portsmouth PO2 ......157 A1
Coronado Rd PO12 ...181 A4
Coronation Ave
Bournemouth BH9 ....189 C1
Upton BH16 ....201 A4
Coronation Cl BH31 ..114 C4
Coronation Eventide Homes
🟥 PO2 ....157 C2
Coronation Homes
SO18 ....104 B4
Coronation Par SO31 .127 C2
Coronation Rd
South Hayling PO11 ...185 C1
Swanmore SO32 ......84 A3
Verwood BH31 ....114 C4
Waterlooville PO7 ....134 C4
Coronation Terr SP6 ...69 A1
Corporation Rd BH1 ..205 B3
Corpus Christi RC Prim Sch
Bournemouth BH5 ....206 A3
Portsmouth PO2 ......157 B1
Corsair Dr SO45 ......125 B2
Corscombe Cl BH17 ..187 C1
Cort Way PO15 ....130 B2
Cortina Way SO30 ....105 B3
Cortry Cl BH12 ....204 A4
Corvette Ave SO31 ...128 C1
Cosford Cl SO50 ....57 A1
Cosham Park Ave PO6 .157 C4
Cosham Sta PO6 .....157 C4
Cossack Gn 🟤 SO14 .103 A2
Cossack La 🟤 SO23 ..11 A4
Cossack Lane Ho 🟤
SO23 ....11 A4
Cosworth Dr SO45 ...125 B2
Cotes Ave BH14 .....203 A3
Cotes Ct BH14 ....203 A3
Cotlands Rd BH1 .....205 A2
Cotsalls SO50 ....57 B1
Cotswold Cl
🟤 Christchurch BH23 .207 C4
🟤 Southampton SO17 ..79 A1
Cotswold Ho 🟤 PO6 ..157 B4
Cotswold Rd SO16 ...101 C4
Cotswold Wlk 🟤 PO14 154 C4
Cott La BH24 ....143 A1
Cott St SO32 ....84 B2
Cott Street La SO32 ...84 C2
Cottage Cl PO7 ....110 C2
Cottage Gdns BH12 ..203 B3
Cottage Gr Gosport PO12 181 A3
Portsmouth PO5 .....215 B2

Court Cl continued
Lymington SO41 ......197 B1
Southampton SO18 ...104 A3
Totton SO40 ....76 B1
Court Cotts SO41 ....197 B1
Court Hill SP6 ....68 C3
Court House Cl 🟤 SO45 126 A2
Court La PO6 ....158 A4
Court Lane Inf Sch PO6 158 A4
Court Lane Jun Sch
PO6 ....158 A4
Court Mead PO6 .....158 A4
Court Rd
Bournemouth BH9 ....190 A1
Kings Worthy SO23 .....2 B3
Lee-on-the-Solent PO13 179 C2
Southampton SO15 ...102 C4
Court Royal Mews SO15 102 C4
Courtenay Ave BH8 ..190 C1
Courtenay Pl SO41 ...197 C2
Courtenay Rd
Poole BH14 ....203 A2
Winchester SO23 ....2 A2
Courthill Fst Sch BH14 .203 B2
Courthill Rd BH14 ....203 B2
Courtier Cl SO45 .....125 B2
Courtland Gdns SO16 ..79 A3
Courtlands SO41 .....197 C2
Courtlands Terr PO8 ..112 A2
Courtleigh Manor 🟤
BH5 ....205 B2
Courtmount Gr PO6 ..158 A4
Courtnay Cl PO15 ....129 B2
Courtney Pl BH21 ....186 B3
Courtyard Cl SO42 ...145 C1
Courtyard Mews SO42 145 C1
Courtyard The
Christchurch BH23 ...207 B3
🟤 Petersfield GU31 ....40 C2
Poole BH12 ....188 B1
🟤 Romsey SO51 ....52 C4
Cousins Gr PO4 ......182 C1
Cove Rd BH10 ....189 B1
Covena Rd BH6 ......206 C3
Coventry Cl BH21 ....186 B2
Coventry Cres BH17 .187 A1
Coventry Ct
Gosport PO13 ....180 B3
🟤 Winchester SO23 ....2 A1
Coventry Rd SO15 ...102 C3
Coverack Way PO6 ..157 A4
Covert Gr PO7 ....135 A3
Covert The SO51 ......53 A3
Covindale Ho 🟤 PO4 .183 A2
Covington Rd PO10 ..137 A3
Cow La Cosham PO6 ..157 B4
Portchester PO16 ....156 B4
Coward Rd PO7 ......134 B3
Coward Rd PO12 ....180 C1
Cowdray Cl
Bishopstoke SO50 .....56 C1
Southampton SO16 ....78 A2
Cowdray Ho PO1 .....215 C3
Cowdray Pk PO14 ...179 A3
Cowdrey Gdns BH8 ..190 C1
Cowdrys Field 🟤 BH21 163 A3
Cowell Dr BH7 ....206 A4
Cowes La SO31 ......152 B3
Cowgrove Rd BH21 ..162 C3
Cowleas Cl SO51 ......26 C3
Cowleas Cotts SO51 ..26 C3
Cowley Cl SO16 ....77 C1
Cowley Rd
Lymington SO41 ......197 B2
Poole BH17 ....202 B4
Cowleys Rd BH23 ....192 B1
Cowper Ave BH25 ...195 A1
Cowper Rd
Bournemouth BH9 ....189 C1
Portsmouth PO1 .....182 C4
Southampton SO19 ..103 B3
Cowpitts La BH24 ....117 B1
Cowplain Sch PO8 ...111 C2
Cowslip Cl Gosport PO13 155 B1
Locks Heath SO31 ....128 C1
Cowslip Rd BH18 ....186 C1
Cowslip Way SO51 ....28 B1
Cox Ave BH9 ....190 A2
Cox Cl BH9 ....190 A2
Cox Dale PO14 ....129 B1
Cox Row SO53 ....55 B2
Cox's Dr SO19 ....104 A1
Cox's La SO19 ....103 B2
Coxes Mdw GU32 .....40 C3
Coxford Cl SO16 ......78 A1
Coxford Dro SO16 ....78 A2
Coxford Rd SO16 ......78 A2
Coxs Hill SO21 ....32 A4
Coxstone La 🟤 BH24 .141 A3
Coy Pond Rd BH12 ..204 A3
Cozens Cl SO19 .....103 C3
Crab Orchard Way
BH21 ....114 C1
Crabapple Cl SO40 ..100 B4
Crabbe Ct PO5 ......215 B2
Crabbs Way SO40 ...100 A4
Crabbswood La SO41 195 C4
Crabden La PO8 ....88 C1
Crableck La SO31 ....128 C2
Crabton Close Rd BH5 205 C2
Crabtree SO16 ....77 C1
Crabtree Cl BH23 ....192 B1
Crabwood Cl SO16 ...77 C1
Crabwood Ct PO9 ...135 C4
Crabwood Dr SO30 ..80 C1
Crabwood Rd SO16 ..77 C1

Cracknore Hard SO40 .102 A1
Cracknore Hard La
SO40 ....102 A1
Cracknore Rd SO15 ..102 B3
Craddock Ho
🟤 Portsmouth PO1 ...182 A3
🟤 Winchester SO23 ...11 B4
Craigmoor Ave BH8 ..190 C1
Craigmoor Cl BH8 ...190 C1
Craigmoor Way BH8 .190 C1
Craigside Rd BH24 ..139 B2
Craigwell Rd PO7 ....134 B2
Craigwood Dr BH22 .165 C2
Crampmoor La SO51 ..28 C1
Cranberry Cl SO40 ...101 C1
Cranborne Cres BH12 203 C4
Cranborne Ct
Bournemouth BH9 ....205 A4
🟤 Bournemouth, Westbourne
BH4 ....204 B2
Cranborne Gdns SO53 .30 A1
Cranborne Pl BH25 ..194 C2
Cranborne Rd
Alderholt SP6, BH21 ..92 A3
Bournemouth BH2 ....204 C4
Cosham PO6 ....134 A1
Wimborne Minst BH21 163 B2
Cranborne Wlk PO14 154 C4
Cranbourne Cl BH17 ..188 A1
Cranbourne Dr SO21 ..31 A2
Cranbourne Pk SO30 ..105 B2
Cranbourne Rd PO12 181 B2
Cranbrook Mews BH12 203 A3
Cranbrook Rd BH12 ..203 A3
Cranbury Ave SO14 ..103 A3
Cranbury Cl Downton SP5 46 C3
Otterbourne SO21 ....31 A2
Cranbury Ct SO19 ...103 C2
Cranbury Gdns SO31 104 C1
Cranbury Pl SO14 ...103 A3
Cranbury Rd
Eastleigh SO50 ....56 A1
Southampton SO19 ..103 C2
Cranbury Terr 🟤 SO14 103 A3
Cranbury The 🟤 SO14 103 A3
Cranbury Twrs 🟤 SO14 103 A3
Crane Cl Gosport PO13 155 A1
Verwood BH31 ......114 C3
Crane Dr BH31 ......114 C4
Crane Way BH23 ....139 A3
Cranemoor Ave BH23 193 C1
Cranemoor Cl BH23 .193 C1
Cranemoor Gdns BH23 193 C1
Cranes Mews BH15 ..202 B2
Craneswater Ave PO4 182 C1
Craneswater Gate 🟤
PO4 ....182 C1
Craneswater Jun Sch
PO4 ....182 C1
Craneswater Mews 🟤
PO4 ....182 C1
Craneswater Pk PO4 .182 C1
Cranfield Ave BH21 ..163 B3
Cranford Gdns SO53 ..55 A4
Cranford Ho 🟤 SO17 ..79 A1
Cranford Rd GU32 .....40 B1
Cranford Way SO17 ..79 A1
Cranleigh Ave PO1 ..182 C3
Cranleigh Cl BH6 ...206 C3
Cranleigh Ct BH6 ...206 C3
Cranleigh Gdns BH6 206 C3
Cranleigh Ho
Hedge End SO30 ......81 B2
Southampton SO17 ..103 A4
Cranleigh Paddock
SO43 ....121 C3
Cranleigh Rd
Bournemouth BH6 ...206 C3
Hedge End SO30 ....105 B3
Portchester PO16 ...156 A4
Portsmouth PO1 ....182 C3
Cranmer Dr SO16 .....77 B3
Cranmer Rd BH9 ....204 C4
Cranmore SO31 .....127 B4
Cransley Ho 🟤 BH4 .204 B1
Crantock Gr BH8 ...190 C1
Cranwell Cl
Bournemouth BH11 .188 C2
Bransgore BH23 .....169 A1
Cranwell Ct SO16 .....77 C3
Cranworth Rd SO22 ...1 C1
Crasswell St PO1 ....215 C4
Craven Ct PO15 .....130 C2
Craven Rd SO53 ......55 B3
Craven St 🟤 SO14 ..103 A3
Crawford Cl SO16 .....77 B3
Crawford Dr PO16 ...130 C2
Crawley Ave PO9 ....136 A3
Crawley Hill SO51 ....50 C1
Crawshaw Rd BH14 .203 A4
Crawte Ave SO45 ...150 B1
Crawters La 🟤 GU31 ..40 C2
Cray Ho PO12 ....181 B2
Creasey Rd BH11 ...189 A3
Credenhill Rd PO6 ...133 B1
Creech Rd BH12 ....203 B3
Creech View PO7 ....110 C2
Creech Wood Forest Wlk*
PO7 ....110 B2
Creedy Gdns SO18 ...80 A2
Creek End PO10 ....160 C4
Creek Rd Gosport PO12 181 B2
South Hayling PO11 ..185 B1
Creekmoor La BH17 ..202 A4
Creighton Rd SO15 ..101 C4
Cremorne Pl 🟤 GU32 .40 C2
Cremyll Cl PO14 .....179 B3

Crescent Cl SO22 ......10 C3
Crescent Cotts SO45 .177 A3
Crescent Ct BH25 ...209 B4
Crescent Dr BH25 ...209 C4
Crescent Ho 🟤 SO50 ..56 A2
Crescent Prim Sch SO50 .56 A2
Crescent Rd
Bournemouth BH2 ...204 C2
Fareham PO16 ....131 A1
Gosport PO12 ....181 A1
Locks Heath SO31 ..128 C1
North Baddesley SO52 53 C3
Poole BH14 ....203 C2
Verwood BH31 ......115 A3
Wimborne Minst BH21 163 B2
Crescent The
Barton on Sea BH25 .209 B4
🟤 Bournemouth BH7 ..205 C2
Eastleigh SO50 ....56 A2
Exbury SO45 ....177 A3
Marchwood SO40 ...101 C1
Netley SO31 ....127 B3
Netley Marsh SO40 ...99 C2
Romsey SO51 ....53 A4
Southampton SO19 ..104 A1
Southbourne PO10 ..161 B4
Twyford SO21 ....32 A3
Upham SO32 ....58 B1
Waterlooville PO7 ...134 C2
Crescent Wlk BH22 .165 C1
Cressey Rd SO51 .....52 C4
Cressy Rd PO2 ......182 A3
Crest Cl PO16 ....131 B1
Crest Rd BH12 ......203 B3
Crest The PO7 ....134 B1
Crest Way SO19 ....104 A3
Cresta Ct 🟤 PO4 ....182 C1
Cresta Gdns BH22 ..165 C1
Crestland Cl PO8 ....112 A2
Crestwood Com Sch
SO50 ....55 C3
Crete Cotts SO45 ...125 C1
Crete La SO45 ......125 C1
Crete Rd SO45 ......125 C1
Cribb Cl BH17 ......202 C4
Crichel Mount Rd BH14 214 B4
Crichel Rd BH9 .....205 A4
Crichton Ho 🟤 SO31 .127 A3
Cricket Cl BH23 ....207 C3
Cricket Dr PO8 .....112 A3
Cricklemede SO32 ...83 B4
Cricklewood Cl SO32 83 B4
Crigdon Cl SO16 ....101 C4
Crimea Rd BH9 .....204 C4
Cringle Ave BH6 ....207 A2
Crinoline Gdns PO4 .183 A1
Cripple Gate La
Beaulieu SO42 ......175 B3
East Boldre SO42 ...175 B3
Cripstead La SO23 ...10 C3
Crispen Cl BH23 ....208 C4
Crispin Cl Fair Oak SO50 .81 B3
Locks Heath SO31 ..129 A2
Crisspyn Cl PO8 ....112 A3
Criterion Arc 🟤 BH1 .204 C2
Crittall Cl SO41 ....172 B1
Crockford Cl BH25 ..195 A3
Crockford Rd PO10 .137 A2
Croft Cl BH21 ......186 B3
Croft Hts SP5 ....24 A2
Croft La PO11 ......159 C1
Croft Rd
Bournemouth BH9 ...189 C1
Bransgore BH23 ....193 A3
Christchurch BH23 ..207 C4
Poole BH12 ....203 B3
Portsmouth PO2 ...157 B1
Ringwood BH24 ....117 B1
Croft The
Chandler's Ford SO53 .55 B3
Crouchheston SP5 ...22 A4
Stubbington PO14 ..154 B2
Totton SO40 ....76 B1
Croftlands Ave PO14 154 B2
Crofton Anne Dale Jun Sch
PO14 ....179 A3
Crofton Ave PO13 ..179 B3
Crofton Cl
Christchurch BH23 .191 C1
Southampton SO17 ..79 A1
Waterlooville PO7 ..134 B3
Crofton Ct PO14 ...179 B3
Crofton Hammond Jun & Inf
Schs PO14 ....179 A3
Crofton La PO14 ...179 A3
Crofton Rd
Portsmouth, Milton PO4 183 A3
Portsmouth, North End
PO2 ....157 C1
Crofton Sch PO14 ..179 C3
Crofton Way
Locks Heath SO31 ..128 B1
Swanmore SO32 .....84 A3
Cromalt Cl SO45 ...125 B1
Cromarty Ave PO4 ..183 A3
Cromarty Cl PO14 ..154 A2
Cromarty Rd SO16 ..77 C3
Crombie Cl PO8 ....111 C2
Cromer Gdns BH12 .203 C3
Cromer Rd
Bournemouth BH8 ..205 B4
Cosham PO6 ....133 C1
Poole BH12 ....203 C3
Southampton SO16 ..77 B1
Cromhall Cl PO14 ..154 B4
Crompton Way PO15 129 B3
Cromwell Pl 🟤 BH5 ..206 A3

Cromwell Rd
Bournemouth BH5 ......206 A3
Poole BH12 ....203 B3
Portsmouth PO4 ......183 A1
Southampton SO15 ....102 C4
16 Wimborne Minst BH21 .163 B2
Winchester SO22 ....10 C3
Crondall Ave PO9 .....135 C3
Crood Ct 7 PO16 .....131 B1
Crooked Hays Cl SO40 .101 C1
Crooked Walk La PO17 .132 C2
Crookham Cl PO9 ......135 B2
Crookham Rd SO19 ....126 C4
Crookhorn Com Sch The
PO7 ....134 C2
Crookhorn La
Soberton SO32 ....85 B4
Waterlooville PO7 ......134 C2
Crosby Rd BH4 ....204 B1
Crosfield Cl SO51 ......51 A1
Cross House Ctr SO14 ..103 C2
Cross Keys Pas 29 SO23 ..11 A4
Cross La
Bishop's Waltham SO32 ..59 A1
Waterlooville PO8 ......112 A3
Cross Lanes BH24 ......117 B4
Cross Rd
Lee-on-the-Solent PO13 ..180 A2
Southampton SO19 .....103 C4
Cross St
6 Bishop's Waltham SO32 .83 B4
Portsmouth PO5 ....215 C2
Portsmouth, Portsea PO1 .182 A3
Winchester SO23 ....10 C4
Cross The Burley BH24 ..143 A4
East Meon GU32 ....38 B1
Cross Trees SP6 ....46 A1
Cross Way
Christchurch BH23 .....191 B1
Compton(Hants) SO21 ...31 B3
Havant PO9 ....135 C1
Cross Ways BH23 ....169 A3
Crossbill Cl PO8 ....112 A4
Crosshouse Rd SO14 ....103 B2
Crossland Cl PO9 ....102 B3
Crossland Dr PO9 ......136 A2
Crossley Cl 6 SO15 ....102 B3
Crossmead Ave BH25 ..195 A1
Crossway The PO16 ....156 B4
Crossways SO41 ....196 B1
Crossways Cl SP5 ....46 C4
Crossways The
Denmead PO7 ....111 A4
Gosport PO12 ....181 B4
Upton BH16 ....201 B4
Crosswell Cl SO19 ......104 B3
Crouch La PO8 ....112 A4
Croucher's Croft SO22 ...1 B1
Crow Arch La BH24 ....141 A3
Crow Arch Lane Ind Est
BH24 ....141 A3
Crow Cotts BH24 ....141 B2
Crow Hill Top BH24 ....142 A3
Crow La BH24 ....141 B3
Crowder Terr SO22 ......10 C4
Crowders 1 SO21 ....56 C4
Crowe Hill Ct 2 BH15 ..202 B4
Crown Cl Poole BH12 ...203 B3
Waterlooville PO7 ......134 C2
Crown Ct
Portsmouth PO1 ....215 C4
8 Wimborne Minst BH21 .163 A3
Crown Mead BH21 ......163 B2
Crown Mews 18 PO12 ..181 B2
Crown St
Portsmouth PO1 ....215 C4
Southampton SO15 ....102 A4
Crown Wlk 9 BH7 ......205 C2
Crows Nest La SO32 .....81 C1
Crowsbury Cl PO10 .....136 C2
Crowsport SO31 ....128 A2
Crowther Cl SO19 ......104 B2
Croydon Cl SO16 ....78 C4
Crummock Rd SO53 .....55 A4
Crusader Ct PO12 ......181 B4
Crusader Rd
Bournemouth BH11 ....188 B2
Hedge End SO30 ......105 B3
Crusader Way SO53 .....54 C3
Cruse Cl SO41 ....172 A1
Cruxton Farm Ctyd
BH21 ....163 B1
Crystal Way PO7 ....135 A4
Cucklington Gdns BH9 ..190 A4
Cuckmere La SO16 ......101 B4
Cuckoo Bushes La SO53 ..55 B4
Cuckoo Hill Rly ★ SP6 ...94 B1
Cuckoo Hill Way BH23 ..169 B1
Cuckoo La
22 Southampton SO14 ...102 C2
Stubbington PO14 .....154 A2
Cuckoo Rd BH12 ....203 A4
Cudnell Ave BH11 ......189 A3
Cudworth Mead SO30 ...81 B1
Cuffnells Cl BH24 ......117 A4
Cul-de-sac BH25 ....209 B4
Culford Ave SO40 ......100 C3
Culford Cl BH8 ....190 C1
Culford Ct 1 BH8 ......205 A3
Culford Way SO40 .....100 C3
Cull Cl BH12 ....204 B4
Cull La BH25 ....195 A4
Culliford Cres BH17 ....187 C1
Culloden Cl PO15 ......130 C1
Culloden Rd PO14 ......154 C3
Cullwood La BH25 ......195 B3
Culver SO31 ....127 B4

Culver Cl SO16 ....77 B1
Culver Dr PO11 ....185 B1
Culver Mews SO23 ......11 A4
Culver Rd
New Milton BH25 ......194 C1
Portsmouth PO4 ....183 A1
35 Winchester SO23 ......11 A4
Culverhayes Pl BH21 ...163 A3
Culverhayes Rd BH21 ...163 A3
Culverin Sq 3 PO23 ....158 A2
Culverlands Cl SO32 ...107 C4
Culverley Cl SO42 .....145 C1
Culverwell Gdns 25 SO23 .10 C4
Culvery Gdns SO18 .....80 A1
Cumber Rd SO31 ....128 C2
Cumberland Ave
Chandler's Ford SO53 ....55 C3
Emsworth PO10 ....136 C2
Cumberland Bsns Ctr
PO1 ....215 C3
Cumberland Cl SO53 ....55 C3
Cumberland Ho PO1 ....182 A4
Cumberland House Natural
History Mus ★ PO5 ....182 C1
Cumberland Inf Sch
PO4 ....183 A2
Cumberland Pl SO15 ...102 C3
Cumberland Rd PO1 ....215 D3
Cumberland St
Portsmouth PO1 ....182 A3
Southampton SO14 ....103 A2
Cumberland Way SO16 .125 B2
Cumbrian Way SO16 ...101 C4
Cummins Gn SO31 .....105 A1
Cumnor Rd BH1 ....205 C3
Cunard Ave SO15 ......102 B4
Cunard Rd SO14 ....103 A1
Cundell Way SO23 ....2 A4
Cunningham Ave SO32 ..83 A4
Cunningham Cl
Bournemouth BH11 ....189 A2
Christchurch BH23 .....208 A3
Portsmouth PO2 ....157 B2
Ringwood BH24 ....141 B4
Cunningham Cres
Bournemouth BH11 ....189 A2
Southampton SO19 ....104 A4
Cunningham Ct
New Milton BH25 ......194 C2
1 Portsmouth PO5 .....182 B1
Cunningham Dr
Gosport PO13 ....155 B2
Locks Heath SO31 .....129 A2
Cunningham Gdns
SO31 ....127 C4
Cunningham Ho SO32 ...83 A4
Cunningham Pl BH11 ...189 A2
Cunningham Rd
Horndean PO8 ....112 B4
Waterlooville PO7 ......134 B3
Cupernham Cl SO51 .....28 A1
Cupernham Inf Sch SO51 .28 A1
Cupernham Jun Sch
SO51 ....28 A1
Cupernham La SO51 .....28 A1
Curdridge Cl 52 PO9 ...136 A4
Curdridge La SO32 ......83 B2
Curdridge Prim Sch
SO32 ....106 B4
Curlew Cl
Emsworth PO10 ....160 C4
Ferndown BH22 ....165 A4
16 Hythe SO45 ....126 A4
Southampton SO16 .....78 A3
Curlew Dr Hythe SO45 ..126 A4
Portchester PO16 ......155 C4
Curlew Gdns PO8 ......111 C2
Curlew Path 7 PO4 .....183 A1
Curlew Rd
Bournemouth BH8 .....190 B1
Christchurch BH23 .....208 A3
Curlew Sq SO50 ....55 C1
Curlew Wlk
Gosport PO13 ....155 A2
Hythe SO45 ....126 A1
Curlews The BH31 ......115 A3
Curlieu Rd BH15 ....202 B3
Curtis Mead PO2 ....157 C2
Curtis Rd BH12 ....203 B3
Curtiss Gdns PO12 .....180 C2
Curve The Gosport PO13 .155 A1
Horndean PO8 ....111 C3
Curzon Ct
32 Bournemouth BH4 ...204 B2
Southampton SO16 .....78 B2
Curzon Howe Rd PO1 ...182 A3
Curzon Pl SO41 ....197 B1
Curzon Rd
Bournemouth BH1 .....205 B3
Poole BH14 ....203 A2
Waterlooville PO7 ......134 C4
Curzon Way BH23 ......208 A3
Custards Rd SO43 ......121 C3
Custards The SO43 .....122 A3
Cut Throat La
Droxford SO32 ....61 A1
Swanmore SO32 ....84 B3
Cutbush La
Southampton SO18 ....104 A4
West End SO18 ....80 A2
Cuthbert Rd PO1 ....182 C4
Cuthburga Rd BH21 ....163 B2
Cuthbury Cl BH21 ......163 A2
Cuthbury Gdns BH21 ...163 A3
Cutler Cl
New Milton BH25 ......195 B2
Poole BH12 ....204 B4
Cutlers La PO14 ....154 B2

Cutlers Pl BH21 ....164 A3
Cutter Ave SO31 ....128 C1
Cutts Arch Droxford SO32 .85 A3
Soberton SO32 ....85 A3
Cygnet Ct PO16 ....155 C4
Cygnet Ho PO12 ....181 A4
Cygnet Rd PO6 ....158 C4
Cygnus Gdns SO45 ....125 B2
Cynthia Cl BH12 ....203 A4
Cynthia Ho BH12 ......203 A4
Cynthia Rd BH12 ......203 A4
Cypress Ave SO19 .....103 C3
Cypress Cres PO8 ......112 A3
Cypress Gdns
Botley SO30 ....106 A4
Totton SO40 ....100 B4
Cypress Gr SO41 ....211 B4
Cyprus Rd
Portsmouth PO2 ....182 C4
Titchfield PO14 ....129 B1
Cyril Rd BH8 ....205 B3

D

D Ave SO45 ....150 C3
D-Day Mus ★ PO5 .....182 B1
Dacombe Cl BH16 .....201 B4
Dacombe Dr BH16 .....201 B4
Dacres Wlk 3 SO41 ....211 B3
Daffodil Rd SO16 ....79 B2
Daggons Rd SP6 ....92 B3
Dahlia Rd SO17 ....79 B2
Daintree Cl SO19 ......104 B2
Dairy Cl
Christchurch BH23 .....207 B4
Corfe Mullen BH21 ....186 A2
Dairy La SO16 ....77 A3
Dairymoor PO17 ....108 A2
Daisy La Gosport PO12 .181 A2
Locks Heath SO31 .....129 B2
Daisy Mead PO7 ....135 A4
Daisy Rd SO16 ....79 A2
Dakota Cl BH23 ....208 A4
Dale Cl Littleton SO22 .....1 A4
Dale Dr PO13 ....155 A3
Dale Park Ho 4 PO1 ...215 B3
Dale Rd Hythe SO45 ...125 C2
Poole BH15 ....202 C3
Southampton SO16 .....78 B1
Stubbington PO14 .....154 B2
Dale The PO7 ....134 B1
Dale Valley Cl SO16 ....78 B1
Dale Valley Gdns SO16 ..78 B1
Dale Valley Rd
Poole BH15 ....202 C4
Southampton SO16 .....78 B2
Dales Cl BH21 ....164 B3
Dales Dr BH21 ....164 A3
Dales La BH23 ....190 C4
Dales Way SO40 ....100 A4
Dalewood Ave BH11 ...188 C3
Dalewood Rd PO15 ....130 B3
Dalkeith Rd
Corfe Mullen BH21 ....186 B2
Poole BH15 ....204 A1
Dalling Rd BH12 ......204 A3
Dallington Cl PO14 ....179 B3
Dalmally Gdns SO18 ...103 C4
Dalmeny Rd BH6 ......207 A2
Dalzell 31 SO23 ....2 A1
Damask Gdns PO7 .....112 A1
Dame Elizabeth Kelly Ct 3
PO2 ....157 C2
Damen Cl SO30 ....105 A3
Damerham Rd BH8 ....190 B2
Damerham Trout Lakes ★
SP6 ....68 B1
Dampier Cl PO13 ......180 B4
Damson Cres SO50 ....57 A1
Damson Hill SO32 ......60 A1
Danbury Ct PO10 .....137 A1
Dances Way PO11 .....184 C2
Dandelion Cl PO13 ....155 A1
Dando Rd PO7 ....111 A2
Dandy's Ford La SO51 ..25 C1
Dane Cl SO45 ....150 C1
Dane Ct BH14 ....203 A2
Dane Dr BH22 ....165 C2
Dane Rd SO41 ....211 A3
Danebury Cl PO9 ......135 C3
Danebury Gdns SO53 ..55 C3
Danebury Way SO16 ....76 B2
Danecourt Cl BH14 ....202 C2
Danecourt Rd BH14 ....202 C2
Danecrest Rd SO41 ....195 C2
Danehurst SO41 ......211 A3
Danehurst New Rd
SO41 ....195 B4
Danemark Ct 4 SO23 ...11 A4
Danes Cl BH25 ....210 A4
Danes Rd Awbridge SO51 .26 B2
Portchester PO16 ......132 A3
28 Winchester SO23 ......2 A1
Danesbrook La PO7 ....135 A4
Danesbury Ave BH6 ...206 C2
Danesbury Mdws SO53 .195 B3
Danestream Cl SO41 ...211 B2
Danestream Ct SO41 ...211 C2
Daneswood Rd BH25 ...195 B4
Daniel Gdns 16 BH15 ..202 B1
Daniell's Cl SO41 ......197 C2
Daniell's Wlk SO41 ....197 C2
Daniels Wlk SO40 ......76 A1
Dansie Cl BH14 ....203 A2
Dapple Pl SO40 ....102 A1
Darby's Cl BH15 ......202 B3

Darby's Cnr BH17 .....187 B1
Darby's La BH15 ......202 B3
Darby's La N BH17 ....202 B4
Dark La Blackfield SO45 .150 C1
Bransgore BH23 ....194 A2
Cheriton SO24 ....14 B3
Darley Rd BH12 ....165 B2
Darlington Gdns SO15 ..78 B3
Darlington Rd PO4 ....182 C2
Darnan Ho 27 SO14 ....103 A4
Darracott Rd BH5 .....206 A3
Darren Cl PO14 ....154 B2
Darren Ct 9 PO16 .....131 B1
Darrian Ct BH16 ......201 A4
Dart Ho SO18 ....103 C4
Dart Rd SO18 ....80 A2
Dartington Rd SO50 ....56 B3
Dartmouth Mews PO5 ..215 A1
Dartmouth Rd PO3 ....158 A1
Darwin Ave BH23 .....191 C1
Darwin Ct 4 BH12 .....204 A2
Darwin Ho PO1 ....215 C4
Darwin Rd Eastleigh SO50 .56 A4
Southampton SO15 ....102 C4
Darwin Way PO13 .....180 B3
Daubney Gdns 3 PO9 ...135 C3
Daulston Rd PO1 ......182 C4
Davenport Cl
Gosport PO13 ....180 B3
Upton BH16 ....201 B4
Daventry La PO3 ......158 B2
David Cl SO51 ....53 A3
David Way BH15 ......201 C1
David's La BH24 ....140 B3
Davidia Ct PO7 ....135 A3
Davidson Ct 27 PO1 ...182 A3
Davis Cl PO13 ....180 B4
Davis Ct BH12 ....203 C3
Davis Field BH25 ......194 C1
Davis Rd BH12 ....203 C3
Davis Way PO14 ......155 A3
Daw La PO11 ....184 C4
Dawkins Bsns Ctr BH15 .201 B2
Dawkins Rd BH15 .....201 B2
Dawkins Way BH25 ...195 A1
Dawlish Ave SO15 .....102 B4
Dawn Chorus BH14 ...203 A2
Dawn Cl BH10 ....189 B1
Dawn Gdns SO22 ......10 B3
Dawnay Cl SO16 ....79 B3
Daws Ave BH11 ....189 A1
Dawson Rd SO19 ......104 B1
Day La PO8 ....111 C4
Day's Ct BH21 ....163 B2
Daylesford Cl BH14 ...203 A1
Dayrell Cl SO40 ....155 A2
Dayshes Cl PO13 ......155 A2
Dayslondon Rd PO7 ...134 B3
De Courtenai Cl BH11 ..188 C3
De Grouchy La SO17 ...79 A1
De Haviland Cl BH21 ..163 C1
De Havilland Ho BH23 .208 A3
De Havilland Way BH23 .208 A3
De La Warr Rd SO41 ...211 B2
De Lisle Cl PO2 ....157 C2
De Lisle Rd BH3 ......204 C4
De Lunn Bldgs 7 SO23 ..11 A4
De Mauley Rd BH13 ...214 C4
De Montfort Rd BH21 ..163 B1
De Mowbray Way SO41 .197 B1
De Port Hts SO32 ......61 B3
De Redvers Rd BH14 ...203 B1
Deacon Cl SO19 ....104 A3
Deacon Cres SO19 ....104 A3
Deacon Gdns BH11 ....189 A3
Deacon Rd
Bournemouth BH11 ....189 A3
Locks Heath SO31 .....129 A1
Southampton SO19 ....104 A3
Deacon Trad Est SO50 ..56 B1
Deadman Hill SP6 ......71 B3
Deal Cl PO14 ....154 B2
Deal Rd PO6 ....133 C1
Dean Cl Hamworthy BH15 .201 C2
Winchester SO22 ....1 B1
Dean Court (Bournemouth
FC) BH7 ....205 C3
Dean Ct Hedge End SO30 .105 B4
2 Southampton SO18 ..104 A4
4 Southampton, Bitterne Manor
SO18 ....103 C4
Dean La
Bishop's Waltham SO32 ..59 C2
Rowland's Castle PO8 ...113 B3
Whiteparish SP5 ....24 A2
Winchester SO22 ....1 A1
Dean Park Cres BH1 ...204 C2
Dean Park Rd BH1 ....204 C2
Dean Rd Cosham PO6 ..157 C4
Fair Oak SO50 ....57 B1
Southampton SO18 ....104 A4
West Dean SP5 ....3 A1
West Tytherley SP5 .....3 C3
Dean St PO1 ....182 A3
Dean Sta SP5 ....3 B2
Dean Swift Cres BH14 ..214 B4
Dean Villas PO7 ....130 C4
Dean's Rd 13 BH5 ......206 A3
Deane Ct 41 PO1 ......182 A3
Deane Down Dro SO22 ...1 A2
Deane Gdns 19 PO13 ..179 C1
Deane's Park Rd PO16 ..131 B4
Deanery The SO53 .....55 A4
Deanfield Cl SO31 .....127 C4
Deans Court La BH21 ..163 B2
Deans Cl SO41 ....211 B4
Deans Dell GU32 ....18 C1

Deans Gate PO14 ......179 B3
Deans Gr BH21 ....163 B2
Deans The BH1 ....204 C2
Deanscroft Rd BH10 ...189 C2
Deansfield Cl SO51 .....53 A4
Deansleigh Rd BH7 ....191 A1
Deanswood Dr PO7 ....111 C1
Dear Hay La BH15 ....202 B1
Dearing Cl SO43 ....121 C2
Debney Lodge PO7 ....134 C4
Decies Rd BH14 ......203 A3
Dee Cl SO53 ....55 A3
Dee Way BH15 ....202 A1
Deep Dell PO8 ....112 A4
Deepdene SO18 ....103 C4
Deepdene La BH11 ....188 C3
Deeping Cl SO19 ......103 C1
Deeping Gate PO7 .....135 A4
Deer Leap PO15 ....130 B3
Deer Park Cl BH25 ....194 C2
Deer Park Farm Ind Est
SO50 ....57 C1
Deer Sanctuary ★ BH24 .119 C3
Deerhurst Cl SO40 ....100 B3
Deerhurst Ho 3 PO6 ...133 C1
Deerleap Cl SO45 .....126 A2
Deerleap La SO40 .....100 B1
Deerleap Way
Hythe SO45 ....126 A2
New Milton BH25 ......195 A3
Defender Rd SO19 .....103 B2
Defender Wlk SO19 ....103 B2
Defoe Cl PO15 ....129 B4
Delamere Gdns BH10 ..189 C2
Delamere Rd PO4 .....182 C2
Delaval Ho 35 PO1 ....182 A3
Delft Cl SO31 ....128 C2
Delft Gdns PO8 ....111 B1
Delft Mews BH23 .....207 B2
Delhi Cl BH14 ....203 B2
Delhi Rd BH9 ....189 C1
Delilah Rd BH15 ......201 B1
Delius Ave SO19 ......104 B2
Delius Wlk SO19 ......104 C3
Delkeith Ct BH22 .....165 B2
Dell Cl Broadstone BH18 .186 C2
Fair Oak SO50 ....57 B1
Waterlooville PO7 ......134 A1
Dell Cotts SO23 ....15 C1
Dell Piece E PO8 ......112 B3
Dell Piece W PO8 .....112 B3
Dell Quay PO13 ......155 A1
Dell Rd Southampton SO18 .79 C1
Winchester SO23 ....11 B3
Dell The
Barton on Sea BH25 ...209 B4
Havant PO9 ....135 A1
Portchester PO16 ......131 B1
Dellcrest Path PO6 ....134 A1
Dellfield Cl 14 PO6 ....133 A1
Delme Dr PO16 ....131 B1
Delme Sq 23 PO16 ....131 B1
Delph Rd BH21 ....187 B4
Delph Woods Woodland
Trail ★ BH21 ....187 B4
Delphi Way PO7 ......134 C1
Delta Bsns Pk PO16 ...155 A4
Delta Cl BH23 ....208 A4
Dempsey Cl SO19 .....104 A2
Denbigh Cl Eastleigh SO50 .55 C3
Totton SO40 ....100 B3
Denbigh Dr PO16 .....130 C1
Denbigh Gdns SO16 ...78 C2
Denby Rd BH15 ....202 C2
Dene Cl Chilworth SO16 .78 C4
Locks Heath SO31 .....128 C2
Ringwood BH24 ....117 B1
Dene Hollow PO6 .....158 B4
Dene Rd SO40 ....100 B1
Dene Way SO40 ......100 B2
Dene Wlk PO13 ......165 C1
Denecote Lo BH13 ....214 D4
Deneside Copse SO41 .197 A1
Deneve Ave BH17 ....187 B1
Denewood Copse BH22 .138 B2
Denewood Rd BH22 ...138 B2
Denewulf Cl 2 SO32 ...83 B4
Denham Cl Poole BH17 .187 C2
Stubbington PO14 .....179 A3
Winchester SO23 ....1 C1
Denham Ct SO23 ....2 A1
Denham Dr BH23 .....193 C1
Denham Fields SO50 ...57 A2
Denham Gdns SO31 ...127 A2
Denham's Cnr SO32 ....81 B3
Denhill Cl PO11 ....184 C3
Denholm Cl BH24 .....117 B1
Denison Rd BH17 .....187 B1
Denmark La BH15 ....202 B2
Denmark Rd
Bournemouth BH9 .....189 C1
Poole BH15 ....202 B2
Denmark Terr BH1 ....205 C3
Denmead BH25 ....195 B2
Denmead Ho PO1 .....215 C4
Denmead Inf Sch PO7 ..111 A1
Denmead Jun Sch PO7 .111 A2
Denmead Rd
Bournemouth BH6 .....206 B4
Southampton SO18 ....104 B4
Dennet Ho SO23 ....2 B1
Dennetts La 19 BH15 ..202 A1
Denning Mews PO1 ...215 B3

Dennis Rd BH21 ....186 B3
Dennis Way GU33 ......21 A2
Dennison Ct 8 SO15 ...102 A4
Dennistoun Ave BH23 ..207 C4
Denny Cl SO45 ....151 A2
Denville Ave PO16 .....156 B3
Denville Cl PO6 ....158 C4
Denvilles Cl PO9 ....136 A1
Denwood Rd BH4 ....204 A1
Denzil Ave Netley SO31 .127 B3
  Southampton SO14 ....103 A3
Depedene Cl SO45 .....150 B2
Derby Ct PO13 ....180 B3
Derby Ho 4 SO50 ....56 A1
Derby Rd
  Bournemouth BH1 .....205 B2
  Eastleigh SO50 ....55 C1
  Portsmouth PO2 ......157 B1
  Southampton SO14 ....103 A3
Dereham Way BH12 ....203 C3
Deridene Ct SO40 .....100 B3
Derlyn Rd PO16 ....131 A1
Derritt La BH23 ....192 B4
Derrybrian Gdns BH25 .195 A1
Dersingham Cl PO6 ....133 C1
Derwent Cl
  Bournemouth BH9 .....190 A1
  Ferndown BH22 ....166 A3
  Horndean PO8 ....88 B1
  Stubbington PO14 ....154 B2
  West End SO18 ....80 A1
Derwent Dr SO40 .....100 A4
Derwent Rd
  Lee-on-the-Solent PO13 .179 C1
  New Milton BH25 .....195 A3
  Southampton SO16 ....77 C1
Derwentwater Rd BH21 .163 B1
Desborough Cl 9 PO6 .133 C1
Desborough Rd SO50 ..56 A1
Devenish Rd SO22 ....1 B2
Deverel Cl BH23 ......207 A4
Deverell Pl PO7 ......134 B2
Devine Gdns 5 SO50 ..56 C1
Devon Cl SO53 ....55 B2
Devon Dr SO53 ....55 B2
Devon Rd
  Christchurch BH23 ....206 C4
  Poole BH15 ....202 C3
  Portsmouth PO3 ......158 A2
Devonshire Ave PO4 ..183 A2
Devonshire Gdns
  Bursledon SO31 ......105 A1
  Hythe SO45 ....150 A4
Devonshire Inf Sch PO4 182 C2
Devonshire Mans 10
  SO15 ....102 C3
Devonshire Rd SO15 ..102 C3
Devonshire Sq PO4 ...182 C2
Devonshire Way PO14 .154 B4
Dew La SO50 ....55 C2
Dewar Cl PO15 ....129 B3
Deweys La BH24 ......140 C4
Dewlands Pk BH31 ....114 B3
Dewlands Rd BH31 ....114 B3
Dewlands Way BH31 ..114 C3
Dewlish Cl BH17 .....188 A1
Dewsbury Ct 3 SO18 .80 A1
Dhekelia Ct PO1 .....215 C4
Dial Cl BH23 ....169 B1
Diamond Cl SP6 ....93 C4
Diamond Ct
  Fordingbridge SP6 ....93 C4
  Waterlooville PO7 ...134 C4
Diamond St 2 PO5 ...215 A1
Diana Cl Gosport PO12 .180 C2
  Havant PO10 ....136 C2
Diana Ct BH23 ....209 A4
Diana Way BH21 ....186 C4
Dibben Wlk SO51 ......28 B1
Dibble Dr SO52 ....53 C2
Dibden Cl
  Bournemouth BH8 ....190 B2
  Havant PO9 ....135 C2
Dibden Lodge Cl SO45 .125 C3
Dibles Rd SO31 ......128 C1
Dickens Cl PO2 ......182 B4
Dickens Dell SO40 ...100 A4
Dickens Dr PO15 .....106 B1
Dickens Rd BH6 ......206 B4
Dickson Pk PO17 .....108 A2
Didcot Rd Poole BH17 .202 B4
  Southampton SO15 ....78 B1
Dieppe Cres PO2 .....157 C2
Dieppe Gdns PO12 ...180 C2
Dight Rd PO12 ....181 B1
Diligence Cl SO31 ...105 A1
Dillington Ho 2 PO7 .134 C4
Dilly La BH25 ....210 A4
Dimond Cl SO18 ......79 C1
Dimond Hill SO18 ....79 C1
Dimond Rd SO18 .....79 C1
Dingle Rd BH5 ......206 A2
Dingle Way SO31 ....129 A3
Dingley Rd BH15 ....202 B3
Dinham Ct BH25 ....195 B2
Dinham Rd BH25 ...195 B2
Dinsey Cl SO16 .....101 C4
Diprose Rd BH21 ...186 C4
Disa Ho SO15 ......102 C3
Discovery Cl PO14 ..154 B3
Disraeli Rd BH23 ...207 B3
Ditcham Cres PO9 ..135 C2
Ditcham Park Sch GU31 .89 C4
Ditchbury SO41 .....197 B3

Ditton Cl PO14 ....154 B2
Ditton Cotts SO42 ...148 C1
Dock La SO42 ....149 A1
Dock Mill Cotts 3 PO5 .182 B1
Dock Rd PO12 ....181 B2
Dockenfield Cl PO9 ..135 B2
Doctor's Hill SO51 ....26 A2
Doctors La GU32 ......37 B3
Dodds La SO32 ....84 B3
Dodgson Cl SP6 ......70 C4
Dodwell La SO31 ....105 A2
Doe Copse Way BH25 .194 C2
Dogdean BH21 ....163 B4
Dogkennel La PO7 ...86 C2
Dogwood Dell 2 PO7 .134 C3
Dogwood Rd BH18 ...186 C1
Dolbery Rd N BH12 ..188 B1
Dolbery Rd S BH12 ..188 B1
Dolman Rd PO12 ....181 B2
Dolphin Ave BH10 ...189 C3
Dolphin Cl 11 SO50 ..56 C1
Dolphin Cres PO12 ..181 B2
Dolphin Ct
  7 Portsmouth PO5 ...182 C1
  Stubbington PO14 ...154 A2
Dolphin Ctr BH15 ...202 B1
Dolphin Hill SO21 ....32 A3
Dolphin Pl BH25 ....210 A4
Dolphin Way PO12 ..181 B1
Dolton Rd SO16 .....77 C2
Dome Alley SO23 ....11 A4
Dominie Wlk 16 PO13 .179 C1
Dominion Ctr BH11 ..188 C2
Dominion Rd BH11 ..188 C2
Dominy Cl SO45 .....126 A2
Domum Rd
  Portsmouth PO2 .....157 C1
  Winchester SO23 .....11 A3
Domvilles App PO2 ..157 A1
Donaldson Rd PO6 ..157 A3
Doncaster Rd SO50 ...80 A4
Donigers Cl SO32 ....84 A3
Donigers Dell SO32 ..84 A3
Donkey La SO30 .....106 A4
Donnelly Rd BH6 ....206 C3
Donnelly St PO12 ...181 A3
Donnington Ct 19 SO23 .2 A1
Donnington Dr
  Chandler's Ford SO53 .55 A2
  Christchurch BH23 ...208 A4
Donnington Gr SO17 .79 B1
Donoughmore Rd 1
  BH1 ....205 C2
Dorcas Cl 1 PO7 ....112 A1
Dorchester Cl SO15 ..102 C4
Dorchester Gdns BH15 .202 C4
Dorchester Mans BH1 .205 B2
Dorchester Rd
  Poole BH15 ....202 C3
  Upton BH16 ....201 A4
Dore Ave PO16 ......132 B1
Dores La Braishfield SO51 .29 A4
  Hursley SO51 ....29 A4
Doric Cl SO53 ....55 C4
Dorking Cres PO6 ...157 C4
Dorland Gdns SO40 .100 B3
Dorlands Rd PO8 ...112 B4
Dormers The BH25 ..194 C1
Dormington Rd PO6 .133 B1
Dormy Cl SO31 .....128 B2
Dormy Way PO13 ...155 A1
Dorney Ct 2 PO6 ...158 A4
Dornie Rd BH13 .....214 C4
Dornmere La PO7 ...135 A4
Dorothy Ct PO5 .....215 C1
Dorothy Dymond St
  PO1 ....215 B3
Dorrick Ct 17 SO15 .102 C4
Dorrien Rd PO12 ....181 A4
Dorrita Ave PO8 ....112 A2
Dorrita Cl PO4 .....182 C1
Dorrits The SO40 ...100 A4
Dorset Ave BH22 ...165 B2
Dorset Cl PO8 ......112 A3
Dorset Grange BH23 .206 C4
Dorset Heavy Horse & Animal
  Ctr* BH21 ....91 B1
Dorset Ho BH13 ....204 A1
Dorset Lake Ave BH14 .214 A4
Dorset Lake Manor
  BH14 ....203 A1
Dorset Rd
  Bournemouth BH4 ....204 B3
  Chandler's Ford SO53 .55 B2
  Christchurch BH23 ...207 C4
Dorset St SO14 .....103 A3
Dorstone Rd PO6 ...133 B1
Dorval Ho 23 SO15 .102 C4
Dorval Manor 24 SO15 .102 C4
Douglas Ave BH23 ..207 A3
Douglas Cl BH16 ....201 B4
Douglas Cres SO19 ..104 B3
Douglas Gdns
  Havant PO9 ....136 A2
  Poole BH12 ....203 C3
Douglas Mews
  Bournemouth BH6 ...206 B3
  Upton BH16 ....201 B4
Douglas Rd
  Bournemouth BH6 ...206 C2
  Poole BH12 ....203 C3
Douglas Way SO45 ..125 C2
Doulton Gdns BH14 .203 A1
Doussie Dr BH16 ....201 A4
Dove Cl PO8 ....111 C4
Dove Dale SO50 .....55 B4
Dove Gdns SO31 ...129 A3
Dove La SO51 ....29 A4

Dover Cl Poole BH13 ..204 A2
  Stubbington PO14 ...154 A2
Dover Ct PO11 ......184 C3
Dover Rd Poole BH13 .204 A2
  Portsmouth PO3 .....183 A4
Dover St SO14 ......103 A4
Dovercourt Rd PO6 ..158 A3
Doveshill Cres BH10 .189 B2
Doveshill Gdns BH10 .189 B2
Doveshill Mobile Home Pk
  BH10 ....189 B2
Doveys Cl BH24 ....143 A2
Dowds Cl SO30 .....105 A4
Dowell Ho PO4 .....183 A1
Dowlands Cl BH10 ..189 B2
Dowlands Rd BH10 .189 B2
Down End PO6 ......134 B1
Down End Rd PO6 ..134 B1
Down Farm La SO22,SO23 .1 C4
Down Farm Pl PO8 ..88 B1
Down Lodge Cl SO45 .93 A3
Down Rd Horndean PO8 .88 A1
  Horndean PO8 ....112 B4
Down's Park Ave SO40 .101 A3
Down's Park Cres SO40 .101 A3
Down's Park Rd SO40 .101 A3
Downend Rd PO16 ..131 C1
Downey Cl BH11 ....188 C1
Downham Cl PO8 ...111 C2
Downhouse Rd PO8 ..88 A2
Downing Cl PO14 ...129 B1
Downland Cl
  Botley SO30 ....105 C4
  Locks Heath SO31 ...129 A2
Downland Pl SO30 ..105 A3
Downlands Cl SP5 ...46 C3
Downlands Rd BH17 .202 C4
Downlands Rd SO22 ..10 A2
Downley Point PO9 ..136 A2
Downley Rd PO9 ....136 A2
Downs Cl PO7 ......134 C2
Downscroft Gdns SO30 .105 A4
Downside PO13 .....155 B1
Downside Ave SO19 .104 A3
Downside Rd
  Waterlooville PO7 ...134 B2
  Winchester SO22 .....1 A1
Downsway The PO7 .156 B4
Downton CE Prim Sch
  SP5 ....46 C4
Downton Cl BH8 ...190 B2
Downton Hill SP5 ....47 B4
Downton Ho 2 PO6 .157 B4
Downton La SO41 ...210 C4
Downton Rd SO18 ...79 C1
Downton Sec Sch SP5 .46 C4
Downview Rd SP6 ...43 A2
Downwood Cl
  Fordingbridge SP6 ...69 B1
  Hythe SO45 ....125 B1
Downwood Way PO8 .88 B1
Doyle Ave PO2 .....157 C2
Doyle Cl PO2 ......157 C2
Doyle Ct
  16 Portsmouth PO2 ..157 C2
  Southampton SO19 ..103 C1
Doyle Ho PO9 ......135 A2
Doyne Rd BH14 ....203 C2
Dradfield La SO32 ..109 B4
Draffatts Ho SO15 ..102 B4
Dragon Est PO6 ....158 C4
Dragon La BH23 ....168 A4
Dragon St GU31,GU32 .40 C4
Dragoon Cl SO19 ...104 B2
Dragoon Way BH23 .206 C4
Drake Cl
  Christchurch BH23 ..207 C3
  Locks Heath SO31 ...129 A3
  Marchwood SO40 ...102 A1
  New Milton BH25 ...194 C2
  Ringwood BH24 ....117 B1
Drake Ct
  Lee-on-the-Solent PO13 .179 B2
  22 Poole BH15 ......202 B1
Drake Ho 4 PO1 ...182 A3
Drake Rd
  Bishopstoke SO50 ...56 C2
  Lee-on-the-Solent PO13 .179 B2
  Poole BH15 ....202 B1
Drakes Cl SO45 ....125 C1
Drakes Ct SO40 ....102 A2
Drakes Rd BH22 ...165 C2
Draper Rd
  Bournemouth BH11 .189 A2
  Christchurch BH23 ..207 C4
Drapers Copse Cvn Site
  SO45 ....125 B2
Draycote Rd PO8 ...88 B2
Draycott Rd BH10 ..189 B1
Drayton Cl 9 SO19 .126 C4
Drayton La PO6 ....134 A1
Drayton Pl SO40 ...100 B4
Drayton Rd PO2 ...157 C1
Drayton St SO22 ....10 B3
Dreadnought Rd PO14 .154 C3
Dresden Pr PO8 ....111 C2
Dreswick Cl BH23 ..191 B2
Drew Cl BH12 .....204 B4
Drewitt Ind Est BH11 .188 C2
Drift Rd Clanfield PO8 .88 B2
Drift The PO9 .....113 A1
Driftwood Gdns
  Portsmouth PO4 ....183 B1
  Totton SO40 ....100 B3
Drill Shed Rd PO2 ..157 A1
Drinkwater Cl SO50 ..55 C2
Drive The Fareham PO16 .131 A1

Drive The continued
  Gosport PO13 ....155 A1
  Havant PO9 ....135 C2
  Poole BH12 ....203 B3
  Sherfield English SO51 .25 A1
  Southbourne PO10 ...161 B4
  Totton SO40 ....100 C3
  West End SO30 ......80 A2
  West Wellow SO51 ...51 A1
Drove Cl SO21 ......31 C3
Drove Rd
  Southampton SO19 ..104 A2
  Southwick PO17 ....133 A2
Drove The
  Blackfield SO45 .....150 C1
  Durley BH30 ....82 B4
  Fair Oak SO50 ......81 B3
  Southampton SO18 ..104 A4
  Swanmore SO32 .....84 A3
  Totton SO40 ....76 A1
  Twyford SO21 ......31 C3
  West End SO30 .....80 C2
  West Wellow SO51 ..50 C2
Droxford Cl PO12 ...180 C2
Droxford Jun Sch SO32 .61 B1
Droxford Rd
  Bournemouth BH6 ...206 A3
  Swanmore SO32 ....84 B3
Druids Cl BH22 ....165 B1
Druitt Rd BH23 ....207 C4
Drum La GU32 .....40 C2
Drum Mead GU32 ..40 C2
Drumlanrig Terr PO12 .181 B4
Drummond Cl SO22 .10 C3
Drummond Ct
  4 Eastleigh SO50 ...56 A3
  8 Hythe SO45 ....126 A3
  Southampton SO19 ..103 C2
Drummond Dr SO14 .103 B4
Drummond Rd
  Bournemouth BH1 ...205 B2
  Hedge End SO30 ....81 B1
  3 Hythe SO45 ....126 A2
  Portsmouth PO1 ....215 C4
Drummond Way SO53 .55 A4
Drury Rd BH4 .....204 A1
Dryden Ave PO6 ...132 C1
Dryden Cl Fareham PO16 .131 A1
  St Leonards BH24 ...139 C3
  Waterlooville PO7 ...111 C1
Dryden Pl 4 SO41 ..211 B3
Dryden Rd SO19 ...104 C3
Drysdale Mews PO4 .183 A1
Duart Ct BH25 .....195 B2
Duck Island La 5 BH24 .141 B4
Duck La BH11 .....188 C2
Ducking Stool La BH23 .207 B3
Duckmead La GU33 .21 A3
Duckworth Ho 23 PO1 .182 A3
Duddon Cl SO18 ...80 A1
Dudleston Heath Dr
  PO8 ....112 A1
Dudley Ave
  Fordingbridge SP6 ...69 C2
  Hordle SO41 ....195 C2
Dudley Gdns BH10 .189 B3
Dudley Pl 29 BH25 .195 A1
Dudley Rd
  Bournemouth BH10 .189 B3
  Portsmouth PO3 ....183 A4
Dudley Terr GU33 ..21 A3
Dudmoor Farm Rd
  BH23 ....191 C2
Dudmoor La BH23 .191 C2
Dudsbury Ave BH22 .165 A3
Dudsbury Cres BH22 .165 C2
Dudsbury Ct 8 BH23 .207 C3
Dudsbury Gdns BH22 .189 C4
Dudsbury Rd BH22 .165 B1
Dudsway Ct BH22 ..165 B2
Duffield La SO32 ...137 C2
Dugald Drummond St
  PO1 ....215 B3
Dugdell Cl BH22 ...165 C3
Duisburg Way PO5 .182 A1
Duke Cres PO1 ....182 B4
Duke of Edinburgh Ho
  PO1 ....182 A3
Duke Rd SO30 .....105 B3
Duke St SO14 ......103 A2
Duke Terr PO9 ....135 B2
Dukes Cl GU32 ....40 B2
Dukes Ct 4 SO32 ..83 B4
Dukes Dr BH11 ....188 C3
Dukes Mill Ctr 11 SO51 .52 C4
  Southampton SO14 ..103 A4
Dukes Wlk 14 PO7 .134 C4
Dukes Wlk Service Rd 13
  PO7 ....134 C4
Dukes Wood Dr SO45 .126 A1
Dukesfield BH23 ...191 B1
Dulsie Rd BH3 .....204 B4
Dumbarton Cl PO2 .182 B4
Dumbleton Cl SO19 .104 C2
Dumbleton's Twrs SO19 .104 C2
Dummer Ct PO9 ...135 B2
Dummer Mews 24 SO23 .10 C4
Dummer Rd SO51 ..28 A2
Dumpers Dro SO32 ..81 B3
Dumpton Sch BH21 .163 B4
Dunbar Cl PO16 ....131 C1
Dunbar Cres BH23 .193 C1
Dunbar Rd
  Bournemouth BH3 ..204 C3
  Portsmouth PO4 ....183 A4
Dunbridge La SO51 ..26 C4
Dunbridge Sta SO51 ..5 B1

Duncan Cl SO19 ....103 C1
Duncan Cooper Ho PO7 134 B4
Duncan Ct SO19 ...104 B3
Duncan Rd
  Locks Heath SO31 ..129 A3
  New Milton BH25 ...195 B2
  Portsmouth PO5 ....182 B1
Duncans Dr PO14 ..154 A4
Duncliff Rd BH6 ...207 A3
Duncombe Dr BH24 .116 B2
Duncombe Rd GU32 .63 B4
Duncton Rd PO8 ...88 B3
Duncton Way PO13 .155 B2
Dundas Cl PO3 ....158 A1
Dundas La PO3 ....158 A1
Dundas Rd BH17 ..202 C4
Dundas Spur PO3 ..158 A1
Dundee Cl PO15 ...130 C2
Dundee Rd SO17 ...79 B1
Dundonald Cl
  South Hayling PO11 .185 A3
  Southampton SO19 ..103 B1
Dundridge La SO32 ..60 B1
Dundry Way SO30 ..105 B4
Dune Crest BH13 ..214 B2
Dunedin Cl BH22 ..165 A2
Dunedin Dr BH22 ..165 A2
Dunedin Gdns BH22 .165 A2
Dunedin Gr BH23 ..208 B3
Dunfield Way SO45 .150 C1
Dunford Cl
  Barton on Sea BH25 .209 C4
  New Milton BH25 ...194 C1
Dunford Rd BH12 ..203 B3
Dunhurst (Bedales Jun Sch)
  GU32 ....40 C3
Dunhurst Cl PO9 ...136 A2
Dunkeld Rd
  Bournemouth BH3 ..204 C3
  Gosport PO12 ......181 A4
Dunkirk Cl SO16 ...78 B2
Dunkirk Rd SO16 ..78 B2
Dunlin Cl
  Christchurch BH23 .208 A3
  Portsmouth PO4 ...183 B3
Dunn Cl PO4 ......183 A2
Dunnings La SO52 ..53 C3
Dunnock Cl
  Ferndown BH22 ...165 A4
  Rowland's Castle PO9 .113 A1
Dunsbury Way PO9 .135 C2
Dunsmore Cl PO5 ..215 B2
Dunstable Wlk PO14 .154 B4
Dunstans La BH15 ..203 A3
Dunster Cl SO16 ...78 B3
Dunster Dr SO16 ...78 B3
Dunvegan Dr SO16 .78 B3
Dunvegan Way SO16 .78 B3
Dunyeats Rd BH18 .187 A2
Dunyeats Rdbt BH18 .187 B2
Durban Cl SO51 ....28 A1
Durban Ct 21 SO15 .102 C4
Durban Ho PO1 ...215 C4
Durban Rd PO1 ...182 C1
Durdells Ave BH11 .189 A3
Durdells Gdns BH11 .189 A3
Durford Ct PO9 ...135 B3
Durford Rd GU31 ..41 B2
Durham Gdns PO7 .134 C3
Durham St Gosport PO12 181 A3
  Portsmouth PO1 ....215 C4
Durland Cl BH25 ...195 A1
Durley Ave PO8 ...111 C2
Durley Brook Rd
  Durley SO32 ....81 C3
  Durley SO32 ....82 A3
Durley CE Prim Sch
  SO32 ....82 A3
Durley Chine Ct BH2 .204 B1
Durley Chine Rd BH2 .204 B1
Durley Chine Rd S BH2 .204 B1
Durley Cres SO40 ..100 A3
Durley Gdns BH2 ..204 B1
Durley Hall Rd SO32 .58 B1
Durley Rd
  Bournemouth BH2 ..204 C1
  Durley SO32,SO50 ..81 C4
  Gosport PO12 ......181 A3
Durley Rd S BH2 ..204 B1
Durley St SO32 ....82 B4
Durlston Court Sch
  BH25 ....210 A4
Durlston Cres BH23 .191 B2
Durlston Rd Poole BH14 .203 B1
  Southampton SO16 ..77 B1
Durnford Rd SO14 .103 A3
Durngate Pl SO23 ..11 A4
Durngate Terr 41 SO23 .11 A4
Durnstown SO41 ...172 B1
Durrant PRU PO9 ..136 A4
Durrant Rd
  7 Bournemouth BH2 .204 C2
  Poole BH14 ....203 B2
Durrant Way SO41 .172 A1
Durrants Gdns PO9 .136 A4
Durrants Rd PO9 ..136 A4
Durrington Pl BH7 ..206 A4
Durrington Rd BH7 .206 A4
Dursley Cres PO6 ..157 C4
Durweston Cl BH9 ..190 A2
Dutton La SO50 ...56 A2
Dutton's Rd SO51 ..52 C4
Dyer Rd SO15 .....102 B4
Dymchurch Ho 3 PO6 .157 C4
Dymewood Rd BH21 .138 C4
Dymoke St PO10 ..136 C2
Dymott Cl SO15 ...102 B3
Dyneley Gn SO18 ..80 A1

Dyram Cl SO50 .....55 C3
Dysart Ave PO6 .....158 A4
Dyserth Cl SO19 .....104 A1
Dyson Dr SO23 .....2 A1

E

E Ave SO45 .....150 C3
Eadens La SO40 .....99 B4
Eagle Ave PO8 .....111 C2
Eagle Cl
  Chandler's Ford SO53 .....55 A2
  Portchester PO16 .....155 C4
Eagle Ct 12 SO23 .....10 C4
Eagle House Sch BH14 .....203 A2
Eagle Rd
  Lee-on-the-Solent PO13 .....179 B2
  Poole BH12 .....204 A2
Eaglhurst 5 BH12 .....204 A2
Eame's Cotts GU32 .....38 C1
Eames La GU33 .....19 C1
Earle Ho 3 SO23 .....11 B4
Earle Rd BH4 .....204 B1
Earley Ct SO41 .....197 C2
Earlham Dr BH14 .....203 B2
Earls Cl SO50 .....57 A1
Earls Rd Fareham PO16 .....155 A4
  Southampton SO14 .....103 A4
Earlsdon St PO5 .....215 B2
Earlsdon Way BH23 .....208 C4
Earlsdown 47 SO23 .....11 A4
Earlswood Dr SP6 .....92 C3
Earlswood Pk BH25 .....195 B2
Earnley Rd PO11 .....185 C1
East Ave
  Barton on Sea BH25 .....209 B4
  Bournemouth BH3 .....204 B3
East Avenue Rdbt BH3 .....204 C3
East Bank Rd SO42 .....173 A4
East Bargate 7 SO14 .....103 A2
East Boldre Rd SO42 .....175 B3
East Borough BH21 .....163 A3
East Cams Cl PO16 .....131 C1
East Cl BH25 .....209 B4
East Cliff Way BH23 .....208 B4
East Cosham Rd PO6 .....158 A4
East Ct Cosham PO6 .....158 A4
  Portsmouth PO1 .....182 C4
East Dean Rd S051 .....4 C1
East Dr SO50 .....56 C2
East Field Cl SO19 .....137 C1
East Hill Lymington SO41 .....197 C2
  Winchester SO23 .....11 A3
East Hill Cl PO16 .....131 B3
East Hill Dr GU33 .....21 A2
East Hoe Rd PO7 .....86 A2
East House Ave PO14 .....179 B3
East Howe La BH10 .....189 B2
East La SO41 .....196 C1
East Links S053 .....55 B1
East Lodge
  Fareham PO15 .....130 B1
  7 Lee-on-the-Solent PO13 .....179 C1
East Lodge Pk PO6 .....158 C4
East Meon CE Prim Sch GU32 .....38 B1
East Meon Rd PO8 .....88 A3
East Overcliff Dr BH1 .....205 B2
East Park Terr SO14 .....103 A3
East Quay BH15 .....202 B1
East Quay Rd BH15 .....202 B1
East Rd Fawley SO45 .....150 B4
  Southwick PO17 .....133 A4
East Shore Sch PO14 .....183 A3
East St Fareham PO16 .....131 B1
  Hambledon PO7 .....86 B2
  Havant PO9 .....135 C1
  Poole BH15 .....202 B1
  Portchester PO16 .....156 C4
  Portsmouth PO1 .....182 A4
  Southampton SO14 .....103 A2
  Titchfield PO14 .....154 A4
  Westbourne PO10 .....137 A2
  Wimborne Minst BH21 .....163 B2
East Street Ctr 16 SO14 .....103 A2
East Surrey St PO1 .....215 B3
East View BH24 .....141 A4
East View Terr 9 PO9 .....135 C1
East Way
  Bournemouth BH8 .....190 B1
  Corfe Mullen BH21 .....186 B3
East Woodhay Rd SO22 .....1 B2
Eastacre SO22 .....1 C1
Eastbourne Ave
  Gosport PO12 .....180 C4
  Southampton SO15 .....102 B4
Eastbourne Rd PO3 .....183 A4
Eastbrook Cl
  Gosport PO12 .....180 C4
  Locks Heath SO31 .....129 A3
Eastbrook Row BH21 .....163 B2
Eastbury Ct BH23 .....207 C2
Eastchurch Cl SO16 .....77 C2
Eastcliff Cl PO13 .....179 C4
Eastcot Cl SO45 .....150 B2
Eastcott Cl BH7 .....206 A4
Eastcroft Rd PO12 .....180 C3
Easter Rd BH9 .....190 A1
Eastern Ave PO4 .....183 A3
Eastern Ind Ctr PO6 .....158 B3
Eastern Par
  Fareham PO16 .....155 A4
  Portsmouth PO4 .....182 C1
Eastern Rd Fawley SO45 .....151 C1
  Havant PO9 .....136 A1
  Lymington SO41 .....197 B2

Eastern Rd continued
  Portsmouth PO3, PO6 .....158 B2
  Portsmouth, Whale Is PO2 .....157 A1
  West End SO30 .....80 B1
Eastern Terr PO4 .....183 A1
Eastern Villas Rd PO4 .....182 B1
Eastern Way
  Fareham PO16 .....131 B1
  Milford on Sea SO41 .....211 C2
Eastfield Ave PO14 .....154 C4
Eastfield Ct BH24 .....141 B4
Eastfield La BH24 .....141 B4
Eastfield Rd
  Portsmouth PO4 .....183 A2
  Southampton SO17 .....103 B4
Eastfields PO5 .....215 C1
Eastgate St
  Southampton SO14 .....103 A2
  Winchester SO23 .....11 A4
Eastlake Ave BH12 .....203 B3
Eastlake Cl GU31 .....41 B2
Eastlake Hts PO4 .....183 B2
Eastlands SO45 .....195 A1
Eastleigh Coll SO50 .....56 A1
Eastleigh Coll of F Ed SO50 .....56 A1
Eastleigh Lakeside Rly★ SO50 .....79 C4
Eastleigh Rd
  Fair Oak SO50 .....57 B1
  Havant PO9 .....136 B2
Eastleigh Sta SO50 .....56 A2
Eastleigh Town Mus★ SO50 .....56 A1
Eastman Cl SP5 .....47 A3
Eastmeare Ct SO40 .....100 B3
Eastney Farm Rd PO4 .....183 B1
Eastney Rd PO4 .....183 A1
Eastney St PO4 .....183 A1
Eastoke Ave PO11 .....185 B1
Easton La SO21 .....2 C2
Easton Lane Bsns Ctr SO23 .....11 A4
Eastover Ct 10 PO9 .....135 B3
Eastville Rd SO50 .....57 B1
Eastways SO32 .....83 B4
Eastwood SO51 .....25 B1
Eastwood Ave BH22 .....165 C3
Eastwood Cl PO11 .....185 A3
Eastwood Rd 5 PO2 .....157 C2
Eastworth Rd BH31 .....114 C4
Eaton Rd BH13 .....204 A1
Ebblake Ent Pk BH31 .....115 B3
Ebblake Ind Est BH31 .....115 B2
Ebden Rd SO23 .....11 A4
Ebenezer La BH24 .....140 C4
Ebery Gr PO3 .....183 B4
Ebor Cl BH22 .....165 C1
Ebor Rd BH12 .....203 B3
Eccles Rd BH15 .....202 A1
Ecton Cl PO3 .....158 B2
Eddystone Rd SO40 .....76 B1
Edelvale Rd SO18 .....80 A1
Eden Ct 20 BH1 .....205 A2
Eden Gr BH21 .....163 B2
Eden Rd SO18 .....80 A1
Eden Rise PO16 .....155 A4
Eden St PO1 .....215 B4
Eden Terr 10 PO2 .....157 B1
Eden Wlk SO53 .....55 A3
Edenbridge Rd PO4 .....183 B3
Edenbridge Way SO31 .....128 C3
Edgar Cres PO16 .....156 B3
Edgar Rd SO23 .....10 C3
Edgar Villas SO23 .....10 C3
Edgarton Rd BH17 .....187 B2
Edgbaston Ho PO5 .....215 B2
Edgecombe Cres PO13 .....180 B4
Edgefield Gr PO7 .....112 A1
Edgehill Rd
  Bournemouth BH9 .....189 C1
  Southampton SO18 .....79 C1
Edgell Rd PO10 .....137 A2
Edgemoor Rd BH22 .....139 A1
Edgerly Gdns PO6 .....157 C3
Edgeware Rd PO4 .....183 A3
Edgewood Ct GU33 .....21 A1
Edifred Rd BH9 .....190 A2
Edinburgh Ct SO15 .....102 A3
Edinburgh Ho 8 SO22 .....10 C4
Edinburgh Rd PO1 .....215 A3
Edington Cl SO32 .....83 A4
Edington Rd SO23 .....2 A1
Edith Haisman Cl SO15 .....102 B3
Edmondsham Ho Gdns★ BH21 .....91 A2
Edmondsham Rd BH31 .....114 C4
Edmonsham Ho 28 BH2 .....204 C2
Edmund Rd PO4 .....182 C1
Edmunds Cl
  Barton on Sea BH25 .....195 A1
  Hedge End SO30 .....105 B3
Edneys La PO7 .....111 A3
Edward Ave SO50 .....56 B2
Edward Church SO45 .....150 C1
Edward Gdns PO9 .....135 B1
Edward Gr PO16 .....132 C1
Edward Rd
  Bournemouth BH11 .....189 A2
  Christchurch BH23 .....207 C4
  Hythe SO45 .....126 A1
  Poole BH14 .....203 B3
  Southampton SO15 .....102 B4
  Winchester SO23 .....10 C3
Edward Way Ct BH11 .....189 A2
Edward's Cl 29 PO6 .....133 A1
Edwards Cl SO41 .....197 A2
Edwin Jones Gn SO15 .....102 C4

Edwina Cl
  North Baddesley SO52 .....54 A2
  Ringwood BH24 .....117 B1
  Southampton SO19 .....104 A3
Edwina Dr BH17 .....187 A1
Edwina Ho BH17 .....187 A1
Effingham Gdns SO19 .....104 B2
Efford Ct SO41 .....197 A1
Efford Farm Cotts SO41 .....197 A1
Efford Way SO41 .....197 A1
Egan Cl PO2 .....157 C2
Egbert Rd SO23 .....2 A1
Egdon Cl BH22 .....165 A2
Egdon Ct BH16 .....201 A4
Egdon Dr BH21 .....187 C4
Egerton Gdns BH8 .....205 B3
Egerton Rd BH8 .....205 B3
Eglantine Cl PO8 .....112 A2
Eglantine Wlk PO8 .....112 B2
Egmont Cl BH24 .....140 B1
Egmont Dr BH24 .....140 B1
Egmont Gdns BH24 .....140 B1
Egmont Rd BH16 .....201 A2
Eight Acres SO51 .....53 A4
Eileen Beard Ho 51 PO9 .....136 A3
Elaine Gdns PO8 .....112 A3
Elan Cl SO18 .....80 A1
Elcombes Cl SO43 .....121 C3
Elder Cl
  Locks Heath SO31 .....128 C1
  Marchwood SO40 .....102 A3
  Winchester SO22 .....10 B2
Elder Gn SO21 .....57 A4
Elder Rd PO9 .....136 A2
Elderberry Cl
  Clanfield PO8 .....88 B2
  Fair Oak SO50 .....57 A1
Elderberry La BH23 .....207 C3
Elderberry Way PO8 .....112 B2
Elderfield Cl PO10 .....137 A2
Elderfield Rd PO9 .....135 B4
Eldon Ave BH25 .....209 A4
Eldon Cl SO40 .....209 C4
Eldon Ct 9 Poole BH14 .....203 A2
  Portsmouth PO5 .....215 B2
Eldon Ho 22 SO14 .....103 A2
Eldon Pl BH4 .....204 A2
Eldon Rd
  Bournemouth BH9 .....189 C1
  Braishfield SO20, SO51 .....7 A3
  King's Somborne SO20 .....7 A3
Eldon St PO5 .....215 B2
Eldridge Gdns SO51 .....52 C4
Eleanor Dr BH11 .....188 B3
Eleanor Gdns BH23 .....206 C4
Electron Way SO53 .....55 B3
Elettra Ave PO7 .....134 B4
Eleven Cross SP6 .....68 A3
Elfin Ct 3 SO17 .....103 A4
Elfin Dr BH22 .....165 B2
Elgar Cl Gosport PO12 .....181 A1
  Portchester PO6 .....156 C4
Elgar Ct SO41 .....197 C2
Elgar Rd
  Bournemouth BH10 .....189 B2
  Southampton SO19 .....104 B2
Elgar Wlk PO7 .....134 C3
Elgin Cl Fareham PO15 .....130 C1
  Hythe SO45 .....126 A2
Elgin Rd
  Bournemouth BH3,BH4 .....204 B3
  Cosham PO6 .....157 C3
  Poole BH14 .....203 B1
  Southampton SO15 .....102 B3
Elijah Cl BH15 .....201 C1
Eling Cl SO22 .....1 B2
Eling Ct PO9 .....135 B3
Eling Hill SO40 .....101 A3
Eling Inf Sch SO40 .....101 A3
Eling La SO40 .....101 A4
Eling Tide Mill★ SO40 .....101 A3
Eling View SO15 .....101 B4
Elingfield Ct SO40 .....101 A4
Eliot Ho
  14 New Milton BH25 .....195 A1
  Southampton SO17 .....79 B1
Elise Cl BH7 .....206 A4
Eliza Pl PO12 .....181 B1
Elizabeth Ave BH23 .....207 B4
Elizabeth Cl Downton SP5 .....46 B4
  West End SO30 .....80 B1
  Wickham PO17 .....107 C2
Elizabeth Cres SO41 .....196 A1
Elizabeth Ct
  12 Bournemouth BH1 .....205 A2
  6 Cosham PO6 .....157 C4
  Eastleigh SO50 .....56 A2
  Fareham PO14 .....154 C4
  4 Gosport PO12 .....181 A3
  11 New Milton BH25 .....195 A1
  Southampton, Aldermoor SO16 .....78 A2
  Southampton, Portswood SO17 .....79 B1
  West End SO30 .....80 B1
Elizabeth Gdns
  Christchurch BH23 .....208 B4
  Hythe SO45 .....126 A1
  Portsmouth PO4 .....182 C1
Elizabeth Ho SO40 .....76 B1
Elizabeth Rd Poole BH15 .....202 B3
  Stubbington PO14 .....179 B3
  Upton BH16 .....201 B4
  Waterlooville PO7 .....134 C3
  Wickham PO17 .....108 A2
  Wimborne Minst BH21 .....163 B4

Elizabeth Way
  Bishop's Waltham SO32 .....83 A4
  Eastleigh SO50 .....56 A3
Elkhams Cl SO41 .....196 B1
Elkstone Rd PO6 .....133 A1
Ellachie Gdns PO12 .....181 A1
Ellachie Mews PO12 .....181 A1
Ellachie Rd PO12 .....181 A1
Elland Cl SO50 .....57 B1
Elldene Ct SO40 .....100 C3
Ellen Gdns SO53 .....55 A3
Ellen Wren Ho SO18 .....79 C2
Ellerslie Ct PO14 .....179 A3
Ellery Gr SO41 .....197 C3
Ellesfield Dr BH22 .....165 B1
Ellesmere Orch PO10 .....137 A3
Ellingham Cross BH24 .....116 C3
Ellingham Dr BH24 .....116 B3
Ellingham Dro BH25 .....209 B4
Elliot Cl SO40 .....100 B4
Elliot Rd BH11 .....188 C4
Elliot Rise SO30 .....81 B1
Ellis Rd SO19 .....104 C3
Ellisfield Rd PO9 .....135 C2
Ellwood Ave SO19 .....104 C3
Ellwood Cl SO19 .....104 C3
Elm Ave
  Christchurch BH23 .....191 C1
  Lymington SO41 .....197 B1
  New Milton BH25 .....195 A4
Elm Cl
  South Hayling PO11 .....185 A2
  Southampton SO16 .....78 C2
Elm Cres Hythe SO45 .....150 A4
  Upham SO32 .....58 C3
Elm Ct
  Chandler's Ford SO53 .....30 B1
  4 New Milton BH25 .....195 A1
  Southampton, Sholing SO19 .....103 C2
  25 Southampton, Westwood Pk SO17 .....79 A1
  Winchester SO22 .....10 C4
Elm Gdns
  Bournemouth BH4 .....204 B3
  West End SO30 .....80 B2
Elm Gr Eastleigh SO50 .....55 C1
  Gosport PO12 .....181 A1
  Portsmouth PO5 .....215 B1
  South Hayling PO11 .....185 A2
Elm La PO9 .....135 C1
Elm Lodge PO5 .....215 C1
Elm Park Rd PO9 .....135 C1
Elm Rd
  Bishop's Waltham SO32 .....83 C4
  Havant PO9 .....160 A4
  Winchester SO22 .....10 C4
Elm St Portsmouth PO1 .....215 A1
  Southampton SO14 .....103 A2
Elm Terr Liss GU33 .....20 C3
  Southampton SO14 .....103 A2
Elm Tree Wlk BH22 .....189 C4
Elmdale GU31 .....41 A2
Elmdale Rd SO31 .....152 B4
Elmdale Gr SO51 .....51 A1
Elmers Way BH23 .....169 A1
Elmes Dr SO15 .....101 C4
Elmes Rd BH9 .....189 C1
Elmeswelle Rd PO8 .....112 A3
Elmfield SP5 .....47 B3
Elmfield La SO45 .....178 C4
Elmgate Dr BH7 .....206 A4
Elmhurst Rd
  Bournemouth BH11 .....189 A3
  Fareham PO16 .....155 A4
  Gosport PO12 .....181 B2
  West Moors BH22 .....138 C1
Elmhurst Way PO12 .....138 C1
Elmleigh Rd PO9 .....135 C1
Elmore Ave PO13 .....180 A3
Elmore Cl PO13 .....179 C1
Elmore Dr BH24 .....139 C3
Elmore Rd PO13 .....179 C1
Elmrise Prim Sch BH11 .....189 A2
Elms Ave BH14 .....203 A1
Elms Cl Fordingbridge SP6 .....69 A1
  Poole BH14 .....203 A1
Elms Rd PO16 .....155 A4
Elms Way BH6 .....206 C2
Elmsdown Ct BH24 .....140 C2
Elmsleigh Ct SO17 .....79 A2
Elmsleigh Gdns SO16 .....79 A2
Elmslie Gdns SO31 .....104 C1
Elmstead Rd BH13 .....214 C4
Elmtree Cl SO40 .....100 A1
Elmtree Gdns
  2 Eastleigh SO50 .....56 A1
  Romsey SO51 .....53 B3
Elmtree Rd PO6 .....158 C4
Elmwood Ave
  Fordingbridge SP6 .....69 B1
  Waterlooville PO7 .....134 C3
Elmwood Ct SO16 .....78 C4
Elmwood Lodge 2 PO16 .....131 A1
Elmwood Rd PO2 .....157 C2
Elmwood Way BH23 .....209 A4
Elphinstone Rd
  Christchurch BH23 .....194 A1
  Portsmouth PO5 .....182 B1
Elsfred Rd PO14 .....179 A3
Elson Inf Sch PO12 .....181 A4
Elson Jun Sch PO12 .....181 A4
Elson La PO12 .....181 A4
Elson Rd PO12 .....181 A4

Elstead Gdns PO7 .....134 C3
Elstree Rd SO19 .....103 C3
Eltham Cl BH7 .....206 A4
Elvin Cl SO41 .....195 C2
Elwell Gn PO11 .....184 C2
Elwyn Rd BH1 .....205 B3
Ely Ct PO13 .....180 B3
Elysium Ct BH22 .....165 C2
Emanuel St PO2 .....157 B1
Embankment Way BH24 .....141 A3
Embassy Ct PO4 .....215 D2
Emberley Cl BH22 .....166 A3
Embley Cl SO40 .....76 B1
Embley La SO51 .....51 C4
Embley Park Ind Est SO51 .....51 C4
Embley Park Jun Sch SO51 .....52 C4
Embley Park Sch SO51 .....51 C3
Embsay Rd SO31 .....128 B4
Emer Rd SO52 .....54 C3
Emerald Cl
  Southampton SO19 .....104 A3
  St Leonards BH24 .....139 C3
  Waterlooville PO7 .....135 A4
Emerald Cres SO45 .....126 A2
Emerson Cl BH15 .....202 B1
Emerson Rd BH15 .....202 B1
Emily Cl BH23 .....192 A1
Emily Ct BH14 .....203 C3
Emily Davis Halls Of Residence 12 SO14 .....102 A3
Emmadale Ct 5 SO14 .....103 A3
Emmanuel CE Mid Sch BH31 .....114 C3
Emmanuel Cl PO14 .....129 B1
Emmett Rd SO16 .....77 C3
Emmons Cl SO31 .....128 A1
Empire Ct 13 PO9 .....135 C1
Empress Pk SO14 .....103 A4
Empress Rd
  Lyndhurst SO43 .....121 C1
  Southampton, Bevois Valley SO14 .....103 A4
Empshott Rd PO4 .....182 C1
Empson Wlk PO13 .....179 C2
Emsbrook Dr PO10 .....136 C1
Emsworth Common Rd PO9,PO10 .....136 C3
Emsworth House Cl PO10 .....136 C1
Emsworth Mus★ PO10 .....160 C4
Emsworth Prim Sch PO10 .....136 C1
Emsworth Rd
  Havant PO9 .....136 A1
  Lymington SO41 .....197 C2
  Portsmouth PO2 .....157 C1
  Southampton SO15 .....102 A4
  Thorney Island PO10 .....161 A1
Emsworth Sta PO10 .....136 C1
Encombe Cl BH12 .....203 C4
Endeavour Cl 17 SO15 .....102 A4
Endeavour Pk BH24 .....141 A3
Endeavour Rd PO12 .....181 B2
Endeavour Way SO45 .....126 A3
Enderleigh Ho PO9 .....135 C1
Enderwood Cl SO40 .....100 A4
Endfield Cl BH23 .....191 C1
Endfield Rd
  Bournemouth BH9 .....190 A1
  Christchurch BH23 .....191 C1
Endle St SO14 .....103 A2
Endofield Cl PO14 .....154 C3
Enfield Cres BH15 .....202 C3
Enfield Gr SO19 .....103 C2
Enfield Rd BH15 .....202 C3
Englands Way BH11 .....188 B2
Englefield Ct 4 SO31 .....127 A3
Englefield Rd SO18 .....103 B4
English Ct 16 SO51 .....52 C3
English Rd SO15 .....102 A4
Enmill La SO22 .....9 C3
Ennel Copse SO52 .....54 A2
Ennerdale Cl PO8 .....88 B1
Ennerdale Gdns SO18 .....80 C1
Ennerdale Rd
  Southampton SO16 .....77 C1
  Stubbington PO14 .....154 B2
Ensbury Ave BH10 .....189 B1
Ensbury Cl BH10 .....189 B1
Ensbury Ct BH10 .....189 B1
Ensbury Park Rd BH9 .....189 C1
Ensign Dr PO13 .....180 B3
Ensign Pk SO31 .....127 C1
Ensign Way SO31 .....127 C1
Enterprise Cl SO31 .....128 C1
Enterprise Ctr
  Fareham PO14 .....155 A3
  Portsmouth PO3 .....158 A2
Enterprise Ind Est PO8 .....112 B4
Enterprise Rd
  Chilworth SO16 .....54 B1
  Horndean PO8 .....112 B4
Enterprise Way
  Hurn BH23 .....190 B4
  Southampton SO10 .....103 A1
Eperston Rd PO8 .....112 A3
Epiphany CE Prim Sch BH9 .....190 A2
Epping Cl SO18 .....80 A1
Epsom Cl SO50 .....81 B4
Epsom Ct PO15 .....129 B4
Epworth Rd PO2 .....157 C1
Erasmus Pk SO23 .....2 B1

Eric Rd PO14 ....179 B3
Erica Cl
  Locks Heath SO31 ....128 C2
  Waterlooville PO8 ....112 A2
Erica Dr BH21 ....186 B3
Erica Way PO8 ....112 A2
Ericksen Rd BH11 ......189 B3
Erinbank Mans BH1 ....205 B2
Ernest Cl PO10 ....136 C1
Ernest Rd Havant PO9 ...135 C2
  Portsmouth PO1 ......182 C4
Erpingham Rd BH12 ....204 A3
Errington Ho 7 SO50 ...56 A1
Erskine Ct SO16 ....77 C3
Erskine Rd SO22 ....10 C4
Escombe Rd SO50 ....56 B2
Escur Cl PO2 ....157 C2
Esdaile La BH24 ....142 C2
Esher Gr PO7 ....111 B1
Eskdale Cl PO8 ....88 B1
Eskdale Ho 16 PO6 .....133 A1
Esmond Cl PO10 ....160 C4
Esmonde Cl PO13 ......179 C4
Esmonde Way BH17 ....202 C4
Esplanade Poole BH13 ..214 C4
  Portsmouth PO4 ......183 A1
Esplanade Gdns PO4 ...183 B1
Esplanade The PO12 ...181 C2
Essex Ave BH23 ....191 C1
Essex Gn SO53 ....55 B1
Essex Rd PO4 ....183 A2
Esslemont Rd PO4 .....182 C2
Estella Rd PO2 ....182 B4
Estridge Cl SO31 ......105 A1
Ethel Rd PO1 ....215 D4
Ethelbert Rd BH21 .....163 B2
Ethelburt Ave SO16 .....79 B3
Ethelred Gdns SO40 ...100 B3
Eton Gdns BH4 ....204 B2
Eton Rd PO5 ....215 D2
Ettrick Rd BH13 ....204 A1
Eucalyptus Ave BH14 ..140 A1
European Way SO14 ...103 A1
Euryalus Rd PO14 .....155 A3
Euston Gr BH24 ....141 A3
Euston Rd PO4 ....183 A3
Eva Allaway Ct 20 PO1 ..182 A3
Evans Cl
  Bournemouth BH11 ...188 C1
  Portsmouth PO2 ......157 A1
  St Leonards BH24 ....139 C3
Evans Rd PO4 ....183 A4
Evans St SO14 ....103 A2
Evelegh Rd PO6 ....158 B4
Evelyn Cl SO32 ....83 C2
Evelyn Cres SO15 .....102 B4
Evelyn Mews 1 BH9 ...189 C1
Evelyn Rd BH9 ....190 A1
Evening Glade BH22 ...165 C2
Evenlode Rd SO16 ......77 C1
Eventide Homes BH8 ...190 C1
Everdene Cl BH22 .....165 B1
Everdon La PO3 ....158 B2
Everest Rd BH23 ......207 C4
Everglades Ave PO8 ...111 C2
Everglades Cl BH22 ...165 B4
Evergreen Cl
  Marchwood SO40 .....101 C1
  Three Legged Cross BH21 138 C4
  Waterlooville PO7 ....134 B4
Evergreens
  St Leonards BH24 ....139 C3
  Totton SO40 ....101 A3
Evering Ave BH12 .....188 B1
Evering Gdns BH12 ....188 B1
Everlea Cl SO41 ....196 B1
Everon Gdns BH25 ....195 A1
Evershot Rd BH8 ......190 C1
Eversleigh BH2 ....204 B1
Eversley Cres PO9 ....135 C2
Eversley Pl SO22 ....10 B3
Everton Rd SO41 ......196 A1
Evesham Cl
  Bournemouth BH7 ....206 A4
  Southampton SO16 ....79 A3
Evesham Ct BH13 .....204 A1
Ewart Ct SO45 ....126 A3
Ewart Rd PO1 ....182 C4
Ewell Way SO40 ....76 B1
Ewhurst Cl PO9 ....135 B2
Exbourne Manor BH1 ...205 B2
Exbury Cl SO50 ....56 C1
Exbury Dr BH11 ....188 C3
Exbury Gdns★ SO45 ...177 A3
Exbury Rd
  Blackfield SO45 ......150 C1
  Havant PO9 ....136 A3
Excellent Rd PO14 ....154 C3
Excelsior Rd BH14 ....203 B4
Exchange Rd PO1 .....215 A3
Exeter Cl Eastleigh SO50 ..55 C1
  Emsworth PO10 ......136 C1
  Locks Heath SO31 ....128 C2
  Southampton SO18 .....80 A1
Exeter Cres BH2 ......204 C2
Exeter Ct
  10 Christchurch BH23 ...209 A4
  Gosport PO13 ....180 B3
Exeter La BH2 ....204 C1
Exeter Park Mans BH2 ..204 C1
Exeter Park Rd BH2 ...204 C1
Exeter Rd
  Bournemouth BH2 ....204 C2
  Portsmouth PO4 ......182 C1
  Southampton SO18 ....104 A4

Exford Ave SO18 ......104 B4
Exford Dr SO18 ....104 B4
Exleigh Cl SO18 ....104 A3
Exmoor Cl
  Swanwick PO15 ......129 A4
  Totton SO40 ....100 A4
Exmoor Rd SO14 ......103 A3
Exmouth Gdns SO50 ....81 B4
Exmouth Rd
  Gosport PO12 ....181 A4
  Portsmouth PO5 ......182 B1
Exton Ave SO14 ....103 A3
Exton Gdns PO16 .....132 B1
Exton Rd
  Bournemouth BH6 ....206 B4
  Havant PO9 ....136 A3
Eyebright Cl SO50 ......81 B3
Eyeworth Wlk SO45 ...125 B2
Eynham Ave SO19 ....104 B3
Eynham Cl SO19 ......104 B3
Eynon Mews BH24 ....140 C3
Eyre Cl SO40 ....100 B3

F

F Ave SO45 ....150 C3
Faber Cl PO9 ....136 A2
Faber Mews SO51 ......53 A4
Fabers Yd 16 SO22 .....10 C4
Fabian Cl PO7 ....135 A4
Factory Rd Eastleigh SO50 56 A1
  Upton BH16 ....201 B3
Fair Field SO51 ....28 A1
Fair Gn SO19 ....104 A3
Fair Isle Cl PO14 .....154 A2
Fair La SO21 ....11 C4
Fair Lea BH2 ....204 C1
Fair Oak Ct
  4 Fair Oak SO50 ....57 B1
  Gosport PO12 ....180 B2
Fair Oak Dr PO9 ......135 C2
Fair Oak Inf Sch SO50 ..57 B1
Fair Oak Jun Sch SO50 ..57 B1
Fairacre Rise PO14 ...154 A4
Fairacre Wlk SO53 .....54 C3
Fairbourne Cl PO8 ....111 C1
Fairclose Dr SO22 ......1 A3
Faircourt 18 BH25 ....195 A4
Faircross Cl SO45 ....150 B2
Fairdown Cl SO23 ......11 B4
Fairfax Cl SO22 ....10 A3
Fairfax Ct SO19 ......104 C3
Fairfax Mews SO19 ...104 C3
Fairfield
  Christchurch BH23 ...207 A4
  Denmead PO7 ....110 C3
Fairfield Ave PO14 ....154 C4
Fairfield Cl
  Christchurch BH23 ...207 A4
  Emsworth PO10 ......136 C1
  Hythe SO45 ....125 C2
  Lymington SO41 .....197 C2
  Wimborne Minst BH21 .163 C3
Fairfield Inf Sch PO9 ..136 A1
Fairfield Rd
  Barton on Sea BH25 ...209 C4
  Compton(Hants) SO21 ..31 B3
  Havant PO9 ....135 C1
  Wimborne Minst BH21 .163 B2
  Winchester SO21 ....1 C1
Fairfield Sq PO6 ......157 C4
Fairgate Ctr The SP6 ...70 A2
Fairhavon Ct 12 BH5 ..205 C2
Fairhome Cl PO12 ....181 A4
Fairies Dr BH22 ......165 C2
Fairisle Inf Sch SO16 ...77 C2
Fairisle Jun Sch SO16 ...77 C2
Fairisle Rd SO16 ......77 C2
Fairlands Montessori Sch
  SO32 ....107 C3
Fairlawn Cl SO16 ......77 C3
Fairlawn Ho 27 SO22 ..10 C4
Fairlea Grange 3 SO16 .78 C2
Fairlea Rd
  Emsworth PO10 ......136 C2
  Lymington SO41 .....197 C3
Fairlead Dr PO13 .....180 B3
Fairlie BH21 ....117 B1
Fairlie Cl SO30 ....81 B2
Fairlie Pk BH24 ....117 A1
Fairlight La SO41 .....195 B4
Fairmead Ct PO11 ....184 C2
Fairmead Way SO40 ...100 A4
Fairmead Wlk PO8 ....112 A2
Fairmile Par BH23 ....191 C1
Fairmile Rd BH23 .....191 C1
Fairoak Rd
  Bishopstoke SO50 ....57 A1
  Fair Oak SO50 ....57 A1
Fairthorn Ct 2 BH2 ..204 C2
Fairthorne Gdns PO12 .181 A2
Fairview Cl Hythe SO45 .126 A2
  Romsey SO51 ....28 A1
Fairview Cres BH18 ...187 A3
Fairview Ct PO12 .....180 C2
Fairview Dr
  Broadstone BH18 ....187 A3
  Hythe SO45 ....126 A2
  Romsey SO51 ....28 A1
Fairview Par 1 SO45 ..126 A1
Fairview Pk BH14 .....203 B2
Fairview Rd BH18 .....187 A3
Fairwater Cl PO13 ....155 A1
Fairway Ave BH14 ....214 B4

Fairway Bsns Ctr PO3 ..158 B1
Fairway Dr BH23 .....206 C3
Fairway Gdns SO16 ....77 C3
Fairway Rd SO45 .....125 C2
Fairway The
  Barton on Sea BH25 ...210 A4
  Gosport PO13 ....155 B1
  Locks Heath SO31 ....128 C1
  Portchester PO16 ....156 B4
  Rowland's Castle PO9 ..113 B1
Fairways PO15 ....165 C3
Fairwinds BH13 ......214 A2
Fairwood Rd BH31 ....115 B3
Fairy Cross Way PO8 ..112 A1
Falaise Rd SO16 ....78 B2
Falcon Cl PO16 ......155 C4
Falcon Dr BH23 ......208 A3
Falcon Fields SO45 ...151 A2
Falcon Gn PO6 ....158 C4
Falcon Rd PO8 ....112 A4
Falcon Sq SO50 ....55 C1
Falcon View SO22 .....10 C2
Falcon Way SO32 .....81 C1
Falconer Ct SO45 ....150 B2
Falconer Dr PO9 .....136 A1
Falconwood Cl SP6 ....69 B1
Falkland Ct SO53 .....55 B2
Falkland Rd
  Chandler's Ford SO53 ..55 B2
  Southampton SO15 ...102 A4
Falkland Sq 2 BH15 ..202 B1
Falklands Cl PO13 ....179 C2
Falklands Rd 1 PO2 ..157 C4
Fallow Field SO22 .....10 B2
Fallows The BH25 ....195 A3
Falstaff Way SO40 ....100 C3
Fancy Rd BH12 ......203 A4
Fanshawe St SO14 ...103 A3
Far Ends 13 BH14 ....203 A2
Far Meadow Way PO10 160 B4
Farcroft Rd BH12 ....203 A3
Fareham Coll PO14 ...130 C1
Fareham Hts PO16 ...131 B2
Fareham Ind Pk PO16 .131 B2
Fareham Park Rd PO15 .130 B2
Fareham Rd
  Gosport PO13 ....155 B2
  Southwick PO17 .....132 C3
  Wickham PO17 ......108 A2
Fareham Sta PO15 ...130 C1
Faringdon Ct 16 SO23 ..2 A1
Faringdon Rd SO18 ...104 B4
Farleigh Cl PO9 ......135 B3
Farley Cl Fair Oak SO50 .57 B1
  Winchester SO22 .....10 A2
Farley Ct SO15 ....78 B1
Farley La SO51 ....7 C1
Farley Mount Nature
  Reserve★ SO21 ....9 A4
Farley Mount Rd SO21 ..9 A2
Farlington Ave PO6 ...134 B1
Farlington Marshes (Nature
  Reserve)★ PO6 ......158 C3
Farlington Rd PO2 ...157 C1
Farm Cl
  Hamble-le-Rice SO31 ..128 A1
  Ringwood BH24 .....141 A4
Farm Edge Rd PO14 ..179 B3
Farm House Cl PO14 .154 B3
Farm La
  Christchurch BH23 ...208 A3
  Southbourne PO18 ...161 C4
Farm La (N) BH25 ....210 A3
Farm La S BH25 .....210 A4
Farm Lane Cl PO7 ....134 B2
Farm Rd
  Titchfield PO14,PO15 ..129 C1
  West Moors BH22 ....138 B1
Farm View PO10 .....136 C2
Farm View Ave PO8 ...88 A3
Farmdene Cl BH23 ...208 B4
Farmers Wlk
  Hordle SO41 ....211 B4
  1 Wimborne Minst BH21 .163 A3
Farmery Cl SO18 ......79 B2
Farmhouse Way PO8 ..112 A2
Farmlea Rd PO6 .....157 A4
Farmside Gdns PO3 ..157 C2
Farnham Rd Liss GU33 ..20 C2
  Poole BH12 ....204 A4
  Steep GU32 ....41 A4
Farnleys Mead SO41 ..197 C1
Faroes Cl PO14 ......154 A2
Farrier Way PO16 ....155 A3
Farriers Cl BH21 .....164 A3
Farriers Way PO7 ....112 B1
Farriers Wlk PO12 ...181 B2
Farringdon Rd PO9 ...136 A2
Farringford Rd SO19 ..104 B3
Farrington BH4 ......204 B1
Farthing La PO1 .....182 A2
Farthings Gate PO7 ..134 C2
Farwell Cl BH23 ......192 B2
Farwell Rd BH12 .....188 B1
Fastnet Cl SO16 ....77 C3
Fastnet Ho 13 PO5 ...182 B1
Fastnet Way PO14 ...154 A2
Fathersfield SO42 ....145 C1
Fathoms Reach PO11 .184 C2
Faulston Cotts SP5 ....22 B4
Faversham BH21 .....204 B1
Fawcett Rd
  Barton on Sea BH25 ..194 C1
  Portsmouth PO4 .....215 D2
Fawley Bsns Ctr SO45 ..151 A2
Fawley By Pass SO45 .151 A2
Fawley Ct 48 PO9 ....136 A3
Fawley Gn BH8 ......190 B2

Fawley Inf Sch SO45 ..151 A2
Fawley La Froxfield GU34 ..17 A2
  Owslebury SO21 ......33 A4
Fawley Rd Fawley SO45 .150 C2
  Hythe SO45 ....150 A4
  Portsmouth PO2 .....157 C3
  Southampton SO15 ...102 A3
Fawn Gdns BH25 .....194 C2
Fay Cl PO14 ....179 B3
Fayre La PO16 ....155 A4
Fayrewood Ct BH31 ..114 C4
Fearon Rd PO2 ......157 C1
Felix Rd PO12 ....181 A4
Fell Cl SO31 ....129 A2
Fell Dr PO13 ....179 C2
Felmer Dr SO23 ....2 B4
Feltham Cl SO51 ......53 B4
Felton Cres BH23 ....208 C4
Felton Ct BH14 ......202 C3
Felton Rd BH14 .....202 C3
Feltons Pl PO3 ......157 C3
Fen Ave PO16 ....155 C4
Fenleigh Cl BH25 ....195 A1
Fennel Gdns SO41 ...197 C3
Fennell Cl PO7 ......111 B1
Fenton Rd BH6 ......206 B3
Fenwick Ct BH8 .....205 A3
Fenwick Hospl SO43 .121 C3
Fern Bank 28 BH2 ...204 C2
Fern Barrow BH2 ....204 A4
Fern Cl Alderholt SP6 ..93 A3
  Burton BH23 ....192 B1
  Petersfield GU31 ....41 B2
Fern Cotts 2 PO16 ...131 B1
Fern Dr PO9 ....136 A1
Fern Rd Hythe SO45 ..125 C2
  Southampton SO19 ...103 C1
Fern Way PO15 .....129 B2
Ferncroft Cl PO14 ...179 B3
Ferncroft Gdns BH10 .189 B3
Ferncroft Rd BH10 ...189 B3
Ferndale Hedge End SO30 105 B3
  Waterlooville PO7 ...135 A4
Ferndale Mews PO13 .155 A2
Ferndale Rd
  Marchwood SO40 .....101 C1
  New Milton BH25 ....195 A4
Ferndene Way SO18 ..103 C4
Ferndown Ct The PO5 ..69 B1
Ferndown Fst Sch BH22 165 B3
Ferndown Ind Est BH22 164 C4
Ferndown Mid Sch
  BH22 ....165 B3
Ferndown Upper Sch
  BH22 ....165 A3
Ferneham Rd PO15 ...130 B2
Fernglade BH25 .....195 A2
Fernheath Cl BH11 ...189 A2
Fernheath Rd BH11 ..189 A2
Fernhill SO53 ....55 C3
Fernhill Cl BH17 .....188 C1
Fernhill Flats 29 BH2 ..204 C2
Fernhill Gate BH25 ...195 A3
Fernhill La BH25 .....195 A2
Fernhill Rd BH25 ....195 A4
Fernhills Rd SO45 ...126 A1
Fernhurst Cl PO11 ...184 B2
Fernhurst Jun Sch PO4 182 C2
Fernhurst Rd PO4 ...182 C2
Fernie Cl PO14 ......179 A3
Fernlea Ave BH22 ...165 B2
Fernlea Cl
  Ferndown BH22 .....165 B2
  St Leonards BH24 ...139 C2
Fernlea Gdns
  Ferndown BH22 .....165 B2
  Southampton SO16 ...78 C2
Fernlea Way SO45 ...125 B2
Fernside Ave BH14 ...202 C2
Fernside Cl
  Holbury SO45 ....150 B2
  Southampton SO16 ..101 C4
Fernside Ct BH15 ....202 C2
Fernside Rd
  Bournemouth BH9 ...204 C4
  Poole BH15 ....202 C2
  West Moors BH22 ...138 C1
Fernside Way SO50 ...57 C1
Fernside Wlk SO50 ...57 C1
Fernway Cl BH21 ....164 C3
Fernwood Cl BH24 ...140 A3
Fernwood Cres SO18 .103 C4
Fernwood Ho PO12 ..112 A1
Ferny Crofts (Scout Ctr)
  SO42 ....148 A4
Fernyhurst Ave SO16 ..77 C1
Ferris Ave BH8 ......190 B1
Ferris Cl BH8 ....190 B1
Ferris Pl BH8 ....190 B1
Ferrol Rd PO12 .....181 B3
Ferry Rd
  Bournemouth BH6 ...206 C2
  Hamworthy BH15 ...202 A4
  Hythe SO45 ....125 C2
  Poole BH19 ....214 A1
  Portsmouth PO4 .....183 B2
  Portsmouth PO4 .....183 C2
  South Hayling PO11 ..184 A2
Ferry Way BH13 .....214 A2
Ferrybridge Gn 4 SO30 105 B3
Ferrymans Quay SO31 .127 A3
Ferrypoint SO41 .....198 A2
Festing Gr PO4 .....183 A1
Festing Rd PO4 .....182 C1
Feversham Ave BH8 ..190 C1
Fey Rd PO12 ....181 B3
Fibbards Rd SO42 ...145 C1

Field Cl
  Compton (Hants) SO21 ..31 B3
  Gosport PO13 ....155 A3
  Locks Heath SO31 ...129 A1
  Romsey SO51 ....53 A4
  Southampton SO16 ....79 B3
Field End SO23 ....2 B4
Field Pl
  Barton on Sea BH25 ..209 B4
  Verwood BH31 ....114 C4
Field View SO53 ......54 C3
Field Way
  Christchurch BH23 ...193 B1
  Compton (Hants) SO21 ..31 B3
  Corfe Mullen BH21 ..186 C4
  Denmead PO7 ....110 C2
  Fordingbridge SP6 ....70 B1
Field Wlk SO41 ......197 B3
Fielden Cl SO22 ......53 C2
Fielder Dr PO14 .....155 A3
Fielders Ct PO7 .....134 B2
Fielders' Way SO51 ...51 A1
Fieldfare Cl PO8 ......88 B2
Fieldfare Ct SO40 ...100 B4
Fieldhouse Dr PO13 ..179 C2
Fieldmore Rd PO12 ..181 A4
Fields Cl SO45 ....150 C1
Fields The BH31 .....114 C4
Fieldway BH24 ......141 A4
Fifth Ave Cosham PO6 ..157 C4
  Havant PO9 ....136 A1
Fifth St PO1 ....182 C3
Filmer Cl PO13 ......180 B4
Filmorehill La GU34 ...17 A2
Filton Cl SO40 ....76 B3
Filton Rd SO41 ......197 B2
Finch Ho PO4 ....183 A1
Finch Rd PO4 ....183 A1
Finch's La SO21 ......31 C3
Finchdean Rd
  Havant PO9 ....135 C2
  Rowland's Castle PO9 .113 B2
Finches The SO17 ....79 A1
Finchfield Ave BH11 ..188 C3
Finchmead La GU34 ...40 A2
Finchwood Farm Ind Units
  PO11 ....160 A1
Findon Rd PO12 .....181 A4
Fineshade 7 BH13 ...214 C4
Finisterre Cl PO14 ...154 A2
Finlay Cl SO19 ......104 B3
Fiona Cl SO23 ....11 B4
Fir Ave BH25 ....195 A1
Fir Cl Lyndhurst SO43 ..121 C2
  West Moors BH22 ...138 C2
Fir Copse Rd PO7 ...134 B2
Fir Croft Dr SO53 .....55 B3
Fir Rd SO40 ....100 A1
Fir Tree Cl Fair Oak SO50 ..81 B4
  St Leonards BH24 ...139 C1
Fir Tree Cotts GU33 ..21 C2
Fir Tree Ct SO18 ....104 A4
Fir Tree Gdns PO8 ...112 B3
Fir Tree Gr SO41 ....150 A4
Fir Tree Hill SP6 ......93 A3
Fir Tree La BH23 ....193 B1
Fir Tree Rd Cadnam SO40 ..99 A4
  South Hayling PO11 ..185 A2
Fir Vale Rd BH1 .....204 C2
Firbank Rd BH9 .....205 A4
Firecrest Cl SO16 .....78 A3
Firgrove Cl SO22 .....53 C2
Firgrove Cres PO3 ...157 C3
Firgrove Ct SO15 ....102 B4
Firgrove La PO17 ....108 C3
Firgrove Rd
  North Baddesley SO52 ..54 A4
  Southampton SO15 ...102 B4
Firlands Rise PO9 ...135 A1
Firmain Rd BH12 ....188 B3
Firmount Cl SO41 ...196 C1
Firs Ave PO8 ....111 C2
Firs Cres SO23 ....2 A4
Firs Dr SO30 ....105 C3
Firs Glen Rd
  Bournemouth BH9 ...204 C4
  Verwood BH31 ......115 A2
  West Moors BH22 ...138 C1
Firs La BH14 ....214 A4
Firs The
  Bournemouth BH1, ...205 A2
  Chandler's Ford SO53 .55 B2
  Gosport PO13 ....155 B1
  Southampton SO16 ...78 C2
Firshill BH23 ....208 C4
Firside Rd BH21 .....186 B2
First Ave Cosham PO6 .157 C4
  Cosham, Farlington PO6 158 C4
  Havant PO9 ....136 A1
  Horndean PO8 ....88 C2
  Southampton SO15 ..101 B4
  Southbourne PO10 ...161 B4
First Marine BH25 ...209 C4
First St SO45 ....150 C4
Firsway PO16 ....201 B4
Firtree Cres SO41 ...195 C2
Firtree La SO50 ....81 C4
Firtree Way SO19 ...104 A3
Firwood Cl SO53 .....55 B4
Fisgard Rd PO12 ....181 A4
Fisher Cl PO14 ......154 A2
Fisher Rd PO13 .....155 B2
Fisher's Rd SO40 ...101 A3
Fisherman's Ave BH5,
  BH6 ....206 A2
Fisherman's Wlk BH5 .206 A2
Fishermans Rd BH15 .202 A2
Fishermans The PO10 .161 A4

Fishermans Wlk PO11 185 C1
Fishers Gr PO6 158 C4
Fishers Hill PO15 130 A1
Fishery La PO11 185 B1
Fishlake Mdws SO51 28 A1
Fitzgerald Cl PO15 129 B4
Fitzharris Ave BH9 205 A4
Fitzherbert Rd PO6 158 B4
Fitzherbert Spur PO6 158 C4
Fitzherbert St PO1 215 B4
Fitzhugh Ho SO15 102 C3
Fitzhugh Pl SO15 102 C4
Fitzhugh St 13 SO15 102 C3
Fitzmaurice Rd BH23 206 C4
Fitzpain Cl BH22 165 B1
Fitzpain Rd BH22 165 B1
Fitzpatrick Ct PO6 133 B1
Fitzroy Cl SO16 78 C4
Fitzroy Wlk PO1 215 C4
Fitzwilliam Ave PO14 179 A3
Fitzwilliam Cl BH11 188 C3
Fitzworth Ave BH16 201 B2
Fitzwygram Cres PO9 135 C2
Five Bridges Rd SO23 10 C2
Five Elms Dr SO51 53 B3
Five Heads Rd PO8 112 B4
Five Post La PO12 181 A3
Fivefields Cl SO23 11 B3
Fivefields Rd SO23 11 B4
Flag Staff Gn PO12 181 B3
Flag Wlk PO8 111 C3
Flaghead BH13 214 C3
Flaghead Chine Rd BH13 214 C3
Flaghead Rd BH13 214 C4
Flambard Ave BH23 192 A1
Flambard Rd BH14 203 B2
Flamborough Cl SO16 77 B2
Flamingo Ct PO16 155 C4
Flamston St SP5 22 A4
Flanders Ho 1 PO14 154 C4
Flanders Ind Pk SO30 105 A4
Flanders Rd SO30 105 A4
Flathouse Rd PO1 182 B4
Flaxfields End SP6 69 C1
Flazen Cl BH11 188 B2
Fleet Cl PO13 155 B1
Fleet End Bottom SO31 152 C4
Fleet End Rd SO31 152 C4
Fleet Terr SO21 31 A1
Fleet's Cnr BH17 202 A4
Fleetend Cl PO9 135 C3
Fleetpoint Bsns Ctr BH15 202 A3
Fleets Est BH15 202 A3
Fleets La BH15 202 B3
Fleetsbridge Bsns Ctr BH17 202 A4
Fleetwood Ct BH15 202 B4
Fleming Ave SO52 54 A2
Fleming Cl PO15 129 B2
Fleming Ct
North Baddesley SO52 54 A2
Southampton SO19 103 B1
Fleming Pl
Colden Common SO21 31 C1
4 Romsey SO51 52 C4
Fleming Rd SO17 79 B2
Fletcher Cl
Bournemouth BH10 189 B2
Hythe SO45 125 B2
Fletcher Rd BH10 189 B2
Fletchwood La SO40 100 A2
Fletchwood Rd SO40 100 A3
Fleuret Cl SO45 126 A1
Flexford Cl SO53 30 A1
Flexford Gdns PO9 136 A2
Flexford La SO41 196 B3
Flexford Rd SO52,SO53 54 C4
Flinders Ct PO4 183 A1
Flint Cl SO19 104 C2
Flint St PO5 215 A1
Floating Bridge Rd SO14 103 B2
Floral Farm BH21 164 A1
Florence Cl SO51 51 A1
Florence Ct 3 SO18 103 C4
Florence Rd
Bournemouth BH5 205 C2
Poole BH14 203 B2
Portsmouth PO5 182 B1
Southampton SO19 103 B1
Florentine Way PO7 135 A4
Florin Mall 7 BH7 205 C2
Florins The
Locks Heath PO14 129 A1
Waterlooville PO7 134 C2
Floriston Gdns BH25 195 B2
Flower Bldgs 6 PO13 179 C1
Flower Ct 10 BH21 163 B2
Flowerdown Cl SO40 100 B4
Flowerdown Cvn Pk SO22 1 B3
Flowerdown Ho SO22 1 B2
Flowers Cl SO31 127 C2
Flowers La SO51 50 B3
Flum' E Rd SO45 151 B2
Flushards SO41 197 C2
Flying Bull Cl 3 PO2 182 B4
Flying Bull Inf Sch PO2 182 B4
Flying Bull Jun Sch PO2 182 B4
Flying Bull La PO2 182 B4
Foldsgate Cl SO43 121 C3
Foley Ho PO1 215 B4
Folkestone Rd PO3 183 A4
Folly Farm La BH24 140 B3
Folly Field SO32 83 B4
Folly La GU32 40 C2
Font Cl PO14 129 B2
Fontley Rd PO15 130 A3
Fontmell Rd BH18 187 B2
Fontwell Cl SO40 76 B1
Fontwell Gdns SO50 81 B4
Fontwell Mews 10 PO7 112 A1
Fontwell Rd 32 PO5 182 B1
Foord Rd SO30 105 A3
Football Gn SO43 98 B2
Footner Cl SO51 28 B2
Footners La BH23 192 B1
Forbes Cl SO16 77 C3
Forbes Rd SO23 2 A4
Forbury Rd 2 PO1 215 C2
Ford Ave SO53 55 B2
Ford Cl BH22 165 C4
Ford La BH22 166 A4
Ford Rd PO12 180 C3
Fordingbridge Bsns Pk SP6 69 B1
Fordingbridge Hospl SP6 69 C1
Fordingbridge Inf Sch SP6 69 C2
Fordingbridge Jun Sch SP6 69 C2
Fordingbridge Rd
Alderholt SP6 93 A4
Portsmouth PO4 183 A2
Fordington Ave SO22 10 C4
Fordington Rd 3 SO22 10 C4
Foreland Cl BH23 191 B2
Foreland Ct PO11 185 B1
Foreland Rd BH16 201 B2
Forelle Ctr The BH31 115 B2
Foremans Cotts PO12 181 C1
Foreshore N SO45 151 A3
Foreshore S SO45 151 A3
Forest Ave PO8 112 A2
Forest Cl
Chandler's Ford SO53 55 B4
Christchurch BH23 193 B1
North Baddesley SO52 53 C3
Verwood BH31 115 B2
Waltham Chase SO32 83 C2
Waterlooville PO8 111 C2
Forest Cnr GU33 21 A4
Forest Ct
Fordingbridge SP6 69 C1
New Milton BH25 195 A1
Forest Edge SO45 151 A2
Forest Edge Cl
St Leonards BH24 139 B3
Sway SO41 172 A2
Forest Edge Dr BH24 139 B3
Forest Edge Rd BH24 141 C3
Forest Edge Sch SO40 100 C4
Forest End PO7 134 B4
Forest Front SO45 150 A4
Forest Gate SO45 177 C4
Forest Gate Gdns SO41 197 B1
Forest Gdns
Lyndhurst SO43 121 C3
Waltham Chase SO32 83 C2
Forest Glade Cl SO42 145 B1
Forest Hall SO42 146 A1
Forest Hill Way SO45 125 C1
Forest Hills Ct BH24 141 B3
Forest Hills Dr SO18 79 C2
Forest La Fareham PO17 131 A4
Holbury SO45 150 A3
Ringwood BH24 141 C3
Verwood BH31 114 C4
Forest Links Rd BH22 138 A1
Forest Mdw SO45 150 A4
Forest Mead PO7 110 C2
Forest Oak Dr BH25 195 A3
Forest Park Rd SO42 145 C1
Forest Pines BH25 195 A2
Forest Rd
Bransgore BH23 169 C2
Burley BH24 142 C3
Chandler's Ford SO53 55 B4
Denmead PO7 110 B2
Liss GU33 21 A3
Nomansland SP5 73 B4
Poole BH13 204 A1
Waltham Chase SO32 83 C2
Waterlooville PO7 134 B4
West Moors BH22 138 C2
Woodgreen SP6 47 C2
Forest Rise
Christchurch BH23 193 B1
Liss GU33 21 A3
Forest View
Brockenhurst SO42 145 B1
New Milton BH25 194 B3
4 Southampton SO14 102 C2
Forest View Cl BH9 190 A1
Forest View Dr BH21 165 A3
Forest View Rd BH9 190 A1
Forest Walks (Rhinefield)★ SO42 145 A1
Forest Way
Christchurch BH23 193 B1
Ferndown BH21 165 A3
Gosport PO13 155 C1
Hordle SO41 196 B1
Totton SO40 76 A1
Forest Wlks (Blackwater)★ SO42 144 C3
Forester Rd SO32 85 A1
Foresters Gate SO45 177 B4
Foresters Pk SO23 2 A2
Foresters Rd SO45 150 C1
Forestlake Ave BH24 141 B3
Forestside Ave PO9 136 A3
Forestside Gdns BH24 117 B1
Forestside The BH31 115 B3
Forge Cl SO31 105 A1
Forge La SO45 151 A2
Forge Rd SO45 177 C4
Forneth Gdns PO15 154 A4
Forres Sandle Manor SP6 69 B1
Forster Rd SO14 103 A4
Forsyth Gdns BH10 189 B1
Forsythia Cl Havant PO9 136 A2
Hedge End SO30 105 A4
Hythe SO45 150 A4
Forsythia Pl SO19 103 C3
Fort Brockhurst★ PO12 155 C1
Fort Cumberland Pl BH15 201 B1
Fort Cumberland Rd PO4 183 B2
Fort Fareham Ind Est PO14 155 A3
Fort Fareham Rd PO14 154 C3
Fort Nelson★ PO16 132 A2
Fort Nelson Mus★ PO17 132 A2
Fort Rd Gosport PO12 181 A1
Southampton SO19 103 C2
Fort Wallington Ind Est PO16 131 B1
Fort Widley Married Quarters PO6 133 C1
Fortescue Rd
Bournemouth BH3 205 A3
Poole BH12 203 B3
Forth Cl
North Baddesley SO53 55 A3
Stubbington PO14 154 A2
Forth Ho 11 SO14 103 B3
Forties Cl PO14 154 A2
Forton Rd Gosport PO12 181 A3
Portsmouth PO1 182 C3
Fortune Ct SO53 55 B3
Fortune Ho PO12 181 A3
Fortunes Way PO9 134 C1
Forum The 6 PO9 135 C1
Forward Dr SO41 197 B1
Foster Cl PO14 154 B2
Foster Rd Gosport PO12 181 A2
Portsmouth PO1 215 C4
Founders Way PO13 155 B1
Foundry Cres SO31 127 C4
Foundry Ct 36 PO1 182 A3
Foundry La SO15 102 A4
Foundry Lane Prim Sch SO15 102 A4
Foundry Rd SP5 47 B4
Fountain Ct
4 Colden Common SO21 31 C1
Hedge End SO30 105 A3
Fountain St PO1 215 B3
Fountain Way BH23 207 A3
Fountains Pk SO31 127 A4
Four Acre SO30 106 A3
Four Cnrs SP6 68 A2
Four Marks Gn 3 PO9 136 A3
Four Wells Rd BH21 164 A4
Fourposts Hill 16 SO15 102 C3
Fourshells Cl SO45 150 C1
Fourth Ave Cosham PO6 157 C4
Havant PO9 136 A1
Fourth St PO1 182 C3
Fowey Cl SO53 55 A3
Fowey Ct PO12 181 B4
Fowey The SO45 150 C1
Fowlers Rd SO30 105 A4
Fowlers Wlk SO16 54 B1
Fox Cl SO50 56 C1
Fox Field SO41 196 B1
Fox La Ferndown BH21 164 B3
Winchester SO22 10 B3
Fox Pond La SO41 197 B1
Fox's Wlk SO45 177 C4
Foxbury Cl SO45 126 A1
Foxbury Gr PO16 156 A4
Foxbury La Gosport PO13 155 B2
Gosport PO13 155 C3
Westbourne PO10 137 B2
Foxbury Rd BH24 166 C4
Foxcombe Cl SO32 84 A3
Foxcote Gdns BH25 194 C2
Foxcote Ho 6 PO6 132 C1
Foxcott Cl SO19 126 C4
Foxcott Gr PO9 135 C3
Foxcroft Dr
Holbury SO45 150 A2
Wimborne Minst BH21 164 A3
Foxes Cl Verwood BH31 114 C3
Waterlooville PO7 134 C3
Foxes La SO51 50 C3
Foxglade SO45 177 C4
Foxglove Cl BH23 208 B4
Foxglove Pl BH25 195 B2
Foxgloves Fareham PO16 131 B2
Upton BH16 201 A4
Foxgloves The SO30 105 B3
Foxhayes La SO45 177 C4
Foxhills Ashurst SO40 100 B2
Verwood BH31 115 A3
Foxhills Cl SO40 100 B2
Foxhills Inf Sch SO40 100 B2
Foxhills Jun Sch SO40 100 B2
Foxholes 1 BH6 206 C2
Foxholes Rd
Bournemouth BH6 206 C2
Poole BH15 202 C3
Foxlands SO45 177 C4
Foxlea 19 SO15 102 C4
Foxlea Gdns PO12 181 A4
Foxlease Terr SO43 121 C2
Foxley Dr PO3 158 A2
Foxtail Dr SO45 125 C1
Foxwood Ave BH23 207 C3
Foxy Paddock SO45 177 C4
Foy Gdns SO31 128 B1
Foyes Ct SO15 102 B3
Foyle Rd SO53 55 A3
Frampton Cl
1 Colden Common SO21 31 C1
New Milton BH25 195 B3
Frampton Pl BH24 141 A4
Frampton Rd BH9 205 A4
Frampton Way
Kings Worthy SO23 2 B4
Totton SO40 100 C3
Frances Ct 18 BH23 209 A4
Frances Rd
Bournemouth BH1 205 B2
Waterlooville PO7 134 B2
Francesca Ct 14 BH23 207 C4
Francesca Grange 13 BH23 207 C4
Francesca Lo 1 BH23 207 C3
Francis Ave
Bournemouth BH11 188 B2
Portsmouth PO4 182 C2
Francis Avenue Ind Est BH11 188 B2
Francis Cl PO13 180 A3
Francis Gdns SO23 2 A2
Francis Pl PO14 179 B3
Francis Rd Horndean PO8 88 B2
Poole BH12 203 C3
Franconia Dr SO16 77 A2
Frank Judd Ct 33 PO1 182 A3
Frank Miles Ho 1 PO5 215 B2
Frank Wareham Cottage Homes The BH9 190 A2
Frankland Cres BH14 203 C2
Frankland Terr 3 PO10 161 A4
Franklin Rd
Bournemouth BH9 190 A2
Gosport PO13 180 B4
New Milton BH25 195 B2
Twyford SO21 32 A4
Franklyn Ave SO19 104 A2
Franklyn Cl BH16 201 A4
Franks Way BH12 203 A4
Frankston Rd BH6 206 B2
Frarydene PO10 161 B4
Fraser Cl SO16 77 C3
Fraser Ct BH25 194 C2
Fraser Gdns PO10 137 C1
Fraser Rd Gosport PO13 155 B2
Havant PO9 135 B1
Kings Worthy SO23 2 B4
Poole BH12 203 C4
Portsmouth PO5 215 C2
Portsmouth,Whale Is PO2 157 A1
Frater La PO12 156 A1
Fratton Ct PO1 215 D3
Fratton Park (Portsmouth FC) PO4 183 A3
Fratton Rd PO1 215 D4
Fratton Sta PO1 182 C3
Fratton Way SO50 57 B1
Frattton Ind Est PO4 183 A3
Frayslea 4 SO45 126 A1
Freda Rd BH23 206 C3
Freda Routh Gdns 12 SO50 57 B1
Frederica Rd BH9 204 C4
Frederick St
Portsmouth PO1 215 B4
Southampton SO14 103 A3
Free St SO32 83 B4
Freedom Ct SO45 126 A2
Freefolk Gn 11 PO9 136 A3
Freegrounds Ave SO30 105 B3
Freegrounds Cl 1 SO30 105 B3
Freegrounds Inf Sch SO30 105 B3
Freegrounds Jun Sch SO30 105 B3
Freegrounds Rd SO30 105 B3
Freemans Cl BH21 164 A3
Freemans La BH21 164 A3
Freemantle Bsns Ctr 12 SO15 102 B3
Freemantle CE Inf Sch SO15 102 B3
Freemantle Cl SO19 103 C3
Freemantle Common Rd SO19 103 C3
Freemantle Rd PO12 181 A4
Freestone Rd 36 PO5 182 B1
Fremington Ct 16 BH25 195 A2
French Rd BH17 187 A1
French St
14 Portsmouth PO1 182 A2
Southampton SO14 102 C2
French's Farm Rd BH16 201 A4
Frenches La SO51 51 B4
Frenchmans Rd GU32 40 C2
Frenchmoor La
East Dean SP5 3 C1
West Tytherley SP5 3 C2
Frendstaple Rd PO7 135 A3
Frensham Cl
Bournemouth BH10 189 C2
Hedge End SO30 105 B3
Frensham Ct
Hedge End SO30 105 B3
Portsmouth PO4 182 C2
Frensham Rd PO4 182 C2
Freshfield Gdns PO7 134 C4
Freshfield Rd SO15 102 A4
Freshfield Sq SO15 102 A4
Freshwater Ct
Chandler's Ford SO53 30 C1
3 Lee-on-the-Solent PO13 179 C1
Freshwater Dr BH15 201 B2
Freshwater Rd
Christchurch BH23 208 B3
Cosham PO6 157 C4
Frewen Liby PO1 182 A2
Friars Croft SO40 76 B1
Friars Gate BH23 208 B3
Friars Pond Rd PO15 130 B1
Friars Rd
Christchurch BH23 208 A3
Eastleigh SO50 55 C1
Friars Way SO18 79 B2
Friars Wlk BH25 210 A4
Friarscroft SO31 127 A4
Friarsgate SO23 11 A4
Friary Cl 31 PO5 182 B1
Friary The 30 PO5 182 B1
Friday's Ct BH24 140 C4
Friendly Societies' Homes PO4 183 A2
Friendship Ho PO5 215 B1
Frimstone Rd SO23 11 B4
Frinton Ct 6 BH14 203 A2
Frith La PO17 108 A4
Frith Lane End PO17 108 A4
Fritham Cl SO40 100 B4
Fritham Gdns BH8 190 B2
Fritham Rd SO18 104 B4
Frobisher Ave BH12 188 C1
Frobisher Cl
Christchurch BH23 207 C3
Gosport PO13 180 B3
Ringwood BH24 117 B1
Frobisher Ct SO40 102 A2
Frobisher Gdns
7 Emsworth PO10 160 C4
Southampton SO19 104 B2
Frobisher Gr PO16 156 B4
Frobisher Ho 9 PO1 182 A3
Frobisher Ind Cntr SO51 27 C1
Froddington Rd PO1 215 C2
Frog La SP6 93 C4
Froghall SO45 126 A1
Frogham Gn PO9 135 B3
Frogham Hill SP6 94 B3
Frogmore PO14 154 B4
Frogmore La
Nursling SO16 77 B2
Waterlooville PO8 112 A3
Frogmore Rd PO4 183 A3
Frome Cl SO40 102 A1
Fromond Cl SO41 197 C3
Fromond Rd SO22 1 B2
Front Lawn Inf Sch PO9 135 C3
Front Lawn Jun Sch PO9 135 C3
Frost La SO45 126 A1
Frost Rd BH11 188 C2
Frosthole Cl PO15 130 C2
Frosthole Cres PO15 130 C2
Froud Way BH21 186 B2
Froude Ave PO12 181 B1
Froude Rd PO12 181 B1
Froxfield CE Inf Sch GU32 18 C1
Froxfield Cl SO22 1 B2
Froxfield Gdns PO16 132 B1
Froxfield Ho PO1 215 C4
Froxfield Rd PO9 136 A3
Froyle Ct 38 PO9 136 A3
Fry Cl Blackfield SO45 150 C1
Hamble-le-Rice SO31 128 A2
Fry's La SO32 61 B2
Fryer Cl BH11 189 A3
Fryern Arc SO53 55 C4
Fryern Cl SO53 55 C3
Fryern Court Rd SP6 69 C3
Fryern Inf Sch SO53 55 C3
Fryern Jun Sch SO53 55 C3
Fryers Cl SO23 2 B4
Fryers Copse BH21 164 B3
Fryers Rd BH21 138 B4
Frys La SO41 196 B1
Fuchsia Gdns SO16 78 B1
Fulflood Ct 2 SO22 10 C4
Fulflood Rd PO9 135 C3
Fullegar Cotts SO32 84 A3
Fullerton Cl
26 Havant PO9 136 A3
Southampton SO19 126 C4
Fullerton Rd SO41 197 B2
Fulmar Cl SO16 78 A3
Fulmar Dr SO45 126 A1
Fulmar Rd BH23 208 A3
Fulmar Wlk PO13 155 A2
Fulmer Wlk PO8 111 C2
Fulwood Ave BH11 188 C3
Funtington Rd PO2 182 C4
Funtley Ct PO16 130 C2
Funtley Hill PO16 130 C2
Funtley La PO17 130 C3
Funtley Rd PO15,PO17 130 C3
Furdies PO7 110 C2
Furley Cl SO23 11 A4
Furlong Mews BH24 140 C4
Furlong The BH24 140 C4
Furlonge Ho PO10 136 C1
Furneaux Gdns PO16 131 A2
Furnell Rd BH15 202 B1
Furness Rd 11 PO5 182 B1
Furniss Way PO11 184 B2

Furnston Gr PO10 ....137 C1
Fury Way PO14 ....154 A2
Furze Cl SO19 ....104 A3
Furze Croft BH25 .....195 A1
Furze Hall PO14 ......131 A2
Furze La PO4 ....183 B2
Furze Rd SO19 ....104 A3
Furze Way PO8 ....112 A2
Furzebrook Cl BH17 ..187 C2
Furzedale Gdns SO45 .126 A1
Furzedale Pk SO45 ...126 A1
Furzedown Cotts SO45 ...7 A4
Furzedown Cres **54** PO9 136 A3
Furzedown Ho SO20 ....7 A3
Furzedown Mews **13**
SO45 ....126 A1
Furzedown Rd
King's Somborne SO20 ...7 A4
Southampton SO17 .....79 A1
Furzehall Ave PO16 ..131 A2
Furzehill BH21 ....163 B4
Furzelands Rd BH21 ..138 C4
Furzeley Rd PO7 .....110 C1
Furzey Ave SO45 .....126 A1
Furzey Cl SO45 ......150 C1
Furzey Gdns* SO43 ....98 A2
Furzey La PO42 ......148 A1
Furzey Rd BH16 ......201 A3
Furzley Ct PO9 ......135 B3
Furzley La SO43 ......74 B3
Furzley Rd SO40, SO43 .74 C2
Furzy Whistlers Cl
BH23 ....169 A1
Fushia Cl PO9 ....136 B2
Futcher Sch PO6 .....158 B4
Fyeford Cl SO16 ......77 C3
Fyfield Cl PO15 ......129 B4
Fyning St PO1 ....215 C4

G

G Ave SO45 ....150 C3
Gable Mews PO11 ....185 A2
Gables Ct SO16 ....78 C3
Gage Cl SO40 ....102 A1
Gain's Rd PO4 ....182 C1
Gainsborough Ave
BH25 ....195 A3
Gainsborough Cl SO19 .104 C3
Gainsborough Ct
11 Bournemouth BH5 .206 A3
Lymington SO41 .....197 B1
North Baddesley SO52 ..54 A2
Gainsborough Mews
PO14 ....153 A2
Gainsborough Rd
Bournemouth BH7 ...205 A4
St Leonards BH24 ....139 C3
Gainsford Rd SO19 ..103 C3
Galaxie Rd PO8 ......112 A2
Gale Moor Ave PO12 .180 B2
Galleon Cl SO31 .....128 C1
Gallia Ct SO17 ....78 C1
Gallop Way BH12 ....204 B4
Gallops The PO14 ....129 B1
Galloway Rd BH15 ...201 B2
Gallows Dr BH22 ....165 C1
Galsworthy Rd SO40 .100 B4
Galt Rd PO6 ....158 B4
Galton Ave BH23 ....206 C3
Gamble Cl SO19 .....103 C2
Gamble Rd PO2 ......182 B4
Gamblins La SO32 ...107 C4
Gang Warily Recn Ctr
SO45 ....150 C2
Ganger Farm La SO51 ..28 B1
Ganger Rd SO51 ......28 B1
Gannet Cl Hythe SO45 .126 A1
Southampton SO16 ....78 A3
Gannets The PO14 ...154 A2
Gar St SO22 ....10 C1
Garage Cotts **2** GU32 ..40 C2
Garbett Rd SO23 .....11 B4
Garden City SO45 ....125 A3
Garden Cl
Lyndhurst SO43 .....121 C3
New Milton BH25 ....195 A1
South Hayling PO11 ..184 C2
Garden Court Cotts
BH22 ....138 B2
Garden Ct
Bournemouth BH1 ...205 B3
Portchester PO16 ....156 B4
Garden Downton Moot*
SP5 ....47 A4
Garden Ho **17** BH1 ...205 A2
Garden La
Portsmouth PO1 .....215 B1
St Leonards BH24 ...139 C3
22 Winchester SO23 ...11 A4
Garden Mews SO31 ..128 B1
Garden Rd BH24 ....142 C2
Garden Terr **5** PO5 ..182 B1
Garden Wlk BH22 ...165 C4
Gardeners Cotts BH24 .141 A2
Gardeners La
Awbridge SO51 ......52 A2
Romsey SO51 ....52 A2
Gardenia Dr PO13 ...129 C2
Gardens Cres BH14 ..214 A4
Gardens Ct **7** BH15 .202 C2
Gardens Rd BH14 ...214 A4

Gardens The
Hambledon PO7 ......86 B2
Havant PO9 ....136 A1
Gardiner Cl SO40 ....102 A1
Gardner Ct BH23 ....206 C4
Gardner Rd
Christchurch BH23 ...206 C4
Ringwood BH24 .....141 A3
Titchfield PO14 .....153 C4
Garendon Ct SP6 .....69 C1
Garfield Ave BH1 ....205 B3
Garfield Cl SO32 .....83 B4
Garfield Rd
Bishop's Waltham SO32 .83 B4
5 Netley SO31 ......127 A3
Portsmouth PO2 .....182 B4
Southampton SO19 ...103 C4
Garland Ave PO10 ...136 C2
Garland Ct **12** PO12 .181 A3
Garland Rd BH15 ....202 B2
Garland Way SO40 ..100 A4
Garnett Cl PO14 .....154 B2
Garnier Pk PO17 ....108 A2
Garnier Rd SO23 .....11 A3
Garnier St PO1 ......215 D3
Garnock Rd SO19 ...103 B1
Garratt Cl SO30 ......81 B1
Garrett Cl SO19 .....104 A1
Garrick Gdns SO19 ..104 A1
Garrick Ho **11** PO2 ..157 C2
Garrison Hill SO32 ...61 A1
Garrow Dr SO41 ....197 C3
Garsdale Cl BH11 ...189 A3
Garsons Rd PO10 ...161 B4
Garston Cl PO14 ....153 C4
Garstons Cl PO14 ...153 C4
Garstons Rd PO14 ...153 C4
Garth Cl BH22 ......139 B2
Garth Rd BH9 ....190 A1
Garton Rd SO19 .....103 B2
Gashouse Hill SO31 .127 B3
Gaston Gdns SO51 ...52 C4
Gatcombe SO31 .....127 B4
Gatcombe Ave PO3 ..158 A1
Gatcombe Dr PO2 ...157 C2
Gatcombe Gdns
Fareham PO14 ......154 A4
West End SO18 ......80 A1
Gatcombe Park Inf Sch
PO2 ....157 C2
Gate House Rd PO16 .156 A4
Gatehouse The
12 Southampton SO18 ..103 C4
West End SO30 ......80 B1
Gatekeeper Cl **10** SO23 .11 B4
Gateway The BH13 ..203 C2
Gatwick Cl SO16 .....78 A2
Gaulter Cl PO9 .....136 C2
Gavan St SO19 .....104 B3
Gayda Ho PO12 .....180 C3
Gaylyn Way PO14 ...154 A4
Gaydon Rise BH11 ..188 C2
Gaza Ave SO42 .....175 B3
Gaza Ho PO15 ......130 B2
Gazelle Cl PO13 ....180 B3
Gazing La SO51 ......50 C2
Gazings The SO51 ...50 C2
Geddes Way GU31 ...41 B4
Gemini Cl SO16 ......77 C2
General Johnson Ct **6**
SO22 ....10 B3
Geneva Ave BH6 ....206 B3
Genoa Cl SO41 .....197 B1
Genoa Ho PO6 ......157 A4
Gento Cl SO30 ......105 C3
Geoffrey Ave PO7 ...134 A1
Geoffrey Cres PO16 .155 A3
George Byng Way PO2 .182 B4
George Ct The **19** PO1 .182 A2
George Curl Way SO18 .79 C3
George Eyston Dr SO22 .10 B3
George Rd SO41 ....211 B3
George Rdbt The BH15 .202 B2
George St Eastleigh SO50 .56 A2
Gosport PO12 ......181 B3
Portsmouth PO1, PO2 .182 C4
Georges Mews BH21 .186 B4
Georgia Cl PO13 ....179 C2
Georgian Cl BH24 ...141 A4
Georgian Way BH10 .189 C2
Georgina Cl BH12 ...204 B4
Georgina Talbot Ho
BH12 ....204 A4
Gerald Rd BH3 .....205 A4
Gerard Cres SO19 ..104 B3
Gerard Ho **6** PO2 ...157 C2
Germaine Cl BH23 ..208 C4
Gervis Cres BH14 ...203 A2
Gervis Pl BH2 ......204 C2
Gervis Rd BH1 .....205 A2
Gibbs Rd SO14 .....102 C3
Gibraltar Cl PO15 ...130 B1
Gibraltar Rd
Gosport PO12 ......154 C3
Portsmouth PO4 ....183 B2
Gibson Cl
Lee-on-the-Solent PO13 .179 C2
Swanwick PO15 .....129 C3
Gibson Rd BH17 ....202 C4
Giddylake BH21 ....163 B3
Gifford Cl PO15 ....130 C2
Gilbert Cl Alderholt SP6 .93 A3
Gosport PO13 ......180 B4
Lymington SO41 ....197 B1
Gilbert Ct **5** BH23 ..207 A4
Gilbert Mead PO11 ..184 C2
Gilbert Rd BH1 .....205 B3

Gilbert Way PO7 ....134 C3
Gilbury Cl SO18 .....79 C2
Gilchrist Gdns SO31 .152 B4
Giles Cl Fareham PO16 .131 A2
Gosport PO12 ......181 A3
Hedge End SO30 .....81 B1
Giles La SP5 ....50 A2
Gilkicker Rd PO12 ..181 B1
Gillam Rd BH10 ....189 B3
Gillcrest PO14 ......129 B2
Gillett Rd BH12 ....204 B4
Gillies The **17** PO16 .131 A1
Gillingham Cl
Bournemouth BH9 ...190 B2
Kings Worthy SO23 ....2 B4
Gillingham Rd SO41 .211 B2
Gillion Ct **2** BH23 ..207 C3
Gilman Rd PO6 .....134 C1
Gilpin Cl Boldre SO41 .173 C1
Southampton SO19 ..104 C3
Gilpin Hill SO41 ....172 A1
Gins La SO42 ......176 C1
Girton Cl PO14 .....129 B1
Gitsham Gdns PO7 ..134 B2
Gladdis Rd BH11 ...188 C2
Glade The
Blackfield SO45 ....177 C4
Chandler's Ford SO53 ..30 C1
Fareham PO15 .....130 B2
South Hayling PO11 .185 B1
St Leonards BH24 ..139 C3
Waterlooville PO7 ..135 A4
Gladelands Cl BH18 .186 B2
Gladelands Mobile Home Pk
BH22 ....186 C2
Gladelands Way BH18 .186 C2
Glades The SO31 ...129 A2
Gladstone Cl BH23 .207 B3
Gladstone Gdns PO16 .156 B4
Gladstone Pl **4** PO2 .182 B4
Gladstone Rd
Bournemouth BH7 ...205 C4
Gosport PO12 ......181 A4
Poole BH12 ....203 B3
Southampton SO19 ..104 A3
Gladstone Rd E BH7 .205 C4
Gladstone Rd W BH1 .205 C3
Gladstone St SO23 ...10 C4
Gladys Ave
Portsmouth PO2 ....157 B1
Waterlooville PO8 ..112 B1
Glamis Ave BH10 ...189 C3
Glamis Cl PO7 .....135 A4
Glamis Ct PO14 ....154 B2
Glamorgan Rd PO8 ..88 A2
Glasgow Rd PO4 ...183 A2
Glasslaw Rd SO18 ..104 A4
Glasspool PO7 .....110 C3
Gleadowe Ave BH23 .206 C3
Glebe Cl PO11 .....184 C3
Glebe Cnr PO17 ....108 A2
Glebe Ct Botley SO30 .106 A4
Fair Oak SO50 ......57 B1
Southampton SO17 ...79 A1
Glebe Dr PO13 .....155 B1
Glebe La SP5 ....49 B2
Glebe Mdw SP5 ......4 A1
Glebe Park Ave PO9 .135 A1
Glebe Rd GU31 ......65 B3
Glebe The PO14 ....179 B3
Glebefield Gdns **1** PO6 157 C2
Glebefields **6** SO41 ..211 B3
Glen Cl BH25 ......209 B4
Glen Dale PO9 .....113 B1
Glen Eyre Cl SO16 ...79 A3
Glen Eyre Dr SO16 ...79 A3
Glen Eyre Hall SO16 .79 A3
Glen Eyre Rd SO16 ...78 C3
Glen Eyre Way SO16 .79 A2
Glen Fern Rd BH1 ...205 A2
Glen Ho PO12 .....180 C2
Glen Rd
Bournemouth BH5 ..205 C2
Locks Heath SO31 ..128 C3
Poole BH14 ....203 A2
Southampton SO19 ..103 B1
Swanwick SO31 ....128 C4
Glen Spey BH25 ...195 B1
Glen The Gosport PO13 .155 C1
Poole BH13 ....203 B3
Poole, Canford Cliffs BH13 214 C4
Glenair Ave BH14 ..203 A2
Glenair Cres BH14 .203 A2
Glenair Rd BH14 ...203 A2
Glenavon BH25 ....195 B1
Glenavon Rd BH23 .193 C1
Glenbrook Wlk PO14 .154 B4
Glencarron Way **11** SO16 .78 C2
Glencoe Rd
Bournemouth BH7 ..205 C4
Poole BH12 ....203 B3
Portsmouth PO1 ...182 C4
Glencoyne Gdns SO16 .77 C1
Glenda Cl SO31 ....152 B4
Glendale
Locks Heath SO31 ..129 A1
Swanmore SO32 ....84 A2
Glendale Ave BH22 .165 C3
Glendale Cl
Christchurch BH23 ..191 B2
Wimborne Minst BH21 .163 B3
Glendale Rd BH6 ...207 A2
Glendon Ave BH10 .189 B3
Glendowan Rd SO53 .55 A4
Glendrive BH25 ....209 B4
Gleneagles BH23 ...206 C3
Gleneagles Ave PO14 .203 B1

Gleneagles Cl BH22 .165 C3
Gleneagles Dr PO7 .112 A1
Glenelg PO15 ......130 C1
Glenesha Gdns PO15 .130 B1
Glenferness Ave BH3,
BH4 ....204 B3
Glenfield Ave SO18 .103 C4
Glenfield Cres SO18 .103 C4
Glenfield Way SO18 .103 C4
Glengariff Rd BH14 .203 B2
Glengarry BH25 ....195 B1
Glengarry Way BH23 .208 B3
Glenhurst Sch PO9 .136 A1
Glenives Cl BH24 ..140 A2
Glenlea Cl SO30 .....80 B1
Glenlea Dr SO30 ....80 B1
Glenleigh Ave **19** PO6 .157 C4
Glenleigh Ct **8** PO6 .157 C4
Glenleigh Pk PO9 ..136 A1
Glenmeadows Dr BH10 .189 A3
Glenmoor (Girls) Sch
BH10 ....189 B1
Glenmoor Cl BH10 .189 B1
Glenmoor Rd
Bournemouth BH9 ..204 C4
Ferndown BH22 ....165 B2
Glenmore Cl SO17 ..103 A4
Glenmount Dr BH14 .203 A4
Glenn Rd SO30 .....80 B1
Glenroyd Gdns BH6 .206 C2
Glenside
Barton on Sea BH25 .209 A4
Hythe SO45 ....125 C2
Glenside Ave SO19 .104 B3
Glenthorne Cl PO14 .179 B3
Glenthorne Mdw GU32 .38 C1
Glenthorne Rd PO3 .158 A1
Glenville Cl SO31 ...194 A1
Glenville Gdns BH10 .189 B1
Glenville Rd
Bournemouth BH10 .189 B1
Christchurch BH23 ..194 A1
Glenwood Ave SO16 .79 A3
Glenwood Cl BH22 ..138 C1
Glenwood Cl SO50 ..57 C1
Glenwood Gdns PO8 .111 C2
Glenwood La BH22 .138 C1
Glenwood Rd
Southbourne PO10 ..137 C1
Verwood BH31 .....114 C3
West Moors BH31 ..138 C1
Glenwood Sch PO10 .136 C1
Glenwood Way BH22 .138 C1
Glidden Cl PO1 ....215 C4
Glidden La PO7 .....86 C2
Glissons BH22 .....165 A1
Globe La BH15 ....202 B1
Gloster Ct PO14 ...129 B3
Gloucester Cl GU32 ..40 C2
Gloucester Ct **8** GU32 ..40 C2
Gloucester Ho **1** PO12 .181 B2
Gloucester Pl PO5 ..215 B1
Gloucester Rd
Bournemouth BH7 ..205 C3
Poole BH12 ....203 C3
Portsmouth PO1 ...182 A3
Waterlooville PO7 ..134 C3
Gloucester Terr PO5 .215 B1
Gloucester View PO5 .215 B2
Glyn Dr PO14 ......179 B3
Glyn Jones Cl SO45 .150 C1
Glyn Way PO14 ....179 B3
Glynville Cl BH21 ..164 A4
Glynville Ct BH21 ..164 A4
Glynville Rd BH21 ..164 A4
Goathorn Cl BH16 ..201 B2
Goathouse La PO17 .109 A2
Goddard Cl SO51 ....50 C2
Godfrey Olson Ho **3**
SO50 ....56 A2
Godfrey Pink Way SO32 .83 B4
Godiva Lawn PO4 ..183 B2
Godmanston Cl BH17 .188 A1
Godshill Cl BH8 ....190 B2
Godson Ho **24** SO23 ..11 A4
Godwin Cl
Emsworth PO10 ....136 C2
Winchester SO22 .....1 B1
Godwin Cres PO8 ...88 B2
Godwins Field SO21 .31 B4
Godwit Cl PO12 ....181 A4
Godwit Rd PO4 ....183 B3
Gofton Ave PO6 ...158 A4
Goggs La SP5 ......47 C3
Gold Mead Cl **3** SO41 .197 C1
Gold Oak SP6 ......91 C4
Gold St PO5 ......215 A1
Goldcrest Cl
Horndean PO8 .....112 A4
Portchester PO16 ..155 C4
Goldcrest Gdns SO16 .78 A3
Goldcrest La SO40 ..100 B4
Golden Cres SO41 ..196 B1
Golden Ct SO30 ....80 C2
Golden Gates BH13 .214 A2
Golden Hind Pk SO45 .125 C1
Golden Sands BH13 .214 A4
Goldenleas Ct BH11 .188 B2
Goldenleas Dr BH11 .188 B2
Goldfinch Cl BH25 ..194 C1
Goldfinch La PO13 ..179 C2
Goldfinch Rd BH17 .201 C4
Goldring Cl PO11 ...185 A2
Goldsmith Ave PO4 .182 C2
Goldsmith Cl SO40 .100 B4
Goldsmith Inf Sch PO4 .182 C2

Goldsmith Rd SO50 ..55 C2
Goldsmiths Ct SO14 .103 A2
Goldwire Dr SO53 ..54 C3
Golf Course Rd SO16 .78 C3
Golf Links Rd
Broadstone BH18 ..187 A3
Ferndown BH22 ...165 C2
Goliath Rd BH15 ...201 B1
Gomer Ct PO12 ....180 C2
Gomer Inf Sch PO12 .180 C2
Gomer Jun Sch PO12 .180 C2
Gomer La PO12 ...180 C2
Good Acre Dr SO53 ..54 C3
Good Rd BH12 ....203 B4
Goodens The SO24 ..14 B3
Goodison Cl SO50 ...57 C1
Goodlands Vale SO30 .105 A4
Goodsell Ct PO14 ..179 A3
Goodwin Cl SO16 ...77 B1
Goodwood Cl
Gosport PO12 .....181 A4
Titchfield PO14 ....129 B3
Waterlooville PO8 ..112 A1
Goodwood Ct PO10 .161 C4
Goodwood Gdns SO40 .100 B4
Goodwood Rd
Eastleigh SO50 .....55 C2
Gosport PO12 .....181 A4
Portsmouth PO5 ..215 D1
Gooseberry La BH24 .140 C4
Gordleton Ind Pk SO41 .196 C2
Gordon Ave
Southampton SO14 .103 A4
Winchester SO23 ....11 B3
Gordon Bldgs SO15 .102 A4
Gordon Ct BH4 ....204 B2
Gordon Mount BH23 .209 A4
Gordon Rd
Bournemouth BH1 ..205 B2
Chandler's Ford SO53 .30 B1
Christchurch BH23 ..209 A4
Curdridge SO32 .....83 B4
Fareham PO16 .....131 A1
Gosport PO12 .....181 A1
Hermitage PO10 ...161 A4
Lymington SO41 ...197 B2
Poole BH12 ....204 A3
Portsmouth PO1 ...182 A2
Waterlooville PO7 ..134 C3
Wimborne Minst BH21 .163 C2
Winchester SO23 ....11 B3
Gordon Rd S BH23 .204 A3
Gordon Terr SO19 ..104 A1
Gordon Way PO12 ..192 B1
Gore Grange BH25 ..194 C1
Gore Rd BH25 .....194 C1
Gore Rd Ind Est BH25 .194 C1
Gorey Ave BH12 ...188 B2
Goring Ave PO8 .....88 B2
Goring Field SO22 ....1 B1
Gorleston Rd BH12 .203 C3
Gorley Cross SP6 ...94 A2
Gorley Ct PO9 .....135 B3
Gorley Lynch SP6 ..94 B2
Gorley Rd BH24 ...117 B1
Gorran Ave PO13 ..155 B1
Gorse Cl
Locks Heath SO31 ..128 C1
New Milton BH25 ..195 B2
St Leonards BH24 ..139 B2
Gorse Down SO21 ..33 A2
Gorse Hill Cl BH15 .202 C3
Gorse Hill Cres BH15 .202 C3
Gorse Hill Rd BH15 .202 C3
Gorse Knoll Dr BH31 .114 C4
Gorse La BH16 ....201 B4
Gorse Rd
Corfe Mullen BH21 ..186 B3
Petersfield GU31 ....41 B2
Gorsecliff Ct **7** BH5 .205 B2
Gorsecliff Rd BH10 .189 B1
Gorsefield Rd BH25 .195 A2
Gorseland Ct BH22 .165 C2
Gorselands Rd SO18 ..80 A1
Gorselands Way PO13 .180 B4
Gorseway PO11 ....184 B2
Gorseway The PO11 .184 B2
Gort Cres SO19 ....104 A2
Gort Rd
Bournemouth BH11 .189 A2
Poole BH17 ....187 A1
Gosling Cl BH17 ...202 C4
Gosport Ho **48** PO9 .136 A3
Gosport La SO43 ...122 A2
Gosport Mus* PO12 .181 B2
Gosport Rd
Fareham PO16 .....155 A4
Lee-on-the-Solent PO13 .179 C1
Stubbington PO14 ..179 C3
Gosport Sh Prec **23**
PO12 ....181 B2
Gosport St SO41 ...197 C2
Gough Cres PO17 ..187 A1
Gover Rd SO16 ....101 B4
Grace Dieu Gdns SO31 .104 C1
Grace La SP6 ......70 C4
Gracefields PO15 ..154 A4
Graddidge Way SO40 .100 B3
Graemar La SO51 ...25 B1
Grafton Cl
Bournemouth BH3 ..205 A4
Christchurch BH23 ..207 B3
Gosport PO12 .....181 B4
Grafton Gdns
Lymington SO41 ...197 B1
Southampton SO16 ..78 B3
Grafton Rd
Bournemouth BH3 ....205 A3

Grafton Rd *continued*
Winchester SO23 . . . .**10** C3
Grafton St PO2 . . . .**182** B4
Graham Ct SO19 . . . .**104** A3
Graham Ho 4 SO14 . . . . .**103** B3
Graham Norris Bsns Ctr The
SO45 . . . .**150** C1
Graham Rd
Gosport PO12 . . . .**181** A4
Portsmouth PO4 . . . .**182** C2
Southampton SO14 . . . . . .**103** A3
Graham St SO14 . . . .**103** B3
Grainger Gdns SO19 . . . . .**104** B2
Grammar School La
BH21 . . . .**163** A2
Granada Cl PO8 . . . .**112** A2
Granada Rd
Hedge End SO30 . . . .**105** A3
Portsmouth PO4 . . . .**182** C1
Granary Mews BH24 . . . .**140** C4
Granary The BH24 . . . . . .**140** C4
Granby Gr SO17 . . . .**79** C4
Granby Rd BH9 . . . .**190** A2
Grand Ave BH6 . . . .**206** B2
Grand Division Row 11
PO4 . . . .**183** A2
Grand Par
20 Poole BH15 . . . .**202** A1
Portsmouth PO1 . . . .**182** A2
South Hayling PO11 . . . . .**185** A1
Grange Ct Gosport PO12 .**180** C3
Havant PO9 . . . .**136** A1
Hordle SO41 . . . .**211** C4
Southampton SO18 . . . . . .**79** C2
Winchester SO23 . . . .**10** C2
Grange Cotts SO30 . . . . . .**105** C4
Grange Cres PO12 . . . . . .**180** C3
Grange Ct
16 Bournemouth BH1 . . . .**205** A2
Netley SO31 . . . .**127** A4
Grange Dr SO30 . . . .**105** B4
Grange Gdns BH12 . . . . . .**203** C4
Grange Inf Sch PO13 . . . .**180** B4
Grange Jun Sch PO13 . . . .**180** B4
Grange La PO13 . . . .**180** B4
Grange Mews SO51 . . . . . .**28** B1
Grange Park Mobile Homes
SO30 . . . .**81** B1
Grange Rd
Bournemouth BH6 . . . . . .**206** B2
Broadstone BH18 . . . .**187** A2
Christchurch BH23 . . . . . .**208** A4
Gosport PO13 . . . .**180** B3
Hedge End SO30 . . . .**105** B4
Netley SO31 . . . .**127** B4
Petersfield GU32 . . . .**40** C1
Portsmouth PO2 . . . .**157** B4
11 Southampton SO16 . . . .**78** A1
St Leonards BH24 . . . . . .**139** C1
Winchester SO23 . . . .**10** C2
Grange Road Bsns Ctr
BH23 . . . .**208** A4
Grange Sch The BH23 . . . .**207** C4
Grange The Hordle SO41 .**211** C4
10 Southampton SO16 . . . .**78** A1
Grangewood Ct SO50 . . . . .**57** A1
Grangewood Gdns SO50 . . .**57** A1
Grangewood Hall BH21 . .**163** B3
Grant Rd PO6 . . . .**158** B4
Grant's Ave BH1 . . . .**205** B3
Grantham Ave SO31 . . . .**127** C2
Grantham Ct 3 SO50 . . . . .**56** A1
Grantham Rd
Bournemouth BH1 . . . . . .**205** C3
Eastleigh SO50 . . . .**56** A1
Southampton SO19 . . . . . .**103** C3
Grantley Rd 16 BH5 . . . .**205** C2
Grants Cl BH1 . . . .**205** C3
Granville Cl PO9 . . . .**136** A1
Granville Pl
32 Bournemouth BH1 . . . .**204** C2
Winchester SO23 . . . .**11** A3
Granville Rd
Bournemouth BH5 . . . . . .**206** A3
Poole BH12 . . . .**203** A3
Granville St SO14 . . . .**103** A2
Grasdean Cl 5 SO18 . . . . . .**80** A1
Grasmere SO50 . . . .**55** C1
Grasmere Cl
Christchurch BH23 . . . . . .**191** B2
West End SO18 . . . .**80** A1
Grasmere Ct SO16 . . . .**77** C1
Grasmere Gdns BH25 . . . .**195** A3
Grasmere Ho 18 PO6 . . . .**133** A1
Grasmere Rd
Bournemouth BH5 . . . . . .**206** A4
Poole BH13 . . . .**214** A2
Grasmere Way PO14 . . . .**154** B2
Grassmere Way PO7 . . . .**112** B1
Grassymead PO14 . . . . . .**129** B2
Grateley Cl 8 SO19 . . . . .**126** C4
Grateley Cres PO9 . . . . . .**135** B2
Gravel Cl SP5 . . . .**46** C2
Gravel Hill
Broadstone BH18 . . . .**187** B3
Swanmore SO32 . . . .**84** A2
Gravel La BH24 . . . .**140** C4
Gray Cl Locks Heath SO31 **128** C1
Poole BH12 . . . .**202** C4
Gray's Yd 23 BH15 . . . . .**202** B1
Graycot Cl BH10 . . . .**189** B3
Grayland Cl PO11 . . . .**184** C2
Grays Ave SO45 . . . .**126** A2
Grays Cl
Colden Common SO21 . . . .**56** C4
Gosport PO12 . . . .**180** C2
Romsey SO51 . . . .**53** A4
Grays Ct PO1 . . . .**182** A2

Grayshott Cl SO22 . . . .**1** B2
Grayshott Rd
Gosport PO12 . . . .**180** C2
Portsmouth PO4 . . . .**182** C2
Grayson Ct BH22 . . . .**165** C2
Great Copse Dr PO9 . . . . .**135** C3
Great Elms Cl SO45 . . . . .**150** A2
Great Field Rd SO22 . . . .**1** B2
Great Gays PO14 . . . .**179** A3
Great Hanger GU31 . . . . . .**41** A2
Great Mead
Denmead PO7 . . . .**111** A2
Lyndhurst SO43 . . . .**121** C1
Great Minster St 34 SO23 **11** A4
Great Posbrook Cotts
PO14 . . . .**153** C3
Great Southsea St PO5 . . .**215** B1
Great Well Dr SO51 . . . . . .**53** A4
Greatbridge Rd SO51 . . . . .**27** C1
Greatfield Way PO9 . . . . .**113** A2
Greatwood Cl SO45 . . . . .**126** A1
Greaves Cl BH10 . . . .**189** B2
Grebe Cl
Broadstone BH17 . . . .**201** C4
Christchurch BH23 . . . . . .**208** A3
Milford on Sea SO41 . . . . .**211** C2
Portchester PO16 . . . .**155** C4
Waterlooville PO8 . . . .**111** C2
Westbourne PO10 . . . .**137** A4
Green Acres BH23 . . . .**207** C4
Green Acres Cl BH24 . . . .**140** B3
Green Bottom BH21 . . . . .**164** A4
Green Cl 11 Hythe SO45 . .**126** C4
Kings Worthy SO23 . . . .**2** A3
Netley Marsh SO40 . . . . . .**99** C2
Poole BH15 . . . .**202** B1
Whiteparish SP5 . . . .**24** C1
Green Cres PO13 . . . .**155** B1
Green Dr SP6 . . . .**93** A3
Green Farm Gdns PO3 . . .**157** C2
Green Gdns BH15 . . . .**202** B1
Green Hollow Cl PO16 . . . .**130** C1
Green Jacket Cl SO22 . . . . .**10** C3
Green La Ampfield SO51 . . .**29** A1
Barton on Sea BH25 . . . . .**210** A4
Bishop's Waltham SO32 . . . .**83** B4
Blackfield SO45 . . . .**177** C4
Bournemouth BH10 . . . . . .**189** B2
Bursledon SO31 . . . .**104** C1
Chilworth SO16 . . . .**54** C1
Clanfield PO8 . . . .**88** B3
Denmead PO7 . . . .**110** C2
Downton SP5 . . . .**46** C4
Ferndown BH22 . . . .**165** A1
Fordingbridge SP6 . . . .**69** C1
Froxfield Green GU32 . . . . .**18** C3
Gosport PO12 . . . .**181** B4
Gosport, Alverstoke PO12 .**181** A2
Hamble-le-Rice SO31 . . . .**128** A1
Hambledon PO7 . . . .**86** A2
Locks Heath SO31 . . . . . .**128** C1
New Milton BH25 . . . .**194** C4
Ower SO40 . . . .**76** A2
Portsmouth PO3 . . . .**158** A4
Ringwood BH24 . . . .**141** A4
Ringwood, Upper Kingston
BH24 . . . .**141** B2
Soberton PO7 . . . .**86** A4
South Hayling PO11 . . . . .**184** C2
Southampton SO16 . . . . . .**77** C1
Swanmore SO32 . . . .**84** B4
Swanwick SO31 . . . .**106** A1
Swanwick, Lwr Swanwick
SO31 . . . .**128** B4
Whitsbury SP6 . . . .**69** B4
Green Loaning 4 BH23 . . .**207** C3
Green Park Cl SO23 . . . .**2** A1
Green Park Rd SO16 . . . . .**101** C4
Green Pk BH1 . . . .**205** B2
Green Pond Cnr 9 PO9 . . .**136** A1
Green Pond La SO51 . . . . . .**29** B2
Green Rd
Bournemouth BH9 . . . . . .**205** A4
Gosport PO12 . . . .**181** A1
Poole BH15 . . . .**202** B1
Portsmouth PO5 . . . .**215** B2
Stubbington PO14 . . . . . .**154** B2
Green The Liss GU33 . . . . . .**20** C3
Locks Heath SO31 . . . . . .**128** C3
Romsey SO51 . . . .**28** B1
Rowland's Castle PO9 . . . .**113** A1
Whiteparish SP5 . . . .**24** A2
Green Wlk PO15 . . . .**130** C2
Green's Cl SO50 . . . .**57** A1
Greenacre BH25 . . . .**210** A4
Greenacre Cl BH16 . . . . . .**201** B3
Greenacre Gdns PO7 . . . .**134** C2
Greenacres Downton SP5 . .**46** B4
Poole BH13 . . . .**204** A2
Greenacres Cl BH10 . . . . .**189** C3
Greenacres Dr SO31 . . . . . .**31** B2
Greenacres Specl Sch
SO22 . . . .**1** C1
Greenaway La
Locks Heath SO31 . . . . . .**128** B1
Locks Heath SO31 . . . . . .**128** C1
Greenbank Cres SO16 . . . .**78** C3
Greenbanks Cl SO41 . . . . .**211** B2
Greenbanks Gdns PO16 . .**131** B1
Greenclose La BH21 . . . . .**163** B2
Greendale Cl
Chandler's Ford SO53 . . . . .**55** C3
Fareham PO15 . . . .**130** C2
Greendale The PO15 . . . . .**130** B2
Greenfield Cres PO8 . . . . .**112** B2
Greenfield Gdns BH25 . . .**210** A4
Greenfield Rd BH15 . . . . .**202** C4
Greenfield Rise PO8 . . . . .**112** B2

Greenfields Liss GU33 . . . . .**21** A2
Poole BH12 . . . .**203** C4
Greenfields Ave SO40 . . . . .**76** C1
Greenfields Cl SO40 . . . . . .**76** C1
Greenfinch Cl
Broadstone BH17 . . . .**186** C1
Eastleigh SO50 . . . .**55** B1
Greenfinch Wlk BH24 . . . .**141** B3
Greenhayes BH18 . . . .**187** B1
Greenhays Rise BH21 . . . .**163** B3
Greenhill Ave SO22 . . . . . .**10** C4
Greenhill Cl
Wimborne Minst BH21 . . .**163** B3
Winchester SO22 . . . .**10** C4
Greenhill La
Rownhams SO16 . . . .**77** C4
Wimborne Minst BH21 . . .**163** B3
Greenhill Rd
Wimborne Minst BH21 . . .**163** B3
Winchester SO22 . . . .**10** C4
Greenhill Terr SO22 . . . . . .**10** C4
Greenlea Cl PO7 . . . .**134** A1
Greenlea Cres SO16 . . . . . .**79** B3
Greenlea Rd PO12 . . . .**180** C4
Greenmead Ave SO41 . . . .**196** B1
Greens Cl SO32 . . . .**83** A4
Greens Meade SP5 . . . .**47** B3
Greenside Ct BH25 . . . . . .**210** A3
Greensleeves Ave BH18 . .**187** A3
Greensome Dr BH22 . . . . .**165** C3
Greenway GU32 . . . .**38** C1
Greenway Cl SO41 . . . .**197** B2
Greenway Cres SO16 . . . .**201** A4
Greenway La GU31 . . . .**65** B3
Greenway Rd PO12 . . . . . .**181** A3
Greenway The PO10 . . . . .**136** C2
Greenways
Chandler's Ford SO53 . . . . .**55** C3
Christchurch BH23 . . . . . .**208** C4
Milford on Sea SO41 . . . . .**211** B3
Southampton SO16 . . . . . .**79** B3
Swanmore SO32 . . . .**84** A3
Greenways Ave BH8 . . . . .**190** B2
Greenways Ct BH22 . . . . . .**165** C2
Greenways Rd SO42 . . . . .**146** A1
Greenwich The
Blackfield SO45 . . . .**150** C1
Southampton SO14 . . . . . .**103** A4
Greenwood Ave
Cosham PO6 . . . .**157** B4
Ferndown BH22 . . . .**165** C3
Poole BH14 . . . .**214** B4
Rownhams SO16 . . . .**77** B3
Greenwood Cl
Eastleigh SO50 . . . .**55** C1
Fareham PO15 . . . .**131** A2
Romsey SO51 . . . .**53** A4
Greenwood Copse
BH24 . . . .**140** A4
Greenwood La SO32 . . . . . .**82** A4
Greenwood Rd BH9 . . . . . .**204** C4
Greenwood Way BH24 . . .**140** A4
Greenwoods 32 BH25 . . . .**195** A1
Greetham St PO1 . . . .**215** B3
Gregory Gdns SO40 . . . . . .**76** B1
Gregson Ave PO13 . . . . . .**155** B2
Gregson Cl PO13 . . . .**155** B2
Grenadier Cl SO31 . . . . . .**129** A1
Grendon Cl SO16 . . . .**79** A3
Grenehurst Way GU31 . . . .**40** C2
Grenfell Rd BH9 . . . .**189** C2
Grenfield Ct PO10 . . . .**136** C2
Grenville Cl BH24 . . . .**117** B1
Grenville Ct
6 Bournemouth BH4 . . . .**204** B2
11 Poole BH15 . . . .**202** B1
Southampton, SO15 . . . . .**102** C4
Southampton, Bitterne Pk
SO18 . . . .**79** C2
Grenville Gdns SO45 . . . . .**126** A1
Grenville Ho 22 PO1 . . . . .**182** A1
Grenville Rd
Portsmouth PO5 . . . .**215** D1
Wimborne Minst BH21 . . .**163** B2
Gresham Rd BH9 . . . .**190** A1
Gresley Gdns SO30 . . . . . .**81** B1
Greville Gn PO10 . . . .**136** C2
Greville Rd SO15 . . . .**102** B4
Grevillea Ave PO15 . . . . . .**129** C2
Greycot Cl BH21 . . . .**138** C2
Greyfriars 26 SO23 . . . . . .**11** A4
Greyfriars Ct PO5 . . . .**215** B1
Greyfriars Rd PO15 . . . . . .**130** B1
Greyhound Cl SO30 . . . . . .**81** A2
Greyladyes SO31 . . . .**128** A4
Greys Farm Cl SO24 . . . . . .**14** C2
Greyshott Ave PO14 . . . . .**154** B4
Greystoke Ave BH11 . . . . .**188** C3
Greywell Ave SO16 . . . . . .**78** B2
Greywell Cl SO16 . . . .**78** B2
Greywell Sq PO9 . . . .**135** C2
Griffen Cl 2 SO50 . . . .**56** C1
Griffin Ct
Southampton SO17 . . . . . .**103** B4
12 Wimborne Minst BH21 .**163** B2
Griffin Ind Pk SO40 . . . . . .**76** C1
Griffin Wlk PO13 . . . .**180** B3
Griffiths Gdns BH10 . . . . .**189** A3
Griffon Cl SO31 . . . .**105** A1
Grigg La SO42 . . . .**146** A1
Grindle Cl PO16 . . . .**132** B1
Gritanwood Rd PO4 . . . . .**183** A2
Grosvenor Cl 19 BH1 . . . .**205** B2
Grosvenor Cl
Southampton SO17 . . . . . .**79** B1
St Leonards BH24 . . . . . .**139** C1

Grosvenor Ct
2 Bournemouth BH1 . . . .**205** B2
Christchurch BH23 . . . . . .**209** A4
Cosham PO6 . . . .**158** C4
Romsey SO51 . . . .**53** B4
7 Southampton SO17 . . . .**79** B1
Stubbington PO14 . . . . . .**179** B3
Grosvenor Dr SO23 . . . .**2** A1
Grosvenor Gdns
Bournemouth BH1 . . . . . .**205** C2
Southampton SO17 . . . . . .**79** B1
West End SO18 . . . .**104** B4
Grosvenor Ho 4 PO5 . . . .**215** B2
Grosvenor Lodge 5
SO17 . . . .**79** B1
Grosvenor Mews
Gosport PO12 . . . .**181** B3
Lymington SO41 . . . .**197** B3
8 Southampton SO17 . . . .**79** B1
Grosvenor Rd
Bournemouth BH4 . . . . . .**204** B2
Chandler's Ford SO53 . . . . .**30** C1
Southampton SO17 . . . . . .**79** B1
Grosvenor Sq SO15 . . . . . .**102** C4
Grosvenor St PO5 . . . .**215** B2
Grove Ave Gosport PO12 .**181** B3
Portchester PO16 . . . .**156** B3
Grove Bldgs 6 PO12 . . . . .**181** B2
Grove Ct 14 PO9 . . . .**135** C1
Grove Gdns SO19 . . . .**104** A1
Grove Ho
Portsmouth PO5 . . . .**215** B1
Portsmouth PO5 . . . .**215** C1
Grove La SP5 . . . .**47** C4
Grove Mans 21 BH1 . . . . .**205** A2
Grove Mews SO19 . . . .**104** A1
Grove Pastures SO41 . . . .**197** C2
Grove Pl Lymington SO41 .**197** C2
Southampton SO19 . . . . . .**104** A1
Grove Rd
Barton on Sea BH25 . . . . .**210** A4
Bournemouth BH1 . . . . . .**205** A2
Compton (Hants) SO21 . . . .**11** A3
Cosham PO6 . . . .**158** B4
Fareham PO16 . . . .**131** A1
Gosport PO12 . . . .**181** A4
Havant PO9 . . . .**135** C1
Lee-on-the-Solent PO13 . .**179** C1
Lymington SO41 . . . .**197** C2
Poole BH12 . . . .**203** A3
Southampton SO15 . . . . . .**102** A4
Wimborne Minst BH21 . . .**163** B2
Grove Rd E BH23 . . . .**207** A4
Grove Rd N PO5 . . . .**215** B1
Grove Rd S PO5 . . . .**215** B1
Grove Rd W BH23 . . . .**206** C4
Grove St SO14 . . . .**103** A4
Grove The
Bournemouth BH9 . . . . . .**189** C4
Bursledon SO31 . . . .**105** A1
Christchurch BH23 . . . . . .**191** C1
Ferndown BH22 . . . .**165** B2
Netley SO31 . . . .**127** B4
Southampton SO19 . . . . . .**104** A1
Stubbington PO14 . . . . . .**179** A3
Verwood BH31 . . . .**115** A3
Westbourne PO10 . . . .**137** A2
Groveburg SO31 . . . .**129** A1
Grovelands Rd SO22 . . . .**1** A1
Groveley Bsns Ctr BH23 **207** C3
Groveley Rd
Bournemouth BH4 . . . . . .**204** A1
Christchurch BH23 . . . . . .**207** C3
Groveley Way SO51 . . . . . .**28** C1
Grovely Ave BH5 . . . .**205** C2
Groves Down SO51 . . . .**50** C2
Grower Gdns BH11 . . . . . .**189** C4
Grundles SP5 . . . .**41** A2
Gruneisen Rd PO2 . . . .**157** C4
Guardhouse Rd PO1 . . . . .**182** A4
Guardian Ct 30 SO17 . . . . .**79** A1
Guardroom Rd PO2 . . . . . .**157** A1
Gudge Heath La
PO15 . . . .**130** C1
Guelders PO7 . . . .**134** C2
Guernsey Cl SO16 . . . .**77** C2
Guernsey Rd BH12 . . . . . .**188** B1
Guessens La PO14 . . . .**153** C4
Guest Ave BH12 . . . .**204** A3
Guest Cl BH12 . . . .**204** A3
Guest Rd
Bishopstoke SO50 . . . .**56** B2
Upton BH16 . . . .**201** A4
Guildford Cl PO10 . . . .**137** C1
Guildford Ct
Bournemouth BH4 . . . . . .**204** B2
Gosport PO13 . . . .**180** B3
Guildford Dr SO53 . . . .**55** A2
Guildford Rd PO1 . . . .**182** C3
Guildford St 30 SO14 . . . .**103** B3
Guildhall Cl 4 BH15 . . . . .**202** A1
Guildhall Sq PO1 . . . .**215** B3
Guildhall Wlk PO1 . . . . . .**215** B3
Guildhill Rd BH6 . . . .**206** C2
Guillemot Cl SO45 . . . . . .**126** A1
12 Wimborne Minst BH21 .**163** B2
Guillemot Gdns PO13 . . . .**155** B2
Gull Cl PO13 . . . .**155** A1
Gulliver Cl BH14 . . . .**214** B4
Gulliver Ct 1 BH21 . . . . . .**163** B2
Gulls The SO40 . . . .**100** C1
Gullycroft Mead SO30 . . .**105** A4
Gunners Bldgs PO3 . . . . . .**157** C2
Gunners Pk SO32 . . . .**83** C4
Gunners Row PO4 . . . .**183** A1
Gunners Way PO12 . . . . . .**155** C1
Gunstore Rd PO3 . . . .**158** A2
Gunville Cres BH9 . . . .**190** A4
Gunwharf Rd PO1 . . . .**182** A2

Gurjun Cl BH16 . . . .**201** A4
Gurkha Mus ★ SO23 . . . .**10** C4
Gurnard Rd PO6 . . . .**157** C4
Gurnays Mead SO51 . . . . . .**50** C2
Gurney Rd
Corfe Mullen BH21 . . . . . .**186** C3
Portsmouth PO4 . . . .**183** A2
Southampton SO15 . . . . . .**102** B4
Gussage Rd BH12 . . . .**203** C4
Gutner La PO11 . . . .**160** B1
Guy's Ct BH1 . . . .**141** A3
Gwatkin Cl PO9 . . . .**135** C2
Gwen-Rhian Ct 10 SO15 .**102** C4
Gwenlyn Rd BH16 . . . .**201** B3
Gwynne Rd BH12 . . . .**203** C3
Gypsy La BH24 . . . .**141** A4

H

H Ave SO45 . . . .**150** C3
Ha'penny Dell PO7 . . . . . .**134** C2
Haarlem Mews BH23 . . . .**207** B4
Hack Dr SO21 . . . .**56** C4
Hackett Way PO14 . . . . . .**155** A3
Hacketts La SO32 . . . .**60** C1
Hackleys La SO31 . . . .**51** A3
Hackupps La SO51 . . . .**6** B1
Hackworth Gdns SO30 . . . .**81** B2
Hadden Rd BH8 . . . .**205** B4
Haddon Cl PO15 . . . .**130** C1
Haddon Dr SO50 . . . .**56** A3
Haddons Dr BH21 . . . .**138** B4
Hadleigh Gdns SO50 . . . . . .**56** A3
Hadleigh Rd 6 PO6 . . . . .**157** B4
Hadley Field SO45 . . . . . .**150** A3
Hadley Way BH18 . . . .**186** C2
Hadow Rd BH10 . . . .**189** B2
Hadrian Cl BH22 . . . .**165** A3
Hadrian Way
Chilworth SO16 . . . .**78** C4
Corfe Mullen BH21 . . . . . .**186** C4
Hadrians Cl SO53 . . . .**55** C4
Haflinger Dr PO15 . . . . . .**129** A4
Haglane Copse SO41 . . . . .**197** B2
Hahnemann Rd BH2 . . . . .**204** C1
Haig Ave BH13 . . . .**203** C1
Haig Rd 21 PO2 . . . .**157** C2
Haig Rd SO50 . . . .**57** A1
Haileybury Gdns SO30 . . . .**81** B4
Hainault Dr BH31 . . . .**115** A3
Haking Rd BH23 . . . .**207** B4
Halcyon Ct BH15 . . . .**202** B3
Halden Cl 2 SO51 . . . .**28** A1
Hale Ave BH25 . . . .**195** A1
Hale Cl PO1 . . . .**182** C4
Hale Gdns BH25 . . . .**195** A1
Hale La SP6 . . . .**47** A2
Hale Prim Sch SP6 . . . .**47** B2
Hale St N PO1 . . . .**215** C4
Hale St S PO1 . . . .**215** C4
Hales Dr SO30 . . . .**105** A3
Halesowen Ho 4 PO5 . . . .**215** B4
Halewood Way BH21 . . . .**206** C4
Half Moon St 2 PO1 . . . . .**182** A3
Halfpenny La PO1 . . . .**182** A2
Halfway Rd SO45 . . . .**151** C1
Halifax Ct SO30 . . . .**80** B1
Halifax Rise PO7 . . . .**134** C4
Halifax Way BH23 . . . .**208** A4
Hall Cl SO32 . . . .**83** B4
Hall Cl SO32 . . . .**107** A4
Hall Lands La SO50 . . . . . .**57** B1
Hall of Aviation (Mus) ★
SO14 . . . .**103** A4
Hall Rd BH11 . . . .**188** C4
Hall Way The SO22 . . . .**1** A3
Hallet Cl SO18 . . . .**80** A1
Hallett Rd PO9 . . . .**136** A1
Halletts Cl PO14 . . . .**154** B2
Halliday Cl PO12 . . . .**181** A3
Halliday Cres PO4 . . . .**183** B2
Halliday Ho PO4 . . . .**183** A1
Hallowell Ho PO1 . . . .**215** B4
Halsey Cl PO12 . . . .**180** C2
Halstead Rd Cosham PO6 .**157** B4
Southampton SO18 . . . . . .**79** C1
Halstock Cres BH17 . . . . .**187** B1
Halter Path BH15 . . . .**201** C2
Halter Rise BH21 . . . .**164** B3
Halterworth Cl SO51 . . . . .**53** B4
Halterworth Com Prim Sch
SO51 . . . .**53** B4
Halterworth La SO51 . . . . .**53** B4
Halton Cl BH23 . . . .**193** A4
Haltons Cl SO40 . . . .**76** B1
Halyard Cl PO13 . . . .**180** B4
Halyards SO31 . . . .**128** A2
Ham La Ferndown BH21 . . .**164** C2
Gosport PO12 . . . .**156** A1
Horndean PO8 . . . .**112** A4
Southbourne PO10 . . . . . .**161** B4
Hambert Way SO40 . . . . . .**100** C3
Hamble Cl SO31 . . . .**128** B1
Hamble Court Bsns Pk
SO31 . . . .**127** C2
Hamble Ct
Chandler's Ford SO53 . . . . .**55** B3
Stubbington PO14 . . . . . .**154** A2
3 Waterlooville PO8 . . . . .**111** C2
Hamble Ho 6 SO16 . . . . . .**155** A4
Hamble House Gdns
SO31 . . . .**128** A1

Hamble La
Bursledon SO31 . . . . .127 C4
Hamble-le-Rice SO31 . . . . .127 C1
Southampton SO31 . . . . . . .104 C1
Waterlooville PO7 . . . . .134 C3
Hamble Manor SO31 . . . . .128 A1
Hamble Prim Sch SO31 127 C2
Hamble Rd Gosport PO12 180 C2
Poole BH15 . . . . .203 A3
Hamble Sec Sch SO31 . . .127 C3
Hamble Springs SO32 . .83 B4
Hamble Sta SO31 . . . . . . .127 C3
Hamblecliff Ho SO31 . . . .127 B2
Hambledon Cl SO22 . . . . . .1 B1
Hambledon Gdns BH6 . .206 B3
Hambledon Inf Sch PO7 .86 B2
Hambledon La PO7,SO32 .85 C2
Hambledon Par PO7 . . . . .111 B1
Hambledon Rd
Clanfield PO8 . . . . .88 A3
Denmead PO7 . . . . .111 A3
Hambledon PO7 . . . . .110 B4
Waterlooville PO7 . . . . .111 A2
Hambleside Ct SO31 . . . . .127 C1
Hambleton Rd BH7 . . . . . .206 A4
Hamblewood SO30 . . . . . .106 A4
Hamblewood Ct SO30 . . .106 A4
Hambrook Rd ☐ PO12 . . .181 A3
Hambrook St PO5 . . . . . . .215 A1
Hamdown Cres SO51 . . . . .51 A1
Hameldon Cl SO16 . . . . . .101 C4
Hamfield Dr PO11 . . . . . . .184 C2
Hamilton Cl
Bournemouth BH1 . . . . .205 B3
Christchurch BH23 . . . . . . .207 C2
Hamworthy BH15 . . . . .201 C1
Havant PO9 . . . . .159 C4
Hamilton Cres BH15 . . . .201 C1
Hamilton Ct
☐ Bournemouth BH8 . . . . .205 A3
Milford on Sea SO41 . . . . . .211 B2
☐ Portsmouth PO5 . . . . . . .182 B1
☐ Southampton SO17 . . . . .79 A1
☐ Wimborne Minst BH21 . .163 A3
Hamilton Gr PO13 . . . . . . .155 A1
Hamilton Ho PO1 . . . . . . .215 D4
Hamilton Mews
☐ Hythe SO45 . . . . .126 A1
Lymington SO41 . . . . .197 C2
Hamilton Pk SP5 . . . . .47 A4
Hamilton Rd
Bishopstoke SO50 . . . . .56 B2
Bournemouth BH1 . . . . .205 B2
Corfe Mullen BH21 . . . . . . .186 C3
Hamworthy BH15 . . . . .201 C1
Hythe SO45 . . . . .150 A4
Portchester PO6 . . . . .156 C4
Portsmouth PO5 . . . . .182 B1
Hamilton Way BH25 . . . .194 C1
Hamlet Ct SO45 . . . . .151 A2
Hamlet Way PO12 . . . . . .156 A1
Hamlon Cl BH11 . . . . .189 A2
Hammond Ho PO12 . . . . .181 C2
Hammond Ind Pk PO14 . .179 B3
Hammond Rd PO15 . . . . .130 C1
Hammond's Gr SO40 . . . .100 B4
Hammonds Cl SO40 . . . . .100 C4
Hammonds La SO40 . . . . .100 C4
Hammonds Way SO40 . . .100 C4
Hampage Gn PO9 . . . . . . .135 B4
Hampden La BH6 . . . . . . .206 A3
Hampreston CE Fst Sch
BH21 . . . . .164 C2
Hampshire Cl BH21 . . . . .191 C1
Hampshire Corporate Pk
SO53 . . . . .55 A1
Hampshire County Cricket
Ground★ SO30 . . . . .80 C1
Hampshire Ct
☐ Bournemouth BH2 . . . . .204 C3
Chandler's Ford SO53 . . . . . .55 B2
Hampshire Ctr The BH8 .190 C1
Hampshire Hatches La
BH24 . . . . .141 A2
Hampshire Ho ☐ BH2 . . .204 C2
Hampshire St PO1 . . . . . .182 C4
Hampshire Terr PO1 . . . .215 A2
Hampton Cl
Blackfield SO45 . . . . .177 C4
Waterlooville PO7 . . . . .135 A4
Hampton Dr BH24 . . . . . . .117 A1
Hampton Gdns SO45 . . . .177 C4
Hampton Gr PO15 . . . . . . .130 A1
Hampton Hill SO32 . . . . .84 A3
Hampton La
Blackfield SO45 . . . . .150 C1
Winchester SO22 . . . . .1 B1
Hampton Twrs ☐ SO19 . .126 C4
Hamptworth Rd SP5 . . . . .48 B2
Hamtun Cres SO40 . . . . . .76 C1
Hamtun Gdns SO40 . . . . . .76 C1
Hamtun Rd SO19 . . . . . . .104 B2
Hamtun St ☐ SO14 . . . . .102 C2
Hamworthy Fst Sch
BH15 . . . . .201 C1
Hamworthy Mid Sch
BH15 . . . . .201 C1
Hamworthy Sta BH16 . . .201 B2
Hanbidge Cres PO13 . . . .155 B2
Hanbidge Wlk PO13 . . . . .155 B2
Handel Rd SO15 . . . . .102 C4
Handel Terr SO15 . . . . . . .102 C3
Handford Pl ☐ SO15 . . . .102 C4
Handley Ct BH24 . . . . . . .140 C4
Handley Lodge BH12 . . . .203 C4

Handley Rd PO12 . . . . . . .180 C3
Handsworth Ho PO5 . . . .215 C2
Handy Villas ☐☐ SO23 . . .11 A4
Hanger Way GU31 . . . . . . .41 A2
Hangers The SO32 . . . . . .59 C1
Hanham Ct BH12 . . . . . . .204 A4
Hanham Rd
Corfe Mullen BH21 . . . . . . .186 B3
Wimborne Minst BH21 . . . .163 B3
Hankinson Rd BH9 . . . . . .205 A4
Hanley Rd SO15 . . . . .102 B4
Hann Rd SO16 . . . . .77 C3
Hannah Gdns PO7 . . . . . .134 C4
Hannah Way SO41 . . . . . .196 C3
Hannay Rise SO19 . . . . . .104 B3
Hannington Pl BH7 . . . . .206 A3
Hannington Rd
Bournemouth BH7 . . . . .206 A3
Havant PO9 . . . . .135 B4
Hanns Way SO50 . . . . .56 A1
Hanover Bldgs SO14 . . . .103 A2
Hanover Cotts SO32 . . . . .36 C2
Hanover Ct
☐ Hythe SO45 . . . . .126 A2
☐ Portsmouth PO1 . . . . . . .182 A2
Hanover Gdns PO16 . . . .131 A2
Hanover Gn BH17 . . . . . . .202 C4
Hanover Ho
Gosport PO13 . . . . .155 A3
Poole BH15 . . . . .202 B2
Totton SO40 . . . . .101 A4
Hanover Lodge SO23 . . . . .10 C3
Hanover St PO1 . . . . .182 A2
Hanoverian Way PO15 . . .129 B4
Hanway Rd PO1, PO2 . . . .182 C4
Harbeck Rd BH8 . . . . .190 B2
Harborough Rd SO15 . . . .102 C3
Harbour Cl BH13 . . . . . . .214 B3
Harbour Cres BH23 . . . . .207 C3
Harbour Ct
Barton on Sea BH25 . . . . . .209 C4
Christchurch BH23 . . . . . . .207 C3
Poole BH13 . . . . .214 C3
Harbour Hill Cres BH15 202 C3
Harbour Hill Rd BH15 . . .202 C3
Harbour Hospl The
BH15 . . . . .202 B2
Harbour Lights BH15 . . . .202 C2
Harbour Par SO15 . . . . . .102 C3
Harbour Prospect BH14 214 B4
Harbour Rd
Bournemouth BH6 . . . . .207 A2
Gosport PO1 . . . . .181 C3
South Hayling PO11 . . . . . .184 B2
Harbour Twr PO12 . . . . . .181 C2
Harbour View PO16 . . . . .156 B3
Harbour View Cl BH23 . . .207 A3
Harbour View Ct BH23 . . .207 A3
Harbour View Rd BH23 . .203 A2
Harbour Watch BH14 . . . .214 B4
Harbour Way
Emsworth PO10 . . . . .161 A4
Portsmouth PO2 . . . . .157 B1
Harbour Wlk PO1 . . . . . . .182 A2
Harbourne Gdns SO18 . .80 A1
Harbourside PO9 . . . . .159 C3
Harbridge Ct PO9 . . . . . . .135 B4
Harbridge Dro BH24 . . . . .93 B2
Harcombe Cl BH17 . . . . . .187 C2
Harcourt Cl PO8 . . . . .112 A2
Harcourt Mews ☐ BH5 . .206 A3
Harcourt Rd
Bournemouth BH5 . . . . .206 A3
Fareham PO14 . . . . .154 A4
Gosport PO12 . . . . .181 A3
Portsmouth PO1 . . . . .182 C4
Southampton SO18 . . . . . . .103 C4
Hard The Gosport PO12 . .181 B3
Portsmouth PO1 . . . . .182 A3
Harding La SO50 . . . . .57 A2
Harding Rd PO12 . . . . . . .180 C3
Hardley Ind Est SO45 . . . .150 A3
Hardley La SO45 . . . . .150 A4
Hardley Rdbt SO45 . . . . . .150 A3
Hardley Sch & Sixth Form
SO45 . . . . .150 B3
Hardman Ct PO3 . . . . .158 A2
Hardwick Rd SO53 . . . . . . .55 B3
Hardwicke Cl SO16 . . . . . .77 C1
Hardwicke Way SO31 . . . .127 C2
Hardy Cl
Locks Heath SO31 . . . . .129 A2
New Milton BH25 . . . . .194 C1
Southampton SO15 . . . . . . .102 A3
West Moors BH22 . . . . .138 C1
Hardy Cres BH21 . . . . . . .163 B2
Hardy Dr SO45 . . . . .126 A1
Hardy Rd Cosham PO6 . . .158 C4
Eastleigh SO50 . . . . .56 A1
Poole BH14 . . . . .203 B2
West Moors BH22 . . . . .138 C1
Hare La Alderholt BH21 . . .91 C3
Hordle SO41 . . . . .195 C2
New Milton BH25 . . . . .195 C2
Harebell Cl PO16 . . . . .131 B2
Harefield Ct SO51 . . . . . . .53 A4
Harefield Inf Sch SO18 . .104 A4
Harefield Jun Sch SO18 104 A4
Harefield Rd SO17 . . . . . . .79 B2
Hares Gn PO7 . . . . .206 A4
Harestock Cl SO22 . . . . .1 B3
Harestock Cnr SO22 . . . . . .1 B4
Harestock Prim Sch SO22 .1 B2
Harestock Rd
Havant PO9 . . . . .135 B2
Winchester SO22 . . . . .1 B1
Harewood Ave BH7 . . . . .206 A3
Harewood Cl SO50 . . . . . . .56 A3

Harewood Cres BH7 . . . . .205 C4
Harewood Gdns BH7 . . . .205 C4
Harewood Gn SO41 . . . . .212 A2
Harewood Pl BH7 . . . . . . .206 A3
Harford Cl SO41 . . . . .197 B1
Harford Rd BH12 . . . . . . .203 B4
Harkness Dr PO7 . . . . .135 A4
Harkwood Dr BH15 . . . . .201 C2
Harland Cres SO15 . . . . . .78 B1
Harland Rd BH6 . . . . .207 A2
Harlaxton Cl SO50 . . . . . . .55 C3
Harlech Dr SO53 . . . . .55 A2
Harlequin Gr PO15 . . . . . .130 C1
Harleston Rd PO6 . . . . . . .133 C1
Harleston Villas ☐☐
BH21 . . . . .163 B2
Harley Cl SO31 . . . . .128 B1
Harley Wlk PO1 . . . . .215 C4
Harlyn Rd SO16 . . . . .77 C1
Harman Rd PO13 . . . . . . .155 B2
Harness Cl BH21 . . . . .164 A3
Harold Cl SO40 . . . . .100 B3
Harold Rd
Portsmouth PO4 . . . . .182 C2
South Hayling PO11 . . . . . .185 A1
Southampton SO15 . . . . . . .102 B4
Stubbington PO14 . . . . .154 B2
Westbourne PO10 . . . . .137 A2
Harold Terr PO10 . . . . . . .136 C1
Harpway La BH23 . . . . . . .192 B3
Harrage The SO51 . . . . . . .52 C4
Harrier Cl Horndean PO8 112 A4
Lee-on-the-Solent PO13 . . .179 C1
Harrier Dr BH21 . . . . .163 B1
Harrier Gn SO45 . . . . .150 A3
Harrier Way
Holbury SO45 . . . . .150 A3
Petersfield SO45 . . . . .41 B1
Harriers Cl BH23 . . . . . . .208 B4
Harriet Cl PO14 . . . . .179 A3
Harrington Ct BH23 . . . . .208 C4
Harris Ave SO30 . . . . .105 B4
Harris Rd PO13 . . . . .155 B2
Harris Way BH25 . . . . . . .195 A3
Harrison Ave BH1 . . . . . . .205 B3
Harrison Cl BH23 . . . . . . .192 B2
Harrison Ho ☐☐ PO2 . . . .157 B1
Harrison Prim Sch
PO16 . . . . .131 A1
Harrison Rd
Fareham PO16 . . . . .131 A1
Southampton SO17 . . . . . . .79 B2
Harrison Way BH22 . . . . .138 C2
Harrison's Cut SO14 . . . . .103 A2
Harrow Cl BH23 . . . . .193 A4
Harrow Down SO22 . . . . .10 B2
Harrow La GU32 . . . . .40 C3
Harrow Rd
Bransgore BH23 . . . . .193 A4
Portsmouth PO5 . . . . .215 D2
Harrowgate La PO7,PO8 .87 A1
Harry Barrow Cl ☐
BH24 . . . . .141 A3
Harry Law Hall PO1 . . . . .215 B3
Hart Cl BH25 . . . . .194 C2
Hart Ct SO19 . . . . .103 C3
Hart Hill SO45 . . . . .126 B1
Hart Plain Ave PO8 . . . . . .111 C1
Hart Plain Jun & Inf Schs
PO7,PO8 . . . . .111 C1
Hartford Ho PO1 . . . . .215 A1
Harthill Dro SP5 . . . . .47 C3
Harting Cl PO8 . . . . .88 B2
Harting Down GU31 . . . . . .41 A2
Harting Gdns PO16 . . . . . .132 B1
Harting Rd BH6 . . . . .206 B4
Hartington Rd
Gosport PO12 . . . . .180 C3
Southampton SO14 . . . . . . .103 A3
Hartland Ct PO10 . . . . . . .137 B1
Hartland's Rd PO16 . . . . .131 A1
Hartley Ave SO17 . . . . . . .79 A2
Hartley Cl
Bishopstoke SO50 . . . . .57 A1
Hythe SO45 . . . . .126 A1
Hartley Ct ☐ SO17 . . . . . .103 A4
Hartley Grange SO16 . . . .79 A2
Hartley Rd
Bishopstoke SO50 . . . . .57 A1
Portsmouth PO2 . . . . .157 C2
Hartley Wlk ☐ SO45 . . . .126 A1
Hartnell Ct BH21 . . . . . . .186 B3
Harts Farm Way PO9 . . . .159 B4
Harts Way SO41 . . . . .196 B1
Hartsbourne Dr BH7 . . . .206 A4
Hartsgrove Ave SO45 . . . .150 C1
Hartsgrove Cl SO45 . . . . .150 C1
Hartwell Rd PO3 . . . . .158 A2
Hartwood Gdns PO8 . . . .111 C1
Harvest Cl SO22 . . . . .10 B2
Harvest Rd
Chandler's Ford SO53 . . . . .54 C3
Denmead PO7 . . . . .110 C2
Harvester Dr PO15 . . . . . .130 A1
Harvester Way SO41 . . . .197 B3
Harvestgate Wlk ☐
PO9 . . . . .135 B3
Harvesting La GU32,PO8 .64 B3
Harvey Brown Ho PO11 .185 A3
Harvey Cres SO31 . . . . . . .128 C1
Harvey Gdns SO45 . . . . . .150 C1
Harvey Ho PO4 . . . . .183 A1
Harvey Rd
Bishopstoke SO50 . . . . .56 C1
Bournemouth BH5 . . . . .206 A3
Oakley BH21 . . . . .187 C4

Harwell Rd BH17 . . . . . . .202 B4
Harwich Rd PO6 . . . . .133 B1
Harwood Cl
Gosport PO13 . . . . .155 B2
Totton SO40 . . . . .100 B4
Harwood Ct BH25 . . . . . . .194 C2
Harwood Pl SO23 . . . . .2 B1
Harwood Rd PO13 . . . . . .155 B2
Haselbury Rd SO40 . . . . .100 C4
Haselfoot Gdns SO30 . . .104 C4
Haselworth Dr PO12 . . . .181 A1
Haselworth Prim Sch
PO12 . . . . .181 A2
Haskells Cl SO43 . . . . .121 C2
Haskells Rd BH12 . . . . . . .203 A4
Haslar Cres PO7 . . . . .111 B1
Haslar Marina PO12 . . . . .181 C2
Haslar Rd PO12 . . . . .181 B1
Haslar Terr PO12 . . . . .181 B1
Haslegrave Ho ☐ PO2 . . .182 B4
Haslemere Ave BH23 . . . .209 A4
Haslemere Gdns PO11 . . .185 C1
Haslemere Pl BH23 . . . . . .209 A4
Haslemere Rd
Portsmouth PO4 . . . . .182 C2
Southbourne PO10 . . . . . . .137 B1
Hasler Rd BH17 . . . . .187 B1
Haslop Rd BH21 . . . . .164 A4
Hassocks The ☐ PO7 . . . .135 A4
Hastings Ave PO12 . . . . . .180 C4
Hastings Ho ☐ PO2 . . . . .157 B1
Hastings Rd
Bournemouth BH8 . . . . .190 C1
Poole BH17 . . . . .187 A1
Hatch La PO7 . . . . .135 B4
Hatch Mead SO30 . . . . . . .80 B1
Hatch Pond Rd BH17 . . . .202 B4
Hatchers La SO21 . . . . . . .33 A3
Hatchet Cl SP6 . . . . .47 B2
Hatchet La
Beaulieu SO42 . . . . .175 B4
East Boldre SO42 . . . . .175 B4
Hatchley La SO21 . . . . .58 A3
Hatfield Ct BH25 . . . . .194 C2
Hatfield Gdns BH7 . . . . . .206 A4
Hatfield Rd ☐ PO4 . . . . . .183 A2
Hathaway Cl SO50 . . . . . . .56 A2
Hathaway Gdns PO7 . . . .112 A1
Hathaway Rd BH6 . . . . . . .206 B2
Hatherden Ave BH14 . . . .202 C3
Hatherell Cl SO30 . . . . . . .80 B1
Hatherley Cres PO16 . . . .156 A4
Hatherley Dr PO16 . . . . . .156 A4
Hatherley Mans ☐
SO15 . . . . .102 B4
Hatherley Rd
Cosham PO6 . . . . .133 A1
Winchester SO22 . . . . .1 C1
Hatley Rd SO18 . . . . .104 A4
Hatt La SO51 . . . . .5 C1
Havant Bsns Ctr PO9 . . . .159 B4
Havant Coll PO9 . . . . .135 C1
Havant Education PRU
PO8 . . . . .111 C1
Havant Farm Cl PO9 . . . .135 C2
Havant Mus & Arts Ctr★
PO9 . . . . .136 A1
Havant Rd Cosham PO6 . .158 B4
Emsworth PO10 . . . . .160 C4
Horndean PO8 . . . . .112 B3
North Hayling PO11 . . . . . .159 C1
Portsmouth PO2 . . . . .182 C4
Havant St PO1 . . . . .182 A3
Havant Sta PO9 . . . . .135 C1
Havant War Meml Hospl
PO9 . . . . .135 C1
Havant-by-pass PO9 . . . .160 A4
Havelock Cl SO31 . . . . . . .128 B1
Havelock Mans PO5 . . . . .215 D2
Havelock Rd
Locks Heath SO31 . . . . .128 B1
Poole BH12 . . . . .204 A3
Portsmouth PO5 . . . . .215 C4
Southampton SO14 . . . . . . .102 C3
Havelock Way BH23 . . . . .193 B1
Haven Cres PO14 . . . . . . .153 C1
Haven Ct
☐ Milford on Sea SO41 . . .211 B2
Poole BH13 . . . . .214 A2
Haven Gdns BH25 . . . . . . .195 A1
Haven Rd
Corfe Mullen BH21 . . . . . . .186 B3
Poole BH13 . . . . .214 C4
South Hayling PO11 . . . . . .185 C1
Haven The Eastleigh SO50 .56 A3
Gosport PO12 . . . . .181 A1
Locks Heath SO31 . . . . .129 A2
Portsmouth PO4 . . . . .183 A3
Southampton SO19 . . . . . . .103 C2
Havendale SO30 . . . . .105 B3
Havenhurst BH13 . . . . . . .214 C4
Havenstone Way SO18 . . .79 B2
Haverstock Rd BH9 . . . . . .190 A2
Haviland Mews BH7 . . . . .205 C3
Haviland Rd
Bournemouth BH1, BH7 . . .205 C3
Ferndown BH21 . . . . .165 A4
Haviland Rd E BH7 . . . . . .205 C3
Haviland Rd W BH7 . . . . .205 C3
Havisham Rd PO2 . . . . . . .182 B4
Havre Twrs ☐ SO19 . . . . .126 C4
Hawden Rd BH11 . . . . . . .189 A1
Hawfinch Cl SO16 . . . . . . .78 A3
Hawk Cl
Stubbington PO14 . . . . .179 A3
Wimborne Minst BH21 . . . .164 A4

Hawkchurch Gdns
BH17 . . . . .187 C1
Hawke St PO1 . . . . .182 A3
Hawker Cl BH21 . . . . .163 C1
Hawkeswood Rd SO18 . .103 B4
Hawkewood Ave PO7 . . . .111 B1
Hawkhill SO45 . . . . .125 B2
Hawkhurst Cl SO19 . . . . .104 A1
Hawkins Cl BH24 . . . . . . .117 B1
Hawkins Ct SO40 . . . . . . .101 C2
Hawkins Rd
Gosport PO13 . . . . .155 B1
Poole BH12 . . . . .188 C3
Hawkley Gn SO19 . . . . . . .126 C4
Hawkley Rd Hawkley GU33 20 B3
Liss GU33 . . . . .20 B3
Hawks Mead GU33 . . . . . .20 C3
Hawkwell PO16 . . . . .155 C4
Hawkwood Rd BH5 . . . . . .205 C2
Hawley Cl PO9 . . . . .135 C3
Haworth Cl BH23 . . . . . . .192 A1
Hawstead Gn ☐☐ PO9 . . .135 B3
Hawswater Cl SO16 . . . . . .77 C1
Hawthorn Cl
Colden Common SO21 . . . . .57 A4
☐ Fair Oak SO50 . . . . .57 B1
Hedge End SO30 . . . . .105 B3
New Milton BH25 . . . . .195 B2
Hawthorn Cres PO6 . . . . .158 A3
Hawthorn Ct ☐ GU31 . . .41 B2
Hawthorn Dr
Broadstone BH17 . . . . .186 C1
Sway SO41 . . . . .172 A1
Hawthorn La SO31 . . . . . .128 C3
Hawthorn Rd
Bournemouth BH9 . . . . .204 C4
Burton BH23 . . . . .192 C2
Denmead PO7 . . . . .110 C2
Horndean PO8 . . . . .88 B1
Hythe SO45 . . . . .125 C2
Southampton SO17 . . . . . . .79 A1
Hawthorn Wlk ☐☐ PO13 .179 C1
Hawthorne Gr PO11 . . . . .185 A2
Hawthorne Rd SO40 . . . .100 B4
Hawthorns The
Bishop's Waltham SO32 . . .83 A4
Christchurch BH23 . . . . . . .207 C3
Eastleigh SO50 . . . . .55 C1
Marchwood SO40 . . . . .102 A4
Hawthorns The Urban
Wildlife Ctr★ SO15 . . . . .102 C4
Hayburn Rd SO16 . . . . . . .77 B1
Haydens Ct SO41 . . . . . . .197 C2
Haydn Cl SO23 . . . . .2 A4
Haydock Cl SO40 . . . . . . .100 B4
Haydock Mews ☐ PO7 . .112 A1
Haydon Rd BH13 . . . . .204 A1
Hayes Ave BH7 . . . . .205 C3
Hayes Cl Fareham PO15 . . .130 B2
Wimborne Minst BH21 . . . .164 A2
Hayes La BH21 . . . . .164 A2
Hayes Mead SO45 . . . . . . .150 A4
Hayes Terr PO12 . . . . .181 A3
Hayeswood Fst Sch
BH21 . . . . .164 A3
Hayeswood Rd BH21 . . . .164 A3
Hayle Rd SO18 . . . . .80 A1
Hayley Cl SO45 . . . . .149 C4
Hayling Ave PO3 . . . . .183 A4
Hayling Cl Fareham PO14 .154 B4
Gosport PO12 . . . . .181 B4
Hayling Sch The PO11 . . .185 A3
Haymoor Mid Sch BH17 187 C1
Haymoor Rd BH15 . . . . . .203 A4
Haynes Ave SO45 . . . . . . .125 C1
Haynes Way SO45 . . . . . . .125 C1
Hays Cotts GU32 . . . . .40 B4
Haysoms Cl BH25 . . . . . . .195 A1
Hayter Gdns SO51 . . . . . . .53 A4
Hayters Way SP6 . . . . .93 A3
Hayton Ct SO40 . . . . .100 C4
Hayward Bsns Ctr PO9 . .136 A2
Hayward Cl SO40 . . . . . . .100 B4
Hayward Cres BH31 . . . . .114 C3
Hayward Ct SO45 . . . . . . .150 B2
Hayward Way BH31 . . . . . .114 C3
Haywards Ct ☐☐ PO1 . . . .182 A2
Haywards Farm Cl
BH31 . . . . .114 C3
Haywards La BH21 . . . . . .186 B4
Hazel Cl Alderholt SP6 . . . .93 A3
Chandler's Ford SO53 . . . . . .30 B1
Christchurch BH23 . . . . . . .193 B3
Colden Common SO21 . . . . .32 A1
Hazel Ct
Bournemouth BH9 . . . . .190 B2
☐☐ New Milton BH25 . . . . .195 A1
Portsmouth PO4 . . . . .182 C2
Hazel Dr BH22 . . . . .165 B4
Hazel Farm Rd SO40 . . . .100 B4
Hazel Gr Ashurst SO40 . . . .99 C2
Clanfield PO8 . . . . .88 B3
Locks Heath SO31 . . . . .129 A1
Winchester SO22 . . . . .10 B3
Hazel Rd Clanfield PO8 . . .88 B3
Lymington SO41 . . . . .197 A2
Southampton SO19 . . . . . . .103 C2
Hazel Wood Inf Sch
SO40 . . . . .100 B4
Hazelbank Cl GU31 . . . . . .41 A2
Hazeldale Villas ☐
SO45 . . . . .126 A3
Hazeldean Ct PO9 . . . . . . .113 A1
Hazeldean Dr PO9 . . . . . . .113 A1
Hazeldene BH18 . . . . .187 A2
Hazeldown Rd SO16 . . . . .77 C3
Hazeleigh Ave SO19 . . . . .103 C1
Hazeley Cotts SO21 . . . . .32 B4

Hazeley Gn PO9 ....136 A3
Hazeley Rd SO21 ....32 B3
Hazelholt Dr PO9 ....135 B2
Hazell Ave BH10 ....189 A1
Hazelton Cl BH7 ....206 A4
Hazelwood PO14 ....154 A3
Hazelwood Ave
Havant PO9 ....135 A2
New Milton BH25 ....194 C2
Hazelwood Dr BH31 ....115 A2
Hazelwood Rd SO18 ....80 A1
Hazlebury Rd BH17 ....202 A4
Hazlemere Dr BH24 ....139 C2
Hazleton Way PO8 ....112 A2
Head Down GU31 ....41 A2
Head's La BH10 ....189 C3
Headbourne Worthy Ho
SO23 ....2 A3
Headland Dr SO31 ....129 A2
Headlands Bsns Pk
BH24 ....117 A1
Headlands The SP5 ....46 C4
Headless Cross BH10 .....189 B3
Headley Cl PO13 ....179 C1
Headon View GU32 ....37 B3
Heads Farm Cl BH10 ......189 C3
Headswell Ave BH10 ......189 C2
Headswell Cres BH10 .....189 C2
Headswell Gdns BH10 .....189 C2
Heanor Cl BH10 ....189 B1
**Hearne Gdns SO32 ....84 A1
Hearts of Oak Mews
SO41 ....197 B2
Heath Ave BH15 ....202 B3
Heath Cl Fair Oak SO50 ...57 B1
Horndean PO8 ....112 A4
Wimborne Minst BH21 ....164 A4
Heath Ct GU31 ....40 C1
Heath Farm Cl BH22 ......165 B2
Heath Farm Rd BH22 ......165 B2
Heath Farm Way BH22 ....165 B2
Heath Gdns SO31 ....127 B4
Heath House Cl SO30 .....105 A2
Heath House Gdns
SO30 ....105 A2
Heath House La SO30 .....105 B2
Heath La BH42 ....175 B4
Heath Lawns PO15 ....130 B1
Heath Lodge GU31 ....40 C1
Heath Rd
Christchurch BH23 ....194 A1
Hordle SO41 ....195 C2
Locks Heath SO31 ....129 C4
North Baddesley SO52 .....54 A2
Petersfield GU31 ....41 A2
Soberton SO32 ....85 A1
Southampton SO19 ....104 A3
St Leonards BH24 ....139 B2
Heath Rd E GU31 ....41 A1
Heath Rd N SO31 ....128 C2
Heath Rd S SO31 ....128 C2
Heath Rd W GU31 ....41 A1
Heath The PO7 ....111 A2
Heathcote Pl SO21 ....30 A4
Heathcote Rd
Bournemouth BH5 ....205 C2
Chandler's Ford SO53 .....55 B3
Portsmouth PO2 ....157 C1
Heathen St SO32 ....82 A2
Heather Chase SO50 ......57 A1
Heather Cl
Bournemouth BH8 ....190 B2
Christchurch BH23 ....194 A1
Corfe Mullen BH21 ....186 C3
Gosport PO13 ....155 A4
Hordle SO41 ....196 A2
St Leonards BH24 ....139 C2
Totton SO40 ....100 C4
Waterlooville PO7 ....134 C3
Heather Ct SO18 ....104 B4
Heather Dell BH31 ....201 A4
Heather Dr BH22 ....165 B4
Heather Gdns PO15 ....130 B2
Heather Lo 2 BH25 ....195 A2
Heather Rd
Blackfield SO45 ....150 C1
Bournemouth BH10 ....189 B2
Petersfield GU31 ....41 B2
Heather View Rd BH12 ....203 C4
Heather Way BH22 ....165 B4
Heatherbank Rd BH4 .....204 B2
Heatherbrae Gdns SO52 ..53 C2
Heatherbrae La BH16 .....201 A3
Heatherdeane Rd SO17 ...79 A1
Heatherdene Rd SO53 ....30 C1
Heatherdown Rd BH22 ....139 A1
Heatherdown Way
BH22 ....139 A1
Heatherfield GU31 ....65 B3
Heatherlands Fst Sch
BH12 ....203 C3
Heatherlands Rd SO16 ...78 C4
Heatherlands Rise
BH12 ....203 B3
Heatherlea Rd BH6 ....206 B2
Heatherley Ct PO5 ....215 C1
Heatherstone Ave SO45 ..125 C1
Heatherton Mews PO10 ...53 C3
Heatherview Cl SO52 .....53 C3
Heathfield SO45 ....125 C1
Heathfield Ave
Fareham PO15 ....130 B1
Poole BH12 ....204 A4
Heathfield Cl
Chandler's Ford SO53 .....30 B1
Southampton SO19 ....104 A2
Heathfield Ho BH23 ......169 C1

Heathfield Jun Sch
SO19 ....104 B1
Heathfield Rd
Chandler's Ford SO53 .....30 B1
Petersfield GU31 ....41 B2
Portsmouth PO2 ....157 B1
Southampton SO19 ....104 B2
West Moors BH22 ....139 A1
Heathfield Specl Sch
PO14 ....154 B4
Heathfield Way BH22 .....138 C1
Heathlands Ave BH22 .....165 B1
Heathlands Cl
Burton BH23 ....192 B2
Chandler's Ford SO53 .....55 B4
Verwood BH31 ....115 A3
Heathlands Prim Sch
BH11 ....189 A2
Heathlands Rd SO53 ......55 B4
Heathwood Ave BH25 .....209 C4
Heathwood Rd BH9 ....204 C4
Heathy Cl BH25 ....209 C4
Heaton Rd
Bournemouth BH10 ....189 A1
Gosport PO12 ....181 A4
Heavytree Rd BH14 ....203 A2
Hebrides Cl PO14 ....154 A2
Heckfield Cl 29 PO9 ......136 A3
Heckford La BH15 ....202 B2
Heckford Rd
Corfe Mullen BH21 ....186 B3
Poole BH15 ....202 B2
Hector Cl PO7 ....134 C1
Hector Rd PO14 ....155 A3
Hedera Rd SO31 ....128 C2
Hedge End Bsns Ctr
SO30 ....81 A1
Hedge End Sta SO30 ......81 B2
Hedge End Wlk 7 PO9 .....136 A3
Hedgerley BH25 ....210 A4
Hedgerow Cl SO16 ....77 C4
Hedgerow Dr SO18 ....80 A1
Hedgerow Gdns PO10 .....136 C2
Hedley Cl SO45 ....150 C1
Hedley Gdns SO30 ....81 A2
Heidelberg Rd PO4 ....182 C2
Heights App BH16 ....201 B4
Heights Rd BH16 ....201 B4
Heights The
Fareham PO16 ....131 B1
Hedge End SO30 ....105 A3
Helena Rd PO4 ....182 C1
Helford Gdns SO18 ......80 A1
Helic Ho 2 BH21 ....163 B3
Hellyer Rd PO4 ....183 C4
Helm Cl PO13 ....180 B3
Helsby Cl PO14 ....154 C4
Helsted Cl PO12 ....180 C2
Helston Dr PO10 ....136 C2
Helston Rd PO6 ....132 C1
Helvellyn Rd SO16 ....101 C4
Helyar Rd BH8 ....190 B4
Hemdean Gdns SO30 ......80 B1
Hemlock Rd PO8 ....111 C2
Hemlock Way SO53 ....54 C1
Hemming Cl SO40 ....100 C3
Hemmingway Gdns
PO15 ....129 B4
Hempland La GU34 ....17 B2
Hempsted Rd PO4 ....133 A1
Hemsley Wlk PO8 ....112 A2
Henbest Cl BH21 ....164 B3
Henbury Cl
Corfe Mullen BH21 ....186 B3
Poole BH17 ....188 A1
Henbury Rise BH21 ......186 B3
Henbury View Fst Sch
BH21 ....186 B3
Henbury View Rd BH21 ...186 B3
Henchard Cl BH22 ....165 B1
Henderson Rd PO4 ....183 B2
Hendford Gdns BH10 .....189 B1
Hendford Rd BH10 ....189 B1
Hendy Cl PO5 ....215 B1
Hengist Rd BH1 ....205 B2
Hengistbury Head Nature
Reserve* BH6 ....207 B2
Hengistbury Head Nature
Trail* BH6 ....207 B2
Hengistbury Rd
Barton on Sea BH25 ......209 C4
Bournemouth BH6 ....207 A2
Henley Ct SO41 ....211 C2
Henley Gdns
Bournemouth BH7 ....206 A4
Fareham PO15 ....130 B2
Henley Rd PO4 ....182 C2
Henning's Park Rd
BH15 ....202 C3
Henry Beaufort Sec Sch
SO22 ....1 C2
Henry Cl SO45 ....150 A3
Henry Cort Com Sch
PO15 ....130 A2
Henry Cort Dr PO15 .....130 A2
Henry Rd
Bishopstoke SO50 ....56 B2
Southampton SO15 ....102 B4
Henry St
9 Gosport PO12 ....181 B2
Southampton SO15 ....102 C3
Henstead Ct 9 SO15 .....102 C3
Henstead Rd SO15 ....102 C3
Hensting La
Colden Common SO21,SO50 .32 C1
Owslebury SO21 ....58 C1
Henty Rd SO40 ....102 A4
Henville Cl PO13 ....180 B4

Henville Rd 6 BH8 ....205 B3
Henwood Down GU31 ......41 A2
Hepworth Cl SO19 ....104 B1
**Herald Ind Est SO30 .....81 A1
Herald Rd SO30 ....81 A1
**Herbert Ave BH12 ....203 B4
Herbert Cl BH12 ....203 B4
Herbert Hospl BH4 ....204 A1
Herbert Rd
Bournemouth BH4 ....204 A1
Gosport PO12 ....180 C3
New Milton BH25 ....195 A2
Poole BH13 ....204 A1
Portsmouth PO4 ....182 C1
Redlynch SP5 ....47 B3
Herbert St PO1 ....182 B4
Herbert Walker Ave
SO15 ....102 B2
Herberton Rd BH6 ....206 B3
Hercules Rd BH15 ....201 B2
Hercules St PO2 ....182 B4
Hereford Ct
Gosport PO13 ....180 B3
Portsmouth PO5 ....215 C1
Hereford Rd PO5 ....215 C1
Hereward Cl SO51 ....53 A4
Heritage Cl BH31 ....214 C4
Heritage Ctr* SO31 ......127 B2
Heritage Gdns PO16 .....156 A4
Heritage Way PO12 ......181 B4
Herm Rd BH12 ....188 B1
Hermes Ct PO12 ....181 B4
Hermes Rd PO13 ....179 B2
Hermitage Cl
Bishop's Waltham SO32 ...83 A4
Havant PO9 ....135 C2
Three Legged Cross BH21 .138 C4
Hermitage Gdns PO7 .....134 C4
Hermitage Rd BH14 ......203 A3
Hermitage The BH14 .....203 A3
**Hern La SP6 ....94 A3
Herne Jun Sch GU31 .....41 A2
**Herne Rd Cosham PO6 ....157 C4
West Meon GU32 ....37 B3
Wimborne Minst BH21 ....163 A4
Winchester SO23 ....11 A4
Heron Cl Portsmouth PO4 183 A3
Sway SO41 ....172 A1
Heron Court Rd BH3,
BH9 ....205 A4
Heron Dr BH21 ....164 A4
Heron La SO51 ....27 B3
Heron Quay PO10 ....161 A4
Heron Sq SO50 ....55 C1
Heron Way PO13 ....155 A2
Herons Cl PO14 ....154 B2
Herons Ct PO11 ....185 A3
Heronswood SO40 ....76 B1
Herrick Cl SO19 ....104 B2
Herriot Cl PO8 ....112 A3
Herriot Ho PO8 ....112 A3
Herstone Cl BH17 ....187 C1
Hertford Cl SP6 ....69 C2
Hertford Ct 12 BH23 .....209 A4
Hertford Pl PO1 ....182 B4
Hertsfield PO14 ....129 B2
Hesketh Cl BH24 ....140 A3
Hesketh Ho 8 SO15 .....102 B3
Hestan Cl BH23 ....191 B2
Hester Rd PO4 ....183 A4
Hestia Cl SO51 ....53 B4
Heston Way BH22 ....138 B2
Heston Wlk PO12 ....180 C2
Hewett Cl PO14 ....153 C4
Hewett Ho PO14 ....153 C4
Hewett Rd
Portsmouth PO2 ....157 C1
Titchfield PO14 ....153 C4
Hewetts Rise SO31 ......152 B4
Hewitt Cl PO12 ....181 A4
Hewitt Rd BH15 ....201 C2
Hewitt's Rd SO15 ....102 B3
Heyes Dr SO19 ....104 B2
Heysham Rd
Broadstone BH18 ....187 A2
Southampton SO15 ....102 A4
Heyshott Gdns PO8 .....88 B2
Heyshott Rd PO4 ....182 C2
Heytesbury Rd BH6 ......206 B3
Heyward Rd PO4 ....182 C2
Heywood Gdns PO9 ......135 B3
Heywood Gr SO19 ....104 C3
Hibberd Way BH10 ......189 B1
Hibbs Cl BH16 ....201 B4
Hickes Cl BH11 ....188 C3
Hickory Cl BH16 ....201 A4
Hickory Dr SO22 ....1 B2
Hickory Gdns SO30 .....80 B2
High Barn Cotts SO32 ...36 C2
High Brow BH22 ....165 B3
High Cross SO32 ....18 C1
High Cross La GU32 .....18 B1
High Ct PO4 ....183 A2
High Firs Gdns SO51 ....53 B4
High Firs Rd Romsey SO51 53 B4
Southampton SO19 ......104 B3
High Howe Cl BH11 ......188 C2
High Howe Gdns BH11 ...188 C2
High Howe La BH11 ......188 C2
High Lawn Way PO9 ......135 C3
High Marryats BH25 .....210 A4
High Mdw SO19 ....104 B3
High Mead
Fareham PO15 ....130 C2
Ferndown BH21 ....165 A1
High Mead La BH22 ......165 A1
High Oaks Cl SO31 ......129 A2
High Oaks Gdns BH11 ...188 C2
High Park Rd BH18 ......186 C2

High Pines BH23 ....208 B4
High Point SO18 ....103 C4
High Rd SO16 ....79 B2
High Ridge Cres BH25 ...195 B4
High St Beaulieu SO42 ...148 C1
Bishop's Waltham SO32 ...83 B4
Botley SO30 ....106 A4
Buriton GU31 ....65 B3
Bursledon SO31 ....128 A4
Christchurch BH23 ......207 A3
Cosham PO6 ....157 C4
Damerham SP6 ....68 B3
Downton SP5 ....47 A4
Droxford SO32 ....61 A1
East Meon GU32 ....38 C3
Eastleigh SO50 ....56 A1
Emsworth PO10 ....160 C4
Fareham PO16 ....131 B1
Fordingbridge SP6 ......69 C1
Gosport PO12 ....181 C3
Hamble-le-Rice SO31 ....128 A1
Hambledon PO7 ....86 B2
Hythe SO45 ....126 A3
Lee-on-the-Solent PO13 .179 C1
Lymington SO41 ....197 C2
Lyndhurst SO43 ....121 C3
Meonstoke SO32 ....61 B2
Milford on Sea SO41 ....211 B3
Petersfield GU32 ....40 C2
Poole BH15 ....202 B1
Portsmouth PO1 ....182 A2
Ringwood BH24 ....140 C4
Shedfield SO32 ....107 C4
Soberton SO32 ....85 A2
9 Southampton SO14 ...103 A3
Southwick PO17 ....132 C3
St Leonards BH24 ......139 C3
Titchfield PO14 ....153 C4
Totton SO40 ....101 A4
Twyford SO21 ....32 A1
Twyford SO21 ....32 A4
West End SO30 ....80 B1
West Meon GU32 ....37 B3
Wimborne Minst BH21 ...163 A4
Winchester SO23 ....11 A4
Woodgreen SP6 ....70 C4
High St N BH15 ....202 B2
High Town Hill BH24 ....141 C4
High Trees Fair Oak SO50 .57 C1
Poole BH15 ....214 D4
Waterlooville PO7 ....134 C4
High Trees Dr SO22 .....1 C1
High Trees Wlk BH22 ....165 B4
High View PO16 ....132 B1
High View Way SO18 ....103 C4
High Walls PO16 ....131 B1
High Way BH18 ....186 C2
High Wlk PO15 ....130 C2
Highbank Ave PO7 ......134 B2
Highbank Gdns SP6 .....69 C1
Highbridge Rd
Colden Common, Highbridge
SO50, SO21 ....56 B4
Colden Common, Twyford Moors
SO21 ....31 C1
Poole BH14 ....203 B2
Highbury Bldgs PO6 .....157 C3
Highbury Cl Fair Oak SO50 57 B1
New Milton BH25 ....195 A1
Highbury Coll PO6 ......158 A3
Highbury Gr PO6 ....158 A3
Highbury Prim Sch PO6 158 A3
Highbury St 6 PO1 ......182 A2
Highbury Way PO6 ......157 C3
Highclere Ave PO9 ......135 C2
Highclere Rd SO16 ......78 B2
Highclere Way SO53 ....55 C4
Highcliff Ave BH1 ....205 A4
Highcliffe Castle* BH23 ...208 C4
Highcliffe Cnr BH23 .....209 A4
Highcliffe Dr SO50 ......56 A4
Highcliffe Jun Sch
BH23 ....193 C1
Highcliffe Rd
Christchurch BH23 ......208 B4
Gosport PO12 ....180 C2
Winchester SO23 ....11 A3
Highcliffe Sch BH23 .....193 B1
Highcroft Ind Est PO8 ...112 B4
Highcroft La PO8 ....112 B4
Highcrown Mews SO17 ..79 A1
Highcrown St SO17 .....79 A1
Higher Blandford Rd
BH18,BH21 ....186 C3
Higher Merley La BH21 ..186 C4
Highfield Lymington SO41 197 B2
Twyford SO21 ....32 A3
Highfield Ave
Fareham PO14 ....154 C4
Lymington SO41 ....197 B2
Ringwood BH24 ....141 A4
Southampton SO16,SO17 .78 C2
Twyford SO21 ....32 A3
Waterlooville PO7 ....111 C1
Highfield Campus (Univ of
Southampton) SO17 ......79 A1
Highfield CE Inf Sch
SO17 ....79 A1
Highfield CE Prim Sch
SO17 ....79 A1
Highfield Cl
Chandler's Ford SO53 ....55 C3
Corfe Mullen BH21 ......186 C3
Southampton SO17 ......79 A1
Sway SO41 ....172 A1
Waterlooville PO7 ....111 C1
Highfield Cres SO17 .....79 A1

Highfield Ct SO32 ....83 A4
Highfield Dr BH24 ......141 A4
Highfield Gdns Liss GU33 21 A1
Sway SO41 ....172 A1
Highfield Hall SO17 .....79 A1
Highfield Ho 12 BH14 ...203 A2
Highfield La Redlynch SP5 47 B3
Southampton SO17 ......79 A1
Highfield Lodge 3 SO17 .79 A1
Highfield Par SO17 .....112 A1
Highfield Rd
Bournemouth BH9 ....189 C1
Chandler's Ford SO53 ....55 C3
Corfe Mullen BH21 ......186 C3
Gosport PO12 ....180 C3
Lymington SO41 ....197 B2
Petersfield GU32 ....40 C2
Portsmouth PO1 ....215 C3
Ringwood BH24 ....141 A4
Southampton SO17 ......79 A1
West Moors BH22 ....138 C2
Highfield Terr 36 SO22 ..10 C4
Highfields SO31 ....128 C1
Highgate Rd PO3 ....158 A1
Highgrove Cl SO40 .....100 B3
Highgrove Ind Pk PO3 ..158 A2
Highgrove Rd PO3 ......183 A4
Highland Ave BH23 .....194 A4
Highland Cl PO10 ......160 C4
Highland Rd
Emsworth PO10 ....136 C1
Poole BH14 ....203 A3
Portsmouth PO4 ....183 A2
Wimborne Minst BH21 ..163 B3
Highland St PO4 ....183 A1
Highland Terr PO4 .....182 C2
Highland View Cl BH21 .163 B3
Highlands Cl Hythe SO45 126 A1
North Baddesley SO51 ...53 C3
Highlands Cres BH10 ...189 B2
Highlands Ho SO19 .....103 B2
Highlands Way
Barton on Sea BH25 ....210 A4
Cosham PO6 ....158 B4
Fareham PO15,PO16 ....130 B2
Highlands Way
Hythe SO45 ....125 C1
Whiteparish SP5 ....24 C1
Highmoor Cl
Corfe Mullen BH21 ......186 B3
Poole BH15 ....203 A2
Highmoor Rd
Bournemouth BH11 ......189 A1
Corfe Mullen BH21 ......186 B3
Poole BH15 ....203 B2
Highmount Cl SO23 .....11 B4
Highnam Gdns SO31 ....128 C2
Hightown Gdns BH24 ...141 B3
Hightown Ind Est BH24 .141 A3
Hightown Prim Sch
SO19 ....104 C2
Hightown Rd BH24 .....141 A3
Hightown Twrs SO19 ...104 C2
Hightrees Ave BH8 .....190 C1
Highview Cl BH23 ......191 C1
Highview Gdns BH12 ...203 B4
Highways Rd SO21 .....31 B3
Highwood SP6 ....92 B3
Highwood La
North Baddesley SO51 ...53 B4
Ringwood BH24 ....117 C2
Highwood Lawn PO9 ....135 B4
Highwood PRU SO42 ...172 C4
Highwood Rd
Brockenhurst SO42 .....172 C4
Gosport PO13 ....180 B4
Poole BH14 ....203 C2
Higworth La PO11 ......184 C3
Hilary Ave PO6 ....158 A4
Hilary Cl SO43 ....122 A2
Hilary Ct PO13 ....180 B3
Hilary Rd BH17 ....187 B1
Hilda Ct 8 SO15 ....102 C4
Hilda Gdns PO7 ....111 A2
Hilda Pl 28 SO14 ......103 B3
Hilda Rd BH12 ....203 C4
Hilden Ct PO11 ....184 C2
Hilden Way SO22 ......1 A3
Hiley Rd BH15 ....202 B3
Hill Brow Rd GU33 ....21 A1
Hill Cl Bransgore BH23 .193 A4
Fair Oak SO50 ....57 B3
Hill Close Est SP6 ......70 C4
Hill Croft PO15 ....129 C2
Hill Dr PO15 ....130 B2
Hill Farm Rd SO15 .....102 C3
Hill Grove La SO32 .....84 B3
Hill Head Rd PO14 .....179 A3
Hill House Sch SO41 ...173 B1
Hill Houses La SO41 ....14 A3
Hill La Bransgore BH23 .193 A4
Burton BH23 ....192 C1
Colden Common SO21 ...31 C1
Southampton SO15 .....78 C4
Hill Park Rd
Fareham PO15 ....130 B2
Gosport PO12 ....180 C2
Hill Pl SO31 ....128 A4
Hill Rd PO15 ....132 B1
Hill Rise Meonstoke SO32 .61 B3
Twyford SO21 ....32 A3
Hill St Ower SO40 .....76 B3
Poole BH15 ....202 B1
Hill Terr SO50 ....57 B3
Hill Top SO22 ....1 B3

Hill View GU32 . . . . .38 B1
Hill View Prim Sch
BH10 . . . . .189 C2
Hill View Rd
Braishfield SO51 . . . . .28 B3
Ferndown BH22 . . . . .165 B4
Michelmersh SO51 . . . . .27 B4
Portchester PO16 . . . . .132 B1
Hill Way BH24 . . . . .139 C3
Hill Wlk PO15 . . . . .130 B2
Hillary Cl PO16 . . . . .130 C1
Hillary Rd BH23 . . . . .207 C4
Hillborough Cres **2**
PO5 . . . . .215 C1
Hillborough Ct **1** PO5 . .215 C1
Hillbourne Fst & Mid Schs
BH17 . . . . .187 A1
Hillbourne Rd BH17 . . . . . .187 A1
Hillbrow Cl
Fareham PO15 . . . . .130 B2
Rowland's Castle PO9 . . . . .113 A1
Hillbrow Rd BH6 . . . . .206 A3
Hillbury Pk SP6 . . . . .93 A3
Hillbury Rd SP6 . . . . .93 A3
Hillcrest Ave
Chandler's Ford SO53 . . . . . .55 C3
Ferndown BH22 . . . . .165 B4
Hillcrest Cl
Bournemouth BH9 . . . . . . .190 A2
North Baddesley SO52 . . . . .53 C3
Hillcrest Dr SO53 . . . . .55 B3
Hillcrest Gdns SO32 . . . . . . .83 B3
Hillcrest Hospl BH10 . . . . .189 B1
Hillcrest Rd
Bournemouth BH9 . . . . . . .190 A2
Corfe Mullen BH21 . . . . . . .186 B3
Hillcroft SP5 . . . . .47 B3
Hilldene Way SO30 . . . . .80 C1
Hillditch SO41 . . . . .197 B3
Hilldown Rd SO17 . . . . .79 A1
Hilldowns Ave PO2 . . . . . . .157 A1
Hiller Wlk **16** PO13 . . . . .179 C1
Hillgrove Rd SO18 . . . . .79 C2
Hillier Way SO23 . . . . .2 A1
Hillman Rd BH14 . . . . .203 B3
Hillmead Gdns PO9 . . . . . .135 A1
Hillmeadow BH31 . . . . .115 A2
Hillside Curdridge SO32 . . .106 C4
Littleton SO22 . . . . .1 B3
Hillside Ave Romsey SO51 53 A4
Southampton SO18 . . . . .79 C1
Waterlooville PO7 . . . . .134 A1
Hillside Cl
Chandler's Ford SO53 . . . . . .55 B3
Horndean PO8 . . . . .88 B2
West Dean SP5 . . . . .3 B1
Winchester SO22 . . . . .1 B1
Hillside Cres PO6 . . . . .132 C1
Hillside Dr BH23 . . . . .191 B2
Hillside First Sch BH14 . . . .114 C4
Hillside Ind Est PO8 . . . . . .112 B4
Hillside Mews BH21 . . . . . .186 B2
Hillside Rd
Corfe Mullen BH21 . . . . . . .186 B3
Lymington SO41 . . . . .197 B2
Poole BH12 . . . . .188 C1
Verwood BH31 . . . . .114 C4
Winchester SO22 . . . . .1 B1
Woodlands BH21 . . . . .114 A3
Hillside Wlk BH21 . . . . .114 A3
Hillsley Rd PO6 . . . . .132 C4
Hillson Dr PO15 . . . . .130 B2
Hillson Ho PO15 . . . . .130 B2
Hillsons Rd SO30 . . . . .106 A4
Hilltop Cl BH22 . . . . .165 A4
Hilltop Cres PO6 . . . . .134 B1
Hilltop Dr SO19 . . . . .104 B2
Hilltop Gdns PO8 . . . . .88 B2
Hilltop Rd
Corfe Mullen BH21 . . . . . . .186 C3
Ferndown BH22 . . . . .165 A4
Hillview PO8 . . . . .112 B3
Hillview Rd
Bournemouth BH10 . . . . . .189 B2
Hythe SO45 . . . . .125 C2
Hillway The
Chandler's Ford SO53 . . . . . .55 B4
Portchester PO16 . . . . .156 B4
Hilly Cl SO21 . . . . .33 A2
Hillyfields SO16 . . . . .77 B2
Hilsea Cres PO2 . . . . .157 C3
Hilsea Mkt PO2 . . . . .157 C3
Hilsea Sta PO3 . . . . .158 A2
Hiltingbury Cl SO53 . . . . . . .30 B1
Hiltingbury Cl SO53 . . . . . . .30 B1
Hiltingbury Inf Sch SO53 30 B1
Hiltingbury Jun Sch
SO53 . . . . .30 B1
Hiltingbury Rd
Chandler's Ford SO53 . . . . . .30 B1
5B Havant PO9 . . . . .136 A3
Hiltom Rd BH24 . . . . .141 A4
Hilton Cl BH15 . . . . .203 A3
Hilton Rd Gosport PO12 . . .181 B2
Hedge End SO30 . . . . .105 B4
New Milton BH25 . . . . .195 A2
Hinchcliffe Cl BH15 . . . . . .201 C1
Hinchcliffe Rd BH15 . . . . . .201 C1
Hinkler Ct SO19 . . . . .104 B2
Hinkler Rd SO19 . . . . .104 C3
Hinton Admiral Mews
BH23 . . . . .193 C1
Hinton Admiral Sta
BH23 . . . . .193 C1

Hinton Ampner Ho★
SO24 . . . . .14 C2
Hinton Cl PO9 . . . . .135 B2
Hinton Cres SO19 . . . . .104 C2
Hinton Hill SO24 . . . . .14 C2
Hinton Ho **1** PO7 . . . . .134 C4
Hinton Manor La PO8 . . . . .87 C1
Hinton Rd BH1 . . . . .204 C2
Hinton Wood BH1 . . . . . . .205 A1
Hinton Wood Ave BH23 . . .193 C1
Hintonwood La BH23 . . . . .193 C1
Hipley Rd PO9 . . . . .136 A2
Hirst Rd SO45 . . . . .126 A2
Hispano Ave PO15 . . . . . . .129 B4
Hither Gn PO10 . . . . .137 C1
Hitherwood Cl **14** PO7 . .112 A1
Hive Gdns BH13 . . . . .214 B3
Hives Way SO41 . . . . .197 B3
HMS Victory★ PO1 . . . . . .181 C3
HMS Warrior★ PO1 . . . . . .181 C3
Hoad's Hill PO17 . . . . .108 A1
Hoadlands GU31 . . . . .41 A2
Hobart Dr SO45 . . . . .126 A2
Hobart Rd BH25 . . . . .194 C1
Hobb La SO30 . . . . .105 B3
Hobbs Ct PO12 . . . . .181 C2
Hobbs Pass PO12 . . . . .181 C2
Hobbs Pk BH24 . . . . .139 C2
Hobby Cl PO3 . . . . .158 A2
Hobson Way SO45 . . . . . . .150 B2
Hoburne Ct BH23 . . . . .193 B1
Hoburne Gdns BH23 . . . . . .193 B1
Hoburne La BH23 . . . . .208 B4
Hockham Ct PO9 . . . . .135 B4
Hockley Cl **7** PO6 . . . . .157 B4
Hockley Cotts
Cheriton SO24 . . . . .13 C2
Twyford SO21 . . . . .32 A4
Hockley Link SO21 . . . . .10 C1
Hocombe Dr SO53 . . . . .30 A1
Hocombe Park Cl SO53 . . . .30 A1
Hocombe Rd SO53 . . . . .30 B1
Hocombe Wood Rd SO53 30 A1
Hodder Cl SO53 . . . . .55 A3
Hodges Cl Havant PO9 . . . .136 A2
Poole BH17 . . . . .202 C4
Hoe La SO52 . . . . .53 B2
Hoe Rd SO32 . . . . .83 C4
Hoe St PO7 . . . . .109 C4
Hoe The PO13 . . . . .155 C1
Hoeford Cl PO16 . . . . .155 A3
Hogarth Cl
7 Romsey SO51 . . . . . . .28 A1
Southampton SO19 . . . . . . .104 B1
Hogarth Way BH8 . . . . .191 A1
Hoggarth Cl GU32 . . . . .41 A2
Hogs Lodge La PO8 . . . . . . .88 C4
Hogue Ave BH10 . . . . .189 B3
Hogwood La SO30 . . . . .80 C3
Holbeach Cl PO6 . . . . .133 C1
Holbein Lodge SO41 . . . . . .198 A2
Holbrook Pl **6** SO51 . . . .52 C4
Holbrook Prim Sch
PO13 . . . . .155 B2
Holbrook Rd
Fareham PO16 . . . . .155 A4
Portsmouth PO1 . . . . .215 C3
Holbury Cl BH8 . . . . .190 C2
Holbury Cl **25** PO9 . . . . .136 A3
Holbury Dro SO45 . . . . .150 B2
Holbury Inf Sch SO45 . . . . .150 B2
Holbury Jun Sch SO45 . . . .150 B2
Holbury La
East Tytherley SO51 . . . . .4 B3
Lockerley SO51 . . . . .4 B2
Holcombe Rd BH16 . . . . . . .201 A3
Holcot La PO3 . . . . .158 B2
Holcroft Rd SO19 . . . . .104 C3
Holdaway Cl SO23 . . . . .2 B4
Holden La SO24 . . . . .34 C4
Holdenbury Ct PO3 . . . . . . .158 B2
Holdenhurst Ave BH7 . . . . .206 B4
Holdenhurst Cl PO8 . . . . . . .88 B1
Holdenhurst Rd
Bournemouth BH8 . . . . . . .205 B3
Bournemouth, Holdenhurst
BH8 . . . . .191 A2
Hole La Curdridge SO32 . . . .83 A1
Soberton PO7 . . . . .110 A4
Holes Bay North Rdbt
BH17 . . . . .202 A3
Holes Bay Rd BH15 . . . . . . .202 A2
Holes Bay Rdbt BH15 . . . . .202 A3
Holes Cl SO41 . . . . .195 C2
Holkham Cl SO16 . . . . .77 C2
Hollam Cl PO14 . . . . .154 A4
Hollam Cres PO14 . . . . .154 A4
Hollam Dr PO14 . . . . .154 A4
Hollam Rd PO4 . . . . .183 A2
Holland Cl SO53 . . . . .55 A2
Holland Pk SO31 . . . . .128 C2
Holland Pl Gosport PO13 155 B1
Southampton SO16 . . . . .78 A1
Holland Rd
Portsmouth PO5 . . . . .215 D2
Southampton SO19 . . . . . . .103 B1
Totton SO40 . . . . .100 B4
Holland Way BH18 . . . . . . .186 C3
Hollands Cl SO21 . . . . .1 A3
Hollands Wood Dr
BH25 . . . . .195 A3
Hollies Cl SO41 . . . . .172 A1
Hollies The SO51 . . . . .55 C2
Hollingbourne Cl SO18 . .103 B4
Hollman Dr SO51 . . . . .52 B4
Hollow La PO11 . . . . .184 C2
Holloway Ave BH11 . . . . . . .188 C3

Holly Cl Hythe SO45 . . . . . .150 A4
Locks Heath SO31 . . . . .128 C2
St Leonards BH24 . . . . .139 B2
Upton BH16 . . . . .201 A4
Holly Ct BH15 . . . . .202 B2
Holly Dell SO16 . . . . .78 C3
Holly Dr PO7 . . . . .135 A3
Holly Gdns Burton BH23 . . .192 B1
Milford on Sea SO41 . . . . . .211 B3
West End SO30 . . . . .80 B2
Holly Gr Fareham PO16 . . . .130 C2
Verwood BH31 . . . . .114 C3
Holly Green Rise BH11 . . . .188 C2
Holly Hatch Rd SO40 . . . . .100 C3
Holly Hedge La BH17 . . . . .202 B4
Holly Hill SO16 . . . . .78 C3
Holly Hill SO16 . . . . .78 C3
Holly Hill La SO31 . . . . . . .128 C2
Holly Hill Mans SO31 . . . . .128 C2
Holly Hill Woodland Pk★
SO31 . . . . .128 B2
Holly Ho SO19 . . . . .103 C1
Holly La Boldre SO41 . . . . .174 A1
Christchurch BH23 . . . . .194 B1
New Milton BH25 . . . . .195 B2
Holly Lo **13** BH12 . . . . .204 A2
Holly Lodge
Chandler's Ford SO53 . . . . . .55 B2
Southampton SO17 . . . . .79 A1
Holly Oak Cl SO16 . . . . .78 A2
Holly Oak Rd SO16 . . . . . . .78 A2
Holly Rd Ashurst SO40 . . . .100 A1
Blackfield SO45 . . . . .177 C4
Holly St PO12 . . . . .181 B2
Hollybank PO13 . . . . .179 C1
Hollybank Cl
12 Hythe SO45 . . . . . . .126 A2
Waterlooville PO8 . . . . .112 B3
Hollybank Cres SO45 . . . . .125 C2
Hollybank La PO10 . . . . . . .136 C2
Hollybank Rd SO45 . . . . . . .125 C2
Hollybrook Ave SO16 . . . . . .78 A2
Hollybrook Cl SO16 . . . . . . .78 A1
Hollybrook Gdns SO31 . . . .129 A3
Hollybrook Inf Sch SO16 . .78 B2
Hollybrook Jun Sch
SO16 . . . . .78 B2
Hollybrook Rd SO16 . . . . . . .78 B1
Hollydene SO45 . . . . .126 A2
Hollywell Dr PO6 . . . . .157 A4
Hollywood Cl SO52 . . . . . . .53 C2
Hollywood Ct SO41 . . . . . . .197 B3
Hollywood La SO41 . . . . . . .197 B3
Holm Cl BH24 . . . . .117 B1
Holm Ct PO11 . . . . .184 C1
Holm Hill La BH23 . . . . . . .194 A4
Holm Oak Cl Littleton SO22 . .1 A3
Verwood BH31 . . . . .114 C4
Holman Ct PO14 . . . . .112 A1
Holmbush Ct PO5 . . . . .215 B1
Holmdale Rd PO12 . . . . . . .180 C4
Holme Cl SO41 . . . . .197 B1
Holmes Cl **8** SO31 . . . . .127 A3
Holmesland Dr SO30 . . . . . .105 C4
Holmesland La SO30 . . . . . .105 C4
Holmesland Wlk SO30 . . . . .105 C4
Holmfield SO43 . . . . .122 A3
Holmfield Ave
Bournemouth BH7 . . . . . . .206 B4
Fareham PO14 . . . . .154 C4
Holmgrove PO14 . . . . .129 B2
Holmhurst Ave BH23 . . . . . .193 C1
Holmsley Cl
Lymington SO41 . . . . .197 A1
Southampton SO18 . . . . . . .104 B4
Holmsley Ct SO40 . . . . .100 A4
Holmsley Pass BH24 . . . . . .170 A4
Holmsley Rd BH25 . . . . . . .170 C1
Holmwood Garth BH24 . . . .141 B4
Holne Ct PO4 . . . . .183 B2
Holnest Rd BH17 . . . . .187 B1
Holst Way PO7 . . . . .134 C3
Holt Cl PO17 . . . . .107 C2
Holt Ct SO19 . . . . .126 C4
Holt Down GU31 . . . . .41 A2
Holt Gdns PO9 . . . . .113 A2
Holt Rd Poole BH12 . . . . . .203 C3
Southampton SO15 . . . . . . .102 C3
Verwood BH21 . . . . .138 B4
Holt View **9** SO50 . . . . . .56 C1
Holworth Cl BH11 . . . . .188 C2
Holy Family RC Prim Sch
SO16 . . . . .77 B1
Holy Rood Est SO14 . . . . . .103 A2
Holyborne Rd SO51 . . . . . . .53 A4
Holybourne Rd PO9 . . . . . .135 C2
Holyrood Ave SO17 . . . . . . .79 A1
Holyrood Cl
Broadstone BH17 . . . . .202 A4
4 Waterlooville PO7 . . . .135 A4
Holyrood Ho **12** SO14 . .103 A2
Holywell Cl BH17 . . . . .187 B2
Home Farm Bsns Ctr SP5 . .4 C3
Home Farm Cl SO45 . . . . . .126 A2
Home Farm Way SO41 . . . .177 C3
Home Farm Office Village
PO16 . . . . .155 B4
Home Field Dr SO16 . . . . . . .77 B3
Home Mead PO7 . . . . .110 C2
Home Rd BH11 . . . . .189 A3
Home Rule Rd SO31 . . . . . .129 A2
Home Way GU31 . . . . .41 B2
Homeborough Ho **7**
SO45 . . . . .126 A3
Homebridge Ho SP6 . . . . . .69 C1

Homedale Ho BH2 . . . . .204 C3
Homedene Ho BH15 . . . . . .202 B2
Homefayre Ho **19** PO16 .131 A1
Homefield SO51 . . . . .28 A1
Homefield Cotts GU33 . . . . .20 C3
Homefield Ho BH15 . . . . . . .195 A1
Homefield Ind Prep Sch
BH6 . . . . .206 C2
Homefield Ind Senior Sch
BH23 . . . . .192 B3
Homefield Rd
Cosham PO6 . . . . .158 B4
Westbourne PO10 . . . . .137 A2
Homefield Way PO8 . . . . . . .88 A3
Homeforde Ho SO42 . . . . . .146 A1
Homefort Ho **2** PO12 . .181 A2
Homegrange Ho **15**
SO41 . . . . .211 B2
Homegrove Ho PO5 . . . . . . .215 C1
Homeheights **28** PO5 . . . .182 B3
Homelake Ho BH14 . . . . . . .203 A2
Homelands Est BH23 . . . . . .206 C3
Homelands Ho BH22 . . . . . .165 B3
Homeleigh Ho **5** BH8 . . .205 B3
Homemead Ho SO51 . . . . . .52 C3
Homemill Ho **5** BH25 . . .195 A2
Homeoaks Ho BH2 . . . . . . .204 C3
Homepoint Ho SO18 . . . . . .104 A4
Homer Cl Gosport PO13 . . . .180 A4
Waterlooville PO8 . . . . .111 C1
Homer Mobile Home Pk
SO45 . . . . .177 C3
Homerise Ho **1** SO23 . . . .11 A4
Homerose Ho PO5 . . . . .215 B2
Homeryde Ho **11** PO13 . .179 C1
Homesea Ho PO5 . . . . .215 B2
Homeside Rd BH9 . . . . .190 A1
Homespinney Ho SO18 . . . .79 B1
Homestour Ho BH23 . . . . . .207 A3
Hometide Ho **13** PO13 . . .179 C1
Homeview Ho BH15 . . . . . . .202 B2
Homewater Ho **7** PO7 . . .134 C4
Homeway Cotts SO40 . . . . .101 A3
Homewell PO9 . . . . .135 C1
Homewood Ho BH25 . . . . . .195 B2
Homewood Ho SO41 . . . . . .197 B1
Honey La Burley BH24 . . . . .142 C1
Honeybourne Cres BH6 . . .207 A2
Honeycritch La GU32 . . . . . .19 B2
Honeysuckle Cl
Gosport PO13 . . . . .155 A2
Locks Heath SO31 . . . . .129 A3
Winchester SO22 . . . . .10 C2
Honeysuckle Ct
Locks Heath SO31 . . . . .129 A3
5 Southampton SO18 . . .104 A4
Waterlooville PO7 . . . . .135 A3
Honeysuckle Gdns
SO41 . . . . .196 B1
Honeysuckle La BH17 . . . . .186 C1
Honeysuckle Rd SO16 . . . . .79 A2
Honeysuckle Way
Christchurch BH23 . . . . .208 A4
North Baddesley SO53 . . . . .55 A3
Honeywood Cl
Portsmouth PO3 . . . . .157 C2
Totton SO40 . . . . .76 B1
Honeywood Ho BH14 . . . . .214 B4
Honister Cl SO16 . . . . .101 C4
Hood Cl
Bournemouth BH10 . . . . . .189 A1
Locks Heath SO31 . . . . .129 A3
Hood Cres BH10 . . . . .189 A1
Hood Rd SO18 . . . . .104 A4
Hook Cl SO51 . . . . .30 A1
Hook Cotts SO31 . . . . .152 C4
Hook Cres SO51 . . . . .30 A1
Hook La SO31,SO51 . . . . . .153 A4
Hook Park Rd SO31 . . . . . .152 C3
Hook Rd Ampfield SO51 . . . .29 C1
Chandler's Ford SO51 . . . . . .29 C1
Hook Water Cl SO53 . . . . . .30 A1
Hook Water Rd SO53 . . . . . .30 A1
Hook with Warsash CE Prim
Sch SO31 . . . . .152 B4
Hook's Farm Way PO9 . . . .135 B2
Hook's La PO9 . . . . .135 B2
Hooke Cl BH17 . . . . .188 A1
Hookpit Farm La SO23 . . . . .2 A4
Hookwood La SO51 . . . . . . .29 C1
Hop Cl BH16 . . . . .201 A4
Hope Lodge Sch SO18 . . . .103 C4
Hope Rd SO30 . . . . .80 C1
Hope St PO1 . . . . .215 B4
Hopfield Cl PO7 . . . . .134 C4
Hopfield Ho PO7 . . . . .134 C4
Hopfield Mews PO7 . . . . . . .134 C3
Hopkins Cl
Bournemouth BH8 . . . . . . .191 A1
Portchester PO6 . . . . .156 C4
Hopkins Ct PO4 . . . . .183 A2
Horace Rd **10** BH5 . . . . .205 C2
Horder Cl SO16 . . . . .78 C2
Hordle CE Prim Sch
SO41 . . . . .196 A2
Hordle Ho Sch SO41 . . . . .210 C3
Hordle La SO41 . . . . .196 A1
Hordle Rd PO9 . . . . .135 C2
Hordle Walhampton Sch
SO41 . . . . .198 A3
Horlock Rd SO42 . . . . .146 A1
Hornbeam Cl **9** SO30 . . .105 B3
Hornbeam Gdns SO30 . . . . .80 B2
Hornbeam Rd
Chandler's Ford SO53 . . . . . .54 C3
Havant PO9 . . . . .136 A2
Hornbeam Way BH21 . . . . .163 C3

Hornby Cl SO31 . . . . .152 B2
Hornchurch Rd SO16 . . . .77 C3
Horndean CE Jun Sch
PO8 . . . . .112 B4
Horndean Com Sch
PO8 . . . . .112 A4
Horndean Ho **6** PO1 . . .215 C4
Horndean Inf Sch PO8 . . . .112 B4
Horndean Prec PO8 . . . . . .112 B4
Horndean Rd
Emsworth PO10 . . . . .136 C3
Horndean PO8 . . . . .112 C4
Hornet Cl Fareham PO15 . . .130 B1
Gosport PO12 . . . . .181 B2
Hornet Rd Gosport PO14 . . .154 C3
Thorney Island PO10 . . . . . .161 A2
Horning Rd BH12 . . . . .203 C3
Horns Dro SO16 . . . . .77 C3
Horns Hill Nursling SO16 . . .77 B3
Soberton SO32 . . . . .85 A1
Horns Hill Cl SO16 . . . . .77 B3
Horsa Cl BH6 . . . . .206 C2
Horsa Ct BH6 . . . . .206 C2
Horsa Rd BH6 . . . . .206 C2
Horse Sands Cl PO4 . . . . . .183 B2
Horsea La PO2 . . . . .157 C2
Horsea Rd PO2 . . . . .157 C3
Horsebridge Rd PO9 . . . . . .136 A2
Horsebridge Way SO16 . . . . .77 C3
Horsecroft **2** SO51 . . . . . .52 C4
Horsefair Ct SO51 . . . . .52 C4
Horsefair Mews SO51 . . . . . .52 C4
Horsefair The SO51 . . . . . . .52 C4
Horsehoe Bridge SO14 . . . .103 B4
Horsepost La PO7,PO8 . . . . .87 A1
Horseshoe Cl
Titchfield PO14 . . . . .129 B1
Wimborne Minst BH21 . . . . .164 A3
Horseshoe Ct
4 Bournemouth BH1 . . . .204 C2
Downton SP5 . . . . .46 C4
Horseshoe Dr
Romsey SO51 . . . . .28 A1
Totton SO40 . . . . .76 A1
Horseshoe Lodge SO31 . . . .128 C1
Horseshoe The BH13 . . . . .214 B2
Horsham Ave BH10 . . . . . . .189 B3
Horton Cl BH9 . . . . .190 B2
Horton Rd Gosport PO13 . . .155 C3
St Leonards BH24 . . . . .139 C3
Verwood BH21 . . . . .114 A1
Horton Way
Bishopstoke SO50 . . . . .56 C1
Verwood BH31 . . . . .114 B3
Hosier's La **23** BH15 . . . .202 A1
Hosker Rd BH5 . . . . .206 A3
Hospital La PO16 . . . . .156 C3
Hospital Rd SO32,PO17 . . .108 A4
Hotspur Cl SO45 . . . . .125 C3
Houchin St SO32 . . . . .83 B4
Houghton Cl **1** PO9 . . . .136 A3
Houlton Rd BH15 . . . . .202 C2
Hound Cl SO31 . . . . .127 B3
Hound Manor SO31 . . . . . .127 C3
Hound Rd SO31 . . . . .127 B3
Hound Road Gdns SO31 127 B3
Hound Way SO31 . . . . .127 B3
Houndells Way BH21 . . . . . .164 A3
Houndwell Pl SO14 . . . . . . .103 A2
Hounsdown Ave SO40 . . . . .100 C3
Hounsdown Cl SO40 . . . . . .100 C3
Hounsdown Sec Sch
SO40 . . . . .100 C2
Hounslow Cl BH15 . . . . . . .201 C1
House Farm Rd PO12 . . . . .180 C2
Hove Ct PO13 . . . . .179 C1
Hoveton Gr SO53 . . . . .55 A4
Howard Cl Burley BH24 . . . .143 C2
Chandler's Ford SO53 . . . . . .55 B2
Christchurch BH23 . . . . .207 C3
Fair Oak SO50 . . . . .57 B1
Southampton SO18 . . . . .79 C2
Howard Oliver Ho SO45 126 A2
Howard Rd
Bournemouth BH8 . . . . . . .205 B4
Portsmouth PO2 . . . . .157 C2
Southampton SO15 . . . . . . .102 B3
Verwood BH31 . . . . .114 C3
Howard's Gr SO15 . . . . . . .102 B4
Howards Mead SO41 . . . . .197 A1
Howe Cl
Christchurch BH23 . . . . .207 C3
New Milton BH25 . . . . .194 C2
Howe La BH31 . . . . .114 C3
Howe Rd PO13 . . . . .180 B3
Howell Ho BH21 . . . . .163 C4
Howerts Cl SO31 . . . . .152 B4
Howeth Cl BH10 . . . . .189 B2
Howeth Rd BH10 . . . . .189 B2
Howlett Cl SO41 . . . . .197 A1
Howton Cl BH10 . . . . .189 B3
Howton Rd BH10 . . . . .189 B3
Hoxley Rd BH10 . . . . .189 B2
Hoyal Rd BH15 . . . . .201 B2
Hoylake Cl PO13 . . . . .155 B1
Hoylake Rd PO6 . . . . .134 B1
Hoyle Cl SO32 . . . . .58 B2
Hoylecroft Cl PO15 . . . . . . .130 C2
Hubert Rd SO23 . . . . .10 C2
Hudson Cl Gosport PO13 . . .180 B3
Poole BH12 . . . . .188 B1
Ringwood BH24 . . . . .141 B4
Hudson Ct SO40 . . . . .100 B3
Hudson Rd PO5 . . . . .215 C2
Hughes Bsns Ctr BH23 . . . .208 A4
Hughes Cl SO45 . . . . .150 C1
Hulbert Jun Sch PO7 . . . .134 C3

Hulbert Rd Havant PO9 . .135 A2
  Waterlooville PO7 . . . . . .134 C4
Hull Cres BH11 . . . . .188 C2
Hull Rd BH11 . . . . .188 C2
Hull Way BH11 . . . . .188 C2
Hulles Way SO52 . . . . . . .53 C2
Hulse Lodge 4 SO15 . .102 C4
Hulse Rd SO15 . . . . .102 C4
Hulton Cl SO19 . . . . .103 B1
Humber Cl PO14 . . . . . .154 A2
Humber Gdns SO31 . . . .105 A1
Humber Rd BH22 . . . . . .166 A3
Hummicks The SO42 . . .176 B4
Hundred Acres PO17 . .108 C2
Hundred Acres Rd
  PO17 . . . . .108 C2
Hundred La SO41 . . . . . .198 A4
Hundred The
  Fordingbridge SP6 . . . . . .69 C1
  Romsey SO51 . . . . .52 C4
  Waterlooville PO7 . . . . . .111 B1
Hunger Hill BH15 . . . . . .202 B1
Hungerfield Cl BH23 . .169 A1
Hungerford SO31 . . . . . .128 A1
Hungerford Hill SP6 . . . .94 B3
Hungerford Rd BH8 . . . .190 B2
Hunt Ave SO31 . . . . .127 B3
Hunt Rd
  Christchurch BH23 . . . . .207 C4
  Poole BH15 . . . . .202 C2
Hunter Cl
  Christchurch BH23 . . . . .208 A4
  Gosport PO13 . . . . .180 B4
  Holbury SO45 . . . . .150 A3
  Wimborne Minst BH21 .164 B3
Hunter Ct 13 SO16 . . . .78 A1
Hunter Rd
  Portsmouth PO4 . . . . . . .183 A2
  Thorney Island PO10 . .161 A2
Hunters Chase SO32 . . .84 B2
Hunters Cl BH31 . . . . . .115 B3
Hunters Cres SO51 . . . . .28 B1
Hunters Ct SO31 . . . . . .105 A2
Hunters Hill SO40 . . . . .100 B2
Hunters Lodge PO15 . .130 B1
Hunters Ride PO7 . . . . .134 C3
Hunters Way SO50 . . . . .57 A1
Huntfield Rd BH9 . . . . .190 A1
Huntingdon Cl
  Titchfield PO14 . . . . . . .129 B1
  Totton SO40 . . . . .76 C1
Huntingdon Dr BH21 . .163 C1
Huntingdon Gdns
  Christchurch BH23 . . . . .192 A1
  Horton Heath SO50 . . . . .81 B4
Huntley 30 PO6 . . . . . . .133 A1
Huntly Rd BH3 . . . . .204 B3
Huntly Way SO19 . . . . . .103 C4
Hunton Cl SO16 . . . . . . .78 B2
Hunts Pond Rd SO31,
  PO14 . . . . .129 B2
Huntsbottom La GU33 . .21 A2
Huntsman Cl PO8 . . . . .111 C3
Huntvale Rd BH9 . . . . . .190 A2
Hurdle Way SO21 . . . . . .31 B4
Hurdles Mead 17 SO41 211 B2
Hurdles The
  Christchurch BH23 . . . . .206 C4
  Titchfield PO14 . . . . . . .129 B1
Hurlingham Gdns SO16 79 A3
Hurn Cl BH24 . . . . .140 B3
Hurn Court La BH23 . .190 C3
Hurn Ct
  Bournemouth BH8 . . . . .191 A2
  15 Havant PO9 . . . . . . .136 A3
Hurn La BH24 . . . . .140 B3
Hurn Rd
  Christchurch BH23 . . . . .191 B4
  St Leonards BH24 . . . . .140 B2
Hurn Way BH23 . . . . . . .191 B1
Hurricane Dr SO16 . . . . .77 C3
Hursley Cl BH7 . . . . . . .206 B4
Hursley Ct SO53 . . . . . . .30 A1
Hursley Dr SO45 . . . . . .177 C4
Hursley Park Rd
  Hursley SO21 . . . . .30 A3
  Hursley SO21 . . . . .30 A4
Hursley Rd
  Chandler's Ford SO53 . . .55 B4
  Havant PO9 . . . . .135 B3
Hurst Cl
  Barton on Sea BH25 . . .209 B4
  Chandler's Ford SO53 . . .55 A4
  Christchurch BH23 . . . . .194 B1
  Stubbington PO14 . . . . .179 A3
  Totton SO40 . . . . .100 C4
Hurst Ct
  6 Christchurch BH23 . .209 A4
  5 Milford on Sea SO41 211 B2
Hurst Gn PO13 . . . . .155 A1
Hurst Green Cl
  Southampton SO19 . . . .104 A1
  Waterlooville PO8 . . . . .112 A1
Hurst Hill BH14 . . . . . . .214 B4
Hurst La
  Colden Common SO21 . .58 A4
  Foxfield GU34 . . . . .18 A2
Hurst Rd
  Milford on Sea SO41 . .211 C2
  Ringwood BH24 . . . . . . .117 A1
Hurstbourne Ave BH23 193 C1
Hurstbourne Cl PO9 . . .135 B3
Hurstbourne Pl SO19 . .126 C4
Hurstdene Rd BH8 . . . .190 B1
Hurstly La SO41 . . . . . .173 A2
Hurstville Dr PO7 . . . . .134 C4
Hurstwood Ave BH23 . .137 C1

Hussar Cl BH23 . . . . . . .206 C4
Hussar Ct PO7 . . . . .111 B1
Hussey Cl 2 SO23 . . . . . .2 A1
Hutfield Ct 8 PO12 . . . .181 A3
Hutwood Rd SO16 . . . . . .79 A4
Huxley Cl SO31 . . . . .129 A1
Huxley Cl SO45 . . . . . . .125 B1
Hyacinth Cl BH17 . . . . .186 C1
Hyde Abbey Rd SO23 . .11 A4
Hyde CE Prim Sch SP6 .94 B3
Hyde Church La SO23 . . .2 A1
Hyde Church Path 24
  SO23 . . . . .2 A1
Hyde Cl Southampton SO15 78 B1
  Sway SO41 . . . . .172 A1
  Totton SO40 . . . . .100 A4
  Winchester SO23 . . . . . . .1 C1
Hyde Gate SO23 . . . . . . .2 A1
Hyde House Gdns 22 SO23 2 A1
  Fordingbridge SP6 . . . . .94 B3
Hyde Lodge SO22 . . . . . .1 C1
Hyde Park Ho PO1 . . . .215 B2
Hyde Park Rd PO1 . . . .215 B3
Hyde Rd BH10 . . . . .189 B3
Hyde St Portsmouth PO5 215 B1
  Winchester SO23 . . . . . . .2 A1
Hyde The BH25 . . . . . . .194 C2
Hyden Cross GU32 . . . . .63 C1
Hyden Farm La PO8 . . . .87 B4
Hyden Wood GU32 . . . . .63 C1
Hylton Rd GU32 . . . . . . .40 C2
Hyman Way SO40 . . . . .100 C4
Hynes Ct 19 SO17 . . . .103 A4
Hynesbury Rd BH23 . .208 B3
Hyssop Cl PO15 . . . . . .129 B4
Hythe By Pass SO45 . .149 C4
Hythe Bypass SO45 . . .150 A4
Hythe Hospl SO45 . . . .126 A1
Hythe Prim Sch SO45 .126 A2
Hythe Rd Cosham PO6 157 C4
  Marchwood SO40 . . . . .124 C4
  Poole BH15 . . . . .203 A4

I

Ibbertson Cl BH8 . . . . .190 C1
Ibbertson Rd BH8 . . . .190 C1
Ibbertson Way BH8 . .190 C1
Ibbett Rd BH10 . . . . . .189 B2
Ibbotson Way SO40 . .100 B3
Ibsen Cl PO15 . . . . .129 B4
Ibsley Cl BH8 . . . . .205 B3
Ibsley Dro BH24 . . . . . .94 A1
Ibsley Gr PO9 . . . . .135 B2
Icarus Pl PO7 . . . . .134 C1
Iddesleigh Rd BH3 . . .205 A3
Ideal Park Homes SO50 .56 C3
Idsworth Cl PO8 . . . . . .112 C3
Idsworth Ho PO1 . . . .215 B4
Idsworth Rd
  Portsmouth PO3 . . . . . .183 A4
  Waterlooville PO8 . . . .112 A1
Iford Bridge Home Pk
  BH6 . . . . .206 B4
Iford Cl BH6 . . . . .206 C3
Iford Ct 18 PO9 . . . . . .136 A3
Iford Gdns BH7 . . . . . .206 B4
Iford La BH6 . . . . .206 C3
Ilex Cres SO31 . . . . . . .128 C2
Ilex Wlk PO11 . . . . .185 B1
Imber Dr BH23 . . . . . . .208 C4
Imber Rd SO23 . . . . .11 B4
Imber Way SO19 . . . . .104 B2
Imbre Ct BH13 . . . . . . .214 C4
Imperial Ave SO15 . . .102 A4
Imperial Ct 4 BH13 . .214 C4
Imperial Pk SO14 . . . .103 A4
Imperial Rd SO14 . . . .103 A4
Imperial Way SO15 . .102 B3
Implacable Rd PO13 . .179 C2
Ingarth 8 BH6 . . . . . . .206 C2
Ingle Glen SO45 . . . . .126 A1
Ingle Gn SO40 . . . . .76 A1
Ingledene Cl
  Gosport PO12 . . . . .181 A2
  Havant PO9 . . . . .135 B1
Inglegreen Cl BH25 . .194 C1
Inglesham Way BH15 .201 C2
Ingleside SO31 . . . . . . .127 B4
Ingleside Cl PO14 . . . .154 A4
Ingleton Rd SO16 . . . . .77 B1
Inglewood Ave BH8 . .190 C1
Inglewood Dr BH25 . .195 A1
Inglewood Gdns SO50 .57 B2
Inglis Rd PO5 . . . . .215 D1
Ingoldfield La
  PO17&SO32 . . . . .109 B4
Ingram Ct SO17 . . . . . .103 B4
Ingram Wlk 13 BH21 .163 B2
Ingworth Rd BH12 . . .204 A3
Inhams La PO7 . . . . . . .110 B3
Inhurst Ave PO7 . . . . .135 A4
Inhurst Rd PO2 . . . . . .157 C1
Inkerman Rd SO14 . . .103 B2
Inkpen Wlk PO9 . . . . .135 B4
Inlands Rd PO18 . . . . .161 C4
Inmans La GU32 . . . . . .41 A3
Insley Cres BH18 . . . .186 C3
International Pk SO18 .79 C3
International Way SO19 126 C4
Inveravon BH23 . . . . . .207 C2
Inverclyde Ho BH14 . .203 B2
Inverclyde Rd BH14 . .203 B2
Invergordon Ave PO6 158 A4
Inverkip Cl PO13 . . . . .179 C2
Inverleigh Rd BH6 . . .206 B3

Inverness Ave PO15 . .130 C2
Inverness Rd
  Gosport PO12 . . . . .181 A3
  Poole BH13 . . . . .214 C4
  Portsmouth PO1 . . . . . .182 C4
Inwood Rd GU33 . . . . . .21 A2
Ionic Cl SO53 . . . . .55 C4
IOW Ferry Terminal
  SO14 . . . . .102 C1
Iping Ave PO9 . . . . .135 C2
Ipley Way SO45 . . . . . .126 A1
Ipswich Rd BH4 . . . . . .204 A2
Ireland Way PO7 . . . . .134 C3
Iris Rd Bournemouth BH9 189 C1
  Southampton SO16 . . . .79 A2
Iron Mill Cl PO15 . . . .130 B2
Ironbridge Cres SO31 129 A3
Ironbridge La PO4 . . .183 B2
Ironmill La SO41 . . . .130 A3
Ironside Ct 12 SO14 . .102 C2
Irvine Cl PO16 . . . . . . .131 A2
Irvine Way BH23 . . . . .207 C4
Irving Rd
  Bournemouth BH6 . . . .206 B3
  Southampton SO16 . . . .77 C1
Irwell Cl SO53 . . . . .55 A3
Irwin Hts PO12 . . . . . .181 A4
Isaacs Cl BH12 . . . . . .204 A4
Isambard Brunel Jun Sch
  PO2 . . . . .182 C4
Isambard Brunel Rd
  PO1 . . . . .215 B3
Isis Cl SO16 . . . . .101 C4
Island Cl PO11 . . . . . . .160 A2
Island Point SO41 . . . .197 C2
Island View SO41 . . . .172 A2
Island View Ave BH23 208 A3
Island View Cl SO41 . .211 C2
Island View Rd BH25 209 B4
Island View Terr PO2 157 B1
Island View Wlk PO16 132 B1
Islay Gdns PO6 . . . . . .133 C1
Itchen Ave SO50 . . . . . .56 C1
Itchen Cl Petersfield GU31 40 C1
  West Wellow SO51 . . . .50 B2
Itchen Ct
  4 Waterlooville PO8 .111 C2
  40 Winchester SO23 . .11 A4
Itchen Valley Ctry Pk
  SO30 . . . . .80 B3
Itchen View SO18 . . . . .79 C2
Itchenor Rd PO11 . . . .185 C1
Itchenside Cl SO18 . . .79 C2
Itchin Cl SO40 . . . . . . .100 B3
Ithica Cl PO11 . . . . . . .185 A4
Ivamy Pl BH11 . . . . . . .188 C4
Ivanhoe Rd SO15 . . . . .78 B1
Ivor Cl SO45 . . . . .150 B2
Ivor Rd
  Corfe Mullen BH21 . . .186 B4
  Poole BH15 . . . . .202 A1
Ivy Cl St Leonards BH24 139 B2
  Totton SO40 . . . . .76 C1
  Winchester SO22 . . . . . .10 C3
Ivy Cotts SO21 . . . . . . .31 A1
Ivy Ct Southampton SO16 78 B2
  Waterlooville PO7 . . . .134 C4
Ivy Dene SO19 . . . . . . .104 B2
Ivy Ho 2 PO12 . . . . . . .181 B4
Ivy La Portsmouth PO1 182 A3
  Ringwood BH24 . . . . . .117 A2
  West End SO18 . . . . . . .80 B1
Ivy Orch PO8 . . . . .88 A3
Ivy Rd Oakley BH21 . .187 B4
  Southampton SO17 . . .103 B4
Ivydene Gdns PO8 . . .112 A2
Ivyhouse La GU32 . . . .18 C2
Iwerne Cl BH9 . . . . . . .190 A2

J

J Ave SO45 . . . . .151 A3
Jacaranda Cl PO15 . .129 C2
Jack Cl SO53 . . . . .54 C3
Jack Cockerill Way 14
  PO5 . . . . .182 B1
Jackdaw Cl PO8 . . . . .111 C2
Jackdaw Rise SO50 . . .55 B1
Jackie Wigg Gdns SO40 101 A4
Jacklin Ct BH18 . . . . .187 A1
Jackman's Hill SO21 . .33 A4
Jackmans Cl SO19 . . .103 B2
Jackson Cl PO6 . . . . . .158 B3
Jackson Gdns BH12 . .203 B3
Jackson Rd BH12 . . . .203 B3
Jacmar Ct 8 BH25 . . .195 A1
Jacob's Gutter La SO40 101 A1
Jacob's St PO1 . . . . . . .215 B4
Jacobean Cl BH23 . . .194 A1
Jacobs Cl Clanfield PO8 .88 B3
  Romsey SO51 . . . . .53 A4
Jacobs Rd BH15 . . . . .201 C1
Jacobs Wlk SO40 . . . .100 C3
Jacqueline Ave PO7 .134 B2
Jacqueline Rd BH12 .203 B4
Jade Ct Gosport PO13 180 B3
  6 Waterlooville PO7 .134 C4
Jago Rd PO1 . . . . .181 C3
Jamaica Pl PO12 . . . .181 B2
James Butcher Ct 12
  PO5 . . . . .182 B1
James Callaghan Dr
  Cosham PO6 . . . . .133 A1
  Portchester PO17 . . . .132 C1

James Cl Gosport PO13 155 B2
  South Hayling PO11 . .184 C1
James Copse Rd PO8 .111 C3
James Ct SO51 . . . . .53 C3
James Grieve Ave SO31 129 A1
James Howell Ct PO7 110 C3
James Rd Gosport PO13 155 B2
  Havant PO9 . . . . .135 C1
  Poole BH12 . . . . .204 A3
James St SO14 . . . . . . .103 A2
Jameson Rd
  Bournemouth BH9 . . . .189 C1
  Southampton SO19 . . .103 C2
Jamica Rd PO12 . . . . .181 B3
Janaway Gdns SO17 .103 B4
Janes Cl SO45 . . . . . . .177 C4
Janred Ct BH25 . . . . .209 C4
Janson Rd SO15 . . . . .102 B4
Japonica Way PO9 . .136 B2
Jarndyce Wlk PO2 . .182 B4
Jarvis Fields SO31 . .128 A4
Jasmine Ct
  Gosport PO13 . . . . .180 B3
  Lymington SO41 . . . . .197 C2
Jasmine Gr PO7 . . . . .135 A3
Jasmine Rd SO30 . . . .105 A4
Jasmine Way PO8 . . . .88 B3
Jasmine Wlk 5 PO14 154 C4
Jasmond Rd PO6 . . . .157 C3
Jason Pl PO7 . . . . .134 C1
Jason Way PO12 . . . .180 C4
Jaundrells Cl BH25 . .195 B2
Java Dr PO15 . . . . .129 B4
Javelin Rd PO10 . . . .161 A2
Jay Cl Horndean PO8 112 A4
  Stubbington PO14 . . .154 A3
Jay's Ct PO13 . . . . . . .209 A4
Jealous La SO41 . . . . .173 A1
Jefferson Ave BH1 . .205 B3
Jeffries Ct SO16 . . . . . .77 C3
Jellicoe Ave PO12 . . .180 C2
Jellicoe Cl BH14 . . . .202 C3
Jellicoe Dr BH23 . . . .207 C3
Jellicoe Ho 8 PO1 . .215 C4
Jenkins Cl SO30 . . . . .106 A4
Jenkins Gr PO3 . . . . .183 A4
Jenner Way SO51 . . . .53 B4
Jennings Rd Poole BH14 203 B1
  Totton SO40 . . . . .101 A4
Jensen Ct SO15 . . . . .102 C4
Jephcote Rd BH11 . .188 C2
Jermyns La SO51 . . . .28 C2
Jerome Ct SO19 . . . . .104 B3
Jerram Ct PO12 . . . . .180 C2
Jerrett's La SO16 . . . .77 B2
Jersey Cl Poole BH12 188 B1
  Southampton SO16 . . .77 C2
  Stubbington PO14 . . .179 B3
Jersey Rd Poole BH12 188 B1
  Portsmouth PO2 . . . . .182 C4
Jervis Court La SO32 .84 A4
Jervis Dr PO12 . . . . . .180 C2
Jervis Rd PO2 . . . . . . .157 B1
Jesmond Ave BH23 . .208 C4
Jesmond Gr SO31 . . .129 A1
Jessamine Rd SO16 . .78 A1
Jessica Ave BH31 . . . .114 B4
Jessica Cl 4 PO7 . . . .112 A1
Jessie Rd Gosport PO12 181 A4
  Havant PO9 . . . . .135 B2
  Portsmouth PO4 . . . . .182 C2
Jessie Terr 28 SO14 .103 A2
Jessop Cl
  Bournemouth BH10 . .189 C2
  Hythe SO45 . . . . .125 C3
Jessop Rd BH21 . . . . .164 A3
Jessop Wlk SO45 . . . .125 C3
Jessopp Ho 6 BH21 .163 B3
Jetty Rd PO13 . . . . . . .155 A3
Jewell Rd BH8 . . . . . .191 A1
Jewry St SO23 . . . . . . .11 A4
Jex Blake Cl SO16 . . .78 A2
Jimmy Brown Ave BH22 138 C3
Jinny La SO51 . . . . . . .27 C3
Joanna Cl SP5 . . . . . . .46 B4
Jockey La SO50 . . . . . .56 C3
Jodrell Cl PO8 . . . . . . .112 B4
Joe Bigwood Cl SO16 .77 B3
John Bunyan Cl PO15 129 B4
John Darling Mall 4
  SO50 . . . . .56 A2
John King Shipyard
  PO10 . . . . .161 A4
John St SO14 . . . . .103 A2
John's Rd SO19 . . . . . .103 B2
Johns Rd PO16 . . . . . .155 A4
Johnson Rd BH21 . . .165 A4
Johnson St 2 SO14 .103 A2
Johnson View PO15 .129 C3
Johnston Rd BH15 . .202 B4
Johnstone Rd BH23 .207 C3
Jolliffe Ave BH15 . . .202 B2
Jolliffe Ct 16 GU32 . .40 C2
Jolliffe Rd BH15 . . . .202 B2
Jonas Nichols Sq SO14 103 A2
Jonathan Cl SO41 . . .197 C3
Jonathan Rd PO15 . .130 C1
Jones La SO45 . . . . . .126 A3
Jopps Cnr BH23 . . . . .192 B2
Jordan Ho PO15 . . . .102 B3
Jordans La Boldre SO41 198 A3
  Sway SO41 . . . . .172 B1
Joseph Nye Ct 30 PO1 182 A3
Joseph St 8 PO1 . . . .181 B2
Joshua Cl BH15 . . . . .201 C1
Josian Wlk 12 SO14 .103 A3
Joslin Block PO12 . . .181 B3
Jowitt Dr BH25 . . . . .194 C1

Joyce Dickson Cl BH24 .141 A3
Joys La SO41 . . . . .198 C4
Joys Rd BH21 . . . . . . .138 C4
Jubilee Ave PO6 . . . .156 C4
Jubilee Bsns Ctr PO7 .134 C4
Jubilee Cl
  Corfe Mullen BH21 . . .186 C4
  Eastleigh SO50 . . . . . . .55 C1
  Fordingbridge SP6 . . . .69 B1
  Ringwood BH24 . . . . .141 B4
Jubilee Cres BH12 . . .203 B3
Jubilee Ct Fareham PO14 155 A4
  Sway SO41 . . . . .172 A1
Jubilee Gdns
  Bournemouth BH10 . .189 B1
  Southampton SO16 . .104 A4
Jubilee Ho PO10 . . . .136 C1
Jubilee Rd
  Corfe Mullen BH21 . . .186 C4
  Fordingbridge SP6 . . . .69 B1
  Gosport PO12 . . . . . . .181 A3
  Poole BH12 . . . . .203 B3
  Portchester PO16 . . . .156 B4
  Portsmouth PO4 . . . . .182 C2
  Romsey SO51 . . . . .52 C4
  Waterlooville PO7 . . . .111 C1
Jubilee Terr
  Portsmouth PO5 . . . . .215 A1
  Westbourne PO10 . . . .137 A2
Julia Cl BH23 . . . . . . .208 A4
Julian Cl SO16 . . . . . . .78 C3
Julian Ct 1 SO18 . . . .79 C1
Julian Rd SO19 . . . . .104 A2
Julian's Rd BH21 . . . .163 A2
Julie Ave PO15 . . . . .130 C1
Juliet Ct PO7 . . . . . . .135 A4
Julius Cl SO53 . . . . . .55 C3
Julyan Ave BH12 . . . .204 A4
Jumar Cl SO31 . . . . . .152 A2
Jumpers Ave BH23 . .206 C4
Jumpers Rd BH23 . . .206 C4
Junction Rd
  Bournemouth BH9 . . .204 C4
  Hamworthy BH16 . . . .201 B4
  Totton SO40 . . . . .101 A4
Juniper Cl
  Ferndown BH22 . . . . . .165 B4
  Lymington SO41 . . . . .197 A1
  North Baddesley SO52 .53 C3
  Three Legged Cross BH21 138 C4
  Winchester SO22 . . . . . .10 B3
Juniper Ct 17 SO18 . .103 C4
Juniper Flats BH23 . .206 C4
Juniper Rd Horndean PO8 88 B3
  Southampton SO18 . .103 C4
Juniper Sq PO9 . . . . .159 C4
Jupiter Cl SO16 . . . . . .77 C2
Jupiter Ct PO1 . . . . . .182 A2
Jupiter Way BH21 . . .186 C4
Jura Cl PO6 . . . . .133 C1
Jurd Way SO31 . . . . .104 C1
Jurds Lake Way SO19 103 C1
Justin PO14 . . . . .154 C4
Justin Gdns BH10 . . .189 C2
Justine Ct 4 SO18 . .104 A4
Justinian Cl SO53 . . .55 C4
Jute Cl PO16 . . . . .132 A1
Jutland Cl PO15 . . . .129 A3
Juventu Cl PO9 . . . . .136 A2

K

Kamptee Copse BH25 .195 A3
Kanes Hill SO19 . . . . .104 C3
Kanes Hill Prim Sch
  SO19 . . . . .104 C3
Kangaw Pl BH15 . . . .201 B1
Karen Ave PO6 . . . . . .158 B3
Kassassin St PO4 . . .183 A1
Kassel Cl PO7 . . . . . . .135 C4
Katherine Chance Cl
  BH23 . . . . .192 B2
Kathleen Rd SO19 . . .104 A2
Katrina Gdns PO11 . .185 A3
Katrine Cres SO53 . . .55 A4
Katterns Cl BH23 . . .191 C1
Kay Cl BH23 . . . . .207 C4
Kayak Cl SO31 . . . . . .128 C1
Kayleigh Cl SO40 . . .100 B3
Kealy Rd PO12 . . . . . .181 A3
Kearsney Ave PO2 . .157 C2
Keast Wlk PO13 . . . .155 B2
Keats Ave
  Milford on Sea SO41 211 B3
  Portchester PO16 . . .132 C1
Keats Cl Swanwick PO15 106 C4
  Waterlooville PO8 . . .111 C2
  Winchester SO22 . . . . .10 A1
Keats Ho Havant PO9 135 C2
  17 New Milton BH25 195 A1
Keats Rd SO19 . . . . . .104 B3
Keble Cl
  Chandler's Ford SO53 .55 B2
  Hursley SO21 . . . . .30 A4
Keble Meml CE Prim Sch
  SO21 . . . . .30 A3
Keble Rd SO53 . . . . . .55 B2
Keble St SO23 . . . . . . .10 B3
Keeble Cl BH10 . . . . .189 B3
Keeble Cres BH10 . . .189 B3
Keeble Rd BH10 . . . .189 B3
Keel Cl Gosport PO13 180 B3
  Portsmouth PO3 . . . . .158 B2
Keelan Ct PO5 . . . . . .182 B1

Keep The PO16 ....156 C4
Keepers Cl SO53 ....55 A3
Keepers La
  Ferndown BH21 ....164 C2
  Mottisfont SO51 ....5 B1
Kefford Cl PO8 ....112 A4
Keighley Ave BH18 ....186 C1
Keith Cl PO12 ....181 A4
Keith Rd BH3 ....204 B4
Kelburn Cl SO53 ....55 A4
Kellaway Rd BH17 .....202 C4
Kellett Rd SO15 ....102 C4
Kelly Cl BH17 ....202 C4
Kelly Ct
  10 Fareham PO16 .....131 A1
  Southampton SO16 ......78 B3
  2 Southampton, Bitterne
  SO18 ....103 C4
Kelly Ho SO18 ....79 C2
Kelly Rd PO7 ....134 C3
Kelmscott Gdns SO53 ...30 A1
Kelsall Gdns BH25 .....195 A2
Kelsey Ave PO10 ......137 C1
Kelsey Cl Liss GU33 ....21 A1
  Locks Heath PO14 .....129 A1
Kelsey Head PO6 ......157 A4
Kelston Cl
  19 Southampton SO15 .102 A4
  Southampton SO15 ....102 A4
Kelvin Cl SO45 ....126 A2
Kelvin Gr Netley SO31 .127 B3
  Portchester PO16 ......156 B4
Kelvin Rd SO50 ....55 C1
Kemp Rd BH9 ....204 C4
Kemp Welch Ct BH12 ..204 A4
Kemps Quay Ind Pk
  SO18 ....103 B4
Kempton Ct PO15 .....129 B4
Kempton Pk **6** PO7 ...112 A1
Kemshott Ct PO9 ......135 B3
Ken Berry Ct PO9 .....136 A3
Ken Rd BH6 ....206 C2
Kench The PO11 ....183 C2
Kendal Ave
  Portsmouth PO3 ....158 A1
  Southampton SO16 ....101 B4
Kendal Cl
  Chandler's Ford SO53 ...55 C4
  Waterlooville PO8 .....112 A2
Kendal Ct SO16 ....77 B1
Kenilworth Cl
  Lee-on-the-Solent PO13 .179 C2
  New Milton BH25 .....195 A4
Kenilworth Ct
  2 Christchurch BH23 ..207 A4
  11 Poole BH15 ....214 C4
  8 Winchester SO23 ....2 A1
Kenilworth Dr SO50 ....56 A3
Kenilworth Gdns SO30 ..80 C1
Kenilworth Ho **15** SO14 .103 B3
Kenilworth Rd
  Portsmouth PO5 ....182 B1
  Southampton SO15 ....102 C3
Kenmore Cl SO40 ......100 C4
Kennard Ct BH25 ......194 C2
Kennard Rd BH25 .....194 C2
Kennart Rd BH17 ......202 A4
Kennedy Ave PO15 ....130 C2
Kennedy Cl PO7 ....134 C2
Kennedy Cres PO12 ...180 C1
Kennedy Rd SO16 ....77 C2
Kennel La SO22 ....1 C2
Kennet Cl Gosport PO12 .181 A1
  Romsey SO51 ....53 B4
  West End SO18 ....80 C2
Kennet Rd
  Petersfield GU31 ....40 C1
  Romsey SO51 ....53 B4
Kenneth Ct **15** BH23 ...209 A4
Kennington La SO40 ....99 A4
Kennington Rd BH17 ..202 A4
Kensington Cl SO50 ....56 B3
Kensington Ct **3** SO17 ..79 B1
Kensington Dr BH2 ....204 B2
Kensington Fields 125 B1
Kensington Gdns PO14 .129 B1
Kensington Pk SO41 ...211 B2
Kensington Rd
  Gosport PO12 ....181 B2
  Portsmouth PO2 ......157 C1
Kenson Gdns SO19 ....104 A2
Kent Gdns SO40 ....100 B3
Kent Gr PO16 ....156 B3
Kent Ho
  20 Bournemouth BH4 ...204 B2
  27 Southampton SO14 .103 B3
Kent La BH24 ....93 B1
Kent Rd
  Chandler's Ford SO53 ...55 B2
  Gosport PO13 ....155 A2
  Poole BH12 ....203 C3
  Portsmouth PO5 ......215 B1
  Southampton SO17 .....79 B1
Kent St Portsmouth PO1 .182 A3
  Southampton SO14 ....103 B3
Kentidge Rd PO7 ......134 C2
Kentish Rd SO15 ......102 B4
Kenwood Rd PO16 ....156 B4
Kenwyn Cl SO18 ....80 A1
Kenya Rd PO16 ....156 A4
Kenyon Cl BH15 ......202 C4
Kenyon Rd Poole BH15 .202 C4
  Portsmouth PO2 ......157 C1
Keppel Cl BH24 ....141 A4
Kerley Rd BH2 ....204 C1

Kern Cl SO16 ....77 C2
Kerrfield SO22 ....10 B4
Kerrfield Mews SO22 ...10 B4
Kerrigan Ct SO17 .....103 A4
Kerry Cl
  Chandler's Ford SO53 ...55 B3
  Lymington SO41 ......197 B2
Kerry Gdns SP6 ....69 A1
Kersley Gdns SO19 ....104 A2
Kesteven Way SO18 ...104 A4
Kestrel Cl
  Bishop's Waltham SO32 ..83 A4
  Botley SO32 ....81 C1
  Clanfield PO8 ....88 B2
  Ferndown BH22 ......165 A4
  Marchwood SO40 .....101 C1
  Southampton SO16 .....78 A3
  Stubbington PO14 ....154 A2
  Upton BH16 ....201 A4
  Winchester SO22 ......10 B2
Kestrel Ct BH24 ......141 A4
Kestrel Dr BH23 ......208 A3
Kestrel Pl PO6 ....158 C4
Kestrel Rd Eastleigh SO50 .55 C1
  Portsmouth PO3 ......158 A2
Kestrel Way SP6 ....93 A3
Keswick Ave SO19 ....183 A4
Keswick Cl BH25 .....195 A3
Keswick Rd
  Bournemouth BH5 .....206 A2
  New Milton BH25 ....195 A3
  Southampton SO19 ...103 B1
Keswick Way BH31 ...114 C3
Keverstone Ct BH1 ...205 B2
Kevlyn Cres SO31 ....104 C3
Kew La SO31 ....128 A4
Kewlake La SO40 ......74 B1
Key La **21** BH15 ......202 A1
Keydell Ave PO8 ......112 A3
Keydell Cl PO8 ....112 A3
Keyes Cl
  Christchurch BH23 ...207 C3
  Gosport PO13 ....155 B2
  Poole BH12 ....188 C1
Keyes Ct **4** PO5 ....215 C1
Keyes Rd PO13 ....155 B2
Keyhaven Cl PO13 ....155 A1
Keyhaven Dr PO9 ....135 B3
Keyhaven Rd SO41 ...211 C2
Keynsham Rd SO19 ...104 A3
Keysworth Ave BH25 .209 C4
Keysworth Rd BH16 ..201 B2
Khandala Gdns PO7 ..134 C2
Khartoum Rd SO17 ....79 A1
Khyber Rd BH12 .....203 B1
Kidmore La PO7 ......110 C3
Kielder Cl SO53 ....55 A4
Kielder Gr **2** PO13 ..155 B1
Kilbride **11** BH12 ...204 A1
Kilbride Path **5** PO2 .182 B4
Kilford Ct SO30 ......106 A3
Kilham La SO22 ....10 B3
Killarney Ct SO19 ....104 C2
Killock **6** BH13 .....214 C4
Kilmarnock Rd BH9 ..189 C1
Kilmeston Rd PO9 ...135 C3
Kilmeston Rd
  Cheriton SO24 ....14 B2
  Kilmeston SO24 ....14 B1
Kilmington Way BH23 .208 C2
Kilmiston Dr PO16 ...132 B1
Kilmiston Rd PO1 ....182 C2
Kiln Acre PO16 ......131 A2
Kiln Cl Corfe Mullen BH21 .186 B2
  Hythe SO45 ....125 C2
Kiln Field GU33 ....20 C3
Kiln Gn SO21 ....57 A4
Kiln Hill SO32 ....109 A4
Kiln La Braishfield SO51 ..28 B3
  Buriton GU31 ....65 B3
  Otterbourne SO21 .....31 B1
  Redlynch SP5 ....47 C4
  Southwick PO17 .....109 B2
Kiln Rd Fareham PO16 .131 A2
  Portsmouth PO3 ......158 A1
Kiln Way BH31 ....115 B2
Kilnside PO7 ....110 C2
Kilnyard Cl SO40 ......76 B1
Kilpatrick Cl **6** PO2 ..182 B4
Kilwich Way PO16 ....156 A3
Kimber Rd BH11 .....188 C2
Kimberley Cl
  Christchurch BH23 ...206 C4
  Fair Oak SO50 ....57 B1
Kimberley Ct SO19 ...103 C1
Kimberley Rd
  Bournemouth BH6 ....206 B3
  Poole BH14 ....203 A2
  Portsmouth PO4 .....183 A1
Kimbers GU32 ....40 C2
Kimbolton Rd SO13 ..183 A3
Kimbridge Cnr SO51 ..27 A3
Kimbridge Cres PO9 .136 A3
Kimbridge La SO51 ...27 A4
Kimmeridge Ave BH12 .203 B4
Kimpton Cl PO13 ....179 C1
Kimpton Ct **9** PO9 ..136 A3
Kineton Rd SO15 .....78 C1
King Albert Ct PO1 ..215 C4
King Albert St PO1 ..215 C4
King Alfred Pl SO23 ...2 A1
King Alfred Terr **7** SO23 ..2 A1
King Alfred's Coll SO22 .10 C4
King Arthur's Ct PO6 .158 B4
King Charles St **9** PO1 .182 A2
King Cl BH24 ....139 C2
King Cote Villas **1** PO5 .182 C1

King Cup Ave SO31 ...128 C2
King Edward Ave
  Bournemouth BH9 ....190 A1
  Southampton SO16 ...102 A4
King Edward Ct BH9 .189 C1
King Edward Pk (Cvn Pk)
  SO53 ....55 A4
King Edward VI Sch
  SO15 ....102 C4
King Edward's Cres
  PO2 ....157 B1
King Fisher Way BH23 .208 A3
King George Ave
  Bournemouth BH9 ....189 C1
  Petersfield GU32 ......40 C2
King George Mews **7**
  GU32 ....40 C2
King George Mobile Home Pk
  BH25 ....194 C1
King George Rd PO16 .156 B4
King George's Ave
  SO15 ....101 C4
King Harold Ct SO23 ..10 C4
King Henry I St PO1 .215 A4
King John Ave
  Bournemouth BH11 ...188 B3
  Portchester PO16 ....156 A4
King John Cl BH11 ...188 B3
King La GU32 ....39 C4
King Richard 1 Rd PO1 .182 A2
King Richard Cl PO6 .157 A4
King Richard Dr BH11 .188 B3
King Richard I Rd PO1 .215 A3
King Richard Sch PO6 .156 C4
King St Emsworth PO10 .161 A4
  Gosport PO12 ....181 B3
  Portsmouth PO5 .....215 B2
  Southampton SO14 ...103 A2
  Westbourne PO10 ....137 A2
  Wimborne Minst BH21 .163 A3
King William St PO1 .182 A3
King's Arms La BH24 .140 C4
King's Arms Row BH24 .140 C4
King's Ave **5** BH23 .206 C3
King's Cl SO53 ....55 B4
King's Copse Rd SO45 .177 B4
King's Cres BH14 ....203 C1
King's Croft La PO9 .135 B1
King's Ho **17** SO14 .103 A2
King La GU32 ....18 B2
Kingsfield
  Lymington SO41 .....198 A1
  Ringwood BH24 .....141 A4
Kingsfold Ave SO18 ...79 C2
Kingsford Cl SP5 .....47 B3
Kingsgate Rd SO23 ...10 C3
Kingsgate St SO23 ...11 A3
Kingsland Cl PO6 ....133 B1
Kingsland Ct Poole BH13 .214 C4
  4 Southampton SO14 ..103 A2
Kingsland Ho **20** SO14 .103 A3
Kingsland Mkt SO14 .103 A2
Kingsland Sq **3** SO14 .103 A2
Kingsleigh Fst Sch
  BH10 ....189 B2
Kingsleigh Jun Sch
  BH10 ....189 B2
Kingsleigh Sec Sch
  BH10 ....189 B2
Kingsley Ave BH6 ...207 A2
Kingsley Cl BH6 .....207 A2
Kingsley Gdns SO40 .100 A4
Kingsley Gn PO9 .....135 C3
Kingsley Pl SO22 ....10 C3
Kingsley Rd
  Gosport PO12 ....180 C4
  Portsmouth PO4 ....183 B2
  Southampton SO15 ..102 A4
Kingsmead PO17 ....108 B4
Kingsmead Ave PO14 .179 B3
Kingsmead Ct
  16 Southampton SO15 ..78 A1
  9 Wimborne Minst BH21 .163 A3
Kingsmill Cl PO12 ...180 C2
Kingsmill Rd BH17 ..202 C4
Kingston SO31 ....127 B4
Kingston Cres PO2 ..182 B4
Kingston Cross PO2 .182 B4
Kingston Ct SO16 .....77 C1
Kingston Gdns PO15 .130 B2
Kingston Lacy Ho (NT)★
  BH21 ....162 A4
Kingston Pk SO41 ....197 B1
Kingston Rd
  Gosport PO12 ....180 C3
  Poole BH15 ....202 B2
  Portsmouth PO1, PO2 .182 C4
  Southampton SO15 ..102 B3
Kingsway
  Chandler's Ford SO53 ..55 C4
  Ferndown BH22 .....165 A4
  North Hayling PO11 ..160 A2
  Southampton SO14 ..103 A3
Kingsway Cl SO31 ...191 C1
Kingsway Ct SO53 ....55 C4
Kingsway Gdns SO53 ..55 C4
Kingsway The PO16 .156 B4
Kingswell Cl BH10 ..189 B1
Kingswell Gdns BH10 .189 A1
Kingswell Gr BH10 ..189 A1
Kingswell Path PO1 .215 B4
Kingswell Rd BH10 .189 B1
Kingswell St PO1 ....215 B4
Kingswood
  Bournemouth BH4 ...204 B1
  Marchwood SO40 ....102 A1
Kingsworthy Rd PO9 .135 C2
Kinloss Ct SO16 ......78 A3
Kinnell Cl PO10 .....160 C4

Kings Field SO31 ....105 A1
Kings Field Gdns SO31 .105 A1
Kings Head Yd **32** SO23 ..11 A4
Kings Huts SO41 ....197 A2
Kings La Chilcomb SO21 .11 C3
  Sway SO41 ....196 C4
Kings Mede PO8 .....112 A3
Kings Mews PO5 .....182 B3
Kings Park Com Hospl
  BH7 ....205 C3
Kings Rd
  Chandler's Ford SO53 ..55 B3
  Gosport PO12 ....181 A3
  Lymington SO41 ....197 B2
  New Milton BH25 ...195 B2
  Petersfield GU32 .....40 B2
  South Hayling PO11 .185 A3
Kings Ride SO45 ....177 C4
Kings Row **7** SO41 ..10 C4
Kings Royal Hussars Mus
  The★ SO23 ....10 C4
Kings Sch The SO50 ..57 A1
Kings Somborne Rd SO51 .7 B1
Kings Way PO9 ....113 A1
Kings Worthy Prim Sch
  SO23 ....2 B3
Kings' Sch SO22 ......10 A4
Kingsbere Ave BH10 .189 A1
Kingsbere Gdns BH23 .209 A4
Kingsbere Rd BH15 ..202 C3
Kingsbridge Rd BH14 .203 B2
Kingsbury Ct PO8 ....88 A3
Kingsbury Rd SO14 .103 A4
Kingsbury's La BH24 .140 C4
Kingsclere Ave
  Havant PO9 ....135 B3
  Southampton SO19 ..126 C4
Kingsclere Cl SO19 ..103 C1
Kingsclere Ho **7** PO6 .132 C1
Kingscote Rd
  Cosham PO6 ....132 C1
  Waterlooville PO8 ...111 B2
Kingscroft Ct PO9 ...135 B1
Kingsdale **13** SO22 ..10 C4
Kingsdown Pl 215 D3
Kingsdown Rd PO7 ..111 B1
Kingsdown Way SO18 ..80 A1
Kingsey Ave PO10 ...160 C4
Kingsfernsden La GU32 .41 A3
King Cl BH24 ....139 C2
King's Park Athletic Ctr★
  BH7 ....205 C3
King's Park Dr BH7 .205 C3
King's Park Rd
  Bournemouth BH7 ...205 C3
  Southampton SO15 ..103 A3
King's Park Sch BH1 .205 C3
King's Rd
  Bournemouth BH3 ...205 A4
  Emsworth PO10 .....160 C4
  Fareham PO16 ......131 A1
  Lee-on-the-Solent PO13 .179 C2
  Portsmouth PO5 ....215 B1
  Winchester SO23 .....10 B3
King's Saltern Rd SO41 .198 A1
King's Sch Prim The
  SO30 ....80 C2
King's Terr
  1 Emsworth PO10 .160 C4
  Portsmouth PO5 ....215 A1
Kingcup Cl BH18 ....186 C1
Kingdom Cl PO15 ...129 B3
Kingfisher Cl
  Bournemouth BH6 ..206 C3
  Hamble-le-Rice SO31 .128 A2
  Rowland's Castle PO9 .113 A1
  South Hayling PO11 .185 B1
  Waterlooville PO8 ...111 C2
  West Moors BH22 ...138 C1
Kingfisher Copse SO31 .129 A2
Kingfisher Ct
  1 Havant PO9 ......136 A1
  Portsmouth PO3 ....158 A2
  1 Southampton SO17 .79 A1
Kingfisher Dr PO10 .137 A2
Kingfisher Park Homes **3**
  BH10 ....189 C2
Kingfisher Pk BH11 .138 C3
Kingfisher Rd SO50 ..55 C1
Kingfisher Way
  Marchwood SO40 ...101 C1
  Ringwood BH24 ....117 A1
  Romsey SO51 ....52 C4
Kingfishers
  9 Christchurch BH23 ..207 A3
  Portchester PO16 ...155 C4
Kingfishers The BH15 .115 A3
Kinghton Heath Ind Est
  BH11 ....188 C2
Kingland Cres BH15 .202 B1
Kingland Rd BH15 ..202 B1
Kings Ave
  Hamble-le-Rice SO31 .127 C2
  Poole BH14 ....203 B1
  Winchester SO22 .....10 C3
Kings Bench Alley PO1 .182 A2
Kings Cl Lymington SO41 .197 B2
  Lyndhurst SO43 .....121 C3
  Rowland's Castle PO9 .113 A1
  Twyford SO21 ....32 A4
  West Moors BH22 ...138 C1
Kings Copse Ave SO30 .105 B3
Kings Copse Prim Sch
  SO30 ....105 B3
Kings Copse Rd SO30 .105 B3
Kings Court Sch PO8 ..88 A1
Kings Cres SO41 ....197 B2
Kings Ct SP6 ....69 C1

Kinross Cres PO6 ...158 A4
Kinross Rd
  Bournemouth BH3 ...204 C3
  Totton SO40 ....100 C3
Kinsbourne Ave BH10 .189 B1
Kinsbourne Cl SO19 .104 C3
Kinsbourne Rise SO19 .104 C3
Kinsbourne Way SO19 .104 C3
Kinsford Ct SO42 ...145 C1
Kinson Ave BH15 ...203 A4
Kinson Gr BH10 ....189 B1
Kinson Park Rd BH10 .189 B1
Kinson Pottery Ind Est
  BH14 ....203 A3
Kinson Prim Sch BH11 .189 A3
Kinson Rd BH10 ....189 B2
Kinterbury Ct **10** SO17 .103 A4
Kintyre Rd PO6 .....133 C1
Kinver Cl SO51 ......28 A1
Kiosks The **20** BH15 .202 B1
Kipling Bldgs **18** PO2 .157 C2
Kipling Cl PO15 ....106 B1
Kipling Ct SO19 ....103 C1
Kipling Rd Eastleigh SO50 .55 C2
  Poole BH14 ....203 A3
  Portsmouth PO2 ....157 C2
Kirby Cl BH15 ......202 C3
Kirby Ct **4** PO2 ...157 C2
Kirby Rd PO2 ......157 C1
Kirby Way BH6 ....206 B2
Kirk Gdns SO40 ...100 C4
Kirkham Ave BH23 .192 B4
Kirkstall Rd PO4 ...182 C1
Kirkway BH18 .....187 A2
Kirtley Cl PO6 .....158 B3
Kirton Rd PO6 .....158 B4
Kitchener Cres BH17 .187 A1
Kitchener Rd SO17 ..79 B1
Kitchers Cl SO41 ...172 A1
Kite Cl PO8 ....111 C2
Kites Croft Cl PO14 .129 B1
Kitnocks Hill SO32 .106 C4
Kitscroft Rd BH10 ..189 B3
Kitt's La SO24 ......16 B1
Kittiwake Cl
  Bournemouth BH6 ..206 C3
  Gosport PO13 .....155 C3
Kitwalls La SO41 ...211 B3
Kitwood Gn **45** PO9 .136 C3
Kiwi Cl BH15 ......202 C2
Kleves Ct SO19 ....104 A3
Knapp Cl BH23 ....207 C4
Knapp La SO51 ....29 B2
Knapps Hard GU32 ..37 A3
Knatchbull Cl SO51 ..52 C4
Knellers La SO40 ...100 B2
Knight Cl SO23 ......2 A1
Knightcrest Pk SO41 .196 C1
Knighton Cnr PO8 ..112 A4
Knighton Heath Cl
  BH11 ....188 C2
Knighton Heath Rd
  BH11 ....188 C2
Knighton La BH21 ..188 B4
Knighton Pk BH25 ..209 C4
Knighton Rd SO19 ..103 C2
Knights Bank Rd PO14 .153 C1
Knights Cl SO31 ...128 C1
Knights Rd BH11 ..188 B3
Knightsbridge Ct BH2 .204 C1
Knightstone Ct **10** PO2 .157 C2
Knightstone Gr BH23 .138 B1
Knightstone Grange **2**
  SO45 ....126 A1
Knightwood Ave
  Havant PO9 ....136 A3
  Lyndhurst SO43 ....121 C3
Knightwood Cl
  Ashurst SO40 ......100 A1
  Christchurch BH23 .208 B4
  Lyndhurst SO43 ....121 C3
Knightwood Oak★
  SO43 ....120 C1
Knightwood Prim Sch
  SO53 ....54 C4
Knightwood Rd
  Chandler's Ford SO52 .55 A3
  Hythe SO45 ....126 A3
  North Baddesley SO52 .55 A3
Knobcrook Rd **3** BH21 .163 A3
Knole Ct **5** BH1 ...205 B2
Knole Gdns BH1 ...205 B2
Knole Rd BH1 .....205 B2
Knoll Gdns★
  Ferndown BH21 ....164 C2
  St Leonards BH24 ..139 C2
Knoll La BH21 .....186 A4
Knoll Manor BH2 ..204 C3
Knotgrass Rd SO41 .128 C1
Knowland Dr SO41 .211 B3
Knowle Hill SO50 ..56 A4
Knowle Hospl PO17 .130 C4
Knowle La SO50 ....57 C1
Knowle Rd SO42 ..145 C1
Knowles Cl
  Christchurch BH23 .207 C4
  Southampton SO16 ..77 B3
Knowles Mdw GU33 .21 A1
Knowlton Gdns BH9 .190 A2
Knowlton Rd BH17 ..187 C1
Knowsley Cres PO6 .158 A4
Knowsley Rd PO6 ..157 C4
Knox Rd Havant PO9 .135 B1
  Portsmouth PO2 ...157 B1
Knyght Cl SO51 ....53 A3

Knyveton Ho BH1 ....205 A2
Knyveton Rd BH1 ....205 B2
Kootenay Ave SO18 .....104 C4
Kooyong Cl SO51 ....51 A1
Kynegils Rd SO22 ....1 C1
Kynon Cl PO12 ....181 B4
Kyrchil La BH21 ....163 C3
Kyrchil Way BH21 ....163 C4
Kytes La SO32 ....82 B3

L

Labrador Dr BH15 ....202 B1
Laburnham Dr SO23 ......2 A4
Laburnum Ave PO6 ....158 B4
Laburnum Cl
  Ferndown BH22 ....165 A3
  North Baddesley SO52 ....54 A3
  Verwood BH31 ....115 B3
Laburnum Cres BH15 ...150 A4
Laburnum Ct SO19 ......103 B2
Laburnum Dr SO41 .....211 C4
Laburnum Gr
  Eastleigh SO50 ....56 A2
  Portsmouth PO2 ....157 C1
  South Hayling PO11 ....185 A4
Laburnum Ho
  8 Bournemouth BH10 ...189 C2
  Hedge End SO30 ....105 B3
Laburnum Rd
  Fareham PO16 ....155 A4
  Hedge End SO30 ....105 B3
  Southampton SO16 ......79 B2
  Waterlooville PO7 .....134 B3
Lacey Cres BH15 ....203 A3
Lackford Ave SO40 .....100 C3
Lacon Cl SO18 ....103 C4
Lacy Cl BH21 ....163 B3
Lacy Dr BH21 ....163 B3
Ladram Rd PO12 ....180 C2
Lady Betty's Dr PO15 ...129 C3
Ladybridge Rd PO7 .....134 B2
Ladycross Rd SO45 .....126 A1
Ladysmith Rd BH23 ....207 C4
Ladysmith Terr SO32 ....83 B4
Ladywood SO50 ....55 C3
Ladywood Ho PO1 ......215 B2
Lagado Cl BH14 ....214 B4
Lagland Ct 12 BH15 ....202 B1
Lagland St BH15 ....202 B1
Lagoon Cl BH14 ....214 A4
Lagoon Rd BH14 ....214 A4
Laidlaw Cl BH12 ....204 A4
Lake Ave BH15 ....201 B1
Lake Cres BH15 ....201 C2
Lake Dr BH15 ....201 B1
Lake Farm Cl SO30 ....105 B4
Lake Grove Rd BH25 ...195 A2
Lake Ho SO15 ....102 B3
Lake Rd
  Bournemouth BH11 ....189 A3
  Chandler's Ford SO53 ...55 C4
  Curdridge SO32 ....106 C4
  Hamworthy BH15 ......201 C1
  Portsmouth PO1 ....215 C4
  Southampton SO19 .....103 B1
  Verwood BH31 ....115 A3
Lake View Manor BH25 .195 A2
Lakeland Gdns SO40 ...101 C1
Lakelands Dr SO15 .....102 B3
Lakes The SO42 ....84 A2
Lakeside Fareham PO17 .130 C3
  Lee-on-the-Solent PO13 ..179 C1
  Ower SO51 ....75 B3
  Ringwood BH24 ....141 B3
Lakeside Ave
  Portsmouth PO3 ....183 A4
  Rownhams SO16 ....77 C3
Lakeside Ctry Pk ★ SO50 .79 C4
Lakeside Gdns PO9 ....136 A1
Lakeside Pines BH25 ...195 A2
Lakeside Rd BH13 .....204 A1
Lakesmere Rd PO8 ....112 B3
Lakeview Dr BH24 .....141 B3
Lakewood Cl SO53 ......55 B4
Lakewood Rd
  Ashurst SO40 ....100 B2
  Chandler's Ford SO53 ...30 C1
  Christchurch BH23 .....193 C1
Lamberhurst Cl SO19 ..127 A4
Lambert Cl PO7 ....134 C3
Lambourn Cl PO14 .....154 B4
Lambourn Sq SO53 .....55 A3
Lambourne Cl SO45 ...125 C1
Lambourne Dr SO31 ...129 A2
Lambourne Ho SO30 ...105 A3
Lambourne Rd SO18 ....80 A1
Lambs Cl BH17 ....187 B1
Lambs Lease GU33 ......21 A2
Lambsgreen La BH21 ..162 C1
Lammas Rd SO45 ......126 A1
Lampeter Ave PO6 ....158 A4
Lampton Gdns BH9 ....189 C1
Lamward Mans 30 SO14 103 A4
Lancaster Cl
  Bursledon SO31 ....105 A1
  Christchurch BH23 .....208 B4
  Corfe Mullen BH18 ....186 C3
  Lee-on-the-Solent PO13 .180 A2
  Portchester PO16 ......132 A1
Lancaster Ct SO30 ......80 B1
Lancaster Dr
  Corfe Mullen BH18 ....186 C3
  Verwood BH31 ....114 C3
Lancaster Rd
  Ferndown BH21 ....165 A4
  Southampton SO16 ......77 C2

Lancaster Way PO7 ....134 C3
Lance's Hill SO18 ......103 C4
Lancer Cl BH23 ....206 C4
Lancer Cl BH15 ....202 B1
Landford CE Prim Sch
  SP5 ....49 B2
Landford Common Farm
  SP5 ....49 C1
Landford Gdns BH8 ....190 B1
Landford Way BH8 ....190 B1
Landguard Rd
  Portsmouth PO4 ....183 A2
  Southampton SO15 .....102 B3
Landon Rd PO13 ....180 B4
Landport St
  Portsmouth PO1 ....215 C4
  Portsmouth, Southsea
    PO5 ....215 A2
Landport Terr PO1 ....215 A2
Landport View PO1 ...215 B4
Lands End Rd SO31 ....128 B4
Landsdowne St PO5 ....215 A2
Landseer Rd
  13 Bournemouth BH4 ..204 B2
  Southampton SO19 ....104 B2
Lane End SO24 ....17 B4
Lane End Cotts SP5 .....49 B2
Lane End Dr PO10 .....160 C4
Lane The
  4 Bournemouth BH8 ...205 B3
  Fawley SO45 ....151 A2
  Gosport PO12 ....181 A1
  Portsmouth PO4 ....182 C1
Lanehays Rd SO45 .....125 C2
Lanes End PO14 ....179 B3
Lanes The BH25 ....195 A3
Lanesbridge Cl SO40 ...99 C3
Langbar Cl SO19 ......103 C3
Langbrook Cl PO9 .....159 C4
Langdale Ave PO6 ....158 A4
Langdale Cl SO16 .....101 C4
Langdon Ct BH14 .....203 B2
Langdon Rd BH14 ....203 B2
Langdown Firs SO45 ..126 A2
Langdown Inf Sch SO45 126 A1
Langdown Jun Sch
  SO45 ....126 A2
Langdown Lawn SO45 .126 A2
Langdown Lawn Cl
  SO45 ....126 A1
Langdown Rd SO45 ...126 A1
Langford La SP5 ....47 C4
Langford Rd PO1 ......182 C4
Langham Cl SO52 ......53 C2
Langham Ct BH23 ....191 C1
Langhorn Rd SO16 .....79 B2
Langley Chase BH24 ..140 A3
Langley Gdn SP6 ....70 A2
Langley Lodge Gdns
  SO45 ....177 C4
Langley Rd
  Christchurch BH23 ....193 C1
  Poole BH14 ....203 C2
  Portsmouth PO2 ....182 C4
  Southampton SO15 .....102 A3
Langrish Cl PO9 ....136 A3
Langrish Hill GU32 .....39 B2
Langrish Prim Sch GU32 .40 A2
Langrish Rd SO16 ......78 A1
Langside Ave PO14 ...204 A4
Langside Sch BH12 ...204 A4
Langstone Ave PO9 ...159 C3
Langstone High St PO9 159 C3
Langstone Ho
  11 Fareham PO16 .....155 A4
  Havant PO9 ....136 A2
Langstone Inf Sch PO3 183 A4
Langstone Jun Sch PO3 183 A4
Langstone Marina Hts
  PO4 ....183 B2
Langstone Rd
  Havant PO9 ....159 C4
  Portsmouth PO3 ....183 A3
Langstone Wlk
  Fareham PO16 ....154 B4
  Gosport PO13 ....155 A1
Langton Cl
  Barton on Sea BH25 ..210 A4
  Winchester SO22 ......1 C1
Langton Dene 27 BH4 .204 B2
Langton Farm Gdns
  PO1 ....182 C4
Langton Rd
  Bishop's Waltham SO32 ..83 B4
  Bournemouth BH7 .....205 C3
Lanham La SO22 ....1 A1
Lankhills Rd SO23 ....2 A1
Lankhills Sch SO22 ......1 C1
Lansdell Ct 6 BH15 ....202 C2
Lansdown Ave PO16 ...156 B3
Lansdown Terr PO10 ..137 A3
Lansdowne Ave
  Waterlooville PO7 .....134 A1
  Winchester SO23 ......10 C3
Lansdowne Cl 3 SO51 ..52 C4
Lansdowne Cres BH1 ..205 A2
Lansdowne Ct
  Romsey SO51 ....52 C4
  3 Winchester SO23 ...10 C3
Lansdowne Gdns
  Bournemouth BH1 .....205 A2
  Romsey SO51 ....52 C4
Lansdowne Hill 9
  SO14 ....102 C2
Lansdowne Ho
  13 Bournemouth BH1 ..205 A2
  3 Gosport PO12 ......181 A3

Lansdowne Rd
  Bournemouth BH1 .....205 A3
  Southampton SO15 ....102 A4
Lansdowne The BH1 ...205 A2
Lantana Cl PO7 ....134 C3
Lantern Ct SO23 ....10 C3
Lanyard Dr PO13 ......180 B3
Lapthorn Cl PO13 .....155 A2
Lapwing Cl
  Gosport PO12 ....181 A4
  Horndean PO8 ....112 A4
  Portsmouth PO8 ....183 B3
Lapwing Dr SO40 .....100 A4
Lapwing Gr PO16 .....155 C4
Lapwing Rd BH21 .....164 A4
Lara Cl BH8 ....190 A2
Larch Ave SO45 ......150 B3
Larch Cl
  Broadstone BH17 .....186 C1
  Hordle SO41 ....195 C2
  Kings Worthy SO23 .....2 A4
  Lee-on-the-Solent PO13 .180 A3
  St Leonards BH24 .....140 A2
  West End SO30 ....80 B1
Larch Ct PO1 ....215 C4
Larch Rd SO16 ....78 A2
Larch Row SP6 ....70 B1
Larch Way
  Bursledon SO31 ......127 C3
  Ferndown BH22 ......165 B4
Larchdale Cl SO31 ....152 B4
Larches Gdns PO15 ...130 B1
Larchfield Way PO8 ..112 B3
Larchwood Ave PO9 ..135 A2
Larchwood Rd SO40 ..100 B3
Larcombe Rd GU32 ....40 B1
Larg Dr SO22 ....1 B2
Lark Hill Rise SO22 ....10 B2
Lark Rd
  Christchurch BH23 ...208 A3
  Eastleigh SO50 ......55 B1
Lark Way PO10 ......137 B2
Larkhill Rd PO3 ......157 C2
Larks Cl BH22 ....165 A4
Larks Rise BH22 .....165 A4
Larksfield Ave BH9 ..190 B2
Larkshill Cl BH25 ....195 A2
Larkspur Chase SO19 .104 C3
Larkspur Cl
  Locks Heath SO31 ....128 C1
  Swanmore SO32 ......84 A3
Larkspur Dr
  Chandler's Ford SO53 ..54 C3
  Marchwood SO40 .....124 C4
Larkspur Gdns
  7 Hedge End SO30 ...105 B3
  Holbury SO45 ....150 A2
Larkwhistle Wlk PO9 .135 B4
Lascelles Ct 1 BH7 ..206 A3
Lascelles Rd BH7 ....206 A3
Laser Cl SO31 ....128 C1
Lasham Gn 47 PO9 ...136 A3
Lasham Ho 3 SO16 ..102 A4
Lasham Wlk PO14 ....154 B4
Latch Farm Ave BH23 207 A4
Latchmore Dr SO45 ..125 B2
Latchmore Forest Gr
  PO8 ....112 A4
Latchmore Gdns PO8 111 C2
Latelie Cl SO31 ......127 B3
Latham Cl SO50 ......57 A1
Latham Ct SO15 .....102 A4
Latham Rd Fair Oak SO50 .57 A1
  Romsey SO51 ....53 A4
Latimer Ct
  Portsmouth PO3 .....158 A2
  11 Southampton SO17 ..79 A1
Latimer Gate 27 SO14 103 A2
Latimer Rd BH9 ......204 C4
Latimer St Romsey SO51 .52 C4
  Southampton SO14 ...103 A2
Latimers BH23 ....193 C1
Lauder Cl PO10 ......137 C1
Launcelyn Cl SO52 ....53 C2
Launceston Cl PO12 ..181 B4
Launceston Dr SO50 ..55 C3
Laundry La SO41 .....211 C2
Laundry Rd SO16 .....78 A1
Laurel Cl
  Christchurch BH23 ...193 B1
  Corfe Mullen BH21 ..186 B3
  Gosport PO12 ....181 B4
  Hordle SO41 ....195 C2
  Hythe SO45 ....125 C2
  Locks Heath SO31 ....129 A2
  Southampton SO19 ...103 B2
  St Leonards BH24 ....139 C2
Laurel Dr BH18 ......187 B4
Laurel Gdns
  Broadstone BH18 ....187 B2
  Locks Heath SO31 ...129 A2
Laurel La BH24 ......139 C2
Laurel Rd
  Locks Heath SO31 ...129 A2
  Waterlooville PO8 ...112 B2
Laurels The
  Brockenhurst SO42 ..172 C4
  Ferndown BH22 .....165 B4
Lauren Mews PO11 ..184 C1
Laurence Ct 2 SO50 ..57 B1
Laurence Gn PO10 ...136 C2
Laurence Mews SO51 ..52 C4
Lauriston Dr SO53 ....30 A1
Laurus Cl PO7 ....135 A3
Laurus Wlk 18 PO13 .179 C1
Lavant Cl PO8 ....112 A1
Lavant Ct 3 GU32 ....40 C2

Lavant Dr PO9 ....136 A2
Lavant St GU32 ....40 C2
Lavender Cl
  Southampton SO19 ...103 C3
  Verwood BH31 ....115 B3
Lavender Rd
  Bournemouth BH8 ....190 B2
  Hordle SO41 ....195 C2
  Waterlooville PO7 ....135 A3
Lavender Villas 1 .....209 A4
Lavender Way BH18 ..186 B2
Laverock Lea PO16 ...132 B1
Laverstock 27 BH5 ...205 B2
Laverstoke Cl SO16 ...77 C3
Lavey's La PO15 .....130 A3
Lavington Gdns SO52 .53 C2
Lavinia Rd Gosport PO12 181 A2
  Poole BH12 ....203 B4
Lawford Rd BH9 ......190 A2
Lawford Way SO40 ...100 C4
Lawn Cl Gosport PO13 .180 B4
  Milford on Sea SO41 .211 C2
Lawn Ct SO17 ....103 A4
Lawn Dr SO31 ....129 A1
Lawn Ho 21 SO23 ....11 A4
Lawn Rd Eastleigh SO50 ..56 A3
  Littleton SO22 ....1 B2
  Lymington SO41 .....197 A2
  Milford on Sea SO41 .211 C2
  Southampton SO17 ...103 A4
Lawn St SO23 ....11 A4
Lawn View BH25 .....194 B3
Lawns Cl BH21 ......164 B3
Lawns Rd BH21 .....164 A3
Lawns The BH23 ....209 A4
Lawnside Rd SO15 ..102 A4
Lawnswood SO50 .....57 B4
Lawnswood Cl PO8 ..111 C1
Lawrence Ave PO8 ..111 C1
Lawrence Ct
  Bournemouth BH8 ...205 B3
  Southampton SO19 ..103 C1
Lawrence Dr BH13 ..203 C1
Lawrence Gr SO19 ..103 C1
Lawrence Ho 6 SO45 126 A2
Lawrence La SP6 ....94 A2
Lawrence Mans PO5 .215 D1
Lawrence Rd
  Fareham PO15 ......130 C1
  Portsmouth PO5 ....215 D1
  Ringwood BH24 .....117 B1
Lawrence Sq 20 PO12 181 B2
Lawrence Wlk PO13 .180 B3
Lawson Cl SO31 .....128 C1
Lawson Ct 12 SO16 ..78 A1
Lawson Rd Poole BH12 203 A3
  Portsmouth PO5 .....215 D2
Laxton Cl
  Locks Heath SO31 ...129 C2
  Southampton SO19 ..104 A1
Layard Dr BH21 .....163 B1
Laymoor La SO31 ...164 B3
Layton Cl BH12 .....203 B3
Layton Rd Gosport PO13 155 B2
  Poole BH12 ....203 B3
Lazy Acre PO10 ....161 B4
Le Patourel Cl BH23 .207 B4
Lea Rd SO45 ....177 C4
Lea The BH31 ......115 A3
Lea Way BH11 .....188 C3
Lea-Oak Gdns PO15 130 B2
Leabrook SO31 ....129 A3
Leacock Cl SO32 ....84 A3
Leafy La PO15 ....129 C3
Lealand Gr PO6 ...158 B4
Lealand Rd PO6 ...158 B4
Leamington Cres PO13 179 C1
Leamington Ho 9 PO5 215 B2
Leamington Rd BH9 .205 A4
Leander Cl SO50 ....56 A3
Leander Dr PO12 ...181 B4
Leaphill Rd BH7 ...206 A3
Lear Rd PO12 ......181 A3
Learoyd Rd BH17 ..202 C4
Leaside Way SO16 ..79 B3
Leatherhead Gdns SO30 ..81 B1
Leaway The PO16 ..156 B4
Lebanon Rd SO15 ..101 B4
Lechlade Gdns
  Bournemouth BH7 ..206 A4
  Fareham PO15 .....130 C2
Leckford Cl
  Portchester PO16 ..132 A1
  Southampton SO18 .104 B4
Leckford Rd PO9 ..136 A3
Ledbury Rd
  Christchurch BH23 .207 C3
  Cosham PO6 ....133 B1
Lederle La PO13 ...155 B3
Ledgard Cl BH14 ..203 A2
Lee Church La SO51 ..76 C4
Lee Ct BH22 ......165 B2
Lee Dro SO51 ......53 A1
Lee La SO51 ....77 A4
Lee Rd PO12 ......181 A3
Lee-on-the-Solent Inf Sch
  PO13 ....179 C1
Lee-on-the-Solent Jun Sch
  PO13 ....179 C1
Leedam Rd BH10 ..189 B4
Leelands SO41 ....197 B1
Leep La PO12 .....181 A1
Lees Cl BH23 .....191 B2
Lees La SO41 ....181 A3
Lees La N PO12 ..181 A3
Leesland CE Inf Sch
  PO12 ....181 A2

Leesland CE Jun Sch
  PO12 ....181 A2
Leesland Rd PO12 ...181 A2
Leeson Dr BH22 .....165 A4
Leeson Rd BH7 .....205 C4
Legg La BH21 ......163 B2
Legion Cl
  Hamworthy BH15 ...201 C1
  Southampton SO16 ...79 B2
Legion La SO23 ....2 B4
Legion Rd
  Hamworthy BH15 ...201 C1
  South Hayling PO11 .185 A4
Leicester Ct PO13 ..180 B3
Leicester Rd Poole BH13 203 C2
  Southampton SO15 ...78 B1
Leicester Way SO23 ...2 B1
Leigh Comm BH21 ..163 C3
Leigh Ct SO50 ......55 C2
Leigh Gdns BH21 ...163 B2
Leigh House Hospl
  Chandler's Ford SO53 .55 B4
  Winchester SO21 ....11 C3
Leigh La BH21 .....163 C3
Leigh Mans 10 SO17 ..79 A1
Leigh Pk SO41 .....197 B2
Leigh Rd
  Eastleigh SO50, SO53 .55 C2
  Fareham PO16 .....131 A1
  Havant PO9 ....135 C1
  New Milton BH25 ..195 A4
  Southampton SO17 ..79 A1
  Wimborne Minst BH21 163 C2
Leigham Vale Rd BH6 206 B2
Leighton Ave 7 SO15 102 A4
Leighton Rd SO19 ..103 C2
Leisure The PO13 ..155 B2
Leith Ave PO16 ....132 C1
Lemon Rd SO15 ...102 A4
Lendorber Ave PO6 158 A4
Lennox Cl
  Chandler's Ford SO53 .55 C4
  Gosport PO12 ......181 B1
  Southampton SO16 ..77 C3
Lennox Rd N PO5 ..182 B1
Lennox Rd S PO5 ..182 B1
Lensyd Gdns PO8 ..111 C3
Lent Hill Ct 5 SO22 .10 B3
Lentham Cl BH17 ..187 B1
Lentune Way SO41 197 B1
Leofric Ct PO4 ....183 B2
Leominster Rd PO6 133 A1
Leonard Rd PO12 ..181 B3
Leonards Ct SO16 .101 B4
Leopold Dr SO32 ..83 A4
Leopold St PO4 ...182 C1
Lepe Ctry Pk ★ SO45 178 A2
Lepe Rd SO45 .....178 A2
Leroux Cl SO15 ...102 C3
Lerryn Rd PO13 ..155 B1
Leslie Loader Ct SO50 .56 A2
Leslie Loader Ho SO19 .103 C3
Leslie Rd
  Bournemouth BH9 ..204 C4
  Poole BH14 ....203 A2
Lester Ave PO9 ...135 B1
Lester Rd PO12 ...180 C3
Lester Sq BH24 ...143 B4
Leven Ave BH4 ...204 B3
Leven Cl
  Bournemouth BH4 .204 B2
  North Baddesley SO53 .55 A4
Leventhorpe Ct PO12 181 B2
Leveson Cl PO12 ..180 C2
Levet's La 5 BH15 .202 A1
Leviathan Cl PO14 .179 B3
Lewens Cl BH21 ..163 B2
Lewens La BH21 ..163 B2
Lewes Cl SO50 ...56 A3
Lewesdon Dr BH18 186 C2
Lewin Cl SO21 ...56 C4
Lewins Wlk SO31 .104 C1
Lewis Cl SO45 ...125 B1
Lewis Ho 19 SO14 103 A3
Lewis Rd PO10 ..137 A2
Lewis Silkin Way SO16 .78 A2
Lewry Cl SO30 ...105 B4
Lexby Rd SO40 ..101 A3
Lexden Gdns PO11 184 C2
Leybourne Ave
  Bournemouth BH10 189 B2
  Southampton SO18 .104 A4
Leybourne Cl BH10 189 B3
Leydene Ave BH8 .190 C1
Leydene Cl BH8 ..190 C1
Leydene Pk GU32 .63 C2
Leyland Cl PO12 ..181 A2
Leyland Rd BH12 .188 C1
Leyside BH23 ....207 C3
Leyton Conyers 16
  BH13 ....214 C4
Leyton Rd SO14 ..103 B3
Liam Cl PO9 ......136 A2
Liberty Cl BH21 ..139 A3
Liberty Ct BH23 ..206 C4
Liberty Rd PO17 ..109 A4
Liberty Row SO31 .128 A1
Library Mews BH12 203 B3
Library Rd
  Bournemouth BH9 ..189 C1
  Ferndown BH22 ....165 B3
  Poole BH13 ....203 C3
  Totton SO40 ....101 A4
Lichen Way SO40 .101 C1
Lichfield Ct PO13 .180 B3

Lichfield Dr PO12 ....181 B4
Lichfield Rd
 Locks Heath PO14 ....129 B2
 Portsmouth PO3 ....183 A3
Liddel Way SO53 ....55 A3
Liddiards Way PO7 ....134 C2
Lidiard Gdns PO4 ....183 A1
Liederbach Dr BH31 ......115 B2
Lightfoot Lawn PO4 ......183 B2
Lightning Cl SO45 ....150 C1
Lilac Cl Havant PO9 ....136 B2
 Ringwood BH24 ....141 A4
Lilac Rd SO16 ....79 C4
Lilies The SO50 ....81 B4
Lilley Cl SO40 ....101 C1
Lilliput CE Fst Sch
 BH14 ....214 B4
Lilliput Ct BH14 ....203 A2
Lilliput Rd BH14 ....214 B4
Lily Ave PO7 ....134 A1
Limberline Rd PO3 ....158 A2
Limberline Spur PO3 ......158 A3
Lime Ave SO19 ....104 C3
Lime Cl
 Colden Common SO21 ....57 A4
 Hythe SO45 ....125 C1
 Poole BH15 ....202 C3
 Southampton SO19 .....104 A3
Lime Gdns SO30 ....80 B2
Lime Gr Cosham PO6 .....133 A1
 Hordle SO41 ....211 B4
 South Hayling PO11 ....184 B2
Lime Kiln La SO45 ....150 A3
Lime Kiln Lane Mobile Home
 Pk SO45 ....150 A3
Lime St SO14 ....103 A4
Lime Tree Cl SP6 ....92 C3
Lime Tree Ho SO41 ......197 C2
Lime Wlk Botley SO30 ....105 C4
 Hythe SO45 ....125 C1
Limekiln La
 Bishop's Waltham SO32 ..59 C2
 East Meon GU32 ....64 B3
Limes Cl GU33 ....20 C2
Limes The Gosport PO13 .155 B1
 Havant PO9 ....159 C4
 Marchwood SO40 ......102 A1
 Waterlooville PO7 .....134 B2
Limetree Wlk **8** SO23 ...11 B4
Limited Rd BH9 ....190 A1
Linacre Rd SO19 ....104 B3
Linbrook Ct BH24 ....117 A1
Lincoln Ave
 Bournemouth BH1 .....205 B3
 Christchurch BH23 ....191 C1
Lincoln Cl
 Locks Heath PO14 .....129 B2
 Romsey SO51 ....28 A1
Lincoln Ct Gosport PO13 .180 B3
 Southampton SO15 .....78 C1
 West End SO30 ....80 B1
Lincoln Rd Poole BH12 ..203 B4
 Portsmouth PO1 ....182 C4
Lincoln Rise PO8 ....112 A2
Lincolns Rise SO50 ....31 A1
Lind Cl PO7 ....134 C2
Lind Rd PO12 ....181 B1
Linda Gr PO8 ....111 C2
Linda Rd SO45 ....151 A2
Lindbergh Cl PO13 ......180 B3
Lindbergh Rd BH21 ......165 A4
Lindbergh Rise PO15 ....129 C3
Linden Cl Ferndown BH22 165 B1
 Waltham Chase SO32 ....83 C2
Linden Ct
 Locks Heath SO31 ......129 B2
 Ringwood BH24 ....140 C4
 12 Romsey SO51 ....52 C4
 West End SO18 ....80 A2
Linden Dr GU33 ....20 C2
Linden Gdns
 Hedge End SO30 ......105 B3
 Ringwood BH24 ....140 C4
Linden Gr
 Chandler's Ford SO53 ...55 B4
 Gosport PO12 ....181 A2
 South Hayling PO11 ...185 A2
Linden Lea PO16 ....132 B1
Linden Rd
 Bournemouth BH9 ....190 A2
 Ferndown BH22 ....165 B1
 Poole BH12 ....203 B3
 Romsey SO51 ....52 C4
 Southampton SO16 .....78 A2
Linden Way Havant PO9 .135 C2
 Lymington SO41 ......197 B2
 Waterlooville PO8 .....112 B3
Linden Wlk SO52 ....53 C3
Lindens Cl PO10 ....136 C1
Lindens The BH23 ....192 B2
Lindisfarne Cl PO6 ......158 A4
Lindley Ave PO4 ....183 A1
Lindsay Ho **35** PO5 ......182 B1
Lindsay Manor **10** BH12 204 A2
Lindsay Pk **15** BH13 ....204 A2
Lindsay Rd Poole BH13 ..204 A2
 Southampton SO19 ...104 C3
Lindum Ct **3** BH12 .....204 A2
Lindway SO31 ....129 A3
Lineside BH23 ....207 B4
Linford Cl BH25 ....195 C4
Linford Cres SO16 ....78 B2
Linford Ct Fair Oak SO50 .57 B1

Linford Ct continued
 Havant PO9 ....135 B4
Linford Ho BH24 ....117 C2
Linford Rd BH24 ....117 B1
Ling Dale SO16 ....78 C4
Ling Rd BH12 ....188 A1
Lingdale Pl **3** SO17 ....103 A4
Lingdale Rd BH6 ....206 B3
Lingfield Ct **20** PO1 ....182 A2
Lingfield Gdns SO18 ......79 C1
Lingfield Grange BH4 ....204 A2
Lingwood Ave BH23 .....207 C3
Lingwood Cl SO16 ....78 C4
Lingwood Wlk SO16 ......78 C4
Linhorns La BH25 ....195 A3
Link Rd Ringwood BH24 .141 B4
 Southampton SO16 .....77 C2
Link Rise BH21 ....186 C3
Link The PO7 ....112 A1
Link Way PO14 ....179 B3
Linkenholt Way PO9 ....135 B2
Linklater Path PO1 ......182 B4
Links Cl PO9 ....113 A1
Links Dr BH23 ....191 B1
Links La
 Rowland's Castle PO9 ..113 A1
 South Hayling PO11 ...184 B2
Links Rd Poole BH14 ....203 B1
 Winchester SO22 ....1 B1
Links The PO13 ....155 B1
Links View Ave BH14 ...203 C1
Links View Way SO16 ....78 C3
Linkside Ave BH8 ....205 C4
Linmead Dr BH11 ....189 A3
Linnet Cl Petersfield GU31 .41 B1
 Ringwood BH24 ....141 B3
 Waterlooville PO8 .....111 C2
Linnet Ct Gosport PO12 .180 C2
 New Milton BH25 .....194 C2
Linnet Rd BH17 ....201 C4
Linnet Sq SO50 ....55 B1
Linnets The
 Portchester PO16 ......155 C4
 Totton SO40 ....100 B4
Linnies La SO41 ....196 A4
Linthorpe Rd BH15 .....202 C2
Linwood Cl SO45 ....126 A1
Linwood Mix Sch BH9 ..205 A4
Linwood Rd BH9 ....205 A4
Lion Brewery The **24**
 PO2 ....182 B4
Lion Ho PO17 ....108 A2
Lion Rd PO1 ....181 C4
Lion St PO1 ....182 A3
Lion Terr PO1 ....182 A3
Lionheart Cl BH11 ......188 B3
Lionheart Way SO31 ....105 A1
Lions Hall **23** SO22 ......10 C4
Lions La BH24 ....139 B3
Lions Wood BH24 ....139 C2
Liphook Ho **40** PO9 .....136 A3
Lipizzaner Fields SO31 ..129 A4
Lippen La SO32 ....36 C2
Lisbon Rd SO15 ....102 B3
Lisle Cl Lymington SO41 .197 B2
 Winchester SO22 ....10 A2
Lisle Court Rd SO41 ....198 B2
Lisle Ct SO22 ....10 C3
Lisle Way PO10 ....136 C2
Liss Inf & Jun Schs GU33 21 A2
Liss Rd PO4 ....182 C2
Liss Sta GU33 ....20 C2
Litchfield Cres SO18 .....79 C1
Litchfield Rd
 Southampton SO18 .....79 C1
 Winchester SO22 ....1 B2
Litchford Rd BH25 ......195 B2
Lith Ave PO8 ....112 B4
Little Abshot Rd PO14 ..153 A4
Little Anglesey PO12 ...181 A1
Little Anglesey Rd
 PO12 ....181 A1
Little Arthur St PO2 ....182 C4
Little Ashton La SO32 ....59 C2
Little Barn Pl GU33 ......21 A2
Little Barrs Dr BH25 ....195 A2
Little Bull La SO32 ....83 B1
Little Burn SO41 ....172 A1
Little Cnr PO7 ....111 C2
Little Coburg St PO1 ....215 C3
Little Croft Rd BH12 ....203 A3
Little Ct Poole BH14 ....214 B4
 Poole, Canford Cliffs BH14 214 C4
Little Dene Copse SO41 197 A1
Little Dewlands BH31 ...114 B3
Little Dro SP6 ....70 C4
Little Forest Mans **10**
 BH1 ....205 A2
Little Forest Rd BH4 ....204 C3
Little Fosters BH13 .....214 C4
Little Gays PO14 ....179 A3
Little George St PO1 ....182 C4
Little Green Orch PO12 .181 A1
Little Gr PO12 ....181 A1
Little Hambrook St **6**
 PO5 ....215 A1
Little Holbury Park Mobile
 Home Pk SO45 ....150 A3
Little Hyden La PO8 ......88 A4
Little Kimble Wlk **3**
 SO30 ....105 B3
Little La PO12 ....181 A1
Little Lance's Hill SO19 103 C3
Little Lonnen BH21 .....163 C4
Little Mead PO7 ....111 A2
Little Minster St SO23 ...11 A4
Little Oak Rd SO16 ......78 C2
Little Park Cl SO30 .....105 A3

Little Park Farm Rd
 PO15 ....129 B3
Little Park Mans PO17 ..107 C2
Little Quob La SO30 ......80 C1
Little Reynolds SO40 ....100 B3
Little Shore La SO32 ......83 B4
Little Southsea St PO5 ..215 A1
Little Toller SO16 ....78 C4
Little Woodfalls Dr SP5 ..47 B2
Little Woodham La
 PO13 ....180 B3
Littlecroft Ave BH9 .....190 A2
Littledown Ave BH7 ....205 C4
Littledown Dr BH7 .....205 C4
Littlefield Cres SO53 .....54 C3
Littlegreen Ave PO9 ....136 A2
Littlegreen Sch PO18 ....90 C2
Littlemead Cl BH17 .....202 A4
Littlemeads SO51 ....52 B4
Littlemoor Ave BH11 ...188 B2
Littlepark Ave PO9 .....135 A2
Littleton Gr PO9 ....135 C2
Littleton La SO21 ....1 A1
Littleton Rd SO22 ....1 A2
Littlewood SO51 ....50 C2
Littlewood Gdns
 Locks Heath SO31 .....128 C2
 West End SO30 ....80 B1
Liverpool Ct PO13 ......180 B3
Liverpool Rd
 Gosport PO14 ....154 C3
 Portsmouth PO1 ......182 C3
Liverpool St SO14 ......103 A4
Livesay Gdns PO1 ......182 C3
Livingstone Ct PO13 ....180 B3
Livingstone Rd
 Bournemouth BH5 ....206 A3
 Christchurch BH23 ...207 B4
 Portsmouth PO5 ......215 C1
 Southampton SO14 ...103 A4
 Wimborne Minst BH21 .163 C2
Llewellin Cl BH16 ......201 B4
Llewellin Ct BH16 ......201 B4
Lloyd Ave SO40 ....101 C1
Loaders Cl BH9 ....205 A4
Loane Rd SO19 ....103 C2
Lobelia Ct PO7 ....135 A3
Lobelia Rd SO16 ....79 B3
Locarno Rd PO3 ....158 A1
Loch Rd BH14 ....203 C3
Lock App PO6 ....157 A4
Lock View PO6 ....157 A4
Lock's Cotts SO45 ......125 B3
Locke Rd SO30 ....105 B4
Lockerley Cl SO41 ......197 C1
Lockerley Cres SO16 .....77 C1
Lockerley Endowed CE Prim
 Sch SO51 ....5 A1
Lockerley Rd PO9 ....136 A2
Lockerly Ct SO15 ....102 C4
Locks Heath Ctr SO31 ..129 A2
Locks Heath Jun & Inf Schs
 SO31 ....129 A1
Locks Rd SO31 ....129 A2
Locksheath Cl **6** PO9 ..135 B3
Locksheath Park Rd
 SO31 ....129 A1
Locksley Dr BH23 ......165 B2
Locksley Rd SO50 ....55 C1
Locksway Rd PO4 ......183 B2
Lockswood Keep SO31 .129 A2
Lockswood Rd SO31 ....128 C2
Lockyer Ct GU32 ....41 A3
Lockyer's Mid Sch BH21 186 B4
Lockyer's Rd BH21 .....186 C4
Lockyers Dr BH22 ......165 C3
Lode Hill SP5 ....47 A4
Loders Cl BH17 ....187 B2
Lodge Ave PO6 ....158 A4
Lodge Cl BH14 ....203 C2
Lodge Ct BH14 ....203 C2
Lodge Dr SO45 ....126 A1
Lodge Dro SP5 ....47 B2
Lodge Gdns PO12 ......181 A2
Lodge Hill PO17 ....109 A3
Lodge Rd
 Christchurch BH23 ....206 C4
 Havant PO9 ....135 A1
 Locks Heath SO31 ....129 A2
 Lymington SO41 ......197 A2
 Southampton SO14 ...103 A4
Lodge The
 Bournemouth BH2 ....204 C2
 Southampton SO15 ...102 C4
 Waterlooville PO7 ....135 A3
Lodge Vale SO51 ....51 A1
Lodgebury Cl PO10 .....161 C4
Lodsworth Cl PO8 ....88 B2
Lodsworth Ho PO1 .....215 C4
Loewy Cres BH12 ....188 B3
Lofting Cl **1** SO50 ....56 C1
Logan Cl SO16 ....77 C3
Lomax St PO1 ....81 B1
Lombard Ave BH6 ......206 B3
Lombard Ct **8** PO1 .....182 A2
Lombard St PO1 ....182 A2
Lombardy
 Gosport PO13 ....155 C1
 Verwood BH31 ....115 A3
Lombardy Rise PO7 ....134 C3
Lomer La BH24 ....93 B2
Lomond Cl PO2 ....182 B4
Londesborough Rd PO4 182 C2
London Ave PO2 ....157 C4
London Ct PO12 ....181 A1

London La BH23 ....167 C1
London Rd Clanfield PO8 ..88 B2
 Cosham PO7 ....134 B2
 Hill Brow GU33 ....21 A1
 Horndean PO8 ....88 B2
 Kings Worthy SO23 ......2 A3
 Petersfield GU31 ....41 A3
 Portsmouth PO2 ......157 C2
 Southampton SO15 ...103 A3
 Steep GU31 ....41 B3
 Waterlooville PO7, PO6 .134 B2
London Tavern Cvn Pk The
 BH24 ....141 B4
Lone Barn La SO32 ....60 C4
Lone Pine Dr BH22 .....165 C2
Lone Pine Way BH22 ...165 C1
Lone Valley PO7 ....134 B2
Long Acre Ct PO7 ......182 C4
Long Beech Dr SO40 ...100 B3
Long Cl Downton SP5 ....46 C3
 Winchester SO23 ....10 C3
Long Copse SO45 ....150 C3
Long Copse Ct PO10 ...136 C2
Long Copse La PO10 ...137 A2
Long Curtain Rd PO5 ..182 A1
Long Down GU31 ....41 A2
Long Dr Gosport PO13 .155 B1
 West End SO30 ....80 C1
Long La Bursledon SO31 .105 A1
 Holbury SO45 ....150 B3
 Marchwood SO40 ....101 B1
 Ringwood BH24 ......141 A2
 Wimborne Minst BH21 .163 C4
Long Lane Cl SO45 .....150 C3
Long Priors GU32 ....37 A3
Long Rd
 Bournemouth BH10 ...189 B3
 Petersfield GU32 ....41 A3
 Soberton SO32 ....85 B3
Long Water Dr PO12 ...181 B1
Long Wlk
 Portsmouth PO1 ......182 B4
 Winchester SO21 ....2 C2
Longacre Cl GU33 ....21 A2
Longacre Dr BH22 .....165 B2
Longacres PO14 ....129 B2
Longbarrow Cl BH8 ....191 A1
Longbridge Cl SO40 .....76 B1
Longbridge Dr SO40 .....76 B1
Longbridge Ho **8** PO5 .215 B2
Longbridge Ind Pk
 SO14 ....103 B2
Longclose Rd SO30 .....105 B4
Longcroft PO9 ....135 C1
Longdean Ct **1** PO6 ...133 A1
Longdown Dairy Farm*
 SO40 ....100 B1
Longespee Rd BH21 ....187 C4
Longfield Ave SO41 ....154 C4
Longfield Cl PO4 ....183 B3
Longfield Dr
 Bournemouth BH11 ...189 A3
 Ferndown BH22 ....189 C4
Longfield Rd
 Emsworth PO10 ....136 C2
 Fair Oak SO50 ....57 B1
 Hordle SO41 ....196 B1
 Winchester SO23 ....11 B4
Longfleet CE Comb Sch
 BH15 ....202 B2
Longfleet Rd BH15 .....202 C2
Longford Pl SO41 ......197 B1
Longhouse Gn **9** SO23 .11 B4
Longlands Rd PO10 ....161 B4
Longleat Gdns
 New Milton BH25 .....194 C2
 Southampton SO16 .....78 A2
Longmead GU33 ....20 C2
Longmead Ave SO50 ....56 B2
Longmead Ct PO9 .....159 C4
Longmead Gdns PO9 ..159 C4
Longmead Rd
 Burley BH24 ....142 C2
 1 Southampton SO18 ..80 A1
Longmeadow Gdns
 SO45 ....126 A2
Longmeadow La BH17 .201 C4
Longmore Ave SO19 ...103 B1
Longmore Cres SO19 ..103 B1
Longmynd Dr PO14 ....154 B4
Longridge Rd SO30 ....105 B3
Longs La PO14 ....154 B2
Longshore Way PO4 ...183 B2
Longspee Sch BH17 ....202 B4
Longstaff Gdns PO16 ..130 C2
Longstock Cl SO19 .....127 A4
Longstock Cres SO40 ..100 C4
Longstock Rd PO9 .....136 A3
Longwood Ave PO8 ....112 A2
Longwood Dean La SO23,
 SO23 ....34 A3
Longwood Rd SO21 ......33 B3
Longworthy **3** SO45 ..125 C1
Lonnen Rd BH21 ....164 A4
Lonnen Wood Cl BH21 .164 A4
Lonsdale Ave
 Cosham PO6 ....158 A4
 Portchester PO16 .....156 B3
Lonsdale Rd BH3 ......204 C3
Looeshanger SP5 ....47 C2
Loperwood SO40 ....76 A1
Loperwood La Ower SO40 76 A1
Loraine Ave BH23 ......209 B4
Lord Cl BH31 ....202 C4
Lord Montgomery Way **1**
 PO1 ....215 A2

Lord Mountbatten Cl
 SO18 ....79 C2
Lord Wilson Sch SO31 .128 C2
Lord's Hill Ctr E SO16 ...77 C2
Lord's Hill Ctr W SO16 ...77 C2
Lord's Hill Way SO16 ....78 A3
Lordington Cl PO6 .....158 A4
Lords Ct PO1 ....215 C4
Lords St PO1 ....215 C4
Lordswood SO50 ....56 C4
Lordswood Cl SO16 .....78 B2
Lordswood Ct SO16 .....78 B2
Lordswood Gdns SO16 ..78 B2
Lordswood Rd SO16 .....78 B2
Loreille Gdns SO16 ......77 C4
Loring Ho **7** PO2 ......157 C2
Lorne Park Rd BH1 .....205 A2
Lorne Pl SO18 ....104 A4
Lorne Rd PO5 ....215 D1
Lortemore Pl **8** SO51 ...52 C4
Loughwood Cl SO50 .....56 A3
Louis Flagg Ho **2** PO5 215 C1
Lovage Gdns SO40 .....100 B4
Lovage Way PO8 ....88 B1
Lovatt Gr PO15 ....130 B2
Love La
 Milford on Sea SO41 ..211 B3
 Petersfield GU31 ......41 A2
 Romsey SO51 ....52 C4
 Twyford SO21 ....32 A3
 Upham SO24,SO32 .....35 A3
 Woodgreen SP6 ....70 C4
Lovedean La
 Horndean PO8 ....111 C3
 Waterlooville PO8 ....111 C3
Lovedon La SO23 ....2 B4
Lovett Rd PO3 ....158 A2
Lovett Wlk SO22 ....1 B2
Lowcay Rd PO5 ....182 C1
Lowden Cl SO22 ....10 B2
Lower Alfred St **10**
 SO14 ....103 A3
Lower Ashley Rd BH25 .195 B1
Lower Banister St **7**
 SO15 ....102 C3
Lower Bartons SP6 ......69 C1
Lower Baybridge La
 SO21 ....33 B1
Lower Bellfield PO14 ...153 C4
Lower Bere Wood PO7 .134 C4
Lower Blandford Rd
 BH18 ....187 A2
Lower Brook St SO14 ....11 A4
Lower Brookfield Rd
 PO1 ....182 C3
Lower Brownhill Rd
 SO16 ....77 B2
Lower Buckland Rd
 SO41 ....197 B3
Lower Canal Wlk SO14 .103 A2
Lower Chase Rd SO32 ...83 C2
Lower Church Path
 PO1 ....215 B3
Lower Church Rd PO14 .129 B2
Lower Common La
 BH21 ....139 A4
Lower Common Rd SO51 50 C2
Lower Crabbick La PO7 110 A3
Lower Densome Wood
 SP6 ....70 C4
Lower Derby Rd PO2 ...157 B1
Lower Drayton La PO6 .158 A4
Lower Duncan Rd SO31 129 A3
Lower Farlington Rd
 PO6 ....158 C4
Lower Farm La SO51 ....29 A4
Lower Forbury Rd PO5 .215 C2
Lower Golf Links Rd
 BH18 ....187 A3
Lower Gr SP6 ....45 A1
Lower Grove Rd PO9 ...160 A4
Lower Heyshott GU31 ...41 A2
Lower La SO32 ....83 B4
Lower Lamborough La
 SO24 ....14 B3
Lower Mead GU31 ....41 A2
Lower Mead End Rd
 SO41 ....171 C1
Lower Moors Rd SO21 ...31 C1
Lower Mortimer Rd
 SO19 ....103 B2
Lower Mullin's La SO45 125 C2
Lower New Rd SO30 .....80 B1
Lower Northam Rd
 SO30 ....105 B4
Lower Pennington La
 SO41 ....212 B4
Lower Quay PO16 ......155 B4
Lower Quay Cl PO16 ...155 A4
Lower Quay Rd PO16 ..155 A4
Lower Rd PO9 ....135 B1
Lower Sandy Down La
 SO41 ....173 B2
Lower Spinney SO31 ...152 B4
Lower St SO51 ....28 A4
Lower St Helens Rd
 SO30 ....105 B3
Lower Stanmore La
 SO23 ....10 C3
Lower Swanwick Rd
 SO31 ....128 B4
Lower Vicarage Rd
 SO19 ....103 B2
Lower Wardown GU31 ...41 A4
Lower William St SO14 .103 B3
Lower William St Ind Est
 SO14 ....103 B3

Lower Wingfield St	
PO1 ....215 C4	
Lower Woodside SO41 ..**212** C4	
Lower York St SO14 ....**103** B3	
Lowesmore Ct BH14 ....**203** B2	
Lowestoft Rd PO6 ......**133** B1	
Loweswater Ho 21 PO6 ..**133** A1	
Lowford Hill SO31 ......**104** C1	
Lowland Rd PO7 ....**110** C2	
Lowry Gdns SO19 ......**104** B1	
Lowther Gdns 3 BH8 ...**205** B3	
Lowther Rd BH8 ....**205** A3	
Loxwood Rd PO8 ....**111** C3	
Luard Ct 11 PO9 ......**136** A1	
Lucas Cl SO16 ....**77** C3	
Lucas Rd Poole BH15 ..**202** A1	
Poole, Upper Parkstone	
BH12 ....**203** B3	
Luccombe Pl SO15 ......**78** B1	
Luccombe Rd SO15 ......**78** B1	
Lucerne Ave	
Bournemouth BH6 ....**206** B3	
Waterlooville PO7 ....**111** B1	
Lucerne Gdns SO30 ....**105** A4	
Lucerne Rd SO41 ......**211** B2	
Luckham Cl BH9 ....**190** A1	
Luckham Gdns BH9 ....**190** B1	
Luckham Pl BH9 ....**190** A1	
Luckham Rd BH9 ....**190** A1	
Luckham Rd E BH9 ....**190** A1	
Lucknow St PO1 ....**215** D3	
Lucky La SO41 ....**174** A1	
Ludcombe PO7 ....**110** C3	
Ludlow Inf Sch SO19 ..**103** C2	
Ludlow Jun Sch SO19 ..**103** C2	
Ludlow Rd Cosham PO6 .**133** B1	
Southampton SO19 ......**103** C2	
Ludwell's La SO32 ......**83** C2	
Lugano Cl PO7 ....**111** B1	
Lukes Cl SO31 ....**128** A1	
Lukin Dr SO16 ....**77** B3	
Lulworth Ave BH15 ....**201** C1	
Lulworth Bsns Ctr SO40 .**76** C1	
Lulworth Cl	
Chandler's Ford SO53 ....**55** A2	
Hamworthy BH15 ....**201** C1	
South Hayling PO11 ....**185** A3	
Southampton SO16 ......**77** C1	
Lulworth Cres BH15 ...**201** C1	
Lulworth Gn SO16 ......**77** C1	
Lulworth Rd PO13 .....**179** C1	
Lumby Dr BH24 ....**141** A4	
Lumby Drive Cvn Pk 3	
BH24 ....**141** A4	
Lumley Gdns PO10 ....**161** A4	
Lumley Rd PO10 ....**137** A1	
Lumley Terr PO10 .....**137** A1	
Lumsden Ave SO15 ....**102** B4	
Lumsden Mans 3 SO15 .**102** B4	
Lumsden Rd PO4 ......**183** B2	
Lundy Cl SO16 ....**77** C3	
Lundy Wlk PO14 ....**154** A2	
Lunedale Rd SO45 .....**149** C4	
Lupin Rd SO16 ....**79** B3	
Luscombe Rd BH14 ....**203** B1	
Luther Rd BH9 ....**204** C4	
Lutman St PO10 ....**136** C2	
Luton Rd SO19 ....**104** A2	
Luxton Cl SO30 ....**105** C4	
Luzborough La SO51 ....**53** B3	
Lyburn Cl SO16 ....**78** B2	
Lyburn Ct SO16 ....**78** B2	
Lyburn Ho SP5 ....**73** A4	
Lyburn Rd SP5 ....**48** C1	
Lych Gate Ct BH24 ....**141** B3	
Lychgate Dr PO8 ......**112** A4	
Lychgate Gn PO14 ....**154** B3	
Lydden Ct 1 PO13 ....**155** B1	
Lydford Gdns BH11 ....**189** A1	
Lydford Rd BH11 ......**189** A1	
Lydgate SO40 ....**100** B4	
Lydgate Cl SO19 ......**104** B2	
Lydgate Gn SO19 ......**104** B2	
Lydgate Rd SO19 ......**104** B2	
Lydgate The SO41 .....**211** A3	
Lydiard Cl SO50 ....**56** A3	
Lydlinch Cl BH22 ......**165** B1	
Lydlynch Inf Sch SO40 .**100** C4	
Lydlynch Rd SO40 .....**100** C4	
Lydney Cl PO6 ....**157** B4	
Lydney Rd SO31 ....**128** C2	
Lydwell Cl BH11 ....**188** C3	
Lyell Rd BH12 ....**203** B3	
Lymbourn Rd PO9 .....**136** A1	
Lyme Cl SO50 ....**55** C3	
Lyme Cres BH23 ......**208** C4	
Lymefields SO41 ......**211** C3	
Lymer La SO16 ....**77** B3	
Lymer Villas SO16 ......**77** B3	
Lymington Cath Sch	
SO41 ....**197** C2	
Lymington CE Inf Sch	
SO41 ....**197** B2	
Lymington Hospl SO41 .**197** B2	
Lymington Infmy & Day Hospl	
SO41 ....**197** C2	
Lymington Jun Sch	
SO41 ....**197** B2	
Lymington Pier Sta	
SO41 ....**198** A2	
Lymington Rd	
Barton on Sea BH25 ....**195** B1	
Brockenhurst SO42 .....**146** A1	
Christchurch BH23 .....**208** C4	
East Boldre SO41 ....**199** A4	
Milford on Sea SO41 ...**211** C3	
Lymington Town Sta	
SO41 ....**197** C2	

Lymington Vineyard ★	
SO41 ....**197** A1	
Lymore La SO41 ......**211** C3	
Lymore Valley SO41 ...**211** C3	
Lynch Cl SO22 ....**1** C1	
Lynch La GU32 ....**37** B2	
Lyndale Cl SO41 ......**211** B3	
Lyndale Rd SO31 ......**129** B2	
Lynden Cl PO14 ......**154** A4	
Lynden Gate SO19 ....**104** A2	
Lyndhurst CE Inf Sch	
SO43 ....**121** C3	
Lyndhurst Cl	
South Hayling PO11 ....**185** A2	
Winchester SO22 ....**1** B2	
Lyndhurst Hill SO40 ....**98** C4	
Lyndhurst Ho PO9 .....**135** C3	
Lyndhurst Jun Sch PO2 **157** C1	
Lyndhurst Rd	
Ashurst SO40 ....**100** A1	
Bransgore BH23 ....**193** B3	
Brockenhurst SO42 ....**146** A1	
Burley BH24 ....**143** B3	
Burton BH23 ....**193** B3	
Cadnam SO40 ....**98** C4	
Christchurch BH23 .....**193** B1	
Gosport PO12 ....**181** A2	
Landford SP5 ....**49** B2	
Portsmouth PO2 ....**157** C1	
Lyndock Cl SO19 ......**103** C1	
Lyndock Pl SO19 ......**103** C1	
Lyndon Ct BH23 ......**191** C1	
Lyndum Cl GU32 ....**40** C2	
Lyne Pl PO8 ....**112** A3	
Lyne's La BH24 ......**140** C4	
Lynford Ave SO22 ....**1** C1	
Lynford Way SO22 ....**1** C1	
Lynn Cl SO18 ....**80** A2	
Lynn Rd Poole BH17 ...**187** C1	
Portsmouth PO2 ....**182** C4	
Lynric Cl BH25 ....**210** A4	
Lynton Cres BH23 .....**191** B2	
Lynton Ct SO40 ....**100** C3	
Lynton Gdns PO16 ....**130** C2	
Lynton Gr PO3 ....**183** A4	
Lynton Rd	
Hedge End SO30 ....**105** B4	
Petersfield GU32 ....**40** C2	
Lynwood Ave PO8 .....**111** B2	
Lynwood Cl BH22 .....**165** B4	
Lynwood Ct	
Lymington SO41 ....**197** B2	
Winchester SO22 ....**1** C1	
Lynwood Dr BH21 .....**187** C4	
Lynx Cl SO50 ....**56** C1	
Lyon Ave BH25 ......**195** A2	
Lyon Rd BH12 ....**188** C1	
Lyon St SO14 ....**103** A3	
Lysander Cl BH23 .....**208** B4	
Lysander Ct PO1 ......**182** A2	
Lysander Way PO7 ....**135** A4	
Lyse Ct GU33 ....**20** C2	
Lysses Ct PO16 ....**131** B1	
Lyster Rd SP6 ....**70** A1	
Lystra Rd BH9 ....**190** A2	
Lytchett Dr BH18 .....**187** A2	
Lytchett Way BH16 ...**201** A3	
Lyteltane Rd SO41 ....**197** B1	
Lytham Rd	
Broadstone BH18 ......**187** A2	
Southampton SO18 ......**80** A1	
Lythe La GU32 ....**40** A3	
Lytton Rd	
Bournemouth BH1 .....**205** B3	
Hythe SO45 ....**126** A1	

M

Mabey Ave BH10 ......**189** B1	
Mabey Cl PO12 ....**181** B1	
Mablethorpe Rd PO6 ..**133** C1	
Macandrew Rd BH13 ..**214** C4	
Macarthur Cres SO18 .**104** A4	
Macaulay Ave PO6 ....**132** C1	
Macaulay Rd BH18 ....**187** A2	
Macklin Ho 35 SO22 ....**10** C4	
Maclaren Rd BH9 .....**189** C2	
Maclean Rd BH11 .....**188** C2	
Macnaghten Rd SO18 .**103** B4	
Madden Cl PO12 ......**180** C2	
Maddison St 5 SO14 ..**102** C2	
Maddoxford La SO32 ...**82** A1	
Maddoxford Way SO32 ..**81** C2	
Madeira Rd	
Bournemouth BH1 .....**205** A2	
Poole BH14 ....**203** B3	
Portsmouth PO2 ....**157** C2	
Madeline Cl BH12 .....**203** A4	
Madeline Cres BH12 ..**203** A4	
Madeline Rd GU31 .....**40** C2	
Madison Ave BH1 .....**205** B3	
Madison Cl PO13 ......**180** C4	
Madison Ct 10 PO16 ..**131** B1	
Madrisa Ct SO41 ......**197** C2	
Mafeking Rd PO4 .....**182** C2	
Maffey Ct SO30 ......**106** A4	
Mag's Barrow BH22 ...**165** C1	
Magazine La SO40 ....**102** C2	
Magdala Rd Cosham PO6 **157** C4	
South Hayling PO11 ....**184** C2	
Magdalen Cl 19 PO12 ..**157** C2	
Magdalen Hill SO23 ....**11** A4	
Magdalen La BH23 ....**207** A3	
Magdalen Mews 45 SO23 .**11** A4	
Magdalen Rd PO2 .....**157** C2	
Magdalene Way PO14 .**129** B1	
Magennis Cl PO13 ....**180** B4	

Magenta Ct PO13 .....**180** B3	
Magna Cl BH11 ......**188** C3	
Magna Gdns BH11 ....**188** C3	
Magna Rd BH11 ......**188** B4	
Magnolia Cl	
Bournemouth BH6 .....**207** A3	
Fareham PO14 ....**154** C4	
Hythe SO45 ....**125** B2	
Verwood BH31 ....**115** B2	
Magnolia Gr SO50 ......**57** C1	
Magnolia Ho 6 BH10 ..**189** C2	
Magnolia Rd SO19 ....**103** C3	
Magnolia Terr PO7 ....**134** C3	
Magnolia Way PO8 ....**112** B2	
Magpie Cl	
Bournemouth BH8 .....**190** B2	
Fareham PO16 ....**131** C1	
Magpie Cotts PO8 ....**113** B2	
Magpie Dr SO40 ......**100** B4	
Magpie Gdns SO19 ....**104** B2	
Magpie Gr BH25 ......**195** C1	
Magpie La Eastleigh SO50 **55** C1	
Lee-on-the-Solent PO13 .**179** C2	
Magpie Rd PO8 ....**113** B3	
Magpie Wlk PO8 ......**111** B2	
Maiden La SO41 ......**197** C1	
Maidford Gr PO3 ......**158** B2	
Maidment Cl BH11 ....**188** C2	
Maidstone Cres PO6 ..**133** C1	
Main Dr PO17 ....**133** A3	
Main Rd	
Colden Common SO21 ....**32** A1	
Compton(Hants) SO21 ...**31** B2	
East Boldre SO41,SO42 .**199** A4	
Fawley SO45 ....**150** B3	
Gosport PO13 ....**155** B3	
Hermitage PO10,PO18 ..**161** B4	
Hythe SO45 ....**125** B3	
Littleton SO22 ....**1** A3	
Marchwood SO40 ......**101** C1	
Otterbourne SO21 ......**31** A2	
Owslebury SO21 ....**33** A3	
Portsmouth PO1 ....**181** C3	
Southbourne PO10,PO18 **161** B4	
Totton SO40 ....**100** C2	
Boldre SO41 ....**198** A4	
Mainline Bsns Ctr GU33 ..**20** C2	
Mainsail Dr PO16 .....**155** A4	
Mainstone SO51 ....**52** B3	
Mainstream SO50 ......**56** B2	
Maisemore Gdns PO10 **160** B4	
Maitland Cres PO1 ....**182** B4	
Maitland Ct SO41 .....**197** B2	
Maitland St 14 PO1 ...**182** B4	
Maitlands The BH2 ....**204** B1	
Maizemore Wlk 21	
PO13 ....**179** C1	
Majestic Rd SO16 ......**77** A2	
Major Cl PO12 ....**181** A4	
Majoram Way PO15 ...**129** B4	
Majorca Mans 11 BH2 .**204** C2	
Malan Cl BH17 ....**202** C4	
Malcolm Cl	
Chandler's Ford SO53 ....**30** C1	
Locks Heath SO31 .....**129** A2	
Malcolm Rd SO53 ......**30** C1	
Malcomb Cl BH6 ......**207** A3	
Malcolm Mews SO40 ..**102** A1	
Maldon Cl SO50 ....**56** B2	
Maldon Rd	
5 Cosham PO6 ....**157** B4	
Southampton SO19 ....**103** C2	
Malibres Rd SO53 ......**55** C4	
Malin Cl	
Southampton SO16 ......**77** C2	
Stubbington PO14 .....**154** A2	
Malins Rd PO2 ....**182** B4	
Mall The Burley BH24 .**143** B4	
Chandler's Ford SO53 ....**55** C4	
Portsmouth PO2 ....**157** B1	
Mallard Bldgs 6 BH25 **195** A2	
Mallard Cl	
Bishop's Waltham SO32 ..**83** A4	
Bournemouth BH8 .....**190** B1	
Christchurch BH23 .....**208** A3	
Hordle SO41 ....**196** A2	
Romsey SO51 ....**52** C4	
Mallard Gdns	
Gosport PO13 ....**155** A1	
Hedge End SO30 ....**81** B1	
Mallard Rd	
Bournemouth BH8 .....**190** B1	
Portsmouth PO4 ....**183** A3	
Rowland's Castle PO9 ..**113** A1	
Wimborne Minst BH21 .**164** A4	
Mallard Way PO10 ....**137** B2	
Mallards Rd SO31 .....**127** C4	
Mallards The	
Fareham PO16 ....**131** A2	
Havant PO9 ....**159** C4	
Mallet Cl SO21 ....**81** C1	
Mallory Cl BH23 ......**207** C4	
Mallory Cres PO16 ....**131** C2	
Mallow Cl	
Broadstone BH18 ......**186** C2	
Christchurch BH23 .....**208** B4	
5 Cosham PO6 ....**157** C4	
Waterlooville PO7 .....**134** C3	
Mallow Rd SO30 ......**105** A3	
Mallows The BH25 ....**195** B2	
Malmesbury Cl SO50 ...**57** B1	
Malmesbury Cl BH8 ...**205** B3	
Malmesbury Gdns SO22 ..**1** B1	
Malmesbury Park Pl 7	
BH8 ....**205** B3	
Malmesbury Park Prim Sch	
BH8 ....**205** A3	

Malmesbury Park Rd	
BH8 ....**205** A3	
Malmesbury Pl SO15 ..**102** B4	
Malmesbury Rd	
Romsey SO51 ....**52** C4	
Southampton SO15 ....**102** B4	
St Leonards BH24 .....**139** C2	
Maloney Mews PO11 ..**185** C1	
Maloren Way BH22 ...**139** A1	
Malory Cl SO19 ......**104** B3	
Malt La SO32 ....**83** B4	
Malta Rd PO2 ....**182** C4	
Malthouse BH15 ......**202** B1	
Malthouse Cl	
Romsey SO51 ....**52** C4	
Winchester SO21 ....**2** C1	
Malthouse Cotts SO51 ..**77** A4	
Malthouse Gdns SO40 .**101** C1	
Malthouse La PO16 ...**131** A1	
Malthouse Rd PO2 ....**182** B4	
Maltings The	
Bournemouth BH11 ....**188** C3	
Fareham PO16 ....**131** B1	
Petersfield GU31 ....**40** C2	
Poole BH15 ....**202** C1	
Malus Cl PO14 ....**154** C4	
Malvern Ave PO14 ....**154** C4	
Malvern Bsns Ctr SO16 ..**78** C1	
Malvern Cl	
Bishop's Waltham SO32 ..**83** B4	
Bournemouth BH9 .....**190** A2	
Malvern Ct	
4 Bournemouth BH9 ...**190** A1	
2 Christchurch BH23 ..**207** C4	
Malvern Dr SO45 .....**125** B2	
Malvern Gdns SO30 ....**81** C3	
Malvern Mews PO10 ..**136** C1	
Malvern Rd	
Bournemouth BH9 .....**190** A1	
Gosport PO12 ....**180** C2	
Hill Brow GU33 ....**21** A1	
Portsmouth PO5 ....**182** B1	
Southampton SO16 ......**78** B1	
Malvern Terr SO16 .....**78** B1	
Malwood Ave SO16 .....**78** B4	
Malwood Cl PO9 ......**136** A3	
Malwood Gdns SO40 ..**100** B4	
Malwood Rd SO45 ....**126** A2	
Malwood Rd W SO45 ..**125** C2	
Manaton Way SO30 ....**81** A1	
Manchester Ct PO13 ..**180** B3	
Manchester Rd	
1 Netley SO31 ....**127** A3	
Portsmouth PO1 ....**182** C3	
Sway SO41 ....**172** A2	
Manchester Terr PO10 .**137** A2	
Mancroft Ave PO14 ...**179** B3	
Mandalay Cl BH31 ....**114** C3	
Mandale Cl BH11 .....**189** A2	
Mandale Rd BH11 .....**188** C2	
Mandarin Way PO13 ..**180** B3	
Mandela Way SO15 ...**102** C3	
Manderley SO41 ......**211** C2	
Manley Rd SO31 ......**104** C1	
Manners La PO4 ......**182** C2	
Manners Rd PO4 ......**182** C2	
Manning Ave BH23 ...**193** B1	
Manning's Heath Rd	
BH12 ....**188** A1	
Manningford SO23 ......**2** C1	
Mannings Heath Rdbt	
BH17 ....**188** A1	
Mannings Heath Works	
BH12 ....**188** A1	
Mannington Pl 19 BH2 **204** C2	
Mannington Way BH22 **138** C3	
Manns Cl SO18 ....**80** B1	
Mannyngham Way SO51 **27** B4	
Manor Ave BH11 ......**188** B1	
Manor Cl Bursledon SO31 **104** C1	
Ferndown BH22 ....**165** C3	
Fordingbridge SP6 ......**69** C1	
10 Havant PO9 ....**135** C1	
Milford on Sea SO41 ...**211** B3	
Totton SO40 ....**100** C3	
Wickham PO17 ....**108** A2	
43 Winchester SO23 ....**11** A4	
Manor Cres	
Bursledon SO31 ....**104** C1	
Cosham PO6 ....**158** A4	
Manor Ct Havant PO9 .**135** B1	
Locks Heath PO15 .....**129** B2	
Ringwood BH24 ....**140** C4	
Verwood BH31 ....**114** C4	
Manor Farm Ctry Pk ★	
SO31 ....**105** B2	
Manor Farm Gn SO21 ..**31** C3	
Manor Farm Gr 3 SO50 .**56** C1	
Manor Farm La SO51 ....**6** C1	
Manor Farm Mus ★	
SO30 ....**105** C2	
Manor Farm Rd	
Bournemouth BH10 ....**189** B4	
Fordingbridge SP6 ......**69** B1	
Southampton SO18 ......**79** B1	
Manor Farmyard BH8 .**191** B4	
Manor Flats SO21 ......**31** C3	
Manor Gdns	
Ringwood BH24 ....**140** C4	
Southbourne PO10 ....**137** A2	
1 Verwood BH31 ......**114** C4	
Manor House Ave SO15 **101** C1	
Manor Inf Sch	
Holbury SO45 ....**150** A2	
Portsmouth PO1 ....**182** C4	

Manor La BH31 ....**114** C3	
Manor Lodge Rd PO9 .**113** A1	
Manor Mews PO6 .....**158** B4	
Manor Park Ave PO3 ..**183** A4	
Manor Park Ho 14 SO18 **103** C4	
Manor Pk BH15 ....**202** A3	
Manor Rd	
Bishopstoke SO50 ......**56** C1	
Bournemouth BH1 .....**205** B2	
Chilworth SO16 ....**54** B1	
Christchurch BH23 .....**207** A3	
Durley SO32 ....**82** B4	
East Tytherley SP5 ....**4** C4	
Holbury SO45 ....**150** B2	
Hythe SO45 ....**125** A2	
Milford on Sea SO41 ...**211** B3	
New Milton BH25 .....**195** A2	
North Hayling PO11 ...**184** C3	
Portsmouth PO1 ....**182** C4	
Ringwood BH24 ....**141** A4	
Southbourne PO10 ....**137** B3	
Twyford SO21 ....**31** C3	
Verwood BH31 ....**114** C3	
Manor Rd N SO19 ....**103** C2	
Manor Rd S SO19 ....**103** C2	
Manor Terr	
Bursledon SO31 ....**104** C1	
Durley SO32 ....**82** C4	
Manor Villas PO17 ....**108** A2	
Manor Way	
Lee-on-the-Solent PO13 .**179** C1	
Lee-on-the-Solent PO13 .**179** C2	
South Hayling PO11 ...**185** A1	
Southbourne PO10 ....**137** B3	
Verwood BH31 ....**114** C4	
Manor Wks SO40 .....**101** A4	
Mansard Ct BH13 .....**214** A2	
Mansbridge Prim Sch	
SO18 ....**79** C2	
Mansbridge Rd	
Eastleigh SO50 ....**56** A1	
Southampton SO18 ......**79** C2	
Mansel Cl BH12 ......**204** B4	
Mansel Ct SO16 ....**77** C1	
Mansel Inf Sch SO16 ....**77** B1	
Mansel Jun Sch SO16 ...**77** B1	
Mansel Rd E SO16 .....**77** C1	
Mansel Rd W SO16 ....**77** B1	
Mansell Cl SO45 ......**125** C1	
Mansergh Wlk SO40 ..**100** A4	
Mansfield Ave BH14 ..**203** B2	
Mansfield Cl	
Ferndown BH22 ....**165** B1	
Poole BH14 ....**203** B2	
Mansfield Rd	
Bournemouth BH9 .....**189** C1	
Gosport PO13 ....**180** B4	
Poole BH14 ....**203** B2	
Ringwood BH24 ....**140** C4	
Mansion Ct 2 PO4 ....**182** C1	
Mansion Rd	
Portsmouth PO4 ....**182** C1	
Southampton SO15 ....**102** B3	
Manston Ct SO16 ......**77** C2	
Mansvid Ave PO6 .....**158** A4	
Mantle Cl PO13 ......**180** B4	
Mantle Sq PO2 ......**157** A1	
Manton Cl BH15 ......**201** C1	
Manton Rd BH15 .....**201** C1	
Maple Cl	
Barton on Sea BH25 ...**210** A4	
Bursledon SO31 ....**127** C4	
Christchurch BH23 .....**208** C4	
Emsworth PO10 ....**136** C1	
Fareham PO15 ....**130** B1	
Lee-on-the-Solent PO13 .**179** C1	
Romsey SO51 ....**53** B3	
Maple Cres PO8 ....**88** B3	
Maple Ct SO19 ......**103** C1	
Maple Dr Denmead PO7 **111** A2	
Ferndown BH22 ....**165** B4	
Kings Worthy SO23 ......**2** A4	
Maple Gdns SO40 ....**100** B3	
Maple Ho SO16 ....**78** C4	
Maple Lo BH16 ......**201** B4	
Maple Rd	
Bournemouth BH9 .....**204** C4	
Hythe SO45 ....**150** A4	
Poole BH15 ....**202** B2	
Portsmouth PO5 ....**182** B1	
Southampton SO18 ....**103** C4	
Maple Sq SO50 ....**55** C4	
Maple Wood PO9 .....**135** A1	
Mapleleaf Gdns 1 SO50 .**56** A1	
Maples The SO53 ......**55** B4	
Mapleton Rd SO30 ...**105** B3	
Mapletree Ave PO8 ..**112** B2	
Maplewood Cl SO40 ..**100** B3	
Maplin Rd SO16 ....**77** B1	
Mapperton Cl BH17 ..**187** C1	
Marabout Cl BH23 ....**207** B4	
Maralyn Ave PO7 .....**134** C3	
Marathon Pl SO50 .....**57** A1	
Marazan Rd PO3 ......**158** A1	
Marbream Cl SP6 ....**69** B1	
Marchesi Cl PO14 ....**154** B2	
Marchwood By Pass	
Marchwood SO40 ......**124** C4	
Totton SO40 ....**101** C4	
Marchwood CE Inf Sch	
SO40 ....**124** C4	
Marchwood Ct PO12 ..**180** B2	
Marchwood Ind Pk	
SO40 ....**102** A2	

Marchwood Jun Sch
SO40 . . . . .101 C1
Marchwood Rd
Bournemouth BH10 . . .189 B2
Havant PO9 . . . . .135 C3
Southampton SO15 . . . .102 A3
Totton SO40 . . . . .101 B2
Marchwood Terr SO40 .101 C1
Marcus Cl SO50 . . . . . . .57 A1
Mardale Rd SO16 . . . . . .101 B4
Mardale Wlk SO16 . . . . .101 B4
Marden Paddock SO42 .145 C1
Mardon Cl SO18 . . . . . . .79 C3
Mare La SO21 . . . . .32 C3
Margam Ave SO19 . . . . .103 C3
Margards La BH31 . . . . .114 C3
Margaret Cl PO7 . . . . . .111 B1
Margarita Rd PO15 . . . .130 C1
Margate Rd PO5 . . . . . .215 C2
Margery's Ct [20] PO1 . .182 A3
Marian Cl BH21 . . . . . . .186 B2
Marian Rd BH21 . . . . . . .186 B2
Marianne Cl SO15 . . . . .101 C3
Marianne Rd Poole BH12 204 B4
Wimborne Minst BH21 . .164 A4
Marie Ave SP5 . . . . .46 B4
Marie Cl BH12 . . . . .203 B4
Marie Ct [5] PO7 . . . . . .134 C4
Marie Rd SO19 . . . . . . .104 B3
Marigold Cl PO15 . . . . .130 C1
Marina Bldgs [3] PO12 .181 A2
Marina Cl PO10 . . . . . . .161 A4
Marina Ct
[21] Bournemouth BH5 . . .205 C2
Christchurch BH23 . . . . .209 A4
Marina Dr
Hamble-le-Rice SO31 . . .128 A1
Poole BH14 . . . . .203 A1
Marina Gr
Portchester PO16 . . . . . .156 B3
Portsmouth PO3 . . . . . . .183 A4
Marina Keep PO6 . . . . .157 A3
Marina The BH5 . . . . . . .205 C2
Marina Twrs [24] BH5 . . . .205 C2
Marina View
[6] Christchurch BH23 . . .207 A3
Netley SO31 . . . . .126 C4
Marine Cotts [14] PO12 .181 A3
Marine Ct
Barton on Sea BH25 . . . .209 B4
Portsmouth PO4 . . . . . . .183 A1
Marine Dr BH25 . . . . . . .209 C4
Marine Dr E BH25 . . . . .210 A3
Marine Drive W BH25 . .209 C4
Marine Par SO14 . . . . . .103 A2
Marine Parade E PO13 .179 C1
Marine Parade W PO13 .179 B1
Marine Rd BH6 . . . . .206 B4
Marine Wlk PO11 . . . . . .185 B2
Mariner's Cl SO31 . . . . .128 A2
Mariners Ct
Christchurch BH23 . . . . .208 A3
Lymington SO41 . . . . . . .197 C1
Mariners Mews [7]
SO45 . . . . .126 A2
Mariners Way
Gosport PO12 . . . . .181 B2
Locks Heath SO31 . . . . .128 B1
Mariners Wlk PO4 . . . . .183 A1
Marion Ct BH23 . . . . . . .207 A4
Marion Rd PO4 . . . . .182 C1
Maritime Ave SO40 . . . .102 A2
Maritime Mus★ SO14 . .102 C2
Maritime Way SO14 . . . .103 A1
Maritime Wlk SO14 . . . .103 A1
Marjoram Cres PO8 . . . .112 A2
Mark Anthony Ct PO11 .184 C2
Mark Cl Portsmouth PO3 .157 C2
Southampton SO15 . . . .102 A4
Mark Ct PO7 . . . . .134 C4
Mark Way SO51 . . . . .4 B2
Mark's La PO14 . . . . . . .195 A4
Mark's Rd PO14 . . . . . . .179 C3
Markall Cl SO24 . . . . .14 B3
Marken Cl SO31 . . . . . . .128 C2
Market Bldgs SO16 . . . . .79 B2
Market Cl BH15 . . . . . . .202 B1
Market La SO23 . . . . .11 A4
Market Par PO9 . . . . . . .135 C1
Market Pl
Fordingbridge SP6 . . . . . .69 C1
Ringwood BH24 . . . . . . .140 C4
Romsey SO51 . . . . .52 C4
[10] Southampton SO14 . .103 A2
Market St Eastleigh SO50 .56 A1
Poole BH15 . . . . .202 A1
Winchester SO23 . . . . . . .11 A4
Market Way BH21 . . . . . .163 B2
Marketway PO1 . . . . . . .215 B4
Markham Ave BH10 . . . .189 B4
Markham Cl BH10 . . . . .189 B4
Markham Rd BH9 . . . . . .205 A4
Marks Rd BH9 . . . . .189 C2
Marks Terr SO32 . . . . . . .83 A4
Marks Tey Rd PO14 . . . .154 B4
Markway Cl PO10 . . . . . .136 B1
Marlands Lawn PO9 . . . .135 B3
Marlands The (Sh Ctr)
SO14 . . . . .102 C2
Marlborough Cl PO7 . . .134 C2
Marlborough Ct
[21] Bournemouth BH4 . . .204 B2
Chandler's Ford SO53 . . . .55 A2
Hythe SO45 . . . . .125 C1

Marlborough Ct continued
[7] Poole BH12 . . . . .204 A2
[3] Wimborne Minst BH21 .163 B3
Marlborough Gdns SO30 .81 B2
Marlborough Gr PO16 . .156 B4
Marlborough Ho SO15 .102 C4
Marlborough Mans [2]
BH7 . . . . .206 A3
Marlborough Pk PO9 . .136 B2
Marlborough Pl
Lymington SO41 . . . . . . .197 B3
Wimborne Minst BH21 . .163 B3
Marlborough Rd
Bournemouth BH4 . . . . .204 B2
Chandler's Ford SO53 . . . .30 C1
Gosport PO12 . . . . .180 C3
Poole BH14 . . . . .203 B2
Southampton SO15 . . . .102 A4
Marlborough Row PO1 .182 A3
Marldell Cl PO9 . . . . . . .136 A3
Marler Ho BH4 . . . . .204 A2
Marles Ct PO13 . . . . . . .180 B4
Marley Ave BH25 . . . . . .194 C2
Marley Cl BH25 . . . . . . .194 C2
Marley Mount SO41 . . .171 C1
Marlhill Cl SO18 . . . . . . .79 C1
Marlin Cl PO13 . . . . .180 B3
Marline Rd BH12 . . . . . .203 B3
Marlott Rd BH15 . . . . . .202 B3
Marlow Cl PO15 . . . . . . .130 C2
Marlow Dr BH23 . . . . . .191 C2
Marlow Rd SO32 . . . . . . .83 A4
Marlowe Ct
Southampton SO19 . . . .103 C1
Waterlooville PO7 . . . . . .111 B1
Marlpit Dr BH23 . . . . . .194 A1
Marlpit La BH25 . . . . . . .195 A4
Marls Rd SO30 . . . . .105 C3
Marmion Ave PO5 . . . . .182 B1
Marmion Gn BH23 . . . . .207 C4
Marmion Rd PO5 . . . . . .182 B1
Marne Ho [9] PO14 . . . . .154 C4
Marne Rd SO18 . . . . . . .104 A4
Marnhull Rd BH15 . . . . .202 B2
Marpet Cl BH11 . . . . . . .188 C3
Marples Way PO9 . . . . .135 B1
Marquis Way BH11 . . . .188 B3
Marram Cl SO41 . . . . . . .197 C3
Marrelswood Gdns PO7 134 B2
Marryat Ct
Christchurch BH23 . . . . .209 A4
New Milton BH25 . . . . . .194 C2
Marryat Rd BH25 . . . . . .194 C2
Marsden Rd PO6 . . . . . .157 A4
Marsh Cl PO6 . . . . .158 B3
Marsh Gdns SO30 . . . . . .81 B1
Marsh Ho [20] SO14 . . . .103 A2
Marsh La Breamore SP6 . .70 A4
Christchurch BH23 . . . . .191 C1
Fawley SO45 . . . . .151 A2
Lymington SO41 . . . . . . .197 C3
Southampton SO14 . . . .103 A2
Upton BH16 . . . . .201 A4
Marsh Par [1] SO45 . . . .126 A2
Marsh The SO45 . . . . . . .126 A2
Marshal Rd BH17 . . . . . .187 A1
Marshall Pl [9] SO16 . . . .78 C2
Marshall Rd PO11 . . . . . .185 B1
Marshfield BH21 . . . . . . .163 C4
Marshfield Cl SO40 . . . .101 B1
Marshfield Ho PO6 . . . .158 B4
Marshlands Cl BH23 . . .207 B3
Marshlands Rd PO6 . . . .158 B4
Marshlands Spur PO6 . .158 C4
Marshwood Ave
Poole BH17 . . . . .187 C2
Waterlooville PO7 . . . . . .135 C4
Marston Cl BH25 . . . . . .195 A3
Marston Gate [5] SO23 . .11 A4
Marston Gr BH23 . . . . . .193 C1
Marston La PO3 . . . . . . .158 A2
Marston Rd
New Milton BH25 . . . . . .195 A3
[2] Poole BH15 . . . . .202 A1
Southampton SO19 . . . .104 C3
Martello Cl PO12 . . . . . .180 B2
Martello Ho [10] BH13 . .214 C4
Martello Pk BH13 . . . . . .214 C4
Martello Rd BH13 . . . . . .203 C1
Martello Rd S BH13 . . . .214 C4
Martello Twrs BH13 . . . .214 C4
Martells Ct [1] PO1 . . . . .182 A2
Martells The BH25 . . . . .210 A4
Martin Ave
Denmead PO7 . . . . .111 A2
Stubbington PO14 . . . . . .179 B3
Martin Cl
Broadstone BH17 . . . . . .201 C4
Lee-on-the-Solent PO13 . .179 C2
Swanmore SO32 . . . . .84 A2
Martin Down National Nature
Reserve★ SP5,SP6 . . . . .42 B2
Martin Kemp-Welch Sch The
BH12 . . . . .203 B4
Martin Rd Havant PO9 . .136 A2
Portsmouth PO3 . . . . . . .183 A4
Stubbington PO14 . . . . . .179 B3
Martin St SO32 . . . . .83 A4
Martin's Rd SO42 . . . . . .146 A1
Martindale Ave BH21 . . .164 A3
Martindale Terr SO16 . . .101 C4
Martingale Cl BH16 . . . .201 B4
Martins Cl BH22 . . . . . . .165 C4
Martins Dr BH22 . . . . . . .165 C4
Martins Fields SO21 . . . . .10 B1
Martins Hill Cl BH23 . . .192 B1
Martins Hill La BH23 . . .192 B1
Martins Rise SP5 . . . . . . .24 A2

Martins The SO50 . . . . . .57 B1
Martins Way BH22 . . . . .165 C4
Martley Gdns SO30 . . . . .81 B1
Marvic Ct PO9 . . . . .135 C3
Marvin Cl SO30 . . . . . . .105 C4
Marvin Way
Hedge End SO30 . . . . . . .105 B4
Southampton SO18 . . . .104 B3
Marwell Cl BH7 . . . . .206 A4
Marwell Zoological Pk★
SO21 . . . . .57 C4
Mary La BH22 . . . . .138 B1
Mary Mitchell Cl BH24 .140 C4
Mary Rose★ PO1 . . . . . .181 C3
Mary Rose Cl PO15 . . . .130 C2
Mary Rose St The PO1 .215 B3
Marybridge Cl SO40 . . .100 C3
Marycourt Sch PO12 . . .181 A1
Maryfield SO14 . . . . .103 A2
Maryland Cl SO18 . . . . . .79 C2
Maryland Ct [3] SO41 . . .211 A2
Maryland Gdns SO41 . . .211 A2
Maryland Rd BH16 . . . . .201 B2
Masefield Ave PO6 . . . . .132 C1
Masefield Cl SO50 . . . . . .55 C2
Masefield Cres PO8 . . . .111 C2
Masefield Gr SO19 . . . . .104 B3
Mason Moor Prim Sch
SO16 . . . . .101 C4
Masseys La SO42 . . . . . .175 B4
Masten Cres PO13 . . . . .180 B4
Masters Ct BH4 . . . . . . .204 B2
Masterson Cl BH23 . . . .207 B4
Matapan Rd PO2 . . . . . .157 C2
Matchams Cl BH24 . . . . .167 A4
Matchams La BH23 . . . .167 A4
Matheson Rd SO16 . . . . .78 A3
Matilda Pl [3] SO23 . . . . .11 A4
Matley Gdns SO40 . . . . .100 A4
Matthews Cl PO9 . . . . . .135 B2
Matthews La SO42 . . . . .175 B3
Maturin Cl SO41 . . . . . . .197 B2
Maundeville Cres BH23 .206 B4
Maundville Rd BH23 . . . .206 C4
Maunsell Way SO30 . . . . .81 B1
Maureen Cl BH12 . . . . . .203 A4
Maurepas Way PO7 . . . .134 C4
Mauretania Ho [13] SO14 .103 B3
Mauretania Rd SO16 . . . .77 A2
Maurice Rd
Bournemouth BH8 . . . . .205 B4
Portsmouth PO4 . . . . . . .183 B2
Maury's La SO51 . . . . . . .50 B2
Mavis Cres PO9 . . . . . . .135 C1
Mavis Rd BH9 . . . . .190 A1
Maxstoke Cl PO1 . . . . . .215 C3
Maxwell Rd
Bournemouth BH9 . . . . .205 A4
Broadstone BH18 . . . . . .186 C2
Poole BH13 . . . . .214 C4
Portsmouth PO4 . . . . . . .183 A4
Southampton SO19 . . . .104 A2
May Ave SO41 . . . . .197 B3
May Bush La SO32 . . . . . .85 A1
May Cl SO45 . . . . .150 B2
May Copse SO45 . . . . . .150 B2
May Cres SO45 . . . . .150 B2
May Gdns
Bournemouth BH11 . . . .188 C2
Christchurch BH23 . . . . .194 A1
May La SO41 . . . . .174 A1
May Rd SO15 . . . . .102 B4
May Tree Cl SO22 . . . . . . .10 B2
May's La PO14 . . . . .154 B2
Maybray King Way
SO18 . . . . .104 A4
Maybush Ct [2] SO16 . . . .78 A1
Maybush Rd SO16 . . . . . .77 C1
Maycroft Ct [3] SO15 . . .102 C4
Maydman Sq PO3 . . . . . .183 A3
Mayfair Ct BH4 . . . . .204 B1
Mayfair Ct SO30 . . . . . . .106 A4
Mayfair Gdns
Bournemouth BH11 . . . .189 A2
Southampton SO15 . . . .102 C4
Mayfield PO13 . . . . .179 C1
Mayfield Ave Poole BH14 203 C2
Totton SO40 . . . . .100 C4
Mayfield Cl
Ferndown BH22 . . . . . . .165 B3
Stubbington PO14 . . . . . .154 B2
Mayfield Dr BH22 . . . . . .165 B3
Mayfield Rd
Bournemouth BH9 . . . . .190 A1
Fordingbridge SP6 . . . . . .69 B1
Gosport PO12 . . . . .181 B2
Portsmouth PO2 . . . . . . .157 C1
Southampton SO17 . . . . .79 B2
Mayfield Sch PO2 . . . . .157 C1
Mayfield Way BH22 . . . .165 B3
Mayflower Cl
Chandler's Ford SO53 . . . .55 A3
Lymington SO41 . . . . . . .198 A1
Stubbington PO14 . . . . . .179 B3
Mayflower Ct [14] SO15 .102 C4
Mayflower Dr PO4 . . . . .183 B2
Mayflower Rd SO15 . . . .102 A4
Mayflowers The SO17 . . .79 A4
Mayfly SP6 . . . . .69 C1
Mayford Rd BH12 . . . . . .204 A3
Mayhall Rd PO3 . . . . . . .158 A1
Mayhill La SO32 . . . . .84 C4
Maylands Ave PO4 . . . . .183 A3
Maylands Rd PO9 . . . . . .135 A1
Mayles Cl PO17 . . . . . . .108 A2
Mayles La PO17 . . . . . . .107 C1
Mayles Rd PO4 . . . . .183 A3

Maylings Farm Rd PO16 130 C2
Maynard Cl PO13 . . . . . .155 C2
Maynard Pl PO8 . . . . . . .112 A4
Maynard Rd SO40 . . . . .100 C4
Mayo Cl PO1 . . . . .182 B4
Maypole Villas SO50 . . . .56 A4
Mayridge PO14 . . . . .129 B2
Mays Firs SP6 . . . . .47 C1
Maytree Cl Fair Oak SO50 .57 B1
Locks Heath SO31 . . . . .129 A2
Maytree Gdns PO8 . . . . .111 C2
Maytree Inf Sch SO14 . .103 A3
Maytree Rd
Chandler's Ford SO53 . . . .30 B1
[16] Fareham PO16 . . . . .131 A1
Southampton SO19 . . . .104 A3
Waterlooville PO8 . . . . . .111 C2
Mayvale Cl SO40 . . . . . .101 C1
Mayville High Sch PO5 .182 B1
Mc William Rd [2] BH9 . .190 A1
McIntyre Rd BH23 . . . . .191 A4
McKinley Rd BH4 . . . . . .204 B4
McWilliam Cl PO12 . . . .204 B4
Meacher Cl SO40 . . . . . .100 C4
Mead Cl
Broadstone BH18 . . . . . .187 B3
Romsey SO51 . . . . .53 A4
Mead Cres SO18 . . . . . . .79 B2
Mead Ct
Chandler's Ford SO53 . . . .55 B3
Southampton SO16 . . . . .78 A2
Mead End Rd
Denmead PO7 . . . . .111 A2
Sway SO41 . . . . .171 C1
Mead Rd
Chandler's Ford SO53 . . . .55 B3
Lymington SO41 . . . . . . .197 A1
Winchester SO23 . . . . . . .10 C2
Mead The Gosport PO13 .155 A2
Hythe SO45 . . . . .125 C2
Mead Way PO16 . . . . . . .131 A2
Meadbrook Gdns SO53 . .55 B3
Meadcrest Wood SO42 .145 B1
Meadcroft Cl SO31 . . . . .152 B4
Meadend Cl PO9 . . . . . .136 A3
Meadow Ave
Fordingbridge SP6 . . . . . .69 C1
Locks Heath SO31 . . . . .129 A2
Meadow Cl
Bransgore BH23 . . . . . . .193 A4
Burley BH24 . . . . .142 C1
Ferndown BH22 . . . . . . .165 B1
Fordingbridge SP6 . . . . . .69 C1
North Baddesley SO52 . . . .54 A2
North Hayling PO11 . . . .159 C2
Ringwood BH24 . . . . . . .141 A4
Sopley BH23 . . . . .192 A4
Totton SO40 . . . . .100 C3
Waltham Chase SO32 . . . .83 C2
West End SO30 . . . . .80 C1
Meadow Court Cl BH9 . .190 A2
Meadow Croft Cl SO21 . .31 B2
Meadow Ct
[6] Bournemouth BH9 . . .190 A2
[2] Emsworth PO10 . . . . .160 C4
Fordingbridge SP6 . . . . . .69 C1
Whiteparish SP5 . . . . .24 B2
[15] Wimborne Minst BH21 .163 B2
Meadow Edge PO7 . . . .134 A1
Meadow Farm La BH21 .186 B4
Meadow Gdns SO32 . . . .83 C2
Meadow Gr
Chandler's Ford SO53 . . . .55 B2
Verwood BH31 . . . . .115 A3
Meadow La Burton BH23 192 B1
Hamble-le-Rice SO31 . . .128 A1
Meadow Rd
Lymington SO41 . . . . . . .197 B1
New Milton BH25 . . . . . .195 A2
Ringwood BH24 . . . . . . .141 A4
Meadow Rise
Corfe Mullen BH18 . . . . .186 C3
Waterlooville PO8 . . . . . .112 A2
Meadow St PO5 . . . . . . .215 A2
Meadow Terr [12] PO16 .131 A1
Meadow The
Denmead PO7 . . . . .110 C2
Romsey SO51 . . . . .28 A1
Meadow View Rd BH11 .188 C2
Meadow Way
Barton on Sea BH25 . . . .210 A4
Fawley SO45 . . . . .151 A2
Ringwood BH24 . . . . . . .141 A4
Verwood BH31 . . . . .115 A3
Winchester SO22 . . . . . . .10 B2
Meadow Wlk
Gosport PO13 . . . . .155 A3
[1] Liss GU33 . . . . .20 C2
Portsmouth PO1 . . . . . . .215 B4
Meadowbank BH16 . . . . .201 B4
Meadowbank Rd PO15 . .130 B1
Meadowhead Rd SO16 . .78 C2
Meadowland
Christchurch BH23 . . . . .207 C3
Kings Worthy SO23 . . . . . .2 C4
Meadowlands
Havant PO9 . . . . .136 A1
Lymington SO41 . . . . . . .197 B2
Ringwood BH24 . . . . . . .141 A2
Rowland's Castle PO9 . . .113 B2
Meadowlands Jun & Inf Schs
PO8 . . . . .111 C3
Meadowmead Ave
SO15 . . . . .102 A4
Meadows Cl BH16 . . . . . .201 B4
Meadows Dr BH16 . . . . .201 B4

Meadows The
Fareham PO16 . . . . .131 B2
Lyndhurst SO43 . . . . . . .122 A2
Waterlooville PO7 . . . . . .134 B4
Meadowside Cl SO18 . . . .79 C2
Meadowsweet PO7 . . . . .112 A1
Meadowsweet Rd BH17 201 C4
Meadowsweet Way
Cosham PO6 . . . . .133 B1
Fair Oak SO50 . . . . .81 B3
Meads The
North Baddesley SO53 . . . .55 A3
Romsey SO51 . . . . .52 B4
Meadway The BH23 . . . .193 B1
Mears Rd SO50 . . . . .57 B1
Meath Cl PO11 . . . . .185 B1
Medina Cl SO53 . . . . .55 C3
Medina Ct PO13 . . . . . . .179 B2
Medina Ho [10] PO16 . . .155 A4
Medina Prim Sch PO6 . .157 C4
Southampton SO15 . . . . .78 A1
Medina Way BH23 . . . . .208 B3
Medlar Cl Burton BH23 . .192 B1
[8] Hedge End SO30 . . . .105 B3
Medley Pl [18] SO15 . . . .102 A4
Medlicott Way SO32 . . . .84 A2
Medstead Rd PO9 . . . . . .135 C2
Medwall Gr SO19 . . . . . .104 B3
Medway Dr SO53 . . . . . . .55 A4
Medway Rd BH22 . . . . . .166 A3
Meerut Rd SO42 . . . . . . .145 C2
Meeting House La
BH24 . . . . .140 C4
Megan Ct [20] PO6 . . . . .157 C4
Megan Rd SO30 . . . . .80 B1
Meggeson Ave SO18 . . . .80 A1
Melbourne Rd BH23 . . . .191 C1
Melbourne Gdns [6]
SO30 . . . . .105 B3
Melbourne Ho PO1 . . . .215 B3
Melbourne Pl PO5 . . . . .215 B2
Melbourne Rd
Bournemouth BH8 . . . . .205 B3
[5] Hedge End SO30 . . . .105 B3
Melbourne St SO14 . . . .103 A2
Melbury Ave BH12 . . . . .203 C4
Melbury Cl
Ferndown BH22 . . . . . . .165 B2
Lymington SO41 . . . . . . .197 B2
Melbury Ct [19] SO17 . . . .79 A1
Melchet Cl SO51 . . . . . . .25 A1
Melchet Rd SO18 . . . . . .104 B4
Melford Ct BH1 . . . . .205 A2
Melick Cl SO40 . . . . .101 C1
Mellor Cl [4] PO6 . . . . . .157 B4
Mellstock Rd BH15 . . . . .202 B3
Melrose Cl PO4 . . . . .183 A2
Melrose Ct
New Milton SO40 . . . . . .195 B2
Totton SO40 . . . . .76 B1
Melrose Gdns PO12 . . . .180 C4
Melrose Rd SO15 . . . . . . .78 B1
Melton Ct BH13 . . . . . . .203 C2
Melverley Gdns BH21 . . .163 B3
Melville Cl SO16 . . . . .78 B1
Melville Rd
Bournemouth BH9 . . . . .204 C4
Gosport PO12 . . . . .181 A4
Portsmouth PO4 . . . . . . .183 B2
Melvin Jones Ho PO14 . .154 B2
Mendip Cl
New Milton BH25 . . . . . .195 B1
Verwood BH31 . . . . .114 C3
Mendip Ct [4] BH23 . . . .207 C4
Mendip Gdns SO45 . . . .125 B1
Mendip Rd
Southampton SO16 . . . .101 C4
Verwood BH31 . . . . .114 C3
Mendips Rd PO14 . . . . . .154 C4
Mendips Wlk PO14 . . . . .154 B4
Mengham Ave PO11 . . . .185 A1
Mengham Ct PO11 . . . . .185 A2
Mengham Inf Sch PO11 185 A2
Mengham Jun Sch
PO11 . . . . .185 A2
Mengham La PO11 . . . . .185 A2
Mengham Rd PO11 . . . . .185 A2
Menin Ho PO15 . . . . . . .130 B1
Menslands La
Hambledon PO7 . . . . . . .86 A1
Soberton PO7 . . . . .109 C4
Mentone Rd [2] BH14 . . .203 A2
Menzies Cl SO16 . . . . . . .77 C3
Meon Cl Clanfield PO8 . . .88 B2
Gosport PO13 . . . . .155 A1
Petersfield GU32 . . . . . . .40 C2
Romsey SO51 . . . . .53 B4
Meon Cres SO53 . . . . . . .55 B3
Meon Ct SO18 . . . . .104 B4
Meon Gdns SO32 . . . . . . .84 A3
Meon Ho [8] PO6 . . . . . .155 A4
Meon Jun & Inf Schs
PO4 . . . . .183 A2
Meon Rd
Bournemouth BH7 . . . . .206 A4
Portsmouth PO4 . . . . . . .183 A2
Romsey SO51 . . . . .53 B4
Meoncross Sch PO14 . . .154 B2
Meonstoke CE Sch SO32 .61 B2
Meonwara Cres GU32 . . .37 B3
Mercer Way SO51 . . . . . .53 A4
Merchants Pl [17] SO23 . .11 A4
Merchants Wlk [21] SO14 102 C2
Merchistoun Rd PO7 . . .112 B4
Mercury Cl SO16 . . . . . . .77 C2
Mercury Gdns SO31 . . . .128 A3

Mercury Pl PO7 . . . . . . .134 C1
Merdon Ave SO53 . . . . . . .55 B4
Merdon Cl SO53 . . . . .55 B4
Merdon Ct SO53 . . . . .55 B4
Merdon Jun Sch SO53 . .55 B4
Mere Croft PO15 . . . . . . .129 C2
Meredith Cl BH23 . . . . . .207 B4
Meredith Gdns SO40 . . . .100 B3
Meredith Inf Sch PO2 . . .182 C4
Meredith Lodge 7 PO7 .135 A4
Meredith Rd PO2 . . . . . . .157 C2
Meredith Twrs SO19 . . . .104 C2
Meredun Cl SO21 . . . . .30 A4
Merepond La GU34 . . . . . .17 C2
Merganser Cl PO12 . . . . .181 B4
Meriden Cl BH13 . . . . . . .214 C4
Meriden Ct 10 SO23 . . . . . . .2 A1
Meriden Rd PO5 . . . . .215 A2
Meridian Ctr 12 PO9 . . . .135 C1
Meridians The BH23 . . . .206 C3
Merino Way BH22 . . . . . .138 C1
Merlewood Cl BH2 . . . . . .204 C4
Merlewood Ct 19 BH25 . .195 A2
Merley Dr BH23 . . . . .209 A4
Merley Fst Sch BH21 . . . .163 B1
Merley Gdns BH21 . . . . . .163 B1
Merley Ho BH21 . . . . .163 B1
Merley House La BH21 . .163 B1
Merley House Mus ★ . . . .
BH21 . . . . .163 A1
Merley La BH21 . . . . .163 C1
Merley Park Rd
Corfe Mullen BH21 . . . . . .186 C4
Wimborne Minst BH21 . . .163 B1
Merley Ways BH21 . . . . . .163 B1
Merlin Cl
Bishop's Waltham SO32 . .83 A4
Ringwood BH24 . . . . .141 B3
Merlin Dr PO3 . . . . .158 A2
Merlin Gdns
Hedge End SO30 . . . . .105 A4
Portchester PO16 . . . . . . .132 A1
Merlin Lodge SO19 . . . . .103 B2
Merlin Way
Chandler's Ford SO53 . . . .54 C4
Christchurch BH23 . . . . . .208 A3
Mermaid Ct 22 BH5 . . . . .205 C2
Mermaid Rd PO14 . . . . . .154 C3
Mermaid Way SO14 . . . . .103 A1
Merrick Way SO53 . . . . . .55 A4
Merridale Rd SO19 . . . . .103 C3
Merriefield Ave BH18 . . .187 A3
Merriefield Cl BH18 . . . .187 A3
Merriefield Dr BH18 . . . .187 A3
Merrieleas Cl SO53 . . . . .55 B4
Merrieleas Dr SO53 . . . . .55 B4
Merriemeade Cl 2
SO45 . . . . .125 C1
Merriemeade Par 1
SO45 . . . . .125 C1
Merrifield BH21 . . . . .163 C4
Merritown La BH23 . . . . .190 B4
Merritt Ct SO53 . . . . .55 B2
Merrivale Ave BH6 . . . . .206 C4
Merrivale Cl SO45 . . . . . .125 C2
Merrivale Ct PO10 . . . . . .137 B1
Merrivale Rd PO2 . . . . . .157 C2
Merrow Ave BH12 . . . . . .204 A4
Merrow Chase 1 BH13 . .214 C4
Merrow Cl PO16 . . . . .156 A4
Merrow Gdns SO52 . . . . . .54 A3
Merryfield PO14 . . . . . . .129 B2
Merryfield Ave PO9 . . . . .135 B3
Merryfield Cl
Bransgore BH23 . . . . .193 A4
Verwood BH31 . . . . .114 C3
Merryfield Ct BH10 . . . . .189 B2
Merryfield La BH10 . . . . .189 B2
Merryfield Rd GU31 . . . . .41 A2
Merryoak Gn SO19 . . . . . .103 C3
Merryoak Rd SO19 . . . . . .103 C3
Merrytree Cl SO51 . . . . . .50 C2
Merryweather Est 3
BH24 . . . . .141 B4
Mersea Gdns SO19 . . . . .104 A2
Mersham Gdns SO18 . . . .104 A4
Merstone Rd PO13 . . . . . .155 B1
Merthyr Ave PO6 . . . . . . .158 A4
Merton Ave PO16 . . . . . . .156 B3
Merton Cl SP6 . . . . .69 C2
Merton Cres PO16 . . . . . .156 B3
Merton Ct
8 Christchurch BH23 . . . .209 A4
3 Poole BH15 . . . . .202 C2
3 Portsmouth PO5 . . . . . .215 C1
Merton Gr BH24 . . . . .140 C4
Merton Rd
Portsmouth PO5 . . . . .215 C1
Southampton SO17 . . . . . .79 A2
Merville Gdns BH9 . . . . .204 C4
Meryl Rd PO4 . . . . .183 B2
Mesh Pond SP5 . . . . .46 B4
Mesh Rd SO15 . . . . .6 A1
Metcalfe Ave PO14 . . . . .154 B2
Meteor Rd PO10 . . . . .161 A2
Methuen Cl 2 BH8 . . . . . .205 B3
Methuen Rd
Bournemouth BH8 . . . . . .205 A3
Poole BH17 . . . . .187 A1
Portsmouth PO4 . . . . .183 A2
Methuen St SO14 . . . . . . .103 A4
Metuchen Way SO30 . . . .105 B2
Mews Ct SO21 . . . . .31 A1
Mews La SO22 . . . . .10 C1
Mews The
Blackfield SO45 . . . . .177 C4
1 Bournemouth BH2 . . . .204 B2
Chandler's Ford SO53 . . . .55 B2

Mews The *continued*
Gosport PO12 . . . . .181 C2
Havant PO9 . . . . .135 C2
Petersfield GU31 . . . . .41 A2
Rownhams SO16 . . . . .77 C3
Mewsey Ct PO9 . . . . .135 B4
Mey Cl PO7 . . . . .135 A4
Meynell Cl SO50 . . . . .55 C2
Meyrick Cl BH23 . . . . .193 A4
Meyrick Ho 15 PO2 . . . . .157 B1
Meyrick Park Cres BH3 .204 C3
Meyrick Park Mans 5
BH2 . . . . .204 C2
Meyrick Rd
Bournemouth BH1 . . . . . .205 A2
Havant PO9 . . . . .135 B1
Portsmouth PO2 . . . . .157 B1
Micawber Ho 12 PO1 . . . .182 B4
Michael Crook Cl PO9 . . .135 B2
Michael's Way SO45 . . . .125 C2
Michaels Way SO50 . . . . .57 B1
Michelgrove Rd BH5 . . . .205 C2
Michelmersh Cl SO16 . . . .77 C3
Michelmersh Gn BH8 . . . .190 B1
Michigan Way SO14 . . . . .100 A4
Mickleham Cl BH12 . . . . .204 A4
Midanbury Cres SO18 . . . .79 C1
Midanbury Ct 10 SO18 . . .103 C4
Midanbury La SO18 . . . . .103 C4
Midanbury Wlk 1 SO18 .103 C4
Midas Cl PO7 . . . . .134 C2
Middle Brook BH11 . . . . .189 A3
Middle Brook St SO23 . . . .11 A4
Middle Common Rd
SO41 . . . . .197 A3
Middle Cl PO1 . . . . .182 C4
Middle La BH24 . . . . .141 A4
Middle Mdw GU33 . . . . . .21 A2
Middle Mead PO1 . . . . . .154 A4
Middle Park Way PO9 . . .135 B3
Middle Rd
Bournemouth BH10 . . . . . .189 B3
Locks Heath SO31 . . . . . .129 A3
Lymington SO41 . . . . .197 B2
New Milton SO41 . . . . . . .195 C4
North Baddesley SO52 . . . .54 A4
Poole BH15 . . . . .202 C3
Southampton SO19 . . . . . .104 A2
Sway SO41 . . . . .172 A1
Sway, Tiptoe SO41 . . . . . .195 C4
Winchester SO22 . . . . .10 C1
Middle St
Portsmouth PO5 . . . . .215 B1
Southampton SO14 . . . . . .103 A4
Middlebere Cres BH16 . . .201 B2
Middlebridge St SO51 . . . .52 C3
Middlebrook 3 SO32 . . . .83 B4
Middlecroft La PO12 . . . .180 C3
Middlehill Dr BH21 . . . . .164 A3
Middlehill Rd BH21 . . . . .164 A3
Middlesex Rd PO4 . . . . . .183 A2
Middleton Cl
Fareham PO14 . . . . .154 C4
Southampton SO18 . . . . . .80 A1
Middleton Rd
Bournemouth BH9 . . . . . .189 B4
Ringwood BH24 . . . . .141 A4
Middleton Rise P08 . . . . . .88 B2
Middleton Wlk 10 PO14 .154 C4
Midfield Cl PO14 . . . . . . .154 C4
Midhurst Ho PO1 . . . . . . .215 C4
Midland Rd BH9 . . . . .189 C1
Midlands Est SO30 . . . . . .80 B1
Midlington Hill SO32 . . . .85 A4
Midlington Ho SO32 . . . . .85 A4
Midlington Rd SO32 . . . . .85 A4
Midway SO45 . . . . .125 C2
Midway Path BH13 . . . . . .214 B2
Midway Rd PO2 . . . . .157 C3
Midways PO14 . . . . .179 B3
Midwood Ave BH8 . . . . . .190 C1
Milbeck Cl P08 . . . . .112 A2
Milborne Cres BH12 . . . .203 C4
Milbourne Rd BH22 . . . . .165 B3
Milburn Cl 12 BH4 . . . . . .204 B2
Milburn Rd BH4 . . . . .204 A2
Milburns The SO51 . . . . . .27 B4
Milbury Cres SO18 . . . . .104 A3
Milbury Ho PO6 . . . . .133 A1
Mildmay Ct 39 SO23 . . . .11 A4
Mildmay St SO22 . . . . . . .10 B1
Mile End Rd PO2 . . . . . . .182 B4
Milebush Rd PO4 . . . . . . .183 B3
Miles Cl PO11 . . . . .185 B1
Miles La SP5 . . . . .24 B3
Milestone Rd BH15 . . . . .202 B3
Milford Cl Havant PO9 . . .135 B2
West Moors BH22 . . . . . . .138 C1
Milford Cres SO41 . . . . . .211 C2
Milford Ct Gosport PO12 .180 B2
Milford on Sea SO41 . . . . .211 C2
6 Portsmouth PO4 . . . . . .183 A2
Milford Dr BH11 . . . . .188 C3
Milford Gdns SO53 . . . . . .55 C3
Milford Ho SO41 . . . . .211 C3
Milford on Sea Prim Sch
SO41 . . . . .211 C3
Milford Rd
Barton on Sea BH25 . . . . .210 A4
Lymington SO41 . . . . .197 A1
Portsmouth PO1 . . . . .215 C4
Milford Trad Est SO41 . . .211 C2
Military Rd
Fareham PO16 . . . . .131 B1
Gosport PO12 . . . . .181 B1
Gosport, Brockhurst PO13 180 C3
Gosport, Clayhall PO12 . . .181 B1
Portsmouth, Hilsea PO3 . . .157 C1

Military Rd *continued*
Portsmouth, Landport PO1 182 A4
Milkwood Ct SO40 . . . . . .100 B4
Milky Down Back La
BH24 . . . . .141 C4
Mill Cl Denmead PO7 . . . .111 A2
North Hayling PO11 . . . . .159 C1
Nursling SO16 . . . . .77 B3
Mill Ct Fordingbridge SP6 .69 C1
4 Southampton SO17 . . . .79 B1
Mill End Damerham SP6 . . .68 B2
Hermitage PO10 . . . . .161 A4
Mill Gate Ho 19 PO1 . . . .182 A3
Mill Hill SO30 . . . . .106 A3
Mill Hill Cl BH14 . . . . . . .203 A2
Mill House Bsns Ctr
SO19 . . . . .103 B2
Mill House Ctr SO40 . . . .101 A4
Mill House Lodge SO50 . . .56 B2
Mill La Boldre SO41 . . . . .198 C3
Brockbridge SO32 . . . . .61 B1
Brockenhurst SO42 . . . . . .146 A1
Burley BH24 . . . . .143 B2
Christchurch BH23 . . . . . .209 A4
Crouchston SP5 . . . . .22 B4
Droxford SO32 . . . . .61 A1
Durley SO32 . . . . .82 B2
Gosport PO12 . . . . .181 A3
Havant PO9 . . . . .159 C3
Hawkley GU33 . . . . .19 C4
Hermitage PO10 . . . . .137 A1
Hurn BH23 . . . . .191 A3
Kings Worthy SO21 . . . . .2 B3
Lymington SO41 . . . . .197 C2
Minstead SO43 . . . . .98 C1
Nursling SO16 . . . . .76 C2
Petersfield GU32 . . . . .41 A3
Poole BH14 . . . . .203 A2
Portsmouth PO1 . . . . .182 B4
Romsey SO51 . . . . .52 B4
Sherfield English SO51 . . . .25 C1
Southwick PO7 . . . . .133 C2
Steep GU32 . . . . .40 C4
Steep Marsh GU32 . . . . . . .19 C1
Sway SO41 . . . . .196 C4
Titchfield PO15 . . . . .130 A1
Westbourne PO10 . . . . . . .137 A1
Wickham PO17 . . . . .108 A3
Wimborne Minst BH21 . . .163 A3
Mill Mdw SO41 . . . . .211 B3
Mill Pond Rd PO12 . . . . .181 A3
Mill Pond The SO45 . . . . .150 A3
Mill Quay PO10 . . . . .161 A4
Mill Race View SP5 . . . . .46 C4
Mill Rd
Christchurch BH23 . . . . . .207 A4
Denmead PO7 . . . . .111 A2
Fareham PO16 . . . . .155 A4
Gosport PO12 . . . . .181 A3
Liss GU33 . . . . .21 A3
Southampton SO15 . . . . . .102 A4
Totton SO40 . . . . .101 A4
Waterlooville PO7 . . . . . . .134 C3
Westbourne PO10 . . . . . . .137 A2
Mill Rd N BH8 . . . . .190 B2
Mill Rd S BH8 . . . . .190 B1
Mill Rise SO51 . . . . .5 B1
Mill Rythe Inf Sch PO11 185 A3
Mill Rythe Jun Sch
PO11 . . . . .185 A3
Mill Rythe La PO11 . . . . .185 A4
Mill St Broadstone BH21 . .162 A1
Eastleigh SO50 . . . . .56 A2
Titchfield PO14 . . . . .154 A4
Mill Way SO40 . . . . .100 C3
Millais Rd SO19 . . . . .103 C3
Milland Rd SO23 . . . . .11 A3
Millbank Ho
14 Southampton SO14 . . .103 A3
5 Wimborne Minst BH21 .163 B3
Millbank St SO14 . . . . . . .103 B3
Millbridge Gdns SO19 . . .104 A2
Millbrook Cl
Chandler's Ford SO53 . . . .55 A3
Liss GU33 . . . . .21 A2
Millbrook Com Sch SO16 77 C2
Millbrook Dr PO9 . . . . . . .136 A3
Millbrook Flyover SO15 . .101 C4
Millbrook Point Rd
SO15 . . . . .102 A3
Millbrook Rd E SO15 . . . .102 B3
Millbrook Rd W SO15 . . .102 A3
Millbrook Sta SO15 . . . . .102 A3
Millbrook Trad Est
SO15 . . . . .101 B4
Millcourt 6 SO50 . . . . .57 B1
Millennium Ct 1 PO7 . . . .134 C3
Miller Cl BH25 . . . . .195 B2
Miller Dr PO16 . . . . .130 C3
Miller Rd BH23 . . . . .207 B4
Miller's Pond Gdns
SO19 . . . . .103 C2
Millers La SO22 . . . . .9 C2
Millers Quay Ho 2
PO16 . . . . .155 A4
Millers Way SO45 . . . . . . .125 C1
Millfield
Broadstone BH17 . . . . . . .202 A2
New Milton BH25 . . . . . . .194 C2
Millhams Cl BH10 . . . . . .189 A3
Millhams Dr BH10 . . . . . .189 A3
Millhams Rd BH10 . . . . . .189 A3
Millhams St BH23 . . . . . .207 A3
Millhams St N BH23 . . . .207 A3
Milliken Cl SO45 . . . . .150 C1
Mills Rd PO2 . . . . .157 B1
Mills The PO12 . . . . .203 C4

Millstream Cl
Broadstone BH17 . . . . . . .202 A2
Wimborne Minst BH21 . . .163 B2
Millstream Rise SO51 . . . .52 B1
Millstream Trad Est
BH24 . . . . .141 A3
Millverton Ct 3 SO18 . . . .104 A3
Millvina Cl SO40 . . . . .99 C2
Millway SO32 . . . . .82 A3
Millyford SO25 . . . . .209 B4
Milman Ct 11 SO23 . . . . . .11 A4
Milne Cl SO45 . . . . .125 B1
Milne Rd BH17 . . . . .187 A1
Milner Cl SO15 . . . . .102 B4
Milner Pl SO22 . . . . .10 C3
Milner Rd BH4 . . . . .204 B1
Milnthorpe La SO22 . . . . .10 C4
Milton Cl BH14 . . . . .203 B2
Milton Ct Ferndown BH22 165 B3
3 Portsmouth PO4 . . . . . .183 A3
Milton Gr
Locks Heath SO31 . . . . . . .129 A1
New Milton SO41 . . . . . . .195 A1
Milton Mead BH25 . . . . . .194 C1
Milton Par PO7 . . . . .111 C1
Milton Park Ave 3 PO4 .183 A2
Milton Park Jun & Inf Schs
PO4 . . . . .183 A2
Milton Rd
Bournemouth BH8 . . . . . .205 A4
Eastleigh SO50 . . . . .56 A4
Poole BH14 . . . . .203 B2
Portsmouth PO3,PO4 . . . .183 A4
Southampton SO15 . . . . . .102 C3
Waterlooville PO7,PO8 . . .111 C1
Wimborne Minst BH21 . . .163 B3
Milton Villas BH8 . . . . . . .205 A3
Miltoncross Sch PO3 . . . .183 A3
Milverton Cl
Christchurch BH23 . . . . . .193 C1
Totton SO40 . . . . .101 A3
Milverton Ho PO5 . . . . . . .215 B2
Milverton Rd
Totton SO40 . . . . .101 A3
Winchester SO22 . . . . .10 C4
Milvil Ct 5 PO13 . . . . .179 C1
Milvil Rd PO13 . . . . .179 C1
Mimosa Ave BH21 . . . . . .187 C4
Mimosa Cl PO15 . . . . .129 C2
Mimosa Dr SO51 . . . . .57 C1
Mincingfield La SO32 . . . .82 B3
Mincingfield Terr SO32 . .82 B3
Minden Ho
Fareham PO14 . . . . .154 C4
Romsey SO51 . . . . .53 A4
Minden Way SO22 . . . . . .10 B3
Minerva Cl PO7 . . . . .134 C1
Minerva Cres PO1 . . . . . .182 A2
Minerva Dr PO12 . . . . . . .181 B4
Minley Ct 35 PO9 . . . . . . .136 A3
Minnitt Rd PO12 . . . . .181 C2
Minstead Ave SO18 . . . . .104 B4
Minstead Cl SO22 . . . . .1 B2
Minstead Ct 4 SO17 . . . . .103 A4
Minstead Rd
Bournemouth BH10 . . . . . .189 B4
Portsmouth PO4 . . . . .183 A2
Minstead Rural Studies Ctr
SO43 . . . . .98 A1
Minster Cl PO15 . . . . .130 B1
Minster Ct 1 SO15 . . . . . .102 B3
Minster 33 SO23 . . . . .11 A4
Minster Pk BH21 . . . . .138 C3
Minster The ★ BH21 . . . . .163 A2
Minster View BH21 . . . . . .163 B3
Minster Way BH16 . . . . . .201 A4
Mint Rd GU33 . . . . .21 A3
Mint The GU31,GU32 . . . .40 C4
Minter's Lepe PO7 . . . . . .134 C2
Mintern Cl SO50 . . . . .56 B2
Minterne Grange BH14 . .214 B4
Minterne Rd
3 Bournemouth BH9 . . . .190 A1
Christchurch BH23 . . . . . .207 C3
Poole BH14 . . . . .214 B4
Minton Mews BH2 . . . . . .204 C3
Mintys Hill SP6 . . . . .68 C4
Mintys Yd 4 BH24 . . . . . .141 A3
Mirror Cl SO31 . . . . .128 C3
Mislingford Rd SO32 . . . .84 B2
Missenden Acres SO30 . . .105 B4
Missenden Pl 5 SO50 . . . .56 A1
Mission La P08 . . . . .112 A2
Mission Rd BH18 . . . . .187 A1
Misslebrook La SO52,
SO16 . . . . .54 B2
Mistletoe Gdns SO31 . . . .128 C3
Mitchell Cl
Barton on Sea BH25 . . . . .210 A4
Locks Heath PO15 . . . . . .129 B3
Mitchell Dr SO50 . . . . .57 B2
Mitchell Point SO31 . . . . .127 C1
Mitchell Rd
Eastleigh SO50 . . . . .56 A1
Ferndown BH21 . . . . .165 A4
Havant PO9 . . . . .135 C2
Poole BH17 . . . . .202 C4
Mitchell Way
Eastleigh SO18 . . . . .79 C4
Portsmouth PO3 . . . . .183 A3
Mitchells Cl Redlynch SP5 .47 B3
Romsey SO51 . . . . .52 C4
Mitre Copse SO50 . . . . . . .56 C1
Mitre Ct 13 PO14 . . . . . . .154 C4
Mizen Ho PO6 . . . . .157 A4
Mizen Way PO13 . . . . .180 B2
Mizoah Villas SO32 . . . . .83 C2
Moat Cl SO45 . . . . .150 A2

Moat Ct
Bournemouth BH4 . . . . . .204 B3
Gosport PO12 . . . . .180 B2
Moat Dr PO12 . . . . .180 B2
Moat Hill SO18 . . . . .79 C2
Moat La BH25 . . . . .209 C4
Moat Wlk PO12 . . . . .180 B2
Mockbeggar La BH24 . . . .117 A4
Moffat Rd BH23 . . . . .207 B4
Moggs Mead GU31 . . . . . . .41 A4
Mole Hill PO7 . . . . .134 C3
Molefields SO41 . . . . .211 C3
Molesworth Rd PO12 . . . .181 B2
Mollison Rise PO15 . . . . . .129 B3
Molyneux Rd BH25 . . . . . .195 B2
Momford Rd SO22 . . . . . . .10 A2
Mon Cres SO18 . . . . .104 B4
Monaco Ct BH9 . . . . .205 A4
Monarch Cl
Locks Heath SO31 . . . . . . .129 A1
5 Waterlooville PO7 . . . . .135 A4
Monarch Way
West End SO30 . . . . .80 C1
Winchester SO22 . . . . .10 B3
Monastery Rd SO18 . . . . .103 C4
Monckton Rd
Gosport PO12 . . . . .181 A1
Portsmouth PO3 . . . . .158 A1
Moneyfield Ave PO3 . . . . .158 A1
Moneyfield La PO3 . . . . . .183 A1
Moneyfly Rd BH31 . . . . . .115 A3
Monk's Hill PO10 . . . . . . .137 A3
Monks Brook Cl SO50 . . . .55 C1
Monks Brook Ind Pk
SO53 . . . . .55 A3
Monks Cl BH22 . . . . .166 A4
Monks Ct 10 SO41 . . . . . .197 C1
Monks Hill PO13 . . . . .179 B2
Monks Orch GU32 . . . . . . .40 C3
Monks Pl SO40 . . . . .100 B3
Monks Rd Netley SO31 . . .127 A3
Winchester SO23 . . . . .2 A1
Monks Way
Bournemouth BH11 . . . . . .188 B3
Eastleigh SO50 . . . . .55 C1
Southampton SO18 . . . . . .79 C2
Stubbington PO14 . . . . . . .179 A2
Monks Wlk SO45 . . . . .149 C4
Monks Wood GU32 . . . . . .40 C3
Monks Wood Cl SO16 . . . .79 A4
Monkshood Cl BH23 . . . . .193 A1
Monkswell Gn BH23 . . . . .207 B3
Monkton Cl BH22 . . . . . . .165 B3
Monkton Cres BH12 . . . . .203 C4
Monkton Ho PO12 . . . . . .181 A1
Monkton La SO40 . . . . . . .100 B3
Monkwood Cl PO9 . . . . . .135 B3
Monkworthy Dr BH24 . . .139 C3
Monmouth Cl
North Baddesley SO53 . . . .55 A3
Verwood BH31 . . . . .115 A2
Monmouth Ct
Lymington SO41 . . . . .197 C2
Ringwood BH24 . . . . .140 C4
Monmouth Dr BH31 . . . . .115 A2
Monmouth Gdns SO40 . . .100 B3
Monmouth Rd PO2 . . . . . .157 B1
Monmouth Sq SO22 . . . . .10 A1
Monnow Gdns SO18 . . . . .80 A1
Monroe Cl PO12 . . . . .180 C2
Mons The 31 SO23 . . . . . .10 C4
Monsal Ave BH22 . . . . . . .165 B4
Montacute Sch BH17 . . . .187 B1
Montacute Way BH21 . . . .187 C4
Montagu Cl PO12 . . . . . . .181 B4
Montagu Pk BH23 . . . . . .209 A4
Montagu Rd BH23 . . . . . .209 A4
Montague Ave SO19 . . . . .104 B2
Montague Cl SO19 . . . . . .104 B2
Montague Ct SO45 . . . . . .149 C4
Montague Gdns GU31 . . . .41 A2
Montague Rd
Bishopstoke SO50 . . . . .56 B2
Bournemouth BH5 . . . . . .206 A2
Portsmouth PO2 . . . . .157 C1
Montague Wallis Ct 31
PO1 . . . . .182 A3
Montana Ct PO7 . . . . .135 A3
Montefiore Ho SO18 . . . . .79 B2
Monterey Dr Havant PO9 136 A2
Hordle SO41 . . . . .195 C2
Locks Heath SO31 . . . . . .129 A1
Montfort Cl SO51 . . . . .53 B4
Montfort Coll SO51 . . . . . .53 B4
Montfort Hts SO51 . . . . . . .53 B4
Montfort Rd SO51 . . . . . . .53 B3
Montgomerie Rd PO5 . . . .215 C2
Montgomery Ave
Bournemouth BH11 . . . . . .189 A2
Totton SO40 . . . . .100 B4
Montgomery Cl SO22 . . . .10 B3
Montgomery Rd
Gosport PO12 . . . . .155 C3
Havant PO9 . . . . .136 A1
Southampton SO18 . . . . . .104 A4
Montgomery Way SO53 . . .55 A2
Montgomery Wlk PO7 . . . .134 B3
Montpelier Cl SO31 . . . . .129 C2
Montrose Ave PO16 . . . . .132 C3
Montrose Cl
Hedge End SO30 . . . . .105 C3
2 Verwood BH31 . . . . . . .114 C3
Montrose Dr BH10 . . . . . .189 A1
Montserrat Rd PO13 . . . . .179 C1
Monument Ct SO14 . . . . .103 A1

Monument La
Boldre SO41 . . . . .198 A3
Southwick PO17 . . . . . . .132 B2
Walderton PO18 . . . . . . .137 C4
Monxton Gn 16 PO9 . . .136 A3
Moody Rd PO14 . . . . . . .179 B3
Moody's Hill SP5 . . . . .3 B1
Moon Cl SO40 . . . . .101 C1
Moonhills La SO42 . . . . .149 A1
Moonrakers BH13 . . . . . .214 C4
Moonrakers Way BH23 .193 C1
Mooncross Ave SO40 . . .100 C2
Moor La SP5 . . . . .48 B4
Moor Pk PO18 . . . . .112 A1
Moor Rd BH18 . . . . .187 A3
Moor View Rd BH25 . . . .202 C4
Moorcroft Ave BH23 . . . .192 B1
Moordown Cl BH9 . . . . . .190 A2
Moordown St John's CE Prim
Sch BH9 . . . . .189 C1
Moore Ave BH11 . . . . . . .189 A2
Moore Cl BH25 . . . . .194 C1
Moore Cres SO31 . . . . . .127 B4
Moore Gdns PO12 . . . . . .180 C2
Moorfield Gr BH9 . . . . . .189 C1
Moorfields Rd BH13 . . . .214 C4
Moorgreen Hospl SO30 . .80 C1
Moorgreen Rd
Havant PO9 . . . . .136 A3
West End SO30 . . . . .80 C1
Moorhaven BH22 . . . . . .165 B3
Moorhead Ct SO14 . . . . .103 B1
Moorhill Gdns SO18 . . . .104 C4
Moorhill Rd Burley BH24 143 A1
West End SO30 . . . . . . .104 B3
Moorhills 14 BH15 . . . . .163 B2
Moorings The
7 Christchurch BH23 . . . .207 A3
Fareham PO16 . . . . .155 A4
Moorings Way PO4 . . . . .183 B3
Moorings Way Inf Sch
PO4 . . . . .183 B3
Moorland Ave BH25 . . . .209 C4
Moorland Cl Hythe SO45 125 B2
Locks Heath SO31 . . . . .129 A2
Moorland Cres BH16 . . . .201 A4
Moorland Gate BH24 . . .141 A3
Moorland Par BH16 . . . .201 A4
Moorland Rd
Bournemouth BH1 . . . . .205 B2
Portsmouth PO1 . . . . . . .182 C3
Moorland Way BH16 . . . .201 A4
Moorlands Cl SO42 . . . . .145 B1
Moorlands Coll BH23 . . .192 A3
Moorlands Cres SO18 . . .104 A4
Moorlands Inf Sch SO18 .80 A1
Moorlands Rd
Swanmore SO32 . . . . . . .84 A4
Verwood BH31 . . . . .114 C4
West Moors BH22 . . . . .138 C2
Moorlands Rise BH22 . . .138 C2
Moorlea 11 BH8 . . . . . . .205 A3
Moors Cl
Colden Common SO21 . . .31 C1
Hurn BH23 . . . . .191 A4
Moors Valley Ctry Park
Visitor Ctr★ BH24 . . . .139 B4
Moors Valley Ctry Pk
St Leonards BH24 . . . . .139 B4
★ Verwood BH24 . . . . . .115 C1
Moors Valley Rly★
BH24 . . . . .115 B1
Moorside Cl BH11 . . . . . .189 A2
Moorside Rd
Bournemouth BH11 . . . .189 A2
Corfe Mullen BH21 . . . . .186 B3
West Moors BH22 . . . . .138 C1
Winchester SO23 . . . . . . .2 B1
Moortown Ave PO6 . . . . .134 B1
Moortown Dr BH24 . . . . .188 A4
Moortown Ho BH24 . . . .141 A3
Moortown La BH24 . . . . .141 B2
Moorvale Rd BH9 . . . . . .190 A1
Moot Cl SP5 . . . . .47 A4
Moot Gdns SP5 . . . . .46 C3
Moot La SP5 . . . . .46 C3
Mopley SO45 . . . . .177 C4
Mopley Cl SO45 . . . . .177 C4
Morant Ct 14 BH25 . . . .195 A2
Morant Rd BH24 . . . . . . .117 A1
Morant Cl PO12 . . . . . . .181 B4
Moray Ct 14 BH25 . . . . .163 A3
Mordaunt Rd SO14 . . . . .103 A4
Morden Ave BH22 . . . . . .165 B2
Morden Rd BH9 . . . . .189 C1
Morecombe Ct 4 PO5 . .215 C2
Moreland Ct PO7 . . . . . . .181 A3
Morelands Ct PO7 . . . . . .134 C2
Morelands Prim Sch
PO7 . . . . .134 C1
Morelands Rd PO7 . . . . .134 C2
Moresby Ct 21 PO16 . . .131 A1
Morestead Rd
Winchester SO21 . . . . . . .11 C2
Winchester SO21 . . . . . . .11 A2
Moreton Rd BH9 . . . . . . .190 A2
Morgan Le Fay Dr SO53 .54 C4
Morgan Rd
Hedge End SO30 . . . . . . .105 B3
Portsmouth PO4 . . . . . . .183 B2
Morgan's La SP5 . . . . . . .42 A1
Morgan's Vale & Woodfall's
Prim Sch SP5 . . . . .47 B4

Morgans Dr PO14 . . . . . .154 B3
Morgans Rise Rd SP5 . . .47 B4
Morgans Vale Rd SP5 . . .47 B3
Moriconium Quay BH15 .201 B1
Morington Ct 8 BH8 . . . .205 A3
Morland Rd SO15 . . . . . . .78 B1
Morley Cl
Bournemouth BH5 . . . . . .206 A3
Burton BH23 . . . . .192 B2
Southampton SO19 . . . . .103 C3
Morley Cres PO8 . . . . . . .112 A2
Morley Dr SO32 . . . . .83 B4
Morley Rd
Bournemouth BH5 . . . . . .206 A3
Portsmouth PO4 . . . . . . .183 A1
Morley Way BH22 . . . . . .165 C2
Morleys La SP5 . . . . .29 B2
Morningside Ave PO16 . .132 C1
Mornington Dr SO22 . . . . .1 B1
Mornish Rd BH13 . . . . . .203 C1
Morpeth Ave SO40 . . . . .100 C4
Morris Cl Gosport PO13 . .155 A3
Hythe SO45 . . . . .125 B2
Morris Rd Poole BH17 . . .202 B4
Southampton SO15 . . . . .102 C3
Morrison Ave PO12 . . . . .203 C3
Morse Ct SO31 . . . . .127 A3
Morshead Cres PO16 . . . .130 C2
Mortimer Cl
Christchurch BH23 . . . . .208 A3
Kings Worthy SO23 . . . . . .2 A1
9 Netley SO31 . . . . .127 A3
Totton SO40 . . . . .76 B1
Mortimer Lawn PO9 . . . .135 B4
Mortimer Rd
Botley SO30 . . . . .106 A3
Bournemouth BH8 . . . . . .190 A1
Cosham PO6 . . . . .133 B1
Southampton SO19 . . . . .103 C2
Mortimer Way SO52 . . . .53 C2
Mortimer's Ind Units
SO51 . . . . .75 C3
Mortimers Dr 10 SO51 . .57 B1
Mortimers La SO32 . . . . .58 A2
Mortimore Rd PO12 . . . .180 C3
Mosaic Cl SO19 . . . . .104 C2
Mosdell Rd PO10 . . . . . . .161 C4
Mosedale Wlk SO16 . . . .101 C4
Moselle Ct SO15 . . . . . . .102 B3
Moss Cl GU33 . . . . .21 A2
Moss Dr SO40 . . . . .101 C1
Moss Rd SO23 . . . . .11 A4
Mossleigh Ave SO16 . . . .77 C3
Mossley Ave BH12 . . . . . .189 A1
Motcombe Rd BH13 . . . .204 A1
Mottisfont Abbey (NT)★
SO51 . . . . .5 C1
Mottisfont Abbey Gdns★
SO51 . . . . .5 C1
Mottisfont Cl SO15 . . . . .102 A3
Mottisfont Rd SO50 . . . . .56 A2
Moulin Ave PO5 . . . . .182 C1
Mound Ct PO12 . . . . .181 A2
Mount Ave BH25 . . . . . . .195 A1
Mount Cl
New Milton BH25 . . . . . .195 A1
Winchester SO22 . . . . . . .1 C2
Mount Dr
Chandler's Ford SO53 . . . .55 C2
Fareham PO15 . . . . .154 A4
Mount Grace Dr BH14 . .214 B4
Mount Heatherbank 30
BH1 . . . . .204 C2
Mount Hospl The SO50 . .56 B3
Mount House Cl 5
SO45 . . . . .126 A3
Mount La SO51 . . . . .25 C4
Mount Pleasant
Christchurch BH23 . . . . .208 A3
Denmead PO7 . . . . .110 C1
Kings Worthy SO23 . . . . . .2 B3
7 Ringwood BH24 . . . . .141 A4
Romsey SO51 . . . . .53 A3
Mount Pleasant Dr BH8 190 C1
Mount Pleasant Ind Pk
SO14 . . . . .103 A4
Mount Pleasant Jun Sch
SO14 . . . . .103 A4
Mount Pleasant La
Lymington SO41 . . . . . . .197 A4
Sway SO41 . . . . .197 A4
Mount Pleasant Rd
Gosport PO12 . . . . .181 A2
Southampton SO14 . . . . .103 A3
Mount Rd
Bournemouth BH11 . . . .189 A2
Poole BH14 . . . . .203 A1
Mount Temple SO51 . . . .53 C4
Mount The Gosport PO13 155 C1
Ringwood BH24 . . . . . . .141 B4
5 Southampton, Bassett
SO16 . . . . .78 C2
9 Southampton, Shirley
SO16 . . . . .78 A1
Mount View SO50 . . . . . .56 A2
Mount View Rd SO22 . . . .10 A2
Mountain Ash Cl SO18 . .104 B4
Mountbatten Ave SO51 . .52 C4
Mountbatten Bsns Ctr
SO15 . . . . .102 B3
Mountbatten Bsns Pk
PO6 . . . . .158 B3
Mountbatten Cl
Christchurch BH23 . . . . .208 A3
Gosport PO13 . . . . .155 B2
Mountbatten Ct
New Milton BH25 . . . . . .194 C2
Winchester SO22 . . . . . . .1 C1

Mountbatten Dr
Ferndown BH22 . . . . .165 B3
Waterlooville PO7 . . . . . .134 B3
Mountbatten Gdns BH8 .190 C1
Mountbatten Pl SO23 . . . .2 B4
Mountbatten Rd
Eastleigh SO50 . . . . .56 A3
Poole BH15 . . . . .204 A1
Totton SO40 . . . . .100 B4
Mountbatten Sch The
SO51 . . . . .53 B3
Mountbatten Sq PO4 . . .183 A1
Mountbatten Way
Portsmouth PO1 . . . . . . .215 A4
Southampton SO15 . . . . .102 B3
Mountfield SO45 . . . . . . .125 C2
Mountjoy Cl BH21 . . . . . .163 C1
Mountview Ave PO16 . . .132 C1
Mountwood Rd PO10 . . .137 B1
Mousehole La
Hythe SO45 . . . . .126 A2
Southampton SO18 . . . . .103 C4
Mousehole Rd PO6 . . . . .132 C1
Mowbray Rd SO19 . . . . .104 A2
Moxhams SP6 . . . . .69 C1
Moyles Court Sch BH24 117 B3
Mt Pleasant Dr BH23 . . .169 B1
Mt Pleasant Rd BH15 . . .202 B2
Muccleshell Cl PO9 . . . . .136 A2
Muddyford Rd SP5 . . . . . .47 B4
Mude Gdns BH23 . . . . . .208 A3
Mudeford BH23 . . . . .207 C3
Mudeford Cty Inf Sch
BH23 . . . . .207 C3
Mudeford Cty Jun Sch
BH23 . . . . .207 C3
Mudeford Green Cl
BH23 . . . . .207 C3
Mudeford La BH23 . . . . .207 C3
Muir Ho SO45 . . . . .125 C1
Muira Est SO14 . . . . .103 B3
Mulberry Ave
Cosham PO6 . . . . .158 A4
Stubbington PO14 . . . . . .179 B3
Mulberry Cl PO12 . . . . . .181 A2
Mulberry Ct 4 BH23 . . . .207 A4
Mulberry Gdns SP6 . . . . .93 C4
Mulberry Gr SO41 . . . . . .211 B4
Mulberry La
Cosham PO6 . . . . .158 A4
Locks Heath SO31 . . . . .128 C3
Mulberry Mews SP6 . . . .93 C4
Mulberry Rd SO40 . . . . .101 C1
Mulberry Wlk SO15 . . . .102 B4
Mullen Cl SO19 . . . . .103 C2
Mullins Cl BH12 . . . . .204 B4
Mullion Cl PO6 . . . . .157 A4
Mumby Rd PO12 . . . . . . .181 B3
Mundays Row PO8 . . . . . .88 B1
Munro Cres SO15 . . . . . .101 C4
Munster Rd Poole BH14 .203 B2
Portsmouth PO2 . . . . . . .157 B1
Murefield Rd PO1 . . . . . .215 C3
Muriel Rd PO7 . . . . .134 C4
Murley Rd BH9 . . . . .205 A4
Murray Cl Fareham PO15 130 C1
Southampton SO19 . . . . .104 C3
Murray Cotts SO32 . . . . .107 B4
Murray Rd PO8 . . . . .112 A3
Murray's La PO1 . . . . . . .181 C3
Murrills Est PO16 . . . . . .156 C4
Mus of Childhood★
BH8 . . . . .205 C4
Mus of Electricity★
BH23 . . . . .207 A4
Muscliffe Prim Sch BH9 .190 B2
Muscliffe Ct 27 PO9 . . . .136 A3
Muscliffe La BH9 . . . . . . .190 A3
Muscliff Rd BH9 . . . . . . .189 C1
Museum of Archaeology★
SO14 . . . . .103 A1
Museum Rd PO1 . . . . . . .182 A2
Mussett Cl SO40 . . . . . . .100 C4
Mustang Ave PO15 . . . . .129 B4
My Lords La PO11 . . . . . .185 A2
Myers Cl SO32 . . . . .84 A3
Myrtle Ave
Portchester PO16 . . . . . .156 B4
Totton SO40 . . . . .100 B3
Myrtle Cl Gosport PO13 . .155 A2
Hordle SO41 . . . . .195 C2
Myrtle Gr PO3 . . . . .183 A4
Myrtle Rd
Bournemouth BH8 . . . . . .205 B3
Southampton SO16 . . . . .78 A2
Myvern Cl SO45 . . . . .150 B2

N

Nada Rd BH23 . . . . .193 B3
Nailsworth Rd PO6 . . . . .133 A1
Nairn Ct BH3 . . . . .204 C4
Nairn Rd
Bournemouth BH3 . . . . .204 C3
Poole BH13 . . . . .214 C4
Naish Ct PO9 . . . . .135 B4
Naish Dr PO12 . . . . .156 A1
Naish Holiday Village★
BH25 . . . . .209 B4
Naish Rd BH25 . . . . .209 C4
Namu Rd BH9 . . . . .189 C1
Nancy Rd PO1 . . . . .215 D3
Nansen Ave BH15 . . . . . .202 B3
Napier Cl PO13 . . . . .180 B3
Napier Cres PO15 . . . . . .130 B1
Napier Rd
Hamworthy BH15 . . . . . .201 B2

Napier Rd continued
Horndean PO8 . . . . .112 B3
Portsmouth PO5 . . . . . . .182 B1
Southampton SO19 . . . . .104 C3
Narrow La
Ringwood BH24 . . . . . . .117 B1
10 Romsey SO51 . . . . . .52 C4
Narvik Rd PO2 . . . . .157 B2
Naseby Cl 5 PO6 . . . . . .133 A1
Naseby Rd BH9 . . . . .190 A1
Nash Cl SO45 . . . . .125 B1
Nash Rd SO45 . . . . .125 B1
Nashe Cl PO15 . . . . .130 B2
Nashe Ho PO15 . . . . .130 B2
Nashe Way PO15 . . . . . .130 B2
Nasmith Cl PO12 . . . . . . .180 B2
Nat Gonella Sq 21 PO12 181 B2
Nathen Gdns BH15 . . . . .201 B1
National Motor Mus The★
SO42 . . . . .148 C1
Nations Hill SO23 . . . . . . .2 B3
Navarac Ct BH14 . . . . . . .203 B2
Navigator's Way SO30 . .105 B4
Navy Rd PO1 . . . . .182 A3
Nea Cl BH23 . . . . .208 B4
Nea Dr BH24 . . . . .116 A3
Nea Rd BH23 . . . . .208 C4
Neacroft Cl BH25 . . . . . .209 B4
Neath Way SO53 . . . . . . .55 A3
Needles Ct 11 SO41 . . . .211 B2
Needles Ho 7 PO16 . . . .155 A4
Needles Point SO41 . . . .211 B2
Neelands Gr PO6 . . . . . . .156 C4
Neighbourhood Ctr
BH17 . . . . .187 C1
Neilson Cl SO53 . . . . .55 B4
Nelson Ave
Portchester PO16 . . . . . .156 A4
Portsmouth PO2 . . . . . . .157 B1
Nelson Cl Holbury SO45 .150 B2
New Milton BH25 . . . . . .194 C2
Romsey SO51 . . . . .52 C4
Nelson Cres PO8 . . . . . . .112 B4
Nelson Ct Fareham PO14 154 C3
12 Hythe SO45 . . . . . . .126 A1
10 Poole BH15 . . . . . . .202 B1
Nelson Ctr The PO3 . . . .158 A1
Nelson Dr BH23 . . . . .207 C3
Nelson Ho PO12 . . . . . . .181 B2
Nelson Ind Pk SO30 . . . . .81 A1
Nelson La PO16 . . . . .132 B1
Nelson Pl SO41 . . . . .197 C2
Nelson Rd
Bishopstoke SO50 . . . . . .56 B2
Bournemouth BH4 . . . . . .204 A2
Gosport PO12 . . . . .181 A2
Poole BH12 . . . . .204 A2
Portsmouth PO5 . . . . . . .215 C1
Southampton SO15 . . . . .102 B3
Winchester SO23 . . . . . . .11 B1
Nelson's Gdns SO30 . . . . .81 B2
Nepean Cl PO12 . . . . . . .181 A1
Neptune Ct
Portsmouth PO1 . . . . . . .182 A2
Southampton SO14 . . . . .77 C2
Neptune Ho 4 PO6 . . . .157 C4
Neptune Rd
Fareham PO15 . . . . .130 B1
Gosport PO14 . . . . .154 C3
Neptune Way SO14 . . . . .103 A1
Nerissa Cl 2 PO7 . . . . . .135 A4
Nerquis Cl SO51 . . . . .53 A4
Nesbitt Cl PO13 . . . . . . .155 A2
Nessus St PO2 . . . . .182 B4
Nest Bsns Pk PO9 . . . . . .136 A2
Nethercliffe Sch SO22 . . .1 C1
Netherfield Cl PO9 . . . . .136 A1
Netherhall Gdns BH4 . . .204 B2
Netherhill La SO32 . . . . .82 A1
Netherton Rd PO12 . . . . .180 C4
Netherwood Pl PO13 . . .163 A3
Netley Abbey Inf Sch
SO31 . . . . .127 A4
Netley Abbey Jun Sch
SO31 . . . . .127 A4
Netley Cl
Chandler's Ford SO53 . . . .55 A2
Poole BH15 . . . . .203 A4
Netley Cliff SO31 . . . . . .127 A3
Netley Court SO31 . . . . . .127 A3
Netley Firs Cl SO19 . . . . .104 C3
Netley Firs Rd SO30 . . . .105 A3
Netley Hill Est SO19 . . . .104 C2
Netley Lodge SO31 . . . . .127 B3
Netley Marsh CE Inf Sch
SO40 . . . . .100 A4
Netley Rd
21 Portsmouth PO5 . . . . .182 B1
Titchfield PO14 . . . . .129 B1
Netley Sta SO31 . . . . . . .127 B3
Netley Terr 20 PO5 . . . . .182 B1
Nettlecombe Ave PO4 . .182 C1
Nettlestone SO31 . . . . . .127 B4
Nettlestone Rd PO4 . . . .183 A1
Nettleton Cl BH17 . . . . . .202 C4
Netton Cl SP5 . . . . .22 A4
Netton St SP5 . . . . .22 A4
Neva Rd SO18 . . . . .103 C4
Neville Ave PO16 . . . . . . .156 B3
Neville Cl PO12 . . . . .181 A2
Neville Gdns PO10 . . . . .136 C2
Neville Lovett Com Sch
PO14 . . . . .154 C4
Neville Rd PO3 . . . . .183 A4
Neville Shute Rd PO3 . . .158 A2
New Borough Rd BH21 .163 B2
New Brighton Rd PO10 .136 C1
New Cliff Ho SO19 . . . .103 C1

New Cliffe Gdns SO30 . .105 A3
New Coll (Univ of
Southampton) SO15 . .102 C2
New Cotts Ashurst SO40 .123 C4
Boldre SO41 . . . . .199 A3
Exbury SO45 . . . . .177 A3
Fareham PO16 . . . . .155 A4
Ferndown BH21 . . . . . . .164 C1
Nursling SO16 . . . . .77 B1
New Ct BH24 . . . . .140 C4
New Cut PO11 . . . . .159 C4
New Down La PO6,PO7 .134 A1
New Fields Bsns Pk
BH17 . . . . .202 B4
New Forest Dr SO42 . . .145 B1
New Forest Ent Ctr
SO40 . . . . .100 C3
New Forest Mus & Visitor
Ctr★ SO43 . . . . .122 A3
New Forest Otter, Owl &
Wildlife Pk★ SO40 . . .123 C4
New Forest Owl Sanctuary★
BH24 . . . . .141 B3
New Forest Reptiliary★
SO43 . . . . .121 A2
New Hall SO23 . . . . .11 A3
New Harbour Rd BH15 .202 A1
New Harbour Rd S
BH15 . . . . .213 A4
New Harbour Rd W
BH15 . . . . .202 A1
New Inn Cotts SO42 . . . .175 B3
East Boldre SO42 . . . . . .175 B3
New Inn Rd SO40 . . . . . . .99 A4
New La Havant PO9 . . . . .136 A2
Milford on Sea SO41 . . . .211 C2
New Milton BH25 . . . . . .194 C3
New Marsh Ho 2 SO45 .126 A2
New Merrifield BH21 . . .163 C4
New Milton Inf Sch
BH25 . . . . .195 A1
New Milton Jun Sch
BH25 . . . . .195 A1
New Milton Sta BH25 . . .195 A2
New Orch BH15 . . . . . . .202 A1
New Par
Bournemouth BH10 . . . .189 C2
Portchester PO16 . . . . . .156 B3
New Park Rd BH6 . . . . .206 B2
New Quay Rd BH15 . . . .202 A1
New Rd Ashurst SO40 . . .100 B1
Bishop's Waltham SO32 . .59 B1
Blackfield SO45 . . . . . . .150 C1
Bournemouth BH10 . . . .189 C2
Clanfield PO8 . . . . .88 B3
Colden Common SO21 . . .31 C1
Fair Oak SO50 . . . . .57 A1
Fareham PO16 . . . . .131 A1
Ferndown BH22 . . . . . . .165 C2
Havant PO9 . . . . .135 C1
Holbury SO45 . . . . .150 B4
Horndean PO8 . . . . .111 C3
Hythe SO45 . . . . .126 A2
Hythe, Hardley SO45 . . . .150 A4
Ibsley BH24 . . . . .117 A4
Landford SP5 . . . . .49 C1
Littleton SO22 . . . . .1 A3
Locks Heath SO31 . . . . .152 C4
Meonstoke SO32 . . . . . . .61 B2
Michelmersh SO51 . . . . . .27 B4
Milford on Sea SO41 . . . .212 A2
Netley SO31 . . . . .127 A3
Poole BH12 . . . . .203 B3
Portsmouth PO2 . . . . . . .182 C4
Ringwood BH24 . . . . . . .141 A2
Rockbourne SP6 . . . . .44 C1
Romsey SO51 . . . . .53 A4
Southampton SO14 . . . . .103 A3
Southbourne PO10 . . . . .161 C4
Swanmore SO32 . . . . . . .84 A3
Swanwick SO31 . . . . . . .128 C3
Westbourne PO10 . . . . . .137 A2
Woodlands BH21 . . . . . .114 A3
New Rd E PO2 . . . . .182 C4
New St Lymington SO41 .197 C2
9 Poole BH15 . . . . .202 A1
Ringwood BH24 . . . . . . .141 A3
New Street Mews SO41 197 C2
New Town PO16 . . . . . . .156 B4
New Valley Rd SO41 . . . .211 B3
Newbarn La PO18 . . . . . .137 C4
Newbarn Rd PO9 . . . . . .135 B2
Newbolt Cl PO8 . . . . .111 C2
Newbolt Rd
13 Cosham PO6 . . . . . . .133 A1
Portchester PO6 . . . . . . .132 C1
Newbridge SO31 . . . . . . .127 B3
Newbridge Jun Sch
PO1 . . . . .182 C4
Newbridge Rd SO40 . . . . .75 A1
Newbridge Way SO41 . . .211 C3
Newbroke Rd PO13 . . . . .180 C4
Newburgh St SO23 . . . . .10 C4
Newbury Cl SO50 . . . . . . .57 A1
Newbury Dr BH10 . . . . . .189 B1
Newbury Pl SO31 . . . . . .128 C1
Newbury Rd SO15 . . . . . .78 B1
Newcombe Rd
Bournemouth BH6 . . . . . .206 C3
Southampton SO15 . . . . .102 C3
West Moors BH22 . . . . .138 B1
Newcome Rd PO1 . . . . . .182 C3
Newcomen Ct 8 PO2 . . .157 B1
Newcomen Rd PO2 . . . . .157 B1
Newcroft Gdns BH23 . . .207 A4
Newenham Rd SO41 . . . .197 C1
Newfield Rd GU33 . . . . . .21 A3

Newfoundland Dr BH15 **202** B1
Newfoundland Drive Rdbt
  BH15 ....**202** B1
Newgate La PO14 .....**155** A2
Newgate Lane Ind Est
  PO14 ....**155** A3
Newland Ave PO12 ....**181** A2
Newlands PO15 ....**130** B1
Newlands Ave SO15 ..**102** B4
Newlands Cl
  Blackfield SO45 ....**150** C1
  Chandler's Ford SO53 ...**54** C3
Newlands Copse SO45 .**150** C1
Newlands Inf Sch SO16 .**77** C1
Newlands Jun Sch SO16 .**77** C1
Newlands La PO7 .....**134** A3
Newlands Manor SO41 .**211** B4
Newlands Rd
  Blackfield SO45 ....**150** C1
  Bournemouth BH7 .....**206** A3
  Christchurch BH23 .....**207** C4
  New Milton BH25 .....**195** A1
  Waterlooville PO7 .....**134** B3
Newlands The ② SO17 ..**79** B1
Newlands Way BH18 ...**186** B2
Newlease Rd PO7 .....**134** C3
Newlyn Way Poole BH12 .**203** C4
  Portsmouth PO6 ......**157** A4
Newlyn Wlk SO51 ....**28** A1
Newman St SO16 ......**102** A4
Newman's La BH22 .....**138** B2
Newmans Cl BH22 .....**138** C3
Newmans Hill PO17 .....**84** B1
Newmarket Cl SO50 .....**81** B4
Newmer Ct ① PO9 ....**135** B3
Newmorton Rd BH9 .....**190** A2
Newney Cl PO2 ....**157** C2
Newnham Ct PO9 ......**136** A3
Newport Cl SO53 ....**55** A2
Newport La SO51 ....**28** B3
Newport Rd PO12 .....**180** C3
Newstead Rd BH6 .....**206** B2
Newton Bglws SP5 ......**24** A2
Newton CE Prim Sch
  PO12 ....**181** B3
Newton Cl
  Stubbington PO14 .....**154** B2
  Whiteparish SP5 ....**24** A2
Newton La Romsey SO51 ..**52** C3
  Whiteparish SP5 ....**24** A2
Newton Morrell BH14 ..**203** B2
Newton Pl PO13 ......**179** C2
Newton Rd
  Barton on Sea BH25 ...**210** A4
  Poole BH13 ....**214** C4
  Southampton SO18 .....**79** C1
  Twyford SO21 ....**32** A4
Newtown Bsns Ctr
  BH12 ....**203** A4
Newtown Ct SO31 .....**128** B1
Newtown La
  Corfe Mullen BH21 ....**186** B4
  Ibsley SP6,BH24 ....**94** B1
  South Hayling PO11 ...**184** C2
  Verwood BH31 ....**115** A3
Newtown Rd
  Eastleigh SO50 ....**56** A2
  Locks Heath SO31 ....**152** B4
  Sherfield English SO51 ..**26** A2
  Southampton SO19 ....**104** A1
  Verwood BH31 ....**115** A3
Newtown Soberton Inf Sch
  PO17 ....**109** B3
Nichol Rd SO53 ....**30** B1
Nicholas Cl BH23 ......**194** A1
Nicholas Cres PO15 ...**130** C1
Nicholas Ct
  ⑩ Lee-on-the-Solent
  PO13 ....**179** C1
  South Hayling PO11 ...**184** C2
Nicholas Gdns BH10 ...**189** B1
Nicholas Rd SO45 .....**177** C4
Nichole Ct BH12 ......**203** A4
Nicholl Pl PO13 ......**155** B1
Nichols Rd SO14 ......**103** A3
Nicholson Cl BH17 .....**202** C4
Nicholson Gdns ① PO1 **215** C3
Nicholson Way PO9 ....**135** C2
Nicholson Wlk SO16 .....**77** B3
Nickel Cl SO23 ....**11** A4
Nickel St ④ PO5 ......**215** A1
Nickleby Gdns SO40 ....**100** A4
Nickleby Ho ⑩ PO1 ...**182** B4
Nickleby Rd PO8 ....**88** A3
Nickson Cl SO53 ....**55** A4
Nightingale Ave SO50 ...**55** B1
Nightingale Cl
  Bursledon SO31 ......**127** C4
  Gosport PO12 ....**180** C3
  Romsey SO51 ....**53** A4
  Rowland's Castle PO9 ..**113** A1
  Verwood BH31 ....**115** A3
  West Wellow SO51 .....**50** B2
  Winchester SO22 ....**10** B3
Nightingale Cres SO32 ..**107** C4
Nightingale Ct SO16 .....**78** A2
Nightingale Dr SO40 ...**100** B4
Nightingale Gr SO15 ...**102** B4
Nightingale Ho SO51 .....**53** A4
Nightingale La BH15 ...**202** B1
Nightingale Mews
  Locks Heath SO31 ....**129** A2
  Netley SO31 ....**127** B3
Nightingale Pk ⑧ PO9 **136** A1
Nightingale Prim Sch
  SO50 ....**55** B1
Nightingale Rd
  Petersfield GU32 ....**40** B1

Nightingale Rd continued
  Portsmouth PO5 ......**182** A1
  Southampton SO15 ....**102** B4
Nightingale Wlk SO31 ..**127** B2
Nightingdale Ct ⑨
  SO15 ....**102** B3
Nightjar Cl
  Broadstone BH17 .....**201** C4
  Waterlooville PO8 ....**112** A3
Nile Rd SO17 ....**79** A1
Nile St PO10 ....**160** C4
Nimrod Dr BH21 ......**180** B3
Nimrod Way BH21 .....**164** C3
Nine Acres GU32 ....**20** A1
Nine Elms La PO17 ....**131** C2
Ninian Cl SO50 ....**57** B1
Ninian Park Rd PO3 ...**158** A1
Niton Cl PO13 ....**155** B1
Noads Cl SO45 ....**125** C1
Noads Way SO45 ......**125** C1
Noadswood Sec Sch
  SO45 ....**125** C1
Nob's Crook SO21 ......**57** A4
Nobbs La PO1 ....**182** A2
Nobes Ave PO13 ......**155** B2
Nobes Cl PO13 ....**155** B1
Noble Cl BH11 ....**188** C1
Noble Rd SO30 ....**105** B3
Noel Cl SO42 ....**146** A1
Noel Rd BH10 ....**189** A1
Noel The BH25 ....**195** B2
Nomansland & Hamptworth
  CE Sch SP5 ....**73** B4
Nook The Eastleigh SO50 ..**56** A3
  Gosport PO13 ....**155** C1
Noon Gdns BH31 .....**115** A3
Noon Hill Dr BH31 ....**115** A3
Noon Hill Rd BH31 ....**115** A3
Norbury Cl SO53 ....**55** A4
Norbury Gdns SO31 ...**127** C1
Norcliffe Cl BH10 .....**189** A2
Norcliffe Rd SO17 .....**103** A4
Norcroft Ct SO15 ....**78** B1
Nordik Gdns SO30 ....**105** A3
Nore Cres PO10 ......**136** B1
Nore Farm Ave PO10 ..**136** B1
Norevil Rd GU32 ....**40** B2
Norfolk Ave BH23 .....**191** C1
Norfolk Cres PO11 ....**184** C1
Norfolk Ct SO53 ....**55** B2
Norfolk Ho ④ PO9 ...**136** A1
Norfolk Mews PO11 ...**184** C1
  Southampton SO15 ...**102** B4
Norfolk St PO5 ....**215** B2
Norgett Way PO16 ....**156** A4
Norham Ave SO16 ......**78** B1
Norham Cl SO16 ....**78** B1
Norland Rd PO4 ......**215** D1
Norlands Dr SO21 ......**31** B2
Norley Cl PO9 ....**135** C3
Norleywood BH23 .....**208** C4
Norleywood Rd SO41 ..**198** C4
Norman Ave BH12 ....**204** A3
Norman Cl PO16 ......**156** B3
Norman Ct ⑥ PO4 ....**182** C1
Norman Gdns
  Hedge End SO30 .....**105** A3
  Poole BH12 ....**204** A3
Norman Ho ⑯ SO14 ..**103** B3
Norman Rd
  Blackfield SO45 ......**177** C4
  Gosport PO12 ....**181** A3
  Portsmouth PO4 .....**182** C2
  South Hayling PO11 ..**185** A1
  Southampton SO15 ...**102** B3
  Winchester SO23 ......**10** C3
Norman Way PO9 .....**135** B1
Normandy Cl
  Rownhams SO16 ......**77** C3
  Sway SO41 ....**172** A1
Normandy Ct
  Locks Heath SO31 ....**128** B1
  Wickham PO17 ....**108** A2
Normandy Dr BH23 ...**207** B4
Normandy Gdns PO12 ..**180** C2
Normandy Ho SO51 .....**53** A4
Normandy La SO41 ....**197** C1
Normandy Rd PO2 ....**157** C2
Normandy Way
  Fordingbridge SP6 .....**69** C1
  Hamworthy BH15 ....**201** B1
  Marchwood SO40 ....**102** A1
Normanhurst Ave BH8 ..**190** C1
Normans SO10 ....**10** C3
Normanton Cl BH23 ...**191** C1
Norris Cl Romsey SO51 ..**28** B1
  St Leonards BH24 ....**139** C2
Norris Gdns Havant PO9 **160** A4
  New Milton BH25 ....**195** A1
Norris Hill SO18 ....**79** C1
Norris Rd PO2 ....**182** C4
Norrish Rd BH12 .....**203** B3
Norset Rd PO15 ......**130** B1
North Ave
  Bournemouth BH10 ...**189** B3
  Portsmouth PO2 .....**157** C3
North Baddesley Inf Sch
  SO52 ....**54** A2
North Baddesley Jun Sch
  SO52 ....**54** A2
North Battery Rd PO2 ..**157** A1
North Bay PO10 ......**161** A2
North Block SO15 ....**102** B3
North Cl Gosport PO12 .**180** C2
  Havant PO9 ....**160** A4
  Lymington SO41 .....**197** C2
  Romsey SO51 ....**28** B1

North Common La
  Landford SP5 ....**49** A3
  Sway SO41 ....**196** C4
North Cres PO11 ......**185** A2
North Cross St PO12 ..**181** B2
North Ct PO1 ....**182** C4
North Dr Littleton SO22 ...**1** A3
  New Milton BH25 ....**170** C1
North East Cl SO19 ...**104** B1
North East Rd SO19 ...**104** A2
North End Ave PO2 ...**157** B1
North End Cl SO53 .....**55** B2
North End Farm Cotts
  SO24 ....**14** B4
North End Gr PO2 ....**157** B1
North End La SP6,BH24 ..**93** B2
North Fields Cotts SO21 ..**32** A4
North Front ⑯ SO14 ..**103** A3
North Greenlands SO41 **197** B1
North Head SO41 .....**211** B3
North Hill PO16 ......**131** A2
North Hill Cl SO22 ......**1** C1
North Hill Ct SO22 ......**1** C1
North La Beaulieu SO42 .**148** C3
  Buriton GU31 ....**65** C3
  Clanfield PO8 ....**88** B4
  East Meon PO8 ....**64** B1
  Nomansland SP5 ......**73** B4
  West Tytherley SP5 .....**4** A4
North Lodge Rd BH14 ..**203** C2
North Millers Dale SO53 ..**55** A4
North Park Bsns Ctr
  PO17 ....**130** B4
North Poulner Rd BH24 **117** A1
North Rd
  Bournemouth BH7 ....**205** C3
  Brockenhurst SO42 ...**146** A1
  Horndean PO8 ....**88** B1
  Hythe SO45 ....**125** C1
  Kings Worthy SO23 .....**2** A4
  Petersfield GU32 ......**40** C2
  Poole BH14 ....**203** B4
  Southampton SO17 ...**103** B4
North Rd E PO17 .....**133** A3
North Rd W PO17 ....**133** A3
North Shore Rd PO11 ..**184** B2
North St Emsworth PO10 **136** C1
  Gosport PO12 ....**181** B2
  Havant PO9 ....**135** C1
  Havant, Bedhampton PO9 **135** A1
  Lymington SO41 .....**197** A1
  Poole BH15 ....**202** B1
  Portsmouth PO1 .....**215** C4
  Portsmouth, Portsea PO1 **182** A3
  Westbourne BH4 .....**137** A2
North Street Arc ⑪
  PO9 ....**135** C1
North Stroud La GU32 ...**39** C2
North Trestle Rd SO45 **151** B3
North View SO22 ......**10** C4
North Wallington PO16 **131** B1
North Walls SO23 ......**11** A4
North Way Gosport PO13 **155** B2
  Havant PO9 ....**135** C1
  Locks Heath SO31 ...**129** C2
North Weirs SO42 ....**145** B1
Northam Bsns Ctr ①
  SO14 ....**103** B3
Northam Mews PO1 ...**215** C3
Northam Prim Sch
  SO14 ....**103** B3
Northam Rd SO14 ....**103** A3
Northam St PO1 ......**215** C4
Northampton La SO45 .**177** C4
Northarbour Rd PO6 ..**157** B4
Northarbour Spur PO6 **157** B4
Northbank Ho PO1 ....**215** C4
Northbourne Ave BH10 **189** B3
Northbourne Cl ⑨
  SO45 ....**126** A1
Northbourne Gdns
  BH10 ....**189** C3
Northbourne Pl ③
  BH10 ....**189** B3
Northbourne Rdbt
  BH10 ....**189** B3
Northbrook Ave SO23 ...**11** B4
Northbrook Cl
  Portsmouth PO1 .....**182** B4
  Winchester SO23 ......**11** B4
Northbrook Ind Est SO16 **78** B1
Northbrook Rd
  Broadstone BH18 ....**187** A1
  Southampton SO14 ...**103** A3
Northbrook Springs
  Vineyard★ SO32 ......**59** A1
Northbrooke Ct ⑪ SO23 ..**11** B4
Northcote Rd
  Bournemouth BH1 ....**205** A2
  Portsmouth PO4 .....**182** C2
  Southampton SO17 ....**79** B1
Northcott Cl PO12 ....**180** C2
Northcroft Rd PO12 ...**180** C3
Northdene Rd SO53 ....**55** B3
Northend La SO32 ......**61** A1

Northern Rd
  Cosham PO6 ....**157** C4
  Fawley SO45 ....**151** C1
Northern Way PO1 ....**181** C4
Northerwood Ave SO43 **121** C3
Northerwood Cl SO52 ...**53** C2
Northerwood Ho SO43 .**121** C3
Northey Rd BH6 ......**206** C3
Northfield Ave PO14 ..**154** C4
Northfield Cl
  Bishop's Waltham SO32 ..**59** A1
  Horndean PO8 ....**88** B1
Northfield Pk PO16 ...**132** A4
Northfield Rd
  Milford on Sea SO41 ..**211** C2
  Ringwood BH24 ......**117** A1
  Southampton SO18 .....**79** C1
Northfields Farm La
  PO17 ....**108** A3
Northgate Ave PO2 ...**182** C4
Northgate Chambers ⑨
  SO23 ....**11** A4
Northlands Cl SO40 ...**100** B4
Northlands Dr SO23 .....**2** C1
Northlands Gdns SO15 **102** C4
Northlands Rd
  Eastleigh SO50 ....**56** A2
  Romsey SO51 ....**53** A4
  Southampton SO15, SO40 **102** C4
  Totton SO40 ....**100** C4
Northleigh Cnr SO18 ...**79** C3
Northleigh La BH21 ...**163** C3
Northmead Dr BH17 ...**201** C4
Northmere Dr BH12 ...**203** C4
Northmere Rd BH12 ...**203** C4
Northmore Cl SO31 ...**129** A3
Northmore Rd SO31 ...**129** A3
Northney La PO11 ....**160** B2
Northney Rd PO11 ....**160** A2
Northolt Gdns SO16 ....**78** A3
Northover BH3 ....**204** C3
Northover La SO41 ...**195** C4
Northover Rd
  Lymington SO41 .....**197** A2
  Portsmouth PO3 .....**183** A4
Northumberland Ct
  BH24 ....**140** C4
Northumberland Rd
  Portsmouth PO1 .....**215** D3
  Southampton SO14 ...**103** A3
Northways PO14 ......**179** B3
Northwood Cl SO16 .....**79** A3
Northwood La PO11 ...**160** A1
Northwood Rd PO2 ....**157** C3
Northwood Sq ⑧ PO16 **131** A1
Nortoft Rd BH8 ......**205** A3
Norton Cl
  Christchurch BH23 ....**207** B4
  Southampton SO19 ...**103** C2
  Southwick PO17 .....**132** C3
  Waterlooville PO7 ...**134** B4
Norton Dr PO16 ......**131** A2
Norton Rd
  Bournemouth BH9 ....**204** C4
  Southwick PO17 .....**132** C3
Norway Cl ③ BH9 ....**189** C1
Norway Rd PO3 ......**158** A2
Norwich Ave BH2 ....**204** B2
Norwich Ave W BH2 ..**204** B2
Norwich Cl SO31 .....**128** C2
Norwich Ct ⑫ BH2 ...**204** C2
Norwich Mans ④ BH2 **204** B2
Norwich Pl PO13 .....**179** C2
Norwich Rd
  Bournemouth BH2 ....**204** C2
  Cosham PO6 ....**133** B1
  Southampton SO18 .....**79** C1
Norwood Pl BH5 .....**206** A3
Norwood Prim Sch SO50 **56** A2
Nottingham Pl PO13 ...**179** C2
Nouale La BH24 ......**141** B4
Novello Gdns PO7 ....**134** C3
Noyce Dr SO50 ....**57** B1
Noyce Gdns BH8 .....**191** A1
Nuffield Hospl BH5 ....**205** C2
Nuffield Ind Est BH17 .**202** B4
Nuffield Rd BH17 .....**202** B4
Nugent Rd BH6 ......**207** A2
Nunns Pk SP5 ....**24** A2
Nuns Rd SO23 ....**2** A1
Nurse's Path SO21 .....**32** A4
Nursery Cl
  Emsworth PO10 ......**136** C2
  Gosport PO13 ....**155** A2
Nursery Field GU33 ....**20** C2
Nursery Gdns
  Chandler's Ford SO53 ...**55** B2
  Romsey SO51 ....**53** A4
  Southampton SO19 ...**104** A3
  Waterlooville PO8 ....**112** A3
  Winchester SO22 ......**10** B4
Nursery Gr SO30 .....**105** B3
Nursery La PO14 .....**179** B3
Nursery Rd
  Bournemouth BH9 ....**190** A2
  Havant PO9 ....**135** B1
  Ringwood BH24 ......**141** A4
  Southampton SO18 .....**79** B1
Nursling CE Prim Sch
  SO16 ....**77** B3
Nursling Cres PO9 ....**136** A3
Nursling Gn BH8 .....**190** B1
Nursling Ind Est SO16 ..**77** A2
Nursling St SO16 ......**77** A3
Nutash PO14 ....**129** B2
Nutbeem Rd SO50 .....**56** A1
Nutbourne Ho PO6 ...**158** B4

Nutbourne Pk PO18 ...**161** C4
Nutbourne Rd
  Cosham PO6 ....**158** B4
  South Hayling PO11 ..**185** C1
Nutburn Rd SO52 ......**54** A3
Nutfield Ct SO16 ......**77** C2
Nutfield Pl PO1 ......**215** C4
Nutfield Rd SO16 ......**77** B3
Nuthatch Cl
  Broadstone BH17 ....**201** C4
  Ferndown BH22 ......**165** A4
  Rowland's Castle PO9 .**113** A1
Nutley Cl BH11 ......**188** C2
Nutley Rd PO9 ....**135** B3
Nutley Way BH11 ....**188** C2
Nutsey Ave SO40 ......**76** B1
Nutsey Cl SO40 ....**76** C2
Nutsey La SO40 ....**76** C1
Nutshalling Ave SO16 ...**77** C3
Nutshalling Cl SO40 .....**76** B1
Nutwick Rd PO9 ......**136** A2
Nutwood Way SO40 .....**76** C1
Nyewood Ave PO16 ...**132** B1
Nyria Way PO12 ......**181** B2

O

O' Jays Ind Pk PO3 ...**158** A1
O'connell Rd SO50 .....**55** C1
Oak Ave BH23 ....**206** B4
Oak Cl Corfe Mullen BH21 **186** B3
  Ferndown BH22 ......**165** C1
  Hythe SO45 ....**125** C1
  Lyndhurst SO43 .....**121** C2
  Southampton SO15 ...**101** B4
  Upham SO32 ....**58** C3
  Waterlooville PO8 ....**111** C1
Oak Coppice Cl SO50 ...**57** A1
Oak Ct Fareham PO15 .**130** B1
  Lymington SO41 .....**197** B1
Oak Dr SO50 ....**57** B1
Oak Gdns SO41 ......**211** B4
Oak Green Way SO18 ..**104** A4
Oak La BH24 ....**141** A4
Oak Lodge ④ PO2 ...**157** B1
Oak Lodge Specl Sch
  SO45 ....**125** B2
Oak Meadow CE Prim Sch
  PO15 ....**130** B3
Oak Mews BH12 ......**203** B3
Oak Park Dr PO9 .....**136** A2
Oak Park Ind Est PO6 .**157** B4
Oak Rd Alderholt SP6 ...**92** C3
  Bishop's Waltham SO32 ..**83** C4
  Bournemouth BH8 ....**205** B3
  Bursledon SO31 .....**127** C4
  Clanfield PO8 ....**88** B3
  Fareham PO15 ......**130** B1
  Hythe SO45 ....**125** C1
  New Milton BH25 ....**195** B4
  Southampton SO19 ...**103** C1
  Upton BH16 ....**201** B3
Oak St PO12 ....**181** B3
Oak Tree Cl SO21 ......**56** C4
Oak Tree Dr
  Emsworth PO10 ......**136** C2
  Liss GU33 ....**21** A2
Oak Tree Gdns SO30 ..**105** A3
Oak Tree Rd SO18 ......**79** C1
Oak Tree Way SO50 .....**56** A3
Oak Vale SO30 ....**80** A2
Oak Wlk SO50 ....**57** B1
Oakapple Gdns PO6 ...**158** C4
Oakbank Rd
  Bishopstoke SO50 ......**56** B2
  Southampton SO19 ...**103** B2
Oakcroft La PO14 .....**154** B3
Oakdale Rd BH15 .....**202** C3
Oakdale South Road Mid Sch
  BH15 ....**202** B3
Oakdene Gosport PO13 .**155** B1
  Totton SO40 ....**100** B4
Oakdene Cl BH21 .....**163** B3
Oakdene Gdns ③ SO31 ..**57** B1
Oakdown Rd PO14 ....**154** B2
Oakenbrow Hythe SO45 .**125** B1
  Sway SO41 ....**172** A1
Oakes The PO14 ......**154** A2
Oakfield Ct ㉜ PO5 ..**215** B1
Oakfield Prim Sch SO40 ..**76** C1
Oakfield Rd Cadnam SO40 **99** A4
  Poole BH15 ....**202** B3
  Totton SO40 ....**100** C4
Oakfields SO50 ....**56** A4
Oakford Ct BH8 ......**190** B2
Oakgrove Gdns SO50 ...**56** C1
Oakgrove Rd SO50 .....**56** C1
Oakham Grange BH22 .**165** C3
Oakhill SO31 ....**105** A1
Oakhill Cl
  Bursledon SO31 .....**105** A1
  Chandler's Ford SO53 ...**55** C3
Oakhill Ct SO53 ....**55** C3
Oakhill Terr SO31 ....**105** A1
Oakhurst Cl Netley SO31 **127** B3
  West Moors BH22 ....**138** C1
Oakhurst Dr PO7 .....**135** A4
Oakhurst Fst Sch BH22 **138** C1
Oakhurst Gdns PO7 ...**134** A1
Oakhurst La BH22 ....**138** C1
Oakhurst Rd
  Southampton SO17 .....**79** A2
  West Moors BH22 ....**138** C1

Oakhurst Way SO31 ....127 B3
Oakland Dr SO40 ....101 C1
Oakland Wlk BH22 ....165 C1
Oaklands
　Chandler's Ford SO53 .....30 A1
　Lymington SO41 ....197 C1
　Waterlooville PO7 ....135 A3
Oaklands Ave SO40 .....100 C4
Oaklands Cl
　Fordingbridge SP6 ....69 C1
　Verwood BH31 ....114 C3
　Winchester SO22 ....10 B3
Oaklands Com Sch SO16 77 C3
Oaklands Gdns PO14 ...129 B1
Oaklands Gr PO8 ......111 C2
Oaklands Ho 9 PO6 ....132 C1
Oaklands RC Comp Sch
　PO7 ....134 C3
Oaklands Rd Havant PO9 136 A1
　Petersfield GU32 ....40 C2
Oaklands The SO53 .....55 B2
Oaklands Way
　Hythe SO45 ....125 B1
　Southampton SO16 ....78 C2
　Titchfield PO14 ....129 B1
Oaklea Cl PO7 ....134 A4
Oakleaf Cl SO40 ....124 C4
Oakleigh Cres SO40 ....100 C3
Oakleigh Dr SP5 ....73 B4
Oakleigh Gdns SO51 .....53 A4
Oakleigh Way BH23 ....208 C4
Oakley Cl SO45 ....150 B2
Oakley Gdns BH16 .....201 A4
Oakley Hill BH21 ......163 B1
Oakley Ho
　Portsmouth PO5 ....215 B1
　11 Southampton, Banister's Pk
　SO15 ....102 C4
　13 Southampton, Shirley
　SO16 ....102 A4
Oakley La BH21 ....163 C1
Oakley Rd Havant PO9 ..135 B3
　Mottisfont SO51 ....5 C2
　Southampton SO16 ......102 A4
　Wimborne Minst BH21 ...163 B1
Oakley Straight BH21 ...163 C1
Oakmead Coll of Tech
　BH11 ....188 C2
Oakmead Gdns BH11 ...188 C2
Oakmead Rd BH17 .....201 C4
Oakmeadow Cl PO10 ...137 A2
Oakmount Ave
　Chandler's Ford SO53 .....55 B2
　Southampton SO17 ....79 A1
　Totton SO40 ....100 C4
Oakmount Dr PO8 ......111 C1
Oakmount Mans SO17 ...78 C1
Oakmount Rd SO53 .....55 C3
Oakridge Rd SO15 .....101 B4
Oaks Coppice PO8 ......112 A3
Oaks Dr BH24 ....139 B2
Oaks Mead BH31 ......115 A3
Oaks The Bursledon SO31 127 C4
　Southampton SO19 ......103 C3
　Verwood BH31 ....114 C4
　Waterlooville PO8 ....112 A1
Oakshott Dr PO9 ....136 A3
Oakthorn Cl PO13 .....180 B3
Oaktree Ct
　Milford on Sea SO41 ....211 B2
　Southampton SO16 ....78 C2
Oaktree Cvn Pk SO30 ...80 B2
Oaktree Par BH23 .....169 A1
Oakum Ho PO3 ....183 A3
Oakville Mans 11 SO15 .102 C4
Oakwood BH3 ....204 C4
Oakwood Ave
　Havant PO9 ....135 A2
　New Milton BH25 ....195 B2
　Otterbourne SO21 ....31 B2
Oakwood Cl
　Bournemouth BH9 ......190 A1
　Chandler's Ford SO53 .....30 A1
　Locks Heath SO31 ......152 B4
　Otterbourne SO21 ....31 B2
　Romsey SO51 ....28 B1
Oakwood Ct
　Chandler's Ford SO53 .....30 B1
　New Milton BH25 ....195 A2
　West End SO30 ....80 C1
Oakwood Ctr The PO9 ..136 A2
Oakwood Dr SO16 ......78 B3
Oakwood Ho SO21 ......31 B2
Oakwood Inf Sch SO16 ...78 A3
Oakwood Jun Sch SO16 ..78 A3
Oakwood Lodge SO21 ...31 B2
Oakwood Rd
　Bournemouth BH9 ......190 A1
　Chandler's Ford SO53 .....55 B4
　Christchurch BH23 .....193 C1
　Portsmouth PO2 ....157 C2
　South Hayling PO11 ....184 C2
Oakwood Way SO31 ....128 A2
Oasis Mews BH16 .....201 A4
Oasis The 12 BH12 ....204 A2
Oates Rd BH9 ....189 C1
Oatfield Gdns SO40 .....76 B1
Oatlands SO51 ....52 C4
Oatlands Cl SO32 ....81 C1
Oatlands Rd SO32 ......81 C1
Oban Rd BH3 ....204 C4
Obelisk Rd SO19 ......103 B1
Obelisk Rd SO19 ......103 C1
Ober Rd SO42 ....145 C2
Oberfield Rd SO42 ....145 B1

Oberland Ct SO41 .....197 B2
Oberon Cl PO7 ....135 A4
Occupation La PO14 ...153 C4
Ocean Ct PO15 ....130 B1
Ocean Ct PO11 ....184 C2
Ocean Hts 28 BH5 ....205 C2
Ocean Pk PO3 ....158 A1
Ocean Ct Gosport PO14 .154 C3
　Southampton SO14 ......103 A1
Ocean Way SO14 ......103 A1
Ockendon Cl PO5 .....215 B2
Ocknell Gr SO45 ....125 B2
Octavia Gdns SO53 .....55 C4
Octavia Hill SO22 ....10 B3
Octavia Rd SO18 ....79 C2
Octavius Ct 5 PO7 ....112 A1
Odell Cl PO16 ....130 C2
Odeon Bldgs 10 PO6 ..157 C4
Odiham Cl
　Chandler's Ford SO53 .....55 A4
　Southampton SO16 ....77 C2
Oelander Cl SO31 .....129 A3
Oglander Rd SO23 ....2 A1
Ogle Rd SO14 ....102 C2
OK Mobile Home Pk
　BH23 ....208 A4
Okeford Rd BH18 .....187 B2
Okement Cl SO18 ....80 A1
Old Agwi Rd SO45 .....151 B3
Old Barn Cl
　Christchurch BH23 .....191 B1
　Ringwood BH24 ....141 B4
Old Barn Cres PO7 ......86 B1
Old Barn Farm Rd BH21 139 A3
Old Barn Gdns PO8 ....113 C3
Old Barn Rd BH23 .....191 B1
Old Bound Rd BH16 ...201 B3
Old Brickyard SP6 ......69 A1
Old Bridge Cl SO31 ....128 A4
Old Bridge House Rd
　SO31 ....128 A4
Old Bridge Rd
　Bournemouth BH6 .....206 B4
　Portsmouth PO4 ....182 C1
Old Canal 5 PO4 .....183 A2
Old Christchurch La 35
　BH1 ....204 C2
Old Christchurch Rd
　Bournemouth BH1,BH2 ..204 C2
　Hordle SO41 ....196 B1
Old Coastguard Rd
　BH13 ....214 A4
Old Comm SO31 ......129 A2
Old Commercial Rd
　PO1 ....182 B4
Old Common Gdns
　SO31 ....129 A2
Old Copse Rd PO9 .....136 A2
Old Cottage Cl SO51 ....50 C2
Old Court Mews BH14 ..203 A2
Old Courts The SO16 ....79 A3
Old Cracknore Cl SO40 .102 A1
Old Cricket Mews SO15 102 C4
Old Farm Cl BH24 .....117 B1
Old Farm Copse SO51 ...50 C2
Old Farm Dr SO18 ......79 C2
Old Farm La
　Stubbington PO14 ......179 B3
　Westbourne PO10 ......137 B3
Old Farm Rd BH15 ....202 C3
Old Farm Way PO6 ....158 C4
Old Farm Wlk SO41 ...197 B2
Old Farmhouse Mews
　SO41 ....197 C3
Old Forge Cl SP6 ....92 C3
Old Forge Ct SO41 ....197 B1
Old Forge Rd BH21 ....164 C3
Old Forge The SO32 ...107 B4
Old Garden Cl SO31 ...129 B1
Old Gdns SO22 ....1 C1
Old Generator Ho The
　BH12 ....204 A3
Old Gosport Rd PO16 ..155 A4
Old Granary The SP5 ...46 C4
Old Ham La BH21 .....164 B2
Old Highway Mews
　BH21 ....163 B2
Old Hillside Rd SO22 .....1 B1
Old Infirmary Ho PO1 ..182 A2
Old Ivy La SO18 ....80 A1
Old Kennels Cl SO22 .....10 A2
Old Kennels La SO22 .....10 A2
Old Kiln Rd BH16 .....201 B3
Old Litten La GU32 ......19 B2
Old London Rd PO2 ....157 C2
Old Lyndhurst Rd SO40 ..98 C4
Old Magazine Cl SO40 ..101 C1
Old Maltings The SO41 .197 B2
Old Manor Cl BH21 ....163 B2
Old Manor Farm PO9 ...135 A1
Old Manor Way PO6 ...158 A4
Old Market Rd BH21 ...186 A4
Old Mill Ho BH24 .....140 C3
Old Mill La
　Hambledon PO8 ....87 B2
　Petersfield GU31 ....41 A3
Old Mill Way SO16 ......78 A1
Old Milton Gn BH25 ...194 C1
Old Milton Rd BH25 ...195 A1
Old Mulberry Cl BH10 ..189 A1
Old Orch BH15 ....202 B1
Old Orchards SO41 ....197 C1
Old Parsonage Ct SO21 ..33 A2
Old Pines Cl BH22 .....165 C2
Old Priory Cl SO31 ....128 A1
Old Priory Rd BH6 ....206 C2

Old Rd Gosport PO12 ...181 B2
　Romsey SO51 ....53 A4
　Southampton SO14 ......103 A1
　Wimborne Minst BH21 ...163 A3
Old Rectory Cl
　Corfe Mullen BH21 .....186 B4
　Westbourne PO10 ......137 A2
Old Rectory Gdns SO21 ...2 B3
Old Rectory La SO21 .....32 A3
Old Rectory Rd PO6 ...158 C4
Old Redbridge Rd SO15 101 B4
Old Reservoir Rd PO6 ..158 B4
Old River PO7 ....110 C2
Old Road The PO6 ....157 C3
Old Romsey Rd SO40 ....98 C4
Old Rope Wlk The BH15 201 C1
Old Ropewalk BH15 ....202 A1
Old Salisbury La SO51 ...27 A1
Old Salisbury Rd SO51 ...75 C4
Old Sandpit La BH16 ...186 A1
Old Sawmill Cl BH31 ..114 B4
Old School Cl
　Ferndown BH22 ....165 B3
　Holbury SO45 ....150 A3
　Netley SO31 ....127 B4
　Poole BH14 ....203 A2
Old School Dr PO11 ...185 A1
Old School Gdns SO30 ...80 C1
Old School Rd SO18 .....20 C2
Old Shamblehurst La
　SO30 ....81 B1
Old Spring La SO32 .....84 A3
Old St PO14 ....154 A2
Old St John's Mews
　BH9 ....189 C2
Old Stacks Gdns BH24 ..141 B3
Old Star Pl 3 PO1 ....182 A3
Old Station App SO23 ...11 A4
Old Swanwick La SO31 .128 B4
Old Timbers PO11 .....184 C2
Old Town Mews 5
　BH15 ....202 B1
Old Turnpike PO16 ....131 A2
Old Turnpike Bsns Pk
　PO16 ....131 A1
Old Van Diemans Rd
　PO7 ....134 B3
Old Vicarage Cl BH10 ..189 C3
Old Vicarage La SO41 ..196 B4
Old Vineries The SP6 ....69 B1
Old Wareham Rd
　Corfe Mullen BH21 .....186 A2
　Poole BH12 ....203 A4
　Cosham PO6 ....157 C4
　Denmead PO7 ....110 C2
　Milford on Sea SO41 ....211 B2
　Southampton SO16 ....79 A3
Old Way SO45 ....125 C1
Old Well Cl The SO19 ..104 B2
Old Winchester Hill La
　Warnford SO32, GU32 ....37 A1
　West Meon GU32 ....37 B1
Old Winchester Hill Nature
　Reserve★ SO32 ....62 B3
Old Winchester Hill Nature
　Trail★ GU32 ....62 B3
Old Wymering La PO6 ..157 C4
Oldbarn Cl SO40 ....76 B1
Oldbury Ct SO16 ....77 B1
Oldbury Ho 6 PO6 ....215 B2
Oldbury Way PO14 ....154 B4
Oldenburg SO31 ....129 A4
Oldgate Gdns 8 PO2 ..157 C2
Oleander Dr SO40 .....100 A4
Olinda St PO1 ....182 C2
Olive Cres PO16 ......156 B3
Olive Ct PO2 ....182 C4
Olive Rd SO16 ....78 A2
Oliver Rd Lymington SO41 196 B4
　Portsmouth PO4 ....183 A2
　Southampton SO18 ....79 B2
Oliver's Battery Cres
　SO22 ....10 A2
Oliver's Battery Gdns
　SO22 ....10 A3
Oliver's Battery Prim Sch
　SO22 ....10 B2
Oliver's Battery Rd N
　SO22 ....10 A3
Oliver's Battery Rd S
　SO22 ....10 A2
Olivers Cl SO40 ....100 A4
Olivers Rd BH21 ......164 B1
Olivers Way BH21 .....164 A3
Olivia Cl 3 PO7 ....112 A1
Olympic Way SO50 ......57 A1
Omdurman Ct 2 SO17 ..79 A1
Omdurman Rd SO17 ....79 A1
Omega Ho PO1 ....215 C3
Omega St PO1 ....215 C3
Onibury Cl SO18 ....80 A1
Onibury Rd SO18 ....80 A1
Onslow Gdns BH21 ....163 B3
Onslow Ho BH21 .....163 B3
Onslow Rd
　Portsmouth PO5 ....182 A1
　Southampton SO14 ......103 A3
Ophir Cl BH8 ....205 B3
Ophir Rd
　Bournemouth BH8 .....205 A3
　Portsmouth PO2 ....157 C2
Oracle Dr PO7 ....134 C2
Orange Gr PO13 ......155 B1
Orange Row PO10 ....160 C4
Oratory Gdns BH13 ....214 C4
Orchard Ave
　Bishopstoke SO50 ....56 C1
　Poole BH14 ....202 C1
Orchard Bglws PO17 ...109 A4
Orchard Cl
　Christchurch BH23 .....207 A3
　Colden Common SO21 ...31 C1

Orchard Cl continued
　Corfe Mullen BH21 .....186 B4
　Edmondsham BH21 ......91 A2
　Fawley SO45 ....151 A2
　Ferndown BH22 ....165 C3
　Fordingbridge SP6 ......69 C1
　Gosport PO12 ....156 A1
　Horndean PO8 ....112 B3
　North Baddesley SO52 ...53 C3
　Ringwood BH24 ....141 A4
　South Hayling PO11 ....184 C1
　Totton SO40 ....100 C3
Orchard Ct Cadnam SO40 .98 C4
　Hedge End SO30 ......105 C4
　10 New Milton BH25 ...195 A2
　Verwood BH31 ....115 A3
Orchard Cvn Pk The
　SO40 ....99 B3
Orchard Gdns SP6 ......69 C1
Orchard Gr
　New Milton BH25 ......195 A1
　Portchester PO16 ......156 A4
　Waterlooville PO8 ......111 C2
Orchard Ho 13 SO14 ..103 A2
Orchard Inf Sch SO45 ..125 C1
Orchard Jun Sch SO45 ..125 C2
Orchard La
　Corfe Mullen BH21 .....186 B4
　Hermitage PO10 ......161 A4
　Romsey SO51 ....52 C4
　Southampton SO14 ......103 A2
Orchard Lea Inf Sch
　PO15 ....130 C2
Orchard Lea Jun Sch
　PO15 ....130 C2
Orchard Leigh 6 BH25 .195 A1
Orchard Mead 5 BH24 ..141 A4
Orchard Mews 2 BH23 .207 A3
Orchard Mount 6 BH24 141 A4
Orchard Pl SO14 ......103 A2
Orchard Rd Fair Oak SO50 57 B1
　Gosport PO12 ....181 B2
　Havant PO9 ....159 C4
　Locks Heath SO31 ......128 C1
　Portsmouth PO4 ....182 C1
　Redlynch SP5 ....47 B3
　South Hayling PO11 ....185 A1
Orchard St BH2 ....204 C2
Orchard The
　Bournemouth BH11 .....188 B3
　Bransgore BH23 ....193 B4
　Chilworth SO16 ....54 C1
　Cosham PO6 ....157 C4
　Denmead PO7 ....110 C2
　Milford on Sea SO41 ....211 B2
　Southampton SO16 ....79 A3
Orchard Way SO45 ....125 C1
Orchard Wlk
　22 Bournemouth BH2 ..204 C2
　Winchester SO22 ....1 B1
Orchardlea SO32 ....84 B2
Orchards Way
　Southampton SO17 ....79 A1
　West End SO30 ....80 B1
Orcheston Rd BH8 ....205 B3
Orchid Way BH23 .....207 B4
Ordnance Ct PO3 ......158 A3
Ordnance Rd
　Gosport PO12 ....181 B2
　Southampton SO15 .....103 A3
Ordnance Row PO1 ....182 A3
Ordnance Way SO40 ...102 A2
Oregon Cl SO19 ......104 A2
Orestes Gate BH23 ....208 A3
Orford Cl BH23 ......191 B2
Orford Ct 17 PO6 ....157 C4
Oriana Way SO16 ......77 A2
Oriel Dr PO14 ....129 A1
Oriel Rd PO2 ....157 B1
Orient Dr SO22 ....1 B2
Orion Cl
　Southampton SO16 ....77 C2
　Stubbington PO14 .....179 B3
Orion Ind Ctr SO18 .....79 C3
Orkney Cl SO16 ....77 C2
Orkney Rd PO6 ....133 C1
Ormesby Dr SO53 ......30 A1
Ormond Cl SO50 ....57 A1
Ormonde Rd BH13 ....204 A1
Ormsby Rd PO5 ......215 B1
Orpen Rd SO19 ....104 B2
Orpine Cl PO15 ....129 C2
Orsmond Cl PO7 .....134 C3
Orwell Cl SO16 ....77 C1
Orwell Cres PO14 .....129 B1
Orwell Rd GU31 ....40 C1
Osborn Cres PO13 ....155 A2
Osborn Ct PO3 ....158 A2
Osborn Mall 6 PO16 ..131 B1
Osborn Rd PO16 ......131 A1
Osborn Sq 5 PO16 ....131 B1
Osborne Rd Netley SO31 .127 B3
　3 Waterlooville PO7 ...135 A4

Osborne Rd continued
　Petersfield GU32 ....40 C2
　Poole BH14 ....203 A2
　Portsmouth PO5 ......182 B1
　Totton SO40 ....101 C1
　Wimborne Minst BH21 ...163 B2
Osborne Rd N SO17 ....79 B1
Osborne Rd S
　Fareham PO16 ....131 A1
　Southampton SO17 .....103 B4
Osborne View Rd PO14 .179 A3
Osbourne Ho 4 BH25 ..195 A2
Osbourne Rd PO12 ....181 B3
Osier Cl PO2 ....157 B2
Osier Rd GU31 ....40 B1
Oslands La SO31 ......128 B4
Oslo Twrs 4 SO19 ....126 C4
Osprey Cl
　Christchurch BH23 .....208 A3
　Cosham PO6 ....158 C4
　Marchwood SO40 ......101 C1
　Southampton SO16 ....78 A3
Osprey Ct PO16 ......155 C4
Osprey Dr PO11 ......185 A2
Osprey Gdns PO13 ....179 C1
Osprey Quay PO10 ....161 A4
Ossemsley Manor Ho
　BH23 ....194 B3
Ossemsley South Dr
　BH25 ....194 C4
Osterley Cl SO30 .....105 C3
Osterly Rd SO19 ......103 C3
Oswald Cl BH9 ....189 C1
Oswald Rd BH9 ....189 C1
Othello Dr PO7 ....113 C3
Otter Cl Bishopstoke SO50 57 A1
　Gosport PO13 ....180 B3
　Upton BH16 ....201 A3
　Verwood BH31 ....115 A3
Otter Rd BH15 ....202 C3
Otterbourne CE Prim Sch
　SO21 ....31 A1
Otterbourne Cres PO9 .135 B3
Otterbourne Hill SO21 ...31 B2
Otterbourne Ho SO21 ....31 A1
Otterbourne House Gdns
　SO21 ....31 A1
Otterbourne Rd SO21 ....31 B3
Otters Wlk BH25 .....195 B3
Ouse Cl SO53 ....55 A4
Outer Circ SO16 ....78 A2
Outlands La SO30 ....106 B4
Outram Rd PO5 ......215 C1
Outwick Cross SP6 .....69 C4
Oval Gdns PO12 ......180 C2
Oval Rd SO51 ....5 A1
Oval The GU33 ....20 C2
Over Links Dr BH14 ...203 B1
Overbrook SO45 ......125 C2
Overbrook Way SO52 ...53 C3
Overbury Rd BH14 ....203 B2
Overcliff Rise SO16 .....78 C2
Overcliffe Mans BH1 ...205 B2
Overcombe Cl BH17 ...187 C1
Overdell Ct 25 SO15 ..102 C4
Overstrand Cres SO41 ..211 B2
Overton Cres PO9 .....135 B3
Overton Rd PO10 .....137 C1
Oviat Cl SO40 ....100 A4
Ovington Ave BH7 ....206 B4
Ovington Ct SO18 .....104 B4
Ovington Gdns BH7 ...206 B4
Ovington Rd SO50 ......56 A1
Owen Cl PO13 ....180 B4
Owen Rd SO50 ....55 C1
Owen St PO4 ....183 A1
Owen's Rd SO22 ....1 C1
Ower La SO45 ....178 C4
Owls Rd
　Bournemouth BH5 .....205 C2
　Verwood BH31 ....115 A3
Owlshotts BH13 ......214 C4
Owlsbury Bottom SO21 .33 A3
Owslebury Gr PO9 ....135 C3
Owslebury Prim Sch
　SO21 ....33 A2
Oxburgh Cl SO50 ......55 C3
Oxenwood Gn 7 PO9 ..135 B3
Oxey Cl BH25 ....195 A1
Oxford Ave
　Bournemouth BH6 .....206 A3
　Southampton SO14 ......103 A3
Oxford Cl PO16 ......131 A1
Oxford La
　Bournemouth BH11 .....189 A3
　Swanmore SO32 ....84 C4
Oxford Rd
　Bournemouth BH1 .....205 A2
　Gosport PO12 ....180 C3
　Portsmouth PO5 ......215 D1
　Southampton SO14 ......103 A4
Oxford St SO14 ....103 A4
Oxford Terr SO41 .....172 A1
Oxlease Cl SO51 ....28 A1
Oxleys Cl PO14 ......154 A4
Oxted Ct 9 PO4 .....183 A3
Oyster Ct PO13 ......179 B2
Oyster Est The PO6 ...158 C3
Oyster Mews
　5 Emsworth PO10 ....160 C4
　13 Portsmouth PO1 ...182 A2
Oyster Quay PO6 .....157 A4
Oyster St PO1 ....182 A2
Ozier Rd SO18 ....80 A1

Pacific Cl SO14 ....103 B1
Packridge La SO51,SO52 ..53 C1
Padbury Cl PO2 ....157 C2
Paddington Cl BH11 ...188 B2
Paddington Gr BH11 ...188 B2
Paddington Rd PO2 ....157 C1
Paddock Cl
　Ferndown BH21 ....165 A3
　St Leonards BH24 ......139 C2
Paddock End PO7 ......110 C2
Paddock Gdns SO41 ...197 B3
Paddock Gr BH31 .....115 A3
Paddock The
　Brockenhurst SO42 ....145 C1
　Eastleigh SO50 ....56 A3
　Fordingbridge SP6 ....94 C3
　Gosport PO12 ....181 A2
　Kings Worthy SO23 ......2 B3
　Stubbington PO14 ....154 B3
　Totton SO40 ....76 B1
Paddock Way GU32 ....40 B1
Paddock Wlk PO6 .....157 A4
Paddocks Cl BH12 ....203 A4
Paddocks The
　Bournemouth BH10 ....189 B2
　Fawley SO45 ....151 A2
Padfield Cl BH6 ....206 C3
Padget Rd BH24 ......117 B3
Padnell Ave PO8 ......112 A1
Padnell Inf Sch PO8 ...112 A2
Padnell Jun Sch PO8 ..112 A2
Padnell Pl PO8 ....112 A1
Padnell Rd PO8 ....112 A2
Padstow Pl PO8 ....93 C4
Padwell Rd SO14 ......103 A4
Padwick Ave PO6 .....158 A4
Padwick Ct PO11 .....184 C2
Paffard Cl PO13 ....180 B4
Page Cl SO45 ....150 A4
Pages La SO42 ....175 B3
Paget Cl BH21 ....164 A4
Paget Rd
　Bournemouth BH11 ....189 A2
　Gosport PO12 ....181 A1
Paget St SO14 ....103 A2
Pagham Cl PO10 ......161 A4
Pagham Gdns PO11 ..185 C1
Paignton Ave PO3 ....183 A4
Paignton Rd SO16 ....77 C1
Paimpol Pl SO51 ......52 C3
Pain's Rd PO5 ....215 C2
Painswick Cl
　Cosham PO6 ....157 B4
　Locks Heath SO31 ....128 C3
Painter Cl PO3 ....158 A2
Painters Field SO23 ....10 C2
Paisley Rd BH6 ....206 B3
Palace Ho ★ SO42 ....148 C1
Palace Mews SO42 ....148 C1
Palace Mews SO32 ....83 B4
Palfrey Rd BH10 ......189 B3
Paling Bsns Pk SO30 ..105 A2
Palk Rd PO9 ....135 B1
Pallant Gdns PO16 ...131 B1
Pallant The PO9 ......135 C1
Pallet Cl SO21 ....56 C4
Pallot Cl SO31 ......104 C1
Palm Ct 16 PO5 ......182 B1
Palm Hall Cl SO23 ....11 B4
Palm Rd SO16 ....78 A2
Palma Ct BH23 ......209 A4
Palmer Pl BH25 ......195 A2
Palmer Rd BH15 ......202 B3
Palmer's Rd PO10 ....136 C1
Palmers Cl SO50 ......57 B1
Palmerston Ave
　Christchurch BH23 ....207 B3
　Fareham PO16 ....131 A1
Palmerston Bsns Pk
　PO14 ....155 A4
Palmerston Cl BH16 ..201 B4
Palmerston Ct 2 SO22,
　SO23 ....10 C1
Palmerston Dr PO14 ...155 A4
Palmerston Mans 28
　PO5 ....182 B1
Palmerston Rd
　Bournemouth BH1 ....205 C3
　Poole BH14 ....203 B2
　Portsmouth PO5 ......182 B1
　South Hayling PO11 ..185 A2
　Southampton SO14 ...103 A2
　Upton BH16 ....201 B4
Palmerston Road Prec 29
　PO5 ....182 B1
Palmerston St SO51 ...52 C4
Palmerston Way PO12 ..180 C2
Palmyra Rd PO12 .....181 A4
Palomino Dr PO15 ....129 A4
Pamphill CE Fst Sch
　BH21 ....162 C3
Pamplyn Cl SO41 .....197 B2
Pan St PO1 ....215 B4
Pangbourne Ave PO6 ..158 A4
Pangbourne Cl SO19 ..104 A2
Pannall Rd PO12 .....181 A4
Panorama Ct 2 PO13 ..179 C1
Panorama Rd BH13 ...214 A2
Pans Cnr BH22 ....165 C2
Pansy Rd SO16 ....79 A2
Pantheon Rd SO53 ....55 C4
Pantiles The SP6 ......69 B1
Panton Cl PO10 ......136 C2
Panwell Rd SO18 .....104 A4
Parade Ct PO2 ....157 C3

Parade The
　Barton on Sea BH25 ...194 C1
　5 Bournemouth BH6 ..206 C2
　Cadnam SO40 ....98 C4
　Gosport PO13 ....155 A2
　New Milton BH25 .....195 B2
　Poole BH17 ....187 A1
　Portsmouth PO1 .....182 A3
Paradise La
　Bishop's Waltham SO32 ..83 C3
　Netley Marsh SO40 ....99 B3
　Portchester PO16 .....131 C1
　Westbourne PO10 ....137 A2
Paradise St
　17 Poole BH15 ....202 A1
　Portsmouth PO1 .....215 B4
Parchment St SO23 ....11 A4
Parchment The PO9 ...135 C1
Pardoe Cl SO30 ......105 B3
Pardys Hill BH21 .....186 B4
Parham Cl BH25 ......194 C2
Parham Dr SO50 ......55 C2
Parham Rd
　Bournemouth BH10 ...189 B1
　Gosport PO12 ....181 B3
Parish Ct SO41 ....197 C2
Parish Rd BH15 ......202 C2
Park Ave
　Bournemouth BH10 ...189 B3
　Lymington SO41 ......197 B2
　Waterlooville PO7 .....134 B2
　Winchester SO23 ......11 A4
Park Cl
　Brockenhurst SO42 ...146 A1
　Burton BH23 ....192 B2
　Gosport PO12 ....180 C3
　Hythe SO45 ....126 A2
　Lyndhurst SO43 ......122 A1
　Marchwood SO40 ....101 B1
　Milford on Sea SO41 ..211 C2
　New Milton BH25 .....195 B3
　Winchester SO23 ......2 A1
Park Com Sch PO9 ....135 B3
Park Cotts PO17 .....108 A2
Park Court Flats 3
　SO15 ....102 B3
Park Cres PO10 ......136 B1
Park Ct
　14 Milford on Sea SO41 ..211 B2
　North Baddesley SO51 ..53 B3
　12 Petersfield GU32 ....40 C2
　Portsmouth PO5 .....215 B1
　1 Winchester SO23 .....2 A1
Park Dr BH31 ....114 C4
Park Farm Ave PO15 ..130 B2
Park Farm Cl PO15 ...130 B2
Park Farm Rd PO7 ....134 B2
Park Gate Bsns Ctr
　SO31 ....129 A3
Park Gate Mews 14
　BH2 ....204 C2
Park Gate Prim Sch
　SO31 ....129 A2
Park Gdns BH23 .....207 C4
Park Glen SO31 ......129 B2
Park Gr PO6 ....157 C2
Park Hill Cl SO45 .....150 B2
Park Ho
　22 Portsmouth PO5 ...182 B1
　Winchester SO23 ......11 A4
Park Homer Dr BH21 ..164 A3
Park Homer Rd BH21 ..163 C3
Park House Farm Way
　PO9 ....135 B3
Park House Prim Sch
　PO9 ....135 B3
Park La Alderholt SP6 ..92 C3
　Beaulieu SO41 ....200 A4
　Bournemouth BH10 ...189 C2
　Cosham PO6 ....158 A4
　Droxford SO32 ....61 A4
　Fareham PO16 ....131 A1
　Havant PO7,PO9 ......135 B4
　Havant PO9 ....135 B2
　Holbury SO45 ....150 A2
　Kings Worthy SO21 .....2 B3
　Marchwood SO40 ....101 B1
　Milford on Sea SO41 ..211 B2
　Otterbourne SO21 ....31 A1
　Rowland's Castle PO10 ..137 B4
　Stubbington PO14 ....154 B2
　Swanmore SO32 ......60 B1
　Twyford SO21 ....32 A3
　Waterlooville PO8 ....112 A1
　Wimborne Minst BH21 ..163 B2
Park Lane Rd BH15 ...202 C1
Park Mans 3 PO6 ....158 A4
Park Par PO9 ....135 C2
Park Pl BH14 ....202 C2
Park Rd
　Barton on Sea BH25 ...194 C1
　Bishop's Waltham SO32 ..83 A4
　Bournemouth BH8 ....205 A3
　Chandler's Ford SO53 ..55 B4
　Denmead PO7 ....110 C3
　Fordingbridge SP6 ....69 C1
　Gosport PO12 ....181 A2
　Lymington SO41 ......197 B2
　Milford on Sea SO41 ..211 C2
　New Milton BH25 .....195 B3
　21 Petersfield GU31 ....40 C1
　Poole BH14 ....202 C2
　Portsmouth PO1 .....182 A3
　South Hayling PO11 ..184 B2
　Southampton SO15 ...102 B3
　Southbourne PO10 ...137 B1
　Waterlooville PO7 ....134 B2
　Winchester SO22,SO23 ..1 C1

Park Rd N PO9 ....135 C1
Park Rd S PO9 ....135 C1
Park Royal 17 PO2 ...157 C2
Park St Gosport PO12 ..181 A3
　Portsmouth PO5 .....215 A2
　Southampton SO15, SO16 ..102 A4
Park Terr 10 PO12 ...181 B2
Park The
　Barton on Sea BH25 ...209 B4
　Droxford SO32 ....61 A1
Park View Botley SO30 ..106 A4
　Compton (Hants) PO1 ..31 C3
　Hedge End SO30 ......105 A4
　Lockerley SO21 ....4 C2
　New Milton BH25 .....195 A1
　Otterbourne SO21 ....31 A1
Park View
　9 Poole BH15 ....202 C2
　Portsmouth PO2 .....157 B2
　Rowland's Castle PO9 ..136 A4
Park View Mews BH25 ..195 A1
Park Villas SO32 ......61 A1
Park Vista GU32 ......38 B1
Park Way Fair Oak SO50 ..57 C1
　Havant PO9 ....135 C1
　West Moors BH22 ....138 C1
Park Wlk Fareham PO15 ..130 B2
　Southampton SO14 ...103 A3
Parker Cl PO12 ......156 A1
Parker Gdns PO7 .....134 B1
Parker Rd BH9 ....204 C4
Parkers Cl BH24 .....117 B1
Parkfield Ho 11 PO6 ..132 C1
Parkland Cl BH31 ....115 B2
Parkland Dr BH25 ....209 C4
Parkland Pl
　New Milton BH25 .....195 A1
　15 Southampton SO17 ..103 A4
Parklands
　Locks Heath SO31 ....129 A2
　6 Southampton SO18 ..79 C1
　Totton SO40 ....101 A4
Parklands Ave PO8 ...112 A3
Parklands Bsns Pk PO7 ..110 C2
Parklands Cl
　Chandler's Ford SO53 ..55 B4
　Gosport PO12 ....181 A3
Parkside
　Christchurch BH23 ....193 B1
　Havant PO9 ....135 B1
　Ringwood BH24 ......141 A3
　Totton SO40 ....100 C3
Parkside Ave SO16 ...101 A4
Parkside Gdns
　Bournemouth BH10 ...189 C1
　Southampton SO1 ......1 B1
Parkside Rd BH14 ....203 B2
Parkside The SO15 ...102 A4
Parkstone Ave
　Poole BH14 ....203 B2
　Portsmouth PO4 .....182 C1
Parkstone Gram Sch
　BH17 ....187 A1
Parkstone Hts
　Poole BH14 ....202 C3
　Poole BH14 ....203 A3
Parkstone Rd BH15 ...202 C2
Parkstone Sta BH14 ..203 A2
Parkview PO4 ....204 C2
Parkville Rd SO16 ....79 B2
Parkway PO15 ....129 C4
Parkway Dr BH8 .....205 C4
Parkway Gdns SO53 ...55 C4
Parkway The
　Gosport PO13 ....155 A1
　Southampton SO16 ....79 A3
Parkwood Cl SO30 ...105 B4
Parkwood Ctr PO7 ...134 C4
Parkwood La 14 BH5 ..206 A3
Parkwood Rd
　Bournemouth BH5 ....206 A2
　Wimborne Minst BH21 ..163 B4
Parley Cl BH22 ......165 C1
Parley Cross BH22 ...189 C4
Parley Fst Sch BH22 ..165 B2
Parley La BH23 ......190 B4
Parley Rd BH9 ....190 A1
Parliament Pl SO22 ....10 B2
Parmiter Dr BH21 ....163 C2
Parmiter Ho 42 SO23 ..11 A4
Parmiter Rd BH21 ....163 C2
Parmiter Way BH21 ..163 C2
Parnell Rd SO50 ......55 C1
Parnholt Rd SO51 ......7 C2
Parr Ho 5 BH14 .....203 A2
Parr Rd PO6 ....157 B4
Parr St BH14 ....203 A2
Parry Cl PO6 ....156 C4
Parry Rd SO19 ....104 B2
Parsonage Barn La
　BH24 ....141 A4
Parsonage Cl
　Fordingbridge SP6 ....69 C1
　Petersfield GU32 ......41 A3
Parsonage Ct 9 BH8 ..205 A3
Parsonage La SO32 ...82 C2
Parsonage Park Dr SP6 ..69 C1
Parsonage Rd
　Bournemouth BH1 ....205 A2
　Southampton SO14 ...103 B3
Parsons Cl PO3 ......157 C2
Partridge Cl
　Christchurch BH23 ....208 A3
　Portchester PO16 ....155 C4
Partridge Down SO22 ..10 C2
Partridge Dr BH14 ...203 B1
Partridge Gdns PO8 ..111 B2
Partridge Gr BH25 ...195 A3
Partridge Hill SP5 .....50 A2

Partridge Rd
　Brockenhurst SO42 ...172 C4
　Hythe SO45 ....125 C1
Partridge Wlk BH14 ...203 A1
Partry Cl SO53 ....55 A4
Pascoe Cl BH14 .....203 A2
Passage La SO31 .....128 A1
Passfield Ave SO50 ....55 C1
Passfield Cl SO50 .....55 C1
Passfield Wlk 40 PO9 ..136 A3
Passingham Wlk PO8 ..112 A2
Pastures The
　Cheriton SO24 ....14 B3
　Denmead PO7 ....110 C2
　Locks Heath PO14 ...129 B2
Pat Bear Cl SO15 ....101 B4
Patchins Rd BH16 ....201 A2
Patchins The BH14 ...214 B4
Pathway Dr PO14 ....154 B4
Paternoster Ho 37 SO23 ..11 A4
Paternoster Row 36
　SO23 ....11 A4
Patricia Cl SO30 ......80 B1
Patricia Dr SO30 .....105 B4
Patrick Howard- Dobson Ct
　6 PO8 ....111 C2
Patrick's Cl GU33 .....21 A2
Patrick's Copse Rd GU33 ..21 A2
Paulet Cl SO18 ....80 A1
Paulet Lecave Ave SO16 ..77 B3
Paulet Pl SO22 ....10 C3
Pauletts La SO40 ......76 A2
Pauls La SO41 ....196 C4
Paulsgrove Ent Ctr PO6 ..157 A4
Paulsgrove Ind Ctr PO6 ..157 A4
Paulsgrove Prim Sch
　PO6 ....157 B4
Paulsgrove Rd PO2 ...182 C4
Paultons Pk ★ SO51 ...75 B3
Pauncefoot Hill SO51 ..52 B3
Pauncefote Rd BH5 ...206 A3
Pauntley Rd BH23 ....207 C3
Pavan Gdns BH10 ....189 B1
Pavilion Cl SO50 ......81 B4
Pavilion Ct 20 SO15 ..102 C4
Pavilion Rd SO30 ....105 B4
Paxton Cl SO30 ......105 B3
Paxton Rd PO14 .....155 A4
Payne Cl PO12 ......138 C3
Payne's La SO50 ......57 B2
Payne's Rd SO15 ....102 B3
Paynes Hay Rd SO51 ..28 C3
Peace Cl BH23 ......193 A4
Peach Rd SO16 ....78 A2
Peacock Cl PO16 ....155 C4
Peacock La PO1 .....182 A2
Peacock Pl 5 SO23 ...11 B4
Peak Cl SO16 ....101 C4
Peak Dr PO14 ....154 B4
Peak La
　Bishop's Waltham SO32 ..59 A2
　Fareham PO14 ....154 B4
Peak Rd PO8 ....88 A3
Peak The PO9 ....113 B1
Peake New Rd SO32 ..61 C4
Peakfield PO7 ....110 C2
Pealsham Gdns SP6 ...69 C1
Pear Cl BH12 ....204 A3
Pear Tree Cl
　Alderholt SP6 ....92 C3
　Botley SO30 ....81 C1
　Bransgore BH23 ......193 A4
Pear Tree Dr SP5 .....73 B4
Pearce Ave BH14 ....203 A1
Pearce Ct PO12 .....181 B3
Pearce Gdns BH14 ...203 A1
Pearce Rd BH16 .....201 A3
Pearce-Smith Cl BH25 ..209 C4
Pearl Gdns BH10 ....189 B1
Pearl Rd BH10 ......189 B2
Pearmain Dr 4 SO41 ..197 C1
Pearman Ct SO41 ...197 B1
Pearson Ave BH14 ...203 A3
Pearson Gdns BH10 ..189 B3
Peartree Ave SO19 ...103 C3
Peartree Cl
　Southampton SO19 ...103 B3
　Stubbington PO14 ....154 B2
　West Wellow SO51 ....50 B2
Peartree Ct
　5 Lymington SO41 ...197 C1
　Southampton SO19 ...103 C3
Peartree Rd Hythe SO45 ..125 C1
　Southampton SO19 ...103 B2
Pebble Cl PO11 .....185 A1
Pebble Ct
　Marchwood SO40 ....101 C1
　South Hayling PO11 ..185 B1
Pebmarsh Rd 8 PO6 ..157 B4
Peckham Ave BH25 ...195 A1
Pedham Cl PO4 ......183 C2
Pedlars Wlk BH24 ....140 C4
Pedula Way SO16 .....56 C3
Peeks Mews BH6 ....206 C3
Peel Cl Poole BH12 ...203 B3
　Romsey SO51 ....28 B1
Peel Common Jun & Inf Schs
　PO13 ....155 A1
Peel Rd PO5 ....215 B2
Peel Rd PO12 ....181 B2
Peel St SO14 ....103 B3
Peewit Hill SO31 .....105 A2
Peewit Hill Cl SO31 ...105 A2
Pegasus Ave SO41 ...196 A4
Pegasus Cl Gosport PO13 ..180 B3
　Hamble-le-Rice SO31 ..127 C1
　Southampton SO16 ....77 C2

Pegasus Ct
　Bournemouth BH1 ....205 A3
　8 New Milton BH25 ...195 A2
Pegasus Lodge BH22 ..165 B3
Peggotty Ho 17 PO1 ..182 B4
Pegham Ind Pk PO15 ..130 A3
Pelham Cl BH23 .....207 B3
Pelham Rd Gosport PO12 ..181 A3
　Portsmouth PO5 .....215 B1
Pelham Terr 2 PO10 ..161 A4
Pelican Cl PO15 ......130 B1
Pelican Ct SO21 ......30 A4
Pelican Mead BH24 ..141 B3
Pelican Rd PO14 .....154 C3
Pembers Cl SO50 .....57 B1
Pemberton Rd SO43 ..122 A3
Pembrey Cl SO16 .....78 A3
Pembridge Rd SP6 ....70 C1
Pembroke Cl
　Eastleigh SO50 ......55 C3
　Portsmouth PO1 .....182 A4
　Romsey SO51 ....52 C4
　Totton SO40 ....101 A4
Pembroke Cres PO14 ..179 A3
Pembroke Ct
　11 Christchurch BH23 ..209 A4
　5 Gosport PO13 ......155 B1
　Southampton SO17 ...79 A1
Pembroke Rd
　Bournemouth BH4 ....204 A1
　Poole BH12 ....203 B4
　Portsmouth PO1 .....182 A2
　Southampton SO19 ...104 A2
Pembury Rd Havant PO9 ..160 A4
　Stubbington PO14 ....154 B2
Pemerton Rd SO22 .....1 B2
Penarth Ave PO6 ....158 A4
Pencraig BH13 ....204 A2
Pendennis Rd PO6 ....132 C1
Pendle Cl SO16 ......101 C4
Pendle Gn SO51 ....4 C1
Pendleton Gdns SO45 ..150 C1
Penelope Ct 18 BH24 ..209 A4
Penelope Gdns SO31 ..104 C1
Penfords Paddock 9
　SO32 ....83 B4
Pengelly Ave BH10 ...189 C3
Penhale Gdns PO14 ..129 A3
Penhale Inf Sch PO1 ..182 C3
Penhale Rd PO1 .....182 C3
Penhale Way SO40 ...100 C3
Penhurst Rd PO9 .....135 A1
Peninsula Rd SO22 ....10 C3
Peninsula Sq SO23 ....10 C4
Penistone Cl SO19 ...104 A1
Penjar Ave PO7 ......134 B2
Penk Ridge PO9 .....158 C4
Penn Cl BH25 ....194 C1
Penn Ct BH22 ....138 B1
Penn Hill Ave BH14 ..203 B2
Penn Way PO12 .....180 C2
Pennant Hills PO9 ...135 A1
Pennant Pk PO16 ....131 B2
Pennant Way BH23 ..207 C4
Pennard Way SO53 ...55 A2
Penner Rd PO9 ......159 C4
Pennerley Ct PO9 ....135 B4
Pennine Ct 8 BH23 ..207 C4
Pennine Gdns SO45 ..125 B1
Pennine Ho SO16 ....101 C4
Pennine Rd SO16 ....101 C4
Pennine Way
　Chandler's Ford SO53 ..55 B2
　Lee-on-the-Solent PO13 ..180 A2
　Verwood BH31 ....114 C3
Pennine Wlk PO14 ...154 C4
Pennington CE Jun Sch
　SO41 ....197 B2
Pennington Cl
　Colden Common SO21 ..56 C4
　Lymington SO41 ......197 B1
　West Moors BH22 ....138 B1
Pennington Cres SO41 ..138 B1
Pennington Cross SO41 ..197 B1
Pennington Inf Sch
　SO41 ....197 B2
Pennington Oval SO41 ..197 A1
Pennington Rd BH22 ..138 B1
Pennington Way PO15 ..130 B2
Penns Rd GU32 ....40 C2
Penny Hedge BH25 ...210 A4
Penny La
　6 Bournemouth BH7 ..205 C2
　Hermitage PO11 ......161 A4
Penny Pl PO7 ....134 C2
Penny St PO1 ....182 A2
Penny Way BH23 .....208 B3
Penny's Cl SP6 ....69 C2
Penny's Cnr SO41 ....195 C2
Penny's Cres SP6 .....69 C2
Penny's Ct BH22 .....165 B3
Penny's Wlk BH22 ....165 B3
Pennycress SO31 ....128 C1
Pennys La SP6 ....69 C2
Pennywell Gdns BH25 ..195 B2
Penrhyn Ave PO6 ....158 A4
Penrhyn Cl SO50 ......55 C3
Penrith Cl BH31 ......114 C3
Penrith Ct SO16 .....101 C4
Penrith Rd BH5 ......206 A2
Penrose Cl 11 PO2 ...157 B1
Penrose Rd BH22 ....165 B3
Penshurst Way SO50 ..56 A3
Pentagon The SO45 ..151 A1
Pentere Rd PO8 .....112 A3

Pentire Ave SO15 . . . . . .78 B1
Pentire Way SO15 . . . . . . .78 B1
Pentland Cl SO45 . . . . .125 B1
Pentland Rise PO16 . . . .132 B1
Penton Ct PO9 . . . . .136 A3
Penton Pl 8 SO23 . . . . . . .11 B1
Penton Rd SO21 . . . . . . .32 A4
Pentons Hill SP6 . . . . . . .94 B3
Pentridge Way SO40 . . .100 C3
Penwood Gn 34 PO9 . . . .136 A3
Peper Harow PO8 . . . . . .112 A3
Peppard Cl SO18 . . . . . .104 A4
Peppercorn Way SO30 . . . .81 B2
Pepys Ave SO19 . . . . . .104 B3
Pepys Cl Gosport PO12 . .181 A4
Portsmouth PO4 . . . . . . .182 C2
Percival Rd PO2 . . . . . . .182 A4
Percivale Rd SO53 . . . . . .54 C2
Percy Chandler St PO1 . .215 C4
Percy Cl SO45 . . . . .125 C3
Percy Rd
Bournemouth BH5 . . . . .205 C2
Gosport PO12 . . . . .181 B2
Portsmouth PO4 . . . . . . .182 C2
Southampton SO15 . . . . .102 A4
Peregrine Cl SO40 . . . . .100 B3
Peregrine Rd BH23 . . . . .208 A3
Peregrines The PO16 . . . .155 C4
Pergin Cres BH17 . . . . . .202 A4
Pergin Way BH17 . . . . . .202 A4
Pern Dr SO30 . . . . .106 A4
Peronne Cl PO3 . . . . . . .157 C3
Peronne Rd PO3 . . . . . . .157 C3
Perran Rd SO16 . . . . .77 B1
Perry Gdns BH15 . . . . . .202 B1
Perry's Ct SO40 . . . . . . .102 A1
Perryfield Gdns BH7 . . . .206 A4
Perrywood Cl SO45 . . . . .150 B2
Perrywood Gdns SO40 . . .100 A4
Perseus Pl PO7 . . . . .134 C2
Perseus Terr PO1 . . . . . .182 A4
Pershore Cl SO31 . . . . . .129 C2
Persian Dr PO15 . . . . . . .129 A4
Persley Rd BH10 . . . . . . .189 C2
Perth Cl BH23 . . . . .191 C1
Perth Ho PO1 . . . . .215 C4
Perth Rd PO13 . . . . .155 B2
Portsmouth PO4 . . . . . . .183 A4
Pervin Rd PO6 . . . . .157 C4
Peststead La SO32 . . . . . .85 B2
Peter Ashley Activity Ctr
PO6 . . . . .134 B1
Peter Ashley Rd PO6 . . . .134 B1
Peter Grant Way BH22 . . .165 B3
Peter Symonds' Coll SO22 . .1 C4
Peterborough Ct PO13 . . .180 B3
Peterborough Rd
Cosham PO6 . . . . .133 C1
Southampton SO14 . . . . .103 A4
Peters Cl
Locks Heath SO31 . . . . .128 C2
Upton BH16 . . . . .201 B3
Peters Rd
Ferndown BH22 . . . . . . .165 C2
Locks Heath SO31 . . . . .128 C2
Peterscroft Ave SO40 . . .100 A4
Petersfield Bsns Pk
GU32 . . . . .40 B2
Petersfield Ho PO1 . . . . .215 C4
Petersfield Hospl GU32 . . .40 C2
Petersfield Inf Sch GU32 .40 C2
Petersfield Pl BH7 . . . . . .206 A4
Petersfield Rd
Bournemouth BH7 . . . . .206 A4
Buriton GU31 . . . . .65 B1
Cheriton SO24 . . . . .14 B2
Clanfield PO8 . . . . .88 B4
Havant PO9 . . . . .136 A3
Winchester SO21, SO23 . . .11 B4
Petersfield Sch The
GU32 . . . . .40 C1
Petersfield Sta GU32 . . . . .40 C2
Petersgate Inf Sch PO8 . . .88 B2
Petersham Rd BH17 . . . . .202 A4
Petit Rd BH9 . . . . .190 A2
Petrel Wlk PO13 . . . . . . .155 A1
Petrie Rd PO13 . . . . .179 C1
Petticoat La SP5 . . . . .47 C4
Pettinger Gdns SO17 . . . .103 B4
Petty Cl SO51 . . . . .53 A3
Pettycot Cres PO13 . . . . .155 A2
Petworth Gdns
Eastleigh SO50 . . . . .56 A3
Southampton SO16 . . . . . .78 B3
Petworth Rd PO3 . . . . . . .183 A4
Petwyn Cl BH22 . . . . . . .166 A3
Pevensey Cl SO16 . . . . . . .77 B1
Peverell Rd BH16 . . . . . .201 A2
Peverells Rd SO53 . . . . . .55 C4
Peverells Wood Ave
SO53 . . . . .55 C4
Peverells Wood Cl SO53 . .55 C3
Peveril Cl BH24 . . . . .139 C3
Peveril Rd SO19 . . . . . . .103 C2
Pewsey Pl SO15 . . . . .78 B1
Phelipps Rd BH21 . . . . . .186 C3
Philip Rd PO7 . . . . .134 C3
Phillimore Rd SO16 . . . . . .79 B2
Phillips Cl SO16 . . . . .77 C3
Philpott Dr SO40 . . . . . . .101 C2
Phoenix Bldgs PO3 . . . .158 A1
Phoenix Cl SO31 . . . . . . .105 A1
Phoenix Pk SO50 . . . . . . .56 B1
Phoenix Pupil Referral Unit
SO45 . . . . .149 C4

Phoenix Sq PO2 . . . . . . .157 C2
Phoenix Way PO13 . . . . .155 B1
Phyldon Cl BH12 . . . . . . .203 A3
Phyldon Rd BH12 . . . . . . .203 A3
Pickard Rd BH22 . . . . . . .165 C4
Pickering Cl BH18 . . . . . .187 A1
Picket Cl SP6 . . . . .69 C1
Pickford Rd BH9 . . . . . . .189 C1
Pickwick Cl SO40 . . . . . .100 A4
Pickwick Ho 13 PO1 . . . .182 B4
Picton Ho 10 PO5 . . . . . .215 B2
Pier Head Rd PO2 . . . . . .157 A1
Pier Rd PO1 . . . . .182 A2
Pier St PO13 . . . . .179 C1
Pig Shoot La BH23 . . . . . .190 C3
Pigeon House La PO7 . . . .133 B2
Pikes Hill SO43 . . . . .121 C3
Pikes Hill Ave SO43 . . . . .121 C3
Pilbrow Ct PO12 . . . . . . .180 C2
Pilchards Ave SO50 . . . . . .57 A2
Pilford Heath Rd BH21 . . .164 A4
Pilgrim Park Homes 1
BH24 . . . . .141 B4
Pilgrim Pl SO18 . . . . .79 C2
Pilgrim's Cl BH25 . . . . . .195 B2
Pilgrims Cl SO53 . . . . .55 A3
Pilgrims Gate SO22 . . . . . .1 C1
Pilgrims Sch The SO23 . . .11 A4
Pilgrims Way
Broadstone BH17 . . . . . .202 A4
Stubbington PO14 . . . . . .179 A3
Pill Hill SP5 . . . . .24 A2
Pilley Bailey SO41 . . . . . .174 A1
Pilley Gn SO41 . . . . .174 A1
Pilley Hill SO41 . . . . .173 C1
Pilley St SO41 . . . . .174 A1
Pilning Ct PO14 . . . . .154 B4
Pilot Hight Rd BH11 . . . . .189 A2
Pilsdon Dr BH17 . . . . . . .187 C2
Pimpern Cl BH17 . . . . . . .187 C1
Pimpernel Cl SO31 . . . . .128 C1
Pine Ave
Bournemouth BH6 . . . . .206 B2
Poole BH12 . . . . .203 C3
Pine Cl Ashurst SO40 . . . .100 A4
Barton on Sea BH25 . . . .209 C4
Ferndown BH22 . . . . . . .165 A4
Hythe SO45 . . . . .125 C1
Landford SP5 . . . . .49 B1
North Baddesley SO52 . . . .53 C3
Winchester SO22 . . . . . . .10 A3
Pine Cotts GU33 . . . . .21 A4
Pine Cres
Chandler's Ford SO53 . . . .30 B1
Christchurch BH23 . . . . .208 C4
Pine Ct PO10 . . . . .136 C2
Pine Dr Clanfield PO8 . . . . .88 B3
Poole BH13 . . . . .203 C2
Southampton SO18 . . . . .104 B4
St Leonards BH24 . . . . . .139 C4
Pine Dr E SO18 . . . . .104 C4
Pine Glen Ave SO16 . . . . .165 B4
Pine Gr PO9 . . . . .136 A1
Pine Grange 4 BH1 . . . . .205 B2
Pine Ho New Milton BH25 195 A2
Southampton SO16 . . . . . .78 C4
Pine Lo 15 BH13 . . . . . . .214 C4
Pine Manor Rd BH24 . . . .139 B3
Pine Mans 3 BH1 . . . . . .205 B2
Pine Park Mans 16
BH13 . . . . .204 A2
Pine Rd Alderholt SP6 . . . .92 C3
Bishop's Waltham SO32 . . .83 B4
Bournemouth BH9 . . . . .205 A4
Broadstone BH21 . . . . . .162 C1
Chandler's Ford SO53 . . . .55 B4
Romsey SO51 . . . . .53 B3
Pine Tree Cl BH21 . . . . . .163 B3
Pine Tree Gdns PO8 . . . . .112 A1
Pine Tree Glen BH4 . . . . .204 B2
Pine Trees Cl PO14 . . . . .154 B4
Pine Vale Cres BH10 . . . .189 C2
Pine View Cl Redlynch SP5 .47 B2
Upton BH16 . . . . .201 B3
Pine View Rd BH31 . . . . .114 B4
Pine Way SO16 . . . . .78 C4
Pine Wlk Chilworth SO16 . .78 C4
Liss GU33 . . . . .21 A3
Locks Heath SO31 . . . . .129 A3
Verwood BH31 . . . . .115 A3
West Moors BH22 . . . . . .138 C2
Pinebeach Ct BH13 . . . . .214 D4
Pinecliff Rd BH13 . . . . . .214 D4
Pinecliffe Ave BH6 . . . . .206 B2
Pinecliffe Rd BH25 . . . . .209 B4
Pinefield Rd SO18 . . . . . . .79 C1
Pinegrove Rd SO19 . . . . .103 C2
Pineholt Cl BH24 . . . . . . .140 A4
Pinehurst
10 Milford on Sea SO41 . .211 B2
13 Southampton SO17 . . . .79 A1
Pinehurst Ave BH23 . . . . .207 C3
Pinehurst Cl PO7 . . . . . . .112 B1
Pinehurst Rd
Southampton SO16 . . . . . .78 C4
West Moors BH22 . . . . . .138 C1
Pinelands Ct SO16 . . . . . . .78 C4
Pinelands Rd SO16 . . . . . .78 C4
Pines The
Fordingbridge SP6 . . . . . .70 B1
Poole BH13 . . . . .204 A1
Portchester SO16 . . . . . .132 A1
Southampton SO16 . . . . . .78 A2
Pineside BH9 . . . . .205 A4
Pinesprings Dr BH18 . . . .186 C1
Pinetops Cl SO41 . . . . . . .197 A2
Pinetree Wlk BH17 . . . . .201 C4

Pineview Cl SO31 . . . . . .105 A1
Pinewood Gosport PO13 . .155 C1
Southampton SO16 . . . . . .78 C3
Pinewood Ave
Bournemouth BH10 . . . . .189 B3
Havant PO9 . . . . .135 A2
Pinewood Cl
Bournemouth BH10 . . . . .189 B3
Christchurch BH23 . . . . .194 A1
Romsey SO51 . . . . .28 B1
Stubbington PO14 . . . . . .154 B2
Upton BH16 . . . . .201 A4
Pinewood Cres SO45 . . . .126 A1
Pinewood Dr SO45 . . . . .126 A1
Pinewood Gdns BH22 . . .165 B4
Pinewood Lodge 5
PO16 . . . . .131 A1
Pinewood Pk SO19 . . . . .104 C3
Pinewood Rd
Christchurch BH23 . . . . .193 C1
Ferndown BH22 . . . . . . .165 B4
Hordle SO41 . . . . .195 C2
St Leonards BH24 . . . . . .139 C2
Upton BH16 . . . . .201 A4
Pink End BH22 . . . . .165 C2
Pink Rd PO2 . . . . .182 A4
Pinkney La SO43 . . . . . . .121 C2
Pinks Hill PO16 . . . . .131 B1
Pinsley Dr PO17 . . . . .133 A3
Pinto Cl PO15 . . . . .129 B4
Pipers Ash 4 BH24 . . . . .141 B4
Pipers Cl SO40 . . . . .100 B3
Pipers Dr BH23 . . . . .208 A4
Pipers Mead PO8 . . . . .88 A3
Pipers Wood Ind Est
PO7 . . . . .134 B4
Piping Cl SO21 . . . . .56 C4
Piping Gn 6 SO21 . . . . . . .56 C4
Piping Rd SO21 . . . . .56 C4
Pipit Cl Gosport PO12 . . . .181 A4
Waterlooville PO8 . . . . . .112 A3
Pippin Cl
Christchurch BH23 . . . . .191 C1
6 Lymington SO41 . . . . .197 C1
Pirelli St SO15 . . . . .102 C2
Pirrie Cl SO15 . . . . .78 B1
Pit Hill La PO7 . . . . .86 C1
Pitcairn Mews PO4 . . . . .183 A1
Pitchponds Rd SO31 . . . .152 B4
Pitcot La SO21 . . . . .33 A2
Pitcroft La GU31 . . . . .65 C3
Pitcroft Rd PO2 . . . . .157 B1
Pitmore Cl SO50 . . . . .56 A4
Pitmore La SO41 . . . . . . .172 B1
Pitmore Rd SO50 . . . . .56 A4
Pitmore Sch SO53 . . . . . . .55 C4
Pitreavie Rd PO6 . . . . . . .157 C3
Pitt Rd SO15 . . . . .102 B3
Pitt Rdbt SO22 . . . . .10 A3
Pitter Cl SO23 . . . . .1 A3
Pittmore Rd BH23 . . . . . .192 B1
Pitts Deep La SO41 . . . . .199 B2
Pitts Pl BH25 . . . . .195 B1
Pitwines Cl BH15 . . . . . .202 B1
Pitymoor La PO17 . . . . . .133 A2
Place Cres PO7 . . . . .134 C3
Place House Cl PO15 . . . .130 B1
Place La SO21 . . . . .31 C4
Plaitford Gr PO9 . . . . . . .135 B3
Plaitford Wlk SO16 . . . . . .77 C1
Plant Park Rd BH24 . . . . .140 B1
Plantaganet Cres BH11 . .188 B3
Plantation SO41 . . . . . . .211 C4
Plantation Ct
Lymington SO41 . . . . . . .197 B2
Poole BH17 . . . . .187 B1
Plantation Dr
Christchurch BH23 . . . . .194 A1
Marchwood SO40 . . . . . .101 C1
Plantation Rd
Hill Brow GU33 . . . . .21 A1
Poole BH17 . . . . .187 B1
West Wellow SO51 . . . . . .74 B4
Plantation The SO32 . . . . .82 C1
Plants Cl SO51 . . . . .51 A1
Plassey Cres BH10 . . . . .189 B3
Platform Rd SO14 . . . . . .103 A1
Platoff Rd SO41 . . . . .212 C4
Player Ct SP6 . . . . .69 C2
Players Cres SO40 . . . . . .100 C3
Playfair Rd PO5 . . . . .215 C2
Playfields Dr BH12 . . . . . .203 C3
Plaza Mews 15 SO51 . . . . .52 C4
Pleasance Way BH25 . . . .194 C2
Pleasant La PO10 . . . . . . .161 B1
Pleasant Rd PO4 . . . . . . .183 A2
Plecy Cl BH22 . . . . .165 B1
Plemont Cl BH12 . . . . . . .188 C1
Pless Rd SO41 . . . . .211 A3
Plough La SO32 . . . . .85 B1
Plough Way SO22 . . . . . . .10 B2
Plover Cl
Southampton SO16 . . . . . .78 A3
Stubbington PO14 . . . . . .179 A3
Plover Dr SO41 . . . . .211 C2
Plover Rd SO40 . . . . .100 B4
Plover Reach PO4 . . . . . .183 A3
Plovers Down SO22 . . . . . .10 A2
Plovers Rd PO8 . . . . .112 A4
PLPH Rd SO45 . . . . .151 A3
Plumer Rd BH17 . . . . . . .187 A1
Plumley Wlk PO9 . . . . . . .135 B4
Plumpton Gdns PO3 . . . .158 A2
Plumpton Gr 7 PO7 . . . . .112 A1
Plymouth Dr PO14 . . . . . .154 A2
Plymouth St PO1 . . . . . . .215 B2
Pococks La GU33 . . . . .19 C4

Poets Way SO22 . . . . .10 B4
Poinsettia Cl PO15 . . . . .129 C2
Pointout Cl SO16 . . . . .78 C2
Pointout Rd SO16 . . . . . . .78 C2
Pokesdown Com Prim Sch
BH5 . . . . .206 A3
Pokesdown Sta BH7 . . . .206 A3
Poles La Hursley SO21 . . . .30 B3
Lymington SO41 . . . . . . .197 C1
Otterbourne SO21 . . . . . .31 A3
Police Station La SO32 . . .61 A1
Police Training Ctr
SO31 . . . . .127 B2
Pollards Moor Rd SO40 . . .75 A1
Pollesden Cl SO53 . . . . . . .55 A4
Polygon Ct SO15 . . . . . . .102 C3
Polygon Special Sch The
SO15 . . . . .102 C3
Polygon The SO15 . . . . . .102 C3
Pomona Cl BH22 . . . . . . .165 B3
Pompey's Cnr BH21 . . . . .165 A2
Pompey's La BH22 . . . . . .165 A1
Pond Cl Marchwood SO40 101 C1
New Milton BH25 . . . . . .195 A2
Pond Cotts GU32 . . . . .39 B1
Pond La PO8 . . . . .88 A3
Pond Piece PO7 . . . . .110 C2
Pond Rd SO31 . . . . .128 C3
Pondhead Cl SO45 . . . . .150 B2
Pondside Flats SO42 . . . .148 C1
Pondside La SO32 . . . . . . .83 B4
Ponsonby Ho PO5 . . . . . .215 B2
Ponsonby Rd BH14 . . . . .203 B2
Pony Dr BH16 . . . . .201 B4
Pook La Fareham PO17 . . .131 B2
Havant PO9 . . . . .160 A4
Pooksgreen SO40 . . . . . .101 B1
Pool La Rdbt BH11 . . . . .188 C2
Poole Aquarium &
Serpentario ★ BH15 . . .202 B1
Poole Commerce Ctr
BH12 . . . . .203 C3
Poole Gram Sch BH17 . . .187 B1
Poole High Sch BH15 . . . .202 B2
Poole Hill BH2 . . . . .204 C2
Poole Hospl BH15 . . . . . .202 B2
Poole La BH11 . . . . .189 A3
Poole Rd
Bournemouth BH2, BH4 . .204 B2
Poole BH12 . . . . .204 A2
Southampton SO19 . . . . .103 C2
Upton BH16, BH17 . . . . .201 B4
Wimborne Minst BH21 . . .163 B2
Poole Sta BH15 . . . . .202 B2
Popes La Totton SO40 . . .100 C4
Upham SO32 . . . . .58 B2
Popes Rd BH15 . . . . .202 B3
Popham Ct PO9 . . . . .135 B3
Poplar Cl
Bransgore BH23 . . . . . . .193 B4
Christchurch BH23 . . . . .209 A4
6 Poole BH15 . . . . .202 A1
Wimborne Minst BH21 . . .163 B3
Poplar Cres BH24 . . . . . .141 A4
Poplar Dr Fareham PO14 154 C4
Marchwood SO40 . . . . . .101 B1
Poplar Gr PO11 . . . . .185 A2
Poplar La BH23 . . . . .193 B4
Poplar Rd
New Milton BH25 . . . . . .195 B2
Southampton SO19 . . . . .103 C3
Poplar Way
Hedge End SO30 . . . . . .105 B3
North Baddesley SO52 . . . .53 C3
Ringwood BH24 . . . . . . .141 A4
Poplars The SO32 . . . . . . .83 C2
Poppy Cl
Christchurch BH23 . . . . .208 B4
Locks Heath SO31 . . . . .128 C1
Poppy Rd SO16 . . . . .79 B3
Poppyfields SO53 . . . . . . .55 A3
Porchester Ct 12 BH1 . . .205 A3
Porchester Pl BH8 . . . . . .205 A3
Porchester Rd
Bournemouth BH8 . . . . .205 A3
Southampton SO19 . . . . .103 C2
Porlock Rd SO16 . . . . .77 B1
Port La Hursley SO21 . . . . .30 B4
Winchester SO22 . . . . . . .10 A1
Port Royal St PO1 . . . . . .215 C3
Port Way PO6 . . . . .157 A4
Portal Rd
Bishopstoke SO50 . . . . . .56 B2
Gosport PO13 . . . . .155 B2
Southampton SO19 . . . . .104 A2
Totton SO40 . . . . .100 B4
Winchester SO23 . . . . . . .11 A3
Portarlington Cl BH2 . . . .204 B1
Portarlington Rd BH4 . . . .204 B1
Portchester Boys Sch
BH7 . . . . .206 A4
Portchester Castle ★
PO16 . . . . .156 C3
Portchester Com Sch
PO16 . . . . .156 B4
Portchester Hts PO16 . . .132 B1
Portchester La PO17 . . . .132 B2
Portchester Rd
Portchester PO16 . . . . . .156 A4
Portsmouth PO2 . . . . . . .182 C4
Portchester Rise SO50 . . .56 A4
Portchester Sta PO16 . . .156 B4
Portcreek Cotts PO6 . . . .158 A3
Portelet Cl BH12 . . . . . . .188 B1
Portelet Ho BH25 . . . . . . .77 B2
Portelet Pl SO30 . . . . . . .105 B3
Porter Rd BH17 . . . . .202 A4
Porter's La SO14 . . . . . . .102 C1

Porters La BH21 . . . . . . .164 B3
Portersbridge St SO51 . . . .52 C4
Portesham Gdns BH9 . . . .190 A2
Portesham Way BH17 . . . .187 C2
Porteus Cres SO53 . . . . . .55 C3
Portfield Cl BH23 . . . . . . .207 A4
Portfield Rd
Christchurch BH23 . . . . .207 A4
Portsmouth PO3 . . . . . . .158 A2
Portfield Sch
Christchurch BH23 . . . . .207 A4
Christchurch BH23 . . . . .207 A4
Portiere Ho BH11 . . . . . .189 A2
Portland Bldgs 5 PO12 181 B2
Portland Dr PO12 . . . . . .180 B2
Portland Ho 24 PO12 . . . .181 B2
Portland Pl BH2 . . . . .204 C2
Portland Rd
Bournemouth BH9 . . . . .205 A4
Portsmouth PO5 . . . . . . .182 B1
Waterlooville PO7 . . . . . .134 C4
Portland Sq 5 GU33 . . . . .20 C1
Portland St
Fareham PO16 . . . . .131 A1
Portsmouth PO1 . . . . . . .182 A3
Southampton SO14 . . . . .102 C2
Portland Terr
27 Portsmouth PO5 . . . .182 B1
Southampton SO14 . . . . .102 C1
Portland's Cl GU32 . . . . . .41 A3
Portman Cres BH5 . . . . . .206 A2
Portman Rd BH7 . . . . . . .205 C3
Portman Terr BH5 . . . . . .206 A2
Portmore Cl BH18 . . . . . .187 B3
Portobello Gr PO16 . . . . .132 C1
Portsdown Ave PO6 . . . . .158 B4
Portsdown Hill Rd
Havant PO9 . . . . .135 A1
Portchester PO17 . . . . . .132 C3
Portsdown Prim Sch
PO6 . . . . .157 C4
Portsdown Rd PO16 . . . . .156 C4
Portside Cl SO40 . . . . . . .102 A2
Portsmouth & Southsea Sta
PO1 . . . . .215 B3
Portsmouth Cath (CE)
PO1 . . . . .182 A3
Portsmouth Cath(RC)
PO1 . . . . .182 A2
Portsmouth City Mus & Art
Gallery ★ PO1 . . . . . . .182 A2
Portsmouth Coll PO3 . . . .183 B4
Portsmouth Gram Sch
PO1 . . . . .182 A2
Portsmouth Harbour Sta
PO1 . . . . .181 C3
Portsmouth High Sch for
Girls PO5 . . . . .215 A1
Portsmouth High Sch for
Girls(Juns) PO5 . . . . . .182 B1
Portsmouth Print Workshop
PO1 . . . . .182 B4
Portsmouth RC Cath ★
PO1 . . . . .215 A4
Portsmouth Rd
Bursledon SO31 . . . . . . .105 A1
Colden Common SO50,
SO21 . . . . .57 B3
Horndean PO8 . . . . .112 A3
Lee-on-the-Solent PO13 . .180 A2
Southampton SO19, SO31 . .104 B1
Portsmouth Sea Life Ctr ★
PO5 . . . . .182 B1
Portsview Ave PO16 . . . . .156 C4
Portsview Gdns PO16 . . .132 C4
Portswood Ave SO17 . . . .103 A4
Portswood Ctr 36 SO17 . . .79 A1
Portswood Dr 2 BH9 . . . .190 A2
Portswood Pk SO17 . . . . .103 A4
Portswood Prim Sch
SO17 . . . . .79 B1
Portswood Rd
Havant PO9 . . . . .135 B3
Portsmouth PO2 . . . . . . .157 C3
Southampton SO17 . . . . . .79 B1
Portuguese Fireplace ★
SO43 . . . . .120 C2
Portview Rd SO18 . . . . . . .79 C1
Portway Cl SO18 . . . . . . .104 A4
Posbrook La PO14 . . . . . .153 C3
Posbrooke Rd PO4 . . . . . .183 A2
Post Office Bldgs BH9 . . .204 C4
Post Office La
6 Poole BH15 . . . . .202 B1
St Leonards BH24 . . . . . .140 A2
Post Office Rd
41 Bournemouth BH1 . . .204 C2
Waterlooville PO7 . . . . . .134 B3
Postern Cl PO16 . . . . . . .156 B4
Postern Ct 14 SO14 . . . . .102 C2
Potash Terr PO9 . . . . .135 C1
Potterdale Ho 17 PO6 . . .133 A1
Potteries The PO16 . . . . .131 A2
Potterne Way BH31 . . . . .115 B2
Potterne Wood Cl BH31 . .115 B2
Potters Ave PO16 . . . . . . .131 A2
Potters Field GU33 . . . . . .21 A2
Potters Heron Cl SO51 . . .29 C2
Potters Heron La SO51 . . .29 C2
Potters Way PO4 . . . . . . .203 B1
Pottery Junc BH14 . . . . . .203 C3
Pottery Rd BH14 . . . . . . .203 A1
Poulner Cl SO19 . . . . . . .104 A1
Poulner Cl PO9 . . . . .135 B3
Poulner Hill BH24 . . . . . .141 C4
Poulner Inf & Jun Schs
BH24 . . . . .117 B1

Poulner Mobile Home Pk
BH24 . . . . .117 B1
Poulner Pk BH24 . . . . .117 B1
Pound Cl Gosport PO13 . .180 B4
Poole BH15 . . . . .202 C3
Ringwood BH24 . . . . .141 A4
Pound Cotts SO32 . . . . .61 B3
Pound Ct SO18 . . . . .104 A4
Pound Gate Dr PO14 . . . .153 B4
Pound Hill SO51 . . . . .50 B3
Pound La Ampfield SO51 . . .29 A1
Ashurst SO40 . . . . .100 C2
Burley BH24 . . . . .142 C1
Cadnam SO40 . . . . .75 B1
3 Christchurch BH23 . . . .207 A3
Damerham SP6 . . . . .68 A3
Meonstoke SO32 . . . . .61 B3
Plaitford SO51 . . . . .50 B3
Poole BH15 . . . . .202 C3
Sherfield English SO51 . . . .25 C1
Pound Lea PO11 . . . . .185 A3
Pound Rd
Bursledon SO31 . . . . .104 C1
Kings Worthy SO23 . . . . .2 B4
Lymington SO41 . . . . .197 A1
Pound St SO18 . . . . .104 A4
Pound Tree Rd SO14 . . . .103 A2
Poundbury Ct SO31 . . . .129 A3
Pounds Terr PO1 . . . . . . .182 A3
Powell Cres SO40 . . . . . . .100 C3
Powell Rd BH14 . . . . .203 A2
Powell Sq 11 PO1 . . . . . . .182 A3
Power Rd PO1 . . . . .182 C3
Powerscourt Rd
Barton on Sea BH25 . . . . .209 C4
Portsmouth PO2 . . . . .182 C4
Powis Cl BH25 . . . . .195 A2
Powlett Rd SO41 . . . . . . .197 C2
Poyner Cl PO16 . . . . .131 A1
Poynings Pl PO1 . . . . .182 A3
Precinct The
Holbury SO45 . . . . .150 B2
10 Waterlooville PO7 . . .134 C4
Precosa Rd SO30 . . . . .105 C3
Prelate Way PO14 . . . . . .129 C3
Premier Ctr The SO51 . . . .53 B3
Premier Par SO18 . . . . .79 C2
Premier Way SO51 . . . . . . .53 B3
Preshaw Cl SO16 . . . . .78 B2
Preshaw Est PO3 . . . . .35 A2
Presseys Cnr SP6 . . . . .93 A4
Preston Cl BH16 . . . . .201 B4
Preston La BH23 . . . . .192 B3
Preston Rd Poole BH15 . . .202 B3
Portsmouth PO2 . . . . .182 C4
Preston Way BH23 . . . . . .208 B4
Prestwood Cl BH25 . . . . .194 C1
Prestwood Rd SO30 . . . . .105 C3
Pretoria Rd
Hedge End SO30 . . . . .105 A3
Portsmouth PO4 . . . . .182 C2
Prettyjohn Ho PO4 . . . . . .183 A1
Pricketts Hill PO17 . . . . .108 A3
Prideaux - Brune Ave
PO13 . . . . .155 B2
Priest Croft PO45 . . . . . . .150 C1
Priest Croft Dr SO45 . . . .150 C1
Priest La BH23 . . . . .192 A4
Priest's House Mus & Gdns★
BH21 . . . . .163 A2
Priestfields PO14 . . . . . . .129 B1
Priestlands SO51 . . . . .52 C4
Priestlands Cl SO40 . . . . .100 A3
Priestlands La SO41 . . . . .197 B2
Priestlands Pl SO41 . . . . .197 B2
Priestlands Rd SO41 . . . . .197 B2
Priestlands Sch SO41 . . . .197 B1
Priestley Cl SO40 . . . . . . .100 B4
Priestley Rd BH10 . . . . . .189 A1
Priestwood Cl SO18 . . . . .104 C1
Primate Rd PO14 . . . . . . .129 C1
Primrose Cl
Chandler's Ford SO53 . . . . .54 C2
Gosport PO13 . . . . .155 B3
Hedge End SO30 . . . . .105 B3
Primrose Ct PO4 . . . . .135 A3
Primrose Gdns BH17 . . . .186 C1
Primrose La Rake GU33 . . .21 B2
Redlynch SP5 . . . . .47 B3
Primrose Rd SO16 . . . . .79 A2
Primrose Terr SO32 . . . . . .59 B1
Primrose Way
Christchurch BH23 . . . . . .208 B4
Corfe Mullen BH21 . . . . . .186 C4
Locks Heath SO31 . . . . . . .128 C1
Romsey SO51 . . . . .28 B1
Prince Albert Rd PO4 . . .183 A2
Prince Alfred St PO12 . . .181 A2
Prince George St PO1 . . .182 A3
Prince George's St PO9 .135 C1
Prince of Wales Ave
SO15 . . . . .102 A4
Prince of Wales Cl 6
PO7 . . . . .135 A4
Prince of Wales Rd
Bournemouth BH4 . . . . . .204 B2
3 Gosport PO12 . . . . . .181 B2
Prince Rd Gosport PO14 . .154 C3
Rownhams SO16 . . . . .77 C3
Prince Regent Ct PO5 . . .215 B2
Prince William Ct 8
SO50 . . . . .56 C1
Prince's Bldgs 18 SO14 . .11 A4
Prince's Mead Sch SO23 . .2 C3
Prince's Pl
New Milton BH25 . . . . . . .195 B2
Portsmouth PO1 . . . . .182 B4
Prince's Rd SO51 . . . . .52 C4

Prince's St
Portsmouth PO1 . . . . .182 B4
Southampton SO14 . . . . . .103 B3
Princes Cl
Bishop's Waltham SO32 . . .83 A4
Ferndown BH22 . . . . .165 B3
Redlynch SP5 . . . . .47 C4
Princes Cotts GU32 . . . . . .63 B4
Princes Cres SO43 . . . . . .122 A3
Princes Ct
Lyndhurst SO43 . . . . .122 A3
6 Poole BH12 . . . . .204 A2
2 Southampton SO14 . .103 B3
Princes Dr PO7 . . . . .112 A1
Princes Hill SP5 . . . . .47 C4
Princes Ho
Portsmouth PO5 . . . . .215 A1
3 Southampton SO14 . .103 B3
Princes Pl SO22 . . . . .10 C3
Princes Rd
Petersfield GU32 . . . . .40 B2
Southampton SO15 . . . . . .102 A3
Princess Anne Hospl
SO16 . . . . .78 A2
Princess Ave BH23 . . . . . .207 A3
Princess Cl SO30 . . . . .80 C1
Princess Ct 10 SO23 . . . . . .11 A4
Princess Gdns PO8 . . . . . .112 B4
Princess Rd
Ashurst SO40 . . . . .100 A1
Bournemouth BH4 . . . . . .204 A3
Poole BH12 . . . . .204 A2
Pringles Cl BH22 . . . . .165 C3
Pringles Dr BH22 . . . . .165 C3
Prinstead Cl 7 SO23 . . . . . .11 A3
Prinsted Cres PO6 . . . . . . .158 B4
Prinsted La PO10 . . . . .161 B4
Prinsted Wlk PO14 . . . . . .154 B4
Printers Row 17 SO23 . . . .10 C4
Priors Barton SO23 . . . . . .10 C3
Priors Cl
Christchurch BH23 . . . . . .208 B4
Southbourne PO10 . . . . . .137 C1
Priors Dean Rd SO22 . . . . .1 B2
Priors Hill La SO31 . . . . . .127 C4
Priors Leaze La PO18 . . . .137 C1
Priors Rd BH17 . . . . .202 A4
Priors Way SO22 . . . . .10 A2
Priors Wlk 7 BH21 . . . . . .163 A3
Priorsdean Ave PO3 . . . . .183 A3
Priorsdean Cres PO9 . . . .135 B2
Priory Ave SO17 . . . . .79 B1
Priory CE Prim Sch The
BH23 . . . . .207 A3
Priory Cl
Bishop's Waltham SO32 . . .83 A4
Southampton SO17 . . . . . . .79 B1
Priory Cres PO4 . . . . .183 A2
Priory Ct
Bishop's Waltham SO32 . . .83 A4
Portchester PO6 . . . . .156 C4
Portsmouth PO5 . . . . .215 D2
Priory Gdns
Portchester PO16 . . . . . . .156 B4
Waterlooville PO7 . . . . . . .111 C1
West Moors BH22 . . . . . . .166 A4
12 Winchester SO23 . . . .11 A4
Priory Ho
Christchurch BH23 . . . . . .207 B3
18 Southampton SO14 . .103 A3
Priory Ind Pk BH23 . . . . .208 A4
Priory Quay BH23 . . . . . . .207 B3
Priory Rd
Bournemouth BH2 . . . . . .204 C1
Eastleigh SO50 . . . . .55 C1
Fareham PO15 . . . . .130 B1
Gosport PO12 . . . . .181 A4
Netley SO31 . . . . .127 A3
Portsmouth PO4 . . . . .183 A1
Southampton SO17 . . . . . .103 B3
West Moors BH22 . . . . . . .166 A4
Priory Sch SO32 . . . . .83 A4
Priory Sec Sch PO5 . . . . . .215 D2
Priory View Ct 5 BH23 . . .207 B3
Priory View Pl 7 BH9 . . . .190 A2
Priory View Rd
Bournemouth BH9 . . . . . .190 A2
Burton BH23 . . . . .192 B1
Private Rd SO41 . . . . .197 C3
Privet Rd BH9 . . . . .204 C4
Privett Ho PO1 . . . . .182 A4
Privett Pl PO12 . . . . .180 C2
Privett Rd Fareham PO15 .130 B1
Froxfield Green GU32 . . . . .18 C1
Gosport PO12,PO13 . . . . .180 C2
Waterlooville PO7 . . . . . . .134 C2
Prochurch Rd PO8 . . . . . . .112 A2
Proctor Cl SO19 . . . . .104 B3
Proctor Dr SO52 . . . . .53 C2
Proctor La PO1 . . . . .182 C3
Promenade BH23 . . . . . . .208 A3
Promenade Ct 4 PO13 . . .179 C1
Promenade The
Emsworth PO10 . . . . .160 C4
Hythe SO45 . . . . .126 A3
20 Portsmouth PO4 . . . .157 B1
Prospect La PO9 . . . . .136 A3
Prospect Pl
Chandler's Ford SO50 . . . . .55 B3
Hythe SO45 . . . . .126 A3
Prospect Rd PO1 . . . . .182 B4
Prosperous St 14 BH15 . .202 B1
Protea Gdns PO14 . . . . . . .130 A1
Provene Cl SO32 . . . . .83 C2
Provene Gdns SO32 . . . . . .83 C2
Providence Ct 8 PO1 . . . .182 B4
Providence Hill SO31 . . . .105 A1
Provost St SP6 . . . . .69 C1

Pruetts La GU33 . . . . .20 C1
Prunus Cl
Ferndown BH22 . . . . .165 A4
Southampton SO16 . . . . . . .78 B3
Prunus Dr BH22 . . . . .165 A4
Pudbrook Ho SO30 . . . . . .106 A3
Pudbrooke Gdns SO30 . . .105 A4
Pudding La SO23 . . . . .2 B2
Puddletown Cres BH17 . . .187 C1
Puffin Cl SO16 . . . . .78 A3
Puffin Cres PO14 . . . . .154 A2
Puffin Gdns PO13 . . . . . . .155 C3
Puffin Wlk PO8 . . . . .111 B2
Pug's Hole SP5 . . . . .4 A3
Pulens Cres GU31 . . . . .41 B2
Pulens La GU31 . . . . .41 A2
Pullman Ct BH22 . . . . .138 B1
Pullman Way BH24 . . . . . .141 B4
Pump La Gosport PO13 . . .155 B1
Waterlooville PO8 . . . . . . .112 A1
Pundle Green Est SO40 . . .98 A3
Punsholt La SO24 . . . . .16 C3
Purbeck Ave BH15 . . . . . .201 C1
Purbeck Cl BH15 . . . . .201 A4
Purbeck Ct
Bournemouth BH5 . . . . . .206 A2
3 Christchurch BH23 . . .207 C4
Purbeck Dr
Fareham PO14 . . . . .154 B4
Verwood BH31 . . . . .114 C3
Purbeck Gdns BH14 . . . . .202 C3
Purbeck Hts BH14 . . . . . . .203 A3
Purbeck Rd
Barton on Sea BH25 . . . . .209 B4
Bournemouth BH2 . . . . . .204 C1
Purbeck St PO1 . . . . .182 A3
Purbeck Wlk PO14 . . . . . .154 B4
Purbrook Chase Prec
PO7 . . . . .134 C2
Purbrook Cl SO16 . . . . .78 B3
Purbrook Gdns PO7 . . . . .134 B3
Purbrook Heath Rd
PO7 . . . . .134 A3
Purbrook Ho PO7 . . . . . . .134 B3
Purbrook Inf Sch PO7 . . . .134 C4
Purbrook Jun Sch PO7 . . . .134 B4
Purbrook Park Sch PO7 . . .134 B2
Purbrook Rd PO1 . . . . .182 B2
Purbrook Way PO7,PO9 . .135 C2
Purcell Cl PO7 . . . . .134 C3
Purcell Rd SO19 . . . . .104 B2
Purchase Rd BH12 . . . . . .204 B4
Purewell BH23 . . . . .207 B3
Purewell Cl BH23 . . . . . . .207 C3
Purewell Cross BH23 . . . .207 C3
Purewell Cross Rd
BH23 . . . . .207 B4
Purewell Ct 11 BH23 . . . .207 C4
Purkess Cl SO53 . . . . .55 B4
Purkiss Cl SO40 . . . . .99 B3
Purley Way SO51 . . . . .50 A2
Purrocks The GU32 . . . . . .40 C3
Purvis Gdns SO19 . . . . . . .104 A1
Pussex La SO31 . . . . .191 A4
Putmans La GU31 . . . . .66 C4
Pycroft Cl
North Hayling PO11 . . . . . .160 B2
Southampton SO19 . . . . . .104 A3
Pye Cl BH21 . . . . .186 C4
Pye Cnr BH21 . . . . .163 A2
Pye La Alderholt BH21 . . . .91 C3
Wimborne Minst BH21 . . .163 A2
Pye St PO1 . . . . .215 B4
Pylands La SO31 . . . . .105 A2
Pyle Cl PO8 . . . . .112 A2
Pylewell Rd SO45 . . . . . . .126 A2
Pyramid Ctr PO3 . . . . .183 A4
Pyramids L Ctr The PO5 .182 B1
Pyrford Cl Gosport PO12 . .180 C2
Waterlooville PO7 . . . . . . .111 C1
Pyrford Gdns 11 SO41 . . .197 C1
Pyrford Mews SO41 . . . . .197 C1
Pytchley Cl PO14 . . . . . . .179 A3

Q

Quadra Point PO3 . . . . . . .158 A2
Quadrangle The
Eastleigh SO50 . . . . .56 A2
North Baddesley SO51 . . . .53 B3
Quadrant SP6 . . . . .93 C4
Quail Way PO8 . . . . .112 A3
Quaker Ct BH24 . . . . .140 C3
Quantock Ct 7 BH23 . . . .207 C4
Quantock Rd SO16 . . . . . .101 C4
Quantocks The SO45 . . . .125 B1
Quarely Rd PO9 . . . . .135 B3
Quarr Ho SO41 . . . . .172 A2
Quarry Chase 7 BH4 . . . .204 B2
Quarry Cl BH21 . . . . .164 A4
Quarry Dr PO21 . . . . .164 A4
Quarry Rd
Wimborne Minst BH21 . . .164 A4
Winchester SO23 . . . . .11 B4
Quarterdeck Ave PO2 . . . .157 A1
Quarterjack Mews 1
BH21 . . . . .163 B2
Quartremaine Rd PO3 . . . .158 A2
Quavey Rd SP5 . . . . .47 C3
Quay 2000 SO14 . . . . .103 B4
Quay Haven SO31 . . . . . . .128 B4
Quay Hill SO41 . . . . .197 C2
Quay Ho SO31 . . . . .128 A1
Quay La Gosport PO12 . . . .181 C2
Gosport, Elson PO12 . . . . .156 A1
Quay Point
19 Poole BH15 . . . . . . .202 B1

Quay Point continued
Portsmouth PO6 . . . . .157 B4
Quay Rd
Christchurch BH23 . . . . . .207 A3
Lymington SO41 . . . . .197 C2
Quay St Fareham PO16 . . .131 B1
Fareham PO16 . . . . .155 B4
Lymington SO41 . . . . .197 C2
Quay The
Hamble-le-Rice SO31 . . . .128 A1
Poole BH15 . . . . .202 B1
Quayle Dr BH11 . . . . .188 C3
Quayside SO30 . . . . .106 A3
Quayside Commerce Ctr **1**
PO16 . . . . .155 A4
Quayside Rd
Fawley SO45 . . . . .151 C1
Southampton SO18 . . . . . .103 B4
Quayside Wlk SO40 . . . . .101 C2
Quebec Gdns SO31 . . . . . .104 C1
Queen Alexandra Hospl
PO6 . . . . .157 C4
Queen Anne Dr BH21 . . . .187 C4
Queen Anne's Dr PO9 . . . .135 B1
Queen Elizabeth Ave
SO41 . . . . .197 B2
Queen Elizabeth Ct
Southampton SO17 . . . . . . .79 B2
Wimborne Minst BH21 . . .163 A2
Queen Elizabeth Ctry Pk★
PO8 . . . . .64 C3
Queen Elizabeth's Sch
BH21 . . . . .162 C3
Queen Katherine Rd
SO41 . . . . .197 C2
Queen Mary Ave BH9 . . . .189 C1
Queen Mary Rd PO16 . . . .156 B4
Queen St Emsworth PO10 .161 A4
Lymington SO41 . . . . .197 B2
Portsmouth PO1 . . . . .182 A3
Twyford SO21 . . . . .31 C3
Woodgreen SP6 . . . . .47 A1
Queen's Ave BH23 . . . . . . .207 A3
Queen's Cl SO51 . . . . .53 A4
Queen's Cres PO5 . . . . . . .215 B1
Queen's Ct SO15 . . . . .102 C3
Queen's Gr PO5 . . . . .215 B1
Queen's Inclosure Prim Sch
PO8 . . . . .112 A1
Queen's Par
Lyndhurst SO43 . . . . .121 C3
8 Waterlooville PO7 . . .134 C4
Queen's Park Ave BH8 . . .205 B4
Queen's Park Gdns BH8 . .205 B4
Queen's Park Rd BH8 . . . .205 B4
Queen's Park South Dr
BH8 . . . . .205 B4
Queen's Park West Dr
BH8 . . . . .205 B4
Queen's Pl PO5 . . . . .215 B1
Queen's Rd
Bournemouth BH4 . . . . . .204 B2
Chandler's Ford SO53 . . . . .31 B1
Christchurch BH23 . . . . . .207 C3
Corfe Mullen BH21 . . . . . .186 B3
Fareham PO16 . . . . .131 A1
Gosport PO12 . . . . .181 B2
Locks Heath SO31 . . . . . . .152 B4
Poole BH14 . . . . .203 B2
Portsmouth PO1 . . . . .181 C3
Portsmouth, Buckland PO2 182 C4
Southampton SO15 . . . . . . .78 B1
Waterlooville PO7 . . . . . . .111 C1
Winchester SO22 . . . . .10 B4
Queen's Terr PO5 . . . . .215 B1
Queen's Terr SO14 . . . . . .103 A2
Queen's Way PO5 . . . . . . .215 B1
Queens Cl Hythe SO45 . . . .126 A2
Lee-on-the-Solent PO13 . . .179 C1
West Moors BH22 . . . . . . .138 C1
Queens Cres
Horndean PO8 . . . . .112 B4
Stubbington PO14 . . . . . . .154 B2
Queens Ct
5 Bournemouth BH4 . . .204 B2
Bournemouth, Charminster
BH9 . . . . .205 A4
New Milton BH25 . . . . . . .195 B2
30 Winchester SO23 . . . .10 C4
Queens Gdns
Bournemouth BH2 . . . . . .204 B2
Fordingbridge SP6 . . . . . . .69 C2
Queens Gr
New Milton BH25 . . . . . . .195 B2
Waterlooville PO7 . . . . . . .134 B3
Queens Ho 15 SO14 . . . . .103 A2
Queens Keep 17 PO5 . . . .182 B1
Queens Mead SO22 . . . . . .10 B3
Queens Par PO12 . . . . . . .180 C2
Queens Rd
Ferndown BH22 . . . . .165 B4
Lee-on-the-Solent PO13 . . .179 C1
Petersfield GU32 . . . . .40 B2
Queens Ride SO52 . . . . . . .53 C2
Queens View SO31 . . . . . .127 A3
Queens Way BH24 . . . . . . .141 B4
Queensbury Mans 7
BH1 . . . . .205 A2
Queensland Rd BH5 . . . . .206 A3
Queensmead 4 BH21 . . . .163 B3
Queenstown Rd SO15 . . . .102 B3
Queensway
New Milton BH25 . . . . . . .194 C2
North Hayling PO11 . . . . . .160 A2
Southampton SO14 . . . . . .103 A2
Queensway The PO16 . . . .156 A4

Pou – Ran | **253**

Queenswood Ave BH8 . . .190 C1
Queenswood Dr BH22 . . . .165 B4
Querida Cl SO31 . . . . .128 B4
Quilter Cl SO19 . . . . .104 B2
Quince La BH21 . . . . .163 C3
Quinton Cl
Christchurch BH23 . . . . . .208 C4
Portsmouth PO1 . . . . .215 C2
Quintrell Ave PO16 . . . . . .156 A4
Quob Farm Cl SO30 . . . . . .80 C2
Quob La SO30 . . . . .80 C2
Quomp The BH24 . . . . . . .141 B4

R

R L Stevenson Ave BH4 . .204 A2
Racecourse View SO43 .121 C3
Rachel Cl Fair Oak SO50 . . .57 A1
Poole BH12 . . . . .203 B4
Rachel Madocks Sch
PO8 . . . . .111 B2
Racton Ave PO6 . . . . .158 A4
Racton Rd PO10 . . . . .136 C2
Radcliffe Ct 11 SO14 . . . .103 A3
Radcliffe Rd SO14 . . . . . . .103 A3
Radclyffe Rd PO16 . . . . . .131 B1
Radipole Rd BH17 . . . . . . .188 C1
Radleigh Gdns SO40 . . . . .100 A4
Radley Cl SO30 . . . . .81 B1
Radnor St PO5 . . . . .215 B2
Radstock Rd SO19 . . . . . . .103 C2
Radway Cres SO15 . . . . . .102 B3
Radway Rd SO15 . . . . .78 C1
Raebarn Cl SO24 . . . . .14 B3
Raeburn Dr SO30 . . . . . . .105 A3
Raglan Cl SO53 . . . . .55 A2
Raglan Ct
3 Eastleigh SO50 . . . . . .56 A3
Gosport PO12 . . . . .181 A2
Locks Heath SO31 . . . . . . .129 A3
Raglan Gdns BH11 . . . . . .189 A1
Raglan St PO1 . . . . .215 C3
Raglan Terr PO10 . . . . . . .137 C1
Ragmore La GU32 . . . . . . .18 C3
Rails La PO11 . . . . .185 B3
Railway Cotts
Southampton SO15 . . . . . .101 A4
West Meon GU32 . . . . .37 B2
West Tisted GU34 . . . . .17 B3
Railway Flats PO1 . . . . . . .182 C3
Railway Terr SO42 . . . . . . .172 C4
Railway Triangle Ind Est
PO6 . . . . .158 A3
Railway View PO1 . . . . . . .215 C3
Railway View Rd SO17 . . . .103 B4
Rainbow Pl SO15 . . . . .102 B3
Rake Bsns Pk GU33 . . . . . .21 C2
Rake CE Prim Sch GU33 . .21 C3
Rake Rd GU33 . . . . .21 A2
Raleigh Cl
Christchurch BH23 . . . . . .207 C3
New Milton BH25 . . . . . . .194 C2
Ringwood BH24 . . . . .141 B4
Raleigh Ho 25 PO1 . . . . . .182 A3
Raleigh Rd BH12 . . . . .188 C1
Raleigh Wlk PO13 . . . . . . .180 B3
Raley Rd SO31 . . . . .129 A1
Ralph La SO51 . . . . .28 A1
Ralph Rd BH21 . . . . .186 C4
Ramalley La SO53 . . . . .55 A4
Rambler Dr PO13 . . . . .180 B3
Ramblers Way PO7 . . . . . .112 B1
Ramillies Ho
11 Fareham PO14 . . . . .154 C4
16 Gosport PO12 . . . . .181 B2
Ramley Rd SO41 . . . . .197 A2
Rampart Gdns PO3 . . . . . .157 C3
Rampart Rd SO18 . . . . . . .103 B4
Rampart Row PO12 . . . . . .181 C2
Rampart The SO41 . . . . . .197 B3
Rams Wlk GU32 . . . . .40 C2
Ramsay Pl PO13 . . . . .155 B1
Ramsay Rd SO23 . . . . .2 B4
Ramsdale Ave PO9 . . . . . . .135 B3
Ramsdean Rd GU32 . . . . . .39 C1
Ramsey Ct BH25 . . . . .194 C2
Ramsey Rd PO11 . . . . .185 A2
Ramshill GU31 . . . . .41 A2
Rances Way SO22 . . . . .10 C3
Randall Cl SO40 . . . . .76 B1
Randall Rd SO53 . . . . .30 B1
Randall's La BH24 . . . . . . .142 C3
Randolph Rd
2 Bournemouth BH1 . . .205 C2
Poole BH14 . . . . .203 B3
Portsmouth PO2 . . . . .157 C2
Randolph St SO15 . . . . . . .102 B4
Ranelagh Ct
Christchurch BH23 . . . . . .208 C4
9 Southampton SO17 . .103 A4
Ranelagh Gdns SO15 . . . .102 C4
Ranelagh Rd
Christchurch BH23 . . . . . .208 C4
Havant PO9 . . . . .135 B1
Portsmouth PO2 . . . . .157 B1
Winchester SO23 . . . . .10 C3
Range Gdns SO19 . . . . . . .104 A2
Range Gn PO2 . . . . .157 B2
Ranmore Cl SO45 . . . . . . .125 B2
Rannoch Cl PO15 . . . . . . .130 C2
Ransome Ct PO14 . . . . . . .153 C4
Ranvilles Jun & Inf Schs
PO14 . . . . .154 B4
Ranvilles La PO14 . . . . . . .154 A4

Rapson Cl PO6 . . . .**133** B1
Rareridge La SO32 . . . .**83** C4
Ratcliffe Rd
 Hedge End SO30 . . . .**105** B4
 Hythe SO45 . . . .**125** C1
Rattigan Gdns PO15 . . .**129** B4
Ravana Ct 4 BH8 . . . . . .**205** A3
Raven Cl PO13 . . . .**180** B3
Raven Croft PO5 . . . .**215** B1
Raven Rd SO14 . . . .**103** A3
Raven Sq SO50 . . . .**55** B1
Raven Way BH23 . . . .**208** A3
Ravens Cl PO14 . . . .**179** B3
Ravens Way SO41 . . . . . .**211** B3
Ravenscourt Rd
 Bournemouth BH6 . . . . . .**206** B3
 Lymington SO41 . . . .**197** B1
Ravenscroft Cl SO31 . . .**104** C1
Ravenscroft Way SO41 . . .**81** C1
Ravensdale Cl BH12 . . . .**203** B3
Ravenshall BH2 . . . .**204** B1
Ravenswood PO14 . . . . . .**129** B2
Ravenswood Gdns 6
 PO5 . . . .**182** B1
Ravine Ct BH13 . . . .**214** C4
Ravine Gdns 5 BH13 . . .**214** C4
Ravine Rd
 Bournemouth BH5 . . . . . .**206** A2
 Poole BH13 . . . .**214** C4
Raymond Cl
 Holbury SO45 . . . .**150** B2
 Verwood BH31 . . . .**115** A3
 West End SO30 . . . .**80** C2
Raymond Rd
 Portchester PO6 . . . .**132** C1
 Southampton SO15 . . . . . .**102** B4
Rayners Dr BH12 . . . .**203** B3
Rayners Gdns SO16 . . . . . .**79** B2
Raynes Rd PO13 . . . .**180** A2
Reading Room La SO32 .**106** B4
Readon Cl GU31 . . . .**41** A2
Readon Ho GU31 . . . .**41** A2
Rebbeck Rd BH7 . . . .**206** A3
Recess The SO50 . . . .**56** A3
Record Rd PO10 . . . .**136** C1
Recreation Cotts SO51 . . .**50** C2
Recreation Rd BH12 . . . .**203** C3
Rectory Ave BH21 . . . . . .**162** B1
Rectory Cl Gosport PO12 .**181** A1
 Stubbington PO14 . . . .**154** B2
Rectory Ct SO30 . . . .**105** C4
Rectory Hill SP5 . . . .**8** A2
Rectory La Breamore SP6 . .**46** A1
 Meonstoke SO32 . . . .**61** B3
Rectory Rd Havant PO9 . .**159** C4
 Poole BH15 . . . .**202** B3
Red Barn Ave PO16 . . . . .**132** B1
Red Barn Com Prim Sch
 PO16 . . . .**156** B4
Red Barn La PO15,PO16 .**130** C2
Red Hill Cres SO16 . . . .**78** C2
Red Hill Way SO16 . . . .**78** C2
Red Horn Cl BH16 . . . .**201** B2
Red House Mews SO41 .**197** C2
Red House Mus & Gdns★
 BH23 . . . .**207** A3
Red La
 Compton (Hants) SO21 . . . .**31** C4
 Corfe Mullen BH21 . . . . . .**186** A4
 Owslebury SO21 . . . .**58** A3
 West Tytherley SP5 . . . .**4** A4
Red Leaves SO32 . . . .**83** C1
Red Lodge SO53 . . . .**55** A2
Red Lodge Sch SO16 . . . . .**78** C2
Red Oaks Cl BH22 . . . . . .**165** A4
Red Oaks Dr SO31 . . . . . .**129** A3
Red Roofs BH22 . . . .**165** C2
Redan Cl BH23 . . . .**208** C4
Redan The PO12 . . . .**181** B1
Redbreast Rd BH9 . . . . . .**190** A2
Redbreast Rd N BH9 . . . .**190** A2
Redbridge Causeway
 SO15,SO40 . . . .**101** A4
Redbridge Com Sch
 SO16 . . . .**101** B4
Redbridge Flyover
 SO15 . . . .**101** B4
Redbridge Gr PO9 . . . . . .**135** B2
Redbridge Hill SO16 . . . . .**77** C1
Redbridge La SO16 . . . .**77** B2
Redbridge Prim Sch
 SO16 . . . .**101** B4
Redbridge Rd SO15 . . . . .**101** B4
Redbridge Sta SO15 . . . . .**101** B4
Redbridge Twrs SO16 . . .**101** B4
Redbrook Cotts SP6 . . . . . .**94** A4
Redcar Ave PO3 . . . .**158** A1
Redcar St SO15 . . . .**102** A4
Redcliffe Cl BH23 . . . .**192** B2
Redcote Cl SO18 . . . .**104** A4
Redcotts La BH21 . . . .**163** A3
Redcotts Rd BH21 . . . .**163** A3
Redcourt 2 SO16 . . . .**78** C2
Redcroft La SO31 . . . .**105** A1
Redfords The SO40 . . . .**76** C1
Redhill SO16 . . . .**78** C2
Redhill Ave BH9,BH10 . . .**189** C2
Redhill Cl
 Bournemouth BH10 . . . . . .**189** C2
 Southampton SO16 . . . .**78** C2
Redhill Cres BH9 . . . .**189** C2
Redhill Ct BH10 . . . .**189** C2
Redhill Dr BH10 . . . .**189** C2
Redhill Ho PO1 . . . .**215** C4

Redhill Park Homes 1
 BH10 . . . .**189** C2
Redhill Rd PO9 . . . .**113** A1
Redhill Rdbt BH10 . . . . . .**189** C2
Redhoave Rd BH17 . . . . . .**187** C1
Redhouse Park Gdns
 PO12 . . . .**180** C4
Redlands
 Christchurch BH23 . . . . . .**208** A4
 Poole BH12 . . . .**203** C3
Redlands Dr SO19 . . . . . .**103** C3
Redlands Gr PO4 . . . .**183** B2
Redlands La
 Emsworth PO10 . . . .**136** C2
 Fareham PO14,PO16 . . . . .**155** A4
Redlands Prim Sch
 PO16 . . . .**155** A4
Redlynch CE Prim Sch
 SP5 . . . .**48** A3
Redlynch Cl PO9 . . . .**136** A2
Redmans View BH31 . . . .**114** C3
Redmoor Cl SO19 . . . .**103** C3
Rednal Ho PO1 . . . .**215** C3
Redoubt Ct PO14 . . . .**154** C3
Redrise Cl SO45 . . . .**150** B2
Redsails BH13 . . . .**214** A2
Redshank Cl BH17 . . . . . .**186** C1
Redshank Rd PO8 . . . .**112** A4
Redvers Cl SO41 . . . .**197** B1
Redvers Rd BH23 . . . .**207** C4
Redward Rd SO16 . . . .**77** C3
Redwing Ct PO4 . . . .**183** B2
Redwing Gdns SO40 . . . .**100** B4
Redwing Rd PO8 . . . .**88** B2
Redwood Cl Hythe SO45 .**125** B2
 Lymington SO41 . . . .**197** B1
 Ringwood BH24 . . . .**141** A4
 West End SO30 . . . .**80** B1
Redwood Ct 3 PO7 . . . . .**134** C4
Redwood Dr
 Ferndown BH22 . . . .**165** B4
 Portchester PO16 . . . .**156** A4
Redwood Gdns SO40 . . . .**100** B4
Redwood Gr PO9 . . . .**136** A2
Redwood Lodge 4
 PO16 . . . .**131** A1
Redwood Park Sch PO6 .**158** A3
Redwood Rd BH16 . . . . . .**201** A4
Redwood Way SO16 . . . . . .**79** A3
Reed Dr SO40 . . . .**101** C1
Reeder Cl SP6 . . . .**69** C1
Reedling Dr PO4 . . . .**183** B3
Reedmace Cl PO7 . . . .**135** A3
Reeds La GU33 . . . .**21** A3
Reeds Pl PO12 . . . .**181** A3
Reeds Rd PO12 . . . .**181** A4
Reeves Cl SO51 . . . .**50** C2
Reeves Way SO31 . . . .**104** C1
Regal Cl PO6 . . . .**157** C4
Regency Cres BH23 . . . . .**206** C4
Regency Ct 12 PO1 . . . . .**182** A2
Regency Gdns PO7 . . . . . .**134** B3
Regency Pl
 Fareham PO15 . . . .**130** C2
 Ringwood BH24 . . . .**141** A4
Regent Cl SO21 . . . .**31** B2
Regent Ct
 24 Southampton SO17 . .**79** A1
 17 Winchester SO23 . . . . .**2** A1
Regent Dr BH7 . . . .**205** C4
Regent Ho SO30 . . . .**81** B2
Regent Mews GU32 . . . . . .**40** B2
Regent Pl PO5 . . . .**215** A1
Regent Rd SO53 . . . .**55** B3
Regent St
 Portsmouth PO1 . . . .**182** B4
 Southampton SO14 . . . . . .**102** C2
Regent Way BH23 . . . .**207** A3
Regent's Gr 1 SO15 . . . .**102** A4
Regent's Park Gdns
 SO15 . . . .**102** A4
Regent's Park Rd SO15 .**102** A4
Regents Ct Havant PO9 . .**159** C4
 6 Southampton SO16 . . .**102** A4
Regents Gate SO31 . . . . . .**128** C3
Regents Park Girls Sch
 SO16 . . . .**102** A4
Reginald Rd PO4 . . . .**183** A2
Reid St BH23 . . . .**207** A4
Reigate Ho PO1 . . . .**215** C4
Relay Rd PO7 . . . .**134** B4
Reldas The 18 PO1 . . . . .**182** A2
Reliant Cl SO53 . . . .**55** A3
Rempstone Rd BH21 . . . .**187** B4
Renault Dr BH18 . . . .**187** A1
Renda Rd SO45 . . . .**150** B2
Renny Rd PO1 . . . .**182** C3
Renouf Cl SO41 . . . .**197** B2
Renown Cl SO53 . . . .**55** A3
Renown Gdns PO8 . . . . . .**111** C3
Renown Ho 14 PO12 . . . .**181** B2
Repton Cl PO4 . . . .**180** C2
Repton Gdns SO30 . . . . . .**81** B1
Reservoir La
 Hedge End SO30 . . . .**105** A3
 Petersfield GU32 . . . .**40** C3
Resolution Ho 13 PO12 .**181** B2
Rest-a-wyle Ave PO11 . .**185** A1
Restharrow BH1, ...**205** A2
Restynge Ho BH31 . . . . . .**114** C4
Retreat Rd BH21 . . . .**163** B2
Retreat The
 Eastleigh SO50 . . . .**56** A1
 Portsmouth PO5 . . . .**215** B1
 Totton SO40 . . . .**101** A3
Revenge Cl PO4 . . . .**183** B3
Revenge Ho 12 PO12 . . .**181** B2

Rewlands Dr SO22 . . . .**1** B2
Rex Est SO53 . . . .**55** B3
Reynard Ct BH15 . . . .**202** C2
Reynolds Cl SO51 . . . .**53** A3
Reynolds Dale SO40 . . . .**100** B3
Reynolds Rd
 Fair Oak SO50 . . . .**57** B1
 Gosport PO12 . . . .**181** B1
 Southampton SO15 . . . . . .**102** B4
Rhinefield Cl
 Bishopstoke SO50 . . . .**56** C1
 Brockenhurst SO42 . . . . . .**145** C1
 Havant PO9 . . . .**135** B2
Rhinefield Ornamental Dr★
 SO42 . . . .**144** C3
Rhinefield Rd
 Brockenhurst SO42 . . . . . .**145** B1
 New Milton BH25 . . . .**170** C1
Rhiners Cl SO41 . . . .**172** A1
Rhyme Hall Mews SO45 .**151** A2
Rhys Ct 1 PO4 . . . .**183** A2
Ribble Cl
 Broadstone BH18 . . . .**187** A1
 Chandler's Ford SO53 . . . . .**55** B3
Ribble Ct SO16 . . . .**77** C1
Ribbonwood Hts BH14 . .**203** A2
Ricardo Cres BH23 . . . . . .**208** A3
Rice Gdns BH16 . . . .**201** B2
Rice Terr BH16 . . . .**201** B2
Richard Cl BH16 . . . .**201** A4
Richard Gr PO12 . . . .**156** A1
Richard Moss Ho 8
 SO23 . . . .**11** A4
Richard Taunton Pl SO17 .**79** A1
Richards Cl
 Blackfield SO45 . . . .**150** C1
 Locks Heath SO31 . . . .**129** A2
Richards Ct 15 SO15 . . . . .**78** A1
Richlans Rd SO30 . . . .**105** B3
Richmond Cl
 Chandler's Ford SO53 . . . . .**30** B1
 South Hayling PO11 . . . . . .**184** C2
 Totton SO40 . . . .**76** A1
Richmond Ct
 15 Bournemouth BH5 . . .**205** C2
 12 Milford on Sea SO41 . .**211** B2
 7 New Milton BH25 . . . .**195** A4
Richmond Dr PO11 . . . . .**184** C2
Richmond Gdns
 Bournemouth BH1 . . . .**204** C2
 Southampton SO17 . . . .**79** A1
 Waterlooville PO7 . . . .**134** A1
Richmond Hall 6 SO17 . . .**79** B1
Richmond Hill BH1,BH2 .**204** C2
Richmond Hill Dr BH2 . .**204** C2
Richmond Ho
 34 Portsmouth PO1 . . . .**182** A3
 5 Southampton SO15 . . .**102** B3
 9 Winchester SO22 . . . . .**10** C4
Richmond La SO51 . . . .**28** A1
Richmond Park Ave
 BH8 . . . .**205** B4
Richmond Park Cl BH8 .**205** B4
Richmond Park Cres
 BH8 . . . .**205** B4
Richmond Park Rd BH8 .**205** B4
Richmond Pk SO21 . . . .**31** B2
Richmond Pl PO1 . . . .**182** A3
Richmond Rd
 Gosport PO12 . . . .**181** A2
 Lee-on-the-Solent PO13 . . .**179** C1
 Poole BH14 . . . .**203** B2
 Portsmouth PO5 . . . .**182** B1
 Southampton SO15 . . . . . .**102** B3
 Wimborne Minst BH21 . . .**163** B2
Richmond Rise
 Bournemouth BH8 . . . .**205** B3
 Portchester BH21 . . . .**132** B1
Richmond St SO14 . . . . . .**103** A2
Richmond Wood Rd
 BH8 . . . .**205** B4
Richville Rd SO16 . . . .**102** A4
Ridding Cl SO15 . . . .**78** B1
Riders Inf Sch PO9 . . . . . .**135** C3
Riders Jun Sch PO9 . . . . .**135** C3
Riders La PO9 . . . .**135** C2
Rideway PO9 . . . .**135** B1
Ridge Cl PO8 . . . .**88** B2
Ridge Common La GU32 . .**40** B3
Ridge La Botley SO30 . . . .**106** B2
 Romsey SO51 . . . .**76** B3
Ridge The SP5 . . . .**47** B3
Ridge Top La GU32 . . . . . .**39** C3
Ridgefield Gdns BH23 . . .**208** B3
Ridgemede Jun Sch
 SO32 . . . .**83** B3
Ridgemount Ave SO16 . . .**78** C3
Ridgemount Gdns BH15 .**201** C2
Ridgemount La SO16 . . . . .**78** C3
Ridgeway
 Broadstone BH18 . . . .**187** A2
 Corfe Mullen BH21 . . . . . .**186** B4
 Ferndown BH22 . . . .**189** C4
 Winchester SO22 . . . .**10** B3
Ridgeway Cl
 Chandler's Ford SO53 . . . . .**55** C3
 Cosham PO6 . . . .**132** C1
 Fair Oak SO50 . . . .**57** B2
Ridgeway House Specl Sch
 SO19 . . . .**103** C3
Ridgeway La SO41 . . . . . .**197** B1
Ridgeway The PO16 . . . .**131** C1
Ridgeway Wlk SO53 . . . . .**55** C3
Ridgewood Cl SO45 . . . . .**125** B2
Ridings The Fair Oak SO50 .**57** A1
 Liss GU33 . . . .**21** A3
 Portsmouth PO2 . . . .**157** C2
 Waltham Chase SO32 . . . . .**83** C2

Ridley Cl SO45 . . . .**150** B2
Ridley Rd BH9 . . . .**204** C4
Ridout Cl BH10 . . . .**189** A1
Rigby Rd SO17 . . . .**103** A4
Riggs Gdns BH11 . . . .**188** C1
Rigler Rd PO15 . . . .**202** A1
Rimbury Way BH23 . . . . .**207** A4
Rimington Gdns 1 SO51 .**28** A1
Rimington Rd PO12 . . . . .**111** C2
Ring The SO16 . . . .**78** C4
Ringbury SO41 . . . .**197** B3
Ringlet Way 6 SO23 . . . . . .**11** B4
Ringwood CE Inf Sch
 BH24 . . . .**141** A4
Ringwood Dr SO52 . . . . . .**53** C3
Ringwood Ho PO9 . . . . . .**135** C3
Ringwood Jun Sch
 BH24 . . . .**141** A3
Ringwood Rd
 Alderholt SP6 . . . .**93** A3
 Bournemouth BH11 . . . . . .**188** C2
 Bransgore BH23 . . . .**193** B3
 Burley BH24 . . . .**142** C3
 Christchurch BH23 . . . . . .**194** A1
 Ferndown BH22 . . . .**165** B3
 Fordingbridge SP6 . . . .**94** A2
 Fordingbridge SP6 . . . .**94** B2
 Poole BH2,BH14 . . . .**203** A4
 Portsmouth PO4 . . . .**183** A2
 Sopley BH23 . . . .**192** A4
 St Leonards BH24 . . . .**139** B1
 Three Legged Cross BH22 .**138** C4
 Totton SO40 . . . .**100** B4
 Verwood BH31 . . . .**115** A3
Ringwood Ret Pk BH11 . .**188** C2
Ringwood Sch BH24 . . . . .**141** A4
Ringwood Terr SO42 . . . .**146** A1
Ringwood Trad Est
 BH24 . . . .**141** A3
Ringwood Waldorf Sch
 BH24 . . . .**140** B3
Ripley Gr PO3 . . . .**183** A4
Ripon Cl SO50 . . . .**81** B4
Ripon Gdns 11 PO7 . . . . .**112** A1
Ripon Rd BH9 . . . .**190** A1
Ripplewood SO40 . . . .**100** A1
Ripstone Gdns SO17 . . . . .**79** A2
Rise The
 Brockenhurst SO42 . . . . . .**145** C1
 Waterlooville PO7 . . . .**134** B1
Ritchie Cl PO11 . . . .**185** A2
Ritchie Ct SO19 . . . .**104** A2
Ritchie Pl BH22 . . . .**138** B2
Ritchie Rd BH11 . . . .**189** A2
Rival Moor Rd GU31 . . . . .**41** B1
River Cl BH21 . . . .**163** B3
River Ct SO41 . . . .**197** C2
River Gdns SO41 . . . .**211** B3
River Gn SO31 . . . .**128** A1
River La PO15 . . . .**130** B3
River Mews SO50 . . . .**56** B2
River Park L Ctr SO23 . . . . .**2** A1
River Pk BH6 . . . .**206** C3
River Rd SP6 . . . .**70** B1
River St PO10 . . . .**137** A2
River View SO19 . . . .**103** B2
River View Rd SO18 . . . . . .**79** B1
River Way
 Christchurch BH23 . . . . . .**191** B1
 Havant PO9 . . . .**136** A2
River Wlk SO18 . . . .**79** C2
River's St PO5 . . . .**215** C2
Riverbourne Ct SO18 . . . .**103** B4
Riverdale Ave PO7 . . . . . .**135** A4
Riverdale Cl SP6 . . . .**69** C1
Riverdale Cotts PO16 . . . .**131** B2
Riverdale La BH23 . . . . . .**207** A3
Riverdene Pl SO18 . . . . . .**103** B4
Riverhead Cl PO4 . . . .**183** A3
Riverlea Rd BH23 . . . .**207** A3
Rivermead Ct SO51 . . . . . .**52** B4
Rivermead Gdns BH23 . .**191** C1
Riverpark Ct SO18 . . . .**79** B1
Rivers Reach SO41 . . . . . .**197** C2
Riversdale Cl BH21 . . . . . .**163** B2
Riversdale Cl SO19 . . . . . .**126** C3
Riversdale 7 PO9 . . . .**135** C1
Riversdale Rd BH23 . . . . .**207** A2
Riverside
 Bishopstoke SO50 . . . .**56** B2
 4 Bournemouth BH10 . . .**189** C2
 Ringwood BH24 . . . .**140** C3
Riverside Ave
 Bournemouth BH7 . . . .**191** B1
 Fareham PO16 . . . .**131** B2
Riverside Bsns Pk SO41 .**197** C2
Riverside Cl Cadnam SO40 .**99** B3
 Liss GU33 . . . .**20** C2
Riverside Cotts SO21 . . . .**31** C3
Riverside Ct SO18 . . . .**103** B4
Riverside Gdns SO51 . . . . .**52** C3
Riverside Ho 44 SO23 . . . .**11** A4
Riverside La BH6 . . . .**206** C3
Riverside Mews PO17 . . .**155** B4
Riverside Pk BH23 . . . . . .**207** A3
Riverside Pk Ind Est
 BH21 . . . .**163** B2
Riverside Pl SP6 . . . .**69** C1
Riverside Rd
 Bournemouth BH6 . . . .**206** C3
 West Moors BH22 . . . .**138** B1
Riverside Sch PO7 . . . . . .**134** C2
Riverside Terr 6 PO10 . . .**161** A4
Riverside Wlk GU31 . . . . . .**41** A2
Riverslea Mews BH23 . . .**207** A3
Riversmeet Ct BH23 . . . .**207** B3
Riverview SO40 . . . .**100** C3

Riverview Terr SO31 . . . .**128** B4
Riviera Ct
 3 Bournemouth BH2 . . .**204** B2
 3 Poole BH13 . . . .**214** C3
Rivirea 22 BH1 . . . .**205** A2
RN Submarine Mus & HMS
 Alliance★ PO12 . . . .**181** C2
Road View PO2 . . . .**182** B4
Roads Hill PO8 . . . .**88** A1
Robere Ho SO19 . . . .**103** B2
Robert Cecil Ave SO18 . . .**79** C2
Robert Mack Ct 32 PO1 .**182** A3
Robert Whitworth Dr
 SO51 . . . .**27** C1
Roberts Cl Hordle SO41 . .**196** C1
 Wickham PO17 . . . .**108** A2
Roberts La BH17 . . . .**202** A4
Roberts Rd
 Bournemouth BH7 . . . .**206** A3
 Gosport PO12 . . . .**180** C1
 Hythe SO45 . . . .**125** C2
 Poole BH17 . . . .**187** A1
 Southampton SO15 . . . . . .**102** C3
 Totton SO40 . . . .**100** C3
Robertshaw Ho SO43 . . . .**121** B4
Robertson Block PO12 . .**181** B3
Robin Cres BH25 . . . .**194** B3
Robin Ct SO15 . . . .**102** C4
Robin Gdns Totton SO40 .**100** B4
 Waterlooville PO8 . . . .**111** B2
Robin Gr BH25 . . . .**194** C1
Robin Sq SO50 . . . .**55** B1
Robina Cl PO7 . . . .**135** A4
Robins Cl PO14 . . . .**154** B2
Robins Ct 7 BH21 . . . . . .**163** B2
Robins Mdw PO14 . . . . . .**129** B1
Robins Way BH23 . . . .**208** A3
Robinson Ct PO16 . . . . . .**132** B1
Robinson Way 7 SO14 . . .**103** A3
Robinson Rd PO14 . . . . . .**179** A3
Robinswood Dr BH22 . . .**165** B4
Robsall Cl BH12 . . . .**203** C4
Robville Ct BH6 . . . .**206** A3
Rochester Ct PO13 . . . . . .**180** B3
Rochester Rd
 Bournemouth BH11 . . . . . .**189** A2
 Portsmouth PO2 . . . .**182** C2
Rochester St SO14 . . . . . .**103** A3
Rochford Rd PO6 . . . .**157** B4
Rockall Cl SO16 . . . .**77** C3
Rockbourne Cl PO9 . . . . .**135** B2
Rockbourne Gdns BH25 .**209** B4
Rockbourne La
 Damerham SP6 . . . .**68** B4
 Rockbourne SP6 . . . .**68** B4
Rockbourne Rd SO22 . . . . .**1** C2
Rockbourne Roman Villa★
 SP6 . . . .**68** C4
Rockery Cl SO45 . . . .**125** C2
Rockford Cl BH6 . . . .**206** C2
Rockford Ho SO50 . . . .**57** A1
Rockingham Way PO16 . .**156** A4
Rockleigh Dr SO40 . . . . . .**100** B3
Rockleigh Rd SO16 . . . .**78** B2
Rockley Rd BH15 . . . .**201** C1
Rockpit Cotts GU33 . . . . . .**21** A4
Rockram Cl SO40 . . . .**99** A4
Rockram Gdns SO45 . . . .**125** B2
Rockrose Way PO6 . . . . . .**133** A1
Rockstone Ct 2 SO14 . . .**103** A3
Rockstone La SO14 . . . . . .**103** A3
Rockstone Pl SO15 . . . . . .**102** C3
Rockville Dr PO7 . . . .**134** C4
Rodbard Ho SO31 . . . .**104** C1
Rodbourne Cl SO41 . . . . .**211** B4
Rodfield La SO24 . . . .**13** B3
Rodlease La SO41 . . . .**173** C1
Rodney Cl Gosport PO13 .**180** B3
 Poole BH12 . . . .**204** A4
Rodney Ct
 Christchurch BH23 . . . . . .**208** A3
 Poole BH15 . . . .**202** B1
 Southampton SO19 . . . . . .**104** B2
Rodney Dr BH23 . . . .**207** C3
Rodney Ho 27 PO12 . . . .**181** B2
Rodney Rd PO4 . . . .**183** A3
Rodney Way PO8 . . . .**112** A3
Rodway BH21 . . . .**163** B2
Rodwell Cl BH10 . . . .**189** B3
Roebuck Ave PO15 . . . . . .**130** B3
Roebuck Cl Cosham PO6 .**157** C4
 New Milton BH25 . . . .**195** A2
Roebuck Dr PO12 . . . .**181** B2
Roeshot Cres BH23 . . . . .**193** C1
Roeshot Hill BH23 . . . . . .**193** B1
Roewood Cl SO45 . . . .**150** B2
Roewood Rd SO45 . . . . . .**150** B2
Rogate Gdns PO16 . . . . . .**132** B1
Rogate Ho 1 PO1 . . . . . .**215** C4
Roger Penny Way
 Brook SO43 . . . .**73** B1
 Fordingbridge, Bramshaw
 SP6 . . . .**72** B3
 Fordingbridge, Godshill SP6 .**71** A3
Rogers Cl
 Bishopstoke SO50 . . . .**56** C2
 Gosport PO12 . . . .**181** A3
Rogers Ho PO13 . . . .**179** C1
Rogers Rd SO50 . . . .**56** C2
Roker Way SO50 . . . .**57** A1
Roland Cl PO8 . . . .**112** A3
Rollestone Rd SO45 . . . . .**150** B1
Rolls Dr BH6 . . . .**207** A2
Roman Cl SO53 . . . .**55** C4
Roman Ct PO10 . . . .**137** B2
Roman Dr SO16 . . . .**78** C4
Roman Gdns SO45 . . . . . .**125** B1

Roman Gn PO7 . . . . .110 C2
Roman Gr PO16 . . . . .156 B3
Roman Ho SO18 . . . . .103 B4
Roman Hts BH21 . . . . . . .186 C4
Roman Mdw SP5 . . . . .46 C4
Roman Quay SP6 . . . . .69 C1
Roman Rd Chilworth SO16 .78 C4
  Corfe Mullen BH18 . . . . .186 C3
  Havant PO10 . . . . .136 B1
  Holbury SO45 . . . . .150 A3
  Hythe SO45 . . . . .125 B1
  Twyford SO21 . . . . .32 A3
Roman Row SO32 . . . . .83 B4
Roman Way Havant PO9 .135 B1
  Hythe SO45 . . . . .125 B1
  Pamphill BH21 . . . . .162 B3
Romans' Rd **1** SO23 . . . . . .11 A3
Romford Rd SO31 . . . . . .152 B4
Romill Cl SO30 . . . . .80 A2
Romney Cl BH10 . . . . . . .189 C2
Romney Rd BH10 . . . . . . .189 C2
Romsey Abbey✶ SO51 . . . .52 C4
Romsey Abbey CE Prim Sch
  SO51 . . . . .52 C4
Romsey Ave
  Portchester PO16 . . . . . .156 A4
  Portsmouth PO3 . . . . . . .183 A3
Romsey Cl SO50 . . . . .56 A2
Romsey Ct **10** SO15 . . . . .102 B3
Romsey Hospl SO51 . . . . . .53 A4
Romsey Ind Est SO51 . . . . .52 C4
Romsey Inf Sch SO51 . . . . .52 C4
Romsey Jun Sch SO51 . . . . .53 A4
Romsey Lodge **8** SO16 . .78 A1
Romsey Rd Cadnam SO40 . .75 C3
  Eastleigh SO50 . . . . .56 A2
  Horndean PO8 . . . . .88 B1
  King's Somborne SO51 . . . . .6 B4
  Lyndhurst SO43 . . . . . . .121 C3
  Ower SO40,SO51 . . . . . . .75 B2
  Southampton SO16 . . . . . .77 C2
  West Wellow SO51 . . . . . .51 A2
  Whiteparish SP5 . . . . .24 C2
  Winchester SO22, SO23 . . .10 B3
Romsey Sch The SO51 . . . .52 C4
Romsey Sta SO51 . . . . . . .52 C4
Romyns Ct PO14 . . . . . . .130 C1
Ronald Bowker Ct **1**
  SO22 . . . . .10 C4
Ronald Pugh Ct SO18 . . . .79 C2
Rookcliff **13** SO41 . . . . . .211 B2
Rookcliff Way SO41 . . . . .211 B2
Rookery Ave
  Swanwick PO15 . . . . . . .129 B4
  Swanwick PO15,SO31 . . .129 A4
Rookery Cotts SP5 . . . . .3 B2
Rookery La SP6 . . . . .45 C1
Rookery Gr PO15 . . . . . . .129 A4
Rookery The PO10 . . . . . .137 A1
Rookes Cl PO8 . . . . .112 A3
Rookes La SO41 . . . . .197 B1
Rookes Mews GU31 . . . . . .41 A2
Rookesbury Park Sch
  PO17 . . . . .108 B2
Rookley SO31 . . . . .127 B4
Rooks Down Rd SO22 . . . .10 B3
Rooksbridge SO45 . . . . . .125 B2
Rooksbury Croft PO9 . . . .136 A3
Rooksway Gr PO16 . . . . . .155 C4
Rookwood **3** SO41 . . . . .211 B2
Rookwood Cl SO50 . . . . . .56 A3
Rookwood Gdns SP6 . . . . .69 B1
Rookwood View PO7 . . . . .110 C3
Roosevelt Cres BH11 . . . .189 A4
Rope Hill SO41 . . . . .173 B1
Rope Wlk SO31 . . . . .128 A1
Rope Wlk The **3** PO16 . .155 A4
Ropers La BH16 . . . . .201 B4
Ropewalk Ho **6** SO23 . . . .11 A4
Ropley Cl SO19 . . . . .127 A4
Ropley Ct PO11 . . . . .184 C2
Ropley Rd
  Bournemouth BH7 . . . . . .206 B4
  44 Havant PO9 . . . . . .136 A3
Rosamund Ave BH21 . . . .163 C1
Roscrea Cl BH6 . . . . .207 A2
Roscrea Dr BH6 . . . . .207 A2
Rose Cl Hedge End SO30 .105 B4
  Hythe SO45 . . . . .126 A1
Rose Cott PO8 . . . . .112 B4
Rose Cres BH15 . . . . .202 C3
Rose Ct BH15 . . . . .202 C2
Rose Gdn Bsh BH23 . . . . .191 B1
Rose Gdns BH9 . . . . .190 A4
Rose Hill PO8 . . . . .112 A3
Rose Rd
  Southampton SO14 . . . . .103 A4
  Totton SO40 . . . . .101 A3
Rosebank Cl SO16 . . . . . . .77 C3
Rosebank Lodge SO16 . . . .77 C3
Rosebay Cl SO50 . . . . .81 B3
Rosebay Ct **3** PO7 . . . .134 C3
Rosebery Ave
  Cosham PO6 . . . . .158 A4
  Hythe SO45 . . . . .126 A1
Rosebery Cl BH31 . . . . . .115 B3
Rosebery Cres SO50 . . . . . .56 A3
Rosebery Rd BH5 . . . . . . .206 A3
Rosebrook **16** SO18 . . . .103 C4
Rosebud Ave **1** BH9 . . .190 A1
Rosecrae **1** BH25 . . . . . .194 C2
Rosedale Ave SO51 . . . . . .53 C4
Rosedale Cl
  3 Christchurch BH23 .207 C4
  Titchfield PO14 . . . . . . .153 C4
Rosehill Cl BH23 . . . . . . .169 A1
Rosehill Dr BH23 . . . . . . .169 A1

Rosehip Cl SO50 . . . . .57 A1
Roselands
  Waterlooville PO8 . . . . . .112 A3
  West End SO30 . . . . .104 B4
Roselands Cl SO50 . . . . . . .57 A2
Roselands Gdns SO17 . . . . .79 A1
Roseleigh Dr SO40 . . . . . .100 C3
Rosemary Ct **14** BH23 . .209 A4
Rosemary Gdns
  Hedge End SO30 . . . . . . .105 B3
  Poole BH12 . . . . .203 A4
  Swanwick PO15 . . . . . . .129 B4
Rosemary La **18** PO1 . . .182 A3
Rosemary Rd BH12 . . . . . .203 B4
Rosemary Way PO8 . . . . .112 A3
Rosemary Wlk **17** PO13 .179 C1
Rosemoor Gr SO53 . . . . . . .30 A1
Rosemount Rd BH4 . . . . .204 A1
Rosendale Rd SO53 . . . . . .55 B2
Rosery The PO12 . . . . . . .181 A4
Rosetta Rd PO4 . . . . .183 A2
Rosewall Rd SO16 . . . . . . .77 C2
Rosewarne Ct **28** SO23 . . .2 A1
Rosewood PO13 . . . . .155 C1
Rosewood Gdns
  Clanfield PO8 . . . . .88 B3
  Marchwood SO40 . . . . . .102 A1
  New Milton BH25 . . . . . .194 C2
Rosina Cl PO7 . . . . .135 A4
Roslin Gdns BH3 . . . . . . .204 B4
Roslin Rd BH3 . . . . .204 C4
Roslin Rd S BH3 . . . . . . .204 C4
Roslyn Ho PO5 . . . . .215 B1
Rosoman Cl SO19 . . . . . . .103 C2
Rosoman Rd SO19 . . . . . .103 C2
Ross Gdns
  Bournemouth BH11 . . . . .188 B3
  Southampton SO16 . . . . . .78 A1
Ross Glades BH3 . . . . . . .204 C3
Ross Mews **2** SO31 . . . .127 A3
Ross Rd BH24 . . . . .117 B1
Ross Way PO13 . . . . .179 C2
Rossan Ave SO31 . . . . . . .152 B4
Rossington Ave SO18 . . . .103 C4
Rossington Way SO18 . . . .103 C4
Rossiters La SO19 . . . . .99 C3
Rossiters Quay BH23 . . . .207 B3
Rossley Cl BH23 . . . . .193 C1
Rosslyn Cl SO52 . . . . .54 A2
Rossmore Par BH12 . . . . .203 A4
Rossmore Rd BH12 . . . . . .203 B3
Rostrevor La **3** PO4 . . . .182 C1
Rostron Cl SO18 . . . . .80 A1
Rosyth Rd SO18 . . . . .103 C4
Rotary Cl BH21 . . . . .163 C4
Rotary Ct SO31 . . . . .127 A3
Rotary Ho SO15 . . . . .102 B4
Rothbury Cl
  Southampton SO19 . . . . .104 A3
  Totton SO40 . . . . .76 B1
Rothbury Pk BH25 . . . . . .195 A1
Rother Cl Petersfield GU31 .41 B4
  West End SO30 . . . . .80 A1
Rother Dale SO19 . . . . . . .104 C2
Rother Ho GU33 . . . . .20 C2
Rotherbank Farm La
  GU33 . . . . .21 A3
Rothercombe La GU32 . . . .40 A2
Rotherfield Rd
  Bournemouth BH5 . . . . . .206 A4
  Christchurch BH23 . . . . . .194 A1
Rotherley **1** GU32 . . . . . .40 C2
Rotherwick Cl PO9 . . . . . .136 A1
Rothesay Dr BH23 . . . . . .208 C4
Rothesay Rd
  Bournemouth BH4 . . . . . .204 B3
  Gosport PO12 . . . . .181 A4
Rothsbury Dr SO53 . . . . . .55 A3
Rothschild Cl SO19 . . . . . .103 C1
Rothville Pl SO53 . . . . .30 A1
Rothwell Cl **12** PO6 . . . .133 A1
Rotterdam Dr BH23 . . . . .207 B3
Rotterdam Twrs **6**
  SO19 . . . . .126 C4
Roughdown La SO45 . . . . .150 B1
Roumelia La BH5 . . . . . . .205 C2
Round Hill SP6 . . . . .69 C1
Roundabouts The GU33 . . .21 A3
Roundcopse PO8 . . . . . . .125 B2
Roundhaye Rd BH11 . . . . .188 C3
Roundhill Cl SO18 . . . . . . .80 A1
Roundhill Cross SP6 . . . . . .45 C1
Roundhouse Ct PO11 . . . .185 A1
Roundhouse Dr SO40 . . . .100 A3
Roundhouse Mdw PO10 . .161 A4
Roundhuts Rise **4** SO23 . .11 B4
Roundway PO7 . . . . .134 C4
Roundways BH11 . . . . . . .188 C2
Routs Way SO16 . . . . .77 C4
Row The SP5 . . . . .47 B4
Row Wood La PO13 . . . . .155 A1
Rowallan Ave PO13 . . . . . .180 A4
Rowan Ave PO8 . . . . .112 A1
Rowan Cl
  Bursledon SO31 . . . . . . .127 C4
  Christchurch BH23 . . . . .208 B4
  Lee-on-the-Solent PO13 .179 C1
  Romsey SO51 . . . . .53 B3
  Southampton SO16 . . . . . .78 A2
  St Leonards BH24 . . . . . .139 B2
  Swanmore SO32 . . . . .84 A1
  Totton SO40 . . . . .100 A3
Rowan Ct
  Portsmouth PO4 . . . . . . .182 C2
  Southampton SO19 . . . . .103 C2
Rowan Dr
  Broadstone BH17 . . . . . .186 C1

Rowan Dr continued
  Christchurch BH23 . . . . . .208 B4
  Verwood BH31 . . . . .115 A2
Rowan Gdns SO30 . . . . . .105 B3
Rowan Tree Cl GU33 . . . . .21 A2
Rowan Way
  Fareham PO14 . . . . .154 B4
  Havant PO9 . . . . .136 A2
Rowans Pk SO41 . . . . . . .197 B2
Rowans The SO40 . . . . . . .101 C1
Rowbarrow Cl BH17 . . . . .187 C1
Rowborough Rd SO18 . . . .103 C4
Rowbury Rd PO9 . . . . . . .135 B3
Rowden Cl SO51 . . . . .50 C1
Rowe Asheway SO31 . . . . .128 C2
Rowena Ct PO5 . . . . .215 C2
Rowena Rd BH6 . . . . .206 C3
Rowes Alley PO1 . . . . . . .181 C2
Rowes La SO41 . . . . .199 A4
Rowhay La SO32 . . . . .58 B3
Rowhill Dr SO45 . . . . .125 B2
Rowin Cl PO11 . . . . .185 B1
Rowland Ave BH15 . . . . . .202 C3
Rowland Rd
  Fareham PO15 . . . . .130 C1
  Portchester PO6 . . . . . . .132 C1
Rowlands Ave PO7 . . . . . .111 C1
Rowlands Castle Rd
  PO8 . . . . .112 C3
Rowlands Castle St John's CE
  Prim Sch PO9 . . . . .136 A4
Rowlands Castle Sta
  PO9 . . . . .113 B1
Rowlands Cl SO53 . . . . . . .55 A2
Rowlands Hill BH24 . . . . .163 B3
Rowlands Wlk **2** SO18 . . .80 A1
Rowley Cl SO30 . . . . .105 C4
Rowley Ct SO30 . . . . .105 C4
Rowley Dr SO30 . . . . .105 C4
Rowlings Rd SO22 . . . . .1 B2
Rowner Cl PO13 . . . . .155 B1
Rowner Jun & Inf Schs
  PO13 . . . . .155 B1
Rowner La Gosport PO13 155 B1
  Gosport, Rowner PO13 . .180 B4
Rowner Rd Gosport PO13 155 A1
  Stubbington PO13 . . . . . .155 A1
Rownhams CE Prim Sch
  SO16 . . . . .77 C3
Rownhams Cl SO16 . . . . . .77 C3
Rownhams Rd SO16 . . . . . .77 C3
Rownhams La SO52,SO16 . .59 C1
Rownhams Pk SO16 . . . . . .77 C4
Rownhams Rd
  Bournemouth BH8 . . . . . .190 B2
  Havant PO9 . . . . .135 B3
  North Baddesley SO52 . . . .54 A2
  Southampton SO16 . . . . . .77 C2
Rownhams Rd N SO16 . . . .77 C3
Rownhams Way SO16 . . . . .77 C3
Roxan Ct **3** SO15 . . . . .102 C4
Roxburgh Ho SO31 . . . . . .129 A4
Royal Arc **5** BH7 . . . . . .205 C2
Royal Bournemouth Gen
  Hospl The BH7 . . . . .191 A1
Royal Crescent Rd
  SO14 . . . . .103 A2
Royal Ct
  Chandler's Ford SO53 . . . .55 B3
  Southampton SO17 . . . . . .79 B1
Royal Gate PO4 . . . . .183 A1
Royal Gdns PO7 . . . . .113 A1
Royal Greenjackets Mus✶
  SO23 . . . . .10 C4
Royal Hampshire Cty Hospl
  SO22 . . . . .10 C4
Royal Hampshire Regiment
  Mus✶ SO23 . . . . .10 C4
Royal London SO15 . . . . .105 A4
Royal Marines Mus✶
  PO4 . . . . .183 A1
Royal Naval Cotts PO17 132 C3
Royal Naval Hospl Haslar
  PO12 . . . . .181 B1
Royal Naval Mus✶ PO1 . .181 C3
Royal Oak Rd BH10 . . . . .189 B3
Royal South Hants Hospl
  SO14 . . . . .103 A3
Royal Sovereign Ave
  PO14 . . . . .155 A3
Royal The PO11 . . . . .184 C1
Royal Victoria Ctry Pk✶
  SO31 . . . . .127 B2
Royal Victoria Hospl
  BH4 . . . . .204 B2
Royal Way PO7 . . . . .135 A4
Royden La SO41 . . . . .173 B2
Roydon Cl SO22 . . . . .10 C3
Royster Cl BH17 . . . . .187 B1
Royston Ave SO50 . . . . . . .56 A3
Royston Cl SO17 . . . . .79 A1
Royston Ct SO40 . . . . .76 C2
Royston Dr BH21 . . . . . . .163 B3
Royston Pl BH25 . . . . . . .210 A4
Rozel Ct SO16 . . . . .77 C2
Rozel Manor BH13 . . . . . .204 A1
Rozelle Cl SO22 . . . . .1 A3
Rozelle Rd BH14 . . . . . . .203 B2
Ruben Dr BH15 . . . . .201 B1
Rubens Cl BH25 . . . . .195 A2
Ruby Ct PO7 . . . . .134 C4
Ruby Rd SO19 . . . . .104 A3
Rudd La SO51 . . . . .27 C4
Rudgewick Cl PO16 . . . . .156 A4
Rudmore Ct **17** PO2 . . .157 B1
Rudmore Rd PO2 . . . . . . .182 B2
Rudmore Sq PO2 . . . . . . .182 B4
Ruffield Cl SO22 . . . . .1 B1

Rufford Cl SO50 . . . . .56 A3
Rufford Gdns BH6 . . . . . .206 C3
Rufus Cl
  Chandler's Ford SO53 . . . .55 C4
  Rownhams SO16 . . . . . . .77 B3
Rufus Ct SO43 . . . . .122 A3
Rufus Gdns SO40 . . . . . . .100 B4
Rufus Stone✶ SO43 . . . . . .98 A3
Rugby Rd Poole BH17 . . .187 A1
  Portsmouth PO5 . . . . . . .215 D2
Rumbridge Gdns SO40 . . .101 A4
Rumbridge St SO40 . . . . .101 A4
Runnymede
  Fareham PO15 . . . . .130 B2
  West End SO30 . . . . .80 B1
Runnymede Ave BH11 . . . .188 C3
Runton Rd BH12 . . . . .203 C3
Runway The BH23 . . . . . .208 A4
Rushall La BH21 . . . . .186 A3
Rushcombe Fst Sch
  BH21 . . . . .186 B3
Rushcombe Way BH21 . . .186 C3
Rushes Farm GU32 . . . . . .40 C2
Rushes Rd GU32 . . . . .40 C2
Rushes The SO40 . . . . . . .101 C1
Rushford Warren BH23 . . .207 C2
Rushin Ho PO16 . . . . .156 B4
Rushington Ave SO40 . . . .100 C3
Rushington Bsns Pk
  SO40 . . . . .100 C3
Rushington La SO40 . . . . .100 C3
Rushmere Gate PO7 . . . . . .86 B1
Rushmere La PO7 . . . . . . .110 C3
Rushmere Rd BH6 . . . . . .206 B4
Rushmere Wlk **11** PO9 .135 B3
Rushpole Ct SO45 . . . . . . .125 B2
Rushton Cres BH3 . . . . . .204 C3
Ruskin Ave BH9 . . . . .190 A2
Ruskin Rd Eastleigh SO50 .56 A3
  Portsmouth PO4 . . . . . . .183 A2
Ruskin Way PO8 . . . . .111 C2
Rusland Cl SO53 . . . . .55 A4
Russel Rd BH10 . . . . .189 B3
Russell Bldgs PO16 . . . . .156 B4
Russell Churcher Ct
  PO12 . . . . .180 C4
Russell Cl PO13 . . . . .179 C1
Russell Cotes Art Gall &
  Mus✶ BH1 . . . . .205 A1
Russell Cotes Rd BH1 . . .205 A1
Russell Ct **3** BH25 . . . .195 A2
Russell Dr
  Christchurch BH23 . . . . .207 B3
  Mottisfont SO51 . . . . .5 B1
Russell Gdns
  Hamworthy BH16 . . . . . .201 B2
  St Leonards BH24 . . . . . .140 A3
  Southampton SO17 . . . . . .79 A1
Russell Pl Fareham PO16 131 A1
  Southampton SO17 . . . . . .79 A1
Russell Rd Havant PO9 . . .135 C1
  Lee-on-the-Solent PO13 .179 C1
  Winchester SO23 . . . . .2 A1
Russell St Gosport PO12 . .181 A3
  21 Southampton SO14 .103 A2
Russell Way GU31 . . . . . . .41 A1
Russet Cl Ferndown BH22 165 B3
  9 Lymington SO41 . . . .197 C1
Russet Gdns PO10 . . . . . .161 A4
Russet Ho SO30 . . . . .105 A3
Russett Cl SO32 . . . . .84 A2
Rustan Cl Fair Oak SO50 . . .57 B1
  Hedge End SO30 . . . . . . .105 A3
Rustington Ho PO1 . . . . . .215 B3
Rutland Cl SO18 . . . . .104 A4
Rutland Gdns SO31 . . . . . .105 A1
Rutland Manor **9** BH12 204 A2
Rutland Rd
  Bournemouth BH9 . . . . . .205 A4
  Christchurch BH23 . . . . . .191 C1
Rutland Way SO18 . . . . . . .80 A1
Ruxley Cl SO15 . . . . .150 B2
Ryall Rd BH17 . . . . .187 B4
Ryan Cl BH22 . . . . .165 B1
Ryan Gdns
  Bournemouth BH11 . . . . .189 A3
  Ferndown BH22 . . . . . . .165 B4
Rydal Cl
  Christchurch BH23 . . . . . .191 B2
  20 Cosham PO6 . . . . .133 A1
Rydal Ho **22** PO6 . . . . .133 A1
Rydal Mews BH21 . . . . . .163 B3
Rydal Rd PO12 . . . . .181 A4
Ryde Pl PO13 . . . . .180 A4
Ryde Terr SO14 . . . . .103 A2
Rye Cl SO53 . . . . .54 C3
Rye Dale SO40 . . . . .100 B2
Rye Paddock La SO45 . . . .151 A2
Ryecroft Havant PO9 . . . . .136 A1
  Titchfield PO14 . . . . .129 B1
Ryecroft Ave BH11 . . . . . .188 C3
Ryedown La SO51 . . . . . . .51 C2
Ryefield Cl GU31 . . . . .41 B2
Ryefield Cotts GU31 . . . . . .41 C1
Rylandes Ct SO16 . . . . . . .77 C2

S

Sabre Rd PO10 . . . . .161 A2
Sackville St PO5 . . . . .215 B2
Saddle Cl BH21 . . . . .164 B3
Saddlers Cl SO50 . . . . .56 A3
Sadlers La SO45 . . . . .126 A1
Sadlers Wlk PO10 . . . . . .161 A4
Saffron Ct
  Bournemouth BH11 . . . . .188 B2
  Locks Heath SO31 . . . . . .128 C1
Saffron Dr BH23 . . . . .208 A4

Saffron Way
  Bournemouth BH11 . . . . .188 B2
  Swanwick PO15 . . . . . . .129 B4
Sage Cl PO7 . . . . .135 A3
Sages La GU34 . . . . .17 B3
Sailors La SO32 . . . . .60 B4
Sainsbury Lodge PO1 . . . .215 D3
Saints Cl BH21 . . . . .138 C4
St Adlem's CE Comb Sch
  BH12 . . . . .204 A3
St Agatha's Rd SO31 . . . .128 A2
St Agathas Way PO1 . . . .215 B4
St Alban's Ave BH8 . . . . .205 B4
St Alban's CE Prim Sch
  PO9 . . . . .136 A2
St Alban's Cres BH8 . . . . .205 A4
St Alban's Rd
  Bournemouth BH8 . . . . . .205 A4
  Havant PO9 . . . . .136 A2
  Portsmouth PO4 . . . . . . .182 C2
  Southampton SO14 . . . . .103 A3
St Albans Ct PO13 . . . . . .180 B3
St Aldhelm's BH14 . . . . . .203 C2
St Aldhelm's Cl BH13 . . . .203 C2
St Aldhelm's Rd BH13 . . .203 C2
St Andrew Cl PO8 . . . . . . .88 B1
St Andrew's Bldgs SO31 128 A1
St Andrew's Cl
  Cosham PO6 . . . . .158 C4
  Gosport PO12 . . . . .181 A2
  Portsmouth PO5 . . . . . . .215 C2
  South Hayling PO11 . . . . .185 A1
St Andrews BH23 . . . . . . .207 A3
St Andrews Cl
  Michelmersh SO51 . . . . . .27 B3
  North Baddesley SO52 . . . .53 C3
St Andrews Gn SO32 . . . . .61 B3
St Andrews Ho **21** SO17 103 A4
St Andrews Pk SO31 . . . . .81 B3
St Andrews Rd
  Broadstone BH18 . . . . . .187 A3
  Southampton SO14 . . . . .103 A3
St Ann's Cres PO12 . . . . .181 A3
St Ann's Ct **1** BH1, ...205 C3
St Ann's Hospl BH13 . . . .214 C3
St Ann's Rd PO8 . . . . .112 B4
St Anne's Ave BH6 . . . . . .207 A3
St Anne's Convent RC Girls
  Sch SO15 . . . . .102 C3
St Anne's Gdns SO19 . . . .103 C1
St Anne's Gr PO14 . . . . . .154 C2
St Anne's Rd
  Portsmouth PO4 . . . . . . .182 C2
  Southampton SO19 . . . . .103 C1
  Upton BH16 . . . . .201 A4
St Annes Cl SO22 . . . . . . .10 B2
St Annes Gdns SO41 . . . . .197 B2
St Annes Ho SO51 . . . . . . .52 C3
St Annes La SO32 . . . . . . .107 C4
St Annes Mews **18** SO14 103 A4
St Anns Ct **7** SO17 . . . . .79 A1
St Anthony's RC Prim Sch
  PO14 . . . . .129 B1
St Anthony's Rd BH2 . . . .204 C3
St Aubin's Ave SO19 . . . . .104 A3
St Aubin's Pk PO11 . . . . .184 B2
St Aubyns Cl **3** BH15 . . .202 A1
St Aubyns La BH24 . . . . . .117 C1
St Augustin's Rd BH2 . . . .204 C3
St Augustine Rd PO4 . . . .182 C2
St Austell Cl SO50 . . . . . . .56 C2
St Barbara Way PO2 . . . .157 C2
St Barbe Cl SO51 . . . . .53 A3
St Barbe Mus✶ SO41 . . . .197 C2
St Bartholomew's Gdns
  PO5 . . . . .215 C1
St Bede CE Prim Sch
  SO23 . . . . .11 A4
St Bede's Ct **26** SO23 . . . .2 A1
St Bernard Ho **24** SO14 .103 A2
St Birinus Rd SP5 . . . . . . .47 B3
St Blaize Rd SO51 . . . . . . .53 B4
St Boniface Cl SO52 . . . . .54 A3
St Bonnet Dr SO32 . . . . . .83 B4
St Brelade Pl SO16 . . . . . .77 B2
St Brelades BH14 . . . . . . .203 B1
St Brelades Ave BH12 . . . .188 B1
St Catherine St PO5 . . . . .182 B2
St Catherine's Par BH23 191 C1
St Catherine's RC Prim Sch
  BH23 . . . . .164 A1
St Catherine's Rd
  Bournemouth BH6 . . . . . .206 C2
  South Hayling PO11 . . . . .184 B2
  Southampton SO18 . . . . . .79 C1
  Winchester SO23 . . . . . . .11 A3
St Catherine's Way
  BH23 . . . . .191 B2
St Catherines BH21 . . . . .163 B2
St Catherines Cl BH21 . . .184 B2
St Catherines Rd SO50 . . .56 A3
St Catherines View
  SO30 . . . . .105 A3
St Catherines Way
  Portchester PO16 . . . . . .131 C1
  Winchester SO23,SO21 . . .11 B3
St Chads Ave PO2 . . . . . .157 C1
St Christopher Ave
  PO16 . . . . .131 B2
St Christopher's Rd
  PO9 . . . . .135 B2
St Christophers Cl SO52 . .54 A2
St Christophers Gdns **4**
  PO13 . . . . .155 B1

St Christophers Hospl
PO16 ....131 A2
St Christophers Sch
SO18 ....103 C4
St Clair Rd BH13 ......214 C4
St Clares Ave PO9 .....135 B4
St Cleeves Way BH22 ...165 B2
St Clement & St John CE Inf
Sch BH8 ....205 B3
St Clement St
21 Winchester SO22 ......10 C4
31 Winchester SO23 ......11 A4
St Clement's Gdns BH1 .205 B3
St Clement's Rd BH8 ....205 B3
St Clements CI SO51 .....52 C4
St Clements La BH15 ....202 A1
St Clements Rd BH15 ....203 A4
St Colman's Ave PO6 ...158 A4
St Cross Ct 4 SO23 ......10 C3
St Cross Hospl★ SO23 ...10 C2
St Cross Mede SO23 .....10 C2
St Cross Rd SO22 ....10 C3
St Cuthberts CI SO31 ...129 A2
St Cuthberts La SO31 ..129 A2
St Cyres Meml Cotts
SO41 ....197 C3
St David's CI SO40 ......76 B1
St David's Ct
3 Bournemouth BH1, ...205 C3
Gosport PO13 ....180 B3
North Baddesley SO52 ...54 A2
St David's Rd
Clanfield PO8 ....88 B3
Portsmouth PO5 ....215 C2
Upton BH16 ....201 A4
St Davids Rd SO31 ......128 C2
St Denys 28 BH15 ....195 A1
St Denys Prim Sch SO17 .79 B1
St Denys Rd SO17,SO18 ..79 B1
St Denys Wlk 13 PO9 ...135 B4
St Denys' Sta SO17 .....103 B4
St Edmondsbury Ct
PO13 ....180 B3
St Edmund CI PO14 .....129 A1
St Edmund's Rd SO16 ..102 A4
St Edmunds RC Sch
PO1 ....215 C3
St Edward's RC/CE Sch
BH15 ....202 C4
St Edward's Rd
Gosport PO12 ....181 A2
Portsmouth PO5 ....215 B1
St Edward's Sch SO51 ...25 A1
St Edward's Terr PO12 ..181 A3
St Edwards Rd SO31 ....127 A4
St Elizabeth's Ave SO18 .104 A4
St Evox CI SO16 ....77 C3
St Faith's CE Prim Sch
SO22 ....10 C2
St Faith's CI PO12 ......181 A3
St Faith's Rd
Portsmouth PO1 ....215 B4
Winchester SO22 ....10 C3
St Francis Ave SO18 ....104 A4
St Francis CE Prim Sch
SO53 ....55 A4
St Francis CI SO45 ......177 C4
St Francis Ct
Locks Heath PO14 ......129 B2
2 Portsmouth PO2 ......157 C2
St Francis PI PO9 ......135 C4
St Francis Rd
Blackfield SO45 ....177 C4
Gosport PO12 ....181 B1
St Francis Specl Sch
PO14 ....154 B4
St Gabriel's Rd SO18 ...104 A4
St George CI SO31 ......104 C1
St George RC Sch (Boys)
SO17 ....79 B3
St George's Almshos 11
BH15 ....202 A1
St George's Ave
Bournemouth BH8 .....205 B4
Havant PO9 ....136 A1
Poole BH12 ....203 A4
St George's Beneficial CE
Prim Sch PO1 ....182 A3
St George's Bsns Ctr 28
PO1 ....182 A3
St George's CI
Bournemouth BH8 .....205 B4
Christchurch BH23 .....208 B4
St George's Cotts SP6 ...47 B2
St George's Cres SP6 ...69 C1
St George's Ct
2 Bournemouth BH1, ..205 C3
North Baddesley SO52 ..54 A2
7 Portsmouth PO5 .....215 A1
St George's Dr BH22 ...165 B2
St George's Ho 14 SO23 .11 A4
St George's Rd
Cosham PO6 ....157 C4
Portsmouth PO1 ....182 A2
Portsmouth, Southsea
PO4 ....183 A1
South Hayling PO11 ...184 B2
St George's Sq 7 SO32 .83 B4
St George's St
Southampton SO14 ....103 A2
Winchester SO23 ......11 A4
St George's Way PO1 ...182 A2
St George's Wlk 11 PO7 134 C4
St Georges CI BH23 ....193 A4

St Georges Cotts
Martin SP6 ....43 B2
Woodgreen SP6 ....70 C4
St Georges Ct 4 PO16 ..155 A4
St Georges Ho 22 SO17 .103 A4
St Georges Ind Est PO4 183 A3
St Georges Mans 18
BH5 ....205 C2
St Georges Rd
Fordingbridge SP6 ......69 C1
Locks Heath SO31 .....128 C2
St Georges Sq PO1 .....182 A3
St Giles CI SO23 ....11 A4
St Giles Hill SO23 ......11 A4
St Giles Way PO8 ....88 B1
St Helen's CI PO4 ......182 C1
St Helen's Par PO4 .....182 C1
St Helen's Rd
Gosport PO12 ....180 C2
South Hayling PO11 ...184 B2
St Helena Gdns SO18 ...79 C2
St Helena Way PO16 ...156 B4
St Helens Mews 8 SO50 .57 B1
St Helier PI SO16 ....77 C2
St Helier Rd BH12 ......188 B1
St Hellen's Rd PO6 .....158 B4
St Hermans Mans PO11 185 B1
St Hermans Rd PO11 ...185 B1
St Hilda Ave PO8 ....88 B1
St Hubert Rd PO8 ....88 B1
St Ives End La BH24 ....140 A2
St Ives Fst Sch BH24 ...140 A3
St Ives Gdns BH24 .....204 C3
St Ives Park BH24 ......140 A3
St Ives Wood BH24 .....140 A3
St James CE Fst Sch SP6 93 A3
St James CE Prim Sch
Bournemouth BH7 .....206 A3
Emsworth PO10 ....136 C1
West End SO30 ....80 C1
St James CI Clanfield PO8 .88 B2
7 Poole BH15 ....202 A1
St James Ho 23 SO14 ...103 A4
St James Hospl PO4 ....183 B3
St James Pk (Cvn Pk)
SO53 ....55 A4
St James Rd
Ferndown BH22 ....165 A3
Sway SO41 ....172 B4
West End SO30 ....80 B1
St James Way PO16 ....156 B4
St James's La SO22,SO23 10 C4
St James's Rd PO10 ....136 C1
St James's Terr SO23 ...10 C4
St James's Villas SO23 ..10 C4
St James's 20 BH5 .....205 C2
St James's CI SO15 ......78 B1
St James's Park Rd SO16 78 B1
St James's Rd
Portsmouth PO5 ....215 B2
Southampton SO15 ....102 A4
St James's Sq BH5 .....206 A3
St James's St PO1 ......182 A3
St John the Baptist CE Prim
Sch
Titchfield PO14 ....129 B1
Waltham Chase SO32 ...83 C1
St John's Ave PO7 ......134 C2
St John's CI
Gosport PO12 ....181 A3
Wimborne Minst BH21 .163 B2
St John's Coll PO5 .....215 C1
St John's Ct
4 Bournemouth BH1, ..205 C3
North Baddesley SO52 ..54 A2
16 Portsmouth PO2 ....157 B1
St John's Ctr SO30 .....105 A3
St John's Gdns 3 BH9 ..189 C1
St John's Hill BH21 .....163 B3
St John's Hospital
(Almshouses)(N) 27
SO23 ....11 A4
St John's Hospital
(Almshouses)(S) 38
SO23 ....11 A4
St Johns CE Fst Sch
BH21 ....163 B2
St Johns CE Prim Sch
PO12 ....181 A4
St Johns CI
Rownhams SO16 ....77 C4
South Hayling PO11 ...184 B2
St Johns Ct SO40 ......101 C1
St Johns Dr SO40 ......101 C1
St Johns Gdns SO51 ....52 C4
St Johns Glebe SO16 ...77 C3
St Johns Inf Sch SO14 ..102 C2
St Johns La SO32 ......107 C4
St Johns Mews SO31 ...129 B2
St Johns RC Prim Sch
PO1 ....215 C3
St Johns Rd BH25 ......195 A4
St Johns Sq 13 PO12 ...181 A3
St Joseph CI SO31 ......129 A2
St Joseph's Mews PO5 .215 C1

St Joseph's RC Comb Sch
BH12 ....203 C4
St Joseph's RC Prim Sch
BH23 ....208 A4
St Jude's CE Prim Sch
PO1 ....182 A2
St Jude's RC Prim Sch
PO14 ....130 C1
St Judes CI PO5 ....215 B3
St Julien's Hospl
(Almhouses) SO14 ....103 A4
St Just CI BH22 ....165 B2
St Katharine's CE Prim Sch
BH6 ....207 B2
St Katherine's CE Prim Sch
BH6 ....206 C1
St Kitts Ho 4 PO6 ......132 C1
St Lawrence CI SO30 ....81 B1
St Lawrence Rd
Eastleigh SO50 ....56 C4
31 Southampton SO14 ..103 A2
St Ledger's PI BH1 .....205 B3
St Ledger's Rd BH8 .....205 B3
St Leonard's Ave PO11 .185 A2
St Leonard's Rd
Bournemouth BH8 .....205 A3
Winchester SO23 ......11 B3
St Leonards CI PO15 ...129 C2
St Leonards Hospl
BH24 ....139 B1
St Leonards Rd SO41 ...199 A4
St Leonards Way BH24 .139 B2
St Lucia Ho 2 PO6 .....132 C1
St Luke's CE Prim Sch
Bournemouth BH9 .....204 C4
Sway SO41 ....172 A1
St Luke's CE Sec Sch
PO1 ....215 B3
St Luke's Rd
Bournemouth BH3 .....204 C4
Gosport PO12 ....181 A3
St Lukes CI SO30 ....81 B1
St Margaret's Almshouses
BH21 ....163 A3
St Margaret's Ave BH23 207 A3
St Margaret's CI SO18 ..104 A4
St Margaret's Cotts SO32 59 B1
St Margaret's Rd
Bishopstoke SO50 ......56 B2
Bournemouth BH10 ....189 B1
Poole BH15 ....202 B2
St Margarets BH2 ......204 C3
St Margarets CI BH21 ..163 A3
St Margarets Hill BH21 .163 B3
St Margarets Ho 6
SO16 ....102 C4
St Margarets La PO14 ..129 C1
St Margarets Rd PO11 ..185 A2
St Mark's CE Jun Sch
SO15 ....102 B4
St Mark's CE Prim Sch
BH10 ....189 B1
St Mark's CI PO12 .....181 A1
St Mark's PI PO12 ......181 A1
St Mark's Rd
Bournemouth BH11 ....189 A2
Gosport PO12 ....181 A1
Portsmouth PO2 ....157 B1
St Marks CI SO53 ....30 C1
St Marks Ct 6 PO12 ...181 A3
St Marks Rd
Lymington SO41 ....197 A2
Southampton SO14 ....103 A3
St Martin CI SO23 ......11 A4
St Martin's CI
Bishopstoke SO50 ......56 B2
Southampton SO16 .....77 C2
St Martin's Ho 15 PO5 .182 B1
St Martins Rd BH10 ....201 A4
St Martins Trad Pk SO23 .11 A4
St Mary Gr SO41 ....196 A1
St Mary Magdalen
Almshouses 50 SO23 ..11 A4
St Mary St
Southampton SO14 ....103 A2
Winchester SO22 ....10 B3
St Mary's SO51 ....52 C3
St Mary's Ave PO12 ....181 A1
St Mary's Church CI
SO18 ....79 B2
St Mary's CI
Droxford SO32 ....61 A1
Kings Worthy SO21 .....2 B3
Redlynch SP5 ....47 C2
St Mary's Coll
Southampton SO18 ....103 C4
Winchester SO23 ......11 A3
St Mary's Ct BH6 ......206 C2
St Mary's Ho PO1 ......182 C3
St Mary's Hospl East Wing
PO3 ....183 A3
St Mary's Hospl West Wing
PO1 ....182 C3
St Mary's Maternity Hospl
BH15 ....202 B2
St Mary's Mews BH22 ..165 B2
St Mary's PI SO14 ......103 A2
St Mary's Prim Sch
SO14 ....103 A2
St Mary's RC Prim Sch
PO12 ....181 A3
St Mary's Rd
Bishopstoke SO50 ......56 B2
Bournemouth BH1 .....205 B3
Ferndown BH22 ....165 B3
Liss GU33 ....20 C2
Netley SO31 ....127 B3
Poole BH15 ....202 C2

St Mary's Rd continued
Portsmouth PO1 ....182 C3
South Hayling PO11 ...184 C2
Southampton SO14 ....103 A3
Stubbington PO14 .....154 A3
St Mary's Stad SO14 ...103 A3
St Mary's Terr SO21 ....32 A3
St Marys BH23 ....193 B4
St Matthew's Rd PO6 ...157 C4
St Matthews Ct 22 SO14 103 A3
St Matthews Ct PO12 ..181 B3
St Matthews Rd SO22 ....1 B1
St Merrin's CI BH10 ....189 B2
St Michael's 2 BH2 ....204 B2
St Michael's CE Mid Sch
BH21 ....163 C4
St Michael's CE Prim Sch
BH2 ....204 B2
St Michael's Ct 28 PO6 .133 A1
St Michael's Gdns 26
SO22 ....10 C4
St Michael's Gr PO14 ...154 C4
St Michael's Ho 8
PO14 ....154 C4
St Michael's Mews 16
BH2 ....204 B2
St Michael's Pas SO23 ..11 A3
St Michael's PI 18 BH2 .204 C2
St Michael's Rd
Bournemouth BH2 .....204 C1
Havant PO9 ....135 B2
Portsmouth PO1 ....215 A2
Winchester SO22 ....10 C3
St Michael's Rdbt BH4 .204 B2
St Michael's Sch SO41 ..150 C1
St Michael's St 18 SO14 102 C2
St Michaels CI
Blackfield SO45 ....150 C1
Hamworthy BH15 ......201 C1
Verwood BH31 ....114 C4
St Michaels Ct 1 BH6 ..206 B2
St Michaels Rd
Locks Heath SO31 .....129 A1
Totton SO40 ....100 C4
Verwood BH31 ....114 C4
St Michaels Way PO8 ...88 B1
St Monica Inf Sch SO19 104 A2
St Monica Jun Sch
SO19 ....104 A2
St Monica Rd SO19 .....104 A2
St Nicholas Ave PO13 ..180 B4
St Nicholas Flats 18
PO2 ....157 B1
St Nicholas Rise SO23 ...2 A3
St Nicholas Row PO17 .108 A2
St Nicholas St PO1 .....182 A2
St Nicholas' Rd PO9 ....135 B2
St Osmund's Rd BH14 ..203 B2
St Patrick's Ct SO22 ....54 A2
St Patrick's La GU33 ....21 B1
St Patrick's RC Prim Sch
SO19 ....103 C2
St Paul's Hill SO22 ......10 C4
St Paul's La BH1 ....205 A2
St Paul's PI BH1 ....205 A2
St Paul's Rd
Bournemouth BH1 .....205 A2
Locks Heath SO31 .....128 C3
Portsmouth PO5 ....215 A2
St Paul's Sq PO5 ....215 A2
St Pauls PI 19 SO22 ....10 C4
St Pauls RC Prim Sch
PO6 ....157 A4
St Peter St SO23 ....11 A4
St Peter's Ave PO11 ....160 B1
St Peter's Cres 36 BH1 .204 C2
St Peter's Ct
17 Petersfield GU32 ....40 C2
7 Poole BH15 ....203 A2
St Peter's Gr PO5 ......215 C1
St Peter's RC Comp Sch
BH6 ....206 C2
St Peter's RC Prim Sch
SO22 ....10 A3
St Peter's RC Sch BH7 .206 A4
St Peter's Rd
Bournemouth BH1 .....205 A2
Petersfield GU32 ....40 C2
Poole BH14 ....203 A2
St Peter's Rdbt BH1 ....205 A2
St Peter's Sq 6 PO10 ..160 C4
St Peter's St SO32 ......83 B4
St Peter's Wlk 38 BH1 .204 C2
St Peters CI SO32 ......106 B4
St Peters Ct
Bournemouth BH1 .....205 A2
4 Emsworth PO10 .....161 A4
St Peters RC Prim Sch
PO7 ....134 C3
St Peters Rd PO11 .....160 B2
St Philip's Way SO18 ..104 A4
St Pirans Rd PO3 ....183 A4
St Quentin Ho 12 PO14 154 C4
St Richards Gdns PO7 ..134 B3
St Ronan's Ave PO4 ....182 C1
St Ronan's Rd PO4 .....182 C1
St Saviors CI BH7 ......206 B4
St Sebastian Cres PO16 131 A2
St Simon CI SO31 ......129 A2
St Simon's Rd PO5 .....182 B1
St Stephen's Ct 6 PO4 .204 C2
St Stephen's Rd
Bournemouth BH2 .....204 C2
Portsmouth PO2 ....182 C4
Winchester SO22 ....1 B1
St Stephen's Way 27
BH2 ....204 C2
St Stephens La BH31 ...115 A4

St Mary's Rd continued
Portsmouth PO1 ....182 C3
South Hayling PO11 ...184 C2
St Swithun CI SO32 .....83 B4
St Swithun St SO23 .....11 C1
St Swithun Wells (RC) Prim
Sch SO53 ....55 C2
St Swithun's CI SO51 ...28 B1
St Swithun's RC Prim Sch
PO5 ....182 B1
St Swithun's Rd BH1 ...205 A2
St Swithun's Rd S BH1 .205 A2
St Swithun's Sch SO21 ..11 A4
St Swithuns Ct 7 SO14 103 A3
St Swithuns Rd PO2 ....157 C1
St Theresas CI PO9 ....135 B2
St Thomas Ave PO11 ...184 B2
St Thomas CI PO16 .....131 B2
St Thomas Ct 7 SO50 ...57 B1
St Thomas Garnet's RC Sch
BH5 ....206 A3
St Thomas Mews 22
SO23 ....10 C4
St Thomas More's RC Prim
Sch PO9 ....135 B2
St Thomas Pk SO41 ....197 B2
St Thomas St SO22 ......10 C4
St Thomas's CI BH10 ...189 C1
St Thomas's Ct 5 PO1 .182 A2
St Thomas's Rd PO12 ..181 A4
St Thomas's St
Lymington SO41 ....197 C2
Portsmouth PO1 ....182 A2
St Tristan CI SO31 .....129 A1
St Ursula Gr PO5 ......215 C1
St Valerie Rd
Bournemouth BH2 .....204 C3
Gosport PO12 ....181 A2
St Vigor Way
Colden Common SO21 ..31 C1
Colden Common SO21 ..57 C1
St Vincent Coll PO12 ...181 A3
St Vincent Cres PO8 ....112 C3
St Vincent L Ctr PO12 ..181 B3
St Vincent Rd
Gosport PO12 ....181 A3
Portsmouth PO5 ....182 B1
St Vincent St PO5 ......215 A2
St Walburga's RC Prim Sch
BH9 ....190 A1
St Winifred's Rd
Bournemouth BH2 .....204 C3
Southampton SO16 .....78 B1
St Winifred's Sch SO17 .79 A1
Salcombe Ave PO3 .....158 A1
Salcombe CI SO53 ......55 A2
Salcombe Cres SO40 ...100 C3
Salcombe Rd
Southampton SO15 ....102 B4
Totton SO40 ....100 C3
Salcot Rd SO23 ....2 A1
Salem St SO15 ....78 B1
Salerno Dr PO12 ....180 C2
Salerno Ho
Fareham PO14 ....154 C2
Romsey SO51 ....53 A4
Salerno PI BH15 ....201 B1
Salerno Rd
Portsmouth PO2 ....157 B2
Southampton SO16 .....78 B2
Salet Way PO7 ....112 A1
Salisbury CI SO50 ......56 A2
Salisbury Ct 1 SO50 ....56 A2
Salisbury Rd
Awbridge SO51 ....52 A3
Bournemouth BH1 .....205 C2
Breamore SP6 ....70 A3
Burton BH23 ....192 B2
Cosham PO6 ....158 A4
Fordingbridge SP6 ......70 A1
Fordingbridge, Ibsley BH24 .94 A1
Ower SO51 ....76 B2
Poole BH14 ....203 B3
Portsmouth PO4 ....182 C1
Ringwood BH24 ....116 C3
Sopley, Winkton BH23 .192 A3
Southampton SO17 .....79 A2
Totton SO40 ....76 B2
West Wellow SO51 .....50 B2
West Wellow SO51 .....51 A1
Salisbury Road Arc
SO40 ....100 C4
Salisbury St
Fordingbridge SP6 .....69 C1
6 Southampton SO15 ..102 C3
Salisbury Terr PO13 ...179 C1
Salmon Dr SO50 ....56 C1
Salt La SO32,SO24 ......34 C2
Salt Meat La PO12 .....181 B3
Salter Rd BH13 ....214 B2
Salterns Ave PO4 ......183 A3
Salterns CI PO11 ....185 B2
Salterns Ct BH14 ......214 A4
Salterns Est PO16 ......155 A4
Salterns La
Bursledon SO31 ....128 A4
Fareham PO16 ....155 A4
South Hayling PO11 ...185 B2
Salterns Point BH14 ...214 A4
Salterns Quay BH14 ...214 A4
Salterns Rd Poole BH14 .203 A2
Stubbington PO13,PO14 .179 A2
Salterns Specl Sch
SO40 ....101 A4
Salterns Way BH14 ....214 A4
Salters Acres SO22 ......1 C1
Salters La SO22 ....1 A1
Saltgrass La SO41 ......212 A2
Saltings Rd BH16 ......201 A3
Saltings The
Cosham PO6 ....158 C4

Saltings The continued
Havant PO9 . . . .**159** C3
Saltmarsh La PO11 . . . . . .**184** C3
Saltmarsh Rd SO14 . . . . .**103** A2
Saltmead SO17 . . . .**79** B1
Salvia Cl PO7 . . . .**135** A3
Salwey Rd SO30 . . . .**105** B3
Samber Cl SO41 . . . .**197** B2
Sammy Miller Motorcycle
  Mus ★ BH25 . . . .**194** C3
Sampan Cl SO31 . . . .**128** C1
Samphire Cl SO41 . . . . . .**197** C3
Samples Way BH17 . . . . .**202** C4
Sampson Rd
  Gosport PO14 . . . .**154** C3
  Portsmouth PO1 . . . .**181** C3
Samson Cl PO13 . . . .**180** B4
Samson Rd BH15 . . . .**201** B1
Samuel Rd PO1 . . . .**182** C3
San Diego Rd PO12 . . . . .**181** A3
San Remo Twrs 28 BH5 . .**205** C4
Sancreed Rd BH12 . . . . . .**203** C4
Sancroft BH21 . . . .**164** A1
Sand Cl SO51 . . . .**50** C2
Sandbanks Bsns Ctr
  BH13 . . . .**214** A2
Sandbanks Rd BH14 . . . . .**203** A1
Sandbourne Rd
  Bournemouth BH4 . . . . . .**204** B1
  Poole BH15 . . . .**202** B2
Sandcroft Cl PO12 . . . . . .**180** C2
Sandecotes Rd BH14 . . . .**203** B2
Sandell Ct SO16 . . . .**79** A3
Sanderling Rd PO4 . . . . . .**183** B3
Sanderlings BH24 . . . . . .**141** B3
Sanderlings The PO11 . . .**185** A1
Sandford Ave PO12 . . . . .**180** B2
Sandford Cl BH9 . . . .**190** B2
Sandford Way BH18 . . . . .**186** C1
Sandhill La PO13 . . . .**180** A3
Sandhills Cl BH17 . . . .**187** B1
Sandhurst Ct PO5 . . . .**215** C1
Sandhurst Dr BH21 . . . . .**139** A4
Sandhurst Rd SO15 . . . . .**102** C3
Sandilands Way 11
  SO45 . . . .**126** A1
Sandisplatt PO14 . . . .**154** B4
Sandle Copse SP6 . . . .**69** A1
Sandleford Rd PO9 . . . . . .**135** B4
Sandleheath Ind Est SP6 **69** A1
Sandleheath Rd SP6 . . . . .**92** C4
Sandlewood Cl
  Clanfield PO8 . . . .**88** B3
  Totton SO40 . . . .**100** B4
Sandmartin BH25 . . . .**209** C4
Sandown Cl PO12 . . . .**180** B2
Sandown Rd
  Christchurch BH23 . . . . .**207** C3
  Cosham PO6 . . . .**157** C4
  Southampton SO15 . . . . . .**78** A1
Sandpiper Cl
  Broadstone BH17 . . . . . .**186** C1
  Horndean PO8 . . . .**112** A4
  Marchwood SO40 . . . . . .**101** C1
Sandpiper Rd SO16 . . . . . .**78** B3
Sandpipers PO6 . . . .**158** C4
Sandpit La
  Beaulieu SO41 . . . .**199** B3
  Poole BH15 . . . .**202** B2
Sandport Gr PO16 . . . . . .**156** A4
Sandringham Cl
  Bournemouth BH9 . . . . . .**190** A2
  Chandler's Ford SO53 . . . .**54** C2
Sandringham Ct
  Bournemouth BH8 . . . . . .**205** B3
  Southampton, Millbrook
    SO15 . . . .**102** A3
  21 Southampton, Westwood Pk
    SO17 . . . .**79** A1
Sandringham Gdns BH9 **190** A2
Sandringham La PO1 . . . .**215** D3
Sandringham Rd
  Fareham PO14 . . . .**154** B4
  Petersfield GU32 . . . .**40** C2
  Poole BH14 . . . .**203** B2
  Portsmouth PO1 . . . .**215** D3
  Southampton SO18 . . . . . .**79** C1
Sandsbury La GU32 . . . . . .**40** B3
Sandy Beach Est PO11 . . .**185** C1
Sandy Brow PO7 . . . .**134** B2
Sandy Cl Petersfield GU31 .**41** B2
  Wimborne Minst BH21 . . .**164** A4
Sandy Down SO41 . . . . . .**173** B2
Sandy La
  Abbotswood SO51 . . . .**28** A2
  Bournemouth BH6 . . . . . .**206** A3
  Christchurch BH23 . . . . .**191** C1
  Fair Oak SO50 . . . .**57** B1
  Lyndhurst SO43 . . . .**121** C4
  North Baddesley SO52 . . . .**54** A3
  Pamphill BH21 . . . .**162** A3
  Rake GU33 . . . .**21** C2
  Redlynch SP5 . . . .**47** C4
  St Leonards BH24 . . . . . .**140** A3
  Three Legged Cross BH21 .**140** A2
  Titchfield PO14 . . . .**153** C4
  Upton BH16 . . . .**201** A3
  Verwood BH31 . . . .**115** A4
  Waltham Chase SO32 . . . . .**83** B1
  Wimborne Minst BH21 . . .**164** A4
Sandy Mead Rd BH8 . . . .**190** C1
Sandy Plot BH23 . . . .**207** B4
Sandy Point Rd PO11 . . . .**185** C1
Sandy Way BH10 . . . .**189** C2
Sandycroft SO31 . . . .**152** B4
Sandyfield Cres PO8 . . . . .**111** C2
Sandyhurst Cl BH17 . . . . .**187** B1
Sanross Cl PO14 . . . .**179** A3

Santoy BH13 . . . .**214** B3
Sapphire Ridge PO7 . . . . .**135** A4
Saracen Cl SO41 . . . .**197** B1
Saracens Rd SO53 . . . .**55** C4
Sarah Cl BH7 . . . .**206** A4
Sarah Robinson Ho 39
  PO1 . . . .**182** A3
Sarah Sands Cl BH23 . . . .**207** A4
Sarisbury CE Jun Sch
  SO31 . . . .**128** C3
Sarisbury Gate SO31 . . . .**129** A3
Sarisbury Inf Sch SO31 . .**128** C2
Sark Rd BH12 . . . .**203** B4
Sarnia Ct SO16 . . . .**77** C2
Sarum Ave BH22 . . . .**138** C2
Sarum Cl SO22 . . . .**10** B4
Sarum Ct BH14 . . . .**203** B2
Sarum Rd
  Chandler's Ford SO53 . . . .**55** C3
  Winchester SO22 . . . .**10** A4
Sarum St 14 BH15 . . . . . .**202** A1
Sarum View SO22 . . . .**10** A4
Sarum Wlk SO41 . . . .**197** B3
Satchell La SO31 . . . .**128** A2
Saturn Cl SO16 . . . .**77** C2
Saulfland Dr BH23 . . . . . .**208** B4
Saulfland Ho BH23 . . . . . .**208** B4
Saulfland Pl BH23 . . . . . .**208** B4
Saunders Ho PO6 . . . .**132** C1
Saunders La SO51 . . . .**26** C3
Saunders Mews PO4 . . . . .**183** A1
Savernake Cl
  Gosport PO13 . . . .**155** B1
  9 Romsey SO51 . . . .**28** A1
Saville Cl
  Bishopstoke SO50 . . . .**56** B3
  Gosport PO12 . . . .**180** C2
Saville Ct 9 BH21 . . . . . .**163** B2
Saville Gdns PO16 . . . . . .**131** A2
Savoy Bldgs 22 PO16 . . . .**131** A1
Savoy Ho SO40 . . . .**101** A4
Sawmills The SO32 . . . . . .**82** A3
Sawyer Cl SO22 . . . .**1** A1
Saxholm Cl SO16 . . . .**78** C3
Saxholm Dale SO16 . . . . . .**78** C3
Saxholm Way SO16 . . . . . .**78** C3
Saxley Ct PO9 . . . .**135** B3
Saxon Cl Horndean PO8 . . .**88** B2
  Locks Heath SO31 . . . . . .**128** C1
  Portchester PO16 . . . . . .**132** A1
Saxon Gdns SO30 . . . .**105** A3
Saxon Ho 17 SO14 . . . . . .**103** B3
Saxon Hts BH6 . . . .**206** C3
Saxon King Gdns BH6 . . . .**207** A2
Saxon Mdw SP5 . . . .**46** C4
Saxon Pl SO41 . . . .**197** B3
Saxon Rd Blackfield SO45 .**150** C1
  Southampton SO15 . . . . .**102** B3
  Winchester SO23 . . . .**2** A1
Saxon Shore Inf Sch
  PO6 . . . .**156** C4
Saxon Sq Sh Ctr 4
  BH23 . . . .**207** A3
Saxon Way Alderholt SP6 . .**93** A3
  Romsey SO51 . . . .**53** A4
Saxon Wlk SO53 . . . .**55** C3
Saxonbury Rd BH6 . . . . . .**206** C3
Saxonford Rd BH23 . . . . .**208** B4
Saxonhurst SP5 . . . .**47** A4
Saxonhurst Cl BH10 . . . . .**189** C3
Saxonhurst Gdns BH10 . .**189** C2
Saxonhurst Rd BH10 . . . .**189** C2
Saxton Ct 15 SO23 . . . . . .**11** A4
Sayers Rd SO50 . . . .**56** C2
Scafell Ave PO14 . . . .**154** B4
Scallops La SO51 . . . .**50** C3
Scantabout Ave SO53 . . . . .**55** C4
Scantabout Prim Sch
  SO53 . . . .**55** C4
Scarf Rd BH17 . . . .**202** C4
Scarff Ct PO11 . . . .**185** A1
Scholars' Wlk PO6 . . . . . .**158** B4
School Cl
  Chandler's Ford SO53 . . . .**55** A3
  Verwood BH31 . . . .**115** A4
School Hill SO32 . . . .**85** B3
School La Boldre SO41 . . . .**197** C4
  Bournemouth BH11 . . . . .**189** A3
  Bransgore BH23 . . . .**169** C2
  Chandler's Ford SO53 . . . .**55** A3
  Compton (Sussex) PO18 . . .**90** C1
  Denmead PO7 . . . .**110** B3
  Emsworth PO10 . . . .**160** C4
  Hamble-le-Rice SO31 . . . .**128** A1
  Kings Worthy SO23 . . . .**2** A1
  3 Liss GU33 . . . .**20** C2
  Lymington SO41 . . . .**197** C2
  Michelmersh SO51 . . . .**6** B1
  Milford on Sea SO41 . . . .**211** C3
  Petersfield GU32 . . . .**41** A3
  Poole BH15 . . . .**202** B3
  Ringwood BH24 . . . .**141** A4
  Southbourne PO18 . . . . . .**161** C4
  St Leonards BH24 . . . . . .**140** A2
  Three Legged Cross BH21 .**138** C4
  Westbourne PO10 . . . . . .**137** A3
  Wimborne Minst BH21 . . .**163** A3
School Pl SO19 . . . .**103** C2
School Rd
  Bransgore BH23 . . . .**169** C2
  Bursledon SO31 . . . .**128** A4
  Fawley SO45 . . . .**151** A2
  Gosport PO12 . . . .**155** C1
  Havant PO9 . . . .**135** C1
  Hythe SO45 . . . .**126** A2
  Nomansland SP5 . . . .**73** B4
  Redlynch SP5 . . . .**48** A3

School Rd continued
  Romsey SO51 . . . .**28** B1
  Totton SO40 . . . .**101** A3
  Twyford SO21 . . . .**31** C3
  West Wellow SO51 . . . . . .**50** C1
  Wickham PO17 . . . .**108** A2
Schooner Way
  Locks Heath SO31 . . . . . .**128** C1
  Portsmouth PO4 . . . .**183** B3
Schooners Cl PO13 . . . . . .**179** C2
Scimitars The PO14 . . . . .**154** A2
Scivier's La SO32 . . . .**58** B1
Scotland Cl SO50 . . . .**57** C1
Scotney Ct 21 PO9 . . . . . .**136** A3
Scott Cl
  Colden Common SO21 . . . .**57** A4
  Poole BH12 . . . .**188** C3
  Stubbington PO14 . . . . . .**154** B2
Scott Ho 2 PO2 . . . .**157** B1
Scott Rd Eastleigh SO50 . . .**55** C1
  Poole BH12 . . . .**188** C1
  Portsmouth PO1 . . . .**181** C3
  Portsmouth, Hilsea PO3 . . .**157** C3
  Southampton SO19 . . . . .**103** C1
Scott's Gn BH23 . . . .**207** C4
Scott-Paine Dr SO45 . . . .**126** A2
Scotter Rd
  Bishopstoke SO50 . . . .**56** B2
  Bournemouth BH7 . . . . . .**206** A3
Scotter Sq SO50 . . . .**56** B2
Scotts Hill La BH23 . . . . .**207** B4
Scratchface La
  Havant PO7 . . . .**135** A1
  Waterlooville PO7 . . . . . .**134** C2
Scullards La 1 SO14 . . . . .**102** C2
Sea Breeze Gdns PO4 . . . .**183** B2
Sea Crest Rd PO13 . . . . . .**179** C1
Sea Front PO11 . . . .**184** C2
Sea Front Est PO11 . . . . .**185** A1
Sea Grove Ave PO11 . . . . .**185** A1
Sea Kings PO14 . . . .**179** A3
Sea La PO11 . . . .**179** B2
Sea Mill Gdns 24 PO1 . . . .**182** A3
Sea Pines SO41 . . . .**211** B2
Sea Point 8 BH13 . . . .**214** C4
Sea Rd
  Barton on Sea BH25 . . . . .**209** C4
  Bournemouth, Boscombe
    BH5, BH6 . . . .**205** C2
  Bournemouth, Southbourne
    BH6 . . . .**206** C2
  Milford on Sea SO41 . . . .**211** C2
  Southampton SO19 . . . . .**103** B2
Sea View Cotts PO10 . . . .**160** C4
Sea View Est SO31 . . . . . .**127** A3
Sea View Rd
  Cosham PO6 . . . .**134** B1
  Poole BH12 . . . .**203** A3
  South Hayling PO11 . . . . .**185** B2
  Upton BH16 . . . .**201** A4
Sea Vixen Ind Est BH23 . .**208** A4
Seabank Cl BH16 . . . .**201** A4
Seabird Way PO16 . . . . . .**155** A4
Seabourne Pl 12 BH5 . . . .**206** A3
Seabourne Rd BH5 . . . . . .**206** A3
Seacombe Gn SO16 . . . . . .**77** B1
Seacombe Rd BH13 . . . . . .**214** A2
Seacroft Ave BH25 . . . . . .**209** C4
Seafarers Wlk PO11 . . . . .**185** C1
Seafield Cl BH25 . . . .**209** C4
Seafield Dr BH6 . . . .**206** C3
Seafield Park Rd PO14 . . .**179** A3
Seafield Rd
  Barton on Sea BH25 . . . . .**209** C4
  Bournemouth BH6 . . . . . .**206** B2
  Christchurch BH23 . . . . .**208** B4
  Portchester PO16 . . . . . .**156** A4
  Portsmouth PO3 . . . .**158** A1
  Southampton SO16 . . . . . .**77** C2
Seafield Terr PO12 . . . . . .**181** B2
Seafields PO10 . . . .**160** C4
Seaford Cl SO31 . . . .**104** C1
Seagarth Cl SO16 . . . .**78** B3
Seagarth La SO16 . . . .**78** B2
Seager's Ct PO1 . . . .**181** C2
Seagrove Rd PO2 . . . .**157** B1
Seagull Cl PO4 . . . .**183** B3
Seagull Ct PO10 . . . .**136** C1
Seagull La PO10 . . . .**136** C1
Seagull Rd BH8 . . . .**190** B1
Seagulls The PO13 . . . . . .**180** A2
Seahorse Wlk PO12 . . . . .**181** B3
Sealark Rd PO12 . . . .**181** B4
Seamans La SO43 . . . .**98** C2
Seamead PO14 . . . .**179** B2
Seamoor La BH4 . . . .**204** A2
Seamoor Rd BH4 . . . .**204** A2
Searles Hill SO21 . . . .**32** A3
Seathrift Cl PO13 . . . .**179** C1
Seathwaite Ho 26 PO6 . . .**133** A1
Seaton Ave PO3 . . . .**183** A4
Seaton Cl
  Christchurch BH23 . . . . .**209** A4
  Lymington SO41 . . . .**197** C3
  West End SO18 . . . .**80** B1
Seaton Rd BH23 . . . .**209** A4
Seatown Cl BH17 . . . .**188** A1
Seaview Ave PO16 . . . . . .**132** A1
Seaview Ct Gosport PO12 **180** B2
  14 Lee-on-the-Solent
    PO13 . . . .**179** C1
Seaview Rd
  Barton on Sea BH25 . . . . .**209** B4
  Christchurch BH23 . . . . .**194** B1
Seaward Ave BH25 . . . . . .**209** C4
Seaward Gdns SO19 . . . . .**103** B2
Seaward Rd Hythe SO45 . .**126** C4

Seaward Rd continued
  Southampton SO19 . . . . .**103** C2
Seaward Twr PO12 . . . . . .**181** C2
Seaway BH25 . . . .**210** A4
Seaway Ave BH23 . . . .**208** B4
Seaway Cres PO4 . . . .**183** B2
Seaway Gr PO16 . . . .**156** B3
Seawinds SO41 . . . .**211** B3
Sebastian Gr PO7 . . . .**135** A4
Second Ave Cosham PO6 . .**157** C4
  Cosham, Farlington PO6 . .**158** C4
  Emsworth PO9 . . . .**136** A1
  Southampton SO15 . . . . .**101** A3
  Southbourne PO10 . . . . . .**161** B4
Second Marine Ave
  BH25 . . . .**210** A3
Second St SO45 . . . .**150** C4
Sedberg Ho SO16 . . . .**77** B1
Sedbergh Rd SO16 . . . .**77** B1
Seddul-Bahr SO30 . . . .**80** C3
Sedgefield Cl
  Portchester PO6 . . . .**156** C4
  Totton SO40 . . . .**100** B4
Sedgeley Gr PO12 . . . . . .**181** A4
Sedgemead SO31 . . . .**127** A3
Sedgemead Ct SO31 . . . . .**127** A3
Sedgewick Cl PO13 . . . . . .**180** B4
Sedgewick Ct SO50 . . . . . .**56** B2
Sedgewick Rd
  Bishopstoke SO50 . . . .**56** B2
  Southampton SO19 . . . . .**104** B3
Sedgley Cl PO5 . . . .**215** C2
Sedgley Rd BH9 . . . .**204** C4
Seed Warehouse The 15
  BH15 . . . .**202** B1
Segars La SO31 . . . .**31** C3
Segensworth E Ind Est
  PO15 . . . .**129** B3
Segensworth N Ind Est
  PO15 . . . .**129** C3
Segensworth Rd PO15 . . .**129** C2
Segensworth W Ind Est
  PO15 . . . .**129** B3
Selangor Ave PO10 . . . . . .**136** B1
Selborne Ave
  Havant PO9 . . . .**135** B3
  Southampton SO18 . . . . .**104** A4
Selborne Ct 3 SO51 . . . . . .**28** B4
Selborne Pl SO22 . . . .**10** B3
Selborne Rd SO40 . . . . . .**100** B4
Selborne Wlk SO18 . . . . .**104** A4
Selbourne Dr SO50 . . . . . .**56** A2
Selbourne Gdns PO12 . . . .**180** C2
Selbourne Rd PO9 . . . . . .**135** C1
Selbourne Terr PO1 . . . . .**215** D3
Selby Cl BH18 . . . .**187** A2
Seldon Cl SO22 . . . .**10** A2
Seldown BH15 . . . .**202** B1
Seldown Bridge BH15 . . . .**202** B1
Seldown La BH15 . . . .**202** B2
Seldown Rd BH15 . . . .**202** B2
Self Rd BH15 . . . .**202** A1
Selfridge Ave BH6 . . . . . .**207** A2
Selfridge Cl BH6 . . . .**207** A2
Selhurst Ho PO1 . . . .**215** C4
Selhurst Way SO50 . . . . . .**57** B1
Seliot Cl BH15 . . . .**202** B3
Selkirk Cl BH21 . . . .**163** C1
Sellwood Rd SO31 . . . .**127** B3
Sellwood Way BH25 . . . . .**209** B4
Selsdon Ave SO51 . . . .**53** A4
Selsey Ave Gosport PO12 **181** A4
  Portsmouth PO4 . . . .**183** A1
Selsey Cl
  South Hayling PO11 . . . . .**185** C1
  Southampton SO16 . . . . . .**77** C1
Selsmore Ave PO11 . . . . . .**185** B2
Selsmore Rd PO11 . . . .**185** A2
Selwood Pk BH10 . . . .**189** B4
Selworth La SO32 . . . .**85** A2
Selworthy Cl BH14 . . . . . .**203** A1
Selwyn Ct 21 PO6 . . . .**157** C4
Selwyn Gdns SO50 . . . .**56** A3
Sengana Cl SO30 . . . .**105** A3
Senlac Rd SO51 . . . .**53** A4
Sennen Pl PO6 . . . .**157** A4
Sentinal Ct BH15 . . . .**202** C2
Sentinel Cl PO7 . . . .**112** A1
Seps 4 Rd SO45 . . . .**151** B2
September Cl SO30 . . . .**80** B1
Serle Cl SO40 . . . .**100** A4
Serle Gdns SO40 . . . .**100** B3
Sermon Rd SO22 . . . .**1** A1
Serpentine Rd
  Fareham PO16 . . . .**131** A1
  Poole BH15 . . . .**202** B2
  26 Portsmouth PO5 . . . . .**182** B1
  Waterlooville PO7 . . . . . .**134** B2
Service Rd PO6 . . . .**157** B4
Set Thorns Rd SO41 . . . . .**172** B1
Setley Gdns BH8 . . . .**190** C2
Setters Cl SO21 . . . .**56** C4
Settle Cl SO16 . . . .**102** A4
Settlers Cl PO1 . . . .**215** C4
Sevenoaks Dr BH7 . . . . . .**206** A4
Sevenoaks Rd PO6 . . . . . .**157** C4
Severn Cl Cosham PO6 . . . .**133** A1
  Portchester PO16 . . . . . .**156** A4
Severn Rd
  Ferndown BH22 . . . .**166** A3
  Southampton SO16 . . . . .**101** C4
Severn Way SO30 . . . .**80** B1
Seward Ave BH6 . . . .**206** B2
Seward Rise SO51 . . . .**53** B4
Seymour Cl
  Chandler's Ford SO53 . . . .**55** C3
  Portsmouth PO2 . . . .**182** B4
  Southampton SO16 . . . . . .**78** C2

Seymour Cl continued
  Totton SO40 . . . .**76** B1
Seymour Ho SO16 . . . .**78** B2
Seymour La SO52 . . . .**53** C2
Seymour Rd
  Lee-on-the-Solent PO13 . .**180** A2
  Ringwood BH24 . . . .**117** A1
  Southampton SO16 . . . . . .**78** B2
Shackleton Ho 2 PO2 . . . .**157** C1
Shackleton Rd PO13 . . . . .**180** B4
Shackleton Sq BH25 . . . . .**169** A1
Shadwell Ct 9 PO2 . . . . . .**157** B1
Shadwell Rd PO2 . . . .**157** B1
Shaftesbury Ave
  Chandler's Ford SO53 . . . .**55** B2
  Southampton SO17 . . . . . .**79** A1
  Waterlooville PO7 . . . . . .**134** C2
Shaftesbury Cl BH22 . . . . .**138** C1
Shaftesbury Rd
  Gosport PO12 . . . .**181** B2
  Poole BH15 . . . .**202** B2
  West Moors BH22 . . . . . .**138** C1
Shaftesbury St SP6 . . . . . .**69** C1
Shaftsbury Rd
  Bournemouth BH8 . . . . . .**205** B3
  Portsmouth PO5 . . . .**182** B1
Shaggs Mdw SO43 . . . . . .**122** A3
Shakespeare Ave SO51 . . .**103** A4
Shakespeare Bsns Ctr
  SO50 . . . .**56** A2
Shakespeare Dr SO40 . . . .**100** B4
Shakespeare Gdns PO8 . .**111** C2
Shakespeare Jun Sch
  SO50 . . . .**56** A3
Shakespeare Mews
  PO14 . . . .**154** A4
Shakespeare Rd
  Bournemouth BH6 . . . . . .**206** B4
  Eastleigh SO50 . . . .**56** A2
  Portsmouth PO1 . . . .**182** C4
  Wimborne Minst BH21 . . .**163** B3
Shakespeare Road Inf Sch
  SO50 . . . .**56** A3
Shalbourne Rd PO12 . . . . .**181** A4
Shalcombe SO31 . . . .**127** B2
Shalden Cl SO16 . . . .**78** B2
Shaldon Rd 8 PO9 . . . . . .**136** A3
Shales Rd SO18 . . . .**104** A4
Shallow La SO41 . . . .**197** C4
Shallows The SO45 . . . .**70** B4
Shamblehurst La N SO32 . .**81** B2
Shamblehurst La S SO30 . .**81** B1
Shamblehurst Prim Sch
  SO30 . . . .**105** B4
Shamrock Cl PO12 . . . . . .**181** B2
Shamrock Ct 2 BH21 . . . .**163** B2
Shamrock Quay SO14 . . . .**103** B3
Shamrock Rd SO19 . . . . . .**103** B2
Shamrock Villas 9 SO17 . .**79** B1
Shamrock Way SO45 . . . . .**126** A3
Shanklin Cres SO15 . . . . . .**78** B1
Shanklin Rd
  Portsmouth PO4 . . . .**182** C2
  Southampton SO15 . . . . . .**78** B1
Shannon Cl PO15 . . . .**130** C3
Shannon Ho 26 SO14 . . . .**103** B3
Shannon Rd
  Gosport PO14 . . . .**155** A3
  Stubbington PO14 . . . . . .**154** A3
Shannon Way SO53 . . . . . .**55** A3
Shapland Ave BH11 . . . . . .**188** C3
Shappen Hill La BH24 . . . .**142** C1
Shapton Cl SO45 . . . .**150** A2
Shapwick Rd BH15 . . . . . .**202** B2
Shard Cl BH31 . . . .**115** A3
Sharlands Cl BH18 . . . . . .**187** B2
Sharlands Rd PO14 . . . . . .**155** A3
Sharon Ct PO12 . . . .**181** B2
Sharon Rd SO30 . . . .**80** B1
Sharp Rd BH12 . . . .**204** A3
Sharp's Copse Inf Sch
  PO9 . . . .**136** A3
Sharp's Copse Jun Sch
  PO9 . . . .**136** A3
Sharp's Rd PO9 . . . .**136** A3
Sharpley Cl SP4 . . . .**69** C2
Sharpness Cl PO14 . . . . . .**154** B4
Sharps Cl PO3 . . . .**158** A2
Sharvells Rd SO41 . . . .**211** B3
Shavard La SO32 . . . .**61** B3
Shaves La BH25 . . . .**195** A3
Shaw Cl Totton SO40 . . . .**100** B4
  West End SO18 . . . .**80** A1
Shaw Rd BH24 . . . .**117** B1
Shawcross Ind Pk PO3 . . .**158** A3
Shawfield Rd PO9 . . . .**160** A4
Shawford Cl
  Ashurst SO40 . . . .**100** A4
  8 Southampton SO16 . . . . .**78** C2
Shawford Gdns BH8 . . . . .**190** B1
Shawford Gr PO9 . . . .**135** C2
Shawford Rd
  Bournemouth BH8 . . . . . .**190** B1
  Twyford SO21 . . . .**31** C3
Shawford Sta SO21 . . . . . .**31** C3
Shayer Rd SO15 . . . .**78** B1
Shear Hill GU31 . . . .**41** A3
Sheardley La SO32 . . . .**62** A1
Shearer Rd PO1 . . . .**182** C4
Shears Brook Cl BH23 . . . .**169** A2
Shears Rd SO50 . . . .**56** C2
Shearwater Ave PO16 . . . .**155** C4
Shearwater Cl PO13 . . . . .**155** A1
Shearwater Ct PO11 . . . . .**185** B1
Shearwater Dr PO6 . . . . . .**158** C4

Sheep Pond La SO32 ....61 A2
Sheep St GU32 ....40 C2
Sheepwash La PO7 ....133 C4
Sheet Prim Sch GU32 ...41 A3
Sheffield Cl SO50 ....56 B3
Sheffield Ct PO13 ......180 B3
Sheffield Rd PO1 ......215 D3
Sheiling Sch The BH24 .140 B3
Shelbourne Cl BH8 .....205 B3
Shelbourne Rd BH8 ....205 A3
Sheldrake Gdns
  Hordle SO41 ....196 A3
  Southampton SO16 ....78 A3
Sheldrake Rd BH23 ....208 A4
Shelford Rd PO4 ....183 A3
Shell Bay Sailing Ctr★
  BH19 ....214 A1
Shell Ct SO40 ....101 C1
Shellcroft SO31 ....152 B4
Shelley Ave PO6 ......132 C1
Shelley Cl
  Bournemouth BH1, ...205 C3
  Christchurch BH23 ....208 B4
  St Leonards BH24 ....139 C3
  Winchester SO22 ......10 A1
Shelley Ct
  Ferndown BH22 ....165 B3
  Southampton SO15 ...102 C3
Shelley Gdns
  Bournemouth BH1, ...205 C3
  Waterlooville PO8 ....111 C2
Shelley Hamlets BH23 .208 B4
Shelley Hill BH23 .....208 B4
Shelley Ho 15 BH25 ...195 A1
Shelley La SO51 ....75 C4
Shelley Park (Bournemouth
  & Poole Coll) BH5 ...205 C2
Shelley Rd
  Bournemouth BH1, BH7 .205 C3
  Eastleigh SO50 ....55 C1
  Poole BH12 ....203 B4
  Southampton SO19 ...104 C3
  Totton SO40 ....76 B1
Shelley Rd E BH7 .....205 C3
Shelley Way SO41 .....211 B3
Shelton Rd BH6 ....206 B3
Shenley Cl PO15 ......130 B1
Shenstone Ct 18 BH25 .195 A1
Shepards Cl PO14 .....154 B4
Shepheard's Way PO12 .181 B1
Shepherd Cl BH23 .....193 C1
Shepherds Cl
  Cadnam SO40 ....99 A3
  Winchester SO22 ......10 A2
Shepherds Down Specl Sch
  SO21 ....31 B1
Shepherds Hey Rd SO40 .76 A1
Shepherds Hill BH24 ..116 B1
Shepherds La
  Compton (Hants) SO21 ..31 B3
  Ibsley BH24 ....116 A1
Shepherds Purse Cl
  SO31 ....128 C1
Shepherds Rd
  Cadnam SO40 ....99 A3
  Winchester SO23 ......11 B4
Shepherds Way
  Bournemouth BH7 .....206 A4
  Nursling SO16 ....77 B3
Sheppard Cl PO8 ......112 A3
Sheppards Field 4
  BH21 ....163 A3
Sherborn Cres BH17 ..188 A1
Sherborne Ct SO50 .....56 A3
Sherborne Dr BH22 ...165 B2
Sherborne House Sch
  SO53 ....55 B4
Sherborne Rd SO17 ....79 A1
Sherborne Way SO30 ..105 B3
Sherbrooke Cl SO23 .....2 A1
Sherecroft Gdns SO30 .106 A4
Sherfield Ave PO9 ....136 A3
Sherfield Cl BH8 ......190 B1
Sherfield English La
  SO51 ....50 B3
Sherfield English Rd SP5 .50 A2
Sherfield Ho 26 SO15 .102 C4
Sheridan Cl
  Southampton SO19 ...104 A3
  Winchester SO22 ......10 B3
Sheridan Gdns
  Swanwick PO15 ......129 B4
  Totton SO40 ....100 B4
Sheringham Rd
  Cosham PO6 ....133 B1
  Poole BH12 ....203 B4
Sherley Gn SO31 ......105 A1
Sherrin Cl BH15 ......202 B3
Sherringham Cl SO45 .151 A2
Sherwin Wlk PO12 ....181 A2
Sherwood Ave
  Ferndown BH22 ......165 B2
  Hedge End SO30 .....105 B2
  Poole BH14 ....203 A2
Sherwood Cl Liss GU33 .21 A1
  13 Southampton SO16 .78 C2
Sherwood Dr BH31 ....115 A3
Sherwood Gdns SO31 .128 C2
Sherwood Rd
  Chandler's Ford SO53 ..30 C1
  Gosport PO12 ....181 A2
Sherwood Way SO45 ..177 C4
Shetland Cl Cosham PO6 133 C1
  Totton SO40 ....100 A4
Shetland Rise PO15 ...129 A4

Shetland View BH31 ..115 A3
Shillinglee PO7 ....134 C2
Shillingstone Dr BH9 ..190 A2
Shillingstone Gdns
  BH12 ....203 C4
Shillito Rd BH12 ......203 B3
Shingle Bank Dr SO41 .211 B2
Shinwell Ct 17 SO15 ...78 A1
Ship Leopard St 12 PO1 182 A3
Shipbuilding Rd PO1 ..181 C4
Shipcote La SO32 ......59 B1
Shipley Rd SO31 ....32 A4
Shipton Gn PO9 ....135 B3
Shipstal Cl BH16 ......201 B2
Shipwrights Wlk SO41 .212 A1
Shire Cl Swanwick PO15 .129 A4
  Waterlooville PO7 ....112 B1
Shires Cl BH24 ....141 A2
Shires Copse BH6 .....206 C2
Shires Mead BH31 ....115 A3
Shires The SO30 ......105 A3
Shires Wlk SO40 ......100 A4
Shirley Ave
  Portsmouth PO4 ......183 B2
  Southampton SO15 ...102 B4
Shirley Cl
  Bransgore BH23 ......169 A1
  West Moors BH22 ....138 C1
Shirley High St SO15,
  SO16 ....102 A4
Shirley Holms SO41 ...173 A1
Shirley Inf Sch SO15 ...78 B1
Shirley Park Rd SO16 .102 A4
Shirley Rd
  Bournemouth BH9 ....190 A1
  Poole BH12 ....203 A3
  Portsmouth PO5 .....182 C1
  Southampton SO15 ...102 B4
  Upton BH16 ....201 B3
Shirley Twrs SO15 ....102 B4
Shirley Warren Prim Sch
  SO16 ....78 A1
Shirrel Ct PO12 ....180 B2
Shoblands Way 10
  SO45 ....126 A1
Shoe La Meonstoke SO32 .61 B3
  Upham SO32 ....58 C3
Sholing Ct PO9 ....135 B3
Sholing Girls Sch SO19 .104 A2
Sholing Inf Sch SO19 .104 A3
Sholing Jun Sch SO19 .104 A3
Sholing Rd SO19 ......103 C2
Sholing Sta SO19 .....103 C1
Shoot Hill PO7&PO17 ..109 B2
Shoot La PO13 ....180 A4
Shooters Hill Cl SO19 .104 A2
Shop La SO19,SO31 ...104 C1
Shore Ave
  Portsmouth PO4 ......183 A3
  Upton BH16 ....201 B3
Shore Cl
  Milford on Sea SO41 .211 B1
  Upton BH16 ....201 B3
Shore Cres SO32 ....83 B4
Shore Gdns BH16 .....201 A3
Shore La
  Bishop's Waltham SO32 .83 B4
  Upton BH16 ....201 B4
Shore Rd Hythe SO45 .126 A2
  Locks Heath SO31 ....128 B1
  Poole BH13 ....214 B3
Shoreacres BH13 .....214 B2
Shorefield Cres SO41 .211 B3
Shorefield Cvn Pk SO41 211 A3
Shorefield Rd
  Marchwood SO40 ....101 C1
  Milford on Sea SO41 .211 B3
  Shorefield Way SO41 .211 B3
Shorehaven PO6 ......156 C4
Shorewell SO31 ....127 B4
Shorewood Cl SO31 ..128 C1
Short Cl BH12 ....204 A4
Short Hill Nomansland SP5 73 A4
  Romsey SO51 ....28 B1
Short Rd PO14 ....179 A3
Short Row PO1 ....182 A3
Shorts Cl BH23 ....192 B1
Shorts Rd SO50 ....57 B1
Shotterfield Terr GU33 ..20 C2
Shotters Hill Cl SO30 ...80 B1
Shotts La SO41 ....198 C2
Shottsford Rd BH15 ..202 B3
Shraveshill Cl SO40 ....76 B1
Shrubb's Ave SO41 ...197 C2
Shrubbery Cl PO16 ...156 B4
Shrubbery The PO12 ..180 C4
Shrubbs Hill Gdns SO43 121 C2
Shrubbs Hill Rd SO43 .121 C2
Shrubland Ct SO18 ...104 A4
Sibland Cl PO14 ......154 B4
Siblings The SO19 ....104 C3
Sicily Ho 16 PO14 ....154 C4
Siddal Ct SO19 ....104 B2
Sidings The Downton SP5 .47 A4
  Netley SO31 ....127 B3
Sidlesham Cl PO11 ...185 C1
Sidmouth Ave PO3 ...183 A4
Sidney Gdns 11 BH9 ..190 A2
Sidney Smith Ct BH17 .187 C1
Silchester Cl BH2 ....204 C3
Silchester Rd PO3 ....183 A4
Silhouette Ct PO11 ...185 B1
Silkin Gdns SO40 .....100 B3
Silksstead Ave PO9 ...135 C3
Silksstead La SO21 .....30 C4
Sillen La SO51 ....43 A2
Silver Birch Ave PO14 .154 C4
Silver Birch Cl Liss GU33 .21 A2

Silver Birch Cl continued
  Poole BH12 ....204 A2
  Southampton SO19 ...104 B2
Silver Birches SO31 ..127 C4
Silver Bsns Pk BH23 ..207 C4
Silver Hill SO23 ....11 A4
Silver St
  Christchurch BH23 ...207 A3
  Hordle SO41 ....196 B3
  Lyndhurst SO43 ......121 B3
  1 Portsmouth PO5 ..215 A1
Silver Way SO19 .....208 C4
Silverdale SO25 ......210 A4
Silverdale Cl BH18 ...186 C2
Silverdale Cres SP6 ...93 A3
Silverdale Ct 22 SO15 .102 C4
Silverdale Rd SO15 ..102 C4
Silverlock Cl 1 PO2 ..182 B4
Silverlock Pl PO10 ...137 A3
Silvers End 6 SO45 ..126 A1
Silvers Wood SO40 ...76 B1
Silversands Gdns PO11 .185 A1
Silverthorne Way PO7 .134 B4
Silvertrees PO10 .....136 C1
Silverweed Ct SO53 ...54 C4
Silverweed Ct SO31 ..128 C1
Silverwood Cl
  Wimborne Minst BH21 .163 B1
  Winchester SO22 ......10 B3
Silvester Rd PO8 .....111 C1
Silwood Cl SO22 ....1 B1
Simmonds Cl BH15 ...202 B3
Simmonds Gn PO11 ..185 B2
Simmons Cl SO30 ....105 B4
Simnel St 18 SO14 ...102 C2
Simon Ct SO18 ....104 C4
Simon Way SO19 .....104 C3
Simonds Cl 5 SO23 .....2 A1
Simpson Cl PO16 .....156 B4
Simpson Rd PO2 ......157 B1
Sinah La PO11 ....184 B2
Sinclair Ct 8 BH14 ..203 A2
Sinclair Inf Sch SO16 ..78 A3
Sinclair Jun Sch SO16 ..78 A3
Sinclair Rd SO16 ......78 A3
Singleton Dr BH10 ...189 B1
Singleton Gdns PO8 ...88 B2
Singleton Way SO40 ..100 A4
Sir Christopher Cl SO45 126 A2
Sir Christopher Ct 5
  SO45 ....126 A2
Sir Galahad Rd SO53 ..54 C3
Sir George's Rd SO15 .102 B3
Sir Harold Hillier Gardens &
  Arboretum★ SO51 ....28 B2
Sir Lancelot Cl SO53 ..54 C3
Sirdar Ho SO17 ....79 B2
Sirdar Rd SO17 ....79 B2
Sirius Ct PO5 ....215 B2
Siskin Cl
  Bishop's Waltham SO32 .83 A4
  Ferndown BH22 ......165 A4
  Southampton SO16 ....78 A3
Siskin Gr PO7 ....135 A3
Siskin Inf Sch PO13 ..180 B3
Siskin Jun Sch PO13 ..180 B3
Siskin Rd PO4 ....183 B3
Sissinghurst Cl SO19 .104 A1
Sissinghurst Rd PO16 .156 A4
Siverdale Dr PO7 .....111 B2
Siward Ho 20 GU32 ...40 C2
Six Dials SO14 ....103 A3
Six Oaks Rd SO52 .....54 A2
Sixpenny Cl
  Locks Heath PO14 ...129 A1
  Poole BH12 ....203 C4
Sixth Ave PO6 ....157 C4
Sizer Way SO45 ......125 A2
Skew Rd PO17 ....132 B1
Skinner St PO1 ......182 B1
Skintle Gn 5 SO21 ....56 C4
Skipper Cl SO40 .....102 A2
Skipper Way PO13 ...180 A3
Skipton Cl BH18 .....187 A1
Skipton Rd SO53 ......55 B2
Sky End La SO41 .....196 A1
Skylark Ct PO4 ......183 B3
Skylark Mdws PO15 ..129 C3
Skys Wood Rd SO53 ..54 C3
Slab La Redlynch SP5 ..47 B3
  West Wellow SO51 ...50 C2
Slade Cl SO41 ....196 A2
Slade's La BH10 .....204 B4
Slades Farm Hostel
  BH11 ....189 B1
Slades Farm Rd BH10 .189 B1
Slades Farm Specl Sch
  BH10 ....189 B1
Slades Hill SO45 .....150 C1
Slater App PO2 ......157 A1
Slater Cl SO40 ....100 A4
Sleepbrook Cl BH31 ..114 C3
Sleeper's Hill Ho SO22 .10 B3
Sleeper's Hill Rd SO22 .10 B3
Sleepers Delle Gdns
  SO22 ....10 C3
Sleepers Hill Gdns SO22 .10 B3
Sleight La BH21 ......186 A4
Slepe Cres BH12 .....203 C4
Slindon Cl PO8 ....88 B3
Slindon Gdns 15 PO9 .135 C1
Slindon St PO1 ......215 B3
Slingsby Cl PO1 .....215 A1
Slinn Rd BH23 ....207 C4
Slip Way BH15 ....202 A1
Slipper Rd PO10 .....161 A4
Slipway The PO6 .....157 A4
Sloane Ave SO45 ....150 B2

Sloane Ct SO45 ......150 B2
Sloane Pk SO32 ......107 B4
Sloane Stanley Ct PO12 181 A3
Slocum Ho 17 PO12 ..181 B2
Sloe Tree Cl PO14 ...129 B1
Slough La BH16 ......201 B3
Smallcutts Ave PO10 .137 B1
Smeaton St 7 PO2 ...157 B1
Smeeton Rd PO13 ....179 C1
Smith Cl SO45 ....150 C1
Smith Gr SO30 ....105 B3
Smith La PO10 ....161 B1
Smith St PO12 ....181 A3
Smith's Field SO51 ...28 A1
Smithe Cl SO50 ....56 A2
Smithfield Pl BH9 ....189 C1
Smithson Ct BH12 ...204 B4
Smiths La SO32 ......107 C3
Smithy La BH25 .....194 C3
Smithy The PO7 .....110 C2
Smugglers La BH21 ..163 C4
Smugglers La N BH23 .193 C1
Smugglers La S BH23 .208 C4
Smugglers Reach BH23 208 A3
Smugglers Wood Rd
  BH23 ....193 B1
Smythe Rd SO19 .....104 B2
Snailing La GU33 .....20 A4
Snails La BH24 ....117 A2
Snakemoor La SO32 ..81 C3
Snapdragon Cl SO31 .128 C1
Snape Cl PO13 ....180 B4
Snellgrove Cl SO40 ...76 B1
Snellgrove Pl SO40 ...76 B1
Snooks La SO41 .....198 A3
Snowberry Cres PO9 .136 B2
Snowdon Dr PO14 ...154 C4
Snowdon Rd BH4 ....204 B2
Snowdrop Cl SO31 ...128 C1
Snowdrop Gdns BH23 .193 A1
Soake Rd PO7 ....111 A2
Soalwood La GU32 ....39 C4
Soberton Ho
  Portsmouth PO1 .....215 C4
  34 Southampton SO17 .79 A1
Soberton Rd
  Bournemouth BH8 ...205 B3
  Havant PO9 ....135 C2
Soberton Twrs SO32 ..85 B3
Solar Ct BH13 ....204 A1
Soldridge Cl 5 PO9 ..136 A3
Solent Ave
  Lymington SO41 .....198 A2
  Southampton SO19 ...104 C3
Solent Bsns Ctr SO15 .102 A3
Solent Bsns Pk PO15 .129 C4
Solent Cl
  Chandler's Ford SO53 ..55 C3
  Lymington SO41 .....197 C2
Solent Ct
  6 Milford on Sea SO41 .211 B2
  Southampton SO19 ...103 C1
  Stubbington PO14 ...179 B3
Solent Ctr PO15 .....129 C4
Solent Dr
  Barton on Sea BH25 .210 A4
  Hythe SO45 ....125 C2
  Locks Heath SO31 ...152 B3
  South Hayling PO11 .184 C1
Solent Gate
  Gosport PO14 ....155 A3
  9 Portsmouth PO5 ..182 B1
Solent Ho
  5 Fareham PO14 ....155 A4
  Havant PO9 ....136 A2
Solent Homes SO19 ..104 C3
Solent Hts
  12 Lee-on-the-Solent
  PO13 ....179 C1
  Portsmouth PO4 .....183 B2
Solent Ind Ctr SO15 ..102 B3
Solent Ind Est SO30 ...81 A1
Solent Inf Sch PO6 ..158 B4
Solent Jun Sch PO6 ..158 B4
Solent Lo 21 BH25 ...195 A1
Solent Mdws SO31 ...128 A1
Solent Pines 2 SO41 .211 A2
Solent Rd
  Barton on Sea BH25 .209 B4
  Bournemouth BH6 ...207 A2
  Christchurch BH23 ...194 A1
  Cosham PO6 ....158 B4
  Havant PO9 ....135 C1
  Hythe SO45 ....149 C4
  Southampton SO15 ...102 C2
  Stubbington PO14 ...129 B1
Solent View Boldre SO41 198 A2
  Bournemouth BH6 ...207 A2
  Fawley SO45 ....178 A4
  Lee-on-the-Solent PO13 179 B2
Solent Village PO15 ..129 C3
Solent Way
  Gosport PO12 ....180 C2
  Milford on Sea SO41 .211 C2
Solihull Ho PO5 .....215 A2
Solly Cl BH12 ....203 C4
Solomon Way BH15 ..201 B1
Solomons Cl SO32 ....83 C1
Solona Ct SO53 ....55 C4
Solway Ho 10 SO14 ..103 B3
Somborne Ct 32 SO17 ..79 A1
Somborne Dr PO9 ...135 C3
Somborne Ho SO19 ..103 C1
Somerby Rd BH15 ...202 B3
Somerford Ave BH23 .208 A4
Somerford Bsns Pk
  BH23 ....208 A4
Somerford Cl SO19 ..104 A3

Somerford Ct BH23 ..208 C4
Somerford Cty Inf Sch
  BH23 ....207 C4
Somerford Cty Jun Sch
  BH23 ....207 C4
Somerford Rd BH23 ..207 C4
Somerford Way BH23 .207 C3
Somerley Rd BH9 ....205 A4
Somerley View 1 BH24 .141 A4
Somers Cl SO22 ....10 B3
Somers Park Prim Sch
  PO1 ....215 C3
Somers Rd
  Portsmouth PO1 .....215 C2
  Portsmouth PO1 .....215 C3
Somers Rd N PO1 ...215 D3
Somerset Cres SO53 ..55 B2
Somerset Ct 4 SO15 .102 B3
Somerset La SO18 ...104 B4
Somerset Rd
  Bournemouth BH7 ...206 A3
  Christchurch BH23 ...206 C4
  Portsmouth PO5 .....182 B1
  Southampton SO17 ...79 B1
Somerset Terr SO15 ..102 B3
Somerstown Flats PO9 .136 B4
Somerton Ave SO18 ..104 A4
Somervell Cl PO12 ...181 A1
Somervell Dr PO16 ...131 A2
Somerville Ct BH25 ..194 C2
Somerville Pl 1 PO2 .157 C2
Somerville Rd
  Bournemouth BH2 ...204 B2
  Kings Worthy SO23 ....2 B4
  Ringwood BH24 .....141 B4
Sommers Ct SO19 ...103 B2
Sonata Ho PO6 ......157 A4
Sonnet Way 1 PO7 ..135 A4
Sonning Way BH8 ...190 A1
Soper's La BH23 .....207 A3
Sopers La BH17 .....187 A1
Sopley Cl BH25 ......209 B4
Sopley Ct 19 PO9 ...136 A3
Sopley Farm Bldgs
  BH23 ....192 A3
Sopley Prim Sch BH23 .168 B1
Sopwith Cl SO31 ....208 A4
Sopwith Cres BH21 ..163 C1
Sopwith Way SO31 ..128 C4
Sorrel Cl Romsey SO51 .28 B1
  Waterlooville PO7 ...135 A3
Sorrel Dr PO15 ......129 B4
Sorrel Gdns BH18 ...186 C1
Sorrell Cl SO31 ......128 C1
Sorrell Ct BH23 .....208 A4
Sorrell Way BH23 ...208 A4
South Ave Fawley SO45 .150 C2
  Holbury SO45 ....150 B3
  New Milton BH25 ...195 A1
  Portsmouth PO2 .....157 C2
South Baddesley CE Prim Sch
  SO41 ....198 C3
South Baddesley Rd
  SO41 ....198 A2
South Bay PO10 .....161 A2
South Cl Gosport PO12 .180 C1
  Havant PO9 ....160 A4
  Romsey SO51 ....28 B1
South Cliff Rd BH2 ..204 C1
South Cross St PO12 .181 B2
South Ct SO31 ....127 C1
South Downs Coll PO7 .135 A2
South Dr Awbridge SO51 .27 A2
  Littleton SO22 ....1 A2
South East Cres SO19 .104 A2
South East Rd SO19 .104 A2
South End Cl SO21 ...30 A4
South Front
  18 Romsey SO51 ....52 C4
  Southampton SO14 ..103 A3
South Gr SO41 ......197 C2
South Hampshire Ind Pk
  SO40 ....76 B2
South Haven Cl BH16 .201 A2
South Hill Alderholt SP6 .93 A3
  Droxford SO32 ....85 A4
  Southampton SO16 ...79 A2
South Kinson Dr BH11 .189 A2
South La Buriton GU31 ..65 B2
  Clanfield PO8 ....88 A3
  Downton SP5 ....46 C4
  Horndean PO8 ....89 A2
  Nomansland SP5 .....73 B4
  Southbourne PO10 ..137 C1
  Westbourne PO10 ...137 B2
South Lo BH13 ......214 D4
South Lodge PO5 ....130 A1
South Mill Rd SO15 ..102 A4
South Millers Dale SO53 .55 C4
South Normandy 4
  PO1 ....182 A2
South Par
  Portsmouth PO5 .....182 B1
  Totton SO40 ....100 C4
South Parade Pier★
  PO4 ....182 C1
South Park Rd BH12 .204 A4
South Pl PO13 ....180 C2
South Rd
  Bournemouth BH1 ...205 C3
  Corfe Mullen BH21 ..186 C3
  Cosham PO6 ....158 B4
  Horndean PO8 ....88 B1
  Poole BH15 ....202 B1
  Portsmouth PO5 .....182 C4
  South Hayling PO11 .184 C2
  Southampton SO17 ..103 B4

South Rd *continued*
Southwick PO17 ....133 A3
South Road Comb Sch
BH15 ....202 B1
South St Eastleigh SO50 ...80 A4
Emsworth PO10 ....160 C4
Gosport PO12 ....181 B2
Havant PO9 ....135 C1
Hythe SO45 ....126 A2
Lymington SO41 ....197 B1
Portsmouth PO5 ....215 B1
Titchfield PO14 ....153 C4
South Stoneham Ho
SO18 ....79 B2
South Sway La SO41 ...196 B4
South Terr PO1 ....182 A3
South Trestle Rd SO45 .151 B3
South View
Bournemouth BH2 .....204 C3
Winchester SO22 ......10 C4
South View Cl PO8 ...112 A2
South View Park Homes
SO22 ....10 B2
South View Pl [17] BH2 .204 C2
South View Rd
Christchurch BH23 ....207 A3
Southampton SO15 ....102 B4
Winchester SO22 ......10 A2
South Way PO15 ......129 C2
South Weirs SO42 ....172 B4
South Western Cres
BH14 ....203 A1
Southampton Airport
Parkway Sta SO18 ....79 C3
Southampton Central Sta
SO15 ....102 A1
Southampton City Coll
SO14 ....103 A2
Southampton Gen Hospl
SO16 ....78 A1
Southampton Hill PO14 153 C4
Southampton Ho [58]
PO9 ....136 A3
Southampton Inst ofH Ed
Marine Operations Ctr
SO40 ....102 A1
Southampton Inst(City
Campus) SO14 ....103 A3
Southampton International
Airport SO18 ....79 C3
Southampton Oceanography
Ctr SO14 ....103 A3
Southampton Rd
Brockenhurst SO41,SO42 .173 A2
Cadnam SO40 ....98 C4
Cadnam, Bartley SO40 ..99 A4
Cosham PO6 ....157 B4
Eastleigh SO50 ....56 A1
Fareham PO14 ....154 A4
Fareham PO16 ....131 A1
Fordingbridge SP6 .....70 A1
Hythe SO45 ....125 C2
Locks Heath SO31,PO14 .129 B2
Lymington SO41 ....197 B3
Lyndhurst SO43 ....122 A1
North Baddesley SO51 ..53 A3
Ringwood BH24 ....140 C4
Romsey SO51 ....53 A3
Southampton St [3]
SO15 ....102 C3
Southbourne Ave
Cosham PO6 ....158 A4
Hermitage PO10 ......161 A4
Holbury SO45 ....150 B2
Southbourne Coast Rd
BH6 ....206 C2
Southbourne Cross Roads [6]
BH6 ....206 C2
Southbourne Gr BH6 ..206 B2
Southbourne Jun & Inf Schs
PO10 ....161 A4
Southbourne Overcliff Dr
BH6 ....206 C2
Southbourne Rd
Bournemouth BH5,BH6 .206 B2
Lymington SO41 ....197 B2
Southbourne Sands
BH6 ....206 B2
Southbourne Sta PO10 .161 C4
Southbrook Cl
Havant PO9 ....159 C4
Poole BH17 ....188 A1
Southbrook Mews [5]
SO32 ....83 B4
Southbrook Rd
Havant PO9 ....159 C4
[15] Southampton SO15 ..102 C3
Southcliff PO13 ....179 C2
Southcliff Rd SO14 ....103 A4
Southcliffe Ho [1] SO14 103 A3
Southcliffe
Barton on Sea BH25 ...209 B4
Christchurch BH23 ....208 B3
Southcote Rd BH1 .....205 B2
Southcroft Rd PO12 ...180 C2
Southdale Ct SO53 ....55 B3
Southdene Rd SO53 ...55 B3
Southdown Ct [1] BH23 207 C4
Southdown Rd
Compton (Hants) SO21 ..31 B3
Cosham PO6 ....158 A4
Horndean PO8 ....88 B2
Southdown View PO7 ..111 B1
Southdown Way BH22 .138 C1
Southend La SO32 .....109 B4
Southern Ave PO4 ....139 A1
Southern Gdns SO40 ...100 C4
Southern La BH25 .....209 C4

Southern Oaks BH25 ...194 C1
Southern Rd
Bournemouth BH6 .....206 B2
Fawley SO45 ....151 C1
Lymington SO41 ....197 B2
Southampton SO15 ....102 C2
West End SO30 ....80 C1
Southernhay PO7 ......110 C2
Southernhay Rd BH1 ...115 A3
Southey Rd BH23 ......207 C4
Southfield BH24 ....141 A3
Southfield La BH24 ....143 B1
Southfield Mews [6]
BH24 ....141 A3
Southfield Wlk PO9 ...135 B4
Southfields Cl SO32 ...83 B4
Southgate St SO23 .....10 C4
Southgate Villas SO23 ..10 C4
Southill Ave BH12 .....203 B3
Southill Gdns BH9 .....190 A1
Southill Rd
Bournemouth BH9 .....190 A1
Poole BH12 ....203 B4
Southlands Cosham PO6 .158 A4
Lymington SO41 ....197 B1
Southlands Ave
Bournemouth BH6 .....206 C2
Corfe Mullen BH21 ....186 C3
Southlands Cl BH21 ....186 B3
Southlands Ct BH18 ....187 A2
Southlands Sch SO41 ..197 C4
Southlawns Wlk BH25 .194 C1
Southlea Ave BH6 .....206 C2
Southleigh Gr PO11 ...184 C2
Southleigh Rd PO9 ....136 B2
Southmead Rd PO15 ...130 C1
Southmoor La PO9 ....159 B4
Southsea Castle ★ PO5 182 B1
Southsea Inf Sch PO4 ..182 C1
Southsea Terr PO5 ....215 A1
Southview SO32 ....61 A1
Southville Rd BH5 .....206 A3
Southwater [1] PO13 ..179 C1
Southway PO13 ....155 B2
Southways PO14 ....179 B3
Southwick Ave PO16 ...132 C1
Southwick Cl SO22 .....1 B2
Southwick Ct PO14 ....155 A3
Southwick Hill Rd PO6 .133 C1
Southwick Ho [5] PO1 .215 C4
Southwick Pl BH6 .....206 B4
Southwick Rd
Bournemouth BH6 .....206 B3
Cosham PO7,PO17 .....133 B1
Denmead PO7 ....110 C2
Wickham PO17 ....108 B2
Southwood Ave
Bournemouth BH6 .....206 B2
Christchurch BH23 ....194 A1
Southwood Cl
Christchurch BH23 ....194 A1
Ferndown BH22 ....165 B3
Southwood Ct BH23 ...194 A1
Southwood Gdns SO31 .128 C2
Southwood Rd
Portsmouth PO2 ......157 C2
South Hayling PO11 ...185 B1
Sovereign Ave PO12 ...181 B4
Sovereign Bsns Ctr
BH15 ....202 A3
Sovereign Cl
Ashurst SO40 ....100 B4
Bournemouth BH7 .....205 C4
Portsmouth PO4 ......183 B3
Sovereign Cres PO14 ..129 A1
Sovereign Ct [20] SO17 .79 A1
Sovereign Ctr BH1 ....205 C3
Sovereign Dr
Hedge End SO30 ......105 B3
Portsmouth PO4 ......183 B3
Sovereign La PO7 .....134 C2
Sovereign Sq [8] BH7 .205 C2
Sovereign Way SO50 ...55 C3
Soverign Dr SO30 .....105 C3
Sowden Cl SO30 ....105 A4
Sowley La SO41 ....199 B3
Spa Rd SO14 ....102 C2
Spain Bldgs [18] GU32 .40 C2
Spain The GU32 ....40 C2
Spalding Rd SO19 .....104 C3
Spaniard's La SO51 ....53 A2
Sparkford Cl
Bournemouth BH7 .....206 A4
Winchester SO22 ......10 C4
Sparkford Rd SO22 ....10 C4
Sparrow Cl PO8 ....111 C2
Sparrow Ct PO13 ......179 C2
Sparrow Sq SO50 ......55 B1
Sparrowgrove SO21 ...31 B1
Sparrowhawk Cl PO3 ..158 A2
Sparsholt Cl PO9 ......135 A3
Sparsholt Rd
Southampton SO19 ....126 C4
Winchester SO21,SO22 ..9 B2
Spartan Cl
Stubbington PO14 .....154 B3
Thorney Island PO10 ..161 A2
Spartina Dr SO41 .....197 C3
Spear Rd SO14 ....103 A4
Specks La PO4 ....183 A3
Speedfields Pk PO14 ..155 A3
Speedwell Cl
Chandler's Ford SO53 ..55 A3
Locks Heath SO31 .....128 C1
Speedwell Dr BH23 ...208 A4
Speggs Wlk [2] SO30 ..105 B3
Speltham Hill PO7 .....86 B1
Spencer Cl PO11 ......185 A2

Spencer Ct
[5] New Milton BH25 ...195 A1
Stubbington PO14 .....179 C3
Spencer Dr PO13 ......179 C1
Spencer Gdns PO8 ....111 C2
Spencer Rd
Bournemouth BH1 .....205 B2
Eastleigh SO50 ....55 C1
Emsworth PO10 ....136 C2
New Milton BH25 .....195 A1
Poole BH13 ....214 C4
Portsmouth PO4 ......182 C1
Southampton SO19 ....104 B3
Spenlow Cl PO2 ....182 B4
Spenser Cl SO31 ......152 B4
Spetisbury Cl BH9 .....190 A2
Spice Quay [18] PO1 ...182 A2
Spicer La BH11 ....188 C3
Spicer's Hill SO40 .....100 C3
Spicer's Way SO40 ....100 C3
Spicers Ct [5] SO22 ...10 C4
Spicewood PO15 ......130 C1
Spinacre BH25 ....210 A4
Spindle Cl
Broadstone BH18 .....186 C1
Havant PO9 ....136 B2
Spindle Warren PO9 ..136 B2
Spindlewood Cl
[26] Barton on Sea BH25 .195 A1
Southampton SO19 ....79 A3
Spindlewood Way SO40 124 C4
Spinnaker Cl
Gosport PO13 ....180 B4
South Hayling PO13 ...184 C2
Spinnaker Dr PO2 .....157 C2
Spinnaker Grange PO11 160 B2
Spinnaker Ho PO6 ....157 A4
Spinnaker View PO9 ..135 A3
Spinners Cl BH22 .....138 C1
Spinners Gdn ★ SO41 .173 C1
Spinney Cl
St Leonards BH24 .....139 B2
Waterlooville PO8 .....111 C2
Spinney Dale SO45 ....126 A1
Spinney Gdns SO45 ...126 A1
Spinney The
Compton (Hants) SO21 ..31 B4
Denmead PO7 ....110 C2
Fair Oak SO50 ....57 A1
Gosport PO13 ....155 B1
Portchester PO16 .....131 C1
Southampton SO16 ....79 A3
St Leonards BH24 .....139 C3
Totton SO40 ....76 B1
Waterlooville PO8 .....112 A1
Spinney Way BH25 ....195 A3
Spinney Wlk SO18 ....79 C2
Spinneys La BH22 .....165 B3
Spinningfield Ho [4]
GU32 ....40 C2
Spitfire Cl SO19 ......103 B2
Spitfire End [7] SO23 ..11 B4
Spitfire Link SO23 .....11 B4
Spitfire Loop SO18 .....80 A4
Spitfire Quay SO19 ....103 B2
Spitfire Rdbt SO23 ....11 B4
Spitfire Way SO31 .....127 C1
Spithead Ave PO12 ...181 B1
Spithead Ho [9] PO16 .155 A4
Spithead Hts PO4 .....183 B2
Spittlefields BH24 .....141 A4
Spouts La SO51 ....50 B3
Spring Cl Fair Oak SO50 .57 B1
Southampton SO19 ....103 C2
Verwood BH31 ....114 C3
Spring Cres SO17 .....103 A4
Spring Ct Poole BH12 ..203 B3
[17] Southampton SO15 .102 C2
Spring Firs SO19 ......103 C2
Spring Garden La PO12 181 B3
Spring Gdns
[1] Emsworth PO10 .....161 A4
North Baddesley SO52 ..54 A2
Poole BH12 ....203 B3
Portsmouth PO1 ......215 A3
Spring Gr SO31 ....105 A1
Spring House Cl SO21 ..32 A1
Spring La
Bishopstoke SO50 .....56 B2
Colden Common SO21 ..31 C1
New Milton BH25 .....195 B1
Swanmore SO32 ......84 A3
Spring Pl [5] SO51 ....52 C4
Spring Rd
Bournemouth BH1 .....205 B3
Hythe SO45 ....126 A2
Locks Heath SO31 .....128 C3
Lymington SO41 ....198 A2
Southampton SO19 ....103 C2
Spring St PO1 ....215 B4
Spring The PO7 ....110 C2
Spring Vale
Swanmore SO32 ......84 A2
Waterlooville PO8 .....112 A2
Spring Wlk PO1 ....215 B4
Springbank Rd BH7 ...205 C4
Springbourne Ct BH1 ..205 B3
Springbourne Mews
BH1 ....205 B3
Springcroft PO13 .....155 A3
Springdale Ave BH18 ..186 C3
Springdale Ct SO40 ...100 C4
Springdale Fst Sch
BH18 ....186 C1
Springdale Gr BH21 ...186 C1
Springdale Rd BH18,
BH21 ....186 C1

Springfield [2] GU33 ...20 C2
Springfield Ave
Bournemouth BH6 .....207 A2
Christchurch BH23 ....191 B1
Holbury SO45 ....150 B2
Springfield Cl
Havant PO9 ....135 A1
Lymington SO41 ....198 A2
Verwood BH31 ....114 C3
Wickham PO17 ....108 A2
Springfield Cres
Poole BH14 ....203 A2
Redlynch SP5 ....47 B3
Springfield Ct SO19 ...103 C1
Springfield Dr SO40 ...100 C3
Springfield Gdns BH25 .195 B1
Springfield Gr SO45 ...150 B2
Springfield Rd
Poole BH14 ....203 A2
Verwood BH31 ....114 C3
Springfield Sch PO6 ...158 B4
Springfield Way PO14 .179 B3
Springfields [3] SO21 ..31 C1
Springford Cl SO16 ....78 A2
Springford Cres SO16 ..78 A2
Springford Gdns SO16 ..78 A2
Springford Rd SO16 ....78 A2
Springhill RC Prim Sch
SO15 ....102 C3
Springhill Rd SO53 ....55 B3
Springles La PO15 .....130 A3
Springvale Ave
Bournemouth BH7 .....206 A4
Kings Worthy SO23 ....2 A3
Springvale Rd SO23 ....2 A4
Springwater Cl BH11 ..189 A2
Springwater Ct BH23 ..207 B3
Springwater Dr BH23 ..207 B3
Springwater Rd BH11 ..189 A2
Springwood Ave PO7 ..134 C3
Spruce Ave PO7 ......135 A3
Spruce Cl
Broadstone BH17 .....186 C1
Locks Heath SO31 .....152 B1
Spruce Dr
Southampton SO19 ....104 C3
Totton SO40 ....100 A4
Spruce Wlk [22] PO13 .179 C1
Spur Cl BH21 ....164 B3
Spur Hill Ave BH14 ...203 B2
Spur Rd Cosham PO6 ..157 C4
Poole BH14 ....203 B2
Waterlooville PO7 .....134 C4
Spur The Gosport PO12 .180 C1
Wickham PO17 ....108 A2
Spurgeon Rd BH7 .....206 A3
Spurlings Rd PO17 ....131 B2
Spurlings Yd PO17 ....131 B2
Square The
Bournemouth BH2 .....204 C2
Compton (Sussex) PO18 .90 C1
Fawley SO45 ....151 A2
Gosport PO12 ....181 B4
Hamble-le-Rice SO31 ..128 A1
Lymington SO41 ....197 B2
Petersfield GU32 ......40 C2
Sherfield English SO51 ..26 A2
Southbourne PO10 ....161 B4
Titchfield PO14 ....153 C4
Westbourne PO10 .....137 A2
Wickham PO17 ....108 A2
Wimborne Minst BH21 .163 B3
Winchester SO23 ......11 A4
Squarey Cl SP5 ....46 C3
Squires Wlk SO19 ....103 C1
Squirrel Cl [7] SO50 ...56 C1
Squirrel Dr SO19 .....104 A2
Squirrel Wlk BH31 ....114 C3
Squirrel's Cl BH23 ....191 B1
Squirrels Wlk SO45 ...125 C1
Stable Cl PO14 ....129 B1
Stable La [23] GU31 ...40 C2
Stables The
Christchurch BH23 ....206 C4
Locks Heath SO31 .....129 C4
Stacey Cl BH12 ....203 B4
Stacey Ct PO9 ....135 B4
Stacey Gdns BH8 .....190 C1
Staff Rd SO51 ....6 C1
Stafford Rd
Bournemouth BH1 .....205 A2
Petersfield GU32 ......40 C3
Portsmouth PO5 ......215 C1
Southampton SO15 ....102 B3
Stag Bsns Pk BH24 ....141 A3
Stag Cl Bishopstoke SO50 .56 C1
New Milton BH25 .....194 C2
Stag Gates SO45 ......150 C1
Stag Way PO15 ....130 B3
Stagbrake Cl SO45 ....150 A2
Stags La SO21 ....33 A3
Stagshorn Rd PO8 ....112 B4
Stagswood BH31 ......114 B3
Stainer Cl SO19 ......104 B2
Staith Cl SO19 ....104 B3
Stake's La SO32 ......59 C4
Stakes Hill Inf Sch PO7 134 C3
Stakes Hill Rd PO7 ....134 C3
Stakes La SO32 ....58 C2
Stakes Rd PO7 ....134 B2
Stalbridge Dr BH22 ...165 B2
Stalbridge Rd BH17 ...202 A4
Stalham Rd BH12 .....203 C3
Stallard Cl PO10 ......136 C1
Stallards La BH24 .....140 C4
Stalybridge Cl SO31 ...129 A3
Stamford Ave PO11 ...184 C2
Stamford Lodge PO11 .184 C2

Stamford Rd BH6 .....206 B3
Stamford St PO1 ......215 D4
Stamford Way SO50 ...57 B1
Stampsey Ct [5] PO2 ..157 B1
Stamshaw Ct [14] PO2 .157 B1
Stamshaw Inf Sch PO2 .157 B1
Stamshaw Jun Sch PO2 157 B1
Stamshaw Rd PO2 .....157 B1
Stanbridge Earls Sch
SO51 ....27 A2
Stanbridge La SO51 ....27 A2
Stanbridge Rd PO9 ....136 A2
Standard Way PO16 ...131 B2
Standen Rd SO16 ......77 B3
Standford St SO14 ....103 A4
Standing Hill SP5 ......3 C4
Stanfield Cl BH12 .....203 B4
Stanford Rd
Bournemouth BH9 .....204 C4
Ferndown BH22 ....165 B3
Poole BH12 ....203 B4
Stanford Cl PO6 ......157 B4
Stanford Ct
[42] Havant PO9 ....136 A3
Southampton SO19 ....104 B2
Stanford Hill SO41 ....197 B2
Stanford Rd SO41 .....197 B2
Stanford Rise SO41 ....172 A1
Stanhope Rd PO1 .....215 B3
Stanier Way SO30 .....81 B1
Staniforth Ct BH23 ....207 B3
Stanley Ave PO3 ......183 A4
Stanley Cl
Croucheston SP5 ......22 A4
Fareham PO15 ....130 C1
Gosport PO12 ....156 A1
Verwood BH31 ....115 A3
Stanley Ct
Bournemouth BH1 .....205 B3
Poole BH15 ....202 B3
Stanley Green Cres
BH15 ....202 B3
Stanley Green Fst Sch
BH15 ....202 B3
Stanley Green Ind Est
BH15 ....202 B3
Stanley Green Rd BH15 202 B3
Stanley La PO5 ....182 B1
Stanley Pearce Ho
BH17 ....187 B1
Stanley Rd
Bournemouth BH1 .....205 B3
Christchurch BH23 ....209 A4
Emsworth PO10 ....161 A4
Holbury SO45 ....150 B2
Lymington SO41 ....198 A1
Poole BH15 ....202 B1
Portsmouth PO2 ......157 B1
Southampton SO17 ....79 B1
Totton SO40 ....76 B1
Stanley St PO5 ....182 B1
Stanmore La SO22 ....10 B3
Stanmore Prim Sch
SO22 ....10 C3
Stannington Cl BH25 ..195 A1
Stannington Cres SO40 .100 C4
Stannington Way SO40 .100 C4
Stanpit BH23 ....207 C3
Stanstead Rd SO50 ....55 C2
Stansted Cl PO9 ......113 B1
Stansted Cres PO9 ....136 A3
Stansted Ct PO9 ......113 B1
Stansted Rd PO5 ......215 D2
Stanswood Rd
Blackfield SO45 ......178 B3
Havant PO9 ....135 B3
Stanton Bldgs [20] SO15 .102 A4
Stanton Lacy [17] BH13 214 C4
Stanton Rd
Bournemouth BH10 ...189 B1
Petersfield GU32 ......40 C2
Southampton SO15 ....102 A4
Stanton Rd Ind Est
SO15 ....102 A4
Stanton Road Ind Est [21]
SO15 ....102 A4
Stapehill Cres BH21 ...164 B3
Stapehill Mus & Gdns ★
BH21 ....164 C3
Stapehill Rd BH21 .....164 C2
Staple Ash La GU32 ...39 B4
Staple Cl PO7 ....111 B1
Staple Close La BH15 .202 B3
Staple Cross
Burton BH23 ....207 C4
Southwick PO17 ......132 A4
Staple Gdns SO23 .....10 C4
Staplecross La BH23 ...207 B4
Stapleford Ave BH22 ..165 C3
Stapleford Cl SO51 ....28 A1
Stapleford La SO32 ....81 C3
Staplehurst Cl SO19 ...104 A1
Staplers Reach PO13 ..155 A1
Stapleton Rd PO3 .....183 A4
Staplewood La SO40 ..124 C4
Star Cottage Gdn ★
BH21 ....162 B3
Star Cotts PO17 ....108 A2
Star La BH24 ....140 C4
Stares Cl PO13 ....180 B4
Starina Gdns PO7 .....135 C4
Starlight Farm Cl BH31 .115 A4
Starling Sq SO50 ......55 B1
Station App
Broadstone BH18 .....187 A2

Station App continued
Brockenhurst SO42 ......146 A1
1 Portsmouth PO1 ......182 A3
Station Cl PO17 ......108 A2
Station Cotts SO42 ......123 B1
Station Hill
Bursledon SO31 ......128 A4
Curdridge SO30 ......106 B4
Eastleigh SO50 ......56 A2
Winchester SO23 ......10 C4
Station La SO53 ......55 B3
Station Rd Alderholt SP6 ......92 C3
Bishop's Waltham SO32 ......83 B4
Burley BH24 ......170 B4
Bursledon SO31 ......128 A4
Christchurch BH23 ......207 A4
Christchurch, Highcliffe
BH23 ......193 B1
Cosham PO6 ......158 B4
Fordingbridge SP6 ......69 B1
Gosport PO12 ......180 C4
Hamworthy BH15 ......202 A1
Liss GU33 ......20 C2
Locks Heath SO31 ......129 A3
Netley SO31 ......127 B3
New Milton BH25 ......195 A1
Nursling SO16 ......77 A3
Petersfield GU31, GU32 ......40 C2
Poole BH14 ......203 A2
Portchester PO16 ......156 B4
Portsmouth PO3 ......183 A4
Romsey SO51 ......52 C4
Soberton SO32 ......85 B4
South Hayling PO11 ......184 C2
Southampton, Redbridge
SO15 ......101 B4
Southampton, Sholing
SO19 ......103 C2
Sway SO41 ......172 A1
Verwood BH31 ......114 C4
West Meon GU32 ......37 B2
West Moors BH22 ......138 B1
Wickham PO17 ......108 A2
Wimborne Minst BH21 ......163 B2
Station Rd N SO40 ......101 A4
Station Rd S SO40 ......101 A4
Station St
Lymington SO41 ......197 C2
Portsmouth PO1 ......215 B3
Station Terr Twyford SO21 ......31 C3
Wimborne Minst BH21 ......163 B2
Station Yd SP6 ......92 C3
Staunton BH2 ......204 C1
Staunton Ave PO11 ......184 B2
Staunton Ctry Pk * PO9 136 A4
Staunton Park Com Sch
PO9 ......136 A4
Staunton Rd PO9 ......135 C1
Staunton St PO1 ......215 B4
Stead Cl PO11 ......185 A2
Stedman Rd BH5 ......206 A3
Steel St PO5 ......215 A1
Steele Cl SO53 ......55 B2
Steels Dro SP6 ......70 C4
Steels La SP6 ......68 B2
Steep CE Prim Sch GU32 40 C4
Steep Cl
Portchester PO16 ......132 B1
Southampton SO18 ......104 B4
Steepdene BH14 ......203 A2
Steeple Cl BH17 ......187 B2
Steeple Way PO14 ......129 B2
Steepleton Rd BH18 ......187 B2
Steerforth Cl PO2 ......182 B4
Stein Rd PO10 ......137 B1
Steinbeck Cl PO15 ......129 B4
Stella Ct
19 Christchurch BH23 ......209 A4
Southampton SO16 ......78 B2
Stem La BH25 ......194 C2
Stenbury Way SO31 ......127 B4
Stenhurst Rd BH15 ......202 A1
Step Terr SO22 ......10 C4
Stephen Cl PO8 ......112 A1
Stephen Langton Dr
BH11 ......188 B3
Stephen Lodge PO5 ......215 B4
Stephen Martin Gdns
SP6 ......69 C1
Stephen Rd PO15 ......130 C1
Stephens Ct SO51 ......52 C3
Stephens Wlk BH24 ......140 C4
Stephenson Cl PO12 ......181 A1
Stephenson Rd
Totton SO40 ......76 B1
Locks Heath PO14,PO15 ......129 C1
Stephenson Way SO30 ......81 A2
Steplake La SO51 ......25 B1
Steplake Rd SO51 ......50 B4
Stepnell Reach BH16 ......201 B3
Sterte Ave BH15 ......202 A2
Sterte Ave W BH15 ......202 A2
Sterte Cl BH15 ......202 B2
Sterte Ct BH15 ......202 A2
Sterte Espl BH15 ......202 B2
Sterte Ind Est BH15 ......202 A2
Sterte Rd BH15 ......202 B2
Steuart Rd SO18 ......103 B4
Stevenson Cres BH14 ......203 C2
Stevenson Rd BH6 ......207 A4
Stevensons Cl **3** BH21 ......163 B2
Steventon Rd SO18 ......104 B4
Stewart Cl **5** BH8 ......205 B3
Stewart Ho SO53 ......30 B1
Stewart Pl PO1 ......182 C4

Stewart Rd BH8 ......205 A3
Stewarts Gn PO7 ......86 B2
Stewarts Way BH22 ......165 C4
Stibbs Way BH23 ......169 B1
Stillmore Rd BH11 ......188 B2
Stinchar Dr SO53 ......55 A3
Stinsford Cl BH9 ......190 A2
Stinsford La BH17 ......202 B3
Stinsford Rd BH17 ......187 B1
Stirling Ave PO7 ......134 C4
Stirling Cl
New Milton BH25 ......195 A2
Totton SO40 ......77 A1
Stirling Cres
Hedge End SO30 ......81 B1
Totton SO40 ......101 A4
Stirling Ct
Bournemouth BH4 ......204 B1
Fareham PO15 ......130 C2
21 New Milton BH25 ......195 A2
Stirling Rd BH3 ......204 C1
Stirling St PO2 ......182 B4
Stirling Way BH23 ......208 A3
Stirling Wlk SO51 ......52 C4
Stirrup Cl Upton BH16 ......201 B4
Wimborne Minst BH21 ......164 B1
Stoborough Dr BH18 ......187 A1
Stock La SP5 ......49 B3
Stock's Cross SO43 ......73 C2
Stock's La SO32 ......61 C3
Stockbridge Cl
Havant PO9 ......136 A3
Poole BH15 ......188 A1
Stockbridge Rd SO21,
SO22, SO23 ......1 B1
Stocker Pl PO13 ......155 B1
Stockers Ave SO22 ......1 B1
Stockheath La PO9 ......135 C2
Stockheath Rd PO9 ......135 C2
Stockheath Way PO9 ......135 C2
Stockley Cl SO45 ......150 B2
Stockton Cl SO30 ......105 B4
Stoddart Ave SO19 ......103 C3
Stodham La GU33 ......20 C1
Stoke Common Rd SO50 ......56 C3
Stoke Gdns PO12 ......181 B2
Stoke Hts SO50 ......57 A2
Stoke Park Dr SO50 ......56 B2
Stoke Park Inf Sch SO50 ......56 C1
Stoke Park Jun Sch
SO50 ......56 C1
Stoke Park Rd SO50 ......56 B2
Stoke Rd Gosport PO12 ......181 B2
Southampton SO16 ......78 A1
Winchester SO23 ......2 A2
Stoke Wood Cl SO50 ......57 A1
Stoke Wood Rd BH3 ......204 C3
Stokes Ave BH15 ......202 B2
Stokes Bay Rd PO12 ......180 C1
Stokesay Cl SO45 ......150 A4
Stokeway **4** PO12 ......181 B2
Stone Crop Cl SO31 ......128 C1
Stone Gdns BH8 ......191 A1
Stone La
5 Gosport PO12 ......181 A2
Wimborne Minst BH21 ......163 A3
Stone Lane Ind Est
BH21 ......163 A3
Stone Sq PO9 ......135 C2
Stone St PO5 ......215 A1
Stone Terr SO21 ......31 C1
Stonechat Cl
Ferndown BH22 ......165 A4
Petersfield GU31 ......41 B1
Stonechat Ct BH23 ......207 C4
Stonechat Dr SO40 ......100 B4
Stonechat Rd PO8 ......112 A4
Stonecrop BH18 ......186 C1
Stoneham Cemetery Rd
SO18 ......79 C2
Stoneham Cl
Petersfield GU32 ......40 B2
Southampton SO18 ......79 B3
Stoneham Ct SO16 ......79 A3
Stoneham Gdns SO31 ......104 C1
Stoneham La
Chilworth SO50 ......79 C4
Southampton SO16 ......79 B3
Stoneham Pk GU32 ......40 B2
Stoneham Way SO16,
SO18 ......79 C3
Stonehills SO45 ......151 B2
Stoneleigh **13** BH13 ......214 C4
Stoneleigh Ave SO41 ......195 C2
Stoneleigh Cl PO16 ......156 A4
Stoner Hill Rd GU32 ......19 A1
Stoners Cl PO13 ......155 A2
Stoney La SO22 ......1 B1
Stony La Burton BH23 ......192 B1
Froxfield Green GU32 ......18 C1
Portsmouth PO1 ......182 A3
Stony La S BH23 ......207 B3
Stonymoor Cl SO45 ......150 B2
Stopples La SO41 ......195 C2
Storrington Rd PO8 ......88 B3
Story La BH18 ......187 A2
Stour Cl Ferndown BH21 ......164 B2
Petersfield GU31 ......40 C1
West End SO18 ......80 A2
West Wellow SO51 ......50 B2
Stour Pk BH10 ......189 C3
Stour Rd
Bournemouth BH8 ......205 B3
Christchurch BH23 ......207 A3
Stour View Gdns BH21 ......162 C1
Stour Way BH23 ......191 B1

Stour Wlk
Bournemouth BH8 ......190 B2
11 Wimborne Minst BH21 ......163 B2
Stourbank Rd BH23 ......207 A3
Stourcliffe Ave BH6 ......206 B2
Stourcroft Dr BH23 ......191 C1
Stourfield Fst & Jun Schs
BH6 ......206 B3
Stourfield Rd BH5 ......206 A2
Stourpaine Rd BH17 ......187 B1
Stourton Ct **17** BH4 ......204 B2
Stourvale Ave BH23 ......206 B4
Stourvale Gdns SO53 ......55 B3
Stourvale Pl **10** BH5 ......206 A3
Stourvale Rd BH5,BH6 ......206 B3
Stourwood Ave BH6 ......206 B2
Stourwood Mans **4**
BH6 ......206 B2
Stourwood Rd BH6 ......206 B2
Stouts La BH21 ......169 A1
Stow Cres PO15 ......130 B1
Stowe Cl SO30 ......81 B1
Stowe Rd PO4 ......183 A2
Stradbrook PO13 ......155 A1
Stragwyne Cl SO52 ......53 C3
Straight Mile The SO51 ......28 C1
Strand SO14 ......103 A2
Strand St BH15 ......202 B1
Strand The PO11 ......185 B1
Stratfield Dr SO53 ......30 A1
Stratfield Gdns PO9 ......135 B4
Stratfield Pk PO7 ......134 B4
Stratfield Pl BH25 ......194 C2
Stratford Ct **9** SO23 ......2 A1
Stratford Ho PO5 ......215 B2
Stratford Pl
Eastleigh SO50 ......56 A2
Lymington SO41 ......197 B3
Stratford Rd PO7 ......135 A4
Strathmore Dr BH31 ......115 A3
Strathmore Rd
Bournemouth BH9 ......190 A2
Gosport PO12 ......181 B2
Stratton Cl PO6 ......157 B4
Stratton Rd
Bournemouth BH9 ......190 B2
Southampton SO15 ......78 B1
Winchester SO23 ......11 B1
Strawberry Fields
East Boldre SO42 ......175 B3
Hedge End SO30 ......105 A3
Strawberry Hill SO31 ......128 C2
Strawberry Mead SO50 ......57 A1
Streamleaze PO14 ......129 B1
Street End SO52 ......54 A3
Street The SP5 ......24 A2
Streets La BH24 ......141 B2
Strete Mount **16** BH23 ......207 C4
Stretton Cl PO9 ......203 A2
Stride Ave PO3 ......183 A3
Strides La BH24 ......140 C4
Strides Way SO40 ......100 A4
Strode Gdns BH24 ......140 A3
Strode Rd PO2 ......157 B1
Strongs Cl SO51 ......53 A4
Stroud Cl BH21 ......164 A3
Stroud End GU32 ......40 A2
Stroud Gdns BH23 ......207 C3
Stroud Green La PO14 ......154 B3
Stroud La BH23 ......207 C3
Stroud Park Ave BH23 ......207 C3
Stroud Sch SO51 ......53 C4
Strouden Ave BH8 ......205 B4
Strouden Court Prec
PO9 ......135 B4
Strouden Ct PO9 ......135 B4
Strouden Rd BH9 ......190 A1
Stroudley Ave PO6 ......158 B3
Stroudley Way SO30 ......81 B1
Stroudwood Rd
Fair Oak SO32 ......58 A2
Havant PO9 ......136 A2
Struan Cl BH24 ......139 C3
Struan Ct BH24 ......140 A3
Struan Dr BH24 ......140 A3
Struan Gdns BH24 ......139 C3
Stuart Bridgewater Ho
SO18 ......104 A4
Stuart Cl
Stubbington PO14 ......179 B3
Upton BH16 ......201 A4
Stuart Cres SO22 ......10 C3
Stuart Ct **7** PO6 ......157 C4
Stuart Rd BH23 ......209 A4
Stubbermere PO10 ......136 C1
Stubbington Ave PO2 ......157 C1
Stubbington Gn PO14 ......154 B2
Stubbington La PO14 ......179 B3
Stubbington Study Ctr
PO14 ......179 B2
Stubbington Way SO50 ......57 B1
Stubbs Dro SO30 ......105 B4
Stubbs Rd SO19 ......104 B1
Stuckton Rd SP6 ......94 A4
Student Village BH12 ......204 B4
Studland Cl SO16 ......77 B1
Studland Ct SO41 ......211 B3
Studland Rd
Bournemouth BH4 ......204 B1
Lee-on-the-Solent PO13 ......179 C1
Southampton SO16 ......77 B1
Studley Ave SO45 ......150 B2
Studley Cl BH23 ......209 B4
Studley Ct BH25 ......209 B4
Sturminster Ho **4** SO16 ......78 A1
Sturminster Rd **10** BH9 ......190 A2
Styles The SP5 ......22 B4
Sudbury Rd PO6 ......157 B4

Suetts La SO32 ......83 C4
Surrey House Inf Sch
SO19 ......104 B2
Surrey Rd
Bournemouth BH2,BH4 ......204 A2
Chandler's Ford SO53 ......55 B2
Poole BH12 ......204 A2
Southampton SO19 ......103 B1
Surrey Rd S BH4 ......204 B2
Surrey St PO1 ......215 B3
Sussex Cl BH9 ......190 A1
Sussex Ct PO5 ......215 B1
Sussex Gdns GU31 ......40 C1
Sussex Pl
Portsmouth PO1 ......215 B4
Portsmouth PO5 ......215 B1
Sussex Rd
Chandler's Ford SO53 ......55 B2
Petersfield GU31 ......41 A1
Portsmouth PO5 ......215 B1
Southampton SO14 ......103 A2
Sussex St SO23 ......10 C4
Sussex Terr PO5 ......215 B1
Sutherland Ave BH18 ......186 C3
Sutherland Cl **6** SO51 ......28 A1
Sutherland Cl SO53 ......55 B3
Sutherland Rd
Portsmouth PO4 ......182 C2
Southampton SO16 ......77 C3
Sutherlands Way SO53 ......55 A4
Sutherlands Way Poole BH17 ......188 B3
Sutton Rd
Portsmouth PO3 ......158 A2
Waterlooville PO8 ......111 B2
Sutton Gdns SO23 ......11 A4
Sutton Pl SO42 ......146 A1
Sutton Rd
Bournemouth BH9 ......190 A1
Totton SO40 ......76 C1
Waterlooville PO8 ......111 B2
Swale Dr SO53 ......55 A4
Swallow Cl
Broadstone BH17 ......201 C4
Havant PO9 ......136 A1
Totton SO40 ......100 A3
Swallow Ct Clanfield PO8 ......88 A3
Lee-on-the-Solent PO13 ......179 C2
Swallow Dr SO41 ......211 C2
Swallow Sq SO50 ......55 B1
Swallow Way BH21 ......164 A4
Swallow Wood PO16 ......131 A2
Swan Cl Emsworth PO10 ......161 A4
Swanwick SO31 ......128 B4
Swan Ct Bursledon SO31 ......128 B4
Gosport PO13 ......155 A2
Swan Ctr The SO50 ......56 A1
Swan Gn **8** BH23 ......207 A3
Swan La SO23 ......10 C4
Swan Mead BH24 ......141 B3
Swan Quay
Portchester PO16 ......155 B4
Southampton SO18 ......103 B4
Swan St GU32 ......40 C2
Swanage Cl SO19 ......103 C2
Swanage Rd PO13 ......179 C1
Swancote PO16 ......155 C4
Swanley Cl SO50 ......56 A3
Swanmore Ave SO19 ......104 B2
Swanmore Bsns Pk SO32 83 C3
Swanmore CE Prim Sch
SO32 ......84 A3
Swanmore Cl
Bournemouth BH7 ......206 A4
Winchester SO22 ......1 B2
Swanmore Park Ho SO32 84 B4
Swanmore Rd
Bournemouth BH7 ......206 A4
Droxford SO32 ......84 C4
Havant PO9 ......135 B2
Swanwick SO32 ......84 A3
Swanmore Sec Sch SO32 84 A2
Swans Wlk PO11 ......185 A2
Swansbury Dr BH8 ......191 A1
Swanton Cl PO14 ......154 B2
Swanton Gdns SO53 ......55 A4
Swanwick Bsns Ctr
SO31 ......128 B4
Swanwick La SO31 ......128 C4
Swanwick Nature Reserve *
SO31 ......128 C4
Swanwick Shore Rd
SO31 ......128 B4
Swanwick Sta SO31 ......129 A3
Swarraton Rd PO9 ......136 A2
Sway Ct **39** Havant PO9 ......136 A3
Sway SO41 ......196 B4
Sway Gdns BH8 ......190 B1
Sway Park Ind Est SO41 172 A1
Sway Rd
Brockenhurst SO42 ......172 C4
Hordle SO41 ......197 A3
Lymington SO41 ......197 A3
New Milton BH25 ......195 B3
Sway SO41 ......172 A1
Swaything Prim Sch
SO17 ......79 A2
Swaything Rd
Havant PO9 ......135 B3
West End SO18,SO30 ......80 A1
Swaything Sta SO18 ......79 B2
Swedish Hos SO41 ......198 C4
Sweep The BH24 ......140 C4
Sweetbriar Gdns PO7 ......134 C3
Sweethills Cres PO15 ......129 B4
Sweyns Lease SO42 ......175 B3
Swift Cl Broadstone BH17 ......201 C4
Eastleigh SO50 ......55 B1
Horndean PO8 ......112 A4
Lee-on-the-Solent PO13 ......179 C2
Winchester SO22 ......10 B3

Stour Wlk
Bournemouth BH8 ......190 B2

Suffolk Ave
Christchurch BH23 ......191 C1
Southampton SO15 ......102 B4
Suffolk Cl
Chandler's Ford SO53 ......55 B1
Wimborne Minst BH21 ......164 B3
Suffolk Dr
Chandler's Ford SO53 ......55 B1
Swanwick PO15 ......129 A4
Suffolk Gn SO53 ......55 B1
Suffolk Rd
Bournemouth BH2 ......204 B2
Bournemouth BH2 ......204 C2
Portsmouth PO4 ......183 A2
Suffolk Rd S BH2 ......204 B2
Sullivan Cl PO6 ......156 C4
Sullivan Rd SO19 ......104 B2
Sullivan Way PO7 ......134 C3
Sultan Rd
Emsworth PO10 ......136 C1
Portsmouth PO1, PO2 ......182 B4
Sumar Cl PO14 ......154 B3
Summer Field Cl BH21 ......164 A2
Summer Flds BH31 ......114 C2
Summerbee Comp Sch
BH8 ......190 B1
Summerbee First Sch
BH8 ......190 B1
Summerbee Jun Sch
BH8 ......190 B1
Summercroft Way
BH22 ......138 C2
Summerfield Cl BH23 ......192 B1
Summerfield Ct PO3 ......158 A2
Summerfield Gdns SO16 ......79 B3
Summerfields
Bournemouth BH7 ......205 C4
Locks Heath SO31 ......129 A4
Summerhill Rd PO8 ......112 A2
Summerlands BH22 ......165 B3
Summerlands Rd SO50 ......57 B1
Summerlands Wlk **36**
PO9 ......136 A3
Summerleigh Wlk PO14 154 B3
Summers Ave BH11 ......189 A3
Summers La BH23 ......192 B1
Summers St SO14 ......103 B3
Summersfield Cl GU33 ......20 C2
Summertrees Ct BH25 ......195 B2
Summit Way SO18 ......79 C1
Sumner Rd GU31 ......65 B3
Sun Ct PO5 ......215 C2
Sun St PO1 ......182 A3
Sunbeam Way PO12 ......181 A2
Sunbury Cl BH11 ......189 A3
Sunbury Ct
8 Bournemouth BH2 ......204 C2
Fareham PO15 ......130 C2
Suncourt Villas PO12 ......181 B2
Sunderland Dr BH23 ......208 A4
Sunderton La PO8 ......88 B3
Sundew Cl
Christchurch BH23 ......193 B1
New Milton BH25 ......195 B2
Sundew Rd BH18 ......186 C1
Sundridge Cl PO6 ......157 C4
Sunningdale
Christchurch BH23 ......206 C3
Hythe SO45 ......125 C2
8 Poole BH15 ......202 C2
Sunningdale Cl
6 Bishopstoke SO50 ......56 C1
Gosport PO13 ......155 B1
Sunningdale Cres BH10 189 B2
Sunningdale Cvn Pk
SO21 ......31 C1
Sunningdale Gdns
Broadstone BH18 ......187 A3
Southampton SO18 ......104 A4
Sunningdale Rd
Portchester PO16 ......156 B4
Portsmouth PO3 ......183 A4
Sunny Hill Ct BH12 ......203 B3
Sunny Hill Rd BH12 ......203 B3
Sunny Way SO40 ......100 C4
Sunny Wlk PO1 ......182 A3
Sunnybank Dr BH21 ......164 A3
Sunnybank Rd BH21 ......164 A3
Sunnybank Way BH21 ......164 A3
Sunnydown Rd SO22 ......10 A2
Sunnyfield BH25 ......210 A4
Sunnyfield Rise SO31 ......105 A1
Sunnyfields PO6 ......158 B4
Sunnyheath PO9 ......135 C2
Sunnyhill Rd BH6 ......206 B3
Sunnylands Ave BH6 ......206 C2
Sunnymead Dr PO7 ......111 B1
Sunnymoor Rd BH11 ......189 A1
Sunnyside Rd BH12 ......203 B3
Sunnyside Wlk PO9 ......135 B4
Sunridge Cl PO14 ......204 A3
Sunrise Ct BH22 ......165 B3
Sunset Ave SO40 ......100 C4
Sunset Lo BH13 ......204 A1
Sunset Rd SO40 ......100 C4
Sunshine Ave PO11 ......185 A1
Suntrap Gdns PO11 ......185 A1
Sunvale Cl SO19 ......104 A2
Sunwood Rd PO9 ......135 B3
Surbiton Rd SO50 ......56 A2
Surrey Cl
Christchurch BH23 ......191 C1
Totton SO40 ......100 B3
Surrey Ct SO15 ......102 B3
Surrey Gdns BH4 ......204 B2
Surrey Ho SO53 ......55 B2

Swift Gdns SO19 ....103 B1
Swift Hollow SO19 ....103 B1
Swift Rd
 Southampton SO19 ....103 B1
 Thorney Island PO10 ....161 A2
Swinburn Gdns PO8 .....111 C2
Swincombe Rise SO18 ...80 A1
Swiss Rd PO7 ....134 C4
Switch House Rd SO45 .151 C1
Swivelton La PO17 .....132 A2
Sword Cl Clanfield PO8 ..88 A3
 Gosport PO12 ....180 C1
Sword Sands Rd PO3 ..183 B4
Swordfish Dr BH23 ....208 A4
Sycamore Ave SO53 ....30 B1
Sycamore Cl
 Broadstone BH17 .....186 C1
 Bursledon SO31 ......127 C4
 Christchurch BH23 ...206 B4
 Clanfield PO8 ....88 B3
 Gosport PO13 ....155 C1
 Milford on Sea SO41 .211 B3
 North Baddesley SO52 .53 C3
 Romsey SO51 ....53 B3
 Titchfield PO14 ......129 B1
 Waterlooville PO8 ....111 C2
Sycamore Ct
 Fordingbridge SP6 .....69 C1
 Ringwood BH24 ....117 B1
Sycamore Dr
 Holbury SO45 ....150 A3
 Kings Worthy SO23 .....2 A4
 South Hayling PO11 ..184 C2
Sycamore Pl BH21 .....164 B3
Sycamore Rd
 Bishop's Waltham SO32 .83 C4
 Hordle SO41 ....195 C2
 Hythe SO45 ....125 C2
 Southampton SO16 .....78 A1
Sycamore Wlk SO19 .....78 A1
Sycamores The 9 SO45 126 A2
Sydenham Ct PO1 .....215 D3
Sydenham Terr
 Portsmouth PO1 ......215 D3
 Westbourne PO10 ....137 A3
Sydling BH17 ....188 A1
Sydmanton Cl SO51 ....53 A3
Sydmonton Ct 2 PO9 .136 A3
Sydney Ave SO31 .....127 C2
Sydney Ho PO1 ......215 B4
Sydney Rd
 Bishopstoke SO50 .....56 B2
 Broadstone BH18 .....187 A2
 Christchurch BH23 ...191 C1
 Gosport PO12 ....181 A2
 Southampton SO15 ....78 A1
Syers Cl GU33 ....20 C2
Syers Rd GU33 ....20 C2
Sylmor Gdns BH9 ....190 A1
Sylvan Ave SO19 .....104 B3
Sylvan Cl Hordle SO41 .196 A1
 St Leonards BH24 ....139 B2
Sylvan Dr SO52 ....53 C2
Sylvan Fst Sch BH12 ..203 A3
Sylvan La SO31 ......128 A1
Sylvan Rd BH12 .....203 A3
Sylvan View PO7 .....134 C3
Sylvans The SO45 ....125 B2
Sylvia Cres SO40 .....76 C1
Symes Rd
 Hamworthy BH15 ....201 C2
 Romsey SO51 ....53 A4
Symonds Cl SO53 .....55 B2
Symonds St SO23 .....11 A4
Sywell Cres PO3 .....158 B2

T

Tadburn Cl
 Chandler's Ford SO53 ..55 B3
 Romsey SO51 ....53 A4
Tadburn Gn SO51 .....52 C3
Tadburn Rd SO51 .....53 A3
Tadden Cotts BH21 ...162 B4
Tadden Wlk BH18 ....186 C1
Tadfield Cres SO51 ....53 A4
Tadfield Rd SO51 .....53 A4
Tadhurst Ho 4 PO1 ..215 C3
Tait Cl BH17 ....202 C4
Tait Pl PO13 ....155 B1
Talbot Ave BH3 .....204 C4
Talbot Cl Havant PO9 .135 B2
 Southampton SO16 ....78 C2
Talbot Comb Sch BH12 204 A4
Talbot Ct
 Bournemouth BH9 ...189 C1
 11 Southampton SO14 103 A2
Talbot Dr
 Christchurch BH23 ...193 C1
 Poole BH12 ....204 A4
Talbot Heath Sch BH4 204 B3
Talbot Hill Rd BH9 ..204 B4
Talbot House Prep Sch
 BH9 ....204 C4
Talbot Manor BH3 ...204 B4
Talbot Mdws BH12 ..204 A4
Talbot Mews BH10 ..189 A1
Talbot Rd
 Bournemouth BH9 ...204 C4
 Havant PO9 ....135 B2
 Hythe SO45 ....125 C2
 Locks Heath PO14 ..129 C1
 Portsmouth PO4 ....182 C2
Talbot Rdbt BH3 ....204 B4
Talbot Rise BH9 ....204 B4
Talisman Bsns Ctr SO31 129 A3
Tall Trees BH14 .....203 A3

Talland Rd PO14 ....129 A1
Tamar Cl Ferndown BH22 166 A3
 Portchester PO16 ...132 A1
Tamar Down PO7 ...135 A4
Tamar Gdns SO18 ....80 A1
Tamar Gr SO45 .....125 C2
Tamarisk Cl
 Portsmouth PO4 ....183 B2
 Stubbington PO14 ..179 B3
 Waterlooville PO7 ..135 A3
Tamarisk Gdns SO18 103 C4
Tamarisk Rd SO30 ..105 A4
Tamella Rd SO30 ...105 C3
Tammys Turn PO14 .154 A4
Tamorisk Dr SO40 ..100 B3
Tamworth Ct 9 PO12 181 A2
Tamworth Rd
 Bournemouth BH7 ..205 C3
 Portsmouth PO3 ....183 A3
Tan Howse Cl BH7 ..206 A4
Tanfield La PO14 ....108 A2
Tanfield Pk PO17 ...108 A2
Tangier La SO32 .....83 A4
Tangier Rd PO3 .....183 A4
Tanglewood
 Fareham PO16 .....131 A2
 Marchwood SO40 ..102 A1
Tanglewood Cl PO7 .134 B2
Tanglewood Oaks 11 BH25 126 A1
Tanglewood Lo BH17 201 C1
Tangley Wlk PO9 ...136 A3
Tangmere Cl BH23 ..208 A3
Tangmere Dr SO16 ...78 A2
Tangmere Pl BH17 ..202 C4
Tangyes Cl PO14 ...154 B2
Tanhouse Cl SO30 ..105 B3
Tanhouse La
 Botley SO30 ....105 B2
 Hedge End SO30 ...105 B3
Tankerdale La GU33 ..41 B4
Tankerton Cl 2 PO6 .157 C4
Tankerville Rd SO19 103 B2
Tankerville Specl Sch
 SO50 ....56 A2
Tanner St 28 SO23 ...11 A4
Tanner's Brook Way
 SO15 ....101 C3
Tanner's La PO7 ....111 A3
Tanner's Ridge PO7 .134 C2
Tanneries Ind Est The
 PO9 ....135 C1
Tanners Brook Inf Sch
 SO15 ....101 C4
Tanners Brook Jun Sch
 SO15 ....101 C4
Tanners La Boldre SO41 199 A2
 Gosport PO14 .....154 C3
 Sandleheath SP6 ....68 C2
 West Wellow SO51 ..51 B4
Tanners Rd SO52 ....54 A2
Tanners The PO14 ..129 B1
Tansy Cl PO7 ......135 A3
Tansy Mdw SO53 ...54 C2
Tanyards The SO53 ..30 A1
Taplin Dr SO30 ....105 B4
Taplings Cl SO22 .....1 B2
Taplings Rd SO22 ....1 B2
Tapper Ct BH21 ....163 C2
Taranto Rd SO16 ....78 B2
Tarbery Cres PO8 ..112 B4
Tardif Ho SO16 .....78 A1
Tarrant Cl BH17 ...187 C1
Tarrant Gdns PO9 ..135 B2
Tarrant Rd BH9 ....190 A2
Tasman Cl
 Christchurch BH23 .206 C4
 Southampton SO14 .103 A1
Tasman Ct SO14 ...103 A1
Taswell Rd PO5 ....182 B1
Tatchbury La SO40 ..99 C4
Tatchbury Mount Hospl
 SO40 ....76 A1
Tate Ct SO15 ......101 B4
Tate Mews SO15 ...101 B4
Tate Rd SO15 ......101 B4
Tates Rd Hythe SO45 126 A1
 Hythe SO45 ....126 A2
Tatnam Rd BH15 ..202 B2
Tattenham Rd SO42 172 C4
Tatum Cres BH15 ..202 B2
Tatwin Cl SO19 ....104 B3
Tatwin Cres SO19 ..104 B3
Taunton Coll SO15 ..78 C1
Taunton Dr SO18 ..104 A4
Taunton Row SO53 ..55 B2
Tavell's La SO40 ...101 C1
Tavells Cl SO40 ....101 C1
Taverner Cl BH15 ..202 B1
Taverners Cl SO19 .104 B2
Tavistock Cl 4 SO51 .28 A1
Tavistock Gdns 10 PO9 136 A3
Tavy Cl SO53 ......55 A3
Taw Dr SO53 ......55 A3
Tawny Owl Cl PO14 154 A2
Taylor Cl SO19 ....103 B1
Taylor Dr BH8 .....190 B2
Taylor Rd PO12 ...181 B1
Taylor Way BH31 ..115 A3
Taylor's Bldgs 21 BH15 202 B1
Taylors Cnr SO23 ...2 A3
Teachers Terr 6 GU33 20 C2
Teachers Way SO45 150 A2

Teak Cl BH13 ......214 D4
Teal Cl Horndean PO8 112 A4
 Portchester PO16 ..155 C4
 South Hayling PO11 185 A2
 Totton SO40 ....100 B4
Teal Wlk PO13 ....155 A2
Teapot Row PO4 ...183 A1
Teasel Way BH22 ..138 C1
Teazle Cl GU31 .....41 B1
Tebourba Cotts SO41 172 A1
Tebourba Dr PO12 ..181 A2
Tebourba Ho 6 PO14 154 C4
Tebourba Way
 Curdridge SO30 ....106 B4
 Southampton SO16 .101 C4
Technology Rd BH17 202 A4
Ted Kelly Ct 29 PO1 182 A3
Tedder Cl BH11 ....189 A2
Tedder Gdns BH11 .189 A2
Tedder Rd
 Bournemouth BH11 189 A2
 Gosport PO13 .....155 B2
 Southampton SO18 .104 A4
Tedder Way SO40 ..100 B4
Teddington Rd PO4 183 A2
Tees Cl SO53 ......55 A4
Tees Farm Rd SO21 56 C4
Tees Gn 2 SO21 ...56 C4
Teg Down GU31 ....41 A2
Teg Down Meads SO22 1 B1
Teglease Gn PO9 ..135 A4
Teignmouth Rd
 Gosport PO12 .....180 C4
 Portsmouth PO3 ...183 A4
Telegraph Rd SO30 .80 C1
Telegraph Way SO21 12 A4
Telephone Rd PO4 .182 C2
Telford Gdns SO30 .81 C1
Telford Rd
 Ferndown BH21 ...165 A4
 Portsmouth PO2 ...157 C2
Telford Way PO15 .129 B3
Teme Cres SO16 ..101 C4
Teme Rd SO16 ....101 C4
Tempest Ave PO7 .135 A4
Templar Ct 29 SO14 103 A4
Templars Mede SO53 55 A2
Templars Way SO53 55 A2
Temple Gdns SO19 103 C1
Temple La GU32 ...63 C4
Temple Mews BH1 .205 B3
Temple Mews PO1 .215 B4
Temple Rd Liss GU33 21 A3
 Southampton SO19 103 C1
Temple St PO1 ....215 B4
Templecombe Rd SO50 56 C1
Templemere PO14 .154 A4
Templer Cl BH11 ..188 C1
Templeton Cl PO2 .157 C2
Tenby Cl SO18 ....104 A4
Tenby Dr SO53 ....55 A2
Tench Way SO51 ..52 C4
Tennyson Cl
 Bishop's Waltham SO32 83 C4
 Holbury SO45 .....150 A3
Tennyson Cres PO7 111 B1
Tennyson Ct
 27 Southampton SO17 79 A1
 37 Southampton SO17 79 A1
Tennyson Gdns PO16 131 A1
Tennyson Rd
 Bournemouth BH9 .189 C1
 Eastleigh SO50 ....55 C1
 1 Poole BH14 .....203 A2
 Portsmouth PO2 ...182 C4
 Southampton SO17 .79 A1
 Totton SO40 ......76 B1
 Wimborne Minst BH21 163 B3
Tensing Cl PO16 ..131 A2
Tensing Rd BH23 ..207 C4
Tenterton Ave SO19 104 A1
Terence Ave BH17 .187 B1
Terence Rd BH17 ..186 B3
Terminus Terr SO14 103 A2
Tern Cl SO45 .....126 A1
Tern Ct BH6 ......206 B3
Tern Wlk PO13 ...155 A2
Terrace Rd BH2 ..204 C2
Terrace The
 Damerham SP6 ...68 B3
 Rockbourne SP6 ..68 C4
Terrier Cl SO30 ...81 B2
Terrington Ave BH23 193 C1
Terriote Cl SO53 ..55 B4
Test Cl GU31 .....40 C1
Test Ho SO51 ....52 B4
Test La SO16 .....77 A1
Test Mills SO51 ..52 B4
Test Rd SO14 ....126 A4
Test Valley Bsns Ctr
 SO16 ....77 B1
Test Valley Bsns Pk
 SO52 ....54 A3
Testbourne Ave SO40 100 B4
Testbourne Cl SO40 100 B4
Testbourne Rd SO40 100 B3
Testcombe Rd PO12 181 A2
Testlands Ave SO16 77 B3
Testwood Ave SO40 76 B1
Testwood Cres SO40 76 B1
Testwood La SO40 101 A4
Testwood Pl SO40 .101 A4
Testwood Rd
 Havant PO9 ....135 B2
 Southampton SO15 102 A3
Testwood Sch SO40 76 C1
Tetbury Dro SP6 ...47 B2
Tetney Cl SO16 ...77 C2
Tetsome Cotts PO17 130 C4

Teviot Ho 9 SO14 .103 B3
Teviot Rd SO53 ...55 A3
Tewkesbury Ave
 Fareham PO15 ....130 B2
 Gosport PO12 .....181 A4
Tewkesbury Cl PO6 157 B4
Texas Dr SO22 ....10 C2
Thackeray Mall 26
 PO16 ....131 A1
Thackeray Rd SO17 103 A4
Thackeray Sq 4 PO16 131 B1
Thacking Gn 3 SO21 56 C4
Thames Alley 13 BH15 202 A1
Thames Cl
 Ferndown BH22 ...166 A3
 West End SO18 ....80 A2
Thames Ct 1 PO8 .111 C2
Thames Dr PO15 ..130 B2
Thames Mews 12 BH15 202 A1
Thames St SO14 ..202 A1
Thamesmead Cl PO12 180 C4
Thatchers La
 Boldre SO41 ......198 C4
 Sopley BH23 ......168 C2
Theatre Mews 2 PO5 182 B1
Theobold Rd BH23 191 A4
Theseus Rd SO17 .179 B2
Thessaly Ct 17 BH5 205 C2
Thetchers Cl BH25 195 A3
Thetford Gdns SO53 55 A4
Thetford Rd
 Gosport PO12 .....180 C4
 Poole BH12 ....203 C4
Thicket The
 Gosport PO13 .....155 C1
 Portchester PO16 .131 C1
 Portsmouth PO5 ..215 C1
 Romsey SO51 .....53 B3
 Waterlooville PO7 134 B2
Third Ave Cosham PO6 157 C4
 Havant PO9 ....136 C1
 Southampton SO15 101 C3
Thirlmere SO50 ...55 C1
Thirlmere Cl PO14 154 B2
Thirlmere Ho 23 PO6 133 A1
Thirlmere Rd SO16 77 C1
Thirlstane Firs SO53 55 A2
Thistle Rd
 Chandler's Ford SO53 54 C3
 Hedge End SO30 ..105 A3
Thistlebarrow Rd BH7 205 C3
Thistledown PO8 ..112 A3
Thistledowne Gdns
 PO10 ....161 A4
Thomas Cl SO40 ..100 B3
Thomas Lewis Way SO16,
 SO17 ....79 B1
Thomas Lockyer Cl
 BH31 ....115 A3
Thomas Rd SO52 ..54 A2
Thompson's La SO21 57 B4
Thoresby Ct BH25 194 C2
Thorn Cl Eastleigh SO50 56 B4
 Petersfield GU31 ..41 B1
Thorn Rd BH17 ...187 B2
Thornbrake Rd PO12 181 B2
Thornbury 15 BH4 204 B2
Thornbury Ave
 Blackfield SO45 ..177 C4
 Southampton SO15 102 C4
Thornbury Cl PO14 154 B4
Thornbury Ho 10 PO6 132 C1
Thornbury Hts SO53 30 C1
Thornbury Rd BH6 207 A2
Thornbury Wood SO53 30 C1
Thornby Ct PO3 ..158 A2
Thorncliffe Cl PO2 157 C2
Thorncombe Cl
 Bournemouth BH9 190 A2
 Poole BH17 ......187 C1
Thorncroft Rd PO1 182 C3
Thornden Sch SO53 55 C4
Thorndike Cl SO16 78 A1
Thorndike Rd SO16 77 C1
Thorne Cl BH31 ..114 C3
Thorne Way BH21 139 A3
Thorner's Homes, Centre Ct
 10 SO15 ....102 A4
Thorner's Homes, North Ct 9
 SO15 ....102 A4
Thorner's Homes, South Ct 11
 SO15 ....102 A4
Thorner's Homes, West Ct 12
 SO15 ....102 A4
Thorners Ct 8 SO15 102 C3
Thorness Cl SO16 .77 B1
Thorney Cl PO14 .154 B4
Thorney Island Com Prim Sch
 PO10 ....161 A2
Thorney Old Pk PO10 161 B1
Thorney Rd
 Hermitage PO10 ..161 A3
 Thorney Island PO10 161 A3
Thorney View PO11 160 B1
Thornfield Cl PO8 .88 B1
Thornfield Dr BH23 193 C1
Thorngate Ct 5 PO12 181 B2
Thorngate Way PO12 181 B2
Thornham La PO10 161 B3
Thornham Rd BH25 195 C2
Thornhill Ave SO19 104 B3
Thornhill Cl SO45 150 C1
Thornhill Park Rd SO18 104 C4
Thornhill Prim Sch
 SO19 ....104 B3
Thornhill Rd
 Blackfield SO45 ..150 C1
 Southampton SO16 78 B2

Swi – Tit 261

Thorni Ave PO15 ..130 B2
Thornleigh Rd SO19 103 C1
Thornley Rd BH10 .189 B2
Thorns La SO41 ...199 C3
Thornton Ave SO31 128 B1
Thornton Cl
 Corfe Mullen BH21 186 B3
 Waterlooville PO7 134 A1
Thornton Rd PO12 181 B4
Thornworthy 4 SO45 125 C2
Thornycroft Ave SO19 103 B1
Thorogood Ct 4 BH15 202 C2
Thorold Ct SO18 ...79 C1
Thorold Rd
 Chandler's Ford SO53 30 C1
 Southampton SO18 79 C1
Three Acre Dr BH25 209 C4
Three Acres PO7 ..111 A2
Three Cross Rd BH21,
 BH22 ....138 C3
Three Horse Shoes La
 SO24 ....16 C1
Three Legged Cross First Sch
 BH21 ....114 C1
Three Lions Cl 12 BH21 163 A3
Three Oaks SO19 .104 C3
Three Tun Cl 21 PO1 182 A3
Threefield La SO14 103 A2
Thresher Cl PO7 ..112 B1
Throop Cl BH8 ...191 A1
Throop Rd
 Bournemouth BH8 190 C2
 Bournemouth BH8 191 A1
Throopside Ave BH9 190 A2
Thrush Rd BH12 ..188 B1
Thrush Wlk PO8 ..111 C2
Thruxton Ct SO19 103 C3
Thruxton Rd PO9 .135 B3
Thurbern Rd PO2 .157 C1
Thurmell Cl SO30 105 B2
Thurmell Wlk SO30 105 B2
Thurmond Cres SO22 10 B3
Thurmond Rd SO22 10 B3
Thursby Rd BH23 .193 C1
Thurston Cl SO53 .55 B4
Thwaite Rd BH12 .204 A3
Thyme Ave PO15 .129 B4
Tichborne Rd
 Eastleigh SO50 ...80 A4
 Southampton SO18 104 B4
Tichborne Way SO19 155 B1
Tichbourne Ho SO30 105 B4
Tickleford Dr SO19 104 A1
Tickner Ct SO30 ..105 C3
Ticonderoga Gdns
 SO19 ....103 C1
Tidcombe Gn PO9 135 B4
Tidemill Cl BH23 ..207 A4
Tides Reach SO18 103 B4
Tides Way SO40 ..101 C1
Tideway Gdns PO4 183 B2
Tidworth Rd PO9 .135 C2
Tiffany Cl SO41 ..195 C2
Tiffield Cl PO3 ...158 B2
Tiger Rd PO1 ....181 C4
Tilbrook Rd SO15 102 A4
Tilburg Rd BH23 .207 B4
Tilden Rd SO21 ...31 B3
Tilebarn La SO42 .173 A3
Tilford Rd PO8 ...111 C3
Tillingbourn PO14 129 B2
Tillinton Gdns PO8 88 B2
Tilmore Gdns GU32 40 C3
Tilmore Rd GU32 .40 C3
Timberlane PO7 ..134 B2
Timberley Ho 2 PO1 215 C3
Timberley La SP5 .48 A3
Timberly Cl SO45 150 B2
Timbermill Ct SP6 93 C4
Timbers The PO15 130 B2
Timor Cl PO15 ...129 B4
Timothy Cl BH10 .189 B3
Timpson Rd PO1 .215 D4
Timsbury Cres PO9 135 C1
Timsbury Ct SO19 103 C2
Timsbury Dr SO16 77 C1
Timson Cl SO40 ..100 B3
Tincleton Gdns BH9 190 A2
Tindale Rd SO16 ..77 C1
Tinker Alley SO18 .80 A4
Tinkers Cross SP6 69 C2
Tinneys Cl SP5 ...47 B2
Tintagel Cl SO16 ..78 B3
Tintagel Way PO6 157 A4
Tintern Cl PO6 ...133 C1
Tintern Gr 18 SO15 102 C3
Tintern Rd PO12 .181 A2
Tipner Gn PO2 ...157 B2
Tipner La PO2 ...157 B2
Tipner Rd PO2 ...157 B1
Tiptoe Gn 20 PO9 136 A3
Tiptoe Prim Sch SO41 195 B4
Tiptoe Rd BH25 ..171 A1
Tipton Ho PO5 ...215 B2
Tiptree Cl SO50 ..56 A3
Tisted Ct 23 PO9 136 A3
Titchborne Gr PO9 135 B3
Titchfield Abbey PO15 130 A1
Titchfield Hill PO14 154 A4
Titchfield Industries
 PO14 ....154 A4
Titchfield La PO15, PO17 107 B2
Titchfield Park Rd PO15 129 B2
Titchfield Prim Sch
 PO14 ....129 C1

Titchfield Rd PO14 .....154 A3
Tithe Barn SO41 ....197 C3
Tithe Mead SO51 ....27 C1
Tithe The PO7 ....110 C2
Tithelands La SO24 .....15 C2
Tithewood Cl SO53 ......30 A1
Titus Gdns PO7 ....135 A4
Tiverton Ct
24 Bournemouth BH4 ....204 B2
1 Fareham PO16 ....131 B1
Tivoli Cl SO53 ....55 C4
Toby St PO1 ....215 B4
Todber Cl BH11 ....188 C2
Tokar St PO4 ....183 A1
Tokio Rd PO3 ....158 A1
Tolefrey Gdns SO53 .....54 C3
Tollard Cl BH12 ....203 C4
Tollbar Way SO30 ....81 A1
Tollerford Rd BH17 .....187 B1
Tollgate SO53 ....55 B1
Tollgate Ests SO51 ....27 A2
Tollgate Rd SO31 ....128 B4
Tollgate The 20 SO23 .....2 A1
Tolpuddle Gdns BH9 ...190 A2
Tolstoi Rd BH14 ....203 A3
Tomkyns Cl SO53 ....54 C3
Toms La BH24 ....118 A4
Tonbridge St PO5 ......182 B1
Tonge Rd BH11 ....189 A3
Tonnant Cl PO14 ....179 B3
Toogoods Way SO16 .....77 B3
Toomer Cl SO45 ....150 C1
Toothill Rd SO51 ....53 B1
Top La BH24 ....141 A4
Topaz Gr PO7 ....135 A4
Topiary Gdns SO31 .....129 A2
Tor Cl Portchester PO16 ..131 C1
Waterlooville PO7 ....134 C2
Tor Way GU31 ....41 A2
Torbay Rd BH14 ....203 B2
Torberry Dr GU31 ....41 A1
Torch Cl SO50 ....57 A1
Torcross Cl SO19 ......103 C1
Torfrida Ct PO4 ....183 B2
Tormead SO45 ....125 C2
Tornay Gr SO52 ....53 C2
Toronto Pl PO12 ....181 A3
Toronto Rd PO2 ....182 C4
Torquay Ave
Gosport PO12 ....181 A4
Southampton SO15 ......102 B4
Torque Cl SO19 ....104 C2
Torre Cl SO50 ....56 A3
Torridge Gdns SO18 .....80 A2
Torrington Cl SO19 .....104 A2
Torrington Rd PO2 .....157 C2
Tortworth Cl PO14 .....154 B4
Torwood Gdns SO50 .....56 C1
Tosson Cl SO16 ....101 C4
Totland Cl SO16 ....101 C4
Totland Ct 8 SO41 .....211 B2
Totland Rd Cosham PO6 .157 C4
Gosport PO13 ....155 B1
Totmel Rd BH17 ....188 A1
Totnes Cl SO50 ....55 C3
Tottehale Cl SO52 ....53 C2
Tottenham Rd PO1 .....215 D4
Totton & Eling Heritage Ctr★
SO40 ....101 A3
Totton By Pass SO40 ...101 A4
Totton Coll SO40 ....100 B4
Totton Recn Ctr SO40 ...100 B4
Totton Sta SO40 ....101 A4
Totton Western By-Pass
SO40 ....100 B3
Totton Wlk 15 PO9 .....135 B3
Tournerbury La PO11 ...185 A2
Tourney Rd BH11 ....188 C3
Tovey Pl SO23 ....2 B4
Towans The BH13 ......214 B2
Tower Cl PO12 ....180 B2
Tower Ct
Bournemouth BH2 ....204 C1
Locks Heath SO31 ....128 B1
14 Winchester SO22 ....10 C4
Tower Gdns 4 SO16 ....78 C2
Tower Ho SO19 ....103 C1
Tower Ind Est The SO50 ..56 B1
Tower La Eastleigh SO50 ..56 B1
Wimborne Minst BH21 ...163 B3
Tower Park Rdbt BH15 .202 C4
Tower Pl SO30 ....80 B1
Tower Rd
Bournemouth BH1 ....205 C3
Poole BH13 ....204 A1
Portsmouth PO4 ....182 C2
Winchester SO22 ....10 C4
Tower Rd W BH13 ......204 A1
Tower St Emsworth PO10 161 A4
Portsmouth PO1 ....181 C2
Winchester SO23 ....10 C4
Tower The 10 PO12 .....181 A3
Towers Farm BH21 .....186 B4
Towers Gdn PO9 ....159 C3
Towers Way BH21 ......186 B4
Town Hall Rd PO9 ......135 C1
Town La GU32 ....41 A3
Town Quay
Portsmouth PO1 ....181 C2
Southampton SO14 ......102 C1
Towngate Bridge BH15 .202 B2
Towngate Sh Ctr 1
BH15 ....202 B1
Townhill Inf Sch SO18 ...80 A1
Townhill Jun Sch SO18 ..80 A1
Townhill Park House (The
Gregg Sch) SO18 ....80 A2
Townhill Way SO18 ......80 A1
Townsend Cl BH11 .....189 A3
Townsend La SP6 ....42 C2
Townsend Prim & Com Sch
BH8 ....191 A1
Townsville Rd BH9 .....190 A1
Towpath Mead PO4 ....183 B2
Toynbee Cl SO50 ....56 A2
Toynbee Rd SO50 ....56 A2
Toynbee Sch The SO53 ...55 C3
Tozer Cl BH11 ....188 C1
Tracey Ct BH23 ....209 A4
Trafalgar Cl SO53 ....55 A3
Trafalgar Ct
Christchurch BH23 ......207 C3
Fareham PO14 ....154 C4
33 Portsmouth PO5 ......182 B1
Trafalgar Pl
Lymington SO41 ....197 C2
Portsmouth PO1 ....215 D4
Trafalgar Rd
Bournemouth BH9 ......204 C4
Southampton SO15 ......102 B3
Trafalgar Sq PO12 .....181 A3
Trafalgar St SO23 ....10 C4
Trafalgar Way 14 SO45 .126 A1
Trafford Way SO50 ......57 B1
Trampers La PO17 .....109 A2
Tranby Rd SO19 ....103 C2
Tranmere Cl SO41 ......197 C1
Tranmere Rd PO4 ......183 A2
Treadwheel Rd PO8 ....113 A3
Treagore Rd SO40 ....76 B1
Trearnan Cl SO16 ......101 C4
Treble Cl SO22 ....10 A2
Tredegar Rd PO4 ....183 A2
Tree Hamlets BH16 ....201 B3
Tree Side Way PO7 .....111 C1
Treebys Cl BH23 ....192 B1
Treeside BH23 ....193 B1
Treeside Ave SO40 .....101 A4
Treeside Rd SO15 ......102 B4
Treetops 9 BH13 ....214 C4
Trefoil Cl 10 PO7 ....135 A4
Trefoil Way BH23 ....208 B4
Tregantle Mews PO12 ..181 A2
Tregaron Ave PO6 ......158 A4
Tregonwell Rd BH2 ....204 C1
Treloar Rd PO11 ....185 C1
Treloen Ct 3 BH8 ....205 A3
Treloyhan Cl SO53 ......55 B2
Tremona Ct SO16 ....78 A1
Tremona Rd SO16 ....78 A1
Trenley Cl SO45 ....150 B2
Trent Cl SO18 ....79 C1
Trent Ho 25 SO14 ......103 B3
Trent Rd SO18 ....79 C1
Trent Way
Ferndown BH22 ....166 A3
Lee-on-the-Solent PO13 ..179 C1
West End SO30 ....80 B1
Trent Wlk PO16 ....156 A4
Trentham Ave BH7 .....206 A4
Trentham Cl BH7 ....206 A4
Tresillian Cl BH23 ......194 A1
Tresillian Gdns SO18 ....80 A1
Tresillian Way BH23 ....194 A1
Trevis Rd PO4 ....183 B2
Trevone 15 BH25 ....195 A2
Trevone Cl SO40 ....100 C3
Trevor Rd PO4 ....182 C2
Trevose Cl
Chandler's Ford SO53 .....55 B2
Gosport PO13 ....155 B1
Trevose Cres SO53 ....55 B3
Trevose Way PO14 ......129 A1
Triangle Gdns SO16 ......77 B2
Triangle La PO14 ....153 C3
Triangle The
Bournemouth BH2 ......204 C2
Upton BH16 ....201 A4
Whiteparish SP5 ....24 A2
Tribe Rd PO12 ....181 A3
Tricketts La BH22 ......165 C3
Tricorn The PO1 ....215 B4
Trigon Rd BH15 ....202 B4
Trimaran Rd SO31 ......128 C1
Trimm's Dro SP6 ....70 C4
Trimmer's Ct PO1 ......181 C2
Trinadad Ho 1 PO6 .....132 C1
Trinidad Cres BH12 ....203 B4
Trinidad Fst Sch BH12 ...203 B4
Trinidad Ho BH12 ....203 B4
Trinity 2 BH1 ....205 A2
Trinity Cl PO12 ....181 C2
Trinity Ct
Chandler's Ford SO53 .....55 B3
2 Southampton SO15 ....102 B3
Totton SO40 ....76 C1
Trinity Gdns PO16 ......131 A1
Trinity Gr PO12 ....181 C2
Trinity Ind Est
Southampton SO15 ......101 C4
Wimborne Minst BH21 ...163 C2
Trinity Rd
Bournemouth BH1 ......205 A2
Southampton SO14 ......103 A3
Trinity St PO16 ....131 A1
Tripps End Cvn Site
SO30 ....105 B4
Tristan Cl SO45 ....178 C4
Tristram Cl SO53 ....54 C2
Triton Ctr The SO51 ....53 B3
Triumph Cl PO15 ....130 B1
Triumph Rd PO14 ....154 C3
Troak Cl BH23 ....207 C4
Trojan Way PO7 ....134 C2
Troon Cres PO6 ....134 B1
Troon Rd BH18 ....187 A3
Trooper Bottom GU32 ...19 A2
Trosnant Inf Sch PO9 ....135 C2
Trosnant Jun Sch PO9 ...135 C2
Trosnant Rd PO9 ....135 C1
Trotters La BH21 ....164 A3
Trotts La
Marchwood SO40 ....101 B1
Totton SO40 ....101 B2
Trowbridge Cl SO16 .....77 C3
Trowbridge Ct 16 SO23 ..11 A4
Truman Rd BH10 ....189 A3
Truro Ct PO13 ....180 B3
Truro Rd PO6 ....132 C1
Truro Rise SO50 ....56 C2
Truscott Ave BH9 ....205 A4
Trussell Cl SO22 ....1 B2
Trussell Cres SO22 ....1 B2
Trystworthy 10 BH2 ....204 C2
Tuckers La BH15 ....201 C1
Tucks Cl BH23 ....193 A4
Tuckton Cl BH6 ....206 B2
Tuckton Rd BH6 ....206 C2
Tudor Ave PO10 ....136 C2
Tudor Cl Alderholt SP6 ....93 A3
Gosport PO13 ....180 B4
Portchester PO16 ....132 A1
South Hayling PO11 .....184 C1
Totton SO40 ....100 B4
Tudor Cres PO6 ....157 C3
Tudor Ct
Bournemouth BH1 ....205 A3
8 Cosham PO6 ....157 C4
18 Fareham PO14 ....154 C4
Poole BH15 ....202 C3
8 Portsmouth PO5 ....182 B1
Tudor Gdns SO30 ....105 A3
Tudor Ho (Mus)★ SO14 102 C2
Tudor Rd BH18 ....187 A2
Tudor Way SO23 ....2 A4
Tudor Wood Cl SO16 .....78 C2
Tuffin Cl SO16 ....77 B3
Tukes Ave PO13 ....155 A2
Tulip Gdns Havant PO9 ..135 B1
Locks Heath SO31 ....128 C2
Tulip Rd SO16 ....79 B2
Tumulus Cl SO19 ....104 C2
Tunstall Rd SO19 ....104 C2
Tunworth Ct PO9 ....136 A3
Tupman Ho 18 PO1 .....182 B4
Tuppenny La PO10 ......161 B4
Turbary Ct
Bournemouth BH12 ......189 A1
Ferndown BH22 ....165 C3
Upton BH16 ....201 B4
Turbary Hts BH11 ....188 C1
Turbary Park Ave BH11 .189 A1
Turbary Rd BH22 ....165 C3
Turbary Ret Pk BH11 ....188 C2
Turbury Cl BH12 ....203 B4
Turbury Rd BH12 ....203 B4
Turf Croft Ct BH23 ......194 A1
Turk's La BH14 ....203 A1
Turlin Moor Fst Sch
BH16 ....201 B2
Turlin Moor Mid Sch
BH16 ....201 B2
Turlin Rd BH16 ....201 B2
Turnberry Cl BH23 ......206 C3
Turner Ave PO13 ....180 C4
Turner Rd PO1 ....182 B4
Turners Farm Cres
SO41 ....196 A1
Turners Oak Ct SO15 ....78 B1
Turnpike Down SO23 .....11 B4
Turnpike Way SO30 .....105 A4
Turnstone Gdns SO16 ....78 A3
Turnworth Cl BH18 ......187 B2
Turtle Cl PO14 ....154 A2
Turvy King Ct PO7 ......110 C2
Tuscan Wlk SO53 ....55 C3
Tuscany Way PO7 ....135 A4
Tussocks The SO40 ......101 C1
Tutland Rd SO52 ....53 C2
Tutt's La SO51 ....50 C2
Tweed Cl SO53 ....55 A4
Tweed La SO41 ....197 B4
Tweedale Rd BH9 ....190 B2
Twemlow Ave BH14 .....202 C2
Twiggs End Cl SO31 .....128 C2
Twiggs La SO40 ....124 C4
Twiggs Lane End SO40 .124 B3
Twin Oaks SO19 ....103 C2
Twin Oaks Cl BH18 .....187 A2
Twittens Way PO9 ......135 C1
Twyford Ave
Portsmouth PO2 ....157 B1
Southampton SO15 ....78 B1
Twyford Cl BH8 ....190 B1
Twyford Ct 15 SO23 ....2 A1
Twyford Dr PO13 ....179 C1
Twyford Ho SO15 ....102 C4
Twyford Rd SO50 ....56 A3
Twyford Sch SO21 ....32 A3
Twyford St Mary CE Prim Sch
SO21 ....31 C3
Twyford Way BH17 ......188 A1
Twynham Ave BH23 ....207 A4
Twynham Cl SP5 ....46 C3
Twynham Rd BH6 ....206 C2
Twynham Sch BH23 ......207 A3
Twynhams Hill SO32 ....108 A4
Tyler Ct PO9 ....135 C3
Tylers Cl SO41 ....197 B3
Tyleshades The SO51 ....53 A3
Tyne Cl SO53 ....55 A3
Tynedale Cl
Bournemouth BH9 ......190 A2
Gosport PO12 ....180 C4
Tyneham Ave BH12 .....203 B4
Tyrells La BH24 ....142 C2
Tyrrel Lawn PO9 ....135 B4
Tyrrel Rd SO53 ....55 B4
Tyrrell Gdns BH8 ....191 A1
Tyrrells Ct BH23 ....169 A1
Tyseley Rd PO1 ....215 B2
Tytherley Gn
Bournemouth BH8 ....190 B1
24 Havant PO9 ....136 A3
Tytherley Rd SO18 ......104 B4

U

Ubsdell Cl BH25 ....195 A2
Uddens Dr BH21 ....164 B4
Uddens Trad Est BH21 ..164 C3
Ullswater SO50 ....56 A1
Ullswater Ave SO18 ......80 A1
Ullswater Ho 15 PO6 ....133 A1
Ullswater Rd
Southampton SO16 ....77 C1
Wimborne Minst BH21 ...163 B1
Undercliff Dr BH1, BH5 .205 B1
Undercliff Gdns SO16 ...78 C2
Undercliff Rd BH5 ......205 C2
Underdown Ave PO7 ....134 B1
Undershore SO41 ....197 C3
Undershore Rd SO41 ...198 A2
Underwood Cl
Poole BH17 ....187 A1
Southampton SO16 ....78 C2
Underwood Rd
Bishopstoke SO50 ....56 C2
Southampton SO16 ....78 C2
Unicorn Rd
Lee-on-the-Solent PO13 ..179 B2
Portsmouth PO1 ....215 A4
Unicorn Trad Ctr The
PO1 ....215 A4
Union La SO32 ....61 A1
Union Pl PO1 ....215 C4
Union Rd Havant PO9 ...135 C1
Southampton SO14 ......103 B3
Union St Fareham PO16 ..131 B1
8 Portsmouth PO1 ....182 A3
Winchester SO23 ....11 A4
Univ of Portsmouth
Portsmouth PO1 ....182 A3
Portsmouth PO1 ....215 B2
Univ of Portsmouth
(Langstone Campus)
PO4 ....183 B3
Univ of Portsmouth (Milton
Campus) PO4 ....183 A2
Universal Marina SO31 .128 B3
University Cres SO17 ....79 A2
University Parkway SO16 54 B1
University Rd SO17 ......79 A2
University Rdbt BH10 ...204 B4
Unwin Cl SO19 ....103 B1
Upham CE Prim Sch
SO32 ....58 C3
Upham St SO32 ....58 B3
Uphill Rd SO22 ....1 B3
Upland La GU33 ....20 A4
Uplands Ave BH25 ....210 A4
Uplands Cl BH22 ....166 A4
Uplands Cres PO16 .....131 A1
Uplands Prim Sch PO16 131 A2
Uplands Rd
Bournemouth BH8 ....190 B1
Cosham PO6 ....158 B4
Denmead PO7 ....110 B3
Rowland's Castle PO9 ...113 B1
West Moors BH22 ....139 A1
Winchester SO22 ....1 C2
Uplands Sch BH14 ....203 B2
Uplands Way SO17 ......79 A1
Uplyme Cl BH17 ....188 A1
Upmill Cl SO18 ....80 A2
Uppark (NT)★ GU31 ......90 C4
Upper Arundel St PO1 ..215 B3
Upper Banister St 1
SO15 ....102 C3
Upper Barn Copse SO50 .57 A2
Upper Bere Wood PO7 .134 C4
Upper Brook Dr SO31 ..128 C1
Upper Brook St SO23 ....11 A4
Upper Brownhill Rd
SO16 ....77 C2
Upper Bugle St SO14 ...102 C2
Upper Church Rd SO32 .107 C4
Upper Common Rd
SO41 ....196 C2
Upper Crabbick La PO7 110 B3
Upper Crescent Rd SO52 53 C3
Upper Deacon Rd SO19 104 B3
Upper Gn GU33 ....19 C4
Upper Golf Links Rd
BH18 ....187 A3
Upper Gordon Rd BH23 194 A1
Upper Heyshott GU31 ...41 A2
Upper High St SO23 .....10 C4
Upper Hinton Rd BH1 ..204 C2
Upper House Ct PO17 ..108 A2
Upper Market St SO50 ..56 A2
Upper Mead Cl 9 SO50 ..57 B1
Upper Moors Rd SO21 ...56 C4
Upper Mount GU33 ....20 C2
Upper Mullins La SO45 .125 C2
Upper New Rd SO30 .....80 B1
Upper Northam Cl
SO30 ....105 A3
Upper Northam Dr
SO30 ....104 C3
Upper Northam Rd
SO30 ....105 A3
Upper Norwich Rd 13
BH2 ....204 C2
Upper Old St PO14 .....154 A2
Upper Piece PO7 ....111 A2
Upper Rd BH12 ....203 B3
Upper Shaftesbury Ave
SO17 ....79 A1
Upper Shirley Ave SO15 .78 B1
Upper Spinney SO31 ...152 B4
Upper St Helens Rd
SO30 ....105 A3
Upper St Michael's Gr
PO14 ....154 C4
Upper Terrace Rd BH2 .204 C2
Upper Toothill Rd SO16 ..77 C4
Upper Wardown GU31 ...41 A2
Upper Weston La SO19 .104 A1
Upper Wharf PO16 .....155 B4
Uppleby Rd BH12 ....203 B3
Upton Cl Havant PO9 ...135 B4
Upton BH16 ....201 A4
Upton Cres SO16 ....77 B4
Upton Cross Mobile Home Pk
BH16 ....201 B4
Upton Ct BH16 ....201 B4
Upton Ctry Pk★ BH17 ..201 C3
Upton Grey Cl SO22 ....1 B2
Upton Heath Est BH16 ..201 B4
Upton Ho 3 SO16 ....78 A1
Upton Inf Sch BH16 .....201 A4
Upton Jun Sch BH16 ....201 A4
Upton La SO16 ....77 B3
Upton Rd
Broadstone BH17 ....202 A4
Poole BH17 ....201 C4
Upton Way BH18 ....186 C2
Upwey Ave BH15 ....201 C2
Utrecht Ct BH23 ....207 B4

V

Vadne Gdns PO12 ......181 A3
Vaggs La Hordle SO41 ...195 C3
New Milton SO41 ....195 B4
Vale Cl BH14 ....203 C2
Vale Dr SO18 ....79 C1
Vale Gr PO12 ....181 A4
Vale Lo BH1 ....205 B3
Vale Mans 4 BH1 ....205 B2
Vale Rd
Bournemouth BH1 ....205 B2
Poole BH14 ....203 C2
Redlynch SP5 ....47 B3
Winchester SO23 ....11 B3
Vale The Horndean PO8 ...88 B1
Hythe SO45 ....125 C2
Locks Heath SO31 ....129 A1
Petersfield GU32 ....41 A3
Portsmouth PO5 ....182 B1
Vale View Pk SO41 .....195 C4
Valencia Cl BH23 ......191 B2
Valentine Ave SO19 ....104 B2
Valentine Cl PO15 ......130 B1
Valentine Ct
Southampton SO19 ......104 B2
Waterlooville PO7 ....135 A4
Valentines Inf Sch SO19 104 B2
Valerian Ave PO15 .....129 C2
Valerian Cl SO50 ....81 B3
Valerian Rd SO30 ......105 B3
Valetta Pk PO10 ....160 C4
Valetta Rd PO10 ....161 B1
Valette Rd BH9 ....190 A2
Valiant Gdns PO2 ......157 B2
Valiant Rd PO10 ....161 B1
Valiant Way BH23 ......208 A4
Valley Cl Blackfield SO45 .150 C1
Christchurch BH23 ......191 C2
Colden Common SO21 .....56 C4
Redlynch SP5 ....47 B3
Waterlooville PO7 ....134 B2
Valley Ct The 4 SO22 ....10 B3
Valley La BH23 ....169 C2
Valley Park Dr PO8 ......88 B2
Valley Rd
Bournemouth BH8 ....190 C2
Chandler's Ford SO53 .....55 B4
Littleton SO22 ....1 A3
Totton SO40 ....100 C3
Valley Rise SO31 ....128 C2
Valley The SO22 ....10 B3
Valley View Poole BH12 .204 A4
Southampton SO19 ......104 A2
Valleydene SO45 ....125 C1
Vallis Cl BH15 ....202 B1
Valsheba Dr PO14 ......179 A3
Vanburgh Way SO53 .....30 A1
Vanguard Rd
Bournemouth BH8 ....190 C1
Gosport PO12 ....181 B4
Poole BH15 ....202 B1
Southampton SO18 ......104 A4
Vanstone Rd PO13 ......180 B4
Vardy Cl SO19 ....104 B2
Varna Rd SO15 ....102 B3
Varsity Rd PO10 ....161 B1
Vaudrey Cl SO15 ....78 B1
Vaughan Cl SO19 ....104 C3
Vaughan Rd SO45 ......125 B2
Vauxhall Way GU32 ......40 C2
Veal's La SO40 ....125 A4
Vear's La SO21 ....57 A4
Vecta Cl BH23 ....208 B3

Vectis Ct 1 SO16 .... 78 C2
Vectis Rd
Barton on Sea BH25 .... 209 B4
Gosport PO12 .... 180 C2
Vectis Way PO6 .... 157 C4
Velder Ave PO4 .... 183 A3
Vellan Ct SO16 .... 77 B1
Velmore Rd SO53 .... 55 A2
Velsheda Ct 2 SO45 .... 126 A3
Velvet Lawn Rd BH25 .... 194 C2
Venator Pl BH21 .... 163 B3
Venerable Rd PO14 .... 155 A3
Vengeance Rd PO13 .... 179 C2
Venice Cl PO7 .... 135 A4
Venning Ave BH11 .... 188 C3
Ventnor Ct SO16 .... 79 B3
Ventnor Rd
Gosport PO13 .... 155 A2
Portsmouth PO4 .... 182 C2
Ventnor Way PO16 .... 131 C1
Ventry Cl BH13 .... 203 C2
Ventura Ctr The BH16 .... 201 B3
Ventura Pl BH16 .... 201 B3
Venture Ct PO3 .... 158 A3
Venture Ind Pk PO3 .... 158 A3
Venture Rd SO16 .... 54 B1
Verbena Cres PO8 .... 112 A2
Verbena Way SO30 .... 105 B3
Verdon Ave SO31 .... 127 C2
Verger Cl PO14 .... 129 B2
Verity Cres BH17 .... 188 A1
Vermont Cl SO16 .... 78 C2
Vermont Sch SO16 .... 78 C2
Vernalls Cl BH10 .... 189 B3
Vernalls Ct BH25 .... 195 B3
Vernalls Gdns BH10 .... 189 B3
Verne Rd BH31 .... 115 A3
Verney Cl BH11 .... 189 A2
Verney Rd BH11 .... 189 A2
Vernham Rd SO22 .... 1 C1
Verno La BH23 .... 193 B1
Vernon Ave PO4 .... 183 A3
Vernon Cl
Bishop's Waltham SO32 .... 59 B1
Gosport PO12 .... 181 A3
Vernon Ct 3 PO2 .... 157 C1
Vernon Hill SO32 .... 59 B1
Vernon Mews 2 PO4 .... 183 A3
Vernon Rd Gosport PO12 181 A3
Portsmouth PO3 .... 158 A1
Vernon Wlk 5 SO15 .... 102 C3
Verona Ave BH6 .... 206 B3
Verona Rd SO53 .... 55 C3
Verulam Pl 31 BH1 .... 204 C2
Verulam Rd Poole BH14 .202 C2
Southampton SO14 .... 103 A4
Verwood CE First Sch
BH31 .... 114 C3
Verwood Cres BH6 .... 207 A2
Verwood Ind Est BH31 .115 A3
Verwood Rd Havant PO9 136 A3
Ibsley BH24 .... 116 A1
St Leonards BH24 .... 140 B4
Three Legged Cross BH21 114 C1
Verwood BH21 .... 114 A4
Woodlands BH21 .... 114 A4
Veryan PO15 .... 130 C1
Vesca Ho SO31 .... 129 A3
Vespasian Ct SO18 .... 103 B4
Vespasian Rd SO18 .... 103 B4
Vespasian Way SO53 .... 55 C4
Vesta Way SO53 .... 55 C4
Vetch Cl BH23 .... 208 B4
Vian Cl PO13 .... 155 B2
Vian Ct BH25 .... 194 C2
Vian Pl SO23 .... 2 B4
Vian Rd PO7 .... 134 C3
Vicarage Cotts BH8 .... 190 C2
Vicarage Dr SO30 .... 105 A3
Vicarage Farm SO50 .... 57 B3
Vicarage Gdns SO41 .... 196 A1
Vicarage La Cadnam SO40 75 A1
Curdridge SO32 .... 106 B4
Hambledon PO7 .... 86 B2
Hordle SO41 .... 196 A1
Stubbington PO14 .... 154 B2
Swanmore SO32 .... 84 B3
Vicarage Pk SP5 .... 47 B3
Vicarage Rd
Bournemouth BH9 .... 189 C1
Marchwood SO40 .... 101 C1
Poole BH15 .... 202 B3
Redlynch SP5 .... 48 A3
Verwood BH31 .... 114 C3
Vicarage Way BH23 .... 192 B1
Vice La SO43 .... 74 A2
Viceroy Rd SO19 .... 104 A2
Vickers Cl BH8 .... 191 A1
Vickery Way BH23 .... 207 B4
Victena Rd SO50 .... 57 B1
Victor Ct SO19 .... 104 B3
Victor Rd
Portsmouth PO1 .... 182 C4
Thorney Island PO10 .... 161 B1
Victor St SO15 .... 78 A1
Victoria Ave
Bournemouth BH9 .... 189 C1
South Hayling PO11 .... 184 C2
Waterlooville PO7 .... 134 A2
Victoria Bldgs SO32 .... 83 A4
Victoria Cl
Corfe Mullen BH21 .... 186 B3
Locks Heath SO31 .... 129 A1
Victoria Cottage Hospl
PO10 .... 160 C4
Victoria Cres BH12 .... 203 B3
Victoria Ct Durley SO32 .. 82 B4
3 Netley SO31 .... 127 A3
Victoria Ct *continued*
South Hayling PO11 .... 184 C2
Victoria Gdns
Ferndown BH22 .... 165 B3
Fordingbridge SP6 .... 69 B1
Ringwood BH24 .... 141 A3
Victoria Glade SO31 .... 127 B3
Victoria Gr PO5 .... 215 C1
Victoria Ho 11 PO16 .... 131 A1
Victoria Hospl BH21 .... 163 A3
Victoria Park Rd BH9 .... 189 C1
Victoria Pl
Bournemouth BH1 .... 205 B3
6 Gosport PO12 .... 181 A2
2 Lymington SO41 .... 197 C1
Romsey SO51 .... 52 C4
Wimborne Minst BH21 .... 163 A3
Victoria Rd
Bishop's Waltham SO32 .... 83 A4
Bournemouth BH1 .... 205 B3
Christchurch BH23 .... 207 C3
Eastleigh SO50 .... 56 A3
Emsworth PO10 .... 136 C1
Ferndown BH22 .... 165 B3
Fordingbridge SP6 .... 69 B1
Milford on Sea SO41 .... 211 B2
Netley SO31 .... 127 A3
North Hayling PO11 .... 159 C1
Poole BH12 .... 203 B3
Portsmouth PO1 .... 182 A3
Southampton SO19 .... 103 B1
Waterlooville PO7 .... 134 C4
Wimborne Minst BH21 .... 163 A3
Winchester SO23 .... 1 C1
Victoria Rd N PO5 .... 215 C2
Victoria Rd S PO5 .... 182 B1
Victoria Sq PO13 .... 179 C1
Victoria St Gosport PO12 181 B3
Portsmouth PO1 .... 182 B4
Southampton SO14 .... 103 B3
Victoria Terr
16 Cosham PO6 .... 157 C4
Hermitage PO10 .... 137 A1
Southbourne PO10 .... 161 B4
Westbourne PO10 .... 137 A2
Victoria Wlk SO30 .... 80 C1
Victory Ave PO8 .... 112 A3
Victory Cl
Chandler's Ford SO53 .... 55 A3
Three Legged Cross BH21 139 A3
Victory Cotts SO31 .... 128 B4
Victory Cres SO15 .... 102 A3
Victory Ct PO13 .... 155 B1
Victory Gn PO2 .... 157 B1
Victory Ho PO6 .... 157 A4
Victory Rd
17 Portsmouth PO1 .... 182 A3
Southampton SO15 .... 102 A3
Stubbington PO14 .... 179 B3
Victory Ret Pk PO2 .... 182 B4
Victory Sq SO15 .... 102 A3
Victory Trad Est PO3 .... 158 A1
Victory Way SO16 .... 77 C4
Viewside Cl BH21 .... 186 B3
Viking Cl Blackfield SO45 177 C4
Bournemouth BH6 .... 207 A2
Southampton SO16 .... 77 C2
Stubbington PO14 .... 154 A2
Viking Way
Bournemouth BH6 .... 207 A2
Christchurch BH23 .... 208 A3
Horndean PO8 .... 88 B2
Vikings The SO51 .... 53 A4
Villa Gdns PO7 .... 134 C4
Village Cl PO14 .... 179 B3
Village Ctr SO40 .... 101 C1
Village Gate PO14 .... 153 C4
Village Rd PO12 .... 180 C1
Village St GU32 .... 41 A3
Ville de Paris Rd PO14 .... 155 A3
Villette Cl BH23 .... 192 A1
Villiers Rd Hythe SO45 .... 149 C4
Portsmouth PO5 .... 182 B1
Southampton SO15 .... 102 B4
Vimoutiers Ct SP6 .... 69 C1
Vimy Ho 3 PO14 .... 154 C4
Vince Cl BH11 .... 189 A3
Vincent Ave SO16 .... 78 B1
Vincent Cl 2 BH25 .... 195 A1
Vincent Gr PO16 .... 156 B4
Vincent Rd
1 New Milton BH25 .... 195 A1
Southampton SO15 .... 102 B4
Vincent St SO15 .... 102 B4
Vincent's Gr SO15 .... 102 A4
Vincent's Wlk SO14 .... 103 A2
Vine Bank SO18 .... 104 A4
Vine Cl Bournemouth BH7 206 A4
Locks Heath SO31 .... 128 B2
Vine Coppice PO7 .... 134 C2
Vine Ct 22 PO6 .... 157 C4
Vine Farm Cl BH12 .... 204 B4
Vine Farm Rd BH12 .... 204 A4
Vine Hill BH21 .... 162 C3
Vine Ho SO31 .... 129 A3
Vine Rd SO16 .... 78 A2
Vinegar Hill SO41 .... 211 B3
Vineries Cl BH21 .... 163 C3
Vineries The BH21 .... 163 C3
Vinery Gdns SO16 .... 78 B1
Vinery Rd SO16 .... 78 B1
Vinery The BH25 .... 195 A1
Vineside PO13 .... 155 C1
Viney Ave SO51 .... 53 A4
Viney Rd SO41 .... 197 C1
Vineyard Cl SO19 .... 103 B2
Vineyards The SO52 .... 54 A2
Vinnells La GU32 .... 37 B3
Vinneys Cl BH23 .... 192 B1
Vinson Rd GU33 .... 21 A2
Violet Ave PO14 .... 179 A3
Violet Cl SO53 .... 55 A3
Violet Farm Cl BH21 .... 186 B4
Violet La BH25 .... 195 A2
Violet Rd SO16 .... 79 A2
Virginia Cl BH12 .... 203 B4
Virginia Park Rd PO12 .180 C3
Viscount Ct BH11 .... 188 B3
Viscount Dr BH23 .... 208 A3
Viscount Wlk BH11 .... 188 B3
Vista Marina BH13 .... 214 B3
Vita Rd PO2 .... 157 C2
Vitre Gdns SO41 .... 197 C1
Vivash Rd PO1 .... 215 D3
Vixen Cl PO14 .... 179 A3
Vixen Wlk BH25 .... 195 A3
Vokes Cl SO19 .... 104 A3
Vulcan Cl SO15 .... 101 C3
Vulcan Rd
Southampton SO15 .... 101 C3
Thorney Island PO10 .... 161 B1
Vulcan Way BH23 .... 208 A4
Vyse La 20 SO14 .... 102 C2

W

Wade Court Rd PO9 .... 160 A4
Wade La PO9 .... 160 A4
Wadham Rd PO2 .... 157 B1
Wadhurst Gdns SO19 .... 127 A4
Wadhurst Rd SO30 .... 105 B3
Wagtail Dr BH25 .... 194 C1
Wagtail Rd PO8 .... 112 A3
Wagtail Way PO16 .... 155 C4
Wainscot Rd PO4 .... 183 A1
Wainsford Cl SO41 .... 197 A1
Wainsford Rd
Hordle SO41 .... 196 C1
Lymington SO41 .... 196 C1
Wainwright Cl PO6 .... 158 B3
Wainwright Gdns SO30 .... 81 B2
Wait End Rd PO7 .... 134 C3
Waite End Prim Sch
PO7 .... 134 C3
Wake Lawn PO4 .... 183 B2
Wakefield Ave
Bournemouth BH10 .... 189 C3
Fareham PO16 .... 130 C2
Wakefield Ct 6 SO18 .... 80 A1
Wakefield Pl PO12 .... 181 A1
Wakefield Rd SO18 .... 80 A1
Wakeford Ct 17 SO51 .... 52 C4
Wakeford Pl SO31 .... 129 A1
Wakefords Way PO9 .... 136 A3
Wakely Gdns BH11 .... 189 A3
Wakely Rd BH11 .... 189 A3
Walberant Bldgs 9
PO3 .... 157 C2
Walberton Ave PO6 .... 158 A4
Walberton Ct 1 PO6 .... 158 A4
Walcheren Pl BH15 .... 201 B2
Walcott Ave BH23 .... 191 C1
Waldegrave Cl SO19 .... 103 B1
Walden Gdns PO8 .... 112 A4
Walden Rd PO2 .... 157 B1
Walditch Gdns BH17 .... 187 C1
Waldon Gdns SO18 .... 80 A1
Waldren Cl BH15 .... 202 C1
Wales St SO23 .... 11 A4
Walford Bldgs PO3 .... 183 A4
Walford Cl BH21 .... 163 B3
Walford Gdns BH21 .... 163 A3
Walford Mill Craft Ctr★
BH21 .... 163 A3
Walford Rd PO6 .... 133 B1
Walhampton Hill SO41 .... 198 A3
Walker Gdns SO30 .... 81 B1
Walker Pl PO13 .... 155 B1
Walker Rd PO2 .... 157 B1
Walker's La S SO45 .... 177 C4
Walkers Cl SO50 .... 57 B1
Walkers La N SO45 .... 150 C1
Walkford La BH25 .... 194 B2
Walkford Rd BH23 .... 194 B1
Walkford Way BH23 .... 194 A1
Walkingfield La BH15 .... 202 B1
Walkwood Ave BH7 .... 206 A4
Wallace La SO42 .... 175 B3
Wallace Rd
Broadstone BH18 .... 187 A2
Portsmouth PO2 .... 182 C4
Southampton SO19 .... 103 C1
Wallington Ct PO14 .... 154 C3
Wallington Dr SO53 .... 55 A4
Wallington Hill 3 PO16 131 B1
Wallington Rd PO2 .... 157 C1
Wallington Shore Rd
Fareham PO16 .... 131 B1
14 Portchester PO16 .... 131 B1
Wallington Way PO16 .... 131 B1
Wallis Bglws PO12 .... 180 C2
Wallis Gdns PO7 .... 111 C1
Wallis Rd
Bournemouth BH10 .... 189 A1
Waterlooville PO7 .... 111 C1
Walliscott Rd BH11 .... 189 A1
Wallisdean Ave PO14 .... 154 C4
Wallisdean Jun & Inf Schs
PO14 .... 154 C4
Wallisdean Rd PO3 .... 183 A4
Wallisdown Rd BH10,
BH11 .... 204 B4
Wallisdown Rdbt BH12 .189 A1
Wallrock Wlk PO10 .... 136 C2
Walmer Cl SO50 .... 56 A4
Walmer Rd PO1 .... 182 C3
Walnut Ave SO18 .... 79 C3
Walnut Cl
Chandler's Ford SO53 .... 30 B1
New Milton BH25 .... 194 C2
Southampton SO16 .... 77 C1
Walnut Dr PO14 .... 179 A3
Walnut Gr SO16 .... 77 C1
Walnut Tree Cl PO11 .... 184 C2
Walnut Tree Dr PO10 .... 137 C2
Walpole La SO31 .... 128 C4
Walpole Rd
Bournemouth BH1 .... 205 C3
Gosport PO12 .... 181 B2
Winchester SO22 .... 10 B3
Walpole Terr 8 PO12 .... 181 A2
Walsall Rd PO3 .... 183 A3
Walsford Rd BH4 .... 204 B3
Walsingham Cl PO6 .... 133 B1
Walsingham Dene BH7 .205 C4
Walsingham Gdns SO18 .79 C2
Waltham Bsns Pk SO32 .. 84 A2
Waltham Cl Droxford SO32 61 A1
Portchester PO16 .... 132 B1
Waltham Cres SO16 .... 78 B2
Waltham Rd BH7 .... 206 A3
Waltham St PO5 .... 215 A2
Walton Cl Gosport PO12 .181 A2
Waterlooville PO7 .... 134 C3
Walton Ct Fareham PO15 130 B2
10 Portsmouth PO1 .... 182 A2
Walton Pl SO22 .... 10 B3
Walton Rd
Bournemouth BH10 .... 189 B1
Cosham PO6 .... 158 B3
Gosport PO12 .... 181 A2
Poole BH15 .... 203 A3
Southampton SO19 .... 104 B2
Waltons Ave SO45 .... 150 B2
Wandesford Pl PO12 .... 156 A1
Wandmore Cl SO45 .... 126 A2
Wangfield La SO32 .... 82 B1
Wansbeck Cl SO53 .... 55 A3
Wanstead Cl BH24 .... 117 A1
War Meml Hospl
Gosport PO12 .... 181 A2
Milford on Sea SO41 .... 211 C2
Warbler Cl
Hamworthy BH16 .... 201 A4
Horndean PO8 .... 112 A4
Southampton SO16 .... 78 A3
Warblington Ave PO9 .... 136 A1
Warblington Cl SO53 .... 55 A2
Warblington Ct 2 PO1 .... 182 A2
Warblington Halt Sta
PO9 .... 136 A1
Warblington Rd PO10 .... 160 C4
Warblington Sch PO9 .... 136 A1
Warblington St PO1 .... 182 A2
Warborne La SO41 .... 198 A4
Warbrook Ct 13 PO9 .... 136 A3
Warburton Cl SO19 .... 104 C2
Warburton Rd
Poole BH17 .... 202 C4
Southampton SO19 .... 104 C2
Warburton Way PO8 .... 88 B2
Ward Block PO12 .... 181 B3
Ward Cres PO10 .... 137 A2
Ward Ct PO11 .... 184 C1
Ward Ho 38 PO1 .... 182 A3
Ward Rd PO4 .... 183 A1
Warden Cl SO30 .... 80 B1
Wardens Cl PO11 .... 184 C3
Warders Ct 9 PO12 .... 181 A3
Wardle Rd SO50 .... 56 B4
Wardroom Rd PO2 .... 157 A1
Wareham Ct BH7 .... 206 A3
Wareham Rd BH21 .... 186 B2
Warfield Ave PO7 .... 134 C4
Warfield Cres PO7 .... 134 C4
Warland Way BH21 .... 186 C4
Warlock Cl SO19 .... 104 B2
Warmwell Cl
9 Bournemouth BH9 .... 190 A2
Poole BH17 .... 187 C1
Warnborough Ct 6
PO9 .... 136 A3
Warner Ct 11 SO23 .... 2 A1
Warnes La BH24 .... 142 C1
Warnford Cl PO12 .... 180 C2
Warnford Cres PO9 .... 135 B3
Warnford Ct SO15 .... 102 C4
Warnford Rd
Bournemouth BH6, BH7 .. 206 B4
Meonstoke SO32 .... 61 B4
Warren Ave
Chandler's Ford SO53 .... 55 C3
Christchurch BH23 .... 207 C3
Portsmouth PO4 .... 183 A3
Southampton SO16 .... 78 A1
Warren Cl
Chandler's Ford SO53 .... 55 C3
South Hayling PO11 .... 184 B2
Southampton SO16 .... 78 A1
St Leonards BH24 .... 140 B3
Warren Cres SO16 .... 78 A1
Warren Dr BH24 .... 140 B3
Warren Edge Cl BH6 .... 206 C2
Warren Edge Ct BH6 .... 206 C2
Warren Edge Rd BH6 .... 206 C2
Warren Gdns SO51 .... 28 A1
Warren La Beaulieu SO42 200 C4
Froxfield Green GU32 .... 19 A3
Owslebury SO21 .... 33 C4
St Leonards BH24 .... 140 B3
Warren Park Prim Sch
PO9 .... 135 B4
Warren Pk SO41 .... 211 A3
Warren Pl SO40 .... 76 B1
Warren Rd
Bournemouth BH4 .... 204 A1
Liss GU33 .... 21 A4
Poole BH14 .... 203 B2
Winchester SO23 .... 11 B4
Warren The SO45 .... 150 A3
Warren Wlk BH22 .... 165 A4
Warrior Bsns Ctr The
PO6 .... 158 C4
Warrior Cl SO53 .... 55 A2
Warrior Pk SO53 .... 55 A2
Warrys Cl SO45 .... 150 A4
Warsash Cl PO9 .... 135 C3
Warsash Ct SO31 .... 128 B1
Warsash Gr PO13 .... 155 A1
Warsash Maritime Ctr (Soton
Inst) SO31 .... 152 B4
Warsash Rd PO14,SO31 .129 A1
Warspite Cl PO2 .... 157 B2
Warton Cl SO42 .... 175 B3
Warwick Ave BH25 .... 195 A2
Warwick Cl
Chandler's Ford SO53 .... 55 A2
Lee-on-the-Solent PO13 .. 180 A2
13 Winchester SO23 .... 2 A1
Warwick Cres PO5 .... 215 B2
Warwick Ct
14 Bournemouth BH5 .... 205 C2
4 Emsworth PO10 .... 160 C4
14 Winchester SO23 .... 2 A1
Warwick Ho 21 SO14 .... 103 B3
Warwick Pl
3 Bournemouth BH7 .... 206 A3
West Wellow SO51 .... 50 C2
Warwick Rd
Bournemouth BH7 .... 206 A3
Poole BH14 .... 203 B2
Southampton SO15 .... 78 B1
Totton SO40 .... 100 C4
Warwick Way PO17 .... 108 A2
Wasdale Cl PO8 .... 88 B1
Washbrook Rd PO6 .... 133 B1
Washington Ave BH8 .... 205 B3
Washington Ct 4 PO4 .... 183 A3
Washington Rd
Emsworth PO10 .... 136 C1
Portsmouth PO2 .... 182 B4
Wastwater Ho 25 PO6 .... 133 A1
Watcombe Rd BH6 .... 206 B3
Water Cl SO23 .... 11 A4
Water La
Bournemouth BH6 .... 206 B4
Hythe SO45 .... 125 C1
Totton SO40 .... 100 C4
Winchester SO23 .... 11 A4
Water Lane Farm BH10 .189 C3
Water's Edge SO30 .... 105 A3
Waterbeech Dr SO30 .... 105 B4
Waterberry Dr PO7 .... 111 B1
Waterditch Rd
Bransgore BH23 .... 193 A2
Burton BH23 .... 193 A2
Waterford Cl
Lymington SO41 .... 197 C2
Poole BH14 .... 203 A1
Waterford Ct SO41 .... 197 B1
Waterford Gdns BH23 .... 209 A4
Waterford La SO41 .... 197 C1
Waterford Lo BH23 .... 208 A3
Waterford Pl BH23 .... 209 A4
Waterford Rd
Christchurch BH23 .... 209 A4
New Milton BH25 .... 195 B2
Waterfront Mus★ BH15 202 A1
Watergate PO12 .... 181 C2
Waterhouse La SO15 .... 102 A4
Waterhouse Way SO15 .... 102 A4
Waterlock Gdns PO4 .... 183 B2
Waterloo Cl PO8 .... 111 B2
Waterloo Ho BH17 .... 187 A1
Waterloo Ind Est SO30 .. 81 A1
Waterloo Rd
Bournemouth BH9 .... 204 C4
Broadstone BH17 .... 202 B4
Corfe Mullen BH21 .... 186 A3
Gosport PO12 .... 181 B1
Havant PO9 .... 135 C1
Lymington SO41 .... 197 C2
Southampton SO15 .... 102 B3
Waterloo Sch The PO7 .... 134 C4
Waterloo St PO5 .... 215 B2
Waterloo Terr SO15 .... 102 C3
Waterloo Way BH24 .... 141 A3
Watermans La SO45 .... 125 C1
Watermead
Christchurch GU21 .... 207 A3
Winchester SO23 .... 10 C3
Watermead Rd PO6 .... 158 C4
Watermill Rd BH23 .... 207 A4
Waters Edge
Lee-on-the-Solent PO13 .. 179 C1
Poole BH13 .... 214 B3
Waters Edge Gdns
PO10 .... 160 C4
Waters Gn SO42 .... 146 A1
Waters Green Ct SO42 .... 146 A1
Waters The PO17 .... 130 C3
Watersedge PO17 .... 108 A2
Watersedge Rd PO6 .... 157 A4
Watershed Ct 2 PO6 .... 133 A1
Watership Dr BH24 .... 141 B3
Waterside
Christchurch BH23 .... 207 C2
4 Hythe SO45 .... 126 A3

Waterside Cl BH24 ......**117** A1
Waterside Gdns PO16 .**131** B1
Waterside La PO16 ......**156** C3
Waterside Rd SO51 ....**28** A1
Waterside Sch PO2 ....**157** A2
Waterside Sch (Unit)
PO4 ....**183** B2
Waterside Sq SO45 .....**125** C3
Watersmeet
Fareham PO16 ....**155** A4
49 Winchester SO23 ....**11** A4
Waterston Cl BH17 .....**187** B1
Waterworks Rd
Cosham PO6 ....**158** B4
Otterbourne SO21 ....**31** B2
Petersfield GU32 ....**41** A3
Watery La
Christchurch BH23 .....**208** B2
Upton BH16 ....**201** A4
Watkin Rd
19 Bournemouth BH5 ..**205** C2
Hedge End SO30 ....**81** B1
Watley Cl SO16 ....**77** B3
Watley La SO21 ....**32** A3
Watson Wlk SO40 ......**100** B4
Watton Cl BH8 ....**191** A1
Watton La SO41 ....**61** C1
Watton Rd SO45 ....**150** B2
Watts Cl SO16 ....**77** C2
Watts Rd
Hedge End SO30 ....**105** B4
Portsmouth PO1 ......**182** B4
Wavecrest Cl SO40 .....**102** A2
Wavell Ave BH17 ....**187** A1
Wavell Rd
Bournemouth BH11 ....**189** A2
Gosport PO13 ....**155** B2
Southampton SO18 ....**104** A4
Wavell Way SO22 ....**10** B3
Wavendon Ave BH25 ..**209** C4
Waveney Cl PO13 ......**179** C1
Waveney Gn SO16 ....**77** C1
Waverley Ave SO31 ....**127** B3
Waverley Cl
Fordingbridge SP6 ......**69** C2
Romsey SO51 ....**28** A1
Waverley Cres BH15 ...**202** B4
Waverley Ct SO31 .....**127** B3
Waverley Gr PO4 ......**182** C1
Waverley Ho **12** BH25 .**195** A1
Waverley Path PO12 ...**180** C2
Waverley Rd
Cosham PO6 ....**158** B4
Fordingbridge SP6 ......**69** C2
New Milton BH25 ......**195** A1
Portsmouth PO4 ......**182** C1
Southampton SO15 ....**102** B3
Wayfarer Cl
Locks Heath SO31 .....**128** C1
Portsmouth PO4 ......**183** B4
Wayfarers PO13 ....**180** B4
Wayground Rd BH21 ..**162** C1
Waylands Pl SO30 .....**105** A2
Wayman Rd BH21 .....**186** C3
Wayne Rd BH12 ....**203** A3
Waynflete Cl **1** SO32 ...**83** B4
Waynflete Pl SO22 ......**10** B3
Wayside SO31 ....**128** B4
Wayside Cl SO41 ......**211** B3
Wayside Rd
Bournemouth BH6 .....**206** C2
St Leonards BH24 .....**166** C4
Wayte St PO6 ....**157** C4
Waytown Cl BH17 .....**187** B1
Weald Cl SO31 ....**129** A2
Weardale Rd SO53 ......**55** B2
Weavers Cl BH22 ......**138** C1
Weavers Gn PO9 ......**136** B2
Weavers Pl SO53 ....**55** A4
Weavills Rd SO50 ....**57** C1
Webb Cl PO11 ....**185** A1
Webb La PO11 ....**185** A1
Webb Rd PO16 ....**156** B3
Webb's Way BH11 .....**188** C1
Webbers Way PO12 ...**181** B1
Webbs Cl BH24 ....**139** B3
Webbs Gn SO32 ....**85** B2
Webbs Way BH24 .....**139** C3
Webburn Gdns SO18 ...**80** A2
Webster Rd
Bournemouth BH9 .....**190** A2
Winchester SO22 ....**1** A1
Wedgewood Cl
Holbury SO45 ....**150** B2
Stubbington PO14 .....**179** A3
Wedgewood Way PO8 ..**111** C1
Wedgwood Dr BH14 ..**203** A1
Wedgwood Gdns BH23 **169** B1
Wedmore Cl SO42 ......**10** A2
Weeke Manor Cl SO22 ..**1** B1
Weeke Prim Sch SO22 ..**1** B1
Weevil La PO12 ....**181** B3
Weirs The **4** SO23 .....**11** A3
Welbeck Ave SO17 ......**79** A1
Welburn Ct SO18 ....**80** A1
Welch Rd Gosport PO12 .**181** A4
Portsmouth PO4 ......**182** C1
Welch Way SO16 ....**77** C2
Welchwood Cl PO8 ....**111** C3
Weldon Ave BH11 .....**188** C3
Well Cl BH25 ....**194** C1
Well Copse Cl PO8 ......**88** B1
Well Hill PO7 ....**110** B4
Well House Cl SP6 ......**45** A2
Well House La SO22 ......**1** C3

Well La
Hamble-le-Rice SO31 ...**128** A1
Poole BH15 ....**202** B2
Swanmore SO32 ....**84** A4
Well Mdw PO9 ....**135** C3
Welland Gdns SO18 .....**80** A1
Welland Gn SO16 .....**101** C4
Welland Rd BH21 .....**163** B3
Wellands Rd SO43 ....**122** A3
Wellbrooke Gdns SO53 .**55** A4
Weller Ho **16** PO1 .....**182** B4
Wellers Cl SO40 ......**100** A4
Welles Rd SO53 ....**55** B3
Wellesley Ave BH23 ..**208** B3
Wellesley Cl PO7 .....**134** C4
Wellington Ave
Christchurch BH23 ....**208** B3
Southampton SO18 ...**104** A4
Wellington Cl
Horndean PO8 ....**112** B3
Hythe SO45 ....**125** B1
Wellington Ct
7 Bournemouth, Deane Pk
BH8 ....**205** A3
Bournemouth, Westbourne
BH2 ....**204** B2
8 Havant PO9 ....**135** C1
New Milton BH25 .....**195** A4
Southampton SO15 ...**102** B3
West End SO30 ....**80** B1
Wellington Gr PO16 ..**156** B4
Wellington Pk SO30 ....**81** A1
Wellington Pl SO40 .....**98** C4
Wellington Rd
Bournemouth BH1, BH8 .**205** A3
Poole BH14 ....**203** B2
Southampton SO18 .....**79** C1
Wellington St PO5 ....**215** B2
Wellington Way **9** PO7 **134** C4
Wellman Ct **10** SO16 ...**78** C2
Wellow Cl Havant PO9 .**135** B3
Southampton SO18 ...**104** B4
Wellow Ct **11** SO18 ...**103** C4
Wellow Dro SO51 ....**50** C4
Wellow Gdns PO14 ...**129** B1
Wellow Sch SO51 ....**50** C2
Wellow Vineyard ★ SO51 .**51** B4
Wellow Wood Rd SO51 .**50** B4
Wellowbrook Cl SO53 ...**55** A3
Wells Cl PO15 ....**129** B4
Wells Pl SO50 ....**56** A1
Wells Rd SO50 ....**56** A1
Wellsmoor PO14 ......**129** B1
Wellswood Gdns PO9 ..**113** B3
Wellsworth La PO9 ...**113** B2
Wembley Gr PO6 .....**158** A3
Wembley Way SO50 ....**57** B1
Wendover Cl BH25 ...**194** C1
Wendover Rd PO9 ....**135** C1
Wendy Cres PO12 ....**165** C2
Wenlock Ct **9** BH23 ..**207** C4
Wensley Gdns PO10 ..**136** C2
Wentwood Gdns BH25 **195** B1
Wentworth BH14 .....**214** B4
Wentworth Ave BH5 ..**206** A2
Wentworth Cl BH5 ...**206** A2
Wentworth Coll BH5 ..**206** A2
Wentworth Dr
Broadstone BH18 .....**187** A3
Christchurch BH23 ...**206** C3
Horndean PO8 ....**112** A4
Wentworth Gdns
Holbury SO45 ....**150** B2
Southampton SO19 ...**104** A1
Wentworth Gr SO45 ..**150** B2
Wentworth Grange SO22 **10** C3
Wescott Way BH11 ...**188** C2
Wesermarsch Rd PO8 ..**112** A2
Wesley Cl
8 Bournemouth BH8 ..**205** B3
Southampton SO19 ...**104** B2
Wesley Ct PO1 ....**215** D3
Wesley Gr PO3 ....**158** A2
Wesley Grange **33** BH4 **204** B2
Wesley Ho **13** SO23 ....**11** A4
Wesley Rd
Kings Worthy SO23 ......**2** B1
Poole BH12 ....**203** B3
Wimborne Minst BH21 .**163** C3
Wessex Ave BH25 ....**195** A1
Wessex Cl
Blackfield SO45 ....**177** C4
Christchurch BH23 ...**208** B4
Wessex Ct
Southampton, Sholing
SO19 ....**104** A2
8 Southampton, Westwood Pk
SO17 ....**103** A4
Wessex Dr SO22 ....**1** C1
Wessex Est BH23 .....**141** A4
Wessex Gate Ind Est
PO8 ....**112** B3
Wessex Gate Ret Pk
BH17 ....**202** A3
Wessex Gdns
Portchester PO16 .....**156** A4
Romsey SO51 ....**53** A4
Wessex La SO18 ....**79** B2
Wessex Maternity Ctr
(private) SO18 ....**80** A2
Wessex Nuffield Hospl
SO53 ....**31** A1
Wessex Rd Horndean PO8 **88** B2
Poole BH14 ....**203** A2
Ringwood BH24 ......**141** A4
Wessex Trad Ctr BH12 **203** A4
Wessex Way
Bournemouth BH8 ....**205** B3

Wessex Way continued
Colden Common SO21 ...**57** A4
West Ave BH21 ....**138** C4
West Bargate **2** SO14 **102** C2
West Battery Rd PO2 ..**157** A1
West Bay Rd SO15 ....**102** B3
West Block SO15 .....**102** B3
West Borough BH21 ..**163** A3
West Butts St **1** BH15 .**202** A1
West Cl Lymington SO41 **197** A1
Verwood BH31 ....**114** B3
West Cliff Cotts BH2 .**204** C1
West Cliff Gdns BH2 .**204** C1
West Cliff Mews BH2 .**204** C1
West Cliff Rd BH2, BH4 .**204** B1
West Close Ct BH6 ...**207** A2
West Close Ho BH6 ..**207** A2
West Comm SO45 .....**177** C3
West Ct Portsmouth PO1 **182** C4
Portsmouth, Southsea
PO4 ....**183** A2
Southampton SO19 ...**103** C1
West Downs Cl PO16 .**131** A3
West Dr SO50 ....**56** B2
West End Cl SO22 .....**10** C4
West End Cotts **18**
PO16 ....**131** A1
West End Rd
Hedge End SO31 .....**104** C3
Southampton SO18 ...**104** A4
West End Terr SO22 ...**10** C4
West Haye Rd PO11 ..**185** B1
West Hayes
Lymington SO41 ......**197** C2
Winchester SO22 ....**10** B4
West Hill Cl SO15 ....**102** C4
West Hill Dr Hythe SO45 .**125** C3
West Hill Pk SO22 .....**10** B4
West Hill Park Sch
PO14 ....**153** C4
West Hill Pk SO22 .....**10** B4
West Hill Pl **15** BH2 ..**204** C2
West Hill Rd BH2 ....**204** C1
West Hoe La SO32 ....**83** C4
West Horton Cl SO50 ..**56** C1
West Horton La SO50 ..**56** C1
West Howe Cl BH11 ..**189** A2
West Howe Ind Est
BH11 ....**188** C2
West La Hordle SO41 .**196** C1
North Baddesley SO52 ...**53** C3
North Hayling PO11 ..**184** C3
West Links SO53 ....**55** B1
West Lodge PO13 ....**179** B2
West Mans **8** BH4 ...**204** B2
West Marlands Rd
SO14 ....**102** C3
West Meon CE Prim Sch
GU32 ....**37** B3
West Mills Rd SP6 .....**69** C1
West Moors Mid Sch
BH22 ....**138** C1
West Moors Rd
Ferndown BH22 ......**165** B4
Three Legged Cross BH21 **138** C4
West Moors BH21 ....**138** C4
West Moors St Mary's CE Fst
Sch BH22 ....**138** B2
West Overcliff Dr BH4 **204** B2
West Park Dr SP6 ......**68** B3
West Park La SP6 ......**68** B3
West Park Rd SO15 ..**102** C4
West Point PO13 .....**179** C1
West Quay (Sh Ctr)
SO15 ....**102** C2
West Quay Rd
Poole BH15 ....**202** A1
Southampton SO15 ..**102** C2
West Rd
Bournemouth BH5 ....**206** A2
Bransgore BH23 ......**193** A4
Emsworth PO10 ......**160** C4
Fawley SO45 ....**150** B4
Hedge End SO30 .....**104** C3
Hythe SO45 ....**125** B1
Milford on Sea SO41 .**211** A3
Southampton, Woolston
SO19 ....**103** C1
Southwick PO17 .....**133** A3
West Row BH21 ......**163** A2
West Row Mews BH21 **163** A2
West St Emsworth PO10 .**160** C4
Fareham PO16 ....**131** A1
Fordingbridge SP6 .....**69** C1
Hambledon PO7 ....**86** B1
Havant PO9 ....**135** C1
Hythe SO45 ....**125** C3
Poole BH15 ....**202** A1
Portchester PO16 ....**156** B4
Portsmouth PO1 .....**181** C2
Ringwood BH24 .....**140** C4
Soberton SO32 ....**85** B3
Southampton SO14 ..**102** C2
Southwick PO17 .....**132** C3
Titchfield PO14 ......**153** C4
Wimborne Minst BH21 **163** A3
West Station Terr BH21 **163** A2
West Street Ct **11** BH21 **163** A3
West Tytherley CE Prim Sch
SP5 ....**4** A4
West View Cotts PO10 .**137** C1
West View Rd
Christchurch BH23 ...**207** C3
Poole BH15 ....**202** B2
West Walk (North) Forest
Wlk ★ PO17 ....**108** C4

West Walk (South) Forest
Wlk ★ PO17 ....**108** C3
West Way
Bournemouth BH9 ....**190** A1
Broadstone BH18 .....**187** A2
Locks Heath PO15 ...**129** C2
Lymington SO41 ......**197** B1
West Way Cl BH9 ....**190** A1
Westbeams Rd SO41 ..**172** A1
Westborn Rd PO16 ...**131** A3
Westbourne Ave
Emsworth PO10 ......**137** A1
Holbury SO45 ....**150** B2
Westbourne Cl
Bournemouth BH4 ...**204** B2
Emsworth PO10 ......**137** A1
Westbourne Cres SO17 .**79** A3
Westbourne Ct **5** PO9 **135** C1
Westbourne Cty Prim Sch
PO10 ....**137** A2
Westbourne Mans **9**
SO17 ....**79** A3
Westbourne Park Rd
BH4 ....**204** B2
Westbourne Rd
Emsworth PO10 ......**137** A2
Portsmouth PO2 .....**182** C4
Westbourne PO10 ....**137** A2
Westbroke Gdns SO51 ..**27** C1
Westbrook Cl
Bournemouth BH10 ..**189** B1
Locks Heath SO31 ...**129** A3
Westbrook Ctr The **12**
PO7 ....**112** A1
Westbrook Gr PO7 ...**134** B2
Westbrook Rd PO16 ..**156** B3
Westbrook Way SO18 ..**79** B2
Westbrooke Cl PO8 ..**112** A3
Westbury Cl
Barton on Sea BH25 .**210** A4
Bransgore BH23 .....**193** A4
Christchurch BH23 ..**193** B1
31 Cosham PO6 ......**133** A3
Westbury Ct
Hedge End SO30 ....**105** B3
10 Poole BH14 ....**203** A2
Westbury Mall **24** PO16 **131** A1
Westbury Manor Mus ★
PO16 ....**131** A1
Westbury Rd
Fareham PO16 ....**131** A1
Ringwood BH24 ......**141** A4
Southampton SO15 ..**101** C4
Westbury Sq **25** PO16 .**131** A1
Westby Rd BH5 ......**205** C2
Westcliff Cl SO17 ....**179** C2
Westcliff Mews SO19 .**103** B2
Westcliff Wlk SO45 ..**125** C3
Westcot Rd SO45 ....**150** A2
Westcroft Par **10** BH25 .**195** A1
Westcroft Pk BH18 ..**187** B2
Westcroft Rd PO12 ..**180** C3
Westdown Rd BH11 ..**189** A3
Westerham Cl PO6 ...**157** C4
Westerham Rd BH4 ..**204** C4
Westering SO51 ....**53** B4
Westerleigh BH4 .....**204** B1
Westerley Cl SO31 ...**128** C1
Western Ave
Barton on Sea BH25 .**209** B4
Bournemouth BH10 ..**189** B2
Emsworth PO10 ......**160** B4
Poole BH13 ....**203** C1
Southampton SO15 ..**102** A3
Western CE Prim Sch
SO22 ....**10** B4
Western Cl BH10 .....**189** B3
Western Com Hospl
SO16 ....**77** C1
Western Ct **14** PO10 ..**131** A1
Western District Cut
SO15 ....**102** B4
Western Downland CE Prim
Sch
Damerham SP6 ....**68** B2
Rockbourne SP6 ......**44** C1
Western Espl SO14 ...**102** C2
Western Par
Emsworth PO10 ......**160** C4
Portsmouth PO5 .....**182** A1
Western Rd
Chandler's Ford SO53 ..**30** C1
Cosham PO6 ....**157** B4
Fareham PO16 ....**131** A1
Fawley SO45 ....**151** C1
Havant PO9 ....**135** C1
Lymington SO41 .....**197** B2
Poole, Branksome Pk
BH13 ....**204** A1
Poole, Canford Cliffs BH13 **214** C4
West End SO30 ....**80** B1
Winchester SO22 .....**10** C4
Western Terr PO2 ...**157** B1
Western Way
Fareham PO16 ....**131** A1
Gosport PO12 ....**180** C1
Portsmouth PO1 .....**181** C4
Westerngate BH13 ..**204** A2
Westfield **13** BH21 ...**163** A3
Westfield Ave
Fareham PO14 ....**154** C4
South Hayling PO11 .**184** C4
Westfield Cl
Fair Oak SO50 ....**81** B4
Hamble-le-Rice SO31 .**127** C1
Wimborne Minst BH21 **163** A3
Westfield Cnr SO18 ...**79** C3

Westfield Comm SO31 .**127** C1
Westfield Cres SO53 ...**55** B2
Westfield Dr SO32 ....**84** B1
Westfield Dro SO24 ...**34** C4
Westfield Gdns BH23 .**193** A1
Westfield Ho SO16 ....**79** C2
Westfield Ind Est
Gosport PO12 ....**181** A2
Horndean PO8 ....**112** B4
Westfield Jun Sch PO6 **156** C4
Westfield Oaks PO11 .**184** C2
Westfield Rd
Bournemouth BH6 ...**206** C2
Chandler's Ford SO53 ..**55** B2
Gosport PO12 ....**181** A2
Littleton SO22 ....**1** A3
Lymington SO41 .....**198** A1
Portsmouth PO4 .....**183** A2
Southampton SO15 ..**102** A4
Totton SO40 ....**100** C4
Westgate PO14 ......**179** B3
Westgate Mews SO30 ..**80** C1
Westgate Mus ★ SO23 ..**10** C4
Westgate Pk BH4 ....**204** A2
Westgate Sec Sch SO22 .**1** C1
Westgate St **19** SO14 .**102** C2
Westgrove SP6 ....**69** C1
Westgrove Gdns PO10 **160** C4
Westham Cl BH17 ....**187** C2
Westheath Rd BH18 ..**187** A2
Westland Dr PO7 ....**134** C2
Westland Gdns PO12 .**181** A2
Westlands Ct BH23 ...**193** A4
Westlands Dr BH13 ..**214** C4
Westlands Gr PO16 ..**156** B4
Westley Cl SO22 ....**1** B1
Westley Gr PO14 ....**154** C4
Westmarch Ct **1** SO17 ..**79** B1
Westmead CI PO11 ..**184** C2
Westminster Ct BH25 **209** C4
Westminster Gate SO22 **10** C3
Westminster Gdns
PO14 ....**129** B2
Westminster Pl PO1 .**182** B4
Westminster Rd
Milford on Sea SO41 .**211** A2
Poole BH13 ....**204** A1
Westminster Rd E BH13 **204** A1
Westmoreland Ct SO41 **195** C2
Westmorland Way SO53 .**55** C2
Weston Ave PO4 .....**183** A2
Weston Cl SO19 .....**103** C1
Weston Cres SO18 ...**104** B4
Weston Dr BH1 .....**205** A2
Weston Grove Rd SO19 **103** B1
Weston Ho **19** GU32 ...**40** C1
Weston La Buriton GU32 ..**65** B4
Nursling SO16 ....**77** A2
Southampton SO19 ..**103** C1
Weston Par SO19 ...**126** C4
Weston Park Boys Sch
SO19 ....**104** A1
Weston Park Inf Sch
SO19 ....**104** A1
Weston Park Jun Sch
SO19 ....**104** A1
Weston Rd Eastleigh SO50 **56** A2
Petersfield GU31 ......**41** A2
Wimborne Minst BH21 **163** C4
Weston Shore Inf Sch
SO19 ....**126** C4
Westons La **8** BH5 ...**205** B1
Westover La BH24 ..**140** B3
Westover Prim Sch
PO3 ....**183** A4
Westover Rd
Bournemouth BH1 ...**204** C2
Milford on Sea SO41 .**211** B2
Portsmouth PO3 .....**183** A4
Southampton SO16 ..**101** B4
Westquay Ho **8** PO16 .**131** B1
Westray Hall BH4 ...**204** B1
Westridge Ct **39** SO17 ..**79** A1
Westridge Rd SO17 ..**103** A4
Westrow Gdns SO15 .**102** C4
Westrow Rd SO15 ...**102** C4
Westside View PO7 ..**111** B1
Westview Rd SO22 .....**1** A1
Westward Rd SO30 ..**105** B4
Westways Cosham PO9 **158** C4
Westways Cl SO16 ....**77** B3
Westwood Ave BH22 .**165** B3
Westwood Cl PO10 ..**137** A1
Westwood Ct
12 Southampton SO17 .**103** A4
Totton SO40 ....**76** C1
West End SO30 ....**80** B1
Westwood Gdns SO53 ..**55** C4
Westwood Mans **28** SO17 **79** A1
Westwood Rd
Lyndhurst SO43 .....**121** C3
Netley SO31 ....**127** A4
Portsmouth PO2 .....**157** C2
Southampton SO17 ..**103** A4
Westwood View SO24 ..**34** C1
Westwoods & Glendene Pk
BH25 ....**194** B3
Wetherby Cl BH18 ...**187** A1
Wetherby Cl SO40 ...**100** B4
Wetherby Gdns SO40 .**100** B4
Wetherdown GU31 ....**41** A2
Weybridge Cl SO31 ..**128** C3
Weyhill Cl Havant PO9 .**135** B3
Portchester PO16 ....**132** B1
Weyman's Ave BH10 .**189** B3
Weymans Dr BH10 ...**189** B3

Weymouth Ave PO12 ...180 C4
Weymouth Rd
Poole BH14 ....203 B3
13 Portsmouth PO2 ....157 B1
Whaddon Chase PO14 ..179 A3
Whaddon Ct PO9 ......135 A2
Whaddon La
Colden Common SO21 ...58 A4
Owslebury SO21 ....33 A2
Whale Island Way PO2 .157 B1
Whalesmead Cl SO50 ...56 C1
Whalesmead Rd SO50 ...56 C1
Whaley Rd PO2 ....157 A1
Wharf Cl BH12 ....203 C3
Wharf Hill SO23 ......11 A3
Wharf Mill 2 SO23 ....11 A3
Wharf Rd
Portsmouth PO2 ......182 B4
Southampton SO19 ....103 B2
Wharfdale Rd
Bournemouth BH4 ....204 B2
Poole BH12 ....203 C3
Wharncliffe Ct BH23 ..208 C4
Wharncliffe Gdns BH23 209 A4
Wharncliffe Ho SO19 ..103 A3
Wharncliffe Rd
Bournemouth BH5 ....205 B2
Christchurch BH23 ...209 A4
Southampton SO19 ....103 A3
Whartons Cl SO40 ....100 B2
Whartons La SO40 ....100 B2
Whatleigh Cl BH15 ...202 B1
Wheat Cl SO53 ....54 C3
Wheatcroft Dr SO18 ...80 A1
Wheatcroft Rd PO13 ..179 C1
Wheatear Dr GU31 .....41 B1
Wheatears Dr SO51 ....50 C2
Wheatland Cl SO22 ....10 B3
Wheatlands PO14 .....129 B2
Wheatlands Ave PO11 .185 C1
Wheatlands Cres PO11 .185 C1
Wheatley Gn 2 PO9 ...135 B3
Wheaton Grange BH4 ..204 B2
Wheaton Rd BH7 .....206 A3
Wheatplot Park Homes 2
BH10 ....189 C2
Wheatsheaf Ct SO30 ..105 A3
Wheatsheaf Dr PO8 ...111 B2
Wheatstone Rd PO4 ..182 C2
Wheeler Cl PO12 .....181 A3
Wheelers La BH11 ....188 B3
Wheelers Wlk SO45 ..177 C4
Wheelwright Mews SP5 .46 C4
Whernside Cl SO16 ...101 C4
Wherwell Ct 33 PO9 ..136 A3
Whichers Cl PO9 .....136 A4
Whichers Gate Rd PO9 136 A4
Whimbrel Cl PO4 .....183 B3
Whimbrel Ct BH23 ...208 A3
Whinchat Cl
Fareham PO15 ....130 B2
Southampton SO16 ....78 A3
Whincroft BH22 ......165 C4
Whincroft Dr BH22 ...165 C3
Whinfield Rd SO45 ...149 C4
Whinwhistle Rd SO51 ..51 A1
Whippingham Cl PO6 .157 B4
Whistler Cl SO19 .....104 B2
Whistler Rd SO19 ....104 B2
Whitaker Cres SO41 ..197 B2
Whitby Ave BH18 ....187 A1
Whitby Cl BH23 ......191 B2
Whitby Cres BH18 ....187 A1
Whitby Ct 4 SO41 ...211 A2
Whitby Rd SO41 .....211 A2
Whitchurch Ave BH18 .187 B2
Whitchurch Ct SO19 ..103 C2
Whitcombe Cl SO40 ..100 C4
Whitcombe Gdns PO12 .182 C3
White Barn Cres SO41 .196 A2
White Cl BH15 ....203 A4
White Cloud Pk 7 PO4 182 C2
White Cloud Pl 8 PO4 182 C2
White Dirt La PO8 .....88 B2
White Farm Cl BH10 ..204 B4
White Gates SO32 .....82 A3
White Harmony Acres Ind Est
SO30 ....80 C3
White Hart La
Cadnam SO40 ....98 C4
Portchester PO16 ....156 B4
White Hart Rd
Fair Oak SO50 ....57 B1
4 Gosport PO12 .....181 A2
Portsmouth PO1 .....182 A2
White Heather Ct 1
SO45 ....126 A3
White Ho The SO41 ...211 B2
White Horse Dr BH15 .202 B3
White Horse La PO7 ..111 A3
White Horses BH25 ...209 C4
White House Gdns GU32 .40 C3
White Knights BH25 ..209 C4
White La SO21 ....32 A4
White Ladies Cl 28 A4
White Ladies Cl PO9 ..136 A1
White Lion Ctyd BH24 .140 C4
White Lion Wlk PO12 .181 B3
White Lodge BH15 ...202 C4
White Lodge Gdns
PO16 ....130 C2
White Oak Wlk 31 PO9 .136 A3
White Rd SO50 ....56 B2
White Row SP5 ....46 B4
White Swan Rd PO1 ..215 C4
White Way SO32 ......61 A4
White Wings Ho PO7 .110 C2

White's Rd SO19 .....104 A3
Whiteacres Cl 11 PO12 .181 A3
Whitebeam Cl
Colden Common SO21 ...57 A4
2 Fareham PO14 ....154 C4
Waterlooville PO8 ....112 B3
Whitebeam Rd SO30 .105 B3
Whitebeam Way
North Baddesley SO52 ...54 A3
Verwood BH31 ......115 A3
Whitechimney Row
PO10 ....137 A2
Whitecliff Cres BH14 .203 A1
Whitecliff Rd BH14 ...202 C1
Whitecliffe Ave PO10 .183 A4
Whitecliffe Ct PO12 ..180 B2
Whitecroft SO45 .....126 A1
Whitecross Cl BH17 ..187 C2
Whitecross Gdns 14
PO2 ....157 C2
Whitefield Lo 1 BH25 .195 A2
Whitefield Rd
Holbury SO45 ....150 B2
New Milton BH25 ....195 A1
Poole BH14 ....203 A1
Whitehall BH23 ......207 B3
Whitehart Fields 2
BH24 ....141 B4
Whitehaugh Ct SO50 ...56 B2
Whitehaven
Horndean PO8 ....112 B3
Portchester PO16 ....156 A4
Whitehaven Home Pk
SO45 ....177 C4
Whitehayes Cl BH23 ..192 B1
Whitehayes Rd BH23 .192 B1
Whitehill Cl SO18 ....104 B4
Whitehorn Dr SP5 .....73 B4
Whitehouse Gdns SO15 102 A3
Whitehouse Rd BH21 .163 B1
Whitelands
Bransgore BH23 .....169 B2
Droxford SO32 ....85 A4
Whitelaw Rd SO15 ...102 A4
Whiteleaf La PO7 .....86 B4
Whitelegg Way BH10 .189 C2
Whiteley La
Locks Heath PO15 ...129 C3
Swanwick PO15,SO31 ..106 B1
Whiteley Prim Sch
PO15 ....129 B4
Whiteley Way PO15 ..129 B3
Whitemoor La SO40,SO51 75 C2
Whitemoor Rd SO42 ..145 B1
Whitenap Cl SO51 ....53 A3
Whitenap La SO51 ....53 B3
Whiteparish All Saints CE
Prim Sch SP5 ....24 A2
Whites Ct 19 PO2 ....157 B1
Whites Hill SO21 .....33 A2
Whites La SO45 .....151 A2
Whiteshoot SP5 ......47 C2
Whiteshoot Hill SP5 ..47 C2
Whiteshute La SO23 ...10 C3
Whitestone Cl SO16 ..101 C4
Whitethorn Rd PO11 .185 A2
Whitewater Rise SO45 .125 C1
Whiteways BH21 .....163 C3
Whitfield Park BH24 ..140 A3
Whitley Cl PO10 .....137 A3
Whitley Row PO4 ....183 B3
Whitley Way BH25 ...195 A3
Whitmore La BH21 ...114 A4
Whitsbury Cl BH8 ....190 B1
Whitsbury Cross SP6 ..69 B4
Whitsbury Rd
Fordingbridge SP6 ...69 C2
Havant PO9 ....136 A2
Whitstable Rd PO6 ...157 C4
Whittington Cl SO45 .125 C2
Whittington Ct PO10 .160 C4
Whittle Ave PO15 ....129 B3
Whittle Rd BH21 .....164 C4
Whittles Way BH15 ..202 A1
Whitwell SO31 ......127 B4
Whitwell Rd PO4 ....182 C1
Whitworth Cl PO12 ..181 A2
Whitworth Cres SO18 .103 B4
Whitworth Ct SO18 ..103 B4
Whitworth Rd
Gosport PO12 ....181 A3
Portsmouth PO2 .....182 C4
Southampton SO18 ..103 B4
Whyke Ct 3 PO9 ....135 C1
Whyte Cl SO45 ......150 A1
Whyteways SO50 .....56 A2
Wick 1 Ind Est BH25 .194 C1
Wick 2 Ind Est BH25 .194 C1
Wick Cl BH25 ....194 C1
Wick Dr BH25 ....194 C1
Wick Farm BH6 .....207 B3
Wick La
Bournemouth BH6 ...207 A3
Christchurch BH23 ..207 A3
Downton SP5 ....46 A4
Wicket Rd BH10 .....189 B3
Wicket The SO45 ....125 C1
Wickfield Ave BH23 ..207 A3
Wickfield Cl BH23 ...207 A3
Wickford Ho BH23 ...207 A3
Wickham CE Prim Sch
PO17 ....108 A2
Wickham Croft PO17 .108 A2
Wickham Ct
Ferndown BH22 .....165 C3
Gosport PO12 ....180 B2
Wickham Dr BH21 ...186 B2

Wickham Ho
17 Southampton SO17 ..79 A1
38 Southampton SO17 ..79 A1
Wickham Rd
Bournemouth BH7 ...206 A3
Droxford SO32 ....85 A3
Fareham PO16,PO17 ..131 A3
Wickham St PO1 .....182 A3
Wickham Vineyard★
SO32 ....107 A4
Wicklea Rd BH6 .....207 A2
Wicklow Dr SO53 .....55 A3
Wickmeads Rd BH6 ..207 A3
Wickor Cl PO10 .....137 A1
Wickor Way PO10 ...137 A1
Wicor Mill La PO16 ..156 A4
Wicor Path PO16 ....156 B3
Wicor Prim Sch PO16 .156 A4
Widbury Rd SO41 ...197 B1
Widden Cl SO41 .....172 A1
Widdicombe Ave BH14 .203 C1
Wide La SO18 ....79 C3
Wide Lane Cl SO42 ..145 C1
Widecombe Dr SO45 .125 C2
Widgeon Cl
Gosport PO12 ....181 A4
Southampton SO16 ....78 A3
Widgeon Ct PO16 ....155 C4
Widget Cl BH11 .....189 A1
Widlers La SO32 .....58 C3
Widley Court Dr PO6 .158 A4
Widley Ct
4 Cosham PO6 ......158 A4
Fareham PO14 ......155 A3
Widley Gdns PO7 ....134 B2
Widley Rd Cosham PO6 .158 A4
Portsmouth PO2 .....157 B1
Widley Wlk PO6,PO7 .133 C2
Widworthy Dr BH18 ..186 C3
Wield Ct PO9 ....135 B2
Wigan Cres PO9 ......135 A1
Wight View
Lee-on-the-Solent PO13 .179 B2
South Hayling PO11 .185 B1
Wight Wlk BH22 .....165 C1
Wightway Mews SO31 .128 C1
Wigmore Ho PO1 ....215 C4
Wilberforce Cl 2 SO22 ..10 B3
Wilberforce Rd
Gosport PO12 ....181 B3
Portsmouth PO5 ....215 B1
Wilby La PO3 ....158 B2
Wild Arum Way SO53 ..54 C3
Wild Cherry Way SO53 ..55 A3
Wild Grounds Nature Reserve
PO13 ....180 B3
Wild Ridings PO14 ...154 B4
Wild Rose Cres SO31 .128 C1
Wildburn Cl SO40 .....76 B1
Wilde Cl SO40 ....100 B4
Wildern Cl SO31 .....128 C2
Wildern Ct SO30 ....105 A4
Wildern La SO30 ....105 A4
Wildern Sec Sch SO30 .105 B4
Wilderness Hts SO18 ..80 B1
Wilderton Rd BH13 ..203 C2
Wilderton Rd W BH13 .204 A2
Wildfell Cl BH23 .....192 A1
Wildground Inf Sch
SO45 ....125 C1
Wildground Jun Sch
SO45 ....125 C1
Wildground La 8 SO45 .126 A1
Wildmoor Wlk PO9 ..136 A3
Wildown Gdns BH6 ..207 A2
Wildown Rd BH6 ....207 A2
Wilfred Rd BH5 .....205 C2
Wilkins Cl PO8 ....88 A3
Wilkins Way BH15 ...202 A1
Wilkinson Dr BH8 ...191 A1
Wilkinson Ho PO4 ...183 A1
Wilks Cl SO15 ....77 B3
Willersley Cl PO6 ....133 B1
Willett Rd BH21 .....163 A1
William Booth Ho 37
PO1 ....182 A3
William Cl
Christchurch BH23 ..194 A1
Stubbington PO14 ...179 B3
William Ct 17 BH23 ..209 A4
William George Ct 9
PO13 ....179 C1
William Gilpin CE Prim Sch
SO41 ....173 C2
William Macleod Way
SO16 ....78 A1
William Price Gdns
PO16 ....131 A2
William Rd
Bournemouth BH7 ...205 C4
Lymington SO41 ....197 B3
William St SO14 .....103 B3
William's Ind Pk BH25 .194 C1
Williams Cl
Gosport PO13 ....180 B4
Holbury SO45 ....150 B2
Williams Rd PO3 ....158 A2
Willis Ave SO52 .....54 A2
Willis Rd Gosport PO12 .181 B2
Portsmouth PO1 .....215 B3
Southampton SO16 ...79 B3
Willis Way BH15 ....202 A3
Willis Waye SO23 .....2 B1
Willment Marine & Bsns Pk
SO19 ....103 B3
Willow Ave SP6 ......69 C2
Willow Cl
Bournemouth BH4 ...204 B2

Willow Cl continued
Havant PO9 ....136 A1
Hedge End SO30 ....105 B3
St Leonards BH24 ...139 B2
Upton BH16 ....201 B3
West End SO30 ......80 C2
Willow Ct
Bournemouth BH7 ...206 B3
Fareham PO14 ......130 B1
Southampton SO16 ...78 A2
Willow Dr
Christchurch BH23 ..207 A3
Marchwood SO40 ...124 C4
Ringwood BH24 .....141 A3
Wimborne Minst BH21 .164 B3
Willow Gdns
North Baddesley SO52 ..53 C3
Westbourne PO10 ...137 A2
Willow Gn SO21 .....57 A4
Willow Gr 11 SO50 ..57 B1
Willow Herb Cl SO31 .128 C1
Willow La BH23 .....169 B2
Willow Lo 1 BH1 ....205 B2
Willow Mead
Bournemouth BH8 ..190 B2
Hedge End SO30 ....105 A4
Willow Pk BH14 .....203 A2
Willow Pl
Christchurch BH23 ..207 B3
Gosport PO12 ....181 A3
Willow Rd
Bishop's Waltham SO32 ..83 C4
Liss SO32 ....21 A2
Willow Tree Ave PO8 .112 A1
Willow Tree Gdns PO14 .154 C4
Willow Tree Ho SO41 .197 B1
Willow Tree Rise BH11 .189 A2
Willow Tree Wlk SO19 .104 A2
Willow View BH16 ...201 B2
Willow Way
Christchurch BH23 ..207 A3
Ferndown BH22 .....165 B4
Willow Wlk BH25 ....210 A4
Willow Wood Rd PO11 .185 A2
Willowdale Ct GU32 ..40 A2
Willowdene Cl
Havant PO9 ....135 C2
New Milton BH25 ...195 B2
Willows The
Barton on Sea BH25 .210 A4
Chandler's Ford SO53 ..55 B2
Denmead PO7 ......110 C2
Wills Cl BH21 ....186 B2
Wills Rd BH12 ......203 B3
Wills Way SO51 .....53 A3
Willwood Cl BH17 ...187 C2
Wilmcote Gdns 5 PO1 .215 C3
Wilmcote Ho PO1 ...215 C3
Wilmer Rd SO50 .....56 A1
Wilmington Cl SO18 ..79 C2
Wilmot Cl SO50 .....56 C1
Wilmott Cl PO12 ....180 C3
Wilmott La PO12 ....180 C3
Wilmur Cres BH15 ...202 C3
Wilson Cl Fair Oak SO50 ..81 B4
Fordingbridge SP6 ...69 C1
Wilson Gr PO5 ......215 C1
Wilson Rd
Bournemouth BH1 ..205 C3
Poole BH14 ....203 B2
Portsmouth PO2 .....157 B1
Wilson St SO14 .....103 B3
Wilton Ave SO15 ....102 C4
Wilton Cl
Christchurch BH23 ..191 B1
Gosport PO12 ......180 C1
Wilton Cres SO15 ....78 C1
Wilton Ct SO15 .....102 B4
Wilton Dr PO8 ......112 A3
Wilton Gdns
New Milton BH25 ...194 C2
Southampton SO15 ...78 B1
Wilton Pl PO5 ......182 B1
Wilton Rd
Bournemouth BH7 ..205 C3
Southampton SO15 ...78 C1
Wilton Terr PO5 .....182 B1
Wiltshire Gdns BH23 .192 C4
Wiltshire Rd
Bransgore BH23 ....192 C4
Chandler's Ford SO53 ..55 B2
Wiltshire St PO5 .....215 A2
Wilverley Ave
Bournemouth BH8 ..190 A2
Havant PO9 ....136 A2
Wilverley Cl SO41 ...197 A1
Wilverley Pl SO45 ...150 C1
Wilverley Rd
Brockenhurst SO42 .145 C1
Brockenhurst, Wootton
BH25 ....170 C2
Christchurch BH23 ..208 A2
Wimbledon Park Rd
PO5 ....182 B1
Wimborne Fst Sch
BH21 ....163 B3
Wimborne Inf & Jun Schs
PO4 ....183 A2
Wimborne Minster Model
Town & Gdns★ BH21 .163 C2
Wimborne Rd
Bournemouth BH10, BH11,
BH2, BH3, BH9 ....204 C3
Bournemouth, Kinson
BH10, BH11, BH2, BH3,
BH9 ....189 B3
Broadstone BH21 ...162 C1

Wimborne Rd continued
Poole BH15 ....202 B3
Portsmouth PO4 ....183 A2
Wimborne Minst BH21 .163 A3
Wimborne Minster, Colehill
BH21 ....163 C3
Wimborne Rd E BH22 .165 B3
Wimborne Rd W
Ferndown BH21 ....164 B3
Wimborne Minst BH21 .164 B3
Wimpole Ct PO1 ....215 C4
Wimpole St PO1 ....215 C4
Wimpson Gdns SO16 ..77 C1
Wimpson La SO16 ...101 C4
Wincanton Way PO7 .112 A1
Winchcombe Rd PO6 .133 A1
Winchelsea Sch BH12 .188 B1
Winchester Cath★ SO23 ..11 A4
Winchester Ct 7 SO31 .127 C1
Winchester Coll
Winchester SO22 ....10 C3
Winchester SO23 ....11 A3
Winchester Ct
Gosport PO13 ......180 B3
5 Romsey SO51 .....28 A1
Southampton SO15 ...78 B1
Winchester Cty Mill★
SO23 ....11 A4
Winchester Cty Mus★
SO23 ....11 A4
Winchester Hill SO51 .53 A4
Winchester Ho 10 PO9 .136 A3
Winchester Pl 3 BH15 .202 B1
Winchester Rd
Bishop's Waltham SO32 ..83 A4
Chandler's Ford SO53 ..55 C4
Durley SO32 ....81 C2
Langrish GU32 ......39 C2
Langrish GU32 ......39 C2
New Milton BH25 ...195 B2
Owslebury SO21, SO32 ..58 B2
Petersfield GU32 ....40 B2
Portsmouth PO2 ....182 C4
Romsey SO51 ....52 C4
Romsey, Woodley SO51 ..28 B1
Southampton SO16 ...78 B1
Upham SO32 ....58 B2
Waltham Chase SO32 ..83 C1
Winchester Sch of Art
SO23 ....11 A4
Winchester St
Botley SO30 ....106 A4
4 Southampton SO15 ..102 C3
Winchester Sta SO22 ..10 C3
Winchester Way SO40 .100 B4
Winchfield Cl SO19 ..104 A1
Winchfield Cres PO9 .135 B2
Winchfield Ho PO12 .181 C2
Wincombe Cl BH21 ..165 B2
Wincombe Dr BH22 ..165 B2
Windbury Rd SO16 ...77 C1
Windermere Ave
Southampton SO16 ...77 C1
Stubbington PO14 ..154 B2
Windermere Gdns SO40 100 C4
Windermere Ho PO6 .157 A4
Windermere Rd
Bournemouth BH3 ..205 A4
Portsmouth PO2 ....157 C2
West End SO18 .....80 A1
Windfield Dr SO51 ....53 A4
Windgreen Est BH21 .186 C4
Windham Mews BH21 .205 B3
Windham Rd BH1 ...205 B3
Windhill Field PO7 ...111 A2
Windmill Cl Clanfield PO8 ..88 B3
5 Milford on Sea SO41 .211 B3
St Leonards BH24 ...140 B2
Windmill Copse SO45 .125 C1
Windmill Gr PO16 ...156 B3
Windmill La
Bursledon SO31 ....105 A1
St Leonards BH24 ..140 B2
Windover Cl SO19 ...104 B3
Windrush Gdns PO7 .134 B4
Windrush Rd SO16 ...101 C4
Windrush Way SO45 .126 A2
Windsor Cl Hordle SO41 .195 C2
St Leonards BH24 ...139 C2
Windsor Ct
5 Christchurch BH23 .209 A4
9 Cosham PO6 ......157 C4
Poole BH14 ....203 A2
14 Southampton SO17 .103 A4
13 Southampton, Bitterne
SO18 ....103 C4
Southampton, Millbrook
SO15 ....102 A3
6 Southampton, Westwood Pk
SO17 ....103 A4
Windsor Gate SO50 ...56 A3
Windsor Ho
3 Portsmouth PO1 ..215 C3
25 Winchester SO23 ..11 A4
Windsor Rd
Bournemouth BH5 ..205 C2
Christchurch BH23 ..206 C4
Cosham PO6 ....157 C4
Gosport PO12 ......181 A2
Petersfield GU32 ....40 C2
Poole BH14 ....203 A2
Portchester PO16 ...156 B3
Windsor Way SP6 ....93 A3
Windward Ct 11 PO12 .181 B2
Wine Cross PO17 ....109 A1

Winecross PO17 ......109 A1
Winfield Way PO10 ...136 C2
Winfrid Ho SO40 ......100 B4
Winfrith Cres BH12 ...203 C4
Winfrith Way SO16 ......77 B3
Wingate Dr SO19 ......104 A3
Wingate Rd
  Gosport PO12 ....155 C1
  Totton SO40 ....100 B4
Wingfield Ave
  Christchurch BH23 ...193 B1
  Poole BH15 ....202 B3
Wingfield Ct BH1 ....205 B2
Wingfield St PO1 ....182 B4
Wingrove Rd SO40 ....100 B2
Winifred Cl SO50 ......57 B2
Winifred Rd Poole BH15 .202 C3
  Waterlooville PO7 ...134 C4
Winkfield Row PO8 ...112 A3
Winkle St SO14 ....103 A1
Winkton Cl Burton BH23 .192 B2
  Havant PO9 ....135 B2
Winkton Ho BH23 .....192 B1
Winn Ct SO17 ....102 C4
Winn Mans 25 SO17 ....79 A1
Winn Rd SO17 ....79 A1
Winnall Cl SO23 ....2 B1
Winnall Manor Rd SO23 .11 B4
Winnall Prim Sch SO23 .11 B4
Winnall Trad Est SO23 .11 B4
Winnall Valley Rd SO23 .11 B4
Winnards Cl BH22 ....165 C1
Winnards Pk SO31 ....128 B2
Winnham Dr PO16 ....132 A1
Winnington PO15 .....130 B2
Winnington Cl PO15 ..130 B2
Winscombe Ave PO8 ..112 A1
Winsford Ave SO50 ....57 A1
Winsford Cl
  Bishopstoke SO50 ....57 A1
  Christchurch BH23 ...193 B1
Winsford Gdns SO50 ..57 A1
Winslade Rd Havant PO9 135 B3
  Winchester SO22 ......1 B2
Winsley Ave BH6 .....206 B4
Winslow St PO6 ......158 B4
Winsor Cl PO11 ......185 B1
Winsor Ct SO40 ....56 B2
Winsor La SO40 ....99 C4
Winsor Rd Cadnam SO40 .75 B1
  Totton SO40 ....101 A3
  Waterlooville PO7 ...111 B1
Winspit Cl BH15 .....201 C2
Winstanley Rd
  Nursling SO16 ....77 B3
  Portsmouth PO2 .....157 B1
Winston Ave BH12 ....204 A3
Winston Churchill Ave
  PO5 ....215 B2
Winston Cl Eastleigh SO50 56 A2
  South Hayling PO11 ..184 C2
  Southampton SO16 ....77 C1
Winston Ct
  1 Christchurch BH23 ...207 A4
  20 New Milton BH25 ...195 A1
Winston Gdns BH12 ..204 A3
Winston Par 22 BH25 ..195 A1
Winston Pk BH12 .....204 A3
Winston Rd BH9 ......190 A2
Winston Way BH24 ...141 A4
Winstone Bldgs SO16 ..78 C2
Winstone Cres SO52 ...54 A2
Winter Rd PO4 ....183 A2
Winterbarrow Cotts
  SO32 ....36 C2
Winterbourne Cl BH15 .202 B2
Winterbourne Rd
  Cosham PO6 ....132 C1
  Poole BH15 ....202 B3
  Romsey SO51 ....28 A1
Winterhayes Ct BH17 .187 C2
Winterhill Rd PO6 ....157 B4
Winters Cl SO45 .....150 B2
Winters Hill
  Bishop's Waltham SO32 ..82 C4
  Durley SO32 ....82 C4
Winters Rd SO32 ......84 A1
Winterslow Dr PO9 ...135 C3
Winton (Boys) Sch
  BH10 ....189 B1
Winton Cl
  Lymington SO41 .....197 C2
  Winchester SO22 ......1 C1
Winton Ct
  11 Petersfield GU32 ...40 C2
  West End SO30 ....80 B1
Winton Prim Sch BH9 .189 C1
Winton Rd
  Petersfield GU32 .....40 C2
  Portsmouth PO2 .....157 C1
Winton St 14 SO14 ...103 A3
Winton Way
  Bournemouth BH10 ..189 B1
  New Milton BH25 ....195 A3
Wisbech Way SO41 ...195 C2
Wisborough Rd PO5 ..182 C1
Wises Ct PO12 ....181 C2
Wish Pl PO5 ....215 D1
Wishart Gdns BH9 ...190 A3
Wistaria Ho 7 BH10 .189 C1
Wisteria Dr BH31 ....115 B2
Wisteria Gdns PO9 ..136 A3
Witchampton Cl PO9 .136 A3
Witchampton Rd BH18 .186 C1
Witham Cl SO53 ......55 A3

Withedwood Ave SO15 .102 B4
Witherbed La
  Locks Heath PO15 ...129 B2
  Locks Heath PO15 ...129 C3
Withermoor Rd BH9 ..204 C4
Withers La SO42 .....175 B4
Withewood Mans 2
  SO15 ....102 B4
Withies Rd PO13 .....180 B4
Withingham Rd BH13 .203 C2
Withington Cl 8 PO6 .133 A1
Withy Cl SO51 ....52 C4
Witley BH14 ....214 B4
Witley Rd PO8 ....111 C3
Witney Rd BH17 .....187 B1
Witt Rd SO50 ....57 B1
Wittensford La SO43 ..98 B4
Wittering Rd
  South Hayling PO11 .185 C1
  Southampton SO16 ...78 A2
Witts Hill SO18 ....79 C1
Woburn Cl SO50 ......56 A3
Woburn Ct PO13 .....179 C1
Woburn Rd SO16 ......78 B3
Wode Cl PO8 ....88 B2
Wodehouse Rd SO19 .103 C2
Woking Rd BH14 .....203 B2
Wolfe Cl
  Christchurch BH23 ...207 B4
  Winchester SO22 .....10 B3
Wollaston Rd BH6 ...206 C2
Wollaton Cres BH22 .165 B2
Wollaton Rd BH22 ...165 B2
Wollstonecraft Rd 25
  BH5 ....205 B2
Wolseley Rd Poole BH12 .203 B3
  Southampton SO15 ..102 B4
Wolsey Way SO41 ...211 B3
Wolterton Rd BH12 ..204 A3
Wolverley Ct
  16 Bournemouth BH4 ..204 B2
  Southampton SO16 ...78 B2
Wolverton Rd
  Bournemouth BH7 ...205 C3
  Havant PO9 ....135 C3
  Southampton SO14 ..103 A3
Wolvesey Castle (Old
  Bishop's Palace)★
  SO23 ....11 A3
Wolvesey Pl SO53 ....55 A2
Wolvesey Terr 3 SO23 ..11 A3
Wonderholm Par BH11 .189 A1
Wonston Ct PO9 .....136 B3
Wonston Rd SO16 ....78 A2
Wood Cl SO19 ....104 B2
Wood End Rd BH24 ..141 C3
Wood End Way SO53 ..55 A3
Wood Glade Cl SO40 .101 C1
Wood House La SO41 .174 A1
Wood La
  Bournemouth BH11 ..188 C3
  Bramdean SO24 ......15 C3
  Milford on Sea SO41 .211 B2
  Southwick PO17 ....133 A3
Wood Lark Gdns GU31 ..41 B2
Wood Lawn Cl BH25 .209 C4
Wood Lodge SO40 ....76 A1
Wood Rd SO40 ......100 A1
Wood Row BH9 .....190 C2
Wood View BH21 ....164 A4
Wood's Cnr BH24 ...143 B3
Woodacre Gdns BH22 .165 C2
Woodberry La PO9,PO10 136 C4
Woodbind Wlk SO31 .128 C1
Woodbourne Cl
  Fareham PO15 ....130 B1
  Liss GU33 ....21 A2
Woodbury
  Bournemouth BH1 ...205 A1
  Brockenhurst SO42 ..145 B1
Woodbury Ave
  Bournemouth BH8 ...190 C1
  Havant PO9 ....159 C4
  Petersfield GU32 .....40 C3
Woodbury Cl BH23 ..191 C2
Woodbury Gr PO8 ...111 C3
Woodcock La SO41 ..196 A4
Woodcocks Cres BH7 .206 A4
Woodcot Cres PO9 ..136 A3
Woodcot Prim Sch
  PO13 ....155 A2
Woodcote Cotts SO24 .15 B3
Woodcote Dr BH16 ..201 A3
Woodcote La PO14 ..155 A2
Woodcote Rd SO17 ...79 B2
Woodcroft Gdns PO8 .111 C3
Woodcroft La PO8 ..111 C3
Woodend Rd BH9 ...204 C4
Wooderson Cl SO50 ..57 A2
Woodfern SP6 ....70 B1
Woodfield Ave PO6 ..134 C1
Woodfield Cotts GU32 ..19 A4
Woodfield Dr SO22 ...10 A3
Woodfield Gdns BH23 .193 B1
Woodfield Ho 22 PO2 .157 C2
Woodfield Park Rd
  PO10 ....161 A4
Woodfield Rd BH11 ..189 A3
Woodford Cl BH24 ..141 B4
Woodford Ho PO15 ..130 B1
Woodford Rd BH1 ...205 B2
Woodgaston La PO11 .160 B1
Woodgreen Ave PO9 .135 B2
Woodgreen Dr BH11 .188 B2
Woodgreen Rd SO22 ..1 B1
Woodgreen Wlk SO40 ..76 A1
Woodhall Way PO15 .130 C3
Woodhay SO43 ......121 C3

Woodhay Wlk 22 PO9 .136 A3
Woodhayes Ave BH23 .193 C1
Woodhill Sch
  Botley SO30 ....105 C4
  Chandler's Ford SO53 ..55 B4
Woodhouse La
  Finchdean PO8 ......113 A3
  Hedge End SO30 .....105 C4
  Rowland's Castle PO8,
    PO9 ....113 B2
Woodhouse Rd PO8 ..112 C4
Woodington Cl 55 PO9 .136 A3
Woodington Rd SO51 ..51 B3
Woodlake BH17 ......187 B1
Woodland Ave BH5 ..206 A2
Woodland Cl
  Southampton SO18 ..104 A4
  Verwood BH31 ......114 C4
  West Wellow SO51 ...51 A1
Woodland Ct BH7 ...205 C3
Woodland Dro SO21 ..32 A2
Woodland Mans BH14 .203 B3
Woodland Mews SO30 ..80 B1
Woodland Pl 18 SO15 .102 C4
Woodland St PO1 ....215 D4
Woodland Vale SO19 .104 A2
Woodland View
  Bursledon SO31 .....127 C4
  Horndean PO8 ......111 C3
Woodland Way
  Christchurch BH23 ...208 B4
  Milford on Sea SO41 .211 B2
Woodland Wlk
  Bournemouth BH5 ...206 A2
  Ferndown BH22 .....165 C3
  ★ Mottisfont SO51 ....5 B2
Woodlands PO16 ....131 B1
Woodlands Ave
  Emsworth PO10 .....136 C2
  Hamworthy BH15 ...201 C2
Woodlands Cl
  Bransgore BH23 .....193 A4
  Chandler's Ford SO53 ..30 B1
  Gosport PO13 ....180 B3
  Hythe SO45 ....125 C1
  Locks Heath SO31 ..128 C3
Woodlands Com Sch
  SO18 ....104 B4
Woodlands Cres BH15 .201 C2
Woodlands Ct
  5 Hythe SO45 ....125 C1
  18 Winchester SO23 ...2 A1
Woodlands Dr SO31 ..127 B3
Woodlands Dro SO40 ..99 C2
Woodlands Gdns 8
  SO51 ....28 A1
Woodlands Gr PO7 ..134 B3
Woodlands La Liss GU33 .21 A2
  South Hayling PO11 ..184 C3
Woodlands Prim Sch
  PO8 ....111 B2
Woodlands Rd
  Ashurst SO40 ....99 C4
  Barton on Sea BH25 .209 C4
  Brockenhurst SO42 ..172 C4
  Netley Marsh SO40 ..99 C2
Woodlands The
  Chandler's Ford SO53 ..30 A1
  Kings Worthy SO23 ...2 B3
Woodlands Way
  Bursledon SO31 ....127 C4
  Havant PO9 ....135 C2
  New Milton BH25 ...195 A3
  North Baddesley SO52 ..53 C2
  Southampton SO15 ..102 C4
  St Leonards BH24 ...139 C2
Woodlane Cl SO24 ....15 B3
Woodlea Cl SO22 ......1 C1
Woodlea Gdns SO30 ..80 C1
Woodlea Ho SO53 ....55 B2
Woodlea Way SO51 ...29 C1
Woodleaze Cl BH18 ..187 A3
Woodleigh Cl PO9 ..136 B2
Woodley Cl SO51 ....28 B1
Woodley Close Flats
  SO51 ....28 B1
Woodley Gdns SO41 .197 B3
Woodley La SO51 .....28 A1
Woodley Rd
  Gosport PO12 ....181 B2
  Southampton SO19 ..103 B2
Woodley Way SO51 ...28 B1
Woodling Cres SP6 ...70 B1
Woodlinken Cl BH31 .115 A2
Woodlinken Dr BH31 .115 A3
Woodlinken Way BH31 .115 B2
Woodmancote La PO10 .137 C2
Woodmancote Rd PO4 .183 A2
Woodmill La SO18 ....79 C1
Woodmoor Cl SO40 .102 A1
Woodpath PO5 ......215 B1
Woodpath Ho PO5 ..215 B1
Woodpecker Cl
  Havant PO9 ....136 A1
  Verwood BH31 ......114 C3
Woodpecker Copse
  SO31 ....129 A2
Woodpecker Dr
  Broadstone BH17 ...201 C4
  Marchwood SO40 ...101 C1
Woodpecker Way
  Eastleigh SO50 ......55 B1
  Portsmouth PO3 ....158 A2
Woodpeckers Dr SO22 ..1 B1
Woodrising BH13 ....214 A4
Woodrisings The BH2 .204 B2
Woodroffe Wlk PO10 .136 C2
Woodrow PO7 ....110 C2

Woodruff Cl BH23 ...208 B4
Woodrush Cres SO31 .128 C1
Woods Ho 5 GU32 ....40 C2
Woods View Rd BH9 .204 B4
Woodsedge PO7 .....135 A2
Woodside
  Brockenhurst SO42 ..173 A4
  Chilworth SO16 .....54 C1
  Gosport PO13 ....155 A3
  Portsmouth PO5 ....215 B1
Woodside Ave
  Eastleigh SO50 ......56 A3
  Lymington SO41 ....197 C1
Woodside Cl
  Ferndown BH22 ....165 C3
  13 Lymington SO41 ..197 C1
  Marchwood SO40 ...101 C1
Woodside Cres SO50 ..54 C1
Woodside Ct 23 SO17 .103 A4
Woodside Gdns SO40 .100 B2
Woodside La SO41 ..197 C1
Woodside Rd
  Bournemouth BH5 ..206 A2
  Eastleigh SO50 ......55 C2
  Ferndown BH22 ....165 C3
  North Baddesley SO52 ..53 C2
  Southampton SO17 ..103 A4
  West Moors BH22 ..138 B2
  Poole BH14 ....203 B2
Woodside Way SO30 .105 A3
Woodstock Ave PO8 .112 A3
Woodstock Cl
  Fareham PO15 ......130 C1
  Hedge End SO30 ....105 B3
  Poole BH14 ....203 A1
Woodstock Ct BH22 .165 C2
Woodstock Dr SO17 ..79 A1
Woodstock La BH24 .141 A3
Woodstock Rd
  Burton BH23 ....192 B1
  Gosport PO12 ......181 B2
  Havant PO9 ....135 B1
  Poole BH14 ....203 A1
Woodthorpe Gdns SO31 128 C3
Woodvale SO15 .....130 B1
Woodvale Gdns BH25 .195 B2
Woodview Cl SO16 ...79 A3
Woodville Dr PO1 ...182 A2
Woodville Rd
  Fawley SO45 ....151 A2
  Havant PO9 ....135 A1
Woodward Cl PO12 ..180 C2
Woofferton Rd PO6 ..133 A1
Wool Rd BH12 ......203 A4
Woolfield La GU32,GU34 .18 A2
Woolford Cl 1 SO22 ..10 B3
Woolley Ho 17 SO14 .103 A3
Woolmer Cl SO19 ...104 B2
Woolmer La BH24 ...117 A1
Woolmer St PO10 ...136 C2
Woolner Ave
  Cosham PO6 ....158 A4
  Petersfield GU32 .....40 C2
Woolsbridge Ind Est
  BH21 ....139 A3
Woolsbridge Rd BH24 .139 C3
Woolslope Cl BH22 ..138 C1
Woolslope Gdns BH22 .138 C1
Woolslope Rd BH22 ..138 C1
Woolston Ct PO12 ..180 B2
Woolston Inf Sch SO19 .103 C1
Woolston Rd Havant PO9 135 B3
  Netley SO31 ....127 B4
Woolston Sch (Annexe)
  SO19 ....103 C2
Woolston Sec Sch SO19 103 C1
Woolston Sta SO19 ..103 B2
Woolven Cl BH14 ...203 A3
Woolwich Cl SO31 ..104 C1
Wootton SO31 ......127 B4
Wootton Farm Rd BH25 170 C1
Wootton Gdns BH1 ..205 A2
Wootton Mount BH1 .205 A2
Wootton Rd
  Lee-on-the-Solent PO13 .180 A2
  New Milton BH25 ...195 B4
Wootton Rough BH25 .195 A4
Wootton St PO6 ....157 C4
Worbarrow Gdns BH12 .203 B4
Worcester Cl 5 PO1 .215 C4
Worcester Ct PO13 ..180 B3
Worcester Pl
  7 Lymington SO41 ..197 C1
  Southampton SO19 .104 A1
Wordsworth Ave
  Bournemouth BH8 ...190 C1
  Portchester PO6 ....132 C1
Wordsworth Cl
  Bishop's Waltham SO32 ..83 C4
  Winchester SO22 .....10 B4
Wordsworth Inf Sch
  SO15 ....78 A1
Wordsworth Pl PO15 .106 B1
Wordsworth Rd SO15 ..78 B1
Worgret Rd BH15 ...202 B4
Workhouse La GU32 ..38 B1
Worldham Rd PO9 ..136 A3
Worrell Dr BH12 ....203 B4
Worsley Rd PO5 ....215 B1
Worsley St PO4 .....183 A1
Worth The PO5 .....182 B1
Worthing Ave PO12 .180 C4
Worthing Rd PO5 ...182 B1
Worthington Cres BH14 203 A2
Worthy Ct 46 PO9 ..136 A3
Worthy Ho SO16 .....78 A1
Worthy La SO23 ......1 C1

Worthy Rd
  New Milton BH25 ...195 A1
  Winchester SO23 .....2 A1
Wortley Rd BH23 ...209 A4
Wr Twr BH18 ....187 B2
Wraxall Cl BH17 ....187 B1
Wraysbury Park Dr
  PO10 ....136 C2
Wren Cl
  Christchurch BH23 ...208 A3
  New Milton BH25 ...194 C1
  Ringwood BH24 ....141 B3
  Winchester SO22 .....10 B3
Wren Cres BH12 ....204 A3
Wren Ctr The PO10 .137 A2
Wren Gdns SP6 ......93 A3
Wren Rd SO50 ....55 C1
Wrenway PO16 .....155 C4
Wrexham Gr PO8 .....88 A3
Wright Way SO45 ...151 C1
Wright's Hill SO19 ..104 A1
Wrights Wlk SO31 ..104 C1
Wriothesley Ct PO14 .153 C4
Wroxham Rd BH12 ..203 C3
Wryneck Cl SO16 .....78 A3
Wuthering Hts SO22 ..10 C3
Wyatts Cl BH21 .....186 B3
Wyatts La BH21 ....186 B3
Wyborn Cl PO11 ....185 A1
Wych Cl PO13 ......155 A2
Wychwood Cl BH2 ..204 C2
Wychwood Dr
  Blackfield SO45 ....177 C4
  Bournemouth BH2 ..204 C2
Wychwood Gr SO53 ..55 C2
Wychwood Grange 1
  BH2 ....204 C2
Wycliffe Rd
  Bournemouth BH9 ..204 C4
  Southampton SO18 ..80 A1
Wycote Rd PO13 ....155 A2
Wyeford Cl 4 PO9 ..136 A3
Wyelands Ave BH21 .164 B3
Wykeham Ave PO2 ..157 C1
Wykeham Cl
  6 Netley SO31 .....127 A3
  Poole BH17 ....202 C4
  Southampton SO16 ...78 C2
Wykeham Field PO17 .108 A2
Wykeham House Sch
  PO16 ....131 B1
Wykeham Ind Est The
  SO23 ....2 B2
Wykeham Lo BH13 ..214 C3
Wykeham Pk SO21 ...12 A4
Wykeham Pl
  Lymington SO41 ....197 C2
  Winchester SO22 ....10 B3
Wykeham Rd
  Netley SO31 ....127 A3
  Portsmouth PO2 ....157 C1
Wyld Green La GU33 ..21 A3
Wylds La GU32 ......65 B4
Wyllie Rd PO2 ......157 C2
Wylye Cl SO18 ....80 A2
Wymering La PO6 ...133 C1
Wymering Manor (Youth
  Hostel) PO6 ....157 B4
Wymering Manor Cl 9
  PO6 ....157 B4
Wymering Rd PO2 ..182 C4
Wyn Sutcliffe Ct 9 PO4 183 C2
Wyncombe Rd BH5 ..206 A3
Wyndcliffe Rd PO4 ..182 C2
Wyndham Cl
  Christchurch BH23 ...194 A1
  Waterlooville PO8 ...112 A2
Wyndham Ct SO15 ..102 C3
Wyndham Mews PO1 .182 A2
Wyndham Pl 14 SO15 .102 C3
Wyndham Rd
  Christchurch BH23 ...194 A1
  Poole BH14 ....203 A2
Wynford Ind Pk SO51 .27 C2
Wynford Rd
  Bournemouth BH9 ..190 A2
  Poole BH14 ....203 B2
Wynne Cl BH18 .....186 C1
Wynter Cl BH7 ......205 C4
Wynter Rd SO18 ....104 A4
Wynton Way PO15 ..130 B2
Wynyards Gap SO52 ..53 C2
Wyre Cl SO53 ....55 A3
Wyvern Cl
  Chandler's Ford SO53 ..55 B3
  Poole BH12 ....203 B4
Wyvern Tech Coll SO50 .57 B1

Y

Yachtsman Cl SO31 ..128 B4
Yaldhurst Ct 28 PO9 .136 A3
Yaldhurst La SO41 ..197 A2
Yapton St PO1 ......215 B3
Yarborough Rd PO5 .215 B1
Yardlea Cl PO9 .....113 A1
Yardley Cl PO3 .....158 B2
Yardley Rd SO30 ...105 B3
Yarmouth Cl BH12 ..204 A3
Yarmouth Gdns 14 SO15 .78 A1
Yarmouth Rd BH12 ..203 C3
Yarrell Mead SO41 ..197 A2
Yarrells Cl BH16 ....201 B3
Yarrells Dr BH16 ....201 A4
Yarrells La BH16 ....201 B3
Yarrells Sch BH16 ..201 A4
Yarrow Cl BH23 ....208 A4

Yarrow Rd BH12 ......203 A4
Yarrow Way SO31 ......128 C1
Yateley Cl PO9 ......135 B3
Yaverland SO31 ......127 B3
Yeatminster Rd BH17 .187 C1
Yeatton Ho SO41 ....196 A1
Yelverton Ave SO45 ...150 A4
Yelverton Rd 38 BH1 ..204 C2
Yeo Ct PO4 ......183 B2
Yeoman Pk SO16 ......77 B1
Yeomans Ind Pk BH8 ..190 C1
Yeomans Rd BH8 .....190 C2
Yeomans Way
  Bournemouth BH8 ....190 C1
  Totton SO40 ....100 C4
Yeovil Chase SO18 ....104 A4
Yeovilton Cl SO41 ....196 C1
Yerville Gdns SO41 ...195 C2
Yew La BH25 ....195 B2

Yew Rd SO18 ....104 A4
Yew Tree Ave PO8 .....112 A1
Yew Tree Cl
  Fair Oak SO50 ....57 B2
  Hedge End SO30 ....105 A3
  Wimborne Minst BH21 ..163 B3
Yew Tree Ct
  Fordingbridge SP6 .....93 C4
  Locks Heath PO15 .....129 A4
  30 New Milton BH25 ....195 A1
Yew Tree Dr PO15 ......129 A4
Yew Tree Gdns
  Denmead PO7 ....110 C2
  3 Ringwood BH24 .....141 A3
Yew Tree Pl GU33 ......21 A2
Yew Tree Rd PO11 .....185 A4
Yewberry Way SO53 ....54 C3
Yews The PO8 ....112 B4
Yewside PO13 ....155 B1

Yewtree Cl SO45 ......150 A4
Yewtree La SO16 ......77 B2
Yoells Cres PO8 ......111 C3
Yoells La PO8 ....111 C3
Yokesford Hill SO51 ....27 C2
Yokesford Hill Est SO51 .27 C3
Yonge Cl SO50 ....56 A2
York Ave BH25 ....195 A2
York Bldgs SO14 ......103 A2
York Cl Broadstone BH18 .187 A1
  Chandler's Ford SO53 ...54 C2
  Christchurch BH23 .....206 C4
  Fair Oak SO50 ....81 B4
  Petersfield GU32 ....40 B2
  Southampton SO14 ....103 B3
  Totton SO40 ....101 A4
York Cres PO13 ......180 A2
York Dro Nomansland SP5 .73 B4
  Southampton SO18 ....104 A4

York Gdns PO16 ......156 C3
York Ho 26 Gosport PO12 181 B2
  7 Southampton SO14 ...103 B3
  32 Winchester SO23 .....2 A1
York Pl Bournemouth BH7 206 A3
  17 New Milton BH25 ....195 A2
  Portsmouth PO1 ....182 A3
York Rd
  Bournemouth BH1 .....205 A2
  Broadstone BH18 ......187 A1
  Eastleigh SO50 ....80 A4
  Netley SO31 ....127 A3
  Southampton SO15 ....102 B4
York Terr PO2 ....157 C3
Yorkdale SO31 ....128 B2
Yorke St PO5 ....215 A2
Yorke Way SO31 ......127 C2
Yorkwood GU33 ....20 C2

Youngbridge Ct 12
  PO16 ....155 A4
Youngs Rd BH11 ......189 A3
Yves Mews PO5 ......182 B1

Z

Zamek Cl BH11 ......189 A3
Zetland Ct BH4 ......204 A1
Zetland Rd Cosham PO6 .158 A2
  Gosport PO12 ....181 A3
Zeus La PO7 ....134 C2
Zinnia Cl BH10 ......189 C1

Any feature in this atlas can be given a unique reference to help you find the same feature on other Ordnance Survey maps of the area, or to help someone else locate you if they do not have a Street Atlas.

The grid squares in this atlas match the Ordnance Survey National Grid and are at 1 kilometre intervals. The small figures at the bottom and sides of every other grid line are the National Grid kilometre values (**00** to **99** km) and are repeated across the country every 100 km (see left).

To give a unique National Grid reference you need to locate where in the country you are. The country is divided into 100 km squares with each square given a unique two-letter reference. Use the administrative map to determine in which 100 km square a particular page of this atlas falls.

The bold letters and numbers between each grid line (**A** to **C**, **1** to **4**) are for use within a specific Street Atlas only, and when used with the page number, are a convenient way of referencing these grid squares.

Example   The railway bridge over DARLEY GREEN RD in grid square A1

Step 1: Identify the two-letter reference, in this example the page is in **SP**

Step 2: Identify the 1 km square in which the railway bridge falls. Use the figures in the southwest corner of this square: Eastings **17**, Northings **74**. This gives a unique reference: **SP 17 74**, accurate to 1 km.

Step 3: To give a more precise reference accurate to 100 m you need to estimate how many tenths along and how many tenths up this 1 km square the feature is. This makes the bridge about **8** tenths along and about **1** tenth up from the southwest corner.

This gives a unique reference: **SP 178 741**, accurate to 100 m.

Eastings (read from left to right along the bottom) come before Northings (read from bottom to top). If you have trouble remembering say to yourself "Along the hall, THEN up the stairs"!

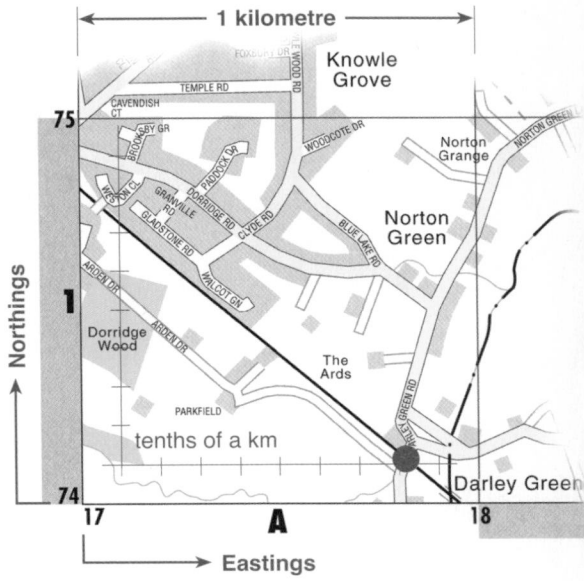

Addresses

Name and Address	Telephone	Page	Grid reference

Name and Address	Telephone	Page	Grid reference

Street Atlases from Philip's

Philip's publish an extensive range of regional and local street atlases which are ideal for motoring, business and leisure use. They are widely used by the emergency services and local authorities throughout Britain.

Key features include:

◆ Superb county-wide mapping at an extra-large scale of 3½ inches to 1 mile, or 2½ inches to 1 mile in pocket editions

◆ Complete urban and rural coverage, detailing every named street in town and country

◆ Each atlas available in two handy sizes – standard spiral and pocket paperback

'The mapping is very clear... great in scope and value'

★★★★ BEST BUY   AUTO EXPRESS

1 Bedfordshire
2 Berkshire
3 Birmingham and West Midlands
4 Bristol and Bath
5 Buckinghamshire
6 Cambridgeshire
7 Cardiff, Swansea and The Valleys
8 Cheshire
9 Cornwall
10 Cumbria
11 Derbyshire
12 Devon
13 Dorset
14 County Durham and Teesside
15 Edinburgh and East Central Scotland
16 Essex
17 North Essex
18 South Essex
19 Fife and Tayside
20 Glasgow and West Central Scotland
21 Gloucestershire
22 North Hampshire
23 South Hampshire
24 Herefordshire and Monmouthshire
25 Hertfordshire
26 East Kent
27 West Kent
28 Lancashire
29 Leicestershire and Rutland
30 Lincolnshire
31 London
32 Greater Manchester
33 Merseyside
34 Norfolk
35 Northamptonshire
36 Nottinghamshire
37 Oxfordshire
38 Shropshire
39 Somerset
40 Staffordshire
41 Suffolk
42 Surrey
43 East Sussex
44 West Sussex
45 Tyne and Wear and Northumberland
46 Warwickshire
47 Wiltshire and Swindon
48 Worcestershire
49 East Yorkshire and Northern Lincolnshire
50 North Yorkshire
51 South Yorkshire
52 West Yorkshire

How to order

The Philip's range of street atlases is available from good retailers or directly from the publisher by phoning 01903 828503